Fodor's 90
Europe

Fodor's Travel Publications, Inc.
New York and London

**Copyright © 1990
by Fodor's Travel Publications, Inc.**

ISBN 0–679–01764–X

Fodor's Europe

Editor: Donna Dailey
Associate Editors: Sean Connolly, Thomas Cussans, Caz Philcox
Contributors: Frances Arnold, Hilary Bunce, Nancy Coons, Asgeir Fridgeirsson, Lisa Gerard-Sharp, Istvan Gyenis, George Hamilton, Simon Hewitt, Alannah Hopkin, Jacqueline Krendel, Robin Neillands, Sylvie Nickels, Tony Peisley, Anita Peltonen, Ken Pottinger, Carla Power, Witek Radwanski, Philip Ray, Linda Stout, Robert Tilley, Fiona Tupper-Carey, Barbara Walsh Angelillo
Art Director: Fabrizio La Rocca
Cartographer: David Lindroth
Illustrator: Karl Tanner
Cover Photograph: Owen Franken

Design: Vignelli Associates

Special Sales

MANUFACTURED IN THE UNITED STATES OF AMERICA
10 9 8 7 6 5 4 3 2 1

Contents

Contents

Maps

Maps

Foreword

This is an exciting time for Fodor's, as we continue our ambitious program to rewrite, reformat, and redesign all 140 of our guides. Here are just a few of the new features:

★ Brand-new computer-generated maps locating all the top attractions, hotels, restaurants, and shops

★ A unique system of numbers and legends to help readers move effortlessly between text and maps

★ A new star rating system for hotels and restaurants

★ Restaurant reviews by major food critics around the world

★ Stamped, self-addressed postcards, bound into every guide, that give readers an opportunity to help evaluate hotels and restaurants

★ Complete page redesign for instant retrieval of information

★ ITINERARIES—The experts help you decide where to go and how to organize your time

★ FODOR'S CHOICE—Our favorite museums, beaches, cafés, romantic hideways, festivals, and more

★ HIGHLIGHTS—An insider's look at the most important developments in tourism during the past year

★ TIME OUT—The best and most convenient lunch stops along the shopping and exploring routes

★ Exclusive background essays that create a powerful portrait of each destination

★ A mini-journal for travelers to keep track of their own itineraries and and addresses

While every care has been taken to assure the accuracy of the information in this guide, the passage of time will always bring change, and consequently, the publisher cannot accept responsibility for errors that may occur.

All prices and opening times quoted here are based on information available to us at press time. Hours and admission fees may change, however, and the prudent traveler will avoid inconvenience by calling ahead.

Fodor's wants to hear about your travel experiences, both pleasant and unpleasant. When a hotel or restaurant fails to live up to its billing, let us know and we will investigate the complaint and revise our entries where the facts warrant it.

Send your letters to the editor of Fodor's Travel Publications, 201 E. 50th Street, New York, NY 10022.

Highlights '90 and Fodor's Choice

Highlights '90

Will 1990 be the boom year for European tourism that many were optimistically forecasting early in 1989? While Europe may still be the ultimate vacation destination for many Americans, the number making the trek in any given year is surprisingly variable and dependent on a series of unpredictable factors. The two most important by far are the health of the dollar and the extent to which Americans consider themselves, rightly or wrongly, at risk from terrorism in Europe. Forecasting just what impact both will have in 1990 is enough to make even the clearest crystal ball cloud over.

But if American tourism remains an unknown quantity, it's beyond question that Europeans themselves are traveling their continent in greater numbers than ever before. Greater prosperity and the approach of 1992 are the essential reasons. 1992? This is the date when all trade barriers between the 12 member states of the E.E.C.—the European Economic Community, or Common Market—are to be dismantled, turning much of Europe into one huge tariff-free market, the largest economic grouping in the world. As the unification nears, there are clear signs of the emergence of a shared "European" identity. And one manifestation of the new view is that Europeans are traveling more.

Transportation For the U.S. visitor, the effects of this mass movement are not entirely academic. For one thing, Europe's transportation network—despite increased capital expenditure—risks becoming grossly clogged. Air travel is the most serious casualty. Many European airports are already near saturation point, and fears exist over their ability to cope with more traffic. Delays, often exacerbated by increased security in the wake of the Pan Am bombing in December 1988, are becoming the norm rather than the exception. Strikes by air-traffic controllers over expanded work loads are commonplace. The likelihood that many of the artificially high airfares throughout Europe will be substantially reduced in the near future will probably add to the congestion.

But it's not all doom and gloom. Greater investment in staff and technology and improved cooperation between governments and their air-traffic controllers, leading eventually to a fully integrated system, are already underway. Similarly, the most obvious physical expression of the move toward a unified Europe—the Channel Tunnel, or Chunnel, between **France** and **Britain**—is expected to help ease pressure on overloaded air routes. But even this massive project is not without its problems. Some fear that the Chunnel will stimulate travel between Britain and the Continent to such an extent that it will be operating at peak capacity from day one (that being May 15, 1993), leading to inevitable delays.

France announced last year that a $3.5 billion expressway will be built *under* **Paris,** with links to all the major routes circling the capital. A less brutal response to the city's traffic problems is the introduction of a new waterbus service along the Seine River.

Rome has banned traffic from ever-larger parts of its downtown area, a step that has made congestion in the immediate vicinity even worse. The Romans have also invested heavily in a new rail-link, scheduled to open by summer 1990, between Fiumicino airport and the downtown Ostiense station. Improvements to the city's metro system are imminent.

Vast schemes are underway for road/rail/air improvements within **Spain** over the next two years. The Madrid–Seville N-IV highway is being upgraded, and many sections are already completed. Due to open in the summer of 1990 is a new 2,000-foot suspension bridge across the Guadiana, which will connect Ayamonte in the Spanish province of Huelva with Portugal's Algarve. The bridge will replace the old car-ferries, which were often crowded and caused long traffic tie-ups in the summer months.

In **Germany,** transportation fares will rise in most places in 1990, but in many Bavarian towns and villages in the Munich area they'll actually come down, as part of a fare restructuring affecting country services. Families heading south to Bavaria and the Alps by train are advised to book seats on the long-distance express "Konigsee," which leaves Hamburg daily for Berchtesgaden. It has a new, well-padded playroom on board.

A new roadway from **Vienna** eastward into Hungary will not be completed this year in its entirety, but as sections are opened the auto trip will be faster and safer. **Austria's** new highway south over the Semmering may also be opened by the end of the year.

Events and **Attractions** Probably the single largest event in terms of anticipated visitors and worldwide interest will be the soccer World Cup series in **Italy.** From June 8 through July 8, 24 nations will battle for the world title. Preliminary matches will be played across the country, and the final will be played in Rome. The Mondiali, as it's known in Italy, may attract sports fans, but others may see the event as a reason to stay away. European soccer fans have an unenviable reputation for hooliganism that can spill over into violence. With an estimated three million visitors, pressure on hotel space will be intense, with consequent hikes in rates.

One of the top amateur gymnastic displays to be seen anywhere will be held in Prague, **Czechoslovakia,** from June 28 through July 1. The spectacular Spartakiada is held every four years, and the 1990 event will involve over 160,000 performers ranging from toddlers to grandmothers, all taking part in breathtaking mass displays.

The Oberammergau Passion Play in **Germany** should be a less frenetic attraction. First performed in 1634 to commemorate the end of a terrible plague, the play has been held just about every 10 years since and will be presented again in 1990. More than 100 performances will be given, each lasting a full day and with a cast of 1,100, and over 500,000 visitors are expected. The artistic merit of the mammoth performances is always a source of debate; some observers think them pure kitsch, others hail them as profoundly moving. Thus far, the real drama has centered around the decision to cast a 35-year-old mother of two as the Virgin Mary. Tradition dictates that a real virgin get the role, and the traditionalists are predictably outraged.

Substantially more in the way of art is promised by the exhibits to be held in Amsterdam and Oterloo in **Holland** to celebrate the 100th anniversary of the birth of Vincent Van Gogh. The exhibits will be held from March 30 to July 29. Paintings and drawings from all over the world will be assembled, with the famous *Sunflowers* making the trek, too, all the way from Japan. The cost of insuring the works is said to be $3.5 billion.

Another must for art lovers is a visit to **Glasgow.** The Scottish city has been designated "Cultural Capital of Europe" for 1990, the sixth to hold the title, following Athens (1985), Florence (1986), Amsterdam (1987), West Berlin (1988), and Paris (1989). Glasgow is home to all but one of Scotland's national performing-arts organizations (among them the Scottish National Opera), and its museums, including the famous Burrell Collection, are among the finest in Britain. This year's events will showcase Glasgow's cultural treasures.

By 1990 the public should be able to view two major additions to the Spanish art world in **Madrid:** the new National Museum of Contemporary Art in the Centro de Arte Reina Sofia, and the famous Thyssen-Bornemisza art collection, housed in the Villahermosa Palace annex to the Prado. In an ancient vein, construction of a $2 million replica of the famous prehistoric Altamira Cave painting in Santander province in northern **Spain** is scheduled for completion in 1990. The replica will stand beside the cave. While the original Altamira Cave can receive only a small number of visitors, by advance application only, the nearby replica will accommodate 2,000 people daily.

More popular appeal is likely to be generated by the miniflood of theme parks sweeping Europe. In first place is the EuroDisneyland park at Marne-la-Vallée, outside **Paris.** This major complex is confidently expected to pull in more than 10 million visitors this year. An equally ambitious leisure park in **London** should be up and running by late 1990, located in the heart of the city, alongside the Thames, on the site of the former Battersea power station.

The Danes have opened Vandland, in Ålborg, the country's first water playground, with chutes and artificial surf galore. Europe's largest planetarium, the Tycho Brahe, in **Copenhagen,** also ranks high among Scandinavia's new attractions. At the most northerly settlement in Europe, Margeroya on **Norway's** North Cape, there's another mighty Nordic attraction: a restaurant/videographic complex overlooking the Arctic Ocean.

Opening in **Sweden** in June is Stockholm's new Wasa Museum, which will feature exhibitions about and tours of the 17th-century warship that is the country's most popular attraction.

Heureka, the new Finnish Science Center near **Helsinki,** offers participatory exhibits, a planetarium, and a robot theater. But southeastern **Finland** is also the only spot in Europe from which to view the most spectacular natural event of 1990. A total eclipse of the sun will occur on July 22, lasting nearly two minutes. The best conditions for observing it may be near Joensuu, though it can also be seen in Helskinki.

On a more down-to-earth note, Icelanders have beeen waiting nearly 70 years for one of the simple pleasures of life—an ice cold beer! Last year the 1922 prohibition was finally lifted, and, although there are only four brands available, demand is great enough to warrant a "beer supermarket" in **Reykjavik.**

Accommodations   **Turkey** is the scene of a massive hotel building program, as the country seeks to become a major tourist destination. Much of the building is being subsidized by British package-tour companies anxious to put a new vacation option on the map. Previous problems with substandard hotels and poor sanitary and power systems are gradually being overcome, and the major hotel groups are moving in, to ensure a good standard of accommodation. Ramada and Sheraton hotels opened in the Antalya region last year, and five more—including a Marriott and a Meridien—are being built. A Novotel has just opened in the Side resort, while, in Istanbul, the Hilton has opened a 100-room extension.

In Turkey, as throughout Europe, hoteliers seem to have noted the excess of hotel building on the Spanish coast and are now creating hotels that blend with, rather than blot out, the landscape. There is, for example, the success of **Spain's** paradors and **Portugal's** pousadas, originally developed for their own people traveling off the beaten track on business. These restored and converted historic buildings (palaces, convents, castles, and monasteries) have been discovered by many tourists. The American Sea Containers Group, which runs the Venice Simplon Orient Express and the famous Hotel Cipriani in Venice, is in the vanguard of the movement. Already restoring Villa San Michele, the 15th-century Franciscan-monastery-turned-hotel in Fiesole, **Italy,** the company is converting a 16th-century villa near Milan into a golf hotel with 40 rooms and 30 cottages.

Sports hotels are in fashion, particularly in **Portugal,** where a new Orient Express hotel has just opened on the Vale de Lobo. At the same upscale resort on Portugal's Algarve, work is well underway on a $525 million development that will include four hotels, 2,000 villas, a 400-berth yacht marina, a conference center, and a golf course. A similar complex is being developed on the Costa Azul, north of Lisbon, while major convention centers will open in Estoril and nearby Lisbon next year.

An interesting development in **Germany's** hotel business last year was the opening of two hotels exclusively for women: the Artemisa in West Berlin and the Haus am Dom in the northern town of Schleswig. And the country's chain of castle hotels acquired another treasure—the 15th-century Schloss Neuhof, near Coburg in Franconia.

Eastern Europe Update   **Glasnost** has moved so fast it is in danger of leaving the various indigenous tourist industries in eastern Europe behind. But there are positive signs that political changes bode well for tourism.

Hungary, which has always welcomed Western visitors, is now welcoming foreign investment in hotels: Gone is the stipulation that such investments must be run as joint ventures with Hungarian interests. Three hotels in Budapest and several throughout the country will open on those terms in the next couple of years. It is, however, a joint British/Hungarian company that operates Budapest's newest attraction: opera cruises on a new Norwegian boat on the Danube.

There were revolutionary political changes in Hungary during 1989. While the future of the one-party–dominated system is clearly in doubt, the makeup of the replacement system is undecided. It is as yet unknown whether or not the Communist Party will share power with some of the quasi parties (which have not been granted party status), and whether or not the transition would be a peaceful one. These questions will be decided by the "free" elections expected to take place in 1990.

Important political reforms, particularly the more democratic elections last year, are making life more liberal in **Poland.** Political tensions persist, however, due to the continuing economic crisis, with inflation approaching 100%. But reforms include the encouragement of private enterprise, and tourist services, such as new restaurants and cafés, are springing up everywhere. Constant devaluation of the złoty currency offsets the effects of inflation for the

Western tourist, and, coupled with new regulations legalizing what were once black-market practices, makes Poland one of the cheapest countries to visit in Europe.

Despite its hard-line image, Poland has always been a relatively easy place to tour. There are no "no-go" areas; but the country's main continuing problem is a shortage of hotels. Three new hotels, including a Holiday Inn and a Trusthouse Forte, opened in Warsaw last year, and these, plus a new Forum Hotel in Cracow, should help. Meanwhile, lack of cash is causing more modest establishments to become ever shabbier, especially in the provinces. Of more serious concern is the pollution problem: 27 regions of the country have been declared ecological danger zones. These include the region of Silesia, as well as the cities of Cracow, Gdańsk, and Toruń.

Bulgaria has similar hotel problems which, in the capital of Sofia at least, are being solved by a major building program. A new Otani and a Novotel have opened in the last couple of years, and negotiations continue with other major groups, such as Sheraton, Hilton, and Hyatt.

A shortage of direct flights into **East Germany** remains a problem for travelers headed there. This year the country will open three new hotels, all in choice sites where accommodation is traditionally tight. But all three—in Berlin, Dresden, and Weimar—will be in the top price-category, with facilities, service, and prices up to Western standards. The demand for more modest hotel accommodations is overwhelming but, alas, is not being met. On the other hand, the new complexes, along with other developments in Berlin, assure a far greater variety of restaurants and food service facilities. Since most of these are open to the local populace as well as visitors, prices are rock-bottom by any standard.

Politics   Financial scandals, political chaos, and confusion plagued **Greece** last year, and the country has been paralyzed by continuous strikes, as the people protest the failing socialist government. Disruption to the already-haphazard Greek daily life has been enormous, and, although the former ruling party was booted out in the last election, it is unlikely that the desired cleanup will happen immediately. Transportation and utility strikes could affect visitors to Greece for some time to come.

Financial sources report that a dramatic devaluation of the drachma of between 20% and 30% is a real possibility. This would, of course, make a holiday budget go that much further. But be careful before you set off for Greece on a cheap, flight-only charter ticket. In an attempt to reduce the numbers of low-budget tourists, Greece will be clamping down on tour operators' "air seat only" deals. Travelers arriving in Greece on a charter flight with no accommodations booked could find themselves sent back on the first available flight. It makes sense to get the Super-apex or excursion fares available with most airlines.

The subject of pollution has become so high-profile in Europe that last year a British hotel promoted "pollution weekends" where guests were promised tours of places hit by acid rain, effluent, and pesticides. Indeed, the "Greens" have become a strong political influence in many countries, putting pressure on governments and developers to look after the environment.

The spotlight has been on the **North Sea** between Britain and Scandinavia, a stretch which has reportedly become heavily contaminated by land and marine waste products. Along the northern **German** beaches, a multi-million–Deutschmark cleanup campaign is underway, although the area already boasts 13 of Europe's cleanest beaches. This follows the 1980s cleanup of the **Mediterranean,** which is now much cleaner off the French and Spanish coasts.

Terrorism, although its outbreaks remain comparatively infrequent, remains a major worry for governments, and security levels at airports only add to the congestion and delays caused by the general increase in traveling. Crime is less well-publicized, but it is, in fact, far more likely to affect the traveler in Europe than terrorism.

Street crime is the biggest problem. Bag and purse snatchers are particularly prevalent in areas of **Italy, Sicily,** and **Spain.** In Rome, steer clear of the gypsy children, who have perfected a swarming technique that allows them to get at your purse or pocket before you realize what's happening. Purse snatching is also common in Barcelona, and petty crime has reached plague proportions in Seville, with much of it directed against tourists. Thefts from cars, frequently when drivers are in them, are depressingly familiar.

In all areas, it pays to take reasonable precautions, especially at night and in crowded places. In general, though, European cities are still safer places in which to walk than their U.S. counterparts.

Fodor's Choice

No two people will agree on what makes a perfect vacation, but it's fun and can be helpful to know what others think. In compiling this list, we've included choices from each of the countries covered in the book, and we hope that you'll have a chance to experience some of them yourself. For more detailed information about each entry, refer to the appropriate chapters within this guidebook.

Sights to Remember

Belgium	Dusk in Bruges
Bulgaria	The panorama from the ramparts of Veliko Tarnovo
France	Mont St-Michel at high tide
Great Britain	Festival fireworks over Edinburgh Castle
Iceland	The midnight sun on Eyjafjordur
Ireland	A jaunting car ride along the lakefront at Killarney
	Slea Head (near Dunquin) after a storm
Italy	Venice Grand Canal at dawn
Malta	The fishing fleet on Valetta Harbor
Norway	The view of the Sør and Hardanger Fjords from Utne
Poland	Wawel Castle and Cathedral in Cracow
Spain	The perched white villages of Andalusia
Turkey	Istanbul skyline at sunset from Camliça Hill
Yugoslavia	The medieval walled city of Dubrovnik

Hotels

Austria	Schlosshotel, Dürnstein (*Very Expensive*)
Denmark	Falsled Kro, Falsled (*Very Expensive*)
France	The Ritz, Paris (*Very Expensive*)
	Any Logis et Auberges (Country Hotels and Inns) de France hotel (*Inexpensive*)
Great Britain	Royal Crescent, Bath (*Very Expensive*)
Holland	Golden Tulip Pulitzer, Amsterdam (*Expensive*)
	Hotel de l'Europe, Amsterdam (*Very Expensive*)
Ireland	Park, Kenmare (*Very Expensive*)
Italy	Hassler-Villa Medici, Rome (*Very Expensive*)
	Monna Lisa, Florence (*Expensive*)
Portugal	The pousadas throughout the country
Spain	Parador Conde de Orgaz, Toledo (*Expensive*)

Sweden	Clas på Hörnet, Stockholm (*Expensive*)
Switzerland	Sonnenberg, Zürich (*Moderate*)
West Germany	Vier Jahreszeiten, Munich (*Very Expensive*)

Restaurants

Austria	Zu den Drei Husaren, Vienna (*Very Expensive*)
Belgium	Comme Chez Soi, Brussels (*Very Expensive*)
France	Tour d'Argent, Paris (*Very Expensive*)
	Louis XV in the Hôtel de Paris, Monaco (*Very Expensive*)
Great Britain	Popjoy's, Bath (*Expensive*)
Hungary	Kisbuda, Budapest (*Moderate*)
Spain	El Caballo Rojo, Córdoba (*Expensive*)
Sweden	Johanna, Gothenburg (*Expensive*)
Switzerland	Bierhalle Kropf, Zürich (*Moderate*)
	Kronenhalle, Zürich (*Expensive*)
West Germany	Aubergine, Munich (for lunch) (*Very Expensive*)

Monuments

Belgium	The Atomium, Laeken, near Brussels
Czechoslovakia	U Stareho Hrbitova (Old Jewish Cemetery), Prague
France	The Arc de Triomphe, Paris
Great Britain	The original Prime Meridian marker, Greenwich
Ireland	The Rock of Cashel
Italy	The Pantheon, Rome
Luxembourg	The Devil's Altar, Diekirch
Norway	The Vigeland Monument, Oslo
Poland	The Solidarity Monument, Gdańsk
Spain	The Valley of the Fallen, near Madrid

Museums and Galleries

East Germany	Pergamon Museum, East Berlin
France	Fondation Maeght, St-Paul-de-Vence
Great Britain	Queen's Gallery, London
Holland	Rijksmuseum Vincent Van Gogh, Amsterdam
Leichtenstein	Prince's Art Gallery, Vaduz
Norway	Munch Museum, Oslo
Portugal	Gulbenkian Foundation, Lisbon
Spain	Prado Museum, Madrid
Switzerland	Villa Favorita, Lugano

| Turkey | Topkapi Saray (Palace) and Harem, Istanbul |
| West Germany | Alte and Neue Pinakotheks, Munich |

Festivals

Austria	Spring Festival (Festspiel), Salzburg
Denmark	Århus Festival
Finland	International Opera Festival, Savonlinna
Great Britain	Edinburgh International Festival
Holland	Holland Festival of Opera and Ballet, Amsterdam
Ireland	St. Patrick's Day Parade, Dublin
Italy	Venice Carnavale
Spain	Easter Celebrations, Seville
Turkey	Istanbul Art Festival
West Germany	Oktoberfest, Munich
Yugoslavia	Dubrovnik Festival

Churches, Temples and Mosques

Austria	Karlskirche, Vienna
France	Chartres Cathedral
Great Britain	York Minster
Hungary	The medieval synagogue, Budapest
Italy	San Lorenzo, Florence
Norway	Medieval stave church, Heddal
Portugal	Jeronimos Monastery, Belem
Spain	The 10th-century Mezquita (Mosque), Córdoba
Turkey	St. Sofia, Istanbul
West Germany	Asamkirche, Munich

Classical Sights

Bulgaria	Roman amphitheater, Plovdiv
Cyprus	Curium
Greece	Delphi
Italy	Herculaneum and the temples of Paestum
Romania	Istria
Turkey	Ruins of Ephesus

Parks and Gardens

Czechoslovakia	Vrtba Zahrada, Prague
France	Monet's "Water Lily" garden, Giverny
Great Britain	Hidcote Manor Garden, near Chipping Campden
	Regent's Park and Queen Mary's Gardens, London
Holland	Het Loo, Apeldoorn
Spain	Generalife, Granada
Sweden	Linné Gardens, Uppsala
West Germany	Alpine Garden, Pforzheim

For Children

Austria	Cable car from Innsbruck to the mountains
Denmark	Legoland, Billund
	Tivoli Gardens, Copenhagen
Finland	Santa Claus's Workshop, Arctic Circle, near Rovaniemi
France	Le Jardin d'Acclimatation, Paris
	Ride to the top of the Eiffel Tower, Paris
Great Britain	The Whispering Gallery of St Paul's, London
Italy	The view from the roof of St Peter's, Rome
Spain	Snowflake, the albino gorilla, Barcelona zoo
	The Barbary Apes in the Apes' Den, Gibraltar
West Germany	Zoologischer Garten (Zoo), Berlin

Shopping

Belgium	Lace from Brussels
East Germany	Classical LPs from East Berlin
France	Chocolates from the Maison du Chocolat, Paris
West Germany	Nymphenburg porcelain from Munich
Great Britain	Cashmere sweaters from Edinburgh
Greece	Natural sponges from Athens
Iceland	Hand-woven woolen goods from Reykjavik
Ireland	Donegal tweeds from Dublin
Italy	Shoes from Florence
Sweden	Crystal from Växjö
Turkey	Hand-woven carpets from Bodrum

Europe

NORWAY

Reykjavik
ICELAND

North Sea

Skagerrat

Edinburgh

Belfast

IRELAND

Irish Sea

DENMARK

Dublin

GREAT BRITAIN

HOLLAND

Cardiff

Amsterdam

London

Rotterdam

ATLANTIC OCEAN

English Channel

Brussels

BELGIUM

Bonn

Frankfurt

Paris

LUXEMBOURG

WEST GERMANY

FRANCE

Munich

Bay of Biscay

Bern

SWITZERLAND

LIECHTENSTEIN

Lyon

Milan

Nice

Marseille

Monaco

PORTUGAL

Madrid

ANDORRA

Barcelona

Florence

Corsica

Lisbon

SPAIN

Seville

Granada

Balearic Islands

Sardinia

Tyrrhenian

Gibraltar

Mediterranean Sea

MOROCCO

ALGERIA

0   400 miles

0   600 km

TUNISIA

World Time Zones

Numbers below vertical bands relate each zone to Greenwich Mean Time (0 hrs.).
Local times may differ, as indicated by lightface numbers on the map.

Algiers, **29**
Anchorage, **3**
Athens, **41**
Auckland, **1**
Baghdad, **46**
Bangkok, **50**
Beijing, **54**

Berlin, **34**
Bogotá, **19**
Budapest, **37**
Buenos Aires, **24**
Caracas, **22**
Chicago, **9**
Copenhagen, **33**
Dallas, **10**

Delhi, **48**
Denver, **8**
Djakarta, **53**
Dublin, **26**
Edmonton, **7**
Hong Kong, **56**
Honolulu, **2**

Istanbul, **40**
Jerusalem, **42**
Johannesburg, **44**
Lima, **20**
Lisbon, **28**
London (Greenwich), **27**
Los Angeles, **6**
Madrid, **38**
Manila, **57**

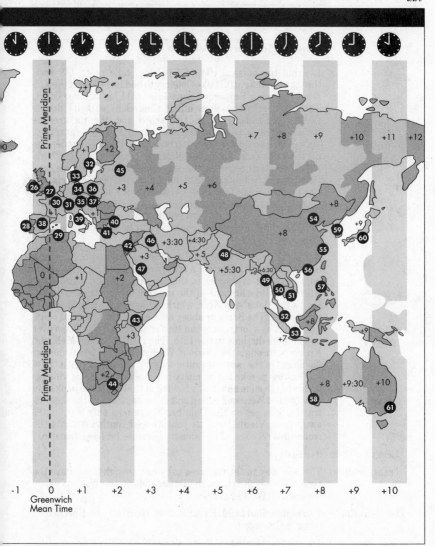

Ten Great Itineraries

Austria: Salzburg to Vienna

Leaving the musical city of Salzburg, take route 158 east, through the delightful Lake Country to Bad Ischel. Visit the Kaiservilla, where Emperor Franz Josef held his summer court. Turning northward, stop off at Gmunden, with its double castle—a Landschloss on the shore and the picturesque Seeschloss on an island in the lake—connected by a causeway. This is an excellent water sports center. From Gmunden, go northeast to Wels, a convenient center for trips into the Danubian hinterland but with its own Romanesque, Baroque, and Renaissance delights. Linz is the capital of Upper Austria, sitting on the banks of the Danube, and is a city of great contrasts —with Austria's largest medieval square, on the one hand, and the country's most modern multipurpose hall, the Brucknerhaus, used for concerts, conventions, and all kinds of gatherings, on the other.

One of the finest examples of Baroque architecture in Austria is to be found at St. Florian, a few miles east of Linz. Among its important art treasures is the Sebastian Altar, painted by Albrecht Altdorfer, one of the masters of the Danube school. Follow the Danube to Melk, which sits on a rocky crag above the great river. The Baroque abbey dominating the town was originally built as a fortress in the 10th century and was taken over by the Benedictines in the 12th. The route between Melk and Krems is through the glorious Wachau Valley—56 kilometers (35 miles) of the most romantic scenery in Austria, with fairy-tale castles perched upon misty hilltops and charming villages dedicated to wine and fruit growing dotted along the banks. Be sure to visit Weissenkirchen and Dürnstein, two of the most attractive villages on the Danube. You're now only 90 minutes away from Vienna, and as you proceed southeastwards the mountains recede and the scenery becomes far less dramatic.

Length of Trip 9 to 14 days.

Transportation The best way to see this area is by car, though if you have the time, take a boat trip on the Danube, down the Wachau Valley between Melk and Krems.

The Main Route **Two nights: Bad Ischl.** Excursions to Hallstatt and Ebensee en route to Gmunden.

Two nights: Gmunden. Relax along the tree-lined promenade, visit the theaters and concert hall, and enjoy the water sports and magnificent scenery. Excursion to Wels en route to Linz.

Three nights: Linz. Visit the old town and its cathedral. Walk along the city ramparts. Excursions to St. Florian and Melk en route to Krems.

Two nights: Krems. Excursions to the medieval towns of Weissenkirchen and Dürstein.

Further Information: *See* Austria.

Danube Cruise

Once the northern border of the Roman Empire, the river Danube is a main artery through Europe's history and geography.

Cruises begin either in Passau or Vienna; choose the former and you'll see the beautiful Wachau region of Austria, characterized by steeply terraced vineyards and craggy castles. Beyond Vienna—one of Europe's most gracious and musical cities—you enter waters shared by Czechoslovakia and Hungary at Bratislava.

There's a stretch of watery wilderness before you round the hilly section of the Danube Bend and, then, the river swings south to divide Hungary's capital into the two towns, Buda and Pest, which form the city of Budapest.

The scene changes as the Danube flows across the vast Hungarian plains that once were exposed to the Mongol warriors sweeping in from the East. The Danube, broader now, crosses the Hungarian frontier into Yugoslavia, where it wends by the imposing fortress of Petrovaradin at Novi Sad before it reaches the country's capital, Belgrade.

Now the dramatic section begins. The river squeezes through a series of gorges that it has carved from the Carpathian mountains. On route, you pass the archaeological site of a Neolithic fishing settlement at Lepenski Vir. This is also the site of Roman military victories, marked by a 2nd-century inscription. While once the fearsome waters rushed through these gorges, the Danube's rush to get to the Black Sea is now controlled by the Iron Gates Hydroelectric Dam on the Yugoslav–Romanian border. This requires the cruise ship to be floated through locks before it continues onward.

The final journey of the Danube is through flat farmland—first in Romania, then Bulgaria, and then back into Romania—until the magnificent wilderness of the delta is reached and the Danube enters the Black Sea.

Length of Trip One or two weeks.

Transportation Soviet Danube Shipping Company is the only cruise company to offer a cruise along the length of the Danube from Passau. Its 10-day trips start at Frankfurt and include a continuation to Istanbul for the flight back. The agents for the Soviet Danube Shipping Company are **United States:** International Cruise Center, 250 Old Country Road, Mineola, NY 11501, tel. 516/747–8880. **United Kingdom:** CTC Lines, 1 Regent Street, London SW1Y 4NN, tel. 01/930–5833.

Local tour companies in Vienna and Budapest also offer cruises along shorter stretches of the Danube.

Further Information: *See* Austria, Hungary, Romania, Yugoslavia.

France: Châteaux of the Loire

Châteaux are all over France, but often they are no more than undistinquished manor houses. That's not so in the Loire valley. Here, not only is there a profusion of châteaux, but they are often architectural masterpieces. Besides the splendid châteaux, the area has old and noble fortresses, such as the castles at Angers and at Chinon. Let us not forget, either, the various and excellent wines of the Loire valley that help to make a picnic on the banks of the Loire or its tributaries a memorable experience.

Start at Angers, with its 13th-century castle-fortress, and head east along the Loire to Saumur and its Renaissance château on a hill overlooking the river. Visit the Cavalry Museum and the curious *maisons troglodytes*, hillside cave dwellings that now serve as mushroom farms and tasting centers for the famous local wines.

Farther east is Chinon, where the large château-fortress perches above the town on a steep hill. Its inside is bare, thanks to Cardinal Richelieu's henchmen in the 17th century. The castle dates from the 12th century and the age of Henry II of England, who died here and is buried, along with Richard the Lionhearted, in the medieval abbey of Fontevraud, a few miles away.

Several miles south of the Loire, on the banks of the little river Indre, lies Azay-le-Rideau, the white fairytale château that is a pure Renaissance pleasure palace with its whimsical turrets. The elegance of its exterior is reflected in the still waters of the moat, and the surrounding park makes an ideal picnic stop. Six miles northeast of Azay-le-Rideau is Villandry, with its château and famous gardens: 1,500 linden trees line the avenue to the terrace in the back.

Amboise is farther along the Loire, beyond the bustling city of Tours and the famous vineyards of Vouvray. The château was a royal palace in the 15th and 16th centuries. Its terrace and park look down on the town, and it is a good base for excursions.

Seven miles from Amboise is Chenonceau, usually described as the most beautiful château of them all. Unlike many châteaux, Chenonceau has an interior that has been undisturbed by the passage of time. It is a showcase of splendid ceilings, huge fireplaces, and famous paintings. These reflect the tastes of some of its famous owners, including Catherine de Medici.

The château of Blois dominates the busy city below: Its construction shows the changing styles from the 13th to the 17th centuries. Inside there are hidden rooms and narrow passages that were conducive to the intrigue that swept the region during the Wars of Religion in the 16th century.

Chambord, on the road east, was built by Francois I in 1519 and, with 440 rooms, is easily the largest of the Loire châteaux. You can wander freely through 3,000 acres of the adjacent forest, formerly the royal hunting grounds. Finish your itinerary in Orléans, with its memories of Joan of Arc.

Length of Trip One week.

Transportation **By Car.** Driving is the best way to explore the châteaux and countryside, particularly because the roads are well marked.

By Public Transportation. Fast trains and buses link all the major towns, from which you can take local buses to visit the sights in the rural areas.

The Main Route **One night: Saumur.** Explore the château, Cavalry Museum, and local cave dwellings. Excursion to Fontevraud en route to Chinon.

Two nights: Chinon. Excursion to Azay-le-Rideau and Villandry en route to Amboise.

Two nights: Amboise. Excursion to Chenonceau en route to Blois.

Two nights: Blois. Excursion to Chambord en route to Orléans.

Further Information: *See* France.

Great Britain: Royal Roads from London

Less than half an hour west of London is Windsor, the home town of the queen of England. Her house is the castle, which sits on a high bluff above the town and overlooks the playing fields of Eton. The castle itself is fascinating, but make sure you see the paintings on exhibit, which represent only a small fraction of the royal collection.

Winchester, an hour west of Windsor, was the capital of England from the 9th to the mid-11th century, and several Saxon kings are buried within its Gothic cathedral. Nearby is the 13th-century Great Hall, the meeting place of medieval parliaments; in it is the supposed Round Table of Arthurian legend.

Farther west is Salisbury. As you approach, you'll see the 404-foot steeple of its 13th-century cathedral, said to be the most complete and perfect English cathedral. On route from Salisbury to Warminster, pay homage to the druids at Stonehenge. Close to Warminster is Longleat House, the best surviving Elizabethan house in the Italianate Renaissance style.

Wells, with England's first completely Gothic cathedral, is the farthest point west on the itinerary. Have a look at one of the few surviving medieval clocks, whose figures strike every quarter hour, then unwind in the peaceful setting amid ancient trees and lawns. A few miles away is Glastonbury, a cradle of early Christian faith and the traditional burial place of King Arthur.

Elegant Bath is north of Wells; handsome Georgian streets run alongside (and above) remains of the Roman occupation. Bath was revitalized in the 18th century when it became the fashion to take the waters in its famous spa.

Head north to Cirencester in the Cotswolds, the region of honey-colored stone villages and rolling pasture land, where rural pleasures are staunchly maintained and nothing changes except the seasons.

Stratford-upon-Avon is the northernmost point on the itinerary; the town of Shakespeare's birth is now England's second most popular tourist destination, after London. Visit the houses and museums related to the great playwright and take in a play at the Royal Shakespeare Theatre. Nearby, you can visit the 14th-century castle at Warwick and Charlecote Park, an Elizabethan mansion where, it is said, Shakespeare poached deer on its estate.

Oxford is your last stop on the way south to London. Some of the most attractive college chapels and courtyards are open to the public, and the Ashmolean Museum has one of the world's foremost collections of antiquities from Greece, Crete, and the Near East. Close to Oxford is Woodstock, the estate village of Blenheim Palace, home of the Dukes of Marlborough and of Churchill. Visit the church at Bladon, on the southeast of the estate, where Churchill is buried.

Length of Trip 10–14 days.

Transportation **By Car.** A rented car is the best way to appreciate the leafy country lanes and smaller villages.

By Public Transportation. Bus and train service between some of the smaller towns is sporadic at best, but recommended overnight stops are well served by trains and buses.

The Main Route **Two nights: Winchester.** Excursion to Salisbury en route to Warminster.

Two nights: Warminster. Excursions to Stonehenge and Longleat House.

One night: Wells. Excursion to Glastonbury.

Two nights: Bath. Explore the Roman and Georgian features of the city.

Three nights: Cirencester. Make this the base for a leisurely discovery of the attractive Cotswold villages and countryside.

Two nights: Stratford-upon-Avon. Visit all the Shakespeare shrines and take in a performance at the Royal Shakespeare Theatre. Excursions to Warwick Castle or Charlecote Park.

Two nights: Oxford. Visit the colleges and the Ashmolean Museum. Excursion to Woodstock and Blenheim Palace.

Further Information: *See* Great Britain.

Ireland: Dingle and the Ring of Kerry

Go south and west from Dublin past the stables and paddocks of Kildare. Beyond Cork City, the scenery grows wilder and, as the shore is washed by the Gulf Stream, the climate becomes appreciably milder. The roads are rarely crowded, and you will enjoy the novelty of almost traffic-free driving. Killarney's lakes are best explored by bicycle or jaunting car (pony and cart) and rowboat; serious climbers will find challenging peaks in the sandstone mountains that encircle the blue island-studded lakes. You'll rarely see greener greens than those on the championship golf courses by the lakes.

The circular coastal road, known as the Ring of Kerry, provides dramatically contrasting views of Dingle Bay and the wide estuary of the Kenmare River. Offshore, the Skellig Rocks, containing early Christian monks' cells, protrude in conical shapes from the pounding Atlantic. Fishing for wild salmon or trout or a day trip afloat in search of shark and other deep-sea specimens tempts many fishermen to the area. The wild, unspoiled Dingle Peninsula is a Gaelic-speaking region, where some of the country's best traditional musicians can be heard giving impromptu concerts in whitewashed pubs. The area is known for its generous hospitality and the spontaneity of its way of life.

Length of Trip One week.

Transportation **By Car.** 815 miles round trip from Dublin.

By Public Transportation. Make your base in Killarney. The train from Dublin to Killarney takes about four hours. From here, you can take local buses or sign up for daily excursions to all points, including the Ring of Kerry and the Dingle Peninsula. Rented bikes are handy in the Killarney area.

The Main Route **One night: Cork.** Day excursion to the Blarney Stone or Gougane Barra National Park.

Two nights: Killarney. Day excursion by bicycle or jaunting car to Muckross House and the Gap of Dunloe; drive through the mountain passes to Kenmare and Glengarriff.

One night: Waterville (Ring of Kerry). Day excursion around the Ring, deep-sea fishing offshore, or (weather permitting) boat trip from Valentia to the Skellig Rocks.

One night: Dingle. Day excursion to Dunquin, the cliffs of Slea Head, and across the Connor Pass to Brandon Bay.

One night: Cashel. Drivers can break the 300-mile Tralee–Dublin journey here to visit the monastic remains on the Rock of Cashel.

Further Information: *See* Ireland.

Italy: Tuscany's Art Treasures

A week's tour of Tuscany will make you want to come back next year for another visit to the famous works of art and architecture, the timeless hill towns, and the glorious scenery of the Tuscan landscape. From Renaissance Florence, home to the works of such masters as Michelangelo and Donatello, head west through sometimes ochre, sometimes green countryside to Lucca. On the way, stop and visit the fine medieval cathedrals of Prato and Pistoia. As if defended by its mighty brick walls, Lucca is still free from the tourist hordes. Here you will see magnificently carved churches in this gracious city with tree-shaded promenades that is set in a luxuriant plain surrounded by hazy blue hills.

On your way to Sienna, drop down to the coast to see Pisa's architectural curiosity, the Leaning Tower, and its white marble companions. Turning inland from Pisa and leaving the flat, coastal plain, proceed through the ageless beauty of the Tuscan countryside and there, awaiting you, will be the Middle Ages, the town of Siena. Gothic palaces and churches are everywhere. Wander through the narrow streets, explore their curves and slopes, and discover for yourself the beauties of the past. For present enjoyment, sip on the local Chianti.

On the way back to Florence, travel up to the hill town of San Gimignano, where turrets were built for noblemen to establish their status in society. Then, while driving through the rolling countryside, blanketed with vineyards, to Florence, plan your return visit to Tuscany.

Length of Trip One week.

Transportation **By Car.** Driving this itinerary makes a 250-kilometer (150-mile) round trip. Connections between most of the main towns can also be made by train or bus.

By Public Transportation. There are no direct trains between Pisa and Siena, but you can take a train from Pisa to Empoli (frequent service) and then from there on to Siena.

The Main Route **Three nights: Florence.** Excursions to Prato and Pistoia en route to Lucca.

Two nights: Lucca. Excursion to Pisa en route to Siena.

Two nights: Siena. Day excursion to San Gimignano.

Further Information: *See* Italy.

Norwegian Coastal Cruise

Every day since 1893, a passenger and car vessel has headed north out of the old Hanseatic port of Bergen for the 4,000-kilometer (2,500-mile) round trip over "the top of Europe" to Kirkenes. The route is called the *Hurtigrute*, and is an adventurous way to explore this northern coast. Scenically, it's of almost unrelieved splendor, reaching its peak north of the Arctic Circle in the fish-rich waters round the Lofoten Islands (where Trollfjord is barely wide enough for the ship to turn around).

Scores of fishing communities cling to the shore of this intricately indented coast, some now also bustling hubs for another harvest: the black gold of North Sea oil. Trondheim, first Viking and royal capital, is the place for history—its glorious medieval Nidaros Cathedral showing striking similarities to England's Lincoln Cathedral. In contrast, Tromsø's Arctic Ocean Cathedral explodes with light from modern stained glass. Farther north, you might see reindeer herds massing across straits and fjords on summer migration. And at Kirkenes, you'll be offered an eight-kilometer (five-mile) bus excursion to the Soviet border.

Each season offers a different thrill: the mists and opening blossoms of the spring, the long days of summer when darkness remains hidden, the blazing colors of the autumn, and the white winter snows contrasting with the long black nights. But the most popular time to make the cruise is between mid-May and July to see the midnight sun at the barren cliffs of the North Cape. Bird life is fascinating throughout the trip, and a pair of binoculars is a priority for the best enjoyment of the ever-passing scene.

Length of Trip   Two weeks.

Transportation   Daily departures from Bergen for the 4,000-kilometer (2,500-mile) round trip, largely through sheltered waters, with 11 nights on board. The vessels vary in size (142–228 berths) and age (1952–1983) and are cozy rather than luxurious; restaurants are licensed for beer and wine. In season, from mid-May through August, shore excursions can be prebooked before you board the cruise ship; at other times, you make the booking on board. Substantial reductions apply in the off-season, with additional discounts if you're 67 years or older.

Further Information: *See* Norway.

Moorish Spain

Heading north from Madrid, your destination is Segovia, but first stop off at the tiny village of San Lorenzo de El Escorial, with its austere monastery, the Escorial, burial place of Spanish monarchs. Then, on route to Segovia, visit the Valle de los Caídos (Valley of the Fallen), a memorial to the dead of the Spanish Civil War and the final resting place of General Franco.

At Segovia, you will encounter the monumental Roman aqueduct, one of the best-preserved Roman remains in the world, and the fairy-tale fortress-palace of the Alcázar. Visit Avila for its imposing city walls, which date from the Middle Ages, and for its shrines to Saint Teresa. The road southeast from Avila leads you to Toledo, in the spectacular setting of the river Tagus. It was once the home of El Greco, and there are many examples of his work in this ancient city.

Heading farther south across the vast plains of La Mancha, following the trail of Don Quixote, and across the infinite vineyards of Valdepeñas, you enter Andalusia, its ancient white villages and great southern cities a living memorial to the 800 years of Moorish occupation. Córdoba is the ancient city of the caliphs: Nowhere else in Europe will you find an 8th-century mosque and a medieval synagogue within a few paces of each other.

South of Córdoba is Seville, on the banks of the Guadalquiver. This was the river from which, downstream at Sanlucar de Barrameda, Columbus sailed his galleons across the Pacific. There are memorabilia from his epic voyage and his tomb is in the cathedral. But the highlight of this Andalusian tour will probably be the magical Alhambra Palace and Royal Chapel in Granada. Complete your tour by returning north to Madrid.

Length of Trip One week.

Transportation This itinerary is best followed by car, but with careful planning, it is possible to go by bus, although it may take more than seven days. The winding route to Granada covers 1,000 kilometers (620 miles), but there is a more direct route back to Madrid, only 430 kilometers (260 miles).

The Main Route **Two nights: Segovia.** Stop at the Escorial on your way to Segovia. Excursion to Avila on the way to Toledo.

One night: Toledo. Wander the ancient streets and go to the cathedral.

One night: Córdoba. Visit the 8th-century Moorish mosque.

Two nights: Seville. Visit the huge cathedral and climb the Giralda Tower. Explore the Alcázar or fortress.

One night: Granada. Explore the Alhambra, seat of the caliphs and kings.

Further Information: *See* Spain.

West Germany's Romantic Road

The 420-kilometer (260-mile) Romantischestrasse (part of it over 1,000 years old) is a north–south procession through a continuous pageant of history, art, and architecture. In this itinerary, start at the northern end of the road and work southward, though you could easily do it the other way around. The first stop after leaving the ancient town of Würzburg, Franconia, is Rothenburg ob der Tauber, an imperial free city and the best-preserved medieval town in Germany. It is renowned for its Pentecost and September festivals. Follow the road south through Feuchtwangen, with its attractive monastery church used as a backdrop for plays in summer, to Dinkelsbühl, another imperial free city, complete with medieval city walls, a moat, bastions, gate, and towers.

Farther south, Nördlingen is described as "the living medieval city." At night, you'll hear the watchman's eerie call echoing through the narrow streets, as it has for centuries. Stop off at the small town of Harburg, Swabia, with its imposing 13th-century hilltop fortress, now a museum of surprising treasures: Romanesque ivory carvings, a fine collection of Gobelin tapestries, and a huge library. Its near neighbor, Donauwörth, is another medieval showpiece.

Venturing into Bavaria, you come to Augsburg, a town founded by the Romans, which grew in status in the early Middle Ages and claims to have been the richest town in Europe during the 15th and 16th centuries. The cathedral, dating from 995, has the oldest stained glass in the world (11th century). It was also the birthplace of both Holbeins and Mozart's father. A little farther south, Landsberg is famous for the Rococo wonders of architect Dominikus Zimmermann. Beyond that is the quiet rural center of Schongau, also known as "The Town in Front of the Mountains." The Alps provide a dramatic backdrop on the horizon and made this town an important staging post in the Middle Ages on the busy trade route between Augsburg and Italy. The city walls, towers, and historic buildings from this era still survive. Complete your journey at the restful spa town of Füssen; the area is dotted with beautiful lakes and spectacular views from Hohenschwangau and Neuschwanstein, the fairy-tale castles built in the 19th century by King Ludwig of Bavaria.

Length of Trip   7 to 10 days.

Transportation   **By Car.** The Romantic Road is a specially designated tourist road and is well maintained and marked.

By Public Transportation. The Europabus route 190/190A runs along the Romantic Road via Frankfurt, Augsburg, and Munich from June to September.

The Main Route   **Two nights: Rothenburg ob der Tauber.** Excursions to Feuchtwangen and Dinkelsbühl.

Two nights: Nördlingen. Excursions to Harburg and Donauwörth.

Three nights: Augsburg. Excursions to Landburg, Schongau, and Füssen.

Further Information: *See* West Germany.

Crossroads in Yugoslavia

From Roman Pula on the coast, you head toward the towering massif of the Julian Alps, pausing on the way at Postojna for a train ride into Europe's grandest limestone caverns. Ljubljana, with its castle and Mestnitrg market, and the Upper Town of Zagreb introduce you to the medieval Slav communities that expanded into major Habsburg cities. Beyond, there are glimpses of the plains that spill over from Hungary before you plunge south into more mountains, this time those of Bosnia, rent by deep, dramatic river gorges.

Huddled at a valley head is Sarajevo. Here, oriental sights and sounds fill the *baščaršija* (bazaar) area threaded by labyrinthine alleys between old mosques and caravansaries, a few blocks from high-rise suburbs and the installations built for the 1984 Winter Olympics. The old town that surrounds Mostar's famous 16th-century bridge echoes over 400 years of Ottoman rule.

From Sarajevo, it's on to the coast for mellow, walled Dubrovnik, which, situated between the rival interests of Venice and the Ottoman Empire, maintained centuries of independence against all odds. From Dubrovnik northward, along the magnificent coast, the road twists and turns between steep mountains and the island-studded sea. The medieval town of Split was built within the walls of Roman Emperor Diocletian's massive palace, and there are more Roman and medieval treasures to be seen in Zadar before you turn inland. At Plitvice, 16 terraced lakes set in beautiful forests spill into each other through a myriad of cascades. From here, you complete the circuit via Rijeka back to Pula.

Length of Trip   Two weeks.

Transportation   **By Car.** A rented car is recommended for this round trip of approximately 1,930 kilometers (1,200 miles).

The Main Route   **Two nights: Kranjska Gora.** Day excursion to explore the Julian Alps.

Two nights: Sarajevo. The *Baščaršija* (bazaar) and trip to the Olympic resort area of Jahorina.

Three nights: Dubrovnik. Walk the walls, explore the old town, take an excursion to the islands.

Two nights: Split. Explore the Diocletian palace (old town) and neighboring medieval Trogir.

Two nights: Plitvice. Ramble along marked forest paths round picturesque terraced lakes.

Further Information: *See* Yugoslavia.

1 Essential Information

Before You Go

Government Tourist Offices

Austria Austrian National Tourist Office. **In the United States:** 500 Fifth Ave., 20th Floor, New York, NY 10110, tel. 212/944–6880; 500 N. Michigan Ave., Suite 544, Chicago, IL 60611, tel. 312/644–5556; 11601 Wilshire Blvd., Suite 2480, Los Angeles, CA 90025, tel. 213/477–3332; 4800 San Felipe, Suite 500, Houston, TX 77056, tel. 713/850–9999.
In Canada: 1010 Sherbrooke St. W., Suite 1410, Montreal, Quebec H3A 2R7, tel. 514/849–3709; 736 Granville St., Suite 1220–1223, Vancouver Block, Vancouver, British Columbia V6Z 1J2, tel. 604/683–5808; 2 Bloor St. E., Suite 3330, Toronto, Ontario M4W 1A8, tel. 416/967–3381.
In the United Kingdom: 30 George St., London W1R OAL, tel. 01/629–0461.

Belgium Belgian National Tourist Office. **In North America:** 745 Fifth Ave., Suite 714, New York, NY 101561, tel. 212/758–8130.
In The United Kingdom: Premier House, 2 Gayton Rd., Harrow, Middlesex HA1 2HU, tel. 01/861–3300.

Bulgaria Bulgarian National Tourist Office. **In North America:** Balkan Holidays (authorized agent), 161 E. 86th St., New York, NY 10028, tel. 212/722–1110.
In the United Kingdom: 18 Princes St., London W1R 7RE, tel. 01/499–6988.

Cyprus Cyprus Tourist Office. **In North America:** 13 E. 40th St., New York, NY 10016, tel. 212/213–9100.
In the United Kingdom: 213 Regent St., London W1R 8DA, tel. 01/734–9822; **North Cyprus Tourist Office,** 28 Cockspur St., London SW1Y 5BN, tel. 01/839–5530.

Czechoslovakia Czechoslovak Travel Bureau and Tourist Office (Cedok). **In North America:** 321 E. 75th St., New York, NY 10021, tel. 212/988–8080.
In the United Kingdom: 17–18 Old Bond St., London W1X 4RB, tel. 01/629–6058.

Denmark Danish Tourist Board. **In the United States:** 655 Third Ave., New York, NY 10017, tel. 212/949–2333.
In Canada: Box 115, Station N, Toronto, Ontario M8V 3S4, tel. 416/823–9620.
In the United Kingdom: 169–173 Regent St., London W1R 8PY, tel. 01/734–2637.

Finland Finnish Tourist Board. **In the United States:** 655 Third Ave., New York, NY 10017, tel. 212/949–2333.
In Canada: 1200 Bay St., Suite 640, Toronto, Ontario M5R 2A5, tel. 416/964–9159.
In the United Kingdom: 66–68 Haymarket, London, SW1Y 4RF, tel. 01/839–4048.

France French Government Tourist Office. **In the United States:** 610 Fifth Ave., New York, NY 10020, tel. 212/315–0888; 645 N. Michigan Ave., Chicago, IL 60611, tel. 312/337–6301; 2305 Cedar Springs Rd., Dallas, TX 75201, tel. 214/720–4010; 9454 Wilshire Blvd., Beverly Hills, CA 90212, tel. 213/271–6665; 1 Hallidie Plaza, Suite 250, San Francisco, CA 94102, tel. 415/986–4174.

In Canada: 1981 McGill College, Suite 490, Montreal, Quebec H3A 2W9, tel. 514/288–4264; 1 Dundas St. W., Suite 2405, Box 8, Toronto, Ontario M5G 1Z3, tel. 416/593–4723.
In the United Kingdom: 178 Piccadilly, London W1V OAL, tel. 01/491–7622 or 01/499–6911.

Germany **German National Tourist Office. In the United States:** 747 Third Ave., New York, NY 10017, tel. 212/308–3300; 444 S. Flower St., Suite 2230, Los Angeles, CA 90071, tel. 213/688–7332.
In Canada: Box 417, 2 Fundy, Place Bonaventure, Montreal, Quebec H5A 1B8, tel. 514/878–9885.
In the United Kingdom: (Federal Republic) 65 Curzon St., London W1Y 7PE, tel. 01/495–3990; (Democratic Republic) Berolina Travel Ltd., 22 Conduit St., London W1R 9TB, tel. 01/629–1664.

Gibraltar **Gibraltar Government Tourist Office. In the United Kingdom:** Arundel Great Court, 179 The Strand, London WC2R 1EH, tel. 01/836–0777.

Great Britain **British Tourist Authority. In the United States:** 40 W. 57th St., New York, NY 10019, tel. 212/581–4700; John Hancock Center, Suite 3320, 875 N. Michigan Ave., Chicago, IL 60611, tel. 312/787–0490; World Trade Center, 350 S. Figueroa St., Suite 450, Los Angeles, CA 90071, tel. 213/628–3525; 2305 Cedar Springs Rd., Suite 210, Dallas, TX 75201, tel. 214/720–4040.
In Canada: 94 Cumberland St., Suite 600, Toronto, Ontario M5R 3N3, tel. 416/925–6326.
In the United Kingdom: Thames Tower, Black's Rd., London W6 9EL, tel. 01/846–9000.

Greece **Greek National Tourist Organization: In the United States:** 645 Fifth Ave., New York, NY 10022, tel. 212/421–5777; 611 W. 6th St., Suite 1998, Los Angeles, CA 90017, tel. 213/626–6696; 168 N. Michigan Ave., Chicago, IL 60601, tel. 312/782–1084.
In Canada: 233 Rue de la Montagne, Montreal, Quebec H3G 1Z2, tel. 514/871–1535; 68 Scollard St., Lower Level, Unit E, Toronto, Ontario M5R 1G2, tel. 416/968–2220.
In the United Kingdom: 195–197 Regent St., London W1R 8DL, tel. 01/734–5997.

Hungary **Hungarian Travel Bureau (IBUSZ). In North America:** 1 Parker Plaza, Fort Lee, NJ, tel. 201/592–8585.
In the United Kingdom: Danube Travel Ltd. (authorized agent), 6 Conduit St., London W1R 9TG, tel. 01/493–0263.

Iceland **Iceland Tourist Board. In North America:** 655 Third Ave., New York, NY 10017, tel. 212/949–2333.
In the United Kingdom: 172 Tottenham Court Rd., 3rd floor, London W1P 9LG, tel. 01/388–5346.

Ireland **Irish Tourist Board. In the United States:** 757 Third Ave., New York, NY 10017, tel. 212/418–0800 or 800/223–6470.
In Canada: 10 King St. E., Toronto, Ontario M5C 1C3, tel. 416/364–1301.
In the United Kingdom: Ireland House, 150 New Bond St., London W1Y OAQ, tel. 01/493–3201.

Italy **Italian Government Travel Office (ENIT). In the United States:** 630 Fifth Ave., Suite 1565, New York, NY 10111, tel. 212/245–4822; 500 N. Michigan Ave., Chicago, IL 60611, tel. 312/644–0990; 360 Post St., Suite 801, San Francisco, CA 94108, tel. 415/392–6206.

In Canada: 3 Place Ville Marie, Montreal, Quebec H3B 2E3, tel. 514/866–7667.
In the United Kingdom: 1 Princes St., London W1R 8AY, tel. 01/408–1254.

Luxembourg **Luxembourg Tourist Information Office. In North America:** 801 Second Ave., New York, NY 10017, tel. 212/370–9850.
In the United Kingdom: 36–37 Piccadilly, London W1V 9PA, tel. 01/434–2800.

Malta **Malta National Tourist Office. In North America:** Maltese Consulate, 249 E. 35th St., New York, NY 10016, tel. 212/725–2345.
In the United Kingdom: College House, Suite 207, Wrights Lane, London W8 5SH, tel. 01/938–2668.

Monaco **Monaco Government Tourist and Convention Bureau. In North America:** 845 Third Ave., New York, NY 10022, tel. 212/759–5227.
In the United Kingdom: 25 Whitehall, London SW1A 2BS, tel. 01/930–4699.

Netherlands **Netherlands Board of Tourism. In the United States:** 355 Lexington Ave., New York, NY 10017, tel. 212/370–7367; 225 N. Michigan Ave., Suite 326, Chicago, IL 60601, tel. 312/819–0300; 90 New Montgomery St., Suite 305, San Francisco, CA 94105, tel. 415/543–6772.
In Canada: 25 Adelaide St. E., Suite 710, Toronto, Ontario M5C 1Y2, tel. 416/363–1577.
In the United Kingdom: 25–28 Buckingham Gate, London SW1E 6LD, tel. 01/630–0451.

Norway **Norwegian Tourist Board. In North America:** 655 Third Ave., New York, NY 10017, tel. 212/949–2333.
In the United Kingdom: 20 Pall Mall, London SW1Y 5NE, tel. 01/839–6255.

Poland **Polish National Tourist Office (Orbis). In North America:** 500 Fifth Ave., New York, NY 10110, tel. 212/391–0844; 333 N. Michigan Ave., Chicago, IL 60601, tel. 312/236–9013.
In the United Kingdom: 82 Mortimer St., London W1N 7DE, tel. 01/637–4972.

Portugal **Portuguese National Tourist Office. In the United States:** 590 Fifth Ave., New York, NY 10036, tel. 212/354–4403.
In Canada: 2180 Yonge St., Toronto, Ontario M4S 2B9, tel. 416/487–3300.
In the United Kingdom: 1–5 New Bond St., London W1Y ONP, tel. 01/493–3873.

Romania **Romanian National Tourist Office. In North America:** 573 Third Ave., New York, NY 10016, tel. 212/697–6971.
In the United Kingdom: 29 Thurloe Place, London SW7 2HP tel. 01/584–8090.

Spain **Spanish National Tourist Office. In the United States:** 665 Fifth Ave., New York, NY 10022, tel. 212/759–8822; 845 N. Michigan Ave., Chicago, IL 60611, tel. 312/644–1992; San Vicente Plaza Bldg., 8383 Wilshire Blvd., Suite 960, Beverly Hills, CA 90211, tel. 213/658–7188.
In Canada: 60 Bloor St. W., Suite 201, Toronto, Ontario MW4 3B8, tel. 416/961–3131.
In the United Kingdom: 57–58 St. James's St., London SW1A 1LD, tel. 01/834–6667.

Sweden Swedish Tourist Board. **In North America:** 655 Third Ave., New York, NY 10017, tel. 212/949–2333.
In the United Kingdom: 3 Cork St., London W1X 1HA, tel. 01/437–5816.

Switzerland Swiss National Tourist Office. **In the United States:** 608 Fifth Ave., New York, NY 10020, tel. 212/757–5944; 260 Stockton St., San Francisco, CA 94108, tel. 415/362–2260.
In Canada: Commerce Court W., Box 215, Commerce Court Postal Station, Toronto, Ontario M5L 1E8, tel. 416/868–0584.
In the United Kingdom: Swiss Center, 1 New Coventry St., London W1V 8EE, tel. 01/734–1921.

Turkey Turkish Tourist Office. **In North America:** 821 UN Plaza, New York, NY 10017, tel. 212/687–2194.
In the United Kingdom: 170–173 Piccadilly, London W1V 9DD, tel. 01/734–8682.

Yugoslavia Yugoslav National Tourist Office. **In North America:** 630 Fifth Ave., Suite 280, New York, NY 10111, tel. 212/757–2801.
In the United Kingdom: 143 Regent St., London W1R 8AE, tel. 01/734–5243.

Tour Groups

The range of tours to Europe is immense, with everything from fully escorted to almost entirely independent trips available, and at prices to suit almost every pocketbook. Whatever your budget, package tours often add value to your trip by providing lower airfares and hotel rates than you would get on your own. There can be trade-offs, of course—you may find yourself dining with 20 strangers and marching to the beat of a tour director's drum.

When considering a tour, be sure to find out: (1) exactly what expenses are included (particularly tips, taxes, side trips, additional meals, and entertainment); (2) government ratings of all hotels on the itinerary and the facilities they offer; (3) cancellation policies for both you and for the tour operator; (4) the number of travelers in your group; and (5) the single supplement cost, should you be traveling alone.

It is beyond the scope of this book to provide a full listing of the many hundreds of tours to Europe currently catalogued. The following is only a sampling of packages from some of the most established, experienced operators. For more information, contact your travel agent. (Most tour operators request that bookings be made through a travel agent—there is no additional charge for this.)

General-Interest Tours American Express Vacations (Box 5014, Atlanta, GA 30302, tel. 800/241–1700 or, in Georgia, 800/637–6200) offers a veritable supermarket of tours. At last count, it had about 100 ways to see Europe, including nearly 20 tours under the general title "Europe in Depth." "Tempo," for example, is a classic grand tour stopping in England, France, Switzerland, Italy, Austria, Germany, and Holland over a frenetic 15 days.
Cosmos/Globus Gateway (150 S. Los Robles Ave., Suite 860, Pasadena, CA 91101, tel. 818/449–0919 or 800/556–5454) has a wide variety of quality tours from the mind-boggling "Super European"—a Globus Gateway tour of 14 countries in 38 days—to regional and city tours. Cosmos is generally the more budget-minded of the affiliated companies.

Caravan Tours (401 N. Michigan Ave., Chicago, IL 60611, tel. 312/321–9800 or 800/621–8338) weighs in with seven grand tours and a variety of regional tours. Caravan's "Two Week Slow and Easy" is a welcome change of pace with only four countries—England, France, Switzerland, and Italy—over 17 days.

If you are willing to pay for luxury, Hemphill/Harris (16000 Ventura Blvd., Suite 200, Encino, CA 91436, tel. 818/906–8086 or 800/421–0454) and Abercrombie & Kent International (1420 Kensington Rd., Oak Brook, IL 60521, tel. 312/954–2944 or 800/323–7308) each offers some posh programs. Other popular operators include Maupintour (Box 807, Lawrence, KA 66044, tel. 913/843–1211 or 800/255–4266) and Olson-Travelworld (5855 Green Valley Circle, Culver City, CA 90230, tel. 213/670–7100 or 800/421–2255).

In the United Kingdom, Thomas Cook (Box 36, Thorpe Wood, Peterborough PE3 6SB, tel. 0733/502200) offers a massive range of European vacations, either escorted tours or packages for the independent traveler, but with a representative on site to help out if needed.

Thomson Holidays (Greater London House, Hampstead Rd., London NW1 7SD, tel. 01/435–8431), another market leader, offers vacations in almost every resort in Europe. A similar company with a wide range of packages is Horizon Holidays Ltd. (Broadway, Edgbaston, Birmingham B15 1BB, tel. 021/616–6222). Check out the brochures from these companies, particularly for fly/drive deals, which are often the best-value options for getting around Europe.

Special-Interest Tours
Adventure

If trekking through the Pyrenees in Spain, France, and Andorra, or a breathtaking (in more ways than one) Alpine pass in Switzerland is your idea of fun, investigate Sobek's International Explorers Society (1089 Angels Camp, CA 95222, tel. 209/736–4524). Various cycling, skiing, backpacking, hiking, and walking tours are also available.

In the United Kingdom, Top Deck Travel (131–133 Earl's Court Rd., London SW5 9RH, tel. 01/244–8641) offers 15 tours to central Europe, with activities including flotilla sailing, a variety of water sports, and rafting.

Art/Architecture

Esplanade Tours (581 Boylston St., Boston, MA 02116, tel. 617/266–7465) and Exprinter Tours (500 Fifth Ave., New York, NY 10110, tel. 212/719–1200) concentrate on Europe's rich heritage. Olson-Travelworld's *(see* General-Interest Tours) "From the Rijksmuseum to the Louvre" covers a staggering range of artistic treasures.

In the United Kingdom, Prospect Art Tours Ltd. (10 Barley Mow Passage, London W4 4PH, tel. 01/995–2163) offers a comprehensive range of art and architecture tours including Great Britain, France, Spain, Italy, Austria, Holland, and East and West Germany.

Ballooning

Buddy Bombard Balloon Adventures (6727 Curran St., McLean, VA 22101, tel. 703/448–9407 or 800/862–8537), offers fine dining and gentle breezes in and above France, Austria, Italy, Switzerland, and England.

Christmas/Culture

"Christmas in Europe and the Kaiserball" is one of Olson-Travelworld's *(see* General-Interest Tours) unique packages. The program includes a traditional white Christmas in the

Swiss Alps, a performance at the marionette theater in Salzburg, and the exclusive Kaiserball in Vienna.

In the United Kingdom, **Page & Moy Ltd.** (136–140 London Rd., Leicester LE2 1EN, tel. 0533/552521) offers nine Christmas tours, including ones with traditional Christmas festivities in the Lake District or the Highlands of Scotland.

Health/Fitness **DER Tours** (11933 Wilshire Blvd., Los Angeles, CA 90025, tel. 213/479–4411 or 800/937–1234) offers a menu of Europe's most heralded spa resorts. Some maintain surprisingly sophisticated medical facilities, others are simply beautiful and healthy places to relax.

In the United Kingdom, **Serena Holidays** (40 Kenway Rd., London SW5 ORA, tel. 01/244–8422) has vacations to a health farm on Malta for one, two, three weeks, or for as long as it takes!

Music **Dailey-Thorp Travel** (315 W. 57th St., New York, NY 10019, tel. 212/307–1555) transforms the traditional grand tour into the "Grand Opera Tour of Europe." Stops on the deluxe program generally include Paris, Milan, Vienna, and London, although itineraries vary according to available performances. "Musical Heartland of Europe" features musical performances in Berlin, Dresden, and Prague, while "Prague, Budapest, Vienna" highlights the historic capitals of the Hapsburg Empire. All tours are deluxe, with generally excellent seats for performances.

In the United Kingdom, **Brompton Travel Ltd.** (206 Walton St., London SW3, tel. 01/584–6143) will arrange tickets and book your flights and accommodations for any musical event in Europe that takes your fancy.

Nature **Questers Tours and Travel** (257 Park Ave. S., New York, NY 10010, tel. 212/673–3120) has an exciting program of worldwide nature tours. Rare birds and animals as well as the ancient sites are the tour stars.

In the United Kingdom, **Ramblers Holidays Ltd.** (Longcroft House, Fretherne Rd., Welwyn Garden City, Herts. AL8 6PQ, tel. 0707/331133) arranges walking tours within Europe with walk leaders to point out natural features of interest.

Rail Climb aboard the *Istanbul Train* with **Olson-Travelworld** *(see* General-Interest Tours) and follow the route of the *Orient-Express* from London's Victoria Station through France, Austria, Hungary, Romania, Bulgaria, and into Istanbul, Turkey.

Singles and Young **Trafalgar Tours** (21 E. 26th St., New York, NY 10010, tel. 212/
Couples 689–8977 or 800/854–0103) offers "Club 21–35," faster paced tours for travelers unafraid of a little physical activity—from bike riding to discoing the night away.

In the United Kingdom, **Club 18–30 Holidays Ltd.** (Academic House, Oval Rd., London NW1 7EA, tel. 01/485–4141) offers much the same activities as Trafalgar Tours, with beach parties, discos, sports, and lots more for those with plenty of energy.

Sports **Travel Concepts** (373 Commonwealth Ave., Suite 601, Boston, MA 02115, tel. 617/266–8450) gives you the choice of the British Open Golf Tournament, the Henley Royal Regatta, or, if you prefer to play rather than sit, the Rangitiki Polo School in Windsor, England, or the SAS Bjorn Borg Tennis Clinic in Stockholm.

In the United Kingdom, **Caravela Tours** (38–44 Gillingham St., London SW1V 1JW, tel. 01/630–9223) has tennis and golf vacations in Austria and Portugal. If you prefer to watch rather than participate, **Page & Moy Ltd.** *(see* Christmas/Culture) arranges vacations to see the international motor racing competitions in Europe.

Wine/Cuisine **Travel Concepts** *(see* Sports) serves up some exceptional food and drink in France, Germany, Italy, Switzerland, Scandinavia, England, and Ireland. Gracious living (and dining) is also available from **Floating Through Europe** (271 Madison Ave., New York, NY 10016, tel. 212/685–5600 or 800/221–3140) with deluxe barge cruises on inland waterways in England, France, Belgium, and Holland.

In the United Kingdom, **World Wine Tours Ltd.** (4 Dorchester Rd., Drayton St. Leonards, Oxon OX9 8BH, tel. 0865/891919) has a six-night wine tasting tour of Germany, along the Rhine, and France in the region of Alsace.

Package Deals for Independent Travelers

Cosmos/Globus Gateway, DER Tours, American Express, and **Abercrombie & Kent** *(see* General-Interest Tours) all offer packages for independent travelers, with choices of hotels, air, ground transportation, and sightseeing. The international airlines are also good sources, particularly **TWA Getaway Vacations** (800–GETAWAY) and **Pan Am Holidays** (800–THE-TOUR). **CIE Tours** (122 E. 42nd St., New York, NY 10168, tel. 212/972–5735) specializes in "fly/drive" tours, as does DER Tours.

In the United Kingdom, the companies mentioned in General-Interest Tours are good for the independent traveler as well as for those who prefer to have their activities organized for them. These companies offer flights and accommodations; tours and activities are offered as optional extras once you arrive at your destination. Company representatives usually are on hand to help you organize anything that may not be covered in their programs.

Festivals and Seasonal Events

The following is just a sampling of the special events in Europe throughout the year; a complete list would fill an entire book. A good overall guide—*Major Events in Europe*—is available from the **European Travel Commission**, 630 Fifth Ave., Suite 565, New York, NY 10111, tel. 212/307–1200.

January **Austria.** Carnival in Vienna; Mozart Week in Salzburg; World Cup Skiing Competition, usually in Kitzbühel.
France. International Circus Festival.
Great Britain. International Boat Show, Earl's Court, London.
Greece. Epiphany celebrations (January 6) nationwide.
Italy. Epiphany celebrations (January 6) nationwide.
Monaco. Monte Carlo Rally (January 19–26).
Norway. Kristiansund Opera Festival, which features original productions, art exhibits, and concerts.
Poland. Golden Washboard Traditional Jazz meet, Warsaw.
Portugal. St. Sebastian Festival, Aveiro.

Switzerland. International Hot Air Balloon Week, Château d'Oex, just east of Montreux.
Turkey. Camel Wrestling Festival, Selçuk.

February **Belgium.** Carnival of the Gilles, Binche.
Finland. Finlandia Ski Race, a 47-mile cross-country marathon from Hameenlinna to Lahti.
France. Carnival celebrations, Nice.
Great Britain. The Jorvik Viking Festival, York; Cruft's Dog Show, Earl's Court, London.
Greece. Carnivals in Patras, Iraklio, Thebes, Lesbos, Skyros, and Hios.
Holland. Carnival celebrations nationwide.
Hungary. Gypsy Festival, Budapest.
Iceland. Feast of Thorri, nationwide.
Italy. Carnivals in Venice and Viareggio.
Malta. Feast of St. Paul's shipwreck (February 10); Valetta Carnival.
Poland. Highland Carnival in the Tatra Mountains, Bukowina Tatrzańska; "Jazz on the Odra" Student Festival, Wroclaw; Festival of Modern Polish Music, Wroclaw.
Portugal. Carnival of Portugal nationwide, with the most famous festivities in the southern Algarve, in Aveiro, and on the island of Madeira.
Sweden. Great Lapp Winter Fair, Jokkmokk.
Switzerland. Carnival, Lucerne; Fasnacht carnival, Basel; Snow Sculpture Contest, Hoch-Ybrig-Schwyz.
Turkey. Folkdance Festival, Ankara.
West Germany. Black Forest Ski Marathon, Schonach-Hinterzarten; Fasching season or Carnival, nationwide.
Yugoslavia. Film Festival, Belgrade.

March **Austria.** Annual Spring Fair, Graz.
Belgium. Arts Festivals in Flanders and Wallonia.
Finland. Lady Day Church Festival, with traditional Lapp dancing and reindeer driving, Enontekio; Ounasvaara Winter Games, Rovaniemi.
France. Prix du Président de la République horse race, Auteuil, Paris.
Great Britain. Shakespeare Season opens in Stratford-upon-Avon; Edinburgh International Folk Festival; Grand National Steeplechase, Aintree Racecourse, Liverpool; The Devizes to Westminster International Canoe Race; the Oxford and Cambridge Boat Race in March or April, depending on tides.
Holland. Amsterdam Arts Weeks, cultural events; Keukenhof Flower Exhibition, Lisse.
Hungary. Spring Festival, Budapest.
Ireland. St. Patrick's Week is celebrated in Dublin, Cork, Galway, and Limerick; International Marching Band Competition and Choral festival, Limerick.
Norway. Holmenkollen Ski Festival and International ski competitions and events, Oslo.
Poland. Jazz Festival and International Festival of Student Theaters, Wroclaw.
Romania. The Kiss Fair, Arad.
Spain. The Fallas de San José are towering papier-mâché caricatures that help celebrate a week-long festival in Valencia.
Sweden. Vasaloppet long-distance ski race from Sälen to Mora, Dalarna.
West Germany. Frankfurt Music Fair; Munich Fashion Week.

April   **Austria.** International Music and Drama Festival, Vienna.
Belgium. International Fairs, Liège and Brussels; Flanders Spring and Summer Festivals, in various towns; Religious processions on Fridays, Veurne.
Finland. Vapunaatto (Walpurgis Night) (April 30), student celebrations to mark the arrival of spring.
France. Le Mans 24-hour motorcycle race; major horse races, Paris.
Great Britain. Camden Festival (London) and London Marathon; International Folk Festival, Eastbourne; the Oxford and Cambridge Boat Race, River Thames, in March or April depending on tides.
Greece. Easter Processions nationwide.
Holland. Flower Parade, Haarlem.
Iceland. Easter weekend festivities, Akureyri and Isafjordur; ski events.
Ireland. Irish Grand National horse race, Easter Monday, Fairyhouse, County Meath; International Choral and Folk Dance Festival, Cork.
Italy. Explosion of the Cart, Easter folklore event, Florence; Good Friday procession, Rome.
Luxembourg. Octave Festival, religious celebrations dating back to 1628.
Monaco. The Monte Carlo Open Tennis Championship.
Norway. Easter Sami Weddings, Karasjok and Kautekeino.
Portugal. The Tertiary Procession by the Franciscans, Ovar; St. Joseph's Festival, Braga.
Spain. April Fair, Seville; Holy Week processions, Seville and nationwide.
Sweden. Walpurgis Night celebrations (April 30), nationwide.
Switzerland. International Choral Festival, Montreux; Sechselauten Spring Festival, Zurich; Easter Festival, Lucerne.
West Germany. Jazz Festival, Stuttgart; Munich Ballet Days; Mannheim May Fair; Walpurgis Festivals in the Harz Mountains, April 30.

May   **Austria.** International Music and Drama Festival, Vienna.
Belgium. Cat Festival, Ieper; the Holy Blood Procession, Bruges, celebrates the vial of holy blood brought by the Count of Flanders from the Second Crusade; Golden Chariot Procession, Mons.
Bulgaria. Sofia Music Weeks; Festival of Arts, Roman Theater, Plovdiv.
Czechoslovakia. Prague Music Festival.
Denmark. Ballet and Opera Festival, Copenhagen.
Finland. May Day is celebrated nationwide.
France. Cannes Film Festival; International Marathon, Paris; French Open Tennis Championship, Paris; May Musical de Bordeaux, Bordeaux.
Great Britain. Royal Windsor Horse Show; Chelsea Flower Show, London; Nottingham Festival.
Holland. National Windmill Day, May 12.
Ireland. Royal Dublin Society Spring Show, Dublin; Norman Festival, Cahir, Co. Tipperary; Pan Celtic Festival, Killarney.
Italy. The Palio of Archers is a medieval crossbow contest, Gubbio; Sardinian Cavalcade, Sassari.
Luxembourg. Procession of St. Willibrod, Echternach; Genzefest celebrates the golden blossoms of the gorse, Wiltz.
Monaco. Formula One Grand Prix (May 24–27).

Norway. Bergen International Festival, with music, drama, folklore, and concerts.
Poland. Chopin celebrations in several locations; International Chamber Music Festival, Lancut.
Portugal. Pilgrimage to Fatima.
Romania. Week of the Lads, Braşov.
Spain. Horse Fair, Jerez de la Frontera; Patio Festival, Córdoba; San Isidro Festival, Madrid.
Switzerland. Annual folklore festival, Vevey.
Turkey. Ephesus Festival of Culture and Art, Selçuk; Kirpinar Wrestling Matches, Edirne.
West Germany. International Theater Festival, Wiesbaden; Annual Summer Festival, Bonn; Spring Folk Festival, Stuttgart.
Yugoslavia. Moreska Sword Dance, on the island of Korcula.

June   **Austria.** Styriarte Music Festival, Graz; Midsummer's Day celebrations nationwide; International Youth Music Festival, Vienna.
Belgium. Annual Chamber Music Festival, Chimay; Flanders Festival with music, ballet, and theater.
Bulgaria. Festival of the Roses, Karlovo and Kazanlak.
Czechoslovakia. Bratislava International Song Festival; Festival of Brass Music, Kolín; Folk Art Festival, Strážnice; the spectacular gymnastic event, Spartakiada, held every five years, (June 27–July 1), Prague.
Denmark. Midsummer's Eve festivals nationwide.
Finland. Kuopio Dance and Music Festival of Central European Dance.
France. Festival du Marais, Paris; International Music Festival, Strasbourg; Grand Steeplechase de Paris and Grand Prix de Paris; Le Mans 24-Hour Endurance Race; Tour de France Cycling Race begins.
Great Britain. Derby Day, Epsom Racecourse; Royal Ascot Horse Race; Wimbledon Lawn Tennis Championships; Henley Royal Regatta, Henley-on-Thames, Oxfordshire; Trooping the Colour at Whitehall, London; Aldeburgh Festival of Music and Arts, Suffolk.
Greece. Arts Festivals in Athens, Epidaurus, Patras, Iraklion, and Ioannina.
Holland. Holland Festival of International Performing Arts, Amsterdam.
Hungary. Sopron Festival Weeks and the Chamber Music Festival, Veszprém.
Iceland. Seaman's Day in Reykjavik and other fishing ports; Iceland National Day (June 17), celebrated nationwide.
Ireland. Festival of Music in Great Irish Houses, performed in several stately homes.
Italy. The Flower Festival, Genzano; medieval Battle of the Bridge is staged at Pisa; Regatta of the Great Maritime Republics, Venice; Festival of Two Worlds, Spoleto; World Cup 1990 (football) (June 8–July 9), nationwide.
Luxembourg. International Festival of Classical Music, Echternach and Luxembourg City.
Malta. Mnarja Folk Festival (June 29).
Norway. Midnight Cup Golf Tournament, Trondheim; Carnival, Oslo; Arts Festival, Harstad.
Poland. Cracow Art Festival; Midsummer Wianki celebrations nationwide (June 23).
Portugal. St. Anthony's Eve processions, Lisbon.

Spain. Rocio Pilgrimage from Huelva, Cadiz, and Seville to Almonte; Corpus Christi in Toledo and Sitges; International Festival of Music and Dance, Granada.

Sweden. Stockholm Marathon; Midsummer celebrations nationwide.

Switzerland. International Music, Theater, and Art Festival, Zurich; Art Fair, Basel; High Alpine Ballooning Week, Murren.

Turkey. Izmir International Culture and Art Festival; Istanbul International Festival.

West Germany. Frankfurt Summertime Festival; Franco-German Folk Festival, Berlin; Nymphenburg Summer Festival; Kiel Week, international sailing regatta; Munich Film Festival.

Yugoslavia. Summer Fair, Budva; International Jazz Festival, Ljubljana.

July **Austria.** Bregenz Festival of opera and concerts; Salzburg Music Festival.

Belgium. Ommegang Pageant, Brussels.

Czechoslovakia. Music Summer, Bratislava.

Denmark. Rebildfest, since 1912, has been the largest celebration of America's independence (July 4) outside the United States; Jazz Festival, Copenhagen.

Finland. Savonlima Opera Festival; Pori Jazz Festival.

France. Festival of Avignon; Festival of Lyric Art and Music, Aix-en-Provence; Festival Estival, Paris; Bastille Day (July 14) is celebrated nationwide.

Great Britain. City of London Festival; the Royal Tournament, Earl's Court, London; Llangollen International Musical Eisteddfod, Llangollen, North Wales.

Greece. Wine Festivals, Daphni and Alexandroupolis; Athens Festival, with opera, ancient drama, ballet, and concerts.

Holland. International Organists' Competition, St. Bavo church, Haarlem.

Hungary. Bartók Choral Festival, Debrecen; Open-Air Opera and Drama Festival, Szeged.

Italy. Palio Horse Race, Siena; Gondolas gather for the Feast of the Redeemer, Venice; Festa de Noantri, with processions, parade of boats, and fireworks, Trastevere quarter, Rome.

Luxembourg. Remembrance Day, Ettelbruck; International Open-Air Theater and Music Theater Festival, Wiltz.

Norway. Molde International Jazz Festival; Peer Gynt Festival, Vinstra.

Portugal. Handicrafts Fair, Estoril; bulls are turned loose in the ring during the Festival of the Red Waistcoat, Vila Franca de Xira.

Spain. San Fermin Festival features bulls and young men running through the streets of Pamplona.

Sweden. Folk Dance Festival, Arbro and other towns.

Switzerland. International Jazz Festival, Montreux International Rowing Regatta, Lucerne.

Turkey. International Bursa Folklore and Music Festival.

West Germany. Folk festivals nationwide; Munich Opera Festival; Richard Wagner Festival, Bayreuth.

Yugoslavia. Balkan Festival of Original Folk Dances and Songs, Ohrid; Dubrovnik Summer Festival; International Summer Cultural Events, Ljubljana.

August   **Belgium.** Planting of the Mayboom Tree, Brussels; Wedding of the Giants, in Ath, pairs a 12-foot image of the patron of cross-bowmen with an equally large bride.
Czechoslovakia. Dvořák Festival, Karlovy Vary.
Finland. Classical and Chamber Music Festival, Turku; Helsinki Festival of art, cinema, opera, and theater.
France. Major parades and celebrations, especially at Lourdes, for Assumption Day (August 15); Music Festival, Cordes; Wine Fair, Colmar.
Great Britain. Battle of Flowers, Channel Islands; Edinburgh International Festival, including the colorful Military Tattoo.
Greece. In Poros, during the Trireme, 170 oarsmen sail a replica of an ancient war galley; Athens Festival at the Acropolis; International Chalkidikis Car Rally.
Hungary. Ethnic Folk Festival, Keszthely; National Flower Festival, Debrecen.
Iceland. Westerman Islands Festival.
Ireland. Dublin Horse Show; Rose of Tralee Festival, Tralee; Puck Fair, Killorgin, County Kerry.
Italy. Joust of the Quintana, a historical pageant in Ascoli and Piceno; Venice Film Festival; Music Weeks in Siena and Stresa.
Luxembourg. Luxembourg City Kermesse.
Poland. International Song Festival, Sopot.
Portugal. Music and Ballet Festival, Estoril; bullfights and bullruns, Alcohete and Barrete Verde.
Spain. Semana Grande celebrations, fireworks, jazz, and carnival, San Sebastián.
Switzerland. Swiss National Day (August 1).
Turkey. Trojan Horse Festival, Çanakkale; International Fair, Izmir.
West Germany. Castle Festival, Heidelberg; wine festivals throughout the Rhineland; Grand Baden-Baden Week, Baden-Baden.
Yugoslavia. International Poetry Evenings, Struga.

September   **Andorra.** National festivities and pilgrimage to the shrine of Meritxell (September 8).
Austria. Harvest and wine festivities nationwide.
Belgium. Festival of Wallonia; Beer Festival, Wieze.
Bulgaria. Plovdiv International Arts Festival.
Czechoslovakia. Wine Festival, Znojmo; International Music Festival, Bratislavia and Brno.
Denmark. Århus Festival Week, with concerts, sports, theater, and exhibitions.
France. Festival of Autumn, Paris; Music Festival of Bresançon and Franche-Comte.
Great Britain. Burghley Horse Trials, Stamford, Lincolnshire; Chelsea Antiques Fair, London.
Holland. The Boulevard of Broken Dreams is a potpourri of theatrical offerings in tents on Amsterdam's Museumplein.
Hungary. Budapest Music Weeks.
Ireland. Dublin Theater Festival; Oyster Festival, Galway.
Italy. Piedigrotta fireworks and parades, Naples; Two-oar gondolas compete in the Historic Regatta in Venice; Joust of the Saracen, Arezzo.
Luxembourg. Grevenmacher Grape and Wine Festival.
Malta. Carnival.
Poland. International Festival of Contemporary Music, Warsaw; International Festival of Song and Dance Ensembles, Zielona Góra.

Portugal. Wine Vintage Festivals nationwide; New Fair, Ponte de Lima; Romaria da Nossa Senhora dos Remedios, processions and fair, Lamego.

Romania. Bucharest Folklore Festival.

Spain. Blessings of the Grapes with flamenco dancing and bullfights, Jerez de la Frontera; International Music Festival and Feast of the Merced, Barcelona.

Switzerland. Knabenschiessen festivities, Zurich.

Turkey. Cappadocian Grape Harvesting Festival, Urgup.

West Germany. Oktoberfest, Munich.

Yugoslavia. Belgrade International Theater Festival.

October   **Austria.** Styrian Autumn Festival, Graz.

France. Prix de l'Arc de Triomphe, Longchamp Racecourse, Paris; International Auto Show, Paris.

Great Britain. Cheltenham Festival of Literature, Gloucestershire; Horse of the Year Show, show jumping, Wembley Arena, London.

Greece. Athens Marathon; Demetria Festival, Thessaloniki.

Hungary. Limestone Cave Concerts, Aggtelek.

Iceland. Leif Erikson's Day (October 9) celebrates his discovery of North America in AD 1,000.

Ireland. Dublin Theater Festival; Dublin International Marathon Road Race; Kinsale Gourmet Festival, County Cork.

Italy. Feast of St. Francis, Assisi; wine festivals nationwide.

Poland. International Jazz Festival, Warsaw.

Portugal. The second yearly pilgrimage to Fatima; Folklore Festival, Nazaré.

Spain. Saffron Rose Festival, Castle of Consuegra, Toledo.

Switzerland. Chestnut Festival, Locarno.

Turkey. Art and Culture Festival, Antalya; Republic Day (October 28–29) nationwide.

West Germany. Berlin International Marathon; Frankfurt Book Fair.

Yugoslavia. Belgrade Music Festival (BEMUS).

November   **Austria.** St. Leopold's Day and Vintage Festival, Klosterneuburg; Advent brings markets and exhibits in Vienna and Salzburg and performances by the Vienna Boys' Choir.

France. Les Trois Glorieuses wine auction, Burgundy; International Dance Festival, Paris; International Food Fair, Dijon.

Great Britain. London–Brighton Veteran Car Run; Lord Mayor's Procession and Show, London.

Italy. Feast of the Salute, Venice.

Portugal. São Martinho Horse Fair, Golegã.

West Germany. Jazz Festival, Berlin; Folk Festival, Hamburg; Antiques Fair, Berlin; St. Martin's Festival, Rhineland; International Six-Day Cycle Race, Munich.

December   **Austria.** The Imperial Ball, Imperial Palace, Vienna; "Silent Night, Holy Night" celebrations (December 24), nationwide.

France. The Shepherd's Festival, Les Baux, Provence.

Great Britain. International Show Jumping Championships, Olympia, London.

Ireland. Horse Racing, Leopardstown; Wren Boys Festivities, County Cork and County Kerry.

Italy. Feast of St. Ambrose celebrations, Milan; Christmas masses in Rome's basilicas.

Norway. Nobel Peace Prize ceremonies, Oslo.

Portugal. Funchal Bay Festivities, with fireworks (December 31), Madeira.

Romania. Winter and New Year Festivals nationwide, especially in Sighetu Marmatiei and Vatra Dornei spa.

Sweden. Santa Lucia Day, Stockholm.

Switzerland. Klausjagen Festival celebrates St. Nicholas, Kuessnacht am Rigi.

Turkey. Festival of Mevlana honors the founder of the order of the Whirling Dervishes, Konya.

West Germany. Christmas markets in Munich, Hamburg, Berlin, Frankfurt, and other cities.

Climate

Current weather information on 235 cities around the world is only a phone call away. Call 800/247-3282 to obtain the Weather Trak telephone number for your area. When you reach that number, a taped message will tell you to dial the three-digit access code to any of the 235 destinations. The code is either the area code (in the United States) or the first three letters of the foreign city. For a list of all access codes send a stamped, self-addressed envelope to Cities, Box 7000, Dallas, TX 75209. For further information, phone 214/869-3035 or 800/247-3282.

For the average daily maximum and minimum temperatures of the major European cities, *see* When to Go in each individual country chapter.

What to Pack

Pack light—porters and baggage trolleys are scarce. The luggage restrictions imposed on international flights help limit what you pack. *(See* Getting to Europe.)

What you pack depends more on the season than on any particular dress code. In general, northern and central Europe have cold, snowy winters, and the Mediterranean countries have mild winters, though parts of southern Europe can be bitterly cold, too. In the Mediterranean resorts you may need a warm jacket for mornings and evenings, even in summer. The mountains usually are warm on summer days, but the weather, especially in the Alps, is unpredictable, and the nights are generally cool. The Pyrenees don't have much snow except in the higher elevations, but they have extremely damp, foggy weather and lots of rain year-round.

For European cities, pack as you would for an American city; formal outfits for first-class restaurants and nightclubs, casual clothes elsewhere. Jeans are as popular in Europe as they are in the rest of the world and are perfectly acceptable for sightseeing and informal dining. Sturdy walking shoes are appropriate for the cobblestone streets and gravel paths that fill many of the parks and surround some of the historic buildings. For visits to churches and cathedrals, especially in southern Europe, avoid shorts and immodest outfits. Italians are especially strict, insisting that women cover their shoulders and arms (a shawl will do). Women, however, no longer have to cover their heads in Roman Catholic churches.

To discourage purse snatchers and pickpockets, take a handbag with long straps that you can sling across your body, bandolier-style, and with a zippered compartment for money and other valuables.

You'll need an electrical adapter for hair dryers and other small appliances. The voltage in most parts of Europe is 220, with 50 cycles. If you stay in budget hotels, take your own soap: Many do not provide soap, and those that do often give guests only one tiny bar per room.

Taking Money Abroad

Traveler's checks and major U.S. credit cards—particularly Visa—are accepted throughout the major cities and resorts of Western Europe and in some cities of Eastern Europe. Even in Western Europe you'll need cash for some of the smaller cities and rural areas and for small restaurants and shops in the major cities. Although you won't get as good an exchange rate at home as abroad, it's wise to change a small amount of money into the currency of the country you're visiting (or the one you'll visit first) to avoid long lines at airport currency exchange booths. Most U.S. banks will exchange your money into foreign currency. If your local bank can't provide this service, contact **Deak International**, 630 Fifth Ave., New York, NY 10111, tel. 212/ 635–0515.

For safety and convenience, it's always best to take traveler's checks. The most recognized traveler's checks are American Express, Barclay's, Thomas Cook, and those issued through major commercial banks such as Citibank and Bank of America. Some banks will issue the checks free to established customers, but most charge a 1% commission fee. Buy some of your traveler's checks in small denominations to cash toward the end of your trip. This will avoid having to cash a large check and ending up with more foreign money than you need. You can also buy traveler's checks in foreign currency, a good idea if the U.S. dollar is falling and you want to lock in the current rate. Remember to take along addresses of offices where you can get refunds for lost or stolen traveler's checks.

Banks and bank-operated exchange booths at airports and railroad stations are the best places to change money. Hotels and privately run exchange firms will give you a significantly lower rate of exchange.

Getting Money from Home

There are at least three ways to get money from home: (1) Have it sent through a large commercial bank with a branch in the European country you're visiting. The only drawback is that you must have an account with the bank; if not, you'll have to go through your own bank and the process will be slower and more expensive. (2) Have it sent through American Express. If you are a cardholder, you can cash a personal check or a counter check at an American Express office for up to $1,000; $200 will be in cash and $800 in traveler's checks. There is a 1% commission on the traveler's checks. American Express has a new service, American Express MoneyGram, that is now available in most major European cities. Through this service, you can receive up to $5,000 cash. To find out the American Express MoneyGram location nearest your home and the addresses of offices in Europe, call 800/543–4080. You do not need to be a cardholder to use this service. (3) Have it sent through Western Union (tel. 800/325–6000). If you have a MasterCard or Visa, you can have money sent for any amount up to your credit limit.

If not, have someone take cash or a certified cashier's check to a Western Union office. The money will be delivered in two business days to a bank in the town where you're staying. Fees vary with the amount of money sent. For $1,000 the fee is $69; for $500, $59.

Passports and Visas

Americans All U.S. citizens need a **passport** to enter the 33 countries covered in this guide. Applications for a new passport must be made in person; renewals can be obtained in person or by mail (*see* below). First-time applicants should apply well in advance of their departure date to one of the 13 U.S. Passport Agency offices. In addition, local county courthouses, many state and probate courts, and some post offices accept passport applications. Necessary documents include: (1) a completed passport application (Form DSP-11); (2) proof of citizenship (either birth certificate with raised seal or naturalization papers); (3) proof of identity (driver's license, employee ID card, or any other document with your photograph and signature); (4) two recent, identical, two-inch-square photographs (black and white or color); (5) $42 application fee for a 10-year passport (those under 18 pay $27 for a five-year passport). Passports are mailed to you in about 10 working days.

To renew your passport by mail, you'll need completed Form DSP-82, two recent, identical passport photographs, and a check or money order for $35.

At press time, U.S. citizens need **visas** to enter Andorra, Bulgaria (if traveling alone but not if part of a group of six or more), Czechoslovakia, France, East Germany, Hungary, Monaco, Poland, Romania, and Yugoslavia. Many countries require visas for stays of three months or longer; apply at the country's embassy in Washington, DC. Since the United States does not have diplomatic relations with Albania, visa applications must go through the Albanian Mission in Paris or Rome. Only Americans of Albanian descent are allowed to enter the country on private visits to their relatives.

Canadians All Canadians need **passports** to enter the 33 countries in this guide. Send the completed application (available at any post office or passport office) to the Bureau of Passports, Complexe Guy Favreau, 200 Dorchester W., Montreal, Quebec H2Z 1X4. Include $25, two photographs, a guarantor, and proof of Canadian citizenship. Applications can be made in person at the regional passport offices in Edmonton, Halifax, Montreal, Toronto, Vancouver, or Winnipeg. Passports are valid for five years and are nonrenewable.

Visas are required by Canadian citizens traveling to Albania, Bulgaria, Czechoslovakia, East Germany, France, Hungary, Poland, Romania, and Yugoslavia. Obtain them from the nearest embassy.

Britons All British citizens need **passports;** applications are available from travel agencies or a main post office. Send the completed form to your nearest regional passport office. The application must be countersigned by your bank manager or by a solicitor, barrister, doctor, clergyman, or justice of the peace who knows you personally. In addition, you'll need two photographs and the £15 fee. The occasional tourist might opt for a British Visitor's Passport. It is valid for one year and allows entry into most European countries (Yugoslavia and Eastern European countries currently excepted). It costs £7.50 and is nonrenewable. You'll need two passport photographs and identification. Apply at your local post office.

Visas are required for British citizens entering Albania, Czechoslovakia, East Germany, Hungary, Poland, and Romania. Apply at the nearest embassy or consulate.

Customs and Duties

On Arrival Arrival formalities vary from country to country and are detailed in each chapter. In addition to specific duty-free allowances, most countries allow travelers to also bring in cameras and a reasonable amount of film and electronic equipment; most do not allow fresh meats, plants, weapons, and narcotics. Eastern European countries generally restrict the importation of Western newspapers, tape and video cassettes, and medicines except those for personal use.

On Departure If you are bringing any foreign-made equipment from home, such as a camera, it's wise to carry the original receipt with you or to register such equipment with U.S. Customs before you leave (Form 4457). Otherwise you may end up paying duty on your return.

U.S. residents may bring home duty-free up to $400 worth of foreign goods, as long as they have been out of the country for at least 48 hours. Each member of the family is entitled to the same exemption, regardless of age, and exemptions may be pooled. For the next $1,000 worth of goods, a flat 10% rate is assessed; duties vary with the merchandise for anything over $1,400. Included for travelers 21 or older are one liter of alcohol, 100 cigars (non-Cuban), and 200 cigarettes. Only one bottle of perfume trademarked in the United States may be brought in. However, there is no duty on antiques or art over 100 years old. Anything exceeding these limits will be taxed at the port of entry and may be taxed additionally in the traveler's home state. Unlimited amounts of goods from designated "developing" or GSP countries also may be brought in duty-free; check with the U.S. Customs Service, Box 7407, Washington, DC 20044. Gifts valued at under $50 may be mailed to friends or relatives at home duty-free, but not more than one package per day to any one addressee and not including perfumes costing more than $5, or tobacco or liquor.

Canadian residents have a $300 exemption and may also bring in duty-free up to 50 cigars, 200 cigarettes, 2 pounds of tobacco, and 40 ounces of liquor, provided these are declared in writing to customs on arrival and accompany the traveler in hand or checked-through baggage. Personal gifts should be mailed as "Unsolicited Gift—Value under $40." Request the Canadian Customs brochure "I Declare" for further details.

British residents, *see* Customs and Duties in Great Britain.

Traveling with Film

If your camera is new, shoot and develop a few rolls before leaving home. Pack some lens tissue and an extra battery for your built-in light meter. Invest about $10 in a skylight filter; it will protect the lens and also reduce haze.

Hot weather can damage film. If you're driving in summer, don't store film in the glove compartment or on the shelf under the rear window. Put it behind the front seat on the floor, on the side opposite the exhaust pipe.

On a plane trip, never pack unprocessed film in check-in luggage; if your bags get X-rayed, you can say good-bye to your pictures. Always carry undeveloped film with you through security and ask to have it inspected by hand (carry your film in a plastic bag for quick inspection). Inspectors at American airports are required by law to honor requests for hand inspection; abroad, you'll have to depend on the kindness of strangers.

The old airport scanning machines use heavy doses of radiation that can turn a family portrait into an early-morning fog. The newer models—used in all U.S. airports—are safe for anything from five to 500 scans, depending on the speed of your film. The effects are cumulative; you can put the same roll of film through several scans without worry. After five scans, though, you're asking for trouble.

If your film gets fogged and you want an explanation, send it to the National Association of Photographic Manufacturers, 600 Mamaroneck Ave., Harrison, NY 10528. Experts will try to determine what went wrong. This service is free.

Photographing trains, junctions, or railway stations can land you in *serious* trouble in Eastern Europe. Turkish and, to a lesser extent, Greek authorities can also be sensitive. This is equally true of airports. Don't take pictures without making sure it is permitted.

Staying Healthy

There are no serious health risks associated with travel in Europe. However, the Centers for Disease Control (CDC) in Atlanta cautions that most of southern Europe is in the "intermediate" range for risk of contracting traveler's diarrhea. Part of this may be due to an increased consumption of olive oil and wine, which can have a laxative effect on stomachs used to a different diet. The CDC also advises that international travelers swim only in chlorinated swimming pools if there is any question about contamination of local beaches and freshwater lakes.

If you have a health problem that might require purchasing prescription drugs while in Europe, ask your doctor to prescribe the drug by its generic name. Brand names vary widely from country to country.

The International Association for Medical Assistance to Travelers (IAMAT) is a worldwide association offering a list of approved English-speaking doctors whose training meets British and American standards. Contact IAMAT for a list of European physicians and clinics that belong to this network. **In the United States:** 417 Center St., Lewiston, NY 14092, tel. 716/ 754–4883. **In Canada:** 188 Nicklin Rd., Guelph, Ontario NIH 7L5. **In Europe:** Gotthardstrasse 17, 6300 Zug, Switz. Membership is free.

Shots and Medications Inoculations are not needed for Europe. The American Medical Association (AMA) recommends Pepto-Bismol for minor cases of traveler's diarrhea.

Insurance

Travelers may seek insurance coverage in three areas: health and accident, lost luggage, and trip cancellation. Your first step is to review your existing health and home-owner policies; some health insurance plans cover health expenses incurred while traveling, some major medical plans cover emergency transportation, and some home-owner policies cover the theft of luggage.

Health and Accident Several companies offer coverage designed to supplement existing health insurance for travelers:

Carefree Travel Insurance (Box 310, 120 Mineola Blvd., Mineola, NY 11501, tel. 516/294–0220 or 800/645–2424) provides coverage for medical evacuation. It also offers 24-hour medical phone advice.

Health Care Abroad, International Underwriters Group (243 Church St. W., Suite 100D, Vienna, VA 22180, tel. 703/281–9500 or 800/237–6615), offers comprehensive medical coverage, including emergency evacuation for trips of 10–90 days.

International SOS Insurance (Box 11568, Philadelphia, PA 19126, tel. 215/244–1500 or 800/523–8930) does not offer medical insurance but provides medical evacuation services to its clients, who are often international corporations.

Travel Guard International, underwritten by Cygna (1100 Centerpoint Dr., Stevens Point, WI 54481, tel. 715/345–0505 or 800/782–5151), offers medical insurance, with coverage for emergency evacuation when Travel Guard's representatives in the United States say it is necessary.

Lost Luggage Airlines are responsible for lost or damaged property only up to $1,250 per passenger on domestic flights, and $9.07 per pound (or $20 per kilo) for checked baggage on international flights, and up to $400 per passenger for unchecked baggage on international flights. If you're carrying valuables, either take them with you on the airplane or purchase additional insurance for lost luggage. Some airlines will issue additional luggage insurance when you check in, but many do not. Insurance for lost, damaged, or stolen luggage is available through travel agents or directly through various insurance companies. Two that issue luggage insurance are **Tele-Trip** (tel. 800/228–9792), a subsidiary of Mutual of Omaha, and the **Travelers Insurance Co.** (Ticket and Travel Dept., 1 Tower Sq., Hartford, CT 06183, tel. 203/277–0111). Tele-Trip operates sales booths at airports, and also issues insurance through travel agents. Tele-Trip will insure checked luggage for up to 180 days and for $500 to $3,000 valuation. For 1–3 days, the rate for a $500 valuation is $8.25; for 180 days, $100. The Travelers Insurance Co. will insure checked or hand luggage for $500 to $2,000 valuation per person, and also for a maximum of 180 days. Rates for 1–5 days for $500 valuation are $10; for 180 days, $85. Other companies with comprehensive policies include **Access America, Inc.,** a subsidiary of Blue Cross-Blue Shield (Box 807, New York, NY 10163, tel. 800/851–2800); and **Travel Guard International** *(see* Health and Accident Insurance).

Before you go, itemize the contents of each bag in case you need to file an insurance claim. Be certain to put your home or business address on each piece of luggage, including carry-on bags.

If your luggage is lost or stolen and later recovered, the airline must deliver the luggage to your home free of charge.

Trip Cancellation   Flight insurance is often included in the price of a ticket when paid for with American Express, Visa, and other major credit cards. It is usually included in combination travel insurance packages available from most tour operators, travel agents, and insurance agents.

Renting, Leasing, and Purchasing Cars

Renting   It's best to arrange a car rental before you leave. You won't save money by waiting until you arrive in Europe, and you may find the type of car you want is not available at the last minute. If you're flying into a major city and planning to spend some time there before using your car, save money by arranging to pick it up on the day of your departure. You'll have to weigh the added expense of renting a car from a major company with an airport office against the savings on a car from a budget company with offices in town. You could waste precious hours trying to locate the budget company in return for only a small financial saving. If you're arriving and departing from different airports, look for a one-way car rental with no return fees. If you're traveling to more than one country, make sure your rental contract permits you to take the car across borders and that the insurance policy covers you in every country you visit. Be prepared to pay more for a car with an automatic transmission; because they are not as readily available as those with manual transmission, reserve in advance.

Rental rates vary widely and depend on size and model, number of days you use the car, insurance coverage, and whether special drop-off fees are imposed. In most cases, rates quoted include unlimited free mileage and standard liability protection. Not included are Collision Damage Waiver (CDW), which eliminates your deductible payment should you have an accident; personal accident insurance; gasoline; or local taxes. European value-added taxes (VAT) vary from country to country, ranging from zero in Switzerland to a whopping 33.3% in France.

Rental companies usually charge according to the exchange rate of the dollar at the time the car is returned or when the credit card payment is processed. Three companies with special programs to help you hedge against the falling dollar, by guaranteeing advertised rates if you pay in advance, are: **Budget Rent-a-Car**, 3350 Boyington St., Carrollton, TX 75006, tel. 800/527–0700; **Connex Travel International**, 983 Main St., Peekskill, NY 10566, tel. 800/333–3949; and **Cortell International**, 17310 Red Hill Ave., Suite 360, Irvine, CA 92714, tel. 800/228–2535.

Other budget rental companies serving Europe include **Europe by Car**, 1 Rockefeller Plaza, New York, NY 10020, tel. 212/245–1713, 800/223–1516, or, in California, 800/252–9401; **Foremost Euro-Car**, 5430 Van Nuys Blvd., Van Nuys, CA 91404, tel. 800/423–3111; and **Kemwel**, 106 Calvert St., Harrison, NY 10528, tel. 800/678–0678. Other major firms with European rentals include **Avis**, tel. 800/331–1212; **Hertz**, tel. 800/223–6472 or, in New York, 800/654–3001; and **National** or **Europcar**, tel. 800/CAR–RENT. If you are looking for a bargain on a car rental, try **Kemwell,** 106 Calvert St., Harrison, NY 10528, tel. 914/835-5555.

In the United Kingdom, there are offices of **Avis** (Hayes Gate House, Uxbridge Rd., Hayes, Middlesex UB40NJ, tel. 01/848-8733); **Hertz** (Radnor House, 1272 London Rd., London SW16 4XW, tel. 01/679-1799); and **Europcar** (Bushey House, High St., Bushey, WD2 1RE, tel. 01/950-4080).

Driver's licenses issued in the United States and Canada are valid in Europe. Non-EEC nationals must have Green Card insurance *(see* By Car: Frontiers in Getting Around Europe). You might also take out an International Driving Permit before you leave in order to smooth out difficulties if you have an accident or as an additional piece of identification. Permits are available for a small fee through local offices of the **American Automobile Association** (AAA) and the **Canadian Automobile Association** (CAA), or from their main offices: AAA, 8111 Gatehouse Rd., Falls Church, VA 22047-0001, tel. 703/AAA-6000; and CAA, 2 Carlton St., Toronto, Ontario M5B 1K4, tel. 416/964-3170.

Britons driving in Europe should have a valid driver's license. Green Card insurance is a wise buy, though not compulsory for EEC nationals. All drivers must carry their car registration documents and a red warning triangle.

Leasing For trips of 21 days or more, you may save money by leasing a car. With the leasing arrangement, you are technically buying a car and then selling it back to the manufacturer after you've used it. You receive a factory-new car, tax-free, with international registration and extensive insurance coverage. Rates vary with the make and model of car and length of time used. Car leasing programs are offered by Renault, Citroën, and Peugeot in France, and by Volkswagen, Ford, Audi, and Opel, among others, in Belgium. Delivery can be arranged outside of France and Brussels for an additional fee. Before you go, compare long-term rental rates with leasing rates. Remember to add taxes and insurance costs to the car rentals, something you don't have to worry about with leasing. Companies that offer leasing arrangements include Kemwel and Europe by Car, listed above.

Purchasing Given the weakness of the dollar on the international market and the logistical complexities of shipping a car home, the option of purchasing a car abroad is less appealing today than it was a decade ago. The advantage of buying a car in Europe is that you'll get what amounts to a free car rental during your stay in Europe. If you plan to purchase a car in Europe, be certain the prices quoted are for cars built to meet specifications set down by the U.S. Department of Transportation. If not, you will have to go through considerable expense to convert the car before you can legally drive it in the United States. You will also be subject to a U.S. Customs duty. For more information, contact Kemwel or Europe by Car, both listed above, or ask your local car dealer to put you in touch with an importer.

Student and Youth Travel

The **International Student Identity Card** (ISIC) entitles students to youth rail passes, special fees on local transportation, Intra-European student charter flights, and discounts at museums, theaters, sports events, and many other attractions. If purchased in the United States, the $10 card also entitles the holder to $2,000 in emergency medical insurance, plus $100 a day for up to 60 days of hospital coverage. Apply to the **Council on International Educational Exchange** (CIEE), 205 E. 42nd St., 16th floor, New York, NY 10017, tel. 212/661–1414. In Canada, the ISIC is also available for $10 from the **Association of Student Councils,** 187 College St., Toronto, Ontario M5T 1P7.

The **Youth International Educational Exchange Card** (YIEE), issued by the **Federation of International Youth Travel Organizations** (FIYTO), 81 Islands Brugge, DK-2300 Copenhagen S, Denmark, provides similar services to nonstudents under 26 years of age. In the United States, the card costs $10 and is available from CIEE (*see* above) or from **ISE,** Europa House, 802 W. Oregon St., Urbana, IL 61801, tel. 217/344–5863. In Canada, the YIEE card is available from the **Canadian Hostelling Association** (CHA), 333 River Rd., Vanier, Ottawa, Ontario K1L 8H9, tel. 613/476–3844.

An **International Youth Hostel Federation** (IYHF) membership card is the key to inexpensive dormitory-style accommodations at thousands of youth hostels around the world. Hostels provide separate sleeping quarters and are situated in a variety of locations, including converted farmhouses, villas, restored castles, and specially constructed modern buildings. IYHF membership costs $20 a year ($10 a year for people under age 18) and is available in the United States through **American Youth Hostels** (AYH), Box 37613, Washington, DC 20013, tel. 202/783–6161. IYHF also publishes an extensive directory of youth hostels around the world. Economical bicycle tours for small groups of adventurous, energetic students are another popular AYH student travel service. The 16-day tour of England for $1,350 (from New York) is typical. For information on these and other AYH services and publications, contact the AYH at the address above.

Council Travel, a CIEE subsidiary, is the foremost U.S. student travel agency and specializes in low-cost charters and serves as the exclusive U.S. agent for many student airfare bargains and student tours. The 70-page *Student Travel Catalog* and *Council Charter* brochure are available free from any Council Travel office in the United States (enclose $1 postage if ordering by mail). Contact CIEE headquarters at the address above, or Council Travel offices in Amherst, Austin, Berkeley, Boston, Cambridge, Chicago, Dallas, La Jolla, Long Beach, Los Angeles, New York, Portland, Providence, San Diego, San Francisco, and Seattle, to name a few.

The **Educational Travel Center,** another student travel specialist worth contacting for information on student tours, bargain fares, and bookings, may be reached at 438 N. Frances St., Madison, WI 53703, tel. 608/256–5551.

Students who would like to work abroad should contact CIEE's **Work Abroad Department,** at the address given above. The council arranges various types of paid and voluntary work experiences overseas for up to six months. CIEE also sponsors study programs in Europe, Latin America, and Asia, and publishes many books of interest to the student traveler, including *Work, Study, Travel Abroad: The Whole World Handbook* ($8.95 plus $1 postage), *The Teenager's Guide to Study, Travel, and Adventure Abroad* ($9.95 plus $1 postage), and *Volunteer!*

The Comprehensive Guide to Voluntary Service in the U.S. and Abroad ($4.95 plus $1 postage).

The Information Center at the **Institute of International Education** (IIE), 809 UN Plaza, New York, NY 10017, tel. 212/883–8200, has reference books, foreign university catalogues, study-abroad brochures, and other materials that may be consulted by students and nonstudents alike, free of charge. The Information Center is open weekdays 10–4.

IIE administers a variety of grant and study programs offered by U.S. and foreign organizations, and publishes a well-known annual series of study-abroad guides, including *Academic Year Abroad, Vacation Study Abroad,* and *Study in the United Kingdom and Ireland.* The institute also publishes *Teaching Abroad,* a book of employment and study opportunities overseas for U.S. teachers. For a current list of IIE publications, along with prices and ordering information, write to the IIE Publications Service at the address given above. Books must be purchased by mail or in person; telephone orders are not accepted. General information on IIE programs and services is available from its regional offices in Atlanta, Chicago, Denver, Houston, San Francisco, and Washington, DC.

For information on the Eurail Youthpass, *see* Rail Passes.

Traveling with Children

Publications   *A Capital Guide for Kids: A London Guide for Parents with Small Children* by Vanessa Miles (Allison & Busby, 6a Noel St., London W1V 3RB; £1.95).
Children's Guide to London by Christopher Pick (Cadogan Books, 16 Lower Marsh, London SE1 7RJ; $8.50).

Europe with Children by K. Appler (Alexandria Press, Alexandria, VA; $12.95) is less a planning guide than an account of one family's trip.
Family Travel Times is an 8- to 12-page newsletter published 10 times a year by TWYCH (Travel with Your Children, 80 Eighth Ave., New York, NY 10011, tel. 212/206–0688). Subscription includes access to back issues and twice-weekly opportunities to call in for specific advice.
Kids' London by Elizabeth Holt and Molly Perham (St. Martin's Press, $5.95).
Young People's Guide to Munich is a free pamphlet available from the German National Tourist Office (747 Third Ave., New York, NY 10017, tel. 212/308–3300).

Family Travel Organizations   **American Institute for Foreign Study** (AIFS; 102 Greenwich Ave., Greenwich, CT 06830, tel. 203/869–9090) offers family vacation programs in England, France, Switzerland, and Austria specifically designed for parents and children.
Families Welcome! (1416 Second Ave., New York, NY 10021, tel. 212/861–2500 or 800/472–8999) is a travel agency that arranges England and France tours brimming with family-oriented choices and activities.
The French Experience (171 Madison Ave., New York, NY 10016, tel. 212/683–2445) is an organization that understands family needs.

Getting There   On international flights, children under two years not occupying a seat pay 10% of the adult fare. Various discounts apply to children 2–12. Reserve a seat behind the plane's bulkhead, where you'll have more leg room and can usually fit a bassinet (supplied by the airline). At the same time, inquire about special children's meals or snacks, offered by most airlines. (For a rundown on children's services offered by 46 airlines, see TWYCH's "Airline Guide," in the February 1988 issue of *Family Travel Times.*) Ask the airline in advance if you can bring aboard your child's carseat. (For the booklet "Child/Infant Safety Seats Acceptable for Use in Aircraft," contact Community and Consumer Liaison Division, APA–400 Federal Aviation Administration, Washington, DC 20591, tel. 202/267–3479.)

Hotels **Novotel** hotels in Europe permit up to two children to stay free in their parents' room and get a free breakfast, too. Many Novotel properties have playgrounds. (International reservations, tel. 800/221–4542.)

Sofitel hotels in Europe offer a free second room for children during July and August and over the Christmas holiday. (International reservations, tel. 800/221–4542.)

Happy Family Swiss Hotels are 22 properties in Switzerland that have joined together to welcome families, offering outstanding programs for children at reduced prices. A brochure on these hotels is available from the Swiss National Tourist Office (608 Fifth Ave., New York, NY 10019, tel. 212/757–5944).

Club Med (40 W. 57th St., New York, NY 10019, tel. 800/CLUB–MED) has "Baby Clubs" (from age four months), "Mini Clubs" (for ages four to six or eight, depending on the resort), and "Kids Clubs" (for ages eight and up during school holidays) at many of its resort villages in France, Italy, Switzerland, and Spain.

In Germany, families should consider any one of the **Schloss** (castle) hotels, many of which are located on parklike grounds. United States representatives: **Europa Hotels and Tours** (tel. 800/523–9570 or, in Washington, 206/485–6985); **DER Tours, Inc.** (tel. 800/937–1234 or, in California, 213/479–4411).

CIGA hotels (Reservations, tel. 800/221–2340) has 22 properties in Italy, all of which welcome families.

Villa Rentals **At Home Abroad, Inc.,** 405 E. 56th St., Suite 6H, New York, NY 10022, tel. 212/421–9165.

Villas International, 71 W. 23rd St., New York, NY 10010, tel. 212/929–7585 or 800/221–2260.

Hideaways, Int'l., Box 1270, Littleton, MA 01460, tel. 508/486–8955.

B. & D. de Vogue, 1830 S. Mooney Blvd., –113, Visalia, CA 93277, tel. 209/733–7119 or 800/727–4748.

Meeting Points, 5515 S.E. Milwaukee Ave., Portland, OR 97207, tel. 503/233–1224.

Vacances en Campagne/Vacanze in Italia/Heritage of England, Box 297, Falls Village, CT 06031, tel. 203/824–5155 or 800/553–5405.

Italian Villa Rentals, Box 1145, Bellevue, WA 98009, tel. 206/827–3694.

Home Exchange See *Home Exchanging: A Complete Sourcebook for Travelers at Home or Abroad* by James Dearing (Globe Pequot Press, Box Q, Chester, CT 06412, tel. 800/243–0495 or in CT 800/962–0973).

Baby-sitting To find out about recommended child-care arrangements, first
Services ask your hotel concierge. Also call the American embassy or consulate for a listing of child-care agencies with English-

speaking personnel. Local tourist offices, especially in Germany, maintain an updated list of local baby-sitters.

Pen Pals For names of children in Europe to whom your children can write before your trip, send a self-addressed, stamped envelope to: **International Friendship League,** 55 Mt. Vernon St., Boston, MA 02108, tel. 617/523–4273.

Hints for Disabled Travelers

The Information Center for Individuals with Disabilities (2743 Wormwood St., Boston, MA 02210, tel. 617/727–5540) offers useful problem-solving assistance, including lists of travel agents who specialize in tours for the disabled.

Moss Rehabilitation Hospital Travel Information Service (12th St. and Taber Rd., Philadelphia, PA 19141, tel. 215/329–5715) provides information on tourist sights, transportation, and accommodations around the world. The fee is $5 for each destination. Allow one month for delivery.

Mobility International (Box 3551, Eugene, OR 97403, tel. 503/343–1284) has information on accommodations, organized study, and so forth, around the world.

The Society for the Advancement of Travel for the Handicapped (26 Court St., Brooklyn, NY 11242, tel. 718/858–5483) offers access information. Annual membership costs $40, or $25 for senior travelers and students. Send a stamped, self-addressed envelope.

The Itinerary (Box 1084, Bayonne, NJ 07002, tel. 201/858–3400) is a bimonthly travel magazine for the disabled.

Access to the World: A Travel Guide for the Handicapped by Louise Weiss is useful. Though out of date, it is available from Facts on File, 460 Park Ave. S., New York, NY 10016, tel. 212/683–2244.

Frommer's Guide for Disabled Travelers is also helpful but dated.

Hints for Older Travelers

The American Association of Retired Persons (AARP, 1909 K St. NW, Washington, DC 20049, tel. 202/662–4850) has two programs for independent travelers: (1) the Purchase Privilege Program, which entitles members to discounts on hotels, airfare, car rentals, and sightseeing; and (2) the AARP Motoring Plan, which offers emergency aid and trip routing information for an annual fee of $33.95 per couple. The AARP also arranges group tours, including apartment living in Europe, through two companies: **Olson-Travelworld** (5855 Green Valley Circle, Culver City, CA 90230, tel. 800/227–7737) and **RFD, Inc.** (4401 W. 110th St., Overland Park, KS 66211, tel. 800/448–7010). AARP members must be 50 or older. Annual dues are $5 per person or per couple.

Elderhostel (80 Boylston St., Suite 400, Boston, MA 02116, tel. 617/426–7788) is an innovative 13-year-old program for people 60 and older. Participants live in dorms on some 1,200 campuses around the world. Mornings are devoted to lectures and seminars; afternoons, to sightseeing and field trips. The all-inclusive fee for trips of 2–3 weeks, including room, board, tuition, and round-trip transportation, is $1,700–$3,200.

Travel Industry and Disabled Exchange (TIDE, 5435 Donna Ave., Tarzana, CA 91356, tel. 818/343–6339) is an industry-based organization with a $15 per-person annual membership fee. Members receive a quarterly newsletter and information on travel agencies and tours.

Travel Tips for Senior Citizens (U.S. Dept. of State Publication 8970, revised September 1987) is available for $1 from the Superintendent of Documents, U.S. Government Printing Office, Washington, DC 20402.

The Discount Guide for Travelers over 55 by Caroline and Walter Weintz (Dutton, $7.95) lists helpful addresses, package tours, reduced rate car rentals, and so forth, in the United States and abroad.

Arriving and Departing

Because the air routes between North America and Europe are among the world's most heavily traveled, the passenger can choose from many airlines and fares. But fares change with stunning rapidity, so consult your travel agent on which bargains are currently available.

From North America by Plane

Be certain to distinguish among (1) nonstop flights—no changes, no stops; (2) direct flights—no changes but one or more stops; and (3) connecting flights—two or more planes, two or more stops.

Airlines The U.S. airlines that serve the major cities in Europe are **TWA,** tel. 800/892–4141; **Pan Am,** tel. 800/221–1111; **American Airlines,** tel. 800/433–7300; **Northwest,** tel. 800/447–4747; and **Delta,** tel. 800/241–4141.

Many European national airlines fly directly from the United States to their home countries. The biggest advantage in arriving on a home airline is that the landing privileges are often better, as are the facilities provided at main airports. Here are the U.S. telephone numbers of those airlines that have representation in the United States; most of the numbers are toll-free.

Austria: Austrian Airlines, tel. 800/843–0002
Belgium: Sabena Belgian World Airlines, tel. 800/632–8050
Cyprus: Cyprus Airways, tel. 212/714–2190
Czechoslovakia: Czechoslovak Airlines (CSA), tel. 212/682–5833
Denmark: Scandinavian Airlines (SAS), tel. 800/221–2350
Finland: Finnair, tel. 800/223–5700
France: Air France, tel. 800/237–2747
Great Britain: British Airways, tel. 800/247–9297; Virgin Atlantic, tel. 800/862–8621
Greece: Olympic Airways, tel. 800/223–1226
Holland: KLM Royal Dutch Airlines, tel. 800/777–5553
Hungary: Malev Hungarian Airlines, tel. 212/757–6446
Iceland: Icelandair, tel. 800/223–5500
Ireland: Aer Lingus, 800/223–6537
Italy: Alitalia, tel. 800/442–5860

Malta: Air Malta, tel. 415/362–2929
Norway: Scandinavian Airlines (SAS), tel. 800/221–2350
Poland: LOT Polish Airlines, tel. 212/869–1074
Portugal: TAP Air Portugal, tel. 800/221–7370
Romania: Tarom Romanian Airlines, tel. 212/687–6013
Spain: Iberia Airlines, tel. 800/772–4642
Sweden: Scandinavian Airlines, tel. 800/221–2350
Switzerland: Swissair, tel. 800/221–4750
Turkey: THY Turkish Airlines, tel. 212/986–5050
West Germany: Lufthansa, tel. 800/645–3880
Yugoslavia: JAT Yugoslav Airlines, tel. 800/752–6528

Flying Time From New York: 6½ hours to London and 7–8 hours to Scandinavian capitals. From Chicago: 8½ hours to London, 10–11 hours to Scandinavian capitals. From Los Angeles: 10 hours to London, 12–13 hours to Scandinavian capitals.

Discount Flights The major airlines offer a range of tickets that can increase the price of any given seat by more than 300%, depending on the day of purchase. As a rule, the further in advance you buy the ticket, the less expensive it is and the greater the penalty (up to 100%) for canceling. Check with airlines for details.

The best buy is not necessarily an APEX (advance purchase) ticket on one of the major airlines, because these tickets carry certain restrictions: They must be bought in advance (usually 21 days); they restrict your travel, usually with a minimum stay of seven days and a maximum of 90; and they also penalize you for changes—voluntary or not—in your travel plans. But if you can work around these drawbacks (and most travelers can), they are among the best-value fares available.

Charter flights offer the lowest fares but often depart only on certain days, and seldom on time. Though you may be able to arrive at one city and return from another, you may lose all or most of your money if you cancel your trip. Travel agents can make bookings, though they won't encourage you, since commissions are lower than on scheduled flights. Checks should, as a rule, be made out to the bank and specific escrow account for your flight. To make sure your payment stays in this account until your departure, don't use credit cards as a method of payment. Don't sign up for a charter flight unless you've checked with a travel agency about the reputation of the packager. It's particularly important to know the packager's policy concerning refunds should a flight be canceled. One of the most popular charter operators is **Council Charter** (tel. 800/223–7402), a division of CIEE (Council on International Educational Exchange). Other companies advertise in Sunday travel sections of newspapers.

Somewhat more expensive—but up to 50% below the cost of APEX fares—are tickets purchased through consolidators, companies that buy blocks of tickets on scheduled airlines and sell them at wholesale prices. Here again, you may lose all or most of your money if you change plans, but at least you will be on a regularly scheduled flight with less risk of cancellation than on a charter. Once you've made your reservation, call the airline to confirm it. Among the best-known consolidators are **UniTravel** (tel. 800/325–2222) and **Access International** (250 W. 57th St., Suite 511, New York, NY 10107, tel. 212/333–7280). Others advertise in newspaper Sunday travel sections.

A third option is to join a travel club that offers special discounts to its members. Three such organizations are **Moments Notice** (40 E. 49th St., New York, NY 10017, tel. 212/486–0503); **Discount Travel International** (114 Forrest Ave., Narberth, PA 19072, tel. 215/668–2182); and **Worldwide Discount Travel Club** (1674 Meridian Ave., Suite 300, Miami Beach, FL 33139, tel. 305/534–2082). These cut-rate tickets should be compared with APEX tickets on the major airlines.

Enjoying the Flight If you're lucky enough to be able to sleep on a plane, it makes sense to fly at night. Many experienced travelers, however, prefer to take a morning flight to Europe and arrive in the evening, just in time for a good night's sleep. Because the air on a plane is dry, it helps, while flying, to drink a lot of nonalcoholic beverages; drinking alcohol contributes to jet lag. Feet swell at high altitudes, so it's a good idea to remove your shoes at the beginning of your flight. Sleepers usually prefer window seats to curl up against; those who like to move about the cabin ask for aisle seats. Bulkhead seats (adjacent to the exit signs) have more legroom, but seat trays are attached to the arms of your seat rather than to the back of the seat in front.

Smoking If smoking bothers you, ask for a seat far from the smoking section. If a U.S. airline representative tells you there are no seats available in the nonsmoking section, insist on one: Government regulations require airlines to find seats for all nonsmokers.

Luggage Regulations Airlines allow each passenger two pieces of check-in luggage and one carry-on piece on international flights from North America. Each piece of check-in luggage cannot exceed 62 inches (length + width + height) or weigh more than 70 pounds. The carry-on luggage cannot exceed 45 inches (length + width + height) and must fit under the seat or in the overhead luggage compartment. On flights within Europe, you are allowed to check a total of 44 pounds, regardless of luggage size. Requirements for carry-on luggage are the same as for those on transatlantic flights.

For information on luggage insurance, *see* Insurance in Before You Go.

Labeling Luggage Put your home or business address on each piece of luggage, including hand baggage. If your lost luggage is recovered, the airline must deliver it to your home, at no charge to you.

From North America by Ship

Cunard Line (555 Fifth Ave., New York, NY 10017, tel. 800/221–4770 or 212/880–7545) operates four ships that make transatlantic crossings. One is the *Queen Elizabeth 2*, the only ocean liner that makes regular transatlantic crossings. The others make repositioning crossings twice a year, as one cruise season ends in Europe and another begins in North America. The *QE2* makes regular crossings April through December, between Baltimore, Boston, and New York City, and Southampton, England. Arrangements for the *QE2* can include one-way airfare. The *Sea Goddess I* and *Sea Goddess II* sail to and from Madeira, Portugal, and St. Thomas in the U.S. Virgin Islands, for their repositioning crossings. The *Vistafjord* sails to and from Marseilles, France, and Fort Lauderdale, Florida, on its repositioning crossings. Cunard Line offers fly/cruise packages and pre- and post-land packages. For the European cruise season, ports of call include Southampton, Madeira, Marseilles, Hamburg, Genoa, Rome, Venice, Naples, Monte Carlo, Malaga, Piraeus (Athens), Copenhagen, and Stockholm. Ports of call vary with the ship.

Royal Viking Line (750 Battery St., San Francisco, CA 94111, tel. 800/634-8000) has three ships that cruise out of European ports. Two of the ships make repositioning crossings to and from Fort Lauderdale and Lisbon, Portugal. Fly/cruise packages are available. Major ports of call, depending on the ship, are Copenhagen, Stockholm, Bergen, Hamburg, Leningrad, Barcelona, Venice, Dubrovnik, Villefranche, Corfu, and Lisbon.

American Star Lines (660 Madison Ave., New York, NY 10021, tel. 800/356-7677 and, in New York, 212/644-7900) makes transatlantic crossings in spring and fall to and from Greece and Barbados (in the British West Indies). The crossings are regular cruises, with ports of call in Portugal, Italy, Turkey, and the Greek islands. Summer cruises are from Piraeus (Athens), to the Greek islands, and Turkey. Fly/cruise packages are available.

Check the travel pages of your Sunday newspaper for other cruise ships that sail to Europe.

From the United Kingdom by Plane

Air travel from Britain to continental Europe has become cheaper, more convenient, and more competitive in recent years, thanks largely to the British government's determination to break down the cozy system of intergovernmental fare setting. This system, which only began to break up in the late 1980s, was aimed at protecting the earnings of national, government-owned airlines. Increasingly, however, while air travel in Europe is still substantially more expensive than in the United States, airlines are being given more freedom to compete without government interference. Britain sold its national carrier, British Airways, (BA), in 1987, and since then BA has pioneered lower fares and better consumer service.

More governments are beginning to let airlines compete—good news for the traveler—and this applies not just to competition between state- and privately owned carriers but also to competition between scheduled and charter airlines. From Britain, for example, rules against "seat-only" charters—that is, tickets for charter flights that are not sold as part of a package tour including prebooked accommodation—have been lifted, and these can be a very cost-effective way of getting to some European destinations, particularly those Mediterranean ones popular with British vacationers.

Scheduled Airlines If time rather than money is your main consideration, then scheduled flights are a better option than charters. London, with its two main airports—Heathrow and Gatwick—and three subsidiary airports—Luton and Stansted farther away from the city, and London City Airport only six miles from the City of London—is Europe's biggest air hub, and frequent scheduled services connect it with virtually every other European capital, most major regional cities, and most resort destinations. Generally speaking, the smaller the city, the less frequently it is likely to be served, but most European cities have daily service by BA and at least one other airline.

New competition by up-and-coming airlines like British Midland and Air Europe, both privately owned, are determined to grab up customers from BA, meaning that there are many options to choose from. Travelers can make substantial savings if they are prepared to accept certain conditions.

These smaller airlines have pioneered routes to European capitals from regional British airports. Manchester, for instance, has become a busy northern hub for several carriers, with shuttle flights to London and several flights a day to Amsterdam and other European points. From Scotland, there are daily flights from Edinburgh to Paris by Air France and to Copenhagen by SAS. Both Glasgow and Edinburgh are linked to London by frequent shuttle flights by BA, British Midland, and others.

Most airline schedules in Europe cater mainly to business travelers who want to fly at clearly defined peak times. But the airlines offer lower fares to leisure travelers who can use off-peak flights. Look for better fares on mid-day flights and ask about cheaper weekend fares. Some of these—called PEX and Super PEX—can be less than half the normal coach-class fare. Most of these bargain rates require a mandatory Saturday night at your destination.

Remember, few flights over Europe last more than four hours; most are less than two hours long. For such short flights, you may feel that flying first or business class, even if it's within your budget, is an unnecessary luxury. Remember, too, that on most European airlines, business class is open to anyone traveling on a normal coach-class fare (called full economy in Europe).

Fares between London and Amsterdam are the cheapest in Europe. Amsterdam's Schiphol Airport also has excellent onward connections to other European cities. Fares from London to Brussels are also lower than the European average, mile for mile, and there is an increasing range of competitive service to Frankfort and to Paris.

The rule of thumb is that the cheaper the fare, the more likely it is to carry a burden of restrictions. *Always* make sure you know what these are—ask the airline or travel agent before you buy the ticket.

Some of the more common conditions include a mandatory overnight stay at your destination; no refund, or reduced refund, if you cancel your reservation; no change of itinerary allowed once you have booked; full payment at time of booking; and, most commonly, a minimum stay requirement—usually seven days or over at least one Saturday night.

Charter Airlines Charter airlines offer much cheaper fares to Europe than the scheduled carriers, but the rules that bind them are more restrictive. While the British government turns a blind eye to sales of seat-only charter tickets, some European governments still require proof that you have bought an inclusive package vacation rather than just a flight.

Most of the seat-only agencies will therefore give you a voucher stating that you have accommodations at a certain hotel. This is to comply with the rules—it won't necessarily get you a bed, even if you can find the hotel in question!

Greece specifically has expressed its determination to stamp out seat-only traffic by threatening passengers using such tickets with fines or deportation under international rules on charter sales. Its implementation of this rule has, though, been patchy so far.

Charter flights are by far the cheapest form of air transportation to main vacation destinations—particularly in the Mediterranean—and some of the charter fares available to last-minute buyers compare favorably even with bus or rail fares. To such destinations as Spain, Greece, Turkey, or Italy, charter flights represent big saavings over scheduled fars because these countries are zealously protective of their national carriers and oppose the introduction of cheap scheduled fares by BA or other British carriers.

The main drawback of traveling by charter is its rigid timetabling. Your return flight will be seven, 14, or 21 days from your departure date. The cheapest flights leave at inconvenient times—mainly in the early hours of the morning—and, in London, from airports a long way from the city center, such as Luton. Another disadvantage to charter flights is that they can be seriously unreliable timekeepers. Delays of several hours are quite common, and a vacation can easily be ruined by the frustration of having to hang around a crowded airport that has inadequate facilities for handling large crowds for long periods.

Air-traffic control systems and staff overloads caused major delays on U.K. flights to Europe in summer 1988 and although steps were taken in 1989 to ease the problems, the various authorities admitted there was no short-term solution and that more delays were inevitable into the 1990s as air traffic continues to grow.

Arrival airports are often resorts rather than capital or major cities. In Spain, most charters fly to the Mediterranean coast rather than to Madrid or Seville; in Portugal, most flights arrive in the Algarve resort area rather than Lisbon. In Greece, this system can be an advantage rather than a drawback—most flights go to the islands rather than to Athens, so if your destination is, for example, Mykonos or Crete, you can fly there direct by charter without having to transfer to domestic flights or ferries at Athens.

Charters bought at the last minute can be extremely cheap—check in travel agents' windows or in the classified sections of the *London Evening Standard* for cheap late-booking deals. Some of these may be so inexpensive that you may consider discarding the round-trip half of the ticket and traveling onward in Europe from your arrival point, rather than coming back to London.

From the United Kingdom by Car

Traveling by car in Europe has outstanding advantages, not the least of which is freedom from dependence on public transportation networks, and the ability to explore off the beaten track and away from major cities.

For advice on whether to bring your own car, or to buy or rent one on your trip, *see* Renting, Leasing and Purchasing Cars in Before You Go.

Most people's reason for traveling by car is to see as much as possible, and for that reason the shortest sea routes—from Dover to Calais and Boulogne—will be the best bet, especially for first-time visitors to Europe. However, if you plan to tour Scandinavia, you may find it worthwhile to travel by sea to Esbjerg in Denmark, or Gothenburg in Sweden; similarly, if your target is the Iberian Peninsula (Spain and Portugal), sailing to Santander cuts out a long drive through France.

Ferries are "ro-ro"—roll-on, roll-off—and you must book ahead if you are traveling by car; rates vary according to the length of your vehicle, the time of your crossing, and whether you plan to travel in peak, shoulder, or low season. Morning and evening crossings in the summer months are most expensive, and national holidays should be avoided where possible.

Both the **Automobile Association** (Fanum House, Basingstoke, Hants. RG21 2EA; tel. 0256/20123) and the **Royal Automobile Club** (RAC Motoring Services Ltd., 49 Pall Mall, London SW1Y 5JG, tel. 0800/400432) operate on-the-spot breakdown repair services and have tow facilities to get you and your car to your destination within the United Kingdom in case of serious breakdown. The cost of basic membership is £26.50 and £32.50, respectively.

From the United Kingdom by Ferry/Ship

Ferry routes for passengers and vehicles link the North Sea, English Channel, and Irish Sea ports with almost all of Britain's maritime neighbors.

The Fast Routes By far the busiest and, for most visitors, the most convenient routes are those connecting the English Channel ports with France and Belgium. The fastest services are the Hovercraft routes between Dover and Calais, making the 22-mile crossing in around 40 minutes with both passengers and cars. Another high-tech route is the passengers-only Dover–Ostend Jetfoil service operated by the Gelbian company RTM that is timed to connect with London–Brussels trains. This is bookable through P&O European Ferries.

While making the crossing in less than half the time of conventional ferry vessels, both the Hovercraft and the Jetfoil are more expensive and more likely to be canceled or delayed by bad weather, especially in winter. It is advisable to book in advance if you're intending to take a car across on peak summer (July and August weekends are the busiest) or Easter sailings. These are also the most expensive times to travel.

To France In addition to the fast route services, travelers to France have a choice of crossings, ranging from the **Sally Lines** service between Ramsgate and Dunkirk in the north, to the **Brittany**

Ferries route between Portsmouth and St. Malo in Brittany. If Paris is your final destination, Calais and Boulogne are the most convenient entry ports; they are linked by an excellent freeway *(autoroute)* to Paris, and ferries connect with trains at the port for travelers without cars.

Sailing to St. Malo cuts out the rather dull drive through northern Franc and delivers you directly to Brittany. The crossing, however, takes about nine hours as compared with two or three hours for the shortest Channel ferry cossings. Furthermore, sailings are much less frequent (every two days as opposed to several times a day), and for passengers without cars the rail connections onward into France are not as good as those at Calais, Boulogne, or Dieppe. There is also a route between Plymouth, in the west of England, and Roscoff in Brittany. It takes six hours.

To Spain and Portugal Brittany Ferries, which runs the St. Malo service, also sails three times a week from Plymouth to Santander in northern Spain. The crossing takes 24 hours and the line's cruise ferries offer economy and luxury cabins as well as entertainment facilities that include a cinema and restaurants. If you are traveling by car and plan to tour Spain, this route offers you the option of looping back through France and returning to Britain without retracing your tracks. Onward travel into Spain without a car, however, will be time-consuming and is really an option only for those with plenty of time to spare.

To Northern Europe For travelers heading north to Germany, the Netherlands, or Scandinavia, there are ferry routes linking British east coast ports with Europe's North Sea coast. Crossings are longer than English Channel routes, and most North Sea ferry lines have adopted the ferry-cruise concept, with cabins in varying degrees of comfort, and on-board facilities that can include duty-free shopping, bars, restaurants, discos, and casinos.

Main operators between the United Kingdom and the Netherlands are **Olau Line,** which sails from Sheerness; **North Sea Ferries,** sailing from Hull; and **Sealink,** sailing from Harwich. The main Dutch ports are Rotterdam, Hook of Holland, and Vlissingen. All three Dutch ports have excellent connections to Amsterdam by road and rail.

Scandinavian Seaways sails from Harwich and Newcastle to the Danish west coast port of Esbjerg and also to Gothenburg in Sweden. The sea voyage to Gothenburg takes just under 24 hours, and the port is an excellent jumping-off place for a tour of Northern Scandinavia—Sweden, Norway, and Finland—by car. **Fred Olsen** has a Harwich-Oslo (Norway) service, and **Norway Line** has a summer-only Newcastle-Stavanger-Bergen (Norway) route.

To Germany If northern Germany is on your itinerary, sail Scandinavian Seaways to Esbjerg and Olau Line, North Sea Ferries, or Sealink to the Dutch ports. For southern Germany and Austria, sail to a northern French port and cut across France to Strasbourg. Scandinavian Seaways has the only direct service (Harwich–Hamburg) to Germany.

Passengers without cars will have little trouble finding berths at short notice at any time of year. Peak traffic is in the summer months and during British school breaks, but the ferry lines increase services accordingly. If you are traveling with a car, book ahead—either directly with the ferry line or through a travel agent. Times to avoid if possible are British national holidays, and the school summer vacation period from late July until early September.

To Ireland Ferry lines (including **B+I Line, Sealink, P&O European Ferries,** and **Belfast Ferries**) also link British west coast ports with the Republic of Ireland and with Northern Ireland. Motorists traveling within the British Isles can cross from Stranraer or Cairnryan in Scotland to Larne in Northern Ireland, drive through the Republic, and re-enter the United Kingdom via the Cork–Swansea route (**Swansea Cork Ferries**)—or vice versa. Cork has a ferry connection to St. Malo as well, so motorists can use this French connection to travel to the Continent.

Cruises Fewer cruise ships proper, as opposed to luxury ferries, now sail from British ports for European waters. However, **CTC Lines** operates a winter cruise from Southampton, England, to Australia, with stops at Naples and Piraeus (Athens). It is possible to book these sectors and travel on independently, or fly back to the United Kingdom as part of the fare package.

Useful Addresses For information on the services mentioned above, contact:

B+I Line (Reliance House, Water St., Liverpool L2 8TP, tel. 051/227–3131).

Belfast Ferries (47 Donegall Quay, Belfast BT1 3ED, tel. 0232/326045).

Brittany Ferries (Brittany Ferry Centre, Wharf Rd., Portsmouth, Hants. PO2 8RU, tel. 0705/819416).

Fred Olsen (Crown House, Crown St., Ipswich, Suffolk IP1 3HB, tel. 0473/233044).

Hoverspeed (Maybrook House, Queens Gardens, Dover, Kent CT17 7UQ, tel. 01/554–7061).

North Sea Ferries (King George Dock, Hedon Rd., Hull HU9 5QA, tel. 0482/796145).

Norway Line (Tyne Commission Quay, North Shields NE29 6EA, tel. 091/296–1313).

Olau Line (Ferry Terminal, Sheerness, Kent ME12 1SN, tel. 0795/666666).

P&O European Ferries (Channel View Rd., Dover, Kent CT17 9TJ, tel. 0800/456456).

Sally Line (Argyle Centre, York St., Ramsgate CT11 9DS, tel. 0800/636465).

Scandinavian Seaways (Scandinavia House, Parkeston Quay, Harwich, CO12 4QG, tel. 0255/554681).

Sealink (163/203 Eversholt St., London NW1 1BG, tel. 01/387–1234).

Swansea Cork Ferries (Box 340, Poole, Dorset BH15 4DD, tel. 0202/681818).

From the United Kingdom by Train

Air travel may offer the fastest point-to-point service, car travel the greatest freedom, and bus transportation the lowest fares, but there is still an unparalleled air of romance about setting off for Europe by train from one of the historic London stations.

Boat trains timed to meet ferries at Channel ports leave London from Victoria, Waterloo, Paddington, and Charing Cross stations and connect with onward trains at the main French and Belgian ports. Calais and Boulogne have the best quick connections for Paris (total journey time about six to seven hours using the cross-Channel Hovercraft); the Dover-Ostend Jetfoil service is the fastest rail connection to Brussels (about 5½ hours, station to station) with good rail connections to Germany, northern France, the German Democratic Republic, Poland, and the U.S.S.R.

Boat trains connecting with ferries from Harwich to the Dutch and Danish North Sea ports leave from London/Liverpool Street; there are good rail connections from the Dutch ports to Amsterdam and onward to Germany and Belgium, and south to France.

For the Republic of Ireland, trains connecting with the ferry services across the Irish Sea leave from London/Paddington.

One-way and return city-to-city tickets, including rail and ferry fares, can be booked in the United States through **BritRail,** either directly or through your travel agent. If you are traveling on one of the European rail passes bookable in the United States or in Britain, you may be entitled to free or discounted ferry crossings (*see* Getting Around Europe By Train).

If all international rail journeys have a certain glamour, the "Venice Simplon-Orient Express," leaving London/Victoria for the Channel crossing and arriving in Venice 32 hours later after a spectacular journey over the Alps, must be the most glamorous of all. This reconditioned vintage train leaves twice weekly and costs upward from £620 for a one-way journey.

Useful Addresses   For European rail information, contact **InterCity Europe,** the international wing of **BritRail,** at London/Victoria station: information, tel. 01/834-2345; reservations, tel. 01/828-9892. Bookings can be made by phone using American Express, MasterCard, and Visa.

From the United Kingdom by Bus

Excellent freeways (motorways) in the United Kingdom link London with the English Channel ferry ports and make bus travel—connecting with fast ferry, Jetfoil, or Hovercraft crossings—only a little slower than rail travel on the shorter routes into Europe.

Bus travel to cities such as Paris, Brussels, Amsterdam, Rotterdam, and Bruges is by fast and comfortable modern buses with reclining seats, air-conditioning, video entertainment, and airplane-style refreshment carts. There ar frequent departures from central London pickup points. Fares by bus are a good deal less than the equivalent rail fare.

Eurolines—a consortium of bus operators that includes the British companies **Wallace Arnold, National Express,** and Grey Green, as well as Dutch, Belgian, and French lines—offers a range of day and night services linking London with Amsterdam, Paris, Antwerp, Brussels, and other points en route. Night services to Paris take about 10¼ hours; overnight journey time to Amsterdam is a little more than 13 hours.

Faster **Citysprint** daytime crossings use the Dover–Ostend Jetfoil service en route to Amsterdam, reducing journey time to a little more than eight hours. The fast Hoverspeed crossing to France cuts the day trip time to Paris to just under seven hours. There are also one-day round-trips to Antwerp and Brussels and "Eurobreakaway" holiday packages with accommodations for two or three nights in Paris, Amsterdam, and Brussels.

National Express uses Sealink British Ferries connections to the Republic of Ireland. A connecting bus service in Ireland is operated by **Bus Eireann.** Sailings are from Fishguard to Rosslare—a 3½-hour crossing. The onward service goes via Waterford and Cork to Killarney and Tralee.

There are summer coach tours to the Spanish vacaton resorts, aimed mainly at British families on a tight vacation budget. If you, too, are on a budget, these can be an inexpensive way of getting to Spain. The same is true for the winter coaches that run to Europe's less expensive ski destinations, notably Andorra and some Italian resorts.

Longer-haul coachs operate to Greece, aiming mainly at the student and backpacker market, but these tend to be less comfortable and, to a certain extent, less safe. Roads deteriorate raplidly once you leave Western Europe, and the overused and narrow main highway through Yugoslavia is to be avoided. Coach travel to Greece and Turkey is only for the really budget-conscious, and even then the savings on the lowest charter airfare are not very great; return bus fare to Athens, costing about £122, or to Istanbul at £175 (low season), is only £30 or so cheaper than the lowest airfare.

Both Eurolines and Hoverspeed City Sprint services are bookable in person at **National Express** offices at Victoria Coach Station (52 Grosvenor Gardens, London SW1, opposite Victoria Rail Station) and at the **Coach Travel Centre** (13 Regent St., London SW1, for credit card reservations, tel. 01/824 –8657; inquiries, tel. 01/730-0202). Or book at any National Express agent throughout Britain.

Getting Around Europe

By Car

Touring Europe by car has tremendous advantages over other ways of seeing the Continent. You can go where you want, when you want, traveling at your own pace, free of the petty restrictions of timetables. But there are pitfalls, too. For the American driver, used to a uniform system of signs and traffic rules from coast to coast, and accustomed to being able to ask directions in English, Europe can be a bewildering experience. On the excellent freeways of northern and central Europe, it's possible to drive through three or four countries in less time than it would take to cross one of the larger of the U.S. states—which means that in one day you may have to cope with perhaps four different languages and four sets of traffic rules!

Road Conditions In general, the richer European countries—France, Germany, Holland, Denmark, the Benelux countries, the United Kingdom, and Italy—all have excellent national highway systems. In Spain, freeway building is proceeding rapidly and roads are much better than they were even 10 years ago.

By contrast, Greece has just two stretches of freeway-type road—the Odos Ethnikos, or National Road, between Athens and Thessaloniki, and the main road between Athens and Patras.

The Irish Republic's nearest equivalent to freeways is its National Primary Routes, but the low speed limit of 55 mph reflects the fact that their general size and standard falls below the usual European freeway network. Of the Western European countries, Portugal still lags furthest behind in freeway building, but the factor that holds it back—it is the poorest country in western Europe—also means that far fewer people own cars, so its relatively poor roads are also less crowded.

In Scandinavia, the roads vary according to how far north they are. The harsh winters crack road surfaces in the far north of Norway, Sweden, and Finland. Minor roads have bumps and dips. Otherwise Scandinavia's main roads are well-surfaced and refreshingly traffic-free.

Traffic Conditions On the freeway, U.S. drivers may find the pace of European traffic alarming. Speed limits in most countries are set much higher than those in the United States. Even on British motorways, where the upper limit is a very conservative 70 mph, it is not uncommon to be passed by vehicles traveling 15–20 mph faster than that. On German *autobahns*, French *autoroutes*, or Italian *autostrade*, cars in the fast lane are often moving at 100 mph. Much of the time traffic is heavier than is common on U.S. freeways outside major city rush hours.

Consequently, most tourists will find it more rewarding to avoid the freeways and use the alternative main routes. On these roads, where traffic moves more slowly, driving at a more leisurely pace is possible, and stopping en route is easier. This can also save money; many European freeways (such as those of France, Spain, Italy, and Greece) are toll roads, and a day's drive on them can be expensive. If you break down on any of the European highways, you can expect to pay a hefty fee for towing unless you have prudently joined one of the motorist plans offered by one of the many national associations such as the AA or RAC in Britain (*see* From the United Kingdom by Car in Getting to Europe).

As in many U.S. states, traffic officers in most European countries (with a few exceptions, such as the United Kingdom) are empowered to fine you on the spot for traffic violations. The language barrier will not make your case any easier.

In Spain and Greece, make sure you carry insurance that provides bail bond in case of an accident. When driving a rental car in Greece, beware of damaging the underside of the vehicle on Greek roads, which are among the worst in Europe. Normal collision damage waiver, even from one of the major international chains, may not cover such damage, and you could face a crippling fine.

In Eastern Europe, police and frontier officials will pay much closer attention to your papers than in the West, but roads are emptier and foreign drivers still a novelty. The language barrier may be greater, but the novelty value has been known to lead to foreigners being let off with a warning where local drivers might be fined for minor offenses.

Road Signs In some European countries—Bulgaria, Greece, and parts of Yugoslavia—the language barrier is compounded by an alphabet barrier. Main road signs in Greece for example, are written in the Greek alphabet. The only solution is to carry a good map.

Rules of the Road In the United Kingdom, the Republic of Ireland, Cyprus, and Gibraltar, cars drive on the left. In other European countries, traffic is on the right. Beware the transition when coming off ferries from Britain or Ireland to the Continent (and vice versa)!

Rush Hours During peak vacation periods, main routes can be jammed with holiday traffic. In the United Kingdom, try to avoid driving during any of the long bank-holiday (public holiday) weekends, when motorways, particularly in the south, can be totally clogged with traffic. In France, where huge numbers of people still take a fixed one-month vacation in August, avoid driving during *le depart*, the first weekend in August, when vast numbers of drivers head south; or *le retour*, when they head back.

Many German families drive to the Yugoslavian or Greek beaches for their summer vacations and, in the months of June and July, the main highways of Yugoslavia—which are at any time among Europe's worst roads—can also be horrendously overcrowded.

Frontiers You may be surprised at the relatively casual approach many European countries have toward border controls for drivers. At many frontiers, you may simply be waved through; it is quite possible, for example, to drive from Amsterdam to the Federal Republic of Germany, via Belgium and France, without once being stopped for customs or immigration formalities. There are, however, spot checks at all borders, and at some—particularly those checkpoints used by heavy commercial truck traffic—there can be long delays at peak times. Ask tourist offices or motoring associations for latest advice on ways to avoid these tie-ups. Remember that, when crossing from western Europe into Eastern Bloc countries, papers are likely to be rigorously inspected at all times. If you are driving a rented car, the rental company will have provided you with all the necessary papers; if the vehicle is your own, you will need proof of ownership, certificate of roadworthiness (known in the United Kingdom as a Ministry of Transport [MOT] road vehicle certificate), up-to-date vehicle tax, and a Green Card proof of insurance, available from the Automobile Association (AA) or Royal Automobile Club (RAC) for a fee of £15.

By Train

European railway systems vary from the sublime to the ridiculous in terms of comfort and convenience. France, Germany, and the United Kingdom led the field in developing high-speed trains; although the latter has fallen behind the other two. The **French National Railroads'** (SNCF's) Train à Grande Vitesse (TGV), for example, takes just 4½ hours to cover the 540 miles from Paris to Marseille on the Mediterranean.

BritRail operates high-speed InterCity 125 trains—with a top speed of 125 mph—on its north-south routes between London and Scotland. Normal fares apply on the BritRail high-speed services, but there is a supplementary fare for travel on French TGV services.

The Federal German rail system **Deutsche Bundesbahn** (DB, known in the United States as GermanRail) last year wrested the world rail speed record from the French, and its high-speed InterCity trains make rail travel the best public transportation option within Germany.

Swiss trains are not the fastest in Europe but they are the most punctual and reliable, making onward travel connections remarkably stress-free.

International trains link most European capital cities, including those of Eastern Europe; service is offered several times daily. Generally, customs and immigrantion formalities are completed on the train by officials who board when it crosses the frontier.

Most European systems operate a two-tier, sometimes three-tier, class system, with first class substantially the most expensive. The only outstanding advantage of first class is that it is likely to be less crowded on busier routes. Train journeys in Europe tend to be shorter than in the United States—trains are much faster and distances much shorter—so first-class rail travel is usually a luxury rather than a necessity. Some of the poorer European countries retain a third class, but avoid it unless you are on a rock-bottom budget.

A number of European airlines and railways operate fast train connections to their hub airports, and these can sometimes be booked though the airline's computer reservation service. The "Lufthansa Express" connects Frankfurt and Köln/Bonn airports and is a splendid two-hour scenic journey along the Rhine valley.

Trains in Sweden and Norway offer supreme comfort, but greater distances and the more rugged terrain make for longer journey times; if you are on a tight schedule you may prefer to take internal flights.

In Italy, there are some excellent rail services between major cities—but be sure that the train you book *is* a main intercity service, not one that stops at every minor station. Off the major lines, Italian rail services are slower and less frequent.

Trains are generally to be avaoided in Spain and Portugal as point-to-point transportation—though there are some attractive scenic routes and special tourist trains. In Greece and Turkey anyone but the most fanatical rail traveler will find the more frequent, modern, and comfortable buses preferable to the trains, which are slow, unreliable, crowded, and dirty.

Rail travel is vital to most Eastern Bloc countries, and services within and between them are better and more comfortable than you might expect. Though usually much slower than the more modern western European trains, service is frequent and reliable.

Scenic Routes While the high-speed expresses are an ideal and comfortable way of getting from one place to another, travelers who delight in train travel for its own sake will find plenty to please them in Europe's smaller rail lines.

In Norway and Sweden, almost any train journey offers a superb view of some of Europe's most grandiose scenery. The trains of Switzerland, Austria, and Czechoslovakia are also a comfortable way to view impressive mountain vistas.

In Switzerland, the *Glacier Express* running between the Alpine resorts of Zermatt, St. Moritz, and Davos is a regular train that has been taken over almost entirely by tourists attracted by the dramatic scenic route. It makes one round-trip a day in winter, and three in summer; reservations are essential.

In Portugal, rail travel is not ideal, but there are some charming journeys to be made on small local trains. For instance, the rail line north from Oporto to Viana do Castelo and the Spanish border, passes through picturesque small towns and crosses over two remarkable river bridges built by Gustav Eiffel, designer of Paris's famed landmark. Branch lines from the same route run through some of Europe's prettiest and least-developed rural countryside.

Special tourist trains operate in many countries in Europe, a number of them using historic rolling stock or original steam engines. The "Venice Simplon-Orient Express" uses the original sleeping and dining cars and coaches of Europe's most romantic train (*see* From the United Kingdom by Train in Getting to Europe). In Scotland, the "Royal Scot" travels the spectacular glens of the Highlands with antique cars from the heyday of rail travel.

In Spain, a tourist special runs in the summer months through the pretty north coast country of Cantabria and Asturias, leaving from Santander. From Seville, the luxurious "Andalus Express" uses four vintage cars built in the 1920s and operates five-day rail cruises via Cordoba and Granada to Málaga. The train features its own bar—open to 3 AM—with live music and dancing, restaurant cars, and a video and game room.

National tourist offices in the United States or in London, and national rail network offices, are the best sources of information on these tourist specials, some of which may operate for one season only.

Rail Passes Almost all European countries offer discount rail passes; details are given in the appropriate country chapter. Here is a listing of the rail passes available before you leave.

The **EurailPass,** valid for unlimited first-class train travel through 17 countries (Austria, Belgium, Denmark, Finland, France, West Germany, Greece, Holland, Hungary, Ireland, Italy, Luxembourg, Norway, Portugal, Spain, Sweden, and Switzerland), is the best-value ticket for visitors from outside Europe. The ticket is available for 15 days ($320), 21 days ($398), one month ($498), two months ($698), and three months ($860). For visitors 26 and under, there is the **Eurail Youthpass,** for one or two months' unlimited second-class train travel, at $360 and $470. The EurailPass does not cover Great Britain and is available only to those who live outside Europe or North Africa. The pass must be bought from an authorized agent before you leave home. Apply through your travel agent, or one of the following: French National Railroads, GermanRail, or Italian State Railways (*see* Useful Addresses, below).

For those who want to spread out their train journeys, there's the new **Eurail Flexipass,** which gives travelers unlimited first-class train travel on any nine days in a 21-day period. The Flexipass costs $340.

For European travelers under 26, the **Inter-Rail card** is an unbeatable value. It is available to people who have been resident in Europe for at least six months, and for one calendar month gives unlimited rail travel in 21 countries—the same as the EurailPass with the addition of Morocco, Romania, European Turkey, and Yugoslavia. It also gives half-price travel within the United Kingdom and discounts of up to 50% on some ferry services to and from the United Kingdom. The card costs around £145 and is available from rail stations.

Useful Addresses Full information on rail services within the countries listed here is available from the addresses below. Otherwise, contact the national tourist office of the country concerned.

In the United States and Canada **Belgian National Railroads,** 745 Fifth Ave., New York, NY 10151.

BritRail Travel International Inc., 630 Third Ave., New York, NY 10017/800 S. Hope St., Los Angeles, CA 90017; Cedar Maple Plaza, 2305 Cedar Springs, Dallas, TX 75201; 94 Cumberland St., Toronto, Ontario M5R 1A3; 409 Granville St., Vancouver, BC V6C 1T2.

French National Railroads, 610 Fifth Ave., New York, NY 10020; 9465 Wilshire Blvd., Beverly Hills, CA 90212; 11 E. Adams St., Chicago, IL 60603; 2121 Ponce de Leon Blvd., Coral Gables, FL 33114; 360 Post St., Union Sq., San Francisco, CA 94108; 1500 Stanley St., Montreal, Quebec H3A 1Re; 409 Granville St., Vancouver, BC V6C 1T2.

GermanRail, 747 Third Ave., New York, NY 10017; 625 Salter Office Bldg., Boston, MA 02116; 95–97 W. Higgins Rd., Suite 505, Rosemont, IL 60018; 112 S. Ervay St., Dallas, TX 75201; 11933 Wilshire Blvd., Los Angeles, CA 90025; 442 Post St., 6th Floor, San Francisco, CA 94102; 8000 E. Girard Ave., Suite 518S, Denver, CO 80231; Bay St., Toronto, Ontario M5R 2C3.

Italian State Railways, 666 Fifth Ave., New York, NY 10103.

In the United Kingdom **Belgian National Railways,** 22–25A Sackville St., London W1X 1DE.

French Railways, French Railways House, 179 Piccadilly, London, W1V 9DB tel. 01/409–1224.

German Federal Railways, 10 Old Bond St., London W1, tel. 01/499–0577.

Netherlands Railways, 25–28 Buckingham Gate, London SW1E 6LD; tel. 01/630–1735.

Norwegian State Railways Travel Bureau, 21–24 Cockspur St., London SW1Y 5BN, tel. 01/930–6666.

Swiss Federal Railways, Swiss Center, 1 New Coventry St., London W1V 8EE, tel. 01/734–1921.

For information about rail networks in other European countries, contact their tourist boards in London.

By Plane

Licenses to operate on a given international or internal route are issued by governments, and international route licenses are in most cases still issued on the basis of bilateral agreements between the two countries in question. This means that bus stop-style services, like those so common in the United States, do not yet exist in Europe, though they may begin to appear in the near future. So-called "fifth freedom" licenses, which grant airlines the right to land and pick up passengers at intermediary points on a given route, are jealously guarded by governments and consequently are hard to come by. This makes touring Europe entirely by air a costly process, and the best bet, if you plan to visit a number of European countries, is to combine air travel with other transport options.

Hub Airports   As in the United States, airlines are developing hub and spoke-style services within Europe. The idea is that you take a transatlantic flight to an airline's hub, then continue on its intra-European services to other European cities. Thus, **SAS** is actively developing Copenhagen as a Scandinavian hub; the Dutch airlin **KLM** is doing the same at Amsterdam Schiphol; **British Airways** at London Heathrow and Gatwick; and **Lufthansa** at Frankfurt. If you plan to fly to other European cities, one of these hubs is your obvious choice.

Domestic Services   Most western European countries have good internal services linking the capital city with major business and industrial centers, and with more remote communities. In West Germany, France, and Spain, regional flights tend to connect major business cities rather than areas of touristic interest—though in Spain there is a considerable overlap between the two.

In such countries as Sweden, Norway, Greece, and to some extent the United Kingdom, however, air services are a vital link between remote island and mountain communities and are often subsidized by the central government. In Greece, for example, you can fly very inexpensively between Athens and the islands—though not *between* islands.

Before booking an internal flight, consider the alternatives. Flights from London to Edinburgh take about one hour—airport to airport—while the competing BritRail InterCity train takes 4½ hours. But if you add in the hour needed to get from central London to the airport, the need to check in as much as one hour before departure, the inevitable flight delays, the time spent waiting for luggage on arrival, and the transfer time back into town from Edinburgh Airport—you'll find you may not have saved any more than an hour in travel time for a considerably higher fare. When looking into air travel as an option, remember that distances between European cities can be deceptively short to an eye accustomed to U.S. routings.

Formalities   For scheduled flights, you will be asked to check in at least one hour before departure; for charter flights, generally two hours. These are guidelines; if you are traveling with just hand luggage, it is possible to check in as late as 30 minutes before takeoff time. European luggage allowances are based on total weight of your checked luggage, not, as in the United States, on the number of bags. The usual allowance is 44 pounds.

You may be pleasantly surprised by the Green Channel/Red Channel customs system in operation at most western European airports and at other international frontier posts. Basically, this is an honor system: If you have nothing to declare, you walk through the Green Channel without needing to open your bags for inspection. There are, however, random spot checks, and penalties for abusing the system can be severe. If in doubt, go through the Red Channel.

Eastern Europe   Eastern European countries need hard Western currency so badly that they try not to set airfares at intolerably high levels. Most routes are operated in tandem with Western carriers, however, and anyone with an eye to comfort and safety will prefer the latter.

Useful Addresses Major national airlines for the following European countries can be contacted at their London addresses:

Aer Lingus (Ireland) (52 Poland St., London W1V 4AA, tel. 01/437–8000).

Aeroflot Soviet Airlines (69/72 Piccadilly, London W1, tel. 01/491–1756).

Air France (158 New Bond St., London W1Y OAY, tel. 01/499–8611).

Alitalia (Italy) (205 Holland Park Ave., London W11 4XB, tel. 01/745–8361).

Austrian Airlines (50/51 Conduit St., London W1R ONP, tel. 01/439–1851).

British Airways (Box 10, Heathrow Airport, Hounslow, Middlesex TW6 2JA, tel. 01/759–5511).

Czechoslovak Airlines (12A Margaret St., London W1, tel. 01/255–1898).

Finnair (14 Clifford St., London W1X 1RD, tel. 01/629–4349).

Iberia (Spain) (29 Glasshouse St., London W1R 5RG, tel. 01/437–9822).

JAT Yugoslav Airlines (2nd floor, Prince Frederick House, 37 Maddox St., London W1R OAQ, tel. 01/629–2007).

KLM Royal Dutch Airlines (Time & Life Building, New Bond St., London, W1Y OAD, tel. 01/750–9200).

LOT Polish Airlines (313 Regent St., London W1R 7PE, tel. 01/580–5037/9).

Lufthansa (Germany) (10 Old Bond St., London W1X 4EN, tel. 01/408–0322).

Olympic Airways (Greece) (Trafalgar House, Hammersmith International Centre, 2 Chalkhill Rd., London W6 8SB, tel. 01/846–9966).

SAS Scandinavian Airlines (52 Conduit St., London W1R OAY, tel. 01/734–6777).

Swissair (Swiss Centre, 10 Wardour St., London W1V 4BJ, tel. 01/734–6737).

Turkish Airlines (11/12 Hanover St., London W1R 9HF, tel. 01/499–9249).

By Bus

If you have opted for land rather than air travel, the choice between rail and bus is a major decision. In countries such as Britain, France, Germany, and Holland, bus travel was, until recently, something of a poor man's option—slow, uncomfortable, and cheap. Today, though, fast modern buses travel on excellent highways and offer standards of service and comfort comparable to those on a train—but still at generally lower fares. Between major cities and over long distances, trains are still preferable and almost always faster, but buses will take you to places that trains often do not reach.

In several southern European countries—including Portugal, Greece, much of Spain, and Turkey—the bus has supplanted the train as the main means of public transportation, and is often quicker, more frequent, and more comfortable than the antiquated rolling stock of the national rail system. Choose the bus over the rail in these countries unless there is a particular scenic rail route or a special tourist train you want to use. But be prepared to discover that the bus is now more expensive than the lowly railway. Competition among lines is keen, so compare services such as air-conditioning or reclining seats before you buy.

Information   Information on bus transportation in most countries is available from national or regional tourist offices. For reservations on major bus lines, contact your travel agent at home. For smaller bus companies on regional routes, you may have to go to a local travel agency or to the bus line office.

Note that travel agencies may be affiliated with a certain line and won't always tell you about alternative services—you may have to do some legwork to be sure of getting the best service.

By Ferry/Ship

Bounded by the sea on three sides and crossed by a number of major rivers, Europe offers an abundance of choice for anyone who loves water travel.

The Baltic   In the north, ferries ply daily between most of the major Baltic ports in western Europe as well as between Finnish ports and those of the Soviet Union. Baltic crossings are not for those in a hurry—several of them last overnight—and shipping lines operate luxury cruise-ferry vessels with all kinds of entertainment facilities and duty-free shopping.

Major lines include **Silja,** which operates between Finland and Sweden/Germany (book through Scandinavian Seaways); **Viking Line,** which operates between Finland and Sweden (book through Scantours); **Jahre Line,** which operates between Sweden and Germany (book through Winge Travel Bureau); **Stena Line,** which operates between Norway and Denmark (book through P&O European Ferries); and **TT-Line,** which operates between Sweden and Germany (book through Olau Lines).

Local ferries ply the Norwegian fjords and are an excellent way of seeing the country, whether you are traveling by car or on public transportation; a fjord trip in mid-summer, the time of the Midnight Sun in northern Norway, should not be missed.

Main international Baltic ports are Copenhagen, Gothenburg, Malmö, Stockholm, Helsinki, Kristiansand, and Oslo—also Travemunde in West Germany.

Useful Addresses   **Jahre Line** (Winge Travel Bureau, 20 Pall Mall, London SW1Y 5NE, tel. 01/839–6604).
Viking Line (Scantours, 8 Spring Gardens, Trafalgar Sq., London SW1A 2BG, tel. 01/930–9510).
For other Baltic ferry lines mentioned here, *see* From the United Kingdom by Ferry/Ship.

Scotland   Ferry services are important, too, in the Scottish Western Isles, where the **Caledonian Macbrayne Ltd.** (The Ferry Terminal, Gourock, Renfrewshire PA19 1QP, Scotland; tel. 0475/34531) has enjoyed a virtual monopoly for many years on its services linking the islands to the mainland port of Oban. The northern Scottish islands of the Orkney and Shetland groups are served by sea from Scrabster on the north coast of mainland Scotland—near John O'Groats.

Greece   Interisland ferries play an important part in the Mediterranean, too, particularly among the Greek islands. Many island communities have formed cooperative companies to operate services linking their island with others and with Piraeus, the port of Athens. While all Baltic ferries offer high standards of comfort, even luxury—at commensurately high fares—Mediterranean ferry lines observe widely differing standards. On Greek ships, for example, you can travel in a first- or second-class cabin, or rough it in deck class for a much lower fare. The same is true for the international ferries plying between the Italian ports of Bari and Brindisi, and the Greek ports of Corfu, Igoumenitsa, and Patras. The age of Greek ferry boats varies widely too. Some are of pre-World War II vintage, while others—like the *Naxos*, which sails between Piraeus and Crete—are modern vessels. For Greek ferry information, contact the **National Tourist Organization of Greece** in New York or London.

Flying Dolphin Lines operates fast hydrofoil service from Piraeus to points popular with Athenian vacationers, including the Saronic Gulf islands and resorts on the eastern Peloponnese.

One luxury sea option in the eastern Mediterranean is the *Orient Express*, owned by the same company that operates the train. The ship connects with the train at Venice, sails to Piraeus, Istanbul, and Kusadasi (Turkey); returns via Patmos and Katakolon in Greece, then meets the train again in Venice. For details, contact: **Venice Simplon-Orient Express** Suite 2565, 1 World Trade Center, New York, NY 10048 or **British Ferries Orient-Express,** 8th Floor, Sea containers House, 20 Upper Ground, London SW1 1JL.

River Travel Major river systems crisscross Europe. Among the many attractive river trips available ar a number of luxury cruises on the Rhine and Danube rivers.

The Danaube passes through European countries in western and eastern Europe, and international cruises are possible. Contact the **German National Tourist Office** for details. There is also an international hydrofoil service that operates several times a day on the Danube between Budapest in Hungary and Bratislava in Czechoslovakia. Information and booking are available through **Ibusz**, the Hungarian state travel agency, or **Cedok**, its Czech equivalent, in New York or London. For details of Rhine trips, contact **K.D. German Rhine Line,** 170 Hamilton Ave., White Plains, NY 10601; or **G.A. Club Rhine Cruise Agency Ltd.,** 80/81 St. Martin's Lane, London WC2N 4AA.

Though a great deal less spectacular than either the Rhine or the Danube, the smaller rivers of Belgium, Holland, France, and other western European countries can also provide a relaxed and fascinating vacation. **Floating Through Europe** (271 Madison Ave., New York, NY 10016) specializes in these kinds of tours.

By Bicycle

Bicycling in Europe can be sheer pleasure or unadulterated torment—depending on when you go, where you go, and what you try to do.

If you're planning a European bike trip, you are probably experienced enough not to need advice on equipment and clothing. But it needs to be said that some European countries are far more user-friendly than others toward bicyclists. In countries like Holland, Denmark, Gemany, and Belgium, bikes are very much part of the landscape—mainly because the landscape tends to be uniformly flat and presents no challenges to even the wimpiest rider. City streets and many main roads in these countries (as well as in the Federal Republic of Germany) have special bike lanes set aside, and car drivers are used to coping with large numbers of bicycle riders.

Cycling is a major sport in Italy, Spain, and Portugal as well as in France, and there are regular "Tour" road races. Cyclists also get a good deal in the Eastern Bloc countries, where for economic reasons, the bicycle is still an everyday form of transportation.

Northern Scandinavia and Iceland, plus the Alpine countries Austria and Switzerland, with their steep terrain, are destinations only for the serious cyclist. The Scandinavian countries have plenty of excellent-value campsites. Ireland has emptier roads and a gentler landscape than Sweden or Norway and is a pleasant country to bicycle in, though the temptation to sample just one more Guinness at each wayside pub can be a hazard in itself.

Of the wealthier European countries, Britain has the most shameful record when it comes to providing facilities for bicyclists or considering their interests. Riding in London traffic is a stomach-churning experience requiring nerves of steel. Except in remoter areas—such as the north of Scotland—main roads are overcrowded and often dangerous to cyclists.

Bicycle Transport Transporting your bicycle from the United Kingdom to Europe holds no big problems—some ferry lines transport bicycles free, others charge a nominal fee. Shop around. Surprisingly, you can transport your bicycle by air as checked baggage—you won't have to pay extra so long as you are within the 44-pound total baggage allowance.

Most European rail lines will transport bicycles free of charge or for a nominal fee, though you may have to book ahead. Check with the main booking office. One of the joys of biking in Europe is being able to bike one way, and to return by train; or to board a train with your bike when you need to cover long distances, or simply when you need to take a rest. SNCF (French Railways) converted wagons on four of its Motorail services from Boulogne to carry bicycles for the first time in 1988. Transporting your bike by bus is also possible but may tax your powers of persuasion, as the bus lines don't seem to have any hard and fast rules but leave the decision to the driver or guide.

Renting Bicycles Bicycles can be rented by the day or week in most European capitals and are most readily available in cities like Amsterdam and Copenhagen, where cycling is part of the way of life. Local tourist boards are the best source of information on reliable rental agencies with safe bicycles to rent; remember to check on local traffic rules and make sure your insurance covers you in case of an accident. **GermanRail (DB)** rents bicycles at selected stations in summer—get further information from GermanRail or the German National Tourist Office in New York.

2 Andorra

Introduction

The coprincipality of Andorra is a country that defies comparison, a political anachronism that has somehow lingered on from the past. This tiny mountain enclave, only 16 miles long and 18 miles wide—about a quarter of the size of the state of Rhode Island—is set in the Pyrenees between France and Spain. To trace its origins one must go back to the 12th century when the French count of Foix ceded the valley of Andorra to the Spanish Bishop of Urgell. Centuries of conflict between France and Spain failed to break the bishops' hold. And so, even today, Andorra enjoys dual protection as a coprincipality, ruled democratically but under the watchful eye of the French government (as descendants of the counts of Foix) and the present-day Bishop of Urgell. This ancient condition has various modern advantages. Andorra is a low-tax, duty-free haven; a popular holiday center, especially for winter sports; and a unique little country, the only one in the world, where Catalan—the language of Barcelona and Roussillon—is the official tongue.

Andorra la Vella, the capital, is now a much-developed tourist center—one vast duty-free shop—but the medieval buildings have been retained and restored. Outside of town, Romanesque churches, bridges, and shrines dot the landscape, and the mountain setting is superb.

Before You Go

When to Go Winter months bring a huge influx of ski buffs, though any time of year suits those with an eye on Andorra's tax- and duty-free shopping status. Andorra is a paradise for lovers of the outdoors. In winter there is reliable snowfall from December to early April, and efficient ski resorts at Soldeu, Arinsal, Pas de la Casa, and La Massana. In summer, hikers will find magnificent trails on the Grande Randonnée (GR) network, and a score of shorter but still demanding routes. Botanists and birdwatchers should arrive by early April, in time for the bird migrations up from Africa, and the first flush of spring flowers on the slopes and in the valleys. Be warned that even in the summer the nighttime temperatures can drop to freezing.

Climate The following are the average daily maximum and minimum temperatures for Andorra.

Jan.	43F	6C	May	62F	17C	Sept.	71F	22C
	30	−1		43	6		49	10
Feb.	45F	7C	June	73F	23C	Oct.	60F	16C
	30	−1		39	10		42	6
Mar.	54F	12C	July	79F	26C	Nov.	51F	10C
	35	2		54	12		35	2
Apr.	58F	14C	Aug.	76F	24C	Dec.	42F	6C
	39	4		53	12		31	−1

Currency The Spanish peseta is the major Andorran currency, but French francs are equally acceptable and all prices are quoted in both currencies in Andorra. For exchange rates and coinage information, *see* Currency in the France and Spain chapters.

What It Will Cost
Sample Prices Andorra's prices are refreshingly easy on the wallet. At press time, some sample costs were as follows: Coca-Cola, 60 ptas.;

cup of coffee, 35–40 ptas.; ham sandwich, 200 ptas.; glass of beer, 75 ptas.; one-mile taxi ride, 125 ptas.

Customs Andorra is unusually lax in the matter of customs, duties, visas, and the like. Non-Europeans can get in with only a passport. Europeans need only an identity card but as visitors are usually just waved in, the card is almost an irrelevance. (On the way *out* of the country, however, be prepared for mega-traffic jams: The French and Spanish customs officers take their jobs far more seriously than do their Andorran counterparts.)

Language Catalan is the official language of Andorra, a tongue shared with the Catalan people who inhabit the area that includes the Pyrenees from Barcelona in Spain to Perpignan in France. French, Spanish, and, increasingly, English are also widely spoken.

Getting Around

By Car Andorran roads vary. The one main artery from France into Spain via Andorra la Vella is excellent and copes with the heaviest traffic, as does the spur north toward the ski resorts at La Massana and Ordino. Elsewhere, roads are narrow, winding, and best suited to four-wheel-drive vehicles or, higher up, mules. In winter, snow tires and chains are essential.

By Bus Minibuses connect the towns and villages, and fares are low; 75 ptas. will take you 30–40 kilometers (18–25 miles). Details on fares and services are available at hotels or from tourist offices (*Sindicat d'Iniciativa*.).

On Foot Mountainous Andorra is a mecca for hikers, hill-walkers, and backpackers. The mountains are high and wild, so a degree of care and experience is advisable. There are two long-distance trails: the GR7, which runs from Portello Blanca on the French frontier to Escaldes on the road to Spain, and the GR75, also called the Ordino Route, a magnificent, high-mountain trail across the central range. Get details on local treks and walks from tourist offices.

Staying in Andorra

Telephones For local inquiries, tel. 11.

Mail You can buy Andorran stamps with French francs or Spanish pesetas, though the postal service within the country is free. The Spanish post office in Andorra la Vella is at Joan Maragall; the French post office is at Avenida Meritxell 39.

Opening and Closing Times **Banks.** Open weekdays 9–1 and 3–5, Saturday 9–noon.

Churches. Most chapels and churches are kept locked around the clock, with the key being left at the closest house. Check with the tourist office for further details.

Shops. Open daily 9–8, though some close 1–3.

National Holidays September 8 (La Verge de Meritxell). Shops open throughout republic except in Meritxell itself, where festival is celebrated.

Local Holidays At Canillo, 3rd Saturday in July and following Sunday and Monday; at Les Escaldes, July 25–27; at Sant Julià de Lòria, last Sunday in July and following Monday and Tuesday; at Andorra la Vella, first Saturday, Sunday, Monday in August; at

Encamp and La Massana, August 15–17; at Ordino, September 16, 17.

Dining Andorra is no gastronomic paradise, but there are good restaurants serving French, Spanish, or Catalan cuisine, and plenty of restaurants where the visitor will eat well at no great cost. Local dishes worth trying include *truites de casseroles* (trout casserole, with mushrooms and eggs); *trixat*, a typical peasant dish of potatoes and cabbage; or local delicacies like jugged *izard* (chamois stew). Although most restaurants offer fixed-price menus, a number of more expensive establishments offer only à la carte.

Meal times True to their Spanish heritage, Andorrans eat late: Dinners don't usually get underway until 8:30 at least, and lunch is a substantial meal often followed by an afternoon siesta.

Dress Jacket and tie is recommended for restaurants in the top-price categories. Casual dress is acceptable elsewhere.

Ratings The following ratings are for a three-course meal for one person, excluding wine. Best bets are indicated by a star ★. At press time (spring 1989), there were 115 pesetas to the dollar.

Category	Cost
Very Expensive	over 5,000 ptas
Expensive	over 2,500 ptas
Moderate	1,000–2,000 ptas
Inexpensive	under 1,000 ptas

Credit Cards The following credit card abbreviations are used: AE, American Express; DC, Diners Club; MC, MasterCard; V, Visa.

Lodging Andorran hotels are increasing in number all the time and standards are improving. The architecture is usually functional, but the service is friendly and the facilities excellent.

Most hotels are open year-round. Reservations are necessary during July and August. Hotel rates often include at least two meals.

Ratings As a general guide, the following price ratings apply for two people in a double room. Best bets are indicated by a star ★. At press time, there were 115 pesetas to the dollar.

Category	Cost
Very Expensive	8,500–9,000 ptas
Expensive	6,000–7,500 ptas
Moderate	4,000–5,500 ptas
Inexpensive	2,500–3,500 ptas

Credit Cards The following credit card abbreviations are used: AE, American Express; DC, Diners Club; MC, MasterCard; V, Visa.

Tipping Restaurants and cafés almost always tack on a 10–15% service charge; if they don't, it's customary to leave a similar amount.

Arriving and Departing

By Plane The closest airport to Andorra la Vella is the Seo de Urgel-Andorra airport (tel. 973/351826), 20 kilometers (12 miles) south over the border in Spain. It is linked to Barcelona International Airport by three daily flights. The nearest international airports are at Barcelona (200 kilometers, 125 miles) and Toulouse-Blagnac (180 kilometers, 112 miles).

A regular bus service shuttles visitors back and forth from Seo de Urgel-Andorra airport; the oneway fare is 3,000 ptas. Taxis are available, too. Bus transit from Barcelona or Toulouse to Andorra la Vella takes from three-and-a-half to four hours.

By Train From Barcelona, take the train to Puigcerdá, then the bus to Seo de Urgel and Andorra la Vella; from Madrid, a train to Lérida and then a bus to Seo de Urgel and Andorra la Vella; from Toulouse, take the train to Ax-les-Thermes or Tour de Carol (on the route to Perpignan), then the bus to Seo de Urgel and Andorra la Vella.

By Bus A bus service runs twice daily from Barcelona (Ronda Universidad 4).

By Car There are only two possible routes—the CG-1, which links Andorra with Spain, or the CG-2, which crosses the French border at the Pas de la Casa. (A third route, CG-3, runs due north from Andorra la Vella and dead-ends a few miles short of the combined French and Spanish borders.)

Important Addresses and Numbers

Tourist Information **Andorra la Vella.** Sindicat d'Iniciativa (National Tourist Office), Dr. Vilanova Street tel. 628/20214. Open Mon.–Sat. 10–1 and 3–7, Sun. and holidays 10–1.
Canillo. Pro-Turism Office, Main Street, tel. 628/51002.
Encamp. Tourist office, Placa Consul General, tel. 31405.
La Massana. Tourist office, Placa l'Hotel Font, tel. 35693.
Ordino. Tourist office, Ring Road, tel. 36963.
St. Julia. Tourist office, Pro-Turism Kiosk, tel. 41352.

Consulates **U.S.:** Via Layetana, Barcelona, tel. 93/319–9550; **Canadian:** Nunez de Balboa 35, Madrid, tel. 91/225–9119; **U.K.:** Apartado de Correos 12111, Barcelona, tel. 93/322–2151.

Emergencies **Doctor:** tel. 628/21905; **Police:** tel. 628/21222; **Ambulance and Fire:** tel. 628/20020.

Travel Agency **American Express:** in the Relax travel agency, Roc dels Escolls 12, Andorra la Vella, tel. 628/22044.

Guided Tours Tours of the capital and surrounding countryside are offered by several firms; check with the tourist office for details.

Exploring Andorra

Exploring Andorra takes time. The roads are narrow and steep, the views compel frequent stops, and every village is worth exploring. If possible, do as much sightseeing on foot as time permits.

Overlooking **Andorra la Vella's main square is the stone bulk of the Casa de la Vall** (House of the Valleys), a 16th-century

Andorra

(map labels) F R A N C E — Pic de Siguer — Pic de Serrera — El Serrat — Valira del Norte — Pic de l'Estanyó — Coma Pedrosa — La Cortinada — Sant Joan de Caselles — Soldeu — Arinsal — Erts — Canillo — Valira del Orient — Ordino — Sanctuary of Meritxell — Port d'Envalira — Pal — La Massana — Sant Roma de les Bons — Pas de la Casa — Pont de St. Antoni — Encamp — Alt del Griu — Andorra la Vella — Sant Miguel d'Engolasters — Pic de Pessons — Santa Coloma — Les Escaldes — Ramio — Valira River — Certers — Sant Julia de Loria — S P A I N — Juverri

0 — 10 miles
0 — 15 km

medieval building that today acts as the seat of the Andorran government. A charmingly rustic spot, the Casa contains many religious frescoes of note, some of which were carefully transported here from village churches high up in the Pyrenees. The kitchen is particularly interesting, with a splendid array of ancient copper pots and other culinary implements. *Vall St. Admission free. Open weekdays 9–10 and 3–4, Sat. 9–10.*

The spa town of **Les Escaldes** is about a 15-minute walk from Andorra la Vella. The Romanesque church of **Sant Miguel d'Engolasters** lies on a ridge northeast of the capital and can be reached on foot—allow half a day for the round-trip—or by taxi up a mountain road. The views are well worth the climb. Just beyond Encamp, 6 kilometers (4 miles) northeast, is the 11th-century church of **Sant Roma de les Bons,** situated in a particularly picturesque spot of medieval buildings and mountain scenery.

Midway between Encamp and Canillo on the CG-2 is the **Sanctuary of Meritxell,** the focal point of the country's prodigious religious fervor. The Blessed Virgin of Meritxell is the principality's patron saint, though oddly enough for such a religious country this patronage was declared only in the late 19th century. The original sanctuary was destroyed by fire in 1972; the new gray stone building looks remarkably like a factory, but the mountain setting is superb. *Admission free. Open weekdays 10–1 and 3:30–6:30, Sat. 10–1.*

Another 3 kilometers (2 miles) farther, just before reaching the town of Canillo, you will see an old stone six-armed cross (actually, five-armed as one has broken off). A mile or so beyond is the Romanesque church of **Sant Joan des Caselles**, whose ancient walls have mellowed with age. The bell tower is stunning, three stories of weathered stone punctuated by rows of arched windows. Inside, the main building is a good example of a *reredos* (a wall or screen positioned behind an altar) dating from 1525 and depicting the life of St. John the Apostle.

Retrace your way back to Andorra la Vella, and this time take the CG-3 due north out of the capital. After just a few miles you'll come to an ancient stone bridge, the **Pont de St. Antoni,** which spans a narrow river. Three kilometers (2 miles) farther is the picturesque mountain town of **La Massana;** take some time to stroll along its quaintly rustic streets. Another 5 kilometers (3 miles) on is the tiny village of **Ordino**. Its medieval church is exceptionally pretty; to see it properly, go at night between 7 and 8 when mass is celebrated.

In **La Cortinada,** a mile or so farther, is the **Can Pal**, another fine example of medieval Andorran architecture. This time the building is a privately owned manor house (strictly no admittance), with a pretty dovecote attached. Note the turret perched high up on the far side.

Backtrack once more to Andorra la Vella, then take the CG-1 south. Within a few miles you'll come to the church of **Santa Coloma,** in the village bearing the same name; parts of the church date from the 10th century.

Shopping

Visitors to Andorra often list the shopping as one of the main attractions, but not all the goods displayed are actually at bargain prices. The French and Spanish come here to buy cigarettes and liquor but find electrical goods and cameras no cheaper than at home. Good buys are consumable items: perfume, cigarettes, whiskey and gin. For cameras, tape recorders, and other imported items, compare prices and models carefully. The main shopping center is Andorra la Vella, but there are shops in all the new developments and in the towns close to the frontiers, at Pas de la Casa and St. Julia de Loria.

Dining and Lodging

For details and price category definitions, *see* Dining and Lodging in Staying in Andorra.

Andorra la Vella
Dining

Chez Jaques. The varied menu features both classical and nouvelle French dishes, though other international cuisines are handled with flair. With good food and a cozy ambience, it's very popular with the locals. *Av. Tarragona, tel. 628/20395. Reservations accepted. AE, DC, MC, V. Expensive.*
Moli del Fanals. This excellent-value restaurant is set in an old windmill and serves mainly classic French dishes. *Dr. Vilanova St. Borda Casadet, tel. 628/21387. Reservations accepted. AE, V. Moderate.*
★ **Versailles.** A tiny and authentic French bistro with only a handful of tables. Versailles is always packed. *Cap del Carrer 1, tel. 628/21331. Reservations advised. DC, MC, V. Moderate.*

Lodging
★ **Andorra Palace.** The large and modern Palace is widely considered one of the capital's best hotels. The outdoor terrace is a

pleasant spot in which to relax and watch the bustle below. *Prat de la Creu, tel. 628/21072. 140 rooms with bath. Facilities: restaurant, parking, bar, sauna, pool. AE, DC, MC, V. Expensive.*

Andorra Park. The Park ranks with the Palace as one of Andorra la Vella's two top hotels. There's a pretty garden, as well as a terrace and private balconies. *Roureda de Guillemo, tel. 628/20979. 75 rooms with bath. Facilities: restaurant, tennis, parking, bar, pool. AE, DC, MC, V. Expensive.*

President. This modern hotel is clean and tidy and offers good value rather than charm. The restaurant commands a particularly dramatic mountain view. *Avda. Sta. Coloma 40, tel. 628/22922. 88 rooms with bath. Facilities: bar, restaurant, sauna, pool. DC, MC, V. Moderate.*

Florida. This is a cheerful, inexpensive hotel. There's no restaurant, but there are several nearby. *Carrer la Llacuna 11, tel. 628/20105. 35 rooms, 32 with bath. Facilities: bar, lounge, DC, MC, V. Inexpensive.*

Les Escaldes
Dining
★

1900. The 1900 is a small, beautifully decorated restaurant serving the best food in the principality, with a mixture of French, Spanish, and Andorran cuisine. It's expensive for Andorra, but the 180 franc (7,600-ptas.) menu is an exceptional value. *Carrer de la Unioll, tel. 628/26716. AE, DC, MC, V. Closed July. Expensive.*

Lodging
★

Roc Blanc. Sleek, modern, and luxurious trappings—and a wealth of facilities to pamper the body—are what the Roc Blanc is all about. Rooms are large, and the hotel's restaurant, El Pi, is consistently good. *Placa Coprinceps 5, tel. 628/21486. 240 rooms with bath. Facilities: 2 pools, sauna, tennis, health club, restaurant, piano bar, hairdresser, terrace. AE, DC, MC, V. Very Expensive.*

Encamp
Lodging

Belvedere. An ex-patriate English couple runs this friendly little inn, which is set in the midst of some amazing mountain scenery. The exceptionally clean rooms tend toward the small side. *Carrer Ballàvista, tel. 628/31263. 10 rooms, 1 with bath. Facilities: restaurant, bar, garden, terrace. No credit cards. Closed mid-Oct.–mid-Dec. Moderate.*

Pas de la Casa
Dining

Le Grizzly. This is a popular French restaurant for lunch or dinner, especially during the ski season. The food is simple but well prepared, and it offers good value, with a choice of four fixed-price menus, from 800 to 1,300 ptas. Try the *entrecote roquefort* (steak) and the thick Provençal soups. *Calle Principal, tel. 628/55227. Reservations advised. AE, V.*

Sant Julia de Loria
Lodging
★

Pol. Gracefully modern surroundings and friendly staff are just two reasons why this hotel is so popular. *Av. Verge de Canolich 52, tel. 628/41122. 71 rooms with bath. Facilities: restaurant, bar, garden, terrace. AE, MC, V. Moderate.*

3   Austria

Introduction

What Austria lacks in size, it more than makes up for in diversity. Its Alps and mountain lakes in the central and southern provinces rival those of neighboring Switzerland; the vast Vienna Woods remind some of the Black Forest; the steppes of the province of Burgenland blend with those across the border in Hungary; and the vineyards along the Danube rival those of the Rhine and Mosel river valleys. In addition, nobody else has a Vienna or a Salzburg—or such pastry shops!

Austria has become considerably more expensive in recent years. But there are still bargains to be found, and one of the diversions of a vacation in Austria can be their discovery.

The country is highly accessible. There are virtually no outposts that are not served by public transport of one form or another. The rail network is well maintained, and trains are fast, comfortable, and punctual. Highways are superb and well marked. Public transportation in the cities, although not cheap, is safe, clean, and convenient. In short, the visitor spends more time in Austria enjoying himself than coping with the logistics of getting from A to B.

The Austrians are, for the most part, friendly and welcoming. They are an outdoor people, given at a moment's notice to head off to the ski slopes, the mountains, the lakes, and the woods. At the same time, they can be as melancholy as some of the songs of their wine taverns would suggest. Communicating with them is not too difficult, since most speak another language beside their native German, and English is the usual choice.

What you'll discover in conversation with Austrians is that they are more for evolution than revolution, so change is gradual and old values tend to be maintained. Graceful dancers do execute the tricky "left waltz" on balmy summer evenings in Vienna, and you may find an entire town celebrating some event, complete with brass band in Lederhosen.

Before You Go

When to Go Austria has two main tourist seasons. The summer season starts at Easter and runs to about mid-October. The most pleasant months weather-wise are May, June, September, and October. June through August are the peak tourist months, and aside from a few overly humid days when you could wish for wider use of air conditioning, even Vienna is pleasant; the city literally moves outdoors in summer. The winter cultural season starts in October and runs into June; the winter sports season gets underway in December and lasts until the end of April, although you can ski in selected areas well into June and on some of the highest glaciers year-round. Some events—the Salzburg Festival is a prime example—make a substantial difference in hotel and other costs. Nevertheless, bargains are available in the (almost nonexistent) off-season.

Climate Summer can be warm; winter, bitterly cold. The southern region is usually several degrees warmer in summer, several degrees colder in winter. Winters north of the Alps can be overcast and dreary, whereas the south basks in winter sunshine.

Austria

The following are the average daily maximum and minimum temperatures for Vienna.

Jan.	34F	1C	May	67F	19C	Sept.	68F	20C
	25	-4		50	10		53	11
Feb.	38F	3C	June	73F	23C	Oct.	56F	14C
	28	-3		56	14		44	7
Mar.	47F	8C	July	76F	25C	Nov.	45F	7C
	30	-1		60	15		37	3
Apr.	58F	15C	Aug	75F	24C	Dec.	37F	3C

Currency The unit of currency is the Austrian schilling (AS), divided into 100 groschen. There are AS 20, 50, 100, 500, and 1,000 bills; AS 1, 5, 10, and 20 coins; and groschen 1, 2, 10, and 50 coins. The 1- and 2- groschen coins are scarce, and the AS 20 coins are unpopular—though useful for some cigarette machines. The 500- and 100-schilling notes look perilously similar; confusing them can be an expensive mistake.

At press time (spring 1989), there were about AS 12.5 to the dollar, and about AS 22.5 to the pound sterling.

Credit cards are widely used throughout Austria, although not all establishments take all cards. American Express has money machines in Vienna at Parkring 10 (actually in Liebengerggasse, off Parkring) and at the airport.

Cash traveler's checks at a bank, post office, or American Express office to get the best rate. All charge a small commission; some smaller banks or "change" offices may give a poorer rate *and* charge a higher fee. All change offices at airports and the main train stations in major cities cash traveler's checks. Bank-operated change offices in Vienna with extended hours are located on Stephansplatz and in the Opernpassage. The Zentralsparkasse machines on Stephansplatz and on Kärntnerstrasse 51 (to the right of the opera) will change bills in other currencies into schillings.

You may bring in any amount of foreign currency or schillings; legally, only AS 50,000 in currency may be taken out.

What It Will Cost Austria is not inexpensive, but since inflation is negligible, costs remain fairly stable. Vienna and Salzburg are the most expensive cities, along with the fashionable resorts such as Kitzbühel, Seefeld, Badgastein, Bad Hofgastein, Velden, Zell am See, and Pörtschach. Many smaller towns offer virtually identical facilities at half the price.

Drinks in bars and clubs are considerably higher than in cafés or restaurants. Austrian prices are inclusive; that is, service and tax are included.

Sample Prices Cup of coffee, AS 22; half-liter of draft beer, AS 26; glass of wine, AS 32; Coca-Cola, AS 20; open sandwich, AS 18; theater ticket, AS 120; concert ticket, AS 170; opera ticket, AS 500; one-mile taxi ride, AS 25.

Customs on Arrival Austria's duty-free allowances are as follows: 200 cigarettes or 100 cigars or 250 grams of tobacco, two liters of wine and one liter of spirits, one bottle of toilet water (about 300-milliliter size); 50 milliliters of perfume for those age 18 and over arriving from other European countries. Visitors arriving from the

United States, Canada, or other non-European points may bring in twice the above amounts.

Language German is the official national language. In larger cities and most resort areas, you will have no problems finding those who speak English; hotel and restaurant staff, in particular, speak English reasonably well. Most younger Austrians speak at least passable English, even if fluency is relatively rare.

Getting Around

By Car
Road Conditions The highway system is excellent, and all roads are well maintained and well marked. Secondary mountain roads may be narrow and winding, but traffic is generally light. Check the condition of mountain roads in winter before starting out: Many mountain passes are closed, though tunnels are kept open.

Rules of the Road Drive on the right. Seat belts are compulsory in front. Speed limits are as posted; otherwise, 130 kph (80 mph) on expressways, 100 kph (62 mph) on other main roads, 50 kph (31 mph) in built-up areas. The right-of-way is for those coming from the right (especially in traffic circles) unless otherwise marked. A warning triangle, standard equipment in rental cars, must be set up in case of breakdown.

Parking Observe signs; tow-away in cities is expensive. Overnight parking in winter is forbidden on city streets with streetcar lines.

Gasoline Prices—AS 9–AS 10 per liter—are fairly consistent throughout the country. Unleaded *(bleifrei)*—regular and premium—is now available almost everywhere.

Breakdowns Emergency road service is available from **ARBÖ** (tel. 123 nationwide) or **ÖAMTC** (tel. 120). Special phones are located along autobahns and major highways.

By Train Trains in Austria are fast and efficient, and most lines have now been electrified. Hourly express trains run on the key Vienna-Salzburg route. All principal trains have first- and second-class cars, and smoking and nonsmoking areas. Overnight trains have sleeping compartments, and most trains have dining cars. If you're traveling at peak times, a reserved seat—available for a small additional fee—is always a good idea.

Fares If you're visiting other European countries, a **Eurail Pass** (*see* Getting Around Europe, in Essential Information, for details), valid throughout most of Europe, is the best deal. Austria has only two discount tickets. The **Austria Ticket** offers unlimited travel for those under 26. The **Kilometerbank** is of value only to natives or visitors planning to travel 2,000 kilometers (1,250 miles) in any one year. Full details are available from travel agents or from the Austrian National Tourist Office.

By Plane Domestic service is expensive. **Austrian Airlines** flies between Vienna and Linz, Salzburg, Graz, and Klagenfurt. **Tyrolean Airlines** has service from Vienna to Innsbruck.

By Bus Service is available to virtually every community accessible by highway. Winter buses have ski racks. Vienna's central bus terminal (Wien-Mitte/Landstrasse Hauptstrasse, opposite the Hilton) is the arrival/departure point for international bus routes; in most other cities the bus station is adjacent to the train station.

By Boat Boats ply the Danube from Passau in West Germany all the way to Vienna and from Vienna to Bratislava (Czechoslovakia), Budapest (Hungary), and the Black Sea. Only East European boats run beyond Budapest. Overnight boats have cabins; all have dining. The most scenic stretches in Austria are from Passau to Linz and through the Wachau valley (Melk, Krems). From Vienna, there are day trips you can take upstream to the Wachau and downstream to Budapest. There are also special moonlight dancing and jazz excursions. Make reservations from **DDSG** in Vienna (tel. 0222/266536) or travel agents.

By Bicycle Bicycles can be rented at many train stations; return them to any other station or the same. Most trains and some postal buses will take bikes as baggage. Bikes can be taken on the Vienna subway on weekends. Marked cycling routes parallel most of the Danube.

Staying in Austria

Telephones Pay telephones take AS 1, 5, 10, and 20 coins. A three-minute
Local Calls local call will cost AS 1. Emergency calls are free. Instructions are in English in most booths. Add AS 1 when time is up to continue the connection. If you will be phoning frequently, get a phone "credit card" at a post office. This works in all "Wertkartentelefon" phones; the cost of the call will be deducted from the card automatically. Card costs are AS 95 for AS 100 worth of phoning.

Phone numbers within Vienna and Innsbruck are being changed. A sharp tone indicates no connection or that the number has been changed.

International Calls It costs more to telephone *from* Austria than it does to telephone *to* Austria. Calls from post offices are least expensive. Hotels time all calls and charge a "per unit" fee according to their own tariff, which can add AS 100 or more to your bill. To avoid this charge, call overseas and ask to be called back. To make a collect call—you can't do this from pay phones—dial the operator and ask for an "R (pronounced "err")-Gespräch."

International Dial 09. Most operators speak English; if yours doesn't, you'll
Information be passed to one who does.

Mail Airmail letters to the United States and Canada cost AS 9.50
Postal Rates minimum; postcards cost AS 7.50. Airmail letters to the United Kingdom cost AS 6; postcards cost AS 5. An aerogram costs AS 11.

Receiving Mail American Express offices in Vienna, Linz, Salzburg, and Innsbruck will hold mail at no charge for those carrying an American Express credit card or American Express traveler's checks.

VAT Refunds Value-added tax (VAT) at 20% (in certain cases, 32%) is charged on all sales and is automatically included in prices. If you purchase goods worth AS 2,000 or more, you can claim back the tax as you leave or once you're back home. Ask shops where you buy the goods to fill out and give you the necessary papers. Get them stamped at the airport or border by customs officials (who may ask to see the goods). You can get an immediate refund of the VAT at the airport or at main border points, less a service charge, or you can return the papers by mail to the shop(s), which will then deal with the details. The VAT refund can be credited to your credit card account or paid by check.

Opening and Closing Times

Banks. Doors open weekdays 8–12:30 and 1:30–3. Principal offices in cities stay open during lunch.

Museums. Opening days and times vary considerably from city to city and depend on season, the size of the museum, budgetary constraints, and assorted other factors. Your hotel or the local tourist office will have current details.

Shops. These open weekdays from 8 or 9 until 6, Saturday until noon or 1 only, except the first Saturday of every month when they stay open until 5. Many smaller shops close for one or two hours at midday.

National Holidays

January 1 (New Year's Day); January 6 (Epiphany); April 15, 16 (Easter); May 1 (May Day); May 24 (Ascension); June 3, 4 (Pentecost); June 14 (Corpus Christi); August 15 (Assumption); October 26 (National Day); November 1 (All Saints); December 8 (Immaculate Conception); December 25, 26 (Christmas).

Dining

Take your choice of sidewalk *wurstl* (frankfurter) stands, quick-lunch stops (*imbisstube*), cafés, Heuriger wine restaurants, self-service restaurants, modest *gasthäuser* neighborhood establishments with local specialties, and full-fledged restaurants in every price category. Most establishments post their menus outside. Shops selling coffee beans (such as Eduscho) also offer coffee by the cup at considerably lower prices than those in a café.

Mealtimes

Austrians often eat up to five meals a day—a very early Continental breakfast of rolls and coffee; a slightly more substantial breakfast *(Gabelfrühstück)* with egg or cold meat, possibly even a small goulash, at mid-morning (understood to be 9, sharp); a main meal at noon; afternoon coffee *(Jause)* with cake at teatime; and, unless dining out, a light supper to end the day. Cafés offer breakfast; most restaurants open somewhat later. Lunches usually cost more in cafés than in restaurants.

Dress

A jacket and tie is generally advised for restaurants in the top price categories. Otherwise, casual dress is acceptable, although in Vienna formal dress is preferred in some moderate restaurants at dinner. When in doubt, it's best to dress up.

Ratings

Prices are per person and include soup and a main course, usually with salad, and a small beer or glass of wine. Meals in the top-price categories will include a dessert or cheese and coffee. Prices include taxes and service (you may wish to leave small change, in addition). Best bets are indicated by a star ★. At press time, there were 12.5 schillings (AS) to the dollar.

Category	Major City	Other Areas
Very Expensive	over AS 800	over AS 600
Expensive	AS 500–AS 800	AS 400–AS 600
Moderate	AS 200–AS 500	AS 170–AS 400
Inexpensive	under AS 200	under AS 170

Credit Cards

The following credit card abbreviations are used: AE, American Express; DC, Diners Club; MC, MasterCard; V, Visa.

Lodging Austrian hotels and pensions are officially classified from one to five stars. These gradings broadly coincide with our own four-way rating system. No matter what the category, standards for service and cleanliness are high. All hotels in the upper three categories will have bath or shower in the room; even the most inexpensive accommodations will have hot and cold water. Accommodations include castles and palaces, conventional hotels, country inns *(Gasthof)*, motels (considerably less frequent), and the more modest pensions.

Ratings All prices quoted here are for two people in a double room. Though exact figures will vary, a single room will generally cost more than 50% of the price of a comparable double room. Breakfast—which can be anything from a simple roll and coffee to a full and sumptuous buffet—is always included in the room rate. Best bets are indicated by a star ★. At press time, there were 12.5 schillings (AS) to the dollar.

Category	Major City	Other Areas
Very Expensive	over AS 2,300	over AS 1,800
Expensive	AS 1,250–AS 2,300	AS 1,000–AS 1,800
Moderate	AS 850–AS 1,250	AS 700–AS 1,000
Inexpensive	under AS 850	under AS 700

Credit Cards The following credit card abbreviations are used: AE, American Express; DC, Diners Club; MC, MasterCard; V, Visa.

Tipping Railroad porters get AS 10 per bag. Hotel porters or bellhops get AS 5 per bag. Doormen get AS 10 for hailing a cab and assisting. Room service gets AS 10 for snacks and AS 20 for full meals. Maids get no tip unless your stay is a week or more, or special service is rendered. In restaurants, 10% service is included. Add anything from AS 5 to AS 50, depending on the restaurant and the size of the bill.

Vienna

Arriving and Departing

By Plane All flights use Schwechat Airport, about 16 kilometers (10 miles) southwest of Vienna (tel. 0222/7770–2231).

Between the Airport and Downtown Buses leave every half-hour from 6 to 8:30 AM, and every 20 minutes from 8:50 AM to 10:10 PM from the airport to the city air terminal by the Hilton on Wien Mitte-Landstrasse Hauptstrasse. Buses also run every hour from the airport to the Westbahnhof (west train station) and the Südbahnhof (south train station). Be sure you get on the right bus! The one-way fare for all buses is AS 50. A taxi from the airport to downtown Vienna costs about AS 330; agree on the price in advance. Cabs (legally) do not meter the drive, as fares are more or less fixed (legally again) at about double the meter fare. A seat in a limousine will cost less; book at the airport. **Mazur** (tel. 0222/604–2530) offers cheaper pickup and delivery service by arrangement. If you are driving from the airport, follow signs to "Zentrum."

By Train Vienna has four train stations. The principal station, Westbahnhof, is for trains to and from Linz, Salzburg, and

Innsbruck. Trains from Germany and France arrive here, too. The Südbahnhof is for trains to and from Graz, Klagenfurt, Villach, and Italy. Franz-Josefs-Bahnhof is for trains to and from Prague, Berlin, and Warsaw. Go to Wien Mitte (Landstrasse) for local trains to and from the north of the city.

By Bus If you arrive by bus, it will probably be at the central bus terminal, Wien Mitte, opposite the city air terminal (and the Hilton).

By Boat All Danube river boats dock at the DDSG terminal on Mexicoplatz. There's an awkward connection with the U–1 subway from here. Some boats also make a stop slightly upstream at Heiligenstadt, Nussdorf, from where there is an easier connection to the U–4 subway line.

By Car Main access routes are the expressways to the west and south (Westautobahn, Südautobahn). Routes to the downtown area are marked "Zentrum."

Getting Around

Vienna is fairly easy to explore on foot; as a matter of fact, the heart of the city—the area within the Ring—is largely a pedestrian zone. The Ring itself was once the city ramparts, torn down just over a century ago to create today's broad, tree-lined boulevard. Public transportation is comfortable, convenient, and frequent, though not cheap.

Tickets for bus, subway, and streetcar are available in most stations. Tickets in multiples of four are sold at cigarette shops, known as Tabak-Trafik, or at the window marked "Vorverkauf" at central stations such as Karlsplatz or Stephansplatz. A strip with four tickets costs AS 56, a single ticket AS 20. If you plan to use public transportation frequently, get a **24-hour ticket** (AS 40), a **three-day tourist ticket** (AS 102), or an **eight-day ticket** (AS 220). Maps and information are available at Stephansplatz, Karlsplatz, and Praterstern U-Bahn stations.

By Bus or Streetcar Inner city buses are numbered 1A through 3A, and operate weekdays to 7:40 PM, Saturday until 2 PM. Lower fares (buy a **Kurzstreckenkarte**; it gives four trips for AS 28) cover these routes as well as designated shorter stretches (roughly two to four stops) on all other bus or streetcar lines. Streetcars and buses are numbered according to route, and run until about midnight. Night buses marked N follow special routes every hour; the fare is AS 25. The central terminal point is Schwedenplatz. The no. 1 and no. 2 streetcar lines run the circular route around the Ring, clockwise and counterclockwise respectively.

By Subway Subway lines (U-Bahn; stations are marked with a huge blue "U") are designated U-1, U-2, and U-4 and are clearly marked and color-coded. Additional services are provided by the city railroad, the Stadtbahn, indicated by a brown "S" symbol, and by a fast suburban train, the S-Bahn, indicated by a stylized blue "S" symbol. Both are tied into the general city fare system.

By Taxi Cabs can be flagged on the street if the "Frei" (free) sign is illuminated. Alternatively, dial 60160'9101, or 4369 to call for one. All rides are metered. The basic fare is AS 22, but expect to pay AS 60 for an average city ride. There are additional charges for bags.

Important Addresses and Numbers

Tourist Information City Tourist Office: Kärntnerstr. 38, behind the opera, tel. 0222/513–8892. Open daily 9–7.

Embassies U.S.: Gartenbaupromenade (Marriott Bldg.), tel. 0222/51451. **Canadian:** Dr. Karl Lueger-Ring, tel. 0222/633691. **U.K.:** Jauresg. 10, tel. 0222/756117.

Emergencies Police: tel. 122; **Ambulance:** tel. 144; **Doctor:** American Medical Society of Vienna, Lazaretteg. 13, tel. 0222/424568; **Pharmacies:** open weekdays 8–6, Sat. 8–noon.

English Bookstores Big Ben Bookshop: Porzellang. 24, tel. 0222/316412; **British Bookshop:** Weihburgg. 8, tel. 0222/512–1945; **English Book Shop:** Plankeng. 7, tel. 0222/512–2993; **Shakespeare & Co.:** Sterng. 2, tel. 0222/535–4376.

Travel Agencies American Express: Kärntnerstr. 21–23, tel. 0222/51540; Parkring 10, tel. 0222/515–1180; **Austrian Travel Agency:** Kärntnerring 3–5, tel. 0222/588000; **Wagons-Lits/Thomas Cook:** Kärntner Ring 2, tel. 0222/50160.

Guided Tours

Orientation Tours Vienna Sightseeing Tours (tel. 0222/712–4683) offers a short highlights tour or a lengthier one to the Vienna Woods, Mayerling, and other areas surrounding Vienna. Tours start in front of or beside the opera house. **Cityrama** (tel. 0222/53413) provides city tours with hotel pickup; tours assemble opposite the InterContinental Hotel. All hotels and travel agencies have details.

Special-Interest Tours Tours are available to the Spanish Riding School, the Vienna Boys Choir, operettas and concerts, the wine suburb of Grinzing, nightclubs, and Vienna by night. Check with the city tourist office or your hotel for details.

Walking Tours *Vienna from A to Z* (in English) is available at most bookstores; it explains the numbered plaques attached to all major buildings in Vienna. *Vienna: Downtown Walking Tours* by Henriette Mandl outlines suggested routes and provides information on sights. For organized walking tours with English-speaking guides, check with the tourist office or your hotel.

Excursions Day bus trips are organized to the Danube valley, the Hungarian border, the Alps south of Vienna, Salzburg, and Budapest; get information from the city tourist office.

Exploring Vienna

Vienna has been described as an "old dowager of a town," not a bad description for this one-time center of empire. It's not just the aristocratic and courtly atmosphere, with monumental doorways and stately facades of former palaces at every turn. Nor is it just that Vienna has a higher proportion of middle-aged and older citizens than any other city in Europe, with a concommitant sense of stability, quiet, and respectability. Rather, it's these factors combined with a love of music, a discreet weakness for rich food (especially cakes), an adherence to old-fashioned and formal forms of address, a high, if unadventurous, regard for the arts, and a gentle mourning for lost glories that combine to produce a stiff but elegant, slightly other-worldly, sense of dignity.

Most main sights are in the inner zone, the oldest part of the city, encircled by the Ring, once the city walls and today a broad boulevard. Before setting out, be sure to check opening times of museums carefully; they can change unpredictably. Carry a ready supply of AS 10 coins, too; many places of interest have coin-operated tape machines providing English commentaries. As you wander around, train yourself to look upward; some of the most memorable architectural treasures are on upper stories and roof lines.

The Heart of Vienna *Numbers in the margin correspond with points of interest on the Vienna map.*

Vienna's role as imperial city is preserved in the complex of buildings that makes up the former royal palace. Start your tour at Albertinaplatz, behind the opera house. Head down

❶ Augustinerstrasse. On your left is the **Albertina,** home to the world's largest collection of drawings, sketches, engravings, and etchings. There are works here by Dürer—these are perhaps the highlight of the collection—Rembrandt, Michelangelo, Corregio, and many others. The holdings are so vast that only a limited number can be shown at one time. Some original works are so delicate that they can only be shown in facsimile. *Augustinerstr. 1, tel. 0222/534830. Admission: AS 30. Open Mon., Tues., Thurs. 10–4; Wed. 10–6; Fri. 10–2; Sat. and Sun. 10–1; closed Sun. in July and August.*

❷ Next door is the 14th-century **Augustinerkirche,** a favorite on Sundays, when the 11 AM mass is sung in Latin. Nearby is the **❸** **Nationalbibliothek** (the National Library), with its stunning Baroque great hall. *Josefsplatz 1, tel. 0222/534100. Admission: AS 15. Open May–Oct., Mon.–Sat. 10–4; Nov.–Apr., Mon.–Sat. 11–12.*

Josefsplatz is where much of *The Third Man* was filmed, specifically in and around the Palais Pallavicini across the street. The **❹** entrance to the **Spanische Reitschule,** the Spanish Riding School, is here, too, though the famed white horses are actually stabled on the other side of the square. For tickets, write the Austrian Tourist Office (Friedrichstr. 7, A–1010 Vienna) *at least* three months in advance. There are performances on Sunday at 10:45 AM and Wednesday at 7 PM year-round. Mid-April through October, there are additional performances on Saturday at 9 AM.

❺ Above the stables is the **Neue Galerie,** housing mainly Impressionist and other 19th- and early 20th-century paintings and sculptures. It's a compact collection, though it contains nothing of outstanding interest. *Reitschulgasse 1, tel. 0222/533–6045. Admission: AS 15. Open Mon.–Thurs., and weekends 10–4.*

From here you're only a few steps from Michaelerplatz, the lit-**❻** tle square that marks the entrance to the **Hofburg,** the royal palace. On one side of the square, opposite the entrance, on the corner of Herrengasse and Kohlmarkt, is the **Loos building** (1911), designed by Adolf Loos. It's no more than a simple brick-and-glass structure, but architectural historians point to it as one of the earliest "modern" buildings in Europe—a building where function determines style. In striking contrast is the

Baroque **Michaelertor** opposite, the principal entrance to the Hofburg.

Time Out Some insist that no visit to Vienna is complete without a visit to **Demel,** on the left just down the Kohlmarkt. Others find the café-pastry shop overpriced—it is expensive even by Vienna standards—and complain of the service. The choice is yours.

Head under the domed entrance of the Michaelertor to visit the ➐ **imperial apartments** of Emperor Franz Josef and Empress Elisabeth. Among the exhibits is the exercise equipment used by the beautiful empress. Here, too, is the dress she was wearing when she was stabbed to death by a demented Italian anarchist on the shores of Lake Geneva in 1898; the dagger marks are visible. *Michaelerplatz 1, tel. 0222/5875-5540. Admission: AS 15. Open Mon.-Sat. 8:30-4, Sun. 8:30-12:30.*

➑ Be sure to see the **Schatzkammer,** the imperial treasury, home of the magnificent crown jewels. *Hofburg, Schweizerhof, tel. 0222/934-5410. Admission: AS 45. Open Nov.-Mar., Mon. and Wed.-Fri. 10-4, weekends 9-4 (Apr.-Oct. until 6).*

➒ The **Hofburgkapelle,** the court chapel, is where the Vienna Boys' Choir sings mass at 11 AM on Sunday. You'll need tickets to attend; these are available at the chapel from 5 PM Friday (expect long lines) or by writing to Burgkapelle, Hofburg, Schweizerhof, A-1010 Vienna. The city tourist office can sometimes help with ticket applications.

➓ Head south to Heldenplatz, the open square in front of the **Neue Hofburg Museums,** a ponderously ornate 19th-century edifice housing a series of museums. Highlights are the Waffensammlung (the weapons collection), the collections of musical instruments (currently closed for reconstruction), the ethnographic museum, and the exciting Ephesus museum, with finds from the excavations at that ancient site.

Walk south again across the Ring, the broad boulevard encircling the inner city, to the imperial museum complex. The ⑪ **Naturhistorisches Museum** (Natural History Museum) is on ⑫ your right, the **Kunsthistoriches Museum** (Art History Museum) is on your left. The latter is one of the great art museums of the world; this is not a place to miss. The collections focus on old-master painting, notably Brueghel, Cranach, Titian, Canaletto, Rubens, and Velazquez. But there are important Egyptian, Greek, Etruscan, and Roman exhibits, too. *Burgring 5, tel. 0222/934-5410. Admission: AS 45; free the first Sun. of each month. Open Wed.-Mon. 9-6.*

Time Out Across the Messeplatz stretches Messepalast, the building that now serves as fair and exhibit space. Inside is one of Vienna's better-kept secrets, the **Glacis-Beisl** restaurant. The garden under the vine-clad arbors has to be experienced. *Tel. 0222/930-7374. Reservations advised. Closed Jan.-Feb.*

At the Mariahilferstrasse end of the Messepalast complex is ⑬ the small and fascinating **Tabak Museum,** the Tobacco Museum. *Mariahilfstr., tel. 0222/961716. Open Wed.-Fri. 10-3, weekends 9-1, Tues. 10-5.*

Head east down the Ring, with the Kunsthistoriches Museum on your right. Looming up to the right, over Karlsplatz, is the

Vienna

heroic facade and dome, flanked by vast twin columns, of the
(14) Karlskirche. It was built around 1715 by Fischer von Erlach.
The oval interior is surprisingly small, given the monumental
facade: One expects something more on the scale of St. Peter's
in Rome. The ceiling has airy frescoes, and stiff shafts of gilt
radiate like sunbeams from the altar.

(15) Take the pedestrian underpass back under the Ring to Opernplatz. This is the site of the **Staatsoper,** the opera house, one of
the best in the world and a focus of Viennese social life. Tickets
are expensive and rare, so you may have to settle for a back-
stage tour. They are given five times daily in July and August,
and once daily in June and September.

Head up Kärntnerstrasse, Vienna's main thoroughfare, now an
elegant and busy pedestrian mall. On your left is the creamy
(16) facade of the **Sacher Hotel.** Take a look inside at the plush red-
and-gilt decor, a *fin de siècle* masterpiece. The hotel is also the
home of the original Sachertorte—the ultimate chocolate cake.
Back on Kärntnerstrasse, around the corner from the Sacher,
is the city tourist office. Leading off Kärtnerstrasse, to the
left, is the little street of Marco d'Aviano-Gasse. Follow it to
(17) Kapuzinerkirche, in whose crypt, called the **Kaisergruft** or the
imperial vault, the serried ranks of long-dead Hapsburgs lie.
The oldest tomb is that of Ferdinand II; it dates from 1633. The
most recent tomb is that of Franz Josef, dating from 1916.

(18) In the center of the square is the ornate 18th-century **Donner
Brunnen,** the Providence Fountain. The figures represent main
rivers that flow into the Danube; Empress Maria Teresa
thought the figures obscene and wanted them removed or properly clothed.

Time Out   Coffee or tea and what are said, even by the French and Belgians, to be the best pastries in the world are available in
staggering quantity at the **Konditorei Oberlaa.** *Neuer Markt
16. Open Mon.–Fri. 9–7, Sat. 9–2.*

(19) Continue north through Neuer Markt to reach pedestrians-
only Graben. The **Pestsäule,** or Plague Column, shoots up from
the middle of the street, looking like a geyser of whipped cream
touched with gold. It commemorates the Black Death of 1697;
look at the graphic depictions of those who fell victim to the
ravages of the terrible disease. A small turning to the right,
(20) just past the column, leads to the Baroque **Peterskirche.** The little church, the work of Johann Lukas von Hildebrandt, finished
in about 1730, has probably the most theatrical interior in the
city. The pulpit is especially fine, with a highly ornate canopy;
but florid and swirling decoration is everywhere. Many of the
decorative elements are based on a tent form, a motif suggested
by the Turkish tents camped outside the city walls during the
great siege of Vienna at the end of the 17th century.

(21) Walk back to Graben and along to Stephansplatz, site of the
Stephansdom (St. Stephen's Cathedral). Its towering Gothic
spires and gaudy 19th-century tiled roof are still the dominant
feature of the Vienna skyline. The oldest part of the building is
the 13th-century entrance, the soaring **Riesentor,** or Giant
Doorway. Inside, the church is mysteriously dark, filled with
an array of monuments, tombs, sculptures, paintings, and pulpits. Despite extensive wartime damage—and numerous

Baroque additions—the building radiates an authentically medieval atmosphere. Climb up the 345 steps of **Alte Steffl,** Old Steve, the south tower, for a stupendous view over the city. An elevator goes up the north tower to **Die Pummerin,** the Boomer, a 22-ton bell cast in 1711 from cannons captured from the Turks. Take a 30-minute tour of the crypt to see the entrails of the Hapsburgs, carefully preserved in copper jars.

㉒ On a narrow street east of the cathedral, is the house where Mozart lived from 1784 to 1787. Today it's the **Mozart Erinnerungsräume,** the Mozart Museum. It was here that he wrote *The Marriage of Figaro,* and here, some say, that he spent the happiest years of his life. *Domgasse 5, tel. 0222/524–0722. Admission: AS 15. Open Tues.–Sun. 10–12:15 and 1–4:30.*

Other Corners of Vienna Walk back down the Graben and the narrow Naglergasse, and turn left into the Freyung. On your left is the **Palais Ferstl,** now a stylish shopping arcade. At the back is the skillfully restored **Café Central,** once headquarters for Vienna's leading literary **㉓** figures. Cross the Freyung to the dominant **Schottenkirche.** The monks brought to found it were actually Irish, not Scottish. They started a school as well, which shares the courtyard to the left with a pleasant garden restaurant in summer. Turn back through the Freyung to **Am Hof,** a remarkable square with the city's Baroque central fire station, possibly the **㉔** world's most ornate. Cross the square to the **Kirche am Hof.** The interior is curiously reminiscent of many Dutch churches.

Time Out For a typical meal or just a beer or coffee, stop at **Gustlbauer.** The restaurant is a regular stop for the Fiaker coachmen, who leave their livery and passengers briefly for a quick Schnapps. The waiter will help you decipher the handwritten menu. Vienna's mayor, who lives nearby, often appears. *Am Hof, Drahtgasse 2, tel. 0222/635889. Open daily 10–midnight, Sat. 10–3.*

㉕ Continue to Judenplatz and turn right into Parisergasse to the **Uhrenmuseum** (Clock Museum), located in a lovely Renaissance house. *Schulhof 2, tel. 0222/533–2265. Admission: AS 15; free Fri. morning. Open Tues.–Sun. 9–12:15 and 1–4:30.*

Turn down the Kurrentgasse and, via Fütterergasse, cross the Wipplingerstrasse into Stoss im Himmel (literally, a "thrust **㉖** to heaven"). To your left down Salvatorgasse is **Mariam Gestade,** originally a church for fishermen on the nearby canal. Note the ornate "folded hands" spire. Return along Wip- **㉗** plingerstrasse, across Marc Aurel-Strasse, to **Hoher Markt,** with a central monument celebrating the betrothal of Mary and Joseph. Roman ruins are displayed in the museum on the south side of the square. *Hoher Markt 3, tel. 0222/5355606. Admission: AS 15; free on Fri. morning. Open Tues.–Sun. 10–12:15 and 1–4:30.*

On the north side of Hoher Markt is the amusing **Anker-Uhr,** a clock that tells time by figures moving across a scale. The figures are identified on a plaque at the lower left of the clock; it's well-worth passing by at noon to catch the show. Go through **㉘** Judengasse to the **Ruprechtskirche** (St. Rupert's). The oldest church in Vienna is small, damp, dark, and, unfortunately, usually closed, though you can peek through a window.

Vienna Environs
29 It's a 15-minute ride from center city on subway line U-4 (stop either at Schönbrunn or Hietzing) to **Schönbrunn Palace,** the magnificent Baroque residence built between 1696 and 1713 for the Hapsburgs. Here Kaiser Franz Josef I was born and died. His "office" (kept as he left it in 1916) is a touching reminder of his spartan life; other rooms, however, reflect the elegance of monarchy. The ornate public rooms are still used for state receptions. A guided tour covers 45 of the palace's 1,441 rooms; among the curiosities are the Chinese room and the gym fitted out for Empress Elisabeth, where she exercised daily to keep her figure. *Schönbrunner Schlosstr, tel. 0222/833646. Admission: AS 50. Open daily, Oct.–Apr. 9–12 and 1–4; May–Sept. 9–12 and 1–5.*

Once at the grounds, don't overlook the **Tiergarten** (Zoo). It's Europe's oldest menagerie and, when established in 1752, was intended to amuse and educate the court. It contains an extensive assortment of animals, some of them in their original Baroque enclosures. *Tel. 0222/821236. Admission: AS 30. Open daily 9–dusk, 6 PM latest.*

Follow the pathways up to the **Gloriette,** that Baroque ornament on the rise behind Schönbrunn, and enjoy superb views of the city. Originally this was to have been the site of the palace, but projected construction costs were considered too high. *Admission: AS 10. Open May–Oct., daily 8–6.*

The **Wagenburg** (Carriage Museum), near the entrance to the palace grounds, holds some splendid examples of early transportation, from children's sleighs to funeral carriages of the emperors. *Tel. 0222/823244. Admission: AS 30. Open Apr.–Oct., Tues.–Sun. 10–4; May–Sept., Tues.–Sun. 10–5.*

30 Take the D streetcar toward the Südbahnhof to reach **Schloss Belvedere** (Belvedere Palace), a Baroque complex often compared to Versailles. It was commissioned by Prince Eugene of Savoy and built by Johann Lukas von Hildebrandt in 1721–22. The palace is made up of two separate buildings, one at the foot and the other at the top of a hill. The lower tract was built first as residential quarters; the upper buildings were reserved for entertaining. The gardens in between are among the best examples anywhere of natural Baroque ornamentation. The buildings hold contemporary significance: The State Treaty that gave Austria its independence in 1955 was signed in the great upper hall. The composer Anton Bruckner lived in an apartment to the north of the upper building until his death in 1896. Both sections now house outstanding art museums: the gallery of 19th- and 20th-century art in the Upper Belvedere (Klimt, Kokoschka, Schiele, Waldmüller, Markart), and the Baroque museum (including medieval Austrian art) in the Lower Belvedere. *Prinz-Eugen-Str. 27, tel. 0222/784158. Admission: AS 30. Open Tues.–Sun. 10–4.*

31 Continue across the Gürtel southward to the **20th Century Museum,** containing a small but extremely tasteful modern art collection. *Schweizer Garten, tel. 0222/782550. Admission: AS 30. Open Thurs.–Tues. 10–4.*

You can reach a small corner of the **Vienna Woods** by streetcar and bus: Take a streetcar or the subway U-2 to Schottentor/University and, from there, the no. 38 streetcar (Grinzing) to the end of the line. Grinzing itself is out of a picture book; alas, much of the wine offered in the taverns is less enchanting. (For better wine and ambience, try the village of Nussdorf, reached by streetcar D.) To get into the woods, change in Grinzing to the no. 38A bus. This will take you to Kahlenberg, which provides a superb view out over the Danube and the city. You can take the bus or hike to Leopoldsberg, the promontory over the Danube from which Turkish invading forces were repulsed in the 16th and 17th centuries.

Off the Beaten Track

Vienna's **Bermuda Triangle** (around Judengasse/Seitenstettengasse) is jammed with everything from good bistros to jazz clubs. Also check the tourist office's museum list carefully: There's something for everyone, ranging from Sigmund Freud's apartment to the Funeral and Burial Museum. The **Hundertwasserhaus** (Kegelgasse/Löwengasse; streetcar N), an astonishing apartment complex designed by artist Friedenreich Hundertwasser, with turrets, towers, odd windows, and uneven floors, will be of interest to those who think architectural form need not follow function.

Shopping

Antiques The best (and most expensive) shops are in the inner city, but there are good finds in some of the outer districts, particularly among the back streets in the **Josefstadt** (eighth) district.

Boutiques Name brands are found along the **Kohlmarkt** and the side streets off the Kärntnerstrasse.

Folk Costumes A good selection at reasonable prices is offered by the **NÖ Heimatwerk** (Herrengasse 6); try also **Trachten Tostmann** (Schottengasse 3a) or **Loden-Plankl** (Michaelerplatz 6).

Shopping Districts Tourists gravitate to the **Kärntnerstrasse,** but the Viennese do most of their shopping on the **Mariahilferstrasse.**

Department Stores **Steffl** (Kärntner Str.), and **Gerngross, Herzmansky,** and **Stafa** (all on Mariahilferstr.) are the major outlets.

Food and Flea Markets The **Naschmarkt** (between Rechte and Linke Wienzeile. Weekdays 6 AM–mid-afternoon, Sat. 6–1) is a sensational open food market, offering specialties from around the world. The **Flohmarkt** (flea market) operates year-round beyond the Naschmarkt (subway U-4 to Kettenbrückengasse) and is equally fascinating (Sat. 8–4). Bargaining here goes on in any number of languages. One of the best seasonal local markets for handicrafts is in **Spittelberggasse.**

Dining

In contrast to many cities, the leading Viennese hotels are in competition for the country's best cooks and so offer some of the city's best dining. Even the chain hotels have joined in the effort to see which can win over the leading chefs. The results are rewarding; you may not even have to leave your hotel to enjoy outstanding food and service. For details and price-category definitions, *see* Dining in Staying in Austria.

Very Expensive **Zu den Drei Husaren.** This is one of Vienna's enduring monu-
★ ments to tradition, complete with candlelight and live piano

(except on Sundays). Casual visitors (as opposed to the "regulars") may have to settle for more atmosphere than service, however. The hors d'oeuvre trolleys are intentionally enticing and can easily double the dinner bill. *Weihburggasse 4, tel. 0222/512–1092. Reservations essential. AE, DC, MC, V.*

★ **Rotisserie Prinz Eugen.** "New Vienna Cuisine"—the Austrian version of nouvelle cuisine—is combined successfully with more usual dishes at the Hilton's Rotisserie Prinz Eugen, which has managed to sustain its initial reputation for outstanding decor, service, and food. Piano accompaniment in the evening. *Hilton Hotel, Am Stadtpark, tel. 0222/752652. Reservations advised. AE, DC, MC, V. Closed Sat. lunch.*

Steirereck. Steirereck boasts the 1988 Chef of the Year, although not all would agree. Some of the standard dishes are more successful than the forays into the "New Vienna Cuisine." No one denies the elegance of the ambience, however. The garden outside in summer is pleasant in the later evening when traffic lets up. *Rasumofskygasse 2, tel. 0222/713–3168. Reservations advised. AE. Closed Sat., Sun., and holidays.*

Expensive   **da Conte.** The newest Italian restaurant on the scene is also the best, set in a series of charming, arched-ceilinged rooms. The same management is responsible for the cheaper, smaller restaurant next door, as well as the Italian gourmet deli on the corner. *Kurrentgasse 12, tel. 0222/533–6464. Reservations advised. AE, DC, MC, V. Closed Sun.*

Demel. One of Vienna's most famous pastry shops offers magnificent snacks of delicate meats, fish, and vegetables, as well as the expected cakes and other goodies. The stuffed mushrooms and vegetable-cheese combinations are especially tempting—as is the hot chocolate. *Kohlmarkt 14, tel. 0222/533–5516. No reservations. AE, DC, MC, V. Closed after 6 PM.*

★ **Korso.** You'll find outstanding food and atmosphere at this gourmet temple of "New Vienna Cuisine." Not all agree with the kitchen's approach to experiments—some say the restaurant really was created for the cook—but few are disappointed. *Mahlerstr. 2, tel. 0222/5151–6546. Reservations advised. AE, DC, MC, V. Closed Sat. lunch and Sun.*

Le Salut. This intimate restaurant offers the best French cuisine in town, with a price tag to match. In summer, the tables outside add to the pleasure. *Wildpretmarkt 3, tel. 0222/533–1322. Reservations advised. AE, DC, MC, V. Closed Sun., also Sat. in July and Aug.*

★ **Vier Jahreszeiten.** This restaurant effortlessly manages to achieve that delicate balance between food and atmosphere. The service is attentive without being overbearing. The lunch buffet offers both excellent food and value. Evening dining includes grill specialties and live piano music (except on Sunday). *Hotel Intercontinental, Johannesgasse 28, tel. 0222/750–5143. Reservations advised. AE, DC, MC, V.*

Moderate   **Bastei-Beisl.** A comfortable, wood-paneled restaurant offering good traditional Viennese fare. Outdoor tables are particularly pleasant on summer evenings. *Stubenbastei 10, tel. 0222/524319. Reservations usually not necessary. AE, DC, MC, V. Closed Sun.*

Franchi's. This place is a good tip for lunch and after concerts. The food is imaginative, with French overtones; the ambience inside is pleasant, and service is attentive—at least until the later hours. Nobody seems to mind the traffic, so the tables outside in summer are always packed. *Schwarzenbergplatz 3, tel. 0222/755334. Reservations advised for dinner and outside lunch. AE, DC, MC, V.*

★ **Gigerl.** It's hard to believe you're right in the middle of the city at this imaginative and charming wine restaurant that serves hot and cold buffets. Rooms are small and cozy but may get smoky and noisy when the place is full—which it usually is. The food is typical of wine gardens on the fringes of the city: roast meats, casserole dishes, cold cuts, salads. The wines are excellent. The surrounding narrow alleys and ancient buildings add to the charm of the outdoor tables in summer. *Rauhen steingasse 3, tel. 0222/513–4431. Reservations advised. DC, V.*

Zur Himmelpforte. This quality restaurant has a deserved reputation for reasonably priced gourmet meals. Standards may not reach the heights of some other Viennese establishments, but then neither do the prices! The house offers the *real* Budweiser beer as well. *Himmelpfortgasse 24, tel. 0222/513–1967. Reservations not essential. AE, DC, MC, V. Closed Sun.*

Melker Stiftskeller. This is one of the city's half-dozen genuine wine taverns, or kellers; the food selection is limited but good, featuring pig's knuckle. House wines from the Wachau are excellent. *Schottengasse 3, tel. 0222/533–5530. Reservations usually not needed. No credit cards. Evenings only; closed Sun.*

★ **Ofenloch.** This place is always packed, which speaks well not only of the excellent specialties from some Viennese grandmother's cookbook but also of the atmosphere. Waitresses are attired in appropriate period costume, and the furnishings add to the color. At times, the rooms may be too smoky and noisy for some tastes. If you like garlic, try *vanillerostbraten*, a rump steak with as much garlic as you request. *Kurrentgasse 8, tel. 0222/637268. Reservations essential. No credit cards. Closed Sun.*

Stadtbeisl. Good standard Austrian fare is served up at this popular eatery, which is comfortable without being pretentious. Service gets uneven as the place fills up, but if you are seated outside in summer, you probably won't mind. *Naglergasse 21, tel. 0222/533–3323. Reservations advised.*

Zu ebener Erde und erster Stock. Ask for a table upstairs in this exquisite, tiny, utterly original Biedermeier house, which serves good, standard Austrian fare; the downstairs space is really more for snacks. *Burggasse 13, tel. 0222/936254. Reservations advised. AE, DC, MC, V. Closed Sun.*

Inexpensive **Figlmüller.** Known for its Schnitzel, Figlmüller is always
★ packed. Guests share the benches, the long tables, and the experience. Food choices are limited, but nobody seems to mind. Only wine is offered to drink, but it is good. The small garden outside in summer is just as popular as the tables inside. *Wollzeile 5 (passageway), tel. 0222/526177. No reservations. No credit cards. Closed Sat. dinner and Sun.*

Ilona-Stüberl. Head to Ilona-Stüberl for a cozy Hungarian atmosphere—without the gypsy music. Be prepared to douse the fire if you ask for a dish with hot peppers! The tables outside in summer are pleasant but somewhat public. *Bräunerstr. 2, tel. 0222/533–9029. Reservations advised. AE, DC, MC, V. Closed Sun.*

Zu den drei Hacken. This is one of the few genuine Viennese *Gasthäuser* in the city center; like the place itself, the fare is solid if not elegant. Legend has it that Schubert dined here; the ambience probably hasn't changed much since. There are tables outside in summer, although the extra seating capacity strains both the kitchen and the service. *Singerstr. 8, tel. 0222/ 525895. No reservations. No credit cards. Closed Sat. dinner and Sun.*

Lodging

Vienna's inner city is the best base for visitors because it's so close to most of the major sights, restaurants, and shops. This accessibility translates, of course, into higher prices. For details and price-category definitions, *see* Lodging in Staying in Austria.

Very Expensive **Bristol.** Opposite the opera house, the Bristol is classic Viennese, preferred by many for the service as well as the location. The bar is comfortable, though not overly private; the restaurants associated with the hotel are outstanding, especially Korso. Back and upper guest rooms are quieter. *Kärntner Ring 1, tel. 0222/515160. 152 rooms with bath. Facilities: bar, restaurants. AE, DC, MC, V.*

★ **Imperial.** This former palace represents elegant old Vienna at its best, with such features as heated towel racks in some rooms. The location could hardly be better, although being on the Ring, the front and lower rooms can be noisy. The bar is intimate and pleasant. Lunch in the café is both reasonable and good; the hotel restaurant is superb. *Kärntner Ring 16, tel. 0222/501100. 151 rooms with bath or shower. Facilities: beauty parlor, conference rooms.*

★ **InterContinental.** Vienna's modern InterContinental has the reputation of being one of the chain's very best. Rooms are spacious, the main restaurant exceptional. But whereas the hotel succeeds in acquiring some Viennese charm, the bar fails hopelessly, as does the Brasserie. Rooms in front overlooking the park are quieter, particularly in winter when the ice-skating rink to the back is in operation. *Johannesgasse 28, tel. 0222/ 75050. 500 rooms with bath. Facilities: sauna, health club, laundry, dry cleaning service, barber, hair stylist, complimentary limo, parking. AE, DC, MC, V.*

Marriott. The one Viennese aspect is the service; all else is global modern. The atrium lobby, while pleasant, is anything but intimate. The restaurants are good, and Sunday brunch at the Marriott has become immensely popular (book at least two days in advance). *Parkring 12A, tel. 0222/515180. 304 rooms with bath. Facilities: sauna, health club, pool, shops, garage. AE, DC, MC, V.*

Palais Schwarzenberg. Rooms are incorporated into a quiet wing of a Baroque palace, a 10-minute drive from the opera. The restaurant enjoys a good reputation. *Schwarzenbergplatz 9, tel. 0222/784515. 38 rooms with bath. Facilities: bar. AE, DC, MC, V.*

Sacher. The hotel's reputation has varied considerably over recent years, but it remains one of the legendary addresses in Europe, with its opulent decor highlighted by original oil paintings, sculptures, and objets d'art. The Blue and Red bars are intimate and favored by nonguests as well, as is the café, or particularly in summer when tables are set up outside. Guest rooms are spacious and elegantly appointed. *Philarmonikerstr. 4, tel. 0222/514560. 117 rooms with bath or shower.*

Facilities: coffee shop, bar. No credit cards, but personal checks accepted.

Expensive   **Astoria.** Though the Astoria is one of Vienna's traditional old
★ hotels, the rooms are considerably modernized. The paneled
lobby has been preserved, however, and retains an unmistakable Old World patina. The location is central, but because of the
street musicians and the late-night crowds in the pedestrian
zone, rooms overlooking the Kärntnerstrasse tend to be noisy
in summer. *Kärntnerstr. 32–34, tel. 0222/515770. 108 rooms
with bath or shower. Facilities: restaurant. AE, DC, MC, V.*

Capricorno. Overlooks the Danube Canal in a fairly central location. Although its facade is modern and somewhat short on
charm, the hotel nonetheless represents good value.
*Schwedenplatz 3–4, tel. 0222/533–3104. 46 rooms with bath or
shower. AE, DC, MC, V.*

Europa. The location—midway between the opera house and
the cathedral—is ideal, but rooms on the Kärntnerstrasse side
are noisy in summer; ask for a room overlooking Neuer Markt.
The building is postwar modern and lacks the charm of older
hotels, but the staff is friendly and helpful. The café is popular,
particularly in summer when tables are put outdoors. *Neuer
Markt 3, tel. 0222/515940. 102 rooms with bath. Facilities: coffee shop, bar, restaurant. AE, DC, MC, V.*

★ **König von Ungarn.** This utterly charming, centrally located hotel is tucked away in the shadow of the cathedral. The historic
facade belies the modern efficiency of the interior, from the
atrium lobby to the guest rooms themselves. The restaurant
(just next door in a house that Mozart once lived in) is excellent,
though not inexpensive, and is always packed at noon.
*Schulerstr. 10, tel. 0222/515840. 32 rooms with bath or shower.
AE, DC, MC, V.*

Mailberger Hof. This is a favorite of opera stars, conductors,
and those who want a central but quiet location. Some rooms
have limited kitchenette facilities. The arcaded courtyard is
very pretty. *Annagasse 7, tel. 0222/512–0641. 80 rooms with
bath or shower. AE, DC, MC, V.*

Central. This older hotel doesn't have quite the downtown location its name suggests, but it is reasonably central, although
across the canal. *Taborstr. 8a, tel. 0222/242405. 60 rooms, 41
with bath or shower. AE, DC, MC, V.*

Pension Christina. This one is gaining a solid reputation, due in
part to its central yet quiet location in the inner city.
Hafnersteig 7, tel. 0222/533–2961. 32 rooms with bath or shower. MC.

★ **Post.** The hotel takes its name from the city's main post office,
opposite. An older but updated hotel that offers fine location,
friendly staff, and a good café. *Fleischmarkt 24, tel. 0222/
515830. 107 rooms, 77 with bath or shower. AE, DC, MC, V.*

Moderate   **Austria.** This older hotel is on a quiet side street in an historic
★ area. It is popular with tourists. *Wolfengasse 3/Fleischmarkt,
tel. 0222/51523. 51 rooms, 40 with bath or shower. Facilities:
bar. DC, MC.*

Kärntnerhof. Though tucked away in a tiny, quiet side street,
Kärntnerhof is nevertheless centrally located. It's known for
its particularly friendly staff. Rooms are functionally decorated but clean and serviceable. *Grashofgasse 4, tel. 0222/512–
1923. 45 rooms, 34 with bath or shower. AE, DC, MC, V.*

Schweizerhof. This is more of a pension than a hotel, but the location is excellent and the smallish rooms are certainly adequate. *Bauernmarkt 22, tel. 0222/533–1931. 55 rooms with bath or shower. AE, DC, MC, V.*

Wandl. The house is old and the rooms small, but the Wandl's location and reasonable prices compensate for most deficiencies. *Petersplatz 9, tel. 0222/534550. 134 rooms with bath or shower. No credit cards.*

★ **Pension Zipser.** This has become a favorite with regular visitors to Vienna. It is slightly less central than some others on our list, but very comfortable. *Lange Gasse 49, tel. 0222/420228. 46 rooms with bath or shower. Facilities: bar. AE, DC, MC, V.*

The Arts

Theater and Opera Check the monthly program published by the city; posters also show opera and theater schedules. Tickets for the Opera, Volksoper, and the Burg and Akademie theaters are available at the central ticket office to the left rear of the Opera (**Bundestheaterkassen,** Hanuschgasse 3, tel. 0222/514440; open weekdays 9–5, weekends 9–1). Tickets go on advance sale a week before performances. Unsold tickets can be obtained at the evening box office. Plan to be there at least one hour before the performance; students can buy remaining tickets at lower prices, so they are usually out in force. Theater is offered in English at **Vienna English Theater** (Josefsgasse 12, tel. 0222/421260) and **International Theater** (Porzellangasse 8, tel. 0222/316272).

Music Most classical concerts are in either the **Konzerthaus** (Lothringerstr. 20, tel. 0222/712–1211) or **Musikverein** Dumbastrasse 3, tel. 0222/505–8190). Tickets can be bought at the box offices. Pop concerts are scheduled from time to time at the **Austria Center** (Am Hubertusdamm 6, tel. 0222/236–9150; U-4 subway to VIC stop).

Film Films are shown in English at **Burg Kino** (Opernring 19, tel. 0222/587–8406), **de France** (Schottenring 5, tel. 0222/345236), and **Film Museum** (Augustinerstr. 1, tel. 0222/533–7054). To find English-language movies, look for "OF" (Originalfassung) or "OmU" (original with subtitles) in the newspaper listings.

Entertainment and Nightlife

Cabarets Most cabarets are expensive and unmemorable. Two of the best are **Cassanova** (Dorotheergasse 6, tel. 0222/512–9845), which emphasizes striptease, and **Moulin Rouge** (Walfischgasse 11, tel. 0222/512–2130).

Discos The **Splendid** (Jasomirgottstr. 3, tel. 0222/533–1515) is the city's oldest dance-bar, open daily to 4 AM. The refurbished **Scotch** (Parkring 10, tel. 0222/512–9417) is going upscale in its efforts to regain its one-time legendary popularity, though it still hasn't quite made it yet. **Queen Anne** (Johannesgasse 12, tel. 0222/512–0203) is central, popular, and always packed. Live bands, dancing, and snacks are offered at **Chattanooga** (Graben 29, tel. 0222/524218).

Nightclubs A casual '50s atmosphere pervades the popular **Café Volksgarten** (Burgring 1, tel. 0222/630518), situated in the city park of the same name; tables are set outdoors in summer. The more formal **Eden Bar** (Liliengasse 2, tel. 0222/512–7450) is considered one of Vienna's classiest nightspots; don't expect to be let in unless you're dressed to kill.

Wine Taverns For a traditional Viennese night out, head to one of the city's atmospheric wine taverns, which sometimes date as far back as the 12th century. You can often have full meals at these taverns, but the emphasis is mainly on drinking. **Melker Stiftskeller** (*see* Dining) is one of the friendliest and most typical of Vienna's wine taverns. Other well-known ones: **Antiquitäten-Keller** (Magdalenenstr. 32, tel. 0222/566–9533; closed Aug.), which has a backdrop of classical music; **Augustinerkeller** (Augustiner Str. 1, tel. 0222/533–1026), open at lunch well as evenings, in the same building as the Albertina collection; **Esterhazykeller** (Haarhof 1, tel. 0222/533–3482), a particularly mazelike network of rooms; **Piaristenkeller** (Piaristengasse 45, tel. 0222/429152), with zither music; and **Zwölf-Apostelkeller** (Sonnenfelsgasse 3, tel. 0222/526777), near St. Stephen's Cathedral.

The Danube Valley

The Danube valley stretches about 88 kilometers (55 miles) west of Vienna, and many visitors enjoy it as part of an excursion from the country's capital. What this region offers is magnificent countryside, some of Austria's best food and wines, and comfortable, in some cases elegant, accommodations. Above the river are the ruins of ancient castles; the one at Durnstein was where the 12th-century English king Richard the Lionhearted was held captive. The abbeys at Melk and Göttweig, with their magnificent libraries, dominate their settings. Vineyards sweep down to the river, which is lined with fruit trees that burst into blossom every spring. People here live close to the land, and at certain times of year vintners open their homes to sell their own wines and produce. Roadside stands offer flowers, fruits, vegetables, and wines. And this is an area of legend: The Danube as well as the Rhine shares the story of the mythical Niebelungen, defenders of Siegfried, hero of German myth.

Getting Around

By Car If pressed for time, take the Autobahn to St. Pölten, turn north onto Route 333, and follow signs to Melk. For a more scenic route, leave Vienna via Klosterneuburg, take S-33 along the south shore of the Danube, cross the Danube at Melk, and then return to Vienna along the north bank of the river.

By Train Depart from the Westbahnhof for Melk; then take the bus along the north bank of the Danube to Dürnstein and Krems. Side bus trips can be made from Krems to Göttweig.

By Boat Travel upstream, with stops at Krems, Dürnstein, Melk, and points between. Return to Vienna by boat or by train from Melk (combination tickets available).

Guided Tours

Vienna travel agencies offer tours of the Wachau, as the Danube valley is known. These range from one-day outings to longer excursions. For details contact the **Lower Austria tourist office** at Heidenschuss 2, tel. 0222/533–3114.

Tourist Information

Dürnstein. Im Rathaus, tel. 02711/219.
Klosterneuburg. Neidermarkt, Postfach 6, tel. 02243/2038.
Krems. Wichnerstr. 8, tel. 02732/2676 (also covers **Stein an der Donau**).
Melk. Im Rathaus, tel. 02752/2307.
Tulln. Nussallee 4, tel. 02272/4285.

Exploring the Danube Valley

North of Vienna lies **Klosterneuburg,** whose huge **abbey** dominates the market town. The abbey's extensive vineyards offer excellent wines; the abbey itself is a major agricultural landowner in the region. *Open Mon.–Sat. 9:30–11 and 1:30–4, Sun. 1:30–4.*

If you are driving, you have the choice of following the river bank or heading up over the village of St. Andrae and down to the river plain again. At **Tulln,** the **town hall** dominates the town square.

You will see **Stift Göttweig** long before you reach it. This impressive, 11th-century Benedictine abbey affords sensational views of the Danube valley; walk around the grounds and view the impressive chapel. *Rte. 303, on the right bank of the Danube, opposite Krems.*

Farther along the valley is the abbey of **Melk,** holding a commanding position over the Danube. The library is rich in art as well as books; the ceiling frescoes are particularly memorable. *Open Palm Sunday–Oct., Mon.–Sat. 9–11:30 and 1–4, Sun. 9:30–11:30 and 1–4; June–Aug. daily 1–5; Nov.–Palm Sunday, daily 11–2.*

Time Out Pay a visit to the Abbey's **Stiftskeller.** The local wines are excellent. Open daily from April through October.

Cross to the north of the river and head back downstream. The beautiful medieval town of **Dürnstein** is known for keeping Richard the Lionhearted imprisoned in its now-ruined castle for 13 months. The town is also known for its fine hotels, restaurants, and wines. Virtually next door is **Stein,** with its former **Imperial Toll House.** Stein and Krems sit at the center of Austria's foremost winegrowing area and are two towns that have grown together.

The road back to Vienna now wanders away from the Danube, crossing through some attractive woodlands. When you reach Leobensdorf you'll spot **Burg Kreuzenstein,** perched to the left upon a nearby hilltop. The castle includes a small museum of armor. *Tours daily 9–4, according to demand.*

Dining and Lodging

For details and price category definitions, *see* Dining and Lodging in Staying in Austria.

Dürnstein   **Schlosshotel.** This early-Baroque castle has been luxuriously
Lodging   converted. Try for a room overlooking the Danube. Eat in the
★   celebrated restaurant and don't miss out on the house wines.

The Danube Valley

0 — 20 miles

0 — 30 km

N

Dürnstein · Krems · Stockerau · Leobensdorf

Spitz · Stein · Danube · Klosterneuburg

Stift Göttweig · Tulln · Wiener Wald · Vienna

Aggsbach Markt

Melk · St. Pölten

Mödling

Mayerling · Baden

Wiener Neustadt

Mariazell

Dürnstein 2, tel. 02711/212. 37 rooms with bath or shower. Facilities: sauna, pool. Closed Nov.–Mar. AE, DC, MC, V. Very Expensive.

Klosterneuburg
Lodging

Schlosshotel Martinschloss. The Martinschloss—a circa 1766 Baroque castle—is romantically set on the banks of the Danube, in the midst of some rolling park land. The real Trapp family lived here until just before the outbreak of World War II. Try for a room overlooking the river. *34–36 Martinstr., tel. 02243/7426. 54 rooms, 24 with bath. Facilities: pool, sauna. AE, DC, MC, V. Expensive.*

Krems
Lodging

Alte Post. A 16th-century house with an arcaded courtyard, the Alte Post is conveniently positioned right in the center of town. In good weather the courtyard is used for dining. *Obere Landstr. 32, tel. 02732/2276. 20 rooms, most with bath. No credit cards. Inexpensive.*

Langelebarn
Dining
★

Zum Roten Wolf. This outstanding, elegant country restaurant serves traditional local foods. *Bahnstr. 58, tel. 02272/2567. Reservations advised. Closed Tues. AE, DC, MC, V. Moderate.*

Mautern
Dining
★

Bacher. The Bacher is one of Austria's best restaurants, elegant but entirely lacking in pretension. Dining in the garden in summer adds to the experience. *Südtirolerplatz 208, tel. 02732/2937. Reservations advised. Closed Mon. May–Oct., Mon. and Tues. Nov.–Apr. Expensive.*

Salzburg

Arriving and Departing

By Plane   For information, phone Salzburg airport, tel. 0662/851204.

Between the Airport and Downtown   Buses leave for the Salzburg train station in Europaplatz every 15 minutes during the day, every half-hour at night. Journey time is 18 minutes. Taxi fare runs about AS 150.

By Train   Salzburg's main train station is at Europaplatz. Train information, tel. 0662/1717; telephone ticket orders and seat reservations, tel. 0622/1700.

By Bus   The central bus terminal (tel. 0662/72150) is in front of the train station.

By Car   Salzburg has several autobahn exits; study the map and decide which one is best for you. Parking is available in the cavernous garages under the Mönchsberg.

Getting Around

By Bus and Trolleybus   Service is frequent and reliable; route maps are available from the tourist office or your hotel.

By Taxi   At festival time, taxis are too scarce to hail on the street, so order through your hotel porter or phone 0662/74400 or 0662/17611.

By Fiaker   Fiakers, or horsedrawn cabs, are available at Residenzplatz.

By Car   Don't even think of it! The old part of the city is a pedestrian zone. Parking anywhere near the center is all but impossible, so if you're driving, leave your car at the hotel or in the vast parking garages under the Mönchsberg.

Guided Tours

Sightseeing Tours   Guided bus tours of the city and its environs are given by **Autoreisebüro Salzkraft** (Mirabellplatz 2, tel. 0662/72656); **Albus** (Markartplatz 9, tel. 0662/73445); and **Albus Kiosk** (Mirabellplatz, tel. 0662/71773). **Salzburg Panorama Tours** (Mirabellplatz, tel. 0662/74029) organizes chauffeur-driven tours for up to eight people. Your hotel will have details.

Tourist Information

Salzburg's official tourist office, **Stadtverkehrsbüro,** has its headquarters at Auerspergstr. 7, tel. 0662/80720. There's also an **information center** at Mozartplatz 5, tel. 0662/847568, and at the main train station, tel. 0662/71712.

Exploring Salzburg

Numbers in the margin correspond with points of interest on the Salzburg map.

Salzburg is best known as the birthplace of Wolfgang Amadeus Mozart and receives its greatest number of visitors during the annual Music Festival in July and August. Dominated by a fortress on one side and a mini-mountain (Mönchsberg) on the other, this Baroque city is best explored on foot. Many areas are pedestrian precincts. Some of the most interesting boutiques and shops are found in the dozens of alleys and passageways that link streets and squares. And take an umbrella: Salzburg is noted for sudden brief downpours that start as abruptly as they stop.

The Salzach river separates the old and new towns; for the best perspective on the old, climb the **Kapuziner** hill (pathways from the Linzerstrasse or Steingasse). Once back down at river level, walk up through Markartplatz, to the **Landestheater,** where light opera and operettas are staged outside at festival time; the larger houses used during the festival are closed most of the year. Wander through the Baroque **Mirabell** gardens in back of the theater and enjoy a dramatic view of the Old City, with the castle in the background. If you are pressed for time, you can pass up the **Baroque Museum.** *Admission: AS 20. Open Sept.– June, Tues.–Sat. 9–12 and 2–5, Sun. 9–12; July and Aug., Mon.–Sat. 9–12 and 2–5, Sun. 9–12.*

However, be sure to look inside **Schloss Mirabell.** It houses public offices, including that of the city's registrar's office; many couples come here to be married in such a sumptuous setting. The foyer and staircase, decorated with cherubs, are good examples of Baroque excess. Chamber music concerts are given in the Baroque hall upstairs in summer. *Mirabellplatz, tel. 0662/ 8072–2258. Open Mon.–Thurs. 8–4, Fri. 8–1.*

Head down Schwarzstrasse, back toward the center of the city. On your left is the famed **Mozarteum,** a music academy (Schwarzstr. 26, tel. 0662/74492) whose courtyard encloses the summer house in which Mozart wrote his opera *The Magic Flute.* Cross over the Markart-Steg footbridge to the "Old City" side of the Salzach river. Turn right and walk a short distance up the Kai to the **Carolino Augusteum Museum.** This is the city museum, whose collections include art, archaeology, and musical instruments. *Museumsplatz 1, tel. 0662/843145. Admission: AS 20; combined ticket with toy museum in Bürgerspital (see below). Open Tues.–Sun. 9–5.*

Time Out From the Carolinum, as the museum is called, turn the corner into Gstattengasse. On your right is the Mönchsberg elevator that will take you to the top of the promontory. Once here, go to the **Café Winkler** (Am Mönchsberg 32, tel. 0662/841215), which is rather commercial but offers superb views of the city, with the fortress in the background. It's a delightful hike over the ridge to the fortress from here (making the trip in reverse, however, will save you an uphill climb).

Down again at city level, follow the Gstattengasse to the **Bürgerspital,** which houses a toy museum within its Renaissance arcades. *Bürgerspitalplatz 2, tel. 0662/847560. Admission: AS 20; combined ticket with Carolino Augusteum. Open Tues.–Sun. 9–5.*

Ahead is Sigmundsplatz, whose central **Pferdeschwemme** (Horse Fountain) is its most notable feature. Built into the side of the mountain itself is the **Festspielhaus,** a huge complex where Salzburg's annual festival, the Festspiel, is held. *Hofstallgasse 1, tel. 0662/842541. Admission: AS 25. Guided tours in May, June, and Sept., weekdays at 11 and 3, Sat. at 11; Oct.–Apr., weekdays at 3, Sat. at 11; during Easter festival, weekdays at 2. No tours in July and Aug.*

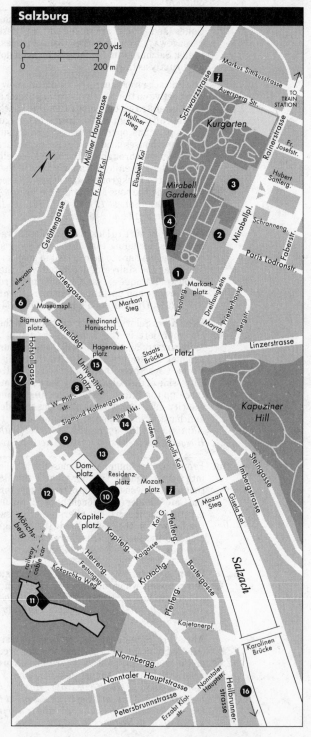

Salzburg

From the Festspeilhaus, turn left into the Wiener-Phil-
(8) harmoniker-Strasse. The **Kollegienkirche** (Collegiate Church)
on the left is the work of Fischer von Erlach and is one of the
best examples of Baroque architecture anywhere; be sure to
look inside. On weekday mornings, the Universitätsplatz, in
front of the church, is crowded with market stands. Cut under
the covered passageway and turn right into Sigmund Haffner-
Gasse. At the corner on the left stands the 13th-century
(9) **Franziskanerkirche** (Franciscan Church), an eclectic mix of architectural styles, with Romanesque and Gothic accents.
(10) Nearby, at Domplatz, is the Salzburg **Dom** (cathedral), a magnificently proportioned building; note the great bronze doors
as you enter.

To reach the fortress on the hill above, walk under the arcade to
the right side of the church and up the narrow Festungsgasse at
the back end of Kapitalplatz. From here, you can either follow
the footpath up the hill or take a five-minute ride on the
Festungsbahn, the inclined railway cable car. On a sunny day, a
far more pleasurable—and strenuous!—route is to hike up the
Festungsgasse, turning frequently to enjoy the changing panorama of the city below.

Time Out **Stieglkeller** (Festungsgasse 10, tel. 0662/842681) offers a wide
choice of good Austrian fare, served outdoors in summer. The
local beer is superb. Try their *Salzburger Nockerln*, a heavenly
meringue dessert. Closed Oct.–Apr.

---

(11) Once at the **Festung Hohensalzburg** itself, you can wander
around on your own (admission: AS 10) or take a tour (AS 30).
The views in all directions from the 12th-century fortress are
magnificent. The main attraction is **St. George's Chapel,** built in
1501. A year later, in 1502, the Festung acquired the 200-pipe
barrel organ, which plays daily in summer at 7 AM, 11 AM, and 6
PM. *Mönchsberg, tel. 0662/843–8213. Open daily, May–Sept. 9–
5:30, Oct.–Apr. 9–4:30.*

(12) Back down in the city, follow the wall to **Stiftskirche St. Peter**
(St. Peter's Abbey). The cemetery lends an added air of mys-
tery to the monk's caves cut into the cliff. The catacombs
attached to the church can be visited by guided tour. *Just off
Kapitelplatz, tel. 0662/844578. Admission: AS 10. Tours daily
May–Sept. 10–5, Oct.–Apr. 11–12 and 1:30–3:30.*

Head around the cathedral to the spacious Residenzplatz, a
(13) vast and elegant square. The **Residenz** itself includes the Bishop's living quarters and representative rooms. *Residenzplatz
1, tel. 0662/8042–2693. Admission: AS 20. Tours Sept.–June
10–11, 2, and 3; July–Aug. every 20 mins. from 10 to 4:40.*

The **Residenzgalerie,** in the same building complex, has an outstanding collection of 16th- to 19th-century European art.
*Residenzplatz 1, tel. 0662/8042–2270. Admission: AS 20. Open
daily 10–5.*

(14) From the lower end of Residenzplatz, cut across into the **Alter
Markt** which still serves as an open market. Salzburg's narrowest house is squeezed into the north side of the square. Turn
left into Griesgasse, a tiny street packed with boutiques and
fascinating shops. At the head of the tiny Rathausplatz is
(15) **Mozart's birthplace,** now a museum. *Getreidegasse 9, tel. 0662/*

844313. Admission: AS 35. Open May–Sept. 9–7, Oct.–Apr. 9–6.

Wander along Getreidegasse, with its ornate wrought-iron shop signs and the Mönchsberg standing sentinel at the far end. Don't neglect the warren of interconnecting side alleys: These include a number of fine shops and often open onto impressive inner courtyards that, in summer, are guaranteed to be filled with flowers.

⑯ One popular excursion from Salzburg is to **Schloss Hellbrunn,** about 5 kilometers (3 miles) outside the city. The castle was built in the 17th century, and its rooms have some fine *trompe l'oeil* decorations. The castle's full name is Lustschloss Hellbrunn—Hellbrunn Pleasure Castle. It was designed for the relaxation of Salzburg's prince bishops and includes the **Wasserspiele,** or fountains, conceived by someone with an impish sense of humor. Expect to get sprinkled as water shoots up from unlikely spots, such as the center of the table at which you're seated. The Baroque fountains are also fascinating. Both castle and fountain gardens can be included on a tour. *Tel. 0662/ 841696. Admission: AS 39. Tours Apr. and Oct. 9–4:30; May and Sept. 9–5; June 9–5:30; July and Aug. 9–6.*

The Hellbrunn complex houses the **Tiergarten** (zoo), which is outstanding because of the way in which the animals have been housed in natural surroundings. (Tel. 0662/841169. Admission: AS 30. Open Oct.–Mar. 9–4; Apr.–Sept. 9–6.) You can also visit the small **folklore museum** (Admission: AS 10. Open Easter–Oct. 9–5).

Dining

Some of the city's best restaurants are in the leading hotels. This is a tourist town, and popular restaurants are always crowded, so make reservations well ahead, particularly during festival time. For details and price category definitions, *see* Dining in Staying in Austria.

Expensive **Goldener Hirsch.** Outstanding creative cuisine is served in a chic atmosphere. Service can be slow, but the grilled hare is well worth any wait. *Getreidegasse 37, tel. 0662/848511. Reservations essential. AE, DC, MC, V.*

Mirabell. Although it's housed in a chain hotel (the Sheraton), some will argue that the Mirabell is the city's top restaurant. The menu mixes international dishes with adventurous versions of local specialties such as Wiener Schnitzel and *wildschwein* (wild boar). *Auerspergstr. 4, tel. 0662/793215. Reservations advised. AE, DC, MC, V.*

★ **Zum Eulenspiegel.** The intimate rooms of an old city house contribute to the charm of this city restaurant. *Hagenauerplatz 2, tel. 0662/843180. Reservations advised. AE, DC, MC, V.*

Moderate **Alt Salzburg.** After an attempt to reach for the stars, this atmospheric restaurant has settled back to offer good local fare in its elegant red-and-white rooms. Try the traditional *tafelspitz* (Austrian pot roast). *Bürgerspitalgasse 2, tel. 0622/841476. Reservations essential. AE, DC, MC, V. Closed Sun.*

Stiftskeller St. Peter. Tucked under the mountain, this vast restaurant offers good food and service in its winding set of rooms. Both fish and game are excellent, or ask the waiter about Salzburg specialties. *By St. Peter's Church, tel. 0662/841268. No credit cards. Closed Mon. in winter.*

Inexpensive **Sternbräu.** If you're not looking for anything too fancy, try the hearty sausages and roasted meats at this vast complex, which has a pleasant garden in summer. *Griesgasse 23, tel. 0662/842140. No credit cards.*

Ratzka. Visitors from all corners of the world come to this café for a taste of Herr Ratzka's *Zwetschkenfleck,* or apple wine cake. His pastries, *torten,* and petit fours are all of unsurpassed quality. *Imbergstr. 45, tel. 0662/70919. No credit cards. Closed Mon. and Tues.*

Lodging

Reservations are always advisable and are essential at festival time (both Easter and summer). For details and price category definitions, *see* Lodging in Staying in Austria.

Very Expensive **Bristol.** The attractive Belle Epoque facade of the Bristol will prepare you for the comfortable rooms and period furnishings inside. One of Austria's classic hotels. *Markartplatz 3, tel. 0662/73557. 90 rooms with bath or shower. AE, DC, MC, V. Closed Jan.–Mar.*

★ **Goldener Hirsch.** This old-timer—800 years old and an inn since 1564—is conveniently set right in the heart of the old city. Arched corridors, vaulted stairs, rustic furniture, and antiques provide a medieval atmosphere; the essential modern appliances stay ingeniously hidden. The restaurant (*see* Dining) is excellent. *Getreidegasse 35–37, tel. 0662/848511. 75 rooms with bath. Facilities: restaurant. AE, DC, MC, V.*

Österreichischer Hof. Salzburg's grande dame occupies a lovely riverside location, and some of the rooms give views of the fortress and the old city. All four restaurants are excellent, but reservations are essential. *Schwarzstr. 5–7, tel. 0662/72541. 120 rooms, 118 with bath or shower. Facilities: 4 restaurants. AE, DC, MC, V.*

Schloss Mönchstein. In a sensational location overlooking the city, this is a top hotel, if expensive. The restaurant is one of the best in the city. *Mönchsberg 26, tel. 0662/848555. 17 rooms with bath. Facilities: garage, restaurant, tennis. AE, DC, MC, V.*

Sheraton. A Sheraton is a Sheraton, but this one has one of Salzburg's best restaurants. The location, beside the Mirabell Gardens, is a plus. *Auerspergstr. 4, tel. 0662/793210. 165 rooms with bath. Facilities: indoor pools, restaurant, laundry, health spa adjacent. AE, DC, MC, V.*

Expensive **Bayrischer Hof.** Not as close to the downtown area as visitors may want but only two blocks from the train station. The modern rooms are very comfortable—which may explain why they're almost always full. *Elisabethstr. 12, tel. 0662/54170. 60 rooms with bath or shower. Facilities: 3 restaurants. AE, DC, MC, V.*

Gablerbräu. A country inn transported to town, the Gablerbräu is cheerful and friendly and an obvious favorite with repeat visitors. *Linzergasse 9, tel. 0662/73441. 51 rooms with bath or shower. AE, DC, MC, V.*

Pitter. Close to the train station, the Pitter is a favorite with business people. The inexpensive restaurant is a definite plus. *Rainerstr. 6–8, tel. 0662/78571. 220 rooms with bath. Facilities: restaurant. AE, DC, MC, V.*

Moderate **Markus Sittikus.** This one is reasonably priced and more than
reasonably comfortable. The train station is near but beyond
walking distance, except for backpackers. *Markus-Sittikus-
Str. 20, tel. 0662/71121. 35 rooms with bath or shower. AE, DC,
MC, V.*

The Arts

Festivals Tickets for the festival performances are almost impossible to
get once you are in Salzburg. Write ahead to **Salzburger
Festspiele,** Postfach 140, A-5010 Salzburg.

Opera, Music, and Theater and opera are presented in the **Festspielhaus** (*see*
Art above); opera and operetta at the **Landestheater** (Schwarzstr.
22, tel. 0662/71512); concerts at the **Mozarteum** (Schwarzstr.
26, tel. 0662/73154). Chamber music—in costume—is performed in **Schloss Mirabell.** Special art exhibits in the **Carolinum** (*see* Exploring) are often outstanding.

Innsbruck

Arriving and Departing

By Plane The airport is 3 kilometers (2 miles) to the west of the city. For
flight information, phone 0512/81777.

Between the Buses go to the main train station; journey time is about 20 min-
Airport and utes. Taxis should take no more than 10 minutes.
Downtown
By Train: All trains stop at the city's main station. Train con-
nections are available to Munich, Vienna, Rome, and Zurich.
For train information, phone 0512/1717. Ticket reservations,
tel. 0512/1700.

By Bus: The terminal is in front of the main train station.

By Car: Exit from the east-west autobahn, or from the Brenner
autobahn running south to Italy. Much of the downtown area is
paid-parking only; get parking vouchers at tobacco shops.

Getting Around

By Bus and Most bus and streetcar routes begin or end at Südtiroler Platz,
Streetcar site of the main train station. The bus is the most convenient
way to reach the five major ski areas outside the city. Many hotels offer free transportation with direct hotel pickup; for those
staying in the Old City, the buses leave from in front of the
Landestheater. Check with your hotel or the tourist offices for
schedules.

By Taxi Taxis are not much faster than walking, particularly along the
one-way streets and in the Old City. To order a radio cab, phone
0512/5311 or 45500.

Guided Tours

Sightseeing Tours Bus tours lasting one and a half hours cover the city's highlights, and leave from the hotel information office at the
railroad station (Südtirolerplatz) daily at noon and at 12:10
from the Hypobank, across from the Tiroler Landesreisebüro
on Boznerplatz. In summer, additional buses are scheduled at

10 and 2. Your hotel or one of the tourist offices will have tickets and details.

Tourist Information

The city's two main tourist offices are at Bozner Platz 7, tel. 0512/59885; and Burggraben 3, tel. 0512/5356.

Exploring Innsbruck

Numbers in the margin correspond with points of interest on the Innsbruck map.

At the center of the province of Tirol lies the quaint and well-preserved capital city of Innsbruck. Squeezed by the mountains and sharing the valley with the Inn river, Innsbruck is compact and very easy to explore on foot. The ancient city—it received its municipal charter in 1239—no doubt owes much of its fame and charm to its unique situation. To the north, the steep, sheer sides of the Alps rise like a shimmering blue-and-white wall from the edge of the city, an awe-inspiring backdrop to the mellowed green domes and red roofs of the picturesque Baroque town.

Modern-day Innsbruck retains close associations with three historical figures: Emperor Maximilian I and Empress Maria Theresa, both of whom are responsible for much of the city's architecture, and Andreas Hofer, a Tirolean patriot. You will find repeated references to these personalities as you tour the city. A good starting point is the **Goldenes Dachl** (the Golden Roof), which made famous the ancient mansion whose balcony it covers (it's actually made of gilded copper tiles). The building now houses an **Olympic Museum,** which features videotapes of the Innsbruck winter Olympics. *Herzog-Friedrich-Str., tel. 0512/53600. Admission: AS 20. Open daily 10–5:30.*

❷ A walk up the Hofgasse brings you to the **Hofburg,** the Rococo imperial palace, with its ornate reception hall decorated with portraits of Maria Theresa's ancestors. *Rennweg 1, tel. 0512/ 587186. Admission: AS 20. Open mid-May–mid-Oct. daily 9–4; mid-Oct.–mid-May, Mon.–Sat. 9–4.*

❸ Close by is the **Hofkirche,** the Imperial Church, built as a mausoleum for Maximilian. The emperor is surrounded by 24 marble reliefs portraying his accomplishments, as well as 28 oversize statues of his ancestors, including the legendary King Arthur. The above-mentioned Andreas Hofer is also buried here. Don't miss the silver chapel with its ornate altar. The **Tiroler Volkskunstmuseum** (Tirolean folk art museum) is housed in the Hofkirche, too, and shows costumes, rustic furniture, and farmhouse rooms decorated in styles ranging from Gothic to Rococo. *Universitätsstr. 2, tel. 0512/584302. Admission: AS 18 (Hofkirche), AS 15 (Volkskunstmuseum); combined ticket AS 25. Hofkirche open May–Sept., daily 9–5, Oct.–Apr., daily 9–12 and 2–5; Volkskunstmuseum open Mon.–Sat. 9–12 and 2–5, Sun. 9–12.*

❹ Follow Museumstrasse to the **Ferdinandeum,** which houses Austria's largest collection of Gothic art, as well as paintings from the 19th and 20th centuries. *Museumstr. 15, tel. 0512/ 594897. Admission: AS 20. Open Tues.–Sat. 10–12 and 2–5, Sun. 9–12 and 2–5.*

Innsbruck

Major Attractions
Annasäule, 6
Ferdinandeum, 4
Goldenes Dachl, 1
Hofburg, 2
Hofkirche, 3
Triumphpforte, 5

Other Attractions
Dom St. Jakob, 9
Helblinghaus, 8
Stadtturm, 7
Tiroler Volkskunst-
museum, 10

⑤ Cut back down Wilhelm Greilstrasse to the **Triumphpforte** (Triumphal Arch), built in 1765, and walk back up Maria Theresien-
⑥ strasse past the **Annasäule** (Anna Column) for a classic "postcard" view of Innsbruck with the Alps in the background.

Off the Beaten Track

Just 3 kilometers (2 miles) southeast of the city and easily reached by either bus or streetcar, is **Schloss Ambras,** one of the country's finest and best-preserved castles. Originally dating from the 11th century, it was later rebuilt as a residence for the Archduke Ferdinand of Tirol (from 1564 to 1582), so most of what you now see is in German Renaissance style. The collection includes numerous pictures, weapons, armor, *objets d'art,* and furniture. *In the village of Ambras (streetcar lines 3 or 6), tel. 0512/41215. Admission: AS 30. Open May–Sept., Wed.– Sun. 10–4.*

Shopping

Shopping Districts Many shops are found in the historic streets of Maria-Theresienstrasse, Museumstrasse, Brixnerstrasse, Meranerstrasse, and among the arcades of Herzog-Friedrichstrasse.

Gift Ideas The best-known and best-loved local specialties include Tirolean hats (those little pointed green felt ones, garnished with a feather), Loden cloth, lederhosen, dirndls, wood-carvings, and mountain and skiing equipment.

Dining

For details and price category definitions, *see* Dining in Staying in Austria.

Expensive **Belle Epoque.** Reestablished in the Alpotel on the edge of the Old City, the outstanding cuisine offered by Chef Wolf has lost none of its imagination or originality. Try his version of standard Tirolean dishes and you will not be disappointed; the French touch combines superbly with venison, veal, and other local favorites, and the atmosphere sets a tone of elegance. *Innrain 13 (Ursulinenpassage), tel. 0512/577931. Reservations essential. AE, DC, MC, V. Dinner only. Closed Sun.*

Domstuben. Now in the capable hands of Chef Peter Beer, the Domstuben is a moderately formal but wholly elegant setting for equally elegant food. The upstairs room is more intimate, if also slightly more Tirolean. *Pfarrgasse 3, tel. 0512/573353. Reservations advised. AE, DC, MC, V.*

Philippine Welser. Regional specialties and swift service are two reasons why the Hotel Europa's restaurant is highly regarded by locals and visitors. *Brixnerstr. 6, tel. 0512/593–1648. Reservations advised. DC.*

Schwarzer Adler. This place drips with atmosphere, its massive-beamed rooms a perfect backdrop to typical Austrian dishes like *knödeln* (dumplings) and *tafelspitz* (a type of pot roast). *Kaiserjagerstr. 2, tel. 0512/587109. Reservations advised. AE, DC, MC, V.*

Moderate **Hirschenstuben.** Old-fashioned hospitality and dark-wood trimmings are found in force at this charming local favorite. *Kiebachgasse 5, tel. 0512/582979. Reservations advised. AE, DC, MC, V. Closed Sun.*

Ottoburg. A rabbit warren of rooms, in a 13th-century building, the Ottoburg is exactly right for an intimate, cozy lunch or dinner. It's packed with Austriana and 100% genuine. Go for the trout if it's available. *HerzogFriedrichstr. 1, tel. 0512/574652. Reservations advised. AE, DC, MC, V.*

Inexpensive   **Goethestube.** The wine tavern of the city's oldest inn, the Goldener Adler (*see* Lodging), is one of Innsbruck's best. It was here that Goethe (who lent his name to the tavern) used to sip quantities of red South Tirolean wine during his stays in 1786 and 1790. *HerzogFriedrichstr. 6, tel. 0512/586334. Reservations not required. AE, DC, MC, V.*

Stieglbräu. Lovers of good beer will be delighted to find this popular rustic spot, which, in addition to its thirst-quenching ales, provides good, solid Austrian fare. Portions are huge, the garden exceptionally pleasant. *WilhelmGreilstr. 25, 0512/584338. No credit cards.*

Lodging

For details and price category definitions, *see* Lodging in Staying in Austria.

Very Expensive   **Europa.** The Europa is a postwar building blessed with a considerable amount of charm. Some rooms have period furnishings; others are 20th-century modern. The restaurant, Philippine Welser (*see* Dining), is highly regarded. *Südtirolerplatz 2, tel. 0512/5931. 132 rooms with bath. Facilities: bar, restaurant, beauty salon. AE, DC, MC, V.*

Scandic Crown. Innsbruck's newest major hotel belongs to the leading Scandinavian chain. Rooms are modern plush; facilities, including sauna, are extensive. The buffet lunch is good value and abundant. The train station is nearby. *Salurnerstr. 15, tel. 0512/59350. 191 rooms with bath. Facilities: restaurants, bar, health club, pool, sauna, garage. AE, DC, MC, V.*

Innsbruck. The city's namesake hotel is modern, comfortably appointed, and the proud possessor of fantastic views of the old city and Nordkette mountains. Its central location is another plus. *Innrain 3, tel. 0512/59868. 90 rooms with bath. Facilities: restaurant, bar, pool, sauna. AE, DC, MC, V.*

Expensive   **Alpotel.** Abundant space, comfort, and modern style are the keys in this new hotel on the edge of the Old City. The Tiroler Stuben and Belle Epoque restaurants are outstanding (*see* Dining); staff is particularly helpful. Many rooms have balconies with splendid views. *Innrain 13 (Ursulinenpassage), tel. 0512/577931. 75 rooms with bath. Facilities: sauna, solarium, 2 restaurants, bar, café, garage, transportation to ski areas. AE, DC, MC, V.*

★ **Goldener Adler.** The Golden Eagle has been an inn since 1390, and over the centuries has welcomed nearly every king, emperor, duke, or poet who passed through the city. The facade looks suitably ancient, and inside passages and stairs twist romantically and rooms crop up when least expected. The several restaurants offer well-prepared seasonal and local dishes, and a good selection of wines from the Tirol. *HerzogFriedrichstr. 6, tel. 0512/586334. 40 rooms. 31 with bath or shower. Facilities: restaurants, bar, coffee shop. AE, DC, MC, V.*

Union. A well-known favorite of many visitors to Innsbruck, the Union commands a loyal following. Very close to the station.

Adamgasse 22, tel. 0512/583313. 60 rooms with bath or shower. Facilities: restaurant, bar. AE, DC, MC, V.

Moderate **Weisses Kreuz.** Occupying an honored position just next to the
★ famous Goldenes Dachl (*see* Exploring), Weisses Kreuz is itself
a lovely old historic building. The staff is unusually welcoming.
HerzogFriedrichstr. 31, tel. 0512/594790. 39 rooms, 28 with bath or shower. AE, V.

Inexpensive **Binder.** A short bus trip from the center of town shouldn't be
too high a price to pay for the less costly comfort at this small,
friendly hotel a short distance from the city's beating heart.
Dr.-Glatzstr. 20, tel. 0512/42236. 32 rooms, some with bath or shower. AE, DC, MC, V.

The Arts

Most hotels have a monthly calendar of events (in English). The
Central Ticket Office is on Centralpassage, tel. 0512/536–0506.
Opera, operetta, musicals, and concerts take place at the
Tiroler Landestheater (Rennweg 2, tel. 0512/520–7430) and
Kongresshaus.

4 Belgium

Introduction

Belgium covers a strip of land just under 320 kilometers (200 miles) long and 160 kilometers (100 miles) wide bordering the North Sea between France and Holland. With more than 10 million people, Belgium is the second most densely populated country in the world. Both Parisians and Amsterdammers tend to sneer at Belgium as a substandard version of "pure" French or Dutch culture. However, Belgium has a distinctive culture, or rather, two: Flemish and Walloon. The Flemish, who speak Dutch (Flemish), inhabit the northern half of the country and account for 56% of the population. The French-speaking Walloons live in the other half. The capital, Brussels, is officially designated a dual-language area.

Belgium is the world's most heavily industrialized country with only 5% of the working population engaged in agriculture (though they still manage to produce two of Europe's greatest pâtés and any number of fine sausages). Besides being natural entrepreneurs, the Belgians also work very hard—partly to make up for what has so long been denied them. In the course of history, the Belgians have been ruled by the Romans, Vikings, French, Spanish, Austrians, Dutch, English, and Germans. Many of Europe's greatest battles have been fought on Belgian soil—from Waterloo and earlier, to the long-slogging encounters of World War I. During World War II, this territory witnessed both the initial blitzkrieg of Nazi Panzer units and Hitler's final desperate counterattack against the advancing Allies in the Ardennes—an offensive that has gone down in history as the Battle of the Bulge.

The south of the country is a wild wooded area, with mountains rising to more than 620 meters (2,000 feet). In the Dutch-speaking north, on the other hand, the land is flat and heavily cultivated, much as in neighboring Holland. Here stand the medieval Flemish cities of Ghent and Bruges, with their celebrated carillons and canals—not to mention the 80 kilometers (50 miles) of sandy beaches that make up the country's northern coastline. To the northeast lies Antwerp, the country's dynamic seaport. This city, where the painter Rubens lived, is now the world's leading diamond-cutting center.

Brussels stands in the very center of the country. A booming, expanding, and often very expensive city, it is now the capital of Europe. Here the Common Market (EEC) has its headquarters, as does NATO. The city boasts more ambassadors than any other in the world—approximately 160. Partly as a result of this concentration of power and partly because of the Belgians' celebrated love of good food, Brussels has become one of the most renowned gastronomic cities in the world. Those without expense accounts, beware! But Belgian cuisine adds French flare to Dutch-size portions—which means that you seldom have to order very much.

As befits a bourgeois culture, the Belgians are great believers in the quality of life. In practice, this means that meals, parks, cars, and houses are large. Homes are highly individualistic yet comfortable; trendy designer bars are cozy as well as chic. Except on the road, Belgians are generous and have time for old-fashioned courtesy.

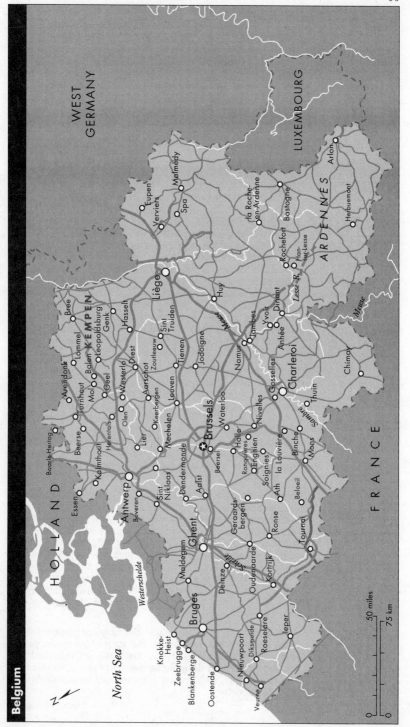

Belgium

WEST GERMANY

LUXEMBOURG

HOLLAND

FRANCE

North Sea

Westerschelde

Arlon

Herbeumont

A R D E N N E S

Malmédy

Eupen

Verviers

Spa

la Roche-
en-Ardenne

Bastogne

Rochefort

Han-
sur-Lesse

Lesse R.

Meuse

Bree

Lommel

Arendonk

KEMPEN

Leopoldsburg

Genk

Hasselt

Sint
Truiden

Liège

Huy

Dinant

Yvoir

Anhée

Meuse

Turnhout

Beerse

Mol

Balen

Geel

Westerlo

Diest

Aarschot

Zoutleeuw

Tienen

Jodoigne

Namur

Jambes

Gosselies

Charleroi

Thuin

Chimay

Baarle-Hertog

Kalmthout

Herentals

Olen

Lier

Ockerbergen

Mechelen

Leuven

Brussels

Waterloo

Nivelles

Sambre

Binche

Mons

Essen

Antwerp

Beveren

Sint
Niklaas

Dendermonde

Aalst

Halle

Beersel

Ronquières

Enghien

Soignies

Ath

la Louvière

Beloeil

Ghent

Geeraards-
bergen

Ronse

Tournai

Maldegem

Deinze

Schelde

Oudenaarde

Kortrijk

Knokke-
Heist

Zeebrugge

Blankenberge

Bruges

Nieuwpoort

Diksmuide

Roeselare

Ieper

Oostende

Veurne

N

50 miles

75 km

0

0

But Belgians are not just creatures of the senses. A robust culture is celebrated in paintings by Brueghel and Rubens, Magritte, and Delvaux; by exciting Gothic, Renaissance, and Art Nouveau architecture; and by the best jazz in Europe. Belgium is no self-publicist, but quietly and confidently waits to be discovered.

Before You Go

When to Go The tourist season runs from early May to late September and peaks in July and August, when the weather is best. In recent years, however, off-season travel has become increasingly popular. Air and hotel rates are considerably cheaper, trains are less crowded, and advance reservations for hotel rooms are not always essential. In the coastal resorts, some hotels and restaurants remain open all year.

Climate Temperatures range from around 65 F in May to an average 73 F in July and August. In winter, temperatures drop to an average of about 40 to 45 F. Snow is unusual except in the mountains of the Ardennes, where cross-country skiing is a popular sport in February and March.

The following are the average daily maximum and minimum temperatures for Brussels.

Jan.	40F	4C	May	65F	18C	Sept.	69F	21C
	30	−1		46	8		51	11
Feb.	44F	7C	June	72F	22C	Oct.	60F	15C
	32	0		52	11		45	7
Mar.	51F	10C	July	73F	23C	Nov.	48F	9C
	36	2		54	12		38	3
Apr.	58F	14C	Aug.	72F	22C	Dec.	42F	6C
	41	5		54	12		32	0

Currency The unit of currency in Belgium is the franc. There are bills of 50, 100, 500, 1,000, and 5,000 francs in addition to coins of 1, 5, 10, 20, and 50 francs. Do not confuse the new 50-franc coin and the old 5-franc coin. At press time (spring 1989), the exchange rate was about BF38 to the dollar and BF66 to the pound sterling.

Traveler's checks and credit cards are the safest and simplest ways to carry money. American Express, Bank of America, Barclays, Eurocheques, and Thomas Cook traveler's checks are all honored in Belgium. American Express and Visa cards are widely accepted, too. Avoid exchanging money on weekends or at hotels and restaurants unless you're prepared to pay a big premium.

What It Will Cost The cost of a hotel stay in Brussels is higher than in many other European cities, largely because of the international role that the city plays. The rates are about the same as in London. Restaurants, however, are less expensive than in surrounding countries. Sales tax on most items ranges from 6% to 33% on luxury items, including jewelry, furs, and a wide selection of electronic goods. Many shops advertise goods "for export"; they provide documents you can use to reclaim the sales tax or VAT when you leave the country. (*See* Shopping below). If you're making substantial purchases, ask the shop to provide the export papers.

Sample Prices A cup of coffee in a café will cost about BF50; a glass of beer, about BF65; and a glass of wine, about BF100. Train travel averages BF6 per mile; the average bus/metro/tram ride costs BF40; theater tickets cost about BF500; and movie tickets about BF200.

Customs on Arrival Visitors from EEC countries can bring in 300 cigarettes or 75 cigars or 400 grams of tobacco; 5 liters of still wine and 1½ liters of spirits or 3 liters of liqueur wine; and 75 grams of perfume. Other goods imported from the EEC may not exceed BF15,800 in value. Visitors from non-EEC countries can bring in 200 cigarettes or 50 cigars or 250 grams of tobacco; 2 liters of still wine and 1 liter of spirits or 2 liters of liqueur wine; 50 grams of perfume. Other goods from non-EEC countries may not exceed BF2,000 in value. There are no restrictions on the import or export of currency.

Language Language is a sensitive subject that has led to the collapse of at least two governments. There are two national languages in Belgium: French, spoken primarily in the south of the country, and Dutch or Flemish, spoken in the north. Brussels is bilingual, with both languages officially recognized, though French predominates. Many people speak English in Brussels and in the north (Flanders). If your French is good but your Flemish nonexistent, it is politic to speak English to Flemings, especially in Antwerp or Flanders. In the south (Wallonia), both French and a dialect are spoken. In major tourist cities you should have no trouble finding people who speak English, but in deepest Wallonia use whatever French you have!

Getting Around

By Car Belgium has an excellent system of expressways, and the main
Road Conditions roads are generally very good. Road numbers for main roads have the prefix N; expressways, the prefix A or E.

Rules of the Road Drive on the right and pass on the left (passing on the right is forbidden). Seatbelts are compulsory in front seats. Each car must have a warning triangle to be used in the event of a breakdown or accident. At intersections, particularly in cities, traffic on the right has priority. Adhere strictly to this rule because there are few stop or yield signs. This also applies to changing lanes in tunnels. In Brussels, the system of tunnels and ring roads is generally effective. Cars within a traffic circle have priority over cars entering it. Buses and streetcars have priority over cars. Maximum speed limits are 120 kph (70 mph) on highways, 90 kph (55 mph) on major roads, and 60 kph (35 mph) in cities.

Road Signs Road signs are written in both languages, so you need to know that Antwerpen (Flemish) is Anvers (French) and Antwerp to us; likewise, Brugge and Brussel (Flemish) are Bruges and Bruxelles (French); Gent (Flemish) is Gand (French) and Ghent (English). Even more confusing, Liège and Luik are the same place, as are Louvain and Leuven and Namur and Namen. Even more difficult is Mons (French) and its Flemish equivalent, Bergen!

Parking Most cities have metered on-street parking (parking meters take 5- or 20-franc coins) and parking lots.

By Train Fast and frequent trains connect all main towns and cities. If you intend to travel frequently, buy a **Tourrail Ticket,** which allows unlimited travel for 16 days, or on five days during a 16-

day period. If you are over 26, the cost of the five-day pass is BF2,550 first class and BF 1,700 second class. For those under 26, the pass costs BF1,700 first class and BF1,300 second class. The 16-day pass costs BF4,580 first class and BF3,050 second class (no reduction for those under 26). The ticket is available from any Belgian train station.

Special weekend round-trip tickets are valid from Friday noon to Monday noon: A 40% reduction is available on the first traveler's ticket and a 60% reduction on companions' tickets. In the tourist season, there are similar weekday fares to the seaside and the Ardennes. Senior citizens can obtain 50% reduction on train fares.

By Bus There is a wide network of local and regional buses throughout Belgium. Details of services are available at train stations and tourist offices.

By Bicycle You can rent a bicycle from Belgian railways at 48 stations throughout the country; train travelers get reduced rates. A special brochure is available at most stations. Bicycling is especially popular in the flat northern and coastal areas. Bicycle lanes are provided in many Flemish cities, but bicycling in Brussels is madness.

Staying in Belgium

Telephones
Local Calls Pay phones work with 5- and 20-franc coins or with Telecards, available in a number of denominations starting from BF200. The Telecards can be purchased at any post office and at many newsstands. Most phone booths that accept Telec rds have a list indicating where these cards are sold. An average local call costs BF10 or BF20.

International Calls The least expensive method is to buy a high-denomination Telecard and make a direct call from a phone booth. A five-minute phone call to the United States at a peak time will cost about BF750 by this method. International calls can also be made at most hotels, but nearly all have a service charge that may double the cost. It's always wise to ask what the service charge is before placing the call. Operator-assisted international calls can also be made at most post offices.

Operators The numbers for operator assistance and information vary from city to city; it's best to ask at a hotel or post office or to consult a telephone directory.

Mail
Postal Rates Airmail letters to the United States cost BF36 for the first 20 grams; postcards, BF24. Airmail letters to the United Kingdom are BF13 for the first 20 grams.

Receiving Mail You can have mail forwarded direct to your hotel. If you're uncertain where you'll be staying, have mail sent in care of **American Express** (1 pl. Louise, B-1000 Brussels). Cardholders are spared the $2 per letter charge.

Shopping
Sales-Tax Refunds When you buy goods for export, you can ask most shops to fill out special forms covering VAT (value-added tax) or sales tax. When you leave Belgium, you must declare the goods at customs and have the customs officers stamp the forms. Once back home, you send the stamped forms back to the shop, and your sales tax will be refunded. This facility is available in most boutiques and large stores and covers most purchases of more than BF2,000.

Opening and Closing Times

Banks. Banks are open weekdays from 9 to 4; some close for an hour at lunch. Exchange facilities are usually open on weekends, but you'll get a better rate during the week.

Museums. Most museums are open from 10 to 5 every day except Monday. Check individual listings.

Shops. Stores are open weekdays and Saturdays from 10 to 6 and generally stay open later on Friday. Hours vary from store to store, so it's best to check in advance. Some small places, mostly food stores, are open on Sunday.

National Holidays

January 1 (New Year's Day); April 16 (Easter Monday); May 1 (May Day); May 8 (Victory 1945); May 24 (Ascension); June 4 (Pentecost Monday); July 21 (National Holiday); August 15 (Assumption); November 1 (All Saints); November 11 (Armistice); November 15 (King's Birthday, stores and banks are open); December 25 (Christmas).

Dining

According to popular legend, the average Belgian is a gourmand not a gourmet, a blatant advertisement for Leonidas chocolates. While it is fair to say that Belgians expect large portions, most people take eating seriously and are discerning about fresh produce and innovative recipes. It is not for nothing that Belgian restaurants have acquired a large number of Michelin stars and Gault Millau recommendations. Regional cuisine is still clearly differentiated and traditions maintained. At the top end of the scale, the *menus de dégustation* offer a chance to sample a large selection of the chef's finest dishes, such as *lapin à la bière* (rabbit in beer) and *faisan à la brabanconne* (pheasant with chicory). Even the simpler restaurants usually have a reputation for one or two special dishes, such as *waterzooi* (a rich chicken or fish hotpot) and *carbonnades* (chunky stews). A Belgian peculiarity is that dogs are allowed into most restaurants; they are often well dressed in coats and booties but not necessarily well mannered.

Local specialties include eels, *boudin* (sausage), and asparagus (Antwerp); *salade Liègoise*, a hot salad with beans and bacon (Liège); wild strawberries and freshwater fish from the Meuse River (Namur); different permutations of sprouts, chicory, and pheasant (Brussels); and shrimps, oysters, and mussels (Flanders).

Belgian snacks are equally appetizing. The waffle *(gaufre/waffel)* has achieved world fame but *couques* (sweet buns), *speculoos* (spicy gingerbread biscuits), and *pain d'amandes* (nutty after-dinner biscuits) are less well known. For lunch, coldcuts, rich pâtés, and *jambon d'Ardenne* (Ardenne ham) are popular, often accompanied by goat's cheese and rye or wholemeal bread.

Mealtimes

Most hotels serve breakfast until 10. Belgians usually eat lunch between 1 and 3, some making it quite a long, lavish meal. However, the main meal of the day is dinner, which most Belgians eat between 7 and 10; peak dining time is about 8.

Dress

Belgians tend to be fairly formal and dress conservatively when dining out in the evenings. Generally speaking, the more prestigious the restaurant, the more formal the dress. Younger Belgians favor stylish, casual dress in most restaurants.

Ratings

Prices are per person and include a first course, main course, and dessert but no wine or tip. Best bets are indicated by a star ★. At press time, there were BF38 to the dollar.

Category	All Areas
Very Expensive	over BF2,500
Expensive	BF1,500–BF2,500
Moderate	BF1,000–BF1,500
Inexpensive	under BF1,000

Credit Cards The following credit card abbreviations are used: AE, American Express; DC, Diners Club; MC, MasterCard; V, Visa.

Lodging You can trust Belgian hotels, almost without exception, to be clean and of a high standard. The more modern hotels in city centers can be very expensive, but there are smaller, well-appointed hotels, offering lodging at excellent rates. However, within the major cities, the moderate and inexpensive hotels are relatively disappointing in terms of charm and even value for money, though not in terms of comfort and location. The family-run establishments in out-of-the-way spots, such as the Ardennes, can be surprisingly inexpensive, especially if you are visiting them out of season. Check in advance, however, since many country hotels close in the off-season.

Pensions Pensions offer a double room with bath or shower and full board from BF2,500 to BF3,500 in Brussels and from BF2,000 to BF3,000 elsewhere. These terms are often available for a minimum stay of three days. The complete list appears in *Hotels 1990*, available from any Belgian tourist office.

Youth Hostels For information about youth hostels, contact **Fédération Belge des Auberges de la Jeunesse** (tel. 02/215–31–00). In the United States: **American Youth Hostels, Inc.,** Box 37613, Washington, DC 20013. In the United Kingdom: **Camping and Caravan Club Ltd.,** 11 Lower Grosvenor Pl., London SW1); **Youth Hostels Association International Travel Bureau,** 14 Southampton St., London WC2.

Camping Belgium is well supplied with camping and caravan sites. For details, contact the **Royal Camping and Caravaning Club of Belgium** (rue Madeleine, 31, B-1000 Brussels, tel. 02/513-12-87).

Ratings Hotel prices are inclusive and are usually listed in each room. All prices are for two people in a double room. Best bets are indicated by a star ★. At press time, there were BF38 to the dollar.

Category	All Areas
Very Expensive	BF6,500–BF10,000
Expensive	BF4,500–BF6,500
Moderate	BF2,500–BF4,500
Inexpensive	under BF2,500

Credit Cards The following credit card abbreviations are used: AE, American Express; DC, Diners Club; MC, MasterCard; V, Visa.

Tipping Tipping has been losing its hold in Belgium over the past few years because a service charge is often figured into the bill. For example, a tip of 16% is included in all restaurant and café bills. The tip is also included in taxi fares. If you want to give more, round the amount up to the nearest BF50 or BF100. Porters in railway stations ask a fixed per-suitcase price, BF30 in the day and BF35 at night. For moderately priced hotels, BF50 should be an adequate tip for bellhops and doormen; in the very expensive hotels, though, BF100 will usually be more appropriate. At the movies, tip the usher BF20, whether or not he or she shows you to your seat. In theaters, tip about BF50 for programs. In restaurants, cafés, cinemas, theaters, train stations, and other public places, you should tip the washroom attendant BF7. Sometimes there is no attendant but simply a plate on which you are expected to leave the tip. In hairdressers' salons, it is usual to tip 20% if service is not included.

Brussels

Arriving and Departing

By Plane All international flights arrive at Brussels's Zaventem Airport, about a 30-minute drive or a 16-minute train trip from the city center. For information on arrival and departure times, call the individual airlines. **Sabena** and **British Airways** dominate the short-haul London–Brussels route, but **Air Europe** is often cheaper and just as good.

Between the Airport and Downtown There is regular train service from the airport to the Gare du Nord (North Station) and the Gare Centrale (Central Station), which leaves every 20 minutes. The trip takes 16 minutes and costs BF200 (first-class round-trip) and BF140 (second-class round-trip); you can buy a ticket on the train. The first train from the airport runs at 6:15 AM and the last one leaves at 11:46 PM. A taxi to the city center will take about half an hour and costs about BF1,000.

By Train There are three main stations in Brussels: the Gare du Nord, Gare Centrale, and Gare du Midi (South Station). There is also a Gare du Quartier Léopold on the east side of the city. The Gare Centrale is most convenient for the downtown area, which includes the Grand' Place. For train information, telephone 02/219-26-40 or inquire at any station.

By Boat/Jetfoil From London, the train service connects with the Dover–Oostende ferry or jetfoil services. From Oostende, the train takes you to Brussels. The whole journey by jetfoil takes just under five hours but is longer by boat. For reservations and times, contact **P & O Ferries** in London (tel. 01/734–4431). A one-way London–Brussels ticket costs £32, excluding the £6.50 jetfoil supplement.

By Bus and Hovercraft From London, the Hoverspeed City Sprint bus connects with the Dover–Calais hovercraft, and the bus then takes you on to Brussels. The journey takes 6¼ hours; a one-way ticket costs £22. For reservations and times, contact **City Sprint** (tel. 01/554–7061).

By Bus There is no central bus depot, but most tour buses stop near the Gare Centrale, a short walk from the Grand' Place.

By Car Follow signs marked "Brussel Centrum" or "Bruxelles Centre." Many of the approaches are via an outer ring road, a beltway surrounding the city, marked "ring" or *"grande ceinture."* The ring takes you through a large number of tunnels but the city center is clearly posted. The same is true of the small ring within the city itself.

Getting Around

By Métro, Tram, and Bus The métro, trams (streetcars), and buses run as part of the same system. All three are clean and efficient, and a single ticket costs BF40. Best buy is a 10-trip ticket, which costs BF210, or a 24-hour card costing BF140. You need to stamp your ticket in the appropriate machine on the bus or tram; in the métro, your card is stamped as you pass through the automatic barrier. You can purchase these tickets in any métro station or at newsstands. Single tickets can be purchased on the bus. All services are few and far between after 10 PM.

Detailed maps of the Brussels public transportation network are available in most métro stations and at the tourist office (rue Marché-aux-Herbes 61, tel. 02/513-89-40).

By Taxi Taxis are expensive, but—as a small plus—the tip is included in the fare. To call a taxi, phone **Taxis Verts** (tel. 02/511-22-44) or **Taxis Oranges** (tel. 02/513-62-00) or catch one at a taxi stand (there are big stands on the Sablon and at all train stations). It is nearly impossible to pick up cruising taxis in Brussels. Hotels and restaurants will phone for taxis at your request. The price per kilometer is BF31, but airport taxis charge higher rates.

Important Addresses and Numbers

Tourist Information The main tourist office for **Brussels** is in the Hôtel de Ville on the Grand' Place (tel. 02/513-89-40), open Mon.-Sat. 9-6. The main tourist office for the rest of **Belgium** is near the Grand' Place (rue Marché-aux-Herbes 61, tel. 02/512-30-30) and has the same opening hours. There is a tourist office at **Waterloo** (chaussée de Bruxelle 149, tel. 02/354-99-10); it is open April-November 15, daily 9:30-6:30; November 16-March, daily 10:30-5.

Embassies U.S.: blvd. du Régent 27, B-1000 Brussels, tel. 02/513-38-30. Canadian: rue de Loxum 6, B-1000 Brussels, tel. 03/513-79-40. U.K.: Britannia House, rue Joseph II 28, B-1040 Brussels, tel. 02/217-90-00

Emergencies Police: tel. 101; Accident: tel. 100; Ambulance: tel. 02/649-11-22; Doctor: tel. 02/648-80-00 and 02/479-18-18; Dentist: tel. 02/426-10-26; Pharmacy: to find out which one is open on a particular night or on weekends, tel. 02/479-18-18.

English Bookstores House of Paperbacks: chaussée de Waterloo 813, Uccle, tel. 02/343-11-22. Open Tues.-Sat. 10-6, Sun. 10-1. W. H. Smith: blvd. Adolfe Max 71-75. Open Mon.-Sat. 10-6. Librairie de Rome: Av. Louise 50b, tel. 02/511-79-37. Open Mon.-Sat. 8 AM-10 PM, Sun. 9-6; the bookshop sells U.S. and U.K. newspapers, periodicals, and paperbacks.

Travel Agencies American Express: pl. Louise 1, B-1000 Brussels, tel. 02/512-17-40. Wagons-Lits: blvd. Adolphe Max 52, tel. 02/217-62-40.

Guided Tours

Traditional guided bus tours are organized by **De Boeck Sightseeing Tours,** (rue de Colline 8, Grand' Place, tel. 02/513-77-

44); and **Panorama Tours** (rue Marché-aux-Herbes 105, tel. 02/
5143–61–54). They charge BF550 for a 2½-hour tour. More
original are the tours run by **Chatterbus,** Agora, rue de la
Madeleine 51 (open weekdays 10–5:30, Sat. 9–noon). For telephone reservations, call 02/512–54–11 (weekdays 9–1:30) or 02/
673–18–35 (weekdays after 7 PM and on weekends). The tours
include a minibus tour of the main sites (BF580), a walking tour
that includes a visit to a bistro (BF220), and an evening tour that
includes a meal with wine and visits to bars (BF920, including
meal and drink).

Special-Interest **ARAU** organizes thematic city bus tours (in English), including
Bus Tours "Brussels 1900: Art Nouveau Brussels"; "Brussels of the '30s:
Art Deco Brussels"; "Industrial Brussels"; and "Hidden Parks
and Gardens." The guides are all enthusiastic architects working to protect the city's heritage. Tours begin in front of the
post office and Bourse (stock exchange), rue Henri Maus; call
02/513–47–61 for times and bookings. Costs are around BF500
for a half-day tour.

Regional Tours **De Boeck Sightseeing Tours** (*see* above) visits Antwerp, the Ardennes, Bruges, Ghent, Ieper, and Waterloo.

Personal Guides Qualified guides for individual tours are available from the
tourist center (tel. 02/513–89–40).

Exploring Brussels

At first sight, the capital of Belgium presents a somber, impersonal exterior, but a little exploration reveals a domestic,
small-town atmosphere seeping through the institutional facade. Walk across the Grand' Place during a *son et lumière*
(sound and light) show and your mood softens, or watch from a
cozy bar, its tables stacked high with pancakes or covered with
bottles of Duvel beer. Brussels is an odd mixture of provincial
and international. Underneath the bureaucratic surface, the
city is a subtle meeting of the Walloon and Flemish cultures. As
the heart of the ancient Duchy of Brabant, Brussels retains its
old sense of identity and civic pride. A stone's throw from the
steel-and-glass towers, there are cobbled streets, canals where
old barges still discharge their freight, and forgotten spots
where the city's eventful and romantic past is plainly visible
through its 20th-century veneer.

The Grand' Place *Numbers in the margin correspond with points of interest on
the Brussels map.*

❶ Begin in the **Grand' Place,** one of the most ornate market
squares in Europe. There is a daily flower market and a colorful
Sunday-morning bird market. On summer nights, the entire
square is flooded with music and colored light. The Grand'
Place also comes alive during local pageants such as the
"Mayboom," the August parade of giants and floats, and the
July "Ommegang," the parade of the Old City guilds.

The bombardment of the city by Louis XIV's troops left only
❷ the **Hôtel de Ville** (town hall) intact. Civic-minded citizens
started rebuilding the Grand' Place immediately, but the highlight of the square remains the Gothic town hall. The central
tower, combining boldness and light, is topped by a statue of
St-Michel, the patron saint of Brussels. Among the magnificent rooms are the Salle Gothique, with its beautiful paneling;
the Salle Maximilienne, with its superb tapestries; and the

Council Chamber, with a ceiling fresco of the *Assembly of the Gods* painted by Victor Janssens in the early 15th century. *Admission: BF50. Open Tues.–Fri. 9:30–5, Sun. 10–4.*

❸ Opposite the town hall is the **Maison du Roi**—(King's House)—though no king ever lived there—a 16th-century palace housing the **City Museum.** The collection includes important ceramics and silverware—Brussels is famous for both—church sculpture, and statues removed from the facade of the town hall. *Grand' Place, tel. 02/511-27-42. Admission: BF50. Open weekdays Apr.–Sept., 10–5, Oct.–Mar., 10–4; weekends and holidays 10–noon.*

Time Out   **La Rose Blanche** (Grand Place 11, tel. 02/511-2754) is situated in a renovated three-story town house beside the town hall. Inside, brightly painted ceilings have been restored, but the minstrel's gallery, the creaking stairs, and the Chimay beer are original enough. Try a *fondue au parmesan* (cheese in batter) with a strong Chimay or a light *bière blanche*. A sweeter combination is a coffee and a *dame blanche* (vanilla ice cream coated with hot chocolate sauce) or a *mousse au chocolat* (chocolate mousse). This is also the spot from which to view a son et lumière display on a summer's evening.

❹ Southwest of the town hall, on the corner of the rue de l'Etuve and rue du Chêne, stands the famous **Manneken Pis,** a fountain with a small bronze statue of a chubby little boy peeing. Made by Jerome Duquesnoy in 1619, the statue is known as "Brussels' oldest citizen" and is often dressed in costumes that are kept in the City Museum. He has quite a wardrobe! The present Manneken is a copy; the original was kidnapped by 18th-century French and English invaders (soldiers, not tourists!).

Leaving the Mannekin, cross the Grand' Place in the direction of the Marché-aux-Herbes. If you are planning to visit the rest of Belgium, stop in at the regional tourist office (rue Marché-aux-Herbes 61).

❺ Opposite the tourist office, take the Petite rue des Bouchers, the main restaurant street in the heart of the tourist maelstrom. In Brussels fashion, each restaurant advertises its wares by means of large signs and carts packed with a selection of fish and animals. From here, explore the network of galleries, including **Galerie du Centre** and **Galerie de la Reine,** built in 1847. Their harmonious glass-top design was the first of its kind in Europe; moreover, the galleries were designed by a 17-year-old. Written on the central galleries is the motto "Omnibus Omnia" (Everything for Everyone), which is not altogether appropriate given the designer prices.

Time Out   **Le Vaudeville** is the most attractive bar in the galleries. Once a historic satirical theater, it is now an Art Deco bistro. In mirrored surroundings, this is the place to watch local trendies discuss art while eating *crêpes* (pancakes) filled with jam, ice cream, or liqueurs. At the back is the **Cocoon Club,** an equally fashionable discothèque *(see* Nightlife). *Galerie de la Reine 15, tel. 02/673-23-78. No credit cards. Inexpensive.*

❻ Head along the rue Marché-aux-Herbes and the rue Madeleine until you come to the **equestrian statue of King Albert.** To the left of the statue is the Central Station and to the right, the

Brussels

107

Bibliothèque
Nationale, **7**
Bois de la Cambre, **24**
Bourse, **19**
Cathédrale de St.
Michel, **17**

Cinquantenaire, **23**
Equestrian Statue of
King Albert, **6**
European Community
Headquarters, **22**
Galerie du Centre, **5**
Grand' Place, **1**

Grand Sablon, **10**
Hôtel de Ville, **2**
Maison du Roi, **3**
Manneken Pis, **4**
Musée d'Art
Moderne, **8**

Musée Royale d'Art
Ancien, **9**
Notre Dame de la
Chapelle, **13**
Palais de Justice, **12**
Palais de la Nation, **16**
Palais Royale, **15**

Petit Sablon, **11**
Place du Jeu de
Balle, **14**
Place des Martyrs, **18**
Place St. Géry, **21**
Tour Noir, **20**

❼ Bibliothèque Nationale (National Library). Walk through the formal gardens next to the National Library and look back at the ornate clock, with moving figures, over the lower archway. Try to hear—and see—it at noon, when it strikes the hour.

Place Royale If you continue walking through the gardens, you will arrive at the **place Royale,** the site of the Coudenberg palace, where the sovereigns once lived. Here you have a superb view over the **❽** lower town. On the northwest corner of the square is the **Musée d'Art Moderne** (Museum of Modern Art), housed in an exciting feat of modern architecture. On entry, a vertiginous descent into the depths reveals a sudden well of natural light. The paintings are displayed with the light and space they deserve. Although there are a few paintings by Matisse, Gauguin, Degas, and Dali, the surprise lies in the quality of Belgian modern art. See Magritte's luminous fantasies, James Ensor's masks and still lifes, and Spilliaert's coastal scenes. Do not miss Permeke's deeply brooding *Fiancés* or Delvaux's Surrealist works. *Pl. Royale 1, tel. 02/513–96–30. Admission: free. Open Tues.–Sun. 10–5.*

❾ Next door is the **Musée Royale d'Art Ancien** (Royal Museum of Ancient Art). Here the collection is of Flemish and Dutch paintings, ranging from magnificent 15th- and 16th-century works—Cranach, Matsys, and Brueghel the Elder among them—to Rubens (several fine canvases), Van Dyck, and David. Do not miss Brueghel's dramatic *La Chute d'Icare* (The Fall of Icarus) or Hieronymous Bosch's *Le Dernier Jugement* (The Last Judgment), a malevolent portrait of humanity. *Pl. Royale. Admission: free. Open Tues.–Sun. 10–5.*

As you stand in the place Royale facing back the way you've come, the rue de la Régence runs on your left up to the Palais de Justice. The Sablon lies along this street, on the right. The **❿ Grand Sablon,** the city's most sophisticated square, is alive with cafés, restaurants, and antiques shops. If you feel tired, have a drink or snack in Le Zavel (*see* Dining). Between the two bars lies the tempting Wittamer, the city's finest cake shop. Toward the end of the square is the **church of Notre Dame du Sablon,** built in flamboyant Gothic style. Although much of the original workmanship was lost in restoration, it remains one of the city's best-loved churches. At night, the brilliant church windows illuminate the Grand Sablon and the Petit Sablon behind.

⓫ A small garden square, the **Petit Sablon** is surrounded by 48 statues representing Brussels's medieval guilds. Each craftsman carries an object that reveals his trade: The furniture maker holds a chair, for instance; the wine merchant, a goblet.

On the Petit Sablon is the **Musée Instrumental** (Museum of Musical Instruments). A huge collection of over 1,000 musical instruments is on display. Half of these are unique, and a few go back to the Bronze Age. The guide can often be persuaded to play one of the pianos. *Petit Sablon 17, tel. 02/512–08–48. Admission: free. Open Tues., Thurs., and Sat. 2:30–4:30, Wed. 4–6, Sun. 10:30–12:30.*

Immediately behind the Petit Sablon is the **Palais d'Egmont,** at different times the residence of Cristina of Sweden, Louis XV, and Voltaire. It is now used by the Belgian Ministry of Foreign Affairs for official meetings. If security allows, you can enter the Jardin d'Egmont, another small park, on this side. Come out of the entrance on rue du Grand Cerf and turn left toward the boulevard de Waterloo, a wide street full of bars and designer shops.

Time Out Among the bars on your left, **Le Nemrod** is the most typical. In summer, there is a sidewalk café. The interior is decorated like a Belgian hunting lodge, with lifelike deer and other stuffed animal heads on the walls. At the first chill, the Nemrod's fireplace is surrounded by drinkers of Gueuze and Kriek beers.

Palais de Justice to the Black Tower
⑫ At the end of the rue de la Régence is the **Palais de Justice.** Often described as the ugliest building in Europe, the palais is designed to impress upon you the majesty of justice. It's located on the site of the former Gallows Hill. If you climb the more than 500 steps to the cupola, you will get an excellent view of the countryside around Brussels, weather permitting.

⑬ Down a rather steep hill from the Palais de Justice is the working-class **Marolles** district, where the artist Pieter Brueghel died in 1569. His imposing marble tomb is in **Notre Dame de la Chapelle,** Brueghel's local church on rue Haute. From the church, head back to the Sablon via the cobbled rue Rollebeek. If you would rather see more of the authentic Marolles district, ignore the cluster of chic restaurants and designer shops on rue Rollebeek. Instead, from place de la Chapelle, take rue Blaes to
⑭ the flea market in **place du Jeu de Balle.** On the way, you will pass a number of rough Belgian bars and North African food shops. Until this century, bourgeois Belgians considered this labyrinth of small alleys a haven for thieves and political refugees. Although the Marolles continues to welcome immigrants and outsiders, it has lost its danger but kept its slightly raffish character. Near Jeu de Balle, you can sometimes see *un gargoteur,* a street vendor with two large baskets, one containing baked potatoes the other, herrings. Before you leave, sample marinated herrings or *caricolles* (water snails) at one of the local bars.

⑮ Return via the Sablon to the place Royale. Directly ahead of you is the **Parc de Bruxelles** (Brussels Park) with the **Palais Royale** (Royal Palace) at the end closer to you. (The palace is usually open during August and a few days before and after. Dates vary from year to year.) You can walk through the park
⑯ to the **Palais de la Nation** (Palace of the Nation) at the opposite end, where the two houses of the Belgian Parliament meet. When Parliament is not sitting, you can visit the building. *Guided tours weekdays 10–4.*

⑰ Surrounding the park are elegant turn-of-the-century houses. The prime minister's office is next to the Parliament building. A walk downhill (rue des Colonies) toward the downtown area and a short right-hand detour brings you to the **Cathédrale de St-Michel.** The cathedral's chief treasure is the beautiful stained-glass windows designed by Bernard van Orley, an early 16th-century painter at the royal court. In summer the great west window is floodlit from inside to reveal its glories.

Time Out Situated between the cathedral and the galleries is **La Mort Subite** (Sudden Death). Little known to outsiders, it is the city's most genuine beer hall. Locals sit on long benches and select drinks from the best beer list in Brussels. Choose a foamy *biere blanche* (white lager beer), a strong *trappiste* (brewed by monks), a *framboise* (made with raspberries), or a heady *kriek* (a cherry beer). Each has its own special glass. To accompany the beer, try the traditional *fromage 1900*, a pot of creamy white cheese and crusty bread. *Rue Montagne-aux-Herbes-Potagères 7, tel. 02/513–13–18.*

⑱ Continue downhill to the **place des Martyrs,** a dignified square over a mass grave for local patriots who died in the 1830 battle to expel the Dutch. This is a mysterious, desolate square, at odds with the rue Neuve, the busy shopping street that runs along one side. Cross the rue Neuve and continue on to the boulevard Adolphe-Max. Turn left and then right, in front of **⑲** the imposing **Bourse** (stock exchange), to place Ste. Catherine.

⑳ The 13th-century **Tour Noir** (Black Tower) here is part of the city's first fortifications. Under the square runs the River Senne, channeled underground in the last century when the pollution of the canal basins and the stench from the open sewers became too great. As a result of its watery past, place Ste. Catherine still holds the city's best seafood restaurants. If you have **㉑** enough energy, take the rue de la Vierge Noire to **place St. Géry,** the next square south. This whole area is undergoing exciting renovation as Bruxellois gradually realize the charms of the 17th-century buildings in this old port setting. Once an island, St-Géry has recently returned to its watery roots: The River Senne has been uncovered and the canalside houses restored. Look at the **Vieux Marché St-Géry** (the Old Market), currently being converted into a galleried indoor garden and crafts center.

Parc du Cinquantenaire and Bois de la Cambre ㉒ Another walk takes you from the Palais de la Nation down the rue de la Loi toward the Cinquantenaire (if the walk is too long for you, take the métro). On the way, you pass in front of the **European Community Headquarters** at the Rond Point Schuman. The vast 13-story cruciform building houses the European Commission. The council offices are located nearby.

㉓ The **Cinquantenaire** is a huge, decorative archway, built in 1905 in a pleasant park. The buildings on either side of the archway house the **Royal Museums of Art and History.** Displays include Greek, Roman, and Egyptian artifacts and toys. Some galleries are closed on even dates, some on odd dates—check locally. *Parc du Cinquantenaire 10, tel. 02/733–96–10. Admission: BF5. Open weekdays 9:30–12:30 and 1:30–4:45; weekends 10–4:45.*

㉔ The **Bois de la Cambre** is a popular, rambling park on the edge of town. Take tram no. 92, 93, or 94 from Sablon or place Stéphanie for a pleasant 10-minute ride along avenue Louise. Just before the bois is the former **Abbaye de la Cambre,** a 14th-century church with cloisters, an 18th-century courtyard, and a terraced park. The park is a good place for a family outing, with a lake, boat trips, pony rides, an outdoor roller-skating rink, and an inviting Swiss chalet bar and restaurant.

Beyond the bois is the **Boitsfort racecourse,** and eastward lies the **Forêt de Soignes,** 27 square kilometers (17 square miles) of forest, mostly beech trees, with walking and riding paths.

Waterloo No history buff can visit Brussels without making the pilgrimage to the site of the **Battle of Waterloo,** where Napoleon was finally defeated on June 18, 1815. It is easily reached from the city and lies 19 kilometers (12 miles) to the south of the Forêt de Soignes; take a bus from place Rouppe or a train from Gare Centrale to Waterloo station. In July and August, a red tourist train runs from Waterloo station to all the main sights (tel. 02/354–78–06).

Wellington's headquarters, now a museum, presents the complex battle through illuminated 3-D maps, scale models, and military memorabilia, including the general's personal belongings. *Admission: BF60. Open Apr.–mid-Nov., Tues.–Sun. 9:30–6:30; mid-Nov.–Mar., Tues.–Sun. 10:30–5.*

The **Battle Panorama Museum,** beside the battlefield, is a rotunda displaying a huge, naturalistic painting of one stage of the battle. *Admission: BF50. Open daily 9:30–6.*

Beside it is the pyramid-shape **Lion Monument,** erected by the Dutch. After you climb 226 steps, one of the bleakest views in the country is before you. With a little imagination, you can quickly conjure up the desolation of the battlefield scene.

Musée du Caillou (Napoleon's Headquarters) is worth visiting to understand the French perspective of the battle. Tours of the site are led by multilingual guides. *Admission: BF60. Open Wed.–Mon. 9–5.*

Time Out For a satisfying lunch of authentic Belgian cuisine, try the **Bivouac de l'Empereur,** an attractive 1720s farmhouse close to the Lion Monument. *Route de Lion 315, tel. 02/384–67–40. AE, DC, MC, V. Moderate.*

If you are in Brussels around June 15, attend the reenactment of the battle. A thousand local citizens dress as French, Prussian, and English soldiers and realistically shoot one another with old muskets. Unlike the real battle, which ended in over 40,000 deaths, this one ends in a large buffet, a son et lumière show, and a fireworks display. Check the dates with the Brussels or Waterloo tourist office.

Off the Beaten Track

Traditional methods are still used to make Gueuze and Lambic beer at the **Brasserie Cantillon** (Cantillon Brewery and Beer Museum). You may have questions about the strange fruit beers, *kriek* (cherry) and *framboise* (raspberry). Your visit includes a guided tour and a beer. *Rue Gheude 56, tel. 02/520–29–91 or 02/521–49–28. Admission: BF70. Open mid-Oct.–Apr., Sat. only, tours at 11, 2, and 3:30; weekdays by request.*

The **Maison d'Erasme** is a beautifully restored 15th-century house where Erasmus, the great humanist, lived in 1521. Every detail of this atmospheric house is authentic, with period furniture and paintings by Holbein, Dürer, and Hieronymous Bosch. The custodian will convince you of the relevance of Erasmus's works to peace in our time. *Rue du Chapitre 31, tel. 02/521–13–83. Admission: BF20. Open Wed. and Fri.–Mon., 10–noon and 2–5.*

The brand-new **Musée de la Bande Dessinée** celebrates the comic strip, emphasizing such famous Belgian graphic artists as

Hergé, Tintin's creator. Hergé apparently invented the *ligne claire*, a simple, bold style of drawing. The display is housed in Victor Horta's splendid Art Nouveau building, once a department store. Horta's juggling of steel, glass, and light has created an exciting backdrop. *Les anciens magasins Waucquez, rue des Sables 20, tel. 02/673-15-06. Tram Nos. 92, 93, 101. Admission: BF100. Open Tues.-Sun. 10-6.*

The **Musée Horta** (Horta Museum) was once a workshop designed by the Belgian master of Art Nouveau, Victor Horta. From the attic to the cellar, every detail of the house displays the exuberant curves of Art Nouveau style. Horta wanted to put nature back into daily life. Here his floral motifs, organic style, and refined curves of iron and stone succeed magnificently. *Rue Américain 25, tel. 02/537-16-92. Admission: BF100. Open Tues.-Sun. 2-5:30. Tram Nos. 81, 92, 50.*

On the outskirts of the city, **Tervuren** has an unspoiled location, bordering the wild Forêt de Soignes. It also has a noble ancestry. As the duke of Brabant's prized estate, it once contained palatial villas and hunting lodges. A few remain, but today's highlights are an attractive park, lakes, and an African museum. At the turn of the century, Leopold II built the **Musée Royale de l'Afrique Centrale,** designed to cover all aspects of life in the Belgian Congo, from geology to flora and fauna, customs, and religion. The museum, set in a classical French park, is a faithful reflection of his hopes. Take the métro to Montgomery station and then change to a No. 44 tram. The pleasant journey is mostly through trees and parkland. By car, take the avenue de Tervuren all the way. *Admission: BF75. Open Mar.-Oct., daily 9-5:30; Oct.-Feb., daily 10-4:30.*

Shopping

Gift Ideas

Crystal　The Val-St-Lambert mark is the only guarantee of hand-blown, hand-carved lead crystal tableware. You can buy it in many stores including **Art and Selection** (Marché-aux-Herbes 83), near the Grand' Place. For cut-price porcelain and china, try the **Vaisselle au Kilo** (rue Bodenbroek 8, near the Sablon district), which is also open on Sunday.

Chocolates　For "everyday" chocolate, try the Côte d'Or variety, available in any chocolate shop or larger store. For the delicious pralines —rich chocolates filled with every fruit, liqueur, or nut imaginable—try the brands made by Godiva, Neuhaus, or Leonidas. Although Godiva is better known abroad, Leonidas is rated more highly by the Belgians. Leonidas shops are scattered throughout the city, but there is one in boulevard Adolphe Max and another in the chaussée d'Ixelles.

Lace　To avoid disappointment, ask the store assistant outright whether the lace is handmade Belgian or made in the Far East. As preparation, visit the **Lace Museum** (6 rue de la Violette, near the Grand' Place). **La Maison F. Rubbricht,** on the Grand' Place, sells authentic, handmade Belgian lace. For a large choice of old and modern lace, try **Manufacture Belge de Dentelles** (Galerie de la Reine 6-8).

Shopping Districts　For boutiques and stores, the main districts are in the **ville basse** (low town), the **Galeries Royales** (luxury goods or gift items), **rue Neuve,** (inexpensive clothes), and **City 2** and the **Anspach Center** (large covered shopping complexes). In City 2,

FNAC is a cherished French institution: as well as being an outlet for books, records, cameras, and stereo equipment at the best prices in town, it is also a trendy cultural and exhibition center.

You'll find designer names and department stores (such as **Inno**), in the **ville haute** (high town). **Avenue Louise** is its center, complete with covered galleries, **Galerie Louise,** and **Galerie de la Toison d'Or,** the appropriately named street of the Golden Fleece! To offset prices, many of these stores operate sales-tax refunds (*see* Shopping in Staying in Belgium). The **place du Grand Sablon** is an equally expensive but more charming shopping district. This is the center for antiques, small art galleries, and designer shops. You'll also find **Wittamer** (12–13 Grand Sablon), Belgium's finest *patisserie* (pastry shop). Around the Sablon and its neighboring streets, **rue des Minimes** and **rue Lebeau,** it is possible to buy anything from Persian carpets and African primitives to 18th-century paintings and Art Nouveau.

Markets On Saturdays (9–6) and Sundays (9–2), the Sablon square is transformed into an **antiques market.** In early December it runs a traditional **Christmas fair** with crafts and food from 12 countries. The **flower market** on the Grand' Place (Tues.–Sun. 8–6) is a colorful diversion. **Midi Market** is far more exotic (by Gare du Midi train station). On Sunday morning (5 AM–1 PM) the whole area becomes a colorful *souk* (bazaar) as the city's large North African community gathers to sell exotic foods and household goods to the Belgians. The **Vieux Marché** (Old Market) in place du Jeu de Balle is a rough flea market worth visiting for the authentic atmosphere of the working-class Marolles district. The market is open daily 7–2.

Dining

Apart from hearty Belgian cuisine, Brussels is proud of its foreign restaurants: Chefs from at least 50 countries work in the city. The local *cuisine bruxelloise* is rich and, in the more expensive restaurants, an imaginative variant of French cuisine. The ambience tends to be formal, dignified, and old-fashioned in the more exclusive restaurants and cozy or jovial in the simpler brasseries or *estaminets*. Servings are plentiful everywhere. If you are interested in local gourmet restaurants, ask the tourist office on the Grand' Place for its booklet *Gourmet Restaurants 1990* (BF50). An independent jury presents awards for excellence: Look for restaurants displaying the iris symbol of quality.

For details and price category definitions, *see* Dining in Staying in Belgium.

Very Expensive **Comme Chez Soi.** Pierre Wynants, the perfectionist owner-
★ chef, has decorated the restaurant in art nouveau style. Every detail is authentic, from the stained-glass panels to the carved mahogany woodwork and the artistic menus. The inventive French cuisine, excellent wine list, and attentive service complement the warm decor. The specialties include seafood, soufflés, and dishes inspired by oysters, endive, and bacon. The restaurant well deserves its three Michelin stars. *Pl. Rouppe, tel. 02/512–29–21. Reservations essential. AE, DC. Closed Sun., Mon., and Aug.*

Écailler du Palais Royal. Situated on the fashionable Grand Sablon square, this dark, clubby restaurant makes a virtue of the gloom to protect its famous guests from prying eyes. Traditional seafood dishes, such as the *ravioli de homard* (lobster ravioli), made the restaurant a society favorite from the first. *Rue Bodenbroek 18–20, tel. 02/512–87–51. Reservations essential. AE, DC, MC, V. Closed Sun. and Aug.*

Maison du Cygne. With decor to match its classical cuisine, this restaurant is set in a grand 19th-century town house on the Grand' Place. Live piano music usually accompanies the evening meal. Typical French-Belgian dishes include *lotte aux blancs de poireaux*, a monkfish and leeks specialty. *Rue Charles Buyls 2, tel. 02/511–82–44. Reservations essential. AE, DC, MC, V. Closed Sat. lunch, Sun., and Aug.*

Expensive **Les Brigittines-Chez Christopher.** Situated near the Sablon area, the restaurant has a quiet setting in a grand old Belgian home. The interior has a fin de siècle atmosphere: Brass lamps, ornate mirrors, period paintings, and heavy drapes give the whole room a slightly somber look. Sound, everyday French cooking is served by lugubrious waiters. Noted dishes include fish soup, pancakes with orange, sole meunière, and asparagus in a mousseline sauce. *Pl. de la Chapelle 5, tel. 02/512–68–91. Reservations essential. AE, DC, MC, V. Closed Wed. and Sun. evening.*

★ **La Porte des Indes.** The city's finest Indian restaurant brings an exotic touch to the bustling avenue Louise business district. Gracious staff, dressed in traditional Indian attire, create a warm, sensitive atmosphere. The plant-filled lobby, wood carvings, soft music, and soothing blue-and-white decor provide a restful backdrop. The cuisine is surprisingly versatile, from a mild pilaf to a spicy *vindaloo* (chili-flavored curry). Exotic fruits complete the meal. If in doubt, ask for a "brass tray," which provides a chance to sample a range of specialties. *Av. Louise 455, tel. 02/647–86–51. Reservations advised. AE, DC, MC, V. Closed Sun.*

Trente Rue de la Paille. Situated just off the Sablon square, this contradictory restaurant serves sophisticated food in a pseudo-rustic setting. The nouvelle cuisine delicacies are anything but simple. These include veal cooked with honey and herbs, *riz de veau pistou* (a rice dish with veal and pine kernels), and monkfish salad. Even if style occasionally wins over content, the food is always imaginative and the service discreet. *Rue de la Paille 30, tel. 02/512–07–15. Reservations advised. AE, DC, MC, V. Closed weekends and July.*

Moderate **Amadeus.** The restaurant occupies a cavernous studio that once belonged to the French sculptor Rodin. It is dramatically lit at night, when the courtyard, statues, and murals are seen at their best. Trendy diners can choose to have a drink, *blinis* (Russian-style pancakes) and caviar in the romantic Wine and Oyster Bar. The bohemian Amadeus restaurant offers spare ribs and unusual salads. Candlelight dinner is accompanied by the music of Mozart. Sunday brunch is a fashionable alternative. The check reflects the atmosphere rather than the food and service, but it would be churlish to complain! *Rue Veydt 13, tel. 02/538–34–27. Reservations advised. AE, DC, MC, V. Wine and Oyster Bar closed Sun. and Mon.*

★ **Aux Armes de Bruxelles.** This restaurant is one of the few to escape the "tourist trap" label in this hectic little street. Inside, a lively atmosphere fills three rooms: The most popular section overlooks the street theater outside, but locals prefer the cozy rotunda. Service is fast and friendly, and portions are large. Specialties include *waterzooi de volaille* (a rich chicken stew) and *moules au vin blanc* (mussels in white wine). Order the *crêpe suzette* if you want to see your table engulfed by brandy flames! *Rue des Bouchers 13, tel. 02/511-21-18. AE, DC, MC, V. Closed Mon.*

Les Petits Oignons. This airy, two-story restaurant has been renovated and furnished with plants and bold modern paintings. There is even a garden for summer dining. Many French-Belgian specialties are on the menu and game dishes are particularly tasty. The à la carte menu and good wines keep prices fairly high, but the fixed menus and the special lunch menu are inexpensive. *Rue Notre-Seigneur 13, tel. 02/512-47-38. AE, DC, MC, V. Closed Wed. and July.*

Inexpensive **La Grande Porte.** An old warren of interconnecting rooms pro-
★ vides a rustic setting for hearty and often rambunctious eating. Dressed in old bibs, the jovial waiters make no concessions to fashion or style; the genuine friendliness attracts Bruxellois from all backgrounds. Part of the appeal lies in the copious portions. The specialties include *risotto à la Provençale* (a simple but tasty risotto with tomato, cheese, and onions); steaks served with rice and/or french fries; and *salade folle* (mixed green salad with cold cuts), a meal in itself. *Rue Notre-Seigneur 9, tel. 02/539-21-32. DC. Closed July.*

★ **Le Paradoxe.** This self-proclaimed "natural"-food restaurant serves unusual seafood and vegetarian dishes in a setting somewhat like an elegant greenhouse. Even the wines are "biologically approved" but taste none the worse for it! Specialties include samosas with rice, scampi with kiwi fruit, exotic vegetables in delicate sauces, and excellent homemade desserts. It is best to go on Friday or Saturday evening, when there is live music ranging from Irish folk or flamenco to New Orleans jazz or Mozart. The Christmas and New Year's musical banquets are particularly good. *Chaussée d'Ixelles 329, tel. 02/649-89-81. AE, DC, MC, V. Reservations advised on musical evenings. Closed Sun.*

Le Zavel. Both a bar and a brasserie, the Zavel is a friendly, unpretentious spot on a pretentious square. Specialties include Belgian waterzooi and salad Liègoise (a warm bacon salad), *tagliatelle au pistou* (noodles with pine kernels), Russian *borsch* (beetroot soup), and *piroghi* (pancakes). The meal can be accompanied by wine or by Belgian beer. You can dine outside in summer. *Pl. du Grand Sablon, tel. 02/512-16-80. No credit cards.*

Lodging

Do not rely on the listings provided by the Brussels tourist office for price information: The entire Benelux classification system is being reorganized, and until this is complete the four official hotel categories bear little relation to price and services. In general, finding accommodation is not difficult but, as a center of business and of the EEC, Brussels has many more choices in the Very Expensive and Expensive ranges. Hotels in categories below these are often comfortable but characterless. The main hotel districts are in the ville basse; near the avenue Louise business district; near Zaventem Airport; and in Brussels's "Silicon Valley." Avoid the cheap hotel districts near

Gare du Midi and Gare du Nord train stations. Hotels can be booked at the tourist office on the Grand' Place (tel. 02/513–89–40), and a deposit is required (deductible from the final hotel bill).

For details and price category definitions, *see* Lodging in Staying in Belgium.

Very Expensive **Alfa Sablon.** The Alfa is a tranquil, new hotel beside the prestigious Sablon area. Unprepossessing from outside, it is quietly elegant within. What the hotel lacks in facilities, it makes up for in location, personal service, and efficiency. Many of the city's finest restaurants are a few minutes away. There are special weekend and group rates. *Rue de la Paille 2–4, tel. 02/513–60–40. 12 rooms with bath. Facilities: bar. AE, DC, MC, V.*

Hilton International. Renovated in 1989, the Hilton now justifies its high prices. This imposing 27-story tower has light, airy, modern rooms. The top-floor restaurant, Plein Ciel, has a terrific view over the city. Centrally located, it is next to the main luxury shopping area and overlooks the quiet Parc d'Egmont. *Blvd. de Waterloo 38, tel. 02/513–88–77. 365 rooms with bath. Facilities: health club, sauna, 2 restaurants, coffee shop, bar, solarium. AE, DC, MC, V.*

★ **Royal Windsor.** This plush hotel is for those who rate a central location and old-fashioned charm above the latest high-tech business facilities. Rooms are decorated in shades of blue or salmon and feature modern conveniences. The Windsor is renowned for its Quatre Saisons restaurant. Wood-paneled public rooms and an intimate bar make this one of the few quiet spots near the Grand' Place. At night, however, the hotel's Crocodile Club (see Nightlife) is considered the city's most sophisticated discotheque. Weekend rates are available. *Rue Duquesnoy 5, tel. 02/511–42–15. 300 rooms with bath. Facilities: restaurant, disco, parking, conference facilities, bar, garden. AE, DC, MC, V.*

Expensive **Amigo.** This world-famous hotel, located off the Grand' Place, was built in the 1950s, but it has the charm of an older age. No one would guess that it was built on the site of the city prison. Each room is individually decorated, often in silk, velvet, and brocades. Prices vary wildly from BF4,500 to BF6,500 and far more for a penthouse suite with terrace. *Rue d'Amigo 1, tel. 02/511–59–10. 183 rooms with bath. Facilities: restaurant, bar, parking. AE, DC, MC, V.*

★ **Hotel Metropole.** Built at the turn of the century, this hotel was designed in Art Nouveau style: great columns towering over palms and a gilt-and-marble decor. Although many of the period features have been wantonly destroyed, they linger in the stylish café and the dining room. Some of the guest rooms have been decorated in Art Deco and Art Nouveau styles, so try to see more than one room. The hotel is centrally located. The candle-lit restaurant offers a live orchestra—and a good set menu for around BF1,000. Á la carte specialties include salmon in light curry, and sole in apricot. The elegant café is worth visiting even if you are not staying here; brunch is also a popular choice. Weekend rates are available. *Pl. de Brouckere 31, tel. 02/217–23–00. 400 rooms with bath. Facilities: restaurant, bar, conference facilities, sauna, garden, sidewalk terrace. AE, DC, MC, V.*

Pullman Astoria. This dignified hotel is situated near the Royal Palace and the main museum district. Decorated in Belle

Époque style, the hotel attracts a loyal following who return for the Old World elegance, the spacious rooms, and the enormous buffet breakfasts. On weekends, classical concerts are often held in a reception room hung with chandeliers. Weekend rates are available. *Rue Royale 103, tel. 02/217-62-90. 128 rooms with bath. Facilities: restaurant, conference facilities, bar, garden. AE, DC, MC, V.*

Moderate   **Alfa Louise.** Situated near the avenue Louise business and shopping district, this convenient hotel is tucked away down a quiet side street. The hotel is modern, service is friendly, and the facilities are above average for a hotel in this price bracket. It is close to a number of good bars and restaurants, including the Amadeus (*see* Dining). Weekend rates are available. *Rue Blanche 4, tel. 02/537-92-10. 83 rooms, most with bath. Facilities: parking, bar, conference facilities, garden. AE, DC, MC, V.*

Arenberg. Recently renovated, this hotel enjoys a central location near the central station. The noted restaurant offers lunch for only BF450 and can cater for special dietary requirements. Weekend rates are available. *Rue d'Assaut 15, tel. 02/511-07-70. 156 rooms with bath. Facilities: restaurant, coffee shop, bar, secretarial service, garden. AC, DC, MC, V.*

Delta. This modern, rather anonymous-looking hotel is located within walking distance of the exclusive place Louise shopping district. The street itself is always busy, so ask for a room at the back. The hotel is comfortable, fairly convenient, but rather colorless. *Chaussée de Charleroi 17, tel. 02/539-01-60. 246 rooms with bath. Facilities: restaurant, bar, parking. AE, DC, MC, V.*

Inexpensive   **Aux Arcades.** Located in a street packed with lively tourist restaurants, the hotel is conveniently near the Grand' Place. Despite its location, Aux Arcades is quiet enough and of good value, though the decor is rather bland. In such an area, the lack of a hotel restaurant is not a problem. *Rue des Bouchers 38, tel. 02/511-28-76. 18 rooms with shower. Facilities: bar. AE, DC, MC, V.*

Arcade Sainte Catherine. This good, reasonably priced hotel is just a few blocks from the Grand' Place. The decor leans toward the motelish. *Rue Joseph Plateau 2, tel. 02/513-76-20. 234 rooms with bath or shower. Facilities: coffee shop, bar. DC, MC, V.*

★ **Marie-José.** Each room is decorated in a different style, most with antiques, in this bargain hotel that is just a five-minute walk from the Parc de Bruxelles. The restaurant, Chez Callens, is moderately priced (a typical meal costs BF1,700) and great for seafood dishes. *Rue du Commerce 73, tel. 02/512-08-42. 17 rooms with bath or shower. Facilities: restaurant. AE, DC, MC, V.*

The Arts

The traditional performing arts—ballet, opera, theater—are well-represented in Brussels. There is also a wide range of English-language entertainment, including movies, and, on occasion, theater. The best way to find out what's going on is to buy a copy of the English-language weekly magazine *The Bulletin.* It's published every Thursday and sold at newsstands for BF65. For a fuller picture, see the Thursday *"Arts et Divertissements"* pull-out section in *Le Soir*, the French-language newspaper. This is often available from the Brussels tourist office.

Dance Resident choreographer Mark Morris and his young American troupe often perform in the **Ancienne Belgique** theater (rue des Pierres 15, tel. 02/512-89-86). Check places and dates in *The Bulletin*.

Music Major classical music concerts are generally held at the **Palais des Beaux-Arts** (rue Ravenstein 23, tel. 02/512-50-45 or 02/513-67-77). Alternatively, there are many free Sunday morning concerts at various churches, including the Cathédrale de St-Michel and the Petite Église des Minimes (rue des Minimes 62).

Opera The national opera company, Compagnie Royale Belge de l'Opera, is based at the **Théâtre Royal de la Monnaie** (pl. de la Monnaie, tel. 02/218-12-02). Major international opera and dance companies also visit. Tickets cost from BF500 to BF2,000.

Theater At Brussels's 30 theaters, actors perform in French, Flemish, and occasionally in English. The loveliest theater is the newly restored **Théâtre du Résidence Palace** (155 rue de la Loi, tel. 02/231-03-05). Avant-garde theater and ethnic music are performed at the cavernous **Halles de Schaerbeck** (rue Royale Ste-Marie 22a, tel. 02/218-00-31). Puppet theater is a Belgian experience not to be missed. In Brussels, visit the intimate **Théâtre Toone VII** (impasse Schuddeveld, petite rue des Bouchers 21, tel. 02/511-71-37). In this atmospheric medieval house, satirical plays are performed in a Bruxellois dialect.

Film Movies are mainly shown in their original language, so many are in English. The **Vendôme Cinéma** (av. Louise 35, tel. 02/537-12-07) shows nothing but the latest American and British imports. For unusual movies or screen classics, visit the **Musée du Cinéma** (Cinema Museum) (rue Ravenstein, tel. 02/537-12-07). Five movies are shown daily, at only BF50 each.

Nightlife

Nightclubs These are not always distinguishable from striptease shows, and lack the Parisian look, verve, and high kicks. **Show Point** (pl. Stéphanie 14, tel. 02/511-53-64) does its best.

Disco The **Crocodile Club** (rue Duquesnoy 5, tel. 02/511-42-15) at the Royal Windsor Hotel appeals to Eurocrats and visiting business executives. **Le Garage,** in a converted garage next door (rue Duquesnoy 16, tel. 02/512-66-22), attracts a younger, more local crowd. Both are closed on Sunday. **Le Cocoon Club** (Ancien Vaudeville, 14 rue de la Montagne, tel. 02/512-49-97) is a trendy spot just off the Galerie de la Reine. It is open on Fridays and Saturdays after 10:30 PM.

Bars The diversity is greater here than in many other European capitals. These are just a few of the best: **La Fleur en Papier Doré** (rue des Aléxiens 53, tel. 02/511-16-59) is a quiet bar that attracts an artistic audience to drink local beer and look at the ancient walls covered with surreal paintings and old etchings.

Falstaff (rue Henri Maus 25, tel. 02/511-98-77 or 02/511-87-89) is a famous Art Nouveau tavern that draws a mixed crowd. **Rick's Café** (av. Louise 344, tel. 02/647-75-30) is as popular with homesick Americans as it is with the British expatriate community. It serves Mexican food.

De Ultieme Hállucinatie (rue Royale 316, tel. 02/217–06–14) is another popular Art Nouveau bar that serves imaginative cocktails, a full range of beers, and a short but appealing menu.

Le Wine Bar (rue des Pigeons 9, tel. 02/511–44–93) is set in 17th-century cellars and offers excellent (mainly French) wines, strong cheeses, and delicate pâtés.

Jazz Brussels lays claim to being Europe's jazz capital. Buy the monthly *Jazz Streets* magazine to find out details. The best-known venue is the smooth **Brussels Jazz Club** (Grand' Place 13, tel. 02/512–40–93), open every night except Wednesday and Sunday. While the Jazz Club attracts a sophisticated clientele, the **Bierodrome** (pl. Fernand Cocq 21, tel. 02/512–04–56) is a smoky rough-and-ready club in Ixelles, a lively part of the city. **La Samaritaine** (rue de la Samaritaine 16, tel. 02/511–33–95) is concealed in a rustic cellar between the Sablon and the Marolles districts. Except for weekend tickets at the Jazz Club, most entrance prices are low—from BF50 to BF500.

Antwerp

Arriving and Departing

By Plane Antwerp International Airport lies just 3 kilometers (2 miles) southeast of the city. For flight information, call 03/218–12–11.

Between the Airport and Downtown Buses bound for Antwerp's central station leave about every 20 minutes; travel time is around 15 minutes. Taxis are readily available as well.

By Train Express trains run between Antwerp and Brussels; the trip takes 35 minutes. Antwerp Central Station is at Koningin Astridplein 27 (tel. 03/231–76–90). Four trains leave every hour from Antwerp's central and north stations.

By Car Several major highways converge on Antwerp's inner-city ring expressway. It's a 10-lane racetrack, so be sure you maneuver into the correct lane well before you exit. Antwerp is an easy 45-kilometer (28-mile) drive from Brussels on A1/E19.

Getting Around

By Streetcar In the downtown area, the streetcar (or tram) is the best, and most usual, means of transportation. Some lines have been rebuilt underground (look for signs marked "Métro"); the most useful line runs between the central station (métro stop Diamant) and the Groenplaats (for the cathedral). For detailed maps of the transportation system, stop in at the tourist office.

Guided Tours

The main tourist office operates a **Guide's Exchange** and, with a week's notice, is able to meet most requirements for city guides.

Tourist Information

There is a tourist office opposite the central station on Koningen Astridplein. The main tourist office is near the cathedral (Grote Markt 15, tel. 03/233–05–70). It is open weekdays 8:30–8, Saturday 9–7, Sunday 9–5.

A booklet on walks, including the famous "Rubens walk," is available from the tourist office. Various other popular walks are signposted throughout the city.

Exploring Antwerp

Antwerp, lying on the Schelde River, is the world's fifth largest port and the main city of Belgium's Flemish region. Its inhabitants, Flemings, speak Dutch—and you would be very foolish to address them in French! Luckily, their English is usually good. Antwerp and Brussels are diametrically opposed in character: No Antwerper would willingly live in Brussels any more than a Bruxellois would live in Antwerp. This difference runs deeper than the age-old linguistic dispute. At best, Antwerp (or more correctly, Antwerpen) is a dynamic, ambitious city. Its citizens are often considered more artistic, active, and politically aware than the more sedate Bruxellois. This bustling sophisticated city has long been used to wealth. With its tradition of Jewish merchants and an ancient diamond-cutting trade, Antwerp has not looked back since the 1860s, when it freed the port from Dutch control.

Numbers in the margin correspond with points of interest on the Antwerp map.

❶ Antwerp's **central station** is a good place to start exploring the city. This once-elegant Art Nouveau building is surrounded by
❷ cafés and cinemas. To the east of the station is **Antwerp Zoo,** one of the world's most reputable. The huge, well-designed zoo complex also includes a winter garden, a planetarium, a good café, and two natural-history museums. *Koningin Astridplein 26, tel. 03/231–16–40. Admission: BF280 adults, BF180 children. Open July–Aug., daily 8:30–6:30; Sept.–Feb., daily 9–5; Mar.–June, daily 8:30–6.*

Near the central station, along the Pelikaanstraat and the streets running off it, lies the **Diamond Quarter.** You can visit the diamond exhibition and see diamond cutters at work at the
❸ **Veiligheidsmuseum** (Security Museum). *Jesusstr. 28–30. Admission: free. Open Wed.–Sun. 10–5.*

The broad De Keyserlei, on the south side of the central station, leads west toward the main shopping area, the **Meir.**
❹ South of the Meir, on Rubensstraat, is **Rubenshuis** (Rubens House). The artist lived here from 1610 until his death in 1640. It's an atmospheric place, very much a patrician's home of the period, enriched with paintings by Rubens and his contemporaries. *Wapper 9. Admission: BF60. Open daily 10–5.*

❺ One of Europe's earliest skyscrapers, the 24-story **Torengebouw,** stands at the end of the Meir. Pass to the left of this building, down the Schoenmarkt, and into the wide Groen-
❻ plaats, with its statue of Rubens. The towering **Onze-Lieve-Vrouw** (Cathedral of Our Lady) stands at the opposite end of the square. Built in Gothic style, it has seven naves and 125 pillars and is the largest church in Belgium as well as Holland. It also has three masterpieces by Rubens. *Admission: BF20. Open mid-Apr.–mid-Oct., weekdays noon–5, Sat. noon–3, Sun. 1–4; mid-Oct.–mid-Apr., weekdays noon–4, Sat. noon–3, Sun. 1–4.*

From the cathedral, walk the short distance along the Suikerrui to the river. To your right is the fortresslike **Steen,** the old-

Antwerp

Antwerp Zoo, **2**

Central Station, **1**

Koninklijk Museum Voor Schone Kunsten, **10**

Nationale Scheepvaart-museum, **7**

Onze-Lieve-Vrouw **6**

Plantin-Moretus Museum, **9**

Rubenshuis, **4**

St. Annatunnel, **8**

Torengebouw, **5**

Veiligheidsmuseum, **3**

Vogelmarkt, **11**

❼ est building in Antwerp. Dating from the 12th century, the Steen now houses the **Nationale Scheepvaartmuseum** (Maritime Museum), which has many beautiful ship models, especially of the East India clippers. *Steenplein 1, tel. 03/232–08–50. Admission: BF60. Open daily 10–5.*

From the terraces around the Steen, you can see the main port installations. For a close look, a **boat excursion** around the port leaves from Quay 13 on weekdays and from Steen Landing stage on Sunday. *Cost: BF300 adults, BF180 children. Information from n.v. Flandria, Steenplein 1, tel. 03/233–74–22.*

❽ Walking along the river south of the Steen, you come to a foot tunnel, the **St. Annatunnel,** leading to the left bank of the river (the entrance is close to the Plantin-Moretus Museum, *see* below). From the riverside park, you get the best view of the city's great spires and wharves.

❾ Return through the tunnel and walk east until you come to the **Plantin-Moretus Museum,** a famous printing works founded in the 16th century. The building is a fine example of Renaissance architecture and is magnificently furnished. Among its treasures are many first editions, engravings, and a copy of Gutenberg's Bible, the *Biblia Regia. Vrijdagmarkt 22. Admission: BF50. Open daily 10–5.*

❿ From the Plantin walk through the Vrijdagmarkt, where there is a **furniture and antiques market** every Wednesday and Friday morning. Continue up the Oude Koornmarkt to the Groenplaats and catch a tram to the **Koninklijk Museum Voor Schone Kunsten** (Royal Museum of Fine Arts). It lies in the southern part of the city and houses more than 1,000 paintings by old masters, including a magnificent array of works by Rubens, Van Dyck, Hals, and Brueghel. The second floor houses one of the best collections of the Flemish school anywhere in the world. The first floor is given over to more modern paintings. The neoclassical building also has an adequate snack bar. *Leopold de Waelplaats 1–9. Admission: free. Open Tues.–Sun. 10–5.*

⓫ On Sunday morning you can see the famous **vogelmarkt,** or bird market, on the south side of the city on the Oude Vaartplaats. You'll find everything from birds and domestic pets to plants, clothes, and food.

Time Out More than 350 kinds of beer are available in **Café Kulminator—** including the lethal EKU-28, claimed by Kulminator to be "the strongest beer on Earth." The beers are best accompanied by the excellent cheeses. *Vleminckveld 32, tel. 03/232–45–38. No credit cards. Closed Sun. Inexpensive.*

Dining

Local specialties include herring and eel dishes and *witloof* (endives) cooked in a variety of ways. As for drink, there are 20 local beers, a city gin called *jenever*, and a strong liqueur, *Elixir d'Anvers*.

For details and price category definitions, *see* Dining in Staying in Belgium.

Very Expensive **La Pérouse.** Seafood is an Antwerp specialty, and here you can sample it in style on a moored ship. It's small, so you *must* reserve ahead. *Steenplain, tel. 03/232-35-28. Reservations necessary. AE, DC, MC, V. Closed Sun., Mon., and May-mid-Sept.*

★ **Sir Anthony von Dijck.** The Sir Anthony is a superb seafood restaurant on an ancient lane near the cathedral. The antiques make dining here a pleasure. Service is deferential and prompt. *Oude Koornmarkt 16, tel. 03/231-61-70. Reservations required. AE, DC, MC, V. Closed Sun. and Mon., most of Aug., and Christmas.*

Expensive **Het Fournis.** There's a heavy country touch in the decor here, and the food matches the ambience, with traditional local dishes and large helpings, all of it cooked with a master's touch. *Reydersstr. 24, tel. 03/233-62-70. Reservations advised. AE, DC, MC, V. Closed Sat., Sun., most of Aug., and Christmas.*
Vateli. It's not fish that rules here (although it is on the menu) but duck—a great favorite in Belgium. One of the special versions that Vateli offers is duck *à la Rouennaise,* as done in Rouen. The cooking is classical and excellent, and the service friendly. *Kidporpvest 50, tel. 03/233-17-81. Reservations advised. AE, DC, MC, V. Closed Sun., Mon., July, and Christmas.*

Moderate **Rooden-Hoed.** Seafood is featured in this traditional cozy restaurant, reputed to be Antwerp's oldest. Specialties include
★ eels and mussels, in season. Try the *paling in t'groen* (eel in green sauce). The restaurant recommends its dry, white wines from Alsace. *Oude Koornmarkt 25, tel. 03/233-28-44. Reservations advised. AE, MC. Closed Wed. and Thurs.*
Sawadee. Evoking a long-standing Far East connection, the menu here is well-stocked with delicious Thai dishes. The restaurant operates on an upper floor of an old house, worth seeing in itself. *Britselei 16, tel. 03/233-08-59. Reservations advised. AE, DC, MC, V. Closed Tues.*

Inexpensive **In de Schaduw van de Kathedraal.** As the name states, this budget restaurant, serving traditional food, lies "in the shadow of
★ the cathedral." Try the seafood dishes, especially mussels in season. There is a terrace for outside dining. *Handshoemarkt 17, tel. 03/232-40-14. Reservations not required. AE, DC, MC, V. Closed Tues.*

Lodging

All hotels are modern, so expect comfort rather than period charm. For details and price category definitions, *see* Lodging in Staying in Belgium.

Very Expensive **Alfa De Keyser.** This well-maintained deluxe hotel is handily
★ situated only 139 meters (150 yards) from the central station and near the diamond center. It has a restaurant that prides itself on its adaptation of local ingredients to nouvelle cuisine. *De Keyserlei 66, tel. 03/234-01-35. 117 rooms with bath. Facilities: airport express bus that stops opposite the hotel, café, bar, nightclub, parking, videos available. AE, DC, MC, V.*

Expensive **Alfa Theater.** This plush, centrally located hotel is part of the reliable Alfa chain. The restaurant offers an appealing blend of nouvelle cuisine presentation and Belgian portions. Try the lobster mousse. *Arenbergstr. 30, tel. 03/232-39-70. 83 rooms* *with bath. Facilities: bar, restaurant, conference facilities. AE, DC, MC.*

Moderate **Columbus.** The main attraction of this hotel is its central location—convenient for sightseeing. It has no restaurant. *Frankrijklei 4, tel. 03/233-03-90. 27 rooms, most with bath or shower. AE, DC, MC, V.*

Inexpensive **Arcade.** This is a modern, impersonal hotel designed along the lines of a university campus. Its location, overlooking the weekend marketplace, makes it ideal for visiting the old district. *Meistr. 39 (Theaterplein), tel. 03/231-88-30. 150 rooms with shower. Facilities: bar, access for the disabled, conference facilities. MC, V.*

Tourist. Situated next to the central station, the Tourist is a budget stalwart, built in 1930, and has long been popular. *Pelikaanstr. 22, tel. 03/232-58-70. 148 rooms, 126 with bath. Facilities: limited restaurant, bar, access for the disabled. AE, MC, V.*

Bruges

Arriving and Departing

By Train Trains run hourly at 46 minutes past the hour from Brussels to Bruges. The London–Brussels service stops here as well. The train station is south of the canal that surrounds the downtown area; for information, tel. 050/38-58-71 or 38-23-82. Travel time from Brussels is 70 minutes.

By Bus National buses do not connect with Bruges, but individual bus tours from Brussels stop here on day excursions.

By Car Bruges lies 97 kilometers (61 miles) northwest of Brussels. The most direct route between the two cities is the A10/E40.

Getting Around

On Foot By far the easiest way of exploring the city is on foot because the downtown sights are fairly close together.

By Horse-Drawn Cab An expensive means of seeing the sights is provided by the horse-drawn cabs that congregate in the market square, March–November, daily 10–6. A 35-minute trip will cost BF480, and the cabs take up to four people.

Guided Tours

Boat Trips Boat trips along the city canals are run by several companies and depart from five separate landings. Boats ply the waters March–November, 10–6. There is no definite departure schedule; boats leave when enough people have gathered, but you'll never have to wait more than 15 minutes or so. The following are just two of the companies operating: **P.C.B. Stael** (tel. 050/33-27-1) and **Coudenys** (tel. 050/33-51-03). During summer months, special evening cruises can be arranged.

Orientation Tours Three-hour bus trips of Bruges and its environs are available July–September. One of the major companies is **Gidsenkring** (tel. 050/82-32-02). Buses leave from Beursplein at 10 and 2:30 on Tuesday, Thursday, and weekends. For further information and a full list of companies, check with the tourist office.

Tour Guides Individual guides can be arranged through the tourist office. Be sure to make your request at least a week in advance.

Tourist Information

The **Bruges Tourist Office** is at Burg 11, tel. 050/44–80–80.

Exploring Bruges

Bruges (or, more correctly, Brugge) is a perfectly preserved medieval museum, deservedly called "the Venice of the North." Bruges was ignored for centuries after the Zwin River silted up, and the port became a romantic Flemish backwater. This past misfortune is its present glory. Little has changed in this city of interlaced canals, overhung with humpbacked bridges and weeping willows. Bruges has a large student population, which is reflected in the lively bars and summer concerts in the historic squares. The **Burg**, an intimate medieval square, is the inspiring setting for summer classical concerts.

Numbers in the margin correspond with points of interest on the Bruges map.

①② The best place to start a walking tour is the **Grote Markt** (Market Square). From the top of the **Beffroi** (Belfry)—"Thrice destroyed and thrice rebuilded," as Longfellow tells us—there's a panoramic view of the town. The belfry has a carillon notable even in Belgium, where they are a matter of civic pride. On summer evenings, the Markt is brightly lit. *The Beffroi. Admission: BF50. Open daily 9:30–12:30 and 1:30–6. Carillon concerts Oct.–mid-June, Sun., Wed., and Sat. 11:45–12:30; mid-June–Sept., Mon., Wed., and Sat. 9–10 PM.*

③ On the eastern side of the Markt stands the **Provinciaal Hof,** the neo-Gothic provincial government building. Walk east from the Markt along Breidlestraat, to the Burg, a square at the center **④** of ancient Bruges. On the left is the **Landshuis** (Provost's House), built in 1622. Across the square is a row of magnificent **⑤** buildings—the **Stadhuis** (town hall), dating from the 14th cen- **⑥** tury, its wonderfully ornate facade covered with statues; **Oude Griffie,** the former Recorder's House dating from the 1530s, and also ornamented with impressive windows; and the **⑦** **HeiligBloed Basiliek** (the Basilica of the Holy Blood), built to enshrine the vial containing Christ's blood, and a church so fascinating that it alone would warrant a visit to Bruges. Here, too, is a **HeiligBloed Museum** (Museum of the Holy Blood), with many treasures associated with the cult. *Stadhuis—Admission: BF30. Open daily 9:30–noon and 2–6. HeiligBloed Basiliek—Worship of the Blood, Fri. 8:30–11:45 and 3–4. Free guided visits daily 2–5. Museum—Admission: BF20. Open daily 9:30–noon and 2–4.*

⑧ Walk through a passage between the town hall and the Oude Griffie and you come to the **Dijver,** the city canal. Canal boat trips leave from here during the day and in the evening from June to September. *Boats leave on demand. Average trip 30 minutes. Cost: BF150.*

⑨ Walking south along the Dijver soon takes you to a group of museums. The **Gruuthuse Museum,** in the 15th-century a former palace of the aristocratic Gruuthuse family, contains archaeological exhibitions and a display of lace from all over Belgium.

Bruges

Beffroi, **2**
Béguinage, **14**
Dijver, **8**
Groeninge
Museum, **10**
Grote Markt, **1**
Gruuthuse Museum, **9**

HeiligBloed Basiliek, **7**
Landshuis, **4**
Memling Museum, **11**
Minnewater, **13**
Onze Lieve
Vrouwekerk, **12**
Oude Griffie, **6**
Provinciaal Hof, **3**
Stadthuis, **5**

*Dijver 17. Admission: BF80; combined ticket for BF200 covers
the Groeninge, Gruuthuse and Memling museums (see below).
Open daily 9:30–noon and 2–6.*

⑩ The **Groeninge Museum,** on the Dijver Canal, has a very rich,
wide-ranging collection of Flemish masterpieces, with works
by van Eyck, Memling, Bosch, and Brueghel, among many
others, plus some contemporary works. *Dijver 17. Admission:
BF80. Open daily 9:30–6.*

⑪ Here, too, is the **Memling Museum,** dedicated to the work of one
of Bruge's most famous sons, the painter Hans Memling (1430–
90), and housed in the former Sint Jans Hospital (Hospital of
St. John), where the artist was nursed back to health after being wounded in France. *Mariastraat 38. Admission: BF80.
Open daily Apr.–Dec. 9–12:30 and 2–6; Jan.–Mar. 10–noon
and 2–5.*

⑫ Next to the Memling Museum is the **Onze Lieve Vrouwekerk**
(Church of Our Lady), with, at 116 meters (375 feet), the highest tower in Belgium, a notable collection of paintings and
carvings—especially a *Madonna* by Michelangelo—and some
splendidly colorful tombs. *Mausoleums—Admission: BF30.
Open weekdays 10–11:30 and 2:30–5, Sun. 2:30–5.*

⑬ Continue south to the enchanting **Minnewater** (Lake of Love)
Park. From the Minnewater visit the adjoining 16th-century
lockkeeper's house, usually surrounded by contented white
swans, the symbol of the city.

⑭ Beside Minnewater, a picturesque bridge leads to the **Béguinage,** the former almshouses and the most serene spot in Bruges. Founded in 1245 by the countess of Flanders, the
Béguinage was a home for religious women who took partial
vows. The nuns lived a devout life while serving the community.
Although the last Béguines left in 1930, a Benedictine community has replaced them. The Béguinage has kept its cloistered
charm. Notice the harmonious pattern made by the gabled
white houses, the expanse of green lawn, and the crooked trees
which stretch diagonally across your view.

Time Out Overlooking the lake is a fairy-tale tower without a princess,
but with a perfect setting in which to enjoy a drink or light
lunch. The romantic **Kasteel** is divided into two sections, for formal and casual dining. Try a tasty ham or mushroom omelet
with crusty bread or a witloof specialty. If you are dining outside, the swans may try to join in. *Tel. 50/33–42–54. DC, V.
Inexpensive–Moderate.*

Explore the medieval ramparts near the Kasteel or retrace
your steps to the Markt. Savor the side streets, the gabled
houses, the lace shops, and the churches along the quay. If you
are tired, take a horse-drawn carriage back to your starting
point.

Dining

For details and price category definitions, *see* Dining in Staying
in Belgium.

Very Expensive **De Witte Poorte.** The fish here, fresh from the North Sea, is in a
★ class by itself; so is the game in season. Family run, and housed
in an old, vaulted warehouse, the de Witte Poorte is *the* place

for a meal you'll remember. *Jan Van Eyckplein 6, tel. 050/33–08–83. Reservations advised. AE, DC, V.*

Expensive **'t Pandreitje.** Here's the place to go for nouvelle cuisine, Belgian-style, in distinctly elegant surroundings. Helpings are larger than one expects from nouvelle dining. There is an excellent selection of French wines. It's handily located just across the canal from the Burg complex. *Pendreitje 6, tel. 050/33–11–90. Reservations advised. AE, DC, MC, V. Closed Sun., Mon., most of Mar., and end of Dec.*

Moderate **Oud Brugge.** Many of the city's restaurants are found in atmospheric ancient buildings, and this is one of them. Tasty local dishes are served under yet more vaulted ceilings. *Kuiperstraat 33, tel. 050/33–54–02. Reservations advised. No credit cards.*

Inexpensive **Gistelhof.** The Gistelhof serves hearty fish stews and other local dishes in historic Flemish surroundings. *West Gistelhof 23, tel. 050/33–62–90. Reservations not necessary. AE, DC, MC, V.*

Lodging

In proportion to its size, Bruges has a large number of hotels; in fact, many more than Antwerp. Prices are relatively high but so are the standards, and you should be rewarded with an elegant hotel in a renovated town house or a rustic hotel on a quiet canal. For details and price category definitions, *see* Lodging in Staying in Belgium.

Very Expensive **Die Swaene.** The Swan, sitting right in the center of town, is a
★ real find. The 15th-century building, lovingly restored by the Hessels-Dutoit husband-and-wife team, has many original features preserved. An ugly former courtyard, for example, is now a pleasant garden. *Steenhouwersdijk 1, tel. 050/34–27–98. 26 rooms with bath and shower. Facilities: bar, restaurant. AE, DC, MC, V.*

Expensive **Duc de Bourgogne.** Set in a stunning location at the bend of a canal, the Duc has rooms that are all tastefully furnished in 17th-century style. There is also a fine restaurant—try the many fish dishes—with a remarkable view. *Huidenvettersplein 12, tel. 050/34–40–37. 18 rooms with bath. AE, DC, MC, V.*

Moderate **Ter Brughe.** If it's atmosphere and period charm you want, you won't be disappointed by this delightful canalside hotel, a 15th-century survival, with friendly service and a cozy atmosphere. There's no restaurant. *Oost-Gisthelhof 2, tel. 050/34–03–24. 17 rooms with bath. DC, MC, V. Closed Jan.–Feb.*

Inexpensive **Van Eyck.** This small, modest hotel, a stone's throw from the market square, makes a fine base for exploring. There's a simple restaurant that gives hearty helpings. *Kotre Zilverstraat 7, tel. 050/33–52–67. 8 rooms, 5 with bath or shower. AE, MC, V.*

5 Bulgaria

Introduction

Bulgaria's close political ties with the U.S.S.R. since World War II have earned the country a reputation in the West as the Soviet Union's closest ally. The tourist should not be deceived, though, by impressions derived from political news coverage of an austere and mysterious land cut off from the Western world.

Bulgaria is one of the best countries to visit in the Eastern Bloc. Economic conditions are better here than in Romania, Poland, and Czechoslovakia, though not as good as in Hungary, and Bulgaria possesses the natural resources to make it Eastern Europe's most popular tourist spot. The Black Sea coast along the country's eastern border is particularly attractive, with secluded coves and old fishing villages, as well as wide stretches of shallow beaches that have been developed into self-contained resorts. The interior landscape offers great scenic beauty, and the traveler who enters it will find a tranquil world of forested ridges, spectacular valleys, and rural communities where folklore is a colorful part of village life.

Bulgaria remains a society made up largely of farmers and shepherds, its economy enriched by attar of roses. "Roses are our golden currency," reads the school sign in a village in the Valley of Roses. In fact, ounce for ounce, rose oil has risen above the price of gold on the international market.

Bulgaria was occupied by the Turks from 1396 to 1898 and was part of the Byzantine Empire from 1018 to 1185; the combined influences are reflected in Bulgarian architecture, which has a truly Eastern feel. Half a century of Muslim rule did not wipe out Christianity, and there are many interesting churches and monasteries to see; the Rila monastery, 118 kilometers (74 miles) south of Sofia, is not to be missed.

The capital, Sofia, is picturesquely situated in a valley near Mount Vitoša. There is much of cultural interest here, and the city has good hotels and restaurants serving international cuisine. Other main towns are Veliko Tărnovo, the capital during the 12th–14th centuries and well worth a visit for the old, characteristic architecture; Plovdiv, southeast of Sofia, which has a particularly interesting old quarter; and Varna, the most important port in Bulgaria.

Before You Go

When to Go   The ski season lasts from mid-December through March, while the Black Sea coast season runs from May to October, reaching its crowded peak in July and August. Fruit trees blossom in April and May; in May and early June the blossoms are gathered in the Valley of Roses (you have to be up early to watch the harvest); the fruit is picked in September, and in October the fall colors are at their best.

Climate   Summers are warm, winters are crisp and cold. The coastal areas enjoy considerable sunshine, though March and April are the wettest months inland. Even when the temperature climbs, the Black Sea breezes and the cooler mountain air prevent the heat from being overpowering.

The following are the average daily maximum and minimum temperatures for Sofia.

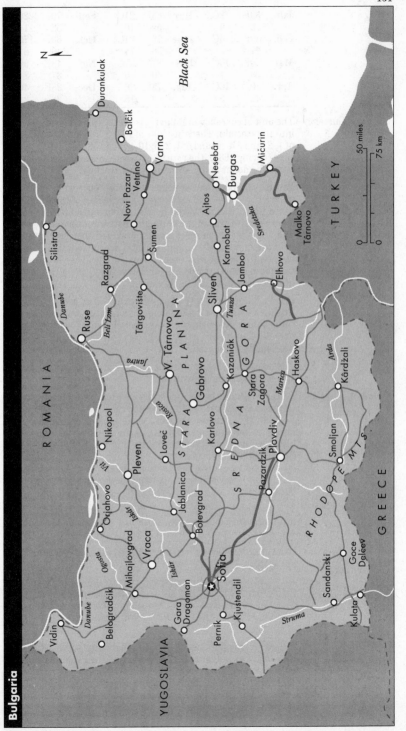

Bulgaria

Jan.	35F	2C	May	69F	21C	Sept.	70F	22C
	25	−4		50	10		52	11
Feb.	39F	4C	June	76F	24C	Oct.	63F	17C
	27	−3		56	14		46	8
Mar.	50F	10C	July	81F	27C	Nov.	48F	9C
	33	1		60	16		37	3
Apr.	60F	16C	Aug.	79F	26C	Dec.	38F	4C
	42	5		59	15		28	2

Currency The unit of currency in Bulgaria is the lev (plural leva), divided into 100 stotinki. There are bills of 1, 2, 5, 10, and 20 leva; coins of 1, 2, and 5 leva, and of 1, 2, 5, 10, 20, and 50 stotinki. At press time (spring 1989), the rate of exchange was approximately 0.9 lev to the dollar and 1.49 to the pound sterling.

You may import any amount of foreign currency, including traveler's checks, and exchange it at branches of the Bulgarian State Bank, Balkantourist hotels, airports, and border posts. Always try to exchange it through a Balkantourist office, which will add a 200% currency bonus, provided that you have prepaid a minimum of two nights' hotel accommodation. Always hold on to your official exchange slips. Avoid the active black market in foreign currency—there are heavy penalties, including imprisonment, for being caught.

It is forbidden either to import or export Bulgarian currency. Unspent leva must be exchanged at frontier posts on departure, before going through passport control. You will need to present your official exchange slips to prove that the currency was legally purchased.

The major international credit cards are accepted in the larger stores, hotels, and restaurants.

What It Will Cost Prices in Bulgaria are generally low and reasonably stable. Bulgaria is best geared to prepaid arrangements, which can be flexible. If you choose the more moderate of the Balkantourist hotels and restaurants, Bulgaria is inexpensive, and it is possible to cut costs still further by staying in a private room in a Bulgarian house or apartment—also arranged by Balkantourist—or by camping. The currency bonus (*see* Currency) can significantly expand your spending power and so can seeking out the duty-free Corecom shops.

Sample Prices Trip on tram, trolley, or bus, .60 lev; theater ticket, 1.20–6 leva; coffee in a moderate restaurant, 1–2 leva; bottle of wine in a moderate restaurant, from 4 leva.

Museums Museum admission is very inexpensive, ranging from .20 lev to .90 lev (25¢–$1).

Visas All visitors need a valid passport; those traveling independently in groups of fewer than six (except families) require a visa as well. Many package tours are exempt from the visa requirement; check with the tour operator or travel agent at the time of purchase.

American travelers needing visas should apply at least two or three weeks in advance to the Embassy of the People's Republic of Bulgaria, 1621 22nd St. NW, Washington, DC 20008. Applicants will need to submit a valid passport, a visa application, one passport-size photo, a self-addressed envelope, and $4–$19 for postage and handling, and the $15 fee.

Canadians in need of visas should apply to the Consulate General of the People's Republic of Bulgaria, 100 Adelaide St. W., Suite 1410, Toronto, Ontario MYH 163. The cost is C$25.

British travelers should apply for visas to the Embassy of the People's Republic of Bulgaria, 186 Queen's Gate, London SW7 5HL. The cost is £20.

Customs on Arrival You may import duty-free into Bulgaria 250 grams of tobacco products, plus one liter of alcohol and two liters of wine. You should declare all items of value—cameras, tape recorders, etc.—so there will be no problem with Bulgarian customs officials when you leave.

Language The official language is Bulgarian, a Slavic language written in the Cyrillic alphabet. English is spoken in the hotels and restaurants, and fairly widely elsewhere, but it is essential to remember that, in Bulgaria, a nod of the head means "no" and a shake of the head means "yes."

Getting Around

By Car
Road Conditions Main roads are generally well engineered, although some routes are narrow for the volume of traffic they have to carry. A large-scale expressway construction program has begun to link main towns. Completed stretches run from Kalotina—on the Yugoslav border—to Sofia, and from Sofia to Plovdiv. Highways are free of tolls, but be prepared for delays at border points (open 24 hours) while documents are checked and stamped.

Rules of the Road Drive on the right, as in the United States. The speed limits are 60 kph (36 mph) in built-up areas, 80 kph (50 mph) elsewhere, except on highways, where it is 120 kph (70 mph). The limit for a car towing a trailer is 50 kph (31 mph), 70 kph (44 mph), and 100 kph (62 mph) respectively. You must obtain a Green Card or Blue Card from your car insurance company, which is recognized international proof that your car is insured. You will be required to show one of these at the frontier. You must also take out insurance providing third-party cover—this you can do at the border checkpoints (Balkantourist recommends Casco Insurance). You are required to carry a first-aid kit in the vehicle and must not sound the horn after dark or in towns. The drinking-driving laws are extremely strict—you are expressly forbidden to drive after consuming any alcohol at all.

Parking Park only in clearly marked parking places. If in any doubt, check with the hotel or restaurant.

Gasoline Stations are regularly spaced on main roads but may be few and far between off the beaten track. All are marked on Balkantourist's free motoring map. Gas can be bought only with vouchers, issued at reduced prices at all border checkpoints, large hotels, and Balkantourist roadside facilities.

Breakdowns In case of breakdown, telephone 146. The **S.B.A.** (Road Air Service) trucks carry essential spares, but it's wise to carry your own spare parts kit.

Car Rental The **Rent-a-Car** organization has offices in most of the major hotels and at Sofia Airport. Rental cars and fly/drive arrangements can be prebooked through Balkantourist agents abroad.

By Train Buy tickets in advance at a ticket office—there is one in each of the major centers—and avoid long lines at the station. Trains are very busy; seat reservations are obligatory on expresses. All medium- and long-distance trains have first- and second-class carriages and limited buffet services; overnight trains between Sofia and Black Sea resorts have first- and second-class sleeping cars and second-class couchettes. From Sofia there are five main routes—to Varna and to Burgas on the Black Sea coast; to Plovdiv and on to the Turkish border; to Dragoman and the Yugoslav border; and to Kulata and the Greek border. Large sections of the main line are powered by electricity. Plans to electrify the rest are under way.

By Plane **Balkanair** (Balkan Bulgarian Airlines) has services from Sofia to Varna and Burgas, and limited services elsewhere within the country. Book through Balkantourist offices, though this can take time, and overbooking is not unusual.

By Bus The routes of the crowded buses are mainly planned to link towns and districts not connected by rail. Within the cities a regular system of trams and trolley buses operates for a single fare of 6 stotinki. Ticket booths, at most tram stops, sell single or season tickets; you can also pay the driver. The tourist information offices have full details of routes and times.

By Boat Hydrofoils link main communities along the Bulgarian stretches of the Danube and the Black Sea, and there are coastal excursions from some Black Sea resorts. A ferry from Vidin to Calafat links Bulgaria with Romania.

Staying in Bulgaria

Telephones Calls can be made from hotels or from public telephones in the post office in each major town or resort. There is direct dialing throughout Europe (the code for the United Kingdom is 0044), but calls to the United States must be placed through the operator.

Mail Letters and postcards cost 60 stotinki to the USA, 45 stotinki to the United Kingdom.

Opening and Closing Times **Banks.** The Foreign Trade Bank is open weekdays 8–noon.
Museums. Museums are usually open 8–6:30, but are often closed Monday or Tuesday.
Shops. Shops are open Monday–Saturday 9–1 and 2–7.

National Holidays January 1; March 3 (Independence Day); May 1, 2 (Labor); May 24 (Bulgarian Culture); September 9, 10 (Liberation); November 7 (October Revolution).

Dining There is a choice of hotel restaurants with their international menus, Balkantourist restaurants, or the inexpensive restaurants and cafeterias run by local authorities. The best bets are the small folk-style restaurants that serve national dishes and local specialties. The word *picnic* in a restaurant name means that the tables are outdoors. Standards are improving, but food is still rarely served piping hot, and visitors should be prepared for loud background music.

Balkantourist operates a prepaid voucher scheme under which you can eat in any Balkantourist restaurant at no extra cost even if you have booked full board in a specific hotel. The vouchers are issued at your hotel or by the tour operator with whom you have booked.

Specialties Balkan cooking revolves around lamb and pork, potatoes, peppers, eggplant, tomatoes, onions, carrots, and spices. Fresh fruit, vegetables, and salads are particularly good, and so are the soups. Bulgaria invented yogurt *(kišalo mleko)* with its promise of good health and longevity, and there are rich cream cakes and syrupy *baklava* to round out a meal.

Bulgarian wines are good, usually full-bodied and inexpensive. The national drink is *slivova*—plum or grape brandy—but vodka is popular, too, and you should try the local rose petal liquor. Coffee is strong; tea is taken with lemon instead of milk.

Dress In Sofia, formal dress (jacket and tie) is customary at Expensive and Very Expensive restaurants. Casual dress is appropriate elsewhere.

Ratings Prices are per person and include first course, main course, dessert, and tip, but no alcohol. Best bets are indicated by a star ★. At press time, there were 0.9 lev to the dollar.

Category	All areas
Very Expensive	over 20 leva
Expensive	15–20 leva
Moderate	7–15 leva
Inexpensive	2–7 leva

Credit Cards The following credit card abbreviations are used: AE, American Express; DC, Diners Club; MC, MasterCard; V, Visa.

Lodging There is a wide choice of accommodations, ranging from hotels —most of them dating from the '60s and '70s—to apartment rentals, rooms in private homes, hostels, and campsites. Although hotels are improving, they still tend to suffer from erratic plumbing and temperamental wiring, and it is a good idea to pack a universal plug, as plugs are often missing in hotel bathrooms.

Hotels Most hotels used by Western visitors are owned by Balkantourist (Interhotels are of the deluxe variety). Others are run by municipal authorities or organizations catering to specific groups (Sipka for motorists, Orbita for young people, Pirin for hikers). Most have restaurants and bars; the large, modern ones have swimming pools, shops, and other facilities. Some coastal resorts have complexes where different categories of hotels are grouped, each with its own facilities.

Rented Accommodations Rented accommodations are a growth industry, with planned, modern complexes as well as picturesque cottages. Cooking facilities tend to be meager and meal vouchers are included in the deal. An English-speaking manager is always on hand.

Private Accommodations Staying in private homes, arranged by Balkantourist, is increasingly popular. Some offer bed and breakfast only, some full board.

Hostels Hostels are basic, but clean and cheap. Contact **Orbita,** 45a Stambolij St., Sofia.

Campsites There are more than 100 campsites, many near the Black Sea coast. They are graded one, two, or three stars, and the best of them offer hot and cold water, grocery stores, and restaurants. Balkantourist provides a location map.

Ratings The following hotel categories are for two people in a double room with half-board (breakfast and a main meal). Best bets are indicated by a star ★. You can pay in either Western or local currency, but if you pay in leva, you must show your exchange slips to prove the money was legally changed.

Category	Sofia	Other Areas
Very Expensive	over 92 leva	over 72 leva
Expensive	56–92 leva	40–72 leva
Moderate	40–56 leva	28–40 leva
Inexpensive	under 40 leva	under 28 leva

Credit Cards The following credit card abbreviations are used: AE, American Express; DC, Diners Club; MC, MasterCard; V, Visa.

Tipping Tipping is officially discouraged but nevertheless acceptable. A safe bet is to tip 10%; foreign coins, which the recipient can spend in foreign currency shops, are particularly welcome.

Sofia

Arriving and Departing

By Plane All international flights arrive at Sofia airport. For information on international flights, tel. 2/72–24–14; domestic flights, tel. 2/54–11–13.

Between the Airport and Downtown Bus no. 84 and bus no. 284 (nonstop) both serve the airport. There is a taxi stand at the airport; be prepared to be patient. The fare is about 3 leva for the 6-mile ride.

By Train The central station is at the northern edge of the city. For information, tel. 2/3–11–11. The ticket offices in Sofia are at Lyudmila Zhivkova National Palace of Culture (1 Bulgaria Sq.) or the Rila International Travel Agency (5 Gurko St., tel. 2/87–07–77). There is a taxi stand at the station.

By Car Heading to or from Yugoslavia, the main routes are E80, going through the border checkpoint at Kalotina on the Nis—Sofia road, or E870 going through the checkpoint at Gyueshevo. Traveling from Greece, take E79, passing through the checkpoint at Kulata, and from Turkey, take E80, passing through checkpoint Kapitan-Andrevo.

Getting Around

By Bus Buses and trolleys run fairly often. Buy a ticket from the ticket stand near the streetcar stop and punch it into the machine as you board. (Watch how the person in front of you does it.) For information, tel. 2/59–71–83.

By Taxi Taxis are cheap but rather rare. Hail them in the street or at a stand—otherwise, ask the hotel to call one.

By Rented Car You can rent a car through Balkantourist and hotel reception desks.

On Foot The main sites are centrally located, so the best way to see the city is on foot.

Important Addresses and Numbers

Tourist Information **Balkantourist Head Office** (tel. 2/4–33–31) is at 1 Vitoša Blvd.; the tourist and accommodation office (tel. 2/88–44–30) is at 37 Dondukov Blvd. It also has offices or desks in all the main hotels.

Embassies **U.S.:** 1 Stamboliiski Blvd., tel. 2/88–48–01. **U.K.:** 65 Tolbukhin Blvd., tel. 2/88–53–61.

Emergencies **Police:** Sofia City Constabulary, tel. 166; **Ambulance:** tel. 150; **Fire:** tel. 160; **Doctor:** Clinic for Foreign Citizens, Mladost 1, 1 Eugeni Pavlovski St., tel. 2/7–53–61: **Pharmacies:** tel. 178 for information about all-night pharmacies.

Guided Tours

Orientation Tours Guided tours of Sofia and environs are arranged by Balkantourist from either of the main Sofia offices or from the Balkantourist desks at the major hotels. Among the possibilities are three- to four-hour tours of the principal city sights by car or minibus; or a longer four- to five-hour tour that goes as far as Mount Vitoša.

Excursions Balkantourist also arranges day trips to the Rila Monastery, to the museum town of Koprivshtitsa, to Plovdiv, or to the Valley of Roses.

Evening Tours Balkantourist has a number of evening tours, from a night out eating local food and watching folk dances to an evening at the National Opera.

Exploring Sofia

Sofia is set on the high Sofia Plain, ringed by mountain ranges: the Balkan range to the north, Ljulin Mountains to the west, part of the Sredna Gora Mountains to the southeast and, to the southwest, Mount Vitoša, the city's playground, which rises to 2,325 meters (7,500 feet). The area has been inhabited for about 5,000 years, but the visitor's first impression is of a modern city with broad streets, light traffic, spacious parks, and open-air cafés. As recently as the 1870s, it was a Turkish capital and two mosques still remain, but most of the city was planned after 1880. There are enough intriguing museums and high-quality musical performances to merit a lengthy stay, but if time is short, you need only two days to see the main sights, and another day, at least, for Mount Vitoša.

Numbers in the margin correspond with points of interest on the Sofia map.

1 **Ploshtad Lenin** (Lenin Square), with its statue of the Russian revolutionary and statesman, is a good starting point for an exploration of the main sights. The south side of the square is **2** dominated by the 19th-century **Tzarkva Sveta Nedelya** (Sveta Nedelja Church). Go behind it to find Vitoša Boulevard, which points directly to the beautiful Mount Vitoša itself.

The first building along this boulevard is the former Courts of **3** Justice, now the **Natzionalen Istoricheski Musei** (National History Museum). Its vast collections, vividly illustrating the creative history of Bulgaria, include priceless Thracian treasures, Roman mosaics, enameled jewelry from the First

Sofia

0 ___ 220 yards
0 ___ 200 meters

Djamiata Banja
Bashi, **16**

Hram-pametnik
Alexander Nevski, **11**

Mavsolei Georgi
Dimitrov, **7**

Naroden Dvoretz na
Kulturata Ljudmila
Zhivkova, **14**

Natzionalen
Archeologicheski
Musei, **6**

Natzionalen
Etnografski Musei, **8**

Natzionalen
Istoricheski Musei, **3**

Natzionalna
Hudozhestvena
Galeria, **9**

Park Na
Svobodota, **13**

Partiyniyat Dom, **5**

Ploshtad Lenin, **1**

Rotonda Sveti
Georgi, **4**

Tzarkva Sveta
Nedelya, **2**

Tzarkva Sveti
Sofia, **12**

Tzarkva Sveti
Nikolai, **10**

Zentralen Universalen
Magazin, **15**

Zentralni Hali, **17**

Bulgarian Kingdom, and glowing religious art that survived the years of Ottoman oppression. *Vitoša Blvd., tel. 2/88–41–60. Open Tues.–Thurs., weekends 10:30–6:30; Fri. 2–6:30.*

Return to the southeast side of Lenin Square and in the courtyard of the Sheraton Sofia Balkan Hotel you will see the **❹ Rotonda Sveti Georgi** (rotunda of Sveti Georgi). Built in the 4th century as a Roman temple, it has served as mosque and church, and recent restoration has revealed medieval frescoes. It is not open to the public. Head east to the vast and traffic-free Deveti Septemvri (September 9th) Place, watched over by **❺** the red star on top of the **Partiyniyat Dom** (Bulgarian Communist Party Headquarters).

Facing the square, but entered via Alexander Stambolijski Boulevard, is the former Great Mosque, now housing the **❻ Natzionalen Archeologicheski Musei** (National Archaeological Museum). The 15th-century building itself is as fascinating as its contents, which illustrate the culture of the different peoples that have inhabited Bulgaria up to the 19th century. *Tel. 2/88–24–05. Open Tues.–Sun. 10–noon and 2–6.*

❼ On the next block to the east is the **Mavsolei Georgi Dimitrov** (Georgi Dimitrov Mausoleum), protected by a military guard that changes every hour on the hour. Inside lies the embalmed body of the famous Bulgarian revolutionary who was the first General Secretary of the Bulgarian Communist Party. He died in Moscow in 1949 and is now known as "Father of the Nation."

❽ Across from the mausoleum is the **Natzionalen Etnografski Musei** (National Ethnographical Museum), with displays of costumes, handicrafts, and tools that illustrate the agricultural way of life of the country people until the 19th century. *Pl. 9 Septemvri, tel. 2/88–51–15. Open Wed.–Sun. noon–12:30 and 1:30–6:30.*

❾ Adjoining this building is the **Natzionalna Hudozhestvena Galeria** (National Art Gallery). It houses a collection of the best works of Bulgarian artists and a foreign art section which contains some graphics of famous artists. *6A Moskovska St., tel. 2/88–35–59. Open Wed.–Mon. 10:30–7.*

❿ Nearby stands the ornate Russian **Tzarkva Sveti Nikolai** (Church of St. Nicholas), erected 1912–14.

From here you enter Ruski Boulevard, with its monument to the Russians, topped by the equestrian statue of Russian Czar Alexander II. It stands in front of the National Assembly. At last you are confronted by the neo-Byzantine structure with glittering onion domes whose image looks out from almost every piece of tourist literature and which really does dominate **⓫** the city. This is the **Hram-pametnik Alexander Nevski** (Alexander Nevski Memorial Church), built by the Bulgarian people at the beginning of this century as a mark of gratitude to their Russian liberators. Inside are alabaster and onyx, Italian marble and Venetian mosaics, and space for a congregation of 5,000. Attend a service to hear the superb choir, and don't miss the fine collection of icons in the **Crypt Museum.** *Open Wed.– Mon. 10:30–6:30.*

Cross the square to the west to pay your respects to the much **⓬** older **Tzarkva Sveta Sofia** (Church of St. Sofia), which dates back to the 6th century, though remains of even older churches have been found during excavations. Its age and simplicity are in stark contrast to its more glamorous neighbor.

⑬ Return to Ruski Boulevard and continue east to the **Park Na Svobodota** (Freedom or Liberty Park), with its lake and fountains, woods and lawns, huge sports stadium, and open-air theater. From the park take Dragan Cankov west (back toward Lenin Square) briefly, before going left on Patriarh Evtimij, toward Juzen Park. The formal gardens and extensive woodlands here are to be extended as far as Mount Vitoša.

At the entrance to the park stands a large modern building, the
⑭ **Naroden Dvoretz na Kulturata Ljudmila Zhivkova** (Ljudmila Zhivkova National Palace of Culture), with its complex of halls for conventions and cultural activities. Its underpass, on several levels, is equipped with shops, restaurants, discos, and a bowling alley. *1 Bulgaria Sq., tel. 2/5-15-01.*

Back at Lenin Square, follow Georgi Dimitrov Boulevard to the train station. The large building on the right is the recently re-
⑮ furbished **Zentralen Universalen Magazin** (Central Department Store). *Open Mon.-Sat. 8-8.*

Just beyond is a distinctive building, a legacy of Turkish domi-
⑯ nation, the **Djamiata Banja Bashi** (Banja Basi Mosque); it is closed to visitors. Close by you will see the Public Mineral
⑰ Baths. Across the boulevard is the busy **Zentralni Hali** (Central Market Hall) with its foodstuffs and household goods.

Time Out Anyone doing the full tour is going to need at least one refreshment stop. There are several eating places on the northern length of Vitoša Boulevard; three of the best cafés are **Magura, Medovina,** and **Kravay.** Across from Lenin's Monument the underpass leading toward the Central Department Store has a café (and the little 14th-century church of Sveta Petka Samardzijska). Or take a break in a café in the underpass at the Palace of Culture, or on Lenin Square itself at the Complex Roubin.

Off the Beaten Track

The little medieval church of **Bojana,** about 10 kilometers (6 miles) south of the city center, is well worth a visit. The church itself is closed for restoration, but a replica, complete with copies of the exquisite frescoes, is open to visitors.

The **Dragalevci Monastery** stands in beechwoods above the nearby village of Dragalevci, and here you can see the actual 14th-century church and its frescoes. From here take the chair lift to the delightful resort complex of **Aleko,** and another nearby chair lift to the top of Malak Rezen. There are well-marked walking and ski trails in the area.

Shopping

Gifts and There is a good selection of arts and crafts at the shop of the
Souvenirs **Union of Bulgarian Artists** (6 Ruski Blvd.). You will find a range of souvenirs at **Sredec** (7 Legue St.), **Souvenir Store** (7 Stambolijski Blvd.), and **Prizma Store** (2 Ruski Blvd). If you are interested in furs or leather, try **4 Slavjanska St., 7 Car**

Kalojan St., or **2 Ruski Blvd.** For recordings of Bulgarian music, go to **Maestro Atanassov** (8 Ruski Blvd.).

Shopping Districts The latest shopping center is in the subway of the modern **Palace of Culture,** where stores sell fashions, leather goods, and all forms of handcrafts. The pedestrians-only area along **Vitoša Blvd.** features many new, small shops.

Department Stores The biggest is the newly renovated **Central Department Store** at 2 Georgi Dimitrov Blvd.

Food Markets All kinds of foods are on sale at the **Central Market Hall,** 25 Georgi Dimitrov Blvd., including excellent fruit and vegetable preserves, local wines, and spirits.

Dining

Eating in Sofia can be enjoyable and even entertaining, if the restaurant has a nightclub or folklore program. Be prepared to be patient and make an evening of it, as service can be slow at times. If you are in a hurry, try a *mehana*, or tavern, where the atmosphere is informal and service is a bit quicker. For details and price category definitions, *see* Dining in Staying in Bulgaria.

Expensive **Berlin.** German food is the specialty in this sophisticated restaurant in the Serdika Hotel. *2 General Zaimov Blvd., tel. 2/ 44–34–11. AE, DC, MC, V.*

★ **Budapest.** This place enjoys a reputation as one of the best restaurants in Sofia for good food, wine, and live music. As the name suggests, Hungarian food takes pride of place. *145 G.S. Rakovski St., tel. 2/82–27–50. AE, DC, MC, V.*

Havana. Cuban food is featured in this popular restaurant near the center of town. *27 Vitoša Blvd., tel. 2/87–01–31. AE, DC, MC, V.*

Moderate **Bojanske Hanche.** Local and national specialties are the main features in this restaurant and folklore center, 6 miles from downtown (take bus no. 63). *Near Bojanske church, tel. 2/56– 30–16. No credit cards.*

Gorubljana. Attached to the motel of the same name, about 9 kilometers (6 miles) southeast of the center, Gorubljana is recommended for a combination of local specialties and folklore presentations. *On E80 southeast of Sofia, tel. 2/72–37–20. No credit cards.*

Rubin. This eating complex in the center of Sofia has a snack bar and an elegant restaurant serving Bulgarian and international food. A full meal can sometimes push the cost into the Expensive bracket. *4 Lenin Sq., tel. 2/87–20–86. No credit cards.*

Inexpensive **Ropotamo.** With its central location, and reasonable prices, Ropotamo is a good bet for visitors on a budget. *63 Lenin Blvd., tel. 2/72–25–16. No credit cards.*

Vodanicarnski Mehani. The English translation is "Miller's Tavern," which is appropriate, since it's made up of three old mills linked together. It is at the foot of Mount Vitoša and features a folklore show and a menu of Bulgarian specialties. *Dragalevic District (bus no. 93), tel. 2/66–50–88. No credit cards.*

Zlatnite Mostove. This restaurant on Mount Vitoša has live music in the evenings. *Vitoša District, 19 km (12 mi) from center. No credit cards.*

Lodging

The following hotels all meet a high standard of cleanliness, and are open year-round unless otherwise stated. If you arrive in Sofia without reservations, go to Interhotels Central Office (4 Sveta Sofia St.), Balkantourist (37 Dondukov Blvd.), Bureau of Tourist Information and Reservations (35 Eksarh Josif St., near Lenin Sq.), National Palace of Culture (1 Bulgaria Sq.), or the central rail station. For details and price category definitions, *see* Lodging in Staying in Bulgaria.

Very Expensive **Novotel Europa.** This member of the French Novotel chain is near the train station and not far from the center of the city. *131 Georgi Dimitrov Blvd., tel. 2/3–12–61. 600 rooms with bath. Facilities: restaurant, cocktail bar, nightclub, shops (including Corecom shop). AE, DC, MC, V.*

★ **Sheraton Sofia Hotel Balkan.** The former Grand Hotel Balkan has been recently done up to Sheraton standards. It is now a first-class hotel with a central location that is hard to match. It also has an excellent restaurant. *1 Lenin Sq., tel. 2/87–65–41. 188 rooms with bath. Facilities: fitness center, nightclub, bars, 3 restaurants. AE, DC, MC, V.*

★ **Vitoša-New Otani.** There is a distinct Oriental flavor to this towering, trim Interhotel, which is not surprising, since it was designed by the Japanese. It is hard to match the range of services and activities available here. And there is a superb Japanese restaurant. *100 Anton Ivanov Blvd., tel. 2/62–41–51. 454 rooms with bath. Facilities: restaurant, health center, pool, nightclub, casino. AE, DC, MC, V.*

Expensive **Grand Hotel Sofia.** This five-story, centrally located Interhotel conveys an atmosphere of relative intimacy, compared with some of its larger rivals in the capital. *1 Nrodno Sobranie Sq., tel. 2/87–88–21. 172 rooms with bath or shower. Facilities: coffee shop, folk tavern, nightclub, shops. AE, DC, MC, V.*

Park Hotel Moskva. The pleasant park setting makes up for the fact that this hotel is not as centrally located as some other comparable hotels. The Russian restaurant has a nightly floor show. *25 Nezabravka St., tel. 2/7–12–61. 390 rooms with bath. Facilities: restaurants, coffee shop, cocktail bar, nightclub, shops. AE, DC, MC, V.*

Rodina. Sofia's newest high-rise hotel is not far from the center and boasts the latest in modern facilities. *8 General Totladen Blvd., tel. 2/53–31. 536 rooms with bath. Facilities: restaurants, coffee shop, summer and winter gardens, pool, gym, nightclub. AE, DC, MC, V.*

Moderate **Bulgaria.** Despite its central location, this small hotel is quiet and a bit old-fashioned. *4 Ruski Blvd., tel. 2/87–19–77. 72 rooms, some with bath or shower. No credit cards.*

Hemus. This is a smaller place near the Vitoša-New Otani. Guests can take advantage of the facilities of its larger neighbor while saving money for the casino or nightclub. *31 Georgi Traikov Blvd., tel. 2/66–13–13. 240 rooms, most with bath or shower. Facilities: folk tavern, nightclub. No credit cards.*

Inexpensive **Serdika.** The centrally located Serdika has an old Berlin-style restaurant serving German specialties. *2 General Zaimov St., tel. 2/44–34–11. 140 rooms, most with bath or shower. No credit cards.*

Slavia. The Slavia is in the southwest, some distance from the center. *2 Sofijski Geroi St., tel. 2/52–55–51. 75 rooms, some with bath or shower. No credit cards.*

The Arts

The standard of music in Bulgaria is high, whether it takes the form of opera, symphonic, or folk music, which has just broken into the international scene with its close harmonies and colorful stage displays. Contact Balkantourist or the **Concert Office** (2 Ruski Blvd., tel. 2/87–15–88) for general information.

You don't need to understand Bulgarian to enjoy a performance at the **Central Puppet Theater** (14 Gourko St., tel. 2/88–54–16) or at the **National Folk Ensemble** (check with the tourist office for details).

There are a number of fine art galleries: The art gallery of the **Ljudmila Zhivkova International Foundation** has a collection of Indian, African, Japanese, and Western European paintings and sculptures (Alexander Nevski Sq., tel. 2/88–21–81; open Wed.–Mon. 10:30–6.). The art gallery of the **Union of Bulgarian Artists** has exhibitions of contemporary Bulgarian art (6 Shipka St., tel. 2/44–61–15; open daily 9–8).

The **Družba cinema** shows relatively recent foreign films.

Entertainment and Nightlife

Nightclubs   The following hotel bars have floor shows and a lively atmosphere: **Bar Sofia,** Grand Hotel Sofia, Narodno Sobranie Sq., tel. 2/87–88–21; **Bar Variety Ambassador,** Vitoša-New Otani Hotel, 100 Anton Ivanov Blvd., tel. 2/62–41–51; **Bar Variety,** Park Hotel Moskva, 25 Nezabrauka St., tel. 2/7–12–61; **Bar Variety,** Grand Hotel Balkan, 2 Lenin Sq., tel. 2/87–65–41.

Discos   There is a disco, nightclub, and bowling alley at the **Ljudmila Zhivkova National Palace of Culture,** 1 Bulgaria Sq., tel. 2/62–41–51.

Casino   Gamblers can try their luck at the casino in the **Vitoša-New Otani Hotel,** 100 Anton Ivanov Blvd., tel. 2/62–41–51.

The Black Sea Golden Coast

Bulgaria's most popular resort area attracts visitors from all over the Eastern bloc and, increasingly, from Western countries. Its sunny, sandy beaches are backed by the easternmost slopes of the Balkan range and the Strandja Mountains. Although the tourist centers tend to be huge state-built complexes, with a somewhat lean feel, they have modern amenities. Sunny Beach, the largest of the resorts with 112 hotels has plenty of children's amusements and play areas; babysitters are also available.

The busy port of Varna is a good center for exploration. It is a focal point of land and sea transportation and has museums, a variety of restaurants, and some nightlife. The fishing villages of Nesebâr and Sozopol are more attractive. Lodgings tend to be scarce in these villages, so private accommodations, arranged by Balkantourist, may be the answer. Whatever resort you choose, all offer facilities for water sports and some have instructors. Tennis and horseback riding are also available.

Getting Around

Bus service is frequenty and inexpensive. Buy your ticket in advance from the kiosks near the bus stops. **Cars** and **bicycles** can be rented; bikes are particularly useful for getting around such spreading resorts as Sunny Beach. A **hydrofoil** service links Varna, Nesebâr, Burgas, and Sozopol. A regular **boat** service travels the Varna-Družba-Golden Sands-Albena-Balcik route.

Guided Tours

A wide range of excursions are arranged from all resorts. There are bus excursions to Sofia from Golden Sands, Družba, Albena, and Sunny Beach; a one-day bus and boat trip along the Danube from Golden Sands, Družba, and Albena; and a three-day bus tour of Bulgaria including the Valley of Roses, departing from Golden Sands, Družba, and Albena. All tours are run by Balkantourist *(see* below, or check with your hotel information desk).

Tourist Information

There is a Balkantourist office in most towns and resorts.
Albena. Tel. 057/22–23–89.
Burgas. 2 Parvi May St., tel. 056/4–55–53.
Družba and Golden Sands. Tel. 052/6–56–27.
Nesebâr. 18 Yana Luskova St., tel. 055/41–38–17.
Sunny Beach. Tel. 055/41–23–46.
Varna. Main office, 3 Moussala St., tel. 52/22–55–24; private accommodations office, 3 Lenin Blvd.

Exploring the Black Sea Golden Coast

Varna **Varna,** Bulgaria's third-largest city, is easily reached by rail (about 7½ hours by express) or road from Sofia. If driving, allow time to see the Stone Forest (Pobiti Kammuni) just off the Sofia-Varna road between Devnya and Varna. The unexpected groups of monumental sandstone tree trunks are thought to have been formed when the area was the bed of the Lutsian Sea. There is plenty to see in the port city of Varna. The ancient city, named Odessos by the Greeks, became a major Roman trading center and is now an important shipbuilding and industrial city. The main sights can be linked by a planned walk.

Begin with the **Museum of History and Art,** one of the great—if lesser known—museums of Europe. The splendid collection includes finds from the Varna necropolis of the 4th millennium BC, as well as Thracian, Greek, and Roman treasures, and richly painted icons. *41 Dimitar Blagoev Blvd., tel. 52/23–70–57. Open Tues.–Sun. 10–5.*

Near the northeastern end of Dimitar Blagoev Boulevard are numerous shops and cafés; the western end leads to Varnenska Komouna Square and the monumental **Cathedral** (1880–86), whose lavish murals are worth a look. Running north from the cathedral is Karl Marx Street, with shops, movie theaters, and

The Black Sea Golden Coast

N

Durankulak

Tolbuhin

Balčik

Šabla

Novi Pazar

Albena

Kavarna

Vetrino

Zlatni Pjasâci
(Golden Sands)

Družba

Varna

Goljama

Staro Orjahovo

Kamčija

Bjala

Kamčija

Obzor

Black Sea

Orizare

Slănčev Brjag
(Sunny Beach)

Ajtos

Nesebâr

Pomorie

Burgas

Sredecka

Sozopol

Djuni

Primorsko

Mičurin

Ahtopol

0   40 miles

0   60 km

TURKEY

eateries. Opposite the cathedral, in the City Gardens, is the
Old Clock Tower, built in 1880 by the Varna Guild Association.
On the south side of the City Gardens, on September 9th
Square, stands the magnificent Baroque **Stoyan Bucharov National Theater.**

Leave the square to the east, and walk past the Moussala Hotel. The tourist information office is at 3 Moussala Street.
Nearby, on the corner of Lenin Boulevard and Shipka Street,
are the remains of the **Roman fortress wall** of Odessos. Lenin
Boulevard is another of Varn'a shopping streets. at no. 44 you
can buy handcrafted souvenirs from one of the outlets of the
Union of Bulgarian Artists.

Walk south along Odessos Street to Han Krum Street. Here
you'll find the Holy Virgin Church of 1602, and the substantial
remains of the **Roman Thermae**—the public baths, dating from
the 2nd-3rd centuries AD. Buy the excellent English guidebook
here to get the most out of your visit.

Not far from the baths, moving west, is old Druzki Street, recently restored and comfortably lined with restaurants, taverns, and
coffee houses.

Head toward the sea and November 8 Street. The old prison
building at no. 5 houses the **Museum of the Revolutionary Movement** (open Tues.–Sun. 10–5). Continue to Cervenoarmejski
Boulevard and follow it, with the sea on your right, to no. 2 for
the **Naval Museum** (0en daily 8–6:30), with its displays of the
early days of navigation on the Black Sea and the Danube. The

museums is at the edge of the extensive and luxuriant **Marine Gardens,** which enjoy wide views over the bay, and have restaurants, an open-air theater, and the fascinating **Copernicus Astronomy Complex** (open weekdays 8–noon and 2–5) near the main entrance.

Druzba Eight kilometers (5 miles) north along the coast from Varna is **Družba** (Friendship), the smallest and most intimate of the Blak Sea resorts, spreads through a wooded park near a series of sandy coves. Warm mineral springs were discovered here in 1947, and the five-star **Grand Hotel Varna,** the most luxurious on the coast, offers all kinds of hydrotherapy under medical supervision *(see* Lodging).

In contrast to the sedate atmosphere of Družba is lively **Zlatni Pjasâci** (Golden Sands), a mere 8 kilometers (5 miles) north, with its extensive leisure amenities, mineral spring medical centers, and sports and entertainment facilities. Just over 4 kilometers (2 miles) inland from Golden Sands is **Aladji Rock Monastery,** one of Bulgaria's oldest, cut out of the cliff face and made accessible to visitors by sturdy iron stairways.

From Družba, if time permits, take a trip 16 kilometers (10 miles) north to **Balcik,** part of Romania until just before World War II, now a relaxed setting where Bulgaria's writers, artists, scientists, and trade unionists can enjoy state-sponsored "R and R." The beautiful **Botanical Gardens** are dotted with curious buildings, including a small Byzantine-style church.

Slancev Brjag Another popular resort, this time south 36 kilometers (22.5 miles) of Varna, is **Slâčev Brjag** (Summy Beach). It is enormous, and especially suited to families because of its safe beaches, activities for children, beachside restaurants, and plenty of gardens and green spaces.

Nesebâr is 5 kilometers (3 miles) south of Sunny Beach, and accessible by regular excursion buses. It would be hard to find a town that exudes a greater sense of age than this ancient settlement, founded by the Greeks 25 centuries ago on a rocky peninsula reached by a narrow causeway. Among its vine-covered houses are richly decorated medieval churches. Don't miss the frescoes.

Still traveling south along the coast, the next place of any size is **Burgas,** Bulgaria's second main port on the Black Sea. Burgas is rather industrial, with several oil refineries, though it does have a pleasant **Maritime Park** with an extensive beach below.

For a more appealing stopover, continue for another 32 kilometers (20 miles) south to **Sozopol,** a fishing port with narrow cobbled streeets leading down to the harbor. This was Apollonia, oldest of the Greek colonies in Bulgaria. It is now a popular haunt for bulgarian and, increasingly, foreign writers and artists who find private accommodations in the pretty stone and wood houses, and sustenance in the restaurants and inns.

Ten kilometers (6 miles) to the south is the vast, modern resort village of **Djuni,** where visitors can stay in up-to-date cottages, in the modern Monastery Compound, or in the Seaside Settlement. The wide range of amenities—cafés, folk restaurants, a sports center, shopping center, yacht club, and marina—make it another attraction spot for families.

Dining and Lodging

For details and price category definitions, *see* Dining and Lodging in Staying in Bulgaria.

Burgas
Dining

Starata Gernia. The name of this restaurant translates as "old boat," appropriate for a beachfront restaurant featuring fish specialties. *39 Parvi May St. No credit cards. Moderate.*

Lodging

Bulgaria. The Bulgaria is a high-rise Interhotel in the center of town. It features its own nightclub with floor show and a restaurant set in a winter garden. *21 Parvi May St., tel. 56/4-28-20. 200 rooms, most with bath or shower. AE, DC, MC, V. Moderate.*

Družba
Dining

Bulgarska Svatba. This folk-style restaurant with dancing is on the outskirts of the resort; charcoal-grilled meats are especially recommended. *Družba Resort. No credit cards. Moderate.*

Manastirska Izba. Centrally located, this eatery is a modest but pleasant restaurant with a sunny terrace. *Družba Resort, tel. 56/6-11-77. No credit cards. Moderate.*

Lodging
★

Grand Hotel Varna. This Swedish-built hotel has a reputation as the best hotel on the coast. It is set just 139 meters (150 yards) from the beach and offers a wide range of hydrotherapeutic treatments featuring the natural warm mineral springs. *Družba Resort, tel. 52/6-14-91. 325 rooms with bath or shower. Facilities: 3 restaurants, nightclub, 2 swimming pools, sports hall, tennis courts, bowling alley. AE, DC, MC, V. Expensive.*

Caika. Caika means "sea gull" in Bulgarian, and this hotel has a bird's-eye view of the whole resort, from its perch above the northern end of the beach. *Družba Resort, 130 rooms, most with bath or shower. No restaurant. No credit cards. Moderate.*

Slânčev Brjag
Dining

Hanska Satra. Situated in the coastal hills behind the sea, this combination restaurant and nightclub has been built to resemble the tents of the Bulgarian khans of old. It has entertainment well into the night. *4.8 km (3 mi) west of Slânčev Brjag. No credit cards. Moderate.*

Ribarska Hiza. This lively beachside restaurant specializes in fish and has music until 1 AM. *Northern end of resort. No credit cards. Inexpensive.*

Lodging

Burgas. Large and comfortable, this hotel lies at the southern end of the resort. *Slânčev Brjag Resort, tel. 0554/23-58. 250 rooms with bath or shower. Facilities: restaurant, 2 pools, sports hall. AE, DC, MC, V. Moderate.*

★

Globus. Considered by many to be the best in the resort, this hotel combines a central location with modern facilities. *Slânčev Brjag Resort, tel. 0554/22-45. 100 rooms with bath or shower. Facilities: indoor pool, restaurant, sports hall. AE, DC, MC, V. Moderate.*

Kuban. Near the center of the resort, this large establishment is just a short stroll from the beach. *Slânčev Brjag Resort, tel. tel. 0554/23-09. 210, most with bath or shower. AE, DC, MC, V. Moderate.*

Caika. This hotel offers the best location at a low cost. *Slânčev Brjag Resort, tel. 0554/23-08. 85 rooms, some with bath or shower. No credit cards. Inexpensive.*

Varna
Dining

Starata Kusta. This restaurant's name means "the old house." Part of a new catering complex along with several bars and restaurants, it provides national specialties in a pseudo old-time atmosphere. *14 Druzki St., tel. 52/23–90–65. No credit cards. Moderate.*

Lodging **Cerno More.** One of the best things about this modern
★ Interhotel is the panoramic view from the 22nd floor; another is the modern facilities. *33 Georgi Dimitrov Blvd., tel. 52/22–01–67. 230 rooms with bath or shower. Facilities: 3 restaurants, ground floor café with terraces, nightclub. AE, DC, MC, V. Expensive.*

Inland Bulgaria

Inland Bulgaria is not as well known to tourists as the capital and coast, and the adventurous traveler, willing to put up with limited hotel facilities and unreliable transportation, will find plenty to photograph, paint, or simply savor. Wooded and mountainous, the interior is dotted with attractive "museum" villages (entire settlements listed for preservation due to their historic cultural value) and ancient towns; the folk culture is a strong survivor from the past, not a tourist-inspired re-creation of it. The foothills of the Balkan Range, marked Stara Planina or "old mountains" on most maps, lie parallel with the lower Sredna Gora mountains, with the verdant Valley of Roses between them. In the Balkan range is the ancient capital of Veliko Târnovo; south of the Sredna Gora stretches the fertile Thracian plain and Bulgaria's second city of Plovdiv. Between Sofia and Plovdiv is the enchanting old town of Koprivštica. To the south, in the Rila Mountains, is Borovec, first of the mountain resorts. A round-trip covering all of these towns, with a side excursion to Rila Monastery, could be made in four or five days, although more time is recommended.

Getting Around

Rail and bus services cover all parts of inland Bulgaria, but the timetables are not easy to follow and there are frequent delays. The best bet is to rent a car; Balkantourist can arrange this.

Guided Tours

Organized tours set out from Sofia, each covering different points of interest. Check with your Sofia hotel information desk or with Balkantourist for specific information.

Tourist Information

Plovdiv. 34 Moskva Blvd., tel. 32/5–38–48.
Veliko Târnovo. 2 Vasil Levski St., tel. 62/2–02–36.

Exploring Inland Bulgaria

Koprivštica **Koprivštica,** one of Bulgaria's showpiece villages, is set in mountain pastures and pine forests, about 930 meters (3,000 feet) up on the Sredna Gora range. It is 103 kilometers (62 miles) from Sofia, reached by a minor road south from the Sofia-Kazanlâk expressway. Founded in the 14th century, it is now a living museum of the carved wood architecture of the National Revival period, or Bulgarian Renaissance, of the 18th and 19th centuries. Many of the houses—several belonging to

Inland Bulgaria

artists and poets—can be visited. Visually, nothing much has changed since the first shots of the tragic April 1876 uprising against the Turks were fired here. A place of pilgrimage for Bulgarians, Koprivštica attracts Western visitors because of its setting and its brightly painted houses, with their distinctive overhanging eaves and broad verandas, their courtyards glimpsed through studded wooden gates.

Return to the main road and turn right. After 15 kilometers (9 miles) you reach **Klisura** and the beginning of the **Rozova Dolina** (Valley of Roses). After another 17 kilometers (11 miles), turn at the village of Karnare, take the winding scenic road north over the Balkan range to the town of Trojan, and, a few miles away, you'll see the **Trojan Monastery**, set in the heart of the mountains. Trojan Monastery Church was painstakingly rebuilt in the 19th century, and its icons, wood carvings, and frescoes are classic examples of National Revival art. Back at Trojan, continue north on the mountain road until it meets highway E771, where you turn right for Veliko Târnovo, 82 kilometers (50 miles) away.

Veliko Târnovo **Veliko Târnovo**, a town of panoramic vistas, rises up against steep mountain slopes through which the River Jantra runs its jagged course. During the 13th and 14th centuries, this was Bulgaria's capital, cradle of its history and consequently the focus of repeated Ottoman attack—not to mention an earthquake in 1913. Fortunately, as much effort hs gone into restoring old buildings as into constructing new ones, and it is now a museum city of marvelous relics. The town warrants two or three days of exploration, but even in a short visit some sights should not be missed. Ideally, begain at a vantage point above town to get an overview of its design and character. Next, seek out **Tsaravec** to the west (Caravec on some maps), protected by a river loop. This is where medieval czars and patriarchs had their palaces. The area is under restoration, with steep paths and stairways for easier viewing of the extensive ruins of the Patriarchite and the royal palace.

The prominent feature to the south is **Baldwin's Tower,** the 13th-century prison of Baldwin of Flanders, one-time Latin Emperor of Constantinople. Nearby are three important churches: the 13th-century **church of the Forty Martyrs,** with its frescoes of the Tarnovo schools and two inscribed columns, one dating back to the 9th century; the **church of Saints Peter and Paul,** with vigorous murals both inside and out; and, across the river, reached by a bridge near the Forty Martyrs, the restored **church of Saint Dimitus,** built on the spot where the Second Bulgarian Kingdom was launched in 1185.

Back toward the center of town, near the Yantra Hotel, is Samovodene Street, lined with restored craft workshops—a fascinating place to linger and a good place to find souvenirs, Turkish candy, or a charming café. On nearby Rakovski Street are a group of buildings of the National Revival period. One of the finest is **Hadji Nikoli,** a museum that was once an inn. *17 Georgi Sava Rakovski, tel. 62/2–17–10 for opening times.*

Leave Veliko Târnovo by E85, and head toward **Plovdiv,** allowing for three stops en route. The first, near the industrial center of Gabrovo—interesting in itself for its House of Humor Museum—is the museum village of **Etur,** 8 kilometers (5 miles) to the southeast. Its mill is still powered by a stream, and local craftsmen continue to be trained in traditional skills. Second is the **Šipka Pass,** with its mighty monument on the peak to the 200,000 Russian soldiers and Bulgarian volunteers who died here in 1877, during the Russo-Turkish Wars. Third is **Kazanlâk,** at the eastern end of the Valley of Roses, where you can trace the history of rose production, Bulgaria's oldest industry. There is also a highly decorated replica of a Thracian tomb of the 3rd or 4th century BC, set close to the original, which remains closed for its preservation.

Plovdiv | From Kazanlâk, take the road west through the **Valley of Roses,** at its fragrant best in May and June, although lavender, sunflowers, vines, and fruit trees are also impressive in season. At either Vasil Levski or Karlovo, turn south for **Plovdiv,** Bulgaria's second-largest city, one of the oldest in Europe, and a major industrial center. The old town, on the hillier southern side of the Marica River, is worth a visit.

Begin at the **National Ethnographical Museum** in the House of Arghir Kovyoumidjioglu, an elegant example of National Revival style that made its first impact in Plovdiv. The museum is full of artifacts from that important period. *2 Comakov St. Open Tues.–Sun. 9–noon and 1:30–5.*

Below the medieval gateway of Hissar Kapiya is the attractive **Georgicdi House** on Starina Street, and the steep, narrow **Strumna Street,** lined with workshops and boutiques, some reached through little courtyards. Follow Maxim Gorki Street westward to its junction with the pedestrians-only Vasil Kolarov Street; here are the remains of a **Roman stadium.** The

Kapana District of restored and traditional shops and restaurants is nearby. Turn east off Vasil Kolarov Street and walk to the fine hilltop **Roman Amphitheater,** sensitively renovated and frequently used for dramatic and musical performances. On the other side of the old town, toward the river, is the **National Archaeological Museum,** which holds a replica of the 4th-century BC Panagjuriste Gold Treasure, the original of which is in Sofia. *1 Suedinie Sq., Open Tues.–Sun. 9–12:30 and 2–5:30.*

Travel west along the E80 Sofia Road. At Dolna Banja, turn off to **Borovec,** about 1,333 meters (4,300 feet) up the northern slopes of the Rila Mountains. This is an excellent walking center and winter sports resort, well-equipped with hotels, folk taverns, and ski schools. The winding mountain road leads back to Sofia from here, past Lake Iskar, the largest in the country.

On the way back to Sofia, you should consider a visit to the **Rila Monastery,** founded by Ivan of Rila in the 10th century. Cut across to E79, travel south to Kocerinovo, and then turn east to follow the steep forested valley past the village of Rila. The monastery has suffered so frequently from fire that most of it is now a grand National Revival reconstruction, although a rugged 14th-century tower has survived. The atmopshere in this mountain retreat, populated by many storks, is still heavy with a sense of the past—although much of the complex has been turned into a museum and the monks' cells are now guest rooms. The visitor can see 14 small chapels with frescoes from the 15th and 17th centuries, a lavishly carved altarpiece in the new Assumption church, the sarcophagus of Ivan of Rila, icons, and ancient manuscripts, a reminder that this was a stronghold of art and learning during the centuries of Ottoman rule. It is well worth the detour—or a special trip from Sofia.

Dining and Lodging

For details and price category definitions, *see* Dining and Lodging in Staying in Bulgaria.

Koprivštica
Dining

Djedo Liben Inn. This attractive folk restaurant is built in the traditional style of the area—with half-timbered, high stone walls. The menu reflects a similar attention to traditional detail. No telephone. No credit cards. Moderate.

Lodging

Koprivštica. This good-value hotel is popular with Bulgarians themselves, and is just over the river from the center of town. Tel. 032/21–18. No credit cards. Inexpensive.

Plovdiv
Dining

Plid. This is an attractive folk restaurant in the center of town. A video presentation in the lobby highlights the city's past. *3 Knyaz Tseretelov St., tel. 032/23–17–20. AE, DC, MC, V. Expensive.*

Alafrangues. This charming folk-style restaurant is located in a restored 19th-century house with wood-carved ceilings and a vine-covered courtyard. *15 Nektariev St., tel. 032/22–98–09. No credit cards. Moderate.*

Rhetora. This coffee bar is in a beautifully restored old house near the Roman amphitheater in the old part of the city. *8 A G. Samodoumov St., tel. 032/22–20–93. No credit cards. Moderate.*

Lodging

Novotel Plovdiv. The large, modern, and well-equipped Novotel is across the river from the main town, near the fairgrounds. *2 Zlatju Boyadjiev St., tel. 032/45–45–95. 322 rooms with bath.*

Facilities: restaurant, folk tavern, nightclub, sports hall, pools. AE, DC, MC, V. Expensive.

Trimontium. This centrally located Interhotel built in the '50s is comfortable and ideal for exploring the old town. *2 Kapitan Raico St., tel. 032/2–55–61. 163 rooms with bath or shower. Facilities: folk tavern, restaurant. AE, DC, MC, V. Expensive.*

Marica. This is a large, modern hotel that offers a less expensive alternative to its neighbor, the Novotel. *5 Georgi Dimitrov St., tel. 032/5–27–35. 171 rooms with bath or shower. Facilities: bar, restaurant. No credit cards. Inexpensive.*

Veliko Târnovo
Dining

Boljarska Izba. In the center of the busy district just north of the river, this place is a folk tavern. *Dimiter Blagoev St., no telephone. No credit cards. Moderate.*

Lodging

Veliko Târnovo. Located right in the middle of the most historic part of the town, this modern Interhotel boasts some of the best facilities for this class of hotel. *2 Emile Popov St., tel. 062/2–05–71. 195 rooms with bath or shower. Facilities: 2 restaurants, coffee shop, disco, sports hall, indoor pool. AE, DC, MC, V. Expensive.*

Yantra. The Yantra has some of the best views in town, looking across the river to Tsaravec. *1 Velchova Zavera Sq., tel. 062/20–30–91. 60 rooms, most with shower. Facilities: restaurant, coffee shop, bar. No credit cards. Moderate.*

Etur. This moderate-size hotel has an address near the more expensive Veliko Târnovo, making it a good base for sightseeing within town. *I. Ivailo St., tel. 062/2–68–51. 80 rooms, most with shower. Facilities: restaurant, coffee shop, bar. Inexpensive.*

6 Cyprus

Introduction

The Mediterranean island of Cyprus was at one time a center for the cult of Aphrodite, the Greek goddess who is said to have risen naked and perfect from the sea near what is now the beach resort of Paphos. Wooded and mountainous, with a 400-mile coastline, Cyprus lies just off the southern coast of Turkey. Oranges, olives, lemons, grapes, and cherries grow here, and fish are plentiful. The summers are hot and dry, the spring, gentle. Snow covers the Troodos Mountains in winter, making it possible to ski in the morning and sunbathe on a beach in the afternoon.

Cyprus's strategic position in the eastern Mediterranean has made it subject to regular invasions by powerful countries. Greeks, Phoenicians, Assyrians, Egyptians, Persians, Romans, and Byzantines—all have ruled here. In the Middle Ages, the English King Richard I took it by force from the Byzantine Empire and gave it to Guy of Lusignan. Guy's descendants ruled until the late 15th century, when it was annexed by the Venetians.

This tragic history adds to the island's appeal—at least for tourists. Many fortifications built by the Crusaders and the Venetians still stand. The tomb of the Prophet Muhammad's aunt (Tekke of Hala Sultan), located on the shores of the great salt lake near Larnaca, is one of Islam's most important shrines. A piece of the true cross is said to exist in the Monastery of Stavrouni, and Paphos has the remains of a pillar where St. Paul was tied and beaten for preaching Christianity.

The upheavals are not over. At present the island consists, politically, of two states. The southern two-thirds, inhabited mainly by Greek Cypriots, forms the Republic of Cyprus, the only part of the island to receive international recognition. The northern third, whose population is almost entirely Turkish Cypriot, is recognized only by Turkey as the Turkish Republic of North Cyprus. The two sections are divided by the UN Green Line, or "Attila Line," which cuts right through the capital city of Nicosia. The origins of this situation go back to 1974, when, fearing that the Greek majority on the island intended to unite Cyprus with mainland Greece, Turkish troops invaded the north and rapidly occupied a third of the island, where they remain.

Talks aimed at uniting the communities into one bizonal federal state have been going on for years, lately under the auspices of the United Nations secretary-general. It is possible to visit the north of the island from the south, on a day trip through the checkpoint in Nicosia, but visitors *must* return to the south by 6 PM. It is not possible to visit the south from the north.

In general, tourism is more thoroughly developed in the south than in the north, though the north is trying to catch up. The south has better facilities, more nightlife, and better beaches. The north shows fewer signs of foreign influence, with an exotic, Eastern flavor. The noticeable military presence shouldn't bother visitors who refrain from taking photographs where the signs prohibit it, and who avoid forbidden areas.

Cyprus

Mediterranean Sea

Before You Go

When to Go
The tourist season runs throughout the year, though prices tend to be lower from November through March.

Climate
The rainy season lasts from December through February, and there is snow on the Troodos Mountains from January through March. January and February can be very cold and wet; July and August, very hot and dry.

The following are the average daily maximum and minimum temperatures for Nicosia.

Jan.	59F	15C	May	85F	29C	Sept.	92F	33C
	42	5		58	14		65	18
Feb.	61F	16C	June	92F	34C	Oct.	83F	28C
	42	5		65	18		58	14
Mar.	66F	19C	July	98F	37C	Nov.	72F	22C
	44	7		70	21		51	10
Apr.	75F	24C	Aug.	98F	37C	Dec.	63F	17C
	50	10		69	21		45	7

Visas
No visas are necessary for holders of valid passports from the United States, Canada, and the United Kingdom.

Customs on Arrival
Customs regulations are minimal, but the export of antiques and historical artifacts, whether gathered on land or during undersea explorations, is strictly forbidden unless a license is obtained from the Ministry of Tourism in Nicosia.

Language English is spoken—to a greater or lesser degree—in hotels, *tavernas*, and other tourist haunts. Off the beaten track, sign language may have to do.

Credit Cards Credit cards are not widely accepted in either the north or the south, though major hotels such as the Hilton will take them. Banks, however, usually allow you to draw cash upon your credit card account, so payment is rarely a problem.

The Republic of Cyprus (Greek)

Currency

The monetary unit in the Republic of Cyprus is the Cyprus pound (C£), which is divided into 100 cents. There are notes of C£10, C£5, C£1, and 50 Cyprus cents and coins of 20, 10, 5, 2, 1, and ½ Cyprus cents. At press time (spring 1989) there were C£0.48 to the U.S. dollar and C£0.82 to the pound sterling. Because of the high rate of inflation of the Turkish lire (the currency of North Cyprus), we have quoted most prices in that section in dollars.

What It Will Cost

A cup of coffee or tea costs Cyprus 30¢–50¢; a glass of beer 50¢–60¢; a kebab around C£1; a bottle of local wine 50¢–70¢. Admission to museums and galleries costs 25¢–80¢.

Arriving and Departing

There are no direct flights from the USA. **Cyprus Airways** and **British Airways** fly direct from London, Birmingham, and Manchester to Larnaca and Paphos. **Alitalia** has a flight from Rome in summer, and **Cyprus Airways** operates from Frankfurt and Munich. There are ferries from Greek and Egyptian ports. An inclusive tour is probably the cheapest and most convenient approach.

Getting Around

By Car International and British driving licenses are acceptable for driving in Cyprus. Roads are generally good, though narrow and winding. Drive on the left. Gas costs around C£1.32 a gallon. Cars are available for rent from C£8.65 a day with unlimited mileage.

By Bus This is the cheapest form of transportation; bus fares are only about 3¢ a mile. The journey from Nicosia to Larnaca (32 miles) costs 55¢.

By Service Taxi These taxis cost about twice as much as buses, and you must reserve seats. No buses or service taxis operate after 6:30 or 7 PM. A service taxi for a 40-mile journey costs C£1.40 per person.

By Private Taxi Private taxis are usually available, very cheap, and always metered. Telephone from your hotel or hail one in the street. Urban taxis cost 35¢ per mile. In-town journeys cost about C£1 for any distance.

On Foot The only way to enjoy nature trails and archaeological sites is on foot. Comfortable shoes are essential. It is unwise to explore remote areas alone—ask the tourist office to recommend safe footpaths.

Staying in the Republic of Cyprus

Telephones Pay phones take 2¢, 10¢, and 20¢ coins. Hotels will add a small service charge for placing a call for you.

Mail At press time (spring 1989), a 10-gram letter to the United States costs Cyprus 25¢, a postcard, 17¢. To the United Kingdom, a 10-gram letter cost Cyprus 18¢, and a postcard, 15¢. Check at your hotel for the latest rates.

Opening and Closing Times **Banks.** Banks are open Monday–Saturday 8:30–noon. Some will cash traveler's checks weekdays 4–6.
Museums. Museums are open from about 8 to 1:30; afternoon hours vary according to the time of year. Most ancient monuments are open from dawn to dusk.
Shops. Shops are open Monday–Saturday 7:30–1. Afternoon hours vary, but many shops close on Wednesday and Saturday afternoons.

National Holidays January 1; January 6 (Epiphany); February 22; March 25 (Independence); April 15–18 (Greek Easter); May 1; June 4 (Pentecost); August 15 (Assumption); October 28 (Oxi); December 25, 26 (Christmas).

Tipping A service charge of 10% is usually added to all bills. If service has been especially good, add 5%.

Important Addresses and Numbers The main **tourist information office** is at 18 Theodotou St., Nicosia, tel. 02/43374. There are local offices at all major resorts.

Embassies or High Commissions **U.S. Embassy:** Dossitheos and Therissos Sts., Nicosia, tel. 02/465151. **British High Commission:** Alexander Pallis St., Nicosia, tel. 02/473131.

Emergencies **Ambulance, Fire Brigade,** and **Police:** tel. 199. **Doctor: Nicosia General Hospital,** tel. 061/32364; **Limassol Hospital,** tel. 051/63111; **Paphos Hospital,** tel. 061/32364. **Pharmacies:** A list, with opening times, appears in the English-language *Cyprus Mail.*

Guided Tours Bus tours and boat trips are run by companies based in Nicosia, Limassol, and Larnaca. Tourist offices have lists of operators and detailed brochures of organized visits to archaeological sites. **Holiday Tours** (C. D. Hay Premises, Ay. Omologitae, Box 1915, Nicosia, tel. 02/445201) has branches in all the main towns. This company offers bus tours to all parts of the island and has rental cars available.

Exploring the Republic of Cyprus

Nicosia, the capital, is twice divided. The picturesque Old City is contained within 16th-century Venetian fortifications, which separate it from the wide tree-lined streets, large hotels, and high rises of the modern section. The second division is political and more noticeable. The so-called Green Line, set up by the United Nations, that divides the island is frustrating to the visitor, because many of the more interesting ancient monuments are in the northern, Turkish sector. As mentioned above, it is possible, at the time of writing (spring 1989), to arrange a day trip from the Greek to the Turkish sector through the official checkpoint in Nicosia, though it is essential to return by 6 PM. Visits in the other direction are not permitted.

There is, however, plenty to see in the Greek sector. A good starting point is **Laiki Gitonia** at the southern edge of the Old City, an area of tree-shaded cafés and restaurants, craft workshops, and the tourist information center. Just to the west lies Ledra Street, where modern shops alternate with yet more craft shops.

Within the walls to the east of the Old City is a cluster of museums. The new **Archbishopric-Makarios Foundation** houses the **European Art Gallery**, with its collection of undistinguished 17th- and 18th-century works; the **Byzantine Art Museum**, with fine displays of icons spanning 1,000 years; and the **Greek War of Independence Gallery**, with a collection of maps, paintings, and mementoes of 1821. *Open weekdays 9:30–1 and 2–5:30, Sat. 9–1.*

Next door, the **Museum of the National Struggle** has dramatic displays of the Greek-Cypriot campaigns against the British in the pre-independence decade 1955–65. *Open Mon.–Sat. 7:30–1:30.*

Close by is the **Cyprus Folk Art Museum** (housed in the old part of the Bishopric, dating from the 14th century), which offers demonstrations of ancient weaving techniques and displays of farm implements, olive and wine presses, and Cypriot costumes. *Open weekdays 8–4, Sat. 8–1.*

Before going outside the walls, visit the **Cathedral of St. John** and look for the paintings depicting the discovery on Cyprus of St. Barnabus's tomb. Outside the walls, to the west, stands the small **Cyprus Museum**. Its archaeological displays range from prehistory to the Romans. A pretty park and café are nearby. *Museum St. Open Mon.–Sat. 7:30–1:30 and 4–6 (winter afternoons 3–5), Sun. 10–1.*

Many visitors choose to stay in the seaside resorts. Both Larnaca and Paphos, each with its airport, make excellent centers. **Larnaca**, 51 kilometers (32 miles) from Nicosia, is famous as the burial place of Lazarus and for its flamboyant Whitsuntide celebration, *Kataklysmos*. It has fine beaches, palm trees, and a modern harbor and marina, the starting point for boat trips. The tourist office is right at the marina, open mornings only, and just a short walk from **Larnaca Museum**, with its displays of finds from the island's archaeological sites. *Open weekdays 7:30–1:30 and 4–6 (in winter 3–5), Sat. 7:30–1 and 3–5, Sun. 10–1.*

A short walk north from the museum, along Kyman Street, will bring you to the site of **Kittium** (the old Larnaca of biblical times), where you can observe the excavations from specially constructed walkways.

Southward from the marina is the 17th-century **Turkish fort**, open the same hours as the museum and with similar, though not as extensive, displays. Walk inland from the fort to the town center and to one of the island's more important churches, **Ayios Lazarus**, resplendent with icons. It has a fascinating crypt containing Lazarus's sarcophagus.

Paphos, 142 kilometers (89 miles) southwest of Nicosia, in the west of the island, has superb sea bathing and numerous historical sights. Begin at the tourist office in Gladstone Street in Upper Paphos.

Don't miss the elaborate mosaics in the **Roman Villa of Theseus** and in the **House of Dionysos,** both in New Paphos. The town bus stops nearby. Also worth seeing are the **Tombs of the Kings,** an early necropolis dating from 300 BC. Natural caves have been extended and linked by passages, and though the coffin niches are empty, a powerful sense of mystery remains.

Limassol, a commercial port and wine-making center on the south coast, 75 kilometers (47 miles) from Nicosia, is also a thriving tourist spot. The modern buildings may be plain and oppressive, but facilities are plentiful and the nightlife is the liveliest on Cyprus. If you're interested in wine making, seek out the **KEO Winery,** just west of town, which welcomes visitors daily. The tourist office is on Spyros Araouzos Street, only a short walk from the **castle,** now restored as a museum of medieval armor and relics. *Open Mon.–Sat. 7:30–1:30.*

Ayia Napa is a fishing village on the south coast, 30 kilometers (20 miles) east of Larnaca, whose extensive sandy beaches led to its development as a tourist center. Its 16th-century **monastery,** now an Ecumenical Conference Center, is in distinct contrast to the plethora of tavernas, bars, and discos and to the tennis, putting, and diving facilities.

The **Troodos Mountains,** north of Limassol, are sought in summer for the shade of their cedar and pine forests and the coolness of their lakes and mineral spas. In winter, skiers take over. **Platres,** in the foothills of Mount Olympus, is the principal resort. Be sure to visit the **Kykko Monastery,** whose prized icon of the Virgin is reputed to have been painted by St. Luke. Though founded in the 12th century, the monastery buildings and lavish church were added in the 19th-century.

Off the Beaten Track

Stavrovouni Monastery stands on a mountain west of Larnaca. It was founded by St. Helena (mother of the Emperor Constantine) in AD 326, though the present buildings date from the 19th century. Ideally, it should be visited in a spirit of pilgrimage rather than sightseeing, out of respect for its monks, though the views of the island are splendid. The monks have decreed that female visitors will not be admitted.

Curium (Kourion), west of Limassol, has numerous Greek and Roman ruins. There is an **amphitheater,** where actors occasionally present classical drama. Next to the theater is the **Villa of Eustolios,** a summer house that belonged to a wealthy Christian; its mosaic floors are still in good condition. A nearby **Roman stadium** has been partially rebuilt. Farther along the main Paphos road is the **Sanctuary of Apollo Hylates** (of the woodlands), an impressive site when viewed through an archaeologist's eye.

Other places to visit include **Kolossi Castle,** a Crusader castle of the Knights of St. John, a 15-minute drive outside Limassol; **Kykko Monastery** in the Troodos Mountains; and the fishing harbor of **Latchi** on the west coast, 32 kilometers (20 miles) north of Paphos.

Dining

Most hotels have restaurants, but these tend to serve bland international-style food garnished with french fries. Visitors with a sense of adventure will want to dine in local restaurants or in one of the informal, family-run tavernas featuring live music. Meals start with a variety of *mezes* (snacks). Kebabs are popular, as are *dolmas*—stuffed grape leaves or cabbage leaves—stews, fresh fish, and various lamb dishes. End with fruit or honey pastries and Turkish coffee, so-named throughout Cyprus. Moderate establishments display a menu; in inexpensive ones it is the custom to go into the kitchen and choose your meal. Food is cheap in Cyprus, and the quality is good.

Prices are for a three-course meal for one person, not including drinks or tip.

Category	All Areas
Expensive	C£3.50–C£6
Moderate	C£2.50–C£3.50
Inexpensive	under C£2.50

Larnaca   **Kellari.** Tournedos is the specialty of the house at this informal seaside taverna, which serves both Cypriot and French foods. There's often live musical accompaniment in the evening. *85 Athens Ave., tel. 041/5166. Inexpensive.*

Nicosia   **The Corner.** This full-fledged restaurant features a traditional decor. Stephanos steak is a favorite of the chef. *Dem. Severi Ave., tel. 02/465735. Closed lunch and Sun. Moderate.*

Plaka. Lovers of hefty lamb dishes will be happy with the *souvla* and *kleftiko* at this large taverna. Tables spill out onto the sidewalk in front. *Archbishop Makarios Sq., Engomi, tel. 02/446498. Closed lunch and Sun. Inexpensive.*

Paphos   **Britannia.** Eat right on the beach at this small restaurant, which provides a wide range of Cypriot and international dishes. *75 Poseidon Ave., tel. 061/36032. Closed Dec.–Mar. Moderate.*

Nautical Club. This huge seaside restaurant seats more than 180. Fresh fish is your best bet. *St. Paul's Ave., tel. 061/33745. Moderate.*

Lodging

Most hotels listed below have private bath or shower, but check when making reservations. Most have at least partial air-conditioning.

Prices are for two people sharing a double room, with breakfast and dinner.

Category	All Areas
Expensive	C£25–C£35
Moderate	C£20–C£25
Inexpensive	C£15–C£20

Ayia Napa **Nissi Beach.** This modern, fully air-conditioned, family-style hotel is set in magnificent gardens overlooking a white sandy beach. *Box 10, Ayia Napa, tel. 037/21021. 251 rooms. Facilities: pool. Expensive.*

Pernara Beach. Those on a budget should enjoy this hotel with a view of the beach. All rooms are air-conditioned. *Tel. 037/21011. 92 rooms. Inexpensive.*

Larnaca **Golden Bay.** Comfort is high on the list at this beach hotel. The extensive range of sports facilities makes it ideal for summer or winter vacations. *Larnaka-Dheklia Rd., Box 741, tel. 041/23444. 194 rooms. Expensive.*

Four Lanterns. Local color, homey atmosphere, and modern comfort are much in evidence at this seafront hotel. There's also a good restaurant. *19 Athens Ave., Box 150, tel. 041/502011. 52 rooms. Moderate.*

Cactus Hotel. This recent addition to Larnaca's hotels is 20 minutes from the seafront, with all its tavernas. *6–8 Shakespeare St., Box 744, tel. 041/27400. 56 rooms. Inexpensive.*

Limassol **Apollonia Beach.** This is a luxury hotel on the beach in the main resort area. The restaurant has an excellent reputation. *Potamos Yermassoyias, Box 594, tel. 051/23351. 204 rooms. Expensive.*

Pamevar. Among this refurbished hotel's attractions are its beach-side setting. *28th October Ave., Box 263, tel. 051/24535. 65 rooms. Facilities: pool. Moderate.*

Nicosia **Cyprus Hilton.** This is among the island's best hotels, with standards you'd expect from a Hilton. It has its own pool, sports facilities, dancing, and more. *Archbishop Makarios Ave., Box 2023, tel. 02/46040. 230 rooms. Expensive.*

Philoxenia. This is a smallish hotel that still has plenty to offer, with its own pool and a variety of sports options, as well as a handy central location. *Eylenia Ave., Box 5466, tel. 02/499700. 35 rooms. Moderate.*

Nicosia Palace. Those seeking a budget option should consider the Nicosia Palace. Located just inside the city walls, it makes an ideal base for exploring the Old City. Some rooms have air-conditioning. *4–6 Pantelides Ave., tel. 02/463718. 42 rooms. Inexpensive.*

Paphos **Paphos Beach.** There are many facilities at this popular hotel surrounded by attractive gardens. Accommodations are either in the main hotel or in spacious bungalows on the grounds. *Posidonos St., Box 136, tel. 061/33091. 190 rooms. Expensive.*

Aloe. On the same street as the Paphos Beach, Aloe has ocean views, a swimming pool, and sports facilities. *Posidonos St., Box 190, tel. 061/34000. 113 rooms. Moderate.*

North Cyprus (Turkish)

Currency

The monetary unit in North Cyprus is the Turkish lire (TL). There are bills for 10,000, 5,000, 1,000, 500, 100, 50, 20, and 10 TL, and coins for lesser sums. The Turkish lire is subject to considerable inflation, so most prices in this section are quoted in dollars.

What It Will Cost

Prices for food and accommodations tend to be lower than in the Republic of Cyprus, and standards dip as well. Wine and spirits, on the other hand, are imported from Turkey and drinks will be slightly more expensive.

Sample Prices A cup of coffee or a glass of beer costs about $1.60. Wine is good and cheap at around $2.10 per bottle. Taxis are also a bargain—a 50-mile ride costs about $13. Admission to museums costs less than $1.

Arriving and Departing

Turkish Airlines and **Cyprus Turkish Airlines** run all flights via mainland Turkey, usually with a change of plane at Istanbul. There are also direct flights from Izmir to Ercan Airport near Nicosia. Ferries run from Mersin and Tasucu in Turkey to Famagusta and Kyrenia, respectively, but in both cases the journey is long and tiring. *It is not possible to enter North Cyprus from the Republic except for a day trip from Nicosia.*

Getting Around

By Car *See* By Car in the Republic of Cyprus.

By Bus Buses and the shared taxi *(dolmus)* are the cheapest forms of transportation. Service is frequent on main routes.

Fares A bus from Nicosia to Kyrenia costs about U.S. 40¢, and to Famagusta about 70¢. A seat in a dolmus for the same trips would cost about 90¢ and $1.70, respectively.

Staying in North Cyprus

Mail Postal rates vary with the rate of inflation; check at your hotel for the latest rates.

Opening and Closing Times **Banks.** Banks are open Monday–Saturday 8:30–noon. Some will cash traveler's checks weekdays 4–6.
Museums. Museums are open from about 8 to 1:30; afternoon hours vary according to the time of year. Most ancient monuments are open from dawn to dusk.
Shops. Shops are open Monday–Saturday 7:30–1. Afternoon hours vary, but many shops close on Wednesday and Saturday afternoons.

National Holidays January 1 (New Year's Day), April 23 (National Independence Day and Children's Day), May 1 (Labor Day), May 19, (Youth and Sports Day), August 30 (Victory Day), October 29 (Republic Day), and various Moslem religious holidays, which vary from year to year.

Credit Cards MasterCard and Diners Club are accepted by all leading hotels, restaurants, and shops in North Cyprus.

Tipping A service charge is usually added, but an additional small tip is expected in better hotels and restaurants.

Important Addresses The main **tourist information office** is at Mehmet Akif Ave., Nicosia. There are local offices at major resorts.

Embassies or High Commissions **The British High Commission** has an office in the Turkish section of Nicosia.

Emergencies **Ambulance, Fire Brigade,** and **Police:** tel. 199. **Doctor: Nicosia General Hospital,** tel. 061/32364.

Exploring North Cyprus

There are two important things to bear in mind in North Cyprus. One is to obey the "no photographs" signs wherever they appear. The other is to note that Turkish names have now been given to all towns and villages. These new names appear on the signposts—not always with the Greek version alongside—so it helps to know that **Nicosia** is known as **Lefkosa, Kyrenia** as **Girne,** and **Famagusta** as **Magosa.** A useful map showing these and other Turkish names is available free from tourist offices.

The Turkish half of **Nicosia** is the capital of North Cyprus. In addition to the Venetian walls already mentioned (*see* Exploring the Republic of Cyprus), it contains the **Selimiyre Mosque,** formerly the 13th-century Cathedral of St. Sophia, and a fine example of Gothic architecture, to which a pair of minarets has now been added. Near the Girne Gate is the former **tekke** (sacred place) of the Mevlevi Dervishes, a Sufi order popularly known as Whirling Dervishes. The building now houses a museum of Turkish history and culture. *Open Mon.–Sat. 8–1, Sun. 10–1.*

A walk around the **Old City,** within the encircling walls, is rich with glimpses from the Byzantine, Lusignan, and Venetian past. There is a great deal of restoration and reconstruction work going on, especially in the parts of the city beyond the walls.

Of the coastal resorts, **Kyrenia,** with its yacht-filled harbor, is the most appealing. There are excellent beaches to the east and west of the town. **Kyrenia Castle,** overlooking the harbor, is Venetian, though on the site of a much older Byzantine defensive structure. It now houses the **Shipwreck Museum,** whose prize possession is the remains of a ship that sank around 300 BC. *Open Mon.–Sat. 8–1, Sun. 10–1.*

Famagusta, the chief port of North Cyprus, has massive and well-preserved Venetian walls and the late 13th-century Gothic Cathedral of St. Nicholas, now **Lala Mustafa Pasha Mosque.** The **Old Town,** within the walls, is the most intriguing part to explore. Elsewhere, many of the hotels lie empty and desolate in a sort of no-man's-land between Greek and Turk, where the military presence cannot be ignored.

Off the Beaten Track

It is well worth making two short excursions from Kyrenia, to **St. Hilarion** and to **Bellapais.** The fantastic ruins of the **Castle of St. Hilarion** stand on a hilltop 11 kilometers (7 miles) to the southwest. It's a strenuous walk, so take a taxi; the views are breathtaking. The ruins of the former **Abbey of Bellapais,** built in the 12th century by the Lusignans, are just as impressive. They lie on a mountainside 6 kilometers (4 miles) to the northeast. The showpiece is the refectory, but there are also dormitories, storerooms, and a church with frescoes.

Salamis, north of Famagusta, is an ancient ruined city, perhaps the most dramatic archaeological site on the island. St. Barnabas and St. Paul arrived in Salamis and set up a church near here. The present ruins date largely from the 12th-century Lusignan rulers of Cyprus, who came from France, and this was their major port before Famagusta was developed by the Turks from the mid-16th century; Salamis does contain relics of earlier civilizations, including Greek and Roman settlements. The city was frequently devastated by earthquakes, but the setting is beautiful, and some of the ruins are sufficiently overgrown to give the visitor a satisfying sense of discovery.

Dining

There is not a great deal of difference between Greek and Turkish cooking on Cyprus, though the Turks don't eat pork and are more sparing in their use of oil. As in the Republic of Cyprus, the larger hotels have dining rooms, but individual restaurants have more local atmosphere. Travelers in North Cyprus should also consider army-run Mucahitler restaurants, which offer excellent value. Try the **Otello** in Famagusta (opposite the Othello Tower), the **Istanbul** along the Bogaz Road, or the **Alsancak** near Kyrenia.

Our ratings reflect prices per person for a three-course meal and do not include drinks.

Category	All Areas
Expensive	over $13.50
Moderate	$6.50–$13.50
Inexpensive	under $6.50

Famagusta **Kemal's Fish Restaurant.** This family-run restaurant specializes, of course, in fresh fish. *Moderate.*
Patek Pastanesi. This is the place to go if you're in the mood for Turkish coffee and honey-drenched cakes. *Opposite Famagusta's Sea Gate. Inexpensive.*

Kyrenia **Harbor Bar.** Surprisingly high-quality French cooking is offered at this little eatery right on the harbor. *Moderate.*
Kyrenia Taverna. This traditional taverna, near the harbor, features fish. *Inexpensive.*

Lodging

There is very little difference between the hotels of North Cyprus and those of the Republic. Prices are per person sharing a double room, including breakfast.

Category	All Areas
Expensive	Over $30
Moderate	$17–$30
Inexpensive	Under $17

Famagusta **Park.** Just outside Famagusta, the Park is handy for those who plan to visit the ruins at Salamis. It has its own private beach and a variety of sports facilities. The restaurant is noted for its excellent cuisine. *Tel. 036/65511. 93 rooms. Expensive.*

Rebecca. This family hotel is situated on the edge of Salamis Forest, five minutes from the sea. The restaurant serves good Turkish and Continental food, and there's an outdoor café in the large shaded courtyard. *Tel. 036/58000. 42 rooms. Moderate.*

Mimosa. This beachfront hotel, best known for its restaurant, specializes in local and Turkish food. Tables are set under a big mimosa tree on the terrace a few yards from the sea. *Tel. 036/56460. 51 rooms. Inexpensive.*

Kyrenia **Dome.** Close to the harbor and within easy distance of Kyrenia is this hotel with a private swimming and sunbathing area built out into the sea. Bedrooms have views of either the bay or the Kyrenia Mountains. *Tel. 081/52453. 161 rooms. Facilities: restaurant, casino. Expensive.*

Club Acapulco Village. Ten kilometers (6 miles) east of town, these simple bungalow-style accommodations are ideal for independent travelers. There's a restaurant and beach bar in the village. *Tel. 081/53510. Moderate.*

Dorana. Located close to the main shopping area and only 300 yards from the sea, the Dorana is a pleasant modern hotel with a bar, restaurant, and 24-hour room service. *Tel. 081/53521. 33 rooms. Moderate.*

Nicosia **Saray.** This hotel overlooks Atatürk Square in the town center. The ninth-floor restaurant has excellent views over the city. There's a casino and live music on weekends. *Tel. 020/71115. 72 rooms. Moderate.*

Picnic. This small hotel, in a quiet area of town, offers a good restaurant and a disco. Snacks are served in the vine-shaded garden. *Tel. 020/72001. 10 rooms. Inexpensive.*

7 Czechoslovakia

Introduction

No country is more centrally European than Czechoslovakia, ringed as it is by Austria, Germany, Poland, the Soviet Union, and Hungary. This central position is a fact of life that has made Czechoslovakia both a cultural crossroads and a frequent political pawn. It has also bred in the Czechs a certain artistic flair and stoic endurance, a good measure of guile, and a neat sense of the ridiculous. This is indeed the land of Kafka and the Good Soldier Švejk.

Invaders and traders have come and gone. Twice an empire was ruled from here. Revolutionary movements have been born and quelled. Above all, the arts have found fertile ground on which to flourish, as did democracy between the two world wars.

In 1938, the British and French sold Czechoslovakia out to Nazi Germany in exchange for a hollow "peace in our time." Thirty years later, Soviet tanks rumbled into Prague (*Praha*, in Czech) and thwarted a brave political experiment combining Communist ideology with democratic rights. Whatever your views, when visiting here it's wise to keep an open mind and to respect the considerable achievements of these intelligent and talented people in this sensitive corner of Europe.

Socialist Czechoslovakia has certain bureaucratic requirements, detailed in the following pages. But you're free to travel where you will and, in the process, may welcome such advantages as streets that are safe to walk at night and a refreshing lack of commercial hype.

Tourist amenities sometimes lack polish, and service can be ungracious. But it is by no means always so, and the loveliness of the countryside and the heritage of history, art, and architecture go a long way to make up for it.

Before You Go

When to Go Organized sightseeing tours run from April or May through October. Some monuments, especially castles, either close or open for shorter hours in winter. Hotel rates drop in the off-season except during festivals. May, the month of fruit blossoms, is the time of the Prague Spring Music Festival. During the fall, when the forests are glorious, Bratislava and Brno hold their music festivals.

Climate The following are the average daily maximum and minimum temperatures for Prague.

Jan.	49F	10C	**May**	82F	28C	**Sept.**	84F	29C
	7	−13		36	2		38	4
Feb.	53F	11C	June	88F	31C	Oct.	71F	22C
	10	−12		44	7		29	−2
Mar.	64F	18C	July	91F	33C	Nov.	57F	14C
	18	−8		49	9		24	−5
Apr.	73F	23C	Aug.	89F	32C	Dec.	50F	10C
	29	−2		47	8		14	−10

Currency The unit of currency is the crown, or koruna, written as Kčs., and divided into 100 haler. There are bills of 10, 20, 50, 100, 500, and 1,000 Kčs., and coins of 5, 10, 20, and 50 halérs and 1, 2, and

Czechoslovakia

EAST
GERMANY

P O L A N D

E R Z G E B I R G E

Cheb

Karlovy Vary

Mariánské
Lázně

Plzeň

Domažlice

B O H E M I A N

F O R E S T

WEST
GERMANY

N

Teplice

Most

Ústí

Litoměřice

Liberec

Mladá
Boleslav

Berounka

Klatovy

Příbram

Tábor

B O H E M I A

Vltava

Prague

Labe
(Elbe)

Hradec-
Králové

Jihlava

Třebíč

Znojmo

Sázava

České
Budějovice

M O R A V I A

Prostějov

Olomouc

Brno

Dyje

Hodonín

Morava

Frýdek Místek

Jičín

Ostrava

Karviná

Gottwaldov

Žilina

Ružomberok

Vah

S L O V A K I A

Trenčín

Nitra

Trnava

Bratislava

Danube

A U S T R I A

H U N G A R Y

Danube

Ipel

Nitra

Hron

Váh

Lučenec

Zvolen

Banská
Bystrica

Poprad

Kežmarok

Levoča

Spišská
n. Ves.

Rožňava

Košice

Prešov

Michalovce

U.S.S.R.

C A R P A T H I A N   M T S.

Elbe

0   100 miles
0   150 km

5 Kčs. At press time (spring 1989), the exchange rate was about 10 Kčs. to the dollar and 16.45 Kčs. to the pound sterling.

If you visit the country on a Čedok tour or prebook hotel accommodations with breakfast and dinner, you'll get a 36% bonus when you cash your traveler's checks or special bonus currency vouchers (buy them from Čedok before you leave) at Čedok offices, Interhotels, and Balnea spa hotels or sanatoriums. This bonus is *not* available at other exchange offices. Note also that Czech currency acquired in this way can't be reconverted into foreign currency.

If you're visiting Czechoslovakia without prepaid arrangements, you must change approximately $15 every day you're in the country. All currency exchanges will be noted on your visa and only amounts *above* the required minimum can be reconverted into hard currencies on departure—and even then there can be problems. Avoid the temptations of the black market: The penalties are severe.

Credit cards are widely accepted in establishments used by foreign tourists.

What It Will Cost Some services and items—hotels or tours, for example—may be less expensive if you haven't paid for them in advance in foreign currency. But in these cases, you lose the advantage of the currency bonus, and there's no doubt that vouchers smooth the way. Costs are highest in Prague and only slightly less in the High Tatra resorts and main spas. The least expensive areas are southern Bohemia and central and eastern Slovakia.

Sample Prices Cup of coffee, 6 Kčs.; beer ([1/2] liter), 6–10 Kčs.; Coca-Cola, 6–9 Kčs.; ham sandwich, 4 Kčs.; one-mile taxi ride, 10 Kčs.

Museums Admission to museums, galleries, and castles ranges from 3 to 5 Kčs.

Visas Visas are required for all visitors. You can get one by sending or bringing a completed visa application form, two photographs, and your passport either directly to one of the Czech embassies, or, in the United Kingdom, to Čedok. Visas are valid for a specified period within three months of the date of issue and are linked with exchange regulations (*see* Currency). They can now be obtained at certain border crossing points with West Germany and Austria at an approximate cost of $20. Visas can be extended during your stay.

Note that if you're staying with friends or relatives in Czechoslovakia, you must register with the local police within 48 hours.

In the United States American citizens pay $16 for a visa. Apply to the **Embassy of the ČSSR,** 3900 Linnean Ave., NW, Washington, DC 20008, tel. 202/363–6308.

In Canada Canadians should apply to the **Embassy of the ČSSR,** 50 Rideau Terrace, Ottawa, Ontario K1M 2A1, tel. 416/234–6581, or 1305 ave. de Pins Ouest, Montreal H3G 1B2, tel. 849–4495.

In the United Kingdom Britons who have booked a Čedok tour can have visa applications processed by Čedok for £14. For independent travelers, the visa fee is £20 plus a £3 service charge through Čedok. The visa section of the **Czech Embassy** is at 28 Kensington Palace Gardens, London W8 4QY, tel. 01/727–3966.

Customs on Arrival Valuable items should be entered on your customs declaration. You can bring in 250 cigarettes (or their equivalent in tobacco), two liters of wine, one liter of spirits, ½ liter of eau de cologne, and gifts to the value of 1,000 Kčs.

On Departure You can take out gifts and souvenirs to the value of 1,000 Kčs., as well as goods bought at Tuzex hard-currency shops (keep the receipts). Crystal and some other items not bought at hard-currency shops may be subject to a tax of 100% of their retail price. Only antiques bought at Tuzex or specially appointed shops may be exported.

Language English is spoken fairly widely among both the young and those associated with the tourist industry. Elsewhere, you will come across English speakers, though not frequently. German is sometimes spoken by older Czechs. Whether a knowledge of German will win you friends is a different matter.

Getting Around

By Car Czech main roads are usually good, if sometimes narrow, and *Road Conditions* traffic is light, especially away from main centers. An expressway links Prague, Brno, and Bratislava. Other highways are single lane only.

Rules of the Road Drive on the right. Speed limits are 60 kph (37 mph) in built-up areas, 90 kph (55 mph) on open roads, and 110 kph (68 mph) on expressways. Seatbelts are compulsory outside built-up areas; drinking and driving is strictly prohibited.

Parking The center of Prague is banned to all cars except those belonging to hotel guests. In other parts of the city, parking is limited to a few specially reserved places. Parking times are limited, however, and you will have to pay for the privilege. If you park anywhere else in Prague, you risk having your car towed away, and getting it back will prove time-consuming and expensive. Elsewhere in the country there's little problem.

Gasoline Gasoline costs about 9 Kčs. per liter. Gas stations are rarer than in the West, but a free map from Čedok shows locations throughout the country. You can buy nonrefundable coupons for gas from Čedok in London before you go, which you can use at all gas stations; cost is about 70¢ a liter. If, however, you are entitled to the currency bonus (*see* Currency, above), gas coupons are of little benefit.

Breakdowns **Autotourist** (head office: Na rybníčku, Prague, tel. 02/203355) operates a patrol service on main highways. The emergency telephone number for motorists is 154; for ambulances, 155; for police (traffic accidents), 02/242424.

By Train There is an extensive rail network throughout the country. As elsewhere in Eastern Europe, fares are low and trains are always crowded. Also, you have to pay a supplement on all express trains (this does not apply if you bought your ticket outside Czechoslovakia). All long-distance trains have dining cars; overnight trains between main centers have sleeping cars.

Fares Eurail pass and Eurail Youthpass tickets are not valid in Czechoslovakia unless you are merely passing through the country.

By Plane Czechoslovakia has a remarkably good internal air service linking Prague with eight other towns, including Brno, Bratislava, Poprad (for the High Tatras), Karlovy Vary, and Pieštany.

Make reservations at Čedok offices or direct with ČSA, Czechoslovak Airlines (tel. 02/2146).

By Bus There's a wide-ranging bus network. Fares are higher than
those on trains. Buses are always full, and, on long-distance
routes especially, reservations are essential.

Staying in Czechoslovakia

Telephones These cost 1 Kčs. from a pay phone. Lift the receiver, insert the
Local Calls coin, and dial.

International Calls You'll pay through the nose if you make calls from your hotel.
There's automatic dialing to many countries, including North
America and the United Kingdom. Special international pay
booths in central Prague will take 5 Kčs. coins, but your best
bet is to go to the main post office (Jindřišská 24, near Wenceslas Square). For international inquiries, dial 0132 for the
United States, Canada, or United Kingdom.

Mail Airmail letters to the United States cost 7 Kčs. up to 10 grams,
Postal Rates postcards 5 Kčs. Airmail letters to the United Kingdom cost 4
Kčs. up to 20 grams, postcards 3 Kčs.

Receiving Mail Mail can be sent to Poste Restante at the main post office in
Prague (Jindřišská 24), or to any other main post office. There's
no charge. The American Express office in Prague will hold letters addressed to cardholders or holders of American Express
traveler's checks for up to one month free of charge.

Opening and **Banks.** Banks are open weekdays 8–2.
Closing Times **Museums.** Museums are usually open Tues.–Sun. 10–5, but
there are many variations.
Shops. Shops are generally open weekdays 9–6 (9–8 on Thurs.);
some close between noon and 2. Many are also open Sat. 9–noon
(department stores, 9–4).

National Holidays January 1 (New Year's Day); April 16 (Easter Monday); May 1
(Labor Day); May 9 (Liberation); December 25, 26.

Dining Independent travelers with prepaid meal vouchers (nonrefundable) are now able to use these at any Čedok hotel or restaurant in the city or region where they are staying. For meals
not limited by vouchers, you can choose among restaurants,
wine cellars *(vinárna)*, the more down-to-earth beer taverns
(pivince), cafeterias, and a growing number of coffee shops and
snack bars. Eating out is popular, and it's wise to make reservations whenever possible.

Prague ham makes a favorite first course, as does soup, which
is less expensive. The most typical main dish is roast pork (or
duck or goose) with sauerkraut and dumplings. Dumplings in
various forms, generally with a rich gravy, accompany many
dishes. Fresh green vegetables are rare, but there are plenty
of the pickled variety.

Mealtimes Lunch is usually from noon to 2 or 3; dinner from 6 to 9:30 or 10.

Dress In Prague, jacket and tie is recommended for Very Expensive
and Expensive restaurants, as well as for some of the stylish
establishments in the Moderate category. Informal dress is appropriate elsewhere.

Ratings Prices are reasonable by American standards, even in the more
expensive restaurants. Czechs don't normally go in for three-

course meals, and the following prices apply only if you're having a first course, main course, and dessert (excluding wine and tip). Best bets are indicated by a star ★ . At press time, there were 10 Kčs. to the dollar.

Category	Prague	Other Areas
Very Expensive	over 150 Kčs.	over 90 Kčs.
Expensive	100–150 Kčs.	60–90 Kčs.
Moderate	50–100 Kčs.	30–60 Kčs.
Inexpensive	under 50 Kčs.	under 30 Kčs.

Credit Cards The following credit card abbreviations are used: AE, American Expres; DC, Diners Club; MC, MasterCard; V, Visa.

Lodging There's a choice of hotels, motels, limited private accommodations, and campsites. Many older properties are gradually being renovated and the best have great character and style. There remains an acute shortage of rooms in the peak season, so make reservations well in advance. The standard of facilities and services hardly match those in the West, so don't be surprised by faulty plumbing or indifferent reception clerks. The prices at least compare favorably.

Hotels These are officially classified from one to five stars. Prices include obligatory half-board, except for five-star hotels, where only breakfast is included. Most hotels used by foreign visitors —Interhotels—belong to Čedok and are mainly in the three- to five-star categories. These will have all or some rooms with bath or shower. Čedok can also handle reservations for some non-Čedok hotels, such as those run by Balnea (the spa treatment organization), CKM (the Youth Travel Bureau), and municipal organizations, some of which are excellent.

Čedok prices are quoted in hard currency. If you haven't reserved in advance, you'll have to pay in hard currency at Interhotels, unless you have met the minimum obligatory exchange requirement.

Private Accommodations Pragotur has the biggest selection in Prague. Čedok can offer some in Prague (minimum stay is three nights) and (on the spot only) in the High Tatras (minimum stay is seven nights).

Camping Campsites are run by a number of organizations. A free map and list are available from Čedok.

Ratings Prices are for double rooms and obligatory half-board for two, except for the Very Expensive and some Expensive places, which include breakfast only. Prices at the lower end of the scale apply to low season. At certain periods, such as Easter or during festivals, there may be an increase of 15–25%. Best bets are indicated by a star ★ . Prices are listed in dollars, since most visitors will prebook their rooms.

Category	Prague	Other Areas
Very Expensive	over $150	over $100
Expensive	$100–$150	$80–$100
Moderate	$66–$100	$55–$80
Inexpensive	under $66	under $55

Credit Cards The following credit card abbreviations are used: AE, American Express; DC, Diners Club; MC, MasterCard; V, Visa.

Tipping Czechs are not usually blatant about the fact that tips are expected. Small sums of hard currency, though not officially encouraged, will certainly be most welcome. Otherwise, in Moderate or Inexpensive restaurants, add a few Kčs.; in more expensive ones, add 10%. For taxis, add 5 Kčs. In the better hotels, doormen should get 2 Kčs. for each bag they carry to the check-in desk; bellhops get up to 5 Kčs. for taking them up to your rooms. In Moderate or Inexpensive hotels, you'll have to lug them yourself.

Prague

Arriving and Departing

By Plane All international flights arrive at Prague's Ruzyně Airport, about 20 kilometers (12 miles) from downtown. For arrival and departure times, tel. 02/367814 or 367760.

Between the ČSA provides bus services linking the airport with Town Ter-
Airport and minal Vltava (Revolučni 25). Departures depend on aircraft
Downtown schedules. The trip costs 6 Kčs. and takes about 30 minutes. A special shuttle service serves main hotels and costs 50 Kčs.; buy the ticket before boarding. The cheapest way to get into Prague is by regular bus 119; the cost is 1 Kčs., but you'll need to change to the subway for the last leg of the trip. By taxi, expect to pay 70–100 Kčs.

By Train The main station for international and domestic routes is Hlavni nádraží (tel. 02/244441), not far from Wenceslas Square.

By Bus The main bus station is Florenc (at Na Florenci, tel. 02/221445), not far from the train station.

Getting Around

Public transportation is a bargain. From special "blue ticket" machines you can buy a one-day ticket for 8 Kčs., giving unlimited use of all public transportation. Otherwise, tickets cost 1 Kčs. and should be obtained before boarding at newsstands, tobacco shops, various stores and hotels, or subway stations. Punch your ticket in the machine as you board.

By Subway Prague's three modern subway lines are easy to use and spotlessly clean. They provide the simplest and fastest means of transportation, and most new maps of Prague mark the routes.

By Tram/Bus You need to buy a new ticket every time you change vehicles. Express buses (marked with green badges) serve the suburbs and cost 2 Kčs.

By Taxi Taxis (tel. 02/202951 or 203941) are inexpensive, but can be difficult to find. The basic charge of 6 Kčs. is increased by 3 Kčs. per kilometer (surcharge at night). Rates are a little higher from the airport and some Interhotels.

Important Addresses and Numbers

Tourist Čedok (Na příkopě 18, tel. 02/212711) is very near Wenceslas
Information Square. For its **Department of Accommodation Services,** go to Panská 5 (tel. 02/227004) just around the corner. Almost next-

door to Čedok is the **Prague Information Service** (Na příkopě 20, tel. 02/544444). Across the road, **Pragotur** (U Obecního domu 2, tel. 02/2317281), near the Powder Tower, provides a variety of services, including reservations in non-Čedok hotels and private accommodations.

Embassies **U.S.:** Tržiště 15, Malá Strana, tel. 02/536641. **Canadian** Mickiewiczova 6, tel. 02/326941. **U.K.:** Thunovská 14, Mala Strana, tel. 02/533347.

Emergencies **Police:** tel. 158; **Ambulance:** tel. 155; **Doctor: Fakultni poliklinika,** Karlovo náměstí 32, tel. 02/299381. **24-Hour Pharmacy:** Na příkopě 7, near Wenceslas Square.

English Bookstores Try Štěpanská 42 or Na příkopě 27. Except in a few top hotels, English-language newspapers are limited to left-wing publications such as *The Morning Star.*

Travel Agencies **American Express** and **Thomas Cook** are both located at the Čedok Foreign Travel Division, Na příkopě 18, tel. 02/224251.

Guided Tours

Čedok arranges a variety of tours in and around Prague; they can be arranged before you leave or can be booked in Prague. Call 02/2318255 or 2316619 for any of the following:

Orientation Tours The "Prague City" tour, departing from three central points, covers the main monuments, including Prague Castle and St. Vitus Cathedral, in half a day.

Special-Interest Tours The "U Fleku" brewery and beer-tasting tour starts at Wenceslas Square 24 and lasts two hours. For cultural tours, call Čedok (*see* above). These include performances of folklore, Laterna Magika (*see* The Arts), opera, and concerts. You can save money by buying tickets—if any are available—at box offices, but this will take time.

Walking Tours A three-hour walk starts at Čedok (Wenceslas Sq. 24) at 8:45 daily, lasts 2¼ hours, and ends at Prague Castle.

Excursions Čedok's one-day tours out of Prague cover main historic and scenic sights, and include lunch. The "Czech Garnet Jewelry" and "Czech Paradise" tours should yield attractive buys as well as good scenery. The "Beauty Spots of South Bohemia" tour focuses on history and medieval architecture among woods and lakes.

Personal Guides Contact **Čedok,** Panská 4, tel. 02/224404.

Exploring Prague

Like Rome, far to the southwest, the city of Prague is built on seven hills, sprawling within the confines of a broad loop of the Vltava River. This riverside location makes a great setting for two of the city's particular features: its extravagant architecture and its memorable music. Mozart claimed that no one understood him better than the citizens of Prague, and he was only one of several great masters who lived or lingered here.

It was under Charles IV (Karel IV) in the 14th century that Prague briefly became the seat of the Holy Roman Empire—

virtually the capital of western Europe—and acquired its distinctive Gothic imprint. At times, you'll need to look quite hard for this medieval inheritance; it's still here, though, under the overlays of graceful Renaissance and exuberant Baroque.

Prague escaped serious wartime damage, but it didn't escape neglect. A long-term restoration program now underway always leaves some part of the city under scaffolding. But what's completed—which is nearly all that's described in the following itineraries—is hard to fault as an example of sensitive and painstaking restoration.

Numbers in the margin correspond with points of interest on the Prague map.

The Nové Město and Staré Město

① ② ③ Václavské náměstí (Wenceslas Square) is the Times Square of Prague. Confusingly, it's not actually a square at all, but a broad boulevard sloping down from the **National Museum** and the equestrian **statue of Wenceslas** (who has yet to fulfill the legend that he will again lead his people in their time of greatest need). The lower end is where all the action is. Na příkopě, once part of the moat surrounding the Old Town, is now an elegant pedestrian mall. Čedok's main office and Prague **④** Information Service are along here, on your way to the **Powder Tower**, a 19th-century neo-Gothic replacement of the medieval original.

⑤ ⑥ ⑦ Turn into Celetná and you're on the old **Royal Route,** once followed by coronation processions through **Staroměstske náměstí** (Old Town Square), **Karlova,** across **Karlův most** (Charles Bridge), and up to the castle. Along this route, you can study every variety or combination of Romanesque, Gothic, Renaissance, and Baroque architecture. Two good examples are the town buildings at 12 Celetná and 8 Karlova. On Staroměstske náměstí, the crowds regularly gather below the famous **Clock Tower,** where, on the hour, the complex 16th-century mechanism activates a procession that includes the Twelve Apostles. Note the skeleton figure of Death that tolls the bell.

⑧ In U Starého Hřbitova (the Old Jewish Cemetery) in the **Prague Ghetto,** ancient tombstones lean and jostle each other; below them, in a dozen layers, are 12,000 graves. As you stand by the tomb of the scholar Rabbi Low, who died in 1609, you may see, stuffed into the cracks, scraps of paper bearing prayers and requests. It's said that many Jews hid their valuables here before being transported to the concentration camps. Their story, and many aspects of the culture of one of the oldest ghettos in Europe, is told in several nearby synagogues that now form part of **⑨** the **State Jewish Museum.** *Jachymova 3. Open Sun.–Fri. 9–4:30; closed Sat. and religious holidays.*

When you stand on Charles Bridge, you'll see views of Prague that would still be familiar to the 14th-century architect Peter Parler and to the sculptors who added the 30 Baroque statues in the early 18th century (a few have been replaced). They're worth a closer look, especially the 12th on the left (St. Luitgarde, by Matthias Braun, circa 1710), and the 14th on the left (in which a Turk guards suffering saints, by F.M. Brokoff, circa 1714).

Prague

HRADČANY

Pod Bruskou

Valdštejnská

Kosártkovo

Náb

Dvořákovo N

Mánesuv Most

Nám
Krasno
Armějcu

Thunovska

Letenská

Vojanovy
Gardens

Veleslavinovč

Malostranské
Nám.

Tržiště

Mostecká

Karlův Most

Nakampě

Križovnicka

Maltézské
Nám.

Velkopřevorske
Nám.

Vltava River

Križovnicke
Nám

N

Karmeliiská

Hellichova

Újezd

Smetanovo Náb

Betlémská

Konvíktská

MALÁ STRANA

Všehrdova

Malostranské Náb

Streiecky
Ostrov

Petřin
Gardens

Vítenzá

Most 1 Máje

Ostrovní

Plaská

Zborovská

Janáčkovo Náb

Pstrossova

0   1/4 mile
0   1/4 km

Peřřinská

Gottwaldovo Náb

Holečkova

Dětský
Ostrov

Vyšehrad

Malátova

Slovanský
Ostrov

⑩ The **museum** devoted to Prague composer **Bedřich Smetana,** located nearby at Novotného lávka, is small, and its exhibits mainly documentary. But it's a lovely quiet oasis in which to listen to tapes of Smetana's music—and admire the views across the Vltava and up to the castle. *Novotného lávka. Open Wed.– Mon. 10–5.*

⑪ **Bethlehem Chapel** has been completely reconstructed since Jan Hus thundered his humanitarian teachings from its pulpit in the early 15th century to congregations that could number 3,000. But the little door through which he came to the pulpit is original, as are some of the inscriptions on the wall. *Betlémské náměstí. Open daily 9–6.*

Malá Strana and Hradčany (Lesser Town and Castle) Cross Charles Bridge and follow Mostecká up to Malostranské náměstí. After the turbulence of the Counter-Reformation at the end of the 16th century, Prague witnessed a great flowering of what became known as Bohemian Baroque. The **⑫** architects (Dienzenhofer, father and son) of the **Church of St. Nicholas** were among its most skilled exponents. If you're in Prague when a concert is being given in this church, fight for a ticket. The lavish sculptures and frescoes of the interior make for a memorable setting. *Malostranskê náměstí. Open daily 9–6.*

⑬ The monumental complex of **Prague Castle** has witnessed the changing fortunes of the city for more than 1,000 years. The scaffolding has only recently been removed from the latest restoration of the castle's **Cathedral of St. Vitus.** It took from 1344 to 1929 to build, so you can trace the whole gamut of styles from Romanesque to 19th-century. This is the final resting place for numerous Bohemian kings. Charles IV lies in the crypt. Good King Wenceslas has his own chapel in the south transept, studded with semiprecious stones. Knightly tournaments often accompanied coronation ceremonies in the castle, hence the broad **Riders' Staircase** leading up to the grandiose Vladislav Hall of the Third Courtyard. Oldest of all the buildings, though much restored, is the Romanesque complex of **St. George's Church and Monastery.** Behind a Baroque facade, it houses a superb collection of Baroque and earlier Bohemian art. *Hradčanské náměstí. All museum buildings in the castle are open Tues.–Sun. 10–5.*

Time Out At the small, pleasant snack bar of **U Ševce Matouše** (At the Cobblers) on Loretánské náměstí, you can get your shoes repaired while you have refreshments.

⑭ The Baroque church and shrine of the **Loretto** is named for the Italian town to which the Virgin Mary's House in Nazareth was supposedly transported by angels to save it from the infidel. The crowning glory of its fabulous treasury is the glittering monstrance of the *Sun of Prague,* set with 6,222 diamonds. *Loreta 12. Admission to Treasury: 3 Kčs. Open Tues.–Sun. 9– noon and 1–5.*

Off the Beaten Track

Take the subway to Malostranská metro station, cross a courtyard, and climb the steps to the **Gardens on the Ramparts** for sweeping views of Prague.

The little-known **Vrtba Zahrada** is a charming retreat of steeply terraced gardens dotted with Baroque statues by Matthias Braun. *Entrance through Karmelitská 25. Open in summer until 9 PM.*

Almost as old as the oldest parts of Prague Castle, the ruins of **Vyšehrad castle** crown a rock bluff rising out of the Vltava, about 2 miles downstream from the Old Town. The quiet cemetery adjoining the **Church of Sts. Peter and Paul** is a place to pay homage to some of the nation's cultural giants, among them Bedřich Smetana and the playwright Karel Čapek.

Across the river, in Prague 5 district, Mozart stayed in the peaceful **Bertramka Villa,** and here composed his opera *Don Giovanni.* With luck, your trip will coincide with a concert here. If not, taped music will accompany your walk through the villa, restored to what it was in his day.

Shopping

Tuzex Stores Ask Čedok for the latest list of these hard-currency-only outlets and their specialties. One of the main ones is at Železná 18, selling imported goods, glass, and porcelain. The branch at Štěpanská 23 specializes in fashion and leather goods. **Moser** (Na příkopě 12) is the most famous for glass and porcelain.

Specialty Shops Look for the name **Dilo** for objects d'art and prints; ULUV or UVA for folk art. At Na příkopě 12 you'll find excellent costume jewelry.

Shopping Districts Many of the main shops are in and around Wenceslas Square (Václavské náměstí) and Na příkopě and along Celetná and Pařížská.

Department Stores Three central ones are **Bilá Labut** (Na poříčí 23), **Družba** (Wenceslas Square 21), and **Kotva** (nám. Republiky 8).

Dining

Eating out in Prague is a very popular pastime, so it's advisable to make reservations whenever possible, especially for dinner. For details and price category definitions, *see* Dining in Staying in Czechoslovakia.

Very Expensive **Klášterní Vinárna.** You'll find this wine restaurant in a former Ursuline convent in the city center. The emphasis is on Czech home cooking—try the house goulash. The menu includes some Moderate dishes. *Národní 8, tel. 02/290596. Reservations accepted. No credit cards. Closed Sun.*

U Labuti. Located in tastefully remodeled stables in the castle area, "At the Swans" has a stylish—if slightly rich and heavy—menu (haunch of venison, goose liver with ham and almonds), which includes some Expensive dishes. The place is rich in atmosphere, too. *Hradčanské náměstí 11, tel. 02/536962. Reservations required. AE, DC, MC, V. Dinner only.*

★ **U Malířů.** This is one of Prague's most picturesque wine taverns, popular with the artist set (the name means "At the Painters"). *Maltézské náměstí 11, Lesser Town, tel. 02/531881. Reservations required. No credit cards. Closed Sun. Dinner only.*

U Mecenáše. This wine restaurant manages to be both medieval and elegant despite the presence of an ancient gallows! Try and get a table in the back room. Moussaka is one of the specialties from an international menu. *Malostranské náměstí 10, Lesser Town, tel. 02/533881. Reservations required. AE, DC, MC, V. Closed Sat. Dinner only.*

Expensive **U Zlaté Hrušky.** Careful restoration has returned this restaurant to its original 18th-century style. It specializes in Moravian wines, which go down well with fillet steaks and goose liver. Some dishes are Moderate. *Nový Svět 3, Castle area, tel. 02/531133. Reservations required. No credit cards. Dinner only.*

Moderate **Opera Grill.** Though called a grill, this is one of the most stylish
★ small restaurants in town, complete with antique Meissen candelabra and Czech specialties. *K. Světlé 35, Old Town, tel. 02/265508. Reservations required. AE, DC, MC, V. Closed weekends. Dinner only.*

U Lorety. Sightseers will find this an agreeable spot—peaceful except for the welcoming carillon from neighboring Loretto Church. Venison and steak are specialties. *Loretánské náměstí 8, near the Castle, tel. 02/531395. Reservations advised. AE, DC, MC, V. Closed Mon. and Tues. in winter.*

U Pastýřky-Koliba. It's worth the trek from the center to enjoy the folk-style decor and specialty dishes of Slovakia here, complete with open fire for spit roasts. *Bělehradská 15, tel. 02/434093. Reservations required. No credit cards. Closed Sun. Dinner only.*

Vikárka. This was an eating house beside St. Vitus Cathedral as far back as the 16th century. It offers good-value local cooking in a historic setting. *Vikářská 6, in the Castle, tel. 02/535150. Reservations accepted. AE, DC, MC, V. Closed Mon. in winter.*

Inexpensive **U Medvídků.** Enjoy South Bohemian and old Czech specialties here in a noisy but jolly atmosphere. *Na perštýně 7, tel. 02/2358904. Reservations not necessary. No credit cards. Closed Sun.*

U Pinkasů. The two great attractions here are the draught beer and the goulash—you can also add your signature to the wall with the countless others before you. *Jungmannovo náměstí 15, tel. 02/265770. Reservations not necessary. No credit cards.*
★ **U Sv. Tomáše.** This restored ancient tavern overflows with atmosphere. Try the famous dark ale and the good down-to-earth fare like roast pork with cabbage and dumplings. *Letenská 12, Lesser Town, tel. 02/530064. Reservations advised. No credit cards. Closed Sun.*

U Zlatého Tygra. This is a favorite with not-so-young beer connoisseurs—a typical no-frills Prague pub. The pork fillet in potato pancake with sauerkraut salad makes a good foundation for the beer. *Husova 17, tel. 02/265219. Reservations not necessary. No credit cards. Closed Sun.*

Lodging

Many of Prague's older hotels—some having great style—have recently been or are due to be renovated. If you haven't prebooked, go to Čedok or Pragotur when you arrive (*see* Tourist Information in Important Addresses and Numbers). For details and price category definitions, *see* Lodging in Staying in Czechoslovakia. Interhotels belong to the Čedok network.

Very Expensive **Forum** (Interhotel). Prague's latest high rise is near ancient Vyšehrad castle. Prices include half-board. *Štětkova ul, tel. 02/ 410111. 531 rooms with bath. Facilities: saunas, pool, bowling alleys, miniature golf, gym, nightclub, roulette. AE, DC, MC, V.*

InterContinental (Interhotel). A fine riverside position in the Old Town makes this an attractive choice. It opened in 1975 and is a favorite with U.S. visitors. *Náměstí Curiových 5, tel. 02/ 2899. 395 rooms with bath. Facilities: saunas, health club, nightclub. AE, DC, MC, V.*

★ **U Tří Pštrosů.** "The Three Ostriches" has a magical location at the Lesser Town end of Charles Bridge: The river views are superb. It's very popular, so you'll need to make reservations well ahead. Prices include half-board. *Dražického 12, tel. 02/536151. 18 rooms with bath. AE, DC, MC, V.*

Expensive **Alcron** (Interhotel). This stylish old town house just around the
★ corner from Wenceslas Square is a favorite with Americans who prefer traditional decor over modern. *Štěpanská 40, tel. 02/2359216–30. 149 rooms with bath. Facilities: 3 restaurants. AE, DC, MC, V.*

Esplanade (Interhotel). Facing a park near the National Museum, this is another favorite with Americans looking for a traditional atmosphere. An old town house, it was last renovated in 1980. The nightclub, Est Bar, has a good local reputation. *Washingtonova 19, tel. 02/222552–4. 65 rooms with bath. AE, DC, MC, V.*

Jalta (Interhotel). The Jalta has a plum location on Wenceslas Square. Despite its five-star status, it's on the shabby side, but comfortable, nevertheless. *Václavské náměstí 45, tel. 02/ 265541. 90 rooms with bath. Facilities: 2 nightclubs. AE, DC, MC, V.*

Panorama (Interhotel). Near Vyšehrad castle, with good subway connections to the center, this hotel makes a practical exploring base. Prices include half-board. *Milevská 7, tel. 02/ 416111. 432 rooms with bath. Facilities: saunas, pool, solarium, nightclub. AE, DC, MC, V.*

Moderate **International** (Interhotel). Situated about 4.8 kilometers (3 miles) from the center, the International is known as the Russian Ritz for its 30-year-old architectural pretensions! High-season prices can edge this one up into the Expensive category. *Náměstí družby 1, tel. 02/321051. 327 rooms with bath. Facilities: garden, miniature golf, nightclub. AE, DC, MC, V.*

★ **Paříž** (Interhotel). This is the pick of the Moderate hotels, despite some small rooms. Its turn-of-the-century Art Nouveau style was tastefully restored in 1985, while the hotel's Old Town location is ideal. Rooms without bath are Inexpensive. *U Obecního domu 1, tel. 02/2322051. 86 rooms, 75 with bath. AE, DC, MC, V.*

Zlatá Husa (Interhotel). Thsi is another oldie from the turn of the century and was renovated in 1983. It's right on Wenceslas Square. *Václavské náměstí 7, tel. 02/221351. 62 rooms with bath. Facilities: disco. AE, DC, MC, V.*

The Arts

Prague's cultural life is one of its top attractions and its citizens like to dress up for it, but performances are usually booked far ahead. You can get a monthly program of events from the Prague Information Service, Čedok, or many hotels. **Čedok**

(Bílkova, tel. 02/2318255) is the main ticket agency for foreigners, but there's a wider choice through **Sluna** (Pasáž Černa Růže, off Na příkopě).

Concerts   Performances are held in the **National Gallery** in Prague Castle; the **National Museum;** the **Gardens** below the castle (where music comes with a view); the **Church of St. Nicholas** in the Lesser Town; and **St. James's Church** on Malá Stupartská (Old Town), where the organ plays amid a flourish of Baroque statuary.

Year-round concert halls include the **House of Artists, Smetana Hall,** and the **Palace of Culture.**

Opera and Ballet   Opera is of an especially high standard in Czechoslovakia. The main venues in the grand style of the 19th century are the beautifully restored **National Theater** and **Smetana Theater.** The even older **Týl Theater** is under restoration until 1992.

Theater   You won't need to know the language at **Divadlo na Zabradlí** (Theater on the Balustrade, Anenské náměstí 5), home of the famous Black Theater mime group when it is (rather rarely) in Prague. **Laterna Magika** (Magic Lantern, Národní 40) is a popular extravaganza combining live actors, mime, and sophisticated film techniques.

Puppet Shows   These are brought to a high art form at the **Špejbl and Hurvínek Theater** (Římská 45).

Nightlife

Cabaret   **The Alhambra** (Václavské náměstí 5) has a three-part floor show. More moderately priced is **Variete Praha** (Vodičkova 30). You'll find plenty of fellow foreigners at both.

Discos   The best-known and most crowded is at the **Zlatá Husa** hotel (*see* Lodging). There's one at each of the three hotels on the Vltava River: **Amirál** (Hořejši nábřeží), **Albatros** (nábřeží L. Svobody), and **Racek** (Dvorecká louka).

Bohemian Spas and Castles

The Bohemian countryside is a restful world of gentle hills and thick woods. It is especially beautiful during fall foliage or in May, when the fruit trees that line the roads are in blossom. In such settings lie the two most famous of Czechoslovakia's scores of spas: Karlovy Vary and Mariánské Lázně. In the 19th and early 20th centuries, the royalty and aristocrats of Europe who came to ease their over indulged bodies (or indulge them even more!), knew these spas as Karlsbad and Marienbad.

To the south, the higher wooded hills of Šumava, bordering West Germany, have their own folklore and give rise to the headwaters of the Vltava. You'll follow its tortuous course toward Prague as you enter South Bohemia, which probably has spawned more castles than any other region of comparable size. The medieval towns of South Bohemia are exquisite, though be prepared to find them in varying stages of repair or decay. In such towns was the Hussite reformist movement born in the early 15th century, sparking off a series of religious conflicts that eventually embroiled all Europe.

Getting Around

Though there are bus connections throughout the area, you may have problems sorting out the timetables. The most convenient way to follow the whole of this itinerary is by car.

Guided Tours

Many of the attractions on this itinerary, and some additional ones in Moravia, are covered by Čedok's escorted seven-day "Short Tour of Czechoslovakia" out of Prague. Most can also be visited on a series of day trips from the capital.

Tourist Information

České Budějovice. Hronznova 21, tel. 038/32381.
Český Krumlov. Gottwaldovo náměstí, tel. 0337/2062.
Domažlice. Náměsti Míru 129, tel. 0189/2713.
Karlovy Vary. Tržiště 23, tel. 017/27798.
Mariánské Lázně. Odborářů 48, tel. 0165/2500.
Tábor. Tř. 9 května 1282, tel. 0361/144585.

Exploring Bohemian Spas and Castles

If you're traveling by car, the best—though not fastest—route is to head south from Prague on Highway 4, then west along minor roads up the Berounka Valley, taking in the castles of **Karlštejn** and **Křivoklát**. The first is an admirable restoration of the 14th-century castle built by Charles IV, but not worth the uphill slog unless the stunning Chapel of the Holy Rood is re-opened, its walls covered with 128 Gothic paintings and encrusted with 2,000 gems. **Křivoklát's** main attractions are its glorious woodlands, a favorite royal hunting ground in times past. *Both castles open Tues.–Sun. 9–6; closed the day after public holidays.*

Karlovy Vary, or Karlsbad, was named after Charles IV who, while out hunting, was supposedly led to the main thermal spring of Vřídlo by a fleeing deer. In due course, the spa drew not only many of the crowned heads and much of the blue blood of Europe but also leading musicians and writers. The same parks, promenades, and colonnades still border the little river Teplá, beneath wooded hills. For all its later buildings and proletarian patients, socialist Karlovy Vary still has a great deal of elegance. The waters from the spa's 12 springs are uniformly foul-tasting. The thing to do is sip them from traditionally shaped cups while nibbling rich Karlovy Vary wafers *(oplatky)*, then resort to the "13th spring," Karlovy Vary's tangy herbal liqueur called *Becherovka.*

Karlovy Vary and **Mariánské Lázně** have Czechoslovakia's two best golf courses. As a spa, Mariánské Lázně is younger and smaller, yet its more open setting gives it an air of greater spaciousness. It was much favored by Britain's Edward VII, though from all accounts, he didn't waste too much time on strict diets and rigorous treatments.

The spas of west Bohemia have long catered to foreign travelers. As you head south to the higher Šumava mountains bordering West Germany, you'll be following much less frequented trails. **Domažlice** is the heart of the region of the

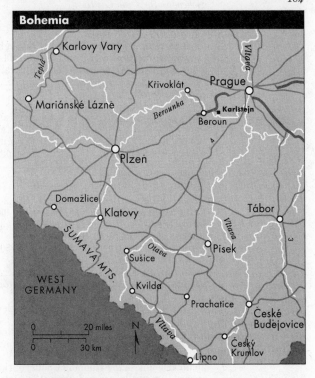

Bohemia

Chods, for centuries guardians of Bohemia's frontiers, a function that earned them a number of privileges. Their special folk culture is still very much alive, not least in their pottery and their contagious dances accompanied by local bagpipes (main festival in mid-August). It is a beautiful little town with a lovely arcaded square, old fortifications, and a castle that houses the **Chod Museum** of local folk culture. *Open Tues.–Sun. 8–noon and 1–4:30.*

From Domažlice runs a tortuous but extremely pretty route, mainly along minor roads, through Sušice along the upper Otava River and over the hills to Prachatice and back to **Kvilda**, where the road joins the young Vltava River. Downstream, the Vltava has been trapped to form the great reservoir and recreational area of **Lipno.** You skirt part of it before turning northeast to Český Krumlov.

The whole of this part of South Bohemia has strong associations with feudal families such as the Rožmberks, who peppered the countryside with their castles and created lake-size "ponds" in which to breed highly prized carp, still the main feature of a Czech Christmas dinner. Once the main seat of the Rožmberks,

Český Krumlov will be a magic place when all the scaffolding has finally been removed. The Vltava River snakes through the town, which is steeply stacked on either bank, with flights of steps linking various levels and with twisting narrow lanes converging on **Gottwaldovo náměstí**, the main square of the Old Town. There are arcades and courtyards and, of course, a Rožmberk Castle, this one with an 18th-century theater.

Ceské Budějovice is on a much larger scale, and here your main stop should be the massive but handsome Žižka Square. The town, originally called Budweis, produces Budvar beer. The townsfolk will be happy to express their own colorful views on its American near-namesake!

Farther north along Highway 3 is Tábor, the very cradle of the Hussite movement. Its twisting streets were designed to confuse the enemy. A labyrinth of tunnels and cellars below the town were used both as living quarters and as links with the outer defenses. Their story is told in the Hussite Museum in the 16th-century town hall on Žižka Square. *It should be open daily 9–5 following restoration in 1991.*

Dining and Lodging

For details and price category definitions, *see* Dining and Lodging in Staying in Czechoslovakia.

Ceský Krumlov
Lodging

Krumlov (Interhotel). This 19th-century town house will be a charmer, once it—and the rest of this town—has been restored. It's in the center of the old town. *Gottwaldovo náměstí 14, tel. 0337/2255–8. 36 rooms, 13 with bath. AE, DC, MC, V. Inexpensive.*

Karlovy Vary
Lodging
★

Grand Hotel Pupp-Moskva (Interhotel). Founded in the early 18th century, the Moskva still features a fine 18th-century hall, Slavností sál. It's one of the oldest surviving hotels in Europe, with a glittering list of guests, both past and present. *Mírové náměstí 2, tel. 017/22121–5. 170 rooms with bath. Facilities: saunas, tennis, golf, riding, 2 nightclubs, several restaurants and taverns. AE, DC, MC, V. Very Expensive–Expensive.*

Parkhotel (Interhotel). This grande dame will soon celebrate its first centenary. One of its two restaurants specializes in Oriental foods, a rarity in this country. Prices decrease to Moderate in low season. *Mírové náměstí 2, tel. 017/22121–5. 117 rooms with bath. Facilities: saunas, nightclub. AE, DC, MC, V. Expensive.*

Mariánské Lázně
Lodging
★

Golf (Interhotel). Built around 1930 and renovated in 1982, this hotel is located a bit out of town by the golf course. The decor is traditional and the restaurant serves good regional dishes such as dumplings. *Zádub 55, tel. 0165/2651–6. 26 rooms with bath. Facilities: pool, tennis, golf, riding. AE, DC, MC, V. Very Expensive, but Moderate in low season.*

Palace Praha (Interhotel). Built in 1875 during the spa's heyday, this elegant building is conveniently situated just within the resort center. French foods are the specialty at one of the hotel's two restaurants. *Třída Odborářů 67, tel. 0165/2222. 35 rooms, 23 with bath. Facilities: nightclub. AE, DC, MC, V. Moderate.*

Highlights of Slovakia

Even if it had not developed quite separately for nearly a millennium under Hungarian or Hapsburg rule, Slovakia would be different from Bohemia in a great many aspects. Its mountains are higher and more rugged, its veneer less sophisticated, its people more carefree. Their talent for spinning a good yarn and their independent spirit have led many to compare them with the Irish. And as with the Irish, Slovakia's folk culture is particularly rich.

Most visitors head for the great peaks of the High Tatras, with their excellent tourist facilities; and this is where most tours will take you. The mountains *are* spectacular, but also worth seeing are the exquisite medieval town of **Spiš** in the plains and valleys below the High Tatras and the beautiful 18th-century country churches farther east. Away from main centers, these areas are short on tourist amenities; so if creature comforts are important to you, stick to the High Tatras.

Getting Around

ČSA's flights from Bratislava to Poprad (for the High Tatras) connect with services from Prague once or twice daily; the journey takes about 40 minutes. From Bratislava to Poprad by bus takes 5–6 hours; by train 6–7 hours. The bus from Poprad to Prešov takes 2[1/2] hours from here it takes about 40 minutes by train, a little longer by bus, to Bardejov. You can then return directly by bus from Bardejov to Poprad.

Guided Tours

Čedok's "Seven-day Tour of Slovakia" leaves from Bratislava and takes in most of the places on this itinerary, plus a few more. From the High Tatras resorts, day trips include either some of the Spiš towns or Červený Kláštor and the Pieniny National Park.

Tourist Information

Bardejov. Námestie osvoboditelov 46, tel. 0935/2134.
Bratislava. Štúrova 13, tel. 07/55280.
Prešov. Ul. Slov. Republiky rád 1, tel. 091/24040.
Smokovec, Starý Smokovec V/22, tel. 0969/2417.
Žilina. Hodžova 9, tel. 089/23347.

Exploring Slovakia

It may come as a surprise that for 300 years **Bratislava** was the capital of Hungary (after Buda and Pest fell to the Turks in the 15th century). The Hungarians knew it as Pozsony and the Hapsburgs, who subsequently took it over, as Pressburg. It wasn't until 1918 that it regained its Slavic name.

In the 18th century, royal and noble families built patrician houses that still add much charm to the narrow streets of the old town, currently undergoing restoration below the **castle.** The castle has been virtually rebuilt since World War II, and is a good point from which to get your bearings as you look down on the broad waters of the Danube, the Gothic spire of the **Cathedral of St. Martin**—where Hungarian kings and queens were crowned—and the huddled roofs of the old town.

Down in the old town there's architectural interest on almost every street, particularly on the square of Primaciálne námestie, with its Gothic-Renaissance **Old Town Hall** and its elegant **Primate's Palace.** The palace has some lovely 17th-century tapestries (made in the royal workshops at Mortlake

Slovakia

near London), depicting the legend of Hero and Leander. *Primaciálne námestie. Open Tues.–Sun. 9–5.*

Whether you travel by car, bus, or train, your route will follow the Vah valley for most of the way to **Poprad,** a transit point for the High Tatras, and, unfortunately, a dreary place. Its suburb of **Spišská Sobota,** however, is a little gem. It was one of 24 small Gothic towns in a medieval region known as Spiš. Steep shingled roofs, high timber-framed gables, and brick-arched doorways are the main features of the rich merchants' dwellings, usually grouped around a main square dominated by a Gothic church, often with a separate Renaissance bell tower. Keep in mind the name Pavol of Levoča, one of the great woodcarvers of the 16th century. The main altar in **Sv. Juraj** (the Church of St. George) is his work.

An electric train network and the so-called Freedom Road link the resorts strung out on the lower slopes of the High Tatras. **Štrbské Pleso** is the highest of the towns and the best launching point for mountain excursions. **Smokovec** is really three resorts in one (Starý, Nový, and Horný) and has the most varied amenities. For the most effortless high-level trip, though, go to **Tatranská Lomnica,** from where a two-stage cable car will take you via Skalnaté pleso (lake) to Lomnický štít, which is 8,635 feet high. The upper stage is being reconstructed but should reopen in 1990. The **Museum of the Tatra National Park** at Tatranská Lomnica offers an excellent introduction to the area's natural and human history. *Admission: 4 Kčs. Open weekdays 8–noon and 1–5, weekends 8–noon.*

Leave Poprad on Highway 18 east. Restoration work on **Levoča**, the most famous of the Spiš towns, is well under way, and the overlays of Renaissance on Gothic are extremely satisfying to the eye (note especially Nos. 43, 45, 47, and 49 on the main square). Pavol of Levoča's work on the main altar of **Sv. Jakub** (the Church of St. James) on the main square is both monumental in size and exquisite in its detail.

The surrounding countryside is dotted with more Spiš towns. About 16 kilometers (10 miles) to the east, the massive, partly restored ruins of **Spiš Castle**, above Spišské Podhradie, dominate the surrounding pastures, orchards, and strawberry fields.

Some of **Prešov's** fortifications survive and its spindle-shaped main square is lined with buildings in the Gothic, Renaissance, and Baroque styles. You are now out of Spiš and into Šariš, a region whose proximity to the Orthodox east has left a unique legacy of both Orthodox and Greek Catholic (Uniat) churches. The latter are particularly interesting because, though acknowledging the pope's supremacy, their clergy retain their own liturgy and are permitted to marry.

Bardejov is a splendid walled town and makes the best center from which to set out on a journey of exploration, as long as you're prepared to get lost along some rough minor roads while seeking out the 17th- and 18th-century wooden churches of **Bodružal, Mirola,** and **Šemetkovce**—and the right person to open them up for you. You'll find these churches east and northeast of **Svidník**, near the border with Poland. Easier to find is the 15th-century wood church of **Hvervartov** (Roman Catholic), 10 kilometers (6 miles) southwest of Bardejov—a fascinating example of timber Gothic with some famous 17th-century frescoes.

Dining and Lodging

For details and price category, definitions, *see* Dining and Lodging in Staying in Czechoslovakia.

Bardejov   **Minerál.** This recently renovated modern hotel lies in a quiet
Lodging   location in the spa town of Bardejovské kúpele, 3½ miles from Bardejov. *Bardejovské kúpele, tel. 0935/4122. 60 rooms with shower. Facilities: tennis. No credit cards. Inexpensive.*

Bratislava   **Kláštorna vináren.** Old-town dining can be a delight in the
Dining   vaulted cellars of an old monastery. Slovak specialties include pork fillet, *Liptovský Hradok*, wrapped in cheese pastry. *Pugačevova 2, tel. 07/330430. Reservations advised. No credit cards. Closed Sun. Expensive–Moderate.*

Rybársky cech. The name means "Fishermen's Guild," and this restaurant is in the guild's house on the river embankment below the castle. It has its own aquarium, and, as you'd expect, the emphasis is on fish specialties, prepared by two award-winning chefs. Try the carp. *Žižkova 1, tel. 07/313049. Reservations advised. No credit cards. Closed Mon. Expensive–Moderate.*

Stará sladovňa. The Old Malthouse has been converted into a series of taverns on three floors, serving the best of Czechoslovak beers. The main restaurant is on the top floor. *Cintorínska 32, tel. 07/51151. Reservations not necessary. No credit cards. Expensive–Moderate.*

★ **Slovenská reštaurácia-Luxor.** This is one of the city's best places to try Slovak specialties, prepared by its award-winning chef, Gašpar Fukas. The folk art decor adds to the atmosphere. Try the *pastierska pochút'ka,* spicy potato pancakes filled with diced meat, mushrooms, and onions. *Štúrova ul. 3, tel. 07/ 52881. Reservations advised. AE, DC, MC, V. Closed Sun. Moderate.*

Lodging **Forum Bratislava** (Interhotel). The Forum opened in 1989 in downtown Bratislava, offering top facilities. It houses a French as well as a Slovak restaurant and several cafés and bars. *Mierove námestie 2. 219 rooms with bath. Facilities: saunas, pool, solarium, health club, nightclub. AE, DC, MC, V. Very Expensive.*

Devin (Interhotel). Many American visitors stay at this recently renovated modern building on the Danube bank, near the old town. Its restaurants serve French, Slovak, and Asian food. *Riečna 4, tel. 07/330851-4. 93 rooms, 87 with bath. Facilities: nightclub, 3 restaurants. AE, DC, MC, V. Expensive.*

Juniorhotel Sputnik. This modern hotel occupies a scenic lakeside position about 3 miles outside the city. The best rooms in the house are 211, 311, and 411, all with good views. *Drieňova 14, tel. 07/288084. 95 rooms with bath. Facilities: disco. No credit cards. Moderate.*

Smokovec **Tatranská kúria.** The Tatranská's rustic decor and Slovak spe-
Dining cialties, prepared by award-winning chef Jan Rogoz, will provide some insight into local life. Dishes include *rezeň kúria* (pork cutlets with a cheese and ham filling in a cheese pastry) and *bryndzove pirohy* (cheese-filled pastry served with cream and bacon). *Starý Smokovec, tel. 0969/2806. Reservations not necessary. No credit cards. Moderate.*

Lodging **Bellevue** (Interhotel). This modern high rise lies about 200 yards from the resort center, with well-appointed rooms. Rates include breakfast and dinner. *Horný Smokovec, tel. 0969/2941-3. 103 rooms, 63 with bath. Facilities: saunas, pool. AE, DC, MC, V. Very Expensive–Expensive.*

Grand Hotel (Interhotel). The town's oldest hotel has maintained its fin-de-siècle atmosphere through frequent renovation. It's right in the resort center, with an excellent restaurant. Rates include breakfast and dinner. Rooms without bath are Moderate. *Starý Smokovec, tel. 0969/2154. 83 rooms, some without bath. Facilities: pool, nightclub. AE, DC, MC, V. Very Expensive–Expensive.*

Tatranská **Zbojnícka koliba.** Slovak specialties are prepared over an open
Lomnica fire, amid rustic decor and accompanied by folk music. *Near*
Dining *Grandhotel Praha, tel. 969/967630. Reservations not necessary. No credit cards. Closed weekends. Expensive–Moderate. Dinner only.*

Lodging **Grandhotel Praha** (Interhotel). A renovated turn-of-the-century building, the Grandhotel has large, comfortable rooms decorated with a traditional touch. Rates include breakfast and dinner. *Tatranská Lomnica, tel. 969/967941-5. 92 rooms with bath. Facilities: nightclub. AE, DC, MC, V. Very Expensive–Expensive.*

8 Denmark

Introduction

Ebullience and a sense of humor have earned the Danes a reputation as "the Italians of Scandinavia." While one might expect
that a country comprising over 400 islands might develop an island mentality, the Danes are famous for their openness and
friendliness, and have even coined a term—*hyggelig*—for the
feeling of well-being that comes from their own brand of lively
hospitality.

The stereotype of melancholic Scandinavia doesn't hold here:
not in the café-studded streets of the larger cities, where musicians and peddlers hawk their wares to passersby; not in the
tiny coastal towns, where the houses are the color of ice-cream
flavors; not in the jam sessions that erupt in the Copenhagen
jazz clubs, nor in the equally joyous "jam" sessions involved in
the production of *smørrebrød* (the famous open-face Danish
sandwich). Even the country's indoor/outdoor museums,
where history is reconstructed through full-scale dwellings out
in the open, indicate that Danes don't wish to keep life behind
glass.

They even joke about their undeniably flat landscape. One of
the country's highest hills—dwarfed by any self-respecting
peak abroad—stands in Jutland, at 139.5 meters (450 feet). The
Danes have dubbed it Himmkelbjerget, or Sky Mountain. Denmark is the only Scandinavian country without wild tracts of
forest and lake. This is a land of well-groomed agriculture,
where every acre is rich in orchard and field. Nowhere are you
far from water, as you drive on and off the ferries and bridges
linking the three regions of Jutland, Funen, and Zealand.

It is the sea surrounding the land that has helped shape
Denmark's history. The Vikings were magnificent seafarers
and had seen much of the world by the 8th century. Today, the
Danes remain expert navigators, using the 4,480 kilometers
(2,800 miles) of coastline for sport—there are regattas around
Zealand and Funen—as well as for fishing and trading.

Long one of the world's most liberal countries, Denmark has a
highly developed social welfare system. The hefty taxes are the
subject of grumbles and jokes, but Danes remain proud of their
state-funded medical and educational systems, as well as of
their high standard of living. Evidence of the strong sense of
community spirit is the uniquely Danish institution of the People's High School, or Folkehøjskole, where pupils live in, and
where the shared experience is deemed as important as the
courses taken. In the summer, adults and even entire families
attend these "schools for life," studying anything from weaving
to the philosopher Wittgenstein.

The country that gave the world Isak Dinesen, Hans Christian
Andersen, and Søren Kierkegaard has a long-standing commit-
ment to culture and the arts. In what other nation does the
royal couple translate the writings of Simone de Beauvoir, or
the queen design postage stamps for Christmas? The Danish
Ballet, founded in Copenhagen in 1722, is world-renowned,
while the provinces boast numerous theater groups and opera
houses.

Perhaps Denmark's greatest charm is its manageable size—
about half the size of Maine. The ferry journey from Esbjerg,

Denmark

North
Sea

Skagerrak

SWEDEN

Hirtshals
Skagen
Hjørring
Frederikshavn
Brønderslev
Sæby
Læsø
Hanstholm
Thisted
*Lim-
fjord*
Limfjord
Ålborg
*Ålborg
Bugt*
Kattegat
Nykøping
Hadsund
Lemvig
Skive
Streier
Holstebro
Randers
Anholt
Viborg
JUTLAND
Grenå
Herning
Silkeborg
Ringkøbing
Århus
Ebeltoft
Skanderborg
Samsø
Tisvildeleje
Hornbaek
Grindsted
Horsens
Nykøbing
Helsingør
Skjern
Frederikssund
Hillerød
Billund
Vejle
*Samsø
Bælt*
Kalundborg
Holbæk
Copenhagen
Esbjerg
Holsted
Fredericia
Middelfart
*Store
Bælt*
Ojyderup
Fanø
Kolding
Kerteminde
Slagelse
Zealand
Roskilde
Ribe
Vojens
Assens
Odense
Køge Bugt
Rømø
Haderslev
Funen
Nyborg
Korsør
Ringsted
Køge
Skærbæk
Åbenrå
Lille Bælt
Fåborg
Næstved
St.
Heddinge
Tønder
Als
Svendborg
Langeland
Karrebæksminde
Sønderborg
Troense
Vordingborg
Møn
Aerøskøbing
Rudkøbing
Tranekær
Stege
Aerø
Marstal
Nakskov
Falster
Bornholm →
Rødby
Maribo
Nykøbing
Nysted
Lolland
Ostsee

WEST
GERMANY

SWEDEN
Baltic Sea

Bornholm

Rønne

0 ———— 50 miles
0 ———— 75 km

on the western coast of Jutland, to Copenhagen, on the eastern coast of Zealand, takes around five hours, and from there, you can make comfortable, unhurried expeditions by boat, car, bus, or train to cover what is one of the world's most civilized countries.

Before You Go

When to Go Most travelers visit Denmark in the warmest months, July and August, but there are advantages to coming in May, June, or September, when sights are less crowded and many establishments offer off-season discounts. However, few places in Denmark are ever unpleasantly crowded, and when the Danes make their annual exodus to the beaches, the cities have even more breathing space. Visitors may want to avoid the winter months, when the days are short and dark, and when important attractions, Tivoli included, close for the season.

Climate The following are the average daily maximum and minimum temperatures for Copenhagen.

Jan.	36F	2C	May	61F	16C	Sept.	64F	18C
	28	−2		46	8		51	11
Feb.	36F	2C	June	67F	19C	Oct.	54F	12C
	28	−3		52	11		44	7
Mar.	41F	5C	July	71F	22C	Nov.	45F	7C
	31	−1		57	14		38	3
Apr.	51F	10C	Aug.	70F	21C	Dec.	40F	4C
	38	3		56	14		34	1

Currency The monetary unit in Denmark is the krone (kr. or DKK), which is divided into 100 øre. At press time (spring 1989), the krone stood at 7.4 to the dollar and 12.3 to the pound sterling. Most well-known credit cards are accepted in Denmark, though the American Express card is accepted less frequently than others. Traveler's checks can be changed in banks or in many hotels, restaurants, and shops.

What it Will Cost Denmark's economy is stable, and inflation remains reasonably low, without wild fluctuations in exchange rates. While Denmark is considerably cheaper than Norway and Sweden, the standard and the cost of living are nonetheless high, especially for luxuries such as alcohol. Prices are highest in Copenhagen, while the least expensive areas are Funen and Jutland.

Sample Prices Cup of coffee, 8–15 kr.; bottle of beer, 15–18 kr.; soda, 10 kr.; ham sandwich 24 kr.; 1-mile taxi ride, 20 kr.

Customs on Arrival If you are entering Denmark from a country that is a member of the European Economic Community (EEC): You may import duty-free one and a half liters of liquor or three liters of strong wine (under 22%), plus four liters of other wine. U.S. residents may import 300 cigarettes or 75 cigars or 250 grams of tobacco; U.K. residents may import 300 cigarettes or 75 cigars or 400 grams of tobacco. Other articles may be brought in up to a maximum of 2,800 kr.; you are also allowed 75 grams of perfume.

If you are entering Denmark from a non-EEC country: You may import duty-free one liter of liquor or two liters of strong wine plus two liters of other wine. Tobacco regulations for U.S. residents are the same as above; U.K. residents may import

200 cigarettes or 50 cigars or 250 grams of tobacco. Other articles (including beer) are allowed up to a maximum of 375 kr.; you are also allowed 50 grams of perfume.

Language A wit once said that Danish was not so much a language as "a disease of the throat." It is a difficult tongue for foreigners, except those from Norway and Sweden, to understand, let alone speak. Danes are good linguists, however, and almost everyone, except elderly people in rural areas, speaks English well.

Getting Around

By Car
Road Conditions Roads here are good and largely traffic-free (except around Copenhagen); you can reach many islands by toll-free bridges.

Rules of the Road The driver needs a valid driver's license, and, if you're using your own car, it must have a certificate of registration and national plates. A triangular hazard-warning sign is compulsory in every car and is provided with a rented car. The driver and front-seat passengers must wear seat belts. Motorcyclists must wear helmets and use low-beam headlights always.

Drive on the right and give way to traffic from the right. A red-and-white triangular Yield sign, or a line of white triangles across the road, means you must yield to traffic on the road you are entering. Do not turn right on a red light, even if the road is clear, unless a green arrow indicates otherwise. Low-beam headlights are compulsory in the dark, mist, or fog; legally, parking lights are not sufficient. Speed limits are 50 kph (30 mph) in built-up areas; on highways, 100 kph (60 mph); and on other roads, 80 kph (50 mph). If you are towing a trailer, you must not exceed 70 kph (40 mph). Speeding and, especially, drinking and driving, are treated severely, even if no damage is caused.

Parking You can usually park on the right-hand side of the road, though not on main roads and highways. "Parkering/Standsning Forbudt" means no parking and no stopping, though you are allowed a three-minute grace period to load and unload. In towns, parking disks are used where there are no parking meters. Get disks from gas stations, post offices, police stations, or tourist offices, and set them to show your time of arrival. Parking for an hour is 9 kr. in Copenhagen, 7 kr. elsewhere.

Gasoline Gas costs around 6.82 kr. a liter.

Breakdowns Before leaving home, consult your insurance company. Members of organizations affiliated with Alliance International de Tourisme (AIT) can get technical and legal assistance from the **Danish Motoring Organization** (FDM) (Blegdamsvej 124, DK 1200 Copenhagen, tel. 01/38–21–12). All highways have emergency phones, and you can even phone the car rental company for help. If you cannot drive your car to a garage for repairs, the rescue corps, **Falck** (tel. 01/14–22–22), can help anywhere, night or day.

By Train and Bus Traveling by train or bus is easy because Danish State Railways (DSB) and a few private companies cover the country with a dense network of services, supplemented by buses in remote areas. Hourly intercity trains connect the main towns in Jutland and Funen with Copenhagen and Zealand, using high-speed diesels, called Lyntog (lightning trains), on the most important stretches. All these trains make the one-hour ferry crossing of the Great Belt, the waterway separating Funen and Zealand. You can reserve seats on intercity trains and Lyntog, and you *must* have a reservation if you plan to cross the Great Belt. Buy tickets at stations for trains, buses, and connecting ferry crossings. You can usually buy tickets on the bus itself. Children under age five travel free and those between five and 12 go half-price. Ask about discounts for senior citizens and groups.

Fares   The **Nordpass** (Nordic Tourist Ticket) is a good buy for 21 days of unlimited travel by rail and on some sea routes in Denmark, Norway, Sweden, and Finland. The price for an adult traveling second-class is 1,550 kr.; 1,160 kr. for young adults (12–26).

By Boat   Denmark has an excellent ferry service, with both domestic and international routes. There is frequent service to Germany, Poland, Sweden, Norway, and the Faroe Islands, as well as to Britain. Domestic ferries provide services between the three areas of Jutland, Funen, and Zealand, and to the smaller islands, 100 of which are inhabited. Danish State Railways and several private shipping companies publish timetables in English, and you should reserve on domestic as well as overseas routes. Ask about off-season discounts.

By Bicycle   It is said that the Danes have the greatest number of bikes per capita in the world, and indeed, with its flat landscape and uncrowded roads, Denmark is a cycler's paradise. You can rent bikes at some train stations and many tourist offices as well as from private firms. Further information on cycling can be supplied by the **Danish Cyclists' Association** (Dansk Cyklist Forbund) (Kjeld Langes Gade 14, DK 1367 Copenhagen). Danish tourist offices publish the pamphlet *Cycling Holiday in Denmark.*

Staying in Denmark

Telephones   Pay phones take 25 øre and 1, 5, and 10 kr. coins. Dial first, then
Local calls   insert your coins when you make your connection. You must use the area codes even when dialing a local number.

International Calls   Dial 009, then the country code, the area code, and the number. Hotels add a hefty service charge, so it's best to use a pay phone.

Operators and   To speak to an operator, most of whom speak English, dial
Information   0033; for an international operator, dial 0039.

Mail   Surface and airmail letters to the United States cost 4.10 kr. for
Postal Rates   20 grams; postcards 3.20 kr.; aerograms 2.40 kr. Letters to the United Kingdom and EEC countries cost 3.10 kr.; postcards 3 kr. You can buy stamps at post offices or from shops selling postcards.

Receiving Mail   If you do not know where you will be staying, have mail sent to American Express or Poste Restante at any post office. American Express charges noncardholders $2 for each letter.

Shopping   Visitors from a non-EEC country can save 18% by obtaining a
VAT Refunds   refund of the value-added tax (VAT), at over 1,500 shops displaying a "Tax Free" sign on the window. If the shop sends your purchase direct to your home address, you pay only the sales price, exclusive of VAT, plus dispatch and insurance costs. If you want to take the goods home yourself, pay the full price

in the shop and get a VAT refund at the Danish duty-free shopping center at the Copenhagen airport. You can obtain a copy of the *Tax-Free Shopping Guide* from the tourist office.

Opening and Closing Times

Banks. In Copenhagen, banks are open weekdays 9:30–4 and Thursdays until 6. Several bureaus de change, including the ones at Copenhagen's central station and Copenhagen's airport, stay open until 10 PM. Outside Copenhagen, banking hours vary, so check locally.

Museums. As a rule, museums are open 10–3 or 11–4. In winter, opening hours are shorter, and some museums close for the season. Check the local papers or ask at tourist offices for current times.

Shops. Shops are generally open weekdays 9–5:30; most stay open on Fridays until 7 or 8, and close on Saturdays at 1 or 2.

National Holidays

January 1 (New Year's Day); April 12–16 (Easter); May 11 (Common Prayer); May 24 (Ascension); June 4 (Pentecost Monday); June 5 (Constitution Day; shops close at noon); December 25, 26 (Christmas).

Dining

Danes take their food seriously, and Danish food, however simple, is excellent, with an emphasis on fresh ingredients and careful presentation. Fish and meat are both of top quality in this farming and fishing country, and both are staple ingredients of the famous smørrebrød. Some smørrebrød are huge meals in themselves: Innocent snackers can find themselves faced with a dauntingly large (but nonetheless delicious) mound of fish or meat, slathered with pickle relish, all atop *rugbrød* (rye bread) and *franskbrød* (wheat bread). Another specialty is *wiener brød* (a Danish pastry), an original far superior to anything that dares call itself "Danish pastry" elsewhere.

All Scandinavian countries have versions of the cold table, but Danes claim that theirs, *det store kolde bord*, is the original and the best. It's a celebration meal; the setting of the long table is a work of art—often with paper sculpture and silver platters—and the food itself is a minor miracle of design and decoration.

In hotels and restaurants, the cold table is served at lunch only, though you will find a more limited version at hotel breakfasts—a good bet for budget travelers because you can eat as much as you like. The price-conscious should also keep their eyes open for establishments displaying the "Danmenu" sign. Wherever you see it, you can be certain of a good two-course meal, either lunch or dinner, for 75 kr.

Liquid refreshment is top-notch, too. Denmark boasts more than 50 varieties of beer made by as many breweries; the best-known come from Carlsberg and Tuborg. Those who like harder stuff should try *snaps*, the famous aquavit traditionally drunk with cold food. Do as the locals do, and knock it back after some herring. The Danes have a saying about the herring-snaps combo: "The fish should be swimming."

Mealtimes

The Danes start work early, which means they generally eat lunch at noon. Evening meals are also eaten early, but visitors can be certain of being able to eat and drink until 10 or 11.

Dress

The Danes are a fairly casual lot; and few restaurants require jacket and tie. Even in the most chic establishments, the tone is elegantly casual.

Ratings Meal prices vary little between town and country. While approximate gradings are given below, remember that careful ordering can get you a Moderate meal at a Very Expensive restaurant. Prices are per person and include a first course, main course, and dessert, plus taxes and tip, but not wine. Best bets are indicated by a star ★. At press time (spring 1989), there were 7.4 kr. to the dollar.

Category	All Areas
Very Expensive	over 330 kr.
Expensive	185–330 kr.
Moderate	100–185 kr.
Inexpensive	under 100 kr.

Credit Cards The following credit card abbreviations are used: AE, American Express; DC, Diners Club; MC, MasterCard; V, Visa.

Lodging Accommodations in Denmark range from the spare and comfortable to the resplendent. Even inexpensive hotels offer simple designs in good materials, and good firm beds. Many Danes prefer a shower to a bath, so if you particularly want a tub, ask for it, but be prepared to pay more. Farmhouse and *kro* (inn) accommodations offer a terrific alternative to more traditional hotels. Except in the case of rentals, breakfast and taxes are usually included in prices, but check when making a reservation.

Hotels Luxury hotels in the city or countryside offer rooms of a high standard, and in a manor-house hotel, you may find yourself sleeping in a four-poster bed. Less expensive accommodations, however, are uniformly clean and comfortable.

Inns A cheaper and charming alternative to hotels are the old stagecoach kro inns scattered throughout Denmark. You can save money by investing in a book of Inn Checks, valid at 66 inns. Each check costs 195 kr. and includes one overnight stay in a double room with bath, breakfast included.

Farm Vacations These are perhaps the best way to see how the Danes live and work. You stay on a farm and share meals with the family; you can even get out and help with the chores. There's a minimum stay of three nights; half board runs around 200 kr., while full board costs 230 kr. Contact the **Horsens Tourist Office** (Søndergade 26, DK 8700 Horsens, Jutland, tel. 75/62–38–22) for details.

Youth Hostels The 95 youth hostels in Denmark are excellent, and are open to all, regardless of age. If you have an International Youth Hostels Association card (obtainable before you leave home), the average rate is 50 kr. Without the card, there's a surcharge of 18 kr.

Rentals Many Danes rent out their summer homes, and a stay in one of these is another good way to see the countryside on your own terms. A simple house with room for four will cost from 1,000 kr. per week. Contact the Danish Tourist Board for details.

Camping Denmark has over 500 approved campsites, with a rating system of one, two, or three stars. You need an International Camping Carnet or Danish Camping Pass (available at any campsite and valid for one year). For more details on camping and discounts for groups and families, contact **Campingradet** (Olof Palmes Gade 10, DK 2100 Copenhagen, tel. 31/42–32–22).

Ratings Prices are for two people in a double room and include service and taxes, and usually breakfast. Best bets are indicated by a star ★. At press time (spring 1989), there were 7.3 kroer to the dollar.

Category	Copenhagen	Other Areas
Very Expensive	over 1,100 kr.	over 700 kr.
Expensive	800–1,100 kr.	550–700 kr.
Moderate	670–800 kr.	345–550 kr.
Inexpensive	under 670 kr.	under 345 kr.

Credit Cards The following credit card abbreviations are used: AE, American Express; DC, Diners Club; MC, MasterCard; V, Visa.

Tipping The egalitarian Danes do not expect to be tipped. Service is included in bills for hotels, bars, and restaurants. Taxi drivers round up the fare to the next krone but expect no tip. The exception is hotel porters, who get around 5 kr. per bag; you should also leave 1 or 2 kr. for the use of a public toilet.

Copenhagen

Arriving and Departing

By Plane The main airport for both international and domestic flights is Copenhagen Airport, 10 kilometers (6 miles) from the center of town.

Between the Airport and Downtown There is frequent bus service to the city; the airport bus to the central station leaves every 15 minutes, and the trip takes about 25 minutes. You pay the 24-kr. fare on the bus. For information, call 01/25–24–20. Public buses are half the price and run as often. Bus no. 32 or no. 32H takes you to Rådhus Pladsen, the city-hall square. A taxi ride takes 15 minutes and costs about 80 kr.

By Train Copenhagen's central station is the hub of the train networks. Express trains leave every hour, on the hour, from 6 AM to 10 PM for principal towns in Funen and Jutland. Find out more from **DSB Information** at the central station (tel. 33/14–17–01). You can make reservations at the central station (tel. 33/14–88–00) and most other stations and through travel agents. In Copenhagen, for those with Inter-Rail cards, there is an Inter-Rail Center (open July–Sept. 17, 7 AM–midnight) that offers rest and a bath, and facilities to cook a meal.

Getting Around

By Bus and Suburban Train The best bet for visitors is the **Copenhagen Card**, affording unlimited travel on buses and suburban trains (S-trains), admission to over 40 museums and sights around Zealand, and a reduction on the ferry crossing to Sweden. You can buy the card, which costs 80 kr. (one day), 140 kr. (two days), or 180 kr.

(three days), at tourist offices and hotels, and from travel agents.

Buses and suburban trains operate on the same ticket system and divide Copenhagen and surrounding areas into three zones. Tickets are validated on the time system: On the basic ticket, which costs 8 kr., for an hour, you can travel anywhere in the zone you started in. You can obtain a discount by buying a packet of 10 basic tickets for 70 kr. Get zone information from the 24-hour information service: tel. 31/95–17–01 for buses, 33/14–17–01 for S-trains. Buses and S-trains run from 5 AM (6 AM on Sundays) to 12:30 AM.

By Car Copenhagen is a city for walkers, not drivers. The charm of its pedestrian streets is paid for by a complicated one-way road system and difficult parking. Leave your car in the garage: Attractions are relatively close together, and public transportation is excellent.

By Taxi Taxis are not cheap, but all are metered. The base charge is 12 kr., plus 8–10 kr. per kilometer. A cab is available when it displays the sign "Fri" (Free); it can be hailed or picked up at a taxi stand, or tel. 31/35–35–35.

By Bicycle More than half the five million Danes are said to ride bikes, which are popular with visitors as well. Bike rental costs 30–50 kr. a day, with a deposit of 100–200 kr. Contact **Danwheel-Rent-a-Bike** (Colbjørnsensgade 3, tel. 31/21–22–27); or **Urania Cykler** (Gammel Kongevej 1, tel. 31/21–80–88).

Important Addresses and Numbers

Tourist Information The main tourist information office is **Danmarks Turistråd** (Danish Tourist Board) (H. C. Andersens Boulevard 22, DK 1553 Copenhagen, tel. 33/11–13–25). Located opposite city hall, it is open May–Sept., weekdays 9–6, Sat. 9–2, Sun. 9–1; Oct.–Apr., weekdays 9–5, Sat. 9–noon, closed Sun. In summer, there are also offices at Elsinore, Hillerød, Køge, Roskilde, Gilleleje, Hundersted, and Tisvildeleje. Youth information in Copenhagen is available at **Huset** (Rådhusstraede 13, tel. 33/15–65–18).

Embassies U.S.: Dag Hammarskjöldsallé 24, tel. 31/42–31–44. **Canada:** Kristen Benikowsgade 1, tel. 33/12–22–99. **U.K.:** Kastelsvej 40, tel. 31/26–46–00.

Emergencies **Police, Fire, Ambulance:** tel. 000. **Doctor:** tel. 0041 (fees payable in cash only; night fees around 250 kr.). **Dentist: Dental Emergency Service,** Tandlægevagten, 14, Oslo Plads, near Østerport station (no telephone; emergencies only; cash only). **Pharmacies:** The following are open 24 hours in central Copenhagen: **Steno Apotek,** Vesterbrogade 6C, tel. 33/14–82–66; **Sønderbro Apotek,** Amagerbrogade 158 (Amager area), tel. 31/58–01–40; **Glostrup Apotek,** Hovedvegen 101 (Glostruup area), tel. 42/96–00–20.

English Bookstores English-language publications can be found at the central-station newsstand and in most bookstores around town. **Boghallen** (Rådhus Pladsen 37), has a particularly good selection.

Travel Agencies **American Express:** Dagmarhus, Amagertorv 18, tel. 33/12–23–01. **Tiaereboro Rejser:** Rådhus Pladsen 75, tel. 33/11–41–00 (arranges charter flights and accommodations all over Europe).

Guided Tours

Orientation Tours Tours are a good way to get acquainted with Copenhagen. From May to September, you can sail on the Öre Sound on board the **Isefjord,** Denmark's oldest schooner. The four-hour tours include lunch or dinner, and leave from Amaliehavn (tel. 33/15–17–29). The "Harbor and Canal Tour" (by boat) leaves from Gammel Strand and the east side of Kongens Nytorv every half hour from 10 AM, while the following bus tours, monitored by the tourist office, leave from the Lur Blower Column in the Rådhus Pladsen: "City Tour" (May 15–Sept. 11, daily at 10; June 15–Aug., daily at 10, 12, 4); "Grand Tour of Copenhagen" (daily at 11, 1:30); "Royal Tour of Copenhagen" (June–Sept. 11, Tues., Thurs., and Sat. at 10); "City and Harbor Tour" (combined bus and boat; May–Sept. 11, daily 9:30, 1, 3). Tickets are available aboard the bus and boat, or from travel agencies.

Special-Interest Tours The "Carlsberg Brewery Tour" meets at the Elephant Gate (Ny Carlsbervej 140), weekdays at 9, 11, and 2:30; or by arrangement for groups (tel. 31/21–12–21, ext. 1312). Tuborg Breweries also provides tours (Strandvejen 54, bus no. 1 or no. 21) weekdays at 10, 12, and 2:30, or by arrangement for groups (tel. 31/29–33–11). The "Royal Copenhagen Porcelain" tour (Smallegade 45, tel. 31/86–48–48), is given on Tuesdays and Thursdays at 9:45.

Walking Tours Two-hour guided walking tours, organized by the Copenhagen Tourist Information Center, operate all year (English-speaking guides are available in July and August only). The tourist office also has information about a taped cassette tour to take on your own. The "Guided Stroll" walking tour has English-speaking guides daily in July and August, and on weekends from April to October (tel. 31/51–25–90, 42/73–00–66).

Regional Tours The Danish Tourist Board has full details of excursions outside the city, including visits to castles (such as Hamlet's castle), the Viking Ship Museum, and Sweden.

Personal Guides The tourist information center can recommend multilingual guides for individual needs, while travel agents have details on hiring a limousine and guide.

Exploring Copenhagen

When Denmark ruled Norway and Sweden in the 15th century, Copenhagen was the capital of all three countries. Today, it is still the liveliest Scandinavian capital, with around a million inhabitants. It's a city meant for walking, the first in Europe to recognize the value of pedestrian streets in fostering community spirit. As you stroll through the cobbled streets and squares, you'll find that Copenhagen combines the excitement and variety of big-city life with a small-town atmosphere. If there's such a thing as a cozy metropolis, you'll find it here.

Nor are you ever far from water, be it sea or canal. The city itself is built upon two main islands, Slotsholmen and Christianshavn, connected by drawbridges. Walk down Nyhavn Canal, an area formerly haunted by a fairly salty crew of sailors. Now it's gentrified, and the 18th-century houses lining it are filled with chic restaurants. You should linger, too, in the five main pedestrian streets collectively known as "Strøget," with shops, cellar galleries and craft workshops, and street musicians and vendors by the dozen. In summer, Copenhagen moves outside, and the best views of city life are from the sidewalk cafés in the shady squares.

Rådhus Pladsen and Slotsholmen *Numbers in the margin correspond with points of interest on the Copenhagen map.*

The best place to start a stroll is the Rådhus Pladsen (City Hall Square), the hub of Copenhagen's commercial district. The mock-Renaissance building dominating it is the **Rådhus** (city hall), completed in 1905. A statue of Copenhagen's 12th-century founder, Bishop Absalon, sits atop the main entrance. Inside, you can see the first World Clock, an astrological timepiece invented and built by Jens Olsen, and put in motion in 1955. If you're feeling energetic, take a guided tour up the 350-foot tower for a panoramic view. *Rådhus Pladsen, tel. 33/15–38–00. Open weekdays 10–3. Tower tours: weekdays at 11 and 2; Sat. at 11.*

On the right of Rådhus Pladsen is **Lur Blower's Column,** topped by two Vikings blowing an ancient trumpet called a *lur.* The artist took a good deal of artistic license—the lur dates from the Bronze Age, 1500 BC, while the Vikings lived a mere 1,000 years ago. The monument is a starting point for sightseeing tours of the city.

If you continue to the square's northeast corner and turn right, you are in Frederiksberggade, the first of the five pedestrian streets that make up the **Strøget,** Copenhagen's shopping district. Walk past the cafés and trendy boutiques to the double square of **Gammel and Nytorv,** where, on April 16, golden apples (really gilded metal balls) dance on the water jets in the fountain to celebrate the queen's birthday.

Turn down Rådhusstræde toward Frederiksholms Kanal. Here you'll find the entrance to the **National museet** (National Museum), with extensive collections that chronicle Danish cultural history to modern times and display Egyptian, Greek, and Roman antiquities. Viking enthusiasts will want to see the Runic stones in the Danish cultural history section. *Frederiksholms Kanal 12, tel. 33/13–44–11. Admission: free. Open June 16–Sept. 15, Tues.–Sun., 10–4; Sept. 16–June 15, Tues.–Fri. 11–3, weekends noon–4.*

Cross Frederiksholms Kanal to Castle Island, dominated by the massive gray **Christiansborg Slot** (Christiansborg Castle). The complex, which contains the Folketinget (Parliament House) and the Royal Reception Chambers, is situated on the site of the city's first fortress, built by Bishop Absalon in 1167. While the castle that stands was being built at the turn of the century, the National Museum excavated the ruins lying beneath the site. *Ruins. Admission: 5 kr. adults, 2 kr. children. Open daily 10–4; closed Sat. Sept. 11–May. Folketinget. Entrance free. Tours every hour on Sun., 10–4. Reception Rooms. Admission: 18 kr. adults, 7 kr. children. Open June–Aug. Tues.–Sun., English tours at 12, 2, and 4; Sept.–May, Tues.–Fri. and Sun., English tour at 2.*

Also on Castle Island, just north of the castle, is **Thorvaldsens Museum.** The 19th-century Danish sculptor Bertel Thorvaldsen, buried at the center of the museum, was greatly

Copenhagen

Hammerskjölds Al.
Farimagsg.
Kristianiag.
Østbaneg.
Langeliniebrd.
Oslo Plads
Folke Bernadottes Al.
Forbindelsesv.
Langelinie

Yderhavn

22

Stockholmsg.
Øster Anlæg
Greningen
St. Kongensg.
21
Churchill Parken

30

29

Selvg.
Rigensg.
Fredericiag.
Esplanaden
20
Bredg.
Amalieg.
19

27
Kongens Have
Kronprincesseg.
Adelg.
Store Kongensg.
Dronningens Tværg.
18
17
Toldbodg.
15
16

Vognmagerg.
Gammelmønt
Pilestræde
Ny Østerg.
Borgerg.
Gothersg.
Bredg.
Sankt Anna's Plads
Amalieg.

HOLMEN
Kr. Bernikg.
Bremerholm
Kongens Nytorv
Nyhavn
Nyhavn
Canal

Inderhavn

2
Amagertorv.
Østerg.
13
Holbro
14
Heibergsg.
Holbergsg.

Læderstr.
Gammel Strand
Holmens
Havnegade

6
Vindelbro
5
10
Børsg.
Chr. IV's Bro
Knippelsbro

CHRISTIANSHAVN

8
Tøjhusgade
7
Sankt Annæg.

9
Frederiksholms Kanal
Christians Brygge
Torveg
11

Voldg.
Blvd.
Langebro
Langerbrog.
Dronningensg.
Princessg.
Christianshavns Voldg.
Torveg.

Amager Blvd.
Stadsgraven
Vermlandsg.

influenced by the statues and reliefs of classical antiquity. In addition to his own works, there is a collection of paintings and drawings by other artists illustrating the influence of Italy on Denmark's Golden Age artists. *Prins Jørgens Gård. Admission: free. Open May–Sept., daily 10–4; Oct.–Apr., Wed.–Mon. 10–3.*

7 Nearby, **Det Kongelige Bibliotek** (Royal Library), houses the country's largest collection of books, newspapers, and manuscripts.

Look for early records of the Viking journeys to America and Greenland, and the statue of the philosopher Søren Kierkegaard in the garden. *Christians Brygge 8. Admission: free. Open weekdays 9–7, Sat. 9–6.*

8 Close to the library is the **Teaterhistorisk Museum** (Theater History Museum), in the Royal Court Theater of 1766. You can see extensive exhibits in theater and ballet history, then wander around the boxes, stage, and dressing rooms to see where it all happened. *Christianborg Ridebane 18, tel. 33/11–51–76. Admission: 10 kr. adults, 5 kr. children. Open June–Sept., Wed., Fri., and Sun. 2–4; Oct.–May, Wed. and Sun. 2–4.*

Also at this address are the Royal Stables, which display vehicles used by the Danish monarchy from 1776 to the present day. *Admission: 5 kr. adults, 2 kr. children. Open Nov.–Apr. 2–4; May–Oct., Fri.–Sun. 2–4.*

9 Across the street that bears its name is **Tøjhuset Museum** (Royal Armory), with impressive displays of uniforms, weapons, and armor in an arched hall 200 yards long. *Tøjhusgade 3, tel. 33/11–60–37. Admission: free. Open May–Sept., Tues.–Sat. 1–4, Sun. 10–4; Oct.–Apr., Tues.–Sat. 1–3, Sun. 11–4.*

10 A few steps from Tøjhuset is the old stock exchange, **Børsen,** believed to be the oldest still in use—though only on special occasions. It was built by the 16th-century monarch King Christian IV, a scholar and warrior, and architect of much of the city. The king is said to have had a hand at twisting the tails of the four dragons that form the structure's distinctive green copper spire. With its steep roofs, tiny windows, and gables, the building is one of Copenhagen's treasures.

From Børsen, look east across the drawbridge (Knippelsbro) that connects Slotsholmen with Christianshavn, one of the old-
11 est parts of Copenhagen, to the green-and-gold spire of **Vor Frelser's Kirke** (Our Savior's Church). The Gothic structure was built in 1696. Local legend has it that the staircase encircling it was built curling the wrong way around, and that when its architect reached the top and saw what he had done, he jumped. The less impulsive will enjoy the spectacular view from the top. *Skt. Annægade, tel. 31/57–27–98. Admission: 10 kr. adults, 4 kr. children. Open Mar. 15–May, Mon.–Sat. 9–5:30, Sun. noon–3:30; June–Aug., Mon.–Sat. 9–4:30, Sun. noon–4:30; Sept.–Oct., Mon.–Sat. 9–3:30, Sun. noon–3:30. Nov.–Mar. 14, Mon.–Sat. 10–1:30, Sun. noon–1:30.*

Head back to Strøget, turning right along the Vimmelskaftet section. Toward the end and to the left is the 18th-century
12 **Helligånds Kirken** (Church of the Holy Ghost). The choir contains a marble font by the sculptor Thorvaldsen.

In Østergade, the easternmost of the streets that make up
⑬ Strøget, you cannot miss the green spire of **Nikolaj Kirke**
(Nikolaj Church). The building that currently stands was built
in the 20th century—the previous structure, which dated back
to the 13th century, was destroyed by fire in 1728. Today, the
church's role is secular—it's an art gallery and an exhibition
center.

Time Out **Café Nikolaj,** inside the old Nikolaj Kirke, is a good place to
stop for a Danish pastry or a light meal. Its long opening hours
(noon–midnight) and central location make it a popular meeting place. *Closed Sun. and Mon. Inexpensive.*

While Strøget is famous as a shopping area, and elegant stores
abound, it's also where Copenhagen comes to stroll. Outside
the posh displays of the fur and porcelain shops, the sidewalks
have the festive aura of a street fair. Arm yourself with an ice
cream or a portable pastry from one of Strøget's many bakeries, and take in the guitar players, flower and fruit stalls, and
peddlers selling trinkets.

Around the Royal Kongens Nytorv (the King's New Market) is the square mark-
Palace ing the end of Strøget. The **Kongelige Teater** (Danish Royal
⑭ Theater), home of Danish opera and ballet as well as theater,
sits on the south side. The Danish Royal Ballet remains one of
the world's great companies, with a repertoire ranging from
classical to modern. On the western side of the square you'll see
the stately facade of the hotel D'Angleterre, the *grande dame*
of Copenhagen hotels. When former president Reagan visited
Denmark, he couldn't stay there owing to security reasons but
asked for a tour of the place just the same.

The street leading southeast from Kongens Nytorv is Nyhavn.
The recently gentrified canal was a longtime haunt of sailors.
Now restaurants and boutiques outnumber the tattoo shops,
but the area retains a genuine charm, with a fleet of old-time
sailing ships and well-preserved 18th-century buildings. Hans
Christian Andersen lived at both numbers 18 and 20. Nearer
the harbor are old shipping warehouses, including two–
Nyhavn 71 and the Admiral–converted into comfortable hotels.

Turn left at the end of Nyhavn to see the harbor front and then
make an immediate left onto Skt. Annæ Plads. Take the third
right onto Amaliegade. Continue straight ahead for
⑮ **Amalienborg Palace,** the principal royal residence since 1784.
When the royal family is in residence during the fall and winter, the Royal Guard and band march through the city at noon
to change the palace guard. The palace interior is closed to the
public.

Rest a moment on the palace's harbor side, amid the trees and
⑯ fountains of **Amaliehavn Gardens.** Across the square, it's just a
⑰ step to Bredgade and the **Marmorikirken** (Marble Church), a
19th-century Baroque church with a dome that looks several
sizes too large for the building beneath it.

⑱ Bredgade is also home to the exotic onion domes of the **Russiske
Ortodoxe Kirke** (Russian Orthodox Church). Farther on is the
⑲ **Kundindustrimuseet** (Museum of Decorative Art), with a large
selection of European and Oriental handicrafts—ceramics, silverware, and tapestry—and an eclectic selection of musical

instruments. *Bredgade 68, tel. 33/14–94–52. Admission: 12 kr. Open Tues.–Sun. 1–4.*

A little farther on, turn right onto Esplanaden, and come to **㉕ Frihedsmuseet** (Liberty Museum), situated in Churchill Parken. It gives an evocative picture of the heroic Danish Resistance movement in World War II, which managed to save 7,000 Jews from the Nazis by hiding them in homes and hospitals, then smuggling them across to Sweden. *Esplanaden, tel. 33/13–77–14. Admission: free. Open Sept. 16–April, daily 11–3; May–Sept. 15, Tues.–Sat. 10–4, Sun. 10–5.*

At the park's entrance stands the English church, St. Alban's, **㉑** and, in the center, the **Kastellet** (Citadel), with two rings of moats. This was the city's main fortress in the 18th century, but, in a grim reversal, during World War II, the Germans used it as the focal point of their occupation of Denmark. *Admission: free. Open 6 AM to sunset.*

Continue on to the Langelinie, which on Sunday is thronged **㉒** with promenading Danes, and at last to **The Little Mermaid** (*Den Lille Havrue*), the 1913 statue commemorating Hans Christian Andersen's lovelorn creation, and the subject of hundreds of travel posters.

Around the Strøget From Langelinie, take the train or bus from Østerport station back to the center. Walk north from the Strøget on Nørregade **㉓** until you reach **Vor Frue Kirke** (The Church of Our Lady), Copenhagen's cathedral since 1924. The site itself has been a place of worship since the 13th century, when Bishop Absalon built a chapel here. The spare neo-classical facade was a 19th-century revamp, repairing damage incurred during Nelson's famous bombing of the city in 1801. Inside, you can see Thorvaldsen's marble sculptures of Christ and the Apostles, and Moses and David in bronze. *Nørregade, Frue Plads. Open Mon.–Sat. 9–5, Sun. 12–5.*

Head north up Fjolstraede until you come to the main **㉔ university** building, built in the 19th century on the site of the medieval bishops' palace. Past the university, turn right onto **㉕** Krystalgade. On the left is the **synagogue**, designed by the famous contemporary architect Gustav Friedrich Hetsch. Hetsch drew on the Doric and Egyptian styles to create the arklike structure.

㉖ Just across Købmagergade is the **Runde Tårn,** a round tower built as an observatory in 1642 by Christian IV. It is said that Peter the Great of Russia drove a horse and carriage up the 600 feet of the inner staircase. You'll have to walk, but the view's worth it. *Købmagergade, tel. 33/93–66–60. Admission: 10 kr. adults, 4 kr. children. Open Dec.–Mar., daily 11–4; Apr.–May and Sept.–Oct., daily 10–5; June–Aug. 10–8.*

Turn right at Runde Tårn onto Landemærket, then left onto Åbenrå. If your appetite for museums is not yet sated, turn right out of Åbenrå until you reach Gothersgade, where anoth-**㉗** er right, onto Øster Voldgade, will bring you to **Rosenborg Slot.** This Renaissance castle was built by Renaissance man Christian IV and is the home of the Crown Jewels as well as a collection of costumes and royal memorabilia. Don't miss Christian IV's pearl-studded saddle. *Øster Voldgade 4A, tel. 33/15–32–86. Admission: May–Sept. 30 kr. adults, 7 kr. children;*

*Oct.–Apr. 20 kr. adults, 7 kr. children. Open May–Sept., daily
10–4; Oct., daily 11–3; Nov.–Apr., Tues.–Sun. 11–3.*

The palace is surrounded by gardens, and just across Øster
Voldgade is **Botansk Have,** Copenhagen's 25 acres of botanical
gardens, with a rather spectacular Palm House containing
tropical and subtropical plants. There's also an observatory
and a geological museum. *Admission: free. Open May–Aug.,
daily 8:30–6; Sept.–Apr., daily 8:30–4.*

Leave the gardens through the north exit to get to the **Statens
Museum for Kunst** (National Art Gallery), where the official
doorman greets you wearing a uniform with buckled shoes and
a cocked hat. The collection ranges from modern Danish art to
works by Rubens, Dürer, and the Impressionists. Particularly
fine are the museum's 20 Matisses. *Sølvgade 48–50, tel. 33/91–
21–26. Admission: free. Open Tues.–Sun. 10–5.*

Time Out The subterranean **cafeteria** in the museum makes an excellent
place to stop for lunch or a coffee. Art posters deck the walls,
and a cheerful staff serves up hearty lunches. *Inexpensive.*

An adjacent building houses the **Hirschprung Collection** of
19th-century Danish art. The cozy museum features works
from the Golden Age, an era characterized by images of the
play of light and water, reminiscent of so much of the Danish
countryside. *Stockholmsgade 20, tel. 31/42–03–36. Admission:
free. Open Wed.–Sun. 1–4.*

From Stockholmsgade, turn right on Sølvgade and then left on
Øster Søgade, just before the bridge. Continue along the canal
(the street name will change from Øster Søgade to Nørre
Søgade to Vester Søgade) until you reach the head of the harbor. Walk straight ahead and turn left onto Vesterbrogade.

On the right lies Copenhagen's best-known attraction, **Tivoli.**
In the 1840s, the Danish architect Georg Carstensen persuaded
King Christian VIII that an amusement park was the perfect
opiate of the masses, preaching that "when people amuse themselves, they forget politics." In the comparatively short season,
from May to September, about four million people come
through the gates. Tivoli is more sophisticated than a mere
funfair: It boasts a pantomime theater and open-air stage, elegant restaurants, and numerous classical, jazz, and rock
concerts. On weekends there are elaborate fireworks displays
and maneuvers by the Tivoli Guard, a youth version of the
Queen's Royal Guard. Try to see Tivoli at least once by night,
when the trees are illuminated along with the Chinese Pagoda
and the main fountain. *Admission: 27 kr. adults, 13 kr. children. Open Apr. 26–Sept. 16, daily 10 AM–midnight.*

At the southern end of the gardens, on Hans Christian
Andersens Boulevard, is the **Ny Carlsberg Glypotek** (New
Carlsberg Picture Hall). This elaborate neoclassical building
houses a collection of works by Gauguin, Degas, and the Impressionists, as well as Egyptian, Greek, Roman, and French
sculpture. *Dantes Plads 7, tel. 33/91–10–65. Admission: 15 kr.
adults, children free; adults free on Wed. and Sun. Open Sept.–
Apr., Tues.–Sat. noon–3, Sun. 10–4; May–Aug., Tues.–Sun.
10–4.*

Off the Beaten Track

Many of Copenhagen's private galleries are in small, out-of-the-way cellars. Two not to be missed are the **Gallerie Peder Oxe,** (Gråbrødre Torv II), attached to a restaurant of the same name, and **Gallerie Asbæk** (89 Gothersgade), a combination café and exhibition of Danish modern painting.

Those nostalgic for the '60s can get a taste of counterculture at Christiania, a community begun in 1971 when students occupied army barracks. Up to 1,400 people live in the shacks and buildings during the summer; the permanent residents number closer to 800. Giant cartoons and grafitti cover the buildings, preaching drugs, love, and peace. Go on a sunny Sunday afternoon, when mellowed Christianians hang out and listen to the street musicians.

City slickers can experience rural life at **Frilandsmuseet,** an 86-acre museum park a half hour outside the city (take bus no. 184 or the S-train to Sorgenfri). Old farmhouses and cottages have been transported from the Danish countryside and set in gardens. During the summer, visitors can watch sheep-shearing, spinning, and folk-dancing sessions. *Kongevejen 100, Lyngby, tel. 42/85–02–92. Admission: 10 kr. adults, 2 kr. children. Open Apr. 16–Sept., daily 10–5; Oct. 1–15, daily 10–3; Oct. 16 –Apr. 15, Sun. 10–3.*

Excursions from Copenhagen

Helsingør–Kronborg Castle Shakespeare immortalized the town and castle when he chose Kronborg Castle as the setting for *Hamlet.* Dating from 1582, the gabled and turreted structure is about 600 years younger than the fortress we imagine from the setting of Shakespeare's tragedy. Well worth seeing is the 200-foot–long dining hall, the luxurious chapel, and the royal chambers. The ramparts and 12 foot walls are a reminder of the castle's role as coastal bulwark —Sweden is only a few miles away. The town of Helsingør has a number of picturesque streets with 16th-century houses. There is frequent train service to Helsingør station. *Helsingør, tel. 49/21–30–78. Admission: 14 kr. adults, 7 kr. children. Open May–Sept. daily 10–5, Oct. and Apr., daily 11–4, Nov.– Mar., daily 11–3.*

Louisiana A world-class modern art collection is housed in a spectacular building on the "Danish Riviera," the North Zealand coast. Even those who can't tell a Rauschenberg from a Rembrandt should make the 35-kilometer (22-mile) trip to see the setting: It's an elegant rambling structure, set in a large park. In the permanent collection, Warhols vie for space with Giacomettis and Picassos. There are temporary exhibits, as well as concerts and films. In the summer, Danes bring their children and picnic in the sculpture garden. There's also a cafeteria, where you get a great view of the Calder mobile, the sound, and, on a clear day, Sweden.

Louisiana is well worth the half-hour train ride from Copenhagen to Humlebæk. The museum is a 10-minute walk from the station. It's also accessible by the E4 highway and the more scenic coastal road, Strandvejen. *Gammel Strandvej 13, Humlebæk, tel. 42/19–07–19. Admission: 35 kr. Open daily 10–5.*

Roskilde History enthusiasts should head 30 kilometers (19 miles) west of Copenhagen to the bustling market town of Roskilde. A key administrative center in Viking times, it remained one of the largest towns in northern Europe through the Middle Ages. Its population has dwindled, but the legacy of its 1,000-year history lives on in the spectacular cathedral. Built on the site of Denmark's first church, the **Domkirke** (cathedral) has been the burial place of Danish royalty since the 15th century. Inside, four chapels house 38 kings and queens. Strewn with marble tombs, the interior has the feeling of a stately but surreal warehouse. The outside, which has received numerous additions over the centuries, provides a crash course in Danish architecture through the ages: The latest chapel dates from 1985. *Domkirkeplasden, Roskilde. Admission: 3 kr. adults, 1 kr. children. Open Apr.–Sept., weekdays 9–5:45, Sat. 11:30–5:45, Sun. 12:30–5:45; Oct.–Mar., weekdays 10–3:45, Sat. 11:30–3:45, Sun. 12:30–1:45.*

A 10-minute walk south and through the park takes you to the water, and to the **Viking Ship Museum.** Inside are five Viking ships, discovered at the bottom of the Roskilde Fjord in 1962. Detailed placards in English chronicle Viking history. There are also English-language films on the excavation and reconstruction. *Strandengen, Roskilde, tel. 42/35–65–55. Admission: 18 kr. adults, 12 kr. children. Open Apr.–Oct., daily 9–5, Nov.–Mar., daily 10–4.*

Shopping

Gift Ideas While Copenhagen is a mecca for shoppers in search of impeccable designs and top-notch quality, budget shoppers may find bargains elusive. Several ideas for inexpensive gifts include simple table decorations—a porcelain candle-holder or ashtray, or the long-lasting candles, often handmade, for which Scandinavia is famous. Denmark also produces tasteful reproductions of Viking ornaments and jewelry, in bronze as well as silver and gold.

Specialty Shops Synonymous with shopping are Strøget's pedestrian streets. For glass, try **Holmegaard** at Østergade. Just off the street is Pistolstræde, a typical old courtyard that's been lovingly restored and filled with intriguing boutiques. **PosterLand** is the home of the largest collection of art prints and posters in northern Europe. There are specialists such as **Royal Copenhagen Porcelain,** which has a small museum attached, as does **Georg Jensen,** one of Denmark's most famous silversmiths.

Off the eastern end of Strøget on Ny Østergade, the **Pewter Center** has a large pewterware collection, and on Gammel Strand there's another pewter designer, **Selangor Designer,** which started in 1885. Back along Strøget, **Birger Christensen** will offer you a glass of sherry while you look at the furs, unless you decide to take your patronage to their competition, **A. C. Bang. FONA** is the place to buy Bang and Olufsen stereo systems, so renowned that they are in the permanent design collection of New York's Museum of Modern Art.

Dining

Food remains one of the great pleasures of a stay in Copenhagen, a city with over 2,000 restaurants. Traditional Danish fare spans all the price categories: You can order a light lunch of the traditional smørrebrød, snack from a *store kolde bord*, or dine out on lobster and Limfjord oysters. Those strapped for cash can enjoy fast food Danish style, in the form of *hapsdogs* (hot dogs) sold from trucks on the street. Team any of this with some pastry from a bakery (look for them under the sign of the upside-down gold pretzel), and you've got yourself a meal on the go.

The Danes are Francophiles when it comes to food, as the French names on menus in the finer restaurants will reveal. "You can't cook a steak in Denmark without calling it French," joked one respected chef. Currently in vogue is a style fusing elements of nouvelle cuisine with traditional Danish ingredients. Copenhagen has also seen an unprecedented rise of international restaurants, so whether you crave Cantonese or kosher cuisine, you can find it here.

For details and price category definitions, *see* Dining in Staying in Denmark.

Very Expensive **Den Gyldne Fortun-Fiskkaelderen.** The lime-and-white color scheme and dark wooden benches lend Copenhagen's number one seafood restaurant an air of minimalist chic, while the menu remains classic, with such elegant dishes as turbot in puff pastry with lobster sauce. *Ved Stannden 18, tel. 33/12–20–11. Reservations advised. AE, DC, MC, V. Closed lunch on weekends.*

Kong Hans Kaelder. Chef Daniel Letz's French-inspired cooking is superb, while the setting is subterranean and mysterious, with whitewashed arching ceilings, candles, and wooden carvings. *Vingårdsstræde 6, tel. 33/11–68–68. Reservations advised. AE, DC, MC, V. Dinner only. Closed Sun. and mid-July–mid-Aug.*

Pakhuskælderen. Cozily situated in the basement of the Nyhavn 71 hotel, with old Pomeranian beams along the ceilings, this is principally a grill house, serving fish as well as meat dishes, both French and Danish style. Look for det store kolde bord at lunchtime. *Nyhavn 71, tel. 33/11–85–85. Reservations required. AE, DC, MC, V.*

★ **Skt. Gertrude's Kloster.** Chef Even Nielsen prepares international cuisine in this 700-year-old cloister. You feast on fish and meat specialties by the light of 1,200 candles, among vaulted spiral stairways and ecclesiastical antiques. *Hauser Plads 32, tel. 33/14–66–30. Reservations required. AE, DC, MC, V. Dinner only.*

Expensive ★ **L'Alsace.** The paintings of Braque and Chagall deck bright, white walls at L'Alsace, and the food matches the understated elegance of the surroundings. Talented chef Franz Stockhammer's French repertoire includes a delicious rendition of quail, as well as some superb fresh-fruit tarts and cakes for dessert. Ask for a seat with a view of the old courtyard on Pistolstraede. *Ny Østergade 9, tel. 33/14–57–43. Reservations advised. AE, DC, MC, V. Closed Sun.*

La Brasserie. This is the place where Copenhagen's see-and-be-seen set goes to eat. Diners enjoy French-inspired food in charming bistro surroundings, under a giant illuminated clock suspended from the ceiling. *Hotel D'Angleterre, Kongens Nytorv 34, tel. 33/32–01–22. Reservations advised. AE, DC, MC, V.*

Els. When it opened in 1853, the intimate Els was the place to be seen before the theater, and the painted muses on the walls still watch diners rush to make an eight o'clock curtain. The antique wooden columns and furniture complement Chef Ole Mathiesen's nouvelle Danish/French menu. It changes daily and incorporates game, fish, and market-fresh produce. *Stora Strandstæde 3, tel. 33/14–13–41. Reservations advised. AE, DC, MC, V.*

Gilleje. Dining at Gilleje is like being in a scene from a Robert Louis Stevenson novel, since this 113-year-old restaurant is decorated with artifacts from old sea expeditions. Under hanging tortoise shells, diners can feast on Danish and international cuisine. Highlights include whiskey steak flambé and Indonesian rijsttafel, which has been on the menu for nearly half a century. *Nyhavn 10, tel. 33/12–58–58. Reservations advised. AE, DC, MC, V. Closed Sun. and July.*

Moderate

★ **Copenhagen Corner.** Diners get a great view of the Rådhus Pladsen here, and terrific smørrebrød besides. Plants hang from the ceiling, waiters hustle platters of herring, steak, and other Danish/French dishes, and businessmen clink glasses. In summer, you can eat outside. *Rådhus Pladsen, tel. 33/91–45–45. Reservations advised. AE, DC, MC, V.*

Havfruen. A life-size wooden mermaid swings langorously from the ceiling in this snug fish restaurant in Nyhavn. Copenhagen natives love the maritime-bistro ambience, and come for the French-inspired fish specialties. *Nyhavn 39, tel. 33/11–11–39. Reservations advised. DC, MC, V. Closed Sun.*

★ **Ida Davidsen.** A Copenhagen institution, this world-renowned lunch place has become synonymous with smørrebrød. The 56-inch menu came into existence at the beginning of the century —Ida is the fourth generation in the sandwich business. The oven in the back smokes fish and meat, while out front, a buffet displays heartbreakingly beautiful sandwiches, piled high with caviar, salmon, smoked duck, and other elegant ingredients. *Skt. Kongensgade 70, tel. 33/91–36–55. Reservations advised. DC, MC, V. Lunch only. Closed weekends and July.*

Peder Oxe. Located in an 18th-century square in the old center of town, the Peder Oxe is classically elegant, with whitewashed walls, wooden floors, an open fireplace, and crisp damask tablecloths. It's usually crowded with diners from every walk of life. All main courses include a self-service salad bar. *Gråbrøde Torv 11, tel. 33/11–00–77. Reservations accepted. DC, MC, V.*

Inexpensive

Café Asbæk. Attached to a modern art gallery, this little establishment makes creative use of fresh ingredients. The menu changes every day, while the art on the walls changes with every new exhibition. The artist showing in the gallery designs the tablecloths and napkins as well! Try the desserts, made on the premises. *Ny Adelgade 8, tel. 33/12–24–16. Reservations not required. AE, DC, MC, V. Lunch only.*

Green's. A vegetarian buffet by day and a restaurant by night, Green's serves up healthy food with much emphasis on grains, natural sweeteners, and fresh fruit and vegetables. It's frequented by chic bohemians who welcome the classical music and friendly service of the youthful staff. *Grønnegade 12–14, tel. 33/15–16–90. No reservations. No credit cards. Closed Sun.*

Krasnapolsky. It's near the university, and there's a brooding youth at every table. Despite the trendy trappings, the food is light and inventive—market-fresh produce is used religiously. Not as healthy as the quiches and sandwiches, but equally delicious, are the cakes and tarts, made in-house. *Vestergade 10, tel. 33/32–88–00. Reservations not required. No credit cards. Lunch only.*

Lodging

Copenhagen is well served by a wide range of hotels. Steer clear of those in the red-light district behind the train station, but otherwise you can expect your accommodations to be clean, comfortable, and well run. Most Danish hotels include a substantial breakfast in the room rate, but this isn't always the case with foreign chains: Inquire when making reservations. During summer, reservations are always recommended, but if you should arrive without one, try the booking service at the *Vaerelseavivisning kiosk* (Rooms Service booth) in the central station. This service will also locate rooms in private homes, with rates starting at about 110 kr. for a single. Young travelers should head for "Use It" (Huset) at Rådhusstraede 13 (tel. 33/15–65–18); after hours, they can check the bulletin board outside for suggestions for accommodations.

For details and price category definitions, *see* Lodging in Staying in Denmark.

Very Expensive ★ **D'Angleterre.** Clint Eastwood and Bruce Springsteen stay here, as do NATO generals and various heads of state. Built in 1755, the place has recently undergone a $10 million renovation, but it retains its Old World, old-money aura. Rooms are done in pinks and blues, with overstuffed chairs and antique escritoires and armoires. There's a liberal use of brass, mahogany, and marble in the bathrooms, all of which are equipped with telephones. *Kongens Nytorv 34, tel. 33/12–00–95. 139 rooms with bath. Facilities: 2 restaurants, bar, barber, beauty salon. AE, DC, MC, V.*

Nyhavn 71. This cozy hotel started life in 1804 as a humble harbor warehouse, though its subsequent metamorphosis has won several design awards. Ask for a room overlooking the harbor —the quaint, porthole-style windows add to the charm. *Nyhavn 71, tel. 33/11–85–85. 82 rooms with bath. Facilities: restaurant, bar. AE, DC, MC.*

SAS Scandinavia. A modern, cloud-scraping tower, the Scandinavia is the city's tallest building. It's set midway between the airport and downtown, facing the old city moats. The prevalent atmosphere is of efficiency and functionality, tempered with expensive plush. *Amager Blvd. 70, tel. 33/11–23–24. 542 rooms with bath. Facilities: sauna, pool, restaurant, bar, coffee shop. AE, DC, MC, V.*

Expensive **Neptun.** The centrally situated Neptun has been in business for nearly 150 years and shows no signs of flagging. Guest rooms are prettily decorated with mahogany touches, and are usually reserved well in advance by American visitors. *Skt. Annæ Plads 18, tel. 33/13–89–00. 66 rooms, 11 apartments, all with bath. Facilities: restaurant, café, travel agency. AE, DC, MC, V. Closed Dec. 24–Jan. 2.*

★ **Savoy.** Tucked behind clothing stores on a busy shopping street, the Savoy is a hidden treasure, an oasis of peace and fin-de-siècle charm. The rooms are quaint, even countrified, with flowered duvets and matching wallpaper, blond-wood beds, and marble bathrooms. It's said to have the largest single beds in the city. *Vesterbrogade 34, tel. 31/31-40-73. Facilities: restaurant (breakfast only). AE, DC, MC, V.*

Webers. The Webers is a modern hotel housed in a century-old building. Decorators have made liberal use of warm peach tones and understated prints. Light sleepers should try for a room at the back, preferably overlooking the courtyard and its fountain. *Vesterbrogade 11b, tel. 31/31-14-32. 80 rooms with bath. Facilities: restaurant (breakfast only), lounge, bar, solarium. AE, DC, MC, V.*

Moderate **Ascot.** A charming old building in the city's downtown area, the Ascot features an elegant wrought-iron staircase and an excellent breakfast buffet. The rooms have cheerful blue bedspreads and cozy bathrooms. Many have been recently remodeled; a few have kitchenettes. *Studiestræde 57, tel. 33/12-60-00. 105 rooms, 10 apartments, all with bath. Facilities: restaurant, bar. AE, DC, MC.*

Copenhagen Admiral. A converted 18th-century granary, the Admiral has a massive and imposing exterior. Inside, sturdy wooden beams harmonize with an ultramodern decor. A few duplex suites are in the Expensive category. *Toldbrogade 24-28, tel. 33/11-82-82. 366 rooms with bath. Facilities: restaurant, bar, café, shop, sauna. MC, V.*

Excelsior. Housed in a circa-1890 building, this hotel was renovated in 1989. The reception room, decorated in bright primary colors, resembles a postmodern playroom, but the bedrooms are slightly subtler, done in bold blue and white, with modern murals on the walls. The tranquil deck-garden in the back is lovely. *Colbjørnsgade 4, tel. 31/24-50-85. 57 rooms, 42 with bath. Facilities: restaurant (breakfast only), bar. AE, DC, MC, V. Closed two weeks at Christmas.*

Triton. Streamlined and modern, the Triton has a cosmopolitan clientele and a central location. The large rooms, in blond wood and warm tones, are equipped with every modern convenience, and many of the bathrooms have been recently updated with state-of-the-art fixtures. The buffet breakfast is exceptionally generous, as is the friendly staff. *Helgolandsgade 7-11, tel. 31/31-32-66. 123 rooms with bath. Facilities: restaurant, bar. AE, DC, MC, V.*

Inexpensive **Skovshoved.** A charming hotel about 8 kilometers (5 miles) from the center of town, the Skovshoved has as neighbors a few old fishing cottages beside the yacht harbor. Licensed since 1660, it has retained its Old World charm, though it is fully modernized. Individual rooms vary from spacious ones overlooking the sea to smaller rooms overlooking the courtyard. The restaurant provides gourmet dishes but ranks in the Expensive category. *Strandvejen 267, Charlottenlund, tel. 31/64-00-28. 20 rooms with bath. Facilities: conference room. AE, DC, MC, V.*

Viking. A comfortable, century-old former mansion close to Amalienborg Castle, Nyhavn, and the Little Mermaid, the Viking is convenient to most sights and public transportation. Rooms are surprisingly spacious. *Bredgade 65, tel. 33/12-45-50. 90 rooms, 19 with bath. Facilities: restaurant. AE, DC, MC.*

The Arts

Copenhagen This Week has good information on musical and theatrical events, as well as on films and exhibitions. Concert and festival information is available from the **Dansk Musik Information Center (DMIC)** (Vimmelskaftet 48, tel. 33/11–20–86). Copenhagen's main theater and concert season runs from September through May, and tickets can be obtained either directly from theaters and concert halls or from ticket agencies; ask your hotel concierge for advice.

Music Tivoli Concert Hall (Vesterbrogade 3, tel. 33/15–10–12), home of the Zealand Symphony Orchestra, offers more than 150 concerts (many free of charge) each summer, featuring a host of Danish and foreign soloists, conductors, and orchestras.

Theater, Opera, and Ballet The **Royal Theater** (Kongens Nytorv, tel. 33/14–10–02), regularly holds performances alternating among theater, ballet, and opera. For English-language theater, attend a performance at the **Mermaid Theater** (27 Skt. Peder Stræde, tel. 33/11–43–03).

Film Copenhagen natives are avid movie buffs, and as the Danes rarely dub films or television imports, you can often see original American and British movies and TV shows.

Entertainment and Nightlife

Many of the city's restaurants, cafés, bars, and clubs stay open after midnight, some as late as 5 AM. Copenhagen is famous for jazz, but you'll find nightspots catering to musical tastes ranging from bop to ballroom music. Younger tourists should make for the **Minefield,** the district around the Nikolaj Kirke, which holds scores of trendy discos and dance spots, with admission only the price of a beer. **Privé** (Ny Østergade 14) and **U-Matic** (Vestergade 10) are particularly popular with the young set.

A few streets behind the railway station is Copenhagen's red-light district, where sex shops share space with Indian grocers. While the area is fairly well lit and lively, women may feel uncomfortable going there alone at night.

Nightclubs Some of the most exclusive nightclubs are in the biggest hotels: **Fellini's** in the SAS Royal (Hammerichsgade 1, tel. 33/14–14–12); **After Eight** at SAS Scandinavia (Amager Blvd. 70, tel. 33/11–23–24); and the **Penthouse** at the Sheraton (Vester Søgade 6, tel. 33/14–35–35).

Jazz Copenhagen has a worldwide reputation for sophisticated jazz clubs. These are a few of the best: **De Tre Musketerer** (Nikolaj Plads 25); **Jazzhus Monmartre** (Nørregade 41), widely held to be one of the best on the Continent; **Jazzhus Slukefter** (Tivoli); and **La Fontaine** (Kompagnistræde 11).

Funen and the Islands

It was Hans Christian Andersen, the region's most famous native, who dubbed Funen "The Garden of Denmark." Part orchard, part farmland, Funen is sandwiched between Zealand and Jutland, and with its tidy, rolling landscape, seaside towns, manor houses, and castles, it is one of Denmark's loveliest islands.

Its capital is 1,002-year-old Odense in the north, one of Denmark's best-known cities and the birthplace of Hans Christian Andersen. It has two museums detailing his life and works.

In a country crowded with castles, Funen has two of the best-preserved ones: the 12th-century castle, Nyborg Slot, in the east, and the famed 16th-century Egeskov Slot, near Svendborg, in the south.

From Svendborg, it's easy to hop on a ferry and visit some of the smaller islands, such as Tåsinge, Langeland, and Ærø, whose main town, Ærøskøbing, with its twisting streets and half-timbered houses, seems caught in a time warp. The local people speak their own dialect and claim it is the tongue spoken by angels on Sundays!

Getting Around

The best starting point from Copenhagen is over the Great Belt, the waterway separating Zealand and Funen, to Nyborg on Funen's east coast. From there, undoubtedly the easiest way to travel is by car, though public transportation is good. (Get details of car rentals from local tourist offices.) Distances in Funen and its islands are short, but there is much to see and you can easily spend two or three days here. The choice is to circle the islands from Nyborg or to base yourself in Odense or Svendborg and make excursions. Whichever you choose, you can use the following itinerary.

Guided Tours

There are few organized tours of any area of Denmark outside Copenhagen. The Funen town of Odense has a two-hour tour that operates Monday through Saturday during July and August. Expect to see anything and everything to do with native son Hans Christian Andersen.

There's also a day trip to Odense from Copenhagen every Sunday from mid-May to mid-September. Lasting about 11 hours, the trip includes stops at several picturesque villages and a lightning visit to Egeskov Slot. Departure is at 8:30 AM from Copenhagen's city-hall square.

Tourist Information

Nyborg. Torvet 9, tel. 65/31–02–80.
Odense. Rådhuset, tel. 66/12–79–10.
Svendborg. Møllergade 30, tel. 66/21–09–80.

Exploring Funen and the Islands

The 13th-century town of **Nyborg** was Denmark's capital during the Middle Ages, as well as an important stop on a major trading route between Zealand and Jutland. From 1200 to 1413, Nyborg housed the Danehof, the early Danish parliament. Nyborg's major landmark is its 12th-century castle, the **Nyborg Slot.** It was here that Erik Glipping granted the first Danish constitution, the Great Charter, in 1282. Several chambers have striking geometric murals on the walls. There is also an arms and armory collection. *Slotspladsen. Admission: 10 kr. adults, 3 kr. children. Open Mar.–May and Sept.–Nov., Tues.–Sun. 10–3; June–Aug., daily 10–5;*

Take Route 160 northwest to the Avnslev junction, where you pick up Route 165, then drive the 15 kilometers (9 miles) along

Funen and the Islands

the coast to **Kerteminde,** Funen's most important fishing village as well as a picturesque summer resort. It's worth strolling down the Langegade to see its half-timbered houses.

Viking enthusiasts will want to head a few kilometers south to the village of **Ladby.** Stop here to see the **Ladbyskibet,** the 1,100-year-old underground remains of a Viking chieftain's burial, complete with his 72-foot-long ship. The warrior was equipped for his trip to Valhalla (the afterlife) with his weapons, four hunting dogs, and 11 horses. *Vikingsvej 12. Admission: 10 kr. adults, 3 kr. children. Open May–Sept., daily 10–6; Oct.–Apr., daily 10–3.*

Twenty kilometers (12 miles) southwest on Route 165 lies **Odense,** Denmark's third largest city. Plan on spending at least one night here; in addition to its museums and pleasant pedestrian streets, Odense gives one a good feel for a provincial capital.

If you can't take quaintness, don't go to the **H. C. Andersens Hus** (Hans Christian Andersen Museum). The surrounding area has been carefully preserved, with cobbled pedestrian streets and low houses with lace curtains. Inside, the detailed exhibits use photos, diaries, drawings, and letters to convey a sense of the man and the time in which he lived. Among the most evocative rooms is one furnished exactly like his Copenhagen study; notice the immense size of his long, narrow boots, casually tossed into a corner. Attached to the museum is an extensive library with Andersen's works in over 100 languages, where you can listen to fairy tales on tape. *Hans Jensenstræde 37, tel. 66/13-13-72. Admission: 15 kr. adults, 3 kr. children. Open Apr., May, and Sept., daily 10-5; June-Aug., daily 9-6; Oct.-Mar., daily 10-3.*

Nearby is the newly opened **Carl Nielsen Museum,** a modern structure with multimedia exhibits on Denmark's most famous composer (1865-1931) and his wife, the sculptress Anne Marie Carl-Nielsen. *Claus Bergsgade, tel. 66/13-13-72. Admission: 12 kr. adults, 2 kr. children; free Thurs. 4-8. Open Fri.-Wed. 10-4, Thurs. 10-8.*

Montegården, Odense's museum of cultural and urban history, fills four houses built from the Renaissance to the 18th century, all grouped around a shady cobbled courtyard. The innovative exhibits inside feature dioramas, old photos, clothed dummies, and tableaux. *Overgade 48-50. Admission: 5 kr. adults, 1 kr. children. Open daily 10-4.*

Brandt's Passage, off Vestergade, is a heavily boutiqued walking street. At the end of it, in what was once a textile factory, is a four-story art gallery, the Brandts Klædefabrik, incorporating the **Museum for Photographic Art,** the **Graphic Museum,** and other spaces, with temporary exhibits for video art. It's well worth the short walk to see Funen's version of a Soho loft. *37-43 Brandts Passage, tel. 66/13-78-97. Admission: 20 kr. Open Tues.-Sun. 10-7.*

Don't neglect **Den Fynske Landsby** (Funen Village), 3 kilometers (2 miles) south; an enjoyable way of getting there is to travel down the Odense River by boat. The open-air museum-village is made up of 20 farm buildings, including workshops, a vicarage, a water mill, and a windmill. There's a theater, too, which in summer stages adaptations of Andersen's tales. *Sejerskovvej 20, tel. 66/13-13-72. Admission: 10 kr. adults, 2 kr. children. Open Apr.-May and Sept.-Oct., daily 9-4; June -Aug., daily 9-6:30; Nov.-Mar., Sun. and holidays only, 10-4.*

Head 30 kilometers (18 miles) south on Route 43 to **Fåborg,** a lovely little town dating from the 12th century. Four times a day, it echoes to the dulcet chiming of the Klokketårnet's (Belfry's) carillon, the largest in Funen. Dating from 1725, **Den Gamla Gård** (the Old Merchant's House) chronicles the cultural history of Funen. *Holkegade 1, tel. 62/61-33-38. Admission: 10 kr. adults, children free. Open May-Sept., daily 10:30-4:30.*

Take time out to visit the **Fåborg Museum for Fynsk Malerkunst** (Art Gallery for Funen Artists), which has a good collection of paintings and sculpture by the Funen Painters, mainly dating from 1880 to 1920, whose works are full of the dusky light that so often illuminates Scandinavian painting. *Grønnegade 75, tel. 62/61-06-45. Admission: 10 kr. adults, 5 kr. children. Open Apr.-Oct., daily 10-4; Nov.-Mar., weekends 11-3.*

From Fåborg, take the car ferry to Søby at the northern tip of Ærø Island, the "Jewel of the Archipelago," where roads wend through fertile fields and past thatched farmhouses. South from Søby on route 16, 13 kilometers (8 miles), is the charming town of Ærøskøbing on the island's north coast. When you've spent an hour walking through its cobbled 17th- and 18th-century streets you will see why it draws visitors back year after year.

From Ærøskøbing, the ferry takes just over an hour to reach Svendborg, Funen's southernmost town. It's also the gateway to the country's southern islands, so leave it for the moment and cross over the bridge onto the tiny island of **Tåsinge.**

Dating from around 1640, **Valdemars Slot,** now a sumptuously furnished naval museum, is one of Denmark's oldest privately owned castles. Most interesting, however, is the castle church, illuminated only by candlelight, and the castle restaurant (*see* Dining and Lodging) situated beneath the church. The Tea Pavilion is now a café overlooking Lunkebugten Bay, with one of south Funen's best stretches of beach. *Slotsalleen 100, Troense, tel. 62/22–61–06. Admission: 20 kr. adults, 10 kr. children. Open May–Sept., daily 10–5; Oct.–Apr., weekends 10–5.*

Pretty **Troense** is one of Denmark's best-preserved villages. Once the home port for many sailing ships, both commercial and Viking, today the harbor is stuffed with pleasure yachts.

Tåsinge is connected with the island of **Langeland** by a causeway-bridge. The largest island in the southern archipelago, Langeland is rich in relics of the past, and the beaches are worth scouting out.

Head back now, passing through Tåsinge, to Funen's **Svendborg.** Just north of town is **Egeskov Slot,** one of the best-preserved island castles in Europe. Egeskov means "Oak Forest," and an entire one was felled around 1540 to form the piles on which the rose-stone structure was built. The park contains noteworthy Renaissance, Baroque, English, and peasant gardens. Unfortunately, few sections of the castle are open to the public.

Dining and Lodging

Funen boasts a wide range of hotels and inns, many of which offer off-season (October through May) rates, as well as special weekend deals. Inquire about the **Funen Combi Pension,** a flexible package that allows visitors to stay at one place but lunch and dine elsewhere en route. The islands are also endowed with numerous campsites and youth hostels, all clean and attractively located. Some, like Odense's youth hostel, are set in old manor houses. For information, contact the local tourist office. For details and price category definitions, *see* Dining and Lodging in Staying in Denmark.

Ærøskøbing
Lodging

Ærøhus. A half-timbered building with a steep red roof, the Ærøhus looks more like a barn than a hotel. Inside, you'll find rustic simplicity in the simple wooden furniture and cheerful curtains and duvets. The garden's five cottages have small terraces. *Vertegade 38 (Ærø), tel. 62/52–10–03. 35 rooms, 12 with bath; 5 cottages. Facilities: restaurant, garden, terrace. Closed Dec. 27–Jan. 20. Moderate.*

Fåborg
Dining and Lodging

Faldsled Kro. This thatched establishment has been a Danish roadside inn since the 15th century, when it doubled as a smuggler's hideaway. Now a member of the Relais et Châteaux group, it's one of the finest inns in Denmark. The rooms are furnished in a mixture of antiques and contemporary Danish designs; most have a sitting area and a fireplace. The superb restaurant specializes in game and seafood. Try the fresh mussels from the local bed, and order some wine from the exceptional selection. *Assensvej 513, Falsled, 13 km. (8 mi.) northwest of Fåborg on the Millinge—Assens highway, tel. 62/ 68–11–11. 14 rooms with bath. AE, DC, MC. Closed Jan.–Feb. Very Expensive.*

Lodging **Steensgård Herregårdspension.** Set in a magnificent manor house dating from the early 1300s, this is the archetypal stately home hotel. The interior elegantly blends wood paneling, parquet floors, antiques, and porcelain stoves—there's even a resident ghost. The grounds contain a deer and wild-boar shelter. The candle-lit restaurant is top-notch. Try the game if it's on the menu. *Steensgård 4 (Funen), in Millinge, 7 km. (4 mi.) northwest of Fåborg, tel. 62/61–94–90. 15 rooms, 13 with bath. Facilities: tennis, horseback riding, restaurant. AE, DC, MC, V. Closed Jan. Expensive.*

Nyborg **Nyborg Strand.** A seaside location adds to the charm of this typ-
Lodging ical Danish hotel. It's clean, bright, and popular. *Østerovej 2, tel. 65/31–31–31. 247 rooms with bath. Facilities: pool, sauna, game room, restaurant, bar, garden. AE, DC, MC, V. Moderate.*

Odense **Den Gamle Kro.** Copper pots, porcelain stoves, even an old
Dining preaching pulpit decorate The Old Inn, which dates from 1683. Diners eat nouvelle Danish/French cuisine in cozy rooms set around a courtyard. There's outside dining in summer. *Overgade 23, tel. 66/12–14–33. Reservations advised. Expensive.*

Under Lindetræt. An award-winning restaurant set in a 240-year-old building, Under Linden Tree serves classic French cuisine in a cozy private-parlor atmosphere, created by the flower arrangements, low-hanging lamps, and a fireplace. *Ramsherred 2, opposite Hans Christian Andersen's house, tel. 66/12–92–86. Reservations advised. DC, MC, V. Closed July. Expensive.*

Rudolf Mathis. You'll enjoy delectable seafood specialties and a splendid view of Kerteminde harbor at this traditional Danish restaurant. *Dosseringen 13, Munkebo, 13 km. (8 mi.) northeast of Odense on Rte. 165, tel. 65/32–32–33. Reservations accepted. No credit cards. Closed Mon. Moderate.*

Målet. A spirited local clientele frequents this sports club and restaurant filled with soccer memorabilia—there's even a goal set against one wall. Schnitzels are the specialty, prepared with mushrooms, paprika, or even Italian and Madagascar style. *Jernbanegade 17, tel. 66/17–82–41. No reservations. No credit cards. Inexpensive.*

Lodging **Grand.** They don't make spacious, gracious places like this anymore. Dating from 1897, the Grand offers spruced-up fin-de-siècle elegance. There's cool, green decor and lovely marble bathrooms in the rooms, as well as a sweeping staircase and a spectacular Pompeiian red dining room. *Jernbanegade 18, tel. 66/11–71–71. 139 rooms with bath. Facilities: sauna, solarium, restaurant, bar, parking. AE, DC, MC, V. Closed Christmas–New Year's. Very Expensive.*

Missionshotellet Ansgar. The rooms are a trifle boxlike but clean and comfortable nonetheless. This hotel offers solid lodging (with satellite television) near the station. *Østre*

Stationsvej 32, tel. 66/11–96–93. 44 rooms with bath. MC, V. Moderate.

Svendborg **Borgen.** You'll find good local fare at reasonable prices at this
Dining cozy corner overlooking the harbor. Try the shellfish (particularly the mussels) or the eels. *Færgevej 34, tel. 62/21–29–76. Reservations advised. Moderate.*

Troense **Valdemars Slot.** Situated in the ancient vaults beneath the
Dining church of Valdemar Castle, this restaurant provides a cool retreat and an excellent meal. Arched ceilings, tiled floors, and candlelight set the elegant tone. *Slotsalleen 100, Tåsinge, tel. 62/22–59–00. Reservations advised. MC. Closed Mon. Expensive.*

Jutland and the Lakes

The peninsula of Jutland is the only part of Denmark attached to the mainland of Europe; its southern boundary is the frontier with West Germany. It's a region of carefully groomed pastures punctuated by stretches of rugged beauty. The windswept landscapes used in *Babette's Feast*, the film version of Isak Dinesen's novel, are in northwest Jutland. One-tenth of the peninsula consists of moors and sand dunes; the remaining land is devoted to agriculture and forestry. To the east of the peninsula, facing Funen, lie the well-wooded fjords, which run for miles inland.

The region of rustic towns and stark countryside also boasts gracious castles, parklands, and the famed Legoland. Ribe, Denmark's oldest town, lies to the south, while to the east is Århus, Denmark's second largest city, with its superb museums and new concert hall.

Getting Around

If you're following this itinerary directly after the tour around Funen, head northwest from Odense through Middlefart, and then on to Vejle. By train, either from Odense or Copenhagen, the starting point is Kolding, to the south of Vejle. While there are good train and bus services between all the main cities, this tour is best done by car. Delightful though they are, the offshore islands are suitable only for those with a lot of time, since many involve an overnight stay.

Guided Tours

Guided tours are scarce in these parts. However, several Jutland towns, such as Århus, Ålborg, and Silkeborg, offer recorded cassette tours from May to August. Århus also offers a "Round and About the City" tour, which leaves from the tourist office daily from June 20 to Sept. 11 at 10 AM, and conducted walks of the old streets, on Thursdays from June 26 to Aug. 25.

Tourist Information

Ålborg. Østerå 8, tel. 98/12–60–22.
Århus. Rådhuset, tel. 86/12–60–00.
Billund. c/o Legoland A/S, tel. 75/33–19–26.
Herning. Bregade 35, tel. 97/12–44–70.
Kolding. Hellingkorsgade 18, tel. 75/53–21–00.

Randers. Hellingandshuset, Erik Menveds Plads 1, tel. 86/42–44–77.
Ribe. Torvet 3–5, tel. 75/42–15–00.
Silkeborg. Torvet 9, tel. 86/82–19–11.
Vejle. Den Smidske Gård, Søndergade 14, tel. 75/82–19–55.
Viborg. Nytorv 5, tel. 86/62–16–17.

Exploring Jutland and the Lakes

If **Kolding** is your starting point, don't miss the well-preserved 13th-century **Koldinghus** castle, a royal residence during the Middle Ages. *Admission: 12 kr. adults, 6 kr. children. Open Apr.–Sept., daily 10–5; Oct.–Mar., Mon.–Sat. noon–3, Sun. 10–3.*

The **Den Geografiske Have** (Geographical Garden) has a rose garden with over 120 varieties, as well as some 2,000 plants from all parts of the world, arranged geographically. *Admission: 14 kr. adults, 7 kr. children. Open June and Aug., daily 9–7; July, daily 9–8; Sept.–May, daily 10–6.*

Vejle, about 20 kilometers (12 miles) to the north of Kolding, is beautifully positioned on the fjord amid forest-clad hills, looking toward the Kattegat, the strait that divides Jutland and Funen. You can hear the time of day chiming on an old Dominican monastery clock; the clock remains, but the monastery has long since given way to the town's imposing 19th-century city hall.

Leaving Vejle, take the road 10 kilometers (6 miles) north to **Jelling** through the Grejs Valley. In Jelling, you'll find two 10th-century burial mounds marking the seat of King Gorm the Old and his wife, Thyra. Between the mounds are the Jelling runic stones, one of which is known as "Denmark's Certificate of Baptism" because it shows the oldest known figure of Christ in Scandinavia. The inscription explains that the stone was erected by Gorm's son, King Harald Bluetooth, who brought Christianity to the Danes in AD 960.

Head north toward **Silkeborg,** set on the banks of the river Gudena in Jutland's lake district. The region stretches from Silkeborg in the west to Skanderborg in the east, and contains some of Denmark's loveliest scenery, as well as one of the country's meager "mountains." Himmelbjerget, measuring 136 meters (438 feet) above sea level, would be a decent-sized hill just about anywhere else. The best way to explore the area is by water, because the Gudena winds its way some 160 kilometers (100 miles) through lakes and wooded hillsides down to the sea. You can take one of the excursion boats, or, better still, the world's last coal-paddle steamer, *Jjejlen,* based at Silkeborg. Since 1861, it has paddled its way through narrow stretches of fjord, where the treetops meet overhead, to the foot of the Himmelbjerget at Lake Julso. From that point, you can clamber up the narrow paths through the heather and trees to the top, where an 80-foot tower stands sentinel, placed there on Constitution Day in 1875 in memory of King Frederik VII.

Silkeborg's other attraction is housed in the **Silkeborg Kulturhistoriske Museum** (Museum of Culture and History): the 2,200-year-old Tollund Man, one of the so-called bog people, whose corpse was preserved by natural ingredients in the soil and water. *Admission: 10 kr. adults, 5 kr. children. Open Apr.*

0   40 miles
0   60 km

Skagen

Hirtshals

Hjørring

Frederikshavn

Sæby

Skagerrak

Brønderslev

N

Hanstholm

Nørresundby

Thisted

Limfjord

*Lim-
fjord*

Løgstør

Nibe

Ålborg

Nykøping

*Djursland
Peninsula*

Hadsund

Limfjord

Lemvig

Skive

Hobro

Mariager Fjord

Mariager

*Venö
Bugt*

Streier

Holstebro

Viborg

Randers

*Nissum
Fjord*

Gudenå

Auning

*Djursland
Peninsula*

Grenå

Storå

Ringkøbing

Silkeborg

Ebeltoft

Herning

Århus

*Ringkøbing
Fjord*

Skjernå

Skjern

Brande

Skanderborg

Samsø

Grindsted

Givskud

Jelling

Horsens

Varde

Billund

Vejle

Vardeå

Vejle Fjord

Esbjerg

Vejnes

Fredericia

Middelfart

Store Bælt

Holsted

Kolding

Funen

Fanø

*Kongeå
Fladså*

Christiansfeld

Odense

Ribe

Haderslev

Nyborg

Rømø

Skærbæk

Fåborg

Åbenrå

Svendborg

15–Oct. 23, daily 10–5; Oct. 24–Apr. 14, Wed., Sat., and Sun. 12–4.

On the coast, lying directly east of Silkeborg, is **Århus,** Denmark's second largest city. The town is at its liveliest during the 10-day Århus Festival in September, which brings together everything from classical concerts to jazz and folk music, clowning, theater, exhibitions, beer tents, and sports. The town's cathedral, the 15th-century **Domkirke,** is Scandinavia's longest church, and contains a beautifully-executed three-paneled altarpiece. Look up at the whimsical sketches around the drains on the ceiling.

Nearby is the **Vor Frue Kirke,** formerly a Dominican abbey. Underneath the 13th-century structure is the eerie but interesting crypt church, rediscovered in 1955 and, dating from 1060, one of the oldest preserved stone churches in Scandinavia. The vaulted room houses a replica of an old Roman crucifix.

Not to be missed is the town's open-air museum, known as **Den Gamle By** (The Old Town). A sophisticated version of Disneyland, it features 65 half-timbered houses, a mill, and a millstream. The meticulously re-created period interiors range from the 17th to the early 20th centuries. *Købstadsmuseet. Admission: 30 kr. adults, 15 kr. children. Open Apr. and Oct., Mon.–Sat. 10–4, Sun. 10–5; May–Sept., daily 10–5; Nov.–Mar., daily 11–3.*

Set in a 250-acre forest in a park south of Århus is the indoor/outdoor **Møesgard Prehistoric Museum,** with exhibits on ethnography and archaeology, including the famed Grauballe Man, an eerie, well-preserved corpse from 2,000 years ago. Take the "Prehistoric Trail" through the forest, which leads past Stone and Bronze Age displays to some reconstructed houses from Viking times. *Admission: 20 kr. adults, children under 15 free. Open Apr.–Sept. 11, daily 10–5; Sept. 12–Mar., Tues.–Sun. 10–5.*

Heading north 21 kilometers (15 miles), you come to the medieval town of **Randers,** where, in 1340, the Danish patriot Niels Ebbesen killed the German oppressor, Count Gert the Bald of Holstein, whose army was then occupying most of Jutland. To the east of Randers is the Djursland Peninsula, a popular vacation area, with fine manor houses open to the public. If time is of the essence, choose **Gammel Estrup,** a grand 17th-century manor in the tiny village of **Auning;** it's full of rich period furnishings, including an alchemist's cellar. *Admission: 10 kr. adults, 2 kr. children. Manor and farm open May–Oct., daily 10–5; Nov.–Apr., (manor) Tues.–Sun. 11–3, (farm) weekends 11–4.*

Aalborg, 55 kilometers (35 miles) to the north, is set at the narrowest point of the Limfjord, the great waterway of northern Jutland, and the gateway between north and south. You'll find charming combinations of new and old; twisting lanes filled with medieval houses and, nearby, broad modern boulevards. Jomfru Ane Gade is a tiny cobbled street in the center of Aalborg, with a number of restaurants, inns, and sidewalk cafés. Major sights include the magnificent **Jens Bangs Stenhus** (Jens Bang's Stone House). A five-story building dating from 1642, it has an atmospheric restaurant and an excellent wine cellar (*see* Dining and Lodging). You'll also want to take in the Baroque cathedral, the **Budolfi Kirke**, dedicated to the English saint Butolph, and the 15th-century **Helligandsklosteret** (Monastery of the Holy Ghost). One of Denmark's best-preserved monasteries, it is now a home for the elderly.

Just to the north, at **Nørresundby**, is **Lindholm Hoje**, a Viking and Iron Age burial ground, where stones placed in the shape of a ship enclose many of the site's 682 graves. *Admission: free.*

If you have some time to spare, head north up to the tip of Jutland, to **Skagen**, where the picturesque streets and the luminous light have inspired painters and writers alike. The 19th-century Danish artist Holger Drachmann (1846–1908) and his friends founded the Skagen School of painting; you can see their efforts on display in the local **Skagens Museum.** *4 Brondumsvej. Admission: 25 kr. adults, children free. Open Apr. and Oct., daily 10–3; May and Sept., daily 10–5; June–Aug., daily 10–6; Nov.–Mar., daily 11–3.*

Heading south once more, you next come to **Viborg**, whose history goes back to the 8th century, when it was a trading post and a place of pagan sacrifice. Later it became a center of Christianity, with monasteries and an episcopal residence. The 1,000-year-old **Haervejen**, the old military road that starts near here, was once Denmark's most important connection with the outside world. Legend has it that in the 11th century, King Canute set out from Viborg to conquer England; he succeeded, and ruled from 1016 to 1035. Today, you can buy reproductions of a silver coin minted by the king, embossed with the inscription "Knud, Englands Konge" (Canute, King of England).

Built in 1130, Viborg's **Domkirke**, the cathedral, was once the largest granite church in the world. Today only the crypt remains of the original building, restored and reopened in 1876. The early 20th-century biblical frescoes are by Danish painter Joakim Skovgaard.

There's terrific walking country 8 kilometers (5 miles) south of Viborg, beside **Hald So** (Hald Lake) and on the heatherclad **Dollerup Bakker** (Dollerup Hills). Next head southwest 45 kilometers (28 miles) to **Herning**, an old moorland town whose flourishing knitwear industry is based on original farmhouse knitting. Don't miss the remarkable circular house, with its 400-foot outer frieze by contemporary artist Carl-Henning Pedersen; it houses the **Carl-Henning Pedersen and Else Afelt's Museum**, set within a sculpture park. *Admission: 20 kr. adults, children free. Open daily 10–4.*

About 100 kilometers (60 miles) to the south, but well worth the extra driving time, is **Ribe**, Denmark's oldest town, whose medieval town center is preserved by the Danish National Trust. From May to mid-September, a night watchman goes around the town telling of its ancient history and singing traditional songs. Visitors can accompany him nightly by gathering at the main square at 10 PM.

The town's present cathedral stands on the site of one of Denmark's earliest churches, built around AD 860. The present structure dates from the 12th century, with a 14th-century bell tower. Note the Cat Head Door: It's said to be for the exclusive use of the devil.

Time Out Hospitality is the rule of the house at the old inn known as **Weis'** **Stue,** on Ribe's market square. Stop in for a meal—or even stay the night in one of the nine bedrooms—and admire the 400-year-old clock in the parlor, a carved cupboard dated 1500, and a candelabrum from 1599. *Torret 2, tel. 75/42–07–00. No credit cards. Inexpensive.*

Devotees of the half-timbered house can get their fill walking down Sønderportsgade, Puggårdsgade, and Sortebrødregade, where the buildings date mainly from the 16th century. Ribe's *Kloster* (Black Friar's Abbey) is among the best preserved monasteries in Denmark.

Before heading back to Vejle, stop off at **Billund** to see the country's most famous tourist attraction. **Legoland** is a park filled with scaled-down versions of cities, towns, and villages, as well as the Pyramids, a statue of Sitting Bull, Mount Rushmore, a safari park, even a Wild West saloon—all constructed of millions of tiny plastic Lego bricks. There are also exhibits of toys from pre-Lego days, including Legoland's high point, Titania's Palace, a sumptuous dollhouse built in 1907 by Sir Neville Wilkinson for his daughter. *Tel. 75/33–13–33. Admission: 40 kr. adults, 20 kr. children. Open Apr. 29–Sept. 17, daily 10–8.*

Dining and Lodging

For details and price category definitions, see Dining and Lodging in Staying in Denmark.

Ålborg **Duus Vinkælder.** Occupying part of Jens Bang's house, and
Dining with 300 years of tradition behind it, Duus Vinkælder is one of
★ Ålborg's best-known restaurants. The wine cellar is phenomenal, a legacy of the days when Bang himself would barter timber for wine and spices in Spain and France. *9 Østerå tel. 98/12–50–56. Reservations required. No credit cards. Closed Sun. Expensive.*

Lodging **Phønix.** A centrally located hotel in a historic building, the Phønix is discreet, traditional, and exceptionally popular. Rooms are comfortable and spacious, the staff pleasant and helpful. One of the Phønix's restaurants, the Halling, serves excellent French and Danish cuisine. *Vesterbro 77, tel. 98/12–00–11. 185 rooms, most with bath. Facilities: sauna, solarium, game room, 2 restaurants, bar, café. AE, DC, MC. Very Expensive.*
Scheelsminde. A pleasantly austere manor house built in 1808, the Scheelsminde was originally a farm. A traditional atmosphere prevails in the public rooms, while bedrooms are Danish modern. The restaurant has fine food and an extensive wine list. *Scheelsmindevej 35, tel. 98/18–32–33. 70 rooms with bath. Facilities: sauna, Jacuzzi, solarium, garden, restaurant. AE, DC, MC, V. Expensive.*

Århus **De Fire Årstider.** The Four Seasons, renowned as one of
Dining Scandinavia's finest restaurants, serves Danish and French
★ nouvelle cuisine behind an unassuming facade on a busy shopping street. Inside, cut flowers, cool blue tones, and crystal complement proprietor Ulrikwitt Pedersen's paintings on the walls. *Aboulevarden 47, tel. 86/19–96–96. Reservations required. AE, DC, MC, V. Closed Sun. Expensive.*

Gammel Aabyhoj. Birthe and Arne Rasmussen run Jutland's only Relais Gourmand, a charming French restaurant set 3.2 kilometers (2 miles) west of Århus. The wine cellar is excellent, the desserts are legendary, and the setting—a house with garden—is cozy and traditional. *Bakke Allé 1, tel. 86/15–77–33. AE, DC, MC, V. Closed Sun. Expensive.*

Lodging　**Royal.** Open since 1838, Århus's grand hotel has welcomed the likes of Arthur Rubenstein and Marion Anderson. It has recently been restored and rebuilt, with its period elegance left intact. Cool pastels abound, as does cheerful chintz. The bathrooms are marble; the service is excellent. *Store Torv 4, tel. 86/12–00–11. 111 rooms with bath. Facilities: 5 cinemas, restaurant, nightclub, sauna, solarium. AE, DC, MC, V. Very Expensive.*

Randers　**Randers.** Anyone who loves pampering would do well to come
Lodging　here. Service is friendly and prompt, decor is as plush as Denmark ever gets, and the Grill Room restaurant regularly produces memorable meals. *Torvegade 11, tel. 86/42–34–22. 82 rooms with bath. Facilities: restaurant. Reservations advised. AE, DC, MC, V. Closed Dec. 23–Jan. 1. Expensive.*

Ribe　**Dagmar.** Occupying a building dating from 1581, the Dagmar is
Lodging　a cozy place, encapsulating all the charm of the 16th century, with stained-glass windows, frescoes, sloping floors, and carved chairs. The restaurant has a delightful central fireplace, and the food is first-class. Try the fillet of veal à la Dagmar. *Torvet 1, tel. 75/42–00–33. 50 rooms with bath. Facilities: restaurant (reservations advised). AE, DC, MC, V. Expensive.*

Skagen　**Brøndums.** With an attractive beachside location, the
Dining and Lodging　Brøndums is a friendly hotel, decorated throughout with paintings by 19th-century artists of the Skagen School. The restaurant puts on a terrific cold table and has lots of fish specialties. There's often music in the evenings, and outside dining. *Anchersvej 3, tel. 98/44–15–55. 14 rooms with bath. Facilities: restaurant (reservations advised). AE, MC, V. Expensive.*

Vejle　**Munkebjerg.** A remote location and marvelous views character-
Lodging　ize this establishment, which dates from 1880. The original building has long since gone, but the nearby beech woods and fjord remain. Guest rooms are modern and light, with fresh colors and stripped-pine decor. The Munkebjerg has two fine restaurants specializing in French cuisine. *Munkebjergvej 125, tel. 75/72–35–00. 148 rooms with bath. Facilities: 2 restaurants, pool, sauna, solarium, game room, tennis, heliport, horseback riding, golf course, and biking, jogging, and walking trails. AE, DC, MC, V. Very Expensive.*

9 Finland

Introduction

If you like majestic open spaces, fine architecture, and civilized living—and can afford the prices—Finland is for you. It is a land of lakes, 187,888 at the last count, and of forests. It is a land where nature is so prized that even the design of city buildings reflects the soaring spaces of the countryside.

The music of Sibelius, Finland's most famous son, tells you what to expect from this Nordic landscape. Both can swing from the somber nocturne of mid-winter darkness to the tremolo of sunlight slanting through pine and bone-white birch or from the crescendo of a sunset before it fades into the next day's dawn. Similarly, the Finnish people reflect the changing moods of their land and climate. They can get annoyed when described as "children of nature," but the description is apt. Their affinity with nature has produced some of the world's greatest designers and architects. Many American cities have buildings designed by Alvar Aalto and the Saarinens, Eliel and son Eero. In fact, Eliel and his family moved to the United States in 1923 and became American citizens—but it was to a lonely Finnish seashore that Saarinen had his ashes returned.

Until 1917, Finland (the Finns call it *Suomi)* was under the domination of its nearest neighbors, Sweden and Russia, who fought over it for centuries. After more than 600 years under Swedish rule and 100 under the tsars, the country inevitably bears many traces of these two cultures, including a small (6%) Swedish-speaking population and a scattering of Russian Orthodox churches.

But the Finns themselves are neither Scandinavian nor Slavic. All that is known of their origins—they speak a Finno-Ugrian tongue, part Finnish, part Hungarian—is that they are descended from wandering groups of people who probably came from west of Russia's Ural mountains before the Christian era and settled on the swampy shores of the Gulf of Finland.

There is a tough, resilient quality in the Finn. No other country that shared its border with the Soviet Union in 1939 now retains its independence. Indeed, no other country has fought the Soviets to a standstill, as the Finns did in the Winter War of 1939–40. This resilience, in part, stems from the turbulence of the country's past but also comes from the people's strength and determination to work the land and survive the long winters. No wonder there is a poet-philosopher lurking in most Finns, one who sometimes drowns his melancholic, darker side in the bottle. For the Finn is in a state of constant confrontation —against the weather, the land, and the Russian bear breathing down his neck. The Finn is stubborn, patriotic, and self-sufficient, yet he is not aggressively nationalistic. On the contrary, rather than being proud of past battles, the Finn is proud of finding ways to live in peace with the Soviet Union. His country's neutrality and his own personal freedom are what he tenaciously holds on to and will never easily relinquish.

The average Finn doesn't volunteer much information, but that's due to reserve, not indifference. Make the first approach and you may have a friend for life. Finns like their silent spaces, though, and won't appreciate back-slapping familiarity—least of all in the sauna, still regarded by many as a spiritual, as well as a cleansing, experience.

Finland

NORWAY

Utsjoki

Inarijärvi

Kilpisjärvi

Inari
Ivalo

Enontekiö
Porttipahdan tekojärvi

Muonio
Lokan tekojärvi

SWEDEN

Kittilä
Södankylä

L A P L A N D
Kemijärvi

Joutsijärvi
Arctic Circle

Arctic Circle
Rovaniemi

Posio
Kuusamo

N

Tornio
Kemi

Pudasjärvi

Oulu
Puolanka
Suomussalmi

Raahe

Oulujärvi
Kajaani
Kuhmo

Kalajoki
Pulkkila
Otanmäki

Kokkola
Nivala
Kärsämäki
Nurmes

Haapajärvi
Iisalmi

Gulf

Kyyjärvi
Pieljnen

Vaasa
Kuopio

Seinäjoki
Äänekoski
Kallavesi
Joensuu

of

Orivesi

Jyväskylä
Varkaus
Savonlinna

Bothnia
Parkano
Pihlajavesi
Punkaharju

Nasijärvi
Päijänne
Mikkeli

Pori
Tampere
Saimaa

Heinola
Imatra
Lake Ladoga

Lahti
Lappeenranta

Ahvenanmaa (Aland)
Hämeenlinna
Kouvola

Turku
Salo
Kotka

Porvoo

Maarianhamina
★ Helsinki
Gulf of Finland

Baltic Sea
Hanko

SOVIET UNION

SOVIET UNION

50 miles
50 km

Before You Go

When to Go   The tourist summer season runs from mid-June until mid-August. Outside this period, many amenities and attractions close or operate on much reduced schedules. But there are advantages to visiting Finland off-season, not the least being that you avoid the mosquitoes, which can be fearsome, especially in the north. Also, hotel rates, especially in vacation villages, may drop by 15% to 40%, and the fall colors (from early September in the far north, October in the south) are spectacular—they even have a special name, *ruskaa*. January through March (through April in the north) is the main cross-country skiing season, and in the lengthening spring days you can get a great suntan. Spring is brief but magical, as the snows melt, the ice breaks up, and nature explodes into life almost overnight. This year there will be a brief eclipse of the sun on July 22, visible from Helsinki and a line northeast to Joensuu. This is the only part of western Europe from which the eclipse can be seen.

Climate   Generally speaking, the spring and summer seasons begin a month earlier in the south of Finland than they do in the far north. You can expect warm (not hot) days in Helsinki from mid-May, in Lapland from mid-June. The midnight sun can be seen from May to July, depending on the region. In mid-winter there is a corresponding period when the sun does not rise at all but when there can be magnificent displays of the Northern Lights. Even in Helsinki, summer nights are brief and never really dark, whereas in mid-winter daylight lasts only a few hours.

The following are average daily maximum and minimum temperatures for Helsinki.

Jan.	26F	−3C	May	56F	14C	Sept.	59F	15C
	17	−9		40	4		46	8
Feb.	25F	−4C	June	66F	19C	Oct.	47F	8C
	15	−10		49	9		37	3
Mar.	32F	0C	July	71F	22C	Nov.	37F	3C
	20	−7		55	13		30	−1
Apr.	44F	6C	Aug.	68F	20C	Dec.	31F	−1C
	30	−1		53	12		23	−5

Currency   The unit of currency in Finland is the Finnmark (FIM), divided into 100 penniä. There are bills of FIM 10, 50, 100, 500, and 1,000. Coins are 5, 10, 20, and 50 penniä, and FIM 1 and FIM 5. At press time (spring 1989), the exchange rate was about FIM 4.1 to the dollar and FIM 7.5 to the pound. Credit cards are widely accepted. Traveler's checks can be exchanged in banks and at bureaux de change at international airports, major train stations, seaports, and hotels, although rates at the latter are about 10% less.

What It Will Cost   The cost of hotels and restaurants in Finland matches the standard of living: Both are high! Expect to spend about 50% more on lodging than in southern Europe, and even more for meals. Prices are highest in Helsinki; otherwise they vary little throughout the country. Taxes are already included in hotel and restaurant charges, and there is no airport departure tax. However, the price of many goods includes an 11% sales tax (*see* Shopping in Staying in Finland).

Sample Prices Cup of coffee, FIM 6; bottle of beer, FIM 13.50; Coca-Cola, FIM 8.70; ham sandwich, FIM 21; one-mile taxi ride, FIM 17.

Customs on Arrival Europeans aged 16 and over entering Finland may bring in 200 cigarettes or 250 grams of other tobacco; visitors from outside Europe may bring in twice as much. All visitors aged 20 or over may also bring in two liters of beer, one liter of alcohol under 18% volume, and one liter over 18% volume. Visitors aged 18 or over may import two liters of beer and two liters of alcohol under 18% volume. Goods up to a value of FIM 1,500 may be imported, but be sure to check restrictions on the amount and type of foodstuffs allowed.

Language The official languages of Finland are Finnish and Swedish, though only a small minority (about 6%) speak Swedish. English is widely spoken among people in the travel industry and by many younger Finns, though they're often shy about using it. Nearly all tourist sites and attractions provide texts in English.

Getting Around

By Car Finland has no superhighways, but there is an expanding net-
Road Conditions work of efficient, major roads, some of them multilane. In some areas, however, especially in the north, you can expect long stretches of dirt road. These are usually adequate to good, although during the spring thaw they become difficult to negotiate. Away from the larger towns, traffic is light, but take moose and reindeer warning signs seriously.

Rules of the Road Drive on the right. At intersections, cars coming from the right have priority. Speed limits (usually marked) are 50 kph (30 mph) in built-up areas, 80 kph (50 mph) in the country, and 110 kph (70 mph) on main roads. Drunk-driving laws are strictly enforced. Low-beam headlights must be used at all times outside city areas, seat belts are compulsory, and you must carry a warning triangle in case of breakdown.

Parking This is a problem only in some city centers. Major cities offer multistory garages; most towns have on-street meters. Make sure that you are legally parked, or your car may be towed away.

Breakdowns The **Automobile and Touring Club of Finland** (ACTF, tel. 90/
and Accidents 694–0022) operates a road patrol service on main roads, where you'll also find a limited number of emergency telephones. If you're involved in an accident, report it without delay to the **Finnish Motor Insurers' Bureau** (tel. 90/19251) as well as to the police.

By Train Finland's extensive rail system reaches all main centers of the country and offers high standards of comfort and cleanliness.

Fares A special **Finnrail Pass** entitles you to unlimited travel for eight, 15, or 22 days. A 15-day second-class ticket costs $135; first class, $203. Children pay half fare. These tickets are available in the USA from **Holiday Tours of America** (tel. 212/832–9072) or **Scantours** (tel. 213/451–0911); in the U.K., from **Finlandia Travel** (tel. 01/839–4741). Other reductions apply to children, groups of three or more, and senior citizens. Reservations are essential on special fast trains.

By Plane **Finnair** (tel. 90/410411) operates an elaborate network of flights linking 21 towns in Finland. For $250, a **Holiday Ticket**

guarantees you unlimited travel for 15 days; visitors aged 12–23 can get a **Youth Holiday Ticket** for $200. Other discounts apply to family groups, children, and senior citizens. These tickets are on sale in most countries, and in Finland from major travel agencies.

By Bus Bus travel plays a leading role in Finland, and the country's bus system provides the most extensive travel network of all; it can take you virtually anywhere. A **Coach Holiday Ticket,** available from bus stations and travel agencies, entitles you to 1,000 kilometers (621 miles) of bus travel for FIM 230. Additional discounts apply for children, family groups, and (*see* Helsinki: Getting Around).

By Boat Helsinki and Turku have regular sea links with the Åland Islands in the Baltic Sea. From mid-June to mid-August you can cruise the labyrinthine lakes of the Finnish interior. Try to include at least one of these trips in your itinerary. Full timetables are available from the Finnish Tourist Board.

By Bicycle Planned bicycle routes, generally following old country roads, are provided in many areas. The main advantages to the cyclist are the lack of hills and the absence of heavy traffic. Bikes can be rented in most tourist centers. The Finnish **Youth Hostel Association** (tel. 90/694–0377) offers accommodation packages of four, seven, or 14 days to tie in with visitors' cycling tours.

Staying in Finland

Telephones
Local Calls Hotels charge a substantial fee for all calls. You can avoid this by using the pay phones provided in most lobbies. Have some FIM 1 and FIM 5 coins ready. Note that the Finnish letters å, ä, and ö come at the end of the alphabet; this may be useful when looking up names in the telephone book.

International Calls The least expensive way to make an international call is to go to a telegraph office; these are marked "Lennätin" and usually adjoin the post office. An operator will assign you a private booth and collect payment at the end of the call. Except in a few remote areas, there is direct dialing to Britain and the USA.

Operators and Information For information about telephone charges, dial 09; for number inquiries in the Helsinki area, 012; for other areas, 020.

Mail
Postal Rates Airmail rates to North America are FIM 3 for a letter of up to 10 grams and FIM 2.50 for postcards. Letters and postcards to the United Kingdom cost FIM 2.50.

Receiving Mail If you're uncertain about where you'll be staying, ensure that mail sent to you is marked "Poste Restante" and addressed to the Main Post Office, Mannerheimintie 11, 00100 Helsinki, or to major post offices in other towns. American Express offers a free clients' mail service and will hold mail for up to one month (*see* Helsinki: Important Addresses). The Finland Travel Bureau also provides a free mail service for foreigners: Mail should be addressed to its Mail Dept., Box 319, 00101 Helsinki, and collected from the office at Kaivokatu 10A.

Shopping
Sales Tax Refunds If you purchase goods worth more than FIM 200 in any of the many shops marked "tax-free for tourists," you can get an 11% refund when you leave Finland. Show your passport and the store will give you a check for the appropriate amount, which you can cash at most departure points.

Opening and Closing Times

Banks. Open weekdays 9:30–4.

Museums. Opening hours vary considerably, so check individual listings. Most close one day a week, usually Monday.

Shops. Most are open weekdays 9–6, Saturday 9–2. Department stores and supermarkets often stay open until 8 on Monday and Friday.

Sightseeing. Hours for most attractions vary widely outside the main tourist season. Check local tourist office for opening days and times.

National Holidays

January 1 (New Year's Day); January 6 (Epiphany); April 13, 16 (Easter); April 30 (May Day Eve); May 1 (May Day); May 19 (Ascension); June 2, 3 (Pentecost); June 22, 23 (Midsummer's Eve and Day); November 3 (All Saints'); December 6 (Independence); December 24–26 (Christmas).

Dining

You can choose among restaurants, taverns, coffee houses, and snack bars. As in other parts of Scandinavia, the cold table (*voileipäpöytä*) is often a work of art as well as a feast. It's usually available at lunchtime. Special Finnish dishes include reindeer casserole (*poronkäristys*; superb in Lapland); salmon, herring, and various freshwater fish; and meatballs (*lihapullia*) with a tasty sauce. Crayfish parties are popular between the end of July and early September. For a delicious dessert, try cloudberries (related to blackberries) and other forest fruits. And if you're heading north and want to find out where you can sample Lapland specialties, get the *Lappi à la Carte* booklet from the Finnish Tourist Board.

Mealtimes

The Finns eat early: lunch runs from 11 or noon to 1 or 2, dinner from 4 to 7. Fixed-price menus, available at these times, are far more moderately priced than the à la carte choices served outside these hours.

Dress

Except for the most elegant restaurants, where a jacket and tie are preferred, casual attire is acceptable for restaurants in all price categories; however, jeans are not allowed in some of the Expensive and Very Expensive establishments.

Ratings

Prices are per person and include first course, main course, dessert, and service charge—but not wine. Most restaurant checks include a service charge (*sisältää palvelupalkkion*). If you want to leave an additional tip—and it really isn't necessary—it's enough to round the figure off to the nearest 5 or 10 FIM. Best bets are indicated by a star ★. At press time, there were 4.1 finnmarks (FIM) to the dollar.

Category	Helsinki	Other Areas
Very Expensive	over FIM 220	over FIM 190
Expensive	FIM 170–FIM 220	FIM 150–FIM 190
Moderate	FIM 110–FIM 170	FIM 90–FIM 150
Inexpensive	under FIM 110	under FIM 90

If one selects the fixed-price menu, which usually covers two courses and coffee and is served between certain hours in many establishments, the cost of the meal can be as little as half these prices.

Credit Cards The following abbreviations are used: AE, American Express; DC, Diners Club; MC, MasterCard; V, Visa.

Lodging The range of accommodations available in Finland includes hotels, motels, boarding houses, private homes, rented chalets and cottages, farmhouses, youth hostels, and campsites. There is no official system of classification, but standards are generally high. If you haven't reserved a room in advance, you can make reservations at the **Hotel Reservation Center** at Helsinki Train Station (tel. 90/171133) or through a travel agency.

Hotels Nearly all hotels in Finland are modern or will have been recently renovated; a few occupy fine old manor houses. Most have rooms with bath or shower. Prices normally include breakfast and often a morning sauna and swim. The **Finncheck** voucher system, operating in many hotels from June through August, offers good discounts. Only the first night can be reserved, but subsequent reservations can be made free from any Finncheck hotel. Ask at the Finnish Tourist Board for further details.

Several hotel groups, such as Rantasipi and Arctia, offer special packages, and some hotels drop their prices substantially in July, unless there's a festival going on.

Summer Hotels University students' accommodations are turned into "summer hotels" from June through August; these offer modern facilities at slightly lower-than-average prices.

Boarding Houses and Private Homes These provide the least expensive accommodations. Local tourist offices have lists.

Rentals The choice is huge, and the chalets and cottages are nearly always in delightful lakeside or seashore settings. For comfortable (not luxurious) accommodations, count on paying FIM 1000–FIM 2500 for a four-person weekly rental. A central reservations agency is **Lomarengas** (tel. 90/441346).

Farmhouses These are located in attractive settings, usually near water. A central reservations agency is **Suomen 4H-liitto** (tel. 90/642233).

Youth Hostels These range from empty schools to small manor houses. There are no age restrictions. You can get a list from the Finnish Tourist Board.

Camping There are about 350 Finnish campsites, all classified into one of three grades. All offer showers and cooking facilities, and many include cottages for rent. A list is available from the Finnish Tourist Board.

Ratings Prices are for two people in a double room, and include breakfast and service charge. Best bets are indicated by a star ★. At press time, there were 4.1 finnmarks (FIM) to the dollar.

Category	Helsinki	Other Areas
Very Expensive	over FIM 750	over FIM 650
Expensive	FIM 550–FIM 750	FIM 440–FIM 650
Moderate	FIM 330–FIM 550	FIM 270–FIM 440
Inexpensive	under FIM 330	under FIM 270

Credit Cards   The following credit card abbreviations are used: AE, American Express; DC, Diners Club; MC, MasterCard; V, Visa.

Tipping   The Finns are less tip-conscious than other Europeans. For restaurant tips, *see* Dining, above. You can give taxi drivers a few small coins, but it's not essential. Train and airport porters have a fixed charge. It's not necessary to tip hotel doormen for carrying bags to the check-in counter, but give bellhops FIM 2–FIM 5 for carrying bags to your room. The obligatory check-room fee of FIM 3–FIM 4 for restaurant doormen is usually clearly indicated; if not, give FIM 3–FIM 10, depending on the number in your party.

Helsinki

Arriving and Departing

By Plane   All international flights arrive at Helsinki's Vantaa Airport, 20 kilometers (12 miles) north of the city. For arrival and departure information, tel. 90/829–2451.

Between the Airport and Downtown   Finnair buses leave two to four times an hour for the city terminal, located at the Inter-Continental hotel (Töölönkatu 21, tel. 90/410111) and the main train station. The trip takes about 25 minutes and costs FIM 13. A local bus service (no. 615) operates on a similar frequency to the train station and costs FIM 10. Expect to pay about FIM 100 for a taxi into the city center. If you are driving, the way is well marked to Highway 137 and Keskusta (downtown Helsinki).

By Train   Helsinki's main train station is in the heart of the city. For train information, phone 90/659411.

By Bus   The terminal for many local buses is the train-station square, Rautatientori. The main bus station is located off Mannerheimintie between Salomonkatu and Simonkatu. For information phone 90/602122.

By Sea   The Silja Line terminal for ships arriving from Stockholm is at Olympialaituri, on the west side of the South Harbor. The Finnjet-Silja Line and Viking Lines terminal for ships arriving from Travemünde and Stockholm is at Katajanokka, on the east side of the South Harbor.

Getting Around

The center of Helsinki is compact and best explored on foot. However, the Helsinki City Tourist Office provides a free Helsinki route map that shows all public transportation. As far as public transportation tickets go, your best buy is the **Helsinki Card,** which gives unlimited travel on city public transportation, as well as free entry to many museums, a free sightseeing tour, and a variety of other discounts. It's available for one, two, or three days (FIM 65, 85, and 105; about half-price for children). You can buy it at most hotels and at the Helsinki City Tourist Office.

By Subway   One subway line links the train station with Itäkeskus, in the eastern suburbs. It runs from 6 AM to 11 PM and each ride costs FIM 6.50.

By Streetcar   These run from 5:30 or 6 AM to 10:30 PM or 1 AM, depending on the line. The fare is the same as for the subway. The 3T streetcar follows a figure-eight circuit around the city center, and, during summer, provides commentary in several languages.

By Taxi Taxis are all marked "taksi." The meters start at FIM 10.50, with the fare rising on a kilometer basis. There is a surcharge after 6 PM and on weekends.

By Boat In summer there are regular boat services from the South Harbor market square to the islands of Suomenlinna and Korkeasaari.

Important Addresses and Numbers

Tourist Information The **Helsinki City Tourist Office** is near the South Harbor, at Pohjoisesplanadi 19, tel. 90/169–3757; open Sept. 16–May 15, Mon. 9:30–4:30, Tues.–Fri. 8:30–4; May 16–Sept. 15, weekdays 8:30–6, Sat. 8:30–1. The **Finnish Tourist Board's Tourist Information Office** (covering all of Finland) is nearby at Unioninkatu 26, tel. 90/144511; open weekdays 9–1 and 2–3:30.

Embassies **U.S.:** Itäinen Puistotie 14A, tel. 90/171931. **Canadian:** Pohjoisesplanadi 25B, tel. 90/171141. **U.K.:** Uudenmaankatu 16 –20, tel. 90/647922.

Emergencies **Police:** tel. 000; **Ambulance:** tel. 000; Doctor, tel. 008; **Dentist:** tel. 90/736166; **Pharmacy: Yliopiston Aptekki,** Mannerheimintie 96 (open 24 hours).

English Bookstores You'll find a good selection of books in English at **Akateeminen Kirjakauppa** (Keskuskatu 1) and **Suomalainen Kirjakauppa** (Aleksanterinkatu 23). English newspapers are on sale at the train station and in major hotels. For news in English, dial 040.

Travel Agencies **American Express:** Travek Travel Bureau, Katajanokan Pohjoisranta 9–13, tel. 90/661631. **Thomas Cook:** Finland Travel Bureau, Kaivokatu 10A, tel. 90/18261.

Guided Tours

Orientation Tours **Suomen Turistiauto** (tel. 90/585166) runs a "City Tour" (1½ hours, starting 1 PM) that covers the main city-center sights and a "Daughter of the Baltic" tour (2¾ hours, starting 10:15 AM) that extends out to the modern suburbs and the island of Suomenlinna. Both start from Asema-aukio, across from the main post office, and you can buy tickets on the bus 15 minutes before departure. **Ageba Travel Agency** (tel. 90/669193) offers a similar but longer combination tour (four hours) including lunch, starting from the Olympic Harbor at 10 AM. **Royal Line Rautakorpi** (tel. 90/652088) operates "Helsinki by Sea" boat tours (1½ hours, starting at 11, 1, and 3) from the South Harbor market square. The same agency runs "Lunch Cruises" to several island restaurants, departing from the South Harbor market square at noon.

Walking Tours You can get an excellent free booklet, *See Helsinki on Foot*, detailing six walking tours of various lengths, from the Helsinki City Tourist Office.

Personal Guides Contact the **Guide Reservation Center** (tel. 90/601966).

Excursions **Finland Travel Bureau** (tel. 90/18261) offers a four-hour trip on Wednesdays to Hvitträsk, for a tour of historic homes of Finnish artists and architects. On Sundays there is a six-hour trip to

Sibelius's home at Ainola and the beautiful old town of Porvoo. No-visa trips by sea to the Soviet Union (Leningrad or Riga, three nights) are offered by **Finnsov Tours** (tel. 90/694–2011). **Saimaa Lines** offers one-day cruises (with visa) to Tallinn (tel. 430–5269).

Exploring Helsinki

Helsinki is a city of the sea. It was built on peninsulas that stab into the Baltic, and streets and avenues curve around bays, bridges arch over to nearby islands, and ferries reach out to islands farther off shore. Sweet-tasting salt air hovers over the city, and the sounds from the vessels steaming into port resonate off the city's buildings.

Like other European capitals, Helsinki has expanded its boundaries and now absorbs about one-sixth of the Finnish population, and the suburbs sprawl from one peninsula to another. The Helsinki resident must know the peninsulas in order to know his city. However, most of the city's sights, hotels, and restaurants cluster on one peninsula, thus forming a compact hub of special interest for the traveler.

Unlike most other European capitals, Helsinki is "new." About 400 years ago, King Gustav Vasa of Sweden decided to woo trade from the Estonian city of Tallinn and thus challenge the monopoly of the Hanseatic League. To do this, he commanded the people of four Finnish towns to pack up their belongings and relocate at the rapids on the river Vantaa. This new town became Helsinki.

For three centuries, Helsinki had its ups and downs as a trading town. Turku, to the west of Helsinki, remained the capital and the center of the country's intellectual pursuits. Ironically, not until Finland was thrust under the dominance of Russia did Helsinki's fortunes improve. Tsar Alexander wanted Finland's political center closer to Russia and, in 1812, selected Helsinki as the new capital. Shortly after the capital was moved from Turku to Helsinki, Turku suffered a monstrous fire. Such was the inferno that the university was also moved to Helsinki. From then on Helsinki's future was secure.

Fire was indeed fortuitous for the future of Helsinki. Just before the tsar's proclamation, a fire had swept through the town, permitting the construction of new buildings suitable for a nation's capital. The German-born architect Carl Ludvig Engel was commissioned to rebuild the city, and, as a result, Helsinki has some of the purest neo-Classical architecture in the world. Add to this foundation the modern buildings designed by talented Finnish architects and you have a European capital city that is as architecturally eye-catching as it is different from its Scandinavian neighbors or the rest of Europe.

Numbers in the margin correspond with points of interest on the Helsinki map.

Helsinki is an easy city to visit on foot. Not only are the key sights on one peninsula but most of them are also contained in the area between the railway station and the central Market Square (Kauppatori).

Across from the city tourist office and beside the South Harbor ❶ is the **Kauppatori.** Sometimes it seems that every Helsinki wife

Ateneum, **12**
Finlandia Hall, **15**
Kauppatori, **1**
Lutheran Cathedral, **5**
Market Hall, **6**
National Museum, **16**
National Theater, **13**
Nordic Arts Center, **8**
Statue of Marshal
Mannerheim, **14**
Presidential Palace, **2**
Senaatintori, **4**
Stockmann's, **10**
Suomenlina, **7**
Swedish Theater, **9**
Temppeliaukio
Church, **17**
Train station, **11**
Uspenski Cathedral, **3**

Helsinki

is here seeking the best buys for the day or simply catching up on the gossip. All around are stalls selling everything from colorful, freshly cut flowers to ripe fruit, from vegetables trucked in from the hinterland to handicrafts made in small villages. Look at the fruit stalls—mountains of strawberries, raspberries, blueberries, and, if you're lucky, cloudberries (*suomuurain*), which mostly grow above the Arctic Circle in the midnight sun. Closer to the dock are fresh fish, caught that morning in the Baltic Sea and still flopping. The market is a hive of activity and, in a sense, the heartbeat of everyday life in Helsinki. Stop at one of the food stalls and, as you sip your coffee, notice the **statue of Havis Amanda** standing in the square. This beautiful lady is loved by all Finns, and every May Day eve she is embraced by students who wade through the protective moat to crown her with their white caps.

The market ends about 1 PM and, in the summer, the fruit and vegetable stalls are replaced with arts and crafts. This happens at about 3 PM and lasts until about 8 PM.

Another heartbeat of Helsinki is across the street, on the other side of Pohjoisesplanadi. The uniformed guards will prevent
❷ you from entering, but the building is the **Presidential Palace** and next to it is the city hall and various administrative offices. Across from the palace is the waterfront, where ferries and sightseeing boats set out into the bay. On a summer's day it is a sailor's vision: sails hoisted and taut to the wind, yacht clubs beckoning, and island waters to explore. The red brick edifice perched above the east side of the market is the Orthodox
❸ **Uspenski Cathedral.**

Just behind the cathedral is the district of **Katajanokka.** Here the 19th-century brick warehouses are slowly being renovated to form a complex of boutiques, arts and crafts studios, and restaurants. One can find innovative designs at these shops, and the restaurants tend to offer lighter fare, which can make this a tempting area to stop for lunch.

A one-minute stroll north of city hall brings you into
❹ **Senaatintori** (Senate Square), the heart of neo-Classical Helsinki and one of the most graceful squares in Europe,
❺ dominated by the domed **Lutheran Cathedral** (Tuomiokirkko). The square is the work of Ludvig Engel. The harmony created with the Tuomiokirkko, the university, and the state council building places you amid one of the purest styles of European architecture. Senaatintor has a dignified, stately air, enlivened in summer by sunworshippers who gather on the wide steps leading up to Tuomiokirkko and, throughout the year by the bustle around the relatively new **Senaati Shopping Center** on the square's south side.

Most of the streets leading off Senaatintori contain government and administrative offices. Worth noting is **Snellmaninkatu,** a street named after J. V. Snellman. Known for awakening the Finnish national spirit, he was instrumental in persuading the Russian overlords to officially recognize the Finnish language and accept the idea of a separate Finnish currency. It is Snellman's statue that stands in front of the Bank of Finland.

Back on the market, head southward along the western shore of the South Harbor on Eteläranta Street. You'll soon come to the
❻ old brick **Market Hall**—it's worth taking a look at the voluminous displays of meat, fish, and other gastronomic goodies. A

little farther on is the **Olympia Terminal,** where the huge ferries from Sweden and Poland berth. Beyond this you enter
Kaivopuisto, the elegant parkland district much favored by
Russian high society in the 19th century. It is now popular as a
strolling ground for Helsinki's citizens and as a residential area
for diplomats. You'll find the U.S. and French embassies and
British ambassador's residence clustered together among the
greenery, interspersed with statues.

Time Out Perched on the shore is the **Ursula café.** However welcome the
refreshments may be, the view of the harbor and waterborne
traffic make it the reason to stop here.

Just around the headland you'll spot a peculiarly Finnish tradition: special platforms jutting out over the water (either the sea
or a lake) on which people gather to scrub their carpets. Laundry, as in other parts of the world, becomes a lively, communal
affair and an occasion to catch up on the latest gossip.

You can avoid the long walk back by cutting across Kaivopuisto
to Tehtaankatu and catching streetcar no. 3T to the marketplace. From here, there's a frequent ferry service to
⑦ Suomenlina. Suomenlina means "Finland's Castle," and for
good reason. In 1748 the Finnish army helped build this fortress, which grew so over the years that today Suomenlina is a
series of interlinked islands. For a long time the impregnable
fortress was referred to as the "Gibraltar of the North." While
it has never been taken by assault, its occupants did surrender
twice without a fight—once to the Russians in the war of 1808–
19 and then to the British, who bombarded the fortress, causing fires.

Although still a fortress, Suomenlina is today a collection of
museums, parks, and gardens. In early summer, it is engulfed
in mauve and purple mists of lilacs, the trees introduced from
Versailles by the Finnish architect, Ehrensvärd. One of the
⑧ museums you may care to visit is the **Nordic Arts Center,** which
exhibits and promotes Scandinavian art. *Admission free. Open
Sept.–Apr., weekdays 10–6; May–Aug., weekdays noon–8,
weekends 10–noon.*

Try to plan your visit to Suomenlina around lunchtime so that
after investigating the ramparts and visiting the museums you
can make your way to the old fort near the historic King's Gate
for a meal at **Walhalla,** located deep in the bastions of the fort
(*see* Dining).

Back on the mainland, head west from the marketplace up
Pohjoisesplanadi (North Esplanade). To your left, the leafy linden trees in the Esplanade gardens provide a peaceful
backdrop for daily concerts at the Esplanade bandstand and
the statues of Finnish writers. On your right are the showrooms and boutiques of some of Finland's top fashion designers
⑨ (*see* Shopping). The circular **Swedish Theater** marks the junction of the Esplanade and Helsinki's main artery,
Mannerheimintie.

⑩ If you take a right up Keskuskatu, you come to **Stockmann's,**
Helsinki's most famous store, well worth a shopping stop. Next
⑪ you come to the **train station** and its square, the bustling com-
muting hub of the city. The station's huge red-granite figures
are by Emil Wikström, but the solid building they adorn was

designed by Eliel Saarinen, one of the founders of the early
⑫ 20th-century National Romantic style. The **Ateneum,** Finland's
central art museum, is on the south side of the square facing the
⑬ **National Theater.** *Admission: FIM 3 adults, children free.*
Open June–Aug. Weekdays 9–5, weekends 11–5; Sept.–May,
Mon.–Sat. 9–5, Sun. 11–5; open Wed. year-round to 8 PM.

Time Out **Café Socis,** in the Seurahuone Hotel opposite the train station,
provides a restful turn-of-the-century atmosphere for a fixed-
price lunch or afternoon tea.

In front of the main post office west of the station, is the eques-
⑭ trian **statue of Marshal Mannerheim** gazing down
Mannerheimintie, the major thoroughfare named in his honor.
Perhaps no man in Finnish history is so revered as Marshal Baron Carl Gustaf Mannerheim, the great leader who guided
Finland through much of the turbulent 20th century. When he
died in Switzerland on January 28, 1951, his body was flown
back to his native land to lie in state in the cathedral. For three
days, young war widows, children, and soldiers with caps in
hand filed past his bier by the thousands. Never in Finland's
history has there been such an expression of national feeling.

About half a mile along, past the colonnaded red-granite Par-
⑮ liament House, stands **Finlandia Hall,** one of the last creations
of Alvar Aalto. If you can't make it to a concert there, take a
guided tour. Behind the hall lies the inland bay of Töölönlahti
⑯ and, almost opposite, the **National Museum,** another example
of National Romantic exotica in which Eliel Saarinen played a
part. *Admission: FIM 5 adults, FIM 2.50 children, free on*
Tues. Open Tues. 11–4 and 6–9, Wed.–Mon. 11–4.

Tucked away in a labyrinth of streets to the west is the strik-
⑰ ingly modern **Temppeliaukio Church.** Carved out of solid rock
and topped with a copper dome, this Helsinki landmark is a
center for religious activities, church services, concerts, and
lectures (Lutherinkatu 3; open Mon.–Sat. 10–8, Sun. noon–2
and 5–8). From here it's only a short distance back to
Mannerheimintie, where you can pick up any streetcar for the
downtown area.

Off the Beaten Track

Located in Espoo, Helsinki's next door neighbor, is **Tapiola**
Garden City, one of Finland's architectural highlights. Designed by Aalvar Aalto, the urban landscape of alternating
high and low residential buildings, fountains, gardens, and
swimming pools blends into the natural surroundings. What
began as an experiment in communal, affordable housing has
now lost its radical appeal, but Tapiola still holds interest for
anyone interested in urban planning. Guides and sightseeing
tours are available from the Espoo City Tourist Office, tel.
467652 or 467692.

Akseli Gallen Kallela (1865–1931) was one of Finland's greatest
artists. His studio-home can be seen at Gallen-Kallelantie 27,
Tarvaspää: To get there, take tram no. 4 to Munkkiniemi, then
it's a one-mile walk through the woods. *Open Tues.–Thurs.*
10–8, Fri.–Sun. 10–5.

Heureka is the new Finnish Science Center at Tikkurila,
Vantaa district, 15 minutes from the city center by train. It of-

fers exciting demonstrations, exhibitions in which adults and children are invited to take part, a planetarium with multimedia programs, computer technology, and a robot theater. There is also an outdoor roof-terrace restaurant for a meal or snack. *Admission: FIM 30–FIM 50. Open May–Sept., weekdays 10–8, weekends 10–6; Oct. 15–Dec. 31 and Jan. 15–Apr. 30, closed Mon. Closed Oct. 1–14 and Jan. 1–14.*

Shopping

Shopping Districts and Specialty Shops
You should find everything you need on **Pohjoisesplanadi** (North Esplanade) and **Aleksanterinkatu;** in the **Forum Shopping Mall** at Mannerheimintie 20; or on the pedestrian mall **Iso Roobertinkatu.** You can make purchases until 10 PM, seven days a week, in the shops along the Tunneli underpass leading from the train station.

The shops in **Senaatti Center** and along Pohjoisesplanadi are open on Sundays from noon to 4 in summer. Along the latter you'll find some of Finland's top design houses: **Metsovaara** fashions at no. 23; **Arabia-Nuutajärvi** ceramics and glass at no. 25; **Pentik** leather, **Aarikka** accessories and wooden toys at no. 27; **Iittala** glass at no. 27A; **Marimekko** fashions at no. 31; and **Studio Tarja Niskanen** furs at no. 33.

Helsinki's three top jewelry boutiques are almost adjacent: **Galerie Björn Weckström,** Unioninkatu 30; **Kalevala Koru,** Unioninkatu 25; and **Kaunis Koru,** Senaatti Center.

Department Stores
Stockmann's, a huge store that fills an entire block between Aleksanterinkatu, Mannerheimintie, and Keskuskatu, is your best bet if you want to find everything under one roof.

Markets
The **Kauppatori market** beside the South Harbor (*see* Exploring Helsinki) is an absolute must. Also try to find time for the **Hietalahti flea market,** located at the southwest end of Bulevardi. Stallholders here include everyone from junk merchants to socialites clearing out their attics, and there is a corresponding variety of goods on offer. *Open Mon.–Sat. 6:30 AM–2 PM.*

Dining

For details and price category definitions, *see* Dining in Staying in Finland.

Very Expensive
★ **George.** George was voted "Restaurant 1987" by a Finnish gourmet club. It is centrally located and offers continental cuisine with soft lights and quiet corners. Try the grilled fillet of lamb with fennel and garlic-butter sauce. *Kalevankatu 17, tel. 90/647662. Reservations advised. AE, DC, MC, V. Closed Sun., Christmas, Easter, and June 22–23.*

★ **Kaivohuone.** Red plush and crystal chandeliers set the mood in this elegant 19th-century restaurant once favored by the Russian aristocracy. Award-winning chef Juha Niemiö adds to its reputation with specialties such as smoked salmon loaf in puff pastry with white-wine butter sauce. *Kaivopuisto, tel. 90/ 177881. Reservations required. AE, DC, MC, V. Closed Sun., Mon., Christmas, and Easter; in winter, open evenings only.*

Savoy. With its airy dining room overlooking the Esplanade gardens, the Savoy is a favorite for business lunches. It was Finnish statesman Marshal Mannerheim's favorite, too, and he introduced the *Vorschmack* (minced lamb meat and anchovies) hors d'oeuvre. *Eteläesplanadi 14, tel. 90/176571. Reservations necessary for lunch, advisable for dinner. AE, DC, MC, V. Closed Christmas, Easter, and June 22–23.*

Walhalla. Deep inside the granite ramparts of suomenlina fortress is a restaurant well worth the 20-minute boat ride from South Harbor. Specialties include whitefish from the stone grill. *Suomenlinna, tel. 668552. Reservations essential. AE, DC, MC, V. Closed mid-Sept.–mid-May.*

Expensive   **Amadeus.** Situated in an old town house near the South Harbor, Amadeus specializes in game dishes, such as baked ptarmigan and reindeer fillets. *Sofiankatu 4, tel. 90/626676. Reservations advised. AE, DC, MC, V. Closed Christmas.*

★ **Bellevue.** Despite its French name, the Bellevue is Russian both in decor and cuisine. Filet à la Novgorod and chicken à la Kiev are the authentic articles here. *Rahapajankatu 3, tel. 90/179560. Reservations advised. AE, DC, MC, V. Closed Sun., Christmas, and June 22–23.*

Kultainen Sipuli. The "golden onion," located in an old brick warehouse in the central Katajanokka district, is one of Helsinki's newest restaurants. The decor is an imaginative combination of timber and leather. Be sure to sample the outstanding crayfish soup. *Kanavaranta 3, tel. 90/179900. Reservations advised. AE, DC, MC, V. Closed Sun., Christmas, and New Year's Eve.*

Troikka. The Troikka takes you back to Tsarist times in decor, paintings, and music, and offers exceptionally good food. If you're reluctant to try bear steak cooked in a clay pot, try the Siberian *pelmens* (small meat pasties). *Caloniuksenkatu 3, tel. 90/445229. Reservations essential in the evening. AE, DC, MC, V. Closed Sun., Christmas, Easter, and June 22–23.*

Moderate   **Omenapuu.** This cozy family restaurant set in the midst of a busy shopping district features special dishes for weight watchers. *Keskuskatu 6, tel. 90/630205. Reservations advisable for lunch. AE, DC, MC, V.*

Perho. This is the restaurant connected to Helsinki's catering school. Visitors are served by friendly students, and in summer the emphasis is on Finnish food, particularly salmon and reindeer. *Mechelininkatu 7, tel. 90/493481. Reservations advised. AE, DC, MC, V. Closed Christmas and June 22–23.*

Wellamo. The decor at this restaurant draws upon changing exhibitions by new artists. The small, subdued dining area extends outside to the shore of the North Harbor where, in the summer, you can enjoy the chef's cooking outside. Try the lamb steak in garlic butter. *Vyökatu 9, tel. 90/663139. No reservations. AE, MC, V. Closed Mon., Christmas, and June 22–23.*

Inexpensive   **Chez Marius.** This cozy French-style bistro is an established favorite, especially for lunch. It's located in the city center, so be prepared for crowds. *Mikonkatu 1, tel. 90/669697. No reservations. No credit cards. Closed weekends, Christmas, and June 22–23.*

Kynsilaukka. The rustic decor suits the menu, which includes juniper-smoked beef. *Fredrikinkatu 22, tel. 90/651939. No reservations. MC, V. DC.*

Lodging

Standards of service and amenities in nearly all Helsinki hotels are reliable. The main criteria for inclusion here are price and location. For details and price category definitions, *see* Lodging in Staying in Finland.

Very Expensive **Hesperia.** Enlarged and redecorated in 1986, the Hesperia is modern in the best Finnish tradition and just a short stroll from the center of the city. *Mannerheimintie 50, tel. 90/43101. 384 rooms with bath. Facilities: sauna, pool, golf simulator, nightclub, helicopter service. AE, DC, MC, V. Closed Christmas.*

★ **Inter-Continental.** This is the most popular hotel in the city—with American visitors, at least. It's modern and close to Finlandia Hall, although its rooms are on the small side. Restaurant noise may disturb guests staying on the top floor. *Mannerheimintie 46–48, tel. 90/40551. 555 rooms with bath. Facilities: sauna, pool, disco, AE, DC, MC, V.*

Palace. The Palace has a splendid location overlooking the South Harbor—but make sure you ask for a room with a view; these are on the 9th floor. *Eteläranta 10, tel. 90/171114. 59 rooms with bath. Facilities: sauna, restaurant. AE, DC, MC, V. Closed Christmas.*

Rivoli Jardin. Rivoli Jardin is a central town house, with all rooms overlooking a quiet courtyard. Rooms are rather small but well equipped and attractively designed. Breakfast is served in the winter garden, but there's no restaurant. *Kasarmikatu 40, tel. 90/177880. 54 rooms with shower. Facilities: sauna. AE, DC, MC, V. Closed Christmas.*

Strand Inter-Continental. Helsinki's latest luxury hotel is centrally located, adjacent to the Old City on the waterfront. The hotel's distinctive use of stone, granite, and marble in the central lobby are accentuated by a soaring atrium and softened by a cozy fireplace. There is a choice of restaurants—from the Vega's elegant gourmet dishes of seafood, steak, and game, to the Atrium's buffet restaurant for light meals. All rooms include the luxury of a heated bathroom floor. The hotel also features an entire floor for nonsmokers. *John Stenbergin ranta 4, tel. 90/39351. 200 rooms with bath. Facilities: sauna, indoor pool, 2 restaurants, lounge-bar. AE, DC, MC, V.*

Expensive **Merihotelli Cumulus.** Located on the seafront, the Merihotelli Cumulus is a 10-minute walk from the center of town. Rooms are somewhat small but modern; those with a sea view get some traffic noise. *Hakaniemenrantu 4, tel. 90/711455. 87 rooms with bath. Facilities: sauna, pool. AE, DC, MC, V.*

Rantasipi Airport Hotel. Just two miles from the airport, the Rantasipi was built in 1981 and expanded in 1986. Although the rooms are rather small, they have forest views. Airport shuttle service is provided, and the hotel features an entire floor for nonsmokers. *Takamaantie 4, Vantaa, tel. 90/826822. 300 rooms with shower. Facilities: sauna, pool, nightclub. AE, DC, MC, V. Closed Christmas.*

★ **Seurahuone.** This is a traditional town house from 1914, renovated in 1982, facing the station. Room decor ranges from sleek modern to crystal chandeliers and brass bedsteads, so specify your preference. Streetside rooms get some traffic noise. *Kaivokatu 12, tel. 90/170441. 118 rooms with bath. Facilities: sauna, disco. AE, DC, MC, V.*

Vaakuna. Located close to the train station, the Vaakuna offers light, airy rooms featuring high-back easy chairs. *Asemaaukio 2, tel. 131181. 288 rooms with bath or shower. Facilities: sauna, solarium, nightclub. AE, DC, MC, V.*

Moderate **Anna.** The Anna, a circa 1935 town house, has light, cheerful rooms well-insulated against traffic noise. It's within easy reach of the town center but has no restaurant (breakfast room only). Nonsmokers will appreciate the designated nonsmoking floor and smoke-free public areas. *Annankatu 1, tel. 90/648011. 58 rooms with shower. Facilities: sauna. AE, MC, V. Closed Christmas and New Year's.*

Helka. The Helka is a town house built in 1925 and extended and renovated in 1985–86. It's convenient to the city center but rooms are rather small. *Pohjoinen Rautatiekatu 23A, tel. 90/440581. 153 rooms, most with bath. Facilities: sauna, solarium. AE, DC, MC, V. Closed Christmas.*

Hospiz. The Hospiz is located on a quiet, central street and is unpretentious but comfortable. *Vuorikatu 17, tel. 90/170481. 163 rooms, with bath or shower. Facilities: sauna. AE, DC, MC, V.*

Inexpensive **Academica.** The Academica is a town house with simple but adequate rooms, 10 minutes' walk from the town center. *Hietaniemenkatu 14, tel. 402–0206. reservations 90/402–0580. 216 rooms, most with shower. Facilities: sauna, pool, indoor tennis, disco. AE, MC, V. Closed Sept.–May.*

Clairet. This is a small, modest, old-fashioned hotel, centrally located close to the train station. There's no restaurant, but breakfast is served in your room. *Itäinen Teatterikuja 3, tel. 90/669707. 15 rooms without bath. MC, V. Closed Christmas.*

★ **Finn.** Occupying the two top floors of a circa 1913 town house, the Finn is the best (and most expensive) hotel in this category. Some rooms are unusually large, but there's no restaurant—breakfast is served in your room on request. *Kalevankatu 3B, tel. 90/640904. 28 rooms, most with bath. Facilities: sauna and pool. MC, V. Closed Christmas, Easter, and June 22–23.*

The Arts

For a list of events, pick up the free publications *Helsinki This Week* or *Helsinki Today* available in hotels and tourist offices. For recorded program information in English, dial 058. A central reservations office for all events is **Lippupalvelu,** Mannerheimintie 5, tel. 90/643043.

Theater Although all performances are in Finnish or Swedish, summertime productions in bucolic settings such as **Suomenlina Island, Kekuspuisto Park, Mustikkamaa Island,** and the **Rowing Stadium** (operettas) make enjoyable entertainment. The splendid new **Opera House** opens in 1992 in a waterside park by **Töölönlahti.**

Concerts The two main locations for musical events are **Finlandia Hall** (tel. 90/40241) and **Temppeliaukio Church** (*see* Exploring). Free organ recitals are given on Sundays at 8 PM in the cathedral, and there's daily entertainment at the bandstand in the **Esplanade** gardens.

Nightlife

Nightclubs **Pressa,** the most popular club in town, is in the Ramada Presidentti Hotel (Eteläinen Rautatiekatu 4, tel. 90/6911). The nightclub in the **Hotel Hesperia** (tel. 90/43101) is more intimate and has the prettiest showgirls in town.

Discos The liveliest and most popular is **Ky Exit** (Pohjoinen Rautatiekatu 21, tel. 90/407238), followed by **Club Anna and Erik** (Eerikinkatu 3, tel. 90/694–4204).

The Lakelands

This is a region of lakes, forests, and islands in southeastern and central Finland. The light in these northern latitudes has a magical softness, and the vistas are constantly changing.

For centuries the lakeland region was a buffer between the warring empires of Sweden and Russia. After visiting the people of the lakelands, you should have a basic understanding of the Finnish word *sisu* (guts), a quality that has kept Finns independent, fiercely guarding their neutrality.

Getting Around

Savonlinna is the best-placed town in the Lakelands and can make a convenient base from which to begin exploring. You can fly to the Savonlinna area from Helsinki in 40 minutes; a connecting bus takes you the remaining 16 kilometers (10 miles) into town. By train, the journey takes 5½ hours, by bus, six hours.

If you travel by car, you can do the lake trips as separate excursions. The alternative is to take advantage of the excellent network of air, rail, bus, and boat transportation. Take the boat from Savonlinna to Kuopio in 12 hours (**Roll Ships**, tel. 971/126744). From Kuopio, take the 320-kilometer (200-mile) cross-country bus ride via Jyväskylä to Tampere. Continue by boat to Hämeenlinna in seven hours (**Silver Line**, tel. 931/124803). The final leg by bus or train back to Helsinki takes about one and a half hours.

Guided Tours

A program of **Friendly Finland Tours,** available through a number of travel agencies, offers escorted lakeland packages from two to 11 days, starting from Helsinki. Brochures are available from the **Finnish Tourist Board** (Unioninkatu 26, Helsinki, tel. 90/144511) and its overseas offices (*see* Chapter 1).

Tourist Information

Hämeenlinna. Raatihuoneenkatu 15, tel. 917/202388. Open May 2–Aug. 13, weekdays 9–6, Sat. 9–4; Aug. 14–May 1, weekdays 8–4.
Kuopio. Haapaniemenkatu 17, tel. 971/182584. Open June 5–Aug. 19, weekdays 8–6, Sat. 8–2; Aug. 20–June 4, weekdays 8:30–4.
Savonlinna. Puistokatu 1, tel. 957/13492. Open Feb.–May, daily 8–6; June–Aug., daily 8 AM–10 PM; Sept.–Oct., daily 6–6; Nov.–Jan., weekdays 9–4.
Tampere. Verkatehtaankatu 2, tel. 931/126652. Open June–Aug., weekdays 8:30 AM–8 PM, Sat. 8:30–6, Sun. 12–6; Sept.–May, weekdays 8:30–4.

The Lakelands

Exploring the Lakelands

The center of **Savonlinna** is a series of islands linked by bridges. First, stop in at the tourist office for information; then cross the bridge east to the open-air **market** which flourishes alongside the main passenger quay. It's from here that you can catch the boat to Kuopio. In days when waterborne traffic was the major form of transport, Savonlinna was the central hub of the passenger fleet serving Saimaa, the largest lake system in Europe. Now the lake traffic is dominated by cruise and sightseeing boats, but the quayside is still bustling with arrivals and departures every summer morning and evening.

A ten-minute stroll from the quay to the southeast brings you to Savonlinna's most famous sight, the castle of **Olavinlinna**. First built in 1475 to protect Finland's eastern border, it retains its medieval character and is one of Scandinavia's best preserved historic monuments. Still surrounded by water that once formed part of its defensive strength, the fortress rises majestically out of the lake. The International Opera Festival is held in the courtyard each July. The combination of music and setting is spellbinding. You will need to reserve well in advance (tel. 957/514700) both for tickets and for hotel rooms, since Savonlinna becomes a mecca for music lovers. And music is not the only activity; arts and crafts are also strongly featured in exhibits around town. *Castle. Admission: FIM 14 adults, FIM 7 children; includes a guided tour. Open June–Aug., daily 9–5; Sept.–May, daily 10–3.*

Close to the castle is the 19th-century steam schooner, **Salama,** which houses an excellent museum on the history of lake traffic, including the fascinating floating timber trains that are still a common sight on Saimaa today. *Admission: FIM 10 adults, FIM 5 children. Open mid-June–mid-Aug., daily 10–8; off-season hours vary, check locally.*

The most popular excursion from Savonlinna is to **Retretti.** You can take either a two-hour boat ride or a 30-minute, 18-mile bus trip. The journey by bus takes you along the five-mile ridge of **Punkaharju.** This amazing ridge of pine-covered rocks, which rises out of the water and separates the lakes on either side, predates the Ice Age. At times it narrows to only 25 feet, yet it still manages to accommodate a road and train tracks. Retretti itself is a modern art complex of unique design, which includes a new cavern section built into Punkaharju ridge. It's also a magnificent setting for concerts in summer. *Admission: FIM 45 adults, FIM 40 seniors and students, FIM 15 children. Special 2-day ticket FIM 55. Open daily 10–8.*

Near Retretti is the **Punkaharju National Hotel.** The building started as a gamekeeper's lodge for Tsar Nicholas I in 1845 but has been subsequently enlarged and restored, and is now a restful spot for a meal or an overnight visit.

The 12-hour boat trip from Savonlinna to **Kuopio** is probably the best opportunity you'll get to feel the soul of the Finnish lakeland. Meals are available on board. The boat arrives at Kuopio passenger harbor, where you'll find a small evening market in action daily from 3 to 10. If you go by car, the best route is by Highways 14, 464, and 5, via Rantasalmi and Varkaus.

The Kuopio tourist office is located close to the **Tori** (market place). The Tori should be one of the places you visit first, for it is one of the most colorful outdoor markets in Finland. *Open weekdays 7–3, Sat. 7–2.*

The **Orthodox Church Museum** has one of the most interesting and unusual collections of its kind in the world. When Karelia was ceded to the Soviet Union after World War II, the religious art was taken out of the monasteries and brought to Kuopio. The collection is eclectic and, of its type, one of the rarest in the world. *Karjalankatu 1, Kuopio, tel. 971/122611. Open Tues.– Sun. 10–4.*

Visitors who are fascinated by the treasures in the museum will want to visit the Orthodox convent of Lintula and the **Monastery of Valamo.** The monastery is a center for Russian Orthodox religious and cultural life in Finland. The precious 18th-century icons and sacred objects are housed in the main church and in the icon conservation center. The Orthodox library is the most extensive in Finland and is open to visitors. Church services are held daily. There is a café-restaurant, and hotel and hostel accommodations are available at the monastery. It can be reached by car and bus routes from Kuopio, Joensuu, and Varkaus. *Uusi-Valamo, tel. 972/61911 (972/61959 for hotel reservations). Guided tours: FIM 15 adults, FIM 5 children. Open daily 10–6.*

The **convent of Lintula** can be reached by boat from Valamo, or you can visit both the convent and monastery by boat on scenic day excursions from Kuopio, which run from June 10 through

August 13. Tickets are available from the tourist office, and cost FIM 170 for adults and FIM 85 for children.

Puijo Tower is best visited at sunset, when the lakes shimmer with reflected light. The slender tower is located three kilometers (two miles) northwest of Kuopio. It has two observation decks and a revolving restaurant on top where you can enjoy the marvelous views. *Open 8 AM—11 PM.*

The 320-kilometer (192-mile) journey from Kuopio to **Tampere** will take four to five hours, whether you travel by car or bus. The train ride from Helsinki to Tampere takes about two hours.

Almost every guide will inform you that Tampere, the country's second largest city, is Finland's Pittsburgh. However, the resemblance begins and ends with the concentrated presence here of industry—the settings themselves have little in common.

From about the year 1,000, this part of Finland was a base from which traders and hunters set out on their expeditions to northern Finland and even to Lapland. But it was not until 1779 that a Swedish king actually founded the town of Tampere. Forty-one years later, a Scotsman by the name of James Finlayson came to the infant city and established a factory for spinning cotton. This was perhaps the beginning of "big business" in Finland. The firm of Finlayson exists today and is still one of the country's leading industrial enterprises.

Artful location is the secret of Tampere's many factories. An isthmus little more than half a mile wide at its narrowest point separates the lakes Näsijärvi and Pyhäjärvi, and at one spot the **Tammerkoski Rapids** provide an outlet for the waters of one to cascade through to the other. Called the "Mother of Tampere," these rapids provide the power on which the town's livelihood depends. Their natural beauty has been preserved in spite of the factories on either bank, and the well-designed public buildings of the city grouped around them enhance their general effect. Also in the heart of town is **Hämeensilta Bridge,** with its four statues by the well-known Finnish sculptor Wäinö Aaltonen.

Close to the Hämeensilta bridge, near the high-rise Hotel Ilves, are some warehouses which have been restored as shops and boutiques. Nearby, at Verkatehtaankatu 2, is the city tourist office, where you can buy a 24-hour **Tampere Service Card** (FIM 40 adults, FIM 25 children) that allows unlimited travel on local city transportation, entrance to museums, and a variety of discounts.

Parts of the ridge of **Pyynikki** separating the two lakes form a natural park, including the Särkänniemi peninsula, about a 20-minute walk northwest of the city center. On the way there, visit one of Tampere's best small museums, **The Workers' Museum of Amuri.** It consists of a block of old timber houses, with descriptions and illustrations of how the original tenants lived; it is so well done that you half expect them to return at any minute. *Makasiininkatu 12. Admission: FIM 10 adults, FIM 3 children. Open June 6–Oct. 3, Tues.–Sun. 12–6.*

At Särkänniemi is Finland's tallest structure, the 560-foot **Nasinnuela Observation Tower** (open daily 10–8). There is an observatory on top, as well as a revolving restaurant. The views are magnificent, commanding the lake, forest, and town.

The contrast between the industrial maze of Tampere at your feet and the serenity of the lakes stretching out to meet the horizon is unforgettable.

The same building complex houses the first **planetarium** in Scandinavia and a well-planned **aquarium,** which includes a separate dolphinarium. Near this complex is another striking example of Finnish architecture, the **Sarah Hildén Art Museum,** where modern Finnish and international artists (including Miro, Leger, Picasso, and Chagall) are on display. *Joint admission: FIM 60 adults, FIM 40 children. Open daily 11–6.*

At the foot of the Pyynikki Ridge is the **Pyynikki Open Air Theater** with a revolving auditorium that can be moved, even with a full load of spectators, to face any one of the sets, ready prepared by nature.

On the east side of the town is the modern **Kaleva Church.** What may appear from the outside to be a grain elevator is in fact, as seen from the interior, a soaring monument to space and light. *Open daily 10–6.*

Most buildings in Tampere, including the cathedral, are comparatively modern. However, though the cathedral was built only in 1907, it is worth a visit to see some of the best known masterpieces of Finnish art, including Magnus Encknell's frescoes, *The Resurrection,* and two works by Hugo Simberg, *Wounded Angel* and *Garden of Death.*

It was in Tampere that Lenin and Stalin first met, and this fateful occasion is commemorated with displays of photos and mementos in the **Lenin Museum.** *Hallituskatsu 19. Admission: FIM 6 adults, FIM 2 children. Open Tues.–Sat. 11–3, Sun. 11–4.*

Just outside of town in Kaukajärvi, about 9 kilometers (6 miles) away, is the charming **Haihara Doll Museum.** The collection features dolls from different parts of the world. *Admission: FIM 15 adults, FIM 5 children. Open Apr. 15–Sept., daily noon–6; Oct.–Nov. and Feb. 11–Mar., Sun. noon–4.*

One of the most popular excursions from Tampere is the **Poet's Way** boat tour along Lake Näsijärvi. The boat passes through the agricultural parish of Ruovesi, where J. L. Runeberg, Finland's national poet, used to live. Shortly before the boat docks at Virrat, you pass through the straights of Visuvesi, where many artists and writers spend their summers. *Finnish Silverline and Poet's Way, Verkatehtaankatu 2, 33100 Tampere, tel. 931/124804. Round-trip fare: FIM 236.*

Not far north of Virrat is **Ahtari,** where Finland's first wildlife park has been established in a beautiful setting, with a holiday village, a good hotel, and recreation facilities.

The Silverline's white motor ships leave Tampere for **Hämeenlinna** from the Laukontori terminal. If you're traveling by car, take Highway 3 and stop en route at the famous **Iittala Glassworks,** which offers guided tours and has a museum and shop. The magnificent glass is produced by top designers, and the "seconds" are bargains you won't find elsewhere. *Open Sept.–Apr., daily 9–6; May–Aug., daily 9–8. Guided tours weekdays at 11, 1, and 3.*

Hämeenlinna's secondary school has educated many famous Finns, among them composer Jean Sibelius (1865–1957). The only timber house surviving in the town center is the **birthplace of Sibelius,** a modest dwelling built in 1834. Here you can listen to tapes of his music and see the harmonium he played when he was a child. *Hallituskatu 11. Admission: FIM 3 adults, FIM 2 children. Open May–Aug., daily 10–4; Sept.–Apr., weekdays and Sun. noon–4.*

The much-altered medieval **Häme Castle,** on the lake shore half a mile north of the town center, doesn't compare with Savonlinna's, but it has seen a lot of action in its time and has been used as a granary and a prison. *Admission: FIM 14 adults, FIM 7 children. Open May–Aug., daily 10–6; Sept.–Apr., daily 10–4.*

Hattula Church, 6 kilometers (3½ miles) to the north, is the most famous of Finland's medieval churches. The interior is a fresco gallery of biblical scenes whose vicious little devils and soulful saints are as clear and fresh as when they were first painted around 1510. There is a regular bus service from the town center. *Admission: FIM 10 adults, FIM 5 children. Open May 7–31, daily 9–6; June–Aug. 15, daily 10–6; Aug. 16–Sept. 3, daily noon–4.*

Rail and bus schedules to Helsinki are frequent. If you're traveling by car, take Highway 3. As you pass by **Riihimäke,** you'll see signs to the **Finnish Glass Museum.** Follow them! It's an outstanding display of the history of glass from early Egyptian times to the present day, beautifully arranged in an old glass factory. *Admission: FIM 8 adults, FIM 4 children. Open Apr.–Sept., Tues.–Sun. 10–6.*

Dining and Lodging

For details and price category definitions, *see* Dining and Lodging in Staying in Finland.

Hämeenlinna
Dining
Häme Castle. Situated on the lake shore half a mile from the town center, Häme Castle is sometimes the setting for medieval banquets. It also has a pleasant coffee house. *Linnantie 6, tel. 917/25928. Reservations essential for banquets. AE, DC, MC, V. Restaurant Expensive; coffee house Moderate.*

Piparkakkutalo. Located in a renovated old timber building, Piiparkakkutalo has a restaurant upstairs, a tavern downstairs. The menu offers fine Finnish fare. *Kirkkorinne 2, tel. 917/121606. Reservations advised. AE, MC, V. Moderate.*

Lodging
★ **Rantasipi Aulanko.** One of Finland's top hotels sits on the lake shore in a beautifully landscaped park 6.4 kilometers (2 miles) from town. *Aulanko, tel. 917/58801. 216 rooms with bath. Facilities: saunas, pool, squash, tennis, golf, riding, boating, swimming beach, nightclub, and tax-free shop. AE, DC, MC, V. Very Expensive (Moderate in July).*

Kuopio
Dining
Mustalammas. Located near the passenger harbor, Mustalammas has been attractively adapted from a beer cellar and features steaks and basic fish dishes. *Satamakatu 4, tel. 971/123494. Reservations advised. AE, DC, MC, V. Expensive.*

Sampo. Situated in the town center, Sampo specializes in vendace (*muikku*), a kind of whitefish. Try the smoked variety. The atmosphere is unpretentious and lively. *Kauppakatu 13, tel. 971/114677. MC, V. Inexpensive.*

Lodging **Rauhalahti.** About 4.8 kilometers (3 miles) from the town center, Rauhalahti is set near the lake shore and has a number of amenities catering to sportsmen and families. The hotel has three restaurants, including the tavern-style Vanha Apteekkari—a local favorite. *Katiskaniementie 6, tel. 971/311700. 126 rooms with bath or shower. Facilities: saunas, swimming pool, solarium, gymnasium, children's playroom, disco, tennis, horseback riding, squash, boat rental. AE, DC, MC, V. Expensive.*

Rivoli. Completed in 1987, the Rivoli is the most modern and best equipped of local hotels. It also has all the advantages of a lakefront location, and is close to the center of town. *Satamakatu 1, tel. 971/195111. 141 rooms with bath or shower. Facilities: sauna, swimming pool, Jacuzzi, solarium, tennis, boat rental. AE, DC, MC, V. Expensive.*

Sport Hotel Puijo. Located next to Puijo Tower, the Sport Hotel Puijo is only four years old but built in the traditional timber style. Rooms are large and very quiet. *Puijo, tel. 971/114841. 20 rooms with shower. Facilities: saunas. AE, DC, MC, V. Moderate.*

Savonlinna
Dining

Rauhalinna. This romantic turn-of-the-century timber villa was built by a general in the Imperial Russian Army. It's 16 kilometers (10 miles) by road, 40 minutes by boat, from town. Both food and atmosphere are old Russian, but some Finnish specialties are also available. *Lehtiniemi, tel. 957/523119. Reservations necessary during festival season. AE, DC, MC, V. Closed Sept.–May. Expensive.*

Snellman. This small 1920s-style mansion is in the center of town. Meals are served against a quiet background of classical music. *Olavinkatu 31, tel. 957/13104. Reservations advised. AE, DC, MC, V. Expensive; Moderate lunches upstairs.*

Majakka. Centrally located, Majakka goes in for home cooking and a family atmosphere. *Satamakatu 11, tel. 957/21456. Reservations necessary during festival season. AE, DC, MC, V. Moderate.*

San Martin. A steak house with a pleasant open courtyard in summer. *Olavinkatu 46, tel. 957/13004. AE, DC, MC, V. Moderate.*

Musta Pässi. Located near the bus station, Musta Pässi serves fresh fish, meatballs, potatoes, and other homemade dishes in a tavern setting. *Tulliportinkatu 2, tel. 957/22228. AE, MC, V. Inexpensive.*

Lodging **Tott.** This is an old favorite, located in the downtown area opposite the passenger harbor. It was completely renovated in 1987. *Satamakatu 1, tel. 957/514500. 60 rooms with bath or shower. Facilities: saunas, pool, nightclub. AE, DC, MC, V. Expensive (Very Expensive in July).*

Casino Spa. Built in the 1960s and renovated in 1986, the Casino Spa has a restful lakeside location on an island linked by a pedestrian bridge to the center of town. *Kasinonsaari, tel. 957/22864. 79 rooms with bath or shower. Facilities: saunas, pool, nightclub, marina, spa treatment. AE, DC, MC, V. Expensive.*

Seurahuone. This old town house is located near the market and passenger harbor. A new extension opened in 1989. Some older rooms are small. *Kauppatori 4, tel. 957/5731. 84 rooms with shower. Facilities: saunas, disco. AE, DC, MC, V. Moderate.*

Vuoilinna Summer Hotel. Guests at this modern hotel use the facilities, including the restaurant, of the nearby Casino Spa

Hotel. *Kasinonsaari, tel. 957/24908. 160 rooms, with shower for every two rooms. AE, DC, MC, V. Closed Sept.–May. Inexpensive (Moderate in July).*

Tampere
Dining

Finlayson Palatsi. Set in its own gardens about one kilometer (one-half mile) from the town center, this elegant restaurant still has many of the original furnishings from the turn of the century, when it was a private residence. *Kuninkaankatu 11, tel. 931/125905. Reservations advised. AE, DC, MC, V. Very expensive.*

Natalie. Russian in atmosphere, cuisine, and background music, Natalie is housed in the old Workers' Theater near the center of town. *Hallituskatu 19, tel. 931/32040. Reservations advised. AE, DC, MC, V. Moderate.*

Salud. Salud has a well-earned reputation for Spanish specialties, though it also features some Finnish dishes. *Otavalankatu 10, tel. 931/35996. Reservations advised. AE, DC, MC, V. Moderate. Closed weekends in July.*

Silakka. Although its atmosphere is casual and unpretentious, Silakka has earned a great reputation for its Finnish fish specialties. *Vuolteenkatu 20, tel. 931/149740. DC, MC, V. Closed Sun. in summer. Inexpensive.*

Lodging

Ilves. The city's newest hotel soars above a newly gentrified area of old warehouses near the city center. It is favored by Americans. *Hatanpään valtatie 1, tel. 931/121212. 336 rooms with bath or shower, special floor for nonsmokers. Facilities: saunas, pool, Jacuzzi, nightclub. AE, DC, MC, V. Very Expensive.*

Cumulus. Overlooking the tamed rapids of Tammerkoski, Cumulus is central and modern. The Finnair terminal is in the same building. *Koskikatu 5, tel. 931/35500. 230 rooms with shower. Facilities: saunas, pool, nightclub. AE, DC, MC, V. Expensive.*

Domus Summer Hotel. About 1.6 kilometers (one mile) from the center of town, in the Kaleva district, this hotel is good value. *Pellervonkatu 9, tel. 931/550000. 200 rooms, 85 with shower. Facilities: saunas, pool, disco. MC, V. Closed Sept.–May. Inexpensive.*

Finnish Lapland

Lapland is often called Europe's last wilderness, a region of endless forests, fells, and great silences. So often the arrival of settlers has obliterated all that came before, but here man has walked gently and left the virgin solitude of this country almost unspoiled. Now easily accessible by plane, train, or bus, this Arctic outpost offers comfortable hotels and modern amenities, yet you won't have to go very far to find yourself in an almost primordial solitude.

The oldest traces of human habitation in Finland have been found in Lapland, and hoards of Danish, English, and even Arabian coins indicate the existence of trade activities many centuries ago. The origins of the Lapps themselves are lost in the mists of history. There are only about 2,500 pure Lapps still living here; the remainder of the province's population of 220,000 are Finns. Until the 1930s, Lapland was still largely unexploited, still a region where any trip was an expedition. Then the Canadian-owned Petsamo Nickel Company (now in Soviet hands) completed the great road that connects

Rovaniemi with the Arctic Sea. Building activities increased along this route (later to be known as the Arctic Highway), the land was turned and sown, and a few hotels were built to cater to increasing numbers of visitors.

In September 1944, in conformity with the terms of the Armistice Treaty with the Soviet Union, the Finns began driving out considerable numbers of German troops then stationed in Lapland. The retreating Germans destroyed all they could; the capital, Rovaniemi, was leveled, and almost every farmhouse, cottage, and cattle shed was burned down or blown up.

Before the ruins ceased smoking, the Finns were already back working to create new communities out of the desolation. Certain areas of Lapland had to be ceded to the Soviet Union (the Arctic coastline, Petsamo, and part of the Salla district on the eastern frontier), but their inhabitants were resettled within the new Finnish boundaries. Among them were 250 Skolt Lapps, a unique tribe who were settled at Sevettijärvi on the northern shores of Lake Inari.

Summer has the blessing of daylight up to 24 hours long and often beautiful weather to go with it—but beware of the mosquitoes. In early fall the colors are so fabulous that the Finns have a special word for it: *ruska*. If you can take the intense but dry cold, winter is also a fascinating time in Lapland, not only for the Northern Lights but for such experiences as the reindeer roundups.

Depending how far north of the Arctic Circle you go, the sun might not rise for several weeks around midwinter. Don't imagine it is pitch dark, though. There is reflected light from the invisible sun below the horizon during the middle of the day and a luminosity from the ever-present snow.

In December and January, reindeer owners round up their herds from all over the country and corral them by the thousands. Sometimes dressed in colorful costumes, the Lapps (and also many Finns) lasso the reindeer in true Wild West fashion, recognizing their own animals by brand marks on the ears. The roundups are attended by many buyers, for reindeer meat is considered a delicacy and is exported to the south and abroad.

To get to some of the remoter roundups you may have to travel by taxi plane, though other corrals are near the road, especially around Ivalo, Inari, and Enontekiö. Most Lapps and northern Finns get there on the motorized sledges that have almost entirely replaced the much more attractive (and silent) reindeer-drawn *pulkka* (a kind of boatshaped sleigh on one runner). In southern Lapland especially, an increasing number of roundups occur in the fall. Finding out exactly when and where a roundup is taking place is not easy, for much depends on the whims of the weather and the reindeer, so you must check locally. The information offices in Rovaniemi, however, will be able to give some guidance.

A few words should be said about the Lapps—a proud, sensitive, and intelligent people who prefer their own name for themselves, Same (pronounced Sah-me)—some of whom resent those visitors who regard them as a tourist attraction put there for their benefit. Modern influences (and intermarriage) have regrettably changed many aspects of their traditional way of life; for example, the attractive costumes are less frequently seen, except on festive occasions. The young, especially, have been affected by the changes, and many of them are far more interested in becoming teachers, lawyers, or engineers than in breeding reindeer or hunting from their remote homesteads. Yet others have found profit from selling souvenirs to the tourists. But most prefer to go about their daily life minding their own business. The Lady Day Church Festival in Enontekiö in March is a particularly colorful event, attended by many Lapps in their most brilliant costumes, and usually feature reindeer racing or lassoing competitions.

The new and the old intermingle in this remote northern corner of Europe. The new Lapland is a place of modern techniques where careful management is gradually driving back the wilderness and creating cornfields beyond the Arctic Circle. The forests are being exploited and managed with expert care, and light industry and hydro-electric projects have added their mark to the Lapland map. Yet gold-panners cut off from the world except for occasional visitors and the aircraft that swoop down with their mail and provisions, still wash the gravel of the Lemmenjoki river, and the rhythm of the seasons still governs the life of all those connected with reindeer. And the experienced traveler who would like to roam through the wilds for days on end without meeting a fellow human being can still do so without any problem at all. Be warned, however, that climatic conditions change rapidly and often unpredictably, especially on those lonely Arctic fells. Always seek local advice and let your hotel and friends know where you are heading and how long you intend to be away. An attractive alternative is provided by organized canoeing or hiking trips with nights in huts or tents in the wilderness.

Getting Around

Rovaniemi is the best base for traveling around the Arctic area. It connects with Helsinki and the south by road, rail, and air links; there is even a car-train from Helsinki. Within the area, driving is the best way to get around, although a regular bus service connects most centers. There are also daily flights from Rovaniemi to Ivalo.

Guided Tours

Friendly Finland Tours features the itinerary (*see* Exploring Lapland below) on an escorted three-day "Arctic Lapland" tour out of Helsinki. You can get details from the Finnish Tourist Board's overseas offices (*see* Chapter 1), or at Unioninkatu 26, Helsinki, tel. 90/144511.

Tourist Information

Ivalo. Bus Station, Piiskuntie 5, tel. 9697/12521.
Rovaniemi. Aallonkatu 1, tel. 960/16270; open June–Aug., weekdays 8–7, weekends 10–7; Sept.–May, weekdays 8–4; also at the train station, tel. 960/22218. For further information on the region, contact **Lapland Travel,** Maakuntakatu 10, tel. 960/16052.
Sodankylä. Jäämerentie 9, tel. 9693/13474.

Exploring Lapland

Your best launching point is the town of **Rovaniemi,** where the Ounas and Kemi rivers meet almost on the Arctic Circle. Rovaniemi is the so-called "Gateway to Lapland" and the administrative hub and communications center of the province.

If you're expecting an Arctic shanty town, you're in for a surprise. Rovaniemi was nearly razed by the retreating German army in 1944, so what you'll see today is a modern city strongly influenced by Aalvar Aalto's architecture. The old way of life is preserved in museums. During the process of rebuilding, the population rose from 8,000 to more than 32,000, so be prepared for a contemporary city on the edge of the wilderness, with various amenities and some incredible architecture—notably **Lappia Hall,** the concert and congress center that also houses the world's northernmost professional theater, designed by Aalto. Rovaniemi also has the best shops in the region.

After collecting information from the tourist office, find a window table in the restaurant of the nearby **Pohjanhovi Hotel,** and plan your itinerary while gazing out at the fast-flowing Kemi River. If it's early July, it will probably be full of floating lumber. Short river cruises are conducted daily in summer.

You can get a good instant introduction to the region and its natural history at the **Museum of the Province of Lapland** at Lappia House. The collection also includes exhibits of Same culture. *Admission: FIM 5 adults, FIM 2 children. Open May–Aug., Tues.–Sun. 10–6; Sept.–Apr., Tues.–Sun. noon–4.*

But you'll get more of a feel for the living past from the **Pöykköla Museum,** located in 18th-century farm buildings 3 kilometers (2 miles) from the town center. *Admission: FIM 3 adults, FIM 1 children. Open June–Aug., daily noon–4; bus service available.*

The Arctic Highway (Highway 4) is the main artery of central and northern Lapland; you'll follow it north for most of this tour. Eight kilometers (5 miles) north of Rovaniemi, right on the Arctic Circle, is **Santa Claus's Workshop,** where gifts can be bought in midsummer for shipping at any time of year, with a special Santa Claus Land stamp. There are various attractions including the **Hundred Elves' House** (an exhibition of Christmas customs) and some reindeer, but for most visitors the main one is to mail postcards home from the special Arctic Circle post office. There's also a very good souvenir shopping complex and the impressive sight of the mountains of mail that pour in from children all over the world. Yes, all of it gets answered. *Admission: free. Open June–Aug., daily 9–8; Sept.–May, daily 9–5.*

After driving north for a couple of hours, you may want to take a short detour to the modern tourist center at **Luostotunturi** in the fell district of southern Lapland—you'll turn right onto a secondary road 16 kilometers (10 miles) south of Sodankylä, and follow it 22 kilometers (13 miles) to the center.

Back on the main road, at **Sodankylä,** there is a **Northern Lights Observatory** (for professionals only) and an ancient wood church.

Continue north, through the village of Vuotso, to **Tankavaara,** the most accessible and the best developed of several gold-

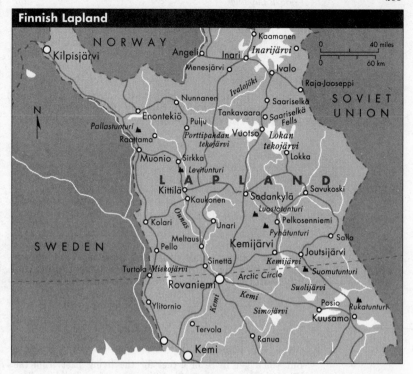

Finnish Lapland

panning areas. The **Gold Museum** tells the century-old story of Lapland's hardy fortune seekers. For a small fee, authentic prospectors will show you how to sift gold dust and tiny nuggets from the dirt of an ice-cold stream. You can keep what you find but don't expect to be able to retire early. *Admission: FIM 12 adults, FIM 5 children. Open June–Aug. 15, daily 9–6; Aug. 16–Sept., daily 9–5; Oct.–May, weekdays 10–4.*

Thirty kilometers (18 miles) north of Tankavaara is the holiday center of **Saariselkä,** which has a variety of accommodations and makes a sensible base from which to set off on a trip (alone or in a group) into the true wilderness. There are marked trails through forests and over fells, where nothing much has changed since the last Ice Age, and where you can experience the timeless silence of the Arctic landscape. More than 965 square miles of this magnificent area has been named the **Urho Kekkonen National Park.**

Just south of the village of Ivalo, the highway passes the **Ivalojoki River.** Canoeing trips are organized on its fast waters down to Lake Inari, returning by bus.

The village of **Ivalo** is the main center for northern Lapland. However, except for a first-class hotel, an airport, and many of the amenities of a modern community, it has little to offer the tourist in search of a wilderness experience.

The huge island-studded expanses of **Lake Inari** (Inarijärvi), north of Ivalo, offer endless possibilities for wilderness exploration. It is a beautiful 40-kilometer (24-mile) drive northwest from Ivalo, along the lakeshore, to **Inari**. This is a good base for summer boat excursions. The **Same Museum**, on the village out-skirts, covers all facets of Lapp culture. *Admission: FIM 12 adults, FIM 5 children. Open June–mid-Aug., daily 8 AM–10 PM; mid-Aug.–mid-Sept., hours vary, check locally.*

In recent years, a growing number of small holiday villages have blossomed near Inari and to the north of it, usually with a small restaurant and shop attached. Amenities are simple, but the locations are often magnificent and bring you very close to the true pulse of Lapland. Usually there will be a boat at your disposal, fishing possibilities, and the experience of preparing your own sauna. From Kaamanen, north of Inari, a side road leads to **Sevettijärvi**, home of the Skolt Lapps, and eventually into Norway.

It is an attractive drive back south from Inari to **Menesjärvi** along a relatively new, secondary road that passes through a wilderness of forest and swamp. Take every opportunity to leave your car and do some walking; it's the only way to experi-ence the vastness of these Arctic spaces. The hills gets gentler and the ride less dramatic as you continue south to Levitunturi, the last of the gently sloping fells before you reach the banks of the Ounas River and return to Rovaniemi via Highway 79.

Dining and Lodging

For details and price category definitions, *see* Dining and Lodg-ing in Staying in Finland.

Inari
Lodging

Kultahovi. This recently renovated old inn is located on the wooded banks of a swiftly flowing river. *Inari, tel. 9697/51221. 29 rooms with shower. Facilities: saunas. MC, V. Moderate.*

Ivalo
Lodging

Hotel Ivalo. Right on the riverside about a kilometer (half a mile) from the village center, Ivalo is modern and well-equipped. One of its two restaurants serves Lapland special-ties, including *poronkäristys*, a reindeer casserole. *Ivalontie 34, tel. 9697/21911. 62 rooms with bath or shower. Facilities: 2 restaurants, saunas, pool, boating, disco. AE, DC, MC, V. Expensive.*

Levitunturi
Lodging

Levitunturi. Built in traditional log style at the foot of the fells, Levitunturi is a particularly well-equipped and modern tourist complex. *Sirkka, tel. 9694/81301. 82 rooms with shower. Facili-ties: special nonsmoking floor, saunas, pool, Jacuzzi, squash, gymnasium, tennis, boating, cross-country skiing, spa facili-ties. AE, DC, MC, V. Expensive.*

Luostotunturi
Lodging

Kantakievari Luosto. Situated amid the fells southeast of Sodankylä, this small-scale hotel is modern and comfortable. It is built in traditional timber style. *Sodankylä, tel. 9693/13681. 32 rooms with shower. Facilities: saunas, boating, disco, cross-country skiing. AE, DC, MC, V. Moderate.*

Rovaniemi
Dining

Bel Giovanni. Northern Finland may be the last place you'd ex-pect to find a lively Italian restaurant, but the atmosphere here is authentic and friendly. The emphasis is on pizzas, pas-tas, and grills. *Valtakatu 34, tel. 960/16406. No reservations. AE, MC, V. Moderate.*

Pinja. Quiet and intimate, Pinja offers good home cooking in a relaxed atmosphere. *Valtakatu 19, tel. 960/14272. No reserva-tions. No smoking. DC, MC, V. Moderate.*

Lodging **Rantasipi Pohjanhovi.** With its pleasant location overlooking the Kemi River, this hotel is an old favorite with travelers to the north. It has been extended and modernized over the years. The hotel offers guests free raft trips. *Pohjanpuistikko 2, tel. 960/313731. 212 rooms with bath or shower. Special floor for nonsmokers. Some rooms in neighboring building. Facilities: saunas, pool, raft trips, boating, disco. AE, DC, MC, V. Very Expensive.*

Ounasvaara. Located on a hilltop three kilometers (two miles) from the center, Ounasvaara is the top choice for views and a tranquil atmosphere, but it's best if you have a car. *Ounasvaara, tel. 960/23371. 52 rooms with bath or shower. Facilities: saunas, cross-country skiing. AE, DC, MC, V. Expensive.*

Gasthof. Built in 1986, the Gasthof is a comfortable small hotel with a restaurant featuring Russian specialties. *Koskikatu 41, tel. 960/23222. 28 rooms with shower. Facilities: special nonsmoking floor, restaurant, saunas, pool. AE, DC, MC, V. Moderate.*

Oppipoika. This hotel belongs to the Hotel School of Rovaniemi. Rooms are spacious and comfortable, but the real reason to come here is the food: Chef Tapio Sointu has created the *Lapland à la Carte* program, featuring a variety of Lapland specialties. *Korkalonkatu 33, tel. 960/20321. 40 rooms with bath or shower. Facilities: restaurant, saunas, pool. AE, DC, MC, V. Moderate.*

Saariselkä **Riekonlinna.** The latest and best-equipped addition to this de-
Lodging veloping tourist complex on the fringes of the wilderness fells, Riekonlinna makes good use of its location. *Tel. 9697/81601. 66 rooms with shower. Facilities: saunas, tennis, boating, squash, cross-country skiing, AE, DC, MC, V. Very Expensive.*

Tankavaara **Wanhan Waskoolimiehen Kahvila.** Lapland specialties are fea-
Dining tured in this attractive café and restaurant; try the braised reindeer with creamed potatoes and lingonberries. Accommodations are limited in the vicinity. *Tankavaara Gold Village, tel. 9693/46158. No reservations. No credit cards. Moderate.*

10 France

Introduction

The French are different. They don't have the Anglo-Saxon outlook you may find reassuring in, say, Germany or Scandinavia. They are a Mediterranean people—temperamental and spontaneous, closer to the Spanish and Italians than to northern Europeans. At the same time, they are heirs to the Cartesian tradition of logic ("I think, therefore I am"), as well as being inveterate theorizers. Their reluctance to take a shortcut to an obvious solution often frustrates English-speaking pragmatists.

One thing the French do well—probably because it's instinctive and they don't need to think about it—is live. The essence of French *savoir-vivre* is simplicity. Everyday things count: eating, drinking, talking, dressing, shopping. Get in the mood: Daily rituals are meant to be enjoyed. Food is the best example. The French don't like rushing their meals. They plan them in advance, painstakingly prepare them, look forward to them over an *apéritif*, admire the loving presentation of each dish, savor each mouthful. The pace is unhurried and the wine flows steadily.

Make the most of the simple pleasure to be had from basking in the sunshine outside a café. Admire the casual elegance of the passersby or the old men in their time-honored berets. Even the most mundane things can become objects of beauty in French eyes. The daily market is a festival of colors and textures, with fruit and vegetable stalls artistically and imaginatively composed. Shop windows are works of art.

Most French towns and villages are quietly attractive and historic. Chances are that the ornate *mairie* (town hall) has been there since the Revolution, and the church or cathedral since the Middle Ages. The main streets tend to be lined with sturdy trees planted before living memory. The 20th century is kept firmly at bay. Modern buildings—such as supermarkets—are banished to the outskirts or obliged to fit in with the architecture of the town center.

At the hub of nearly every town you can expect to find an "eternal triangle" of buildings. The church and mairie, representing God and the State, are the first two. The third—representing the tourist—is the Syndicat d'initiative. The Syndicat d'initiative (marked on signs with an *i* and sometimes more helpfully known as the Office de tourisme, or tourism office) should be your first stop when visiting any French town. At the very least, you'll come away with a street map and list of hotels —if you're lucky, reservations can be made for you on the spot —plus plenty of brochures about other towns and regions.

There is a bewildering variety of man-made marvels in France. Southern France is rich in Roman remains: Try not to miss the triumphal arch in Orange, the amphitheater in Arles, or the Pont du Gard aqueduct near Nîmes. Western France is dotted with Romanesque churches from the 10th and 11th centuries, with some of the best examples in Poitiers.

Gothic architecture was born in the Ile de France around Paris: The huge cathedrals of Amiens, Reims, Bourges, and Chartres—not to forget Notre-Dame in the capital—rank among the world's finest. The Renaissance yielded the sumptuous Loire châteaux and the Palace of Fontainebleau, paving the way for the haughty Baroque of Versailles.

Bordeaux is an elegant example of the more restrained Classicism prevalent in the 18th century. Paris contains masterly demonstrations of 19th-century architecture and city planning. The 20th century has been as productive as its predecessors—take the futuristic steel and glass of La Défense, west of Paris, the space age Pompidou Center, or the glass pyramid of the Louvre.

France boasts as much natural as man-made variety. There's just about every type of landscape except desert. You'll find ski slopes and towering peaks in the Alps or Pyrenees; beaches and cliffs in Brittany or along the Mediterranean; extinct volcanoes in Auvergne; limitless horizons beyond the golden grain fields of the Beauce or the misty plains of the north; haunting evergreen forests stretching from the Ardennes, near Belgium, down to the Midi (south); marsh and canals in the Marais Poitevin, the "Green Venice" of the west; barren, rock-strewn wilderness in the southern Causses; lush, softly lit valleys along the Seine or Loire; steep-climbing terraces above the Rhône; and wherever you go, the swirl and sway of ripening vines.

Although its regional differences are tangible, France remains a well-knit nation. Its boundaries are largely natural and undisputed. It is a manageable size and a sensible shape (Frenchmen refer to their country as the Hexagon). Not that all Frenchmen are the same. Along the south coast, exuberant Latins live in tune with the sun-and-siesta rhythms of the Mediterranean. Nice, after all, was an Italian city until 1860. The southwest of France looks toward Spain: Basque territory extends on either side of the Pyrenees. The wine regions of Bordeaux and Cognac have centuries-long links with Britain, and it is no coincidence that their inhabitants are comparatively calm and "phlegmatic" (a Frenchman's favorite adjective for the average Englishman). The people of Brittany proudly defend their Celtic heritage and feel as much affinity with the Cornish and Welsh as with their fellow French. Don't forget the Viking origins of the Normans who conquered England or the historical German influence on Alsace. And the French of the north have plenty in common with their Belgian neighbors, beginning with a mutual craving for beer and french fries.

Whatever you may have been led to believe, France is a welcoming country. Don't be misled by the superficial coldness of the French: They are a formal people who don't go out of their way to speak to strangers (except in anger). Above all, don't suppose that all Frenchmen are like Parisians—it's not true. Most of the French are more approachable and friendly. One of the reasons is that a great many have foreign origins themselves. France has always attracted immigrants from less affluent countries: Italy, Spain, Portugal, Poland, and North Africa. More than a million Frenchmen were brought up in Algeria and came home only in the early 1960s after Algerian independence.

Despite the parochial inertia you may find in rural areas, many of the French can be remarkably outward looking. Their unique geographical position has a lot to do with that. France considers itself to be, above all, a European power. It borders

France

N

ENGLAND

La Manche
(English Channel)

Boulogne

Cherbourg

Dieppe

Le Havre

Rouen

Seine

Caen

Roscoff

St-Malo

Brest

Morlaix

St-Brieuc

Chartres

Quimper

Rennes

Le Mans

Orléans

Lorient

Vannes

Angers

Blois

Nantes

Loire

Tours

ATLANTIC
OCEAN

Poitiers

La Rochelle

Niort

Limoges

Bay of Biscay

Angoulême

Périgueux

Bordeaux

Garonne

Brive-la-Gaillarde

Dordogne

Langon

Cahors

Montauban

Bayonne

Albi

Pau

Tarbes

Toulouse

Carcassonne

S P A I N

ANDORRA

Calais
BELGIUM
Lille
Arras
Amiens
Cambrai
St. Quentin
Beauvais
LUXEMBOURG
Reims
Metz
Paris
Châlons-sur-Marne
Nancy
Strasbourg
Troyes
GERMANY
Auxerre
Mulhouse
Belfort
Bourges
Dijon
Beaune
Besançon
Nevers
SWITZERLAND
Montluçon
Mâcon
Bourg-en-Bresse
Saône
Clermont-Ferrand
Lyon
Rhône
Chambéry
Aurillac
Le Puy
Grenoble
Rhône
ITALY
Rodez
Montélimar
Millau
Avignon
Nîmes
Aix-en-Provence
Monte Carlo
Nice
Montpellier
Cannes
Marseille
Narbonne
Toulon
Perpignan
Mediterranean Sea
Corsica

Corsica
Calvi
Bastia
Corte
Ajaccio

0   50 mi
0   75 km

seven countries (Belgium, Luxembourg, West Germany, Switzerland, Italy, Spain, Andorra) and looks across the Channel at an eighth (Great Britain). France played a crucial role in the creation of the European Economic Community and, since the admission of Spain and Portugal, can claim more than ever to be the crossroads of Western Europe. Everywhere you go you will hear talk of 1992—the date when internal trade barriers between members of the EEC will be abolished, an event anticipated by the French as a watershed in modern history. The French cannot understand why the British cling to their insularity and have dragged their feet so long over the Channel Tunnel.

Still, deep down, most of the French are chauvinists who are proud of *La douce France*, worship Napoleon, and feel that the Liberty-Equality-Fraternity motto of the French Revolution confers moral superiority upon their country—as they showed during the patriotic celebrations in 1989 that marked the bicentennial of the Revolution.

Before You Go

When to Go On the whole, June and September are the best months to be in France. Both months are free of the mid-summer crowds. June offers the advantage of long daylight hours, while slightly cheaper prices and frequent Indian summers (often lasting well into October) make September an attractive proposition. Try to avoid the second half of July and all of August, or be prepared for inflated prices and huge crowds on the beaches. Don't travel on or around July 14 or August 1, 14, or 31 (national holidays). In addition, July and August heat can be stifling in southern France. Paris can be stuffy in August, too. But, on the other hand, it's pleasantly deserted (although many restaurants, theaters, and small shops are closed).

The skiing season in the Alps and Pyrenees lasts from Christmas through Easter—steer clear of February (school vacation time) if you can. Anytime between March and November will offer you a good chance to soak up the sun on the Riviera. If you're going to Paris or the Loire, remember that the weather is unappealing before Easter. If you're dreaming of Paris in the springtime, May (not April) is your best bet.

Climate Be prepared for changes in climate if you wish to visit different parts of France. North of the Loire (including Paris), France has a northern European climate—cold winters, pleasant if unpredictable summers, and frequent rain. Southern France has a Mediterranean climate: mild winters, long, hot summers, and sunshine throughout the year. The more continental climate of eastern and central France is a mixture of these two extremes: Winters can be very cold and summers very hot. France's Atlantic coast has a temperate climate even south of the Loire, with the exception of the much warmer Biarritz.

The following are the average daily maximum and minimum temperatures for Paris.

Jan.	43F	6C	May	68F	20C	Sept.	70F	21C
	34	1		49	10		53	12
Feb.	45F	7C	June	73F	23C	Oct.	60F	16C
	34	1		55	13		46	8
Mar.	54F	12C	July	76F	25C	Nov.	50F	10C
	39	4		58	15		40	5
Apr.	60F	16C	Aug.	75F	24C	Dec.	44F	7C
	43	6		58	14		36	2

The following are the average daily maximum and minimum temperatures for Marseille.

Jan.	50F	10C	May	71F	22C	Sept.	77F	25C
	35	2		52	11		58	15
Feb.	53F	12C	June	79F	26C	Oct.	68F	20C
	36	2		58	15		51	10
Mar.	59F	15C	July	84F	29C	Nov.	58F	15C
	41	5		63	17		43	6
Apr.	64F	18C	Aug.	83F	28C	Dec.	52F	11C
	46	8		63	17		37	3

Currency The unit of French currency is the franc, subdivided into 100 centimes. Bills are issued in denominations of 20, 50, 100, and 500 francs (frs); coins are 5, 10, 20, and 50 centimes, and 1, 2, 5, and 10 francs. The small, copper-colored 5-, 10-, and 20-centime coins have considerable nuisance value but can be used for tips in bars and cafés.

International credit cards and traveler's checks are widely accepted throughout France, except in rural areas. At press time (spring 1989), the dollar was worth 6.2 frs, and the pound sterling was worth 11 frs.

What It Will Cost Gasoline prices are above the European average, and there are tolls on major highways. Train travel, though, is a good buy.

Hotel and restaurant prices compensate for travel expense. Prices are highest in Paris, on the Riviera, and in the Alps during the ski season. But even in these areas, you can find pleasant accommodations and excellent food for surprisingly reasonable prices.

All taxes must be included in posted prices in France. The initials TTC (*toutes taxes comprises*—taxes included) are sometimes included on price lists but, strictly speaking, they are superfluous. Restaurant and hotel prices must *by law* include taxes and service charges: If they are tacked on your bill as additional items, you should complain.

Sample Prices Cup of coffee, 3.50–6 frs; glass of beer, 6–8.50 frs; soft drink, 8–12 frs; ham sandwich, 12–15 frs; one-mile taxi ride, 20–25 frs.

Visas Citizens of the United States and Canada—but not Britain—need a visa as well as a passport to visit France. Completed application forms should be submitted along with your passport to the nearest French consulate. U.S. citizens must pay $3 for a 72-hour transit visa, $9 for a three-month multiple-entry visa, and $15 for a five-year multiple-entry visa. Canadians must go through the same process. Check with travel agents for the latest costs.

Customs on Arrival   Travelers from the United States and Canada may bring into France 400 cigarettes or 100 cigars or 100 grams of tobacco, one liter of liquor of 22% volume and two liters of wine, 0.50 liters of perfume and 0.25 liters of toilet water, and other goods to the value of 300 frs.

Adults traveling from the United Kingdom may bring into France 300 cigarettes or 150 cigarillos or 75 cigars or 400 grams of tobacco; 1.5 liters of liquor over 22% volume or three liters of liquor under 22% volume or three liters of fortified/sparkling wine, plus four liters of still wine; 0.9 liters of perfume and 0.375 liters of toilet water; plus other goods to the value of 2,400 frs.

Language   The French study English for a minimum of four years at school, but few are fluent in their conversation. English is widely understood in major tourist areas, and in most tourist hotels there should be at least one person who can converse with you. Be courteous, patient, and speak slowly: France, after all, has visitors from many countries and is not heavily dependent for income on English-speaking visitors as, for example, is Spain.

Even if your own French is rusty, try to master a few words: The French are more cooperative when they think you are at least making an effort to speak their language.

Getting Around

By Car
Road Conditions   France's roads are classified into five types, numbered and prefixed A, N, D, C, or V. Roads marked A *(Autoroutes)* are expressways. There are excellent links between Paris and most French cities, but poor ones between the provinces (the principal exceptions being A62 between Bordeaux and Toulouse and A9/A8 the length of the Mediterranean coast). It is often difficult to avoid Paris when crossing France—this need not cause too many problems if you steer clear of the rush hours (7–9:30 AM and 4:30–7:30 PM). A *péage* (toll) must be paid on most expressways: The rate varies but can be steep. The N *(Route Nationale)* roads—which are sometimes divided highways—and D *(Route Départementale)* roads are usually wide and fast, and driving along them can be a real pleasure. Don't be daunted by smaller (C and V) roads, either. The yellow regional Michelin maps—on sale throughout France—are an invaluable navigational aid.

Rules of the Road   You may use your own driver's license in France but must be able to prove you have third-party insurance. Drive on the right. Be aware of the French tradition of yielding to drivers coming from the right. Seat belts are obligatory, and children under 12 may not travel in the front seat. Speed limits are 130 kph (80 mph) on expressways, 110 kph (70 mph) on divided highways, 90 kph (55 mph) on other roads, 60 kph (40 mph) in towns. French drivers break these limits and police dish out hefty on-the-spot fines with equal abandon.

Parking   Parking is a nightmare in Paris and often difficult in other large towns. Meters and ticket machines (pay and display) are common: Make sure you have a supply of 1-fr coins. In smaller towns, parking may be permitted on one side of the street only—alternating every two weeks—so pay attention to signs. The French sometimes ignore them, but don't follow their example; if you're caught, your vehicle may unceremoniously be hauled off to the dreaded compound (from where it will cost you 500 frs to retrieve it).

Gasoline Fuel is more expensive on expressways and in rural areas. Don't let your tank get too low—you can go for many miles in the country without passing a gas station—and keep an eye on pump prices as you go. These vary enormously; anything from 4.70 to 5.30 frs per liter. Be careful to choose the right gas for your automobile: "Super" is premium and "essence" is regular.

Breakdowns If you break down on an expressway, go to the nearest roadside emergency telephone and call the breakdown service. If you break down anywhere else, find the nearest garage or contact the police.

By Train France's SNCF is generally recognized as Europe's best national train service: fast, punctual, comfortable, and comprehensive. The high-speed TGVs, with a top speed of 160 mph, are the best domestic trains, operating between Paris and Lyon, the Riviera, and Switzerland, with a new link to Nantes and Bordeaux scheduled for 1990. As on other express trains, you may need to pay a small supplement when taking a TGV at peak hours. Also, you need a seat reservation—easily obtained at the ticket window or from an automatic machine. Seat reservations are reassuring but seldom necessary on other French trains, except at certain busy holiday times.

You need to punch your train ticket in one of the waist-high orange machines you'll encounter alongside platforms. Slide in your ticket face up and wait for a "clink" sound. If nothing happens, try another machine. (The small yellow tickets and automatic ticket barriers used for most suburban Paris trains are similar to those in the métro/RER).

It is not necessary to take an overnight train, even if you are traveling from one end of France to the other; but if you take one, you have a choice between *wagons-lits* (sleeping cars), which are expensive, and *couchettes* (bunks), which sleep six to a compartment (sheet and pillow provided) and are more affordable (around 75 frs). Ordinary compartment seats do not pull together (as in West Germany) to enable you to lie down. There are special summer night trains from Paris to Spain and the Riviera geared for a younger market, with discos and bars to enable you to dance the night away.

Fares Various reduced-fare passes are available from major train stations in France and from travel agents acting as agents for SNCF. If you are planning a lot of train travel, we suggest you buy a special **France Vacances** card (around 1,350 frs for nine days). Families and couples are also eligible for big discounts. So are senior citizens (over 60) and young people (under 26), who qualify for different discount schemes. Having paid for your pass, you can get 50% reductions during blue periods (most of the time) and 20% most of the rest of the time (white periods: noon Friday to noon Saturday; 3 PM Sunday to noon Monday). On major holidays (red periods) there are no reductions. A calendar showing the red, white, and blue periods is available at any station. Note there is no reduction for booking an *aller-retour* (round-trip) ticket rather than an *aller simple* (one-way).

By Plane **Air France** operates France's domestic airline service, called

Air Inter. Most domestic flights from Paris leave from Orly. Contact your travel agent or Air Inter (tel. 45–39–25–25). Train service may be faster, though, particularly when you consider the time it takes to travel between the airport and city center, so check train schedules before committing yourself to a flight.

By Bus Because of excellent train service, long-distance buses are rare and found mainly where train service is inadequate. Bus tours are organized by the **SNCF** and other tourist organizations, such as **Horizons Européens:** Ask for their brochures at any major travel agent, or contact France-Tourisme at 214 rue de Rivoli, 75001 Paris, tel. 42–60–30–01.

By Boat France has Europe's busiest inland waterway system. Canal and river vacations are popular: Visitors can either take an organized cruise or rent a boat and plan their own leisurely route. Contact a travel agent for details or ask for a *Tourisme Fluvial* brochure in any French tourist office. Some of the most picturesque stretches are to be found in Brittany, Burgundy, and the Midi. The Canal du Midi between Toulouse and Sète, constructed in the 17th century, is an historic marvel. Further information is available from French national tourist offices; **France-Anjou Navigation,** Quai National, 72300 Salbé-sur-Sarthe; or **Bourgogne Voies Navigables,** Maison du Tourisme, 89000 Auxerre.

By Bicycle There is no shortage of wide empty roads and flat or rolling countryside in France suitable for bike riding. The French themselves are great cycling enthusiasts—witness the Tour de France. Bikes can be rented from many train stations for around 30 frs a day; you need to show your passport and leave a deposit of about 200 frs (unless you have a Visa or MasterCard). You do not always need to return the bike to the same station. Bikes may be sent as accompanied luggage from any station in France; some trains in rural areas don't even charge to transport bikes. Tourist offices will supply details on the more than 200 local shops that have bikes for rent, or obtain the SNCF brochure *Guide du Train et du Vélo.*

Staying in France

Telephones The French telephone system is modern and efficient. Phone
Local Calls booths are plentiful; they are nearly always available at post offices and cafés. A local call in France costs 12 centimes per minute (minimum tariff 73 centimes); half-price rates apply between 9:30 PM and 8 AM and between 1:30 PM Saturday and 8 AM Monday.

Pay phones work with 1-, 2-, and 5-fr coins (1 fr minimum). Lift the receiver, place the coin(s) in the appropriate slot, and dial. Unused coins are returned when you hang up. Many French pay phones are now operated by *télécartes* (phone cards), which you can buy from post offices and some shops (cost: 40 frs for 50 units; 96 frs for 120). These cards save money and time.

All French phone numbers have eight digits; a code is required only when calling the Paris region from the provinces (dial 16–1 and then the number) and for calling the provinces from Paris (dial 16, then the number). Note that the number system was changed in 1985 and that you may come across some seven-digit numbers in Paris and some six-digit ones elsewhere. Add 4 to the front of such Paris numbers and the former two-digit area code to provincial ones.

International Calls Dial 19 and wait for the tone, then dial the country code (1 for the United States and Canada, 44 for the United Kingdom), area code (minus any initial 0), and number. If you make phone calls from your hotel room, expect to be greatly overcharged.

Operators To find a number within France, or to request other information, dial 12. For international information, dial 19–33 plus the country code.

Mail
Postal Rates Airmail letters to the United States cost 4.20 frs for five grams, to Canada 2.80 frs for five grams; these prices increase by 60 centimes per five grams up to 20 grams total. Letters to the United Kingdom cost 2.20 frs for up to 20 grams, as they do within France. Postcards cost 2 frs within France and if sent to Canada and EEC countries; 2.80 frs to the United States and elsewhere. Stamps can be bought in post offices and cafés sporting a red "Tabac" sign outside.

Receiving Mail If you're uncertain where you'll be staying, have mail sent to American Express, Thomas Cook, or Poste Restante at most French post offices. American Express has a $2 service charge per letter.

Shopping
VAT Refunds A number of shops, particularly large stores in cities and holiday resorts, offer value-added tax (VAT) refunds to foreign shoppers. You are entitled to an export discount of 13% or 23%, depending on the item purchased, though this often applies only if your purchases in the same store reach a minimum 2,400 frs (for residents of EEC countries) or 1,200 frs (all others, including Americans and Canadians).

Bargaining Shop prices are clearly marked and bargaining is not a way of life. Still, at outdoor markets, flea markets, and in antiques stores, you can try your luck. If you're thinking of buying several items in these places, you have nothing to lose in cheerfully suggesting to the proprietor, *"Vous me faites un prix?"* ("How about a discount?").

Opening and Closing Times **Banks.** In general, banks are open weekdays 9:30–4:30, but times vary. Most close for an hour to an hour and a half for lunch.

Museums. Most museums are closed one day a week (usually Tuesday) and on national holidays. Usual times are from 9:30 to 5 or 6. Many museums close for lunch (noon–2); many are open afternoons only on Sunday.

Shops. Large shops in big towns are open from 9 or 9:30 to 6 or 7 without a lunch break. Smaller shops often open earlier (8 AM) and close later (8 PM), but take a lengthy lunch break (1–4). This siesta-type schedule is more typical in the south of France. Corner grocery stores, often run by immigrants, frequently stay open until around 10 PM.

National Holidays January 1 (New Year's Day); April 16 (Easter Monday); May 1 (Labor Day); May 8 (VE Day); May 24 (Ascension); June 4 (Pentecost Monday); July 14 (Bastille Day); August 1; August 14; August 15 (Assumption); August 31; November 1 (All Saints); November 11 (Armistice); December 25 (Christmas Day).

Dining Eating in France is a serious business, at least for two of the three meals each day. For a light meal, try a *brasserie* (steak and french fries remain the classic), a picnic (a *baguette* loaf with ham, cheese, or pâté makes a perfect combination), or one of the fast-food places that have sprung up in urban areas over recent years.

French breakfasts are relatively modest—strong coffee, fruit juice if you insist, and croissants. International chain hotels are likely to offer American or English breakfasts, but in cafés you will probably be out of luck.

Mealtimes Dinner is the main meal and usually begins at 8. Lunch begins at 12:30 or 1.

Dress Jacket and tie are recommended for Very Expensive and Expensive restaurants, and at some of the more stylish Moderate restaurants as well. When in doubt, it's best to dress up. Otherwise, casual dress is appropriate.

Precautions Tap water is perfectly safe, though not always very appetizing (least of all in Paris). Mineral water is a palatable alternative; there is a vast choice of *eau plate* (plain) as well as *eau gazeuse* (fizzy).

Ratings Prices are per person and include a first course, main course, and dessert plus taxes and service (which are always included in displayed prices), but not wine. Best bets are indicated by a star ★. At press time, there were 6.2 frs to the dollar.

Category	All Areas
Very Expensive	over 400 frs
Expensive	250–400 frs
Moderate	150–250 frs
Inexpensive	under 150 frs

Credit Cards The following credit card abbreviations are used: AE, American Express; DC, Diners Club; MC, MasterCard; V, Visa.

Lodging France has a wide range of accommodations, from rambling old village inns to stylishly converted châteaux. Prices must, by law, be posted at the hotel entrance and should include taxes and service. Prices are always by room, not per person. Ask for a *grand lit* if you want a double bed. Breakfast is not always included in this price, but you are usually expected to have it and often are charged for it whether you have it or not. In smaller rural hotels, you may be expected to have your evening meal at the hotel, too.

The quality of rooms, particularly in older properties, can be uneven; if you don't like the room you're given, ask to see another. If you want a private bathroom, state your preference for *douche* (shower) or *baignoire (bath)*—the latter always costing more. Tourist offices in major train stations can reserve hotels for you, and so can tourist offices in most towns.

Hotels Hotels are officially classified from one-star to four-star-deluxe. France has—but is not dominated by—big hotel chains: Examples in the upper price bracket include Frantel, Holiday Inn, Novotel, and Sofitel. The Ibis and Climat de France chains are more moderately priced. Chain hotels, as a rule, lack atmosphere, with the following exceptions:

Logis de France. This is a group of small, inexpensive hotels that can be relied on for comfort, character, and regional cuisine. Look for its distinctive yellow and green sign. The Logis de France paperback guide is widely available in bookshops (cost: around 45 frs) or from Logis de France (23 rue Jean-Mermoz, 75008 Paris).

France-Accueil is another chain of friendly low-cost hotels. You can get a free booklet from France-Accueil (85 rue Dessous-des-Berges, 75013 Paris).

Relais et Châteaux. You can stay in style at any of the 150 members of this prestigious chain of converted châteaux and manor houses. Each hotel is distinctively furnished, provides top cuisine, and often stands in spacious grounds. A booklet listing members is available in bookshops or from Relais et Châteaux, 10 pl. de la Concorde, 75008 Paris.

Rentals *Gîtes Ruraux* offers families or small groups the opportunity for an economical stay in a furnished cottage, chalet, or apartment. These can be rented by the week or month. Contact either the **Fédération Nationale des Gîtes Ruraux,** 35 rue Godot de Mauroy, 75009 Paris (indicate the region that interests you), or the French Government Tourist Office in New York or London (*see* Before You Go, Chapter 1).

Bed and Breakfast These are known in France as *chambres d'hôte* and are increasingly popular in rural areas. Check local tourist offices for details.

Youth Hostels With inexpensive hotel accommodations in France so easy to find, you may want to think twice before staying in a youth hostel—especially as standards of French hostels don't come up to those in neighboring countries. Contact **Fédération Unie des Auberges de Jeunesse** (10 rue Notre-Dame de Lorette, 75009 Paris).

Villas The French Government Tourist Offices in London and New York publish extensive lists of agencies specializing in villa rentals. You can also write to **Rent-a-Villa Ltd.,** 3 W. 51st St., New York, NY 10019; or, in France, **Interhome,** 88 blvd. Latour-Maubourg, 75007 Paris.

Camping French campsites have a good reputation for organization and amenities but tend to be crowded in July and August. More and more campsites now welcome advance reservations, and if you're traveling in summer, it makes sense to book in advance. A guide to France's campsites is published by the **Fédération Française de Camping et de Caravaning,** 78 rue de Rivoli, 75004 Paris.

Ratings Prices are for double rooms and include all taxes. Best bets are indicated by a star ★. At press time (spring 1989), there were 6.2 francs to the dollar.

Category	All Areas
Very Expensive	over 850 frs
Expensive	450–850 frs
Moderate	250–450 frs
Inexpensive	under 250 frs

Credit Cards   The following credit card abbreviations are used: AE, American Express; DC, Diners Club; MC, MasterCard; V, Visa.

Tipping   The check in a bar or restaurant will include service, but it is customary to leave some small change unless you're dissatisfied. The amount varies, from 30 centimes for a beer to a few francs after a meal. Tip taxi drivers and hairdressers about 10%. Give ushers in theaters 1–2 frs. Cloakroom attendants will expect nothing if there is a sign saying *Pourboire interdit*—no tip; otherwise give them 5 frs. Washroom attendants usually get 5 frs—a sum that is often posted.

Bellhops should get 10 frs per item.

If you stay more than two or three days in a moderately priced hotel, it is customary to leave something for the chambermaid—perhaps 10 frs per day. Expect to pay 10 frs for room service—but nothing is expected if breakfast is routinely served in your room. If the chambermaid does some ironing or laundering for you, leave an additional 5 frs in the room.

Service station attendants get nothing for giving you gas or oil, and 5 or 10 frs for checking tires. Train and airport porters get a fixed sum (6–10 frs) per bag. Museum guides should get 5–10 frs after a guided tour. It is standard practice to tip guides (and bus drivers) after an excursion.

Paris

Arriving and Departing

By Plane   International flights arrive at either Charles de Gaulle Airport (Roissy), 24 kilometers (15 miles) northeast of Paris, or at Orly Airport, 16 kilometers (10 miles) south of the city. For information on arrival and departure times, call individual airlines.

Between the Airport and Downtown   **From Charles de Gaulle:** Buses leave every 12 minutes from 5:45 AM to 11 PM. The fare is 35 frs and the trip takes 40 minutes (up to 1½ hours during rush hour). You arrive at Porte Maillot, on the Right Bank by the Hotel Concorde-Lafayette, a half-mile west of the Champs-Elysées (two stops by métro).

From Orly: Buses leave every 12 minutes from 5:50 AM to 11 PM and arrive at the Air France terminal near Les Invalides on the Left Bank. The fare is 28 frs, and the trip takes between 30 and 60 minutes, depending on traffic.

Both airports provide free bus shuttles to the nearest train stations, where you can take the RER service to Paris. The advantages of this are speed, price (25 frs to Paris from Charles de Gaulle in Roissy, 20 frs from Orly), and the fact that the RER trains link up directly with the métro system. The disadvantage is having to lug your bags around. Taxi fares from airports to Paris range from 150 to 200 frs.

By Train   Paris has five international stations: Gare du Nord (for northern France, northern Europe, and England via Calais or Boulogne); Gare de l'Est (for Strasbourg, Luxembourg, Basle, and central Europe); Gare de Lyon (for Lyon, Marseille, the Riviera, Geneva, Italy); Gare d'Austerlitz (for the Loire Valley, southwest France, Spain); Gare St-Lazare (for Normandy, England via Dieppe). The Gare Montparnasse currently serves only western France (mainly Nantes and Brittany) but is scheduled as the terminus for the new TGV Atlantic service that should link Paris to Bordeaux and Spain by 1990. For train information, tel. 45–82–50–50. You can reserve tickets at any Paris station regardless of the destination. Go to the Grandes Lignes counter for travel within France or to the Billets Internationaux (international tickets) desk if you're heading out of France.

By Bus Long-distance bus journeys within France are rare compared with train travel, and Paris has no central bus depot. The two leading Paris-based bus companies are **Eurolines Nord** (7 av. de la Villette, 19e, tel. 42–05–12–10) and **L'Autobus** (4 bis rue St-Sauveur, 2e, tel. 42–33–86–72).

By Car It is no surprise in a country as highly centralized as France that the highway system fans out from Paris. You arrive from the north (England/Belgium) via A1; from Normandy via A13; from the east via A4; from Spain and the southwest via A10; from the Alps, the Riviera, and Italy via A7. Each of these expressways connects with the *Périphérique* (beltway) that encircles Paris. Note that exits here are named by "Porte," and are not numbered. The "Périphe" can be extremely fast—but it gets very busy and is best avoided between 8 and 10 AM and between 5 and 7:30 PM.

Getting Around

Paris is relatively small as capital cities go, and most of its prize monuments and museums are within walking distance of one another. A river cruise is a pleasant way to get an introductory overview. The most convenient form of public transportation is the métro, with stops every few hundred yards; buses are a slower alternative, though they do let you see more of the city. Taxis are not expensive but not always easy to hail, either. Car travel within Paris is best avoided because parking is chronically difficult.

By Métro There are 13 métro lines crisscrossing Paris and the nearby suburbs, and you are seldom more than 465 meters (500 yards) from the nearest station. It is essential to know the name of the last station on the line you take, since this name appears on all signs within the system. A connection (you can make as many as you please on one ticket) is called a *correspondance*. At junction stations, illuminated orange signs, bearing the names of each line terminus, appear over the corridors leading to the various correspondances. Illuminated blue signs, marked *sortie*, indicate the station exit.

The métro service starts out from each terminus at 5:30 AM and continues until 1:15 AM—when the last métro on each line reaches its terminus. Some lines and stations in the seedier parts of Paris are a bit risky at night—in particular Line 2 (Porte-Dauphine–Nation) and the northern section of Line 13 from St-Lazare to St-Denis/Asnières. The long, bleak corridors at Jaurès and Stalingrad are a haven for pickpockets and purse snatchers. But the Paris métro is a relatively safe place, as long as you don't walk around with your wallet hanging out of your back pocket or (especially women) travel alone late at night.

The métro network connects at several points in Paris with RER trains that race across Paris from suburb to suburb: RER

Paris Metro

trains are a sort of supersonic métro and can be a great time-saver. All métro tickets and passes are valid for RER and bus travel within Paris. Second-class métro tickets cost 5 frs, each, though a *carnet* (10 tickets for 29.60 frs) is a far better value. Alternatively, you can buy a *coupon jaune* (weekly) or *carte orange* (monthly) ticket, sold according to zone. Zones 1 and 2 cover the entire métro network (cost: 48 frs per week or 168 frs per month). If you plan to take a suburban train to visit monuments in the Ile de France, you should consider a four-zone ticket (Versailles, St-Germain-en-Laye; 86 frs per week) or five-zone ticket (Rambouillet, Fontainebleau; 102 frs per week). For these weekly or monthly tickets, you need to obtain a pass (available from train and major métro stations) and provide two passport-size photographs.

There are also so-called *Sesame* tickets valid for two, four, or seven days (cost: 59, 89, and 148 frs, respectively) entitling you to first-class travel on the métro, buses, and RER A and RER B (south of the Gare du Nord only).

Access to métro and RER platforms is through an automatic ticket barrier. Slide your ticket in flat and pick it up as it pops up farther along. Keep your ticket; you'll need it again to leave the RER system.

By Bus   Most buses run from around 6 AM to 8:30 PM; some continue until midnight. Night buses operate from 1 AM to 6 AM between Châtelet and nearby suburbs. They can be stopped by hailing them at any point on their route. The buses and the métro use the same tickets, but they must be bought either from métro stations or tobacco shops. You need to show weekly/monthly/Sesame tickets to the driver as you get on; if you have individual yellow tickets, you should state your destination and be prepared to punch one or more tickets in the red and gray machines on board the bus.

By Taxi   There is no standard vehicle or color for Paris taxis, but all offer good value. Daytime rates (6:30 AM to 9 PM) within Paris are about 2.50 frs per kilometer, and nighttime rates are around 3.75 frs, plus a basic charge of 10 frs. Rates outside the city limits are slightly higher. It is best to ask your hotel or restaurant to call for a taxi, since cruising cabs can be hard to find. There are numerous taxi stands, but you have to know where to look. Note that taxis seldom take more than three people at a time.

Important Addresses and Numbers

Tourist   **Paris Tourist Office,** 127 av. des Champs-Elysées, tel. 47–23–
Information   61–72. Open daily 9 AM–8 PM. (Closed Dec. 25, Jan 1.) Offices in major train stations are open daily 8–8.

Embassies   **U.S.:** 2 av. Gabriel, 75008 Paris, tel. 42–96–12–02. **Canada:** 35 av. Montaigne, 75008 Paris, tel. 42–25–99–55. **U.K.:** 35 rue du Faubourg St-Honoré, 75008 Paris, tel. 42–66–91–42.

Emergencies   **Police:** dial 17 for emergencies. Automatic phone booths can be found at various main crossroads for use in police emergencies *(Police-Secours)* or medical help *(Services Medicaux);* **Ambulance:** tel. 18 or 43–78–26–26; **Doctor:** tel. 47–07–77–77; **Hospitals: American Hospital,** 63 blvd. Victor-Hugo, Neuilly, tel. 47–47–53–00; **British Hospital,** 48 rue de Villiers,

Levallois-Perret, tel. 47–58–13–12; **Dentist**, tel. 43–37–51–00 (24-hours).

Pharmacies: Dhéry, Galerie des Champs, 84 av. des Champs-Elysées, tel. 45–62–02–41 (open 24 hours); **Drugstore,** corner of blvd. St-Germain and rue de Rennes, 6e (open until 2 AM); **Pharmacie des Arts,** 106 blvd. Montparnasse 6e (open until midnight).

English Bookstores   **W. H. Smith:** 248 rue de Rivoli; **Galignani:** 224 rue de Rivoli; **Brentano's:** 37 av. de l'Opéra; **Shakespeare & Co.:** rue de la Bûcherie.

Most newsstands in central Paris sell *Time, Newsweek,* and the *International Herald Tribune,* as well as the British dailies.

Travel Agencies   **American Express:** 11 rue Scribe 75009 Paris, tel. 42–66–09–99. **Thomas Cook:** 32 rue du 4 Septembre 75002 Paris, tel. 42–63–48–48.

Guided Tours

Orientation Tours   Bus tours of Paris offer a good introduction to the city. The two largest operators are **Cityrama** (tel. 42–60–30–14) and **Paris Vision** (tel. 42–60–30–01). Tours start from their respective offices, 4 pl. des Pyramides and 214 rue de Rivoli. Both addresses are in the first *arrondissement* (ward), opposite the Tuileries Gardens (toward the Louvre end). Tours are generally given in double-decker buses with either a live guide or tape-recorded commentary (English, of course, is available). They last three hours and cost about 150 frs). The same operators also offer a variety of other tours with a theme (Historic Paris, Modern Paris, Paris by Night, etc.) lasting from 2½ hours to all day and costing between 120 and 300 frs.

Boat Trips   Boat trips along the Seine are a must for first-time Paris visitors. The two most famous services are the **Bâteaux Mouches,** which leaves from the Pont de l'Alma, at the end of the avenue George V, and the **Vedettes du Pont-Neuf,** which sets off from the square du Vert Galant, on the western edge of the Ile de la Cité. Price per trip is around 25 frs. Boats depart in season every half-hour from 10:30 AM to 5 PM (slightly less frequently in winter). Evening cruises are available most of the year and, thanks to the boats' powerful floodlights, offer unexpected views of Paris's riverbanks.

Canauxrama (tel. 46–07–13–13) organizes canal tours in flat-bottom barges along the picturesque but relatively unknown St-Martin and Ourcq Canals in East Paris. Departures from 5 bis quai de la Loire, 19e (métro Jaurès), or the Bassin de l'Arsenal, opposite 50 blvd. de la Bastille, 12e (métro Bastille). Times vary, so phone to check hours. Tours cost from 60 frs, depending on the time of day and length of trip.

Walking Tours   There are numerous special-interest tours concentrating on historical or architectural topics. Most are in French, however. Charges vary between 30 and 50 frs, depending on fees that may be needed to visit certain buildings. Tours last about two hours and are generally held in the afternoon. Details are published in the weekly magazines *Pariscope* and *L'Officiel des Spectacles* under the heading "Conférences."

Excursions   The **RATP** (Paris Transport Authority) organizes many guided excursions in and around Paris. Ask at its tourist service on the place de la Madeleine (north of place de la Concorde), or at the RATP office at St-Michel (53 quai des Grands-Augustins). **Cityrama** and **Paris Vision** *(see* Orientation Tours) organize half- or full-day trips to Chartres, Versailles, Fontainebleau, the Loire Valley, and the Mont St-Michel at a cost of between 150 and 750 frs.

Personal Guides **International Limousines** (182 blvd. Péreire 17e, tel. 45–74–77–12) has luxury cars and minibuses that take up to seven passengers around Paris or to surrounding areas for a minimum of three hours. The cost is about 200 frs per hour. Phone for details and reservations.

Exploring Paris

Paris is a compact city. With the possible exception of the Bois de Boulogne and Montmartre, you can easily walk from one sight to the next. Paris is divided in two by the River Seine, with two islands (Ile de la Cité and Ile St-Louis) in the middle. The south—or Left—Bank has a more intimate, bohemian flavor than the haughtier Right Bank. The east–west axis from Châtelet to the Arc de Triomphe, via the rue de Rivoli and the Champs-Elysées, is the principal thoroughfare for sightseeing and shopping on the Right Bank.

Monuments and museums are sometimes closed at lunchtime (usually noon–2) and one day a week (Monday or Tuesday): Check before you make the trip. A special **Carte Musées** pass, covering access to Paris museums and monuments, can be obtained from museums or métro stations (price: one-day pass, 50 frs; three days, 100 frs; five days, 150 frs). And remember that cafés—unlike British pubs, for example—stay open all day, making them the goal of foot-weary tourists in need of coffee, a beer, or a sandwich. Bakeries are another reliable source of sustenance.

Though attractions are grouped in four logical touring areas, there are several "musts" that most first-time visitors will not want to miss: the Eiffel Tower, the Champs-Elysées, the Louvre, and Notre-Dame. If time is a problem, you can explore Notre-Dame and the Latin Quarter; head to place de la Concorde and enjoy the vista from the Champs-Elysées to the Louvre; then take a boat trip along the Seine for a waterside rendezvous with the Eiffel Tower and a host of other monuments. You could finish off with dinner in Montmartre and consider it a day well spent.

Notre-Dame and the Left Bank *Numbers in the margin correspond with points of interest on the Paris map.*

❶ The most enduring symbol of Paris, and its historical and geographical heart, is **Notre-Dame Cathedral,** around the corner from Cité métro station. This is the logical place to start any tour of the city—especially as the tour starts on the Ile de la Cité, one of the two islands in the middle of the Seine, where Paris's first inhabitants settled around 250 BC. Notre-Dame has been a place of worship for more than 2,000 years; the present building is the fourth on this site. It was begun in 1163, making it one of the earliest Gothic cathedrals, although building dragged on until 1345. The facade seems perfectly proportioned until you notice that the north (left) tower is wider than the south.

The interior is at its lightest and least cluttered in the early morning. Bay-by-bay cleaning is gradually revealing the original honey color of the stone. Window space is limited and filled with shimmering stained glass; the circular rose windows in the transept are particularly delicate. The 387-step climb up the towers is worth the effort for a perfect view of the famous gargoyles and the heart of Paris. *Towers open 10–5. Admission: 22 frs adults, 12 frs children. Treasury (religious and vestmental relics) open 10–1, Sun. 2–6. Admission: 15 frs adults, 10 frs students, 3 frs children.*

The pretty garden to the right of the cathedral leads to a bridge that crosses to the city's second and smaller island, the **Ile St-Louis,** barely 372 meters (400 yards) long and an oasis of inner-city repose.

② The rue des Deux Ponts bisects the island. Head left over the Pont de la Tournelle. To your left is the **Tour d'Argent,** one of the city's most famous restaurants (*see* Dining).

③ Continue along quai de la Tournelle past Notre-Dame, then turn left at rue St-Jacques. A hundred yards ahead, on the right, is the back end of the **Eglise St-Séverin,** an elegant and unusually wide 16th-century church. Note the spiraling column among the forest of pillars behind the altar.

④ Turn left out of the church, cross the bustling boulevard St-Germain and take rue de Cluny to the left. This leads to the **Hôtel de Cluny.** Don't be misled by the name. This is a museum devoted to the late Middle Ages and Renaissance. Look for the *Lady with the Unicorn* tapestries and the beautifully displayed medieval statues. *6 pl. Paul-Painlevé. Admission: 15 frs, Sun. 8 frs. Open Wed.–Mon. 9:45–12:30 and 2–5:15.*

⑤ Head up rue de la Sorbonne to the **Sorbonne,** Paris's ancient university. Students here used to listen to lectures in Latin, which explains why the surrounding area is known as the *Quartier Latin* (Latin Quarter). The Sorbonne's pompous 17th-century buildings hardly foster a campus atmosphere, as a quick stroll into the main courtyard (off place de la Sorbonne) will bear out.

⑥ Walking up rue Victor-Cousin and turning left into rue Cujas, you come to the **Panthéon.** Its huge dome and elegant colonnade are reminiscent of St. Paul's in London but date from a century later (1758–89). The Panthéon was intended to be a church, but during the Revolution it was swiftly earmarked as a secular hall of fame. Its crypt contains the remains of such national heroes as Voltaire, Rousseau, and Zola. The interior is empty and austere, with principal interest centering on Puvis de Chavanne's late 19th-century frescoes, relating the life of Geneviève, patron saint of Paris. *Admission: 22 frs adult, 12 frs children. Open daily 10–noon and 2–5.*

Behind the Panthéon is **St-Etienne du Mont,** a church with two claims to fame: its ornate facade and its curly Renaissance rood-screen (1521–35) separating nave and chancel—the only one of its kind in Paris. Don't forget to check out the fine 17th-century glass in the cloister at the back of the church.

⑦ Take the adjoining rue Clovis, turn right into rue Descartes, then left at the lively place de la Contrescarpe down rue Rollin. Cross rue Monge to rue de Navarre. On the left is the **Arènes de**

Paris

Lutèce (always open during daylight hours, admission free), a Gallo-Roman arena rediscovered only in 1869; it has since been landscaped and excavated to reveal parts of the original amphitheater, and counts as one of the least-known points of interest in Paris.

❽ Rue de Navarre and rue Lacépède lead to the **Jardin des Plantes** (Botanical Gardens), which have been on this site since the 17th century. The gardens have what is reputedly the oldest tree in Paris, a robinia planted in 1636 (allée Becquerel), plus a zoo, Alpine garden, hothouses, aquarium, and maze. Natural science enthusiasts will be in their element at the various museums, devoted to insects (Musée Entomologique), fossils and prehistoric animals (Musée Paléontologique), and minerals (Musée Mineralogique). *Admission: 10–16 frs. Museums open Wed.– Mon. 2–5.*

Head back up Rue Lacépède from the Jardin des Plantes. Turn left into rue Gracieuse, then right into rue Ortolan, which soon crosses the rue Mouffetard—site of a colorful market and many restaurants. Continue along rue du Pot-de-Fer and rue Rataud. At rue Claude-Bernard, turn right; then make your first left up rue St-Jacques.

❾ Set slightly back from the street is the **Val de Grâce,** a domed church designed by the great architect Jules Hardouin-Mansart and erected in 1645–67 (after the Sorbonne church but before the Invalides). Its two-tiered facade, with capitals and triangular pedestals, is directly inspired by the Counter-Reformation Jesuit architectural style found more often in Rome than in Paris. The Baroque style of the interior is epitomized by the huge twisted columns of the baldachin (ornamental canopy) over the altar.

Time Out If you're feeling thirsty (and rich), continue to the **Closerie des Lilas** along nearby boulevard de Port-Royal. This celebrated brasserie retains more style than some of its cousins farther down the once bohemian, now unexciting, boulevard du Montparnasse, whose modern landmark, the 203-meter (656-foot) Tour Montparnasse, is visible in the distance. *171 blvd. du Montparnasse, tel. 43–26–70–50. Reservations advised for meals. AE, DC, V.*

From the crossroads by the Closerie des Lilas, there is an enticing view down the tree-lined avenue de l'Observatoire toward
❿ *the* **Palais du Luxembourg.** The palace was built by Queen Maria de' Medici at the beginning of the 17th century in answer to Florence's Pitti Palace. It now houses the French Senate and is not open to the public. In the surrounding gardens, mothers push their baby carriages along tree-lined paths among the majestic fountains and statues.

Head through the gardens to the left of the palace into rue de Vaugirard. Turn left, then right into rue Madame, which leads
⓫ down to the enormous 17th-century church of **St-Sulpice.** Stand back and admire the impressive, though unfinished, 18th-century facade, with its unequal towers. The interior is overwhelmingly impersonal, but the wall paintings by Delacroix, in the first chapel on the right, are worth a visit.

Rue Bonaparte descends to boulevard St-Germain. You can
⓬ hardly miss the sturdy pointed tower of **St-Germain-des-Prés,**

the oldest church in Paris (begun around 1160, though the towers date back to the 11th century). Note the colorful nave frescoes by the 19th-century artist Hippolyte Flandrin, a pupil of Ingres.

Time Out The spirit of writers Jean-Paul Sartre and Simone de Beauvoir still haunts the **Café de Flore** opposite the church, though this, and the neighboring **Aux Deux Magots,** have more tourists than literary luminaries these days. Still, you can linger over a drink while watching what seems to be all of Paris walking by. *Blvd. St-Germain. No credit cards.*

Rue de l'Abbaye runs along behind St-Germain-des-Prés to place Fürstenberg, a charming little square where fiery Romantic artist Eugène Delacroix (1798–1863) had his studio. If you go there on a summer evening you'll often find young Frenchmen singing love songs to guitar accompaniment. Turn left into rue Jacob and continue along rue de l'Université. You are now in the heart of the Carré Rive Gauche, the Left Bank's district of art dealers and galleries.

About 232 meters (250 yards) along rue de l'Université, turn
⑬ down rue de Poitiers. Ahead is the sandstone bulk of the **Musée d'Orsay.** Follow it around to the left to reach the main entrance. The new Musée d'Orsay—opened in late 1986—is already one of Paris's star tourist attractions, thanks to its imaginatively housed collections of the arts (mainly French) spanning the period 1848–1914. Exhibits take up three floors, but the visitor's immediate impression is one of a single, vast hall. This is not surprising: The museum was originally built in 1900 as a train station. The combination of hall and glass roof with narrow, clanky passages and intimate lighting lends Orsay a human, pleasantly chaotic feel. You may get lost inside, but you won't mind too much.

The chief artistic attraction, of course, is the Impressionist collection, transferred from the inadequate Jeu de Paume museum across the river. Other highlights include Art Nouveau furniture, a faithfully restored Belle Epoque restaurant (formerly part of the station hotel), and a model of the Opéra quarter beneath a glass floor. *62 rue de Lille, tel. 45–49–48–14. Admission: 23 frs, 12 frs Sun. Open Tues., Wed., Fri., Sat. 10–5:30; Thurs. 10–9; Sun. 9–5:30.*

If the lines outside the Musée d'Orsay prove daunting, take a peek into the **Légion d'Honneur** museum opposite, a stylish mansion with a collection of French and foreign medals and decorations. *Admission: 10 frs. Open Tues.–Sun. 2–5.*

⑭ Return to the Seine and follow its bank to the 18th-century **Palais Bourbon,** home of the French National Legislature. (Assemblée Nationale) The colonnaded facade commissioned by Napoleon is a sparkling sight after a recent cleaning program (jeopardized at one stage by political squabbles as to whether cleaning should begin from the left or right). There is a fine view from the steps across to place de la Concorde and the Madeleine.

Follow the Seine down to the exuberant **Pont Alexandre III.** The Grand and Petit Palais are to your right, across the river. To the
⑮ left, the silhouette of **L'Hôtel des Invalides** soars above expansive if hardly manicured lawns. The Invalides was founded by

Louis XIV in 1674 to house wounded (or "invalid") war veterans. Although only a few old soldiers live here today, the military link remains in the form of the **Musée de l'Armée**—a vast collection of arms, armor, uniforms, banners, and pictures. The **Musée des Plans-Reliefs** contains a fascinating collection of scale models of French towns made by the military architect Vauban in the 17th century.

The museums are far from being the only reason for visiting the Invalides. It is an outstanding Baroque ensemble, designed by Bruand and Mansart, and its church possesses the city's most elegant dome as well as the tomb of Napoleon, whose remains are housed in a series of no less than six coffins within a tomb of red porphyry. A *son-et-lumière* (sound and light) performance in English is held in the main courtyard on evenings throughout the summer (Admission: 30 frs). *Admission to museums and church: 23 frs adults, 12 frs children. Open daily 10–6 (10–5 in winter).*

🔟 Alongside is the **Musée Rodin.** Together with the Picasso Museum in the Marais, this is the most charming of Paris's individual museums, consisting of an old house (built 1728) with a pretty garden, both filled with the vigorous sculptures of Auguste Rodin (1840–1917). The garden also has hundreds of rosebushes, with dozens of different varieties. *77 rue de Varenne. Admission: 16 frs, 8 frs Sun. Open Tues.–Sun. 10–5.*

Take avenue de Tourville to avenue de La Motte-Picquet. Turn left, and in a few minutes you will come face to face with the 🔟 **Eiffel Tower.** It was built by Gustave Eiffel for the World Exhibition of 1889. Recent restorations haven't made the elevators any faster—long lines are inevitable—but decent shops and two good restaurants have been added. Consider coming in the evening, when every girder is lit in glorious detail. Such was Eiffel's engineering precision that even in the fiercest winds the tower never sways more than 11½ centimeters (4½ inches). Today, of course, it is the most well known of Parisian landmarks, and exudes an air of permanence. Standing beneath it, you may have trouble believing that it nearly became 7,000 tons of scrap-iron when its concession expired in 1909. Only its potential use as a radio antenna saved the day; it now bristles with a forest of radio and television transmitters. If you're full of energy, you can stride up the stairs as far as the tower's third floor, but only the elevator will take you right to the top. The view from 1,000 feet up will enable you to appreciate the city's layout and proportions. *Admission: on foot, 7 frs; elevator, 12–44 frs, depending on level. Open July–Aug., daily 10 AM–midnight; Sept.–June, Sun.–Thurs. 10 AM–11 PM, Fri., Sat. 10 AM–midnight.*

West Paris and the Louvre

Our second itinerary starts at the **Musée Marmottan.** To get there, take the métro to La Muette, then head down chaussée de la Muette, through the small Ranelagh park to the corner of rue Boilly and avenue Raphaël. The museum is a sumptuous early 19th-century mansion, replete with many period furnishings, and probably is the most underestimated museum in Paris. It houses a magnificent collection of paintings by Claude Monet—including some of his huge, curving *Waterlily* canvasses—along with other Impressionist works and some delicately illustrated medieval manuscripts. *2 rue Louis-Boilly. Admission: 18 frs adults, 8 frs children and seniors. Open Tues.–Sun. 10–5:30.*

Continue along rue Boilly and turn left on boulevard Suchet. The next right takes you into the **Bois de Boulogne.** Class and style have been associated with "Le Bois" (The Woods) ever since it was landscaped into an upper-class playground by Haussmann in the 1850s. The attractions of this sprawling 891-hectare (2,200-acre) wood include cafés, restaurants, gardens, waterfalls, and lakes. You could happily spend a day or two exploring, but for the moment we suggest you pass Auteuil racetrack on the left and then walk to the right of the two lakes. An inexpensive ferry crosses frequently to an idyllic island. Rowboats can be rented at the far end of the lake. Just past the boathouse, turn right on the route de Suresnes and follow it to Porte Dauphine, a large traffic circle.

Cross over to avenue Foch, with the unmistakable silhouette of the Arc de Triomphe in the distance. Keep an eye out for the original Art Nouveau iron-and-glass entrance to Porte Dauphine métro station, on the left. Then continue along avenue Foch, the widest and grandest boulevard in Paris, to the **Arc de Triomphe.** This 51-meter (164-foot) arch was planned by Napoleon to celebrate his military successes. Yet when Empress Marie-Louise entered Paris in 1810, it was barely off the ground, and an arch of painted canvas had to be strung up to save appearances. Napoleon had been dead for more than 20 years when the Arc de Triomphe was finally finished in 1836. In 1988–89 it underwent a thorough facelift to ward off signs of decay.

Place Charles de Gaulle, referred to by Parisians as **L'Etoile** (The Star) is one of Europe's most chaotic traffic circles. Short of a death-defying dash, your only way to get over to the Arc de Triomphe is to take the pedestrian underpass from either the Champs-Elysées (to your right as you arrive from avenue Foch) or avenue de la Grande Armée (to the left). France's Unknown Soldier is buried beneath the archway; the flame is rekindled every evening at 6:30.

From the top of the Arc you can see the "star" effect of Etoile's 12 radiating avenues and admire two special vistas: one, down the Champs-Elysées toward place de la Concorde and the Louvre, and the other, down avenue de la Grande-Armée toward La Tête Défense, a severe modern arch surrounded by imposing glass and concrete towers. Halfway up the Arc there is a small museum devoted to its history. *Museum and platform. Admission: 12 frs. Open daily 10–5:30.*

The Champs-Elysées is the site of colorful national ceremonies on July 14 and November 11; its trees are often decked out with French tricolors and foreign flags to mark visits from heads of state. It is also where the cosmopolitan pulse of Paris beats strongest. The gracefully sloping 2-kilometer (1¼-mile) boulevard was originally laid out in the 1660s by André Le Nôtre as a garden sweeping away from the Tuileries. There is not much sign of that as you stroll past the cafés, restaurants, airline offices, car showrooms, movie theaters, and chic arcades that occupy its upper half. Farther down, on the right, is the **Grand Palais,** which plays host to Paris's major art exhibitions. Its glass roof makes its interior remarkably bright. *Admission varies. Usually open 10:30–6:30.*

The Grand Palais also houses the **Palais de la Découverte,** with scientific and mechanical exhibits and a planetarium. Entrance is in the avenue Franklin-Roosevelt. *Admission: 15 frs adults, 10 frs students; additional 11 frs for planetarium. Open Tues.–Sun. 10–6.*

22 Directly opposite the main entrance to the Grand Palais is the **Petit Palais,** built at the same time (1900) and now home to an attractively presented collection of French painting and furniture from the 18th and 19th centuries. *Admission: 12 frs adults, 6 frs students. Open Tues.–Sun. 10–5:40.*

The flowerbeds, chestnut trees, and sandy sidewalks of the lower section of the Champs-Elysées are reminders of its original leafy elegance. Continue down to place de la Concorde, built around 1775 and scene of more than a thousand deaths at the guillotine, including those of Louis XVI and Marie-Antoinette. The obelisk, a gift from the viceroy of Egypt, was erected in 1833.

23 To the east of the place de la Concorde is the **Jardin des Tuileries:** formal gardens with trees, ponds, and statues. Standing guard on either side are the **Jeu de Paume**—former home of the Impressionist collection and now the home of temporary exhibitions—and the **Orangerie,** recently restored to contain some early 20th-century French works by Monet, Renoir, Marie Laurencin, and others. *Admission: 15 frs, 8 frs Sun. Open Wed.–Mon. 9:45–5.*

Pass through the Tuileries to the Arc du Carrousel, a rather small triumphal arch erected more quickly (1806–08) than its big brother at the far end of the Champs-Elysées. Towering be-**24** fore you is the **Louvre,** with its glass pyramids. The Louvre, originally a royal palace, is today the world's largest and most famous museum. I. M. Pei's pyramids are the highlight of a major modernization program; in the course of their construction the medieval foundations of the palace were unearthed and are maintained and displayed as an integral part of the museum's collection. The pyramids stand as the easternmost landmark of a majestic vista stretching through the Arc du Carrousel, Tuileries, place de la Concorde, the Champs-Elysées, and the Arc de Triomphe all the way to the giant arch of La Défense, 4 kilometer (2½ miles) west of the capital.

The Louvre was begun as a fortress in 1200 (the earliest parts still standing date from the 1540s) and completed under Napoleon III in the 1860s. The apparent harmony of its buildings belies their diverse construction dates. The Louvre used to be even larger; a wing facing the Tuileries Gardens was razed by rampaging revolutionaries during the bloody Paris Commune of 1871.

Whatever the aesthetic merits of Pei's new-look Louvre, the museum has emerged less cramped and more rationally organized. Yet its sheer variety can seem intimidating. The main tourist attraction is Leonardo da Vinci's *Mona Lisa* (known in French as *La Joconde),* painted in 1503. The latest research, based on Leonardo's supposed homosexuality, would have us believe that the subject was actually a man! The *Mona Lisa* may disappoint you; it's smaller than most imagine, it's kept behind glass, and it's invariably encircled by a mob of tourists.

Turn your attention instead to some of the less-crowded rooms and galleries nearby, where Leonardo's fellow-Italians are strongly represented: Fra Angelico, Giotto, Mantegna, Raphael, Titian, and Veronese. El Greco, Murillo, and Velázquez lead the Spanish; Van Eyck, Rembrandt, Frans Hals, Brueghel, Holbein, and Rubens underline the achievements of northern European art. English paintings are highlighted by works of Lawrence, Reynolds, Gainsborough, and Turner. Highlights of French painting include works by Poussin, Fragonard, Chardin, Boucher, and Watteau—together with David's *Coronation of Napoleon*, Géricault's *Raft of the Medusa*, and Delacroix's *Liberty Guiding the People*.

Famous statues include the soaring *Victory of Samothrace* (3rd century BC), the celebrated *Venus de Milo* (end of 2nd century BC), and the realistic Egyptian *Seated Scribe* (C. 2000 BC). Be sure to inspect the Gobelins tapestries, the Crown Jewels (including the 186-carat Regent diamond), and the 9th-century bronze statuette of Emperor Charlemagne. *Admission 20 frs, free Sun. Open Wed.–Mon. 9:45–6:30.*

Montmartre If you start at the Anvers métro station and head up rue de Steinkerque, with its budget clothing shops, you will be greeted by the most familiar and spectacular view of the Sacré Coeur basilica atop the Butte Montmartre. The **Sacré-Coeur** was built in a bizarre, mock-Byzantine style between 1876 and 1910. It is no favorite with aesthetes, yet it has become a major Paris landmark. It was built as an act of national penitence after the disastrous Franco-Prussian War of 1870—a Catholic show of strength at a time when conflict between Church and State was at its most bitter.

The large, rather gloomy interior is short on stained glass but long on golden mosaics; *Christ in Glory*, above the altar, is the most impressive. The basilica's many cupolas are dominated by a dome and an 80-meter (260-foot) bell tower that contains the Savoyarde, one of the world's largest bells, cast in Annecy, Savoy, in 1895. The view from the dome is best on a clear day, when all the sights of Paris are spread out before you.

Around the corner is the **place du Tertre,** full of would-be painters and trendy, overpriced restaurants. The painters have been setting up their easels on the square for years; don't be talked into having your portrait done unless you really want to—in which case, check the price first.

Despite its eternal tourist appeal and ever-growing commercialization, Montmartre has not lost all its traditional bohemian color. Walk down rue Norvins and descend the bustling rue Lepic to place Blanche and one of the favorite haunts of Toulouse-Lautrec and other luminaries of the Belle Epoque— the legendary **Moulin Rouge** cabaret.

Montmartre is some distance from the rest of the city's major attractions, so go left up boulevard de Clichy as far as **place Pigalle,** then take the métro to Madeleine.

Central Paris The **Eglise de la Madeleine,** with its array of uncompromising columns, looks like a Greek temple. The only natural light inside comes from three shallow domes; the walls are richly but harmoniously decorated, with plenty of gold glinting through the dim interior. The church was designed in 1814 but not consecrated until 1842, after efforts to turn the site into a train station were defeated. The portico's majestic Corinthian colonnade supports a huge pediment with a sculptured frieze of the *Last Judgment*. From the top of the steps you can admire the vista down rue Royale across the Seine. Another vista leads up boulevard Malesherbes to the dome of **St-Augustin,** a mid-19th-century church notable for its innovative use of iron girders as structural support.

㉙ ㉚ Place de la Madeleine is in the heart of Paris's prime shopping district: Jewelers line rue Royale; **Fauchon's,** behind the Madeleine, is a high-class delicatessen; **Aux Trois Quartiers,** at the start of boulevard de la Madeleine, is a stylish department store.

㉛ ㉜ Continue down boulevard de la Madeleine and turn right into boulevard des Capucines. This nondescript street leads to rue de la Paix. Immediately to the right is **place Vendôme.** This is one of the world's most opulent squares, a rhythmically proportioned example of 17th-century urban architecture that shines in all its golden-stoned splendor since being sandblasted several years ago. Other things shine here, too, in the windows of jewelry shops that are even more upscale (and discreet) than those in rue Royale—fitting neighbors for the top-ranking **Ritz** hotel. The square's central column, topped by a statue of Napoleon, is made from the melted bronze of 1,200 cannons captured at the Battle of Auschwitz in 1805.

Time Out Rue de la Paix leads, logically enough, to the **Café de la Paix** on the corner of the place de l'Opéra. There are few grander cafés in Paris, and fewer places where you can perch with as good a tableau before you.

㉝ Dominating the northern side of the square is the imposing **Opéra,** the first great work of the architect Charles Garnier, who in 1860 won the contract to build the opera house. He used elements of neoclassical architecture—bas reliefs on facades and columns—in an exaggerated combination that borders on parody. The lavishly upholstered auditorium, with its delightful ceiling painted by Marc Chagall in 1964, seems small—but this is because the stage is the largest in the world, accommodating up to 450 players. *Admission: 17 frs. Open daily 11–4:30.*

㉞ Behind the Opéra are **les grands magasins,** Paris's most venerable department stores. The nearer of the two, the **Galeries Lafayette,** is the more outstanding because of its elegant turn-of-the-century glass dome. But **Printemps,** farther along boulevard Haussmann to the left, is better organized and has an excellent view from its rooftop cafeteria.

㉟ Take the métro at Chaussée d'Antin, near the Galeries Lafayette, and travel three stops (direction Villejuif) as far as **Palais-Royal.** This former royal palace, built in the 1630s, has a charming garden, bordered by arcades and boutiques, that many visitors overlook.

㊱ On the square in front of the Palais-Royal is the **Louvre des Antiquaires,** a chic shopping mall full of antiques dealers. It deserves a browse whether you intend to buy or not. Afterward, head east along rue St-Honoré and left into rue du Louvre. Skirt the circular **Bourse du Commerce** (Commercial Exchange) and head toward the imposing church of **St-Eustache,** **㊲** (1532–1637), an invaluable testimony to the stylistic transition between Gothic and Classical architecture. It is also the "cathedral" of **Les Halles**—the site of the central market of Paris until **㊳** the much-loved glass-and-iron sheds were torn down in the late

'60s. The area has since been transformed into a trendy—and already slightly seedy—shopping complex, Le Forum.

Head across the topiary garden and left down rue Berger. Pass the square des Innocents, with its Renaissance fountain, to boulevard de Sébastopol. Straight ahead lies the futuristic, **(39)** funnel-topped **Centre Pompidou** (Pompidou Center)—a must for lovers of modern art. The Pompidou Centre, also known as the Beaubourg, was built in the mid-1970s and named in honor of former French president Georges Pompidou (1911–74). This "cultural Disneyland" is always crowded, housing a **Museum of Modern Art,** a huge library, experimental music and industrial design sections, a children's museum, and a variety of activities and exhibitions. Musicians, magicians, fire-eaters, and other street performers fill the large forecourt near the entrance. *Admission: Museum of Modern Art, 20 frs, free Sun.; 40 frs for daily pass covering all sectors of the center. Open Mon., Wed.–Fri. noon–10; weekends 10–10.*

Continue east to the **Marais,** one of the most historic quarters of Paris. The spacious affluence of its 17th-century mansions, many restored to former glory, contrasts with narrow winding streets full of Jewish shops and restaurants. Rue de Rambuteau leads from the Centre Pompidou into rue des Francs-Bourgeois. Turn left on rue Elzivir to rue Thorigny, where you **(40)** will find the Hôtel Salé and its **Musée Picasso.** This is a convincing experiment in modern museum layout, whether you like Picasso or not. Few of his major works are here, but many fine, little-known paintings, drawings, and engravings are on display. *5 rue Thorigny. Admission: 21 frs. Open Thurs–Mon. 9:15–5:15; Wed. 9:15 AM—10 PM.*

Double back down rue Elzivir and turn left along rue des **(41)** Francs-Bourgeois until you reach the **place des Vosges.** Built in 1605, this is the oldest square in Paris. Its harmonious proportions, soft pink brick, and cloisterlike arcades give this square an aura of calm. In the far corner is the **Maison de Victor Hugo,** containing souvenirs of the great poet's life and many of his surprisingly able paintings and ink drawings. *6 pl. des Vosges. Admission: 9 frs. Open Tues.–Sun. 10–5:40.*

Time Out   The shops on nearby rue St-Antoine (see below) have all the makings for a first-class picnic, which you can have in the shade of the square inside place des Vosges.

Rue Birague leads from the middle of the place des Vosges down to rue St-Antoine. About 93 meters (100 yards) along on **(42)** the left is the **place de la Bastille.** Unfortunately, there are no historic vestiges here; not even the soaring column, topped by the figure of Liberty, commemorates the famous storming of the Bastille in 1789 (the column stands in memory of Parisians killed in the uprisings of 1830 and 1848). Only the new **Opéra de la Bastille,** which opened in 1989, can be said to mark the bicentennial.

Retrace your steps down rue St-Antoine as far as the large Baroque church of **Saint-Paul-Saint-Louis** (1627–41). Then **(43)(44)** continue down the rue de Rivoli to the **Hôtel de Ville.** This magnificent city hall was rebuilt in its original Renaissance style after being burned down in 1871, during the violent days of the Paris Commune. The vast square in front of its many-statued facade is laid out with fountains and bronze lamps.

Avenue de Victoria leads to place du Châtelet. On the right is
the **Tour St-Jacques.** This richly worked 52-meter (170-foot)
stump is all that remains of a 16th-century church destroyed in
1802.

From Châtelet take the pont-au-Change over the Seine to the
Ile de la Cité and the **Palais de Justice** (law courts). Visit the
turreted **Conciergerie,** a former prison with a superb vaulted
14th-century hall (Salles des Gens d'Armes) that often hosts
temporary exhibitions. The **Tour de l'Horloge** (clock tower)
near the entrance on the quai de l'Horloge has a clock that has
been ticking off time since 1370. Around the corner in the boulevard du Palais, through the imposing law court gates, is the
Sainte-Chapelle, built by St-Louis (Louis IX) in the 1240s to
house the Crown of Thorns he had just bought from Emperor
Baldwin of Constantinople. The building's lead-covered wood
spire, rebuilt in 1854, rises 77½ meter (250 feet). The somewhat
garish lower chapel is less impressive than the upper one,
whose walls consist of little else but dazzling 13th-century
stained glass. *Conciergerie and Sainte-Chapelle. Admission:
joint ticket 22 frs; single ticket 12 frs. Open daily 10–6; winter
10–5.*

From boulevard du Palais turn right on quai des Orfèvres. This
will take you past the quaint place Dauphine to the **square du
Vert Galant** at the westernmost tip of the Ile de la Cité. Here,
above a peaceful garden, you will find a statue of the Vert
Galant: gallant adventurer Henry IV, king from 1589 to 1610.

Off the Beaten Track

Few tourists venture into east Paris, but there are several points of interest tucked away here. The largest is the **Bois de
Vincennes,** a less touristy version of the Bois de Boulogne,
with several cafés and lakes. Rowboats can be taken to the two
islands in Lac Daumesnil or to the three in Lac des Minimes.
There is also a zoo, cinder racetrack *(hippodrome)*, and an extensive flower garden (Parc Floral, route de la Pyramide). The
Château de Vincennes (av. de Paris) is an imposing, high-walled
castle surrounded by a dry moat and dominated by a 53-meter
(170-foot) keep. It contains a replica of the Sainte-Chapelle on
Ile de la Cité and two elegant classical wings added in the mid-
17th century. *Best métro access to the woods is at Porte Dorée;
to the flower garden and castle (admission: 22 frs; open 10–6),
at Château de Vincennes.*

Cemeteries aren't every tourist's idea of the ultimate attraction, but **Père Lachaise** is the largest, most interesting, and
most prestigious in Paris. It forms a veritable necropolis with
cobbled avenues and tombs competing in pomposity and originality. Steep slopes and lush vegetation contribute to a
powerful atmosphere; some people even bring a picnic lunch.
Leading incumbents include Chopin, Molière, Proust, Oscar
Wilde, Sarah Bernhardt, Jim Morrison, and Edith Piaf. Get a
map at the entrance and track them down. *Av. du Père-
Lachaise, 20e; métro Gambetta. Open daily 8–6, 8–5 in winter.*

The **Canal St-Martin** starts life just south of the Place de la Bastille but really comes into its own during the 1.2-kilometer (¾-
mile) stretch north across the 10th arrondissement. It has an
unexpected flavor of Amsterdam, thanks to its quiet banks,

locks, and footbridges. *Closest métro stations: Jaurès to the north and Jacques Bonsergent to the south.*

If you're intrepid and don't mind the smell, a glimpse—and a good whiff—of subterranean Paris can be had in the sewers, **Les Egouts.** *Meet at the angle of quai d'Orsay and pl. de la Résistance on the Left Bank just east of Pont de l'Alma. Admission: 8 frs. Open Mon., Wed., and last Sat. of the month 2–5; métro Alma-Marceau.*

Hidden away in a grid of narrow streets not far from the Opéra is Paris's central auction house, the **Hôtel Drouot.** It is open six days a week (except at Christmas, Easter, and midsummer), and its 16 salesrooms make a fascinating place to browse, with absolutely no obligation to bid—though you may well wish to do so! Everything from stamps and toy soldiers to Renoirs and 18th-century commodes is available. The mixture of fur-coated ladies with money to burn, penniless art lovers desperate to unearth an unidentified masterpiece, and scruffy dealers trying to look anonymous makes up Drouot's unusually rich social fabric. *Viewing takes place 11–noon and 2–6, with auctions starting at 2. Entrance at the corner of rue Rossini and rue Drouot, métro Richelieu-Drouot.*

Shopping

Gift Ideas
Paris is the home of fashion and perfumes. Old prints are sold in *bouquinistes (stalls) along the Left Bank of the Seine. For state-of-the-art home decorations, the shop in the* **Musée des Arts Décoratifs** in the Louvre (107 rue de Rivoli) is worth visiting.

Antiques
Antique dealers proliferate in the **Carré Rive Gauche** between St-Germain-des-Prés and the Musée d'Orsay. There are also several dealers around the Drouot auction house near Opéra (corner of rue Rossini and rue Drouot métro: Richelieu-Drouot). The **Louvre des Antiquaires,** near the Palais-Royal (*see* Exploring), and the **Village Suisse,** near the Champ de Mars (78 av. de Suffren), are stylish shopping malls dominated by antiques.

Boutiques
Only Milan can compete with Paris for the title of Capital of European Chic. The top shops are along both sides of the Champs-Elysées and along the avenue Montaigne and the rue du Faubourg St-Honoré. If you're on a tight budget, search for bargains along the shoddy streets around the foot of Montmartre (*see* Exploring), or near **Barbès-Rochechouart** métro station. The streets to the north of the Marais, close to **Arts-et-Métiers** métro, are historically linked to the cloth trade, and many shops offer garments at wholesale prices.

Department Stores
The most famous department stores in Paris are **Galeries Lafayette** and **Printemps,** on boulevard Haussmann. Others include **Au Bon Marché** near Sèvres-Babylone (métro on the Left Bank); the **Samaritaine,** overlooking the Seine east of the Louvre (métro Pont-Neuf); and **Aux Trois Quartiers,** near the Madeleine.

Food and Flea Markets
The sprawling **Marché aux Puces de St-Ouen,** just north of Paris, is one of Europe's largest flea markets. Best bargains are to be had early in the morning (open Sat.–Mon.; métro Porte de Clignancourt). There are smaller flea markets at the Porte de Vanves and Porte de Montreuil (weekends only).

Dining

Eating out in Paris should be a pleasure, and there is no reason why choosing a less expensive restaurant should spoil the fun. After all, Parisians themselves eat out frequently and cannot afford five-star dining every night, either. For details and price category definitions, *see* Dining in Staying in France.

Left Bank
Very Expensive

Jules Verne. The sensational view from this restaurant on the third floor of the Eiffel Tower is a fitting accompaniment to the subtle flavors of Louis Grondard's cuisine. The elegant gray-and-black decor is at its best at night, but prices are most accessible on a weekday at lunch, when there is a good fixed-price menu. *Eiffel Tower, 7e, tel. 45–55–61–44. Reservations essential. AE, DC, MC, V.*

★ **Tour d'Argent.** Discretion is the key at this temple of French gastronomy, on the Left Bank opposite the Ile St-Louis. The restaurant's exterior is plain; inside, however, a plush elevator whisks you to the top and to a memorable view of Notre-Dame and the Ile de la Cité. Waiters materialize in anticipation of your slightest wish. Parisians are relieved that the food has maintained its high standards under new chef Manuel Martinez. There is a fixed-price lunch menu (330 frs) every day except Sunday. *15 quai de la Tournelle, 5e, tel. 43–54–23–31. Reservations essential. AE, DC, MC, V. Closed Mon.*

Expensive

Le Coupe-Chou. Uneven floors, bare stone walls, and candlelit alcoves make this many-roomed restaurant, in a rickety old town house near the Panthéon, popular for its atmosphere. The service can seem desultory, but the competent cuisine and magical setting compensate. Coffee amid the cushions and flickering shadows of the after-dinner lounge makes a romantic end to the evening. *11 rue de Lanneau, 5e, tel. 46–33–68–69. Reservations advised. V. Closed Sun. lunch.*

Moderate

Petit Zinc. This is a long-established haunt on the lively rue de Buci. Its imperturbable white-aproned waiters and unpretentious Belle Epoque decor lend it an authentically Parisian atmosphere, especially on the bustling, green-walled first floor; the room upstairs is larger but more discreetly lit. The seafood is good here; *pintade* (guinea fowl) is recommended, and game and poultry are served up in robust sauces. It is open until 3 AM. *25 rue de Buci, 6e, tel. 46–33–51–66. Reservations advised. AE, DC, MC, V.*

Suffren. Next to the Ecole Militaire at the far end of the Champ de Mars, is this anarchetypal brasserie: lively, good value, with oysters, fish, and other seafood in abundance. Foreigners are treated with a welcome lack of condescension. *84 av. de Suffren, 15e, tel. 45–66–97–86. Reservations not required. V. Closed Mon.*

Vagenende. Dark wood, gleaming mirrors, and obsequious waiters take the Vagenende dangerously close to turn-of-the-century pastiche. It claims to be a bustling brasserie, but don't believe it: Service is far too unhurried and the dining room far too cozy. You can be sure of having a copious and enjoyable meal (foie gras, oysters, and chocolate-based desserts are outstanding), with a stroll outside along the cheerful boulevard St-Germain to walk it off. *142 blvd. St-Germain, 6e, tel. 43–26–68–18. Reservations advised. AE, DC, MC, V. Closed Feb. 1–8.*

West Paris
Very Expensive

Maxim's. Eating here is a once-in-a-lifetime experience for two reasons: first, the plush velvet interior, with its curly riot of Art Nouveau furnishings; second, Maxim's international reputation for luxurious abandon. Unfortunately, the check—and not the cuisine—is the most lasting reminder of a dinner here, but that seems not to bother most customers. *3 rue Royale, 8e, tel. 42–65–27–94. Reservations essential. AE, DC, MC, V. Closed Sun. in July, Aug.*

★ **Robuchon.** Virtuoso chef Joël Robuchon is a cult figure in epicurean circles and a worthy successor to the great Jamin, previous owner of this elegant restaurant near the Trocadero. To get a table here—there are only 45 seats—you need to make a reservation well in advance, but it is worth it: The menu changes constantly as Robuchon concocts new works of edible art. *32 rue de Longchamp, 16e, tel. 47–27–12–27. Reservations essential. MC, V. Closed Sat., Sun., Aug.*

Expensive

Chez Edgard. Some come here for the reliable French cuisine, accompanied by a fine wine list. But most are eavesdroppers, picking up the crumbs from the whispered conversations of senior politicians and journalists amid the discreet warmth of the restaurant's deep red decor. It is a place to watch Paris power brokers in action—with a handy address close to the Champs-Elysées. *4 rue Marbeuf, 8e, tel. 47–20–51–15. Reservations advised. AE, DC, MC, V. Closed Sun.*

Inexpensive

★ **Relais de la Sabretèche.** It's worth traveling deep into the residential 16th arrondissement, near the Porte de St-Cloud, for a restaurant that offers both unbeatable value and appealing, country-house decor. Consider the four-course set menu (served lunchtimes and at dinner until 9 PM) for about 90 frs. For a similar sum, you can wash the meal down with a St-Estèphe or Châteauneuf-du-Pape (ask for a bottle from the cellar or it will be too warm). The service is discreet to the point of forgetfulness. *183 blvd. Murat, 16e, tel. 46–47–91–39. Reservations advised. V. Closed Sun. dinner, Mon.*

Montmartre and Central Paris
Expensive

Au Quai des Ormes. Sometimes you're better off at a restaurant that seems to make no concessions to tourists. Au Quai des Ormes is one of these. Most of its business comes from Parisians who put the quality of food—particularly the game entrées—before strained attempts at atmosphere. A special low-calorie menu (rare in Paris) indicates a further concern for the customer. An attractive and convenient setting on the Right Bank, by the Ile St-Louis, adds to its popularity. *72 quai de l'Hôtel de Ville, 4e, tel. 42–74–72–22. Reservations essential. V. Closed Sat., Sun., and Aug.*

Escargot Montorgueil. Traditional French favorites—such as snails, of course—help the Escargot Montorgueil maintain its reputation as one of the most reliable restaurants in Les Halles. The extravagant turn-of-the-century decor, with mirrors and traditional wall sofas, recalls the time before this area underwent its dramatic facelift. *38 rue Montorgueil, 1er, tel. 42–36–83–51. Reservations essential. AE, DC, MC, V. Closed for one week in mid-Aug.*

Moderate

Brasserie Flo. Flo is an authentic, bustling brasserie that effortlessly recaptures the spirit of 1900. Sausages and sauerkraut are served with large glasses of Alsatian beer. The atmosphere gets livelier (some would say noisier) through the evening. Closing time is 1:30 AM. *7 cour des Petites-Ecuries, 10e, tel. 47–70–13–59. Reservations essential. AE, DC, V.*

Clodenis. A small, elegant restaurant down the slope from the Sacré Coeur, Clodenis serves excellent fish dishes and has some fixed-price menus for less than 200 frs. The decor—soft lighting, small tables, and beige wallpaper—is easy on the eye. *57 rue Caulaincourt, 18e, tel. 46-06-20-26. Reservations advised. AE, DC, MC, V. Closed Sun., Mon.*

Inexpensive **Chartier.** This is the down-to-earth Belle Epoque cousin of the Vagenende (*see* Left Bank). Again, there are mirrors and fancy lamps, but here you'll be rushed and crowded; the waiter's white apron will be stained; and your check will be written on the tablecloth. This is the gastronomic equivalent of roughing it, but as this is Paris, you can have steak, fries, and a glass of wine for the same price as the burger meal at the fast-food places nearby. The good food belies the price. *7 rue du Faubourg-Montmartre, 9e, tel. 47-70-86-29. No reservations. No credit cards. Closes 9:30 PM.*

Jo Goldenberg. The doyen of Jewish eating places in Paris, Jo Goldenberg is in the heart of that most Jewish district, the Marais. Its two-level restaurant, with modern paintings, is always good-natured and crowded. The food is solid and cheap and heavily influenced by Central Europe (ground beef and salami). This makes it a great place to dine on a winter evening, but a bit heavy going in summer. The Israeli and Eastern European wines are rarely available elsewhere in France. *7 rue Rosiers, 4e, tel. 48-87-20-16. Reservations advised. AE, DC, V.*

Lodging

Paris is popular throughout the year, so make reservations early. The cost of renovating many hotels for the 1989 bicentennial celebrations has been passed on to the consumer, so be prepared for higher prices. For details and price category definitions, *see* Lodging in Staying in France.

Left Bank and Ile St-Louis **Lutétia.** Looking across a leafy square at the Bon Marché department store, the Lutétia maintains its excellent reputation for old-fashioned service. The building was renovated from top to bottom only four years ago, under the eagle eye of top fashion designer Sonia Rykiel. The facade shines again, and the elegant interiors are full of Art Deco touches. *45 blvd. Raspail, 6e, tel. 45-44-38-10. 300 rooms with bath. AE, DC, MC, V.*
Very Expensive

Expensive **Hôtel d'Angleterre.** Some claim the Hôtel d'Angleterre is the
★ ultimate Left Bank hotel: a little shabby, but elegant, small, and perfectly managed. The 18th-century building was originally the British ambassador's residence; later, Ernest Hemingway made it his Paris home. Room sizes and rates vary greatly, and all rooms are individually decorated. Some are imposingly formal, others are homey and plain. Ask for one overlooking the courtyard. There's no restaurant, but a small bar has been installed. *44 rue Jacob, 6e, tel. 42-60-34-72. 30 rooms with bath. Facilities: bar. AE, DC, MC, V.*

Moderate **Esméralda.** You'll find this delightful 17th-century inn just across the river Seine from Notre-Dame. The rooms are small but full of character: Don't be afraid to ask for one with a view of the cathedral. There are also three inexpensive singles in the eaves. *4 rue St-Julien-le-Pauvre, 5e, tel. 43-54-19-20. 19 rooms, with bath or shower. Facilities: sauna. No credit cards.*

Marronniers. There are few better places in Paris for great value and great atmosphere. Located on appealing rue Jacob, the hotel is reached through a small courtyard. All the rooms are light and full of character. Those on the top floor have sloping ceilings, uneven floors, and terrific views over the church of St-Germain-des-Prés. The vaulted cellars have been converted into two atmospheric lounges. There's a bar but no restaurant. *21 rue Jacob, 6e, tel. 43-25-30-60. 37 rooms with bath or shower. Facilities: bar. No credit cards.*

St-Louis. This is another of the Ile-St-Louis's elegantly converted 17th-century town houses, and antique furniture and oil paintings decorate the public areas. The bedrooms are elegantly simple, with exposed beams and stone walls. Blue-gray or light brown tiles add a classy accent to the bathrooms. Breakfast is served in the ancient cellar, but there's no restaurant or bar. *75 rue St-Louis-en-l'Isle, 4e, tel. 46-34-04-80. 21 rooms with bath. No credit cards.*

Inexpensive **Vieux Paris.** Low rates and a handy location on a side street leading to the Seine make the Vieux Paris a winner. The hotel is tiny and is set in a late 15th-century building. You won't find great comfort in the rooms—some of them are *very* small—but the combination of age and slightly musty French charm is hard to resist. *9 rue Gît-le-Coeur, 6e, tel. 43-54-41-66. 21 rooms, 11 with bath. MC, V.*

West Paris **Le Bristol.** Luxury and discretion are the Bristol's trump
Very Expensive cards. The understated facade on rue du Faubourg St-Hon-
★ oré might mislead the uninformed, but the Bristol ranks among Paris's top four hotels. The spaciously elegant and air-conditioned rooms all have authentic (or good imitation) Louis XV and Louis XVI furniture. Moreover, the management has filled the public room with paintings, sculptures, sumptuous carpets, and tapestries. The marble bathrooms are magnificent. Nonguests can have tea in the vast garden or dine in the summer restaurant; the piano bar is open till 1 AM. For hotel guests, there's a pool on the roof, complete with solarium and sauna. Service throughout is impeccable. *112 rue du Faubourg St-Honoré, 8e, tel. 42-66-91-45. 155 rooms and 45 suites with bath. Facilities: 2 restaurants, bar, pool, sauna, solarium, parking, conference facilities for 400. AE, DC, MC, V.*

Crillon. There can surely be no more sumptuous hotel than this regal mansion overlooking place de la Concorde. The Crillon was founded in 1909 by the Champagne family Taittinger, with the express intention of creating the best hotel in the city. They chose as their setting two adjoining town houses built by order of Louis XV. Renovations in the '80s have seen great additional comfort—all rooms are air-conditioned—though not at the expense of the original imposing interior. Mirrors, marble, tapestries, sculptures, great sprays of flowers, and glistening floors are found in all the public rooms. The expansive bedrooms have judicious mixtures of original and reproduction antiques and are hung with beige velvet. The bathrooms, of course, are marble. Of the three restaurants, the best is Les Ambassadeurs, offering some of the best hotel food in the city. *10 place de la Concorde, 8e, tel. 42-65-24-24. 189 rooms and suites with bath. Facilities: 3 restaurants, bars, private reception rooms. AE, DC, MC, V.*

George V. Some say that the George V lacks the style of its super deluxe Parisian counterparts. Others value its unashamedly international atmosphere. There's no lack of authentic period furniture or of highly trained staff. All the rooms are imposing, though the penthouse suites are the only ones to enjoy a commanding view over the city. There are a number of restaurants, the best of which is Les Princes; in summer, you can eat on the leafy patio. *31 av. George V, 8e, tel. 47–23–54–00. 292 rooms and 42 suites with bath. Facilities: 3 restaurants, bars, shopping mall, hairdresser, conference facilities. AE, DC, MC, V.*

Moderate **Bradford.** The Bradford prides itself on providing slightly old-fashioned, well-polished service in an appealing, fusty atmosphere, the kind that has guests coming back year after year. An old wooden elevator takes you up from the flower-filled lobby to the rooms. Some are vast, with brass beds and imposing fireplaces. None has TV; that's not the Bradford style. Drinks are served in the soothing Louis XVI-style lounge on the first floor; there's no restaurant. *10 rue St-Philippe-du-Roule, 8e, tel. 43–59–24–20. 46 rooms with bath or shower. MC, V.*

Queen's Hotel. Queen's is one of only a handful of hotels located in the desirable residential district around rue la Fontaine, within walking distance of the Seine and the Bois de Boulogne. The hotel is small and functional, but standards of comfort and service are high. Flowers on the facade add an appealing note. *4 rue Bastien-Lepage, 16e, tel. 42–88–89–85. 22 rooms with bath or shower. AE, MC, V.*

Montmartre and Central **Grand.** The restoration in 1988 of the Grand's honey-colored facade put the final touch to a three-year renovation program

Very Expensive that has transformed this 19th-century palace backing onto place de l'Opéra. All rooms have been lavishly redecorated in Art Nouveau style and are air-conditioned. Of its three restaurants, the Opéra is the most formal and imposing, while the Relais Capucines offers less intimidatingly grand meals. Le Patio serves buffet lunches and breakfast. *2 rue Scribe, 9e, tel. 42 –68–12–13. 515 rooms and suites with bath. Facilities: 3 restaurants, 2 bars, 13 conference rooms, secretarial services, travel agency, shops, parking. AE, DC, MC, V.*

Ritz. The Paris Ritz is one of the world's most famous hotels, located on the most famous and elegant square in the city, place Vendôme. Millions of dollars have been lavished on the hotel by Egyptian-born owner Mohammed al-Fayed (the owner of Harrods in London). The building is a sumptuous 18th-century town house, a delightful combination of elegance and comfort. The luxurious suites are named after just some of the guests who have stayed here—Coco Chanel, Marcel Proust, and Edward VII among them. The restaurant L'Espador maintains the luxurious note. *15 pl. Vendôme, 1er, tel. 42–60–38–30. 143 fully equipped rooms and 46 suites. Facilities: health and sports complex, 2 restaurants. AE, DC, MC, V.*

Expensive **Bretonnerie.** You'll find this small, three-star hotel on a tiny street in the Marais, a couple of minutes' walk from the Beaubourg. Rooms are decorated in elegant Louis XIII-style but vary considerably in size. The largest is room 1, a duplex; others are definitely cramped. The bar and breakfast rooms in the vaulted cellar have been completely renovated, but there is no restaurant. *22 rue Ste-Croix-de-la-Bretonnerie, 4e, tel. 48–87–77–63. 27 rooms with bath or shower. Facilities: bar. MC, V.*

Régina. The historic place des Pyramides is the location of this late 19th-century hotel. The building is somewhat old-fashioned and formal, but the rooms are spacious and the service is excellent—friendly but efficient. Ask for a room overlooking the Louvre and the Tuileries Gardens. *2 pl. des Pyramides, 1er, tel. 42–60–31–10. 130 rooms and 15 suites with bath. Facilities: restaurant, bar. AE, DC, MC, V. Restaurant usually closed in Aug.*

Moderate **Family.** A few minutes' walk from the Tuileries Gardens will get you to this small two-star hotel near the Madeleine. It was entirely renovated in 1988, but the rooms have kept their stylish '30s look. There's no restaurant, but breakfast and snacks can be served in your room. Service is exceptionally friendly. *35 rue Cambon, 1er, tel. 42–61–54–84. 24 rooms and 1 suite with bath. AE, MC, V.*

Place des Vosges. A loyal American clientele swears by this historic little hotel, located on a charming street just off the exquisite square of the same name. The grand entrance hall is decorated in Louis XIII style; some of the rooms, however, are little more than functional, and a number of the smaller ones fall into the inexpensive category. There's no restaurant, but there's a welcoming little breakfast room. *12 rue de Birague, 4e, tel. 42–72–60–46. 11 rooms with bath or shower. AE, DC, MC, V.*

Regyn's Montmartre. Despite small rooms (all recently renovated), this small, owner-run hotel in Montmartre's place des Abbesses is rapidly gaining an enviable reputation for simple but stylish accommodation. A predominantly young clientele and a correspondingly relaxed atmosphere have made the hotel very popular. Try for one of the rooms on the upper floors for great views over the city. *18 pl. des Abbesses, 18e, tel. 42–54–45–21. 14 rooms with bath or shower. DC, MC, V.*

The Arts

The monthly magazine *Passion* (in English) and the weekly magazines *Pariscope, L'Officiel des Spectacles,* and *7 à Paris* give detailed entertainment listings. The best place to buy tickets is at the place of performance. Otherwise, try hotels, travel agencies (try **Paris-Vision** at 214 rue de Rivoli), and special ticket counters (in the **FNAC** stores at 26 av. de Wagram, near the Arc de Triomphe and the Forum des Halles). Half-price tickets for same-day theater performances are available at the ticket stand at the west side of the Madeleine church.

Theater There is no Parisian equivalent to Broadway or the West End, although a number of theaters line the grand boulevards between Opéra and République. Shows are mostly in French; classical drama is at the distinguished **Comédie Française** (by Palais-Royal). A completely different charm is to be found in the tiny **Théâtre de la Huchette,** near St-Michel, where Ionesco's short modern plays make a deliberately ridiculous mess of the French language.

Concerts The principal venues for classical music are the **Salle Pleyel** (252 rue du Faubourg St-Honoré), near the Arc de Triomphe, and the new **Opéra de la Bastille.** You can also attend one of the many inexpensive organ or chamber music concerts in churches throughout the city.

Opera The **Opéra** itself is a splendid building, and, with Rudolf Nureyev as artistic director, its dance program has reached new heights. Getting a ticket for an opera or ballet performance is not easy, though, and requires either luck, much preplanning, or a well-connected hotel receptionist. The **Opéra Comique** (the French term for opera with spoken dialogue), close by in the rue Favart, is more accessible. The new **Opéra de la Bastille** opened in 1989 and stages both traditional opera and symphony concerts.

Film There are hundreds of movie theaters in Paris and some of them, especially in principal tourist areas such as the Champs-Elysées and the boulevard des Italiens near Opéra, run English films marked "V.O." *(version originale*—i.e., not dubbed). Admission is around 30–35 frs, with reduced rates on Monday. Movie fanatics should check out the **Centre Pompidou** and **Musée de Cinéma** at Trocadéro, where old and rare films are often screened.

Entertainment and Nightlife

Cabaret This is what Paris is supposed to be all about. Its nightclubs are household names—more so abroad than in France, it would seem, judging by the hefty percentage of foreigners present at most shows. Prices range from 150 frs (basic admission plus one drink) up to 510 frs (dinner included). For 250–350 frs, you can get a good seat plus half a bottle of Champagne.

The **Crazy Horse** (12 av. George V, tel. 47–23–32–32) is one of the field leaders in pretty women and dance routines: It features lots of humor and a lot less clothes. The **Moulin Rouge** (place Blanche, tel. 46–06–00–19) is an old favorite at the foot of Montmartre. Nearby is the **Folies-Bergère**, (32 rue Richer, tel. 42–46–77–11), not as it once was but still renowned for its glitter and vocal numbers. The **Lido** (116 bis av. des Champs-Elysées, tel. 45–63–11–61) is all razzle-dazzle.

Bars and Nightclubs Upscale nightclubs are usually private, so unless you have a friend who is a member, forget it. A good bet, though, for drinking and dancing the night away, is the **Club 79** (79 av. des Champs-Elysées). For a more leisurely evening in an atmosphere that is part bar and part gentlemen's club, try an old haunt of Hemingway, Fitzgerald, and Gertrude Stein: **Harry's Bar** (5 rue Danou), a cozy wood-paneled spot for Americans, journalists, and sportsmen.

Jazz Clubs The Latin Quarter is a good place to track down Paris jazz, and the doyen of clubs is the **Caveau de la Huchette** (5 rue de la Huchette), where you can hear Dixieland in a hectic, smoke-filled atmosphere. **Le Slow Club** (130 rue de Rivoli), another favorite, tries to resurrect the style of early Bourbon street, and nearly succeeds.

Rock Clubs **Le Sunset** (60 rue des hombards) is a small, whitewashed cellar with first-rate live music and a clientele that's there to listen. **New Morning** (7 rue des Petites Ecuries) is a top spot for visiting American musicians and good French bands.

Discos **Club Zed** (2 rue des Anglais off bd. St. Germain), is the best place for lively dancing. **Memphis** (3 impasse Bonne Nouvelle) boasts some impressive lighting and video gadgetry.

Ile de France

The area surrounding Paris is called the Ile (island) de France, reflecting the role it has played over the centuries as the economic, political, and religious center of the country. For many visitors to Paris, it is the first taste of French provincial life, with its slower pace and fierce devotion to the soil.

Although parts of the area are fighting a losing battle to resist the encroaching capital, you can still see the countryside that was the inspiration for the Impressionists and other 19th-century painters, and is home to a wealth of architecture dating back to the Middle Ages. The most famous buildings are Chartres—one of most beautiful of French cathedrals—and Versailles, the monumental château of Louis XIV, the Sun King.

Before the completion of Versailles, king and court resided in the delightful château of St-Germain-en-Laye, west of Paris. This is within easy day-trip range from Paris, as are the châteaux of Vaux-le-Vicomte, Rambouillet, and Fontainebleau.

Getting Around

The attractions below can all be reached easily from Paris by car and by regular suburban train services. But you might find it convenient to group some of them together: Versailles, Rambouillet, and Chartres are all on the Paris–Chartres train line; Fontainebleau, Barbizon, and Vaux-le-Vicomte are all within a few miles of each other.

By Train Three lines connect Paris with Versailles; on each, the trip takes about 30 minutes. Best for the château is RER C2 (Express métro line) to Versailles Rive Gauche station. Trains from Gare St-Lazare go to Versailles Rive Droite. Trains from Gare Montparnasse go to Versailles Chantiers and then on to Rambouillet and Chartres. Fontainebleau is served by 20 trains a day from Gare de Lyon; buses for Barbizon leave from in front of the main post office in Fontainebleau.

By Car Expressway A13, from the Porte d'Auteuil, followed by A12, will take you from Paris to Versailles. Alternatively, you can get to Chartres on A10 or N10 south from Porte d'Orleans. For Fontainebleau, take A6 from Porte d'Orleans or, for a more attractive route through the forest of Sénart and the northern part of the forest of Fontainebleau, take N6 from Porte de Charenton via Melun. Vaux-le-Vicomte is 6 kilometers (4 miles) northeast of Melun via N36 and D215.

Guided Tours

Two private companies, **Cityrama** and **Paris Vision**, organize regular half-day and full-day tours from Paris with English-speaking guides. Times and prices are identical. Cityrama tours depart from 4 place des Pyramides 1er, tel. 42–60–30–14. Paris Vision leaves from 214 rue de Rivoli 1er, tel. 42–60–31–25.

Versailles and the Les Trianons. Daily excursions starting at 9:30 include a complete tour of Paris in the morning followed by an afternoon at Versailles. Half-day excursions of Versailles leave mornings and afternoons daily (9:30 and 1:30. Admission: 160 frs) and include a guided tour of the château, Hall of Mirrors, and Queen's Suite. On Thursday only, a daylong excursion (280 frs) extends the tour to include an afternoon visit (starting 1:30) to the Trianons. Separate afternoon visits to the Trianons, again on Thursday, start at 1:30 (140 frs).

Chartres. Both companies organize half-day tours to Chartres on Tuesday and Saturday afternoons (departure at 1 PM, 180 frs), but if you're short of time or cash, you'd be better off taking the **Versailles-Chartres** day trips, also on Tuesday and Saturday (departure at 9:30).

Fontainebleau and Barbizon. Half-day trips (departure at 1:30, 160 frs) on Wednesday, Friday, and Sunday run to Fontainbleau and nearby Barbizon (which is otherwise difficult to reach), but can be linked to a Versailles tour leaving at 9:30 on the same days.

Tourist Information

Barbizon. 41 rue Grande, tel. 60–66–41–87.
Chartres. 7 Cloître Notre-Dame, tel. 37–21–54–03.
Fontainebleau. 31 pl. Napoléon Bonaparte, tel. 64–22–25–68.
Rambouillet. Pl. de la Libération, tel. 34–83–21–21.
Versailles. 7 rue des Réservoirs, tel. 39–50–36–22.

Exploring the Ile de France

Versailles **Versailles** is the location of one of the world's grandest palaces and one of France's most popular attractions. Wide, tree-lined avenues, broader than the Champs-Elysées and bordered with massive 17th-century mansions, lead directly to the Sun King's château. From the imposing place d'Armes in front of the château, you enter the Cour des Ministres, a sprawling cobbled forecourt. Right in the middle, the statue of Louis XIV stands triumphant, surveying the town that he built from scratch to house those of the 20,000 noblemen, servants, and hangers-on who weren't lucky enough to get one of the 3,000 beds in the château.

The building of the château in its entirety took 50 years. Hills were flattened, marshes drained, forests transplanted, and water for the magnificent fountains was channeled from the Seine several miles away. Visit the **Grands Appartements,** the six salons that made up the royal living quarters, and the famous **Galerie des Glaces** (Hall of Mirrors). Both can be visited without a guide, but you can get a cassette in English. There are also guided tours of the **petits appartements,** where the royal family and friends lived in relative intimacy, and the miniature opera house—one of the first oval rooms in France, built on the north wing *(aile nord)* for Louis XV in 1770. *Grands Appartements and Galerie des Glaces. Admission: 23 frs. adults, 12 frs students and seniors citizens. Open Tues.–Sun. 9:45–5.*

The château's vast grounds are masterpieces of formal landscaping. At one end of the Petit Canal, which crosses the Grand Canal at right angles, is the **Grand Trianon,** a scaled-down pleasure palace built in the 1680s. The **Petit Trianon,** nearby, is a sumptuously furnished 18th-century mansion, commissioned by Louis XVI for Marie-Antoinette, who would flee here to

Ile de France

avoid the stuffy atmosphere of the court. Nearby, she built the village, complete with dairy and mill, where she and her companions would dress as shepherdesses and lead a make-believe bucolic life. *Château* grounds. Admission: free. Open 8:30–dusk. Grand Trianon. Admission: 15 frs. Open 9:45–5:30. Petit Trianon. Admission: 10 frs. Open 2–5:30. Joint ticket: 18 frs adults, 9frs children and senior citizens.

Rambouillet Just a little more than 20 kilometers (12 miles) southwest of Versailles is the small town of **Rambouillet,** home of a château, adjoining park, and 13,770 hectares (34,000 acres) of forest. Since 1897, the château has been a summer residence of the French president; today, it is also used as a site for international summits. You can visit the château only when the president is not in residence—fortunately, he's not there often.

French kings have lived in the château since it was built in 1375. Highlights include the **Appartements d'Assemblée,** decorated with finely detailed wood paneling, and Napoleon's bathroom, with its Pompeii-inspired frescoes. The park stretches away behind the château. Beyond the **Jardin d'Eau** (Water Garden) lies the English-style garden and the **Laiterie de la Reine** (Marie-Antoinette's Dairy). This was another of her attempts to "get back to nature." *Château. Admission: 6 frs. Open Apr.–Sept., Wed.–Mon. 10–12 and 2–6; Oct.–Mar., 10–12 and 2–5. Park. Admission: free. Open sunrise–sunset. Marie-Antoinette's Dairy. Admission 9 frs. Open same hours as Château, closes at 4 in winter.*

The **Forest of Rambouillet** stretches more than 13,770 hectares (34,000 acres). By car, you can visit the 20 attractive ponds and **étangs** (small lakes). The **Etang de Hollande,** near St-Leger-en-Yvelines, is the most popular but gets overcrowded on weekends and during the summer. There is a good walking route from the town; get details from the tourist board.

Chartres   From Rambouillet, N10 will take you straight to **Chartres.** Long before you arrive you will see its famous cathedral towering over the plain of the Beauce, France's granary. The attractive old town, steeped in religious history and dating back to before the Roman conquest, is still laced with winding medieval streets.

Today's Gothic cathedral, **Notre-Dame de Chartres,** is the sixth Christian church on the site; despite a series of fires, it has remained virtually the same since the 12th century. The **Royal Portal** on the main facade, presenting "the life and triumph of the Savior," is one of the finest examples of Romanesque sculpture in the country. Inside, the 12th-and 13th-century rose windows come alive even in dull weather, thanks to the deep Chartres blue of the stained glass: Its formula remains a mystery to this day. *Cathedral tours available: Ask at the Maison des Clercs, 18 rue du Cloître Notre-Dame.*

Since the rest of the tour is on another side of Paris, and it is probably easier to return to the capital to continue (*see* Getting Around).

Fontainebleau   In the early 16th century, the flamboyant Francis I transformed the medieval hunting lodge of **Fontainebleau** into a magnificent Renaissance palace. His successor, Henry II, covered the palace with his initials, woven into the *D* for his mistress, Diane de Poitiers. When he died, his queen, Catherine de' Médicis, carried out further alterations, later extended under Louis XIV. Napoleon preferred the relative intimacy of Fontainebleau to the grandeur of Versailles. Before he was exiled to Elba, he bade farewell to his Old Guard in the courtyard now known as the **Cour des Adieux** (Farewell Court). The emperor also harangued his troops from the **Horseshoe Staircase.** Ask the curator to let you see the **Cour Ovale** (Oval Court), the oldest and perhaps most interesting courtyard. It stands on the site of the original 12th-century fortified building, but only the keep remains today.

The **Grands Appartements** (royal suites and ballroom) are the main attractions of any visit to the château. The **Galerie de François I** is really a covered bridge (built 1528–30) looking out over the Cour de la Fontaine. The overall effect inside the Galerie—and throughout Fontainebleau—is one of classical harmony and proportion, combining to create a sense of Renaissance lightness and order. Francis I appreciated the Italian Renaissance, and the ballroom is decorated with frescoes by Primaticcio (1504–70) and his pupil, Niccolò dell'Abbate. If you're there on a weekday, you will also be able to join a guided tour of the Petits Appartements, used by Napoleon and Josephine. *Fontainebleau. Admission: 21 frs. Open 9:30–12:30 and 2–5. Closed Tues. and holidays.*

The huge **Forest of Fontainebleau** is a favorite spot for walkers, horseback riders, and climbers. The French Alpine club started using the famous *rochers* (outcrops) for training back in

1910 and still climb the best known: Plutus and Gargantua. There are more than 144 kilometers (90 miles) of paths, so before you go, invest in a Touring Club map at the tourist office. One of the best views in the forest is from the **Hauteurs de la Solle,** within easy walking distance of Fontainebleau itself.

Barbizon The **Rochers des Demoiselles,** just south of the town, are also good for an afternoon stroll. The **Gorges d'Apremont,** which offer the best views of the rocks, are located near **Barbizon,** on the edge of the forest, 10 kilometers (6 miles) northwest of Fontainebleau. This delightful little village is scarcely more than a main street lined with restaurants and boutiques, but a group of landscape painters put it on the map in the mid-19th century. Théodore Rousseau and Jean-François Millet both had their studios here. Sculptor Henri Chapu's bronze medallion, sealed to one of the famous sandstone rocks in the forest nearby, pays homage to the two leaders of what became known as the Barbizon group.

Drop in at the **Ancienne Auberge du Père Ganne** (Pere Ganne's Inn), where most of the landscape artists ate and drank, while in Barbizon. They painted on every available surface, and even now you can see some originals on the walls and in the buffet. Today, the back room is devoted to modern landscape artists. *Rue Grande, tel. 60–66–46–73. Admission: free. Guided visits mid-Mar.–Oct., Wed.–Mon. 9:45–6; Nov.–mid-Mar., Fri. 2–6, weekends 10–6.*

Next to the church, in a barn that Rousseau used as a studio, you'll find the **Musée de l'Ecole de Barbizon** (Barbizon School Museum), containing documents of the village as it was in the 19th century as well as a few original works by Rousseau, Diaz, Troyon, and Charles Jacque. *Rue Grande, tel. 60–66–22–38. Admission: 7 frs adults, children free. Open Apr.–Sept., Mon. and Wed.–Fri.; 10:30–12:30 and 2–6, weekends 2–6; Oct.–Mar., Mon and Wed.–Fri. 10:30–12:30 and 2–5, weekends 2–5.*

From Barbizon, D64 offers a pleasant shortcut to Melun and then on to the château of **Vaux-le-Vicomte,** one of the greatest monuments of 17th-century French architecture. It was to have been Nicolas Fouquet's pride and joy, but turned out to be his downfall. This superintendent of France's finances under Louis XIV tended to use state resources for his own benefit—the château itself is damning evidence—and the Sun King eventually had him imprisoned for life. From the visitor's point of view, though, Fouquet's *folie de grandeur* is a treat. He had excellent taste (and a large budget) and chose the best-qualified team to build Vaux-le-Vicomte. Louis liked the results enough to reemploy them all when he built Versailles. Visit the kitchens, which have been preserved just as they were in the 17th century. The **gardens** (admission: 15 frs) are open all day. *Guided tours of château. Admission: 40 frs. Open Apr.–Oct., daily 10–6; Nov.–Mar., daily 10–5. Candlelit visits. Admission: 50 frs. Open May–Sept., Sat. 8:30–11:30.*

Dining and Lodging

For details and price category definitions, *see* Dining and Lodging in Staying in France.

Barbizon **Le Relais.** The delicious specialties—particularly the beef and
Dining the game (in season)—are served in large portions and there is
a good choice of fixed-price menus. The Relais is spacious, with
walls covered with paintings and hunting trophies, and there is
a big open fire. The owner is proud of the large terrace where
you can eat in the shade of lime and chestnut trees. *2 av.
Charles de Gaulle, tel. 60–66–40–28. Weekend reservations essential. MC, V. Closed Tues., Wed., Aug. 20–Sept. 5, Dec. 18–
Jan. 6. Moderate.*

Lodging **Auberge des Alouettes.** This delightful, 19th-century inn, is set
on 8,094 square meters (two acres) of grounds. The interior has
been redecorated in '30s style, but many rooms still have their
original oak beams. The restaurant, with a large open terrace,
features nouvelle cuisine in sizable portions. *4 rue Antoine
Barye, tel. 60–66–41–98. 23 rooms with bath or shower. Facilities: tennis, parking. Reservations essential for restaurant.
AE, DC, MC, V. Moderate.*

Chartres **Vieille Maison.** Located in a recently refitted 14th-century
Dining building only 46½ meters (50 yards) from the cathedral, Vieille
Maison serves excellent nouvelle cuisine as well as more traditional dishes. Try the regional *menu beauceron* for the
homemade foie gras and duck dishes, or the mouth-watering
menu gourmand, if the wallet allows. *5 rue au Lait, tel. 37–34–
10–67. Reservations essential. AE, DC, MC, V. Closed Sun.
evening, Mon., and Jan. 1–15, July 15–31. Expensive.*
Buisson Ardent. Set in an attractive old oak-beamed building
within sight of the cathedral's south portal, Buisson Ardent is a
popular restaurant providing inexpensive fixed-price menus
(especially good on weekdays) and a choice of imaginative à la
carte dishes with delicious sauces. The wine list is comprehensive. *10 rue au Lait, tel. 37–34–04–66. Reservations advised.
AE, DC, MC, V. Closed Sun. and Tues. evenings, Wed. Moderate.*

Lodging **Grand Monarque.** The Monarque is an 18th-century coaching
inn that has had a recent face-lift: 11 rooms were added in 1988
in a separate turn-of-the-century building overlooking a small
garden, and the entrance hall was completely renovated. The
rooms have the level of comfort and consistency you would expect from a Best Western. It also has an excellent moderately
priced restaurant. *22 pl. des Epars, tel. 37–21–00–72. 57
rooms, 52 with bath or shower. Facilities: restaurant. AE, DC,
MC, V. Moderate.*

Fontainebleau **Le Dauphin.** Prices are reasonable in this homey, rustic restau-
Dining rant located near the town hall and just five minutes from the
château. Specialties include snails, *confit de canard* (duck preserve), and a variety of homemade desserts. *24 rue Grande, tel.
64–22–27–04. Reservations advised, especially on Sun. AE,
MC, V. Closed Tues. evening, Wed., Feb., and Sept. 1–8. Inexpensive.*

Lodging **Londres.** The balconies of this tranquil, family-style hotel look
out over the palace and the Cour des Adieux; the 19th-century
facade is preserved by government order. Inside, the decor is
dominated by the Louis XV-style furniture. *1 pl. Général de
Gaulle, tel. 64–22–20–21. 22 rooms, most with bath or shower.
Facilities: restaurant, tea room, bar, parking. AE, MC, V.
Closed Dec. 20–Jan. 31. Inexpensive/moderate.*

Rambouillet **La Poste.** Traditional, unpretentious cooking is the attraction
Dining of this former coaching inn, close to the château. Until 1988, it
could seat only 36 people, but a new upstairs dining room has
been opened, doubling the capacity. The service is good, as is
the selection of inexpensive fixed-price menus, even on Sunday. *101 rue du Général-de-Gaulle, tel. 34-83-03-01.
Reservations advised. AE, MC, V. Moderate.*

Versailles **Trois Marches.** This, the best-known restaurant in Versailles, is
Dining also recognized as one of the best in France for its nouvelle cuisine. Don't miss Gerard Vié's bisque of lobster, salmon with
fennel, or turbot *galette*, served in this magnificent late-18th-
century *hôtel particulier* (town house) decorated with Old Masters. *3 rue Colbert, tel. 39-50-13-21. Reservations essential.
AE, DC, MC, V. Closed Sun., Mon. Expensive.*

Boule d'Or. Built in 1696, this restaurant claims to be the
second-oldest house in Versailles, as well as the oldest inn. Its
friendly owner, Claude Saillard, loves to reproduce 17th- and
18th-century dishes in the appropriately oak-beamed surroundings. His specialty is the "Trilogy" (served evenings
only): It includes sole in a sauce introduced in 1733; braised
beef, created in 1742; and a duck fricassé first served in 1654.
There are simpler lunchtime fixed-price menus. *25 rue du
Maréchal Foch, tel. 39-50-22-97. Reservations essential. AE,
DC, MC, V. Closed Sun. evening, Mon. Moderate.*

Potager du Roy. There is excellent value in this restaurant run
by Philippe Letourneur, former colleague of Gerard Vié (*see*
Trois Marches). The cuisine gets better each year, yet the
prices remain reasonable. It is hardly surprising that this bistro and the enclosed terrace are often crowded and that
reservations are a must. *1 rue du Maréchal Joffre, tel. 39-50-
35-34. Reservations essential. MC, V. Closed Sun., Mon.
Moderate.*

Normandy

Jutting out into the Channel, Normandy probably has more
connections with the English-speaking world than any other
part of France. The association continues until this day. Visitors flock to Normandy not only to see historic monuments;
they also come simply to relax in the rich countryside with its
apple orchards, lush meadows, and sandy beaches.

The historic cities of Rouen and Caen, capitals of Upper and
Lower Normandy respectively, are full of churches, well-
preserved buildings, and museums. The Seine Valley is lined
with abbeys and castles from all periods: St-Wandrille, for example, dates back to the 7th century. Richard the Lionhearted's 12th-century Château Gaillard, at Les Andelys, is
still imposing. Normandy also has one of France's most enduring tourist attractions: Mont St-Michel, a remarkable Gothic
abbey perched on a rocky mount off the Cotentin peninsula.

Etretat and Fécamp on the Alabaster coast and Deauville,
Trouville, and Honfleur on the Côte Fleurie (Flowered Coast)
are among Normandy's many seaside resorts. Hotels, restaurants, and beaches cater to the simpler pleasures of life, while
casinos make the rich poor—and sometimes the other way
around, too. Normandy is also recognized as one of France's
finest gastronomic regions; try some of the excellent cheeses

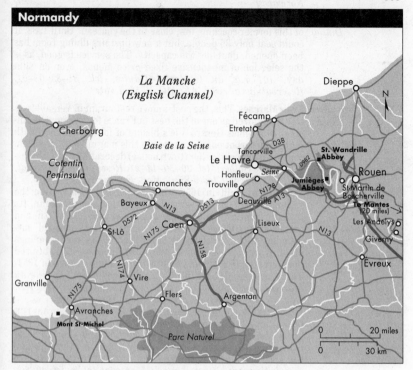

washed down with local cider, the apple brandy (Calvados), or the wide range of seafood dishes.

Getting Around

Normandy is best visited by car, although there are regular daily trains from Paris to Rouen, Caen, and Bayeux. Limited train connections make cross-country traveling difficult. Many historic monuments and some towns—such as Honfleur, which has no train station—are off the beaten track.

Guided Tours

Cityrama (214 rue de Rivoli, Paris 1er, tel. 42–60–31–25) and **Paris Vision** (4 pl. des Pyramides, Paris 1er, tel. 42–60–30–14) organize identical one-day excursions to Mont St-Michel from Paris, leaving at 7:15 Saturday morning and taking you by bus to Mont St-Michel in time for lunch at the Terrasse Poulard restaurant (*see* Mont St-Michel). There is a guided tour of the mount and the abbey, and you return by first-class train from Laval to Gare Montparnasse. Cost: 750 frs.

Tourist Information

Regional Centers   **Caen** (Lower Normandy). Pl. du Canada, tel. 31–86–53–30.
Rouen (Upper Normandy). 2 rue du Petit Square, tel. 35–88–61–32.

Local Offices **Les Andelys.** Rue Philippe Auguste, tel. 32–54–41–93.
Bayeux. 1 rue des Cuisiniers, tel. 31–92–16–26.
Caen. Pl. St-Pierre, tel. 31–86–27–65.
Deauville. Pl. de la Mairie, tel. 31–88–21–43.
Etretat. Pl. de la Mairie, tel. 35–27–05–21.
Fécamp. Front de Mer, tel. 35–29–16–34.
Honfleur. 33 cour des Fosses, tel. 31–89–23–30.
Mont St-Michel. Corps de Garde des Bourgeois, tel. 33–60–14–30.
Rouen. Pl. de la Cathédrale, tel. 35–71–41–77.

Exploring Normandy

Take Expressway A13 from Paris (Porte d'Auteuil) as far as Meulan or Mantes and cross the Seine to the right (north) bank. Then follow D913 or make a short stop in the little village of **Giverny,** where you can visit the house and gardens in which the Impressionist painter Claude Monet lived and worked. *Admission: 25 frs. Open Apr.–Oct., Tues.–Sun. 10–noon and 2–6.*

D313 goes to **Les Andelys,** a small town on the banks of the Seine, dominated by the imposing **Château Gaillard,** a fortress built in 1196 by English king and duke of Normandy, Richard the Lionhearted. *Admission: 10 frs. Open mid-Mar.–mid-Nov., Thurs.–Mon. 10–12:30 and 2–5, Wed. 2–5.*

Numbers in the margin correspond with points of interest on the Rouen map.

Rouen **Rouen,** the capital of Upper Normandy, has a remarkable num-
① ber of historic churches, from the city's **Cathédrale Notre-Dame,** dating from the 12th century, to the modern, fish-
② shaped **Eglise Jeanne d'Arc** on the old market square, where Joan of Arc was burned at the stake in 1431. The tourist office organizes a guided tour leaving from the place de la Cathédrale
③ and visiting the city's main churches, the **Palais de Justice,** and the lively old quarter around the rue du Gros-Horloge, where you can see the giant Renaissance clock that was built in 1527. The most noteworthy churches are located on the right bank, around the old quarter, and can be visited on foot. Try to visit
④ ⑤ **Eglise St-Maclou,** with its five-gabled facade; **'Abbaye St-Ouen,**
⑥ a beautifully proportioned 14th-century abbey; and the **Eglise St-Godard,** with well-preserved stained-glass windows.

One ticket will get you into several of Rouen's best museums,
⑦ notably the **Musée des Beaux Arts** (Fine Arts Museum), near Eglise St-Godard (on Square Vedral). This specializes in 17th- and 19th-century French paintings, with a particular emphasis on artists who lived and worked locally. There is an outstanding collection of macabre paintings by Romantic painter Géricault.
⑧ Nearby museums include the **Musée Le Secq des Tournelles** (rue Jacques Villon, in the Eglise St-Laurent), which has an unusual
⑨ collection of wrought iron; the **Musée de la Céramique** (rue Faucon 1), which now houses Rouen's porcelain collections; and
⑩ the **Musée du Gros-Horloge** (rue du Gros-Horloge), where you can study the mechanism of the Renaissance clock that gives its name to the museum. *Museums. Admission: 11 frs. Open Thurs.–Mon. 10–noon and 2–6, Wed. 2–6.*

Follow D982 across the Forest of Roumare and along the Seine via St-Martin de Boscherville, with its mighty 11th-century Romanesque abbey church of St-Georges, to **Jumièges Abbey,**

Abbaye St-Ouen, **5**

Cathédrale
Notre-Dame, **1**

Eglise Jeanne d'Arc, **2**

Eglise St-Godard, **6**

Eglise St-Maclou, **4**

Musée des Beaux-
Arts, **7**

Musée de la
Céramique, **9**

Musée du Gros-
Horloge, **10**

Musée Le Secq des
Tournelles, **8**

Palais de Justice, **3**

Rouen

once a powerful Benedictine center. The abbey was dismantled
during the Revolution, but you can still wander through the remains of the chapter house and several of the chapels.
*Admission: 15 frs adults, 9 frs senior citizens, 5 frs children,
Open Apr.–Sept. daily 10–noon and 2–6; Oct.–Mar., weekdays 10–noon and 2–4; weekends 2–5.*

The nearby **St-Wandrille Abbey,** off D982, was founded a few
years before—in 649—and still has a Benedictine community.
Arrive early in the morning to hear the Gregorian chants at
Mass. *Morning Mass Mon.–Sat. at 9:30; Sun. and holidays at
10.*

Fécamp **Fécamp,** at the foot of the highest cliffs in Normandy, was the
region's first place of pilgrimage. Legend has it that in the first
century, an abandoned boat washed ashore here with a bottle
containing Christ's blood. The 11th-century **Eglise de la Trinité**
was built to accommodate all the pilgrims. *Admission: 10 frs.
Guided tours May–Oct., Sun. at 11, 3, and 5.*

Fécamp is also home of the famous Bénédictine liqueur. The
museum devoted to its production—rebuilt in 1892 after a
fire—is one of the most popular attractions in Normandy.
*Musée de la Bénédictine. 110 rue Alexandre-le-Grand. Admis-
sion: 22 frs. Open Easter–Oct., daily 9:30–11:30 and 2–5:30;
Nov.–Mar., daily 10–1:30 and 3:30–4:30.*

Follow the pretty coast road about 12 kilometers (7 miles) to
Etretat, where the sea has cut into the cliff to create two im-

mense archways that lead to the neighboring beaches at low tide. For a view over the bay and the **Aiguille,** which is an enormous rock towering in the middle, take the little path up the Falaise d'Aval cliff.

To avoid doubling back to Fécamp, take D39 to the Tancarville Bridge, which links Upper and Lower Normandy. Have some small change ready for the toll. Turn right on D178 and drive south for 14 kilometers (9 miles) to a major crossroads. Turn right and drive the same distance to Honfleur.

Honfleur Once an important port for maritime expeditions, **Honfleur** became a favorite spot for painters, including the Impressionists. Today, Honfleur's lively cobbled streets, inland harbors full of colorful yachts, and the Eglise Ste-Catherine, a little 15th-century wooden church, make it very popular with tourists. In the summer or on weekends, be prepared for lines at restaurants and cafés.

The popular resorts of **Trouville** and **Deauville** are 16 kilometers (10 miles) along the Côte de Grâce, on D513. Deauville is the swankier of the two, with its palaces, casino, horse racing, and film festival. Its more modest neighbor, Trouville, with its active fighting fleet, is a better place to get a feel for traditional Normandy.

Caen, slightly inland from these resorts, is the capital of Lower Normandy. It was badly bombed in 1944 but has been rebuilt with care and imagination. William the Conqueror was responsible for Caen's large **fortress** perched on a hill behind the town: Its ramparts now encircle the public garden. William and his queen, Mathilde, also built Caen's "his and hers" abbeys— **Abbaye aux Hommes** and **Abbaye aux Femmes.** The city hall is alongside the Abbaye aux Hommes, which has hourly guided tours (Admission: 5 frs); Abbaye aux Femmes is now a hospital and only the church is open to visitors.

Bayeux **Bayeux,** a few miles inland from the D-Day beach via N13, was the first French town freed by the Allies in June 1944. But it is known primarily as the home of **La Tapisserie de la Reine Mathilde** (known to us as the Bayeux Tapestry), which tells the epic story of William's conquest of England in 1066. It is on show at the **Centre Culturel Guillaume le Conquérant** (William the Conqueror Cultural Center). *Rue St-Exupère. Admission: 20 frs. adults, 10 frs students. Open June–Sept., daily 9–7; Oct.–May, daily 9:30–12:30 and 2–6 and 2–7. Closed Dec. 25, Jan. 1.*

The new **Musée de la Bataille de Normandie** (Museum of the Battle of Normandy) traces the history of the Allied advance against the Germans in 1944. It overlooks the British Military Cemetery. *Blvd. Général-Fabian-Ware. Admission: 16 frs adults, 9 frs students. Open June–Aug., daily 9–7; Sept.–mid-Oct. and mid-Mar.–May, daily 9:30–12:30 and 2:30–6:30; mid-Oct.–mid-Mar., daily 10–12:30 and 2–6.*

Bayeux is a good starting point for excursions to the coast. In **Arromanches** harbor, you can see the remains of **Mulberry B,** an artificial port built for the British D-Day landings. Mulberry A, where American troops landed farther up the coast on what is now known as **Omaha Beach,** was destroyed by a storm a few months after the landings. The **Musée du Débarquement** (Landings Museum) on Arromanches seafront shows the landing plan and a film (in English) on the operation. *Admission: 16 frs. Open June–mid-Sept., daily 9–6:30; mid-Sept.–mid-Apr., daily 9–11:30 and 2–5:30. Closed Dec. 25, Jan. 1–18.*

Mont St-Michel Drive through the fertile heartland of Normandy, among the rolling hills and orchards that produce Calvados and cider. Take D972 to **St-Lô** and then D999 and N175 to **Avranches,** where you will have your first view of **Mont St-Michel,** the Gothic abbey and village rising up from the sea. The mount's fame comes not just from its location—it's cut off from the mainland at high tide—but from the dramatic nature of its construction in the 8th century, when tons of granite were brought from the nearby Chausey Islands and Brittany and hauled up the 265-foot peak. It has been a pilgrimage center ever since.

For most of the year, Mont St-Michel is surrounded by sandy beach. The best time to see it is during the high tides of spring and fall, when the sea comes pounding in—dangerously fast—and encircles the mount. **La Merveille** (the Wonder) is the name given to the collection of Gothic buildings on top. What looks like a fortress is in fact a series of architectural layers that trace the evolution of French architecture from Romanesque to late-Gothic. You can join a guided tour (in English). *Admission: 23 frs adults, 13 frs students and senior citizens, 5 frs children. Open mid-May–Sept., daily 9–11:30 and 1:30–6; Oct.–mid-May, Wed.–Mon. 9:30–11:45 and 1:45–4:15.*

The **village,** with its steep streets, is best visited off-season when the souvenir sellers and tourists have departed. The ramparts, and the North Tower in particular, offer the best views over the bay.

Dining and Lodging

For details and price category definitions, *see* Dining and Lodging in Staying in France.

Bayeux **Lion d'Or.** Flower-filled balconies and a courtyard full of palm
Lodging trees adorn this '30s property in the center of Bayeux. The rooms are all well equipped and the recently redecorated restaurant serves Norman specialties. *71 rue St-Jean, tel. 31–92–06–90. 28 rooms with bath or shower. Facilities: indoor garage. AE, DC, MC, V. Closed mid-Dec.–mid-Jan. Moderate.*

Caen **Bourride.** Michel Bruneau, owner and chef of this famous res-
Dining taurant set in one of the oldest streets near the castle, bases his inventive recipes almost exclusively on local and regional produce. Specialties include skate caramelized in honey and cider and meat pastry cooked in cider vinegar. *15 rue du Vaugueux, tel. 31–93–50–76. Reservations advised. AE, DC, MC, V. Closed Sun., Mon., Jan. 1–24 and Aug. 15–31. Expensive.*

Lodging **Le Dauphin.** Although small, the rooms in this old priory near the citadel are clean and renovated. Many of them overlook the quiet hotel courtyard. Le Dauphin also has an excellent restaurant serving Norman dishes topped by unusually light sauces, with an emphasis on seafood. *29 rue Gémare, tel. 31–86–22–26. 21 rooms with bath or shower. Facilities: parking. AE, DC, MC, V. Closed part of Feb. and mid-July–mid-Aug.; restaurant closed Sat. Inexpensive.*

Deauville **Spinnaker.** Here is a handy—and affordable—restaurant in
Dining the center of this chic resort. The atmosphere is informal and

the food is local, with special emphasis on seafood. Try the delicious fresh pasta and crab salad. *52 rue Mirabeau, tel. 31–88–24–40. Reservations advised. MC, V. Closed Wed. out of season, Thurs., and Nov. 15–Dec. 15. Moderate.*

Etretat
Dining

Roches Blanches. A warm welcome is the rule in this family-run seafood restaurant near the ocean. The restaurant is particularly popular on Sunday. Try the fixed-price menus or the *plat du terroir* (veal escalope *flambée* with Calvados). *Rue Abbé Cochet, tel. 35–27–07–34. Reservations essential. MC, V. Closed Wed. in summer, Tues.–Thurs. in winter, and Oct. and Jan. Moderate.*

Fécamp
Dining

Martin. This is the sort of unpretentious restaurant that only the French seem to know how to run. The food—seafood is a good bet—is of a high standard. For dessert try the *soufflé à la Bénédictine* or the *soufflé au Calvados. 18 pl. St-Etienne, tel. 35–28–23–82. Reservations not necessary. Closed Sun. evening, Mon.; Mar. 1–15, Sept. 1–15. Inexpensive.*

Lodging

Hotel d'Angleterre. Oak beams and wood paneling set the tone in the lobby of this comfortable hotel near the sea, glowing now, thanks to the 1988 renovations carried out by the new owners. Its restaurant is good and has four fixed-price menus. *93 rue de la Plage, tel. 35–28–01–60. 30 rooms, 23 with bath or shower. Facilities: garage. AE, DC, MC, V. Closed Dec. Inexpensive.*

Honfleur
Dining

Absinthe. The magnificent 17th-century dining room dominates the ground floor, where you will also find the pub-style bar, the Ivanhoe. But in warm weather, the place to be is on the sunny terrace on the quayside. The menu features both nouvelle and traditional cuisines, with the accent on seafood. *10 quai de la Quarantaine, tel. 31–89–39–00. Reservations advised. AE, DC, MC, V. Closed Mon. evening and Tues., except in midsummer. Expensive.*

Ancrage. Vast seafood platters are the specialty in this charming old restaurant overlooking the Vieux Bassin (old harbor), but meat dishes are good, too, particularly the calf sweetbreads braised in cider. *12 rue Montpensier, tel. 31–89–00–70. Reservations advised in summer. MC, V. Closed Tues. evening, Wed.; Jan. 2–Feb. 2. Moderate.*

Lodging

Ferme St-Simeon. One of the most luxurious hotels in Normandy, St-Simeon is set in an impressive 17th-century farmhouse on the edge of Honfleur, overlooking the Seine estuary. There are several rooms in the nearby manor house and in a recently converted cider press. Its restaurant is known for its fresh seafood, sophisticated desserts, and excellent wine list. *Route Adolphe-Marais, tel. 31–89–23–61. 38 rooms with bath, 4 with Jacuzzi. Reservations essential in restaurant. MC, V. Very Expensive.*

Mont St-Michel
Lodging

Terrasses Poulard. This delightful, 19th-century hotel was completely renovated in 1986; each room was given the name of a famous local Norman personality and decorated accordingly. Several rooms have breathtaking views of the bay, while others look out onto a little garden. The restaurant, with superb fresh lobster, has its best views upstairs. *Rue Principale, tel. 33–60–14–09. 29 rooms with bath. Facilities: restaurant. AE, DC, MC, V. Expensive.*

Rouen **La Couronne.** Built in 1345, La Couronne claims to be the oldest
Dining inn in France. The oak beams, leather upholstery, and woodwork provide an attractive setting for a collection of sculptures.
The traditional cuisine features homemade foie gras, duck *à
l'orange,* and turbot in flaky pastry. *31 pl. du Vieux Marché,
tel. 35–71–40–90. Reservations essential. AE, DC, MC, V. Expensive.*

Lodging **Hotel de Dieppe.** A newly renovated 19th-century hotel opposite the train station, Hotel de Dieppe offers two types of room:
modern and period-style. The buffet-style breakfast is
substantial—unlike most in France—and the popular restaurant serves a range of grilled meats as well as *canard au sang*
(duck cooked in its own blood). *Pl. Bernard Tissot, tel. 35–71–
96–00. 42 rooms with bath or shower. AE, DC, MC, V. Moderate.*

Burgundy and Lyon

For a region whose powerful medieval dukes held sway over
large tracts of Western Europe and whose current image is
closely allied to its expensive wine, Burgundy is a place of surprisingly rustic, quiet charm.

Despite the mighty Gothic cathedrals of Sens and Auxerre,
Burgundy's leading religious monument is the Romanesque basilica at Vézelay. Once one of Christianity's most important
pilgrimage centers, Vézelay is today a tiny village hidden in
the folds of rolling, verdant hills. In its time, the abbey of Cluny
farther south was equally important, but few of its buildings
remain.

The heart of Burgundy consists of the dark, brooding Morvan
Forest. Dijon is the region's only city and retains something of
its medieval opulence. Its present reputation is essentially gastronomic, however; top-class restaurants abound, and local
"industries" involve the production of mustard, *cassis* (black-
currant liqueur), snails, and—of course—wine. The vineyards
extending down toward the ancient town of Beaune are among
the world's most distinguished and picturesque.

The vines continue to flourish as you head south along the
Saône Valley, through the Mâconnais and Beaujolais, toward
Lyon, one of France's most appealing cities. The combination of
frenzied modernity and unhurried *joie de vivre* give Lyon a
sense of balance. The only danger is a temptation to overin-
dulge in its rich and robust cuisine.

Burgundy's winters are cold, its summers hot. The ideal times
to come are late May, when the countryside is in flower, and
September or October, for the wine harvest.

Getting Around

Burgundy is a region best visited by car. Its meandering country roads invite leisurely exploration. There are few big towns,
and traveling around by train is unrewarding, especially since
the infrequent cross-country trains steam along at the speed of
a legendary Burgundy snail.

Guided Tours

The Dijon branch of the regional tourism office organizes a series of tours using Dijon as a base. These include wine tastings and historic tours of the famous religious centers. Write to Comité Régional de Tourisme, 4 rue Nicolas-Berthot, 21000 Dijon.

Tourist Information

Auxerre. 1 quai de la République, tel. 86–52–06–19.
Beaune. Rue de l'Hôtel-Dieu, tel. 80–22–24–51.
Dijon. Pl. Darcy, tel. 80–43–42–12.
Lyon. Pl. Bellecoeur, tel. 78–42–25–75.
Sens. Pl. Jean-Jaurès, tel. 86–65–19–49.

Exploring Burgundy and Lyon

It makes sense for **Sens** to be your first stop on the way down to Burgundy, since it lies just 120 kilometers (70 miles) from Paris on N6—a fast, pretty road that hugs the Yonne Valley south of Fontainebleau. Sens is home to France's senior archbishop and is dominated by the 12th-century **Cathédrale St-Etienne.** This is one of the oldest cathedrals in France and has a foursquare facade topped by towers and an incongruous little Renaissance campanile. The vast, harmonious interior contains outstanding stained glass of various periods.

The 13th-century **Palais Synodal** alongside, now a local museum, provides a first encounter with Burgundy's multicolored tiled roofs; from its courtyard, there is a fine view of the cathedral's south transept, constructed in the fluid Flamboyant Gothic style of the 16th century. *Rue des Déportés de la Résistance. Admission: 10 frs. Open Mar.–mid-Dec. daily 10–noon and 2–5; mid-Dec.–Feb., Thurs.–Tues. 2–4:30.*

Auxerre   N6 continues to **Auxerre,** a small, peaceful town with its own **Cathédrale St-Etienne,** perched on a steepish hill overlooking the Yonne. The muscular cathedral, built between the 13th and 16th centuries, has a powerful north tower similar to that at Clamecy. The former **abbey of St-Germain** nearby contains an underground church dating from the 9th century. *Rue Cochois. Guided tour of crypt. Admission: 8 frs. Open Wed.–Mon. 10–noon and 2–5.*

Chablis, famous for its dry white wine, makes an attractive excursion 16 kilometers (10 miles) to the east of Auxerre, along N65 and D965. Beware of village tourist shops selling local wines at unpalatable prices. The surrounding vineyards are dramatic: Their towering, steeply banked hills stand in marked contrast to the region's characteristic gentle slopes.

Clamecy   From Auxerre, take N151 43 kilometers (27 miles) south along the Yonne to **Clamecy.** This sleepy town is not on many tourist itineraries, but its tumbling alleyways and untouched, ancient houses epitomize *La France profonde.* The many-shaped roofs of Clamecy, dominated by the majestic square tower of the **church of St-Martin,** are best viewed from the banks of the Yonne. The river played a crucial role in Clamecy's development: Trees from the nearby Morvan Forest were cut down and floated in huge convoys to Paris. The history of this curious

Burgundy

form of transport *(flottage)*, now extinct, is detailed in the town **museum**. *Rue Bourgeoise. Admission: 5 frs. Open July–Sept. Wed.–Mon. 10–noon and 2–5; rest of the year by appointment.*

Vézelay lies 24 kilometers (15 miles) east of Clamecy, along D951. The **Basilica** is perched on a rocky crag, with commanding views of the surrounding countryside. It rose to fame in the 11th century as the resting place of the relics of St. Mary Magdalene and became a departure point for the great pilgrimages to Santiago de Compostela in northwest Spain. The church was rescued from decay by the 19th-century Gothic Revival architect Eugène-Emmanuel Viollet-le-Duc and counts as one of the foremost Romanesque buildings in existence. Its interior is long and airy, with superbly carved column capitals; the facade boasts an equally majestic tympanum.

Avallon is 13 kilometers (8 miles) farther along from Vézelay, via D957. Its site, on a promontory, is spectacular, and its old streets and ramparts make agreeable places to stroll. The imagination of medieval stone carvers ran riot at the portals of the venerable church of **St-Lazarus**.

The expressway passes close by Avallon and can whisk you along to Dijon, 96 kilometers (60 miles) away, in less than an hour. If you're in no rush, take the time to explore part of the huge **Morvan Regional Park**; the road twists and turns through lakes, hills, and forests. Take D10 south to **Quarré-les-Tombes**—so called because of the empty prehistoric stone tombs discovered locally and eerily arrayed in a ring around the church—before continuing southeast toward Saulieu. The **Rocher de la Pérouse,** 8 kilometers (5 miles) from Quarré-les-Tombes, is a mighty outcrop worth climbing for the view of the Cousin Valley. Continue to **Saulieu** via the D6, D264, and D977.

Saulieu's reputation belies its size (just 3,000 inhabitants). It is renowned for good food (Rabelais, that 16th-century authority, extolled its hospitality) and Christmas trees (a million are harvested each year). The **Basilica of St-Andoche** is almost as old as Vézelay's, though less imposing and much restored. The adjoining town **museum** (Admission: 5 frs. Open Wed.–Mon., 10–noon and 2–5) contains a room devoted to François Pompon, a sculptor whose smooth, stylized creations smack of state-of-the-art yet predate World War II.

Dijon N6 and then D977 link Saulieu to the Dijon-bound A38 expressway to the east. **Dijon** is capital of both Burgundy and gastronomy. Visit its restaurants and the **Palais des Ducs** (Ducal Palace), testimony to bygone splendor and the setting for one of France's leading art museums (Admission: 8 frs. Open Wed.–Mon. 10–6). The tombs of Philip the Bold and John the Fearless head a rich collection of medieval objects and Renaissance furniture. Outstanding features of the city's old churches include the stained glass of **Notre-Dame,** the austere interior of the **cathedral of St-Bénigne,** and the chunky Renaissance facade of **St-Michel.** Don't miss the exuberant 15th-century gateway at the **Chartreuse de Champmol**—all that remains of a former charterhouse—or the adjoining **Puits de Moïse,** a "well" with six large, compellingly realistic medieval statues on a hexagonal base.

Beaune A31 connects Dijon to **Beaune,** 40 kilometers (25 miles) to the south, but you may prefer a leisurely trip through the vineyards. Take D122, then N74 at Chambolle-Musigny; just to the south is the Renaissance **Château du Clos de Vougeot,** famous as the seat of Burgundy's elite company of wine tasters, the Confrérie des Chevaliers du Tastevin, who gather here in November at the start of the three-day festival Les Trois Glorieuses—which includes a wine auction at the Hospices de Beaune. *Château du Clos de Vougeot. Admission: frs. Guided tours daily 9–11:30 and 2–5:30. Closed Dec. 24–Jan. 3.*

The **Hospices** (or Hôtel-Dieu) **de Beaune** owns some of the finest vineyards in the region yet was founded in 1443 as a hospital. Its medical history is retraced in a **museum** that also features Roger van der Weyden's medieval Flemish masterpiece *The Last Judgment,* plus a collection of tapestries, though a better series (late 15th century, relating the *Life of the Virgin*) hangs in Beaune's main church, the **Collégiale Notre-Dame,** which dates from 1120. *Hospices de Beaune. Admission: 20 frs adults, 8 frs children. Open daily 9–11:30 and 2–5:30.*

The history of local wines can be explored at the **Musée du Vin de Bourgogne,** housed in a mansion built in the 15th and 16th centuries (Admission: 9 frs. Open Apr.–Oct., daily 9–noon and 1:30–6; Nov.–Mar., daily 10–noon and 2–5:30). The place to drink the stuff is in the candle-lit cellars of the **Marché aux Vins** (wine market), on rue Nicolas Rolin, where you can taste as much as you please for around 30 frs.

Autun Autun is 48 kilometers (30 miles) west of Beaune along D973 but is worth a detour, if only for the Renaissance **château of Sully**

on the way (Admission: 6 frs. Visits to grounds only, daily in summer, 10–noon and 2–5). The leading monument in Autun is the church of **St-Lazarus,** a curious Gothic cathedral redone in the Classical style by 18th-century clerics trying to follow fashion. The building actually dates back to the first half of the 12th century. Note the majestic picture by Ingres, the *Martyrdom of St-Symphorien,* in one of the side chapels. Across from the cathedral is the **Musée Rolin** (Admission: 8 frs. Open Wed.–Mon. 10–noon and 2–5; Sun. 2–5), with several fine paintings from the Middle Ages, although the town's importance dates back to Roman times, as you can detect at the **Porte St-André,** a well-preserved archway, and the **Théâtre Romain,** once the largest arena in Gaul.

From Autun, head southeast along N80 and D980, via industrial Montceau-les-Mines, to **Cluny,** 80 kilometers (50 miles) away. The **Abbey** of Cluny, founded in the 10th century, was the largest church in Europe until Michelangelo built St. Peter's in Rome in the 16th century. The ruins give an idea of its original grandeur. Note the **Clocher de l'Eau-Bénite** (a majestic bell tower) and the 13th-century **Farinier** (flour mill) with its fine chestnut roof and collection of statues. *Guided tours of ruins. Admission: 22 frs. adults, 5 frs children. Open Easter–Oct., daily 9–noon and 2–5; Nov.–Easter, daily, late morning–early afternoon.*

A model of the original abbey can be seen in the **Musée Ochier,** the 15th-century abbot's palace. *Rue Conant. Admission: 4 frs. Open Wed.–Mon. 10–noon and 2–5. Closed Jan. 1–15.*

Cluny is a mere 28 kilometers (16 miles) northwest of **Mâcon,** a bustling town best known for its wine fair in May and for its stone bridge across the Saône; the low arches are a headache for large river barges. At Mâcon take N6 or A6 due south to Lyon, where the river Rhône runs parallel to the Saône before the two converge south of the city center.

Lyon In recent years, **Lyon** has solidified its role as one of Europe's leading commercial centers, thanks to France's policy of decentralization and the TGV train that puts Paris at virtual commuter distance (two hours). Much of the city has an appropriate air of untroubled prosperity, and you will have plenty of choices when it comes to good eating.

The clifftop silhouette of **Notre-Dame de Fourvière** is the city's most striking symbol: an exotic mish-mash of styles with an interior that's pure decorative overkill. Climb the Fourvière heights for the view instead and then go to the nearby Roman remains. *Théâtres Romains. Admission: free. Open Mar.–Oct., 8–noon and 2–5, Sat. 9–noon and 3–6, Sun. 3–6; Nov.–Feb., weekdays 8–noon and 2–5.*

The medieval **Primatiale St-Jean** (closed noon–2) is Lyon's disappointing cathedral. Note the Romanesque chancel, the 14th-century astronomical clock in the north transept (chimes at 3 **PM**), and the variety of styles of window and vaulting in the lateral chapels. Lyon's oldest sectors—St-Jean, St-Paul, and St-Georges—run north of the cathedral along the west bank of the Saône. Their narrow streets and medieval/Renaissance houses are crowded with cheap restaurants and cafés.

The pick of Lyon's museums is the **Musée des Beaux-Arts** (open Wed.–Mon. 11–6). It houses sculpture, classical relics, and an extensive collection of Old Masters and Impressionists. Don't miss local artist Louis Janmot's 19th-century mystical cycle *The Poem of the Soul*, 18 canvases and 16 drawings that took nearly 50 years to complete. *Admission: free. Open Wed.–Sun. 10:30–6.*

Dining and Lodging

For details and price category definitions, *see* Dining and Lodging in Staying in France.

Auxerre **Jardin Gourmand.** As its name implies, the Jardin Gourmand
Dining has a pretty garden where you can eat *en terrasse* during the summer. The interior, dominated by light-colored oak, is equally congenial. The cuisine is innovative—try the ravioli and foie gras or the duck with black currants—and the service is discreet. *56 blvd. Vauban, tel. 86-51-53-52. Reservations advised. AE, DC, MC, V. Closed Sun. evening (winter), Mon., Feb. 1–7, and Nov. 1–22. Moderate.*

Lodging **Normandie.** This picturesque creeper-covered construction is right in the town center, with its own garden but no restaurant. The rooms are well equipped and unpretentious. *41 blvd. Vauban, tel. 86-52-57-80. 48 rooms, some with bath or shower. AE, DC, MC, V. Inexpensive.*

Avallon **Moulin des Ruats.** The hotel is housed in an old flour mill just
Lodging southwest of Avallon along D427. The rooms, many with their own balcony, are rustic. Most look onto the sparkling river Cousin, and in the summer you can eat on the riverbank. Dishes served in the wood-paneled restaurant are sturdy and copious; try the *coq au vin* (chicken) done in local Burgundy wine. This hotel is popular, so make sure to have a reservation in July or August. *Vallée du Cousin, tel. 86-34-07-14. 27 rooms, some with shower or bath. AE, DC, MC, V. Closed winter. Moderate.*

Beaune **L'Ecusson.** Despite its unprepossessing exterior, L'Ecusson is
Dining a comfortable, friendly, thick-carpeted restaurant, with four fixed-price menus offering outstanding value. For around 170 frs, you can have rabbit terrine with tarragon followed by leg of duck in oxtail sauce, then cheese, and dessert. *2 rue du Lieutenant-Dupuis, tel. 80-22-83-08. Reservations advised. AE, DC, MC, V. Closed mid-Feb.–mid-Mar. Moderate.*

Cluny **Bourgogne.** It is hard to find a better place to get into the med-
Lodging ieval mood of Cluny than this old-fashioned hotel, right next door to the ruins of the famous abbey. There is a small garden and an excellent restaurant with sober pink decor and refined cuisine (foie gras, snails, and fish with ginger are specialties). *Pl. de l'Abbaye, tel. 85-59-00-58. 14 rooms with bath or shower. AE, DC, MC, V. Closed mid-Nov.–mid-Mar. Moderate/Expensive.*

Dijon **Jean-Pierre Billoux.** M. Billoux's restaurant is reputedly the
Dining best of all in this most gastronomic of French cities. It is magnificently situated in a spacious, restored town house with garden, bar, and stone-vaulted restaurant. Service is charming. Specialties include steamed frogs' legs served with cress pancakes, and guinea fowl with foie gras. *14 pl. Darcy, tel. 80-30-11-00. Reservations essential. AE, DC, MC, V. Closed Sun. evening, Mon., and mid-Feb.–mid-Mar. Expensive.*

Lodging **Chapeau Rouge.** This is a good choice if you want to be sure of getting a quiet, well-appointed room in the center of town—it's close to Dijon cathedral. The Chapeau is even a better choice for its restaurant, renowned as a haven of regional cuisine. New chef Bernard Noël, formerly of the top-ranking Tour d'Argent in Paris, creates a marvelous, saucy menu. *5 rue Michelet, tel. 80–30–28–10. 30 rooms with bath or shower. Reservations essential. AE, DC, MC, V. Moderate.*

Lyon **Léon de Lyon.** A mixture of regional tradition (dumplings, hot **Dining** sausages) and eye-opening innovation keep Léon de Lyon at the forefront of Lyon's restaurant scene. It consists of two floors in an old house full of alcoves and wood paneling. The blue-aproned waiters melt into the old-fashioned decor, and dishes such as fillet of veal with celery or leg of lamb with fava beans will linger in your memory. *1 rue Pléney, tel. 78–28–11–33. Reservations essential. MC, V. Closed Sun., Mon. lunch, and Dec. 24–Jan. 6. Expensive.*

A Ma Vigne. Here is a restaurant that's popular with readers; it provides straightforward meals as a break from too much gourmet Lyonais dining. French fries, *moules* (mussels), roast ham, and tripe lead the menu. Locals appreciate this, too, so get there early, especially at lunchtime. *23 rue Jean-Larrivé, tel. 78–60–46–31. Reservations not needed. MC, V. Moderate.*

Lodging **Royal.** The Royal is located on the spacious and elegant place Bellecoeur in the very heart of Lyon. Beware of the huge range in room prices (250–700 frs); many rooms have been stylishly renovated and some of the most expensive are positively luxurious. *20 pl. Bellecoeur, tel. 78–37–57–31. 90 rooms, most with bath or shower. Facilities: parking. AE, DC, MC, V. Moderate.*

Sens **Paris et Poste.** This is a newly modernized hotel and makes a **Lodging** pleasant stopping point on the way to Burgundy from Paris. The helpful service and sumptuous breakfasts (rare in France) confirm a sense of well-being created by the robust evening meal (with fixed-price menus including duck, snails, and steak) served in the large, solemn restaurant, whose decor can be described as rustic Burgundian. *97 rue de la République, tel. 86–65–17–43. 30 rooms with bath or shower. AE, DC, MC, V. Moderate.*

Vézelay **L'Espérance.** Located in the small neighboring village of St-**Dining** Père-sous-Vézelay, L'Espérance is one of France's premier restaurants. Chef Marc Meneau is renowned for the subtlety and originality of his cuisine. Parisian gourmets think nothing of driving down to Burgundy to eat here: Madame Meneau is a charming hostess, and the setting—by a park and stream with Vézelay's hill and basilica in the background—makes even a long trip worth it. *St-Père-sous-Vézelay, tel. 86–33–20–45. Reservations essential. AE, DC, MC, V. Closed Tues., Wed. lunch, and Jan. 1–Feb. 15. Very Expensive.*

Loire Valley

The Loire is the longest river in France, rising near Le Puy in the east of the Massif Central and pursuing a broad northwest curve on its 1,008-kilometer (630-mile) course to the Atlantic Ocean near Nantes. The region traditionally referred to as the Loire Valley—château country—is the 224-kilometer (140-mile) stretch between Orléans, 70 miles south of Paris and Angers, 96 kilometers (60 miles) from the Atlantic coast. Thanks to its mild climate, soft light, and lush meadowland, this area is known as the Garden of France. Its leading actor—the wide, meandering Loire—offers two distinct faces: fast-flowing and spectacular in spring, sluggish and sandy in summer.

To the north lies the vast grain plain of the Beauce; to the southeast the marshy, forest-covered Sologne, renowned for mushrooms, asparagus, and game. The star attractions along the rocky banks of the Loire and its tributaries—rivers Cher, Indre, Vienne, and Loir (with no *e*)—are the famous châteaux: stately houses, castles, or fairy-tale palaces. Renaissance elegance is often combined with fortresslike medieval mass. The Loire Valley was fought over by France and England during the Middle Ages. It took the example of Joan of Arc, the "Maid of Orléans" (scene of her most rousing military successes), for the French finally to expel the English.

The Loire Valley's golden age came under Francis I (1515–47), France's flamboyant contemporary of England's Henry VIII. He hired Renaissance craftsmen from Italy and hobnobbed with the aging Leonardo da Vinci, his guest at Amboise. His salamander emblem is to be seen in many châteaux, including Chambord, the mightiest of them, begun in 1519.

The best months to come are June to October, though the weather can sometimes be hot and sticky in midsummer. Nature in the region is at its best in late spring and early fall, when there are fewer crowds. In peak season (especially August), it is essential to have your accommodations reserved.

Getting Around

The easiest way to visit the Loire châteaux is by car; N152 hugs the riverbank and offers excellent sightseeing possibilities. Trains run along the Loire Valley every two hours, supplemented by local bus services. A peaceful way to explore the region is to rent a bicycle at one of the SNCF train stations (some trains even transport bikes for free.)

Guided Tours

Bus tours for the main châteaux leave daily in summer from Tours, Blois, Angers, Orléans, and Saumur: Ask at the relevant tourist office for latest times and prices. Most châteaux insist that visitors follow one of their own tours anyway, but try to get a booklet in English before joining the tour, as most are in French only.

Tourist Information

Angers. Pl. du Président Kennedy, tel. 41–88–12–43.
Blois. 3 av. du Docteur Jean-Laigret, tel. 54–74–06–49.
Orléans. Blvd. Aristide-Briand, tel. 38–53–05–95.
Tours. Pl. du Maréchal Leclerc, tel. 47–05–58–08.

Exploring the Loire Valley

Châteaudun Orléans, little more than an hour away by expressway (A10) or train, is the most obvious gateway to the Loire Valley if you're coming from Paris. Apart from its arts museum and august

Ste-Croix cathedral, however, Orléans has little going for it. We suggest instead that you take the expressway from Paris to Chartres, then N10 along the undisturbed Loir valley to **Châteaudun,** whose colossal château stands resplendent on a steep promontory and houses graceful furniture and lavish tapestries. Its chapel contains 15 statues produced locally in the 15th century. *Admission: 22 frs. Open mid-Mar.–Sept. 9:30– 11:45 and 2–6; Oct.–mid-Mar. 10–11:45 and 2–6.*

Continue along N10 to **Vendôme,** 40 kilometers (25 miles) to the southwest, where the Loire splits into many arms, lending the town a canal-like charm that harmonizes with its old streets and bridges. Architecture buffs will pinch themselves as they inspect the large but little-known main church, **Eglise de la Trinité,** an encyclopedia of different styles with brilliantly carved choir stalls and an exuberant west front—the work of Jean de Beauce, best known for his spire at Chartres Cathedral. Vendôme also has a ruined **castle** with ramparts and pleasant, uncrowded gardens. *Admission: 5 frs. Open Mar.– June, Wed.–Mon. 10–noon and 2–6; July and Aug., daily 10– noon and 2–6.*

Blois   Blois lies 32 kilometers (20 miles) southeast of Vendôme along D957. It is the most attractive of the major Loire towns, with its tumbling alleyways and its château. The **château** is a mixture of four different styles: Feudal (13th-century); Gothic-Renaissance transition (circa 1500); Renaissance (circa 1520); and Classical (circa 1635). *Admission: 21 frs. Open May–Aug., daily 9–6:30; Sept.–Apr., daily 9–noon and 2–5.*

Blois makes an ideal launching pad for a visit to the châteaux of Chambord and Cheverny. **Chambord** (begun 1519) is 20 kilometers (11 miles) east of Blois along D33, near Bracieux. It stands in splendid isolation in a vast forest and game park. There's another forest on the roof: 365 chimneys and turrets, representing architectural self-indulgence at its least squeamish. Grandeur or a mere 440-room folly? Judge for yourself, and don't miss the superb spiral staircase or the chance to saunter over the rooftop terrace. *Admission: 22 frs adults, 5 frs children. Open July–Aug., daily 9:30–6:30; Sept.–June, daily 9:30–11:45 and 2–sunset.*

A pleasant 20-kilometer (12-mile) drive through the forest leads you southwest to **Cheverny,** which can also be reached along D765 from Blois. This white, symmetrical château in the disciplined Classical style (built 1620–34) has ornate painted and gilded paneling on its walls and ceilings. Hunting buffs will thrill at the sight of the antlers of 2,000 hapless stags in the Trophy Room. Hordes of hungry hounds lounge around outside dreaming of their next kill. *Admission: 22 frs adults, 13 frs students and senior citizens. Open mid-June–mid-Sept., daily 9– 6:30; mid-Sept.–mid-June, daily 9:30–noon and 2:30–5.*

About 20 kilometers (12 miles) south of Blois, along D751, stands the sturdy château of **Chaumont,** built between 1465 and 1510—well before Benjamin Franklin became a regular visitor. There is a magnificent Loire panorama from the terrace, and the stables—where thoroughbreds dined like royalty—show the importance attached to fine horses, for hunting or just prestige. *Admission: 22 frs adults, 12 frs students and senior citizens. Open Apr.–Sept., daily 9:30–12:30 and 2–4:30; Oct.– Mar., daily 9:30–12:30 and 2–3:30.*

The Loire Valley

Amboise Downstream (westward) another 16 kilometers (10 miles) lies the bustling town of **Amboise,** whose **château,** with charming grounds, a rich interior, and excellent views over the river from the battlements, dates from 1500. It wasn't always so peaceful: In 1560, more than 1,000 Protestant "conspirators" were hanged from these battlements during the Wars of Religion. *Admission: 25 frs adults, 8 frs children. Open July–Aug., daily 9–6:30; Sept.–June, daily 9–noon and 2–5.*

The nearby **Clos-Lucé,** a 15th-century brick manor house, was the last home of Leonardo da Vinci, who was invited to stay here by Francis I. Da Vinci died here in 1519, and his engineering genius is illustrated by models based on his plans and sketches. *Admission: 26 frs adults, 17 frs students and senior citizens. Same hours as château, but open till 6:30 in winter. Closed. Jan.*

The early 16th-century château of **Chenonceau,** 16 kilometers (10 miles) south of Amboise along D81 and then D40, straddles the tranquil river Cher like a bridge. It is surrounded by elegant gardens and a splendid avenue of plane trees. Inside, note the fine paintings, colossal fireplaces, and richly worked ceilings. A waxworks museum lurks in an outbuilding. *Admission: 30 frs adults, 20 frs children. Open mid-Feb.–mid-Mar., daily 9–sunset; mid-Nov.–mid-Feb., daily 9–4:30.*

Tours **Tours,** 25 kilometers (15 miles) farther on, is the unofficial capital of the Loire. It retains a certain charm despite its sprawling size (250,000 inhabitants) and extensive postwar reconstruction. Its attractive old quarter has been tastefully restored, while the **Cathedral of St-Gatien** (1239–1484) numbers among France's most impressive churches. The influence of local Renaissance sculptors and craftsmen is much in evidence on the ornate facade, and the stained glass in the choir is particularly delicate: Some of it dates from 1320.

The château of **Villandry**, 16 kilometers (10 miles) southwest of Tours along the river Cher, is known for its painstakingly relaid 16th-century gardens, with their long avenues of 1,500 manicured lime trees. The château interior, restored like the gardens in the mid-19th century, is equally beguiling. Note the painted and gilded ceiling from Toledo and the collection of Spanish pictures. *Admission: 24 frs. Open daily 9–6; gardens open 8–dusk.*

Langeais **Langeais** is just 14 kilometers (9 miles) west of Villandry: Keep on D7 to Lignières before turning right onto D57 and crossing the Loire. A massive **castle**, built in the 1460s and never altered, dominates this small town. Its apartments contain a superb collection of tapestries, chests, and beds. *Admission: 20 frs adults, 10 frs children. Open Easter–Oct., daily 9–6:30; Nov.–Easter, Tues.–Sun. 9–noon and 2–5. Closed Mon.*

Azay-le-Rideau (1518–29), one of the prettiest of the Loire châteaux, lies on the river Indre 10 kilometers (6 miles) south of Langeais along D57. It has harmonious proportions and exquisite grounds, with a domesticated moat that is really a lake. This graceful ensemble compensates for the château's spartan interior, as does the charm of the surrounding village. *Admission: 22 frs adults, 12 frs senior citizens, 5 frs children. Open Apr.–Sept., daily 9:30–noon and 2–6; Oct.–Mar., daily 9:30–noon and 2–4:15.*

A short ride down the Indre Valley (on D17 and then D7) from Azay will help you judge whether Ussé really is, as the brochures claim, the fairy-tale setting that inspired *Sleeping Beauty*. Its bristling roofs and turrets, flowered terraces, and forest backcloth have undeniable romance. Don't forget the **chapel** in the park, built 1520–38 in purest Renaissance proportions. *Admission: 34 frs adults, 20 frs students. Open mid-Mar.–Nov., daily 9–noon and 2–6.*

Chinon **Chinon**, 13 kilometers (8 miles) from Ussé via D7 and D16, is an ancient town nestled by the River Vienne, with a rock-of-ages **castle** patrolling the horizon. This 12th-century fortress, with walls 372 meters (400 yards) long, is mainly in ruins, though small museums are installed in the Royal Chambers and sturdy Tour de l'Horloge (clock tower). There are excellent views from the ramparts over Chinon and the Vienne Valley. *Admission: 16 frs. Open June–Sept., daily 10–6; Oct., Wed.–Mon. 10–noon and 2–5; Feb.–mid-Mar., Wed.–Mon. 10–noon and 2–6; closed Nov.–Feb.*

From just south of Chinon, D751 heads off up the Vienne Valley toward **Fontevraud**, 13 miles (21 kilometers) away. This quiet village is dominated by its medieval **abbey**, where English kings Henry II and Richard the Lionhearted are buried. The church, cloisters, Renaissance chapter house, long-vaulted refectory, and octagonal kitchen are all still standing. The guided tours are in French, but you can get a brochure in English to keep track of where you are. *Admission: 22 frs. adults, 12 frs senior citizens, 5 frs children. Open June–mid-Sept., daily 9–noon and 2–6:30; Sept.–Apr., daily 9:30–12:30 and 2–5.*

Saumur, 16 kilometers (10 miles) west along the Loire from Fontevraud via D947, is a prosperous town famous for its riding school, wines, and château—a white 14th-century castle that towers above the river. The château contains two outstanding museums: the **Musée des Arts Décoratifs** (Decorative Arts Museum), featuring porcelain and enamels; and the **Musée du Cheval** (Equine Museum) with saddles, stirrups, skeletons, and Stubbs engravings. *Admission: 18 frs adults, 10 frs students and senior citizens. Open July–Sept., daily 9–6:30; Nov.–Mar., Weds.–Mon. 10–5.*

Angers **Angers** is a large, historic town on the river Maine just to the north of the Loire. D952 runs along the Loire Valley from Saumur, 45 kilometers (28 miles) away. The feudal **château** was built by St-Louis (1228–38) and has a dry moat, drawbridge, and 17 round towers along its half-mile-long walls. A modern, well-integrated gallery houses an exquisite tapestry collection, notable for the enormous *Tapestry of the Apocalypse,* woven in Paris around 1380. *Admission: 22 frs adults, 12 frs students and senior citizens, 5 frs children. Open July–Aug., daily 10–7; Sept.–June, daily 9:30–noon and 2–5:30.*

The substantial 12th–13th century **St-Maurice Cathedral** has early Gothic vaulting and masterly stained glass of various eras. Also of interest is the **Musée David d'Angers,** where works by the distinguished local 19th-century sculptor are displayed in a ruined church with a modern glass roof. *33 rue Toussaint. Admission: 10 frs adults, children free. Open Tues.–Sun., 10–noon and 2–6.*

Dining and Lodging

For details and price category definitions, *see* Dining and Lodging in Staying in France.

Angers **Le Quéré.** Despite a curious upstairs setting (in a former bar-
Dining bershop), Le Quéré is rated one of the region's finest eating places. The large dining room has brass chandeliers and lace tablecloths. Fish from the Loire and foie gras with asparagus can be admirably accompanied by any of a vast selection of local wines. *9 pl. du Ralliement, tel. 41–87–64–94. Reservations advised. AE, DC, MC, V. Closed Tues. evening, Wed., part of Feb., and July 1–20.*

Lodging **Hôtel d'Anjou.** An old friend of a hotel, this has spacious, well-modernized rooms and is handily situated by the Jardin du Mail, a pleasant park. It has its own parking facilities and a good restaurant, La Salamandre (tel. 41–88–99–55), with a Renaissance-style dining room. *1 blvd. du Mal-Foch, tel. 41–88–24–82. 51 rooms with bath or shower. Facilities: restaurant, parking. AE, DC, MC, V. Restaurant closed Sun. Moderate.*

Blois **Bocca d'Or.** The old 14th-century stone vaults at this restau-
Dining rant, in the heart of Blois, provide a historical atmosphere that contrasts with its nouvelle cuisine, though both are refined. Fish, shellfish, and poultry figure prominently, and the wine list is comprehensive. *15 rue Haute, tel. 54–78–04–74. Reser-*

vations advised. AE, MC, V. Closed Sun., Mon. lunch; Feb.–Mar. 5. Moderate.

Lodging **Anne de Bretagne.** An unpretentious hotel without a restaurant, Anne de Bretagne is conveniently situated on a broad avenue close to the tourist office and château. Parking is less of a headache here than it can be in the narrow streets of old Blois, but you may feel cheated of some of the atmosphere. *31 av. du Dr. Jean-Laigret, tel. 54–78–05–38. 29 rooms, some with bath or shower. AE, DC, MC, V. Closed mid-Feb.–early Mar. Moderate.*

Chambord **Hôtel St-Michel** offers good value, considering its location right
Lodging across from the château. Some of its rooms afford splendid views
★ of the château, its lawns, and the forest backcloth, as does the conveniently situated terrace, an ideal place for summer morning coffee before the tourist hordes arrive. *Bracieux, tel. 54–20–31–31. 38 rooms, some with bath or shower. Facilities: tennis court, parking, restaurant. MC, V. Closed Nov. 12–Dec. 19. Moderate.*

Chinon **Auberge du Haut Clos.** Situated 4.8 kilometers (3 miles) south of
Lodging Chinon (via D751), this hotel stands on a steep hill. You will enjoy the views from the terrace—a great place for an aperitif—before moving inside to the large dining hall with its huge fireplace and vast serving table festooned with salads and cuts of meat. The hotel is something of a letdown, being inexpensive and adequate, rather than memorable, although the flowered wallpaper in some rooms is overpowering. *La Roche-Clermault, tel. 47–95–94–50. 15 rooms, some with shower. MC, V. Closed Jan., Feb. Restaurant closed Sun. evening, Mon. off-season. Inexpensive.*

Saumur **Le Prieuré.** Five miles northwest of Saumur via D751, Le
Lodging Prieuré is a neo-Renaissance manor house perched high above the south bank of the Loire. It has its own restaurant overlooking the river, a heated swimming pool, and vast park. The rooms are large and luxuriously furnished, most with a view of the Loire. A reservation is advised, or you may find yourself in one of the less attractive houses in the park. *Chênehutte-les-Tuffeaux, Gennes, tel. 41–67–90–14. 35 rooms with bath. MC, V. Closed Jan., Feb. Expensive.*

Tours **Jean Bardet.** The restaurant takes its name from the chef, one
Dining of the finest in France, who moved from Châteauroux to Tours in 1987. His new restaurant is situated just north of the Loire in an early 19th-century mansion. The dining room overlooks a large garden (planted by a previous English owner) and is decorated with colorful chairs and carpets. There is a superb wine list and each dish is a work of art and originality: Try the eel fricassée or lobster in wine spiced with lime and ginger. Doing it all justice doesn't come cheap, but you can get a glimpse with a set menu for around 200 frs. *57 rue Groison, tel. 47–41–41–11. AE, DC, MC, V. Expensive.*

Lodging **Domaine de la Tortinière.** Ten kilometers (six miles) due south of Tours along N10, this turreted building dates from the mid-19th century. It stands proudly on a hill amid vast fields and woodland. The bedrooms are individually decorated in styles ranging from conventionally old-fashioned to brash ultramodern. The airy restaurant looks out over the gardens. Salmon, pigeon, and rabbit with truffles are menu highlights. *Les Gués* *de Veigné, 37250 Montbazon, tel. 47-26-00-19. 14 rooms with bath. MC, V. Closed mid-Dec.–Feb. Restaurant closed Wed. lunch and Tues. in Nov., Dec., and Mar. Expensive.*

Vendôme
Lodging
Hôtel Vendôme. Near the banks of the Loir, Hôtel Vendôme makes a handy base for exploring the pedestrian streets of the old town. It is stylish and appropriately priced, with excellent, modernized rooms, though lacking a little in character. There is a trustworthy restaurant with quietly efficient English-speaking service. *15 Faubourg Chartrain, tel. 54-77-02-88. 35 rooms with bath or shower. Facilities: restaurant, parking. MC, V. Closed Dec. 23–Jan. 6. Restaurant closed Sun. evening Dec.–Mar. Moderate.*

The Riviera

Few places in the world have the same pull on the imagination as France's fabled Riviera, the Mediterranean coastline stretching from St-Tropez in the west to Menton on the Italian border. Cooled by the Mediterranean in the summer and warmed by it in winter, the climate is almost always pleasant. Avoid the area in July and August, however—unless you love crowds. To see the Riviera at its best, plan your trip in the spring or fall, particularly in May or September.

The Riviera is a land of contrasts. While the coastal resorts seem to live exclusively for the tourist trade and have often been ruined by high-rise blocks, the hinterlands remain relatively untarnished. The little villages perched high on the hills behind medieval ramparts seem to belong to another century. One of them, St-Paul de Vence, is the home of the Maeght Foundation, one of the world's leading museums of modern art.

Artists, attracted by the light, have played a considerable role in popular conceptions of the Riviera, and their presence is reflected in the number of modern art museums: the Musée Picasso at Antibes, the Musée Renoir and the Musée d'Art Moderne Mediterranéan at Cagnes-sur-Mer, and the Musée Jean Cocteau near the harbor at Menton. Wining and dining are special treats on the Riviera, especially if you are fond of garlic and olive oil. *Bouillabaisse*, a spicy fish stew, is the most popular regional specialty.

The tiny horseshoe-shaped principality of Monaco, which lies between Nice and Menton, is included in this section despite the fact that it is a sovereign state. Although Monaco has its own army and police force, its language, food, and way of life are French. Its famous casino, the highly visible royal Grimaldi family, and the wealth of jetsetters, chic fashions, and opulent yachts all ensure that it maintains its reputation as a "golden ghetto."

Getting Around

By Car Expressway A8 is the only way to get around the Riviera quickly, but for the drama of mountains and sea, take one of the famous Corniche roads.

By Train The train line follows the coast from Marseille to the Italian border, providing excellent access to the seaside resorts and some inland towns such as Grasse, but you will have to take local buses (marked *Gare Routière*) or guided tours to visit the perched villages.

Guided Tours

SNCF, the French national railroad company, runs the greatest number of organized tours. For information, contact the Nice Tourist Office (*see* Tourist Information). Tours are most valuable to areas otherwise impossible to reach by public transportation: St-Paul-de-Vence, Upper Provence, and the spectacular Verdon Gorges.

Boats operate from Nice to Marseille; from St-Tropez to the charming Hyères Islands; and from Antibes, Cannes, and Juan-les-Pins to the Lérins Islands.

Tourist Information

Antibes. Pl. du Général de Gaulle, tel. 93–33–95–64.
Cagnes-sur-Mer. 26 av. Renoir, tel. 93–20–61–64.
Cannes. Palais des Congrès, La Croisette, tel. 93–39–24–53.
Fréjus. Blvd. de la Libération, tel. 94–51–48–42.
Grasse. 3 pl. Foux, tel. 93–36–03–56.
Menton. Palais de l'Europe, tel. 93–35–77–23.
Monaco. 2A blvd. des Moulins, tel. 93–50–60–88.
Nice. Av. Thiers, tel. 93–87–07–07; av. Gustave Flaubert, tel. 93–87–60–60.
St-Paul-de-Vence. Maison Tour, rue Grande, tel. 93–32–86–95.
St-Tropez. Quai Jean-Jaurès, tel. 94–97–45–21.
Vence. Pl. du Grand Jardin, tel. 93–58–02–02.

Exploring the Riviera

St-Tropez   **St-Tropez** was just another pretty fishing village until it was "discovered" in the 1950s by the "beautiful people," a fast set of film stars, starlets, and others who scorned bourgeois values while enjoying bourgeois bank balances. Today, its summer population swells from 6,000 to 60,000. In season, its top hotels, restaurants, nightclubs, and chic little shops are jammed. In the winter, it's hard to find a restaurant open. The best times to visit, therefore, are early summer or fall. May and June are perhaps the best months, when the town lets its hair down during two local festivals.

The **old port** is the liveliest part of town. You can kill time here at a café terrace, watching the rich and famous on their gleaming yachts. Between the old and new ports is the **Musée de l'Annonciade,** set in a cleverly converted chapel, which houses paintings by artists drawn to St-Tropez between 1890 and 1940—including Paul Signac, Matisse, Derain, and Van Dongen. *Quai Gabriel-Péri. Admission: 16 frs adults, 8 frs children. Open June–Sept., Wed.–Mon. 10–noon and 3–7; Oct.–May, Wed.–Mon. 10–noon and 2–6.*

Across the place de l'Hôtel de Ville lies the old town, where twisting, narrow streets, designed to break the impact of the terrible mistral wind, open on to tiny squares and fountains. A long climb up to the **citadel** is rewarded by a splendid view over the old town and across the gulf to **Ste-Maxime,** a quieter, more working-class family resort with a decent beach and reasonably priced hotels. St-Tropez is also a good base for visiting **Port**

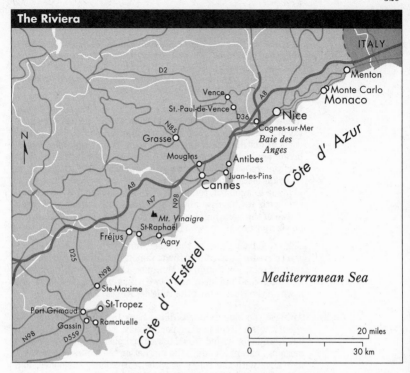

The Riviera

Grimaud, a pastiche of an Italian fishing village (take D558) and the nearby hilltop villages: the old Provençal town of **Ramatuelle** and the fortified village of **Gassin.**

The **Corniche des Issambres** (N98) runs along the coast from Ste-Maxime to **Fréjus,** a Roman town built by Julius Caesar in 49 BC, standing on a rocky plateau between the Maures and Esterel hills. Two main roads link Fréjus and Cannes. Tortuous N7, originally a Roman road, skirts the northern flank of the rugged Esterel hills. Look for an intersection called the "carrefour du Testannier" and follow the signs to **Forêt Domaniale de l'Esterel** and **Mont Vinaigre** for a magnificent view over the hills. The **Corniche d'Or** coast road (N98) takes you past **St-Raphaël** to the little resort of **Agay,** whose deep bay was once favored by ancient Greek traders.

Cannes   In 1834, a chance event was to change the lifestyle of **Cannes** forever. Lord Brougham, Britain's lord chancellor, was en route to Nice when an outbreak of cholera forced the authorities to freeze all travel to prevent the disease from spreading. Trapped in Cannes, he fell in love with the place and built himself a house there as an annual refuge from the British winter. The English aristocracy, czars, kings, and princes soon caught on, and Cannes became a community for the international elite. Grand palace hotels were built to cater to them, and Cannes came to symbolize dignified luxury. Today, Cannes is also synonymous with the **International Film Festival,** which celebrated its 40th anniversary in 1987 in the controversial **Palais des Festivals,** often known by its critics as the "Bunker."

Cannes is for relaxing—strolling along the seafront on the **Croisette,** and getting tanned on the beaches. Almost all the beaches are private, but that doesn't mean you can't use them, only that you must pay for the privilege. The Croisette offers splendid views of the **Napoule Bay.** Only a few steps inland is the old town, known as the **Suquet,** with its steep, cobbled streets and its 12th-century watchtower.

Grasse is perched in the hills behind Cannes. Take N85 or just follow your nose to the town that claims to be the perfume capital of the world. A good proportion of its 40,000 inhabitants work at distilling and extracting scent from the tons of roses, lavender, and jasmine produced here every year. The various perfumers are only too happy to guide visitors around their fragrant establishments. Fragonard is the best known (20 blvd. de Fragonard, tel. 93–36–44–65). The old town is attractive, with its narrow alleys and massive, somber **cathedral.** Three of the paintings inside the cathedral are by Rubens and one is by Fragonard, who lived here for many years.

Take N85 back down to the coast, but fork left at **Mougins,** an attractive fortified hilltop town, famous for one of France's best restaurants, Le Moulin de Mougins. D35 takes you to **Antibes** and **Juan-les-Pins,** originally two villages that now form one town on the west side of the **Baie des Anges** (Angels' Bay).

Antibes   **Antibes,** the older village, dates back to the 4th century BC, when it was a Greek trading port. Today, it is renowned throughout Europe for its industrial flower and plant production. Every morning, except Monday, the market on the Cours Masséna comes alive with the colors of roses, carnations, anemones, and tulips. The Grimaldis, the family that rules Monaco, built **Château Grimaldi** here in the 12th century on the remains of a Roman camp. Today, the château's main attraction is the **Musée Picasso**—a bounty of paintings, ceramics, and lithographs inspired by the sea and Greek mythology. *Admission: 20 frs adults, 8 frs students and senior citizens. Open Dec.–Oct., Wed.–Mon. 10–noon and 2–6.*

St-Paul-de-Vence   The 20-kilometer (13-mile) stretch of flat coast between Antibes and Nice lacks charm, but the hinterland makes up for it. The picture-book medieval village of **St-Paul-de-Vence** (via D2 and D7) stands hidden behind its ramparts. A prosperous town in the Middle Ages, it was rediscovered only in the 1920s by a group of painters who met at the **Colombe d'Or,** now a popular inn with its walls covered with their paintings. Today, the village is full of artists' studios, antique shops, and craft galleries, and is one of the most visited in France.

The **Fondation Maeght** is less than a mile away. This temple of modern art is an attractive ensemble in a pinewood setting. Giacometti's figures stride the courtyard between the white concrete and rose-colored brick buildings, which house an excellent collection of modern art and sculpture, studios, a library, cinema, and auditorium. *Admission: 35 frs adults, 25 frs children. Open July–Sept., daily 10–7; Oct.–June, daily 10–2:30 and 2:30–6.*

The larger village of **Vence** lies farther along D2. Like St-Paul, it has its share of artists' studios and galleries, but its major contribution to modern art is the **Chapelle du Rosaire,** the Rosary Chapel designed and decorated by Henri Matisse in the late 1940s. *Admission: free. Open Tues. and Thurs., 10–11:30 and 2:30–5:30.*

Nice Take D36 back down to the coast and join A8 or N7 into **Nice.** With its population of 400,000, its own university, new congress hall, and nearby science park, Nice is the undisputed capital of the Riviera. Founded by the Greeks as Nikaia, it has lived through several civilizations and was attached to France only in 1860. It consequently boasts a profusion of Greek, Italian, British, and French styles. Tourism may not be the main business of Nice, but it is a deservedly popular center with much to offer. The double blessing of climate and geography puts its beaches within an hour-and-a-half's drive of the nearest ski resorts. There is an eclectic mixture of old and new architecture, an opera house, museums, flourishing markets, and regular concerts and festivals, including the Mardi Gras festival and the Battle of Flowers.

Numbers in the margin correspond with points of interest on the Nice map.

❶ The **place Masséna** is the logical starting point for an exploration of Nice. This fine square was built in 1815 to celebrate a local hero: one of Napoleon's most successful generals. The
❷ **Promenade des Anglais,** built by the English community here in
❸ 1824, is only a short stroll past the fountains and the **Jardin Albert 1er.** It now carries heavy traffic but still forms a splendid strand between town and sea. The narrow streets in the old town are the prettiest part of Nice: Take the rue de l'Opéra to
❹ ❺ see **St-François-de-Paule** church (1750) and the **opera house.** At
❻ the northern extremity of the old town lies the vast **place Garibaldi** —all yellow-ocher buildings and formal fountains.

❼ The **Musée Chagall** is on the boulevard de Cimiez, near the Roman ruins. The museum was built in 1972 to house the Chagall collection, including the 17 huge canvases of *The Message of the Bible,* which took 13 years to complete. *Admission: 15 frs adults, 8 frs students and senior citizens. Open July–Sept., Wed.–Mon. 10–7; Oct.–June, Wed.–Mon. 10–12:30 and 2–5:30.*

Monaco *Numbers in the margin correspond with points of interest on the Monaco map.*

Sixteen kilometers (10 miles) along the coast from Nice is **Monaco.** For more than a century Monaco's livelihood was centered
❶ around its splendid copper-roof **casino.** The oldest section dates from 1878 and was and was conceived by Charles Gariner, architect of the Paris opera house. It's as elaborately ornate as anyone could wish, bristling with turrets and gold filigree, and masses of interior frescoes and bas-reliefs. There are lovely sea views from the terrace, and the gardens out front are meticulously tended. The main activity is in the American Room, where beneath the gilt-edged ceiling busloads of tourists feed the one-armed bandits. *Pl. du Casino, tel. 93–50–69–31. Persons under 21 not admitted. Admission for American Room free. Open daily 10 AM– 4 AM. Closed May 1.*

❷ The **Musée National des Automates et Poupées d' Autrefois** (Museum of Dolls and Automatons) has a compelling collection of 18th-and 19th-century dolls and mechanical figures, the latter

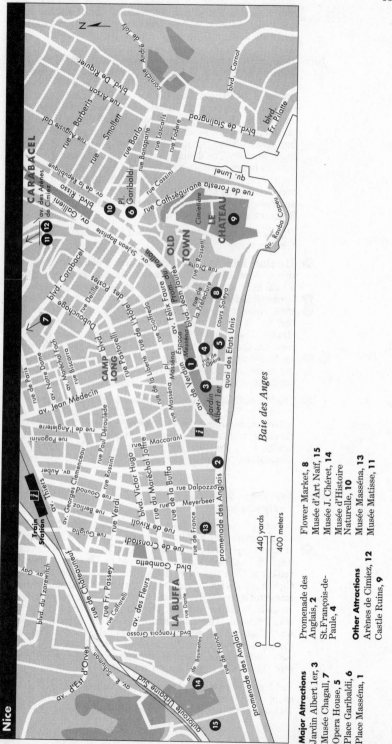

Major Attractions
Jardin Albert 1er, **3**
Musée Chagall, **7**
Opera House, **5**
Place Garibaldi, **6**
Place Masséna, **1**

Promenade des Anglais, **2**
St.François-de-Paule, **4**

Flower Market, **8**
Musée d'Art Naïf, **15**
Musée J. Chéret, **14**
Musée d'Histoire Naturelle, **10**
Musée Masséna, **13**
Musée Matisse, **11**

Other Attractions
Arènes de Cimiez, **12**
Castle Ruins, **9**

Monaco

MONTE CARLO

LA CONDAMINE

FONTVIEILLE

0   220 yards
0   200 meters

Casino, **1**
Cathedral, **4**
Fort Antoine
Theater, **7**
Jardin Exotique, **8**
Musée Historial des
Princes de Monaco, **5**

Musée National des
Automates et Poupées
d'Autrefois, **2**
Musée
Océanographique, **6**
Museum of Prehistoric
Anthropology, **9**
Palais du Prince, **3**

shamelessly showing off their complex inner workings. It's magically set in a 19-century seaside villa (designed by Garnier). *17 av. Princesse Grace, tel. 93-30-91-26. Admission: 22 frs adults, 12 frs children. Open daily 10-12:15 and 2:30-6:30.*

Monaco Town, the principality's old quarter, has many vaulted passageways and exudes an almost tangible medieval feel. The ❸ magnificent **Palais du Prince** (Prince's Palace), a grandiose Italianate tructure with a Moorish tower, was largely rebuilt in the last century. Here, since 1297, the Grimaldi dynasty has lived and ruled. The spectacle of the **Changing of the Guard** occurs each morning at 11:55; inside, guided tours take visitors through the state apartments and a wing containing the **Palace Archives** and **Musée Napoléon** (Napoleonic Museum). *Pl. du Palais, tel. 93-25-18-31. Admission: 30 frs. Palace open July-Sept., daily 9:30-12:30 and 2-6:30. Musée Napoléon and Palace Archives open year-round, Tues.-Sun. Admission: 15 frs adults, 7 frs children.*

❹ Monaco's **cathedral** (4 rue Colonel Bellando de Castro) is a late 19th-century neo-Romanesque confection where Philadelphia-born Princess Grace lies in splendor along with past members ❺ of the Grimaldi dynasty. Nearby is the **Musée Historial des Princes de Monaco** (Waxworks Museum), a Monégasque Madame Tussauds, with none-too-realistic wax figures stiffly portraying various episodes in the Grimaldi history. The waxworks may not convince, but the rue Basse is wonderfully atmospheric. *27 rue Basse, tel. 93-30-39-05. Admission: 18 frs. Open May-Sept., daily 9-8; Oct.-Dec., daily 10:30-5:30; Jan.-Apr., daily 9-6:30.*

Next to the **St-Martin Gardens**—which contain an evocative bronze monument in memory of Prince Albert 1 (Prince Rainier's great-grandfather, the one in the sou'wester and fly-❻ ing oil skins, benignly guiding a ship's wheel)—is the **Musée Océanographique** (Oceanography Museum and Aquarium). This fascinating museum is also an internationally renowned research institute founded by the very Prince Albert who is remembered outside for being an eminent marine biologist in his day; the well-known underwater explorer Jacques Cousteau is the present director. The aquarium is the undisputed highlight, however, where a collection of the world's fish and crustacea live out their lives in public, some colorful, some drab, some the stuff nightmares are made of. *Av. St-Martin, tel. 93-30-15-14. Admission: 45 frs adults, 23 frs children. Open Sept.-June, daily 9:30-7; July and Aug., daily 9-9.*

Time Out Take the elevator to the aquarium's roof terrace for a fine view of the sea—which may look a little different now that you know what's lurking down there—and have a restorative drink at the bar.

Before heading back inland, take a short stroll to the eastern ❼ tip of the rock, to the **Fort Antoine Theater,** a converted 18th-century fortress that certainly looks a lot prettier now than it would have in more warlike times, covered as it is in ivy and flowering myrtle and thyme. In the summer, this is an open-air theater seating 350. **Av. de la Quarantaine, tel. 93-30-19-21.**

❽ The Moneghetti area is the setting for the **Jardin Exotique** (Tropical Garden), where 600 varieties of cacti and succulents cling to the rock face, their improbable shapes and sometimes violent coloring a further testimony to the fact that Mother Nature will try anything once. Your ticket also allows you to explore the **caves,** adjacent to the gardens, and to visit the **Museum of Prehistoric Anthropology,** adjacent. *Blvd. du Jardin Exotique, tel. 93–30–33–65. Admission: 27.50 frs adults, 18 frs senior citizens, 14 frs children. Open Oct.–May, daily 9–5:30; June–Sept., daily 9–7.*

Menton **Menton** also once belonged to the Grimaldis and, like Nice, was attached to France only in 1860. Because of its popularity among British visitors, the western side of the town was developed at the turn of the century to cater to the influx of the rich and famous, with spacious avenues, first-class hotels, and the inevitable casino. The eastern side of town long remained the domain of the local fishermen but has more recently been developed to cater to the needs of tourists. A large marina was built and the **Sablettes,** once a tiny beach, has been artificially extended.

Down by the harbor stands a small 17th-century fort, where Jean Cocteau, the artist, writer, and filmmaker once worked. It now houses the **Musée Jean Cocteau,** with a collection of his work. *111 quai Napoléon. Admission: free. Open mid-June–mid-Sept., Wed.–Sun. 10–noon and 3–6; mid-Sept.–mid-June, 10–noon and 2–6.*

Menton's Lemon Fair in February celebrates the town's vast production of excellent citrus fruits. In August, its popular chamber music festival holds concerts in the attractive Italianate churches in the old town.

Dining and Lodging

For details and price category definitions, *see* Dining and Lodging in Staying in France.

Antibes **Auberge Provençale.** André Martin is rightly proud of his con-
Lodging verted abbey in the old town near the harbor, with its gardens in the former cloisters. The rooms and service are sunny, partly a reflection of the manageable size of the hotel. Its popular restaurant serves lobster and shellfish as well as *boudin de rascasse,* a minced fish shaped into a sausage. *61 pl. Nationale, tel. 93–34–13–24. 6 rooms with bath. Restaurant reservations required. AE, DC, MC, V. Closed mid-Nov.–mid-Dec. Restaurant closed Mon., Tues. lunch. Moderate.*

Cagnes **Cagnard.** This hotel is in an attractive 15th-century building in
Lodging the old village. The restaurant—once the Grimaldi Château Guards Room—dates back to the early 14th century. The hotel has several suites in two houses in the garden and a third up the road. The view from them all—over the Cap d'Antibes—is memorable. *Rue du Pontis-Long, tel. 93–20–73–21. 19 rooms and suites with bath. AE, DC, MC, V. Closed Nov.–Dec. 20. Restaurant closed Thurs. lunch. Expensive.*

Cannes **Mirabelle.** For many, this is a favorite restaurant in the Suquet.
Dining Mirabelle was entirely redecorated in 1988 and now has a more countrified atmosphere, reflecting the new menu with specialties from all over France. The cuisine is inventive, the sauces light, and the desserts special. *24 rue St-Antoine, tel. 93–38–72–75. AE, MC, V. Closed Tues., Dec., Mar. 1–15. Expensive.*

Lodging **Majestic.** Unlike most of its neighbors among the luxury hotels lining the Croisette on the seafront, the Majestic has a discreet atmosphere. The rooms are spacious and traditional but refreshingly decorated in pastels. It also offers a reasonably priced evening meal in winter. *14 blvd. Croisette, tel. 93–68–91–00. 249 rooms with bath. Facilities: private beach, swimming pool, air-conditioning, parking lot, access to tennis, golf, and horseback riding. AE, DC, MC, V. Closed Nov. 15–Dec. 20. Very Expensive.*

Roches Fleuries. A pretty little hotel near the Suquet and the old port, the Roches Fleuries is set on several levels, with stairs leading up from its garden to two terraces, where you can have breakfast while looking down on the sea. Rooms vary in size and style: Some are genuinely Provençal, and several have balconies. *92 rue Georges Clemenceau, tel. 93–39–28–78. 24 rooms, 15 with bath or shower. No credit cards. Closed Nov. 15–Dec. 27. Inexpensive.*

Grasse **Panorama.** The excellent views of the Massif d'Estérel and
Lodging right across to Cannes are the vindication of this hotel's name. It is modern and well run and has ample parking. Most rooms have good views, but there is no restaurant. *2 pl. du Cours, tel. 93–36–80–80. 36 rooms with bath. AE, MC, V. Moderate.*

Menton **Chez Mireille-l'Ermitage.** Best known for its restaurant, this el-
Lodging egant yet cozy hotel stands on the promenade du Soleil, overlooking the beach. Each room has its own style and all are different, although many have good views. The restaurant is a favorite for local specialties: *bourride (fish soup)* and bouillabaisse, salmon, and bass fillets. *1080 promenade du Soleil, tel. 93–35–77–23. 21 rooms with bath or shower. AE, DC, MC, V. Restaurant closed Mon. evening, Tues. mid-Nov–mid-Apr. Moderate.*

Monaco **Louis XV.** A strong contender for the best-in Monaco award,
Dining Louis XV's opulent decor and chef Alain Ducasse's beautifully conceived dishes, such as ravioli with foie gras and truffles, contribute to the formal atmosphere. The wine cellar is exceptional. *Hôtel de Paris, pl. du Casino, tel. 93–50–80–80. Reservations advised. AE, DC, MC, V. Very Expensive.*

Bec Rouge. This is where all the best Monégasques can be observed relishing their *gratin de langoustes* (lobster) at dinnertime, linen napkins billowing. Food is classic French, decor *le plus chic. 11 av. de Grande Bretagne, tel. 93–30–74–91. Reservations essential. AE, DC. Closed Jan. and mid.–June. Expensive.*

Polpetta. This popular trattoria is close enough to the Italian border to pass for the real thing. It's excellent value for the money, with delicious home cooking to boot. *2 rue Paradis, tel. 93–50–67–84. Reservations essential in high season. V. Closed Tues., Feb. 15–Mar. 15, and Oct. 15–30. Expensive.*

Lodging **Hôtel de Paris.** An exceptional establishment, where elegance,
★ luxury, dignity, and Old World charm are the watchwords. Built in 1864, it still exudes the gold-plated splendor of an era when kings and grand dukes stayed here. *Pl. du Casino, tel. 93–50–80–80. 255 rooms with bath. Facilities: 2 restaurants, bar, pool, health club, shops, tennis court. AE, DC, MC, V. Very Expensive.*

Balmoral. Despite the name, there's nothing even vaguely Scottish about this somewhat old-fashioned hotel overlooking the harbor. Rooms are a reasonable size, if blandly decorated;

many have balconies. *12 av. de la Costa, tel. 93–50–62–37. 75 rooms with bath or shower, half with air conditioning. Facilities: restaurant. AE, DC, MC, V. Restaurant closed Nov. Moderate.*

France. The modest hotel France, near the train station, can't begin to compete with the opulence of some of the others listed here, but it's one of the cheapest around and worth a look if you are on a tight budget. *6 rue de la Turbie, tel. 93–30–24–64. 26 rooms, 18 with bath or shower. DC, MC, V. Inexpensive.*

Mougins
Dining

Le Moulin de Mougins. Roger Vergé has created one of France's finest restaurants in a converted mill about 1½ miles from the village along D3. The cuisine ranges from some apparently simple salads to some rich, complicated sauces for lobster, salmon, or turbot. Considering that it is a gourmet favorite, the restaurant has a surprisingly informal atmosphere. *Quartier Notre-Dame-de-Vie, 424 Chemin du Moulin, tel. 93–75–78–24. Reservations essential. AE, DC, MC, V. Closed Mon. (except summer), Thurs., lunch, and Feb. 1–Mar. 20. Very Expensive.*

Nice
Dining

Ane-Rouge. Famous for generations as *the* place for Nice's best fish and seafood, this tiny, family-run restaurant is popular with locals, not least for the Vidalots, the pleasant couple who run it. *7 quai des Deux-Emmanuels, tel. 93–89–49–63. Reservations advised. MC, V. Closed Sat., Sun., mid-July–end of-Aug. Expensive.*

Lodging

Negresco. Opened in 1912, the Negresco is officially listed as a historic monument and is a byword for Old World elegance. The public rooms have antique coffered ceilings and magnificent fireplaces. No two bedrooms are alike, but they all have antique furniture and paintings. Its main restaurant, Le Chanteclerc, is, without doubt, the best in Nice: Young chef Dominique Le Stanc made a brilliant name for himself in Monaco before joining the Negresco in 1988. *37 promenade des Anglais, tel. 93–88–39–51. 130 rooms with bath. Facilities: 2 restaurants (reservations required). AE, DC, MC, V. Restaurants closed Nov. Very Expensive.*

St-Tropez
Lodging

Byblos. This hotel is unique. Its luxury rooms and suites are built around tiled courtyards, fragrant with magnolia and orange trees, like a miniature Provençal village. Each room is different, with amusing touches and subtle lighting. Les Caves du Roy, one of its two nightclubs, and Le Chabichou an independent restaurant within the complex, are considered among the best in town. Chef Michel Rochedy is famous for his delicate, inventive touches. Specialties include foie gras and lobster. The more adventurous should try the baby squid stew with pigs' feet and fava beans. La Braiserie, the hotel's other restaurant, offers slightly more moderately priced meals. *Av. Paul Signac, tel. 94–97–00–04. 59 rooms and 48 suites with bath. Facilities: 2 restaurants, 2 nightclubs, sauna, pool, hairdresser. AE, DC, MC, V. Closed Nov.–Feb. Very Expensive. Le Chabichou, tel. 94–54–80–00. Reservations essential. AE, DC, MC, V. Closed Oct. 10–May 1. Very Expensive.*

11 East Germany

Introduction

East Germany, or the German Democratic Republic, divides a nation otherwise united by language and cultural heritage. Though the standard of living here is the highest of all the Communist countries, the urban centers are unmistakably Eastern Bloc, with drab apartment blocks housing a populace exhorted by banner and slogan to do its best for the development of socialism and "the common good." Outside the cities, however, villages and their residents appear to the casual visitor to be not much different from their Western counterparts. East Germany has been spared most of the worst aspects of modernization that have blighted so much of West Germany. The countryside is attractive, and great effort has been put into removing the devastating effect of the last war.

The Prussian mentality that in past centuries built disciplined armies that swept across Europe is still evident in the determination with which the government has placed East Germany among the top-ranking industrial nations in the world. The same purposeful effort has gone into creating world champions in various sports, rebuilding whole sections of cities, and carrying subsidies to such extremes that the prices of some goods and services are so low they bear no relationship to their real cost.

These are the features that make East Germany both interesting and a challenge to the tourist. Every corner offers a contrast—or a mirror reflection—when seen against the rest of Europe, whether the Europe of today or that of an elegant past.

Before You Go

When to Go The main tourist season runs from late April to early October. Berlin, however, is active year-round. The weather is best in the spring and fall; summer can be muggy, except along the Baltic coast or in the southern mountains. Avoid Leipzig around the first weeks in March and September; the trade fair commandeers all accommodations and prices soar. Off-season prices are not substantially lower.

Climate The following are the average daily maximum and minimum temperatures for Berlin.

Jan.	35F	2C	May	66F	19C	Sept.	68F	20C
	26	−3		47	8		50	10
Feb.	37F	3C	June	72F	22C	Oct.	56F	13C
	26	−3		53	12		42	6
Mar.	46F	8C	July	75F	24C	Nov.	45F	7C
	31	0		57	14		36	2
Apr.	56F	13C	Aug.	74F	23C	Dec.	38F	3C
	39	4		56	13		29	−1

Currency The monetary unit of East Germany is the Mark der DDR (M), divided into 100 pfennigs. There are banknotes of 100, 50, 20, 10, and 5 marks and coins of 20, 10, 5, 2, and 1 mark and 50, 20, 10, and 1 pfennig. The exchange rate for the East German mark is the same as that for the West German deutschmark (DM). At press time (spring 1989), it was M1.86 to the dollar and M3.27 to the pound sterling.

East Germany

DENMARK

Baltic Sea

Rügen

Barth
Stralsund
Greifswald
Rostock
Anklam
Wismar
Güstrow
Teterow
Schwerin
Neubrandenburg
Waren
Neustadt-Glewe
Neustrelitz
Ludwigslust
Pritzwalk
Elbe
Perleberg
Neuruppin
Wittenberge
Oranienburg
Salzwedel

WEST
GERMANY

POLAND

Oder

Stendal
West Berlin
East Berlin
Potsdam
Brandenburg
Frankfurt
Magdeburg
Halberstadt
Lübben
Dessau
Wittenberg
Cottbus
Bernburg
Bitterfeld
Nordhausen
Halle
Leipzig
Mühlhausen
Meissen
Görlitz
Erfurt
Weimar
Dresden
Eisenach
Gera
Karl Marx Stadt
(Chemnitz)
Suhl
Saalfeld
Zwickau
Meiningen
Plauen

CZECHOSLOVAKIA

N

WEST
GERMANY

0   50 miles
0   75 km

You may bring in as much foreign currency as you wish, but you must declare it upon arrival. What you fail to declare, you may not be able to take out. East German currency may not be exported.

Currency and traveler's checks can be exchanged at nearly all banks and larger hotels; airports and main train stations also have money-changing facilities. Resist any offers for unofficial exchange by private individuals: If caught, you not only lose the money but run the risk of fine and arrest.

Visitors are required to change DM25, or its equivalent in another Western currency, per day per person; DM7.50 for children 6–15 years of age. If you have prepaid hotel or camping vouchers, you probably have already met the minimum exchange requirement. When changing currency or paying in Western currency, or with a credit card, get a receipt. This will serve as proof that you have met the minimum exchange requirement.

Credit Cards All Interhotels, Intershops, and some independent shops and restaurants accept American Express, Diners Club, MasterCard, or Visa. These cards are also valid for car rentals. Save all charge slips as evidence of currency exchange.

What It Will Cost By Western standards, East Germany is not an expensive country to visit. The major exception is hotel lodging. The main hotels in the larger cities are very much up to Western standards and are priced accordingly. Off the beaten track, prices drop, but accommodations are more modest.

Sample Prices Cup of coffee in a cafe, M1.50–M2; draft beer in a Bierkeller, M2–M3; vodka or schnapps, M2.50–M4; half-bottle of wine in a restaurant, M20–M30; Coca-Cola, M1–M2; movie ticket, M3–M4; theater ticket, M5–M10; concert or opera ticket, M5–M15; one-mile taxi ride, M.70–M1.10; streetcar, bus, subway or city railway ticket, M.20–M.50.

Museums Admission charges to museums in East Germany vary greatly, and can change from day to day, even from morning to afternoon. But expect to pay only a nominal fee of M.50–M2.

Visas Visas are required of all visitors to East Germany. East German consulates in the United States and the United Kingdom do not issue visas to individuals, only to accredited travel agencies. The procedure takes 6–8 weeks and costs the equivalent of DM15. A travel agent in the USA will charge $16–$20 for the visa and handling, $26–$30 for rush service. You will also need a voucher confirming your hotel reservations; this can be arranged with the travel agent at the same time.

Visitors from the USA or Canada can find out the names and addresses of accredited travel agencies by writing the **East German Consulate** (1717 Massachusetts Ave. NW, Washington, DC 20036). In the United Kingdom, East German tourist affairs, including visa assistance, are handled by **Berolina Travel** (20 Conduit St., London W1R 9TD, tel. 01/629–1664).

Upon entering East Germany, you will be given a small form to fill out that will be stamped with the entry date. This form must be surrendered when you leave the country, so be careful not to lose it.

You can visit East Berlin from West Berlin on a daily pass card good for a 24-hour stay. The visa costs DM5 or its equivalent and can be extended for up to a week, either by an Interhotel or by the Reisebüro der DDR once you are in the country. Note that the minimum currency exchange requirement applies to shorter visits as well (*see* Currency). Transit visas for stays of up to 72 hours are available at border crossing points, provided you have a valid visa for the country to be visited next (usually Poland or Czechoslovakia). Obtaining a day pass from West Berlin into East Berlin is no major problem but may take time at the border. It is far preferable to make arrangements in advance and have the visa and other papers ready when you reach the border. You can obtain a visa from any of the GDR consulates in Western Europe (except in the United Kingdom and West Germany, where only travel agencies issue visas); usually only two or three days are required. Visas are included as part of the half-day tour packages operated by travel agencies from West Berlin.

If you are staying in East Germany, you must be registered with the police; your hotel management will normally take care of this, but it's best to check.

Customs
On Arrival
Customs procedures vary from casual to meticulous, but it is wisest to follow the rules and not take chances. You may import any amount of tobacco, spirits, or wine. You may also bring in gifts to the value of M200 duty-free per person for visits of up to five days. If your visit will last longer than five days, this amount is increased to M100 for each day of your stay, to a maximum of M1,000. Note that the value of the goods brought in is based on their price in East Germany, not necessarily on what you paid for them. Customs regulations have now been somewhat relaxed regarding publications, but some Western magazines and newspapers may not be allowed, and officials may hesitate over tape- and videocassettes. If you are carrying such valuables as a video recorder, special photo equipment, or a fur coat, avoid possible problems when leaving the country by having these items noted in your passport when you arrive.

On Departure
When you leave, duty may be charged on goods you take out beyond the value of M20 per person per day's stay for up to five days, or M100 for a longer stay. This regulation is rarely enforced and is designed mainly to keep Poles from coming across the border and buying up East German goods 'on the cheap.' If you buy antiques or anything else of substantial value, you will get an official receipt (assuming you bought it from an authorized source), which will solve any export problems, should customs officials ask. For regulations covering the import and export of money, *see* Currency.

Language
English is widely spoken in the main city centers, but is far less common in other areas than it is in West Germany.

Getting Around

By Car
Road Conditions
Nearly 1,600 kilometers (1,000 miles) of expressway and 11,200 kilometers (7,000 miles) of secondary roads crisscross the country. Highways are constantly being improved, but many roads other than main routes are in poor condition.

Rules of the Road
Drive on the right-hand side of the road. Traffic regulations, from parking rules to speed limits, are strictly enforced. The police levy fines—in West German currency, for foreigners—for the slightest offense. Driving while intoxicated is strictly

forbidden, and fines are heavy. If not otherwise indicated, cars coming from the right have the right-of-way. Speed limits on the autobahn (expressway) are 100 kph (62 mph); on other roads, 80 kph (50 mph); and in towns, 50 kph (30 mph).

Gasoline Gas is available at either **Minol** or **Intertank** stations; both chains sell regular and premium grades by the liter. Diesel fuel is not available at all stations, and distribution of unleaded fuel is limited to expressways and main centers. Minol stations supply gasoline for either East German marks (you may be asked to show your currency exchange receipt) or coupons, which may be bought at a discount at the border. Otherwise, the Intertank stations sell gasoline at reduced prices for West German deutschmarks.

Road Tax Foreign drivers must pay a tongue-twisting *Strassenbenützungsgebühr*, or road-users' tax, at the rates of M5 for up to 200 kilometers (125 miles), M15 for up to 300 kilometers (190 miles), M20 for up to 400 kilometers (250 miles), or M25 for up to 500 kilometers (310 miles). The tax must be paid in equivalent foreign currency.

By Train The government runs three types of trains: express, the fastest, shown as *IEx* or *Ex* in timetables; fast, shown as *D;* and slightly slower services, indicated with an *E*. These categories have varying supplementary fares; local trains do not. Most long- and medium-distance trains have both first- and second-class cars, and many have either dining or buffet cars, although these may be open only to and from specific destinations. Trains are usually full, so reservations—made either via the Reisebüro der DDR travel agency or at any major train station —are recommended.

By Boat "White Fleets" of inland boats, including paddleboats, ply the inland lakes around Berlin and on the Elbe river. Dresden is the major starting point; from there, boats go upstream to Meissen or downstream and on into Czechoslovakia.

Staying in East Germany

Telephones Pay phones require a 20-pfennig coin. Long-distance calls are not possible from a pay phone, but may be made from your hotel or from any post office. Connections within Europe are immediate; overseas calls may take longer. Some hotels have international direct dialing. To call the USA or Canada, dial 012–1 followed by the area code and number. For the United Kingdom, dial 0644 plus the city code and the number.

Mail Airmail letters to the USA and Canada cost M1.40; postcards,
Postal Rates 90 pfennig. Airmail letters to the United Kingdom cost 80 pfennig; postcards, 60 pfennig. Some hotels may ask for West German currency in payment for stamps; post offices deal only in local currency.

Receiving Mail Hotels will hold mail for visitors who have reservations; envelopes should indicate the date of expected arrival.

Opening and **Banks.** Banks are generally open Monday to Saturday from 8 to
Closing Times 11:30. Some have afternoon hours.
Museums. Museums are generally open from 10 to 6 daily except Monday.
Shops. Most Berlin shops are open weekdays from 10 to 7 (8 on Thursday); shops outside Berlin, from 9 to 6. Only department

stores and other large shops are open on Saturday, and then mornings only.

National Holidays January 1 (New Year's Day); April 13 (Good Friday); May 1 (Labor Day); June 4 (Pentecost Monday); October 7 (Republic); December 25, 26 (Christmas).

Dining Dining possibilities range from the street stands offering frankfurters and various types of very tasty sausages; the "quick lunch" stops (mainly stand-up snack bars), called *Imbiss-stube*, which specialize in local favorites such as knuckle of pork; cafés, most of which have at least a limited lunch menu; *Bierkeller*, which offer hearty local fare and tankards of beer; and restaurants, which can be divided between *SB (Selbstbedienung*, or self-service cafeterias) and the more traditional establishments in all price ranges. If not eaten in a hotel, breakfast is a café affair; restaurants generally do not open until about 10 AM. The country's Eastern Bloc ties are reflected in restaurants featuring the national cuisines of other socialist states, although such exotica as Japanese, Chinese, Indonesian, and French dishes are now appearing.

Specialties National favorites include, *Eisbein mit Sauerkraut* (knuckle of pork with pickled cabbage), *Rouladen* (rolled stuffed beef), *Berliner Schüsselsülze* (potted meat in aspic), and *Kartoffelpuffer* (fried potato cakes). Regional specialties are finding wider acceptance. Typical dishes are *Thüringer Sauerbraten mit Klössen* (roast corned beef with dumplings), *Bärenschinken* (cured ham), and *Harzer Köhlerteller mit Röstkartoffeln* (charcoal-grilled meat with roast potatoes).

Mealtimes The main meal of the day is traditionally taken at noon. Restaurants are crowded then and reservations are necessary. Evening dining usually begins at 7 or 7:30.

Dress People tend to dress formally for dinner in East German cities. In the upper price categories, jacket and tie is expected. Otherwise, casual but neat dress is appropriate.

Ratings Prices are per person. In the lower-priced establishments, they include a main course and a small beer or possibly a glass of wine. In the top two categories, meals will be at least three courses. Prices include tax and tip, but it is customary to leave a small extra tip of M1–M3. In Very Expensive establishments, double this tip. Best bets are indicated by a star ★ . At press time, there were 1.86 East German marks to the dollar.

Category	City	Country
Very Expensive	over M40	over M30
Expensive	M30–M40	M25–M30
Moderate	M20–M30	M15–M25
Inexpensive	under M20	under M15

Credit Cards The following credit card abbreviations are used: AE, American Express; DC, Diners Club; MC, MasterCard; V, Visa.

Lodging Western visitors to East Germany are effectively obliged to stay in the hotels of the state-run Interhotel chain; these include the major hotels in all cities and other tourist centers. Interhotels such as the Grand, Palast, and Metropol in Berlin,

Merkur in Leipzig, and Bellevue in Dresden measure up to the highest international standards, including prices. Tourists seeking more moderate accommodations may try the H-O chain or the hostels run by the Evangelical church. The few private hotels are real bargains but are almost impossible for a Western visitor to book. East German travel officials will try to steer you to one of the best hotels; if you want more moderate accommodations, be prepared to argue your point at some length.

Ratings Prices indicated here are for double rooms, with full bath in the top two categories. A single room with bath will cost about M5 –M10 more than half the double rate shown. Breakfast is included in room rates. Best bets are indicated by a star ★. At press time, there were 1.86 East German marks to the dollar.

Category	City and Country
Very Expensive	over M250
Expensive	M170–M250
Moderate	M130–M170
Inexpensive	under M130

Credit Cards The following credit card abbreviations are used: AE, American Express; DC, Diners Club; MC, MasterCard; V, Visa.

Tipping The official line on tipping is *nein*, but tips are generally accepted, indeed expected, in major hotels and better restaurants. Tip in West German deutschmarks if possible, otherwise in U.S. currency. When paying by credit card, leave the tip in cash. Tip porters and doormen DM1, $1, or, as a last resort, M1 if you don't have any deutschmarks left. Taxi drivers do not expect a tip, but round up the fare to the nearest mark or to the next M.50.

East Berlin

Arriving and Departing

By Plane All flights arrive at Schönefeld airport, about 24 kilometers (15 miles) outside the downtown area. For information on arrival and departure times, tel. 02/672–4031.

Between the Airport and Downtown A shuttle bus (fare 20 pfennigs) leaves every 10–15 minutes for the nearby S-Bahn train station. S-Bahn trains (fare 30 pfennigs) leave every 20 minutes for the Friedrichstrasse station. The trip takes about 30 minutes, and you can get off at whatever stop is nearest your hotel. Taxis are usually available at the stops from Ostbahnhof onward. You can also take a taxi from the airport; fare to your hotel will be about M30–M35, and the trip will take about 40 minutes. By car, follow the signs for "Stadtzentrum Berlin."

By Train International trains arrive at Friedrichstrasse or the Ostbahnhof. For train information, tel. 02/49541 for international trains, 02/49531 for domestic services. Trains coming from or via West Berlin arrive at the Friedrichstrasse station.

By Bus Berlin has no scheduled intercity or international bus service.

By Car Expressways lead to Berlin via Magdeburg, Leipzig, Rostock,

Dresden, and Frankfurt-Oder. Road crossings also go to and from West Berlin. The downtown is marked "Stadtzentrum."

Getting Around

Most tourist goals are easily reached on foot, and walking is recommended as the best way to see the city. But public transportation is good and wonderfully cheap.

By Bus and Streetcar Buses and streetcars are often crowded, and route maps, posted at each stop (marked H or HH), are not particularly clear to the uninitiated. Fares on buses and streetcars are a uniform 20 pfennigs within the main city area, allowing transfer from one line or from one form of transport to another. Get a ticket by dropping coins into the dispenser on the bus or tram; you'll have to pull the lever several times until the machine produces your ticket. If you transfer, put the first ticket into the dispenser and get yourself a new one for the next leg. A one-day tourist ticket (**Touristenfahrkarte**) is available for M2; it's good on all transportation, including the trip to Schönefeld airport. You can get several in advance and have them dated for any day you want.

By U-Bahn and S-Bahn All city guides and maps show the subway (U-Bahn) and city train (S-Bahn) routes and stops. The system is simple to understand. The U-Bahn ticket system is the same as for the trams and buses (see above). The elevated electric line (S-Bahn) is fast and frequent. Tickets are issued from a dispenser (exact change!) for 20 pfennigs, good for most destinations (fares are posted). The ticket is validated by poking it into a stamping device at the end of each platform: Take your cue from other passengers. The M2 full-day Touristenfahrkarte avoids all the hassle.

By Taxi Finding a taxi in Berlin can be an adventure, but try the ranks at such busy points as the Friedrichstrasse and Alexanderplatz stations. Taxis can be flagged on the street and are nearly always available around major hotels. If the "Taxi" light is on, the cab is available. Order a cab by phoning 02/3646 for immediate or same-day reservations, 02/365–4176 for service during the coming week. Taxi fares are low, with a typical downtown fare costing M2–M4.

By Car Arrangements can be made through any of the Interhotels. Rental headquarters is at the **Metropol Hotel** (tel. 02/220-4695); cars can be rented at **Schönefeld airport** as well (tel. 02/672–2418).

Important Addresses and Numbers

Tourist Information **Reisebüro der DDR:** Alexanderplatz 5, tel. 02/215–4328; special service office for foreign visitors on second floor (tel. 02/215–4402); Schönefeld airport, tel. 02/678–8248.

Embassies **U.S.:** Neustädtische Kirchstr. 4–5, tel. 02/220–2741. **U.K.:** Unter den Linden 32–34, tel. 02/220–2431. **Canadian:** There is no Canadian Embassy in East Berlin at present. If circumstances demand, call the Canadian Embassy in Warsaw (from East Berlin, phone 064822/029–8051; address: Ulica Matejika 1–5, PL-00481 Warsaw, Poland). Alternatively, try the Canadian Military Mission in West Berlin (tel. 849/261–1161). If that fails, the British Embassy will help, provided the people know that you have made an effort to contact the other two.

Emergencies **Police:** tel. 110; **Ambulance:** tel. 115; **Doctor, Dentist:** tel. 1259, or call the U.S. or U.K. Embassy for assistance; **Pharmacies:** tel. 160; **Motorist's assistance:** tel. 02/524–3565, 6 AM–10PM.

Guided Tours

Eleven different guided city tours, lasting from one hour to nearly four hours, can be booked through your hotel or the Reisebüro der DDR; fares range from M3 to M12. Taxi sight-seeing tours of the city cover six fixed routes, starting and ending at Alexanderplatz. Tours last from 40 minutes to two and a half hours and cost M16.50–M55, depending on the route, for up to four persons; tel. 02/246–2255 for details.

Exploring East Berlin

The infamous wall seems ever-present, but bear in mind it sur-rounds West, not East, Berlin, much as you may have a slightly claustrophobic feeling when you're in the eastern sector of the city. Stark contrasts exist between West and East. In the lat-ter, discipline, orderliness, and the lack of traffic are immediate impressions, as is the overall subdued tone. The stately buildings of the city's past are not as overwhelmed by new high-rise construction as in West Berlin, but East Berlin's postwar architectural blunders are just as monumental in their own way. These will be obvious—along with the sad shabbi-ness of years of neglect—as you explore the side streets together with the main thoroughfares.

Historic East Berlin *Numbers in the margin correspond with points of interest on the East Berlin map.*

❶ As you head up the Friedrichstrasse from **Checkpoint Charlie,** your initial impression will be that the differences between East and West Berlin are minimal: Both sides of the street are lined with attractive new shops and trendy restaurants. Turn right onto Johann-Dieckmann-Strasse and you'll arrive at the Platz der Akadamie, with its beautifully reconstructed ❷ **Schauspielhaus**—built in 1818, and now the city's main concert hall—and the rebuilt **German and French cathedrals.** In the lat-❸ ter, you'll find the **Huguenot Museum,** which has some interesting collections of the history and art of the French Protestant Huguenots who took refuge in Germany after being expelled from Catholic France in 1685. *Platz der Akadamie. Open weekdays 10–5.*

Time Out The **Arkade Café** on the northwest corner of the plaza (Französischer Str. 25) is perfect for a light snack, some excel-lent pastry, and a beer, coffee, or tea.

Continue east along the Französischer Strasse to Babelplatz. ❹ The peculiar round shape of **St. Hedwigs Kathedrale** (St. Hedwig's Cathedral) calls to mind Rome's Pantheon. The tiny street named Hinter der Katholische Kirche (Behind the Cath-olic Church) is a reminder that though Berlin was very much a Protestant city, St. Hedwig's was built (about 1747) for Catho-lics.

East Berlin

Altes Museum, **9**
Berlin Cathedral, **13**
Bodemuseum, **12**
Brandenburger Tor, **6**
Centrum department store, **17**
Checkpoint Charlie, **1**
Huguenot Museum, **3**

Humboldt University, **7**
Marienkirche, **15**
Märkisches Museum, **20**
Museum für Deutsche Geschichte, **8**
Nationalgalerie, **10**
Nikolaikirche, **19**
Palast der Republik, **14**

Pergamon Museum, **11**
Rathaus, **18**
Schauspielhaus, **2**
St. Hedwigs Kathedrale, **4**
State Opera, **5**
TV Tower, **16**

Walk north on Unter den Linden, the elegant central thorough-
⑤ fare of old Berlin, to the **State Opera,** the great opera house of
Berlin, now with an entirely new interior. Next door is the former crown prince's palace, the **Palais Unter den Linden,** now
restored and used to house official government visitors.

Look back down toward the western sector and you'll see, just
⑥ inside the wall, the monumental **Brandenburger Tor** (Brandenburg Gate), its chariot-and-horses sculpture now turned to face
the east. Cross Unter den Linden and look into the courtyard of
⑦ **Humboldt University:** It was built as a palace for the brother of
Friedrich II of Prussia but became a university in 1810, and today is the largest in East Germany. Marx and Engels were its
two most famous students. Next door, housed in a one-time ar-
⑧ senal (1695–1705) is the **Museum für Deutsche Geschichte**
(Museum of German History), which traces events from 1789 to
the present—with a pronounced Marxist bias. *Unter den Linden 2. Open Mon.–Thurs. 9–7, weekends 10–5.*

Turning left along the Spree canal will bring you to East Berlin's museum complex, at the northern end of what is known as
Museumsinsel (Museum Island). The first of the Big Four that
⑨ you'll encounter is the **Altes Museum** (entrance on Lustgarten),
an austere neoclassical building just to the north of Marx-
Engels-Platz. The collections here include postwar art from
some of East Germany's most prominent artists, and numerous
etchings and drawings from the Old Masters. Next comes the
⑩ **Nationalgalerie,** on Bodestrasse, which features 19th and 20th-
⑪ century painting and sculpture. The **Pergamon Museum** on Am
Kupfergraben, is one of Europe's greatest. Its name derives
from the museum's principal exhibit and the city's number-one
attraction, the **Pergamon Altar,** a monumental Greek temple
dating from 180 BC that occupies an entire city block. Almost as
impressive is the **Babylonian Processional Way.** The Pergamon
Museum also houses vast Egyptian, early-Christian, and Byzantine collections, plus a fine array of sculpture from the 12th
⑫ to the 18th centuries. To the north is the **Bodemuseum** (also on
Am Kupfergraben, but with its entrance on Monbijoubrücke),
with an outstanding collection of early-Christian-Byzantine
and Egyptian art, as well as special exhibits of Italian Old Masters. *Museum complex open Wed., Thurs., weekends 9–6, Fri.
10–6; closed Mon. and Tues. (except Pergamon Museum,
whose Pergamon Altar and architectural rooms remain open
9–6).*

From the museum complex, follow the Spree canal south to
⑬ Unter den Linden and the vast and impressive **Berlin cathedral.**
The hideous modern building across the way is the **Palast der
⑭ Republik** (Palace of the Republic), a postwar monument to socialist progress, also housing restaurants, a theater, and a
dance hall.

Time Out The cafeteria-style **Quick restaurant** in the Palast Hotel, although mobbed at noon, is a good spot for lunch or a snack
(entrance on Karl-Liebknecht-Strasse).

Cross the street for a closer look at the 13th-century
⑮ **Marienkirche** (Church of St. Mary), especially noting its late-
Gothic *Dance of Death* fresco. You are now at the lower end of
Alexanderplatz, easy to find from any part of the city: Just
⑯ head in the direction of the massive **TV tower,** an East Berlin
⑰ landmark. A focal point for shopping is the **Centrum depart-**

ment store, alongside the Hotel Stadt Berlin, at the very top of
the plaza.

⑱ The area adjacent to the **Rathaus** (City Hall)—itself somewhat
of a marvel for its red-brick design and the frieze depicting
scenes from the city's history—has been handsomely rebuilt.

⑲ **Nikolaikirche** (on Spandauerstrasse), dating from about 1200,
is Berlin's oldest building. It was heavily damaged in the war,
but has been beautifully restored. The quarter surrounding
the church is filled with delightful shops, cafés, and restaurants. Wander back down Muhlendamm into the area around
the Breite Strasse—there are some lovely old buildings here—
and on over to the **Fischerinsel** area. The throbbing heart of Old
Berlin of 750 years ago, Fischerinsel retains a tangible medieval flavor.

Time Out | The **Alt-Cöllner Schankstuben,** overlooking the Spree canal
(Friedrichsgracht 50), is as charming and friendly a café as
you'll find in East Berlin. On a sunny day, enjoy a glass of beer
at an outdoor table.

⑳ Nearby is the **Märkisches Museum** (Museum of Cultural History), which has an amusing section devoted to automaphones—
"self-playing" musical instruments. *Am Kollnischen Park 5.
Open Wed. and Sun. 9–6, Thurs. and Sat. 9–5, Fri. 9–4.*

Shopping

Shopping Districts | Good shops in Berlin are found along the **Friedrichstrasse,
Unter den Linden,** and around **Alexanderplatz.** Shops run by
other socialist countries along the north side of Alexanderplatz
may have some interesting offerings. The **Palast** and **Grand** hotels both contain small shopping malls.

Department Stores | For basic local goods, including souvenirs, try the **Centrum** de-
partment store at the north end of Alexanderplatz. The
subsidized prices for some items make them very cheap,
though style is not a strong point.

Dining

Most menus are translated into English. In general, the smaller the establishment, the more limited the choice. Unfortunately, the custom of posting a menu outside seems to be disappearing, but no one will mind if you ask to see a menu before
being seated—even if you then decide to go elsewhere. For details and price category definitions, *see* Dining in Staying in
East Germany.

Very Expensive
★ | **Ermeler Haus.** The wine restaurant in a series of upstairs
rooms reflects the elegance of this restored patrician house,
which dates from 1567 (it was moved to its present location in
1969, however). The atmosphere is subdued, the wines are imported, and the service matches the excellent German
specialties. There's dancing on Saturday evening. *Märkisches
Ufer 10–12, tel. 02/279–4036. Reservations advisable. AE, DC,
MC, V.*

Ganymed. Velvet draperies, oil paintings, and brass chandeliers adorn this particularly attractive restaurant, whose
choice of dishes ranges from cold plates to cordon bleu, with
even a few Indonesian specialties thrown in. The front room has

piano music in the evening. *Schiffbauerdamm 5, tel. 02/282–9540. Reservations essential. No credit cards. Closed Mon. lunch.*

Expensive **Schwalbennest.** This is a fairly new restaurant on the edge of
★ the Nikolai quarter, overlooking the Marx-Engels-Forum. Both food and service are outstanding; the choice is wide for both main dishes and wines. The grilled meats are wonderful, but note that no additional price is indicated on the menu for the flambéed dishes—ask about this, or you could be in for a surprise when the bill arrives! *Am Marstall, Rathausstr. at Marx-Engels-Forum, tel. 02/212–4569. Reservations essential, even for lunch. AE, DC, MC, V.*

Moderate **Moskau.** Some may mutter that Moskau is overpriced for what it offers—superb Soviet dishes like chicken Kiev, and real Russian vodka—but it has nevertheless been voted top choice among Berliners for several years running. However, it is less centrally located and offers considerably less in the way of atmosphere than many other city eateries. *Karl-Marx-Allee 34, tel. 02/279–4052. Reservations advised. No credit cards.*
Ratskeller. This is actually two restaurants in one—a wine and a beer cellar, both vast, atmospheric, and extremely popular. Menus are limited, but offer good, solid Berlin fare. The beer cellar is guaranteed to be packed at main dining hours, and attempts at reservations may be ignored (locals simply line up and wait). *Rathausstr. 14, in basement of the City Hall, tel. 02/212–4464. Reservations advisable, though not always possible. No credit cards.*
Wernesgrüner Bierstube. Wernesgrüner beer is considered one of the city's best, and this cozy, pine-paneled beer cellar serves plenty of it alongside heaping portions of *Eisbein* (knuckle of pork) and *Schlachteplatte* (a variety of grilled meats). Lunchtime brings a ban on smoking in the right-hand room. *Karl-Liebknecht-Str. 4, tel. 02/282–4268. Reservations advisable, especially at lunch. No credit cards.*

Inexpensive **Alt-Cöllner Schankstuben.** A charming and genuine old Berlin house is the setting for this conglomerate of no less than four tiny restaurants, all of which provide exceptionally friendly service. *Friedrichsgracht 50, 02/212–5972. No reservations. No credit cards.*
★ **Zur letzten Instanz.** Established in 1525, this place combines the charming atmosphere of Old-World Berlin with a limited (but tasty) choice of dishes. Napoleon is said to have sat alongside the tiled stove in the front room. The emphasis here is on beer, both in the recipes and in the mug. Service can be erratic, though engagingly friendly. *Waisenstr. 14–16 tel. 02/212–5528. Reservations essential for both lunch and dinner. No credit cards.*

Lodging

All of the newer hotels in Berlin are in the Very Expensive category; if you prefer more modest and less expensive accommodations, you will have to argue for it. Travel officials will encourage bookings in the fancier Interhotels and often tell you that the less expensive hotels are fully booked. If you name a particular establishment and are patient, you may win out.

You cannot get into East Germany—other than on a 24-hour pass from West Berlin—without a hotel reservation, but should you find yourself needing a hotel room, check with the **Reisebüro der DDR** at Alexanderplatz 5, tel. 02/212–4328, and ask for the "Zimmervermittlung."

For details and price category definitions, *see* Lodging in Staying East Germany.

Very Expensive   **Grand Hotel** (Interhotel). Berlin's newest is also its most expensive. There's nothing of Eastern Europe here: Facilities range from the plush atrium lobby, four restaurants, winter garden, beer stube, bars, and a concert café to a swimming pool, sauna, and squash courts. *Friedrichstr. 158–164, corner Behrenstr., tel. 02/20920. 350 rooms with bath. Facilities: shopping arcade, hairdresser, theater ticket office, car and yacht rental. AE, DC, MC, V.*

★ **Metropol** (Interhotel). This is the businessperson's choice, not least for its excellent location opposite the Friedrichstrasse train station and the International Trade Center. The staff is particularly helpful and friendly. Best rooms are those in front, with a view toward the north. While none of the three restaurants is especially notable (except for price), the nightclub is excellent. *Friedrichstr. 150–153, tel. 02/22040. 320 rooms with bath. Facilities: pool, sauna, health club, shops; car, horse-drawn carriage, and yacht rental. AE, DC, MC, V.*

Palast (Interhotel). This is another of Berlin's mega-facility hotels. Ask for a room overlooking the Spree river; those on Alexanderplatz can be noisy if you like your windows open. The shopping arcade includes an antiques gallery and the main central theater ticket office. *Karl-Liebknecht-Str. 5, tel. 02/2410. 600 rooms with bath. Facilities: 6 restaurants, 4 bars, beer stube, nightclub, pool, sauna, health club, bowling, car and yacht rental. AE, DC, MC, V.*

Expensive   **Stadt Berlin** (Interhotel). With its 40 stories (it's the city's largest hotel), the Stadt Berlin, at the top end of Alexanderplatz, competes with the nearby TV tower for the title of City Landmark. The roof dining room, Panorama, features not only good food and service but stunning views as well; reservations are essential. *Alexanderplatz, tel. 02/2190. 975 rooms with bath. Facilities: 4 restaurants, beer garden, 3 bars, sauna, shops. AE, DC, MC, V.*

★ **Unter den Linden** (Interhotel). The class may be missing, but the location couldn't be better. The restaurant is known for the best food on what was once Berlin's most elegant boulevard. *Unter den Linden 14, corner Friedrichstr., tel. 02/220–0311. 307 rooms with bath. Facilities: souvenir shop. AE, DC, MC, V.*

Moderate   **Adria** (H-O). This hotel tends to be fully booked well in advance, attesting to its less expensive prices rather than to any particular charm. Rooms in back are quieter, if you have any choice. *Friedrichstr. 134, tel. 02/282–5451. 70 rooms with bath. Facilities: restaurant. No credit cards.*

Newa (H-O). The Newa—an older hotel just a 10-minute streetcar ride from downtown—is popular, but, as with the Adria, this is mainly due to the price. Rooms in front can be noisy. *Invalidenstr. 115, tel. 02/282–5461. 57 rooms, some with bath. No credit cards.*

Inexpensive   **Hospiz am Bahnhof Friedrichstrasse.** For reasons of both price and convenience, this Evangelical church-run hostel tends to be heavily booked months in advance. It appeals to families, so public rooms are not always restful. *Albrechtstr. 8, tel. 02/282–5396. 110 rooms, some with bath. Facilities: restaurant. No credit cards.*

Hospiz Auguststrasse. Another church-run hostel, this one with comfortable rooms and a particularly friendly staff. It's about a 10-minute streetcar ride to the downtown sights. Only breakfast is served. *Auguststr. 82, tel. 02/282–5321. 70 rooms, some with bath. No credit cards.*

The Arts

The quality of opera and classical concerts in Berlin is impressively high. Tickets are available at the separate box offices, either in advance or an hour before the performance. Tickets are also sold at the central tourist office of the Reisebüro der DDR (Alexanderplatz 5), at the ticket offices in the Palast and Grand hotels, or from your hotel service desk. Check the monthly publication *Wohin in Berlin?*

Concerts **Schauspielhaus,** Platz der Akadamie, tel. 02/227–2156; **Palast der Republik,** Marx-Engels-Platz, tel. 02/238–2354.

Opera and Ballet **Deutsche Staatsoper,** Unter den Linden 7, tel. 02/20540; **Komische Oper,** Behrenstr. 55–57, tel. 02/220–2761; **Metropol Theater,** Friedrichstr. 101, tel. 02/200–0651.

Entertainment and Nightlife

The nightlife here is more modest than in West Berlin—but the prices are less extravagant, too. An evening of dancing, entertainment, and wine at the Stadt Berlin hotel can cost as little as DM25 (payable in hard currency or with a credit card). Other Interhotels offer dinner-dancing as well, but are more expensive. Music in the hotels is generally live; clubs have discos with DJs. For nightclubs with music and atmosphere, try one of the following: **Club Metropol** in the Metropol Hotel; **Panorama Bar** atop the Hotel Stadt Berlin; **Hafenbar,** Chauseestr. 20; **Haifishbar,** Unter den Linden 5, in the Opern Café complex; **Sinusbar** in the Palast Hotel.

Dresden

Arriving and Departing

By Plane Dresden Airport (tel. 051/589141) lies about 10 kilometers (6 miles) north of the city. Buses are available into the downtown area, leaving 45 minutes to an hour after each flight arrives; travel time is half an hour. Taxis are available as well.

By Train Dresden is easily reached by direct train connections with East Berlin; travel time is anywhere from 2½ to 3 hours.

By Car Dresden is about 160 kilometers (100 miles) south of Berlin. Leave Berlin on the E22. Exit at Lübbenau for the E15, which leads directly to Dresden.

Getting Around

Local public transport in the form of buses and streetcars is both cheap and efficient. Taxis, too, are inexpensive, but the city is small and walking is the best way to discover its hidden surprises.

Guided Tours

Dresden tours are often reserved well in advance by groups, so their availability will vary. In general, **walking tours** of the city sights depart daily (check with the tourist office for details). **Streetcar tours** leave from Postplatz Tuesday to Sunday, at 9, 11, and 1:30. **Bus tours** leave from Dr.-Kulz-Ring on Tuesday, Wednesday, and Thursday at 11.

Tourist Information

For information and reservations on city tours, contact the Dresden tourist office: **Reisebüro der DDR,** Prager Str. 11, tel. 051/495-5025. Open Monday–Wednesday 9–6, Thursday 9–6:30, Friday 9–7, and weekends and holidays 9–2.

Exploring Dresden

Dresden, splendidly situated on the banks of the Elbe river, was devastated during World War II but has been lovingly rebuilt. Italianate influences are everywhere, most pronounced in the city's glorious Rococo and Baroque architecture.

The **Semper Opera House,** at Theaterplatz, in the center of Dresden, is a mecca for music lovers. Named for its architect, Gottfried Semper, and opened in 1850, its conductors have included Wagner and von Weber. The original building was destroyed in the 1945 bombings, but Semper's architectural drawings had been preserved and it was rebuilt following his plans and reopened in 1985. Tickets are in great demand and hard to come by. Try booking through your travel agent before you go or ask at your hotel.

The city's other main attraction is the **Zwinger Palace,** with its wonderful portrait gallery. The building itself, like most of old Dresden, is a restored masterpiece, dating from 1710. It now contains a brilliant collection of paintings (few other museums can match its collection of 16th- and 17th-century Italian and Dutch masterpieces by Raphael, Rembrandt, Rubens, and Tintoretto), weapons, coins, armor, and Meissen china. The art gallery is closed for renovations through 1990, but the most famous pieces can be found in the Alterbinum, part of the Gallery of New Masters. *Postplatz. Porcelain collection open Mon.–Thurs. 9:30–4, weekends 9–4; Gallery of New Masters open Fri.–Wed. 10–5, Tues. 10–6.*

An unusual attraction is the **Deutches Hygiene-Museum** (German Museum of Health), reflecting Dresden's position of importance in medicine. *Lingnerplatz 1. Open Sat.–Thurs. 9–6.*

Two fine examples of Baroque architecture, both built by Pöppelman, designer of the Zwinger Palace, are the Oriental-influenced **Schloss Pillnitz** (open May–Sept.) and the **Schloss Moritzburg** hunting lodge (tel. 0297/439. Open Wed.–Sun. 9–11 and 1–4), which now houses an excellent **Baroque Museum.** Both places can be reached by streetcar or river boat.

Dining

For details and price category definitions, *see* Dining in Staying in East Germany.

Moderate **Café Pöppelmann.** There's a splendid Baroque atmosphere in
★ this restored old city house, now cleverly incorporated into the Hotel Bellevue. Try the hearty *Eisbein mit Sauerkraut* (knuckle of pork, accompanied by Germany's favorite side dish). *Grosse Meissner-Gasse 15, tel. 051/56620. Dinner reservations advised. AE, DC, MC, V.*

Sekundogenitur. This wine restaurant is situated right on the bank of the Elbe. If the weather allows, ask for an outside table so you can observe the tranquil flow of the river while you eat. The Wiener Schnitzel is great. *Brühlsche Terrasse, tel. 051/495 –1435. Reservations advised. No credit cards. Closed Mon.*

Inexpensive **Kügeln Haus.** Actually a combination grill-coffee shop-restaurant-and-beer keller, Kügeln Haus is extremely popular, so either get there early or reserve your table in advance. You'll find the usual local hefty dishes, but prepared with a deft touch. *Str. der Befreiung 14, tel. 051/52791. Reservations advised. No credit cards.*

Lodging

For details and price category definitions, *see* Lodging in Staying in East Germany.

Very Expensive **Hotel Bellevue** (Interhotel). A modern hotel opened in 1985, but combining new sections with some older city architecture, the Bellevue is just across the river from the Zwinger Palace and the Semper Opera House; the views are terrific. One of the hotel's five restaurants, Café Pöppelmann (*see* Dining), is recommended both for its atmosphere and its hearty dishes. *Kopckestr., tel. 051/56620. 328 rooms with bath. Facilities: 5 restaurants, wine cellar, café, bars, nightclub, shops, pool, sauna, solarium jogging course. AE, DC, MC, V.*

Expensive **Newa** (Interhotel). A sleek, ultramodern construction close to the train station, the Newa is a good choice for comfort, though slightly anemic in decoration. Its main restaurant accepts only hard currency or credit cards. The hotel is on the package tour route and is often booked well in advance. *Leningrader Str. 34, tel. 02/496–7112. 314 rooms with bath. Facilities: restaurant, café, 2 bars, sauna, shops, AE, DC, MC, V.*

Moderate **Astoria** (Interhotel). Somewhat away from the center, close to the Dresden zoo, the Astoria is a modern, five-story, cream-colored hotel with a garden terrace. You'll find nothing fancy as far as decor (Minimalist would describe it best), but the hotel staff is pleasant. *Ernst-Thälmann-Platz, tel. 051/475–5851. 84 rooms, most with bath. Facilities: 2 restaurants, bar, shop. AE, DC, MC, V.*

Leipzig

Arriving and Departing

Frequent trains run between Berlin and Leipzig. At fair time (the first weeks of March and September), there are flights from most West European cities to Schkeuditz airport, but only for a limited period extending a few days before and after the fairs. The airport is about 20 minutes from the city center, with regular bus connections. Rental cars are available at the airport.

Getting Around

By Public Transportation Leipzig itself sprawls, but most tourist attractions are within walking distance. Otherwise, buses, streetcars and the S-Bahn city railway are available. Tickets for both must be obtained in advance, at various prices according to the number of rides in a block. Get S-Bahn tickets at the main railway station. For ticket and other information on public transportation, tel. 041/795-9331. Nearby communities can be reached by train or S-Bahn.

By Taxi Taxis are more abundant than in other GDR cities because of the number needed to cope with peak traffic at fair time. For a taxi, call 7160 or 70171.

Guided Tours

Orientation Tours City sightseeing tours by bus run daily at 10, 1:30, and 4 March to mid-October (10 and 1:30 only in winter). The starting point is the Information Building in the city center (tel. 795-9329).

Excursions Tours are available to the nearby city of Halle, where the composer Händel was born and lived, and to Wittenberg, where Martin Luther taught and posted his theses. Tours are also available to the castle at Altenburg, with its playing-card museum. For information, contact the **Reisebüro der DDR** or **Leipzig Information** (see below). For those who choose Leipzig as a base, Dresden is only about an hour's drive away.

Tourist Information

You can get information on local events as well as on tours and excursions from the **Reisebüro der DDR,** Katharinenstrasse 1, (tel. 041/79210), open weekdays 9–5; or **Leipzig Information,** Sachsenplatz 1 (tel. 041/79590), open weekdays 9–7 (theater tickets until 6), Sat. 9:30–2.

Exploring Leipzig

Numbers in the margin correspond with points of interest on the Leipzig map.

An important market town since the Middle Ages, Leipzig has long been a center of printing and the book and fur trades. The twice-yearly trade fairs in March and September bring together buyers and sellers from East and West, and is the most important single meeting place for East European and Western commerce and trade.

Those who know music and German literature will know Leipzig for its associations with composer Johann Sebastian Bach (1685–1750), who was organist and choir director at the St. Thomas Church. In 1813, the composer Richard Wagner was born here. The names of the German poets and authors Johann Wolfgang von Goethe (1749–1832) and Friedrich von Schiller (1759–1805) and the composer Georg Friedrich Händel (1685–

1759) are also closely associated with the city and its immediate area.

But trade and the arts are only two aspects of the city's fame: One of the greatest battles of the Napoleonic Wars—the Battle of the Nations—was fought here in 1813 and was instrumental in leading to the French general's defeat. That battle is commemorated today by several monuments in Leipzig.

Following devastation during World War II, little is left of old Leipzig, although the GDR has undertaken considerable and successful restoration in the old city center. Nevertheless, the city retains touches of its medieval and Renaissance character, which even today penetrates the heart of the city center.

Railroad buffs may want to start their tour of Leipzig at the ❶ **Hauptbahnhof,** the main rail station. With its 26 platforms, it is the largest in Europe. From there, cross the Platz der Republik to enter the pedestrian area. This leads to Sachsenplatz and on to the Markt, or old city market square. Here, in the rebuilt ❷ 12th-century marketplace, you will find the **Altes Rathaus,** the Renaissance town hall, now housing the city museum. *Markt 1, tel. 041/209766. Admission: M3. Open Tues.–Sun. 9–5.*

You will be tempted to wander through the passageways and windowshop in the complex ahead. Tucked away here is the ❸ **Auerbachs Keller** restaurant, built in 1530 and made famous in Goethe's tale of *Faust.* But instead, turn right onto ❹ Thomasgasse to reach the **Thomaskirche,** where the composer Johann Sebastian Bach worked. The Thomaskirche is a point of pilgrimage for many. Originally the center of a 13th-century monastery which was rebuilt in the 15th century, the tall Gothic church now stands by itself, but the names of adjacent streets recall the cloisters that once surrounded it. The church is also Bach's burial place, and, to this day, home to the Thomas choir and a center of Bach tradition. *Thomaskirchhof 16. Admission: free. Open Tues.–Sun. 9–12, Mon. 2–4.*

From this point, Leipzig's other attractions are scattered. If you're feeling energetic, you can take a long walk out across the Martin-Luther-Ring and head up the Harkortstrasse to the ❺ **Georgi Dimitrov Museum,** the city's outstanding fine arts museum, with a graphic arts collection. *Georgi-Dimitrov-Platz 1, tel. 041/32600. Admission: M3. Open Tues.–Sat. 9–noon and 1–5; picture gallery open Tues.–Fri. 9–6, Sat. 9–5, Sun. 9–1.*

❻ By noting the enormous tower which marks **Karl Marx University,** you will come to a large square, **Karl-Marx-Platz,** on which ❼ ❽ stand the **Opera House** and the **Neues Gewandhaus** (concert hall), both centers of Leipzig's musical life. Head across the Ring and up the short Grimmaisch Steinweg to reach the ❾ **Grassimuseum** complex. It includes the **Museum of Arts and Crafts** (open Tues.–Fri. 9:30–6, Sat. 10–4, Sun. 9–1); The **Geographical Museum** (open Tues.–Fri. 10–3, Sun. 9–1); and the **Musical Instruments Museum** (enter from Täubchenweg 2; open Tues.–Thurs. 3–6, Fri. and Sun. 10–1, Sat. 10–3). *Grassimuseum. Johannesplatz 5–11, tel. 041/209024 or 291043. Admission: M3.*

❿ The **Botanischer Garten** (Botanical Gardens) is a set of splendid open-air gardens and greenhouses. *Linnestr. 1. Admission: M2. Open weekdays 9–4, Sun. 10–4; greenhouses Sun. 10–12:30 and 2–4.*

Leipzig

Altes Rathaus, **2**
Auerbachs Keller, **3**
Botanischer
Garten, **10**
Exhibition
Pavillion, **11**
Georgi Dimitrov
Museum, **5**
Gohliser
Schlösschen, **13**

Grassimuseum, **9**
Hauptbahnhof, **1**
Karl Marx
University, **6**
Neues Gewandhaus, **8**
Opera House, **7**
Schiller's House, **14**
Schloss Dölitz, **15**
Thomaskirche, **4**
Völkerschlacht-
denkmal, **12**

⑪ Still farther out, via streetcars No. 15, 20, 21, or 25, is the **Exhibition Pavillion** at Leninstrasse 210. It's main feature is a vast diorama portraying the Battle of the Nations of 1813 (open Tues.–Sun. 9–4). Slightly farther on Leninstrasse is the mas-
⑫ sive **Völkerschlachtdenkmal,** a memorial in the formal park; it, too commemorates the battle (open daily 9–4).

Outside of the center of Leipzig but reachable by public transportation (streetcars No. 20 and 24, then walk left up Poetenweg, or streetcar No. 6 to Menckestr.) is the delightfully
⑬ Rococo **Gohliser Schlösschen** (Gohliser House), which contains the Bach archive. *Menckestr. 23. Open Mon. and Fri. 1–5, Tues., Thurs., and Sat. 9–1, Wed. 1–8.*

⑭ Beyond that is **Schiller's House,** for a time the home of the German poet and dramatist Friedrich Schiller. *Menckestr. 21. Open Tues., Wed., Fri., and Sat. 11–5.*

⑮ **Schloss Dölitz** (streetcars No. 22 or 24, walk up Helenstrasse) contains an exhibition of *Zinnfiguren,* historical tin soldiers. *Torhaus, Schloss Dölitz, Helenstr. 24. Admission: M3. Open Sun. 9–1.*

Dining

For details and price category definitions, *see* Dining in Staying in East Germany.

Expensive **Sakura.** Located in the Hotel Merkur, Sakura offers good Japanese cuisine, perhaps out of respect for the Japanese firm that designed and built the hotel. *Gerberstr., in Hotel Merkur, tel. 041/7990. Reservations essential. AE, DC, MC, V.*

Moderate **Altes Kloster.** This restaurant, set in a former cloister, features
★ game in an appealing Old World environment. *Klostergasse 5, tel. 041/282252. Reservations advised. No credit cards.*
★ **Auerbachs Keller.** This historic restaurant (built 1530) in the city center is immortalized in Goethe's *Faust.* Both a visit and a prior reservation are "musts." The menu features regional dishes from Saxony, often with Faustian names. There is a good wine list. *Grimmaischestr. 2–4, tel. 041/209131. Reservations essential. AE, DC, MC, V.*
Burgkeller. Romanian national specialties are served here in the Doina restaurant; the keller, at least, is authentic. *Naschmarkt 1–3, tel. 041/295639. Reservations not necessary. No credit cards.*
★ **Paulaner.** This intimate, attractive restaurant is recommended for its quiet atmosphere and good regional-style food. *Klostergasse 3, tel. 041/281985. Reservations advised. No credit cards.*

Inexpensive **Kaffeebaum.** Allegedly the country's oldest café (established 1694), Kaffeebaum has a limited menu, but the atmosphere of this nearly 500-year-old Bürgerhaus, plus its "regulars," makes a visit worthwhile. *Fleischergasse 4, tel. 041/20452. No credit cards.*
Panorama Café. Atop the university building, this café offers a remarkable view of the city, somewhat broader than the limited food menu. *Karl-Marx-Platz, tel. 041/7466. No reservations. No credit cards.*

Lodging

During fair time, Very Expensive and Expensive hotels increase their prices significantly. Hotels in lower price categories increase prices only less significantly, possibly pushing them temporarily into the next higher price group.

For details and price category definitions, *see* Lodging in Staying in East Germany.

Very Expensive
★

Hotel Astoria (Interhotel). While this is an older hotel, it is still preferred by many for its ambience and central location next to the main rail station. Traffic in the area is considerable, so rooms on the back side are quieter. *Platz der Republik 2, tel. 041/71710. 309 rooms with bath. Facilities: 2 restaurants, bar, dance café, nightclub, sauna, car rental, parking. AE, DC, MC, V.*

Hotel Merkur (Interhotel). The city's newest and by far most luxurious accommodation is central, close to the main rail station, and fully air-conditioned. A Japanese garden acknowledges the nationality of the hotel's builders. *Gerberstr., tel. 041/7990. 440 rooms with bath. Facilities: 4 restaurants, 2 bars, coffee bar, nightclub, pool, sauna, solarium, bowling, jogging course, boutiques, car rental, parking. AE, DC, MC, V.*

Expensive

Hotel am Ring (Interhotel). This is the choice for those who want to be close to opera and the concert hall. The hotel is modern and efficient. Rooms on the back side are quieter. *Karl-Marx-Platz 5–6, tel. 041/79520. 276 rooms with bath. Facilities: 2 restaurants, bar, nightclub, sauna, shops, car rental, parking. AE, DC, MC, V.*

Hotel Stadt Leipzig (Interhotel). The hotel is surprisingly quiet considering its central location, which is very close to the main rail station. The style is postwar modern; public rooms are air-conditioned. *Richard-Wagner-Str. 1, tel. 041/288814. 340 rooms with bath. Facilities: 3 restaurants, café, bar, nightclub, sauna, shops, car rental, parking. AE, DC, MC, V.*

Moderate
★

International (Interhotel). This charming older hotel, with friendly personnel, is located close to the rail station. There is a pleasant sidewalk café, weather permitting. *Tröndlinring 8, tel. 041/71880. 104 rooms, some with bath. Facilities: restaurant, beer stube, bar, shops, car rental, parking. AE, DC, MC, V.*

★

Hotel zum Löwen (Interhotel). This is another modern hotel, built to handle fair traffic. It's less impersonal than most—almost cheerful—if not opulent. It is around the corner from the Astoria, close to the rail station. *Rudolf-Breitscheid-Str., tel. 041/7751. 108 rooms with bath. Facilities: restaurant, shops, car rental, parking. AE, DC, MC, V.*

Inexpensive

Parkhotel (H-O Group). The location, directly across from the rail station could hardly be better, but with few rooms with baths, the accommodations are inconvenient, if not downright spartan. *Richard-Wagner-Str. 7, tel. 041/7821. 174 rooms, few with bath. Facilities: restaurant, shop, parking. No credit cards.*

12 West Germany

Introduction

West Germany is a challenge to the visitor. At first glance, it is the most American of European countries, with an efficient network of highways linking cities with modern shopping complexes, chain hotels, and extensive sports facilities. Work seems to be taken more seriously than in France or Italy, where long lunches are still the norm, or in Great Britain, where a busy day at the office begins sometime around 9:30 AM. Americans can also understand a country where the capital concentrates on federal administration but is overshadowed by regional giants in other areas, such as commerce and industry.

At the same time, though, West Germany is steadfastly European. Officially the Bundesrepublik Deutschland, it was a founding member of the European Common Market, now the European Economic Community (EEC), and its government has always championed efforts to expand the "club." Bordered by more countries than any other EEC member, West Germany has led the way to the dismantling of trade frontiers— now set to take effect in 1992.

A fact of life about West Germany is its sometimes daunting prosperity. Look at the taxis lined up outside a major train station and you'll think you've found the assembly line of the Mercedes-Benz factory. Top-flight restaurants in Munich (München) and Frankfurt turn away customers every night. Electronics shops are full of expensive gadgets geared for the spoiled child or pampered business executive. The economy is healthy, and it shows.

Luckily, the Germans also know the importance of good value and a good time. Like a rich person who still clips shopping coupons, the prosperous West German will insist on attractively priced travel, food, and accommodations, which are there for the visitor as well. Always check to see if your train ticket or overnight stay in a hotel falls within the boundaries of some special deal. And, as in other countries, exploring the out-of-the-way regions has the bonus of turning up the real bargains. Remember, too, that inflation has long been held in check in West Germany, and domestic prices have risen only slightly in the past year.

There's no question about "All work and no play makes Johann a dull boy," either. A series of holidays and festivals throughout the country and the calendar helps see to that. Moreover, apart from the five weeks of vacation that a typical West German white-collar worker can expect, there is often an extra two weeks of "rest" time to be spent in the revivifying air of a spa or mountain resort. While you're likely to see groups of Germans being put through their paces on the exercise trail through a forest, you're just as likely to see some others toning up their drinking arms in preparation for the next *Oktoberfest* in Munich.

The great outdoors have always been an important escape hatch for the Germans, and *Lebensraum* (living space) is even more highly prized in the era of high technology and pressurized urban life. West Germany does its best to meet the needs of its hardworking inhabitants. A Bavarian mountain inn, the glow of its lights reflected on the blanket of snow outside, may be only a short drive from Munich. The busy industrial city of Stuttgart lies at the gateway to the Black Forest (Schwarzwald), the popular region of spas, hiking trails, and its tempting cake. Even West Berlin, a hectic enclave well inside East Germany, is surrounded by its own lakes and green parklands. The Green Party is a political expression of this environmental concern.

West Germany's size—less than half that of France—belies its social and geographical diversity. Everyone knows that Germany was divided into West and East after World War II, but few realize that the prewar state of unity was in fact only recent and was preceded by a long period of fragmentation and bitterness. Semiautonomous states were political and economic rivals, united—only to an extent—by a shared language and culture. A trip down the now peaceful Rhine (Rhein) would have meant having to pay a series of tolls to anyone who felt he could collect it. Religious differences were often settled by the sword.

Things are a lot quieter now, but you'll still meet cold stares if you sing the praises of Rhine wines in beer-drinking Munich or tell a Berliner that you intend to visit the "capital": To him Bonn is a sleepy provincial town in the middle of nowhere. Instead, make the most of each city or region and welcome the differences you'll find up the river, across the lake, or farther along the mountain road.

The transportation system needed to link these important regions is a godsend to the visitor. West German trains are fast, clean, and punctual, and a drive on a speed limit-free autobahn will give you an idea of just how fast all those BMW and Mercedes sports cars are meant to go. Maybe the best way to soak in the flavors and sights of West Germany is to float along the Rhine, past the vineyards and medieval castles, viewing it all from the deck of a steamer. Whichever way you go, take some time to reflect on the achievements of this hardworking people, who have produced an economic miracle on a grand scale, while at the same time nurturing one of the most vigilant environmental pressure groups in the world. Anomalies like this are typical of a country that has made a selling point of its diversity and turned conflict into consensus.

Before You Go

When to Go The main tourist season in Germany runs from May to late October, when the weather is naturally at its best. In addition to many tourist events, this period has hundreds of folk festivals. The winter sports season in the Bavarian Alps runs from Christmas to mid-March. Prices everywhere are generally higher during the summer, so you may find considerable advantages in visiting out of season. Most resorts offer out-of-season *(Zwischensaison)* and "edge-of-season" *(Nebensaison)* rates, and tourist offices can provide lists of hotels offering special low-price inclusive weekly packages *(Pauschalangebote)*. Similarly, many winter resorts offer lower rates for the periods immediately before and after the high season (*Weisse Wochen*, or "white weeks"). The other advantage of out-of-season travel is that crowds, which in major destinations are often thick on the ground, are very much less in evidence. The disadvantages of visiting out of season, especially in winter, are that the

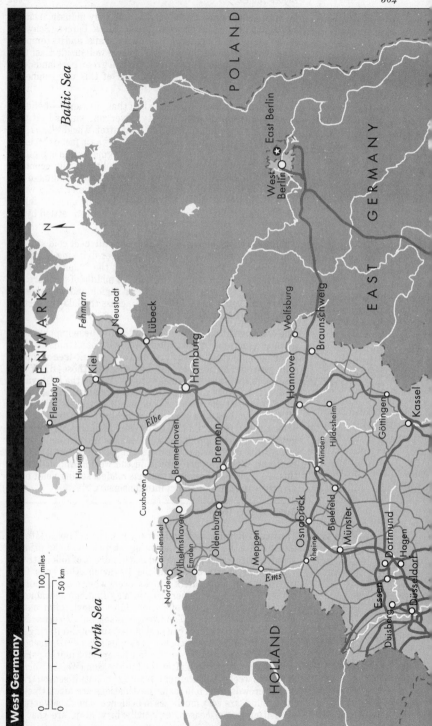

West Germany

weather, which is generally good in summer, is often cold and gloomy, and many tourist attractions, especially in rural areas, are closed.

Climate Germany's climate is generally temperate. Winters can be dull though never particularly cold, except in the Alps, the Harz region of Lower Saxony, and the higher regions of northern Franconia. Summers are usually sunny and warm, though be prepared for a few cloudy and wet days. The south is normally always a few degrees warmer than the north. As you get nearer the Alps, however, the summers get shorter accordingly, often not beginning until the end of May. Fall is sometimes spectacular in the south: warm and soothing. The only real exception to the above is the strikingly variable weather in southern Bavaria (Bayern) caused by the *Föhn*, an Alpine wind that gives rise to clear but oppressive conditions in summer and, in winter, can cause snow to disappear overnight.

The following are the average daily maximum and minimum temperatures for Munich.

Jan.	35F	1C	May	64F	18C	Sept.	67F	20C
	23	−5		45	7		48	9
Feb.	38F	3C	June	70F	21C	Oct.	56F	13C
	23	−5		51	11		40	4
Mar.	48F	9C	July	74F	23C	Nov.	44F	7C
	30	−1		55	13		33	0
Apr.	56F	14C	Aug.	73F	23C	Dec.	36F	2C
	38	3		54	12		26	−4

Currency The unit of currency in Germany is the Deutschmark, written as DM and generally referred to as the Mark. It is divided into 100 pfennigs. There are bills of 5 (rare), 10, 20, 50, 100, 500, and 1,000 Marks, and coins of 1, 2, 5, 10, and 50 pf and 1, 2, and 5 Marks. At press time (spring 1989), the Mark stood at DM 1.85 to the dollar and DM 3.19 to the pound sterling.

Major credit cards are widely accepted in Germany, though not universally so. You can buy a seat on a Lufthansa flight with a credit card but not on a German train, for example. Most hotels, a significant number of restaurants, and all leading car rental companies accept credit cards, however. A growing number of shops also honor them, but don't be surprised if you are offered a discount for cash. As a general rule, always check that your own piece of plastic will be accepted before ordering a meal or checking into a hotel.

What It Will Cost After three years of virtually zero inflation, West Germany's annual cost-of-living increase crept back above the 2% level in 1989. Higher taxes on gasoline and home-heating fuel, tobacco, and some luxury goods, and increases in public transportation and postage charges were mostly responsible for the rise, which is still small in comparison with most other European countries. Unfortunately, the strength of the Deutschmark, particularly against the dollar, counteracts the potential benefits for visitors of this price stability.

The most expensive areas to visit are the major cities, notably Düsseldorf, Hamburg, and Munich. Out-of-the-way rural regions, such as north and east Bavaria, the Saarland on the

French border, and parts of central Germany, offer the lowest prices.

The only tax occasionally levied on visitors is the modest Kurtax, a nominal DM 1 or DM 2 per person per night; because only a handful of spas and resorts levy the tax in the first place, however, it is unlikely to upset your vacation budgeting.

Sample Prices Cup of coffee in a café, DM 2.50, in a stand-up snack bar DM 1; bottle of beer in a beer hall, DM 3, from a supermarket, DM 1.5; soft drink, DM 2; ham sandwich, DM 3; one-mile taxi ride, DM 7.

Customs on Arrival There are three levels of duty-free allowance for visitors to West Germany.

Entering West Germany from a non-European country, the allowances are (1) 400 cigarettes or 100 cigars or 500 grams of tobacco, plus (2) one liter of spirits more than 22% proof or two liters of spirits less than 22% proof, plus (3) two liters of wine, plus (4) 50 grams of perfume and a quarter-liter of toilet water, plus (5) other goods to the value of DM 115.

Entering West Germany from a country belonging to the EEC, the allowances are (1) 200 cigarettes (300 if not bought in a duty-free shop) or 75 cigars or 400 grams of tobacco, plus (2) one liter of spirits more than 22% proof (1.5 liters if not bought in a duty-free shop) or three liters of spirits less than 22% proof, plus (3) five liters of wine, plus (4) 75 grams of perfume and one-third of a liter of toilet water, plus (5) other goods to the value of DM 780.

Entering Germany from a European country not belonging to the EEC (Austria or Switzerland, for example), the allowances are (1) 200 cigarettes or 50 cigars or 250 grams of tobacco, plus (2) one liter of spirits more than 22% proof or two liters of spirits less than 22% proof, plus (3) two liters of wine, plus (4) 50 grams of perfume and one-quarter of a liter of toilet water, plus (5) other goods to the value of DM 115.

Tobacco and alcohol allowances are for visitors aged 17 and over. Other items intended for personal use may be imported and exported freely. There are no restrictions on the import and export of West Germany currency.

Language English is a compulsory subject in German high schools other than those in the Saarland (where pupils can study French instead). As a result, most Germans under age 40 can speak passable English, though a staggering number are practically fluent. Older people in rural areas are less likely to speak English, but there are few hotels and restaurants anywhere in Germany where English is not spoken, in however rudimentary a fashion. For the most part, however, the German cab driver who can discuss Shakespeare with his English-speaking passenger is not an exception.

If you speak some German, you may find some regional dialects hard to follow, particularly in Bavaria. At the same time, however, all Germans can speak "high," or standard, German; even in the backwoods of Bavaria, the locals can alternate between dialect and standard German at will. Don't be shy about trying out whatever German you can muster. Your efforts will be appreciated by your *Gesprächspartner* (literally, "conversation partner").

Getting Around

By Car
Road Conditions
West German autobahns (turnpikes) are marked either A (on blue signs), meaning inter-German highways, or E (on green signs), meaning they form part of the Europe-wide *Europastasse* network. All autobahns are toll-free. Local roads are called *Bundestrassen* and are marked by their number on a yellow sign. All local roads are single lane and slower than autobahns.

Rules of the Road
Drive on the right, as in the United States. Always give way to traffic from the right unless traffic signs indicate otherwise. There is no speed limit as such on autobahns—Germans like to drive fast, and speeds over 160 kph (100 mph) are common—but there is a recommended limit of 130 kph (80 mph). The speed limit on Bundestrassen is 100 kph (60 mph). In built-up areas, speed limits vary between 30 kph (18 mph) and 80 kph (50 mph). Limits are shown on the side of the road.

Parking
Daytime parking in cities is very difficult. If you can find one, use a parking lot or you'll risk having your car towed. Parking restrictions are not always clearly marked, but can be hard to understand when they are. At night, parking meter spaces are free.

Gasoline
Leaded, low-octane gas is no longer available in Germany, so if you have an older model car, you'll have to fill it with high-octane gas. In spring 1989, a liter of gas cost DM 1.2.

Breakdowns
The **ADAC,** the major West German automobile organization, gives free help and advice to tourists, though you have to pay for any spare parts and labor you need. All autobahns have regularly spaced telephones with which you can call for help. The contact address for the ADAC is Am Westpark 8, 8000 Munich 70 (tel. 089/76760).

By Train
West Germany has one of the most comprehensive and efficient rail systems in Europe. All German cities are linked by fast Inter-City trains; principal services run hourly. In addition, the domestic network is fully integrated with the Europe-wide Euro-City system, which joins most major cities in 13 European countries. Both services have first- and second-class cars, though some Euro-City trains have first-class cars only. A supplement of DM 6 (DM 10 for first class) is payable on Euro-City trains, but this includes the seat-reservation charge. Overnight trains have sleeping cars. These range from private compartments in first class to six-bunk couchette (sleeper) cars. All overnight Euro-City services depart before midnight and arrive after 6 AM, meaning you're assured of a good night's sleep. There are no nighttime stops, and any frontier formalities are handled by sleeping-car attendants. All daytime Inter-City and Euro-City trains have dining or buffet cars, while light refreshments, drinks, and breakfast are available on night trains.

Other trains are D trains (regular express services); E trains (short-distance services); local trains, sometimes supplemented by buses; and FD trains, which connect some German cities with resort areas such as the Alps.

Fares
German Railways offers a bewildering range of special fares. If you're visiting other European countries, a **EurailPass** *(see* Getting Around Europe in Chapter 1), valid for most other rail systems in Europe, too, is the best deal. If you're visiting West

Germany only, German Railways' **Tourist Card** offers the simplest and most inexpensive way of traveling around the country. The card is available for four, nine, or 14 days and allows unlimited travel on virtually all trains, most long-distance buses, and riverboats on the Rhine, Moselle, and Main. The cost at press time (spring 1989), was DM 164 for the four-day card and DM 339 for the 14-day card. If you plan to visit West Berlin using the card, a supplement is payable (on the other hand, you do get a complementary tour of the city).

By Bus Long-distance bus services in Germany are part of the Europe-wide Europabus network. Services are neither as frequent nor as comprehensive as those on the rail system, so make reservations. Be careful in selecting the service you travel on: All Europabus services have a bilingual hostess and offer small luxuries that you won't find on the more basic, though still comfortable, regular services. For details and reservations, contact **Deutsche Touring Gesellschaft** (am Römerhof 17, 6000 Frankfurt/Main 90, tel. 069/79030). Reservations can also be made at any of the Deutsche Touring offices in Cologne (Köln), Hanover, Hamburg, Munich, Nuremberg (Nürnberg), and Wuppertal and at travel agents.

Rural bus services are operated by local municipalities and some private firms, as well as by German Railways and the post office. Services are variable, however, even when there is no other means to reach your destination by public transportation.

By Plane West Germany's national airline, **Lufthansa,** serves every West German city other than Berlin. Services are frequent and efficient, if expensive by U.S. standards. Check out the *Flieg und Spar* ("fly and save") round-trip tickets; you can save between 35% and 40% on the full fare. Contact Lufthansa at Frankfurt International Airport (6000 Frankfurt 65 (tel. 069/6961).

By Boat For a country with a small coastline, West Germany is a surprisingly nautical nation: You can cruise rivers and lakes throughout the country. The biggest fleet, and most of the biggest boats, too, belongs to the Cologne-based KD line, the Köln-Düsseldorf Rheinschiffahrt. It operates services on the rivers Rhine, Moselle, and Main, ranging from luxurious five-day trips from Amsterdam or Rotterdam in Holland all the way down the Rhine to Basel in Switzerland, to short "riverboat shuffles" with jazz bands and freely flowing wine. For details, write **Rhine Cruise Agency,** Dietrich Neuhold Corp., 170 Hamilton Ave., White Plains, NY 10601, or **KD Line,** Frankenwerft 15, 5000 Köln 1.

Services on the 160 kilometer (100 miles) stretch of the Danube (Donau) between the spectacular Kelheim gorge and Passau on the Austrian border are operated by **Donauschiffahrt Wurm & Köck** (Höllgasse 26, D-8390 Passau). The company has daily summer cruises on the rivers Danube, Inn, and Ilz, which meet at Passau; some two-day cruises are also offered. Bodensee (Lake Constance), the largest lake in Germany, located at the meeting point of Germany, Austria, and Switzerland, has up to 40 ships crisscrossing it in summer, the so-called Weisse Flotte, or white fleet. Write **Deutsche Bundesbahn,** Bodensee-Schiffsbetriebe, D-7750 Konstanz. Bavaria's five largest lakes —Ammersee, Chiemsee, Königsee, Tegernsee, and Starnbergersee—have regular summer cruises and excursions. Details are available from local tourist offices.

By Bicycle Bicycles can be rented at more than 280 train stations throughout Germany. Cost is DM 10 per day, or DM 5 if you have a train ticket. You can return your bike at any other train station. Bicycles can be carried free on all trains except Inter-City services and some local trains. Most cities also have privately run bike rental companies; ask at local tourist offices for details.

Staying in West Germany

Telephones Local calls cost a minimum of 23 pf. Public phones take 10 pf, 50
Local Calls pf, and DM 1 coins. If you plan to make an out-of-town call, take along a good supply of DM 1 coins. Most phone booths have instructions in English as well as German; if yours doesn't, simply lift the receiver, put the money in, and dial.

International Calls These can be made from public phones bearing the sign "Inlands und Auslandsgespräche." They take 10 pf, DM 1, and DM 5 coins; a four-minute call to the United States costs DM 15. To avoid weighing yourself down with coins, however, make international calls from post offices; even those in small country towns will have a special booth for international calls. You pay the clerk at the end of your call. Never make international calls from your hotel room; rates can be double the regular charge.

Operators and The West German telephone system is fully automatic, and it's
Information unlikely that you'll have to employ the services of an operator. If you do, dial 1188, or 00118 for international calls. If the operator doesn't speak English (also unlikely), you'll be passed to one who does.

Mail Airmail letters to the United States and Canada cost DM 1.40;
Postal Rates postcards cost 80 pf. Airmail letters to the United Kingdom cost DM 1; postcards cost 60 pf.

Receiving Mail You can arrange to have mail sent to you in care of any West German post office; have the envelope marked "Postlagernd." This service is free. Alternatively, have mail sent to any American Express office in Germany. There's no charge to cardholders, holders of American Express traveler's checks, or anyone who has booked a vacation with American Express. Otherwise, you pay DM 2 per collection (not per item).

Shopping German goods carry a 14% value-added tax (VAT). You can
VAT Refunds claim this back either as you leave the country or once you're back home. When you make a purchase, ask the shopkeeper for a form known as an "Ausfuhr-Abnehmerbescheinigung"; he or she will help you fill it out. As you leave the country, give the form, plus the goods and receipts, to German customs. They will give you an official export certificate or stamp. In the unlikely event that there's a branch of the Deutsche Bank on the spot, you can take the stamped form to it, where you will receive the refund on the spot. Otherwise, send the form back to the shop, and it will send the refund.

Opening and **Banks.** Times vary from state to state and city to city, but
Closing Times banks are generally open weekdays from 8:30 or 9 to 3 or 4 (5 or 6 on Thursday). Branches at airports and main train stations open as early as 6:30 AM and close as late as 10:30 PM.

Museums. Most museums are open Tuesday–to Sunday 9–6. Some close for an hour or more at lunch, and some are open on Monday.

Shops. Times vary, but shops are generally open weekdays from 8:30 or 9 until 5:30 or 6, and on Saturday mornings. On the first Saturday of each month, larger shops and department stores are open until 6 or 6:30.

National Holidays January 1; April 13, 16 (Easter); May 1 (May Day); May 24 (Ascension); June 4 (Pentecost); June 14 (Corpus Christi, southern Germany only); June 17 (German Unity Day); August 15 (Assumption Day, Bavaria and Saarland only); November 1 (All Saints); November 21 (Day of Prayer and Repentance); December 25, 26.

Dining It's hard to generalize about German food beyond saying that standards are high and portions are large. In fact, the range of dining experiences is vast: everything from highly priced nouvelle cuisine to hamburgers. As a visitor, you should search out local restaurants if atmosphere and regional specialties are your priority. Beer restaurants in Bavaria, *Apfelwein* taverns in Frankfurt, *Kneipen*—the pub on the corner cum local café— in Berlin nearly always offer best value and atmosphere. But throughout the country you'll find *Gaststätten* and/or *Gasthöfe* —local inns—where atmosphere and regional specialties are always available. Likewise, just about every town and many villages, too, will have a *Ratskeller*, a cellar restaurant in the town hall, where exposed beams, huge fireplaces, sturdy tables, and immense portions are the rule.

The most famous German specialty is sausage. Everyone has heard of frankfurters, but if you're in Munich, try *Weisswurst*, a delicate white sausage traditionally eaten only between midnight and noon. Nuremberg's sausage favorite is the *Nürnberger Bratwurst;* its fame is such that you'll find restaurants all over Germany serving it. Look for the "Bratwurststube" sign. Dumplings *(Knödel)* can also be found throughout the country, though their natural home is probably Bavaria; farther north, potatoes often take their place.

The natural accompaniment to German food is either beer or wine. Munich is the beer capital of Germany, though there's no part of the country where you won't find the amber nectar. Say "Helles" if you want light beer; "Dunkles" if you want dark beer. In Bavaria, try the beer brewed from wheat, called *Weissbier*. Germany is a major wine-producing country, also, and much of it is of superlative quality. You will probably be happy with the house wine in most restaurants or with one of those earthenware pitchers of cold Moselle wine. If you want something more expensive, remember that all wines are graded in one of three basic categories: *Tafelwein* (table wine); *Qualitätswein* (fine wines); and *Qualitätswein mit Prädikat* (top-quality wines).

Mealtimes Lunch is served from around 11:30 (especially in rural areas) to around 2; dinner from around 8 to 10:30 (and sometimes later in cities). Lunch tends to be the main meal, a fact reflected in the almost universal appearance of a lunchtime *Tageskarte*, or suggested menu; try it if you want maximum nourishment for minimum outlay. This doesn't mean that dinner is a rushed or skimpy affair, however; the Germans have too high a regard for food for any meal to be underrated. Breakfast, served anytime from 6:30 to 10, is often a substantial affair, with cold meats, cheeses, rolls, and fruit.

Dress Jacket and tie are recommended for restaurants in the Very Expensive and Expensive categories. Casual dress is appropriate elsewhere.

Ratings Prices are per person and include a first course, main course, dessert, and tip and tax. Best bets are indicated by a star ★. At press time (spring 1989), there were DM 1.85 to the dollar.

Category	Major Cities and Resorts	Other Areas
Very Expensive	over DM 95	over DM 90
Expensive	DM 65–DM 95	DM 55–DM 90
Moderate	DM 45–DM 65	DM 35–DM 55
Inexpensive	under DM 45	under DM 35

Credit Cards The following credit card abbreviations are used: AE, American Express; DC, Diners Club; MC, MasterCard; V, Visa.

Lodging The standard of German hotels, from top-notch luxury spots (of which the country has more than its fair share) to the humblest pension, is generally excellent. Prices can be high, but not disproportionately so in comparison to other northern European countries. You can expect courteous service, clean and comfortable rooms, and, in rural areas especially, considerable old-German atmosphere.

In addition to hotels proper, the country also has numerous *Gasthöfe* or *Gasthäuser* (country inns); pensions or *Fremdenheime* (guest houses); and, at the lowest end of the scale, *Zimmer*, meaning, quite simply, rooms, normally in private houses. Look for the sign "Zimmer frei" or "zu vermieten," meaning "for rent." A red sign reading "besetzt" means there are no vacancies.

Lists of hotels are available from the German National Tourist Office and from all regional and local tourist offices. Tourist offices will also make reservations for you—they charge a nominal fee—but may have difficulty doing so after 4 PM in peak season and on weekends. A reservations service is also operated by **ADZ** (Beethovenstr. 61, 6000 Frankfurt/Main, tel. 069/740767). The reservation fee is DM 3 per person.

Most hotels have restaurants, but those describing themselves as *Garni* will provide breakfast only.

Romantik Hotels Among the most delightful places to stay and eat in Germany are the aptly named Romantik Hotels and Restaurants. All are in historic buildings—this is a precondition of membership—and are personally run by the owners. The emphasis generally is on solid comfort, good food, and style. A detailed listing of all Romantik Hotels is available from **Romantik Hotel Reservations,** Box 1278, Woodinville, WA 98072, tel. 800/826–0015.

Castle Hotels This is a similar hotel association, though you may find that some of the simpler establishments lack a little in the way of comfort and that furnishings can be basic. But most can be delightful, with antiques, imposing interiors, and out-of-the-way locations setting the tone. Prices are mostly moderate. Ask the German National Tourist Office or your travel agent for the *Castle Hotels in Germany* brochure. It details a series of good-value packages, most for stays of four to six nights.

Landidyll Hotels This newly formed hotel association groups establishments in the medium price range. They are good-value hotels, and often situated in beautiful areas of the country (Landidyll means "country idyll"). Contact Landidyll (Steinacherstr. 8, 8500 Nürnberg 90).

Rentals Apartments and hotel homes, most accommodating from two to eight guests, can be rented throughout Germany. Rates are low, with reductions for longer stays. Charges for gas and electricity, and sometimes water, are usually added to the bill. There is normally an extra charge for linen, but not if you bring your own. Local and regional tourist offices have lists of apartments in their areas; otherwise write the **German Automobile Association** (ADAC), Am Westpark 8, 8000 Munich 70, tel. 089/76760.

Farm Vacations *Urlaub auf dem Bauernhof,* as the Germans know them, have increased dramatically in popularity over the past four or five years. Almost every regional tourist office has listings of farms by area offering bed and breakfast, apartments, or whole farmhouses to rent. Alternatively, write the **German Agricultural Association** (DLG), Rüsterstr. 13, D-6000 Frankfurt/Main 1. It produces an annual listing of more than 1,500 farms, all of them inspected and graded, that offer accommodations.

Camping There are more than 2,000 campsites in Germany, about 1,600 of which are listed by the **German Camping Club** (DCC), Mandlstr. 28, D-8000, Munich 40. The German National Tourist Office also publishes an annually updated listing of sites. Most are open from May through October, with about 400 staying open year-round. They tend to become crowded during the summer, so it's always worthwhile to make reservations a day or two ahead. Prices range from DM 10 to DM 15 per night for two adults, a car, and trailer (less for tents). If you want to camp away from an official site, you must get permission beforehand; if you can't find the owner, ask the police. You're allowed to spend no more than one night in parking lots on roadsides if you're in a camper, and you may not set up any camping equipment.

Youth Hostels Germany's youth hostels—*Jugendherberge*—are probably the most efficient, up-to-date, and proportionately most numerous of those in any country in Europe. There are 600 in all, many located in castles, adding a touch of romance to otherwise utilitarian accommodations. There's an age limit of 27 in Bavaria; elsewhere, there are no restrictions, though those under 20 take preference if space is limited. You'll need an International Youth Hostel card to stay in a German youth hostel; write **American Youth Hostels Association**, Box 37613, Washington DC 20013, or **Canadian Hostelling Association**, 333 River Rd., Ottawa, Ontario K1L 8H9. For full listings, write **Deutsches Jugendherbergswerk Hauptverband,** Bülowstr. 26, D-4930 Detmold, tel. 05231/74010, or contact the German National Tourist Office.

Ratings Service charges and taxes are included in all quoted room rates. Similarly, breakfast is usually, but not always, included—large breakfasts are always extra—so check before you book in. Rates are often surprisingly flexible in German hotels, varying considerably according to demand. Major hotels in cities often have lower rates on weekends or other periods when business is quiet. If you're lucky, you can find reductions of up to 60%. Likewise, rooms reserved after 10 PM will often carry a discount, on the basis that an occupied room at a reduced rate is better than an empty one. Although it's worthwhile asking if your hotel will give you a reduction, don't count on finding rooms at lower rates late at night, especially in the summer. Prices are for two people in a double room. Best bets are indicated by a star ★. At press time (spring 1989), there were DM 1.85 to the dollar.

Category	Major Cities or Resorts	Other Areas
Very Expensive	over DM 200	over DM 180
Expensive	DM 160–DM 200	DM 120–DM 180
Moderate	DM 100–DM 160	DM 80–DM 120
Inexpensive	under DM 100	under DM 80

Credit Cards The following credit card abbreviations are used: AE, American Express; DC, Diners Club; MC, MasterCard; V, Visa.

Tipping The Germans are as punctilious about tipping as they are about most facets of life in their well-regulated country. Overtipping is as frowned upon as not tipping at all, though the kind of abuse you risk in some countries for undertipping is virtually unknown here. Nonetheless, tips are expected, if not exactly demanded. Follow these simple rules and you won't go wrong.

In restaurants, service is usually included (under the heading *Bedienung*, at the bottom of the check), and it is customary to round out the check to the next mark or two, but never to more than 5% of the total. In cafés and beer halls, where it may not always be clear if service is included, give 10%. Taxi drivers also get 10%. Railway and airport porters (if you can find any) have their own scale of charges, but round out the requested amount to the next mark. Hotel porters get DM 1 per bag. Doormen are tipped the same amount for small services, such as calling a cab. Room service should be rewarded with at least DM 2 every time you use it. Maids should get about DM 1 per day. Double all these figures at luxury hotels. Service station attendants get 50 pfennigs or DM 1 for filling the tanks, checking oil and tires, or cleaning windshields.

Munich

Arriving and Departing

By Plane Munich (München) airport, Riem, is located about 10 kilometers (6 miles (10 kilometers) from downtown. Conditions can be chaotic in summer and around Christmas, and the airport authorities are periodically driven to appeal to overseas visitors for patience. A new, much larger, airport is scheduled to open in 1991.

**Between the
Airport and
Downtown**
Buses leave Riem for Munich every half hour between 6 and 8 AM and every 15 minutes between 8 AM and 9 PM. Thereafter, buses run according to aircraft arrivals. Buses to Riem leave from the north of the main train station in Munich, opposite the hotel Deutscher Kaiser, every 15 minutes between 5 AM and 9 PM. The 30-minute ride costs DM 5. At rush hours, a taxi can take just as long as the bus; other times, the trip should take about 15 minutes. The one-way fare is around DM 20. If you're picking up a rental car from the airport, simply take the main road out of the airport and follow the "Stadtmitte" signs (meaning "downtown)." The autobahn will take you right into Munich.

By Train
All long-distance services arrive at and depart from the main train station, the Hauptbahnhof. Trains to and from destinations in Bavaria use the adjoining Starnbergerbahnhof. For information on train times, tel. 089/592991; English is spoken by all the railroad staff. For tickets and information, go to the station or to the ABR travel agency right by the station on Bahnhofplatz.

By Bus
Munich has no central bus station. Long-distance buses arrive at and depart from the north side of the train station. A taxi stand is 20 yards away.

By Car
From the north (Nuremberg, Frankfurt), leave the autobahn at the Schwabing exit and follow the "Stadtmitte" signs. The autobahn from Stuttgart and the west ends at Obermenzing; again, follow the "Stadtmitte" signs. The autobahns from Salzburg and the east, from Garmisch and the south, and from Lindau and the southwest all join up with the city beltway, the Mittlere Ring. The city center is well posted.

Getting Around

Downtown Munich is only about one mile square, so it can easily be explored on foot. Other areas—Schwabing, Nymphenburg, the Olympic Park—are best reached on the efficient and comprehensive public transportation network. Munich's public transportation system is, in fact, a model of its kind: clean, fast, and ultra-reliable. It incorporates buses, streetcars, subways (U-Bahn), and suburban trains (S-Bahn). Tickets are good for the entire network, and you can break your trip as many times as you like using just one ticket, provided you travel in one direction only and within a given time limit. If you plan to make only a few trips, buy individual tickets; the cost is DM 2.40 (DM 2 for children under 15) for a single-zone ride. Otherwise, buy the 24-hour (24-Stunden) ticket, which allows unlimited travel on all public transportation in any 24-hour period. Costs are DM 6.50 (children under 15 DM 2) for an inner-zone card and DM 12 (children under 15 DM 4) for the entire network. Holders of a EurailPass, a Youth Pass, an Inter-Rail Card, or a DB Tourist Card travel free on all S-Bahn trains.

By Taxi
Munich's cream-colored taxis are numerous. Hail them in the street or call 089/21611 (there's an extra charge for the drive to the pickup point). Rates start at DM 2.90 and rise by DM 1.70 per kilometer (about DM 2.75 per mile). There are additional charges of 50 pf for each piece of luggage. Figure on paying DM 7 to DM 10 for a short trip within the city.

Important Addresses and Numbers

Tourist Information
The main tourist information office is in the heart of the city at Sendlingerstrasse 1, tel. 089/23911. It's around the corner from Marienplatz. Open Monday–Thursday 8:30–3, Friday 8:30–2. Longer opening hours are kept by the city tourist office at the Hauptbahnhof, tel. 089/239–1256. Open Monday–Saturday 8:30–10 PM, Sunday and holidays 1 PM–9:30 PM.

Consulates
U.S.: Königinstrasse 5, tel. 089/23011. **U.K.:** Amalienstrasse 62, tel. 089/394015).**Canadian:** Maximiliansplatz 9, tel. 089/222661.

Emergencies
Police: tel. 089/110. **Ambulance** and **emergency medical attention:** tel. 089/558661. **Dentist:** tel. 089/723–3093. **Pharmacies:** The **Internationale Inter-Apotheke,** corner of Luisenstrasse and Elisenstrasse, stocks American and British products; tel. 089/595444. Open weekdays 8–5:30, Saturday 8–1. Outside these hours, call 089/594475.

English Bookstores
The **Anglia English Bookshop,** Schellingstrasse 3, tel. 089/283642, has the largest selection of English-language books in Munich. A library of English-language books is kept in **Amerika Haus,** Karolinenplatz 3, tel. 089/595369.

Travel Agencies
American Express: Promenadenplatz 6, tel. 089/21990. **ABR,** the official Bavarian travel agency, has outlets all over Munich; tel. 089/12040 for information.

Guided Tours

Orientation Tours
City bus tours are operated by **Münchner Fremden-Rundfahrten.** Contact them at the ABR office at the train station (tel. 089/12040). Tours run daily and take in the city center, the Olympic Park, and Nymphenburg. Departures are at 10 AM from outside the Hertie department store across from the train station, and the cost is between DM 13 and DM 23 per person, depending on the duration of the tour.

Walking Tours
The Munich tourist office (*see* above) organizes guided walking tours, for either groups or individuals, on demand; no regular walking tours are offered. Tours will be tailored to suit individual requirements, and costs vary accordingly.

Excursions
Münchner Fremden-Rundfahrten (*see* above) organizes bus trips to most leading tourist attractions outside the city. A tour of the royal palaces of Ludwig II, for example, costs DM 46 per person. All tours leave from outside the Hertie department store. Other tours are offered by **Reisebüro Autobus Oberbayern,** Lenbachplatz 1, tel. 089/558061. Among the offerings is a "Late Riser's Excursion," which departs at 10 AM. All tours leave from Elisenstrasse, in front of the Old Botanical Garden.

Exploring Munich

Even in Bonn—the real capital of Germany—they grudgingly call Munich the nation's "secret capital." This sly compliment may reflect the importance of Munich—it's far and away the most important tourist destination in Germany, as well as being probably the most attractive major German city—but there's nothing "secret" about the way the Münchner makes this brave claim. Indeed, the noise with which the people of Munich trumpet the attractions of their city could be dismissed as so much Bavarian bombast were it not for the fact that it is so enthusiastically endorsed by others. Flamboyant, easygoing Munich, city of beer and Baroque, is light-years away from the dour Prussian glumness of Berlin, the gritty industrial drive of Hamburg, or the hardheaded commercial instincts of high-rise Frankfurt. This is a city to visit for its good-natured and relaxed charm—*Gemütlichkeit* they call it here—and for its beer halls, its museums, its malls, its parks, and its palaces.

Munich has been described as a mixture of corn and class, a juxtaposition epitomized by the fanciful and extravagant buildings of its most famous 19th-century son, the "Dream King," Ludwig II, ruler of Bavaria from 1864 to 1886, champion of Wagner and builder of fantasies. By turns elegant, opulent, and just a little bit vulgar, Munich is a city that's easy to like.

The Historic Heart *Numbers in the margin correspond with points of interest on the Munich map.*

① Begin your tour of Munich at the **Hauptbahnhof,** the main train station and an important orientation point. The city tourist office is here, too, ready with information and maps. Cross the street and you're at the start of a mile and a half of pedestrian shopping malls. Facing you are **Hertie,** Munich's leading department **②** store, and **Karlsplatz** square, known locally as Stachus—though no one seems to know why for certain—and one of Europe's busiest traffic intersections. The huge, domed building on your left is the late-19th-century **Justizpalast** (Palace of Justice), now fresh from a seven-year clean-up. It's one of Germany's finest examples of *Gründerzeit*, the display of 19th-century reproductions of Medieval and Renaissance architectural styles.

Head down into the pedestrian underpass—it's another extensive shopping area—to reach the other side and one of the **③** original city gates, **Karlstor.** The city's two principal shopping streets—**Neuhauserstrasse** and **Kaufingerstrasse**—stretch away from it on the other side. Two of the city's major churches **④ ⑤** are here, too: the **Bürgersaal** and the **Michaelskirche.** The latter is one of the most magnificent Renaissance churches in Germany, a spacious and handsome structure decorated throughout in plain white stucco. It was built for the Jesuits in the late 16th century and is closely modeled on their church of the Gesù in Rome. The intention was to provide a large preaching space, hence the somewhat barnlike atmosphere. Ludwig II is buried here; his tomb is in the crypt. The large neoclassical tomb in the north transept is the resting place of Eugène de Beauharnais, Napoleon's stepson. The highly decorated Rococo interior of the Bürgersaal makes a startling contrast with the simplicity of the Michaelskirche.

A block past the Michaelskirche to your left is Munich's 14th-**⑥** century cathedral, the **Frauenkirche,** or Church of Our Lady. Towering above it are two onion-shaped domes, symbols of the city (perhaps because they resemble brimming beer mugs, cynics claim). They were added in 1525 after the body of the church had been completed. Step inside and you'll be amazed at the stark simplicity of the church; it's very different from the darkly mysterious interiors of other Gothic cathedrals. In part, this is the result of the terrible damage the church suffered in the

war: A series of photographs at the main entrance show the building as it was just after the war, a gaunt skeleton filled with rubble. Look for the Baroque tomb of Ludwig the Bavarian by the west door, put up in 1662. In the crypt, you'll find an assortment of other Wittelsbach tombs (the Wittelsbachs were rulers of Bavaria until the early years of this century).

7 From the Frauenkirche, walk to the **Marienplatz** square, the heart of the city, surrounded by shops, restaurants, and cafés. It takes its name from the 300-year-old gilded statue of the Virgin in the center. When it was taken down to be cleaned in 1960, workmen found a small casket containing a splinter of wood said to have come from the cross of Christ. The square is dominated **8** by the 19th-century **Neues Rathaus,** the new town hall, built in **9** the fussy, turreted style so loved by Ludwig II. The **Altes Rathaus,** or old town hall, a medieval building of great charm, sits, as if forgotten, in a corner of the square. At 11 and 5 daily the **Glockenspiel,** or chiming clock, in the central tower of the town hall, swings into action. Two tiers of dancing and jousting figures perform their ritual display. It can be worthwhile scheduling your day to catch the clock. Immediately after the war, an American soldier donated some paint to help restore the battered figures and was rewarded with a ride on one of the knight's horses, high above the cheering crowds.

Time Out Duck into the arcades at **Donisl,** on your left as you face the town hall, for the first beer of your Munich visit. This is one of the most authentically Bavarian of the city's beer halls, where the beer flows freely all day—and night—long. You can grab a bite to eat, too. *Weinstr. 1.*

Heading south down Sendlingerstrasse from Marienplatz, you **10** come to the **Asamkirche** on your right. Some consider the Asamkirche a preposterously overdecorated jewelbox; others consider it one of Europe's finest late-Baroque churches. One thing is certain: If you have any interest in church architecture, this is a place you shouldn't miss. It was built around 1730 by the Asam brothers—Cosmas Damian and Egid Quirin—next door to their home, the Asamhaus. They dedicated it to St. John Nepomuk, a 14th-century Bohemian monk who was drowned in the Danube. Pause before you go in to see the charming statue of angels carrying him to heaven from the rocky riverbank. Inside, there is a riot of decoration: frescoes, statuary, rich rosy marbles, billowing clouds of stucco, and gilding everywhere. The decorative elements and the architecture merge to create a seamless sense of movement and color.

11 Go back to Marienplatz and turn right for the **Viktualienmarkt,** the food market. Open-air stalls sell cheese, wine, sausages, fruit, and flowers. Fortified with Bavarian sausage and sauer-**12** kraut, plunge into local history with a visit to the **Residenz,** home of the Wittelsbachs from the 16th century to their enforced abdication at the end of World War I. From Max-Joseph-Platz you enter the great palace, with its glittering Schatzkammer, or treasury, and gloriously Rococo theater, designed by court architect François Cuvilliès. Also facing the **13** square is the stern neoclassical portico of the **Nationaltheater,** built at the beginning of the 19th century and twice destroyed. *Residenz and Residenz Museum, Max-Joseph-Platz 3. Admission: DM 2.50 adults, DM 1.50 children. Open Tues.–Sat. 10–4:30, Sun. and holidays 10–1.*

❶ To the north of the Residenz is the **Hofgarten,** the palace gardens. Two sides of the gardens are bordered by sturdy arcades designed by Leo von Klenze, whose work for the Wittelsbachs in the 19th century helped transform the face of the city. Dominating the east side of the Hofgarten are the bombed-out ruins of what was once the War Museum. Next to its gaunt silhouette, work is proceeding apace on one of the most controversial building projects Munich has seen for many years, the new State Chancellery.

Time Out Munich's oldest café, the **Annast,** is located on Odeonsplatz, right by the west entrance to the Hofgarten. Sit at one of the tables under the Hofgarten trees, and the downtown bustle can seem miles away.

Odeonsplatz itself is dominated by two striking buildings. One
❶ is the **Theatinerkirche,** built for the Theatine monks in the mid-17th century, though its handsome facade, with twin eye-catching domes, was added only in the following century. Despite its Italian influences, the interior, like that of the Michaelskirche, is austerely white. The other notable building
❶ here is the **Feldherrnhalle,** an open loggia built by Ludwig I and modeled on the Loggia dei Lanzi in Florence. Next to it is the site of Hitler's unsuccessful *putsch* of 1923, later a key Nazi shrine.

The Feldherrnhalle looks north along one of the most imposing boulevards in Europe, the **Ludwigstrasse,** which in turn becomes the **Leopoldstrasse.** Von Klenze was responsible for much of it, replacing the jumble of old buildings that originally stood here with the clean, high-windowed lines of his restrained Italianate buildings. The state library and the university are
❶ located along it, while, halfway up it, is the **Siegestor,** or Arch of Victory, modeled on the Arch of Constantine in Rome. Beyond it is **Schwabing,** once a sort of combination Latin Quarter and Greenwich Village. It's much glossier these days, but still has an unmistakable vigor and spontaneity. Explore the streets around Wedekindplatz to get the feel of the place.

Back on Leopoldstrasse, wander down to the university, turn on to Professor-Huber-Platz (he was a Munich academic executed by the Nazis for his support for an anti-Hitler movement), and take Veterinärstrasse. It leads you to Munich's
❶ largest park, the magnificent **Englischer Garten.** You can rent a bike from Dr. Buss's stand at the entrance to the park on summer weekends. Cost is DM 5 per hour and DM 15 for the day.

The Englischer Garten, 4½ kilometers (three miles) long and over a ½ kilometer (one mile) wide, was laid out by Count Rumford, a refugee from the American War of Independence. He was born in England, but it wasn't his English ancestry that determined the park's name as much as its open, informal nature, a style favored by 18th-century English aristocrats. You can rent boats, visit beer gardens—the most famous is at the foot of a Chinese Pagoda—ride your bike (or ski in winter), or simply stroll around. Ludwig II used to love to wander incognito along the serpentine paths. What would he say today, now that so much of the park has been taken over by Munich's nudists? This is no misprint. Late 20th-century Germans have embraced nature worship with almost pagan fervor, and large sections of the park have been designated nudist areas. The biggest is behind the **Haus der Kunst,** Munich's art gallery, one of the few Hitler-era buildings left in the city. If you prefer the idealized version of the human body to the real thing, head inside. Unusually, the museum also houses one of the city's most exclusive discos, the PI. *Haus der Kunst, Prinzregentenstr. 3. Admission: DM 3.50 adults, 50 pf children; Sun. and holidays free. Open Tues.–Sun. 9–4:30, and Thurs. 7–9.*

You'll find more culture in Munich's two leading picture galleries, the Alte (meaning "old") and the Neue (meaning "new") Pinakothek. They are located on Barerstrasse, just to the west of the university. The **Alte Pinakothek** is not only the repository of some of the world's most celebrated old masters, but an architectural treasure in its own right, though much scarred from wartime bomb damage. It was built by von Klenze at the beginning of the 19th century to house Ludwig I's collections. Early-Renaissance works, especially by German painters, are the museum's strongest point, but there are some magnificently heroic works by Rubens, too, among much else of outstanding quality. *Barerstr. 27. Admission: DM 4, adults, 50pf children; free Sun. and holidays. Open Tues.–Sun. 9–4:30; Tues. and Thurs. 7 PM–9 PM.*

The **Neue Pinakothek** was another of Ludwig I's projects, built to house his "modern" collections, meaning, of course, 19th-century works. The building was destroyed in the last war, and today's museum opened in 1981. Whatever you think of the low, brick structure—some have compared it with a Florentine palazzo—it is an unparalleled environment in which to see one of the finest collections of 19th-century paintings in the world. *Barerstr. 29. Admission: DM 4 adults, 50 pf children; free Sun. and holidays. Open Tues.–Sun. 9–4:30, and Tues. and Thurs. 7–9 PM.*

There are two trips you can take to attractions just out of Munich. One is to the **Olympic Park,** a 20-minute U-Bahn ride north of the city; the other is to Nymphenburg, 6 kilometers (4 miles) northwest and reached by the no. 12 streetcar or 41 bus.

Suburban Attractions **Schloss Nymphenburg** was the summer palace of the Wittelsbachs. The oldest parts date from 1664, but construction continued for more than 100 years, the bulk of the work being undertaken in the reign of Max Emmanuel between 1680 and 1730. The gardens, a mixture of formal French *parterres* (trim, ankle-high hedges and gravel walks) and English parkland, were landscaped over the same period. The interiors are exceptional, especially the Banqueting Hall, a Rococo masterpiece in green and gold. Make a point of seeing the Schönheits Galerie, the **Gallery of Beauties.** It contains more than 100 portraits of women who had caught the eye of Ludwig I; duchesses rub shoulders with butchers' daughters. Among them is Lola Montez. Seek out the **Amalienburg,** or Hunting Lodge, on the grounds. It was built by Cuvilliès, architect of the Residenz Theater in Munich. That the hunting the lodge was designed for was often the indoor variety can easily be guessed by the sumptuous silver and blue stucco and the atmosphere of courtly high life. The palace also contains the **Marstallmuseum** (the Museum of Royal Carriages), containing a sleigh that belonged to Ludwig II, among the opulently decorated vehicles, and, on the floor above, the **Nymphenburger Porzellan,** where examples of the gorgeous porcelain produced here between 1747 and the 1920s, when the factory closed, can be seen. *Schloss Nymph-*

enburg. Admission: DM 5, children free. Open Apr.–Sept., Tues.–Sun. 9–12:30 and 1:30–5; Oct.–Mar., 10–12:30 and 1:30–4.

Of all the controversial buildings that mark Munich's skyline none outdoes the circus tent-shaped roofs of the **Olympic Park.** Built for the 1972 Olympics, the park, with its undulating, transparent tile roofs and modern housing blocks, represented a revolutionary marriage of technology and visual daring when first unveiled, though it all seems a little bit dated now. Sports fans might like to join the crowds in the Olympic stadium when the local soccer team, Bayern Munich, has a home game. Call 089/3061–3577 for information and tickets. There's an amazing view of the stadium, the Olympic Park, and the city from the Olympic tower. An elevator speeds you to the top in seconds. *Admission: DM 4 adults, DM 2.50 children. Open mid-Apr.–mid-Oct., daily 8 AM–midnight; mid-Oct.–mid-Apr., daily 9–midnight.*

Off the Beaten Track

Even though the Olympic Tower is higher, romantics say the best view of Munich and the Alps is from the top of the **Alte Peter** church tower; it's just off Marienplatz. Check that a white disk is hanging on the wall outside the entrance: It means that visibility is good. There are 302 steps to climb to the top. For the most inexpensive sightseeing tour of the center, take a no. 19 streetcar from outside the train station at Bahnhofplatz and ride it to **Wienerplatz,** itself located in Haidhausen, one of Munich's most interesting areas. On a fine day, join the chess players at their open-air board in Schwabing's **Münchner Freiheit** square. On a rainy day, pack your swimsuit and splash around in the Art Nouveau setting of the **Müllersches Volksbad** pool; it's located on the corner of the Ludwigsbrücke, one of the bridges over the Isar.

Shopping

Gift Ideas Munich is a city of beer, and beer mugs and coasters make an obvious gift to take home. There are many specialist shops in downtown Munich, but **Ludwig Mory,** located in the town hall on Marienplatz, is about the best. Munich is also the home of the famous Nymphenburg porcelain factory; its major outlet is on Odeonsplatz.

Shopping Districts From Odeonsplatz you are poised to plunge into the heart of the huge pedestrian mall that runs through the center of town. The first street you come to, **Theatinerstrasse,** is also one of the most expensive. In fact, it has only one serious rival in the money-no-object stakes: **Maximilianstrasse,** the first street to your left as you head down Theatinerstrasse. Both are lined with elegant shops selling desirable German fashions and other high-priced goods from around the world. Leading off to the right, you'll find **Maffeistrasse,** where **Loden-Frey** has Bavaria's most complete collection of traditional wear, from green "loden" coats to Lederhosen. Maffeistrasse runs parallel to Munich's principal shopping streets: **Kaufingerstrasse** and **Neuhauserstrasse,** the one an extension of the other.

Department Stores All the city's major department stores—other than **Hertie** (*see* Exploring)—are along Maffeistrasse, Kaufingerstrasse, and

Neuhauserstrasse. **Kaufhof** and **Oberpollinger** are probably the best. Both have large departments stocking Bavarian arts and crafts, as well as clothing, household goods, jewelry, and other accessories.

Antiques Antique hunters should make for **Karlstrasse** and **Türkenstrasse,** or to the flea markets held on weekends on **Dachauerstrasse,** beyond Leonrodplatz.

Dining

If it's generally true that the Germans take their food seriously, then it's unquestionably true that it's the Müncheners who take it most seriously of all. In fact, you can probably eat as well here as in any other city in Europe, Paris perhaps excepted. It's no surprise that Munich boasts what, by common consent, are generally held to be the two best restaurants in the country. If you're interested in haute cuisine, however, don't come expecting to find it dressed in Bavarian garb. The best Bavarian food has unmistakable Teutonic elements, but otherwise has much more in common with the sort of sophisticated nouvelle offerings you find in Paris than with wholesome and hearty German specialties. It would be wrong, though, to give the impression that the only food you'll find in Munich is light and sophisticated. Those with a taste for the kind of time-honored, traditional eating places that have been pulling in the crowds for years will not be disappointed. The city's beer and wine restaurants offer great atmosphere, low prices, and as much wholesome German food as you'll ever want. If there's one specialty you shouldn't miss it's *Weisswurst, the traditional sausage. Wash it down with a large glass of cold beer. Leberkäs,* meat loaf made with pork and beef, is another celebrated favorite.

For details and price category definitions, *see* Dining in Staying in West Germany.

Very Expensive **Aubergine.** German gourmets swear by the upscale nouvelle
★ cuisine of Eckart Witzigmann, chef and owner of the most sophisticated, restaurant in town. The decor is streamlined modern—white and glittery. The service is appropriately polished. If you want a gastronomic experience on the grand scale, try the turbot in champagne or the breast of pigeon with artichoke and truffle salad. *Maximilianplatz 5, tel. 089/598171. Reservations essential. MC. Closed Sun., Mon., Christmas and New Year's Day, and first 3 weeks of Aug.*
Boettner's. This is the oldest of Munich's classy restaurants, in business since 1905. There's a time-honored and quiet quality to its gracious bar and dark, wood-paneled dining room. Seafood dominates the menu; try the lobster and sole served on a bed of tomato-flavored pasta. *Theatinerstr. 2, tel. 089/221210. Reservations essential. AE, DC, MC, V. Closed Sat. for dinner, Sun., and holidays.*
Sabitzer's. Further evidence of upscale Munich's love affair with nouvelle cuisine, though with Bavarian influences, is provided by the classy offerings at Sabitzer's. Within its elegant gold-and-white 19th-century interior, you dine on specialties such as wild salmon with stuffed goose livers and lamb with venison. *Reitmorstr. 21, tel. 089/298584. Reservations essential. AE, DC, MC. Closed Sat., Sun., July and Aug.*

Tantris. Chef Heinz Winkler presides almost regally over what some consider Munich's top restaurant. Here, too, nouvelle cuisine, served with great panache, reigns supreme. Try the pigeon breast for a remarkable gastronomic experience. The downside is the setting, which bears an uncanny resemblance to an airport departure lounge, albeit one for VIPs. *Johann-Fichter-Str. 7, tel. 089/362061. Reservations essential. AE, DC, MC. Closed Sat. lunch, Sun., Mon., 1st week in Jan., and 3 weeks in Aug.*

Expensive **Austernkeller.** The nautical decor of this centrally located,
★ vaulted cellar-restaurant provides an appropriate setting for the classy seafood specialties of the Austernkeller. Oysters—*Austern* in German—dominate the menu, but there's a wide range of other shellfish featured, too. *Stollbergstr. 11, tel. 089/298787. Reservations advised. AE, DC, MC, V. Closed Mon. and Christmas.*

Bouillabaisse. There's little point eating here if your tastes run to German specialties. Pungent and rich *bouillabaisse*, the garlicky fish stew from Provence in the south of France, is the star attraction here. The decor is striking, with imposing chandeliers to lighten up the otherwise somber and heavy-beamed dining room. *Falkenturmstr. 10, tel. 089/297909. Reservations advised. AE, DC, MC, V. Closed Sun., Mon. lunch, and Aug.*

Le Gourmet. Imaginative combinations of French and Bavarian specialties have won the little Gourmet substantial praise from local critics. Try chef Otto Koch's oxtail in champagne sauce or his zucchini and truffle salad. *Ligsalzstr. 46, tel. 089/503597. Reservations advised. AE, DC, MC. Closed Sun. and 1st week in Jan.*

Käferschanke. Fresh fish, imported daily from the south of France, is the attraction here. Try the grilled prawns in a sweet-sour sauce. The rustic decor, complemented by some fine antique pieces, is a delight. The restaurant is located in the classy Bogenhausen suburb, a 10-minute taxi ride from downtown. *Schumannstr. 1, tel. 089/41681. Reservations advised. AE, DC, MC. Closed Sat. and holidays.*

★ **Preysing Keller.** Devotees of all that's best in modern German food—food that's light and sophisticated but with recognizably Teutonic touches—will love the Preysing Keller, the best hotel-restaurant in the city. The restaurant is in a 16th-century cellar, though this has been so overrestored that there's practically no sense of its age or original character. Never mind; it's the food, the extensive wine list, and the perfect service that make this somewhere special. Try the fixed-price seven-course menu—a bargain at DM 100 per person—for best value and an all-around taste of the most underrated restaurant in Munich. *Innere-Wiener-Str. 6, tel. 089/481015. Reservations essential. No credit cards. Closed Sun., Christmas, and New Year's Day.*

Moderate **Bistro Terrine.** The name may make you think that this is no more than a humble, neighborhood French-style restaurant. In fact, excellent classic French dishes are served within its appealing Art Nouveau interior. Order the fixed-price menu to keep the check low; *à la carte* dishes are appreciably more expensive. *Amalienstr. 40, tel. 089/281780. Reservations advised. AE, MC. Closed Sun.*

★ **Nürnberger Bratwurst Glöckl.** This is about the most authentic old-time Bavarian sausage restaurant in Munich, and it's always crowded. Wobbly chairs, pitch-black wooden paneling, tin plates, monosyllabic waitresses, and, downstairs, some seriously Teutonic-looking characters establish an unbeatable mood. If you want undiluted atmosphere, try for a table downstairs; if you want to hear yourself speak, go for one upstairs. The menu is limited, with *Nürnberger Stadtwurst mit kraut*—finger-size Nürnberg sausages—taking pride of place. The beer, never in short supply, is served straight from wooden barrels. The restaurant is right by the Frauenkirche—the entrance is set back from the street and can be hard to spot—and makes an ideal lunchtime layover. *Frauenplatz 9, tel. 089/ 220385. Reservations advised. No credit cards.*

Welser Küche. You eat here in medieval style, in a red-brick vaulted banqueting hall and with only a dagger to tackle the roast meat. It sounds tourist-trail fare, but in fact it's fun and the food's good. *Residenzstr. 27, tel. 089/296565. Reservations advised. AE, DC, MC, V.*

Inexpensive **Donisl.** Ranking high among the beer restaurants of Munich, Donisl is located just off Marienplatz, and in summer, its tables spill out onto the sidewalk. But the real action is inside. The large central hall, with garlands of dried flowers and painted and carved booths lining the walls, is animated night and day. The atmosphere, like the food, is rough and ready. *Weinstr. 1, tel. 089/220184. No reservations. AE, DC, MC, V.*

Dürnbräu. A fountain plays outside this picturesque old Bavarian inn. Inside, the mood is crowded and noisy. Expect to share a table; your fellow diners will range from millionaires to students. The food is resolutely traditional. Try the cream of spinach soup and the boiled beef. *Dürnbräugasse 2, tel. 089/ 222195. Reservations advised. AE, DC, MC, V.*

Franziskaner. Vaulted archways, cavernous rooms interspersed with intimate dining areas, bold blue frescoes on the walls and long wooden tables create a spin-and-span medieval atmosphere—the look without the dirt. This is the place for an early morning *Weisswurst* and a beer; the Bavarians swear it will banish all trace of that morning-after feeling. Perusastr. 5, tel. 089/645548. No reservations. No credit cards.

★ **Haxnbauer.** This is about the most sophisticated of the beer restaurants. There's the usual series of interlinking rooms—some large, some small—and the usual sturdy/pretty Bavarian decoration. But there is much greater emphasis on the food than in other similar places. Try *Leberkäs* or *Schweinshaxe*, pork shank. *Münzstr. 2, tel. 089/221922. Reservations advised. MC, V.*

Hofbräuhaus. The heavy stone vaults of the Hofbräuhaus contain the most famous of the city's beer restaurants. Crowds of singing, shouting, swaying beer drinkers—make no mistake; this is a place where beer takes precedence over food—fill the atmospheric and smoky rooms. Picking their way past the tables are hefty waitresses in traditional garb bearing frothing steins. Some people love it. Others deplore the rampant commercialization and the fact that the place is now so obviously aimed at the tourist trade. It's just north of Marienplatz. *Platzl 9, tel. 089/221676. No reservations. No credit cards.*

Hundskugel. This is Munich's oldest tavern, dating back to 1640; history positively drips from its crooked walls. The food is surprisingly good. If *Spanferkel*—roast suckling pig—is on the menu, make a point of ordering it. This is simple Bavarian fare at its best. *Hotterstr. 18, tel. 089/264272. Reservations advised. No credit cards.*

Max Emanuel Bräuerei. Folk music and theater are featured in this time-honored Munich institution, located just by the university. The clientele is predominantly young, and the atmosphere is always lively. In summer, you can eat in the delightful little beer garden. The food is wholesome Bavarian, with some Greek and French touches. *Adalbertstr. 33, tel. 089/271–5158. Reservations advised. DC, MC.*

★ **Pfälzer Weinprobierstube.** A warren of stone-vaulted rooms of various sizes, wooden tables, glittering candles, dirndl-clad waitresses, and a vast range of wines add up to an experience as close to your picture of timeless Germany as you're likely to get. The food is reliable rather than spectacular. Local specialties predominate. *Residenzstr. 1, tel. 089/225628. No reservations. No credit cards.*

Lodging

Make reservations well in advance and be prepared for higher-than-average rates. Though Munich has a vast number of hotels in all price ranges, most are full year-round; this is a major trade and convention city as well as a prime tourist destination. If you plan to visit during the "fashion weeks" (Mode Wochen) in March and September or during the Oktoberfest at the end of September, make reservations at least two months in advance. The tourist office at Rindermarkt 5 has a reservations office, but note that personnel will not accept telephone reservations. There's also a reservations office at the airport. Your best bet for finding a room if you haven't reserved is the tourist office at Bayerstrasse by the train station. The staff will charge a small fee, but are supremely well organized.

The closer to the city center you stay, the higher the price. Consider staying in a suburban hotel and taking the U-Bahn or S-Bahn into town. Rates are much more reasonable, and a 15-minute train ride is no obstacle to serious sightseeing. Check out the city tourist office "Key to Munich" packages. These include reduced-rate hotel reservations, sightseeing tours, theater visits, and low-cost travel on the U- and S-Bahn. Write to the tourist office at Rindermarkt 5.

For details and price category definitions, *see* Lodging in Staying in West Germany.

Bayerischer Hof. This is one of Munich's most traditional luxury hotels. Public rooms are decorated with antiques, fine paintings, marble, and painted wood. Old-fashioned comfort and class abound in the older rooms; some of the newer rooms are rather functional. *Promenadenplatz 2–6, tel. 089/21200. 440 rooms with bath. Facilities: 3 restaurants, nightclub, rooftop pool, garage, sauna, masseur, hairdresser. AE, DC, MC, V.*

City Hilton. Munich's second Hilton is right next door to the Gasteig cultural center. Ticket bookings are no problem. The hotel has all the expected Hilton comforts and services—it even has a selection of track suits and shoes for joggers. *Rosenheimerstr. 15, tel. 089/48040. 680 rooms and suites with bath. Facilities: piano bar, restaurant, access to body-building center and public pool. AE, DC, MC, V.*

★ **Vier Jahreszeiten.** The Vier Jahreszeiten—it means the Four Seasons—has been playing host to the world's wealthy and titled for more than a century. It has an unbeatable location on Munich's premier shopping street, and is only a few minutes' walk from the heart of the city. Elegance and luxury set the tone throughout; many rooms have handsome antique pieces. Dine in one of Munich's finest restaurants, the Walterspiel. *Maximilianstr. 17, tel. 089/230390. (Reservations in the U.S. from Kempinski International, tel. 800/426–3135). 341 rooms with bath, 25 apartments, presidential suite. Facilities: restaurant, nightclub, rooftop pool, garage, sauna, car rental, Lufthansa check-in desk. AE, DC, MC, V.*

Expensive   **Eden Hotel Wolff.** Chandeliers and dark wood paneling in the public rooms underline the old-fashioned elegance of this downtown favorite. It's close to the train station and the fairgrounds. Rooms are comfortable, and most are spacious. Dine on excellent Bavarian specialties in the intimate Zirbelstube restaurant. *Arnulfstr. 4, tel. 089/551150. 210 rooms with bath. Facilities: restaurant. AE, DC, MC, V.*

Excelsior. The Excelsior is very much a businessperson's hotel, with a sense of functional comfort and a pedestrian mall location, close by the train station, that makes it ultraconvenient for downtown. Renovations in 1986 have helped maintain its reputation for efficiency and good service. *Schützenstr. 11, tel. 089/551370. 116 rooms with bath or shower. Facilities: restaurant, bar. AE, DC, MC, V.*

Palace. The Palace is a modern hotel that opened in 1986. Decor and mood lean toward old-fashioned elegance, with the accent firmly on Louis XVI styles and plush luxury. Most rooms overlook the little courtyard. The hotel is located in Alt-Bogenhausen, 6½ kilometers (4 miles) from the airport. Downtown Munich is a 10-minute tram ride away. *Trögerstr. 21, tel. 089/4705091. 73 rooms and suites with bath. Facilities: bar, roof garden, Jacuzzi, sauna, gym. AE, DC, MC, V.*

Prinzregent. An air of Bavarian rusticity pervades this small, new hotel. Carved wood, gilt angels, Rococo-style sconces and mirrors, and rough white plaster walls predominate. There's no restaurant, but the breakfast room is decked out with woods taken from an old farmhouse The hotel is just a 10-minute ride from downtown. *Ismaningerstr. 42–44, tel. 089/4702081. 70 rooms with shower. Facilities: sauna, pool, bar. AE, DC, MC, V.*

★ **Splendid.** Chandelier-hung public rooms, complete with antiques and Oriental rugs, give the small Splendid something of the atmosphere of a spaciously grand 19th-century hotel. Service is attentive and polished. Have breakfast in the small courtyard in summer. There's no restaurant, but the bar serves snacks as well as drinks. It's close to classy shops and the Isar River. *Maximilianstr. 54, tel. 089/296606. 37 rooms with bath and 1 suite. Facilities: bar. AE, MC, V.*

Trustee Park Hotel. Located close to the exhibit grounds, this newly opened businessperson's hotel is functional in decor; high season coincides with trade fairs and conventions. Check out weekend rates: Special family deals are often available. Rooms are spacious, and many have balconies or terraces. *Parkstr. 31, tel. 089/519950. 40 rooms with bath. Facilities: restaurant, bar. AE, DC, MC, V.*

Moderate   **Adria.** A modern and comfortable hotel, the Adria is located on the edge of Munich's museum quarter, in the attractive Lehel district, a short walk from the Isar River and the Englischer Garten. There's no restaurant, but there's a large and bright breakfast room. *Liebigstr. 8, tel. 089/293081. 51 rooms with bath. AE, DC, MC, V. Closed Dec. 24–Jan. 6.*

Braüfpanne. The plain concrete exterior of the Braüfpanne belies the functional comforts within. Though the rooms are sparsely furnished, they are intelligently designed, with writing desks and sofas. The restaurant offers excellent local specialties at affordable prices. Don't stay here if you want to be close to the center of things; it's in the northeast suburbs, a 25-minute tram ride from downtown. *Oberföhringerstr. 107, tel. 089/951095. 25 rooms with bath. Facilities: restaurant, bar, skittle alley. AE, DC, MC, V.*

Domus. Head here for home comforts and friendly, personal service. All rooms have balconies. There's no restaurant, but drinks and snacks are available in the Tyrolean Room bar, decked out in rough-hewn and snug Alpine style. The hotel is close to many museums and the Englischer Garten. *St. Anna-Str. 31, tel. 089/221704. 45 rooms with bath. Facilities: bar, garage. AE, DC, MC, V. Closed Christmas.*

★ **Gästehaus am Englischer Garten.** Despite the slightly basic rooms, you need to reserve well in advance to be sure of getting one in this converted, 200-year-old watermill. The hotel, complete with ivy-clad walls and shutter-framed windows, stands right on the edge of the Englischer Garten, no more than a 5-minute walk from the bars and shops of Schwabing. Be sure to ask for a room in the main building; the modern annex down the road is cheaper but charmless. There's no restaurant, but in summer, breakfast is served on the terrace. *Liebergesellstr. 8, tel. 089/392034. 34 rooms, some with bath. No credit cards.*

Intercity. Despite its proximity to the train station, double-glazing in all rooms ensures peace in this longtime downtown favorite. Try for one of the Bavarian-style rooms; others are basic and little more than adequate. There's an excellent restaurant offering good-value Bavarian specialties. *Bahnhofplatz 2, tel. 089/558571. 208 rooms and 4 apartments with bath. Facilities: restaurant, bar, skittle alley. DC, MC, V.*

Inexpensive **Ariane.** Make reservations well in advance for this small pension; it's located a 5-minute walk due south of the train station. Standards of comfort are high, and many appreciate the excellent central location. *Pettenkoferstr. 44, tel. 089/535529. 12 rooms, most with bath. No credit cards.*

Kriemhild. If you're traveling with children, you'll appreciate the low rates of this welcoming, family-run pension in the western suburb of Nymphenburg. It's just a few minutes' walk from the palace itself and from one of the city's best beer gardens. It's a 30-minute tram ride from downtown. There's no restaurant, but an extensive breakfast buffet is included in the room rate. *Guntherstr. 16, tel. 089/170077. 40 rooms, half with bath. Facilities: bar. MC.*

★ **Monopteros.** There are few better deals in Munich than the little Monopteros. It's located just south of the Englischer Garten, with a tram stop for the 10-minute ride to downtown right by the door. Rooms may be basic, but the excellent service, warm welcome and great location more than compensate. There's no restaurant. *Oettingenstr. 35, tel. 089/292348. 11 rooms, 3 with shower. No credit cards.*

The Arts

Details of concerts and theater performances are available from the *Vorschau* or *Monatsprogramm* booklets obtainable at most hotel reception desks. Some hotels will make ticket reservations; otherwise use one of the ticket agencies in the city center, such as **Radio-Rim** or the **Residenz Bücherstube,** both on Theatinerstrasse.

Concerts Munich's Philharmonic Orchestra has a new home, the concert hall of the **Gasteig Cultural Center.** Tickets can be bought directly at the box office (the Gasteig center is on Rosenheimerstrasse, on a hill above the Ludwigsbrücke bridge). The Bavarian Radio Orchestra performs Sunday concerts here. In summer, concerts are held at two Munich palaces, **Nymphenburg** and **Schleissheim,** and in the open-air interior courtyard of the **Residenz.**

Opera Munich's **Bavarian State Opera** company is world famous, and tickets for major productions in its permanent home, the State Opera House, are difficult to obtain. Book far in advance for the annual opera festival held in July and August. The box office, (Maximilianstr. 11, tel. 089/221316) takes reservations one week in advance. It's open weekdays 10:30–1:30 and 3:30–5:30, Saturday 10–12:30.

Dance The ballet company of the Bavarian State Opera performs at the **State Opera House.** Ballet productions are also staged at the attractive late 19th-century **Gärtnerplatz Theater.**

Film Munich has an annual film festival, usually held in June. English-language films are shown regularly at the **Atlantic Palast** (Schwantalerstr. 2–6), **Cinema** (Nymphenburgerstr. 31), the **Film Museum** (St. Jakobs Platz), and the **Museum Lichtspiele** (Ludwigsbrücke).

Theater There are two state theater companies, one of which concentrates on the classics. More than 20 other theater companies (some of them performing in basements) are to be found throughout the city. An English-speaking company, called the **Company** (tel. 089/343827) presents, about four productions a year.

Nightlife

Bars, Cabaret, Nightclubs Although it lacks the racy reputation of Hamburg, Munich has something for just about all tastes. For spicy striptease, explore the regions south of the train station (Schillerstrasse, for example), or in the neighborhood of the famous Hofbräuhaus (Am Platzl).

Jazz The best jazz can be heard at the **Allotria** (Türkenstr. 33), the **Domicile** (Leopoldstr. 19), and the **Podium** (Wagnerstr. 1). **Jenny's Place** (Georgenstr. 50) is run by an English actress-singer who has a great voice and a warm welcome for any visitor from the United States or Britain.

Discos Schwabing is disco-land. Try the **Circo Valentino** on Occamstrasse (a fun street at all times of day).

For singles Every Munich bar is singles territory. Three you might like to try are: **Schumann's** (Maximilianstr. 36) any time after the curtain comes down at the nearby opera house; **Alter Simpl**

(Türkenstr. 57) but not before midnight, and **Harry's New York Bar** (Falkenturmstr. 9), which offers an escape from the German bar scene *and* serves genuine Irish Guinness. Ernst Polomsky used to be butler in the Bush family home. He now has his own bar, the **Bistro Polo** (Mühlbauerstr.), but George Bush's favorite cocktail is a closely guarded secret.

Frankfurt

Arriving and Departing

By Plane Frankfurt airport, the busiest in central Europe, is about 10 kilometers (6 miles) southwest of the city.

Between the Airport and Downtown There are several ways to get into town. Two suburban (S-Bahn) lines connect the airport and the center. The S-14 runs between the Hauptwache station and the airport, and the S-15 from the main train station, the Hauptbahnhof. The S-14 runs every 20 minutes and takes 15 minutes; the S-15 leaves every 10 minutes and takes 11 minutes. The trip costs DM 3.10 (DM 4.20 in rush hour). Inter-City trains also stop at Frankfurt airport train station on hourly direct runs to Cologne, Dortmund, Hamburg, and Munich. A no. 61 bus runs from the airport to the Sudbahnhof station in Sachsenhausen, where there is access to the U-Bahn (subway) lines U-1 and U-3; the fare is DM 3.10. Taxi fare from the airport to downtown is DM 35. By rented car, follow the signs to Frankfurt ("Stadtmitte") via the B-43 main road.

By Train Frankfurt's main train station, the Hauptbahnhof, and the airport station are directly linked with all parts of the country by fast Euro-City and Inter-City services. For train information, tel. 069/2651. For tickets and general information, go directly to the station or to the DER travel office at the Hauptbahnhof.

By Bus Long-distance buses connect Frankfurt with more than 200 European cities. Buses leave from the south side of the Hauptbahnhof. Tickets and information are available from **Deutsche Touring GmbH.** (Am Römerhof 17, tel. 069/79030).

By Car From the north, leave autobahn A5 at the Nordwestkreuz, join A66 and follow it to its end, in the Nordend district. From the east, A66 brings you into Enkheim, from where you follow the signs to the downtown area, the "Stadtmitte." From the west, leave autobahn A3 at the Frankfurt-south ("Frankfurt-Süd") exit and enter the city on B43/44. From the south, leave the autobahn at the Offenbach exit (the "Anschluss-stelle Offenbach") and enter the city on B459.

Getting Around

By Public Transportation A combination of subway and suburban train, streetcar, and bus services provides speedy and efficient public transportation. Tickets cover travel on the complete network, which is divided into two tariff zones. A 24-ticket booklet costs DM 8, less than the cost of four single tickets in the inner (city) tariff zone. The 24-hour ticket is available at all ticket-selling points; single tickets from the blue automatic dispensing units are at all major stops. For further information or assistance, call 069/26940.

By Taxi Taxi meters start at DM 3.60, and the fare is DM 1.80 per kilometer (about DM 2.90 per mile). Count on paying DM 10 to DM 12 for a short city ride. Taxi drivers charge 50 pf for each piece of luggage carried. To order a taxi, call 069/250001 or 069/545011.

Important Addresses and Numbers

Tourist Information The main tourist information office is at the Hauptbahnhof, across from platform 23 (tel. 069/2128849). It's open Monday–Saturday 8 AM–10 PM (November–March until 9 PM), Sunday and holidays 9:30 AM–8 PM. Another information office is at the Hauptwache (tel. 069/2128708). It's open weekdays 9–6, Saturday 9–2. There are three information offices at the airport (in departure hall B, arrival hall B, and transit hall B). For information in advance of your trip, contact the **Verkehrsamt Frankfurt/Main** (Gutleutstr. 7–9, 6000 Frankfurt, tel. 069/2128849).

Consulates **U.S.:** Seismayerstrasse 21, tel. 069/74007. **U.K.:** Bockenheimer Landstrasse 51–53, tel. 069/72046.

Emergencies **Police:** tel. 110. **Doctor or Ambulance:** tel. 069/792–0200. **Dentist:** tel. 069/660727. **Pharmacy Information:** tel. 069/11500.

English Bookstores **British Bookshop:** Börsentrasse 17, tel. 069/280492. **Internationale Buchhandel:** Münchnerstrasse 56, tel. 069/252914.

Travel Agencies **American Express:** Steinweg 5, tel. 069/210548. **Thomas Cook:** Kaiserstrasse 11, tel. 069/13470.

Guided Tours

Orientation Tours Bus tours of the city, with English commentary, start at the north side of the main train station, at 10 and 2 daily from March through October; at 2 only from November to mid-December and from mid-January through February. The tour takes about three hours and costs DM 26 (half-price for children and senior citizens). A tour that takes in not only the main city sights but also some of the Taunus countryside starts at 11 daily from January through November (DM 34, half-price for children and senior citizens). On weekend afternoons, a gaily painted old streetcar, "The Ebbelwei Express", trundles around the city and Sachsenhausen, on the south side of the Main. The 40-minute ride—starting and ending at the Ostbahnhof train station, at Danzigerplatz in Frankfurt's Ostend district—includes a glass of apple cider (**Ebbelwei**) and a pretzel in the DM 3 fare. Further information and tickets can be obtained from the **Stadtwerke** (Rathenauplatz 3, tel. 069/13682425).

Excursions Bus tours of the surrounding countryside, as far as the Rhine, are offered by the **Reisebüro Wagon-Lits** (Kaiserstr. 72, tel. 069/7530010); the **Deutsche Touring GmbH.** (Am Römerhof 17, tel. 069/79031); and **DEMA Reisen GmbH.** (Tour Center, Karlsruhestr. 18, tel. 069/231322). One-day excursions are also offered by German Railways, the Bundesbahn. These are described in a brochure, *Der Schöne Tag*, obtainable from the main train station and the DER tourist office. A "Casino-Express" bus service runs daily from Frankfurt (departing from Baselerplatz) to the casino at Bad Homburg in the Taunus Mountains. The fare is deducted from the entrance charge to the casino. The bus departs hourly, from 2:15 to 11:15 PM.

Exploring Frankfurt

Numbers in the margin correspond with points of interest on the Frankfurt map.

At first glance, Frankfurt-am-Main doesn't seem to have much to offer the tourist. Virtually flattened by bombs during the war, it now bristles with skyscrapers, the visible sign of the city's role as West Germany's financial capital. Yet the inquisitive and discerning visitor will find many remnants of Frankfurt's illustrious past (besides being well placed for excursions to other historic cities, such as Heidelberg and Würzburg, and within easy reach of the Rhine).

Originally a Roman settlement, Frankfurt was later one of Charlemagne's two capitals (the other being Aachen). Still later, it was for centuries the site of the election and coronation of the emperors of that unwieldy entity, the Holy Roman Empire, which was the forerunner of a united Germany. It was also the birthplace of the poet and dramatist Goethe (1749–1832). The house in which he was born is one of many restored and reconstructed old buildings that inject a flavor of bygone days into the center of this busy modern city.

Although the true center of Frankfurt is its ancient **Römerberg Square,** where the election of Holy Roman emperors was traditionally proclaimed and celebrated, this tour of the city begins
➊ slightly to the north, at the **Hauptwache,** an 18th-century guardhouse that today serves a more peaceful purpose as a café, with a city information center on the lower ground floor. The printed material you can pick up here is in English and includes a recommended tour of the city, which is followed on these pages for much of its route.

➋ Head south along Kornmarkt, passing on the left the **Church of St. Catherine**—historic center of Frankfurt Protestantism. After crossing Berlinerstrasse, and still heading south, you'll
➌ pass the **Paulskirche** (Church of St. Paul): It was here that the first all-German parliament convened in 1848, and the church is therefore an important symbol of German unity and democracy. Continue down Buchgasse and within a few minutes you're on the north bank of the river **Main.** Turn left toward the great iron bridge known as the **Eiserne Steg** and at the **Rententurm,** one of the city's medieval gates, bear left again and you'll arrive
➍ at the massive **Römerberg,** center of Frankfurt civic life over the centuries. In the center of the square stands the 16th-century **Fountain of Justitia** (Justice): At the coronation of Emperor Matthias in 1612, wine instead of water spouted from the stonework. The crush of people was so great, however, that the Germans have not repeated the trick since.

➎ Compared with many city halls, Frankfurt's **Römer** is a modest affair, with a gabled Gothic facade. It occupies most of one side of the square and is actually three patrician houses (the Alt-Limpurg, the Römer—from which it takes its name—and the Löwenstein). The mercantile-minded Frankfurt burghers used the complex not only for political and ceremonial purposes, but for trade fairs and commerce.

The most important events to take place in the Römer, however, were the elections of the Holy Roman emperors. The **Kaisersaal** (banquet hall) was last used in 1792 to celebrate the

Frankfurt

election of Emperor Francis II, who was later forced to abdicate by arch-egomaniac Napoleon Bonaparte. (A 16-year-old Goethe smuggled himself into the banquet celebrating the coronation of Emperor Joseph II in 1765 by posing as a waiter.) Today, visitors can see the impressive full-length 19th-century portraits of the 52 emperors of the Holy Roman Empire that line the walls of the banqueting hall. *Admission: DM 1 adults, 25 pf children. Open Mon.–Sat. 9–5, Sun. 10–4.*

Charlemagne's son, Ludwig the Pious, established a church on the present site of the Römerberg in AD 850. His church was replaced by a much grander Gothic structure, one used for imperial coronations; it became known as the **Kaiserdom,** the Imperial Cathedral. The cathedral suffered little damage in World War II, and it still contains most of its original treasures, including a fine 15th-century altar.

On the south side of the square stands the 13th-century **Nikolaikirche** (St. Nicholas's Church). It's worth trying to time your visit to the square to coincide with the chimes of the glockenspiel carillon, which ring out three times a day. *Carillon chimes daily at 9, noon, and 5.*

From the Römerberg, stroll back down to the river, but turn right this time, past the riverside **Leonhardskirche** (St. Leonhard's Church), which has a fine 13th-century porch and a beautifully carved circa 1500 Bavarian altar, then into the narrow Karmelitergasse to the **Carmelite Monastery.** Within its quiet cloisters is the largest religious fresco north of the Alps, a 16th-century representation of the birth and death of Christ. *Open weekdays 8–4.*

From here, it's only a short way to the **Goethehaus und Goethemuseum** (Goethe's House and Museum). It was here that the poet was born in 1749, and though the house was destroyed by Allied bombing, it has been carefully restored and is furnished with pieces from Goethe's time, many belonging to his family. The adjoining museum contains a permanent collection of manuscripts, paintings, and memorabilia documenting the life and times of Germany's most outstanding poet. *Grosser Hirschgraben 23, tel. 069/282824. Admission: DM 3 adults, DM 1.50 children. Open Apr.–Sept., 9–5:30, Sun. 10–1; Oct.–Mar., 9–4, Sun. 10–1.*

From the Goethehaus, retrace your steps to the Hauptwache via Rossmarkt. From there, take a window-shopping stroll past the elegant boutiques of Goethestrasse, which ends at Opernplatz and Frankfurt's reconstructed opera house, the **Alte Oper.** Wealthy Frankfurt businessmen gave generously for the construction of the opera house in the 1870s (provided they were given priority for the best seats), and Kaiser Wilhelm I traveled from Berlin for the gala opening in 1880. Bombed in 1944, the opera house remained in ruins for many years while controversy raged over its reconstruction. The new building, in the classical proportions and style of the original, was finally opened in 1981, but burned down six years later. It has again been reconstructed, and opens to the public on January 1, 1991.

Time Out For a quick, tasty snack, make for nearby **Fressgass** (literally "Food Street"), a gourmet shopper's paradise.

12 Just around the corner from Fressgass is the Frankfurt **Börse,** Germany's leading stock exchange and financial powerhouse. It was founded by Frankfurt merchants in 1558 to establish some order in their often chaotic dealings. Today's dealings can also be quite hectic; see for yourself by slipping into the visitors' gallery. *Gallery open weekdays 11:30–1:30.*

From the stock exchange, turn south again and retrace your steps via the Hauptwache to the river (if you have the energy, Frankfurt's main shopping street, the **Zeil,** stretches eastward from the Hauptwache). Across the Main lies the district of **Sachsenhausen.** It's said that Charlemagne arrived here with a group of Saxon families in the 8th century and formed a settlement on the banks of the Main. It was an important bridgehead for the crusader Knights of the Teutonic Order, and, in 1318, officially became part of Frankfurt. Cross to Sachsenhausen
13 over the **Alte Brücke.** Along the bank to your left you'll see
14 the 15th-century **Kuhhirtenturm,** the only remaining part of Sachsenhausen's original fortifications. The composer Paul Hindemith lived and worked in the tower from 1923 to 1927.

The district still has a medieval air, with narrow back alleys and quiet squares that have escaped the destructive tread of the city developer. Here you'll find Frankfurt's famous *Ebbelwei* taverns. Look for a green pine wreath over the entrance to tell passersby that a freshly pressed—and alcoholic —apple juice is on tap. You can eat well in these little inns, too.

Time Out The locals have been eating and drinking well for more than a century in **Zum Fichtekränzl** (Wallstr. 5). Join them in the tavern's cozy dining room, and you'll soon understand why the place is so popular.

No fewer than seven top-ranking museums line the Sachsenhausen side of the Main, on **Schaumainkai** (locally known as the Museum Bank). These range from exhibitions of art
15 and architecture to the German Film Museum. The **Städelsches Kunstinstitut und Städtische Galerie** (Städel Art Institute and Municipal Gallery) has one of the most significant art collections in Germany, with fine examples of Flemish, German, and Italian old masters, plus a sprinkling of French Impressionists. *Schaumainkai 63. Admission: DM 2. Open Tues.–Sun. 10–5 (Wed. until 8).*

Dining

Several Frankfurt restaurants close for the school summer vacation break, a six-week period that falls between mid-June and mid-September. Always check to avoid disappointment.

For details and price category definitions, *see* Dining in Staying in West Germany.

Expensive **Brückenkeller.** *Keller* is German for cellar, and that's where the Brückenkeller is situated. The ancient vaulted interior (the restaurant has been in business since 1652) is set off by carefully selected antiques. The wine-list choice of 180 different labels is supported by an extraordinary stock of 85,000 bottles. Ask for a look at the wine cellar—and ask, too, for *Tafelspitz* (a version of pot roast) with *grüner* sauce. *Schützenstr. 6, tel. 069/ 284238. Reservations advised. AE, DC, MC, V. Dinner only. Closed Sun. and 3 weeks in July.*

Gutsschanke Neuhof. About 12½ kilometers (8 miles) south of Frankfurt (take the A661 to the Dreieich exit), Gutsschanke Neuhof is part of a country estate. The elegant dining room offers an eclectic mix of German and international dishes. The estate farm supplies the restaurant with home-cured meats, which can be bought and taken home as well as ordered from the extensive menu. *6072 Dreieich-Götzenhain, tel. 06102/3214. Reservations advised. AE, DC, MC, V.*

Humperdinck. The nouvelle dishes of chef Willi Tetz depend on what he finds in the market each morning; everything, from salads to soup, is of guaranteed freshness. Engelbert Humperdinck—the 19th-century composer *(Hänsel und Gretel)*—used to live and work in the Grüneburg house it occupies. *Grüneburgweg 95, tel. 069/722122. Reservations advised. AE, DC, MC, V. Closed Sat. lunch, Sun., and summer school vacation.*

Moderate   **Bistrot 77.** Mainly Alsatian specialties are served at this bright,
★   light, and cheerful French restaurant in Sachsenhausen. Ask chef/owner Dominique Mosbach for her advice on what to order, and you won't go wrong. *Ziegelhüttenweg 1–3, tel. 069/614040. Reservations accepted. AE, DC, MC, V. Closed Sat. lunch, Sun., and mid-June–mid-July.*

Börsenkeller. French dishes dominate the menu of this centrally located eatery, which is on a pedestrian-only street close to the stock exchange. *Schillerstr. 11, tel. 069/281115. Reservations accepted. AE, DC, MC, V. Closed Sun.*

Casa Nova. The inviting exterior is fully matched by the cozy interior of this superior Italian restaurant, in an attractive Sachsenhausen house. Fish is prepared with imagination and skill, and if the pasta proves too plentiful, half-portions are willingly served. *Stresemannallee 38, tel. 069/632473. Weekend reservations required. MC. Closed Sat. and 2 weeks in Aug.*

Zum Bären. It's said that Geothe was a regular visitor to this popular 18th-century inn in the suburb of Hoechst. The menu has changed a lot since his time and is now under the excellent direction of Pauline Lauterbach. If it's a fine summer or autumn day, choose a table in the garden. *Schlossplatz 8, 6230 Hoechst, tel. 069/301524. Reservations advised. Dinner only. Closed Mon.*

Inexpensive   **Atschel.** A blackboard announces specialties of the day at this former apple-cider tavern in Sachsenhausen. If fish soup is chalked up, you're in luck—it's delicious. Atschel is not for the shy. Expect to eat at one of the long tables that retain the tavern style of this friendly restaurant. *Wallstr. 7, tel. 069/619201. No reservations. No credit cards.*

★   **Zum Gemalten Haus.** This is the real thing, a traditional wine tavern in the heart of Sachsenhausen. Its name means "At the Painted House," a reference to the frescoes that cover the place inside and out. In the summer and on fine spring and autumn days, the courtyard is the place to be (the inner rooms can get a bit crowded). But if you can't at first find a place at one of the bench-lined long tables, order an apple cider and hang around until someone leaves: It's worth the wait. *Schweizerstr. 67, tel. 069/614559. Reservations not needed. No credit cards. Closed Mon. and Tues.*

Zum Rad. This 19th-century apple-cider tavern serves inexpensive but tasty local dishes in the picturesque village of Seckbach on the outskirts of Frankfurt (take the subway line 4 to Seckbacher Landstrasse and then bus no. 43 or 12). In summer and on fine spring and autumn days, the tree-shaded courtyard is a delight. *Leonhardtsgasse 2, tel. 069/479128. Reservations not needed. No credit cards. Dinner only.*

Zur Eulenburg. Take the subway or a streetcar to Seckbacher Landstrasse, in the district of Bornheim, to visit this popular apple-cider tavern. You'd better be hungry, though: portions are on the caveman side. Meat dishes cram the menu—try the Frankfurt-style *Rippchen* (ribs). *Eulengasse 46, tel. 069/451203. Reservations not needed. No credit cards. Dinner only. Closed Mon. and Tues.*

Lodging

For details and price category definitions, *see* Lodging in Staying in West Germany.

Very Expensive
★

Gravenbruch Kempinski. This spacious, elegant hotel retains the atmosphere of the manor house that once stood on its parkland site in leafy Neu Isenburg (a 15-minute drive south of Frankfurt). Some of its luxuriously appointed rooms and suites are arranged as duplex penthouse apartments. Make sure you get a room overlooking the lake. *6078 Neu Isenburg 2, tel. 06102/5050. 317 rooms with bath. Facilities: restaurant, indoor and outdoor pools, tennis, health spa, hairdresser, Lufthansa check-in service, limo service to airport and city (both 15 minutes away). AE, DC, MC, V.*

Hessischer Hof. This former palace is still owned by a prince of Hesse, and fine antiques are deftly positioned in many guest rooms. A daily supply of fresh fruit delivered to all rooms is part of the outstanding service. One of the two bars, Jimmy's, numbers among Frankfurt's best, and the hotel restaurant is highly prized both for its gourmet cuisine and refined ambience. *Friedrich-Ebert-Anlage 40, tel. 069/75400. 167 rooms with bath. Facilities: restaurant, 2 bars. AE, DC, MC, V.*

Steigenberger Hotel Frankfurter Hof. The presidential suite here is as spacious as a house, while the other guest rooms and suites are by no means cramped. All are impeccably furnished in teak and cherry wood. A majestic building in true "grande dame" style, the hotel stands in the downtown area. *Am Kaiserplatz 17, tel. 069/21502. 359 rooms with bath. Facilities: restaurant, shopping arcade. AE, DC, MC, V.*

Expensive

Palmenhof. The city's west end houses this turn-of-the-century hotel that has recently been renovated to a very high standard. In the basement is a cozy restaurant, the Bastei, which has an expensive nouvelle menu. *Bockenheimer Landstr. 89–91, tel. 069/7530060. 50 rooms with bath. Facilities: restaurant. AE, DC, MC, V.*

Moderate

Arcade. The modern Arcade is situated on the north bank of the Main river, just 5 minutes' walk from the train station. Rooms are furnished basically, though all have TV, and two are specially equipped for disabled guests. *Speicherstr. 3–5, tel. 069/273030. 193 rooms with bath. Facilities: restaurant, bar. MC, V.*

Liebig. A comfortable, family-run hotel, the Liebig has spacious, high-ceilinged rooms and a friendly feel. Be sure to ask for a room at the back—they're much quieter. The Weinstube restaurant serves an excellent Hessen wine. *Liebigstr. 45, tel.*

069/727551. 20 rooms with bath. Facilities: restaurant. DC, MC, V.

★ **Maingau.** This excellent-value hotel is in the city's Sachsenhausen district, within easy reach of the downtown area and just a stone's throw from the lively Altstadt quarter, with its cheery apple-cider taverns. Rooms are spartanly furnished, though clean and comfortable, and some even have TV. *Schifferstr. 38–40, tel. 069/617001. 100 rooms with bath. Facilities: restaurant. AE, MC.*

Neue Kräme. This small, friendly hotel is located on a quiet pedestrians-only street right in the downtown area. Rooms are basic, but all have TV and minibar. There's no restaurant, but drinks and snacks are available. *Neue Kräme 23, tel. 069/284046. 21 rooms with bath. AE, DC, MC, V.*

Inexpensive **Diana.** A pleasant residential area is the location of this family-run pension, convenient both for the Frankfurt fairground and the downtown area. *Westendstr. 83, tel. 069/747007. 29 rooms, 9 with bath. AE, DC, MC, V.*

Pension Uebe. This one occupies the top three floors of an office building on a street favored with some excellent restaurants. The elevator stops at the fourth floor, though by walking up just one extra flight of steps, you'll find yourself on the top floor, whose rooms are cozily and atmospherically set under the inclined eaves. *Grüneburgweg 3, tel. 069/591209. 18 rooms with bath. AE, DC, MC, V.*

Hamburg

Arriving and Departing

By Plane Hamburg's international airport, Fuhlsbüttel, is 11 kilometers (7 miles) northwest of the city. Lufthansa flights connect Hamburg with all other major German cities.

Between the Airport and Downtown A bus service between Hamburg's central bus station and the airport (stopping also at the hotels Atlantic and Plaza and the Schauspielhaus Theater) operates daily at 20-minute intervals between 5:15 AM and 9:30 PM. The first bus leaves the airport for the city at 6:30 AM. It takes about 25 minutes. One-way fare, including luggage, is DM 7. There is also an "Airport Express" bus, no. 110, which runs between the airport and the Ohlsdorf S-Bahn (suburban line) and U-Bahn (subway) station. The fare is DM 2.80. Taxi fare from the airport to the downtown area is about DM 25. By rented car, follow the signs to "Stadtmitte" (Downtown), which appear immediately outside the airport area.

By Train Hamburg is a terminus for mainline services to northern Germany; trains to Schleswig-Holstein and Scandinavia also stop here. There are two principal stations: the main train station (Hauptbahnhof) and Hamburg-Altona. Euro-City and Inter-City services connect Hamburg with all German cities and the European rail network. For train information, tel. 040/19419.

By Bus Hamburg's bus station, the Zentral-Omnibus-Bahnhof, is in Adenauerallee, behind the Hauptbahnhof. For tickets and information, contact the **Deutsche Touring Gesellschaft** (Am Römerhof 17, 6000 Frankfurt/Main, tel. 069/79030).

By Car Hamburg has proportionately fewer cars than most other German cities and an urban road system that is the envy of many of them. Incoming autobahns end at one of Hamburg's three beltways, which then connect easily with the downtown area ("Stadtmitte").

Getting Around

By Public Transportation The comprehensive city and suburban transportation system includes a subway network (U-Bahn), which connects efficiently with S-Bahn (suburban) lines, and an exemplary bus service. Tickets cover travel by all three, as well as by harbor ferry. A ticket costs DM 2 and can be bought at the automatic machines found in all stations and most bus stops. A 24-hour ticket for the central city zone costs DM 10 (children under 12 free). A 24-hour ticket covering the entire Hamburg urban area is DM 14 (children under 12 free). The all-night buses (nos. 600–640) tour the downtown area, leaving the Rathausmarkt and the Hauptbahnhof every hour. Information can be obtained from the **Hamburg Passenger Transport Board** (HHV), tel. 040/322911.

By Taxi Taxi meters start at DM 3.60, and the fare is DM 1.80 per kilometer (or about DM 2.88 per mile). To order a taxi, phone 040/441011, 040/656211, or 040/682001.

Important Addresses and Numbers

Tourist Information The principal Hamburg tourist office is at Bieberhaus, Hachmannplatz, near the Hauptbahnhof. It's open weekdays 7:30–6, Saturday 7:30–3 (tel. 040/300510). There's also a tourist information center inside the Hauptbahnhof itself (open daily 7 AM–11 PM, tel. 040/24870240) and in the arrivals hall of Hamburg Airport (open daily from 8 AM to 11 PM, tel. 040/50080). The last two centers will reserve hotel accommodations. **Hafen Tip** (at the St. Pauli-Landungsbrücken, tel. 040/30051200) provides information about the harbor and sells cruise tickets. It's open weekdays 9–6.

Consulates U.S.: Neuer Jungfernstieg 6a, tel. 040/411710. **U.K.:** Hervestehuder Weg 8a, tel. 040/446071.

Emergencies Police: tel. 110. **Doctor:** tel. 040/228022. **Dentist:** tel. 040/468-3260. **Dentist:** tel. 040/468-3260. **Ambulance:** tel. 112. **Pharmacy Information:** tel. 040/228022.

English Bookstores Frensche: Spitalerstrasse 26e, tel. 040/327585.

Travel Agencies **American Express:** Rathausmarkt 5, tel. 040/331141.

Guided Tours

Orientation Tours Bus tours of the city, with an English-speaking guide, leave from Kirchenallee (across from the Hotel Europäischer Hof and next to the Hauptbahnhof) at 11 and 3, from late March until the end of October, and at 2 during the winter months. The two-hour tour costs DM 18 for adults, DM 9 for children. A 2½-hour tour, taking in more of the city, starts at 10 and 2 daily from the same place. The fare is DM 22 for adults, DM 11 for children. A night tour of the city sets off from the Kirchenallee at 8 and returns shortly after midnight. The fare of DM 80 includes a drink at each stop and a short boat ride.

Boat Tours Hamburg is a city dominated by water, and one of the best ways of getting a feel of the place is by taking one of the many boat trips offered. From mid-March through November, tours of the harbor (with English-speaking guides) start twice a day (11:15 and 3:15) from pier 1 on the Landungsbrücken; the one-hour tour costs DM 11 for adults, DM 5.50 for children. During the winter months, tours with an English-speaking guide can be organized in advance (tel. 040/564523).

From Easter to Christmas, you can combine a nighttime cruise on the harbor, a lavish buffet, and a shuffle around the dance floor of the party boat, which leaves the HADAG pavilion on the Landungsbrücken every evening at 8 (tel. 040/313687). Cost is about DM 50.

Cruises of the Binnenalster and Aussenalster leave from the Jungfernstieg every half hour between 10 and 6, April–October. The fare is DM 9 for adults, DM 4 for children. A tour including canals leaves every 40 minutes (DM 15 and DM 7, respectively). For information, tel. 040/341141.

For general information on boat tours of Hamburg, tel. 040/2201201.

Excursions Bus tours of the surrounding countryside are offered by **Jasper-Reisebüro** (Colonnaden 72, tel. 040/343751).

Exploring Hamburg

The comparison that Germans like to draw between Hamburg and Venice is—like all such comparisons with the *Serenissima*—somewhat exaggerated. Nevertheless, Hamburg is, like Venice, a city on water: the great river Elbe, which flows into the North Sea; the small river Alster, which has been dammed to form two lakes, the Binnenalster and Aussenalster; and many canals. Once a leading member of the Hanseatic League of cities, which dominated trade on the North Sea and the Baltic during the Middle Ages, Hamburg is still a major port, with 33 individual docks and 500 berths for oceangoing vessels.

Apart from its aquatic aspects, the most striking thing about Hamburg is its contradictions. Within the remaining traces of its old city walls, Hamburg combines the seamiest, steamiest streets of dockland Europe with the sleekest avenues to be found anywhere between Biarritz and Stockholm. During World War II and afterward, Hamburg was wrecked from without and within—by fire, then by Allied bombing raids, and finally by philistine town planners, who tore down some of the remaining old buildings to make way for modernistic glass-and-steel boxes. The result is a city that is, in parts, ugly, but still a fascinating mixture of old and new.

It is also a city in which escaping the urban bustle is relatively easy, since it contains more than 800 kilometers (500 miles) of riverside and country paths within its boundaries. The following itinerary includes a few detours, some by boat, which will enhance your enjoyment of Hamburg.

Numbers in the margin correspond with points of interest on the Hamburg map.

❶ Hamburg's main train station, the **Hauptbahnhof,** is not only the start of the city tour but very much part of it. It's not often you are tempted to linger at a train station, but this is an exception. Originally built in 1906 and modernized since, it has a remarkable spaciousness and sweep, accentuated by a 148-meter (160-yard) wide glazed roof, the largest unsupported roof in Germany. Gather city travel guides and maps from the city tourist office here and ride one stop on the S-Bahn (suburban railroad) to the Dammtor station. Compare this Art Nouveau—style building with the one you've just left. You'll find splendid examples of Germany's version of Art Nouveau, the *Jugendstil*, throughout your tour of Hamburg.

The Dammtor station brings you out at a narrow stretch of parkland that runs for more than a mile alongside what was once the western defense wall of the city. The first two sections **②** of the park—the **Alter Botanischer Garten** (Old Botanical **③** Garden) and the **Planten un Blomen**—have lots to attract the attention of gardeners and flower lovers. In summer, the evening sky over the Planten un Blomen lake is lighted up by the colored waters of its fountain, dancing what the locals romantically call a "water ballet."

The park is interrupted abruptly by the northern edge of the **St. Pauli** district and its most famous—or infamous— **④** thoroughfare, the **Reeperbahn** *(see* Nightlife). Unlike other business sections of Hamburg, this industrious quarter works around the clock; although it may seem quiet as you stroll down its tawdry length in broad daylight, any male tourist who stops at one of its bars will discover that many of the girls who work this strip are on a day shift.

If it's a Sunday morning, join the St. Pauli late revelers and the **⑤** early joggers and dog-walkers for breakfast at the **Fischmarkt** (fish market), down at the Elbe riverside between the St. Pauli Landungsbrücken (the piers where the excursion boats tie up) and Grosse Elbstrasse. The citizens of Hamburg like to breakfast on raw herring, but if that's not to your taste, there's much more than fish for sale, and the nearby bars are already open. *The fish market is held every Sun., 5 AM–9:30 AM, starting an hour later in winter.*

⑥ The nearby **Landungsbrücken** is the start of the many boat trips of the harbor that are offered throughout the year *(see* Guided Tours).

Along the north bank of the Elbe is one of the finest walks Hamburg has to offer. The walk is a long one, about 13 kilometers (eight miles) from the St. Pauli Landungsbrücken to the **⑦** attractive waterside village of **Blankenese,** and that's only three-quarters of the route. But there are S-Bahn stations and bus stops along the way, to give you a speedy return to the downtown area. Do, however, try to reach Blankenese, even if you have to catch an S-Bahn train from downtown to Blankenese station and walk down to the riverbank from there.

Blankenese is another of Hamburg's surprises—a city suburb that has the character of a fishing village. If you've walked all the way from St. Pauli, you may not be able to face the 58 flights of stairs (nearly 5,000 individual steps) that crisscross through Blankenese between its heights and the river. But by all means attempt an exploratory prowl through some of the tiny lanes,

Hamburg

Tiergartenstr.
Moorwei
Lagerstr.
Jungiusstrasse
Planten un Blomen **3**
Schulterblatt
Stresemannstrasse
Schanzenstr.
Grabenstr.
Karolinenstrasse
Marseillerstr.
ES
Botanischer Garten **2**
Jungiusstrasse
Lerchenstr.
Marktstr.
Glashutten str.
B. D. Kirchhofen
Dammtorwall
Wohlwillstr.
Budapesterstr.
Neuer Kamp
Feldstrasse
Hölstenglacis
Gorch-Fock-Wall
Caffamacherreihe
Fuhlenwiete
Karl-Muck-Platz
Valentinskamp
Backerbreiterg
Paulinen-pl.
Heiligengeistfeld
Glacischaussee
Grasse Wallenlagen
Holstenwall
Speck str.
Pool-Str.
Kohlhofen
Hüten Pilatuspool
Neustädtstr.
Wohlwillstr.
Kurze-str.
Thielbeck
Rademacher Gang
Clemens Schultzstr.
ST. PAULI
Holstenwall
Peterstr.
Neanderstr.
Wexstrasse
Simon Von Utrechtstr.
Detlev Brennerstr.
Budapesterstr.
9
Hüten
Ater Steinweg
Reeperbahn
Hein Hoyerstr.
Millerntor Pl.
Reeperbahn
Neuer Steinweg
Stadthu
Ost-West-Str.
10
Spielbudenplatz
Davidstr.
Zirkusweg
Helgoländer Allee
Ost-West-Str.
Dustern
4
Gerstackerstr.
8
Herbstr.
Elb Park
Rothesoodstr.
Böhmkenstr.
Ro Mo
Bernhard Notchstr.
Seewartenstr.
Venusberg
Martin-Luther-str.
Herrengraben
Admiralität Str.
Rödings-Markt
7
5
Schaarsteinweg
Rödings-Markt
St-Pauli Hafenstr.
Stubbenhuk
Kajen
6
Ditmar Koelstr.
Johannis Bollwerk Vorsetzen
Neue Neuerweg
Stein Hof
Dr
0   1/4 mile
0   1/4 km
Elbe
Baumwall
Binnenhafen

Alter Botanishcer Garten, **2**
Bismarck Memorial, **8**
Blankenese, **7**
Fischmarkt, **5**
Hauptbahnhof, **1**
Jungfernstieg, **13**
Kunsthalle, **14**

Landungsbrücken, **6**
Museum für Hamburgische Geschichte, **9**
Planten un Blomen, **3**
Rathaus, **12**
Rathausmarkt, **11**
Reeperbahn, **4**
St. Michaelis, **10**

lined with the retirement retreats of Hamburg's sea captains and the cottages of the fishermen who once toiled here.

Time Out For a fine view and fine refreshment to accompany it, stop in at **Sägebiel's Fährhaus,** a former farmhouse, where Kaiser Wilhelm once celebrated his birthday. If you're lunching, fish is the natural choice. *Blankenese Hauptstr. 107, tel. 040/861514.*

A ferry connects Blankenese with Hamburg's St. Pauli, although the S-Bahn ride back to the city is much quicker. Back at St. Pauli, resume your tour at the riverside and head back toward the downtown area through the park at the side of the
❽ Helgolander Allee, to the **Bismarck Memorial**—an imposing statue of the Prussian "Iron Chancellor," the guiding spirit of the 19th-century unification of Germany. Cross the square
❾ ahead of you and make for the **Museum für Hamburgische Geschichte** at Holstenwall 24. This fascinating display of Hamburg's history has a feature of great interest to American descendants of German immigrants, who can arrange to have called up from the microfilm files information about any ancestors who set out for the New World from Hamburg. *Holstenwall 24, tel. 040/349122360. Admission: DM 3 adults, 70 pf. children. Open Tues.–Sun. 10–5.*

Cross Holstenwall to Peterstrasse, where you'll find a group of finely restored, 18th-century half-timbered houses. Turn right down Neanderstrasse and cross Ost-West-strasse to
❿ Hamburg's principal Protestant church, **St. Michaelis,** decorated in a florid Baroque style. Twice in its history, this well-loved 17th-century church has given the people of Hamburg protection—during the Thirty Years' War and again in World War II. From its 440-foot (134-meter) tower, there is a magnificent view of the city and the Elbe, and twice a day the watchman blows a trumpet solo from up there. *Cost for the elevator up to the tower: DM 2.50 adults, DM 1.50 children.*

From St. Michaelis, recross Ost-West-strasse and turn left down Brunnenstrasse to Wexstrasse. At the end of Wexstrasse, cross the Bleichenbrücke and Adolphsbrücke (Bleichen and Adolph bridges), over two of Hamburg's canals (known as the Fleete), turn left into Alter Wall, and you'll come
⑪ to the **Rathausmarkt,** the town hall square. The designers of the square deliberately set out to create a northern version of the Piazza San Marco in Venice and, to a certain extent, suc-
⑫ ceeded. The 100-year-old **Rathaus** is built on 4,000 wooden piles sunk into the marshy ground beneath. It is the home not only of the city council but of the Hamburg state government, for Hamburg is one of West Germany's federal, semiautonomous states. The sheer opulence of its interior is hard to beat. Although visitors can tour only the state rooms, the tapestries, huge staircases, glittering chandeliers, coffered ceilings, and gilt-framed portraits convey forcefully the wealth of the city in the last century and give a rich insight into bombastic municipal taste. *Marktplatz. Admission: DM 1. Guided tours in English weekdays every halfhour 10:15–3:15, weekends 10:15–1:15.*

If you've had enough sightseeing by this time, you've ended up at the right place, for an arcade at the western edge of the Rathausmarkt signals the start of Europe's largest undercover shopping area, nearly a mile of airy arcades, cool in summer and warm in winter, bursting with color and life. Three hundred shops, from cheap souvenir stores to expensive fashion boutiques, are crammed into this consumer-age labyrinth. There are expensive restaurants and cozy cafés, and one of the rare opportunities in Germany (or anywhere) to eat lobster and sip good wine at a fast-food outlet. It's easy to get lost here, but all the arcades lead at some point to the wide, seasidelike promenade, the **Jungfernstieg**, which borders Hamburg's two artificial lakes, the **Binnenalster** and the **Aussenalster.** Although called lakes, they are really dammed-up sections of the Alster River, which rises only 56 kilometers (35 miles) away in Schleswig Holstein. The river was originally dammed up at the beginning of the 13th century to form a millrace before it spilled into the Elbe. The original muddy dam wall is today the elegant Jungfernstieg promenade. From the Jungfernstieg, you can take a boat tour of the two Alster lakes and the canals beyond (*see* Guided Tours), passing some of Hamburg's most ostentatious homes, with their extensive grounds rolling down to the water's edge (the locals call it "Millionaires' Coast").

Hamburg has its share of millionaires, enriched by the city's thriving commerce and industry. But they, in turn, can claim to have enriched the artistic life of Hamburg. For example, it was a group of wealthy merchants who, in 1817, founded the Kunstverein, from which grew Hamburg's famous Kunsthalle collection. The **Kunsthalle** is well placed at the end of our Hamburg tour, next to the Hauptbahnhof, and its collection of paintings is one of Germany's finest. You'll find works by practically all the great northern European masters from the 14th to the 20th centuries, as well as by painters such as Goya, Tiepolo, and Canaletto. For many visitors, the highlight of the entire collection is the *Grabow Altarpiece*, painted in 1379 by an artist known only as Master Bertram; the central scene is the Crucifixion, but numerous side panels depict the story of man from genesis to the nativity. *1 Glockengiesserwall, tel. 040/248251. Admission: DM 4 adults, DM 1 children. Open Tues.–Sun. 10–5.*

Dining

For details and price category definitions, *see* Dining in Staying in West Germany.

Expensive **L'Auberge Française.** Generally regarded as Hamburg's most authentic French restaurant, L'Auberge Française specializes in traditional seafood dishes and fine wines. *Rutschbahn 34, tel. 040/4102532. Reservations required. DC, MC, V. Closed weekends in summer.*

Landhaus Dill. Situated in a former coaching inn on the road to Blankenese (*see* Exploring), Landhaus Dill is an informal restaurant with an imaginative and varied menu. In summer, specialties include lobster salad, prepared at your table; in fall, wild duck with port wine sauce. *Elbchaussee 404, tel. 040/828443. Reservations advised. AE, DC, MC, V. Closed Mon.*

Landhaus Scherrer. A popular, country house-style restaurant located in the city's Altona district, Landhaus Scherrer specializes in fine regional cuisine and prides itself on its extensive wine list. It offers a separate bistro for lunches. *Elbchaussee 130, tel. 040/8801325. Reservations required. AE, DC, MC. Closed Sun.*

★ **La Mer.** Located in the elegant Hotel Prem, on the southwest bank of the Aussenalster, La Mer offers a fine and varied menu. Chef Rainer Wolter, Germany's 1986 New Chef of the Year, serves a host of sumptuous specialties. Try the marinated inoki mushrooms with imperial oysters and salmon roe or the spring venison with elderberry sauce. *An der Alster 9, tel. 040/ 241726. Reservations advised. AE, DC, MC, V. Closed Sat. and Sun. lunch.*

Peter Lembcke. This formal, traditional restaurant offers the best of German cuisine. The imaginative menu features such Hamburg delicacies as eel soup and *Röte Grütze*, a mélange of sweet and sour berries. Steaks are another specialty. *Holzdamm 49, tel. 040/243290. Reservations advised. AE, DC, MC. Closed Sun.*

Moderate **Ahrberg.** Located on the river in Blankenese, the Ahrberg has a
★ pleasant terrace for summer dining, and, for a warm retreat on cooler days, a cozy, wood-paneled dining room. The menu features a range of traditional German dishes and seafood specialties—often served together. Try the shrimp and potato soup and fresh carp in season. *Strandweg 33, tel. 040/860438. Reservations advised. AE, DC, MC.*

★ **Le Château.** Visitors to this traditional French restaurant, located in a modernized, 19th-century mansion in fashionable Poseldorf, can enjoy cuisine prepared by a former chef at Maxim's in Paris—for a fraction of the price. *Milchstr. 19, tel. 040/ 444200. Reservations advised. Closed Sat. and Sun. lunch.*

Marktplatz. It takes some finding in the suburb of Nienstedten, but it's well worth the search. The restaurant is in a traditional old farmhouse, and the menu matches its authentic rustic style. *Nienstedtener Marktplatz 21, tel. 040/829848. Reservations advised at weekends.*

Tre Fontane. At this fine Italian restaurant, the lady of the house prepares all the dishes herself, and she and her husband are happy to advise guests on the specials of the day. Be prepared for portions. *Mundsburger Damm 45, tel. 040/223193. Reservations advised. No credit cards. Closed Tues.*

Inexpensive **At Nali.** This is one of Hamburg's oldest and most popular Turkish restaurants. It is friendly and comfortable and offers a very reasonable and extensive menu. It stays open late—until 2 AM. *Rutschbahn 11, tel. 040/4103810. Reservations advised. AE, DC, MC, V.*

Avocado. This popular, modern restaurant offers excellent value and an imaginative menu. Try the salmon in Chablis. *Kanalstr. 9, tel. 040/2204599. Reservations required. No credit cards. Diner only. Closed Sun.*

Lodging

For details and price category definitions, *see* Lodging in Staying in West Germany.

Very Expensive **Atlantic.** Since it first opened in 1909, the luxuriously appointed Atlantic has been a focal point of the Hamburg social scene. Two restaurants offer a choice between haute cuisine and traditional German fare. *An der Alster 72, tel. 040/28880. 265 rooms with bath. Facilities: rooftop pool, nightclub, bar, beer tavern, Lufthansa check-in desk. AE, DC, MC, V.*

Hamburg Marriott. The U.S. Marriott group chose downtown Hamburg as the site of its first hotel in West Germany. It opened in 1988 amid the city's shopping arcades and smart restaurants. Among its many refinements is a floor reserved for nonsmokers. *ABC-Str. 52, Kleiner Gänsemarkt, tel. 041/ 35050. 278 rooms with bath. Facilities: pool, sauna, solarium, fitness center, restaurant, sea grill, piano loungs, café. AE, DC, MC, V.*

★ **Vier Jahreszeiten.** This hotel, with its antique-style rooms, impeccable service, and excellent food, is rated among the world's best. It is currently being remodeled to increase the size of the rooms. Centrally located, it offers scenic views of the Binnenalster. An attractive, wood-paneled lounge provides a welcome haven for weary sightseers. *Neuer Jungfernstieg 9– 14, tel. 040/34941. 150 rooms with bath. Facilities: two restaurants, nightclub, pâtisserie, farm. AE, DC, MC, V.*

Expensive **Abtei.** Located on a quiet, tree-lined street near the Alster lakeside park, the Abtei occupies an elegant period house with a tea salon and pretty garden. *Abteistr. 14, tel. 040/345-7565. 14 rooms with bath. AE, DC, MC, V.*

Aussen Alster. Only seven minutes from the train station and 46½ meters (50 yards) from the Alster Lake, the Aussen Alster is a small, tranquil hotel occupying a gracious 19th-century house. Many of the rooms have balconies with scenic views. Bicycles and sailboats stand ready for sporting guests, and the hotel will even provide tracksuits for joggers. *Schmilinskystr. 1, tel. 040/241557. 27 rooms with bath. Facilities: sauna, solarium. AE, DC, MC, V.*

Moderate **Baseler Hospiz.** Centrally located near the inner lake and the State Opera House, the Baseler Hospiz offers friendly and efficient service and neatly furnished rooms. There is no charge for children under 10 sharing a room with parents. *Esplanade 11, tel. 040/341921. 160 rooms, most with bath. Facilities: restaurant, meeting rooms. AE, DC, MC, V.*

Steen's. This is a small, intimate hotel decorated in a light, airy Scandinavian style. It is conveniently located, close to the main train station. Guests enjoy breakfast in a pleasant garden. *Holzdamm 43, tel. 040/244642. 11 rooms with bath. AE, MC.*

Wedina. This is a somewhat old-fashioned but comfortable hotel. It has a bar, pool, sauna, and garden but no restaurant. *Gurlittstr. 23, tel. 040/243011. 23 rooms, most with bath. AE, DC, MC, V. Closed Dec. 18–Jan. 1.*

Inexpensive **Alameda.** The Alameda offers guests good, basic accommodations. All rooms feature TV and radio. *Colonnaden 45, tel. 040/ 344290. 18 rooms with shower. AE, DC, MC, V.*

Metro Merkur. Centrally located near Hamburg's main train station, the recently renovated Metro Merkur is a convenient, functional hotel. There is no restaurant, but the bar offers a selection of evening snacks and warm dishes. *Bremer Reihe 12– 14, tel. 040/247266. 109 rooms, most with bath. AE, DC, MC, V.*

Nightlife

Few visitors can resist taking a look at the Reeperbahn, if only by day. At night, however, from 10 onward, the place really shakes itself into life, and *everything* is on sale. Among the Reeperbahn's even rougher side streets, the most notorious is the Grosse Freiheit, which means "a lot of freedom." A stroll through this small alley, where the attractions are on display behind plate glass, will either tempt you to stay or send you straight back to your hotel. Three of the leading clubs on the Grosse Freiheit are the **Colibri** (No. 34, tel. 040/313233), the **Safari** (no. 24, tel. 040/315400), and the **Salambo** (no. 11, tel. 040/315622).

A few tips for visiting the Reeperbahn: Avoid going alone; demand a price list whenever you drink, keep firm hold of it, and pay as soon as you're served; if you have trouble, threaten to call the cops. If that doesn't work—call the cops.

West Berlin

Arriving and Departing

By Plane Because of West Berlin's unique position in the heart of the foreign territory of the German Democratic Republic, the easiest way to arrive is by plane. Tegel Airport is centrally located, only seven kilometers (four miles) from downtown.

Between the Airport and Downtown An airport bus, city line no. 9, runs at 10-minute intervals between the airport and central Kurfürstendamm and Budapesterstrasse. The fare for the 40-minute trip is DM 2.20. The taxi fare runs between DM 15 and DM 20. If you've rented a car at the airport, take the "Stadtautobahn" highway, which runs directly from the airport to the center.

By Train A transit visa is required for train travel to West Berlin; this is obtained on the train. The train service is run by the East German railways, called the Deutsche Reichsbahn, although half the rolling stock is West German. There are five rail crossing points from West Germany into East Germany, and the West Berlin terminus for all lines is the Bahnhof Zoologischer Garten (the Bahnhof Zoo), the main train station. The Bahnhof Zoo connects directly with the U-Bahn (subway) and S-Bahn (metropolitan railway) networks and the city bus system. For information or bookings in West Berlin, call the Deutsche Reichsbahn (030/313–3055 or 030/300–433).

By Bus Long-distance bus services connect West Berlin with all West German cities and, through the Europabus network, with the rest of Europe. A transit visa is issued at the border; have your passport ready. The city's bus station is at the corner of Masurenallee and Messedamm. For information, call 030/30882.

By Car The officially designated transit roads between West Germany and West Berlin must be strictly followed by drivers, and stops can be made only at clearly marked parking areas and service stations. There are four road-crossing points, and the necessary transit visa is obtained at the border before the driver from the west is allowed through. Western motorists must also produce a passport, driver's license, and car registration papers.

Getting Around

By Public Transportation West Berlin is surprisingly large, and only the center can comfortably be explored on foot. Fortunately, the city is blessed with excellent public transportation, a combination of U-Bahn (subway) and S-Bahn (metropolitan train) lines, bus services, and even a ferry across the Wannsee lake. The eight U-Bahn lines alone have 116 stations. An all-night bus service (the buses are marked by the letter N next to their number) is also in operation. A ticket (DM 2.30 adults, DM 1.50 children) covers travel on the entire system. A multiple ticket, valid for five trips, costs DM 10.50 (DM 6.50 children), but the best deal for visitors is the 24-hour inner-city ticket, costing DM 8 (DM 5 children). A two-day ticket costs DM 16 (DM 9.50 children) and a four-day ticket costs DM 32 (DM 19 children). A 24-hour ticket covering the entire area of West Berlin (including lake travel) costs DM 14.50 (DM 7.30 children). Information can be obtained from the office of the city transport authority, the Berliner Verkehrsbetriebe (BVG) at Hardenbergplatz, in front of the Bahnhof Zoo, or by calling 030/216–5088.

By Taxi Taxi meters start at DM 3.40 and the fare is DM 1.58 per kilometer (DM 1.69 after midnight). Taxi drivers charge 50 pf for each piece of heavy luggage carried. A drive along the Kurfürstendamm will cost about DM 10. Taxis can be ordered by telephone: Call 030/6902, 030/216–060, 030/261–026, or 030/240–202.

Important Addresses and Numbers

Tourist Information The main tourist office is at the Europa Center, Budapesterstrasse, tel. 030/262–6031. It's open daily 7:30 AM–10:30 PM. There are other offices at the main hall of Tegel airport, tel. 030/41012306, open daily 8 AM–11 PM; the Bahnhof Zoo, the main train station, tel. 030/313–9063, open daily 8 AM–11 PM; and at the border crossing point Dreilinden, tel. 030/803–9057, open daily 8 AM–11 PM. Accommodations can be reserved at all offices, which also issue a free English-language information brochure, *Berlin Turns On*. Pretravel information on Berlin can be obtained by writing to the Verkehrsamt Berlin, Europa Center, D-1000 Berlin 30.

Consulates U.S.: Clayallee 170, tel. 030/832–4087. **Canada:** Europa-Center, tel. 030/261–1161. **U.K.:** Uhlandstrasse 7/8, tel. 030/309–5292.

Emergencies Police: tel. 030/110. **Ambulance and emergency medical attention:** tel. 030/310–031. **Dentist:** tel. 030/1141. **Pharmacies:** for emergency pharmaceutical assistance, tel. 030/1141.

English Bookstores **Marga Schoeller,** Knesebeckstrasse 33, tel. 030/881–1112; **Buchhandlung Kiepert,** Hardenbergstrasse 4–5, tel. 030/311–0090.

Guided Tours

By Bus Bus tours of West and East Berlin are offered by a number of West Berlin operators, the chief of which are **Severin & Kühn,** Kurfürstendamm 216, Charlottenburg, tel. 030/883–1015; **Berliner Bären Stadtrundfahrt,** Rankestrasse 35 (corner of Kurfürstendamm), tel. 030/213–4077; **Reisebüro Berolina,** Kurfürstendamm 220, tel. 030/883–3131; and **Bus Verkehr Berlin (BVB),** Kurfürstendamm 225, tel. 030/882–2063 or 030/882–6847). A two-hour tour of West Berlin costs about DM 20 and a combined tour of West and East Berlin about DM 50 (plus a fee of about DM 15 levied by the East Germans). There are also half-day tours to Potsdam and the SansSoucis palace, favorite residence of Frederick the Great, now in East German territory. Lunch is included in the DM 99 cost of the tour. Passports and early booking are essential for tours to East Berlin and Potsdam.

By Boat West Berlin is a city of waterways, and boat trips can be made on the Spree and Havel rivers and on the city's canals. For details, contact the city tourist office at the Europa Center, Budapesterstrasse, tel. 030/262–6031.

Exploring West Berlin

Visiting West Berlin is a bittersweet experience, as so many of the triumphs and tragedies of the past are tied up with the bustling present. The result can be either dispiriting or exhilarating. And by European standards, Berlin isn't that old: Cologne was more than 1,000 years old when Berlin was born from the fusion of two tiny settlements on islands in the river Spree. Although already a royal residence in the 15th century, Berlin really came into its own three centuries later, under the rule of King Friedrich II—Frederick the Great—whose liberal reforms and artistic patronage led the way as the city developed into a major cultural capital.

The events of the 20th century would have crushed the spirit of most other cities. Hitler destroyed the city's reputation for tolerance and plunged Berlin headlong into the war that led to wholesale destruction of monuments and houses. And after World War II, Berlin was still to face the bitter division of the city and the construction of the infamous wall.

Despite all this, West Berliners can revel and party as if there were no tomorrow—or perhaps as if there had been no yesterday. The city has recovered much of the artistic energy and social whirl of better times. In its crowded bars, cafés, and nightclubs and in the lake-studded parks and woodland, you can recall that this was once the capital of a free Europe.

Numbers in the margin correspond with points of interest on the West Berlin Map.

Bustling Kurfürstendamm, or Ku'damm as the Berliners call it, is one of Europe's greatest thoroughfares, throbbing with activity day and night. At its eastern end is the **Kaiser Wilhelm Gedächtniskirche** (Kaiser Wilhelm Memorial Church Tower). This landmark has come to symbolize not only West Berlin, but the futile destructiveness of war. The shell of the tower is all that remains of the church that was built at the end of the 19th century and dedicated to the memory of Kaiser Wilhelm. Inside is a historical exhibition of the devastation of World War II. *Admission: free. Open Tues.–Sat. 10–6, Sun. 11–6.*

Cross Budapesterstrasse to enter the **Zoologischer Garten,** Berlin's zoo. It has the world's largest variety of individual types of fauna along with a fascinating aquarium. *Admission: DM 9 adults, DM 5 children. Open daily from 9 to dusk or 7 PM (whichever is later).*

The zoo is set in the 255-hectare (630-acre) **Tiergarten Park,** which has at last recovered from the war, when it was not only ripped apart by bombs and artillery, but was stripped of its wood by desperate, freezing Berliners in the bitter cold of 1945–46. In the northern section of the park is the **Englischer Garten** (English Garden), which borders the riverside **Bellevue**

Schloss, a small palace built for Frederick the Great's brother: It is now the official West Berlin residence of the West German president.

④ The column in the center of a large traffic circle in the Tiergarten is the **Siegessäule** victory column, erected in 1873 to commemorate four Prussian military campaigns against the French. The granite and sandstone monument originally stood in front of the Reichstag (parliament), which was burned by Hitler's men in 1933. Climb the 285 steps to its 65-meter (210-foot) summit and you'll be rewarded with a fine view of West Berlin and, across the wall, East Berlin. *Admission: 50 pf adults, 10 pf children. Open Tues.–Sun. 9–6, Mon. 1–6.*

⑤ The Berlin Wall, ugly as it is, exerts a magnetic pull on any visitor to Berlin, so at the base of the Siegessäule, go east down the wide Strasse des 17 Juni, named in memory of the day, in 1953, when 50,000 East Germans staged an uprising that was put down by force. On the left, you'll pass the **Soviet Victory** monument, a semicircular colonnade topped with a statue of a Russian soldier and flanked by what are said to be the first Soviet tanks to have fought their way into Berlin in 1945. This monument is an important Soviet toehold in West Berlin: Red Army troops are permitted to guard it and the guard is changed every hour. (You can watch the goose-stepping ceremony from a discreet distance.)

⑥ Ahead of you is **Brandenburger Tor** (Brandenburg Gate), built in 1788 as a victory arch for triumphant Prussian armies. The horse-drawn chariot atop the arch was reerected after the war, still facing west, although the great monument is now some way into East German territory. The wall is at its thickest here, more than 1 meter (three feet) of tank-proof concrete. Viewing platforms allow you to peer over the ugly mass into East Berlin.

⑦ The most famous crossing point, **Checkpoint Charlie,** is a half-hour walk south then east along the wall. It's much easier to save time and effort and go by taxi from Brandenburg Gate. At Checkpoint Charlie, there's a museum that tells the history of the wall and describes (with exhibits and models) the ingenious escapes that have been made since it was built in 1961. *Checkpoint Charlie Museum, Friedrichstr. 44, tel. 030/251–4569. Admission: free. Open daily 9–8.*

⑧ Find the nearby Kochstrasse U-Bahn station and go two stops south on the U-6 line to Mehringdamm. Head for Kreuzbergstrasse. Just on the left is the 62-meter (200-foot) **Kreuzberg,** West Berlin's highest natural hill. (There are higher hills made of the rubble gathered from the bombed-out ruins of the city when reconstruction began in 1945.) On the sheltered southern slopes of the Kreuzberg is a vineyard that produces some of Germany's rarest wines: They are served only at official Berlin functions.

⑨ Bordering Kreuzberg to the west is the Schöneberg district, where you'll find the seat of the city and state government of West Berlin, the **Rathaus Schöneberg** (City Hall). In the belfry of the Rathaus is a replica of the Liberty Bell, donated to Berliners in 1950 by the United States and rung every day at noon. In a room at the base of the tower are stored 17 million American signatures expressing solidarity with West

West Berlin

Ägyptisches
Museum, **11**

Brandenburger Tor, **6**

Checkpoint Charlie, **7**

Englischer Garten, **3**

Gemädegalerie, **13**

Gipsformerei, **12**

Grunewald, **14**

Kaiser Wilhelm
Gedächtniskirche, **1**

Kreuzberg, **8**

Rathaus
Schöneberg, **9**

Schloss
Charlottenburg, **10**

Siegessäule (Victory
Column), **4**

Soviet Victory, **5**

Zoologischer Garten, **2**

Berlin, some, no doubt, inspired by President Kennedy's famous "Ich bin ein Berliner" speech, which he made here in 1963.

Time Out | While at the Rathaus, go downstairs to the **Ratskeller Schöneberg,** an inexpensive place to get a good, filling set-price lunch. The atmosphere is busy and friendly.

Take the U-Bahn north one stop from Rathaus Schöneberg station and change to the U-7 line for eight stops, to Richard-Wagner-Platz station. From the station, walk left for about 465 ⑩ meters (500 yards) to the handsome **Schloss Charlottenburg** (Charlottenburg Palace). Built at the end of the 17th century by King Frederick I for his wife, Queen Sophie Charlotte, the palace was progressively enlarged for later royal residents. Frederick the Great's suite of rooms can be visited; in one glass cupboard, you'll see the coronation crown he inherited from his father—stripped of jewels by the ascetic son, who gave the most valuable diamonds and pearls to his wife. *Schloss Charlottenburg, Luisenplatz, Charlottenburg. Admission: DM 4.50 adults, DM 2 children. Open Tues.–Sun. 10–5.*

⑪ Opposite the palace is the **Ägyptisches Museum** (Egyptian Museum), home of perhaps the world's best-known portrait sculpture, the beautiful Nefertiti. The 3,300-year-old Egyptian queen is the centerpiece of a fascinating collection of Egyptology that includes one of the finest preserved mummies outside Cairo. *Ägyptisches Museum, Schlossstr. 70, Charlottenburg. Admission: free. Open Sat.–Thurs. 9–5.*

If you like, you can take Nefertiti home with you. Behind ⑫ Schloss Charlottenburg is the **Gipsformerei** (State Museum Plaster Foundry), which will turn out a copy of any of a dozen masterpieces in stock. They're not cheap (portrait busts cost between DM 700 and DM 900), but how can you put a price on having Nefertiti on the mantelpiece? *Gipsformerei, Sophie-Charlotten-Str. 17/18, Charlottenburg. Open weekdays 9–4.*

Take U-Bahn line U-7 back toward Schöneberg until Fehrbelliner Pl., where you change to line U-2 southwest for five stops to Dahlem-Dorf station. This is the stop for West-⑬ Berlin's leading art museum, the **Gemädegalerie,** in the district of Dahlem. The collection includes many works by the great European masters, with 26 Rembrandts and 14 by Rubens. Or is it 25 Rembrandts? *The Man in the Golden Hat,* until recently attributed to Rembrandt, has now been ascribed to one of the great Dutch master's pupils. Does it really matter? Maybe not to the public, which still sees it as a masterpiece, but it could affect the value of the painting by a million or two. *Gemäldegalerie, Arnimallee 23/27, Dahlem. Admission: free. Open Tues.–Sun. 9–5.*

No visit to West Berlin is complete without an outing to the ⑭ city's outdoor playground, the **Grunewald** park. Bordering the Dahlem district to the west, the park is a vast green space, with meadows, woodlands, and lakes.ald park. Bordering the Dahlem district to the west, the park is a vast green space, with meadows, woodlands, and lakes. The city's total waterfront of 208 kilometers (130 miles) is longer than West Germany's Baltic Coast. There's even space for nudist beaches on the banks of the Wannsee lake, while in winter a downhill ski run and even a ski jump operate on the modest slopes of the Teufelsberg hill.

Dining

For details and price category definitions, *see* Dining in Staying in West Germany.

Expensive **Alt-Luxembourg.** There are only nine tables at this popular restaurant in the Charlottenburg district, and you'll receive attentive service. Chef Kurt Wannebacher uses only fresh ingredients and announces his daily specials on the blackboard. If lobster lasagna is chalked up, look no further. *Pestalozzistr. 70, tel. 030/323-8730. Reservations required. No credit cards. Closed Sun., Mon., two weeks in Jan., three weeks in July.*

★ **Bamberger Reiter.** Considered by Berliners to be the city's best restaurant, Bamberger Reiter is the pride of its chef, Franz Raneburger. He relies heavily on fresh market produce for his *neue deutsche Küche* (new German cuisine), so the menu changes from day to day. Fresh flowers, too, abound in his attractive, oak-beamed restaurant. *Regensburgerstr. 7, tel. 030/ 244282. Reservations required. No credit cards. Dinner only. Closed Sun., Mon., Aug. 1-20.*

Frühsammer's Restaurant an der Rehwiese. From your table, you can watch chef Peter Frühsammer at work in his open kitchen. He's ready with advice on the daily menu: Salmon is always a treat here. The restaurant is located in the annex of a turn-of-the-century villa in the southern district of Zehlendorf (U-Bahn to Krumme Lanke and then bus no. 53 to Rehwiese). *Matterhornstr. 101, tel. 030/803-2720. Reservations required. AE, DC, MC, V. Closed Dinner only. Sun., Mon.*

Moderate **Alt-Nürnberg.** Step into the tavernlike interior and you could be in Bavaria: The waitresses even wear dirndls. The Bavarian colors of blue and white are everywhere, and such Bavarian culinary delights as *Schweinshaxe* (knuckle of pork) are well represented on the menu. If you prefer to eat in the Prussian style, the calves' liver *Berliner Art* is recommended. *Europa Center, tel. 030/261-4397. No reservations. AE, DC, MC, V.*

★ **Blockhaus Nikolskoe.** Prussian King Wilhelm III built this Russian-style wooden lodge for his daughter Charlotte, wife of Russia's Czar Nicholas I. It's located in the south of the city, on the eastern edge of Glienicker Park. In summer, you can eat on the open terrace overlooking the Havel River. In character with its history and appearance, the Blockhaus features game dishes. *Nikolskoer Weg, tel. 030/805-2914. No reservations. AE, DC, MC, V.*

Forsthaus Paulsborn. Game is the specialty in this former woodsman's home deep in the Grunewald Forest. You dine here as the forester did—from an oak table in a great dining room and under the baleful eye of hunting trophies on the wall. Apart from game, the menu extends to various German and international dishes. *Am Grunewaldsee, tel. 030/813-8010. Reservations advised on weekends. AE, DC, MC, V. Closed Mon., dinner in winter (Oct.-Mar.).*

Hecker's Deele. You could find yourself seated in one of the antique church pews that complete the oak-beamed interior of this restaurant that features Westphalian dishes. The *Westfälische Schlachtplatte* (a variety of meats) will set you up for a whole day's sightseeing—the Ku'damm is right outside.

Grolmannstr. 35, tel. 030/88901. No reservations. AE, DC, MC, V.

Mundart Restaurant. Too many cooks don't spoil the broth (and certainly not the excellent fish soup) at this popular restaurant in the Kreuzberg district. Five chefs are at work in the spacious kitchen. Fortunately, they all agree on the day's specials, and you can follow their advice with impunity. *Muskauerstr. 33/34, tel. 030/612–2061. No reservations. No credit cards. Dinner only. Closed Mon., Tues.*

Inexpensive **Alt-Berliner Weissbierstube.** A visit to the Berlin Museum (a permanent historical exhibition on Berlin) must include a stop at this pub-style restaurant in the museum building. There's a buffet packed with Berlin specialties, and a jazz band plays on Sunday morning. *Berlin Museum, Lindenstr. 14, tel. 030/251–0121. No reservations. No credit cards. Closed Mon.*

Thürnagel. Also located in the Kreuzberg district, Thürnagel is a vegetarian restaurant where it's not only healthy to eat, but fun. The seitan in sherry sauce or the tempeh curry are good enough to convert a seasoned carnivore. *Gneisenaustr. 57, tel. 030/691–4800. No reservations. No credit cards. Dinner only.*

Lodging

For details and price category definitions, *see* Lodging in Staying in West Germany.

Very Expensive **Bristol Hotel Kempinski.** Located in the heart of the city, this grand hotel has the best of Berlin's shopping on its doorstep. English-style furnishings give the "Kempi" an added touch of class. All the rooms and suites are luxuriously decorated and equipped, with marble bathrooms, air-conditioning, and cable TV. Children under 12 stay for free if they share their parents' room. *Kurfürstendamm 27, tel. 030/884340. 325 rooms with bath. Facilities: 2 restaurants, indoor pool, sauna, solarium, masseur, hairdresser, limousine service. AE, DC, MC, V.*

CC-City Castle Apartment Hotel. The CC (short for "Congress Center," which is nearby) is a fine fin-de-siècle Berlin mansion, commanding a corner on the Ku'damm (ask for one of the many quiet rooms at the back). *Kurfüstendamm 160, tel. 030/8918005. 36 rooms with bath. Facilities: bar, restaurant. AE, DC, MC, V.*

★ **Intercontinental Berlin.** The "Diplomaten Suite" is expensive, but it is in a class of its own: It's as large as a suburban house and furnished in the Oriental style. The other rooms and suites are not so exotically furnished but still show individuality and exquisite taste. The lobby is worth a visit even if you're not tempted to stay overnight: It's a quarter the size of a football field, opulently furnished, and just the place for afternoon tea and pastries. *Budapesterstr. 2, tel. 030/26020. 600 rooms with bath. Facilities: 3 restaurants (including a rooftop garden), indoor pool, sauna, 24-hour room service, boutiques, Pan-Am check-in service. AE, DC, MC, V.*

Expensive **Berlin Excelsior Hotel.** Fixed rates that don't fluctuate with the seasons are offered by this modern, well-run establishment only five minutes from the Ku'damm. That means, however, that there are no special weekend offers (a usual feature of top German hotels). The comfortable rooms are furnished in dark teak, and the helpful front-office staff will arrange sightseeing tours and try to obtain hard-to-get theater and concert tickets.

Hardenbergerstr. 14, tel. 030/31991. 320 rooms with bath. Facilities: garden terrace, winter garden. AE, DC, MC, V.

★ **Palace.** The rooms here are comfortable and adequately furnished, but can't quite match the scale of the palatial lobby. Ask for a room on the Budapesterstrasse: The view is memorable. Or even take a suite with a whirlpool bath. The Palace is part of Berlin's Europa Center, and guests have free use of the center's pool and sauna. The Palace is popular with Americans. *Europa Center, tel. 030/269111. 160 rooms with bath. AE, DC, MC, V.*

Schweizerhof Berlin. There's a rustic, Swiss look about most of the rooms in this centrally located hotel, but they have a high standard of comfort and facilities. Ask to be placed in the west wing, where rooms are larger. Children stay for free if they are in their parents' room. The indoor pool is the largest of any Berlin hotel, and the hotel is opposite Tiergarten Park. *Budapesterstr. 21–31, tel. 030/26960. 430 rooms with bath. Facilities: sauna, solarium, fitness room, hairdresser, beauty salon. AE, DC, MC, V.*

Moderate **Casino Hotel.** The owner of the Casino is Bavarian, so his restaurant serves south German specialties. The hotel itself is a former Prussian military barracks but bears little evidence of its former role: Rooms are large and comfortable and well equipped. The hotel is located in the Charlottenburg district. *Königin-Elisabeth-Str. 47a, tel. 030/303090. 24 rooms with bath. AE, DC, MC, V.*

Ravenna. This small, friendly hotel is located in the Steglitz district, close to the Botanical Garden and the Dahlen Museum. All the rooms are well equipped, but suite 111B is a bargain: It includes a large living room and kitchen for the rate of only DM 200. *Grunewaldstr. 8–9, tel. 030/792–8031. 45 rooms with bath or shower. AE, DC, MC, V.*

Riehmers Hofgarten. Located in the interesting Kreuzberg district, this hotel in a late-19th-century building is a short walk from the Kreuzberg hill and has fast connections to the center of town. The high-ceilinged rooms are elegantly furnished. *Yorckstr. 83, tel. 030/781011. 21 rooms with bath or shower. AE, DC, MC, V.*

Inexpensive **Econtel.** Families are well cared for at this hotel that's situated within walking distance of Charlottenburg Palace. Lone travelers also appreciate the touches in the single rooms, which come with a trouser press and hair dryer. *Sommeringstr. 24, tel. 030/344001. 205 rooms with bath or shower. Facilities: snack bar. MC.*

The Arts

Today's Berlin has a tough task in trying to live up to the reputation it gained from the film *Cabaret*, but if nightlife is a little toned down since the '20s, the arts still flourish. Apart from the many hotels that book seats, there are three main ticket agencies: **Theaterkasse,** Kurfürstendamm 24; **Theaterkasse im Europa-Center;** and **Theaterkasse Centrum,** Mienekestrasse 25.

The Berlin Philharmonic, one of the world's leading orchestras, performs in the **Philharmonie,** Matthaikirchstrasse 1, tel. 030/254880. It plays a leading role in the annual festival months of August, September, and October. The **Deutsche Oper** (Opera House), by the U-Bahn stop of the same name, is the home of the opera and ballet companies. Tickets are hard to obtain, but call 030/341–4449 for information.

West Berlin is still Germany's drag-show capital, as you'll see if you go to **Chez Nous**, Marburgerstrasse 14. Next door (no. 15) the girls are for real at the **Scotch Club 13.**

Nightlife

Dschungel at Nürnbergerstrasse 53, is the number-one disco, and is funky and fun. For an escape from the usual disco sounds, try the **Blue Note** (Courbierestr. 13), which mixes jazz, bebop, and Latin American rhythms.

One of the best ways to feel the pulse of this exciting city is to visit one of the *Kneippen,* bars with a relaxed feel where you might hear some music or just sit outside with a beer or coffee.

The Rhine

None of Europe's many rivers is so redolent of history and legend as the Rhine, known in German as the Rhein. For the Romans, who established forts and colonies along its western banks, the Rhine was the frontier between civilization and the barbaric German tribes. Roman artifacts can be seen in museums throughout the region. The Romans also introduced viticulture—a legacy that survives in the countless vineyards along the riverbanks—and later, Christianity. Throughout the Middle Ages, the river's importance as a trade artery made it the focus of sharp, often violent, conflict between princes, noblemen, and archbishops. Many of the picturesque castles that crown its banks were the homes of robber barons who held up passing ships and barges and exacted heavy tolls to finance even grander fortifications.

For poets and composers, the Rhine—or "Vater (Father) Rhine," as the Germans call it—has been an endless source of inspiration. As legend has it, the Loreley, a treacherous, craggy rocks, was home to a beautiful and bewitching maiden who lured sailors to a watery grave. Wagner based four of his epic operas on the lives of the medieval Nibelungs, said to have inhabited the rocky banks. To travel the Rhine by boat, especially in autumn, when the rising mists enshroud the castles high above, is to understand the place the river occupies in the German imagination.

The Rhine does not belong to Germany alone. Its 1,312-kilometer (820-mile) journey takes it from deep within the Alps through Switzerland and Germany, into The Netherlands, and out into the North Sea. But it is in Germany—especially the stretch between Mainz and Bonn known as the Middle Rhine—that the riverside scenery is most spectacular. This is the "typical" Rhine: a land of steep and thickly wooded hills, terraced vineyards, tiny villages hugging the shore, and a succession of brooding castles.

A nine-hour steamer trip between Mainz and Bonn will give you a taste of this fabled region. But in order to really experience it, you will need to spend several days in the area. A town such as Koblenz provides a convenient base for excursions up and down the river and into the lovely Moselle Valley.

Getting Around

By Train One of the best ways to visit the Rhineland in very limited time is to take the scenic train journey from Mainz to Bonn along the western banks of the river. The views are spectacular, and the entire trip takes less than two hours. You can get on and off the train along the route. Most of the Rhine towns are also connected by bus services originating in Frankfurt and other major cities. For information about both train and bus services, contact **German National Railways** in Frankfurt, Reisedienst Friedrich-Ebert-Anlage 35, tel. 069/2651.

By Boat Passenger ships traveling up and down the Rhine and its tributaries offer a pleasant and relaxing way to see the region. **Köln-Düsseldorfer Steamship Company (KD)** operates a fleet of ships that travel between Düsseldorf and Mainz, daily from Easter to late October, and along the Moselle and Main rivers. They also offer cruises along the entire length of the Rhine. Passengers have a choice of buying an excursion ticket or a ticket to a single destination. For information about services, tel. 0221/20880. From March through November, **Hebel-Line** (tel. 06742/2420) offers a scenic cruise of the Loreley Valley; night cruises feature music and dancing. For information about Neckar River excursions, contact **Neckar Personen Schiffahrt** in Stuttgart, tel. 0711/541073 or 0711/541074.

By Car If you prefer to drive, the Rhineland offers a comprehensive highway network that takes in some of the region's most spectacular scenery. Roads crisscross the entire province, from the historic vineyards of the Mosel Valley to the beautiful castle and wine-growing country of the Rhine's west bank. For information about routes available, contact the **German Automobile Club**, Lyonerstr. 16, Frankfurt-am-Main 71, tel. 069/66061.

By Bicycle Another enjoyable and inexpensive way to see the country is by bicycle. Tourist offices in all the larger towns will provide information and route maps. German Railways also provides bicycle rental facilities on some of its routes. For information, tel. 069/2651. You can also take advantage of the myriad *Wanderwegen* (walking paths) running throughout the region. These are marked with signs depicting red or green grapes. Contact local tourist offices for information.

Tourist Information

Bacharach. Fremdenverkehrsamt, Oberstrasse 1, tel. 06743/2968.

Bonn. 2 Munsterstrasse 20, tel. 0228/773466 and LVV Rheinland, Rheinallee 69, Bad Godesberg, Bonn, tel. 0228/362921.

Boppard. Verkehrsamt, Karmeliterstrasse 2, tel. 06742/10319.

Koblenz. Fremden Verkehrsamt, Verkehrspavillon, tel. 0261/31304 and Fremdenverkehrsverband Rheinland-Pfalz, Postfach 1420, tel. 0261/31079.

Königswinter. Verkehrsamt, Drachenfelsstrasse 7, tel. 02223/21048.

Mainz. Verkehrsverein, Bahnhofstrasse 15, tel. 06131/233741.

Rüdesheim. Verkehrsamt, Rheinstrasse 16, tel. 06722/2962.

Guided Tours

In addition to a number of special-interest cruises, **KD** (Köln-Düsseldorfer) operates a series of guided excursions covering the towns along its routes (*see* above). The British-run **European Yacht Cruises Ltd.** conducts a variety of Rhine cruises, some with optional shore excursions (tel. in London 01/462–8843). The tourist offices in Mainz and Koblenz also offer tours (in English) of their respective cities.

Exploring the Rhine

Bonn **Bonn,** West Germany's capital city, marks the northern boundary of the Middle Rhine region. It offers a number of interesting historical sights and is a convenient spot from which to begin your tour of the Rhineland.

Like so many Rhine cities, Bonn began as a Roman settlement—called Castra Bonnensia—and last year celebrated its 2,000th anniversary. For 500 years—the 13th through the 18th centuries—it was the seat of power for the prince electors of Cologne. Its many Baroque monuments date from this later period. The most impressive Baroque building, the **Kurfürstliches,** houses the university. Other notable buildings include the **Rathaus** (City Hall), in the marketplace, the **Poppelsdorf Schloss** (Castle), and the **Kreuzberg Church.**

The center of Bonn is a maze of picturesque, winding streets and historic houses. Among them is Beethoven's birthplace. This is now a museum brimming with objects, instruments, and documents associated with the great composer. Among the most poignant are the ear trumpets he used in his battle against deafness. *Bonngasse 20, tel. 0228/635188. Admission: DM 1.50. Open Apr.–Sept., Mon.–Sat. 9–1, Sun. 9–1 and 3–6; Nov.–Mar., Mon.–Sat. 9:30–1 and 3–5, Sun. 10–1. Closed holidays.*

While you are in the Old Town center, stop in at the **Marktplatz,** the site of a colorful vegetable market. Nearby, on Münsterplace, is Bonn's oldest church, the **Münster of St. Martin.** Although it had to be heavily restored following severe bombing in World War II, it remains one of the Rhineland's best examples of Romanesque architecture. Bonn also offers a number of noteworthy museums. The **Rheinisches Landesmuseum** is a good place to get acquainted with the history and culture of the Rhine region. Exhibits include the famous Neanderthal skull. *Colmanstr. 16. Admission: DM 2. Open Tues.–Fri. 9–5 (9–8 Wed.) weekends and holidays 10–5.*

Just south of Bonn on the west side of the Rhine is **Bad Godesberg,** an ancient spa town and the center of Bonn's diplomatic community. The 32½ meter (105-foot) **Godesburgwatch Tower** is one of the last remaining fortifications of a 13th-century castle that stood here. Most of the fortress was destroyed in the 16th century.

Across the river from Bad Godesberg—accessible by bridge or car ferry—is **Königswinter,** site of one of the most-visited castles on the Rhine. The ruins of **Drachenfels** crown the highest hill in the **Siebengebirge** (Seven Hills) area, commanding a spectacular view of the river. The castle was built in the 12th

The Rhine

century by the archbishop of Köln. Its name—Drachenfels—
commemorates a dragon said to have lived in a nearby cave. As
legend has it, the dragon was slain by Siegfried, the
Niebelunglied hero. While you are in the area, visit the **Kloster
Heisterbach,** a Cistercian monastery about two miles from
Königswinter. This is a fine example of late Romanesque
church architecture, characteristic of the ruins that fired the
imagination of the Romantic poets and painters of the 19th century.

Continuing south along the west bank, you come to the ancient,
half-timbered town of **Remagen.** Originally a Roman village
built near the source of a mineral spring, where the Ahr River
meets the Rhine, Remagen was an important bridgehead during World War II. Here, American forces were able to capture
the bridge and speed their advance into Germany. The Ahr Valley, lined with picturesque, terraced vineyards, produces some
of Germany's finest red wines.

Koblenz In the heart of the Middle Rhine region, at the confluence of the
Rhine and Moselle rivers, lies the city of **Koblenz,** the area's
cultural and administrative center and the meeting place of the
two great wine-producing districts. It is also one of the most
important traffic points along the Rhine. Here you are ideally
placed to sample and compare the light, fruity Moselle wines
and the headier Rhine varieties. The city's **Weindorf** area, just
south of the **Pfaffendorfer Bridge,** has a wide selection of taverns, where you can try the wines in traditional Römer glasses,
with their symbolic amber and green bowls.

The city of Koblenz began as a Roman camp—Confluentes—more than 2,000 years ago. The vaults beneath **St. Florin Church** contain an interesting assortment of Roman remains. In the 12th and 13th centuries, the city was controlled by the archbishop-electors of Trier, and a host of fine churches and castles were built.

A good place to begin your tour of Koblenz is the **Deutches Eck,** or "Corner of Germany," the tip of the sharp peninsula separating the Rhine and Moselle rivers. In the 12th century, the Knights of the Teutonic Order established their center here. The towering equestrian statue of Kaiser Wilhelm that once stood here was destroyed by Allied bombs during World War II, but the base remains as a monument to German unity. On summer evenings, concerts are held in the nearby **Blumenhof Garden.** Most of the city's historic churches are also within walking distance of the Deutsches Eck. The **Liebfrauenkirche** (Church of Our Lady), completed in the 13th century, incorporates Romanesque, late Gothic, and Baroque elements. **St. Florin,** a Romanesque church built around 1100, was remodeled in the Gothic style in the 14th century. Gothic windows and a vaulted ceiling were added in the 17th century. The city's most important church, **St. Kastor,** also combines Romanesque and Gothic elements and features some unusual altar tombs and rare Gothic wall paintings.

Although the city lost 85% of its buildings during wartime air raids, some of the old buildings survived and others have been built in complementary styles. Much of the **Old Town** of Koblenz is now a pedestrian district, and an attractive area for a leisurely stroll. Many of the ancient cellars beneath the houses have been rediscovered and now serve as wine bars and jazz clubs.

Koblenz also offers an assortment of castles and palaces. The former residence of the archbishop of Trier now houses the city administrative offices. The original 18th-century building was demolished during the war; today only the interior staircase remains. Across the river, on the Rhine's east bank, towers the city's most spectacular castle, the **Ehrenbreitstein,** now a youth hostel and a museum of ethnography and prehistory. The fortifications of this vast structure date back to the 1100s, although the bulk of it was built much later, in the 16th and 17th centuries. To reach the fortress, take the cable car *(Sesslebahn)* or, if you're in shape, try walking up. The view alone is worth the trip. On the second Saturday in August, a magnificent fireworks display, "The Rhine Aflame," is presented here. Before you leave, visit the **Mittelrhein Museum** for a look at Rhenish art and artifacts from the Middle Ages to the present day. *15 Florinsmarkt. Admission: free. Open Tues.–Sat. 10–1 and 2:30–5:30; Sun. 10–1.*

Rhine Gorge Between the cities of Koblenz and Mainz, the Rhine flows through the 64-kilometer (40-mile) stretch known as the **Rhine Gorge.** It is here that the Rhine lives up to its legends and lore and where the river, in places, narrows to a width of 200 yards. Once it was full of treacherous whirlpools, sudden shallows, and stark rock outcroppings that menaced passing ships. Today, vineyards occupy every inch of available soil on the steep, terraced slopes. High above, ancient castles crown the rocky shelves.

South of Koblenz, at a wide, western bend in the river, lies the quiet old town of **Boppard,** once a bustling city of the Holy Roman Empire. Now the remains of its Roman fort and castle are used to house a museum of Roman artifacts and geological specimens. There are also several notable churches, including the **Carmelite Church,** with its fine Baroque altar, and the Romanesque Church of **St. Severus.** Boppard also offers a wonderful view across the Rhine to the ruined castles of **Liebenstein** and **Sterrenberg,** known as the "hostile brothers." As legend has it, the castles were built by two feuding brothers to protect their respective interests. The Boppard riverbanks also feature two miles of pleasure grounds and an extensive municipal forest.

Continuing south from Boppard, you come to the little town of **St. Goar,** crowded against the steep gorge cliff and shadowed by the imposing ruin of **Rheinfels Castle.** A steep, narrow road takes you up to the castle—a fine spot for scenic river vistas. Rheinfels was built in the mid-13th century by Count Dieter von Katzenelnbogen (whose name means "cat's elbow"). The count's enormous success in collecting river tolls provoked the other river barons to join together and lay siege to his castle. What transpired is unclear, but through the years Rheinfels survived numerous sieges. It was finally destroyed by the French in 1797. During the 19th century, the ruins served as a source of inspiration for a host of Romantic poets and artists. It is now in the process of restoration, and a luxury hotel has been built on the site *(see* Dining and Lodging). *Admission: DM 2.50. Open Apr.–Oct., daily 9–5.*

On the east bank of the river, just across from the town of St. Goar, lies its sister village, **St. Goarshausen.** An hourly ferry service links the two. St. Goarshausen is dominated by **Burg Katz** (Cat Castle), a massive fortress built by a later Count von Katzenelnbogen. Today it is a government-run youth facility. Tourists are not permitted inside, but the top of the cliff offers a lovely view of the famous Loreley rock. About 3.2 kilometers (two miles) north of St. Goarshausen is the **Burg Maus,** or Mouse Castle. Legend has it that an archbishop of Trier built the fortress to protect a strip of land he owned at the base of the cliff. The Count von Katzenelnbogen, annoyed at what he considered an intrusion into his territory, sent the archbishop a message explaining that his "Cat" (Burg Katz) was sufficient to protect the electoral "Mouse." Hence the nickname, Burg Maus.

Many tourists visit St. Goarshausen for its location—only a few miles from the legendary **Loreley rock.** To get to Loreley, follow the road marked with "Loreley-Felsen" signs. Here the Rhine takes a sharp turn around a rocky, shrub-covered headland. This is the narrowest and shallowest part of the Middle Rhine, full of treacherous currents. According to legend, the beautiful maiden, Lore, sat on the rock here, combing her golden hair and singing a song so irresistible that passing sailors forgot the navigational hazards and were swept to their deaths.

Oberwesel, on the west bank, is a medieval wine town encircled by ancient walls and towers. Sixteen of the original 21 towers remain. Two churches deserve a visit: **St. Martin,** built in the 14th and 15th centuries, features a distinctive, brightly painted nave; the **Liebfrauen Kirche** (known as the "red church" because of its fiery facade) contains a magnificent choir screen, some fine sculpture, and an altarpiece depicting the magnanimous deeds of St. Nicholas.

One of the most photographed sites of the Middle Rhine region is the medieval village of **Kaub,** just south of Oberwesel on the east side of the river. Its unusual castles are well worth a visit. The **Pfalzgrafenstein,** situated on a tiny island in the middle of the Rhine, bristles with sharp-pointed towers and has the appearance of a small sailing ship. In the 14th century, the resident graf, or count, was said to have strung chains across the Rhine in order to stop riverboats and collect his tolls. A special boat takes visitors to the island. *Admission: DM 1.50. Open Tues.–Sun. 9–noon and 2–5:30.*

On a hillside above Kaub hovers another small castle: **Burg Gutenfels.** Built in the 13th century, Gutenfels was renovated completely at the end of the 18th century and is now an exquisite hotel *(see* Dining and Lodging).

The picturesque little village of **Bacharach,** encircled by 15th-century walls, is the best-preserved town of the Middle Rhine. It takes its name from the Roman "Baccaracum," or "altar of Bacchus"—a great stone that stood here until it was dynamited by river engineers during the last century. As its name implies, Bacharach is also a wine-trade center. Like many small towns of the Middle Rhine and Moselle valleys, the village holds a colorful wine festival each October. In addition to providing an excellent opportunity for liberal imbibing, Rhine wine festivals often feature lively displays of folk crafts and traditions.

Farther south, on the Rhine's east bank and at the center of the Rheingau region, lies another famous wine town. According to legend, **Rüdesheim's** first vines were planted by Charlemagne. More recent vintages can be enjoyed in the many taverns lining **Drosselgasse,** a narrow, colorful street in the heart of town. Rüdesheim is a tourist magnet—about the most popular destination on the Rhine—so if you plan to stay overnight, be sure to reserve well in advance. Besides its half-timbered houses, hidden courtyards, and medieval castles, Rüdesheim offers an interesting museum, **Rheingau und Weinmuseum,** devoted to the history of wine making and local lore. *Rheinstr. Admission: DM 2.50. Open Mar.–mid-Nov., 10–12:30 and 1:30–6.*

Mainz On the west side of the Rhine, at the mouth of the river Main, stands the city of **Mainz,** an old university town that's the capital of the Rhineland-Palatinate state. During Roman times, Mainz was a camp called Moguntiacum. Later it was the seat of the powerful archbishops of Mainz. But it is perhaps best known as the city in which, around 1450, printing pioneer Johannes Gutenberg established his first movable press. He is commemorated by a monument and square bearing his name and a museum containing his press and one of his Bibles. *Liebfrauenplatz 5. Admission: free. Open Tues.–Sat. 10–6, Sun. and holidays 10–1. Closed Jan.*

Today, Mainz is a bustling, modern city of nearly 200,000 inhabitants. Although it was heavily bombed during the war, many of the buildings have been faithfully reconstructed, and the city retains much of its historic charm. On **Gutenbergplatz** in the **Old Town** stand two fine Baroque churches, **Seminary Church** and **St. Ignatius.** The Gothic church of **St. Stephan** features six windows by the French artist Marc Chagall. The city's **(Dom)** cathedral is one of the finest Romanesque churches in Germany. The Old Town also boasts the country's oldest Renaissance fountain—**the Marktbrunnen**—and the **Dativius-Victor-Bogen Arch,** dating back to Roman times. The **Römisch-Germanisches Museum,** in the **Kürfürstliches Schloss,** contains a notable collection of archaeological finds. *Rheinstr. Admission: free. Open Tues.–Sun. 10–6.*

Dining and Lodging

When it comes to cuisine, the Rhineland offers a number of regional specialties. Be sure to sample the wide variety of sausages available, the goose and duck dishes from the Ahr Valley, and Rhineland *Sauerbraten*—accepted by many as the most succulent of pot roasts. Hotels in the Rhineland range from simple little inns to magnificent castle hotels. Many smaller towns have only small hotels and guest houses, some of which close during the winter months. During the peak summer season and in early autumn—wine festival time—accommodations are scarce, so it is advisable to reserve well in advance.

For details and price category definitions, *see* Dining and Lodging in Staying in West Germany.

Bacharach **Altkölnischer Hof.** The Altkölnischer Hof is a small guest house
Lodging with a rustic air. *Am Marktplatz, tel. 06743/1339. 20 rooms, some with bath. No credit cards. Moderate.*

Bonn **Rheinterrassen.** Located near the city's diplomatic center, in
Dining Bad Godesberg, Rheinterrassen offers a lovely terrace and scenic views of the Rhine. *Ruengsdorf, Rheinstr. 82, tel. 0228/ 334494. Reservations advised. No credit cards. Closed in winter. Expensive.*

★ **Schaarschmidt.** Situated on one of the Old Town's most charming streets, Schaarschmidt offers fine German cuisine and a wide selection of Rhine wines. *Brudergasse 14, tel. 0228/ 654407. Reservations advised. DC. Closed Sun. Expensive.*
Zum Kapellchen. This is a colorful wine tavern featuring fine German and French cuisine. *Brudergasse 12, tel. 0228/651052. Reservations advised. AE, DC, MC, V. Closed Sun. Moderate.*

Lodging **Maritim.** Opened in 1988, the Maritim is already an established part of the Bonn hotel scene. It's located directly on the Rhine and beneath Königswinter's Petersberg heights. *Rheinallee 3, 5330 Königswinter 1, tel. 02223/7070. 250 rooms and suites with bath. Facilities: pool, sauna, bar, riverside terrace restaurant. AE, DC, MC, V. Expensive.*

★ **Königshof.** The sleek, modern Königshof is a favorite hotel among diplomatic visitors only partly for its convenient location near the Old Town and close to the Rhine. Patrons of the fine terrace restaurant enjoy an excellent river view. There is also a well-stocked wine cellar. *Adenauerallee 9, tel. 0228/ 26010. 139 rooms, with bath. AE, DC, MC, V. Expensive.*
Haus Daufenbach. Located on a narrow, winding road in the heart of the Old Town, Haus Daufenbach has a friendly, hearty atmosphere. *Brudergasse 6, tel. 0228/637444. 22 rooms, some with shower. Facilities: wine bar and restaurant. No credit cards. Moderate.*
Schlosspark. In a modern building close to the botanical gardens, the Schlosspark is a comfortably appointed, attractive hotel located only a short distance from the town center.

Venusbergweg 27–31, tel. 0228/217036. 67 rooms with bath. Facilities: restaurant, pool, sauna, solarium. AE, DC, MC, V. Moderate.

Boppard **Klostergut Jakobsberg.** This hotel is set in a handsome castle,
Lodging formerly a monastery, overlooking the Rhine Valley. Horseback riding and a wedding chapel top the list of facilities. *Boppard, tel. 06742/3061. 110 rooms with bath. Facilities: restaurant, tennis court, pool, game park. AE, DC, MC, V. Closed in winter. Very Expensive.*

Kaub **Burg Gutenfels.** The terrace of this luxurious castle hotel offers
Lodging one of the finest views in the Rhine Valley. Guests can also en-
★ joy wine from the hotel's own vineyard. Be sure to reserve well in advance. *Kaub, tel. 06774/220. 12 rooms with bath. Facilities: restaurant, private chapel. AE, DC, MC. Very Expensive.*

Koblenz **Weinhaus Hubertus.** This restaurant, named for the patron
Dining saint of hunting, lives up to its sporting image. Its decor is 17th-century rustic, its specialty, fresh game in season. Guests enjoy generous portions and a congenial atmosphere. *Florinsmarkt 6, tel. 0261/31177. Reservations advised. No credit cards. Moderate.*

Lodging **Scandic Crown.** This elegant, modern hotel has a lovely garden and terrace overlooking the river. *Julius-Wegeler-Str., tel. 0261/1360. 170 rooms with bath. Facilities: 2 restaurants, bar, sauna, whirlpool. AE, DC, MC, V. Expensive.*
Hohenstaufen. Hohenstaufen is located in a modern building near the train station. Facilities include a restaurant and garage. *Emil-Schuller-Str. 41–43, tel. 0261/37081. 65 rooms with bath. AE, DC, MC, V. Moderate.*

Königswinter **Zum Alten Bräuhaus.** Located in a pleasant, shady garden in
Dining the center of town, Zum Alten Bräuhaus features hearty German fare, served with a selection of local wines and beers. *Hauptstr. 454, tel. 02223/22528. No credit cards. Moderate.*

Lodging **Günnewig Rheinhotel.** A modern hotel situated right on the banks of the Rhine, Günnewig Rheinhotel offers pleasant river views. *Rheinallee 9, tel. 02223/24051. 110 rooms with bath. Facilities: restaurant, bar, pool, sauna, solarium. AE, DC, MC, V. Expensive.*

Mainz **Drei Lilien.** This beautifully appointed restaurant offers an-
Dining tique furnishings and excellent nouvelle cuisine. *Ballplatz 2,*
★ *tel. 06131/225068. Reservations advised. AE, DC, MC, V. Expensive.*
Rats und Zunftstuben Heilig Geist. Although the decor is predominantly modern, this popular restaurant also incorporates some Roman remains and offers a traditional atmosphere. The cuisine is hearty German fare. *Rentengasse 2, tel. 06131/225757. Reservations required. AE, DC, MC, V. Moderate.*

Lodging **Bristol.** Located near the city's picturesque Weisnaur Rhine Bridge, the Bristol is a new luxury hotel with comfortable rooms and good facilities. *Friedrich Ebert-Str., tel. 06131/8060. 57 rooms with bath. Facilities: restaurant, bar, pool, sauna. AE, DC, MC, V. Expensive.*
Hilton International. This enormous, glossy hotel presents a number of attractive public rooms, including a rooftop restaurant and Roman wine cellar. The bedrooms are tastefully furnished. *Rheinstr. 68, tel. 06131/2450. 435 rooms with bath.*

Facilities: pool, sauna, health club, conference center. AE, DC, MC, V. Expensive.

Rüdesheim
Lodging

Central. This is a friendly, family-run hotel. It also has a fine restaurant. *Kirchstr. 6, tel. 06722/2391. 53 rooms with bath. AE, DC, MC, V. Moderate.*

Hotel und Weinhaus Felfenkeller. Located just around the corner from Drosselgasse, Hotel and Weinhaus Felfenkeller is a traditional 18th-century establishment offering modern comforts. *Oberstr. 64, tel. 06722/2094. 64 rooms with bath. AE, MC, V. Inexpensive.*

St. Goar, St. Goarshausen
Dining

Roter Kopf. This is a historic wine restaurant brimming with rustic Rhineland atmosphere. *Burgstr. 5, St. Goarshausen, tel. 06771/2698. No credit cards. Moderate.*

Lodging

Schlosshotel–Burg Rheinfels. Situated high above St. Goar, on a hill commanding spectacular river views, the Schlosshotel–Burg Rheinfels rises from the ruins of the adjacent castle *(see* Exploring). During the spring and fall, the hotel organizes medieval banquets. *Schlossberg 47, tel. 06741/2071. 48 rooms with bath. Facilities: restaurant, pool, sauna. AE, DC, MC, V. Very Expensive.*

Pohl's Rhein Hotel Adler. Perched right on the edge of the Rhine, this is a turn-of-the-century, family-run establishment. Facilities include an attractive garden and terrace. *St. Goarshausen, tel. 06771/2613. 73 rooms with bath. Facilities: restaurant, pool, solarium. AE, DC, MC, V. Closed Nov.–Feb. Moderate.*

The Black Forest

Only a century ago, the Black Forest (Schwarzwald) was one of the wildest stretches of countryside in Europe. It had earned its somber name because of the impenetrable stretches of dark forest that clothed the mountains and shielded small communities from the outside world. Today, it's a friendly, hospitable region, still extensively forested but with large, open valleys and stretches of verdant farmland. Among the trailblazing tourists of the adventurous 19th century was Mark Twain, who wrote enthusiastically about the natural beauty of the region. The deep hot springs first discovered by the Romans were rediscovered, and small forgotten villages became wealthy spas. Hikers treasured the lonely trails that cut through the forests and rolling uplands, skiers opened the world's first lift on the slopes of the region's highest mountain, and horseback riders cut bridle paths through the tangle of narrow river valleys.

The Black Forest is the southernmost German wine region and the custodian of some of the country's best traditional foods. (Black Forest smoked ham and Black Forest cake are world-famous.) It retains its vibrant clock-making tradition, and local wood-carvers haven't yet died out. Best of all, though, it's still possible to stay overnight in a Black Forest farmhouse and eat a breakfast hearty enough to last the day, all for the price of an indifferent meal at a restaurant in, say, Munich or Frankfurt.

Getting Around

Today the Black Forest is easily accessible from all parts of the country. The Rhine Valley autobahn, the A5, runs the entire

length of the Black Forest and connects at Karlsruhe with the
rest of the German expressway network. Well-paved, single-
lane highways traverse the region. A main north–south train
line follows the Rhine Valley, carrying Euro-City and Inter-
City trains that call at hourly intervals at Freiburg and Baden-
Baden, connecting those two centers directly with Frankfurt
and many other German cities. Local lines connect most Black
Forest towns, and two east–west services, the Black Forest
Railway and the Höllental Railway, are spectacular scenic
runs. The nearest airports are at Stuttgart and the Swiss border city of Basel, just 64 kilometers (40 miles) from Freiburg.

Tourist Information

Baden-Baden. Augustaplatz 8, tel. 07221/275200.
Freiburg. Rotteckring 14, tel. 0761/32657.
Freudenstadt. Promenadenplatz 1, tel. 07441/8640.
Pforzheim. Marktplatz 1, tel. 07231/302314.

Guided Tours

Guided bus tours of the Black Forest begin in both Freiburg
and Baden-Baden. In Freiburg, day tours are organized by the
city tourist office (*see* Tourist Information) and include excursions into neighboring Switzerland (a day tour to the foot of the
Eiger costs DM 40). In Baden-Baden, tours are offered by the
Deutsches Reisebüro (Sofienstr. 1b, tel. 07221/24666) and concentrate on the Black Forest, although one afternoon tour has
the French border city of Strasbourg as its destination.

Exploring the Black Forest

The regional tourist authority has worked out a series of scenic
routes covering virtually every attraction the visitor is likely to
want to see (obtainable from the **Fremdenverkehrsverband,**
Bertoldstrasse 45, 7800 Freiburg, tel. 0761/31317). Routes are
basically intended for the motorist, but most points can be
reached by train or bus. The following itinerary is accessible by
all means of transportation and takes in parts of the Black Forest High Road, Low Road, Spa Road, Wine Road, and Clock
Road.

The ancient Roman city of **Pforzheim** is the starting point here,
accessible either from the Munich–Karlsruhe autobahn or by
train from Karlsruhe/Frankfurt. Known even beyond Germany's borders as the Gold City because of its association with
the jewelry trade, Pforzheim has the world's finest museum collection of jewelry in the **Reuchlinhaus,** spanning four centuries
(Am Stadtgarten; closed Monday). Pforzheim was almost completely destroyed by wartime bombing and is a fine example of
reconstruction work: Visit the centrally located parish church
of **St. Michael** to see how faithfully the experts stuck to the
original mixture of sturdy Romanesque and later, finer Gothic
styles. For a contrast, take a look at Pforzheim's **St. Matthew's
Church,** a tentlike construction erected in 1953 when the designers of the similarly styled Olympic stadium in Munich were
still at the drawing board.

On the way out of Pforzheim, toward B463, the Nagold Valley
road, gardeners should make a detour to the **Alpine Garden** on
the Tiefenbronn road. More than 100,000 varieties of plants,

The Black Forest

0 20 miles
0 30 km

FRANCE

Karlsruhe

Pforzheim
Bad Liebenzell

Baden-Baden   Calw   Stuttgart

B463

Zavelstein   Talmühle

Kehl   *Mummelsee*

Baiersbronn   Nagold

Offenburg   Freudenstadt

Neckar

B415   Zell   Alpirsbach

Lahr   Wolfach   B294   Schiltach

B294   *Gutach-tal Valley*

Kaiserstuhl   Triberg

Freiburg   Furtwangen   *Danube*   Rottweil

Titisee   Tuttlingen

Himmelreich

Staufen   *Schluchsee*

Zell   Radolfzell

Rheinfelden   Friedrichshafen

Bodensee

N

SWITZERLAND

including the rarest Alpine flowers, are found here, and many are for sale. *Open daily Apr.–Sept.*

Bad Liebenzell, our first stop on B463, is one of the oldest spas of the Black Forest, with the remains of 15th-century installations. Visitors are welcome to take the waters at the **Paracelsus baths** on the Nagold riverbank. *Admission: DM 9.80 for 2 hours. Open Apr.–Oct., from 7:30; Nov.–Mar., from 8:30.*

Leave plenty of time to explore **Calw** (pronounced Calve), the next town on the road south. Its famous native son, the poet Hermann Hesse, called it the "most beautiful [town] of all I know." And Hesse, who died in Switzerland in 1962, had seen more than a few in his extensive travels. Pause on the town's 15th-century bridge over the rushing Nagold River—if you're lucky, you'll see a local tanner spreading hides over the river wall to dry, as his ancestors did for centuries past. Pause, too, in the town's market square and reflect on all the sights and sounds those 18th-century half-timbered houses, whose sharp gables stab the sky on all sides, must have been witness to in their time.

If you're traveling in spring, watch for a sign to **Zavelstein,** some 5 kilometers (3 miles) out of Calw. Take the short detour up a side-valley to see the greatest natural display of wild crocuses Germany has to offer. Don't pick any of the flowers, however—the meadows are officially protected.

Back on the main road south, turn off at Talmühle for the **Neubulach silver mine.** Once the most productive workings of the Black Forest, the mine is now open to visitors—and is also home for an asthma therapy center thanks to its dry, dust-free interior. *Admission: DM 4 adults, DM 3 children (includes entry to mineral museum). Open Apr.–Oct., Mon.–Sat. 10–4, Sun. 9:30–5.*

Time Out In **Nagold,** the town that gave the river and the valley their name, drop in at the half-timbered **Alte Post** inn on the main street. Kings and queens have taken refreshment here on journeys through the Black Forest. Enjoy the local beer and a plate of Black Forest smoked ham or a pot of strong coffee and a slice of delectable Black Forest cake.

From Nagold, the road travels on through lush farmland to **Freudenstadt,** another war-flattened German city that has been painstakingly restored. It was originally built in the early 17th century as a model city to house not only workers in nearby silver mines but refugees from religious persecution in what is now Austrian Carinthia. The streets are still laid out in the grid pattern decreed by the original planners, while the vast central square continues to wait for the palace that was intended to stand here. It was to have been built for the city's founder, Prince Frederick I of Württemberg, but he died before work could begin. Don't miss Freudenstadt's **Protestant parish church,** just off the square. It's L-shaped, a rare architectural liberty in the early 17th century, when this imposing church was built.

A fine introduction to the history and traditions of the Black Forest can be obtained at the **Black Forest Museum** at Lossburg, 8 kilometers (5 miles) south of Freudenstadt. For the past two years the museum has been looking for a new home. It hopes to be installed in new quarters sometime in 1990. Call the Lossburg tourist office, tel. 07446/2156, for its new address.

Quench your thirst at nearby **Alpirsbach,** where the unusually soft water gives the local beer an especially smooth quality. South of Alpirsbach, stop at **Schiltach** to admire (and possibly giggle at) the frescoes on the 16th-century town hall that depict the history of this exceptionally pretty village. The devil figures prominently in the frescoes: He was blamed for burning Schiltach down on several occasions.

From here, take B294 to **Wolfach** to visit the last Black Forest factory, where glass is blown by centuries-old techniques once common throughout the region. *Die Wolfacher Glashütte, Glashüttenweg 4, tel. 07834/751. Admission: DM 2.50 adults, DM 1.50 children. Open Apr.–Oct., 9–3:30.*

Just outside Wolfach is the **Vogtsbauernhof Open-Air Museum** of Black Forest farmhouses, dismantled at their original sites and rebuilt here, complete with authentic interiors. *Admission: DM 4 adults, DM 2 children. Open Apr.–Oct., daily 8:30–6.*

The **Gutachtal Valley,** south of Wolfach, is famous for its traditional costumes, and if you're there at the right time (holidays and some Sundays), you'll see the married women sporting black pompoms on their hats to denote their matronly status (red pompoms are for the unmarried). At the head of the valley, at **Triberg,** are Germany's highest waterfalls, which reach a height of nearly 155 meters (500 feet). This is also cuckoo clock country. The Black Forest **Museum of Furtwangen,** south of Triberg, has lots of examples, plus one of the oldest wooden clocks in existence. It has just seven wheels and was carved (with a bread knife, no less!) in 1640. *Admission: DM 3 adults, DM 1 children. Open Apr.–Oct., daily 10–5.*

From Furtwangen, the road leads to the lakeland of the Black Forest. The two largest lakes, Titisee and Schluchsee, are beautifully set amid fir-clad mountains, but try to avoid them at the height of the summer holidays, when they are quite crowded. From here, it's a short run to Freiburg, capital of the Black Forest. The most direct route goes via the aptly named Höllental (Hell Valley). The first stop outside the narrow, gorgelike valley is called, appropriately enough, Himmelreich, meaning "Kingdom of Heaven." The village is said to have been given the name by railway engineers grateful finally to have run a line through Hell Valley. The Black Forest railway, more than 100 years old, still tackles the mountainous route, connecting Freiburg and the resort of Hinterzarten; details and tickets are available from the **Bundesbahn** (German Railways) in Freiburg (tel. 0761/19419).

Perched on the western slopes of the Black Forest, **Freiburg** was founded as a free market town in the 12th century, fought over by various rival armies throughout history, and badly bombed in World War II. Towering over the rebuilt, medieval streets of the city is its most famous landmark, the cathedral, or **Münster.** The cathedral took three centuries to build: Visitors can trace the progress of successive generations of builders through the changing architectural styles of the times, from the fat, 11th-century Romanesque columns and solid, rounded arches to the lofty 13th-century Gothic windows, interior, and 115-meter (370-foot) tower and delicately perforated spire, described by some art historians as the world's finest.

Try to visit Freiburg on a Friday, which is market day. The square in front of the cathedral then becomes a mass of color and movement, while a fitting backdrop is provided by **Kaufhaus,** the 16th-century market house.

Time Out Stroll up to the Oberlinden Square and call in at one of Germany's most ancient inns, **Zum Roten Bären** (the Red Bear) (*see* Dining, below). Order a "Viertel" of the local wine and perhaps a plate of locally smoked ham—and if you like the atmosphere, why not stay the night?

Having braved Hell Valley to get to Freiburg, a visit to the nearby town where Dr. Faustus is reputed to have made his deal with the devil should hold no horrors. **Staufen,** which claims the inquisitive doctor as one of its early burgers, is some 19 kilometers (12 miles) south of Freiburg. Local records show there really was an alchemist named Faustus who blew himself up in his laboratory. According to legend, the devil dragged him off to hell from the **Löwen** (Lion) tavern, which you can still visit on the market square.

Staufen is on the **Wine Road** and is the turning point of this tour. Now head north toward Baden-Baden, through the southernmost vineyards of Germany, source of the prized Baden wine. Some of the best vineyards are situated on a volcanic outcrop known as the **Kaiserstuhl** (Emperor's Chair). Sample a glass in the village of **Achkarren,** which has a fascinating **wine**

museum. *Admission: DM 2 adults, DM 1 children. Open Apr.–Oct., weekdays 2–5, weekends 10:30–4.*

All the vineyards along the Wine Road offer tastings, so don't hesitate to drop in and try one or two. Leave the Wine Road at the town of Lahr and head inland, on B415, through the narrow Schuttertal valley to Zell, and from there to the Black Forest **High Road.** This is the land of fable and superstition, and if you're here during the mist-days of autumn, stop off at the mystery-shrouded **Mummelsee Lake,** immortalized by the poet Mörike in his ballad *The Spirits of the Mummelsee.* Legend has it that sprites and other spirits of the deep live in the cold waters of the small, round lake in its forest setting. It's true that no fish are found in the lake, but scientific sorts say this is a result of the high mineral content of the water.

From the Mummelsee, it's downhill all the way to fashionable **Baden-Baden,** idyllically set in a wooded valley of the northern Black Forest. The town sits on top of extensive underground hot springs that gave the city its name *(Bad,* German for "spa"). The Romans first exploited the springs, which were then rediscovered by wealthy 19th-century travelers. By the end of the 19th century, there was scarcely a crowned head of Europe who had not dipped into the healing waters of Baden-Baden. The town became the unofficial summer residence of numerous royal and titled families, and they left their imprint in the form of palatial houses that grace its tree-lined avenues. Some are hotels: Brenner's Park Hotel, in particular, is world-famous *(see* Dining and Lodging), though if the price of a room is too high, you can soak up the atmosphere over a cocktail in its piano bar.

One of the grand buildings of Baden-Baden's Belle Epoque is the pillared **Kurhaus,** home of Germany's first casino, which opened its doors to the world's gamblers in 1838. Entrance costs a modest DM 5, though visitors are required to sign a declaration that they enter with sufficient funds to settle subsequent debts! *Jacket and tie required. Passport necessary as proof of identity. Open Sun.–Fri. 2 PM–2 AM, Sat. 2 PM–3 AM. Daily tours (DM 2) from Apr.–Sept., daily 9:30–noon; Oct.–Mar., 10–noon.*

If jackets and ties are customary attire at the casino, no clothes at all are de rigueur at Baden-Baden's famous Roman baths, the **Friedrichsbad.** You "take the waters" here just as the Romans did nearly 2,000 years ago—nude. Römerplatz 1, tel. 07221/275940. *Admission: DM 25. Children under 16 not admitted. Open Mon. and Wed.–Sat. 8 AM–10 PM, Tues. 8–4.*

The remains of the Roman baths that lie beneath the Friedrichsbad can be visited in summer (April–October). *Admission: DM 2.*

Time Out   Step into the warm elegance of the **Café König** in the nearby Lichtentalerstrasse pedestrian zone. Order a pot of coffee and a wedge of Black Forest cake and listen to the hum of contentment from the monied spa crowd who have made this quiet corner their haunt.

The attractions of the Friedrichsbad are rivaled by the neighboring **Caracalla baths,** opened in 1985. The huge, modern complex has five indoor pools, two outdoor ones, numerous whirlpools, a solarium, and what is described as a "sauna landscape"—you look out through windows at the countryside while steaming. Römerplatz 11, tel. 07221/275940. *Admission: DM 13 for 2 hours. Open daily 8 AM–10 PM.*

Dining and Lodging

For details and price category definitions, *see* Dining and Lodging in Staying in West Germany.

Baden-Baden
Dining
★ **Merkurius.** The owner-chef of the Merkurius is Czech-born, and his menu features the best of Bohemian cooking. The comfortably appointed restaurant, its homey atmosphere completed by an open fire, is part of a small country-house hotel 8 kilometers (5 miles) south of Baden-Baden; it's well worth the journey. Bohemian dumplings tussle with German potato pancakes for top honors. *Klosterberg 2, tel. 07223/5474. Reservations required. AE, DC, MC. Closed all day Mon., Sun. and Tues. dinner. Expensive.*

Stahlbad. The Gallo-Germanic menu here is echoed by the restaurant's furnishings—19th-century French oils adorn the walls, while French and German china are reflected in the mahogany gleam of antique tables and sideboards. An abundance of green velvet catches the tone of the parklike grounds of the stately house that accommodates this elegant restaurant. *Augustaplatz 2, tel. 07221/24569. Reservations advised. AE, DC, MC, V. Closed Sun. dinner and Mon. Expensive.*

Zum Alde Gott. A tiny rustic and comfortable (lots of wood, but cushions, too) restaurant in the Neuweier district, Zum Alde Gott specializes in traditional Baden dishes that are topped with imaginative touches. Try the lamb "pot au feu" and, as dessert, figs in beer pastry. *Weinstr. 10, Neuweier, tel. 07223/5513. Reservations advised. AE, DC, MC, V. Closed Thurs. and Fri. lunch. Moderate.*

Lodging
Brenner's Park Hotel. This exceptional stately mansion, on Baden-Baden's leafy Lichtentaler Allee, is set in spacious private grounds. All rooms are luxuriously furnished and appointed—as they should be, since they cost up to DM 1,950 per day. *An der Lichtentaler Allee, tel. 07221/3530. 101 rooms with bath. Facilities: health club, pool, sauna. No credit cards. Very Expensive.*

★ **Der Kleine Prinz.** Each room of this beautifully modernized 19th-century mansion is decorated in a different style, from romantic Art Nouveau to Manhattan modern (owner Norbert Rademacher was director of New York's Waldorf-Astoria for several years). Some rooms have whirlpool baths. The hotel's elegant restaurant offers "new German cuisine" with a French touch. *Lichtentalerstr. 36, tel. 07221/3464. 30 rooms with bath. Facilities: restaurant. AE, DC, MC, V. Restaurant closed Jan. Very Expensive.*

Laterne. Dating from the late 17th century, Laterne is one of Baden-Baden's oldest hotels. Public rooms, the restaurant, and some bedrooms have original beams and woodwork, as well as antique Black Forest furnishings. The hotel is central but quietly situated in a pedestrian zone, with a café-terrace at the front. *Gernsbacherstr. 10, tel. 07221/29999. 10 rooms with bath. Facilities: café, restaurant. AE, DC, MC, V. Moderate.*

Hotel am Markt. The Bogner family has run this historic, 250-year-old hotel for more than 30 years. It's friendly, popular, and right in the center of town. *Marktplatz 17–18, tel. 07221/ 22747. 27 rooms, 9 with bath. Facilities: restaurant and terrace. AE, DC, MC, V. Inexpensive.*

Baiersbronn   **Bareiss.** The mountain resort of Baiersbronn is blessed with
Dining   two first-class restaurants that have become gastronomic
★   shrines, pulling pilgrims from as far away as the French Alsace. The more famous of the two, the Bareiss, confines itself almost exclusively to French cuisine, although chef Manfred Schwarz is undeniably German (and has been voted one of Germany's top 10 cooks). *Kurhotel Mitteltal, Gärtnerbuhlweg 14, tel. 07442/471. Reservations required. AE, DC. Closed end-Nov.–Christmas, and Mon. and Tues. Very Expensive.*
Traube Tonbach. French cuisine is also the specialty of the Traube Tonbach, where diners are settled at antique tables beneath a ceiling of gnarled beams and straw thatch. Try for a table by the large picture window overlooking the Tonbach valley. *Tonbachstr. 237, tel. 07442/4920. Reservations required. AE, DC, MC, V. Closed Jan. 10–Feb. 10, Thurs. and Fri. lunch. Expensive.*

Freiburg   **Falkenstube.** A 10-course "gourmet menu" is one of the many
Dining   attractions of the softly lit and oak-paneled Falkenstube restaurant in Freiburg's luxurious Colombi Hotel. The French influence is evident, from the snail and frog-leg delicacies (including a delicately spiced snail soup) to a dish for two that dresses a whole veal fillet with pâté de foie gras and truffles. *Colombi Hotel, Rotteckring 16, tel. 0761/31415. Reservations required. AE, DC, MC, V. Expensive.*
Kühler Krug. Venison is the staple dish here, though the restaurant's variety of fish dishes is large and imaginative. It makes its own pâté de foie gras. *Torplatz 1, tel. 0761/29103. Reservations advised. AE. Closed Thurs. and 3 weeks in June. Moderate.*
Ratskeller. In the shadow of the cathedral, the popular Ratskeller has a typical Black Forest ambience (lots of wood paneling and beams), which is matched by a menu of mostly traditional dishes (roasts and rich sauces). *Münsterplatz 11, tel. 0761/37530. Reservations advised. AE, DC, MC, V. Closed Sun. dinner, Mon. Moderate.*
Zum Roten Bären. The Red Bear claims to be the oldest inn in Germany (it was first mentioned in official documents in 1311). True or not, it's the archetypal German history-book inn, with a traditional menu to match. Demand Swabian *Spätzle* (a delicious variety of noodle) with everything. *Oberlinden 12, tel. 0761/36913. Reservations advised. AE, DC, MC, V. Moderate.*

Lodging   **Panorama Hotel am Jägerhäusle.** This hotel is situated high above Freiburg, although it's only a few minutes by car to the downtown area. All rooms have south-facing balconies, with fine views of the city and surrounding countryside. *Wintererstr. 89, tel. 0761/51030. 85 rooms with bath. Facilities: pool, sauna, solarium, tennis, ping-pong. AE, DC, MC, V. Very Expensive.*
Novotel. One of a European chain of modern hotels offering a high degree of comfort and conveniences at relatively modest rates, the Novotel is only a few minutes' walk from the old city. City tours and Black Forest excursions are willingly organized by the reception staff. *Am Karlsplatz 1, tel. 0761/31295. 112 rooms with bath. Facilities: garden terrace, conference room. AE, DC, MC, V. Expensive.*

★ **Romantik Hotel Stollen.** Run by the same family for the past 140 years, this half-timbered country house offers rooms decorated to a sophisticated standard; some have romantic detailing like canopied beds. The restaurant has won awards for its excellent concoctions. Located in Gutach im Elztal, 9 kilometers (6 miles) from Freiburg, the hotel is best reached from the Karslrühe–Basle autobahn by taking the Freiburg north exit and following the Waldkirch road. *7809 Gutach im Elztal, tel. 07685/207. 10 rooms with bath. AE, DC, MC, V. Expensive.*

Rappen Hotel. You'll sleep like a pampered farmhouse guest here, in brightly painted rustic beds, beneath soft feather quilts. It's as quiet as a country village, too: The Rappen is in the center of the traffic-free old city. In the countrified but comfortable restaurant, patrons have the choice of more than 200 regional wines. *Am Münsterplatz 13, tel. 0761/31353. 20 rooms, most with bath. Facilities: bar-restaurant, terrace. AE, DC, MC, V. Moderate.*

Freudenstadt
Dining

Bären. Fish is the Bären's strength (with local trout a specialty), but simple, traditional Swabian dishes find a prominent place on the menu, too. If you like tripe, this is *the* place to indulge yourself. *Langestr. 33, tel. 07441/6585. Reservations advised. AE, DC, MC, V. Closed Sun. dinner, Mon., and last 2 weeks in Jan. Moderate.*

Ratskeller. If it's cold outside, ask for a place near the Ratskeller's *Kachelofen*, a large, traditional, tiled heating stove. Swabian dishes and venison are prominent on the menu, but if the homemade trout roulade with crab sauce is featured, go for it. *Marktplatz 8, tel. 07441/2693. Reservations advised. AE, DC, MC, V. Closed Tues. and Feb. Moderate.*

Lodging

Golfhotel-Waldlust. A spacious villa set in its own extensive grounds, the Waldlust is equipped with fine views of the Black Forest countryside. In its pillared lounge, tea dances are held most days and an orchestra plays in the evening. Its guest rooms are traditionally furnished and sport carefully selected antiques. *Lauterbachstr. 92, tel. 07441/4051. 110 rooms with bath. Facilities: bar, terrace. No credit cards. Expensive.*

Schwarzwaldhotel Birkenhof. This hotel describes itself as a sports hotel, although its old-fashioned comfort and woodland setting have appeal for the less active. The town center is, however, a 15-minute walk away. The hotel's two restaurants offer a choice of French or Black Forest cuisine. *Wildbaderstr. 95, tel. 07441/4074. 60 rooms with bath. Facilities: squach court, miniature golf, ping-pong, bowling, indoor pool, sauna, solarium, steambath, whirlpool, massage and beauty treatments. AE, DC, MC, V. Expensive.*

Hotel Schwanen. The Schwanen has been efficiently managed by the capable Bukenberger family since 1900. Centrally situated, only two minutes' walk from the train station, it gives excellent value and above-average comfort. *Forststr. 6, tel. 07441/2267. 17 rooms with bath. No credit cards. Inexpensive.*

Landhaus Bukenberger. The Bukenbergers run this one, too. Its country-lodge exterior is picked up by lots of wood inside: The paneled television and reading room is a particularly snug retreat. *Herrenfelderstr. 65, tel. 07441/2771. 14 rooms with bath. No credit cards. Inexpensive.*

Hinterzarten
Lodging
★

Park Hotel Adler. This hotel has been in the possession of the Riesterer family for more than five centuries: Since 1446, when an early ancestor gave 17 schillings for the original property, it has been developing into one of Germany's finest hotels. The hotel complex stands in nearly 8 square kilometers (two acres) of grounds ringed by the Black Forest. Among the seven rooms devoted to eating and drinking are a French restaurant and a paneled 17th-century dining room. An orchestra accompanies dinner and later moves to the bar for dancing. *Adlerplatz 3, tel. 07652/711. 75 rooms with bath. Facilities: pool, sauna, solarium, tennis (indoor and outdoor), ping-pong, golf. AE, DC, MC, V. Very Expensive.*

Nagold **Romantik Restaurant Alte Post.** This centuries-old half-tim-
Dining bered inn has the kind of atmosphere lesser establishments believe can be built in with false beams. The menu ranges from Swabian traditional to pricey French, so stay with the local dishes (veal in a rich mushroom sauce or, in season, venison in the Baden-Baden style) and you won't be shocked by the bill. *Bahnhofstr. 2, tel. 07452/4221. Reservations essential. AE, DC, MC, V. Closed for 2 weeks in Jan., and on Sat. morning. Moderate.*

Lodging **Hotel Post Gästehaus.** Run by the former proprietors of the adjacent Alte Post restaurant, the Post Gästehaus is a modern, ivy-clad hotel offering a high degree of comfort—and homemade preserves for breakfast. *Bahnhofstr. 3, tel. 07452/4048. 24 rooms with bath. Facilities: English-language cable TV. AE, DC, MC, V. Expensive.*

Pforzheim **Rôtisserie Le Canard.** A little corner of France right in
Dining Pforzheim's Gute Hoffnung Hotel, this French country house–style restaurant doesn't restrict its menu solely to French cuisine but pays just as much attention to local Swabian fare. The home-made Spätzle with fresh herbs is first-rate. *Dillsteinerstr. 9–11, tel. 07231/26459. Reservations advised. AE, DC, MC, V. Closed Sun. Expensive.*

Titisee **Romantik Hotel Adler Post.** This hotel is in the Neustadt dis-
Lodging trict of Titisee, about 4½ kilometers (3 miles) from the lake. The solid old building has been in the possession of the Ketterer family for nearly 140 years. Guest rooms are comfortably and traditionally furnished. The hotel's restaurant, the Rôtisserie zum Postillon, has built up a good name locally. *Hauptstr. 16, tel. 07651/5066. 32 rooms with bath. Facilities: pool, sauna, solarium. AE, DC, MC, V. Expensive.*

13 Great Britain

Introduction

Great Britain is a small country with a long history spread out for all to see. Two factors have helped to ensure the preservation of so much of the nation's past. First is the absence of fighting on British soil. While for centuries Britain's armies crossed the channel to take part in European wars and during the 18th and 19th centuries it won for itself an extensive worldwide empire, the physical fact of the English Channel has kept its shores from invasion for more than 900 years, thus avoiding the process of destruction and reconstruction seen in much of the rest of Europe. In addition, the nation's internal conflicts, though bloody, have generally been brief. The second factor is the innate sense of history (some would call it conservatism) of the British, who generally prefer the old to the new and are often reluctant to contemplate any kind of change, especially in their physical surroundings.

All this means that Great Britain is an ideal holiday destination for anyone with a feel for the past. Here are soaring medieval cathedrals, tributes to the faith of the churchmen and masons who built them; grand country mansions of the aristocracy filled with treasures—paintings, furniture, tapestries—and set in elegantly landscaped grounds; and grim fortified castles, their gray stone walls set fast against all challengers.

But Britain is not merely a historical theme park, and the visitor who concentrates solely on such traditional sights misses the essence of the land and the people. Many of the pleasures of exploration away from the main tourist routes derive from the constantly changing variety of the countryside. A day's drive from New York, for example, will take you through long stretches of wild, heather-covered moorland, ablaze with color in the fall, or past the steep, sheep-covered mountainsides of the Dales, cut by deep valleys and scattered with isolated stone-built hamlets.

Wandering off the beaten track will also let you discover the distinctive character of Britain's many small country towns and villages. A medieval parish church, a high street of 18th-century buildings interrupted by occasional survivors from earlier centuries, and a grandiose Victorian town hall, all still in use today, help to convey a sense of a living past.

This direct continuity of past and present can be experienced in such a celebrated and tourist-filled place as Startford-upon-Avon, but even more in such communities as the little town of Chipping Campden, set in the rolling Cotswold Hills, and Bury St. Edmunds, in the gentle Suffolk countryside east of Cambridge. In such places, the visitor's understanding is often helped by small museums devoted to explaining local history, full of intriguing artifacts and information on trade, traditions, and social life. Such towns, too, are the places to look for specialty goods, such as knitwear, pottery, glass and pictures, the product of a 1980s renaissance in craftsmanship.

In contrast is the hectic, at times aggressive, pace of life in London, still one of the world's great metropolises. This is a city that scarcely seems to sleep, with a vibrant artistic, cultural, and commerical life. Yet here, too, the links with the past are numerous and plain for all to see. For instance, despite all the recent rebuilding, the basic street pattern of the city (the financial quarter between St. Paul's Cathedral and the Tower of London) is the one that evolved in the Middle Ages, more than 600 years ago; and still standing is much of the work of Christopher Wren, the master architect chiefly responsible for reconstruction after the disastrous fire of 1666. Most notable of these works is St. Paul's itself. Here again, exploration off the beaten track will reward you with the discovery of a London relatively untouched by tourists.

Finally, it is important to remember that Great Britain consists of three nations—England, Scotland, and Wales—and that 640 kilometers (400 miles) north of London lies another capital city, Edinburgh, whose streets and monuments bear witness to the often turbulent and momentous history of the Scottish people. Cardiff, 272 kilometers (170 miles) west of London, is a busy port and the focal point of two of the famous Welsh passions—singing and rugby.

Before You Go

When To Go The main tourist season runs from mid-April to mid-October. In recent years, however, parts of the winter—especially December—have been almost as busy. Winter is also the height of London's theater, ballet, and opera season. Springtime reveals the countryside at its most verdant and beautiful, while fall offers soft vistas of muted, golden color. September and October are the months to visit the northern moorlands and Scottish highlands, while June is best for Wales and the Lake District. Most British people take their vacations during July and August, when costs and accommodations are at a premium.

Climate On the whole, Britain's climate is a temperate one: Winters are rarely bitter and summers are unlikely to be scorchers. But wherever you are, and whatever the season, be prepared for sudden changes. What begins as a brilliant, sunny day often turns into a damp and dismal one by lunchtime. Take an umbrella and raincoat wherever you go, particularly in Scotland. In general, temperatures in the north are somewhat cooler.

The following are the average daily maximum and minimum temperatures for London.

Jan.	43F	6C	May	62F	17C	Sept.	65F	19C
	36	2		47	8		52	11
Feb.	44F	7C	June	69F	20C	Oct.	58F	14C
	36	2		53	12		46	8
Mar.	50F	10C	July	71F	22C	Nov.	50F	10C
	38	3		56	14		42	5
Apr.	56F	13C	Aug.	71F	21C	Dec.	45F	7C
	42	6		56	13		38	4

Currency The British unit of currency is the pound sterling, divided into 100 pence (p). Bills are issued in denominations of 5, 10, 20, and 50 pounds (£). Coins are £1, 50p, 20p, 10p (the same as the old two-shilling piece, still in circulation), 5p (the old one-shilling piece), 2p and 1p. Scottish banks issue Scottish currency, and all coins and notes—with the exception of the £1 notes—are accepted in England. At press time (spring 1989), the exchange rate was approximately $1.70 to the pound.

Great Britain

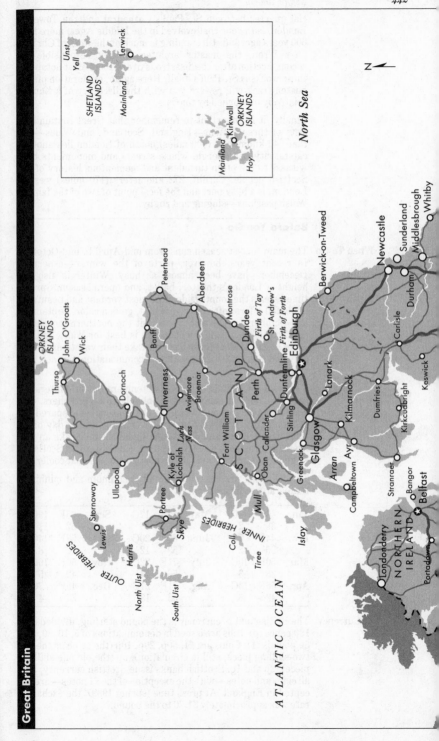

N

North Sea

Unst
Yell
Lerwick
SHETLAND
ISLANDS
Mainland

ORKNEY
ISLANDS
Kirkwall
Mainland
Hoy

ORKNEY
ISLANDS
John O'Groats
Wick
Thurso
Dornoch
Peterhead
Aberdeen
Banff
Montrose
Inverness
Aviemore
Braemar
Firth of Tay
Dundee
St. Andrew's *Firth of Forth*
Perth
Edinburgh
Loch Ness
Fort William
Dunfermline
Stirling
Berwick-on-Tweed
Oban Callander
Lanark
Newcastle
Sunderland
Middlesbrough
Whitby
Durham
Carlisle
SCOTLAND
Glasgow
Kilmarnock
Keswick
Greenock
Ayr
Dumfries
Kirkcudbright
Stornoway
Lewis
Ullapool
Kyle of
Lochalsh
Portree
Skye
Harris
North Uist
INNER HEBRIDES
Mull
Coll
Tiree
Islay
Arran
Campbeltown
Stranraer
Bangor
Belfast
NORTHERN
IRELAND
Londonderry
Portadown
OUTER HEBRIDES
South Uist
ATLANTIC OCEAN

Credit cards and traveler's checks are widely accepted in Britain, and many banks, hotels, and shops offer currency-exchange facilities. You will probably lose from 1¢ to 4¢ on the dollar, however, depending on where you change them; banks offer the best rates. In London and other big cities, Bureaux de Change abound, but beware: They usually have a minimum change of 50p, and often a great deal more.

What It Will Cost In general, transportation in Britain is expensive in comparison with other countries. You would be well advised to take advantage of the many reductions and special fares available on trains, buses, and subways. Always ask about these when buying your ticket. Gasoline prices are about the same as those on the Continent.

London now ranks with Tokyo as one of the world's most expensive hotel capitals. Finding budget accommodations—especially during July and August—can be difficult. Many London hotels offer special off-season (October-March) rates, however. Dining out, even in moderate restaurants, can be prohibitively expensive, though a large number of pubs offer excellent food at reasonable prices, and fast-food facilities are widespread. Many ethnic restaurants also tend to be better value for money.

Remember that the gulf between prices in the capital and outside is wide, so try to divide your time between London and the rest of the country. But take advantage of one ubiquitous bargain: Nearly all state-owned museums are free to visitors. Be prepared to pay a value-added tax (VAT) of 15% on almost everything you buy, however.

Sample Prices For London: Cup of coffee, 70p; pint of beer, £1.20; glass of wine, £1.10; soda, 50p; 1-mile taxi ride, £2.20; ham sandwich, £1.

Customs on Arrival There are two levels of duty-free allowance for people entering the United Kingdom; one, for goods bought outside the European Economic Community (EEC), or for goods bought in a duty-free shop within the EEC; two, for goods bought in an EEC country but not in a duty-free shop.

In the first category, you may import duty-free 200 cigarettes or 100 cigarillos or 50 cigars or 250 grams of tobacco *(Note:* If you live outside Europe, these allowances are doubled), plus one liter of alcoholic drinks over 22% volume or two liters of alcoholic drinks not over 22% volume or fortified or sparkling wine, plus two liters of still table wine, plus 50 grams of perfume, plus nine fluid ounces of toilet water, plus other goods to the value of £32.

In the second category, you may import duty-free 300 cigarettes or 150 cigarillos or 75 cigars or 400 grams of tobacco, plus 1.5 liters of alcoholic drinks over 22% volume or three liters of alcoholic drinks not over 22% volume or fortified or sparkling wine, plus four liters of still table wine, plus 75 grams of perfume, plus 13 fluid ounces of toilet water, plus other goods to the value of £250. *(Note:* Though it is not classified as an alcoholic drink by EEC countries for customs' purposes and is thus considered part of the "other goods" allowance, you may not import more than 50 liters of beer.)

In addition, no animals or pets of any kind may be brought into the United Kingdom. The penalties for doing so are severe and are strictly enforced.

Getting Around

By Car
Road Conditions

Britain has superhighways (called motorways) running almost the length of the country, with links connecting them in the South, Midlands, and North. Motorways, given the prefix M on maps and road signs, have two or three lanes in each direction and are designed for high-speed, rather than scenic, travel.

The main north—south road between London and Leeds is M1. Other principal routes are M5, running from the Midlands to the Southwest, and M6, from the Midlands north to Scotland. M4 covers the route from London to Wales via Bristol. Encircling London is M25, which, outside peak traveling times, provides easy access to the countryside and southeast coast. Divided A roads are usually shown on maps as thick, red lines, and, except for occasional traffic lights, are similar to motorways. Most other major routes are the 19th-century coach and turnpike roads designed for horses and carriages. Although they—and the even narrower, winding village roads—will allow you to see much more of the real Britain, your journey could end up taking twice the time. In remote country areas, road travel can be slow, especially in icy winter. Good planning maps are available from the **AA** (Automobile Association) and the **RAC** (Royal Automobile Club); for in-depth exploring, try the Ordinance Survey 1:50,000-series maps. These show every road, track, and footpath in the country.

Rules of the Road

You can use either your driver's license or an International Driving Permit in Britain. Drive on the left-hand side of the road and pay close attention to the varying—and abruptly changing—speed limits. Seat belts are obligatory for frontseat passengers. In general, speed limits are 30 mph in the center of cities and built-up areas, 40 mph in suburban areas, 70 mph on motorways and divided highways, and 60 mph on all other roads.

Parking

Parking in London and other large cities can be a nightmare. On-street meters are hard to find, and lots, though available, can be very expensive. Cheaper pay-and-display lots (the driver inserts money into a machine to receive a sticker for the car with the amount of time allowed for parking) are common in smaller towns and suburban areas. But wherever you are, in town or city, beware of yellow lines. A single yellow line denotes a loading zone—you may park for no longer than 20 minutes during daytime hours—and a double one means no parking anytime, day or night. In many parts of London, as well as in some large northern cities, illegal parking can result in having your car towed away by the police, and wheel clamping is also on the rise as a parking penalty. Retrieving your car from the pound or getting it unclamped entails a hefty fine, so be sure to read street signs carefully before parking.

Gasoline

In Britain, gas (called petrol) comes in three grades, though the price difference between them is negligible. Strangely enough, though most gas stations advertise prices by the gallon, pumps actually measure in liters. A British Imperial gallon is larger than its American equivalent—four of the former equal five of the latter. Most British people solve the dilemma by buying gas by the tankful, or several pounds' worth. At press time (spring 1989), the price of gasoline was about £1.80 per gallon.

By Train Despite severe financial restrictions and frequent complaints from commuters, Britain offers one of the fastest, safest, and most comfortable rail services in the world. All trains are run by the state-owned **British Rail.**

The country's principal—and most efficient—service is the InterCity network, linking London with every major city in the country. The most modern high-speed trains travel up to 125 mph and offer comfortable, fully air-conditioned cars, both first- and second-class, with restaurant or buffet facilities. Local train services are not quite as reliable, particularly around congested city centers such as London. In general, seat reservations are not necessary except during peak vacation periods and on popular medium- and long-distance routes. Reserving a standard-class ticket costs £1.

Fares British Rail fares are high when compared with those in other countries. However, the network does offer a wide, and often bewildering, range of ticket reductions, and these can make a tremendous difference. The information office in each station is generally the most reliable source of information. Information and tickets can also be obatined from British Rail Travel Centers within the larger train stations and from selected travel agents displaying the double arrow British Rail logo.

One of the best bargains available to overseas visitors is the **BritRail Pass** or the **BritRail Youth Pass,** the U.K. equivalent of the Eurail ticket. It provides unlimited travel over the entire British Rail network (and associated ferry and bus routes) for periods of eight, 14, or 22 days, or one month. The cost of a **BritRail economy ticket** for eight days is $179; for 14 days, $259; for 22 days, $339 and for a month, $389. The **Youth Pass,** for those aged 16 to 25, provides unlimited second-class travel, and costs $149 for eight days, $219 for 14 days, $289 for 22 days, and $329 for one month. The **Senior Citizen Pass** entitles pasengers over 65 to unlimited first-class travel. It costs $210 for eight days, $310 for 14 days, $400 for 22 days, and $460 for one month. These passes can be purchased only outside Britain, either in the United States, before you leave, or in one of 46 other countries. British Rail has its own information offices in New York, Los Angeles, Chicago, Dallas, Vancouver, and Toronto.

If you are planning to travel only short distances, be sure to buy inexpensive same-day return tickets. These cost only slightly more than ordinary one-way, standard-class tickets, but can be used only after 9:30 AM and at weekends. Other speical offers are regional **Rover** tickets, giving unlimited travel within local areas, and **Saver** returns, allowing greatly reduced round-trip travel during off-peak periods. For information about routes and fares, contact the **British Travel Centre** (12 Regent Street, London SW1, tel. 01/730–3400). Also inquire at main rail stations for details about reduced-price tickets to specific destinations.

By Plane For a comparatively small country, Britain offers an extensive network of internal air routes. These are run by about a dozen different airlines. Hourly shuttle services operate every day between London and Glasgow, Edinburgh, Belfast, and Manchester. Seats are available on a no-reservations basis, and you can generally check in about half an hour before flight departure time. Keep in mind, however, that Britain's internal air services are not as competitive as those in the United States. And with modern, fast trains and relatively short distances, it is often much cheaper—and not much more time-consuming—to travel by train.

By Bus Buses provide the most economical form of public transportation in Britain. Prices are invariably half that of train tickets, and the network is just as extensive. In recent years, both short- and long-distance buses have improved immeasurably in speed, comfort, and frequency. There is one important semantic difference to keep in mind when discussing bus travel in Britain. Buses (either double- or single-decker) are generally part of the local transportation system in towns and cities, and make frequent stops. Coaches, on the other hand, are comparable to American Greyhound buses and are used only for long-distance travel.

National Express offers the largest number of routes of any coach operator in Britain. It also offers a variety of discount tickets, including the **BritExpress Card** for overseas visitors, which covers all the National Express and Scottish Citylink services. This ticket entitles you to one-third off standard fares for any number of trips made during 30 consecutive days on services throughout England and Wales and selected services in Scotland. You can buy it from travel agents in the United States; in London, at the Victoria Coach Station, Buckingham Palace Road, SW1; or at main train stations in Edinburgh and Glasgow. Information about all services—including bargain fares and special Rover and Explorer tickets—can be obtained from the National Express Information Office at Victoria Coach Station or from **Scottish Omnibuses** (Buchanan Bus Station, Killermont Street, Glasgow G2 3NP).

By Boat Britain offers more than 2,400 kilometers (1,500 miles) of navigable inland waterways—rivers, lakes, canals, locks, and loughs—for leisure travel. Particular regions, such as the Norfolk Broads in East Anglia, the Severn Valley in the West Country, and the sea lochs and canals of Scotland, are especially popular among the nautically minded. Although there are no regularly scheduled waterborne services, hundreds of yachts, canal boats, and motor cruises are available throughout the year. The British Tourist Authority's booklet *UK Waterway Holidays*, is a good source of information. You can also contact the **Inland Waterways Association** (114 Regents Park Road, London NW1 8UQ, tel. 01/586–2510).

By Bicycle Cycling provides an excellent way to see the countryside, and most towns—including London—offer bike rental facilities. Any bike shop or tourist information center should be able to direct you to the nearest rental firm. Rental fees generally run from £5 to £7.50 per day, plus deposit. If you're planning a tour and would like information on rental shops and special holidays for cyclists, contact a British Tourist Authority office in the United States before you leave home. An additional incentive: Except on InterCity 125 trains and selected London services, British Rail will carry bicycles free of charge.

On Foot Many organizations conduct group walking holidays during the summer months. These are especially popular in the Welsh mountains, the Lake District, Dartmoor, and Exmoor. Details are available from the British Tourist Authority.

Staying in Great Britain

Telephones For years, both foreign tourists and the British themselves have cursed the country's inefficient and antiquated phone system. The recent privatization of British Telecom has brought little improvement, though the system is gradually being modernized. Making a phone call in Britain—especially from a public booth—remains a frustrating experience at best.

Local Calls Public telephones are plentiful in British cities, especially London, although you will ordinarily find a high proportion out of order. Other than on the street, the best place to find a bank of pay phones is in a hotel or large post office. As part of Telecom's modernization efforts, the distinctive red boxes are gradually being replaced by generic glass and steel cubicles, but the red boxes still remain in more remote areas of the country. The workings of coin-operated telephones vary, but there are usually intructions in each unit. The oldest kind takes only 10p coins; the new ones take 10p, 20p, 50p, and £1 coins. But the newest innovation is the Phonecard, which comes in denominations of 10, 20, 40, and 100 units, and can be bought in a number of retail outlets. Cardphones are clearly marked with a special green insignia, and they will not accept coins.

A local call during the peak period (9 AM–1 PM) costs about 10p, or 1 unit. Each large city or region in Britain has its own numerical prefix, which is used only when you are dialing from outside the city. In provincial areas, the dialing codes for nearby towns are often posted in the booth, and some even list international codes.

Note: Effective from May 6, 1990, London's 01 prefix will be replaced by two three-digit prefixes: 071 for inner London and 081 for the outer zones.

International Calls The cheapest way to make an overseas call is to dial it yourself. But be sure to have plenty of coins or Phonecards close at hand. After you have inserted the coins or card, dial 010, the international code, then the country code—for the United States, it is 1—followed by the area code and local number. To make a collect or other operator-assisted call, dial 155.

Operators and Information For information anywhere in Britain, dial either 142 or 192. For the operator, dial 100.

Mail
Postal Rates Airmail letters to the Untied States and Canada cost 32p for the first 10 grams and 15p for each additional gram. Postcards and aerogrammes go for 27p. First-class letters within the United Kingdom cost 19p; second-class letters and postcards, 14p. (in October 1989 these prices will rise to 20p and 15p respectively). Airmail rates, too, may well increase by early 1990.

Receiving Mail If you're uncertain where you'll be staying, you can arrange to have your mail sent to American Express, 6 Haymarket, London SW1. The service is free to cardholders; all others pay a small fee. You can also collect letters at London's main post office. Ask to have them sent to Poste Restante, Main Post Office, London. The point of collection is King Edward Building, King Edward Street, London EC1A 1AA. Hours are Monday, Tuesday, Thursday, and Friday 8 AM–7 PM, Wednesday 8:30 AM–7

PM, and Saturday 9 AM–12:30 PM. You'll need your passport or other official form of identification.

Shopping
VAT Refunds
Foreign visitors can avoid Britain's crippling 15% value-added tax (VAT) by taking advantage of a variety of special refund and export schemes. The easiest and most usual way of getting a refund is the Over the Counter method. To qualify for this, you must buy goods worth £75 or more. The shopkeeper will attach a special paper—Form VAT 407—to the invoice, and upon leaving the United Kingdom, you present the goods, form, and invoice to the customs officer. The form is then returned to the store, and the refund forwarded to you, minus a small service charge. The Direct Export method is another option. With this method, you are also issued Form VAT 407, but your purchases are sent home separately, and upon returning home, you must have the form certified by customs or a notary public. You then return the form to the store, and your money is refunded.

Opening and Closing Times
Banks. Banks are open weekdays 9:30–3:30. Some have extended hours on Thursday evenings, and a few are open on Saturday mornings.
Museums. Museum hours vary considerably from one part of the country to another. In large cities, most open weekdays 10–5; many are also open on Sunday afternoons. The majority close one day a week. Holiday closings vary, so be sure to check individual listings.
Shops. Usual business hours are Monday–Saturday 9–5:30. Outside the main centers, most shops observe an early closing day once a week, often Wednesday or Thursday; they close at 1 PM and do not reopen until the following morning. In small villages, many also close for lunch. In large cities—especially London—department stores stay open for late-night shopping (usually until 7:30 or 8) one day a week. Apart from some newsstands and small food stores, almost all shops are closed on Sunday.

National Holidays
England and Wales: January 1; April 13 (Good Friday); April 16 (Easter Monday); May 7 (May Day); May 28 (Spring Bank Holiday); August 27 (Summer Bank Holiday); December 25 and 26 (Christmas). Scotland: January 1 and 2; April 13; May 7; May 28; August 6; December 25 and 26.

Dining
Until relatively recently, British food was condemned the world over for its plainness and mediocrity. But an influx of foreign restaurants and the birth of the New British Cuisine have had a noticeable effect on the quality of the nation's food. Nowadays, the problem is not so much bad food as expensive food. The best of traditional British cooking is solid and straightforward and dependent on top-quality, fresh materials, such as succulent spring beef and seasonal vegetables. The worst consists of heavy, starchy foods, overboiled and deep-fat fried.

Mealtimes
These vary somewhat, depending on the region of the country you are visiting. But in general, breakfast is served between 7:30 and 9, and lunch between noon and 2. Tea—an essential and respected part of British tradition and often a meal in itself—is generally served between 4:30 and 5:30. Dinner or supper is served between 7:30 and 9:30, sometimes earlier, but rarely later. High tea, at about 6, replaces dinner in some areas, and in large cities, after-theater suppers are often available.

Dress   Jacket and tie are suggested for the more formal restaurants in the top-price categories, but in general, casual chic or informal dress is customary in most establishments.

Ratings   Prices quoted here are per person and include a first course, main course, and dessert, but not wine or service. Best bets are indicated by a star ★. At press time (spring 1989), the pound was equal to $1.70.

Category	London	Other Areas
Very Expensive	over £40	over £38
Expensive	£25–£40	£24–£38
Moderate	£12–£25	£12–£24
Inexpensive	under £12	under £12

Credit Cards   The following credit card abbreviations are used: AE, American Express; DC, Diners Club; MC, MasterCard; V, Visa.

Lodging   Britain offers a wide variety of accommodations, ranging from enormous, top-quality, top-price hotels to simple, intimate farm and guest houses.

Hotels   British hotels vary greatly, and there is no official system of classification. Most have rooms with private bathrooms, although there are still some—usually older hotels—that offer rooms with only wash basins; in this case, showers and bathtubs (and toilets) are usually just down the hall. Many also have "good" and "bad" wings. Be sure to check before you take the room. Generally, British hotel prices include breakfast, but beware: Many offer only a Continental breakfast—often little more than tea and toast. A hotel that includes a traditional English breakfast in its rates is usually a good bet. Hotel prices in London are significantly higher than in the rest of the country, and often the quality is not as good. Tourist information centers all over the country will reserve rooms for you, usually for a small fee. A great many hotels offer special weekend and off-season bargain packages. For extra thrills (or chills) the British Tourist Authority can recommend overnight accommodation in one of Britain's "haunted" hotels.

Bed and Breakfasts   These small, simple establishments are a special British tradition, and the backbone of budget travel. They offer modest, inexpensive accommodations, usually in a family home. Few have private bathrooms, and most offer only breakfast. Guest houses are a slightly larger, somewhat more luxurious, version. Both provide the visitor with an excellent glimpse of everyday British life that's seldom seen in large city hotels.

Farmhouses   Such accommodations have become increasingly popular in recent years. Farmhouses do not usually offer top hotel standards, but have a special appeal: the rustic, rural experience. Prices are generally very reasonable. Ask for the British Tourist Authority booklets. Farmhouse Vacations and Stay on a Farm.

Holiday Cottages   Furnished apartments, houses, cottages, and trailers are available for weekly rental in all areas of the country. These vary from quaint, cleverly converted farmhouses to brand-new buildings set in scenic surroundings. For families and large groups, they offer the best value-for-money accommodations.

Lists of rental properties are available free of charge from the British Tourist Authority. Discounts of up to 50% apply during the off-season (October to March).

Stately Homes It is possible to stay as a paying guest in a number of the famous stately homes scattered throughout the countryside. Styles range from Jacobean castles and manors to Regency houses. The equally stately prices usually include both meals and lodging. Reservations are essential. For details, contact the **British Travel Centre** (tel. 01/730–3400) or write to the **British Tourist Authority** (Thames Tower, Blacks Road, London W6).

University Housing In larger cities and in some towns, certain universities offer their residence halls to paying vacationers. The facilities available are usually compact sleeping units, and they can be rented on a nightly basis. For information, contact the **British Universities Accommodation Consortium,** (University Park, Nottingham).

Youth Hostels There are more than 350 youth hostels throughout England, Wales, and Scotland. They range from very basic to very good. Many are located in remote and beautiful areas; others can be found on the outskirts of large cities. Despite the name, there is no age restriction. The accommodations are inexpensive and generally reliable and usually include cooking facilites. For further information, contact the **YHA Headquarters** (Trevelyan House, 8 St. Stephen's Hill, St. Albans, Hertfordshire).

Camping Britain offers an abundance of campsites. Some are large and well equipped; others are merely small farmers' fields, offering primitive facilities. For information, contact the British Travel Authority in the United States, or the **Camping and Caravan Club, Ltd.** (11 Lower Grosvenor Place, London SW1, tel. 01/828–1012).

Ratings Prices are for two people in a double room and include all taxes. Best bets are indicated by a star ★. At press time (spring 1989), the pound was equal to $1.70.

Category	London	Other Areas
Very Expensive	over £120	over £110
Expensive	£75–£120	£70–£110
Moderate	£40–£75	£35–£70
Inexpensive	under £40	under £35

Credit Cards The following credit card abbreviations are used: AE, American Express; DC, Diners Club; MC, MasterCard; V, Visa.

Tipping Some restaurants and most hotels add a service charge of 10–15% to the bill. In this case you are not expected to tip. If no service charge is indicated, add 10% to your total bill. Taxi drivers should also get 10%. You are not expected to tip theater or cinema ushers, elevator operators, or bartenders in pubs. Hairdressers and barbers should receive 10–15%.

London

Arriving and Departing

By Plane   International flights to London arrive at either Heathrow Airport, 12 miles west of London, or at Gatwick Airport, 25 miles
south of the capital. Most—but not all—flights from the United
States go to Heathrow, while Gatwick mostly serves European
destinations, often with charter flights.

Between the   The Piccadilly Line serves Heathrow (all terminals) with a di-
Airport and   rect Underground (subway) link. The 40-minute ride costs
Downtown   £1.90. Three special buses also serve Heathrow: A1 leaves every 20 minutes for Victoria Station; A2 goes to Euston Station
every 20 minutes and takes 80 mintues; night bus N97 runs
hourly from midnight to 5 AM into central London. The one-way
cost is £4.

By Train   London is served by no fewer than 15 train stations, so be absolutely certain of the station for your departure or arrival. All
have Underground stations either in the train station or within
a few minutes' walk from it, and most are served by several bus
routes. British Rail controls all major services. The principal
routes that connect London to other major towns and cities are
on an InterCity network; unlike its European counterparts,
British Rail makes no extra charge for the use of this express
service network.

Seats can only be reserved by phone with a credit card. You
can, of course, apply in person to any British Rail Travel Centre
or directly to the station from which you depart. Below is a list
of the major London rail stations and the areas they serve.

Charing Cross (tel. 01/928–5100) serves southeast England, in-
cluding Canterbury, Margate, Dover/Folkestone.
Euston/St. Pancras (tel. 01/387–7070) serves East Anglia,
Essex, the Northeast, the Northwest, and North Wales, in-
cluding   Conventry,   Stratford-upon-Avon,   Birmingham,
Manchester, Liverpool, Windermere, Glasgow, and Inverness.
King's Cross (tel. 01/278–2477) serves the east Midlands; the
Northeast, including York, Leeds, and Newcastle; and north
and east Scotland, including Edinburgh and Aberdeen.
Liverpool Street (tel. 01/928–5100) serves Essex and East An-
glia.
Paddington (tel. 01/262–6767) serves the south Midlands, west
and south Wales, and the west country, including Reading,
Bath, Bristol, Oxford, Cardiff, Swansea, Exeter, Plymouth,
and Penzance.
Victoria (tel. 01/928–5100) serves southern England, including
Gatwick Airport, Brighton, Dover/Folkestone (from May), and
the south coast.
Waterloo (tel. 01/928–5100) serves the southwestern United
Kingdom, including Salisbury, Bournemouth, Portsmouth,
Southampton, Isle of Wight, Jersey, and Guernsey.

Fares   There is a wide, bewildering range of "savers" and other ticket
bargains. Unfortunately, ticket clerks cannot always be relied
on to know which type best suits your needs, so be sure to ask at
the information office first. **Cheap Day Returns** are best if
you're returning to London the same day, and many family and
other discount railcards are available. You can hear a recorded
summary of timetable and fare information to many InterCity

destinations by dialing the appropriate "dial and listen" numbers listed under British Rail in the telephone book.

By Bus The **National Express** coach service has routes to over 1,00 major towns and cities in the United Kingdom. It's considerably cheaper than the train, although the trips will usually take longer. National Express offers two types of service: an ordinary service, which makes frequent stops for refreshment breaks, and a Rapide service, which has hostess and refreshment facilities on board. Day returns are available on both, but booking is advised on the Rapide service. National Express coaches leave Victoria Coach Staion (Buckingham Palace Rd.) at regular intervals, depending on the destination. For travel information, dial 01/730–0202.

In addition to National Express, **Greenline** operats bus services within a 30–40 mile radius of London. A **Golden Rover** ticket, which allows unlimited travel, is available. Contact Greenline for more information, tel. 01/668–7261.

From Gatwick, the quickest way to London is the nonstop Gatwick Express, costing £5 one-way and taking 30 minutes to reach Victoria Station. Regular bus services are provided by Greenline Coaches, including the Flightline 777 to Victoria Station. This takes about 70 minutes and costs £5 one-way.

From Heathrow, take M4 into London; the trip can take more than an hour, depending on traffic. The taxi fare is about £25. If you are driving from Gatwick, take M23 and then A23 to central London. The taxi fare is about £35.

Getting Around

By Underground Known as "the tube," London's extensive Underground system is by far the most widely used form of city transportation. Trains run both beneath and above ground out into the suburbs, and all stations are clearly marked with the London Underground circular symbol. (A "subway" sign refers to an under-the-street crossing.) Trains are all one class; smoking is *not* allowed on board or in the stations.

There are nine basic lines—all named—plus the East London line, which runs from Shoreditch and Whitechapel across the Thames south to New Cross, and the Docklands Light Railway, which is the best way to travel around the Isle of Dogs in London's East End. The trains on the light railway are computer-operated and run from Tower Gateway to Island Gardens. The Central, District, Northern, Metropolitan, and Piccadilly lines all have branches, so be sure to note which branch is needed for your particular distination. Electonic platform signs tell you the final stop and route of the next train, and some signs also indicate how many minutes you'll have to wait for the train to arrive.

From Monday to Saturday, trains begin running around 5:30 AM; the last services leave central London between midnight and 12:30 AM. On Sundays, trains start two hours later and finish about an hour earlier. The frequency of trains depends on the route and the time of day, but normally you should not have to wait more than 10 minutes in central areas.

A pocket map of the entire tube network is available free from most Underground ticket counters. There should also be a large

London Underground

454

© Copyright London Regional Transport

map on the wall of each platform—though often these are defaced beyond recognition.

Fares For both buses and tube fares, London is divided into five concentric zones; the fare goes up the farther afield you travel. Ask at Underground ticket counters for the London Regional Transport (LRT) booklet "Tickets," which gives details of all the various ticket options and bargains for the tube; after some experimenting, you'll soon know which ticket best serves your particular needs. Till then, here is a brief summary of the major ticket categories, but note that these prices are subject to increase.

Singles and Returns. For one trip between any two stations, you can buy an ordinary single for travel anytime on the day of issue; if you're coming back on the same route the same day, then an ordinary return costs twice the single fare. Singles vary in price from 60p in the central zone to £1.90 for a five-zone journey—not a good option for the sightseer who wants to make several journeys.

Cheap Day Return. Issued weekdays Monday–Friday after 9:30 AM and anytime on weekends, these are basically good for one return journey within the five zones.

One-Day Off-Peak Travelcards. These allow unrestricted travel on the tube, most buses, and British Rail trains in the Greater London zones, and are valid weekdays after 9:30 AM, weekends, and all public holidays. They cannot be used on airbuses, night buses, Route 128, for special services, or on tours and excursions. The price is £2.30 for adults, 80p for children under 16 (no photograph is required except for children aged 14–15, who must show child-rate photocards).

Other Travelcards. These can be purchased for seven days, one month, or up to one year and are valid for unlimited travel on the tube, most buses, and British Rail trains in the zones specified. Photographs are required. Prices for a weekly ticket range from £6.40 for the central zone to £17.70 for all five zones.

Visitor's Travelcard. These must be bought before leaving home and are available both in the United States and Canada. They are valid for periods of one, three, four, or seven days and can be used on the tube and virtually all buses and British Rail services in London. This card also includes a set of money-saving discounts to many of London's top attractions. Apply to travel agents or to BritRail Travel International.

For more information, there are **LRT Travel Information Centres** at the following tube stations: Euston, *open Sat.–Thurs. 7:15–6, Fri. to 7:30;* King's Cross, *open Sat.–Thurs. 8:15–6, Fri. to 7:30;* Oxford Circus, *open Mon.–Sat. 8:15–6;* Piccadilly Circus, *open Mon.–Sun. 8:15–6;* Victoria, *open Mon.–Sun. 8:15–9:30;* and Heathrow, *open Mon.–Sun. (to 9 or 10 PM* in Terminals 1 and 2). For information on all London bus and tube times, fares, etc., dial 01/222–1234; the line is operated *24 hours.*

By Bus London's bus system now consists of the bright red double- and single-deckers, plus, in the outer zones, other buses of various colors. Destinations are displayed on the front and back, with the bus number on the front, back, and side. By no means do all buses run the full length of their route at all times, so always check the termination point before boarding, preferably with the conductor or driver. Many buses are still operated with a conductor whom you pay after finding a seat, but there is now a move to one-man buses, in which you pay the driver upon boarding.

Buses stop only at clearly indicated stops. Main stops—at which the bus *should* stop automatically—have a plain white background with a red LRT symbol on it. There are also request stops with red signs, a white symbol, and the word "Request" added; at these you must hail the bus to make it stop. Smoking is not allowed on the lower deck of a double-decker, and is discouraged on the top deck, except at the back. Although you can see much of the town from a bus, *don't* take one if you want to get anywhere in a hurry; traffic often slows travel to a crawl, and during peak times you may find yourself waiting at least 20 minutes for a bus and then not being able to get on it once it arrives. If you do go by bus, ask at a Travel Information Centre for a free London Wide Bus Map.

Fares Single fares start at 40p for short distances (60p in the central zone). Travelcards are good for tube, bus, and British Rail trains in the Greater London Zones. There are also a number of bus passes available for daily, weekly, and monthly use, and prices vary according to zones. A photograph is required for weekly or monthly bus passes; this also applies to children and older children who may need a child-rate photocard to avoid paying the adult rate.

By Taxi London's black taxis are famous for their comfort and for the ability of their drivers to remember the mazelike pattern of the capital's streets. Hotels and main tourist areas have ranks (stands) where you wait until you get to the front of the line. You can also hail a taxi if the flag is up or the yellow "for hire" sign is lit. Fares start at £1 and increase by units of 20p per 495 yards or 60 seconds. A surcharge of 60p or 80p is added in the evenings until midnight and on holidays.

By Car The best advice is to avoid driving in London because of the illogical street patterns and the chronic parking shortage. A constantly changing system of one-way streets adds to the confusion.

Things are a lot easier outside the rush hours (8AM–10AM and 4PM–6PM), and if you drive through central London in the early hours of the morning, you'll see that the traffic-choked arteries of daytime (such as the Strand and Oxford Street) are convenient ways to cross London.

By Boat The **Thamesline Riverbus** operates between Chelsea and Greenwich, with seven stops between. For information, tel. 01/897–0311.

Important Addresses and Numbers

Tourist Information The main **London Tourist Information Centre** at Victoria Station Forecourt provides details about London and the rest of Britain, including general information; tickets for tube and bus; theater, concert, and tour bookings; and accommodations. Telephone information service: 01/730–3488. Open Apr.–Oct., daily 9–8:30; rest of the year, Mon.–Sat. 9–7, Sun. 9–5.

Other information centers are located in **Harrods** (Brompton Rd., SW3) and **Selfridges** (Oxford St., W1) and are open store hours only; at **Tower of London** (West Gate, E1), open summer months only; and **Heathrow Airport** (Terminals 1, 2, and 3). The **City of London Information Centre** (St. Paul's Churchyard, EC4, tel. 01/606–3030) has information on sights and events in the City. Open May–Oct., daily 9:30–5; Nov.–Apr., weekdays 9:30–5, Sat. 9:30–12:30.

The **British Travel Centre,** (12 Regent St., W1, tel. 01/730–3400), provides details about travel accommodations, and bookings for the whole of Britain. Open weekdays 9–6:30 and weekends 10–4.

Embassies and Consulates **American Embassy:** 24 Grosvenor Sq., W1A, 1AE, tel. 01/499–9000. Located inside the embassy is the **American Aid Society,** a charity set up to help Americans in distress. Dial the embassy number and ask for extension 570 or 571.

Canadian High Commission: Canada House, Trafalgar Sq., London SW1 Y 5BJ, tel. 01/629–9492.

Emergencies For police, fire brigade, or ambulance, dial 999.

The following **hospitals** have 24-hour emergency rooms: **Guys,** St. Thomas St., SE1, tel. 01/407–7600; **Royal Free,** Pond St., Hampstead, NW3, tel. 01/794–0500; **St. Bartholomew's,** West Smithfield, EC1, tel. 01/601–8888; **St. Thomas's,** Lambeth Palace Rd., SE1, tel. 01/928–9292; **University College,** Gower St., W1, tel. 01/387–9300; **Westminster,** Dean Ryle St., Horseferry Rd., SW1, tel. 01/828–9811 (adults only).

Pharmacies Chemists (drugstores) with late opening hours include: **Bliss Chemist,** 50–56 Willesden Lane, NW6, tel. 01/624–8000, open daily 9 AM–2 AM, also the branch at 5 Marble Arch, W1, tel. 01/723–6116, open daily 9 AM–midnight; **Boots,** 44 Piccadilly Circus, W1, tel. 01/734–6126, open Mon.–Sat. 8:30–8, also the branches at 439 Oxford St., W1, tel. 01/409–2857, open Thurs. 8:30–7, and 114 Queensway, W2, tel. 01/229–4819, open Mon.–Sun. 10–10.

Travel Agencies **American Express:** 6 Haymarket, SW1, tel. 01/930–4411, and at 89 Mount St., W1, tel. 01/499–4436. **Hogg Robinson Travel/Diners Club:** 176 Tottenham Court Rd., W1, tel. 01/580–0437. **Thomas Cook:** 45 Berkeley St., Piccadilly W1, tel. 01/499–4000.

Credit Cards Should your credit cards be lost or stolen, here are some numbers to dial for assistance: **Access (MasterCard),** tel. 0702/352244 or 352255; **American Express,** tel. 01/222–9633 (24 hours) or 0273/696933 (8–6 only) for credit cards, tel. 0800/521313 for traveler's checks; **Barclaycard (Visa),** tel. 0604/230230; **Diners Club,** tel. 0252/516261.

Guided Tours

Orientation Tours **London Regional Transport's** official guided sightseeing tours
By Bus (tel. 01/222–1234) offer passengers a good introduction to the city from double-decker buses (seating capacity 64–72). Tours run daily every half hour 10–5, from Marble Arch (top of Park Lane near Speakers' Corner), Victoria Station, and Piccadilly Circus (Haymarket). The route covers roughly 18–20 miles and lasts 1½ hours; no stops are included. Tickets may be bought from the driver, any London Transport Travel Information Centre (ticket price reduced by £1), or in advance from the London Tourist Information Centre at Victoria. Other agencies offering half- and full-day bus tours include **Evan Evans** (tel. 01/930–2377), **Frames Rickards** (tel. 01/837–3111), and **Travellers Check-In** (tel. 01/580–8284). These tours have a smaller seating capacity of approximately 50 passengers and include stops at places of special interest, such as St. Paul's Cathedral and Westminster Abbey. Prices and pick-up points vary according to the sights visited, but many pick-up points are at major hotels.

By River From April to October, boats cruise up and down the Thames, offering a different view of the London skyline. Most leave from Westminster Pier (tel. 01/930–4097), Charing Cross Pier (Victoria Embankment, tel. 01/839–3572), and Tower Pier (tel. 01/488–0344). Downstream routes go to the Tower of London, Greenwich, and Thames Barrier; upstream destinations include Kew, Richmond, and Hampton Court. Most of the launches seat between 100 and 250 passengers, have a public address system, and provide a running commentary on passing points of interest. Depending upon the destination, river trips may last from one to four hours. For more information, call **Catamaran Cruises,** tel. 01/839–2349, or **Travel Cruises,** tel. 01/928–9009.

By Canal During summer, narrow boats and barges cruise London's two canals, the Grand Union and Regent's Canal; most vessels (seating about 60) operate on the latter, which runs between Little Venice in the west (the nearest tube is Warwick Ave. on the Bakerloo Line) and Camden Lock (about 200 yards north of Camden Town tube station). **Jason's Canal Cruises** (tel. 01/286–3428) operates one-way and round-trip narrow boat cruises on this route. During April, May, and September, there are two cruises per day; from June to August there are four. Trips last 1½ hours and cost £2.95 for adults, £1.50 for children and senior citizens.

Canal Cruises (tel. 01/485–4433) also offers cruises from March to October on the *Jenny Wren* (£2.40 adults, £1.20 children and senior citizens), and all year on the cruising restaurant *My Fair Lady* (Tues.–Sat. dinner £17.95, Sun. lunch £12.75).

Walking Tours One of the best ways to get to know London is on foot, and there are many guided walking tours from which to choose. **London Walks** (tel. 01/441–8906), **Cockney Walks** (tel. 01/504–9159), **City Walks** (tel. 01/937–4281), **Footloose in London** (tel. 01/435–0259), and **Discovering London** (tel. 0277/213704) are just a few of the better-known firms, but your best bet is to peruse a variety of leaflets at the London Tourist Information Centre at Victoria Station. The duration of the walks varies (usually 1–3 hours), and you can generally find one to suit even the most specific of interests—Shakespeare's London, say, or a Jack the Ripper tour. Prices range around £3 for adults.

If you'd rather explore on your own, then the City of London Corporation has laid out a **Heritage Walk** that leads through Bank, Leadenhall, and Monument; follow the trail by the directional stars set into the sidewalks. A map of this walk may be found in *A Visitor's Guide to the City of London*, available from the City Information Centre across from St. Paul's Cathedral. Another option is to follow the **Silver Jubilee Walkway,** created in 1977 in honor of the 25th anniversary of the reign of the present queen. The entire route covers 10 miles and is marked by a series of silver crowns set into the sidewalks; Parliament Square makes a good starting point. Several books are available from the British Travel Centre (12 Regent St., W1) that also list a number of different walks to follow.

Excursions **LRT, Evan Evans, Frames Rickards,** and **Travellers Check-In** (*see* Orientation Tours) all offer day excursions (some combine bus and boat) to places of interest within easy reach of London, such as Windsor, Hampton Court, Oxford, Stratford, and Bath. Prices vary and may include lunch and admission prices or admission only.

Personal Guides **Prestige Tours** (tel. 01/584–3118) operates a fleet of standard London taxis, each driven by a qualified guide. Tours are available all year, and a day's advance booking is usually enough to arrange an expert tour of the capital. There are three basic tours: full-day (around six hours) for £130; half-day (three hours) for £80; and the two-hour "Easy Rider" for £55. Alternatively, you can arrange an out-of-town trip, such as Stratford combined with Oxford. Rates may seem high, but are for up to four people.

With 30 years' experience of providing a customized sightseeing service, **British Tours** (tel. 01/629–5257) will pick you up from your hotel and take you anywhere in the United Kingdom. Tour prices include car and driver-guide expenses and range from £55 for two people in a medium-size car going on a two-hour tour of London, to £200 for one to four people in a large car taking in both Oxford and Cambridge (10 hours). A good choice of tours, for one to six people, is available all year. Details of similar private operators may be found at the London Tourist Information Centre in Victoria Station or at the British Travel Centre.

Exploring London

Traditionally, London has been divided between the City, to the east, site of the original Roman settlement of Londinium, where its banking and commercial interests lie, and Westminster to the west, the seat of the royal court and of government. Today the distinction between the two holds good, and even the briefest exploration will demonstrate that each enjoys a quite distinct atmosphere. It is in these two areas also that you will find most of the grand buildings that have played a central role in British history: the Tower of London and St. Paul's Cathedral, Westminster Abbey and the Houses of Parliament, Buckingham Palace and the older royal palace of St. James's.

These sites are natural magnets for visitors to London, as the crowds of people and the ubiquitous tourist coaches demonstrate. But visitors who restrict their sightseeing to these well-known tourist traps miss much of the best the city has to offer. Within a few minutes' walk of Buckingham Palace, for instance, lie St. James's and Mayfair, two neighboring quarters of elegant town houses built for the nobility in the 17th and early 18th centuries, and now full of stylish shops patronized by an international, jet-setting clientele. The same lesson applies to the City, where, tucked away in quiet corners, stand many of the churches Christopher Wren built to replace those destroyed during the Great Fire of 1666.

Other parts of London worth exploring include Covent Garden, where a former fruit and flower market has been converted into a lively shopping and entertainment center with a bazaar where craftspeople sell their own wares. The atmosphere here is informal, and you can stroll for hours enjoying the friendly bustle of the streets. Hyde Park and Kensington Gardens, by contrast, offer a great swathe of green parkland across the city center, preserved by past kings and queens for their own hunting and relaxation. A walk across Hyde Park will bring you to the museum district of South Kensington, with the four major national collections: the Natural History Museum, the Science Museum, the Geological Museum, and the Victoria and Albert Museum, which specializes in costume and the fine and applied arts.

The south side of the River Thames has its treats as well. A short stroll across Waterloo Bridge brings you to the South Bank Arts Complex, which includes the National Theatre, the Royal Festival Hall, the Hayward Gallery (with changing exhibitions of international art), the National Film Theatre, and the recently opened Museum of the Moving Image (MOMI)—a must for movie buffs. The views from here are stunning—to the west are the Houses of Parliament and Big Ben, to the east the dome of St. Paul's is just visible on London's changing skyline.

The key to London is thus a simple one. Explore for yourself off the beaten track. Use your feet, and when you are tired, take to the bus or the Underground. And look around you, for London's centuries of history and its vibrant daily life are revealed as much in the individual streets and houses of the city as in its grand national monuments and galleries.

Numbers in the margin correspond with points of interest on the London map.

Westminster   **Westminster** is the royal backyard—the traditional center of the royal court and of government. Here, within a mile or so of each other, are virtually all London's most celebrated buildings (St. Paul's Cathedral and the Tower of London excepted), and there is a strong feeling of history all around you. Generations of kings and queens and their offspring have lived here since the end of the 11th century, in no less than four palaces, three of which (Buckingham, St. James's, and Westminster) still stand.

❶ Start at **Trafalgar Square,** which is on the site of the former Royal Mews. Both the square's name and its present appearance date from about 1830. A statue of Lord Nelson, victor over the French in 1805 at the Battle of Trafalgar, at which he lost his life, stands atop a 57-meter (185-foot) column. Lions guard the base of the column, which is decorated with four bronze panels depicting naval battles against France and cast from French cannons captured by Nelson. The bronze equestrian statue on the south side of the square is of the unhappy Charles I; he is looking down Whitehall toward the spot where he was executed in 1649.

❷ In the **National Gallery,** which occupies the long neoclassical building on the north side of the square, is a comprehensive collection of paintings, with works from virtually every famous artist and school from the 14th to the 19th centuries. The gallery is especially strong on Flemish and Dutch masters, Rubens and Rembrandt among them, and on Italian Renaissance works. *Trafalgar Sq., tel. 01/839-3321; 01/839-3526 (recorded information). Admission free. Open Mon.–Sat. 10–6, Sun. 2–6; June–Aug., Wed. until 8.*

Around the corner, at the foot of Charing Cross Road, is a second major art collection, the **National Portrait Gallery,** which
❸ contains portraits of well-known (and not so well-known) Brit-

ons, including monarchs, statesmen, and writers. *2 St. Martin's Pl., tel. 01/930–1552. Admission free. Open weekdays 10–5, Sat. 10–6, Sun. 2–6.*

④ The Gallery's entrance is opposite the distinctive neoclassical church of **St. Martin-in-the-Fields,** built in about 1730. Regular lunchtime music recitals are held here.

Time Out Both the **National Gallery Restaurant** and **Field's Restaurant** in the crypt of St. Martin's serve light lunches and a good selection of salads, sandwiches, and pastries.

⑤ **Admiralty Arch** guards the entrance to **The Mall,** the great ceremonial way that leads alongside **St. James's Park** to Buckingham Palace. The Mall takes its name from a game called "pell mell," a version of croquet that society people, including Charles II and his courtiers, used to play here in the late 1600s. The park, one of central London's smallest and most attractive, with superbly maintained flowerbeds, was developed by successive monarchs, most recently by George IV in the 1820s, having originally been used for hunting by Henry VIII. Join office workers relaxing with a lunchtime sandwich, or stroll here on a summer's evening when the illuminated fountains play and Westminster Abbey and the Houses of Parliament beyond the trees are floodlit.

⑥ On the other side of the Mall, you pass along the foot of the imposing **Carlton House Terrace,** built in 1827–32 by John Nash. A right turn up Marlborough Road brings you to the complex of
⑦ royal and government buildings known collectively as **St. James's Palace.** Although the earliest parts of this lovely brick building date from the 1530s, it had a relatively short career as the center of royal affairs, from the destruction of Whitehall Palace in 1698 until 1837, when Victoria became queen and moved the royal household down the road to Buckingham Palace. A number of royal functionaries have offices here, however, and various court functions are held in the state rooms. Foreign ambassadors are still accredited to the "Court of St. James's."

⑧ At the end of Marlborough Road, beyond the open-sided **Friary Court,** turn left along **Cleveland Row,** and walk past **York House, the London home of the Duke and Duchess of Kent.** An-
⑨ other left turn into **Stable Yard Road** takes you to **Lancaster House,** built for the Duke of York by Nash in the 1820s and used today for government receptions and conferences. On the other
⑩ side of Stable Yard is **Clarence House,** so called because it was designed and built by Nash in 1825 for the Duke of Clarence, who later became King William IV. It was restored in 1949 and is now the home of the Queen Mother. Inside the palace is the **Chapel Royal,** said to have been designed for Henry VIII by the painter Holbein; it was heavily redecorated in the mid-19th century. The ceiling still has the initials H and A, intertwined, standing for Henry VIII and his second wife, Anne Boleyn, the mother of Elizabeth I and the first of his wives to lose her head. The public can attend Sunday morning services here between the first week of October and Good Friday.

⑪ **Buckingham Palace,** at the end of the Mall, is the London home of the queen and the administrative hub of the entire royal family. When the queen is in residence (on weekdays except in January, August, September, and part of June), the royal stan-

London

dard flies over the east front. Inside, there are dozens of splendid state rooms used on such formal occasions as banquets for visiting heads of state. The private apartments of Queen Elizabeth and Prince Philip are in the north wing. Behind the palace lie some 16 hectares (40 acres) of private gardens, a haven for wildlife in the midst of the capital.

The ceremony of the **Changing of the Guard** takes place in front of the palace at 11:30 daily April through July and on alternate days during the rest of the year. It's advisable to arrive early; the Queen Victoria Memorial in the middle of the traffic roundabout provides a grandstand view.

⑫ Buckingham Palace is not open to the public. The former chapel, bombed during World War II and rebuilt in 1961, has been converted into the **Queen's Gallery**, however, where there are regular exhibitions drawn from the vast royal art collections. *Buckingham Palace Rd., tel. 01/930–4832. Admission: £1.20 adults, 60p children and senior citizens. Open Tues.–Sat. 10:30–4:30, Sun. 2–4:30; closed between exhibitions.*

⑬ Just along Buckingham Palace Road from the Queen's Gallery is the **Royal Mews,** where some of the queen's horses are stabled and the elaborately gilded state coaches are on view. *Tel. 01/930–4832. Admission: £1 adults, 50p children and senior citizens. Open Wed. and Thurs. 2–4; closed during state occasions involving royal carriage processions and during Royal Ascot week (June).*

⑭ **Birdcage Walk,** so called because it was once the site of the royal aviaries, runs along the south side of St. James's Park, past the **Wellington Barracks.** These are the regimental headquarters of the Guards Division, the elite troops that traditionally guard the sovereign and mount the guard at Buckingham Palace. The **Guards Museum** relates the history of the Guards from the 1660s to the present day; paintings of battle scenes, uniforms, and a cat o'nine tails are among the items on display. *Tel. 01/930–4466, ext. 3271 or 3253. Admission: £2 adults, £1 children under 16 and senior citizens. Open Sat.–Thurs. 10–4.*

⑮ The **Cabinet War Rooms,** between the Foreign Office and the House Office, are the underground offices used by the British High Command during World War II. Among the rooms on display are the Prime Minister's Room, where Winston Churchill made many of his inspiring wartime broadcasts, and the Transatlantic Telephone Room, from which he spoke directly to President Roosevelt in the White House. *Clive Steps, King Charles St., tel. 01/930–6961 or 01/735–8922. Admission: £2.80 adults, £1.50 children under 16, students, and senior citizens. Open daily 10–5:15.*

⑯ **Parliament Square** is the large open space flanked, on the river side, by the Palace of Westminster. Among the numerous statues of statesmen long since dead are those of Churchill, Abraham Lincoln, and Oliver Cromwell, the Lord Protector of England during the country's sole, brief republican period (1648–60).

⑰ The **Palace of Westminster** was the monarch's main residence from the 11th century until 1512, when the court moved to the newly built Whitehall Palace. The only part of the original building to have survived, however, is **Westminster Hall,** which has a fine hammer-beam roof. The rest was destroyed in a disastrous fire in 1834 and was rebuilt in the newly popular mock-medieval Gothic style with ornate interior decorations. The architect, Augustus Pugin, provided many delightful touches, such as Gothic umbrella stands. In addition to Westminster Hall, which is used only on rare ceremonial occasions, the palace contains the debating chambers and committee rooms of the two Houses of Parliament—the Commons (whose members are elected) and the Lords (whose members are appointed or inherit their seats). There are no tours of the palace, but the public is admitted to the Public Gallery of each House; expect to wait in line for several hours (the line for the Lords is generally much shorter than that for the Commons).

The most famous features of the palace are its towers. At the south end is the 104-meter (336-foot) **Victoria Tower.** At the other end is **St. Stephen's Tower,** better known, but inaccurately so, as Big Ben. That name properly belongs to the 13-ton bell in the tower on which the hours are struck; Big Ben himself was Sir Benjamin Hall, commissioner of works when the bell was installed in the 1850s. A light shines from the top of the tower during a night sitting of Parliament.

18 **Westminster Abbey** is the most ancient of London's great churches and the most important, for it is here that Britain's monarchs are crowned. The abbey dates largely from the 13th and 14th centuries, although **Henry VII's Chapel,** an exquisite example of the heavily decorated late Gothic style, was not built until the early 1600s and the twin towers over the west entrance are an 18th-century addition. There is much to see inside, including the memorial to Winston Churchill; the tomb of the Unknown Warrior, a nameless World War I soldier buried in earth brought with his corpse from France; and Poets' Corner, where some of the country's finest writers are commemorated. Behind the high altar are the royal tombs, including those of Queen Elizabeth I, Mary Queen of Scots, and Henry V. In the Chapel of Edward the Confessor stands the Coronation Chair. Among the royal weddings that have taken place here are those of the present queen and most recently, in 1986, the Duke and Duchess of York.

It is all too easy to forget, amid the crowds trying to see the abbey's sights, that this is a place of worship. Early morning is a good moment to catch something of the building's atmosphere. Better still, take time to attend a service. *Broad Sanctuary, tel. 01/222–5152. Admission to the nave is free, to Poets' Corner and Royal Chapels, £2 adults, £1 students and senior citizens, 50p children (Royal Chapels, free Wed. 6–7:45 PM). Open weekdays 9–4, Sat. 9–2 and 3:45–5; Sun. all day for services only; museum and cloisters open Sun.; closed weekdays to visitors during services; Royal Chapels closed Sun. No photography except Mon. evening.*

The Norman **Undercroft,** off the original monastic cloisters, houses a small museum with exhibits on the abbey's history. In the **Pyx Chamber** next door are fine examples of silver vessels and other treasures. The nearby **Chapter House** was where the English Parliament first met. *Tel. 01/222–5152. Joint admission: £1.50 adults, 75p students and senior citizens, 40p children. Open daily 10:30–4.*

From Parliament Square, walk up **Parliament Street** and **Whitehall** (this is a single street—its name changes), past gov-

⑲ ernment offices, toward Trafalgar Square. The **Cenotaph** is the national memorial to the dead of both world wars. On the left is the entrance to **Downing Street,** an unassuming row of 18th-century houses. The prime minister's office is at No. 10 (she has a private apartment on the top floor). The chancellor of the exchequer, the finance minister, occupies No. 11.

⑳ On the right side of Whitehall is the **Banqueting House,** built by the architect Inigo Jones in 1625 for court entertainments. This is the only part of Whitehall Palace, the monarch's principal residence in the 16th and 17th centuries, that was not burned down in 1698. Outside there is an inscription that marks the window through which King Charles I stepped to his execution. *Tel. 01/930–4179. Admission: £1.60 adults, £1.20 students and senior citizens, 80p children. Open Tues.–Sat. 10–5, Sun. 2–5.*

㉑ Opposite is the entrance to **Horse Guards Parade,** the former tilt yard of Whitehall Palace. This is the site of the annual ceremony of Trooping the Colour, when the queen takes the salute in the great military parade that marks her official birthday on the second Saturday in June (her real one is on April 21). There is also a daily guard-changing ceremony outside the guard house, at 11 AM, 10 on Sunday.

After such a concentrated dose of grand, historical buildings, it's time to explore two of London's elegant shopping areas, **St. James's** and **Mayfair.** Start by walking west from Piccadilly Circus along **Piccadilly,** which contains a mixture of airline offices, shops (including **Hatchards,** the booksellers, and **Fortnum and Mason,** the queen's grocer) and academic societies.

㉒ **St. James's Church** was designed by the 17th-century architect Christopher Wren and contains beautiful wood carvings by Grinling Gibbons.

Time Out | The Wren at St. James's is a friendly café in the church precincts. Coffee, pastries, and light lunches are served.

Jermyn Street, south of Piccadilly, is famous for upscale shops selling costly shirts, ties, and sweaters. **Paxton & Whitfield** sells an extraordinary variety of cheeses. Shops along **Duke Street** and **Bury Street** specialize in paintings, the former in Old Masters, the latter in early English watercolors. Don't be put off by the exclusive appearance of these establishments—anyone is free to enter, and there is no obligation to buy. **King Street** is home to **Christie's,** the fine art auctioneer, and to **Spink and Son,** renowned for Oriental art.

On the north side of Piccadilly, **Burlington House** contains the offices of many learned societies and the headquarters of the **㉓** **Royal Academy.** The RA, as it is generally known, stages major visiting art exhibitions. The best known is the Summer Exhibition (May–Aug.), featuring works by living British artists.

Burlington Arcade is a covered walkway with tiny shops selling primarily jewelry and craft goods, such as woolens. Built in 1819, it was the first shopping precinct in the country, and it retains something of its original atmosphere. A uniformed beadle is on duty to ensure that no one runs, whistles, or sings here.

㉔ The **Museum of Mankind** contains the British Museum's ethnographic collection. There are displays on the South Seas, the Arctic, and other regions of the world. *6 Burlington Gardens, tel. 01/437–2224. Admission: free. Open Mon.–Sat. 10–5, Sun. 2:30–6.*

There are three special shopping streets in this section of Mayfair, each with its own specialties. **Savile Row** is the home of gentlemen's tailors. Nearby **Cork Street** has many dealers in modern and classical art. **Bond Street** (divided into two parts, Old and New, though both are some 300 years old) is the classiest shopping street in London. This is haute couture, with famous names such as **Gucci, Hermès,** and **St. Laurent,** and costly jewelry from shops such as **Asprey, Tiffany,** and **Cartier.**

Some of the original 18th-century houses survive on the west side of **Berkeley Square.** Farther along is **Curzon Street,** which runs along the northern edge of **Shepherd Market,** a maze of narrow streets full of antique shops, restaurants, and pubs that retain something of a village atmosphere.

Time Out L'Artiste Musclé is a popular bistro serving French food; the *boeuf bourguignonne* is very tasty. *1 Shepherd Market.*

㉕ **Hyde Park Corner** is the start of a great expanse of green parkland that cuts right across the center of London. **Hyde Park,** which covers about 137 hectares (340 acres), was originally a royal hunting ground, while **Kensington Gardens,** which adjoins it to the west, started life as part of the royal Kensington Palace. These two parks contain many fine trees and are a haven for wildlife. **Rotten Row** is the sandy track that runs along the south edge of Hyde Park. There's nothing rotten about it; in fact, for several hundred years it has been one of the most fashionable places to go riding. The name derives from *route du roi* (the King's Way)—the route William III and Queen Mary took from their home at Kensington Palace to the court at St. James's. There is boating and swimming in the **Serpentine,** the S-shaped lake formed by damming a river that used to flow here. Refreshments can be had at the Serpentine bars, buffet, and restaurant complex, and the **Serpentine Gallery** holds temporary exhibitions of modern art.

Leave the park at **Exhibition Road** and visit three of London's **㉖** major museums. The **Science Museum** is the major national collection of science and technology, with extensive hands-on exhibits on outer space, astronomy, computers, transportation, and medicine. *Tel. 01/589–3456; 01/938–8123 (recorded information). Admission: £2 adults, £1 children under 15 and senior citizens. Open Mon.–Sat. 10–6, Sun. 11–6.*

㉗ The **Natural History Museum** is housed in an ornate late-Victorian building with striking modern additions. As in the Science Museum, its displays on topics such as human biology and evolution are designed to challenge visitors to think for themselves. *Cromwell Rd., tel. 01/589–6323; 01/725–7866 (recorded information). Admission: £2 adults, £1 children under 15 and senior citizens; free weekdays 4:30–6. Open Mon.–Sat. 10–6, Sun. 2:30–6.*

㉘ The **Victoria and Albert Museum** (or V & A) originated in the 19th century as a museum of ornamental art and has extensive collections of costumes, paintings, jewelry, and crafts from every part of the globe. The collections from India, China, and the Islamic world are especially strong. *Cromwell Rd., tel. 01/938–8500; 01/938–8441 (recorded information). For admission, a donation is requested but is not essential. Open Mon.–Sat. 10–5:50, Sun. 2:30–5:50.*

Time Out The **V & A restaurant** is just the place to recuperate after visiting the museum. You can enjoy morning coffee, hot lunchtime dishes, or afternoon tea.

㉙ Back in Kensington Gardens, the **Albert Memorial** commemorates Queen Victoria's much-loved husband, Prince Albert, who died in 1861 at the age of 42. The monument, itself the epitome of high Victorian taste, commemorates the many socially uplifting projects of the prince, among them the Great Exhibition of 1851, whose catalog he is holding.

From the **Flower Walk,** behind the Albert Memorial, carefully planted so that flowers are in bloom virtually throughout the **㉚** year, strike out across Kensington Gardens to the **Round Pond,** a favorite place for children to sail toy boats.

㉛ **Kensington Palace,** across from the Round Pond, has been a royal home since the late 17th century—and is one still, for the Prince and Princess of Wales and Princess Margaret. From the outside, it looks less like a palace than a country house, which it was until William III bought it in 1689. Inside, however, are state rooms on a grand scale, mostly created in the early 18th century. Such distinguished architects as Wren, Hawksmoor, Vanbrugh, and William Kent were all employed here. Queen Victoria lived at Kensington as a child, and several rooms are furnished as they were in her time. The public part of the palace also contains an exhibition of court dress. *Tel. 01/937–9561. Admission: £3 adults, £2 students and senior citizens, £1.50 children. Open Mon.–Sat. 9–5, Sun. 1–5.*

North of Kensington Gardens are two lively districts, **Bayswater** and **Notting Hill,** both full of restaurants and cafés where young people gather. The best-known attraction in this area is **㉜** **Portobello Road,** where the celebrated antiques and bric-a-brac market is held each Saturday (arrive early in the morning for the best bargains). The street is also full of regular antiques shops that are open most weekdays.

Time Out **Geales** (2 Farmer St.) is a superior Notting Hill fish-and-chips establishment, popular with locals and the rich and famous alike. The fish really is fresh.

Covent Garden You could easily spend a half-day exploring the block of streets **㉝** north of the Strand known as **Covent Garden.** The heart of the area is a former wholesale fruit and vegetable market, established in 1656. The market moved to more modern and accessible premises only in 1974. The Victorian **Market Building** is now an elegant and fashionable shopping center, with numerous boutiques, craft shops, and health-food bars. On the south side of the market building is the lively and much less formal **Jubilee open-air market,** where artists and craftspeople sell their wares at stalls.

The atmosphere in Covent Garden is friendly and informal. Look for the open-air entertainers performing under the porti-

�['34'] co of **St. Paul's Church**—you can enjoy an excellent show for the price of a few coins thrown in the hat that's passed among the onlookers. The church, entered from Bedford Street, is known as the Actors' Church. The **Royal Opera House** and the **Theatre Royal Drury Lane,** two of London's oldest theaters, are close by, and inside are numerous memorials to theater people.

Time Out There's a good selection of eating places in and around the Market Building. **Crank's,** at No. 11, serves delicious quiches, salads, and cakes. The **Calabash,** in the basement of the Africa Center at 38 King Street, serves authentic African dishes at reasonable prices.

For interesting specialty shops, head north of the market building. Shops on **Long Acre** sell maps, art books, and glass; shops on **Neal Street** sell clothes, pottery, and jewelry, and goods from the East.

㉟ The collection of vehicles at the **London Transport Museum** includes a steam locomotive, a tram, a subway car, and an Underground train simulator. Visitors are encouraged to operate many of the vehicles. The shop sells T-shirts, books, souvenirs, and current and historic London Transport posters. *The Piazza (southeast corner), tel. 01/379–6344. Admission: £2.40 adults, £1.10 children under 16 and senior citizens. Open daily 10–5:15.*

㊱ The **Theatre Museum** contains a comprehensive collection of material on the history of the English theater—not merely the classic drama but also opera, music hall, pantomime, and musical comedy. Scripts, playbills, costumes, and props are displayed; there is even a re-creation of a dressing room filled with memorabilia of former stars. *Russell St., tel. 01/831–1227. Admission: £2.25 adults, £1.25 children under 14, students, and senior citizens. Open Tues.–Sun. 11–7.*

㊲ On **Bow Street** is the **Royal Opera House,** home of the Royal Ballet and the Royal Opera Company. The plush interior captures the richness of Victorian England.

Bloomsbury **Bloomsbury** is a semiresidential district to the north of Covent Garden that contains some spacious and elegant 17th- and 18th-century squares. It's generally thought of as the intellectual center of London, since both the British Museum and the University of London are found here. The area also gave its name to the Bloomsbury Group, a clique of writers and painters that thrived here in the early 20th century. The antiquarian and specialist bookshops, publishing houses, restaurants, and pubs frequented by the local literati add to the academic-cum-bohemian ambience of the area.

㊳ The **British Museum** houses a vast and priceless collection of treasures, including Egyptian, Greek, and Roman antiquities; Renaissance jewelry; pottery; coins; glass; and drawings from virtually every European school since the 15th century. It's best to pick out one section that particularly interests you—to try to see everything would lead to an attack of cultural indigestion! Some of the highlights are the **Elgin Marbles,** sculptures that formerly decorated the Parthenon in Athens; the **Rosetta Stone,** which helped archaeologists to interpret Egyptian script; a copy of the **Magna Carta,** the charter signed by King John in 1215 to which is ascribed the origins of English liberty;

and the **Mildenhall treasure,** a cache of Roman silver found in East Anglia in 1842. *Great Russell St., tel. 01/636–1555; 01/ 580–1788 (recorded information). Admission: free. Open Mon.–Sat. 10–5, Sun. 2:30–6.*

39 The **Jewish Museum** has a small but interesting collection of antiquities illustrating Judaism, Jewish life, and history. There are also audio-visual programs on Jewish festivals and ceremonies. *Woburn House, Upper Woburn Pl., tel. 01/388–4525. Admission: free. Open Tues.–Thurs. (and Fri. in summer) 10–4, Sun. (and Fri. in winter) 10–12:45.*

The City   The **City,** the traditional commercial center of London, is the most ancient part of the capital, having been the site of the great Roman city of Londinium. Since those days, the City has been built and rebuilt several times. The wooden buildings of the medieval City were destroyed in the Great Fire of 1666. There were further waves of reconstruction in the 19th century, and then again after World War II, to repair the devastation wrought by air attacks. The 1980s have seen the construction of many mammoth office developments, some undistinguished, others incorporating adventurous and exciting ideas.

Throughout all these changes, the City has retained its unique identity and character. The lord mayor and Corporation of London are still responsible for the government of the City, as they have been for many centuries. Commerce remains the lifeblood of the City, which is a world financial center rivaled only by New York, Tokyo, and Zurich. The biggest change has been in the City's population. Until the first half of the 19th century, many of the merchants and traders who worked in the City lived there, too. Today, despite its huge daytime population, scarcely 8,000 people live in the 274 hectares (677 acres) of the City. Try, therefore, to explore the City on a weekday morning or afternoon. On weekends, its streets are deserted, and many of the shops and restaurants, even some of the churches, are closed.

40 Following the Great Fire, **St. Paul's Cathedral** was rebuilt by Sir Christopher Wren, the architect who was also responsible for designing 50 City parish churches to replace those lost in the Fire. St. Paul's is Wren's greatest work. Fittingly, he is buried in the crypt, under the simple epitaph composed by his son: "Reader, if you seek his monument, look around you." The cathedral has been the site of many famous state occasions, including the funeral of Winston Churchill in 1965 and the marriage of the Prince and Princess of Wales in 1981. There is much fine painting and craftsmanship—the choir stalls are by the great 17th-century wood carver Grinling Gibbons—but overall the atmosphere is somewhat austere and remote. The cathedral contains many monuments and tombs. Among those commemorated are George Washington; the essayist and lexicographer Samuel Johnson; and two military heroes—Nelson, victor over the French at Trafalgar in 1805, and Wellington, who defeated the French on land at Waterloo 10 years later. In the ambulatory (the area behind the high altar) is the American Chapel, a memorial to the 28,000 U.S. citizens stationed in Britain during World War II who lost their lives while on active service.

The greatest architectural glory of the cathedral is the dome. This consists of three distinct elements: an outer, timber-framed cone covered with lead; an interior dome built of brick and decorated with frescoes of the life of St. Paul by the 18th-century artist Sir James Thornhill; and, in between, a brick cone that supports and strengthens both. There is a good view of the church from the **Whispering Gallery,** high up in the inner dome. The gallery is so called because of its remarkable acoustics, whereby words whispered on one side can be clearly heard on the other, 35 meters (112 feet) away. Above this gallery are two others, both external, from where there are fine views over the City and beyond. *Tel. 01/248-2705. Admission to Ambulatory (American Chapel): 60p adults, children free; to Crypt and Treasury: 80p adults, 40p children; to galleries: £1 adults, 50p children. Tours of the cathedral weekdays at 11, 11:30, 2, and 2:30, £3.60 adults, £1.60 children. Cathedral open Mon.–Sat. 7:30–6, Sun. 8–6; the Ambulatory, Crypt, and Galleries weekdays 10–4:15, Sat. 11–4:15.*

Time Out **Balls Brothers Wine Bar** is a good place for a bite and a drink. Freshly made soup and grilled steak in a French bread sandwich are two specialties. Aim to arrive early to beat the crowds of lunchtime City workers. *2 Old Change Court, St. Paul's Churchyard, EC4. Closed weekends.*

A short walk north of the cathedral, to **London Wall,** so called because it follows the line of the wall that surrounded the Roman settlement, brings you to the **Museum of London.** Its displays enable you to get a real sense of what it was like to live in London at different periods of history, from Roman times to the present day. Among the highlights are the Lord Mayor's Ceremonial Coach, an imaginative reconstruction of the Great Fire, and the Cheapside Hoard, jewelry hidden during an outbreak of plague in the 17th century and never recovered by its owner. A new gallery devoted to the 18th century was opened in 1989. The 20th-century exhibits include a Woolworth's counter and elevators from Selfridges; both stores were founded by Americans and had an immense impact on the life of Londoners. *London Wall, tel. 01/600-3699. Admission: free. Open Tues.–Sat. 10–6, Sun. 2–6.*

Royal Britain is a newly opened exhibition using all the latest audiovisual techniques to re-create more than 1,000 years of royal history from semi-mythical figures, such as King Arthur, to the royal family of today. *Aldersgate St., tel. 01/588-0588. Admission: £3.95 adults, £2.95 students, £2.50 children and senior citizens. Open daily 9–5:30.*

The **Barbican** is a vast residential complex and arts center built by the City of London. It takes its name from the watchtower that stood here in the Middle Ages, just outside the City walls. The arts center contains a concert hall, where the London Symphony Orchestra is based. It also has two theaters, an art gallery, a cinema, and several cafés and restaurants. The theaters are the London home of the Royal Shakespeare Company.

On the south side of London Wall stands the **Guildhall,** the much reconstructed home of the Corporation of London; the lord mayor of London is elected here each year amid much ceremony. *King St., tel. 01/606-3030. Admission: free. Open weekdays 9–5.*

Now walk south to **Cheapside.** This was the chief marketplace of medieval London (the word *ceap* meant market), as the street names hereabouts indicate: Milk Street, Ironmonger Lane, etc. Despite rebuilding, many of the streets still run on the medieval pattern. The church of **St. Mary-le-Bow** in Cheapside was rebuilt by Christopher Wren after the Great Fire; it was built again after being bombed during World War II. It is said that to be a true Cockney, you must be born within the sound of Bow bells.

A short walk east along Cheapside brings you to a seven-way intersection. The **Bank of England,** which regulates much of Britain's financial life, is the large windowless building on the left. At the northern side of the intersection, at right angles to the bank, is the **Royal Exchange,** originally built in the 1560s as a trading hall for merchants. The present building, opened in 1844 and the third on the site, is now occupied by the **London International Financial Futures Exchange.** You can watch the hectic trading from the Visitors' Gallery. *Tel. 01/623–0444. Admission: free. Visitors' Gallery open weekdays 11:30–2.*

The third major building at this intersection, on its south side, is the **Mansion House,** the official residence of the lord mayor of London.

Continue east along **Cornhill,** site of a Roman basilica and of a medieval grain market. Turn right into Gracechurch Street and then left into **Leadenhall Market.** There has been a market here since the 14th century; the present building dates from 1881.

Just behind the market is one of the most striking pieces of contemporary City architecture: the headquarters of **Lloyd's of London,** built by the modernist architect Richard Rogers. Its main feature is a 62-meter-high (200-foot) barrel vault made of sparkling glass. The underwriters of Lloyd's provide insurance for everything imaginable, from oil rigs to a pianist's fingers. An exhibit traces the history of Lloyd's from the 17th century. *1 Lime St., tel. 01/623–7100, ext. 6210 or 5786. Admission: free. Open weekdays 10–2:30.*

Time Out   Lloyd's was founded in a coffee house, and so **Lloyd's Coffee House,** at the foot of the modern building, is an apt place for coffee and pastries, a full lunch, or afternoon tea.

From here, it's a short walk east to the **Tower of London,** one of London's most famous sights and one of its most crowded, too. Come as early in the day as possible and head for the Crown Jewels, so you can see them before the crowds arrive.

The tower served the monarchs of medieval England as both fortress and palace. Every British sovereign from William the Conqueror in the 11th century to Henry VIII in the 16th lived here, and it remains a royal palace. The **History Gallery,** south of the White Tower, is a walk-through display designed to answer questions about the inhabitants of the tower and its evolution over the centuries.

The **White Tower** is the oldest and also the most conspicuous building in the entire complex. Inside, the **Chapel of St. John** is one of the few unaltered parts. A structure of great simplicity, it is almost entirely lacking in ornamentation. The **Royal Armories,** England's national collection of arms and armor, occupies the rest of the White Tower. Armor of the 16th and

17th centuries forms the centerpiece of the displays, including pieces belonging to Henry VIII and Charles I.

Among other buildings worth seeing is the **Bloody Tower.** This name has been traced back only to 1571; it was originally known as the Garden Tower. Sir Walter Raleigh was held prisoner here, in relatively comfortable circumstances, between 1603 and 1616, during which time he wrote his *History of the World;* his rooms are furnished much as they were during his imprisonment. The little princes in the tower—the boy king Edward V and his brother Richard, Duke of York, supposedly murdered on the orders of Gloucester, later crowned Richard III— certainly lived in the Bloody Tower, and may well have died here, too. Another bloody death is alleged to have occurred in the **Wakefield Tower,** when Henry VI was murdered in 1471 during England's medieval civil war, the Wars of the Roses. It was a rare honor to be beheaded in private inside the tower; most people were executed outside, on **Tower Hill,** where the crowds could get a much better view. Important prisoners were held in the **Beauchamp Tower;** the walls are covered with graffiti and inscriptions carved by prisoners.

The **Crown Jewels,** housed in the **Jewel House,** are a breathtakingly beautiful collection of regalia, precious stones, gold, and silver. The Royal Scepter contains the largest cut diamond in the world. The Imperial State Crown contains some 3,000 precious stones, largely diamonds and pearls; it was made for the coronation of Queen Victoria in 1838. Look for the ravens whose presence at the tower is traditional. It is said that if they leave, the tower will fall and England will lose her greatness. *Tower Hill, tel. 01/709-0765. Admission: £4.80 adults, £3 students and senior citizens, £2 children under 16. Reduced admission charges apply during Feb. when the Jewel House is closed. Small additional admission charge to the Fusiliers Museum only. Open Mar.-Oct., Mon.-Sat. 9:30-5:45, Sun. 2-5:45; Nov.-Feb., Mon.-Sat. 9:30-4:30.*

Yeoman Warder guides conduct tours daily from the Middle Tower, no charge, but a tip is always appreciated. Subject to weather and availability of guides, tours are conducted about every 30 minutes until 3:30 in summer, 2:30 in winter.

Off the Beaten Track

Walk along the bank of the **Regent's Park Canal** to **Camden Lock,** where there are lots of little shops selling gifts, secondhand clothes, crafts, and antiques. On weekends, there's an outdoor market as well.

You can extend the excursion in two different directions from Camden Lock. Either walk east along the canal towpath through the elegant streets of Islington and then through increasingly less prosperous areas until you reach the Thames at Limehouse or turn north to **Hampstead** and **Hampstead Heath.**

Hampstead is a village within the city, where many famous poets and writers have lived. Today it is a fashionable residential area, with a main shopping street and some rows of elegant 18th-century houses. The heath is one of London's largest and most attractive open spaces. In **Keats Grove,** on the southern edge of the heath, is the house where the Romantic poet John Keats (1795–1821) lived. *Wentworth Pl., tel. 01/435-2062. Ad-*

mission: free. Visitors are advised to call in advance for exact opening times.

Standing alone in its own landscaped grounds on the north side of the heath is **Kenwood House,** built in the 17th century and remodeled by Robert Adam, the talented exponent of classical decoration, at the end of the 18th. The house contains a collection of superb paintings by such masters as Rembrandt, Vermeer, Turner, Reynolds, Van Dyck, and Gainsborough, which gain enormously by being displayed in the grand country-house setting for which they were originally intended. The lovely landscaped grounds, with lake, provide the setting for symphony concerts in summer (tel. 01/734–1877 for details). *Hampstead Lane, tel. 01/348–1286. Admission: free. Open Apr.–Sept., daily 10–6; Oct. and Feb.–Mar., daily 10–5; Nov.–Jan., daily 10–4.*

The historical and maritime attractions at **Greenwich,** on the Thames, some 8 kilometers (5 miles) east of central London, make it an ideal place for a day out. Visit the **National Maritime Museum,** a treasure house of paintings, maps, models, sextants, and, best of all, ships from all ages, including the ornate royal barges. *Romney Rd., tel. 01/858–4422. Joint admission with the Royal Observatory: £3 adults, £1.50 children and senior citizens. Open late Mar.–late Oct., Mon.–Sat. 10–6, Sun. 2–6; late Oct.–late Mar., Mon.–Sat. 10–5, Sun. 2–5.*

Two ships now in dry dock are the glorious 19th-century clipper ship *Cutty Sark* and the tiny *Gipsy Moth IV,* which Sir Francis Chichester sailed single-handed around the world in 1966. *Cutty Sark, King William Walk, tel. 01/858–3445. Admission: £1.40 adults, 70p children under 16 and senior citizens. Open late Mar.–late Oct., Mon.–Sat. 10–5:30, Sun. noon–5:30; late Oct.–late Mar., Mon.–Sat. 10–4:30, Sun. noon–4:30. Gipsy Moth IV, King William Walk, tel. 01/853–3589. Admission: 20p adults, 10p children and senior citizens. Open Apr.–Oct., Mon.–Sat. 10–5:30, Sun. noon–5:30.*

The **Royal Naval College** was built from 1694 as a home, or hospital, for old sailors. You can see the magnificent **Painted Hall,** where Nelson's body lay in state following the Battle of Trafalgar, and the College Chapel. *Tel. 01/858–2154. Admission: free. Open Fri.–Wed. 2:30–4:30.*

Behind the museum and the college is **Greenwich Park,** originally a royal hunting ground and today an attractive place to wander and relax. On top of the hill is the **Old Royal Observatory,** founded in 1675, where original telescopes and other astronomical instruments are on display. The prime meridian —zero degrees longitude—runs through the courtyard of the observatory. *Greenwich Park, tel. 01/858–4422. Joint admission with National Maritime Museum: £3 adults, £1.50 children and senior citizens. Open Apr.–Oct., Mon.–Sat. 10–6, Sun. 2–6; Nov.–Mar., Mon.–Sat. 10–5, Sun. 2–5.*

You can get to Greenwich by riverboat from Westminster and Tower Bridge piers, by ThamesLine's high-speed river buses, or by train from Charing Cross station. You can also take the Docklands Light Railway from Tower Gateway to Island Gardens and walk a short distance along a pedestrian tunnel under the river.

Shopping

Shopping is one of London's great pleasures. Different areas retain their traditional specialties, as described below, but part of the fun is to seek out the small craft, antiques, and gift stores that have sprung up all over the city during the past few years.

Shopping Districts   **Chelsea** is a mecca for those in search of up-to-the-minute fashions, antiques, and classy home furnishings. A Saturday stroll along the **King's Road** will reveal some of the weirder fashion trends among London's youngsters.

Covent Garden is the home of craft shops and trendy boutiques. Antiques are the main draw in **Kensington,** especially along **Kensington Church Street.** There are some good clothes stores on **Kensington High Street.**

The great Edwardian bulk of Harrods dominates **Knightsbridge,** but don't neglect the boutiques and art galleries on other shopping streets in the area, such as **Sloane Street, Beauchamp Place,** and **Walton Street.**

In **Mayfair,** the area between **Piccadilly** and **Oxford Street,** the emphasis is on traditional British clothing for men and women. **South Molton Street** adds a modern, raffish accent. Go to **Bond Street** for designer-label fashions and world-famous jewelry. Both quality and prices are tops here.

Noisy, crowded **Oxford Street** is to be endured rather than enjoyed. **Selfridges, Marks and Spencer,** and **John Lewis** are all good department stores here, and little **St. Christopher's Place,** almost opposite Bond Street tube, adds a chic touch.

There are still a number of classy stores along **Piccadilly,** including **Simpsons** (clothes), **Hatchards** (books), and **Fortnum and Mason** (foodstuffs, fashions). Side streets lead to several elegant shopping arcades, the best-known of which is the **Burlington Arcade.**

China, clothes, fabrics, and good department stores help to make **Regent Street** an appealing alternative to neighboring Oxford Street. The crowds are just as thick, but the presence of **Liberty's**—the city's most appealing department store, still with its original emphasis on Oriental goods—helps to compensate.

Though his suits may be made in Savile Row, the English gentleman comes to **St. James's** for the rest of his outfit, which includes shoes, shirts, silk ties, hats, and all manner of accessories. The prices mirror the quality.

Markets   Street markets are one aspect of London life not to be missed. Here are some of the more interesting markets:

Bermondsey. Arrive as early as possible for the best treasure— or junk. *Tower Bridge Rd., SE1. Open Fri. 4:30 AM–noon.* Take the tube to London Bridge and walk or take the no. 15 or 25 bus to Aldgate and then a no. 42 bus over Tower Bridge to Bermondsey Square.

Camden Lock. This is just the place for an unusual and inexpensive gift; it's also a picturesque place to wander around. There's an open-air antiques market on weekends, but it gets horribly crowded. *Chalk Farm Rd., NW1. Open Tues.–Sun. 9:30–5:30. Take the tube or the no. 24 or 29 bus to Camden Town.*

Camden Passage. The rows of little antique shops are a good hunting ground for silverware and jewelry. Saturday is the day for stalls; shops are open during the rest of the week. *Islington, N1. Open Wed.–Sat. 8:30–3. Take the tube of no. 19 or 38 bus to the Angel.*

Petticoat Lane. Look for good-quality, budget-priced leather goods, dazzling knitwear, and bargain-price fashions, plus cameras, videos, and stereos at budget prices. *Middlesex St., E1. Open Sun. 9–2. Take the tube to Liverpool Street, Aldgate, or Aldgate East.*

Portobello Market. Saturday is the best day to search the stalls for not-quite-bargain-priced silverware, curios, porcelain, and jewelry. It's always crowded, with an authentic hustle-and-bustle atmosphere, and firmly on the tourist route. *Portobello Rd., W11. Open Fri. 5–3, Sat. 8–5. Take the tube, no. 52 bus to Notting Hill Gate or Ladbroke Grove, or no. 15 bus to Kensington Park Road.*

VAT Refunds   Foreign visitors to Britain need not pay the 15% value added tax (VAT) added to every purchase if they take advantage of the Personal Export Scheme. Most main stores have export departments that will give you all the help you need.

Dining

For details and price category definitions, *see* Dining in Staying in Great Britain.

Bloomsbury   **The White Tower.** The most upscale Greek restaurant in town
Expensive   has barely changed since it first opened in 1939. There are portraits on the walls, glass partitions between the tables, and an entertainingly rhapsodic menu. Dishes range from the traditional—*taramasalata*—to the more creative—roast duckling with crushed wheat. *1 Percy St., tel. 01/636–8141. Reservations essential. AE, DC, MC, V. Closed weekends, 3 weeks in Aug., 1 week at Christmas, holidays.*

Moderate   **Auntie's.** Come to Auntie's for authentic English food—"the General's curried egg mayonnaise," Barnsley lamb chop with Durham mustard sauce, tipsy fruit trifle—served in an intimate Edwardian atmosphere of dark green walls hung with theater bills. *126 Cleveland St., tel. 01/387–1548. Reservations advised. AE, DC, MC, V. Closed Sat. lunch, Sun., 2 weeks in mid-Aug., 1 week at Christmas.*

Inexpensive   **The Agra.** This Indian restaurant is popular with media folk for its good value and wide choice of meat and vegetarian curries. Overhead fans, low lighting, and attentive waiters add a touch of class. *135–137 Whitfield St., tel. 01/387–8833. Reservations advised for dinner. AE, DC, MC, V. Closed Dec. 25.*

The North Sea Fish Restaurant. Only freshly caught fish is served in this popular haunt. Recommended are the seafood platter and Dover sole. You can eat in or take out. *7–8 Leigh St., tel. 01/387–5892. Reservations advised. AE, DC, MC, V. Closed Sun., holidays, 10 days at Christmas.*

Chelsea   **La Tante Claire.** Though cripplingly expensive, this spot is
Very Expensive   justly famous for its superb haute cuisine: hot foie gras on shredded potatoes with a sweet wine and shallot sauce, and pig's trotter studded with mousse of white meat with sweet-

breads and wild mushrooms. *68 Royal Hospital Rd., tel. 01/ 352-6045. Reservations 3-4 weeks in advance. AE, DC, MC, V. Closed weekends, 10 days at Easter and Christmas, 3 weeks in Aug.-Sept.*

Expensive **English House.** This charming private house is decorated in
★ chintz with antiques and cream linen tablecloths. Authentic recipes include Holm Oak smoked pigeon breasts with rhubarb and ginger preserve and hot toffee and apple tart. *3 Milner St., tel. 01/584-3002. Reservations essential for dinner. AE, DC, MC, V. Closed Dec. 25, Good Friday.*

Moderate **19.** This popular, informal Anglo-French bistro serves consistently high-standard mega-portions (fresh salmon and halibut terrine, venison casserole) in attractive country-cottage surroundings. *19 Mossop St., tel. 01/589-4971. MC, V. Closed Sat. lunch, Christmas, Easter.*

Inexpensive **Henry J. Bean's.** Hamburgers and Tex-Mex food are served to American oldies music. There's American-bar decor: the walls are covered with newspapers and other ephemera. *195-197 King's Rd., tel. 01/352-9255. Closed Dec. 25, 26, 31.*

The City **Bill Bentley's.** Once a wine merchant's vaults with bare walls
Expensive and arched ceiling, this atmospheric spot is recommended for the seafood platters and Bill Bentley's special oysters. There are two other branches, at Beauchamp Place and Baker Street. *Swedeland Ct., 202 Bishopsgate, tel. 01/283-1763. Reservations essential. AE, DC, MC, V. Closed weekends, holidays.*

Gallipoli. A 200-year-old Turkish bathhouse, with gleaming mosaics, has been transformed into a stylish restaurant with a live band from 9 PM to 2:30 AM. The clientele is a mix of City people and tourists, and the food has a marked Turkish flavor—try the yogurt kebab or the fillet of duck with honey, lime, and orange. It's less expensive at lunchtime. *8 Bishopsgate Churchyard, tel. 01/588-1922. Reservations advised. AE, DC, MC, V. Closed Sat. lunch, Sun., Dec. 25, 26, and holidays.*

★ **Le Poulbot.** This is one of the best fixed-price lunches in the entire city; it's also part of the Roux Brothers' empire. Top-class, well-balanced food is served in an intimate red-plush setting. There is a good choice of dishes for each course and an aperitif is included in the price. *45 Cheapside, tel. 01/236-4379. Reservations 2-3 days in advance. AE, DC, MC, V. Open weekdays for lunch only.*

Moderate **Sweetings.** City gents stand in line to lunch at this tiny, basic Victorian restaurant close to a Roman temple. The service is Old World courteous; the fish, cheese, and puddings are comforting and well prepared. *39 Queen Victoria St., tel. 01/248-3062. No credit cards. Open weekdays for lunch only; closed Christmas, holidays.*

Covent Garden **Inigo Jones.** This is *the* place for beautifully presented French
Very Expensive modern cuisine. You'll pay dearly for the saddle of hare with
★ pumpkin mousseline in a ginger and citrus sauce, but it is a gourmet's paradise—even though the bare brick and glass surroundings don't encourage you to linger. *14 Garrick St., tel. 01/ 836-6456. Reservations advised. AE, DC, MC, V. Closed Sat. lunch, Sun., Christmas-New Year, holidays.*

The Savoy Grill. Continuing to attract more than its fair share of literary and artistic names, as well as the odd tycoon, this French-English place guarantees top-notch cooking. Order an omelet Arnold Bennett (seafood is the extra ingredient) or a fillet of pork with fresh cranberries. *Strand, tel. 01/836–4343. Reservations advised for lunch and for Thurs.–Sat. dinner. AE, DC, MC, V. Closed Sat. lunch, Sun.*

Expensive **Rules.** This is a London institution with a splendid Edwardian atmosphere; it features good roast beef, lamb, and Dover sole, as well as game in season. Try the homemade whiskey-and-ginger ice cream for dessert. *35 Maiden La., tel. 01/836–5314. Reservations at least 1 day in advance. AE, DC, MC, V. Closed Dec. 25.*

Moderate **Bertorelli's.** Opposite the stage door of the Royal Opera House, Bertorelli's is a favorite with opera goers. Chic, postmodern decor complements the traditional Italian food—try the hot mushroom and garlic salad and the *saltimbocca alla romana* (veal and ham in a butter and wine sauce). *44a Floral St., tel. 01/836–3969. Reservations advised. AE, DC, MC, V. Closed Sun., Dec. 25.*

★ **Joe Allen.** This basement restaurant behind the Strand Palace Hotel follows the style of its New York counterpart. It's a great place to spot stage or screen stars. The barbecued ribs and Caesar's salad are a real treat. There's a pianist after 9 PM, if you can hear through the surrounding decibels. *13 Exeter St., tel. 01/836–0651. Reservations essential. Closed Christmas.*

Inexpensive **Food for Thought.** This is a simple downstairs vegetarian restaurant, with seats for only 50, so there's almost always a waiting line. The menu—stir fries, casseroles, salads, and dessert—changes daily, and each dish is freshly made. There's no alcohol served here. *31 Neal St., tel. 01/836–0239. No credit cards. Closed Sun., Sat. after 4:30 PM, weekdays after 8 PM, 2 weeks at Christmas, holidays.*

Porter's. Traditional but filling English fare is served here, with pies the specialty. Try the lamb and apricot or steak and mushroom, followed by bread-and-butter pudding or potted Stilton cheese. *17 Henrietta St., tel. 01/836–6466. MC, V. Closed Dec. 25, 26.*

Kensington **Bombay Brasserie.** Here's one of London's most fashionable
Expensive and stylish Indian restaurants. The fine menu, drawn from dif-
★ ferent regions, includes Bombay thali (small bowls of vegetables or meat), Kashmiri lamb, and Goan fish curry. The Sunday lunch buffet is particularly popular. *140 Gloucester Rd., tel. 01/370–4040. Reservations essential for dinner. AE, DC, MC, V. Closed Christmas.*

Drake's. Watch the chefs preparing the best of traditional English fare at this two-level, bare-brick basement restaurant. Spit-roast boar with mustard sauce, beef Wellington, or roast duck on a bed of mushrooms with calvados sauce are tempting specialties. *2a Pond Pl., tel. 01/584–4555. Reservations advised. AE, DC, MC, V. Closed lunch (except Sun.), Dec. 25.*

Reeds. This small Anglo-French restaurant has a country-house feel (lots of plants and wickerwork). Salmon galet is the house specialty–raw, marinated salmon, cooked at the table by your good self, and then wrapped in seaweed pancakes. There is also succulent roast beef and an excellent cheeseboard. *152 Old Brompton Rd., tel. 01/373–2445. Reservations advised. AE, DC, MC, V. Closed Sun. dinner, holidays, 2 weeks in Aug. and 2 weeks at Christmas.*

Moderate **Lou Pescadou.** Ring the bell for admission to this Provencal res-
★ taurant with a boating theme—there are pictures of boats,

boats as lamps, and so on. Fish is the specialty: Try the petite bouillabaisse (fish soup) or red mullet poached in tarragon sauce. *241 Old Brompton Rd., tel: 01/370–1057. AE, DC, MC, V. Closed Aug., Dec. 25.*

Knightsbridge
Very Expensive

Waltons. Formal and sumptuous, this Anglo-French restaurant with soft lighting and miles of mirrors has an imaginative, constantly changing menu. The seafood sausage and the roast duck are a must. *121 Walton St., tel. 01/584–0204. Reservations advised. AE, DC, MC, V. Closed Dec. 25, 26, and Easter.*

Expensive
★

Ménage à Trois. Appetizers and desserts only are served at this stylish pink-and-gray restaurant. Recommended are the terrine of leeks and duck confit served with grilled foie gras and, to top it off, the chocoholics anonymous—six chocolate puddings on one plate! *15 Beauchamp Pl., tel. 01/589–4252. Reservations essential for dinner. AE, DC, MC, V. Closed Sat. and Sun. lunch, Dec. 25 and 26, Good Friday.*

Moderate

Luba's Bistro. Long wooden tables, basic decor, and authentic Russian cooking—chicken Kiev, beef Stroganoff—give this spot a relaxed, informal atmosphere. Bring your own wine. *6 Yeoman's Row, tel. 01/589–2950. Reservations advised. AE, MC, V. Closed Sun., Dec. 25, holidays.*

Inexpensive

Stockpot. Speedy service is the mark of this large, jolly restaurant full of young people. The food is filling and wholesome; try the homemade soups, Lancashire hot pot, or the apple crumble. Breakfast is also served Monday–Saturday. *6 Basil St., tel. 01/589–8627. Closed Dec. 25, New Year's day.*

Mayfair
Very Expensive
★

Le Gavroche. Generally regarded as London's finest restaurant, Le Gavroche has excellent service, discreetly sumptuous decor, and lavish haute cuisine—duck with foie gras, lobster and champagne mousse. It's near the U.S. embassy. *43 Upper Brook St., tel. 01/408–0881. Reserve at least 1 week in advance. AE, DC, MC, V. Closed weekends, 10 days at Christmas, holidays.*

Expensive

Jam's. Colorful fresh food with a sense of humor is served in this stylish, split-level dining room (the parent restaurant is in New York). The most popular dish on the menu is an extravaganza—red-pepper pancakes filled with sweetcorn sauce, salmon caviar, *crème fraîche*, and smoked salmon. Also try rack of lamb on Chinese leaves with butter sauce and roasted pine nuts. *42 Albemarle St., tel. 01/493–3600. Reservations essential for lunch, advised for dinner. AE, MC, V. Closed Sat. lunch., Sun., holidays.*

Langan's Brasserie. It's rather exclusive, with wall-to-wall celebrities, but if you do manage to get in, you'll be impressed by the modern art on the walls, the vast menu, the frank service (the waiters sometimes advise against certain dishes), and the top-quality food. Try the spinach soufflé with anchovy sauce and the stuffed artichokes with hollandaise sauce. *Stratton St., tel. 01/491–8822. Reservations necessary up to 6 weeks in advance. AE, DC, MC, V. Closed Sat. lunch, Sun., holidays.*

Moderate

Pizzeria Condotti. Run by the cartoonist Enzo Apicella, the walls here are lined with cartoons and modern paintings. The pizzas are first-class, if calorific; the figure-conscious can choose salads instead, such as the *insalata Condotti* (mixed salad with mozzarella and avocado). *4 Mill St., tel. 01/499–1308. AE, DC, MC, V. Closed Sun., holidays, Dec. 25, 26.*

Smollensky's Balloon. This is an American-style bar-restaurant with fine food, good service, and air-conditioning. The menu changes weekly, but five types of steak and vegetarian dishes are standard. Calves' liver with couscous is recommended, as is the peanut butter cheesecake. Saturday and Sunday lunch are for families, always with live entertainment. *1 Dover St., tel. 01/491–1199. Reservations advised. Thurs.–Sun. AE, DC, MC, V. Closed Christmas.*

Inexpensive **The Chicago Pizza Pie Factory.** Huge pizzas with salad and garlic bread are served at reasonable prices in this bright basement spot. The choice of toppings is somewhat limited, but try the American sausage and mushroom version. There's also a cocktail bar, rock music, and videos. *17 Hanover Sq., tel. 01/ 629–2669. Reservations advised for lunch. Closed Dec. 25, 26.*

Justin de Blank's. This attractive, upscale, self-service spot is ideal for a break from Oxford Street shopping. The food is all homemade. Favorites include the crab and cucumber mousse, fruit brûlé, and chocolate roulade. *54 Duke St., tel. 01/629– 3174. MC, V. Closed after 9 PM, Sat. dinner, Sun., holidays.*

Notting Hill Gate **Clarke's.** There's no choice of dishes at dinner at all (and only a
Expensive limited choice at lunch); chef Sally Clarke plans the meal according to what is fresh in the market each day, using the freshest herbs and the best olive oils. It's fine cuisine. *124 Kensington Church St., tel. 01/221–9225. Reservations advised. MC, V. Closed weekends, 10 days at Christmas; Easter, 3 weeks in Aug.*

Moderate **L'Artiste Assoiffé.** The parrots Stanley and Sally will amuse
★ you in the bar of this eccentric Victorian house before you escape to eat in the can-can room or the merry-go-round room to the accompaniment of operatic music. Pop stars, actors, and royals come here for the unique atmosphere and the French food: fillet of steak caramelized with Dijon mustard and spinach pancakes with nuts and cheese. It's open for lunch on Saturdays only. *122 Kensington Park Rd., tel. 01/727–4714. Reservations essential. AE, DC, MC, V. Closed Sun., holidays.*

Inexpensive **Gate Diner.** This American-owned, New York–style eatery on three floors is right by Portobello Road antiques market. The Sunday brunch washed down with a pitcher of Bucks Fizz is great. Generous portions of chili, ribs, steak, and hamburgers are accompanied by real French fries. *184A Kensington Park Rd., tel. 01/221–2649. Reservations essential for Sunday brunch. MC, V. Closed Dec. 26.*

Wine Gallery. This is an art gallery where you have to eat and drink if you want to view the pictures. The food, too, is creative (pastry parcels with duck, shallots, and garlic; blinis with sour cream, smoked salmon, and caviar), and the wine is reliable. Traditional English lunch is served on Sundays. *294 Westbourne Grove, tel. 01/229–1877. MC, V. Closed holidays.*

Soho **Alastair Little.** A favorite among media people, chef Alastair
Expensive serves nouvelle British designer and international food, such as venison terrine with orange marmalade and mascarpone tart with figs. The customers' favorite is terrine of fresh foie gras with wafer-thin poilaine toast. Drawbacks include the paper napkins, functional decor, and closely packed tables. *49 Frith St., tel. 01/734–5183. Reservations advised. Closed Sat. lunch, Sun., Christmas, Easter.*

Lindsay House. Inside this restored 16th-century town house, mouth-watering traditional English 17th-century recipes, such as "Brye favors" (Brie in pastry with fresh tomato sauce), are served amid opulent decor, with hunting scenes and oil portraits on the walls. *21 Romilly St., W1, tel. 01/439–0450. Reservations advised. AE, DC, MC, V. Closed Christmas.*

Moderate **Chiang Mai.** The interior is modeled on a traditional Thai stilt
★ house. The food is delicious and spicy, all easy to order from an English menu. Try a *Tom Yum* (hot and sour soup) or a *Pad Kra Prow* (beef, pork, or chicken with fresh Thai basil and chili). *48 Frith St., tel. 01/437–7444. Reservations advised for dinner. AE, MC, V. Closed Sun. and holidays.*

Manzi's. This is one of London's oldest and most traditional fish restaurants. The downstairs restaurant is the more lively and atmospheric; decor is kitsch Moulin Rouge murals and monstrous plastic lobsters. *1–2 Leicester St., tel. 01/734–0224. Reservations advised. AE, DC, MC, V. Closed Dec. 25, 26.*

Inexpensive **Crank's.** One restaurant of a popular vegetarian chain (other branches are at Covent Garden, Great Newport Street, Adelaide Street, Tottenham Street, and Barrett Street), Crank's has a nutritious and tasty menu. Lunch is self-service, dinner candlelit waiter-service (many branches, though not this one, close at 8 PM). *8 Marshall St., tel. 01/437–9431. Reservations advised for dinner. AE, DC, MC, V. Closed Sun., Dec. 25.*

Poon's. A popular Chinese restaurant (there are long lines in the evening), Poon's specializes in wind-dried meats. There is a sister restaurant in Covent Garden, but this one is cheaper and more authentic. *4 Leicester St., tel. 01/437–1528. Reservations essential. Closed Sun., Dec. 25, 26.*

St. James's **Suntory.** Frequented by ministers and officials from the Japa-
Very Expensive nese embassy, this is a gracious place to appreciate the delicacy of Japanese cuisine. There's a *teppanyaki* bar, where fresh meat or fish is cooked in front of you. The main dining room is where you can choose from an extensive menu of exotic dishes. There are also private *tatami* rooms, where seating is on the floor. *72 St. James's St., tel. 01/409–0201. Reservations essential. AE, DC, MC, V. Closed Sun., holidays, Christmas and New Year's day.*

Expensive **Le Caprice.** Furnished in sophisticated black-and-white decor, Le Caprice caters to equally stylish patrons. The menu should appeal to all tastes, from hamburgers to elaborate dishes such as salmon fishcakes with sorrel sauce. Finish with a mousse of dark and white chocolate. *Arlington House, Arlington St., tel. 01/629–2239. Reservations required. AE, DC, MC, V. Closed 10 days at Christmas.*

The Veeraswamy. London's oldest Indian restaurant, founded in 1927, having shed its colonial trappings, now has a modern European-style ambience. The king prawn masala (medium hot prawn curry) and the lamb kadai ghost (curried lamb with capsicums) are both recommended. *99 Regent St., tel. 01/734–1401. Reservations advised. AE, DC, MC, V. Closed Dec. 25, 26, and New Year's.*

Wilton's. Traditional British fare—turtle soup, sausage and mashed potatoes, partridge, Stilton—is served here in Edwardian surroundings. Each day has its own specialty. The oysters are London's best—all the seafood arrives fresh up to four times a day. *55 Jermyn St., tel. 01/629–9955. Reservations* advised 2 days in advance. AE, DC, MC, V. Closed Sat. lunch, Sun., last week in July and 1st 2 weeks in Aug., 10 days at Christmas.

Lodging

Although British hotels traditionally included breakfast in their nightly tariff, these days many of London's most expensive establishments charge extra for breakfast. For details and price category definitions, *see* Lodging in Staying in Great Britain.

Bayswater
Very Expensive
★

Whites. This cream-faced Victorian "country mansion" has a wrought-iron portico and a view of Kensington Gardens, especially grand when floodlit at night. Thick carpets, gilded glass, marble balustrades, swagged silk draperies, and Louis XV-style furniture all help to give a sense of deep luxury. Some of the bedrooms have balconies, seating areas, and personal safes. Colors are muted: powder blue, old rose, and pale green. *Lancaster Gate, W2 3NR, tel. 01/262–2711. 54 rooms with bath. Facilities: restaurant, lounge, valet service, free in-house movies. AE, DC, MC, V.*

Expensive

Abbey Court. A short walk from Kensington Gardens brings you to this luxury bed-and-breakfast establishment in a historic 1850 building. Each bedroom is individually designed with 19th-century French furniture, Venetian mirrors, and oil portraits; some have four-poster beds. *20 Pembridge Gardens, W2 4DU, tel. 01/221–7518. 22 rooms with bath. Facilities: Jacuzzis, drawing room. AE, DC, MC, V.*

Portobello. A faithful core of visitors return again and again to this tiny hotel in a Victorian terrace near the Portobello Road antiques market. Some rooms are tiny, but the suites have sitting rooms attached, and the atmosphere is relaxed and informal. *22 Stanley Gardens, W11 2NG, tel. 01/727–2777. 25 rooms with bath or shower. Facilities: 24-hour bar, restaurant. AE, DC, MC, V. Closed 10 days at Christmas.*

Moderate
★

Camelot. This affordable hotel, recently refurbished and extended, has beautifully decorated rooms. The breakfast room has a large open fireplace with wooden trestle tables and a polished wood floor. *45–47 Norfolk Sq., W2 1RX, tel. 01/723–9118. 44 rooms, 39 with bath or shower. Facilities: lounge, free in-house videos. MC, V.*

Edward Lear. The former home of Edward Lear, the artist and writer of nonsense verse, this hotel has an imposing entrance leading to a black-and-white tiled floor. Ask for one of the quieter rooms to the rear. The breakfast room has huge French windows. *28–30 Seymour St., W1H 5WD, tel. 01/402–5401. 30 rooms, 15 with bath or shower. V.*

Prince William. This is a handsome, mid-19th-century building near Paddington Station. Most rooms have the original high ceilings, and some have balconies that catch the elusive London sun. *42–44 Gloucester Terrace, W2 3DA, tel. 01/724–7414. 42 rooms with bath. Facilities: bar, restaurant, free in-house movies. AE, DC, MC, V.*

Inexpensive

Ashley. The hotel consists of three handsome terraced houses in a slightly shabby neighborhood. Although some rooms are small and simply furnished, the very friendly and conscientious managers (two brothers) make this a decidedly good choice. *15*

Norfolk Sq., W2 1RX, tel. 01/723–3375. 52 rooms, 18 with bath or shower. Facilities: lounge. Closed Christmas and New Year's.

Norfolk. Though small, this is a modest, pleasant Regency hotel near Paddington Station. Some rooms have French windows and balconies overlooking the square. *20 Norfolk Sq., W2 1RS, tel. 01/723–4963. 28 rooms, 9 with bath. MC.*

Bloomsbury
Expensive
★
Grafton. This hotel of great style features an Edwardian drawing room with red-plush armchairs, classical columns, and an open fireplace. The recently refurbished bedrooms are more modern. The Grafton's location makes it convenient for Euston and King's Cross stations. *130 Tottenham Court Rd., W1P 9HP, tel. 01/388–4131. 236 rooms with bath or shower. Facilities: bar, lounge, restaurant, laundry, free in-house movies. AE, DC, MC, V.*

Moderate
White Hall. Beyond the imposing entrance here, there's an elegant lobby with arched windows and a marble floor and a garden bar leading on to a patio and not-too-manicured garden. *2–5 Montague St., WC1B 5BU, tel. 01/580–5871. 74 rooms, 32 with bath. Facilities: bar, restaurant. AE, DC, MC, V.*

Morgan. This charming family-run hotel in an 18th-century terrace house has rooms that are small and comfortably furnished, but friendly and cheerful. The tiny paneled breakfast room is straight out of a doll's house. The back rooms overlook the British Museum. *24 Bloomsbury St., WC1B 3QU, tel. 01/636–3735. 14 rooms with shower. No credit cards.*

Inexpensive
Ridgemount. The public rooms here have a friendly, cluttered feel, especially the family-style breakfast room. Some rooms overlook a leafy garden. *65 Gower St., WC1E 6HJ, tel. 01/636–1141. 15 rooms, none with bath. Facilities: lounge. No credit cards.*

Ruskin. Family-owned, pleasant and quiet, this popular hotel is immediately opposite the British Museum. All front windows are double-glazed. Bedrooms are clean though nondescript; back ones overlook a pretty garden. *23–24 Montague St., WC1B 5BN, tel. 01/636–7388. 35 rooms, 7 with shower. Facilities: lounge. AE, DC, MC, V.*

Chelsea and Kensington
Very Expensive
★
Blakes. Patronized by musicians and film stars, this hotel is one of the most exotic in town. Its Victorian exterior contrasts with the 1980s ultra-chic interior, with an arty mix of Biedermeier, leather, and bamboo furniture; rich fabrics; four-posters; and Oriental enameled screens. The bedrooms have individual designs, ranging from swaths of black moiré silk to a more severe plain gray. *33 Roland Gardens, SW7 3PF, tel. 01/370–6701. 50 rooms with bath. Facilities: restaurant, bar, satellite TV. AE, DC, MC, V.*

Eleven Cadogan Gardens. There's scarcely a sign of the 1980s in this aristocratic, late Victorian gabled town house hotel that's popular with international antiques dealers. There is fine period furniture, landscape paintings, and portraits throughout; the bedrooms have mahogany furniture, restful color schemes, and pretty bedspreads and draperies. *11 Cadogan Gardens, Sloane Sq., SW3 2RJ, tel. 01/730–3426. 60 rooms with bath. Facilities: garden, lounge, chauffeur-driven car. No credit cards.*

Expensive
London Tara. This vast, fully air-conditioned, functional international hotel has a cordial atmosphere and light and colorful rooms. *Scarsdale Pl., W8 5SR, tel. 01/937–7211. 831 rooms*

with bath; 10 converted for the disabled. Facilities: 3 restaurants, lounge, bars. AE, DC, MC, V.

Moderate **Annadale.** This comfortable hotel is efficiently run and good for the money, as the many repeat visitors attest. Breakfast is traditional British: kippers, Welsh rarebit, cereal, and genuine Scottish porridge. *39 Sloane Gardens, SW1 8DG, tel. 01/730–5051. 12 rooms, 10 with bath. No credit cards.*

Prince. Unashamedly upscale, yet reasonably priced, with original cornices in the bathrooms and a high standard of furnishings, this hotel is a good accommodation for the money. The hall is papered in a pleasant mint-green Regency stripe. *6 Sumner Pl., SW7 3AB, tel. 01/589–6488. 20 rooms, 14 with bath. Facilities: garden, lounge. AE, MC, V.*

Inexpensive **Abbey House.** Standards are high and the rooms unusually spacious in this hotel in a fine residential block near Kensington Palace and Gardens. *11 Vicarage Gate, W8 4AG, tel. 01/727–2594. 15 rooms, none with bath. Facilities: orthopedic beds. No credit cards.*

Oakley House. Impeccably Victorian outside and a bit dark inside—but not at all dreary—the rooms here are small yet pleasant, with attractive moldings and colorful Indian print bedspreads. The public showers are clean and gigantic. Breakfast is self-service. Located in the heart of Chelsea, the Oakley House is not near a tube station. *71–72 Oakley St., SW3 5HF, tel. 01/352–7610. 24 rooms, 2 with bath. No credit cards.*

Vicarage Hotel. This genteel establishment, run by the same husband-wife team for the last 25 years, has high standards of cleanliness throughout. Bedrooms are traditional and comfortable with solid English furniture. It attracts many repeat visitors from the United States and welcomes single travelers. *10 Vicarage Gate, W8 4AG, tel. 01/229–4030. 20 rooms, none with bath. Facilities: small TV lounge. No credit cards.*

Knightsbridge and Victoria **Cadogan Thistle.** This turreted Edwardian building has teak furniture and pretty fabrics in the bedrooms and boldly colored *Very Expensive* hand-painted tiles in the bathrooms. There's a fascinating collection of Edwardian photos in the cocktail bar. The front part of the hotel was once the home of Lily Langtry, the actress who was Edward VII's mistress while he was Prince of Wales. *75 Sloane St., SW1X 9SG, tel. 01/235–7141. 72 rooms with bath. Facilities: bar, lounge, restaurant. AE, DC, MC, V.*

Goring. Around the corner from Buckingham Palace and often used by visiting VIPs, this hotel was built in 1910 and is now run by the third generation of Gorings. The atmosphere remains Edwardian: marble fittings in the bathrooms, with brass fittings and the original fitted closets in some of the bedrooms. *Beeston Pl., Grosvenor Gardens, SW1W 0JW, tel. 01/834–8211. 87 rooms with bath. Facilities: bar, restaurant, lounge. AE, DC, MC, V.*

Hyde Park Hotel. In the 1920s, this was the favored accommodation of Rudolph Valentino and of sultans and maharaiahs, who would book whole floors. The decor is high Victorian, with sumptuous green-veined marble, gold-topped columns, potted palms, and sparkling chandeliers. The bedrooms are furnished in the best of English taste: Edwardian darkwood furniture and pretty arrangements of fresh flowers. It's well placed for shopping and Hyde Park; some rooms have good views. *66 Knightsbridge, SW1Y 7LA, tel. 01/235–2000. 186 rooms with* *bath. Facilities: bar, 2 restaurants, lounge, hairdresser. AE, DC, MC, V.*

St. James Court. This elegant 1900 apartment block has been converted into a stylish hotel with a stately courtyard adorned by a fountain and a brick frieze portraying Shakespearean scenes. The reception area is grand, all marble and wood and lots of greenery. The bedrooms are appealingly decorated in different color schemes; the bathrooms are well equipped. *Buckingham Gate, SW1E 6AF, tel. 01/834–6655. 390 rooms with bath. Facilities: 2 restaurants, coffee shop, fitness center with sauna, spa pools. AE, DC, MC, V.*

Expensive **Basil Street.** Women guests here are granted automatic mem-
★ bership in the ladies' organization called "Parrot Club." Family-run for some 75 years, this is a gracious Edwardian hotel on a quiet street. The rooms are filled with antiques. The Gallery is a writing area, with desks in the window alcoves, unusual paintings on glass, polished wooden floors, and fine red and blue carpets. *Basil St., SW3 1AH. tel. 01/581–3311. 92 rooms, 70 with bath. Facilities: wine bar, lounge, ladies' club, 2 restaurants. AE, DC, MC, V.*

★ **Knightsbridge Green.** There are more suites than bedrooms at this recently refurbished 18th-century hotel just two minutes' walk from Harrods. The style of the second floor is French with white furniture; the third is English, in beech. Breakfast is served in your room—there's no restaurant. *159 Knightsbridge, SW1X 7PD, tel. 01/584–6274. 22 rooms/suites with bath. Facilities: club room. AE, MC, V. Closed 5 days at Christmas.*

Stakis St. Ermins. Convenient for Westminster Abbey, this is a Victorian hotel with high ceilings, a fine curved stairwell, and roomy bedrooms brightened by floral fabrics. Most of the guests are businesspeople. *Caxton St., SW1 K0QW, tel. 01/222 –7888. 290 rooms with bath or shower. Facilities: bar, coffee lounge, 2 restaurants. AE, DC, MC, V.*

Moderate **Ebury Court.** This small, old-fashioned, country house–style hotel is near Victoria Station. The rooms are small, with chintz and antique furniture to give them extra character. *26 Ebury St., SW1W 0LU, tel. 01/730–8147. 38 rooms, 11 with bath. Facilities: club with bar and lounge (membership fee payable), restaurant. MC, V.*

West End **Berkshire.** Ideally situated for Oxford Street shopping, this un-
Very Expensive usual flatiron building was totally renovated in 1987–88. The
★ decor is in Chinese style throughout, with exquisite Oriental vases and lamp shades. The bedrooms have richly decorated cream walls and ceilings, red or blue carpets, and tasteful paintings. In the drawing room, you can doze peacefully in front of the open fire, browse along the bookshelves, or enjoy the afternoon with tempting cream cakes. *350 Oxford St., W1N 0BY, tel. 01/629–7474. 147 rooms with bath. Facilities: restaurant, free in-house videos. AE, DC, MC, V.*

Brown's. Close to Bond Street, Brown's is like a country house in the middle of town, with wood paneling, grandfather clocks, and large fireplaces. The elegant furnishings of the bedrooms include brass chandeliers and matching olive carpets, and velour armchairs, and sweeping curtains. *34 Albemarle St., W1A 4SW, tel. 01/493–6020. 133 rooms with bath. Facilities: restaurant, lounge, writing room, cocktail bar. AE, DC, MC, V.*

Duke's. This small Edwardian hotel is situated in a cul-de-sac in St. James's and enjoys a distinct Old World character, helped by the portraits of dukes adorning the walls. The top-floor bedrooms are the most spacious. *5 St. James's Pl., SW1A 1NY, tel. 01/491–4840. 36 rooms with bath, 22 suites. Facilities: bar, restaurant. AE, DC, MC, V.*

Inn on the Park. Said to be one of Howard Hughes's hideaways, this opulent hotel, with its polished marble entrance hall, is close to Hyde Park. The rooms are exquisitely furnished with gigantic beds and plenty of extras, such as guest bathrobes and phone extensions in the bathrooms. *Hamilton Pl., Park Lane, W1A 1AZ, tel. 01/499–0888. 228 rooms with bath. Facilities: bar, lounge, 2 restaurants, shopping arcade, free in-house movies, garden. AE, DC, MC, V.*

★ **Savoy.** This grand, historic late-Victorian hotel has long been the byword for luxury. The best rooms, with antiques and cream plasterwork, overlook the Thames; others are in 1920s style with the original splendid bathroom fittings. *Strand, WC2R 0EU, tel. 01/836–4343. 200 rooms with bath. Facilities: 2 bars, restaurant, grill room, hairdresser, florist, theater-ticket desk, free in-house movies. AE, DC, MC, V.*

Expensive **Clifton-Ford.** This is one of central London's most peaceful hotels, situated in an 18th-century street north of Oxford Street. The public rooms have comfortable armchairs, chandeliers, and marble floors. Bedrooms are in light colors and have all the latest accessories. *47 Welbeck St., W1M 8DN, tel. 01/486–6600. 245 rooms with bath. Facilities: restaurant, bar, laundry, lounge with pianist, free in-house movies. AE, DC, MC, V.*

Pastoria. A recently refurbished hotel, the Pastoria stands on a quiet street only yards away from the restaurants and bright lights of Soho. The limed oak bedrooms have light pink walls and navy blue carpets. *3–6 St. Martin's St., WC2H 7HL, tel. 01/930–8641. 58 rooms with bath. Facilities: restaurant, bar, lounge. AE, DC, MC, V.*

Moderate **Bryanston Court.** Three 18th-century houses have been converted into a traditional English family-run hotel with open fires and comfortable armchairs; the bedrooms are more contemporary. *56–60 Great Cumberland Pl., W1H 7FD, tel. 01/262–3141. 56 rooms with bath. Facilities: bar, lounge, restaurant. AE, DC, MC, V.*

The Arts

For a list of events in the London arts scene, visit a newsstand or bookstore to pick up any of the weekly magazines: *Time Out, What's On,* or *City Limits* (the last is best for fringe events). The city's evening paper, the *Evening Standard,* carries listings, as do the major Sunday papers, the daily *Independent* and *Guardian,* and, on Friday, *The Times.* Further information on any aspect of the arts in the capital is available from **Greater London Arts,** 9 White Lion St., tel. 01/837–8808. Open weekdays 9:30–5:30.

Theater London's theater life can broadly be divided into three categories: the national, subsidized, companies; the commercial, or "West End," theaters; and the fringe.

The main national companies are the **National Theatre** (NT) and the **Royal Shakespeare Company** (RSC). Each has its own custom-designed facilities, in the South Bank arts complex and in the Barbican Arts Centre, respectively. Each presents a variety of plays by writers of all nationalities, ranging from the classics of Shakespeare and his contemporaries to specially commissioned modern works. Box office information: N.T., tel. 01/928–2252; RSC, tel. 01/628–8795.

The West End theaters largely stage musicals, comedies, whodunits, and revivals of lighter plays of the 19th and 20th centuries, often starring television celebrities. Occasionally, there are more serious productions, and sometimes successful productions from the subsidized theaters, such as RSC's hugely successful musical *Les Misérables*.

The dozen or so established fringe theaters, scattered around central London and the immediate outskirts, frequently present some of London's most intriguing productions, if you're prepared to overlook occasional rough acting and uncomfortable seating.

Most theaters have an evening performance at 7:30 or 8 daily, except Sunday, and a matinee twice a week (Wednesday or Thursday and Saturday). Expect to pay from £6 for a seat in the upper balcony to £18.50 for a good seat in the stalls or dress circle (mezzanine). Tickets may be booked in person at the theater box office, over the phone by credit card, or through ticket agents such as **Keith Prowse** (tel. 01/741–9999, or look in the phone book under *Keith* for the nearest office). In addition, the ticket booth in Leicester Square sells half-price tickets on the day of performance for about 45 theaters; there is an 80p service charge. Beware of unscrupulous ticket agents who sell tickets at four or five times their box office price (a small service charge is legitimate) and scalpers, who stand outside theaters offering tickets for the next performance; they've been known to charge £200 for a sought-after show.

Concerts Ticket prices for symphony orchestra concerts are still relatively moderate—between £3 and £12, although you can expect to pay more to hear big-name artists on tour. If you can't book in advance, arrive half an hour before the performance for a chance at returns.

The London Symphony Orchestra is in residence at the **Barbican Arts Centre** (tel. 01/628–8795), although other top symphony and chamber orchestras also perform here. The **South Bank arts complex** (tel. 01/928–3191), which includes the **Royal Festival Hall** and the **Queen Elizabeth Hall,** is another major venue for choral, symphony, and chamber concerts. For less expensive concert going, try the **Royal Albert Hall** (tel. 01/589–8212) during the summer Promenade season; special tickets for standing room are available at the hall on the night of performance. Inexpensive lunchtime concerts take place all over the city in smaller halls and churches, often featuring string quartets, singers, jazz ensembles, and gospel choirs. St. John's (tel. 01/222–1061) and St. Martin-in-the-Fields (tel. 01/839–1930) are two of the more popular sites.

Opera The **Royal Opera House** ranks alongside the New York Met in cost. Prices range from £2.50 (in the upper balconies, from where only a tiny portion of the stage is visible) to £300 for a box in the Grand Tier. Bookings are best made at the box office (tel. 01/240–1066). The **Coliseum** (tel. 01/836–3161) is the home of the English National Opera Company; productions are staged in English and are often a good deal more exciting than those at the Royal Opera House. The prices, which start at £5, are generally lower, too.

Ballet The Royal Opera House also hosts the **Royal Ballet.** The prices are slightly more reasonable than for the opera, but be sure to book well ahead. The **London Festival Ballet** and visiting companies perform at the Coliseum from time to time. **Sadler's Wells Theatre** (tel. 01/278–8916) hosts various ballet companies —including the Royal and the Rambert—as well as regional ballet and international modern dance troupes. Prices here are reasonable.

Film Most West End cinemas are in the Leicester Square Piccadilly Circus area. Tickets average £3.50–£4.50, but can run twice as high. Matinees and Monday evenings are cheaper. Cinema clubs screen a wide range of films: classics, continental, underground, rare, or underestimated masterpieces. The membership fee is usually about £1. One of the best-value clubs is the **National Film Theatre** (tel. 01/928–3232), part of the South Bank arts complex.

Nightlife

London's night spots are legion, and there is only space here to list a few of the best known.

Jazz **Bas Clef** (35 Coronet St., tel. 01/729–2440), situated in an out-of-the-way warehouse on the northern edge of the City, offers some of the best live jazz in town and a gourmet Anglo-French menu. **Ronnie Scott's** (47 Frith St., tel. 01/439–0747) is the legendary Soho jazz club where a host of American performers have played.

Nightclubs **Legends** (29 Old Burlington St., tel. 01/437–9933) has an impressive high-tech interior; a large choice of cocktails is served at the upstairs bar, while the downstairs area is graced with a large cool dance floor and central bar. Celebrity-packed **Stringfellows** (16 Upper St. Martin's Lane, tel. 01/240–5534) has an Art Deco upstairs restaurant, mirrored walls, and a dazzling light show in the downstairs dance floor. **The Limelight** (136 Shaftesbury Ave., tel. 01/434–1761) is one of London's most fashionable night spots, with lots of one-nighter shows and special events. A good place for celebrity-spotting. **Xenon** (196 Piccadilly, tel. 01/734–9344) has a luxurious ground-floor piano bar with live music and a sophisticated lower-level disco where specialty circus acts and Xenon dancers are featured nightly. No restaurant, but good, substantial snacks are served.

Disco Wednesday nights have made the **Café de Paris** (3 Coventry St., tel. 01/437–2036) one of London's hottest spots; dinner is served on the balcony overlooking the dance floor, where you can people-spot in comfort. There is a disco-dance on Friday and Saturday for the more mellow. The **Hippodrome** (Cranbourn St., tel. 01/437–4311) is a hugely popular and lavish disco with an exciting sound and laser light system, live bands and dancing acts, video screen, bars, and restaurant. Trendy, chic dress will help you to gain entrance.

Casinos By law, you must apply in person for membership in a gaming house; in many cases, clubs prefer an applicant's membership to be proposed by an existing member. Approval usually takes about two days.

Crockford's (30 Curzon St., tel. 01/493–7771) is a civilized and unflashy 150-year-old club with a large international clientele; American roulette, punto banco, and blackjack are played.

Sportsman Club (3 Tottenham Court Rd., tel. 01/637–5464) is one of the few gaming houses in London to have a dice table as well as punto banco, American roulette, and blackjack.

Rock   **Dingwalls** (Camden Lock, Chalk Farm Rd., tel. 01/267–1430) is a long-established music venue where a good selection of live bands play everything from rock to jazz every night of the week.

The Rock Garden (The Piazza, Covent Garden, tel. 01/240–3961) is famous for encouraging younger talent; Talking Heads, U2, and The Smiths are among those who played here while still virtually unknown. Music is in the standing-room-only basement, so eat first in the American restaurant upstairs. The **Marquee** (105 Charing Cross Rd., tel. 01/437–6601), Soho's original rock club, is now in new premises; at least two live bands perform every night.

Cabaret   The best comedy in town can be found in the small, crowded basement of the **Comedy Store** (28 Leicester Sq., tel. 01/839–6665). There are two shows, 8 and midnight, with the famous improvised show *Comedy To Go* on Sunday. **Gaslight of St. James's** (4 Duke of York St., tel. 01/930–1648) is a basement night spot with attractive hostesses and three striptease cabarets each night.

Windsor to Stratford

The Thames, England's second-longest river, winds its way toward London through an accessible and gracious stretch of countryside. An excursion west from the capital, roughly following the river toward its source in the Cotswold Hills, allows you to explore historic townships such as Windsor, where the castle is still regularly used by the royal family; Oxford, home of the nation's oldest university; and Shakespeare's birthplace at Stratford-upon-Avon. Traveling south, Bath's 18th-century streets recall an age more elegant than our own.

Getting Around

By Train   Suburban services run from London (Waterloo and Paddington stations) to Windsor. Regular fast trains run from Paddington to Oxford and Bath, and less frequent and slower services requiring at least one change, to Stratford. For information, call 01/262–6767. An alternative route to Stratford is from London's Euston Station to Coventry, from where Guide Friday operates bus connections (summer five times daily, winter three times daily); telephone 0789–294466 for details.

By Bus   Regular long-distance services leave from Victoria Coach Station. For information, call 01/730–0202.

By Car   The M4 and the M40 are the main highways out of London serving Oxford, the Cotswolds, and Bath. Once you're clear of London, take to the country roads and explore tiny villages and the countryside—your trip may take a bit longer, but you'll be rewarded by the best of the English countryside.

Tourist Information

Bath. Abbey Churchyard, tel. 0225/462831.
Oxford. St. Aldate's, opposite the town hall, tel. 0865/726871.
Stow-on-the-Wold. Public library, St. Edwards Hall, tel. 0451/
30352 (summer only).
Stratford. Judith Shakespeare's House, on the corner of High
Street and Bridge Street, tel. 0789/293127/67522.
Windsor. Central station, tel. 0753/852010.

Guided Tours

National Holidays operates five-day trips in the Cotswolds,
some in Bath. There are agents throughout the country.
Frames Rickards runs full-day sightseeing tours to Windsor,
Stratford-upon-Avon, and Bath, (tel. 01/837–3111). **Evan
Evans** offers a variety of one- and two-day tours to Oxford and
the Cotswolds, Stratford and Warwick Castle, Windsor, and
Bath (tel. 01/930–2377). **White's of Oxford** runs daily coach
tours of the Cotswolds from April through September and
minibus and chauffeured car tours to a selection of stately
homes (tel. 0865/61295).

Exploring Windsor to Stratford

Windsor **Windsor,** some 40 kilometers (25 miles) west of London, has
been a royal citadel since the days of William the Conqueror in
the 11th century. In the 14th century, Edward III revamped
the old castle, building the Norman gateway, the great round
tower, and new apartments. Almost every monarch since then
has added new buildings or improved existing ones; over the
centuries, the medieval fortification has been transformed into
the lavish royal palace the visitor sees today. Windsor Castle
remains a favorite spot of Queen Elizabeth and Prince Philip;
they spend most weekends here, and there is a grand celebration with all the family at Christmas. Naturally, the royal
family's private apartments are closed to the public, but you
can see the State Apartments, where visiting heads of state are
sometimes entertained.

The following are some of the highlights of the castle: **St.
George's Chapel,** more than 71 meters (230 feet) long with two
tiers of great windows and hundreds of gargoyles, buttresses,
and pinnacles, is one of the noblest buildings in England. Inside, above the choir stalls, hang the banners, swords, and
helmets of the Knights of the Order of the Garter, the most senior Order of Chivalry. The many monarchs buried in the chapel
include Henry VIII and George VI, father of the present
queen. The **State Apartments** indicate the magnificence of the
queen's art collection; here hang paintings by such masters as
Rubens, Van Dyck, and Holbein; drawings by Leonardo da
Vinci; and Gobelin tapestries, among many other treasures.
There are splendid views across to Windsor Great Park, the remains of a former royal hunting forest. Make time to view
Queen Mary's Dolls' House, a charming residence with every
detail complete, including electricity, running water, and miniature books on the library shelves. It was designed in 1921 by
the architect Sir Edwin Lutyens for the present queen's grandmother. *Windsor Castle, tel. 0753/868286. Precincts open daily
10–4:15 (till 7:15 mid-May–Aug.). St. George's Chapel. Ad-*

Windsor to Stratford

mission: *£1.50 adults, 60p children under 16 and senior citizens. Open Mon.–Sat. 10:45–3:45, Sun. 2–3:45. State Apartments. Admission: £2 adults, £1 children under 16 and senior citizens. Open Mon.–Sat. 10:30–5 (until 3, Nov.–Apr.), Sun. (May–Oct. only) 1:30–5. Queen Mary's Dolls' House. Admission: £1 adults, 50p children under 16 and senior citizens. Open daily 10:30–5 (Oct.–Mar. until 3).*

After seeing the castle, stroll around the town and enjoy the shops; antiques are sold in cobbled Church Lane and Queen Charlotte Street. Opposite the castle, the **Royalty and Empire Exhibition** in part of the central station re-creates in waxworks the arrival at the station of Queen Victoria to celebrate her Diamond Jubilee in 1897; the scene is incredibly lifelike. *Thames St., tel. 0753/857837. Admission: £3.55 adults, £2.55 children under 16 and senior citizens. Open Apr.–Oct., daily 9:30–5:30, Nov.–Mar., daily 9:30–4:30.*

Time Out The **Adam and Eve** pub opposite the walls of Windsor Castle serves hot snacks and plowmen's lunches, while the **Chocolate House** in Market Street is an inviting place for morning coffee, lunch, or a cream tea.

A short walk over the river brings you to **Eton,** Windsor Castle's equally historic neighbor and home of the famous public school. (In Britain, so-called "public" schools are private and charge fees.) Classes still take place in the distinctive red-brick Tudor-style buildings; the oldest buildings are grouped around a quadrangle called School Yard. The **Museum of Eton Life** has displays on the school's history, and a guided tour is also available. *Brewhouse Yard, tel. 0753/863593. Admission: £1.80 adults, £1.20 children under 16. Open daily during term 2–4:30, 10:30–4:30 on school holidays. Guided tours Mar.– Oct., daily at 2:15 and 3:15; charge: £2.40 adults, £1.80 children under 16, including admission to museum.*

A relatively uncrowded route from Windsor to Oxford is along the river through Marlow and Henley on roads A4094, then A4155 and A423. Both these riverside towns contain numerous historic buildings, many still in private residential use. In **Marlow,** there are some stylish 18th-century houses on Peter and West Streets, and several Princes of Wales have lived in Marlow Place on Station Road, which dates from 1721. Mary Shelley wrote her celebrated horror story *Frankenstein* in the town.

Henley has been famous since 1839 for the rowing regatta it holds each year around the first Sunday in July. For the spectators, the social side of the regatta is as entertaining as the races themselves; elderly oarsmen wear brightly colored blazers and tiny caps, businessmen entertain wealthy clients, and everyone admires the ladies' fashions. The town is worth exploring for its small but good selection of specialty shops, such as Saffron on Bell Street (craft items) and Thames Gallery on Thameside (Georgian and Victorian silver). The Red Lion Hotel near the 200-year-old bridge has been visited by kings, dukes, and writers; the Duke of Marlborough stayed there while Blenheim Palace was being built. St. Mary's Church has a 16th-century "checkerboard" tower made of alternate squares of flint and stone, and the **Chantry House,** built in 1420 as a school for poor boys, is an unspoiled example of the rare overhanging timber-frame design. *Hart St. Admission: free. Open Thurs. and Sat. 10–noon.*

Numbers in the margin correspond with points of interest on the Oxford map.

Oxford Continue along A423 north to **Oxford.** The surest way to absorb Oxford's unique blend of history and scholarliness is to wander around the tiny alleys that link the honey-colored stone buildings topped by elegant "dreaming" spires, exploring the colleges where the undergraduates live and work. Oxford University, like Cambridge University, is not a single building but a collection of 35 independent colleges; many of their magnificent chapels and dining halls are open to visitors—times are

❶ displayed at the entrance lodges. **Magdalen College** is one of the most impressive, with 500-year-old cloisters and lawns leading

❷ down to the river Cherwell. **St. Edmund Hall,** the next college up the High Street, has one of the smallest and most picturesque quadrangles, with an old well in the center; **Christ**

❸ **Church,** on St. Aldate's, has the largest quadrangle, known as Tom Quad; in the medieval dining hall hang portraits of former pupils, including John Wesley, William Penn, and no less than 14 prime ministers. The doors between the inner and outer

❹ quadrangles of **Balliol College,** on Broad Street, still bear the scorch marks from the flames that burned Archbishop Cranmer and Bishops Latimer and Ridley at the stake in 1555 for their Protestant beliefs.

❺ The **Oxford Story** on Broad Street is a brand-new multimedia presentation of the university's 800-year history, in which visi-

Oxford

Major Attractions
Ashmolean Museum, **7**
Balliol College, **4**
Christ Church, **3**
Magdalen College, **1**
Oxford Story, **5**
St. Edmund Hall, **2**
Sheldonian Theatre, **6**

Other Attractions
All Souls College, **13**
Bodleian Library, **16**
Exeter College, **17**
Jesus College, **19**
Keble College, **10**
Radcliffe Camera, **15**
St. Giles' Church, **9**
St. Mary Magdalen Church, **20**

Trinity College, **18**
University Church (St. Mary's), **14**
University Museum, **11**
Wadham College, **12**
Worcester College, **8**

tors travel through depictions of college life. *Broad St., tel. 0865/728822. Admission: £2.50 adults, £1.25 children. Open Apr.–Oct., daily 9:30–5, Nov.–Mar., daily 9–5.*

6 Also on Broad Street is the **Sheldonian Theatre,** which St. Paul's architect Christopher Wren designed to look like a semi-circular Roman amphitheater: It's one of his earliest works. Graduation ceremonies are held here. *Sheldonian Theatre, Broad St., tel. 0865/277299. Admission: 30p adults, 15p children. Open Mon.–Sat. 10–12:45 and 2–4:45; closes at 3:45 Dec.–Feb.*

7 The **Ashmolean Museum,** which you encounter by turning right out of Broad Street, into Magdalen Street then taking the first left, is Britain's oldest public museum, holding priceless collections of Egyptian, Greek, and Roman artifacts; Michelangelo drawings; and European silverware. *Beaumont St., tel. 0865/278000. Admission: free. Open Tues.–Sat. 10–4, Sun. 2–4.*

For a relaxing walk, make for the banks of the river Cherwell, either through the University Parks area or through Magdalen College to Addison's Walk, and watch the undergraduates idly punting a summer's afternoon away. Or rent one of these narrow flat-bottomed boats yourself. But be warned: Navigating is more difficult than it looks!

Time Out The **Queen's Lane Coffee House** on High Street offers inexpensive snacks and is popular with undergraduates. The **Eagle and Child** is a historic pub in St. Giles. On the outskirts of the city are two excellent pubs, the **Perch** at Binsey and the **Trout** at Godstow. Connoisseurs go to the former at lunchtime to sit on the wide lawn, savor the exotic sandwiches, and listen to the cooing of white doves. In the evening, they visit the Trout for a meal or simply to enjoy a drink while watching the peacocks strutting by the tumbling weir.

Blenheim Palace, 12.8 kilometers (8 miles) north of Oxford on the main A34 road, is a large and imposing mansion in neoclassical style built in the early 18th century by the architect Sir John Vanbrugh; it stands in 2,500 acres of beautiful gardens landscaped later in the 18th century by "Capability" Brown, perhaps the most famous of all English landscape gardeners. The house was built by the soldier and statesman John Churchill, 1st Duke of Marlborough, on land given to him by Queen Anne and with money voted him by Parliament on behalf of a "grateful nation" as a reward for his crushing defeat of the French at the Battle of Blenheim in 1704. The house is full of fine paintings, tapestries, and furniture. Winston Churchill, a descendant of Marlborough, was born in the palace; some of his paintings are on display, and there is an exhibition devoted to his life. *Woodstock, tel. 0993/811325. Admission: £4.50 adults, £2.20 children under 15, £3.20 senior citizens. Open mid-Mar.–Oct., 10:30–4:45. Grounds open all year 9–5.*

Sir Winston Churchill (1874–1965) is buried in the nearby village of **Bladon.** His grave in the small tree-lined churchyard is all the more touching for its simplicity.

The Cotswolds The A34 runs northwest from Oxford and Blenheim across the Cotswold Hills to Stratford-upon-Avon. The **Cotswolds** are high, bare hills patterned by stones walls that protect the sheep that have grazed here from the earliest times. In the

Middle Ages, English wool commanded high prices, and the little towns and villages nestling in valleys and on hillsides grew in prosperity. Although the wool trade has now dwindled in importance, the legacy of those days remains in the solid, substantial churches, cottages, and manor houses built of the mellow, golden-gray local stone. Burford, Stow-on-the-Wold, Upper Slaughter, Bourton-on-the-Water, Broadway, and Moreton-in-Marsh are just a few of the picturesque villages connected by pleasant country roads that are well worth the detour off the main road.

Stratford-upon-Avon Even without its most famous son, **Stratford-upon-Avon** would be worth visiting. Its timbered buildings bear witness to its prosperity in the 16th century, when it was a thriving craft and trading center, and attractive 18-century buildings are also of note.

Numbers in the margin correspond with points of interest on the Stratford-upon-Avon map.

❶ ❷ There are four main Shakespearean places of interest. The **Shakespeare Centre** and **Shakespeare's Birthplace** contain the costumes used in the BBC's dramatization of the plays and an exhibition of the playwright's life and work. *Henley St., tel. 0789/204016. Admission: £1.90 adults, 80p children. Open Apr.–Sept., Mon.–Sat. 9–6, Sun. 10–6; Oct., Mon.–Sat. 9–5, Sun. 10–5; Nov.–Mar., Mon.–Sat. 9–4:30, Sun. 1:30–4:30.*

Time Out **Mistress Quickly** in Henley Street serves light refreshments and meals throughout the day; an unusual feature is the jigsaw tree sculpture. The **Black Swan**—better known locally as the Dirty Duck—is a riverside pub serving good ales and bar meals.

❸ Two very different attractions reveal something of the times in which Shakespeare lived. Originally a farmhouse, the girlhood home of Shakespeare's mother, **Mary Arden's House,** is now an extensive museum of farming and country life. It was built in the 16th century and many of the original outbuildings are intact, together with a 600-nesting-hole dovecote. *Wilmcote (4.8 km [3 mi.] northwest of Stratford, off A34 and A422), tel. 0789/204016. Admission: £1.60 adults, 70p children. Open Apr.–Sept., Mon.–Sat. 9–6, Sun. 10–6; Oct., Mon.–Sat. 9–5, Sun. 10–5.*

❹ A complete contrast is **Hall's Croft,** a fine Tudor town house that was the home of Shakespeare's daughter Susanna and her doctor husband; it is furnished in the decor of the day, and the doctor's dispensary and consulting room can also be seen. *Old Town, tel. 0780/292107. Admission: £1.10 adults, 50p children. Open Apr.–Sept., Mon–Sat. 9–6, Sun. 10–6; Oct., Mon.–Sat. 9–5, Sun. 10–5.*

❺ The **Royal Shakespeare Theatre** occupies a perfect position on the banks of the Avon—try to see a performance if you can. The company (always referred to as the RSC) performs five Shakespeare plays each season, between March and January. It has ❻ two other theaters in Stratford: The **Swan,** where plays by con- ❼ temporaries of Shakespeare are staged, and **The Other Place,** where lesser-known Shakespeare plays are performed in repertory with new studio plays and fringe productions. It's best to book well in advance, but tickets for the day of performance

Major Attractions

Anne Hathaway's Cottage, **9**

Hall's Croft, **4**

Holy Trinity Church, **8**

Mary Arden's House, **3**

The Other Place, **7**

Royal Shakespeare Theatre, **5**

Shakespeare's Birthplace, **2**

Shakespeare Centre, **1**

Swan, **6**

Other Attractions

American Foundation, **16**

Grammar School and Guildhall, **11**

Guild Chapel, **12**

Harvard House, **15**

New Place, **13**

Shakespeare Institute, **10**

Town Hall, **14**

are always available, and it is also worth asking if there are any returns. *Programs are available starting in February from the Royal Shakespeare Theatre, Stratford-upon-Avon, Warwick-shire CV37 6BB, tel. 0789/205301.*

8 In **Holy Trinity Church,** close the Royal Shakespeare Theatre, Shakespeare and his wife are buried.

9 **Anne Hathaway's Cottage,** in Shottery on the edge of the town, is the early home of the playwright's wife. *Admission: £1.60 adults, 60p children. Open Apr.–Sept., Mon.–Sat. 9–6, Sun. 10–6; Oct., Mon.–Sat. 9–5, Sun. 10–5; Nov.–Mar., Mon.–Sat. 9–4:30, Sun. 1:30–4:30.*

Warwick **Warwick,** some 12.8 kilometers (8 miles) north of Stratford along A46, is an unusual mixture of Georgian red-brick and Elizabethan half-timbered buildings, although some unattractive postwar developments have spoiled the town center. **Warwick Castle** is one of the finest medieval structures of its kind in England, towering on a precipice above the river Avon. Most of the present buildings date from the 14th century; look for the remarkable gate house, which consists of a pair of towers above the doorway passage, and two massive towers, Guy's and Caesar's, both about 40 meters (130 feet) tall, the latter with a system of double battlements. The interior contains magnificent collections of armor, paintings, and furniture, while, outside, peacocks strut in the 24 hectares (60 acres) of landscaped riverside gardens. Recently more battlements have been opened to the public and there is a newly restored Victorian boathouse which features a flora and fauna exhibition and a nature walk. *Castle Hill, tel. 0926/495421. Admission: £4.50 adults, £3 children under 16, £3.50 senior citizens. Open Mar.–Oct., daily 10–5:30, Nov.–Feb., daily 10–4:30.*

Chipping Campden From Stratford take A46, take an easy detour to **Chipping Campden.** If you have time to visit only one Cotswold town, make it this one. The broad High Street is lined with houses in an attractive disarray of styles, many dating from the 17th century. Look for the group of almshouses built in 1624 and raised above street level and for the gabled **Market Hall** built three years later for the sale of local produce.

One of the town's earliest building, dating from the 14th century, is the **Woolstaplers Hall,** which contains a museum of local history; besides material on the wool trade, there is a 1920s cinema and collections of medical equipment. *Admission: 80p adults, 40p children. Open Apr.–Oct., daily 11–6.*

Five kilometers (three miles) outside Chipping Campden is **Hidcote Manor Garden,** a 20th-century garden created around a Cotswold manor house (not open to the public). The garden consists of a series of rooms divided by walls and hedges and each in a different style. *Hidcote Bartrim, tel. 0386/438333. Admission: £2.90 (£3.20 Sun.) adults, £1.45 children. Open Apr.–Oct., Sat.–Mon., Wed., Thurs. 11–8.*

A46 runs along the western edge of the gently rolling Cotswold hills, through Cheltenham, once the rival of Bath in its Georgian elegance, now marred by modern developments. There are still unsurpassed examples of Regency style in its graceful secluded villas, lush gardens, and leafy crescents and squares.

Bath Bath lies at the southern end of the Cotswolds (at the end of A46), some 112 kilometers (70 miles) from Stratford. A perfect 18th-century city, perhaps the best-preserved in all Britain, it is a compact place, easy to explore on foot; the museums and elegant shops and terraces of magnificent town houses are all close to each other.

Numbers in the margin correspond with points of interest on the Bath map.

It was the Romans who first took the waters at Bath, building a temple in honor of their goddess Minerva and a sophisticated series of baths to make full use of the curative hot springs. To this day, these springs gush from the earth at a constant temperature of 115.7°F (46.5°C). In the **Roman Baths Museum,** underneath the 18th-century Pump Room, you can see the ex-

Bath

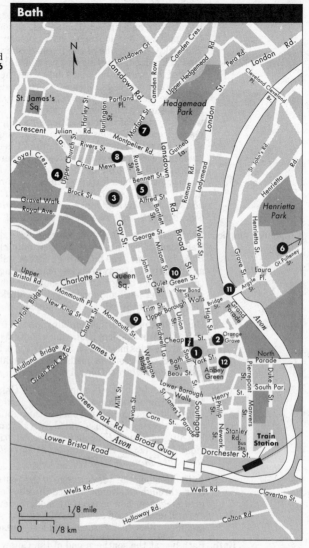

cavated remains of almost the entire baths complex. *Abbey Churchyard. Admission: £2.70 adults, £1.40 children. Open Mar.–Oct. daily 9–6 (July–Aug. 9–7); Nov.–Feb., Mon.–Sat. 9–5, Sun. 10–5.*

2 Next to the Pump Room is the **Abbey,** built in the 15th century. There are superb fan-vaulted ceilings in the nave.

In the 18th century, Bath became the fashionable center for taking the waters. The architect John Wood created a harmonious city from the mellow local stone, building beautifully executed terraces, crescents, and villas. The heart of Georgian

3 Bath is the perfectly proportioned **Circus** and the Royal Cres-
4 cent. On the corner, **No. 1 Royal Crescent** is furnished as it might have been when Beau Nash, the master of ceremonies

and arbiter of 18th-century Bath society, lived in the city. *Admission: £1.50 adults, £1 children and senior citizens. Open Mar.–Oct., Tues.–Sat. 11–5, Sun. 2–5; Nov.–Dec., weekends 11–3.*

⑤ Also near the Circus are the **Assembly Rooms,** frequently mentioned by Jane Austen in her novels of early 19th-century life. This neoclassical villa now houses a Museum of Costume, which is temporarily closed. Across the Avon, in an elegant 18th-
⑥ century building, is the **Holburne Museum and Crafts Study Centre,** which houses a superb collection of 17th- and 18th-century fine art and decorative arts. There is also work by 20th-century craftsmen in the study center. *Great Pulteney St., tel. 0225/466669. Admission: £1 adults, 50p children and senior citizens. Open Easter–Oct., Mon.–Sat. 11–5, Sun. 2:30–6; Nov.–mid-Dec. and mid-Feb.–Easter, Tues.–Sat. 11–5, Sun. 2:30–6.*

Time Out | Bath has a good selection of spots for coffee or lunch. Try the **Pump Room** (Abbey Churchyard) for morning coffee or afternoon tea in grand surroundings, perhaps listening to the music of a string quartet, or, in nearby North Parade Passage, **Sally Lunns,** where the famous Sally Lunn bun is still baked. The **Theatre Vaults** in Sawclose is a good place for a pre- or post-theater drink or meal; the theater itself is one of the finest surviving Georgian theaters in England.

Dining and Lodging

For details and price category definitions, *see* Dining and Lodging in Staying in Great Britain.

Windsor and Eton
Dining
The Cockpit. Cockfighting once took place in the courtyard of this smart 500-year-old inn with oak beams, located on Eton's quiet main street. Specialties include guinea fowl and a casserole of bacon in mushroom sauce. *High Street, Eton, tel. 0753/860944. AE, DC, MC, V. Expensive.*

The House on the Bridge. Looking out across the river from Eton to Windsor Castle, this house was built as a boat house. Traditional English food is served here. *Windsor Bridge, Eton, tel. 0753/860914. AE, DC, MC, V. Expensive.*

Bensons. Chicken in mushroom sauce and panfried sirloin with parsley butter are among the specialties at this oak-beamed restaurant in the oldest part of town. Downstairs there is a less formal champagne and wine bar. *Church Lane, Windsor, tel. 0753/858331. MC, V. Moderate.*

Lodging
Oakley Court. This Victorian mansion is set in leafy grounds beside the river, just outside Windsor. Some of the bedrooms are in a bright modern annex. *Windsor Rd., Water Oakley, tel. 0628/74141. 92 rooms with bath. AE, DC, MC, V. Very Expensive.*

Sir Christopher Wren's House. As the name suggests, this house was built by the famous architect, though modern additions have been made to turn it into a hotel. The restaurant overlooks the river, and the cream teas served on the terrace are renowned. *Thames St., Windsor, tel. 0753/861354. 39 rooms with bath. AE, DC, MC, V. Expensive.*

Ye Harte and Garter. Originally two Tudor taverns, this hotel was rebuilt during the last century. It is in a busy position im-

mediately opposite the castle. *High Street, Windsor, tel. 0753/
863426. 50 rooms, 43 with bath. AE, DC, MC, V. Moderate.*

Oxford
Dining

Elizabeth's. These small, elegant dining rooms in a 16th-
century bishop's palace overlook Christ Church and have the
best views of any restaurant in Oxford. Salmon rolls and roast
lamb are among the Spanish chef's specialties and there are
outstanding wines. *St. Aldates, tel. 0865/242230. MC, V. Expensive.*

Fifteen North Parade. Just outside the city center, this is an intimate, stylish restaurant with cane furniture and plants. The
menu changes regularly and may feature steamed breast of
chicken with morel mousse, served with truffle noodles, or venison with Madeira sauce and celeriac. *North Parade, tel. 0865/
513773. MC, V. Moderate.*

Munchy Munchy. A daily changing menu of spicy Malaysian
dishes and a good selection of fresh fruit and vegetables makes
this a refreshing and popular spot. The surroundings are unpretentious and the prices reasonable. *Park End St., tel. 0865/
245710. Inexpensive.*

Lodging

Cotswold Lodge. This is a privately owned hotel about half a
mile from the city center. There is a modern wing behind the
original Victorian building. *Banbury Rd., tel. 0865/512121. 52
rooms with bath. AE, DC, MC, V. Expensive.*

The Eastgate Hotel. This welcoming hotel has the traditional
style of an inn. Its bar is a favorite with undergraduates and is
a good place for getting an insight into university life. *The
High, tel. 0865/248244. 43 rooms with bath. AE, DC, MC, V.
Expensive.*

The Randolph. Oxford's only large central hotel is particularly
grand, with an elaborate Victorian Gothic interior. It's across
from the Ashmolean Museum. *Beaumont St., tel. 0865/247481.
109 rooms with bath. AE, DC, MC, V. Expensive.*

Stratford
Dining

Box Tree Restaurant. In the Royal Shakespeare Theatre, this
elegant restaurant overlooks the river and is a favored spot for
pre- and post-theater dining. Specialties include noisettes of
lamb Box Tree and poached Scotch beef fillet. *Waterside, tel.
0789/293226. AE, MC, V. Expensive.*

The Slug and Lettuce. Don't let the name put you off. This is a
pine-paneled pub that serves excellent meals; the long-standing favorite is chicken breast baked in avocado and garlic. *38
Guild St., tel. 0789/299700. MC, V. Moderate.*

The River Terrace. For less expensive fare at the theater, this
spot provides informal meals and light refreshments. Hot
dishes include lasagna and shepherd's pie, and there are also
salads, cakes, and sandwiches. *Waterside, tel. 0789/293226. Inexpensive.*

Lodging

The Falcon Hotel. Licensed as an ale house since 1640, its atmosphere is still that of a friendly inn. The heavily beamed
rooms in the older part are small and quaint, those in the modern extension are in typical standard international style.
*Chapel St., tel. 0789/205777. 73 rooms with bath. Facilities:
garden. AE, DC, MC, V. Expensive.*

The Shakespeare Hotel. For a touch of typical Stratford, stay at
this timbered Elizabethan town house in the heart of the town,
close to the theater and to most of the attractions. It has been
luxuriously modernized while still retaining its Elizabethan
character. *Chapel St., tel. 0789/294771. 70 rooms with bath.
AE, DC, MC, V. Expensive.*

Arden Hotel. Across from the theater, these 18th-century town houses have been successfully converted into a comfortable Old World hotel with beamed bedrooms. *Waterside, tel. 0789/294949. 65 rooms with bath. Facilities: garden. AE, DC, MC, V. Moderate.*

Caterham House. Situated in the town center near the theater, Caterham House was built in 1830. Its pretty bedrooms are all decorated in period style and have brass beds and antique furniture. *Rother St., tel. 0789/67309/297070. 14 rooms, 2 with bath. MC, V. Inexpensive.*

Bath
Dining

Popjoys Restaurant. Beau Nash entertained the best of 18th-century society here, and Popjoys retains its air of elegance. *Sawclose, tel. 0225/460494. AE, MC, V. Expensive.*

Peking. The excellent and well-presented Chinese food served here more than makes up for the waiters' rather brusque attitude. The sizzler dishes—served sizzling hot on an iron griddle —are exceptional. *New St., Kingsmead Sq., tel. 0225/466377/461750. AE, DC, MC, V. Moderate.*

Pasta Galore. Fellow diners here may include actors from the nearby Theatre Royal after a performance. Best choices on the menu include tagliatelle marinara and tagliatelle with chili and bacon in tomato sauce. *Barton St., tel. 0225/463861. AE, MC, V. Inexpensive.*

Lodging

Royal Crescent. The ultimate in luxurious living is what the famous Royal Crescent is all about. Each bedroom has been individually designed to recapture the elegance of Bath's heyday. *Royal Crescent, tel. 0225/319090. 45 rooms, including 13 suites, all with bath. Facilities: whirlpool bath, garden, croquet. AE, DC, MC, V. Very Expensive.*

Francis Hotel. Overlooking one of Bath's attractive Georgian squares, the Francis consists of six Georgian houses and a new wing. Bedrooms in the old building are decorated in period style. *Queen Sq., tel. 0225/24257. 94 rooms with bath. AE, DC, MC, V. Expensive.*

Royal York. The young Queen Victoria (whose room is still furnished as it was during her visit), the novelist Charles Dickens, and the statesman Benjamin Disraeli stayed here. The Royal York has been welcoming guests since 1759. *George St., tel. 0225/461541. 53 rooms, 44 with bath. AE, DC, MC, V. Moderate.*

The Tasburgh Hotel. This spacious and beautifully refurbished Victorian house, set in delightful gardens with beautiful views over the Avon Valley, has tastefully furnished rooms complete with all modern comforts. It's situated a mile from city center. *Warminster Rd., tel. 0225/25096. 14 rooms, 10 with bath. Facilities: extensive gardens, paddocks, fishing and mooring rights. AE, DC, MC, V. Moderate.*

Cambridge

Cambridge, home of England's second-oldest university, is an ideal place to explore. Students began studying here in the late 13th century, and virtually every generation since then has produced fine buildings, often by the most distinguished architects of their day. The result is a compact gallery of the best of English architecture. There is also good shopping in the city, as well as relaxing riverside walks.

A short excursion outside Cambridge will introduce you to some characteristic East Anglian landscapes. To the north, on the edge of the Fens, is **Ely,** which boasts an impressive medieval cathedral. To the east is **Bury St. Edmunds,** a bustling market town rich with 17th- and 18th-century buildings and surrounded by cornfields, gentle hills, and tiny villages, each with its medieval church.

Getting Around

By Train Regular fast trains from London's Liverpool Street Station take an hour to Cambridge; there's somewhat slower service from London's King's Cross Station. For information, call 01/928–5100. Local services connect Cambridge with both Ely and Bury St. Edmunds.

By Bus There's regular long-distance service from Victoria Coach Station that takes about two hours. Tel. 01/730–0202.

By Car The M11 is the main highway from London to Cambridge. This connects with the fast A45 road east to Bury St. Edmunds. Ely is reached along the A10 from Cambridge. The main car rental companies have offices in Cambridge.

Tourist Information

Bury St. Edmunds. Angel Hill, tel. 0284/763233.
Cambridge. Wheeler Street, off King's Parade, tel. 0223/322640.
Ely. Public Library, Palace Green, tel. 0353/662062.

Guided Tours

The **Cambridge Tourist Information Center** offers two-hour walking tours of the city and the colleges Monday–Saturday. It also runs excursions to Ely and the Fens.

Exploring Cambridge

The university is in the very heart of **Cambridge.** It consists of a number of colleges, each of which is a separate institution with its own distinct character and traditions. Undergraduates join an individual college and are taught by dons attached to the college, who are known as "fellows." Each college is built around a series of courts, or quadrangles; because students and fellows live in these courts, access is sometimes restricted, especially during examination weeks in early summer. Visitors are not normally allowed into college buildings other than chapels and halls.

Numbers in the margin correspond with points of interest on the Cambridge map.

● **King's College,** off King's Parade, is possibly the best known of all the colleges. Its chapel, started by Henry VI in the mid-1500s, is a masterpiece of late Gothic architecture, with a great fan-vaulted roof supported only by a tracery of soaring side columns. Behind the altar hangs Rubens's painting of the *Adoration of the Magi.* Every Christmas Eve the college choir sings the Festival of Nine Lessons and Carols, which is broadcast all over the world.

Cambridge

Clare College, **2**
Downing College, **13**
Emmanuel College, **14**
Fitzwilliam Museum, **12**
Kettle's Yard, **8**
King's College, **1**
Magdalene College, **7**

Merton Hall, **6**
Pembroke College, **10**
Peterhouse, **11**
Queen's College, **9**
St. John's, **5**
Silver Street Bridge, **15**
Trinity, **4**
Trinity Hall, **3**

King's runs down to the famous "Backs," the tree-shaded grounds on the banks of the River Cam, onto which many of the colleges back. From King's make your way along the river and through the narrow lanes past **Clare College** and **Trinity Hall** to **Trinity.** This is the largest college, established by Henry VIII in 1546. It has a handsome 17th-century Great Court around which are the chapel, hall, gates, and a library by Christopher Wren, who also designed St. Paul's Cathedral, London. In the massive gatehouse is Great Tom, a large clock that strikes each hour with high and low notes. Prince Charles was an undergraduate here in the late 1960s.

Beyond Trinity lies **St. John's,** the second-largest college. The white crenellations of the enormous mock-Gothic **New Building** of 1825 have earned it the nickname "the wedding cake." It is reached across a facsimile of the Bridge of Sighs in Venice. Behind St. John's is the oldest house in Cambridge, the 12th-century **Merton Hall.**

Across **Magdalene** (pronounced maudlin) **Bridge** you come to **Magdalene College** with its pretty red-brick courts. The **Pepys Library** contains the 17th-century diarist's own books and desk. *Admission: free. Open mid-Jan.–mid-Mar. and mid–Sept.–mid–Dec., Mon.–Sat. 2:30–3:30, mid–Apr.–Aug., Mon.–Sat. 11:30–12:30 and 2:30–3:30.*

Beyond Magdalene is **Kettle's Yard.** This was originally the home of Jim Ede, a connoisseur of 20th-century art. Here, he displayed his collections to the public; a gallery extension now houses temporary exhibits. *Castle St., tel. 0223/352124. Admission: free. House open Tues.–Sun. 2–4; gallery open Tues.–Sat. 12:30–5:30 (Thurs. to 7:30), Sun. 2:30–5:30.*

Returning the way you've just come, along the Backs from King's, you come to **Queen's College,** where Isaac Newton's **Mathematical Bridge** crosses the river. This arched wooden structure was originally held together by gravitational force; when it was taken apart to see how Newton did it, no one could reconstruct it without using nails.

Back from the river, on Trumpington Street, stand **Pembroke College,** which contains some 14th-century buildings and a chapel by Wren, and **Peterhouse,** the oldest college, dating from 1281. Next to Peterhouse is the **Fitzwilliam Museum,** which contains outstanding art collections (including paintings by Constable) and antiquities (especially from ancient Egypt). *Trumpington St., tel. 0223/332900. Admission: free. Open Tues.–Sat. 10–5, Sun. 2:15–5.*

Other colleges worth visiting include **Downing College,** which has a unique collection of neoclassical buildings dating from about 1800, and **Emmanuel College,** whose chapel and colonnade are by Christopher Wren. Emmanuel's spacious gardens have a pretty duck pond with several unusual breeds. Among the portraits of famous Emmanuel men hanging in the hall is one of John Harvard, founder of Harvard University.

If you have time, hire a punt at **Silver Street Bridge** or at **Magdalene Bridge** and navigate down past St. John's or upstream to **Grantchester,** the pretty village made famous by the Edwardian poet Rupert Brooke. On a sunny day, there's no better way to absorb Cambridge's unique atmosphere—somehow you will seem to have all the time in the world.

Time Out The coffee shop in the **Fitzwilliam Museum** is an excellent choice for a pastry or a light lunch. So is **Henry's** on Pembroke Street. **The Pickerel,** on Bridge Street beyond St. John's, is a pleasant pub with a small garden.

From Ely to Bury St. Edmunds Some 24 kilometers (15 miles) north of Cambridge, on A10, is the small, compact town of Ely. Dominating the town is the **Cathedral,** whose commanding position atop one of the few Fenland ridges makes it visible from miles away; not for nothing is it nicknamed "the ship of the Fens." Within the cathedral, which was begun by the Normans in 1081, is one of the marvels of medieval construction: a vast stained-glass skylight that replaced the central tower when it collapsed in 1322. The **Lady Chapel,** restored during the 1970s with financial help from the United States, contains delicate decorative carving and a superb fan-vaulted ceiling. There is also a **Stained-Glass Museum.** *Chapter Office, The College, tel. 0353/667735. Cathedral admission: £2 adults, £1.20 children over 7, students, and senior citizens, free on Sun. Open Apr.–Oct., Mon.–Sat. 7–7, Sun. 9–9; Nov.–Mar. Mon.–Sat. 7–6:30, Sun. 9–5. Stained-Glass Museum admission: £1 adults, 50p children. Open May–Oct., daily 11–4.*

Around the cathedral are the well-preserved buildings of the cathedral courtyard, where many of the clergy live, and of the **King's School,** which provides the cathedral with its choristers. To the north is the little market square and shopping streets leading down to the attractive riverside.

Time Out The **Steeplegate Café and Gallery** in the 16th-century Steeplegate is a convenient spot for lunch.

The route from Cambridge to Bury St. Edmunds, along A1303, passes by **Newmarket,** headquarters of British horse racing. The town is known both for its first-class race course and as a breeding and training center. The **National Horseracing Museum** traces the history of the sport and has a fine collection of paintings. *High St., tel. 0638/667333. Admission: £1.60 adults, 80p children and senior citizens. Open Apr.–Dec., Tues.–Sat. 10–5; Aug., Mon.–Sat. 10–5, Sun. 2–5.*

Tours can be made of the **National Stud,** one of Britain's principal racing stables, where you can see the stallions being trained. *Tours offered from the end of Mar.–Nov., weekdays 11:15 and 2:30 and also on some summer Sats. at 11:15. Admission: £2.50 adults, £1.25 children, students, and senior citizens. Advance booking essential. Tel. 0638/663464.*

Bury St. Edmunds is a quintessential English country town with a picturesque gate tower and the ruins of a great 11th-century Norman abbey, **Angel Hill.** Medieval buildings along one side of the street face elegant 18th-century houses on the other; there are also some striking public buildings along **Abbeygate Street.**

The early 17th-century house on Angel Hill, known as **Angel Corner,** houses a fine collection of "time-measuring instruments." *Gershom-Parkington Memorial Collection of Clocks and Watches, 8 Angel Hill, tel. 0284/757071. Admission: free, but donations welcome. Open Mon.–Sat. 10–5, Sun. 2–5.*

The **Theatre Royal,** built in 1819, is a perfect example of a working Regency theater and a delightfully intimate place to watch a performance. If rehearsals are not taking place, you can look around during the day. *Westgate St., tel. 0284/755127. Open Mon.–Sat. 9–8. Advance booking advised for tours.*

As if to remind visitors that Bury St. Edmunds remains a working town, not a museum piece, a livestock market is held every Wednesday and Saturday off **Risbygate.**

Time Out The **Harvest Café** on Abbeygate Street serves good-quality self-service lunches and snacks in a timbered building.

Dining and Lodging

For details and price category definitions, *see* Dining and Lodging in Staying in Great Britain.

Dining **Twenty-Two.** This intimate restaurant occupies a modest house a half-mile from the city center. The proprietor cooks the set dinner. Fish and game are the specialties. *Chesterton Rd., tel. 0223/351880. Reservations advised. MC, V. Moderate.*

Upstairs. Moroccan furnishings provide the backdrop for such specialties as lamb couscous and *kala josh* (beef with cloves and yogurt). *Castle Hill, tel. 0223/312569. No credit cards. Moderate.*

Flames. The accent is on romantic, candlelit evenings in this renovated 18th-century building. Fondues of all kinds are the specialty—from fillet steak to chocolate. *53 Castle Hill, tel. 0223/60723. Reservations advised. No credit cards. Inexpensive.*

Pentagon Restaurant. At the Arts Theatre, this spot has a suitably theatrical feel, with lots of signed photographs of actors who have played here. The menu changes daily according to the foods in season. *6 Edwards Passage, tel. 0223/359302. Reservations advised. DC, MC, V. Inexpensive.*

Lodging **The Garden House.** This fairly luxurious establishment is set among the colleges. The gardens back onto the river, and there is a large new extension. *Granta Pl., tel. 0223/63421. 117 rooms with bath. Facilities: restaurant, bar, in-house movies, garden. AE, DC, MC, V. Expensive.*

Arundel House. This hotel occupies an elegant Victorian house overlooking the river. The recently redecorated bedrooms are comfortably furnished with locally made mahogany furniture. *Chesterton Rd., tel. 0223/67701. 90 rooms, 73 with bath. Facilities: restaurant, bar, videos, garden. AE, DC, MC, V. Moderate.*

Royal Cambridge. Seven renovated Victorian terraced town houses were renovated to form this hotel with spacious rooms decorated in period style. *Trumpington St., tel. 0223/351631. 63 rooms, 48 with bath. Facilities: restaurant, bar. AE, DC, MC, V. Moderate.*

York and Environs

Once England's second city, the ancient town of York has survived the ravages of time, war, and industrialization to remain one of the most perfectly preserved walled cities in Europe. It was King George VI, father of the present queen, who once remarked that the history of York is the history of England. Even in a brief visit to the city, you can see evidence of life from every era since the Romans, not only in museums, but in the very streets and houses. On a more contemporary note, the city also boasts one of the most fashionable shopping centers in this part of the country.

York is surrounded by some of the grandest countryside England has to offer. A fertile plain dotted with ancient abbeys and grand aristocratic mansions leads both westward to the hidden valleys and jagged, windswept tops of the Yorkshire Dales and northward to the brooding mass of the North York Moors. This is a land quite different from the south of England —it's friendlier, emptier, and less aggressively materialistic. No visitor to Britain should overlook it.

Getting Around

By Train Regular fast trains run from London's King's Cross Station to York. The trip takes two hours. For information, call 01/278–2477.

By Bus Regular long-distance buses leave from Victoria Coach Station. The trip takes 4½ hours. For information, call 01/730–0202.

By Car Take A1, the historic main route from London to the north, which branches east onto the A64 near Tadcaster for the final 12 miles to York. Alternatively, take the M1, then the M18, and finally the A1. The drive from London takes a minimum of four hours. The main car rental companies have offices in York.

The best way to explore the area around York is by car— although it's inadvisable to take a car into the crowded city center. Coach tours (see below) visit most of the nearby attractions.

Tourist Information

There is a tourist information office at De Grey Rooms, Exhibition Square, tel. 0904/621756.

Guided Tours

The **York Association of Voluntary Guides** arranges short walking tours around the city (free, but a gratuity is appreciated) each morning and afternoon, April–October, and in the evening June–August; the departure point is Exhibition Square. Contact the tourist information office for details.

Yorktour (12 Coney St., tel. 0904/645151) operates a "SuperCity" tour by open bus, by boat, and on foot. It departs each morning from major hotels, March–October. Excursions to attractions outside the city are also available.

Exploring York

Numbers in the margin correspond with points of interest on the York map.

❶ York's greatest glory is the **Minster,** the largest Gothic church in England and one of the greatest in Europe. Take time to gaze at the soaring columns and intricate tracery of the 14th-

York

Major Attractions:
Castle Museum, **3**
Jorvik Viking
Centre, **2**
Merchant
Adventurers' Hall, **6**
Minster, **1**
National Railway
Museum, **7**
Shambles, **4**
Stonegate, **5**

Other Attractions:
All Saints, **8**
Assembly Rooms, **9**
Cholera Burial
Ground, **13**
St-Michael-le-
Belfry, **10**
Theater Royal, **11**
York Story (Heritage
Center), **12**

century nave, the choir screen portraying the kings of England, and the rose window that commemorates the marriage of Henry VII and Elizabeth of York. Visit the exquisite 13th-century **Chapter House** and the Roman and Saxon remains in the **Undercroft Museum and Treasury.** Climb the 275 steps of the **Central Tower** for an unrivaled view of the city and the countryside beyond. *York Minster Undercroft Museum and Treasury, Chapter House, and Central Tower, tel. 0904/624426. Admission: Undercroft £1.30 adults, 60p children; Chapter House 50p adults, 20p children; Central Tower £1 adults, 50p children. Open Mon.–Sat. 10–6, Sun. 1–6.*

② At the **Jorvik Viking Centre,** south of the Minster through tiny medieval streets, you can take another journey into history—traveling in little "time cars" back to the sights, sounds, and even the smells of a Viking street, which archaeologists have re-created in astonishing detail. *Coppergate, tel. 0904/643211. Admission: £2.75 adults, £1.35 children. Open Apr.–Oct., daily 9–7, Nov.–Mar., daily 9–5:30.*

Walk south down Castlegate and onto Tower Street, where **③** you'll find the **Castle Museum,** housed in an 18th-century prison. It has a series of realistic period displays that bring the past to life. Highlights include a Victorian street scene, an 18th-century dining room, and a moorland farmer's cottage. Don't miss the Coppergate Helmet, one of only three Anglo-Saxon helmets ever found. *Clifford St., tel. 0904/653611. Admission: £2.50 adults, £1.25 children. Open Apr.–Oct., Mon.–Sat. 9:30–5:30, Sun. 10–5:30; Nov.–Mar., Mon.–Sat. 9:30–4, Sun. 10–4.*

Even more than the wealth of museums, it is the streets and city walls that bring the city's past to life. A walk along the **walls,** most of which date from the 13th century, though with extensive restoration, provides delightful views across rooftops and gardens and the Minster itself. The narrow paved path winds between various fortified gates where the old roads ran out of the city.

Within the walls, the narrow streets still follow the complex **④** medieval pattern. The **Shambles,** in the heart of this walled city, is a perfectly preserved example; the half-timbered shops and houses have such large overhangs that you can practically **⑤** reach from one second-floor window to another. **Stonegate** is a narrow pedestrian street of 18th-century (and earlier) shops and courts. Along a narrow passage off Stonegate, you will find the remains of a 12th-century Norman stone house—one of the very few surviving in England.

⑥ The **Merchant Adventurers' Hall** is a superb medieval building (1357–68) built and owned by one of the richest medieval guilds; it contains the largest timber-framed hall in York. *Fossgate, tel. 0904/654818. Admission: £1 adults, 50p children under 16, 80p senior citizens. Open Easter–Aug., daily 9:30–5; Sept.–Easter, Mon.–Sat. 9:30–3.*

⑦ One very different attraction is the **National Railway Museum,** just outside the city walls, by the train station. This houses Britain's national collection of railway locomotives, including such giants of the steam era as *Mallard,* holder of the world speed record for a steam engine (126 mph), early rolling stock, and pioneer diesel and electric locomotives. *Leeman Rd., tel. 0904/621261. Admission: £2 adults, £1 children under 16 and*

senior citizens, £5.50 family ticket. Open Mon.–Sat. 10–6,
Sun. 11–6.

Time Out   York's eating places tend to specialize in wholesome, traditional English cooking. Try **Hudson's Below Stairs** (60 Bootham) for
morning coffee, lunch, and afternoon tea. The historic **Black
Swan** pub on Peaseholme Green does genuine Yorkshire pudding, served, as it should be, with onion gravy.

Outside York   Traveling west on A59, you soon reach the **Yorkshire Dales,**
made world-famous by the writings of a local veterinarian,
James Herriot. The fertile river valleys of the Dales are separated from one another by areas of wild, high moorland that
offer many opportunities for exhilarating walks and drives. At
Bolton Abbey, about 57 kilometers (36 miles) west of York, the
ruins of a 13th-century priory lie on a grassy embankment contained within a great curve of the river Wharfe. (There's
unrestricted access during daylight.) Explore the ruins and
walk through some of the most romantic woodland scenery in
England, past the legendary **Strid,** where the river plunges
through a rocky chasm only a few yards wide.

North from Bolton Abbey, on B6160, is **Grassington,** a village of
stone houses with an ancient, cobbled marketplace—a convenient center to explore the wild landscapes of Upper
Wharfedale. The **National Park Centre** has a wide choice of
guidebooks, maps, and bus schedules to help you enjoy a day in
the Dales. Organized tours depart from the center with qualified guides who explain the botanical and geological features of
the area. *Colvend, Hebdon Rd., tel. 0756/752748. Open Apr.–
Oct., daily 10–5.*

About 24 kilometers (15 miles) east from Grassington, along
B6265, across the moors, is **Fountains Abbey and Studley Royal,**
on the very edge of the hills. Here, the ruins of a 12th-century
monastery are set in an 18th-century landscaped water garden
and deer park, complete with lakes, half-moon ponds, statuary,
and pseudo-Greek temples. *Tel. 076586/333. Admission: £1.90
adults, 90p children. Open daily Oct.–Mar., 10–5 (or dusk),
Apr.–June and Sept., 10–7, July–Aug., 10–8. Closed Fri. in
Nov. and Dec.*

Nearby **Newby Hall**—5 kilometers (3 miles) south of Ripon
along a pleasant country road—has some celebrated interiors
by the 18th-century master architect Robert Adam and some
equally celebrated gardens with a collection of old breeds of
roses and rare shrubs. Children will enjoy the adventure playground, steam railway, and river steamer. *Skelton-on-Ure, tel.
0423/322583. Admission: £3.20 adults, £1.60 children. Open
Easter–Oct., Tues.–Sun., grounds 11–5:30, house noon–5.*

To the northeast, across the Vale of York, lie the **North York
Moors,** dominated by a vast expanse of dense woodland and
heather moorland that in late summer turns a rich blaze of
crimson and purple. Nestled in deep valleys are charming villages built of brownstone—a contrast with the gray stone of
the Dales.

Helmsley is a pleasant market town on the southern edge of the
Moors, a good starting point for a more detailed exploration. It
is not far, by road (B1257 north) or footpath, to the ruins of
Rievaulx Abbey, a medieval seat of monastic learning whose

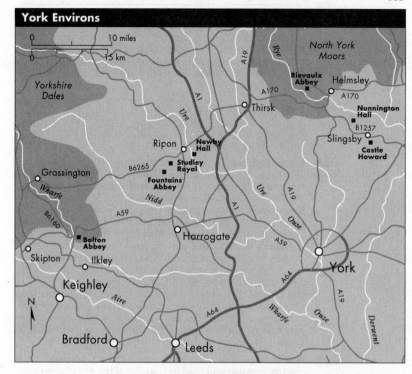

York Environs

graceful arches occupy a dramatic riverside setting. The ruins
are best seen from the **Rievaulx Terraces,** a long grassy walkway on the hillside above, terminating in the remains of several
classical temples. *Rievaulx Abbey, tel. 04396228. Admission:
£1.30 adults, 65p children, £1 senior citizens. Open 10–6
(closes at dusk in winter). Rievaulx Terraces. Admission:
£1.30 adults, 60p children. Open Easter–Oct., 10–5:30.*

Returning south to York, stop off at **Nunnington Hall** (off
B1257), a largely late 17th-century manor house set on the river Rye containing a paneled hall with a carved chimneypiece,
fine tapestries and china, and a superb collection of miniature
rooms with intricate dollhouse furniture of different periods.
*Nunnington, tel. 04395/283. Admission: £1.80 adults, 90p chil-
dren. Open July–Aug., Tues.–Thurs. 2–6, weekends noon–6;
May, June, Sept., Oct., Tues.–Thurs. and weekends 2–6; Apr.,
weekends 2–6, Easter week 2–6.*

Time Out   Teas (and light lunches on summer weekends) can be enjoyed at
Nunnington Hall's excellent **tearoom.**

In marked contrast to Nunnington is the palatial majesty of
Castle Howard (south off B1257 at Slingsby), the setting for the
TV series "Brideshead Revisited." The great central domed
tower, flanked by two huge and richly decorated wings, took 60
years—from 1699 to 1759—to build. The central hall, with its
spectacular painted ceiling, leads to a series of grand state-
rooms and galleries, filled with paintings, sculpture, furniture,

and porcelain. On the grounds is a mock classical landscape, with bridges, obelisks, even pyramids—more a conceit than a natural English country landscape. There's also an attractive collection of period costumes in the adjoining Stable Court. *Coneysthorpe, tel. 065384/333. Admission: £4 adults, £2 children, £3 senior citizens. Open late Mar.–Oct., daily, grounds 10–4:30, house 11–4:30.*

Dining and Lodging

For details and price category definitions, *see* Dining and Lodging in Staying in Great Britain.

York
Dining

Judges Lodging. This is a first-rate hotel restaurant. The fine 18th-century building, once a judge's house, is an ideal setting for a candlelit dinner of classic French cuisine. *9 Lendal, tel. 0904/38733. Reservations advised. AE, DC, V. Expensive.*

Freshneys. Fish is the name of the game here—salmon, lemon and Dover sole, local fresh trout and, when available, lobster. *Galtres Hotel, Petergate, tel. 0904/622478. MC, V. Moderate.*

Giovanni's Restaurant. Delicious pasta, veal, and beef dishes are served with Italian wine in this typical small Italian restaurant. It's close to the minster. *Goodramgate, tel. 0904/623539. Reservations advised. AE, MC, V. Moderate.*

Oat Cuisine. Homemade soups, unusual salads, quiches, and sweets are served in a vegetarian restaurant with modern decor. The cashew nut slice and enchiladas with mozzarella are particularly worth trying. *High Ousegate, tel. 0904/627929. Reservations advised. AE, MC, V. Moderate.*

Lodging

Middlethorpe Hall. This handsome, superbly restored 18th-century mansion is located on the edge of the city. Rooms have antique furnishings, paintings, and flower arrangements, and you can eat by candlelight in the original dining room. The extensive gardens boast a lake and a 17th-century dovecote. *Bishopthorpe Rd., tel. 0904/641241. 31 rooms with bath. AE, DC, MC, V. Very Expensive.*

Mount Royale Hotel. Two elegant town houses, dating from the 1820s, are comfortably furnished in a traditional country-cottage style. It's about a 15-minute walk from the city center. *The Mount, tel. 0904/628856. 21 rooms with bath. Facilities: outdoor pool, garden, sauna. AE, DC, MC, V. Expensive.*

The Churchill. Rooms are in a large 18th-century house with many period features and lots of character. *Bootham, tel. 0904/644456. 11 rooms, 10 with bath. AE, DC, MC, V. Moderate.*

Wheatlands Lodge Hotel. This small hotel-guest house occupies a handsome 19th-century bay-windowed house with a reputation for warm Yorkshire hospitality. The rooms are simple but of a high standard. *Scarcroft Rd., tel. 0904/654318/628601. 32 rooms, most with bath. MC, V. Inexpensive.*

Edinburgh

Scotland and England *are* different—and let no Englishman tell you otherwise. Although the two nations have been united in a single state since 1707, Scotland retains its own marked political and social character, with, for instance, legal and educational systems quite distinct from those of England. And by virtue of its commanding geographical position, on top of a long-dead volcano, and the survival of a large number of outstanding buildings carrying echoes of the nation's history, Edinburgh proudly ranks among the world's greatest capital cities.

Getting Around

By Train Regular fast trains run from London's King's Cross Station to Edinburgh Waverley; the fastest journey time is about 4½ hours. For information, call, in London, 01/278–2477; in Edinburgh, 031/557–3000.

By Plane **British Airways** operates a shuttle service from London's Heathrow Airport to Edinburgh; reservations are not necessary, and you are guaranteed a seat. Flying time from London is one hour 10 minutes. British Airways also runs bookable services from Gatwick. For information, call 01/897–4000 or 031/225–2525. **British Midland** (01/589–5599 or 031/447–1000) also flies from Heathrow. Transatlantic flights direct to Scotland use Prestwick Airport on the west coast.

By Bus Regular services are operated by **Citylink Coaches** (01/636–9373/9374 and 031/556–9630) and **Stagecoach** (01/930–5781 and 0738/33481) between Victoria Coach Station, London, and St. Andrew Square bus station, Edinburgh. The journey takes approximately eight to nine hours.

By Car London and Edinburgh are 640 kilometers (400 miles) apart; allow a comfortable nine hours for the drive. The two principal routes to the Scottish border are the A1 (mostly a small but divided road) or the eight-lane M1 then M6. From there, the choice is between the dual-carriageway A74, which can be unpleasantly busy, followed by the A701 or A702, and the slower but much more scenic A7 through Harwick. All the main car rental agencies have offices in Edinburgh.

Tourist Information

City Information (3 Princes Street, tel. 031/557–1700) is the main tourist center for Edinburgh. The **Scottish Travel Centre,** South St. Andrew Street, tel. 031/332–2433 (individuals only), offers a travel service for those going beyond Edinburgh.

Guided Tours

Both **Lothian Regional Transport** (deep-red-and-white buses) and **Eastern Scottish** (green buses) operate tours in and around the city. For information, call 031/226–5087 or 031/554–4494 (Lothian), or 031/556–8464 or 031/558–1616 (Eastern Scottish). Tickets allowing unlimited travel on city buses for various periods are also available.

The Cadies (Upper Bow, tel. 031/225–6745) offers a highly popular murder and mystery tour, historical, and other special-interest tours. **Ghillie Personal Travel** (Silverknowes Rd., tel. 031/336–3120) provides luxury personal tours by car, minibus, yacht, train, and air.

Exploring Edinburgh

The key to understanding Edinburgh is to make the distinction between the Old and New Towns. Until the 18th century, the city was confined to the rocky crag on which its castle stands, straggling between the fortress at one end and the royal residence, the Palace of Holyroodhouse, at the other. In the 18th century, during a civilizing time of expansion known as the "Scottish Enlightenment," the city fathers fostered the construction of another Edinburgh, one a little to the north. This is the New Town, whose elegant squares, classical facades, wide streets, and harmonious proportions remain largely intact and lived-in today.

Numbers in the margin correspond with points of interest on the Edinburgh map.

The Royal Mile
❶ **Edinburgh Castle,** the brooding symbol of Scotland's capital and the nation's martial past, dominates the city center. The castle's attractions include the city's oldest building—the 11th-century **St. Margaret's Chapel**—the **Crown Room,** where the Regalia of Scotland are displayed, **Old Parliament Hall,** and **Queen Mary's Apartments,** where Mary, Queen of Scots, gave birth to the future King James VI of Scotland (who later became James I of England). In addition, there are excellent views. *Tel. 031/225-9847. Admission: £2.20 adults, £1.10 children and senior citizens, £5 families. Open Apr.–Sept., Mon.–Sat. 9:30–5:05; Sun. 11–5:05; Oct.–Mar., Mon.–Sat. 9:30–4:20, Sun. 12:30–3:35.*

❷ The **Royal Mile,** the backbone of the Old Town, starts immediately below the **Castle Esplanade,** the wide parade ground that hosts the annual Edinburgh Military Tattoo—a grand military display. The Royal Mile consists of a number of streets, running into each other—**Castlehill, Lawnmarket, High Street,** and **Canongate**—leading downhill to the Palace of Holyroodhouse, home to the Royal Family when they visit Edinburgh. Tackle this walk in leisurely style; the many original Old Town "closes," narrow alleyways enclosed by high tenement buildings, are rewarding to explore and give a real sense of the former life of the city.

❸ In Lawnmarket, the six-story tenement known as **Gladstone's Land** dates from the 17th century. It has a typical arcaded front and first-floor entrance and is furnished in the style of a merchant's house of the time; there are magnificent painted ceilings. *483 Lawnmarket, tel. 031/226-5856. Admission: £1.60 adults, 80p children and senior citizens. Open Apr.–Oct., Mon.–Sat. 10–5, Sun. 2–5.*

❹ Close by is **Lady Stair's House,** a town dwelling of 1622 that now recalls Scotland's literary heritage with exhibits on Sir Walter Scott, Robert Louis Stevenson, and Robert Burns. *Lady Stair's Close, Lawnmarket, tel. 031/225-2424, ext. 6593. Admission: free. Open May–Sept., Mon.–Sat. 10–6; Oct.–Apr., Mon.–Sat. 10–5, Sun. 2–5 during festival.*

A heart shape set in the cobbles of the High Street marks the
❺ site of the **Tolbooth,** the center of city life until it was demol-
❻ ished in 1817. Nearby stands the **High Kirk of St. Giles,** Edinburgh's cathedral; parts of the church date from the 12th century, the choir from the 15th. *High St., Admission: free. Open Mon.–Sat. 9–7, Sun. for services.*

❼ Farther down High Street you come to **John Knox's House.** Its traditional connections with Scotland's celebrated religious reformer are tenuous, but it is said to be the only 15th-century building surviving in Scotland and gives a flavor of life in the

Edinburgh

N

Holyrood Park

Salisbury Crags

Queen's Dr.

Calton Hill, **14**

Pleasance St.

Regent Rd.

Calton Rd.

Canongate

St. Mary's St.

Waverley Station

Leith St.

E. Market St.

South Bridge

Potterow

Waterloo Pl.

North Bridge

Cowgate

Chambers St.

Dublin St.

High St.

George IV Br.

Lawnmarket

Laurision Pl.

St. David's St.

Queen St.

Mound

The

Grassmarket

West Port

Hanover St.

Johnston Ter.

Lady Lawson St.

Howe St.

Frederick St.

Thistle St.

Rose St.

Princes St.

King's Stables Rd.

Bread St.

Fountainbridge

Heriot Row

Castle St.

George St.

Lothian Rd.

Morrison St.

India St.

Gloucester Ln.

Charlotte Square

Canning St.

Dean Br.

Queensferry St.

Standrick Pl.

Melville St.

Morrison St.

Queensferry Rd.

Belford Rd.

Walker St.

Chester St.

Manor Pl.

W. Maitland St.

Palmerston Pl.

Dalry

Haymarket

0   220 yards

0   200 meters

Arthur's Seat, **11**
Calton Hill, **14**
Canongate Kirk, **9**
Edinburgh Castle, **1**
Edinburgh
International Festival
Office, **17**

Fringe, **18**
Georgian House, **16**
Gladstone's Land, **3**
High Kirk of
St. Giles, **6**
Huntly House, **8**
John Knox's House, **7**

Lady Stair's House, **4**
National Gallery of
Scotland, **12**
Palace of
Holyroodhouse, **10**

Royal Mile, **2**
St. Andrew Square, **15**
Scott Monument, **13**
Tolbooth, **5**

Old Town in the Middle Ages. *45 High St., tel. 031/556–6961. Admission: £1 adults, 70p children and senior citizens. Open Mon.–Sat. 10–5.*

Canongate was formerly an independent burgh, or trading ⑧ community, outside the city walls of Edinburgh. **Huntly House,** built in 1570, is a museum featuring Edinburgh history and social life. *142 Cannongate, tel. 031/225–2424, ext. 6689. Admission: free. Open Jun.–Sept., Mon.–Sat. 10–6; Oct.– May, Mon.–Sat. 10–5, Sun. 2–5 during the Edinburgh International Festival.*

Some notable Scots are buried in the graveyard of the ⑨ **Canongate Kirk** nearby, including the economist Adam Smith and the poet Robert Fergusson.

Time Out Two places that serve a good cup of tea and a sticky cake (a notable Scottish indulgence) to weary walkers are **Clarinda's** in Canongate and the **Abbey Strand Tearoom,** near the palace gates. The **crypt of St. Giles** also has a popular lunch and tearoom.

⑩ The **Palace of Holyroodhouse,** still the Royal Family's official residence in Scotland, was founded by King James IV at the end of the 15th century and was extensively remodeled by Charles II in 1671. The state apartments, with their collections of tapestries and paintings, can be visited. *Tel. 031/556–7371. Admission: £1.80 adults, £1 children and senior citizens. Open Apr.–Oct., Mon.–Sat. 9:30–5:15, Sun. 10:30–4:30; end Oct.– Mar., Mon.–Sat. 9:30–3:45; closed during royal and state visits.*

The open grounds of **Holyrood Park** enclose Edinburgh's dis-
⑪ tinctive originally volcanic mini-mountain, **Arthur's Seat,** with steep slopes and miniature crags.

In 1767, the competition to design the New Town was won by a young and unknown architect, James Craig. His plan was for a grid of three east-west streets, balanced at each end by a grand square. The plan survives today, despite all commercial pressures. Princes, George, and Queen Streets are the main thoroughfares, with St. Andrew Square at one end and Charlotte Square at the other.

⑫ The **National Gallery of Scotland,** on the Mound, the street that joins the Old and New Towns, contains works by the Old Masters and the French Impressionists and has a good selection of Scottish paintings. *Tel. 031/556–8921. Admission: free; charge for special exhibitions. Open Mon.–Sat. 10–5, Sun. 2–5. Print Room, weekdays 10–12:30 and 2–4:30.*

To the east along Princes Street is the unmistakable soaring ⑬ Gothic spire of the 62-meter (200-foot) high **Scott Monument,** built in the 1840s to commemorate the celebrated novelist of Scots history. There is a statue of Sir Walter and his dog within. The views from the top well are worth the 287-step climb. *Admission: 45p. Open Apr.–Sept., Mon.–Sat. 9–6; Oct.–Mar. Mon.–Sat. 9–3.*

⑭ There are more splendid views from **Calton Hill:** north across the Firth (or estuary) of Forth to the Lomond Hills of Fife and also to the Pentland Hills that enfold the city from the south. Among the various monuments on Calton Hill are a partial reproduction of the **Parthenon** in Athens begun in 1824 but left incomplete because the money ran out, the **Nelson Monument,** and the **Royal Observatory.**

⑮ Make your way to **St. Andrew Square,** then along George Street, where there is a wide choice of shops, and on to **Charlotte Square,** whose north side was designed by the great Scottish classical architect Robert Adam. The rooms of the ele-
⑯ gant **Georgian House** are furnished to show the domestic arrangements of a prosperous late 18th-century Edinburgh family. *7 Charlotte Sq., tel. 031/225–2160. Admission: £1.70 adults, 85p children and senior citizens. Open Apr.–Oct., Mon.–Sat. 10–4:30, Sun. 2–4:30.*

Time Out **La Lanterna,** at 9–11 Hope Street, offers no-nonsense, good-value Italian home cooking with self-service at lunchtime, waitress service at dinner. **Bianco's,** at 83 Hanover Street, close to the Georgian House, is good for coffee and croissants.

Finally, a word about the **Edinburgh International Festival,** the annual celebration of music, dance, and drama that the city stages each summer (the 1990 dates are Aug. 12–Sept. 1), featuring international artists of the highest caliber. The **Festival Fringe,** the unruly child of the official festival, spills out of halls and theaters all over town, offering visitors a cornucopia of theatrical and musical events of all kinds—some so weird that they defy description. While the official festival is the place to see top-flight performances by established artists, at a Fringe event you may catch a new star, or a new art form, or a controversial new play in the making. Or then again, you may not; it's very much up to luck. Advance information, programs, and
⑰ ticket sales for the festival are available from the **Edinburgh International Festival Office,** 21 Market St. (tel. 031/226–4001);
⑱ for the **Fringe,** from 180 High St. (tel. 031/226–5257/5259).

Dining and Lodging

For details and price category definitions, *see* Dining and Lodging in Staying in Great Britain.

Dining **The Pompadour.** The decor here is inspired by the France of Louis XV, with ornate gilts and reds prevailing. A sophisticated French menu in the evening is balanced by a Scots flavor at lunchtime. *Princes St., tel. 031/225–2433. AE, DC, MC, V. Expensive.*

The Vintners Room. Away from the city center, the ornate plasterwork here is a complete surprise. The atmosphere is one of relaxed good taste, with such specialties as sautéed scallops with smoked salmon and grilled oysters with bacon and hollandaise sauce. Prime Angus beef is also served. *Giles St., Leith, tel. 031/554–6767. AE, DC, MC, V. Expensive.*

Cousteau's. Enjoy fresh fish and seafood in a traditional dining room with cane furniture and an open fire in winter. The house specialty is the hot seafood platter, but the menu also features a few meat dishes. There's an oyster bar as well. *Hill Street North Lane, tel. 031/226–3355. AE, DC, MC, V. Moderate.*

The Indian Cavalry Club. This restaurant has a cool and sophisticated atmosphere, with a confident, up-to-date approach—almost Indian nouvelle cuisine. Its specialties are mainly steam-cooked dishes. *Atholl Pl., tel. 031/228–3282. AE, DC, MC, V. Moderate.*

Jackson's Restaurant. Intimate and candlelit in an historic Old Town close, Jackson's offers good Scots fare. Aberdeen Angus steaks and Border lamb are excellent; there are vegetarian and seafood specialties, too. *Jackson Close, High St., tel. 031/225–1793. MC, V. Moderate.*

Henderson's Salad Bowl. This friendly place claims to be the city's original vegetarian restaurant, long before such places became fashionable. Try the vegetarian haggis! *Hanover St., tel. 031/225–2131. AE, DC, MC, V. Inexpensive.*

Ristorante Tinelli. A little away from the fashionable center, Tinelli has a chef who offers authentic Italian cooking in a relaxed atmosphere, amid pine and Hessian decor. *Easter Rd., tel. 031/652–1932. MC, V. Inexpensive.*

Lodging **The Caledonian Hotel.** Popularly known as "the Caley," this hotel echoes the days of the traditional great railway hotel, though its neighbor station has long since closed. The imposing Victorian decor has been preserved in the recent total refurbishment. There's also an excellent restaurant. *Princes St., tel. 031/225–2433. 238 rooms with bath. Facilities: hairdresser, in-house movies. AE, DC, MC, V. Very Expensive.*

George Hotel. This extensively refurbished city-center hotel has elegant 18th-century features in the public rooms and up-to-date bedrooms. Though busy, the staff takes time to be helpful. *George St., tel. 031/225–1251. 195 rooms with bath. Facilities: restaurant. AE, DC, MC, V. Very Expensive.*

Bruntisfield. All the rooms have their own style and character, with the lavish use of floral patterns and antiques. *Bruntisfield Pl., tel. 031/229–1393. 51 rooms with bath. AE, DC, MC, V. Expensive.*

Mount Royal Hotel. This modern hotel overlooks Edinburgh Castle. The public areas have recently been refurbished, while the bedrooms have been totally redecorated and modernized. It has a friendly staff. *Princes St., tel. 031/225–7161. 159 rooms with bath. AE, DC, MC, V. Expensive.*

The Albany Hotel. Three fine 18th-century houses with many original features have been carefully converted into a comfortable city-center hotel. *Albany St., tel. 031/556–0397/0398. 22 rooms with bath. AE, DC, MC. Moderate.*

Braid Hills Hotel. This comfortable, old-fashioned hotel is conveniently situated near the city center and the golf course. The turreted and gabled building dates back to 1886 and affords fine views over the city. *Braid Rd., tel. 031/447–8888. 68 rooms with bath. AE, DC, MC, V. Moderate.*

Dorstan Private Hotel. A Victorian villa in a quiet area, the Dorstan has fully modernized rooms decorated in bright, country-cottage colors. *Priestfield Rd., tel. 031/667–6721. 14 rooms, 9 with bath. No credit cards. Inexpensive.*

Salisbury Hotel. Another successful 18th-century building conversion, this quiet hotel is situated in a pleasant area. It's good value and a convenient location for city sightseeing. *Salisbury Rd., tel. 031/667–1264. 14 rooms, 11 with bath. No credit cards. Inexpensive.*

14 Greece

Introduction

You cannot travel far across the land in Greece without meeting the sea, or for long across the sea without meeting one of its 1,425 islands. About the size of New York state, Greece has 15,019 kilometers (9,387 miles) of coastline, more than any other country of its size in the world. The sea is everywhere, not on three sides only but at every turn, reaching through the shoreline like a probing hand. The land itself is stunning, dotted with cypress groves, oleander, and olive trees, carved into gentle bays or dramatic coves with startling white sand, rolling hills, and rugged mountain ranges that plunge straight into the sea. This natural beauty and the sharp, clear light of sun and sea, combined with plentiful archaeological treasures, make Greece one of the world's most inviting countries, and one of its greatest sightseeing targets.

Poetry, music, architecture, politics, medicine, law—all had their Western birth here in Greece centuries ago, alongside the great heroes of mythology who still seem to haunt this sun-drenched land. The Pindus range runs north to south, containing the fabled peak of Mount Olympus, home of the Greek gods; and Mount Parnassus, favorite haunt of the sun-god Apollo and the nine Muses, goddesses of poetry and science. The remains of the ancient civilizations—the Acropolis and the Parthenon, the temples of Delphi, the Tombs of the Kings in Mycenae—and a later procession of Byzantine churches, Crusader castles and fortresses, and Turkish mosques are spread throughout the countryside.

Of the hundreds of islands and islets scattered across the Aegean Sea in the east and the Ionian Sea in the west, only 130 have ever been inhabited. This world of the fisherman is being quickly replaced by the world of the tourist. Over eight million holiday-makers visit Greece each year, almost as many as the entire native population; in fact, tourism has overtaken shipping as the most important element in the nation's economy. On some of the islands, the impact of the annual influx of visitors has meant the building of a new Greece, more or less in their image. Pubs and bars have replaced *ouzeris*, discos have replaced *kafenions*, and pizza and hamburger stands have overtaken tavernas; once-idyllic beaches have become overcrowded and noisy, and fishing harbors have become flotilla sailing centers. Prices are beginning to go up, and the simplicity has long disappeared from the islands' way of life.

As mass tourism takes effect in the main centers, strike out and find your own place among the smaller islands and the miles of beautiful mainland coastline. Except for some difficulty in finding accommodations, since Greek families on vacation tend to fill the hotels in out-of-the-way places, this is the ideal way to see traditional Greece. Those who come only to worship the classical Greeks and gaze at their temples, seeing nothing but the glory that was, miss today's Greece. If you explore this fascinating country with open eyes, you'll enjoy it in all its forms: its slumbering cafés and buzzing tavernas; its elaborate religious rituals; its stark, bright beauty; and the generosity, curiosity, and kindness of its people.

Before You Go

When to Go Although the tourist season runs from May to October, the heat can be unpleasant in July and August, particularly in Athens. On the islands, a brisk northerly wind, the *meltemi*, can make life more comfortable. If you want to move about the country and avoid all the other tourists, the ideal months are May, June, and September. The winter months are likely to be damp and cold virtually everywhere.

The following are the average daily maximum and minimum temperatures for Athens.

Jan.	55F	13C	May	77F	25C	Sept.	84F	29C
	44	6		61	16		67	19
Feb.	57F	14C	June	86F	30C	Oct.	75F	24C
	44	7		68	20		60	15
Mar.	60F	16C	July	92F	33C	Nov.	66F	19C
	46	8		73	23		53	12
Apr.	68F	20C	Aug.	92F	33C	Dec.	58F	15C
	52	11		73	23		47	8

Currency The Greek monetary unit is the drachma (dr.). Bank notes are in denominations of 50, 100, 500, 1,000, and 5,000 dr.; coins, 1, 2, 5, 10, 20, and 50. At press time (spring 1989), there were 154.50 dr. to the U.S. dollar and 263 dr. to the pound sterling. Daily exchange rates are prominently displayed in banks. You'll get a better exchange rate at banks than from hotels or stores.

What It Will Cost Inflation in Greece is high, about 20% to 25% a year, and fluctuations in currency make accurate budgeting long in advance an impossibility, so keep an eye on the exchange rates before and during your vacation. On the whole, Greece offers good value compared with many other European countries. The values are especially good for modest hotels and restaurants, transportation, and entertainment.

There are few regional price differences for hotels and restaurants. A modest hotel in a small town will charge the same rates as a modest hotel in Athens, with the same range of amenities. The same is true of restaurants. Rhodes, Corfu, and Crete are more expensive than other islands, but justifiably so. Car rentals are expensive in Greece, but taxis are inexpensive, even for long-distance runs.

Sample Prices At a central-city café, you can expect to pay about 200 dr. for a coffee or a beer, 140 dr. for a soft drink, and 240 dr. for a toasted cheese sandwich. These prices can, of course, vary considerably from place to place. A 1½-kilometer (one-mile) taxi ride will cost about 200 dr.

Customs on Arrival You may take in 200 cigarettes or 50 cigars or one-quarter pound smoking tobacco; one liter of alcohol, or two liters of wine; and gifts up to a total value of 5,000 dr. There's no duty on articles for personal use. Your car, camping and sport equipment, and items such as typewriters and cameras are registered in your passport upon entry to prevent their sale within the country. Foreign bank notes in excess of $1,000 (about £560) must be declared for re-export. There are no restrictions on traveler's checks. Only 10,000 dr. may be imported or exported.

Greece

BULGARIA

YUGOSLAVIA

ALBANIA

Stavróupoli
Sidirókastro
Séres
Philippi
Kilkis
Eleftheroúpoli
Amfípoli
Kavala
Edessa
Gianitsa
Thessaloniki
Florina
Alexandria
Thérmi
Nea
Appolonia
Kastoria
Ptolemaïda
Veria
Polygyros
Ormylia
Vatopedia
Ivirion
Kozani
Katerini
Dafni
Siatista
Grevena
Mount
Olympus ▲
Gulf of
Thermaikos
Athos
Kónitsa
Gulf of Kassandra
Delvinákio
Elassóna
Kalithéa
Métsovo
Palioúri
Kerkira
Kalambaka
Tirnavos
Corfu
Igoumenitsa
Ioanina
Agia
Paramythia
Trikala
Larissa
Parga
Karditsa
Volos
SPORADES
Arta
Stavros
Farsala
Skiathos
Aliki
Almiros
Preveza
Lamia
Skópelos
N
Karpenissi
Skyros
Lefkas
Vassiliki
Orhomenós
ÉVIA
Kymi
Kephalonia
Ithaki
Agrinio
Itea
Delphi
Nefpaktos
Galaxidi
Livadia
Halkida
Lixouri
Sami
Messolongi
Patras
Thebes
Gulf of Corinth
Diakofto
Kárystos
Killini
Megara
Athens
Loutra
Corinth
Piraeus
Zákynthos
Amalias
Nemea
Egina
Voula
Lavrio
Kéa
Zákynthos
Pyrgos
Argos
Poros
Sounio
Kaiafas
Olympia
Náfplio
Er
Andritsena
Tripoli
Toló
Ermioni
Kythnos
Kyparissia
PELOPONNESE
Ydra
Spetses
Serifos
Ionian Sea
Messini
Sparta
Leonidio
Gargaliani
Kalamata
Geraki
Pilos
Mystras
Kyparíssi
Methoni
Skala
Koroni
Gythio
Monemvassía
Milos
Areopoli
Agía Pelagia
Kythira
Kythira
Haniá
CRETE

0   100 miles
0   300 km

Black Sea

THRACE   T U R K E Y

Kastaniés

Xanthi
Didymótiho

Avdira   Mákri   Alexandróupoli

Thassos

Samothrace

Sea of Marmara

Límnos

■ Troy

Aegean Sea

Lesvos   Mytilíni

Plomári

T U R K E Y

Hios   Hios
Mésta
Pyrga

Izmir (Smyrna)

Andros
Andros

■ Ephesus

Sámos   Sámos

Ikaria   Pythagório

Tinos
Ermoúpoli   Tinos
Syros   *Mykonos*
Delos

Agios
Kirykos

Pátmos

Paros

Náxos

Leros

Bodrum
(Halicarnassus)

C Y C L A D E S   *Amorgós*

Kos   Kos

Ios

Astypalea

Nissyros   *Symi*

Rhodes

Thira
Santorini   *Anafi*

Tilos   Kámiros

Halki

Rhodes   Lindos

D O D E C A N E S E

Sea of Crete

Kárpathos

Iraklio   Mallia
■ Knossos

Kassos

■ Phaestos   Ierapetra

Language English is widely spoken in hotels and at major tourist sites. Although waiters, taxi drivers, and sales clerks may speak little English, there will always be someone around who is delighted to help, even in relatively out-of-the-way places.

In this guide, names are given in the Roman alphabet according to the Greek pronunciation except when there is a familiar English form, such as "Athens."

Getting Around

By Car
Road Conditions Driving in Greece is not to be recommended unless you have iron nerves. As a ratio of collisions to the number of cars on the road, Greece has the worst accident rate in Europe, due in part, it seems, to a combination of national temperament and road conditions. The latter vary. Motorways tend to be good; tolls are 100 dr. and are charged according to distance. Many country roads are poorly maintained but free of traffic. If you do decide to drive in Greece, keep your wits about you and expect the unexpected. Red traffic lights are frequently ignored and passing on hills and corners is not unusual.

Rules of the Road Unless you are a citizen of an EEC country, you must have an International Driver's License. Driving is on the right, and although the vehicle on the right has the right of way, as mentioned above, don't expect this or any other driving rule to be obeyed. The speed limit is 110 kph (68 mph) on the open road, 50 kph (31 mph) in town. The wearing of seat belts is compulsory.

Parking Parking spaces are hard to find; thousands park illegally. In Athens or Thessaloniki, you can pay to use one of the many temporary parking lots set up in vacant lots, but you're better off leaving your car in the hotel garage and walking or taking a cab.

Gasoline At press time gas costs about 75 dr. a liter (about 320 dr. a gallon). Gas pumps and service stations are everywhere, and lead-free gas is widely available.

Breakdowns **The Automobile and Touring Club of Greece** (ELPA, Athens Tower, 2 Mesagoiu St., Athens, tel. 01/779–1615) assists tourists free of charge.

By Bicycle Mopeds and bikes can be rented on the islands, the only places where biking is relatively safe.

By Train Few tourists use the trains because they are slow and railway networks are limited. The main line runs north from Athens to Yugoslavia. It divides into three lines at Thessaloniki. The main line continues on to Yugoslavia, a second line goes east to the Turkish border and Istanbul, and a third line heads northeast to Bulgaria. The Peloponnese in the south is served by a narrow-gauge line dividing at Corinth into the Mycenae-Argos section and the Patra-Olympic-Kalamata section. A **run-about ticket,** available only in Greece, gives unlimited second-class travel on trains and express buses operated by the railway (tel. 6/362–4402, for tickets and information).

By Plane **Olympic Airways** (6 Othonos, Syntagma, Athens, tel. 01/929–2247) has service between Athens and most towns and islands. Thessaloniki is also linked to the main islands, and there are many inter-island connections.

By Bus Travel by bus is inexpensive, usually comfortable, and relatively fast. Buses operated by the Greek railways are particularly good. Bus information and timetables are available at tourist information offices throughout Greece. Make reservations at least one day before your planned trip. Railway-operated buses leave from the main railway station in Athens. All other buses leave from one of two bus stations: 260 Liossiou—for central and eastern Greece and Evvia; 100 Kifissou—for the Peloponnese and northwestern Greece.

By Boat There are frequent car ferries from Piraeus, the port of Athens, to central and southern Aegean islands and Crete. Nearby islands also are served by hydrofoils from Rafina, east of Athens. Ships to other islands sail from ports nearer to them. Connections between the islands of a group, such as the Cyclades, are good. But between islands of different groups or areas, such as Rhodes and Crete, the service is less frequent. Travel agents and shipping offices in Athens and Piraeus, and in the main towns on the islands, have details. Buy your tickets two or three days in advance, especially if you are traveling in summer or taking a car. Reserve or confirm your return journey or continuation soon after you arrive.

Staying in Greece

Telephones
Local Calls Most curbside booths have pay telephones for local calls only. You pay the man inside the booth after the call.

International Calls The easiest way to make and pay for international and long-distance calls is to go to a Telecommunications Office (OTE), usually located in the center of towns and villages. There are several branches in Athens. There are also a few special telephone booths (distinguished by their orange band) for international and long-distance calls. The standard charge is 400 dr. per minute or part of a minute for a call to the United States or Canada. Hotels tend to add a hefty service charge for long-distance calls.

Operators and Information There are English-speaking operators on the International Exchange. Ask your hotel reception desk or an employee at the OTE for help in reaching one.

Mail
Postal Rates Letters or postcards within Greece cost 26 dr. for 20 grams; within Europe, 60 dr.; and to the rest of the world, 70 dr.

Receiving Mail You can have your mail sent to Poste Restante, Aeolou 100, Athens (take your passport to pick up your mail), or to American Express, Syntagma Square 2, Athens. For holders of American Express cards or traveler's checks, there is no charge for the service. Others pay 250 dr. per item.

Shopping
VAT Refunds Prices quoted in shops include the value-added tax (VAT). There are no VAT refunds.

Bargaining Prices in large stores are fixed. Bargaining may take place in small owner-managed souvenir and handicraft shops and in antique shops. In flea markets, bargaining is expected.

Export Permits Antiques and Byzantine icons require an export permit (not normally given if the piece is of any value), but beautiful replicas can be bought fairly cheaply, although even these require a certificate stating they are copies.

Opening and Closing Times The government is attempting to abolish the midday closing of businesses and shops, in an effort to cut down on the number of daily rush hours. It is also trying to stagger hours to alleviate the crush. Gradually, office, bank, and shopping hours are changing, but not all Greeks favor these changes. Check with your hotel for up-to-the-minute information on opening and closing times. Below is a rough guide:

Banks. Banks are open weekdays, 8–2:30; closed weekends and public holidays.

Museums. Most major museums are open 8–6; some smaller ones close earlier. Generally, museums are closed Tuesday and have shorter hours on Sunday and holidays. Archaeological sites are generally open 8–6 (in midsummer they tend to open earlier and close at sunset). Hours vary according to the importance of the site and the time of year—everything closes earlier in winter. *See* Exploring for hours of individual museums and sites; also check hours with your hotel.

Shops. Most shops are open weekdays from 8 to 2:30, but hours vary according to the type of shop. Some are open different hours on alternate days: Tuesday, Thursday, and Friday, 8–1:30 and 5–8; Monday, Wednesday, and Saturday, 8–2:30.

National Holidays January 1 (New Year's Day); January 6 (Epiphany); March 25 (Greek Revolution Memorial Day); April 13 (Greek Orthodox Good Friday); April 16 (Easter Monday); May 1 (May Day); (Pentecost); August 15 (Feast of the Assumption); October 28 (Oxi Day); December 25–26 (Christmas).

Dining Greek cuisine cannot be compared to that of France, and few visitors would come to Greece for its food alone. You'll certainly be able to find a delicious and inexpensive meal, but don't look in hotel restaurants, where the menus usually consist of bland, unimaginative international fare (although it's only here that you will find a reasonably priced fixed menu. Your best bet is to look for tavernas, *psistarias*, and *estiatorions* (restaurants), and choose the one frequented by the most Greeks. If there is much distinction between a taverna and a restaurant, it is that the former is less formal, generally has plastic tablecloths, and is frequently outdoors. The latter may have subdued lighting, possibly even a pianist, and will of course be slightly more expensive. The principal elements of Greek cuisine are vegetables, such as eggplants, tomatoes, and olives, fresh and inventively combined with lots of olive oil and seasonings, such as lemon juice, garlic, basil, and oregano. Meat dishes are limited (mutton and poultry being the most common), and fish is often a better choice, particularly on the coast. Seaside fish tavernas may *look* ramshackle but serve excellent—though expensive—fish.

Fast-food bars have sprung up all over Greece in recent years and serve *souvlaki* (slices of grilled meat with tomato and onions in pita bread), pastries filled with a variety of stuffings (spinach, cheese, or meat), and the ubiquitous hamburgers and pizza.

Mealtimes Lunch in Greek restaurants is served from 12:30 until 3. Dinner begins at about 9 and is served until 1 in Athens and until midnight outside Athens.

Precautions Tap water is safe to drink everywhere, but it is often heavily chlorinated. Excellent bottled mineral water, such as *Loutraki*, is available.

Dress Throughout the Greek islands you can dress informally for dinner, even at Expensive restaurants; in Athens, you may want to wear a jacket and tie at some of the top-price restaurants.

Ratings Prices are per person and include a first course, main course, and dessert (generally fruit and cheese). They do not include drinks or the 12%–15% service charge. Best bets are indicated by a star ★. At press time, there were 154.50 drachma to the dollar.

Category	Athens/Thessaloniki	Other Areas
Very Expensive	over 5,000 dr.	over 4,000 dr.
Expensive	2,500 dr.–5,000 dr.	2,000 dr.–4,000 dr.
Moderate	1,200 dr.–2,500 dr.	1,200 dr.–2,000 dr.
Inexpensive	under 1,200 dr.	under 1,200 dr.

Credit Cards The following credit card abbreviations are used: AE, American Express; DC, Diners Club; MC, MasterCard; V, Visa.

Lodging Most accommodations are in standard hotels, sometimes called motels. There are a number of "cottage" complexes, especially at the beaches, and as part of some hotels. Some private houses, especially those on the islands, offer accommodations, usually a double room with shower. These are often better than accommodations at the local hotel. In a very few places, there are state-organized "traditional settlements"—fine old houses with guest accommodations.

Greek hotels are classified as Deluxe, A, B, C, etc. (a star system is about to be introduced). These classifications do not always indicate price. A Deluxe hotel, for example, may charge less than some B-classified hotels. In this guide, hotels are classified according to price: Very Expensive, Expensive, Moderate, and Inexpensive. All Very Expensive and Expensive hotels have air-conditioning, so our listings in these categories only mention the absence of air-conditioning. If a Moderate or an Inexpensive hotel is air-conditioned, this is indicated. All have been built or completely renovated in the past 20 years, and all have private baths.

Prices quoted by hotels usually include service, local taxes, and VAT. Some may also include breakfast. Prices quoted are for double occupancy. Single occupancy is slightly less. The official price should be posted on the back of the door or inside a closet. Seaside hotels, especially those in the Very Expensive and Expensive categories, will frequently insist on guests taking half-board (lunch or dinner included in the price).

Ratings Prices quoted are for a double room in high season, including taxes and service, but not breakfast. Rates are the same throughout the country for each category. Best bets are indicated by a star ★. At press time, there were 154.50 drachma to the dollar.

Category	All Areas
Very Expensive	over 20,000 dr.
Expensive	8,000 dr.–16,000 dr.

Moderate	5,000 dr.–8,000 dr.
Inexpensive	under 5,000 dr.

Credit Cards   The following credit card abbreviations are used: AE, American Express; DC, Diners Club; MC, MasterCard; V, Visa.

Tipping   There are no absolute rules for tipping. In restaurants, cafés, and tavernas, in addition to the 15% service charge, you should leave a tip for the waiter of around 10% in the better restaurants and between 5% and 10% in cheaper tavernas. This should be left on the table for your waiter and not on the plate, where it will be taken by the head waiter. In hotels, tip porters 50 dr. or 100 dr. per bag for carrying your luggage—more in a top hotel. Taxi drivers don't expect tips, but Greeks usually give something, especially to round off the fare or if the driver has been especially helpful. Hairdressers usually get 10% or slightly more. In legitimate theaters, tip ushers 20 dr. to 40 dr. if you are shown to your seat. In movie theaters, tip about the same if you receive a program from the usher. On cruises, cabin and dining-room stewards get about 250 dr. to 300 dr. per day.

Athens

Arriving and Departing

By Plane   Most visitors arrive by air at Ellinikon Airport. All Olympic Airways flights, both international and domestic, use the Western terminal next to the ocean. All other flights arrive and depart from the Eastern terminal on the opposite side of the airport.

Between the Airport and Downtown   From the Western terminal buses run every 20 minutes to the Olympic Airways office at 96 Syngrou (fare: 125 dr.); from the Eastern terminal, they run every 20 minutes to 4 Amalia Avenue, near Syntagma Square (fare: 100 dr.). A taxi to the center of Athens costs about 600 dr.

By Train   Athens has two railway stations, side by side, not far from Omonia Square. International trains from the north arrive at, and depart from, Stathmos Larissis, and trains from the Peloponnese use the marvelously ornate and old-fashioned Stathmos Peloponnisos next door.

By Bus   Greek buses arrive at the Athens bus station at 100 Kifissou. International buses drop their passengers on the street, usually in the Omonia Square area.

By Car   Whether you approach Athens from the Peloponnese or from the north, you enter by the National Road and then follow signs for the center. Leaving Athens, routes to the National Road are well marked; signs usually name Lamia for the north and Corinth or Patras for the southwest.

By Ship   Except for cruise ships, few passenger ships from other countries call at Piraeus, the port of Athens, 10 kilometers (6 miles) from Athens' center. If you do dock at Piraeus, you can take the metro right into Omonia Square. The trip takes 20 minutes and costs 50 dr. Alternatively, you can take a taxi, which may well take longer due to traffic and will cost a great deal more, around 650 dr.

Getting Around

Many of the sights you'll want to see, and most of the hotels, cafés, and restaurants, are within a fairly small central area. It's easy to walk everywhere.

By Metro An electric (partially underground) railway is under construction. At present, it runs from Piraeus to Omonia Square and then on to Kifissia. It is not useful for getting around the central area. The standard fare is 50 dr. There are no special fares or day tickets for visitors, and there is, as yet, no public transport map.

By Bus The fare on blue buses and the roomier yellow trolley buses is 50 dr. You must have the exact change. Buses run from the center to all suburbs and suburban beaches until after midnight. For suburbs beyond central Kifissia, you have to change at Kifissia. Attica is well served by brown buses. Most buses, including those for Sounion, leave from Platia Aigyptou, at the corner of Patission and Alexandras Avenues.

By Taxi Taxis are plentiful except during rush hours and rainstorms. But they are often on strike. Also, drivers seem to lead a maverick life—those without occupants often refuse to pick up passengers, while those with occupants often stop to pick up more. Many drivers are unfamiliar with the city; some automatically deposit every American at the Hilton Hotel. Fares are low, starting at 25 dr. and rising roughly 30 dr. per kilometer (0.6 mile). There is a 200-dr. minimum and a small surcharge for luggage and for travel after midnight. Some drivers overcharge foreigners, especially on trips from the airport or from Piraeus; insist that they turn on the meter as soon as you get in.

Important Addresses and Numbers

Tourist Information There are **Greek National Tourist Offices** at Karageorgi Servias 2, in the bank, tel. 01/322–2545; at Ellinikon Airport, tel. 01/979–9500; and at Piraeus, Vasilissis Sofias 91, tel. 01/412–1400.

Embassies U.S.: Vasilissis Sofias 91, tel. 01/721–2951; **Canadian:** Gennadiou 4, tel. 01/723–9511; and **U.K.:** Ploutarchou 1, tel. 01/723–6211.

Emergencies **Police:** Tourist Police, tel. 171; Traffic Police, tel. 01/523–0111; and City Police, tel. 100. **Ambulance:** tel. 166. **Doctors:** Top hotels usually have one on staff; any hotel will call one for you. You can also call your embassy. **Dentist:** Ask your hotel or embassy. **Pharmacies:** Most pharmacies in the central area have someone who speaks English and knows all the usual medical requirements. Try **Marinopoulois,** Kanari 23, tel. 01/361–3051.

English Bookstore **Pantelides:** Amerikas 11, tel. 01/364–5161.

Travel Agencies **American Express:** Ermou 2, tel. 01/324–4975; **Wagons-Lits Travel:** Karageorgi Servias 2, tel. 01/324–2281; **CHAT Tours:** Stadiou 4, tel. 01/322–2886, and **Viking Tours,** Filellinon 3, tel. 01/322–9383.

Guided Tours

Orientation Tours All tour operators offer a four-hour morning bus tour of Athens, including a guided tour of the Acropolis, for around 1,300 dr. Make reservations at your hotel or at a travel agency; besides those agents already mentioned, there are hundreds of others, many situated around Filellinon and Nikis Streets off Syntagma Square. **Key Tours** (Ermou 2, tel. 01/323–2520) offers a one-day tour of Athens, including all ancient and modern points of interest, for around 5,000 dr.

Special-Interest Tours For those interested in folk dancing, there is a four-hour evening tour (May–Sept.) that begins with a sound and light spectacle at the Acropolis and then goes on to a performance of Greek folk dances in the open-air theater nearby. Another evening tour offers a dinner show at a taverna in the Plaka area. Any travel agency can arrange these tours—and the excursions below—for you, but go first to **CHAT Tours** or **Viking Tours** (*see* Travel Agencies) for reliable and efficient service.

Excursions The choice is almost unlimited. A one-day tour to Delphi will cost up to 3,250 dr., with lunch included; a two-day tour to Corinth and Mycenae, around 6,500 dr., with meals and accommodations included. A full-day cruise from Piraeus, visiting three nearby islands—Aegina, Poros, and Ydra—is around 5,625 dr., and a two-day cruise, including Mykonos and Delos, costs up to 15,500 dr.

Personal Guides All the major tourist agencies can provide English-speaking guides for personally organized tours.

Exploring Athens

Athens is essentially a village that outgrew itself, spreading out from the original settlement at the foot of the Acropolis. Back in 1834, when it became the capital of modern Greece, it had a population of 20,000. Now it houses more than a third of the Greek population—around four million—and 100,000 more join the masses every year. A modern concrete city has engulfed the old village and now sprawls for 388 square kilometers (150 square miles), covering almost all the surrounding plain from the sea to the encircling mountains.

The city is very crowded, very dusty, and overwhelmingly hot in summer. It also has an appalling air-pollution problem, mainly caused by traffic fumes; in an attempt to lessen the congestion, it is forbidden to drive private cars in central Athens on alternate working days. Despite the smog, heat, and dust, Athens is an experience not to be missed. It has a tangible vibrancy that makes it one of the most exciting cities in Europe, and the sprawling cement has failed to overwhelm the few striking and astonishing reminders of ancient Athens, most of which are on the steep-sided, flat-topped hill of the Acropolis or around its base. It was here that the ancient Athenians laid the foundation for Western civilization, with their towering achievements in philosophy, literature, drama, art, and architecture.

The central area of modern Athens is small, stretching from the Acropolis to Mount Lycabettos, with its small white church on top. The layout is simple—three parallel streets, Stadiou, Venizelou, and Academias, link two main squares, Syntagma and Omonia. Do wander off this beaten tourist track to catch some of the real flavor of living Athens. Seeing the Athenian butchers in the market near Monastiraki sleeping on their cold, marble slabs during the heat of the afternoon siesta, may give you more of a feel for the city than seeing hundreds of fallen pillars.

The Historic Heart *Numbers in the margin correspond with points of interest on the Athens map.*

At the center of modern Athens is **Syntagma (Constitution) Square.** It has several leading hotels, airline and travel offices, and numerous cafés. Along one side of the square stands the **Parliament Building,** completed in 1838 as the royal palace for the new monarchy. In front of the palace, you can watch the changing of the vividly costumed **Evzone guard** at the Tomb of the Unknown Soldier. Amalias Avenue, leading out of Syntagma will take you to the **National Gardens,** a large oasis in the vast sprawl of this largely concrete city.

Time Out There are several breakfast/lunch spots around Syntagma Square. **Brazilian,** at Voukourestiou 1B, one block from the square, is ideal for a quick coffee and snack (there are no tables or chairs). Just off the National Gardens, at Xenofontos 10, is **Diros,** efficiently serving good Greek food and steaks.

Across the street, at the far end of the National Gardens, you will see the columns of the once huge **Temple of Olympian Zeus.** This famous temple was begun in the 6th century BC, and when it was finally completed 700 years later, it exceeded in magnitude all other temples in Greece. It was destroyed during the invasion of the Goths in the 4th century, and today only the towering sunbrowned columns remain. *Admission: 250 dr. Open Apr.–Oct., Mon.–Sat. 9–3, Sun. and holidays 9–2:45.*

To the right stands **Hadrian's Arch,** built at the same time by the Roman Emperor. It consists of a Roman archway, with a Greek superstructure of Corinthian pilasters. Visiting heads of state are officially welcomed here; it is not open to the public.

About three-quarters of a kilometer (a half mile) to the left, down Leoforos Olgas Avenue, you come to the marble **stadium,** built for the first modern Olympic Games in 1896; it is a blindingly white, marble reconstruction of the ancient Olympic stadium of Athens and can seat 70,000 spectators. Greece hopes to be chosen to host the games in the centennial year 1996.

From Hadrian's Arch, take the avenue to the right, Dionysiou Areopagitou, past the Acropolis to the **Theater of Dionysos,** built in the 6th century BC. Here, the famous ancient dramas and comedies were originally performed in conjunction with bacchanalian feasts. *Tel. 01/321–0219. Admission: 300 dr. Open Apr.–Oct., Mon.–Sat. 7:30–7:30; Sun. and holidays, 9–2.*

A little higher up, on the right, you'll see the massive back wall of the much better preserved **Theater of Herodes Atticus,** built by the Romans in the 2nd century AD. Here, on pine-scented summer evenings, the **Athens Festival** takes place. It includes opera, ballet, drama, and concerts (*see* The Arts). *Tel. 01/321–0219. Admission: 250 dr. Open Apr.–Oct., Mon.–Sat. 9–2:45, Sun. and holidays, 9–1:45.*

Beyond the theater, a steep, zigzag path leads to the **Acropolis.** Though the Sacred Rock had been a center of worship for 5,000 years, the Athenians built this complex in the 5th century BC to commemorate the Greek naval victory at Salamis over the Per-

Athens

sians. The first ruins you'll see are the **Propylaea**, the monumental gates that led worshippers from the temporal world into the spiritual world of the sanctuary; now only the columns of Pentelic marble remain. Above, to the right, stands the graceful **Temple of Wingless Victory** (or Athena Nike), so called because the sculptor depicted the goddess of victory without her wings to prevent her from flying away. The elegant and architecturally complex **Erechtheion temple**, most sacred of the shrines of the Acropolis and later turned into a harem by the Turks, has now emerged from extensive repair work. Dull, heavy copies of the infinitely more beautiful Caryatids (draped maidens) now support the roof. The Acropolis Museum houses five of the six originals, their faces much damaged by acid rain. The sixth is in the British Museum in London.

9 The **Parthenon** dominates the Acropolis and indeed the Athens skyline. Designed by Ictinus, with Phidias as master sculptor, it is the largest Doric temple ever built and the most architecturally sophisticated. Even with hordes of tourists wandering around the ruins, you can still feel a sense of wonder. The temple was originally painted in vivid reds and blues, but time and neglect have given the marble pillars their golden-white shine and the beauty of the building is all the more stark and striking. The British Museum houses the largest remaining part of the original 162-meter (523-foot) frieze (The Elgin Marbles). The building has 17 fluted columns along each side and 8 at the ends, and these lean slightly inward and bulge to counterbalance cleverly the natural optical distortion. The Parthenon has had a checkered history: It was made into a brothel by the Romans, a church by the Christians, a mosque by the Turks. The Turks also stored gunpowder in the Propylaea, and when this was hit by a Venetian bombardment in 1687, a fire raged for two days and 28 columns fell, leaving the Parthenon in its present condition. *Admission: 625 dr., joint ticket to Acropolis and museum. Open Apr.–Oct., 7:30–7:30; Nov.–Mar., 8–5; closed full-moon nights.*

10 The **Acropolis Museum,** just below the Parthenon, contains some superb sculptures from the Acropolis, including the Caryatids and a large collection of colored *kore* (statues of women in attendance to Athena). *Tel. 01/323–6665. Admission: 625 dr., joint ticket to the Acropolis. Open Apr.–Oct., Mon.–Sat. 7:30–7:30, Sun. and holidays, 8–6; Nov.–Mar., Wed.–Mon. 8–5, Tues. 11–5.*

On the rocky outcrop facing the Acropolis, St. Paul preached to the Athenians; the road leading down between it and the hill of Pnyx is called Agiou Pavlou (St. Paul). To the right stands the **11** **Agora,** which means "marketplace," the civic center and focal point of community life in ancient Athens. The sprawling confusion of stones, slabs, and foundations is dominated by the **12** best-preserved temple in Greece, the **Hephestaion** (often wrongly referred to as the Theseion), built in the 5th century BC. Nearby, the impressive Stoa of Attalus II, reconstructed by the American School of Classical Studies in Athens with the help of the Rockefeller Foundation, houses the **Museum of the Agora 13 Excavations**. *Tel. 01/321–0185. Admission: 400 dr. Open Mon. and Wed.–Sat. 8:45–3, and Sun. and holidays 9:30–2:30.*

Next to the Agora you'll find the **Plaka,** almost all that's left of 19th-century Athens. In the 1950s and '60s, the area became garish with neon as nightclubs moved in and residents moved out. Renovation in recent years has restored the Plaka, and it is again lined with attractive houses and the vine-shaded court-yards of open-air tavernas and bars.

⑭ Below the Plaka, in Cathedral Square, stands a charming 12th-century Byzantine church known as the "Old" or **"Little Cathedral,"** nestling below the vast structure of the 19th-century **Cathedral of Athens.** From here, a short walk up Mitropoleos will take you back to Syntagma.

Time Out Visit the **De Profundis Tea Room** in an old mansion at Hatzimichali 1. Classical music plays softly as you drink fruit juice, herbal tea, or coffee in this sedate café; the homemade pastries are delicious. Other favorite places in the Plaka are **Paragoti,** at Appollonos 11, where you can sit out on the pave-ment and watch the world go by, and the **American Restaurant,** at Mitropoleos 3. Both are ideal for breakfast or a quick snack during the day; the latter serves excellent eggs, toast, jam, and coffee as well as such American fare as burgers, fries, and chili.

Downtown Athens If you walk along Venizelou Avenue (also known as Pane-pistimiou Avenue) from the square, you will pass, on the right, **⑮** three imposing buildings in Classical style: the **Academy,** the **⑯ ⑰** **Senate House of the University,** and the **National Library.** When you reach **Omonia Square,** a bedlam of touts and tourists, you are in the heart of downtown Athens.

⑱ Try to spare time to see the **Archaeological Museum.** Despite being somewhat off the tourist route, a good 10-minute walk north of Omonia Square, it is well worth the detour. This is by far the most important museum in Athens. It houses one of the most exciting collections of antiquity in the world, including sensational archeological finds made by Heinrich Schliemann at Mycenae, a 15th-century BC fresco from the Akrotiri ruins on Santorini, and the 6½-foot-tall bronze sculpture *Poseidon,* an original work of circa 750 BC, possibly by the sculptor Kalamis, which was found in the sea off Cape Artemision in 1928. *Tossitsa 1, off 28 Oktovriou, tel. 01/821–7717. Admission: 500 dr. Open Tues.–Sat. 8–7, Sun. 8–6.*

⑲ Alternatively, from Syntagma you can take Vassilissis Sofias Avenue along the edge of the National Gardens to reach the **Ev-zone Guards' barracks.** From here you have several options. If you continue farther along Vassilissis Sofias, it will bring you eventually to the Hilton Hotel and the U.S. Embassy. Or, turn **⑳** right onto Herodes Atticus, which leads to the **Presidential Palace,** a neo-Renaissance building.

㉑ Opposite the Evzone Guards' barracks, on the corner of Vassilissis Sofias and Herodes Atticus, is the **Benaki Museum,,** with an eclectic and interesting hodgepodge of objects from dif-ferent countries and periods, ranging from ancient sculpture, through Byzantine pieces, Ottoman ceramics, and Chinese jades, to modern paintings. There is also a fabulous collection of genuine Greek national costumes and folk art and embroi-dery. *Koumbari 1, tel. 01/361–1617. Admission: 200 dr. Open Wed.–Mon. 8:30–2.*

㉒ The new **Museum of Cycladic Art** is up the next street to the left. The collection spans 5,000 years, with 230 exhibits of the Cycladic civilization (3,000–2,000 BC) in comparison with modern primitives. *Neofytou Douka 4, tel. 01/321-3018. Admission: 200 dr., free on Sat. Open Mon. and Wed.-Fri. 10-4, Sat. 10-3.*

㉓ A little farther along is the **Byzantine Museum,** housed in an 1840 mansion that was built by an eccentric French aristocrat. It has a unique collection of icons and the very beautiful 14th-century Byzantine embroidery of the body of Christ in gold, silver, yellow, and green. Sculptural fragments provide an excellent introduction to Byzantine architecture.

㉔ **Kolonaki,** the chic shopping district and one of the most fashionable residential areas, occupies the lower slopes of **Mount Lycabettos** and is only a 10-minute walk northwest of Syntagma; it's worth a stroll around if you enjoy window-shopping and people-watching. Three times the height of the Acropolis, Lycabettos can be reached by funicular railway from the top of Ploutarchou Street (a 23 bus from Kolonaki Square will drop you at the station). The view from the top—pollution permitting—is the finest in Athens. You can see all of Athens, Attica, the harbor, and the islands of Aegina and Poros laid out before you.

Off the Beaten Track

Outside central Athens, on the slopes of Mount Ymitos (ancient Mount Hymettus), is one of the city's most evocative Byzantine remains, the **Kaisariani monastery.** Take a taxi or the bus from the university (halfway up Venizelou Avenue) for 6 kilometers (4 miles) east of central Athens until you pass through the working-class suburb of Kaisariani to the monastery. The well-restored 11th-century church, built on the site of a sanctuary of Aphrodite, has some beautiful frescoes dating from the 16th century. Outside, there are plenty of shady places under the trees to sit and contemplate the view over Athens. If you feel particularly energetic, you can keep on walking up Mount Ymitos—the roads wind through the forested slopes for 19 kilometers (12 miles)—and take your pick of the many picnic spots. *Tel. 01/723-6619. Admission: free. Open Mon.-Sat. 9-3, Sun. 9-2.*

Beyond the port of Piraeus, the little harbor of **Mikrolimano** is a must. This crescent-shaped gem of a harbor is crowded with small yachts, and its restaurants—22 at the last count—are famous for fish and seafood. While it's not a particularly cheap place to eat, the freshness and quality will not be found elsewhere in Greece. If you don't like seafood, you'll still be enchanted by the terraces of lovely houses tucked up against the sloping hillsides, the elegant yachts, and the sturdy fishing craft. To get there from Athens, take the train from Omonia Square to New Phaleron or a bus from Filellinon Street to the New Phaleron train station; it's only five minutes' walk from there. Alternatively, a relatively expensive (700 dr.) taxi ride will take you 16 kilometers (10 miles) along the new coast road and will give you wonderful views of the Saronic Gulf.

Shopping

Gift Ideas Better tourist shops sell copies of traditional Greek jewelry, silver filigree, enamel, Skyro pottery, onyx ashtrays and dishes, woven bags, attractive rugs (including *flokates—*

shaggy wool rugs, often brightly colored), good leather items, and furs. Furs made from scraps are inexpensive. Some museums sell replicas of small items that are in their collections. The best handicrafts are sold in **National Welfare Organization shops** (Voukourestiou 24a and Ypatias 6) near the cathedral. Other shops sell dried fruit, packaged pistachios, and canned olives. For books in English, go to **Pantelides** (Amerikas 11 or Eleftheroudakis, Nikis 4). Most large hotels also maintain good English-language bookstores.

Antiques Many shops, especially in **Pandrossou Street** sell small antiques and icons. Keep in mind, however, that there are many fakes around and remember that you must have permission to export genuine objects from the Greek, Roman, or Byzantine periods.

Shopping Areas The central shopping area lies between Syntagma and Omonia. The **Syntagma** area has good jewelers, shoe shops, and handicraft and souvenir shops, especially along **Voukourestriou.** **Stadiou Street** is the best bet for men's clothing. Try **Ermou Street** and the fascinating small streets that lead off it for fabrics and housewares. Go to **Mitropoleos** for rugs and souvenirs. This is also the main furrier street and most of the moderately-priced fur shops are here, including Hydra, Mitsakou, Maoum, Samaras, and Voula. Ermou runs west to **Monastiraki,** a crowded market area popular with Athenians. Below the cathedral, **Pandrossou** has antiques, sandals (an especially good buy), and inexpensive souvenirs. **Kolonaki,** just beyond central Athens, has the best shops for gifts and shoes. Its boutiques include branches of some of the top French fashion houses such as Dior (Kriezotou 7), Yves St. Laurent (Kriezotou 10), and Lanvin (Anagnostopoulou 3), with prices lower than those in Paris.

Department Stores The few that exist are neither large nor good. The best is **Lambropoulos** (Aeolou 99–101). **Marinopoulos** shops (Kanari 9, Kifissias 16, and elsewhere) specialize in toiletries and inexpensive casual clothing.

Flea Market The flea market, based on **Pandrossou** and **Ifestou Streets,** operates on Sunday mornings and sells almost anything: secondhand clothes, daggers, cooking pots and pans, old books, guitars, *bouzouki* (stringed instruments), old furniture and carpets, backgammon sets. However little it costs, you should haggle. Ifestou Street, where the coppersmiths have their shops, is more interesting on a weekday and you can pick up copper wine jugs, candlesticks, cooking ware, etc. for next to nothing.

Dining

Although hotel dining rooms are generally the only places that have fixed-price menus, they also have fairly unimaginative international food. Your best bet might be to eat out in the innumerable tavernas and fish restaurants offering typically Greek food. Be adventurous and go looking for the places that have at least half a dozen tables occupied by Athenians—they're discerning customers. Alternatively, if you would like a change of cuisine, there are plenty of French, Italian, Lebanese, Chinese, and Japanese restaurants, all to be found in the same area as the hotels around Syntagma and Omonia Squares, and all fairly expensive. The Greek tavernas may not aspire to their culinary heights, but then, they don't cost as much. For details and price-category definitions, *see* Dining in Staying in Greece.

Very Expensive **L'Abreuvoir.** This restaurant, outstanding among the many average French restaurants, is ideal for a romantic candlelit dinner. The classic French dishes are served on a terrace under the leaves of a mulberry tree. Frequented by wealthy Athenians and resident expatriates wanting a break from Greek cuisine, it has an elegant, dressed-up ambience. Specialties include spinach tart, steak *au poivre* (with pepper), and *entrecôte* (steak) *Provençale. Xenokratous 51, tel. 01/722–9061. Reservations advised. AE, DC, MC, V. Closed Mon.*

Bajazzo. This elegant wood-paneled restaurant, in a converted neoclassical mansion in fashionable Kolonaki, has a moving theater to entertain its guests. The food is exquisitely presented and specialties include duck in mousseline sauce, salmon roulade, and a Fisherman's Dream soup with clams, langoustines (crayfish), *moules* (mussels), and ouzo. *Ploutarchou 35, tel. 01/ 729–1420. Reservations advised. AE, DC, MC, V.*

Expensive **Aglamair.** The most civilized and expensive of the fish restaurants lining the picturesque Mikrolimano harbor, this is also one of the best in Athens. Practically on the water's edge, you can dine watching the lights shimmer across the bay. The decor is cheerful but sophisticated, with red tablecloths and green and black chairs. The menu includes lobster, shrimps, prawns, octopus, and squid. *Akti Koumoundourou 54, tel. 01/411–5511. Reservations advised. AE, DC, MC, V.*

Dionyssos. You may be able to get better food at better prices elsewhere in Athens, but the view of the Acropolis is unbeatable and the food is usually of a high standard. Try to go for dinner when there is a *son-et-lumière* (sound-and-light show) performance on the Parthenon; the sight is unforgettable. The best view is from the terrace upstairs. *Robertou Gali 43, tel. 01/923–3182. Reservations advised. AE, DC, MC, V.*

G.B Corner. High standards and good service are the trademark of this independently run restaurant in the Grande Bretagne Hotel. Centrally located opposite Parliament, it has a civilized, quiet, essentially British atmosphere accentuated by polished wood paneling and tartan carpeting. The menu offers a representative selection of Greek and Continental dishes; the sherbets are, by repute, excellent. *Grande Bretagne Hotel, Platia Syntagma, tel. 01/323–0251. Reservations advised. AE, DC, MC, V.*

★ **Gerfinikas.** This cheerful and bustling restaurant, tucked away in a narrow alley off a street leading up to Kolonaki, has a loyal expense-account clientele. The two-tier dining room, with sun terrace on one side, has glass-fronted cases with inviting displays of Greek and Turkish specialties and seafood dishes. *Pinadrou 10, tel. 01/362–2719. Reservations advised. AE, DC, MC, V.*

Moderate **Dionyssos.** Located on top of Mount Lycabettos, this restaurant has a sweeping view of Athens and Piraeus, down to the sea. Take the funicular railway from the top of Ploutarchou Street, in Kolonaki. In addition to the restaurant, which serves Continental and Greek cuisine, there is a cafeteria and patisserie, open from the earliest to the latest cablecar run (check the time of the last one!). *Mount Lycabettos, tel. 01/722–6374. Reservations not necessary. AE, DC, V.*

Hermion. An English-language menu, a shady courtyard, and a location on a street below the cathedral make this restaurant very popular with visitors. It has two or three fixed-price menus, all offering excellent Greek and international fare. *Pandrossos 15, tel. 01/324–6725. Reservations not necessary. AE, DC, MC, V.*

Ideal. This typically old-style Athenian restaurant still displays its day's specialties in the front window, as it has done since 1922. The busy all-wood dining room is filled with Athenians of all ages, as well as students from the nearby university. It has an extensive menu featuring high-quality Greek and Continental dishes. *Venizelou 46, tel. 01/361–4604. Reservations not necessary. DC.*

★ **Kostoyannis.** If you're looking for authenticity, this is the place to go. One of the oldest and most popular tavernas in the area, located behind the Archaeological Museum, it has an impressively wide range of Greek dishes including excellent shrimp and crab salads, stuffed mussels, and fried brains. The new extension should help to accommodate the crowds. *Zaimi 37, tel. 01/822–0624. Reservations advised in summer. AE, DC, MC, V. Dinner only. Closed Sun.*

Xynus. A large, tumbledown taverna, with three rooms and a tree-covered patio, the Xynus is hidden in a narrow pebble-paved lane in the Plaka. The food is much more pleasing than the decor—exposed pipes and stoves, and cretonne curtains—and is highly recommended by Athenians, who consider it one of the finest restaurants in the city. A trio of musicians wanders from room to room playing folk melodies. *Angelou Geronta 4, Plaka, tel. 01/322–1065. Reservations advised. AE, DC, MC, V. Dinner only. Closed Sun.*

Inexpensive **Delphi Restaurant.** Very popular with businessmen wanting a quick, cheap meal, this restaurant serves excellent Greek and international food and is always crowded. It may be a little touristy and service can be slow, but the food is worth the wait. The front part of the restaurant is rustic, while the back-room decor is more refined. *Nikis 13, tel. 01/323–4869. No reservations. AE, DC. Closed Sun.*

Eden. This vegetarian restaurant, in a converted old Plaka villa, serves superb vegetable pies and spinach burgers in yogurt sauce—a delightful experience for those tired of seeing lamb roasted on a spit at every corner. You can sit outside at wrought-iron tables on a rooftop terrace. *Flessa 3, tel. 01/324–8858. Reservations not necessary. AE, DC. Closed Tues.*

O Platanos. Set in a picturesque corner of the Plaka, this is one of the oldest tavernas in the area. It has a shady garden for outdoor dining. There's no music, so prices are low. Although it's extremely friendly, not much English is spoken. *Diogenous 4, tel. 01/322–0666. Reservations not necessary. AE, DC, MC, V.*

Syntrivani. Well established and reliable, Syntrivani offers a good range of traditional Greek dishes. It's near Syntagma and has a small garden for outdoor dining. *Filellinon 5, tel. 01/323–8662. Reservations not necessary. AE, DC, MC, V.*

Lodging

As Athens is the starting point for so many travelers, its hotels are very full, and it's always advisable to reserve a room in advance. Which type of hotel you choose is really a matter of personal taste. Basically, the style of hotels in Athens can be

divided into two neat brackets—traditional and modernistic—
and these can be found both in the center of town, around
Omonia and Syntagma Squares, near the U.S. Embassy, and
further out along the seacoast and near the airport. In the heat
of the summer, it might be preferable to go for the fresh, clean
lines of a more modern-style hotel, leaving the older hotels for
winter visits. Hotels in the center of Athens can be so noisy
that it's difficult to get a good night's sleep, while those out on
the coast become more expensive, as you spend more money on
taxis getting to and from town. For details and price category
definitions, *see* Lodging in Staying in Greece.

Very Expensive **Aphrodite Astir Palace.** Located in a coastal area 25 kilometers
(16 miles) from Athens, this is actually three hotels called Aphrodite, the newest and least expensive; Arion, the most
exclusive; and Nafsika, the most chic and perhaps the most
beautiful. The complex, on a pine-covered promontory, has its
own beach and helicopter pad. This is Greece's most prestigious seaside hotel complex and is highly recommended.
*Vouligmeni, tel. 01/896–210/9. 570 rooms with bath. Facilities:
restaurants, 3 outdoor pools, miniature golf, nightclub. AE,
DC, MC, V.*

★ **Athens Hilton.** Set in a commanding position on a hill near the
U.S. Embassy, the Hilton is about a 10-minute walk from
Syntagma Square. All rooms and suites have fine views and
soundproof windows; some have balconies and black Carrara
baths. On Monday evening in summer, there's a poolside barbe-
cue. Lunch is served at the Galaxy on the roof (a piano bar by
night), wines and appetizers at the new Kellari, and dinner at
Ta Nissia, a Greek-style taverna. *Vasilissis Sofias 46, tel. 01/
722–0201. 480 rooms with bath. Facilities: 2 restaurants, a
lounge, nighttime piano bar; outdoor pool with food and beverage service; shops. AE, CB, DC, MC, V.*

★ **Grande Bretagne.** G.B., as it is known, is centrally located on
Syntagma Square. An internationally famous landmark, this
distinguished hotel was modernized a few years ago but still
has its vast high-ceilinged, elegant lobby and lounges, decorated with tapestry wall-coverings, and its own particular
friendly atmosphere. Ask for an inside room to escape the noise
of the traffic. The hotel houses the excellent G.B. Corner Restaurant (*see* Dining). *Syntagma Square, tel. 01/323–0251/9. 394
rooms with bath. Facilities: restaurant, rooftop garden. AE,
DC, MC, V.*

Ledra Marriott. Between Athens center and the sea, this is a
popular chain hotel known for standard comfort and service.
There's a very attractive Polynesian restaurant called Kona
Kai, complete with waterfall, or the Zephyros Café, which
serves an outstanding Sunday buffet brunch, and a spectacular
rooftop swimming pool with a snack area. *Syngrou 115, tel. 01/
934–7711. 258 rooms with bath. Facilities: 4 restaurants, rooftop garden, outdoor pool, shops. AE, DC, MC, V.*

Expensive **Athens Chandris.** Located near the sea and the race course, the
★ Athens Chandris offers all the comfort, service, and facilities of
a very expensive hotel, but at more reasonable prices. Visitors
on combined flight-cruise tours stay here, and the individual
traveler may feel a little overwhelmed and lost. The hotel runs
a complimentary shuttle service to and from Syntagma. It has a
fine Continental restaurant, the Four Seasons; a poolside snack
bar, and a lounge. *Syngrou 385, tel. 01/941–4824. 386 rooms*

with bath. Facilities: restaurant, lounge, snack bar, rooftop garden, outdoor pool. AE, DC, MC, V.

Divani-Zafolia Palace. On a small street near the Acropolis and other ancient sites, this hotel seems to be gaining in popularity. It is also an ideal base from which to stroll and explore. The public areas are clean and attractive and the upper-story bedrooms have excellent views. *Parthenos 19, tel. 01/922–2945. 193 rooms with bath. Facilities: restaurant, rooftop garden, outdoor pool. AE, DC, MC, V.*

Holiday Inn. Centrally located, less than a mile from city center, this is a good base for sightseers and a typical, comfortable, though anonymous, example of the chain. Its restaurant, the Bistro Greek, offers mainly French cuisine. *Mihalakopoulou 50, tel. 01/724–8322. 198 rooms with bath. Facilities: restaurant and lounge, bowling alley, disco. AE, DC, MC, V.*

★ **St. George Lycabettos Hotel.** Situated on the wooded slopes of Mount Lycabettos, this hotel has a splendid view. Getting there, however, involves a steep short walk or a ride up (remember, taxis are inexpensive). It is friendly and has, as its trump card, Le Grand Balcon, a two-tiered rooftop restaurant with excellent food and a marvelous panoramic view. It also has terraces with snack tables, a lower-level restaurant, an intimate, cozy grill-room, and a very attractive coffee shop. *Kleomenous 2, tel. 01/729–0710. 149 rooms with bath. Facilities: restaurants, nightclub, outdoor pool, roof garden. AE, DC, MC, V.*

Moderate   **Athens Gate Hotel.** This hotel looks across a busy street to the Arch of Hadrian. Front rooms have the view, but also the traffic noise; back rooms are quiet. The hotel is conveniently located between the center of town and the Acropolis. The restaurant is only mediocre, but it serves a good, American-style buffet breakfast. *Syngrou 10, tel. 01/923–8302/9. 106 rooms with bath. Facilities: restaurant, roof garden, air-conditioning. AE, DC, MC, V.*

Ilissia Hotel. This small, but rather shabby, friendly hotel is located near the Hilton, in an area where there are many good restaurants and night spots. Generally, it could use a good spring-cleaning, but the location makes up for its dowdy appearance. *Mihalakopoulou 25, tel. 01/724–4051. 60 rooms with bath. Facilities: restaurant, air-conditioning. AE, DC, MC, V.*

La Mirage. Conveniently located, this hotel overlooks busy Omonia Square. Rooms are comfortable, but ask for one that's soundproof. *Mirakis Kotopouli 3, tel. 01/523–4072/3. 208 rooms with bath. AE, DC, MC, V.*

Inexpensive   **Alkistis Hotel.** The market area, where the Alkistis is located, is full of life and color by day, but deserted at night. The hotel is pleasant and well run and was recently redecorated. The roof garden has a fine view of the Acropolis and seating for sunbathers. Try to get a room overlooking the Acropolis, if you can, as the other rooms have terraces over the street. *Platia Theatrou 18, tel. 01/321–9811/9. 120 rooms with bath. Facilities: restaurant, roof garden, outdoor pool. AE, DC, MC, V.*

Aphrodite Hotel. This is near Syntagma and perfectly comfortable. With all the facilities of other, more costly hotels, it offers excellent value for money. Don't be put off by it's cold-looking entrance. *Apollonos 21, tel. 01/323–4354. 84 rooms with bath. Facilities: bar, roof garden. AE, DC, MC, V.*

★ **Austria.** This small, unpretentious hotel is on Filopappou Hill, opposite the Acropolis, ideal as a base for wandering around the heart of ancient Athens. It has no restaurant and is at the top of the inexpensive category, but is well worth considering. *Mouson 7, tel. 01/923–5151. 40 rooms with bath. AE, DC, MC, V.*

The Arts

The **Athens Festival** runs from late June through September and includes concerts, recitals, opera, ballet, folk dancing, and drama. Performances are in various locations, including the open-air theater of Herodes Atticus at the foot of the Acropolis, nearby Philopappou Hill, and Mount Lycabettos. Tickets are available a few days before the performance from the festival box office in the arcade at Stadiou 4 (tel. 01/322–1459). Admission ranges from 500 dr. to 3,000 dr.

For those disappointed with the daytime view of the Acropolis, the **Son-et-Lumière** (Sound-and-Light) shows bring history to life. Performances are given nightly from April to October, in English, at 9:15 (the time is liable to change), and admission is 500 dr. The entrance is on Dion Areopagitou, opposite the Acropolis, and from your seat on the top of Philopappou Hill, you watch the changing lighting of the monuments.

In winter, cultural activities are much less frequent and rarely planned far in advance. Daily listings are published year-round in *The Athens News* and weekly listings in *This Week in Athens*, both available in hotels.

Concerts Winter concerts are given at the **Pallas** by the State Orchestra and the Radio/TV Orchestra. Information and tickets are available from the theater box office on Voukourestiou, near Syntagma Square. Contact the **NTOG**, tel. 01/322–2545, for up-to-date information and further details.

Opera The **Lyriki Skini Opera Company** has a winter season and a small—not very good—ballet season at the Olympia Theater, Akademias 59, tel. 01/361–2461. The top seat costs about 800 dr.

Films There are several cinemas that show foreign films and *The Athens News* lists them in English. Try the **Elena Cinema** (Antifilon 47, tel. 01/778–9120) for new American films and the **Cinema Thission** (Pavlou 7, tel. 01/347–0980) for American and European classics.

Nightlife

Athens has an active nightlife, with hundreds of places offering some sort of entertainment, much of it distinctly Greek. One way to get a taste is to take an "Athens by Night" guided tour, which takes in a number of clubs. This can be arranged for you by any good travel agent (*see* Important Addresses) but try Viking Tours first. If you want to go on your own, try a *bouzoukia*, or a taverna with a floor show. Most are closed Sunday. Tavernas with floor shows are concentrated in the Plaka area. Be forewarned that you will have to pay for an overpriced, second-rate meal at most places. The name, style, and quality of tavernas and bouzoukias change frequently. Ask your hotel for recommendations.

Tavernas

Palia Taverna Kritikou. Here's a fun taverna where there's room for you to indulge in Greek dances to the amusement of the few Greek customers. *Mniskleous 24, tel. 01/322-2809. Reservations advised. AE, DC, V. Expensive.*

Psarra. The specialty in this taverna is swordfish kabob. Customers are invited to play the guitar themselves and to join in the Greek dances. *Erehtheou 16, tel. 01/325-0285. Reservations advised. AE, DC, MC, V. Expensive.*

Bouzoukias

Athinaia. Highly prized and priced, it's the real thing, where you'll find an orchestra, female vocalist, and lots of clanging of the *bouzouki*, an Oriental mandolin. *Leoforos Posidonos 63, tel. 01/942-3089. Reservations advised. AE, DC, MC, V. Very Expensive.*

Diogenes. Currently the "in" place with chic Greeks, and very ritzy, it's also the most expensive. *Leoforos Syngrou 255, tel. 01/942-4267. Reservations necessary. AE. Very Expensive.*

The Peloponnese

Suspended from the mainland of Greece like a large leaf, with the isthmus of Corinth as its stem, the ancient land of Pelops offers beautiful scenery—rocky coasts, sandy beaches, and mountains—and a fascinating variety of ruins: temples, theaters, mosques, churches, palaces, and medieval castles built by crusaders.

Legend and history meet in Mycenae, where Agamemnon, Elektra, and Orestes played out their grim family tragedy. This city dominated the entire area from the 16th to the 12th centuries BC, even conquering Minoan Crete. According to Greek mythology, Paris, son of the king of Troy, abducted the beautiful Helen, wife of Menelaus, the king of Sparta. Agamemnon, the king of Mycenae, was his brother. This led to the Trojan War in which Troy was defeated. The story of the war is told in Homer's *Iliad.* Following Heinrich Schliemann's discoveries of tombs, palaces, and aqueducts during excavations in 1874, Mycenae has become a world-class archeological site and, of all the sites in the Peloponnese, is most worthy of a visit.

Sparta, once a powerful city-state, contributed decisively to the defeat of the Persians who invaded Greece in the 5th century BC. Later, Athens and Sparta and their respective allies fought each other from 461 BC to 404 BC, in the two Peloponnesian Wars, for dominance of the Greek world. Sparta emerged the victor. In the 2nd century BC, both Sparta and Athens fell before the might of Macedon, whose king, Alexander the Great, was to take Hellenic civilization to the limits of the known world, from Europe to India. There is virtually nothing in situ from Sparta's ancient past, however; the Spartans were always better at destroying than building. The town today is, unfortunately, devoid of charm or character and the ruins are disappointing.

Corinth was the largest, richest, and most pleasure-loving city of Greece in the 3rd century BC, a reputation it continued to enjoy after the Roman conquest. It gave St. Paul plenty to denounce when he came here in the 1st century AD. Now, it is lifeless and unattractive, bearing no relation whatsoever to the original vibrant city. This is due in part to the fact that when the new town was destroyed by earthquakes in 1858 and 1928, each time more practical and dull-looking apartment blocks were built.

In the Middle Ages, the Peloponnese was conquered by leaders of the Fourth Crusade and ruled as a feudal state by French and Italian nobles. It formed the cornerstone of the Latin (Christian) power in the eastern Mediterranean in the 13th and 14th centuries. In 1821, when the bishop of Patras raised the standard of revolt against Turkish domination, the Peloponnese played a key role in the Greek War of Independence. Nafplio was, for a short time in the 1800s, the capital of Greece. Among the region's many fine contributions to humanity are the Olympic Games, founded in 776 BC in Olympia.

Getting Around

The best way to see all the important sights of the Peloponnese at your own pace is by car. If you take the car ferry from Italy to Patras, capital of the Peloponnese, or if you rent a car in Patras, you can tour the area on the way to Athens. Otherwise, your tour will begin in Athens. Take the route suggested in the itinerary below. You could encounter a shortage of hotel rooms in summer, especially at Nafplio, so plan in advance.

Guided Tours

CHAT Tours (4 Stadiou, Athens, tel. 01/322–2886) and **Wagons-Lits Travel** (Karageorgi Servias 2, Athens, tel. 01/324–2281) both organize tours in the Peloponnese. **Viking Tours** (Filellinon 3, tel. 01/322–9383) can book other companies' tours. A four-day tour of the Peloponnese and Delphi, including the sites, qualified guide, and accommodations at first-class hotels, costs around 40,000 dr. A two-day tour, again including accommodations to Corinth, Mycenae, and Epidauros will cost around 7,000 dr.

Tourist Information

In Patras, visit the **Greek National Tourist Organization** (Iroon Polytechniou, Glyfada, tel. 061/420–305); or **American Express,** inside the National Bank of Greece (Amalias St. 46, at corner of Othonos St., tel. 061/220–902). The **Tourist Police** are at Othonos Amalias 14, on the seafront. There are hundreds of tourist offices along this street; **K. Tsimara Tour Office** (tel. 061/277–783) deals specifically with excursions to the Ionian islands but should be able to help you with other arrangements, too. The **Olympic Airlines** office is at Agios Andreou 16 (tel. 061/222–901). The **Greek Automobile and Touring Club** (ELPA) has a branch office at Korinthou 127 in Patras (tel. 061/425–411).

Exploring the Peloponnese

Eleven kilometers (7 miles) northwest of Athens, after you have passed the last houses of the Athenian urban sprawl, you come to the 6th-century monastery of **Daphni**. It was sacked in 1205 by Frankish crusaders, who later installed Cistercian monks from Burgundy to rebuild it. The monastery has superb mosaics. *tel. 01/581–1558. Admission: 300 dr. Open Mon. and Wed.–Sat. 8:45–3, Sun. and holidays 9:30–2:30.*

Descending from Daphni to the sea, you face the narrow straits where the Persian fleet of Xerxes was defeated in 480 BC by

The Peloponnese

Delphi
Itea
Livadia
Thebes (Thiva)
Nefpaktos
Messolongi
Galaxidi
Patras
Dafne
Gulf of Corinth
Diakofto
Killini
Loutra
Amalias
Corinth Canal
Megara
Eleusis Daphni
Piraeus
Corinth
Nemea
Acrocorinth
Egina
Athens
Mycenae
Argos
Epidauros
Pyrgos
Olympia
Nafplio
Poros
Kaiafas
Trípoli
Toló
Andritsena
Ermioni
Ydra
Kyparissia
PELOPONNESE
Spetses
Messini
Sparta
Leonidio
Gargaliani
Kalamata
Mystras
Geraki
Pilos
Kyparíssi
Methoni
Skala
Koroni
Gýthio
Monemvassía
Areopoli

Kýthira
Agía Pelagia

N

| 0 | 50 miles |
| 0 | 75 km |

Sparta. Shortly beyond are the ruins of **Eleusis**, site of antiquity's most important harvest celebrations, the Eleusinian Mysteries, where participants underwent rites commemorating the gift of corn cultivation given by Demeter, goddess of corn. Now the area is unattractive, surrounded by factories and their pollution, and there is almost nothing left of the ancient Eleusis, but for a few fallen pillars and overgrown pathways. Admission to the site includes entrance to a small museum. *Admission: 250 dr. Open Mon. and Wed.–Sat. 8:45–2:30, Sun. and holidays 9:30–2:30.*

When you cross the **Corinth Canal**, about 88 kilometers (55 miles) from Athens, you enter the **Peloponnese**. Modern **Corinth** lies by the sea; the ancient Greek city stood higher up. All that remains is the **Doric Temple of Apollo,** built in the 6th century BC and restored by Julius Caesar. In AD 51, St. Paul fulminated against the sacred prostitutes who served Aphrodite on the **Acro-Corinth,** the peak behind the ancient city. A museum beside the ruins contains finds from the excavations. Be sure to see the fine display, next to the museum, of the evolution of Greek columnar architecture. Drive to a tourist pavilion below the imposing Franco-Turkish fortifications on the mountain and explore the **Fort of AcroCorinth** on foot. *Tel. 0741/31–207. Admission: 400 dr. Open Apr.–Oct., Mon. and Wed.–Sat. 8–7, Sun. and holidays 8–6; Nov.–Mar., Wed.–Mon., 8–5.*

Mycenae, 48 kilometers (25 miles) from Corinth, was the fabulous stronghold of the Achaean kings of the 13th century BC. Destroyed in 468 BC, it was forgotten until 1874 when German archaeologist Heinrich Schliemann, who discovered the ruins of ancient Troy, uncovered the remains of this ancient fortress city. Mycenae was the seat of the doomed House of Atreus—of King Agamemnon and his wife, Clytemnestra, sister of Helen of Troy, and of their tragic children, Orestes and Elektra. When Schliemann uncovered six shaft graves (so named because the kings were buried standing up) of the royal circle, he was certain that one was the tomb of Agamemnon. The gold masks and diadems, daggers, jewelry, and other treasures found in the graves are now in the Athens Archaeological Museum; the new local museum is dedicated to archaeological studies. Along with the graves, you'll find the astounding beehive tombs built into the hillsides outside the reconstructed wall, the **LionGate**, dating to 1250 BC, and the castle ruins crowning the bleak hill, all remnants of the first great civilization in Continental Europe. The tombs, the acropolis, the palace, and the museum can all be explored for the cost of admission. *Admission: 500 dr. Open Apr.–Oct., Mon.–Sat. 8–7, Sun. and holidays 8–6; Nov.–Mar. daily 8–5.*

Moving south, 11 kilometers (7 miles) from Mycenae, you pass **Argos**, Europe's oldest continuously inhabited town, and the Cyclopean ramparts (huge, irregular stones) of **Tiryns**. One version of the legend has Tiryns as the birthplace of Hercules, but the present remains, including the walls, date mostly from the 13th century BC when Tiryns was one of the most important Mycenaean cities.

Farther on is **Nafplio**, a picturesque town below the Venetian fortifications. Modern Greece's first king lived for a year or two within the walls of the higher fortress when Nafplio was capital of Greece. His courtiers had to climb 999 steps to reach him; you can still climb the long staircase or drive up to the fortress. The **Venetian naval arsenal** on the town square houses a museum crowded with Mycenaen finds. *Tel. 0752/27–502. Admission: 300 dr. Open Mon. and Wed.–Sat. 8:45–3, Sun. and holidays 9:30–2:30.*

Epidauros, 29 kilometers (18 miles) east of Nafplio, was the sanctuary of Aesculapois, the Greek god of healing. You can visit the foundations of the temples and ancient hospitals. The most important site is the ancient open-air theater, which seats 16,000. In summer, during the **Epidauros Festival**, ancient Greek plays are staged here (*see* the Arts). The theater merits a visit any time of year. The acoustics are so good that you can sit in the top row and hear a whisper on stage. *Tel. 0753/22–009. Admission: 500 dr. Museum and theater open Apr.–Oct., Mon.–Sat. 8–7, Sun. and holidays 8–6; Nov.–Mar., daily 8–5. Museum closed Tues.*

You can return from here to Athens along the coast, a lovely drive, or continue on to **Olympia** by way of the rugged mountains of Arcadia. The site of ancient Olympia lies a few miles from the sea, northeast of **Megalopolis**, once the largest town in ancient Greece. The first Olympic Games were held in Olympia in 776 BC and continued to be celebrated every four years until AD 393, when the Roman Emperor, Theodosius I, with his Christian sensibility, banned these "pagan rites." Women were excluded from the games under penalty of death. Archaeologists are still uncovering statues and votive offerings among the olive groves and pine trees surrounding **Olympic Stadium** and the imposing **ruins of the temples of Zeus and Hera** within the sacred precinct. The **International Olympic Academy,** 6.4 kilometers (4 miles) east, houses the **Museum of the Olympic Games.** *Tel. 0624/22–742. Admission: 400 dr. Open Apr.–Oct., Mon.–Wed.–Sat. 8–7, Tues. noon–7, and Sun. and holidays 8–6; Nov.–Mar., Wed.–Mon. 9–5, Tues. 11–5.*

Northeast of Olympia, 119 kilometers (74 miles) away, is **Patras,** the third-largest city in Greece, its main western port, and the hub of the business world in the Peloponnese. Walk up to the **Byzantine kastro,** built on the site of the ancient acropolis, to take a look at the fine view along the coast. The **Cathedral of St. Andrew's,** reputedly the largest in Greece and built on the site of the crucifixion of St. Andrew, is also worth exploring. Its treasure is the saint's silver-mounted skull, returned to Patras in 1964 after 500 years in St. Peter's, Rome. You'll find the cathedral on Odios Trion Navarkon. Apart from the kastro and the cathedral there is little here of particular interest. The city's prettiest features are its squares, surrounded by neoclassical-style buildings, and its arcaded streets.

The shortest route back to Athens follows the National Road along the southern shore of the Gulf of Corinth, an exceptionally beautiful drive. You could choose instead to cross the entrance to the gulf and visit Delphi (*see* Exploring in Mainland Greece) on your way back to Athens.

Dining and Lodging

Many of the hotels in the Peloponnese have good dining rooms so try these, as well as the usual tavernas serving their traditional Greek cuisine and fresh seafood. For details and price category definitions, *see* Dining and Lodging in Staying in Greece.

Napflio
Dining

Savouras. Fresh seafood is served in this unpretentious taverna overlooking the bay; it is generally regarded as one of the best fish restaurants in the area. *Akti Miaouli, no telephone. Reservations not necessary. No credit cards. Inexpensive.*

Lodging
★

Amalia. The attractive hotel occupies a fine neo-classical building in large gardens 4 kilometers (2½ miles) outside town, near ancient Tiryns. The public rooms are spacious and comfortable, the service attentive, and the swimming pool very inviting. With a beach nearby, this makes the ideal base for a relaxing stay. *Tel. 0752/24–401, 173 rooms with bath. Facilities: restaurant, outdoor pool, gardens. AE, DC, V. Expensive.*

Agamemnon. Located on the waterfront, this hotel has a large, cool lobby overhung with vines, a superb spot from which to watch the action. The double rooms have marble terraces overlooking the water. *Akti Miaouli 3, tel. 0752/28–021. 40 rooms with bath. Facilities: restaurant, roof garden, pool. DC. Moderate.*

Olympia
Dining

Pete's Den. Owned by a Greek-German couple, this restaurant mixes traditional Greek and German cuisine, with sensational results. *Saganaki* (a cheese, leek, and eggplant omelet) is served hot and bubbling with brandy, and the toasted bread—complete with hot garlic butter—is a delightful change from the usual heavy white bread. *Main St. Tel. 0642/22–066. Reservations not necessary. No credit cards. Inexpensive.*

Taverna Pritannio. With its bright lighting and plastic tablecloths, this is a decent and unpretentious taverna in the center of town. The grilled meat and salads are good, plentiful, and satisfying. *Main St., no telephone. Reservations not necessary. No credit cards. Inexpensive.*

Lodging
★
Amalia. Pleasantly situated a little outside the village near the museum, the Amalia is comfortable and well run. Unfortunately, the Greek- and European-style fare in the restaurant is served with little panache, but the other facilities of the hotel make up for this drawback. *Main St., tel. 0642/22-190. 147 rooms with bath. Facilities: restaurant, pool. AE, DC, MC, V. Expensive.*

Apollon. This hotel's contemporary decor has become rather shabby and worn but it is still very clean; don't be put off. The amenities are good for the price: the rooftop swimming pool is a definite plus and the self-service restaurant is very convenient. *Douma 13, tel. 0624/22-522. 110 rooms with bath. Facilities: restaurant, outdoor pool, roof garden. AE, DC. Closed Nov.-March. Moderate.*

Patras
Dining
Evangelatos. This reliable Greek restaurant, near the sea on the road that runs up to the Acropolis, is renowned for its good service and its fresh and simply-cooked local fare. *Ag. Nikolaou 7, tel. 061/27-777/2. Reservations not necessary. AE, DC, V. Moderate.*

Bieneza. It's good to find a cheap, traditional taverna like this one, still serving Greek specialties. Dishes include fish and noodles as well as the more usual salad, grilled meat, and fries. *Kolokotroni 18, tel. 061/221-209. Reservations not necessary. No credit cards. Inexpensive.*

Lodging
Astir. This large hotel enjoys an excellent location on the waterfront near the center of town. Spacious and pleasant, it looks out on the busy harbor and across to the mountains on the other side of the gulf. *Ag. Andreou 16, tel. 061/277-502. 121 rooms with bath. Facilities: restaurant, roof garden, outdoor pool. AE, DC, MC, V. Very Expensive.*

★ **Porto Rio.** There's a large and varied selection of rooms and cottages with a wide range of prices at this hotel complex on the sea at Rion, about 10 kilometers (6 miles) from Patras. Rooms over the front have outstanding views across the narrow entrance to the Gulf of Corinth. *Tel. 061/992-212. 267 rooms and cottages with bath. Facilities: restaurant, 2 outdoor pools, tennis, miniature golf, children's playground, nightclub. AE, DC, MC, V. Closed Nov.—Mar. Moderate and Expensive.*

The Arts

The **Festival of Ancient Drama** in the theater at Epidauros takes place from mid-July to mid-September, Saturday and Sunday only, at 9 PM. Tickets can be bought either at the theater itself before performances, or in advance from the festival box office at Stadious 4, Athens, tel. 01/322-3111.

Mainland Greece

A rugged land of eagles and ancient gods, mainland Greece has many ranges of high, barren mountains enclosing narrow, wooded valleys. The massive Pindus range in the west and rocky Mount Olympus in the east have snowcapped peaks for much of the year. Mount Parnassus and nearby Elikon, sacred to Apollo and the Muses, rise in the south. Mount Pelion, near the eastern coast, looms over nearby Ossa.

The dramatic rocky heights of Greece provide an appropriate setting for man's attempt to approach divinity. The ancient Greeks placed their gods on Mount Olympus and chose the precipitous slopes of Parnassus, "the navel of the universe," as the site for Delphi, the most important religious center of the ancient world. Many centuries later, pious Christians built a great monastery (Ossios Loukas) in a remote mountain valley. Others settled on the rocky mountain peninsula of Athos, the Holy Mountain. Later, devout men escaping from Turkish persecution established themselves precariously on top of strange, towerlike rocks and built monasteries, such as those at Meteora. In fact, all of mainland Greece's most memorable sights are closely connected with religion—including the remarkable Byzantine churches of Thessaloniki. Of course, there are remains of palaces and cities, but these do not have the impact of the great religious centers.

In this land of lonely mountain villages, narrow defiles, and dark woods, bands of *klephts* (a cross between brigands and guerrillas) earned their place in folk history and song during the long centuries of Turkish rule. The women of Souli, one of the mountain strongholds of the klephts, threw themselves dancing and singing over a cliff rather than be captured by the Turks. In these same mountains during the German occupation of Greece in World War II, guerrilla bands descended to the valleys and plains to assault the occupying army and drive it from their land.

Now the land is peaceful again and the villages, tucked away in the hills, seem almost asleep, their shops and their tavernas as they have been for 100 years. This is a beautiful area to explore; the mainland Greeks see fewer tourists and have more time for those they do see, hotels are unlikely to be full, and the sights —steep, wooded mountains, cypress trees like candles, narrow gorges, the soaring monasteries of Meteora—are beautiful.

Getting Around

This proposed itinerary begins in Athens. It can be done by public transportation, by car, or by guided tour. A one-day trip to Delphi is rushed; two days will give you more leisure time. Your best bet is a three-day trip that includes Delphi and Meteora. A longer trip through the Peloponnese should include Ossios Lukas. Thessaloniki is usually included only in lengthy guided tours of northern Greece. If you don't have a car, you can leave the Delphi-Meteora tour at Trikala, take the train to Thessaloniki, and return to Athens by plane or train. You can also take a guided tour of northern Greece and leave the group at Thessaloniki. In September, during the Thessaloniki International Trade Fair, there are no hotel rooms to be had; make reservations well in advance.

Guided Tours

Travel agencies in Athens with tours of mainland Greece include **American Express** (Syntagma Sq. and in the Hilton Hotel), **Wagons-Lits Travel** (Karageorgi Servias 2), **Key Tours** (Ermou 2), and **Viking Tours** (Filellinon 3). A one-day tour to

Delphi, with lunch, will cost around 3,500 dr. Other, lengthier tours will cost considerably more.

Tourist Information

In **Delphi,** visit the New Delphi Tourist Office on Frederikis, open daily 9–7 (tel. 0265/82–900); the Tourist Police is at Pavlou and Frederikis 25. At **Kalambaka,** the Tourist Police can be found at Rammidi 33. In **Thessaloniki,** visit the Greek National Tourist Organization (Platia Aristotelous 8, tel. 031/271–888); here, the Tourist Police is at Egnatia 10.

Exploring Mainland Greece

To get from Athens to Delphi, take the National Road toward Thessaloniki and turn off to **Thebes** (Thiva), the birthplace of the legendary Oedipus, who unwittingly fulfilled the prophesy of the Delphic Oracle by slaying his father and marrying his mother. Little now remains of the ancient city. At **Livadia,** 45 kilometers (28 miles) farther along the road, the ruins of a medieval fortress tower above the springs of Lethe (Oblivion) and Mnemosyne (Remembrance). Halfway between Livadia and Delphi is the crossroads where, according to mythology, Oedipus killed his father.

The road to the left leads to a serene upland valley and the **Monastery of Ossios Loukas**, a fine example of Byzantine architecture and decoration. Built in the 11th century to replace the earlier shrine of a local saint, it has some of the world's finest Byzantine mosaics. *Tel. 0265/321–3571. Admission: 300 dr. Open Mon. and Wed.–Sat. 8:45–3, Sun. and holidays 9:30–2:30.*

Back on the road to Delphi, you climb a spur of Mount Parnassus to the village of **Arahova**, 38 kilometers (23 miles) from Livadia, known for its brightly colored woolen handicrafts, especially rugs. From Arahova, a short, spectacular drive down to Delphi crosses the gorge of the Pleistos. You'll see a great cliff called Phaedriades and a deep, narrow chasm, at the bottom of which the **Castalian spring** gushes with cool, pure water. It was here that pilgrims to the Delphic Oracle came for purification.

The ancient Greeks believed that **Delphi** was the center of the universe because two eagles released by the gods at opposite ends of earth met here. For hundreds of years, the worship of Apollo and the pronouncements of the Oracle here made Delphi the most important religious center of the ancient world. As you walk up the Sacred Way to the **Temple of Apollo,** the **theater,** and the **stadium** that comprise the **Sanctuary of Apollo,** you have Mount Parnassus above, silver-green olive trees below, and, in the distance, the blue gulf of Itea. This is one of the most rugged and lonely sites in Greece, and one of the most striking; if you can get to the site in the early morning or evening, avoiding the busloads of tourists, you will feel the power and beauty of the place. You may even see an eagle or two. First excavated in 1892, most of the ruins date from the 5th to the 3rd centuries BC. *Admission (includes Delphi museum): 400 dr. Open Apr.–Oct., Mon.–Sat. 8–7, Sun. and holidays 8–6; Nov.–Mar., daily 8–5.*

Mainland Greece

Don't miss the famous bronze charioteer (early 5th century BC) in the **Delphi Museum.** Other interesting and beautiful works of art here include the column of the dancers (or Caryatids), 4th century BC; a statue of Antinous, Emperor Hadrian's lover; and the stone representing the naval of the earth. *Tel. 0265/82–313. Admission: joint ticket 400 dr. Open Apr.–Oct., Mon, and Wed.–Sat. 8–7, Sun. and holidays 8–6; Nov.–Mar., daily 8–5.*

From Delphi, the road descends in sharp bends past groves of gnarled, ancient olive trees. Continue 23 kilometers (14 miles) to Amphissa and over the Pourmaraki (Bralos) Pass to the town of Lamia. Follow the road to Karditsa and around the Thessalian plain to Trikala. You will then arrive at **Kalambaka,** the base for visits to the monasteries of **Meteora,** which sit atop gigantic rocks above the town. Monks and supplies once reached the top of the slopes by ladders or nets. Today steps are cut in the boulders, and some of the monasteries can be reached easily by car now. Not all of them are open to the public, however.

One of the more accessible monasteries, **Aghios Stephanon,** has a notable church. The fortresslike **Aghios Varlaam** monastery is also easy to reach. To get a better idea of what living in these monasteries was like 300 years ago, climb the steep rock steps to the **Great Meteoron,** the largest of the rocks. The monasteries are all closed during midday. The hours vary from place to place but they are generally open 9–1 and 3–6, although to complicate matters the Stephanon is closed on Monday, Varlaam on Friday, and Great Meteoron on Tuesday. Admission free.

Leaving Kalambaka for Thessaloniki, you find the road crosses the plain of Thessaly, one of Europe's hottest places in summer, and joins the National Road at Larissa. Ahead you will see Mount Olympus, Greece's highest mountain. The road runs for 154 kilometers (96 miles) through the valley of Tempe and then on up the coast to **Thessaloniki,** the birthplace of Aristotle. This is Greece's second-largest city, its second port after Piraeus, capital of Northern Greece and cocapital of the country as a whole, and as a shopping center, it is possibly superior to Athens.

Although Thessaloniki still has some remains from the Roman period, the city is best known for its fine Byzantine churches. The city is compact enough for you to see the main sights on foot. Start at the 15th-century grayish **White Tower,** landmark and symbol of Thessaloniki, previously named "Tower of Blood," referring to its use as a prison. Now it houses a museum, with an exhibition on the history and art of Byzantine Thessaloniki, including pottery, mosaics, and ecclesiastical objects. *Tel. 031/267–832. Admission: 350 dr. Open Wed.–Mon. 2:45–9.*

Then walk up Davlou Mela toward Tsimiski, the elegant tree-lined shopping street, and cut across to the green-domed basilica-style church of **Aghia Sophia,** which dates from the 8th century and has beautifully preserved mosaics.

Walk up Egnatia, which traces the original Roman road leading from the Adriatic to the Bosporous. You will pass the **Roman Agora** (town center) and come to **Agios Dimitrios,** the principal church. Though it is only a replica of the original church that burned down in 1917, it is adorned with many 8th-century mosaics that were in the original building. Follow Aghiou Dimitriou to **Agios Georgios,** a rotunda built by Roman Emperor Galerius as his tomb in the 4th century AD. His successor, Constantine the Great, the first Christian emperor, turned it into a church. Particularly interesting are its 4th-century mosaics of Roman buildings.

Return to Egnatia and the **Arch of the Emperor Galerius,** built shortly prior to the rotunda to commemorate the Roman victories of Emperor Galerius over forces in Persia, Armenia, and Asia Minor. A short walk downhill toward the sea wall will bring you to the **Archaeological Museum.** Among its many beautiful objects are a huge bronze vase and a delicate, gold myrtle wreath from Deryeni and gold artifacts from recent excavations of the royal tombs of Vergina, including an 11-kilogram gold casket standing on lions' feet, containing bones thought to be those of Philip II, father of Alexander the Great. *Tel. 031/830–583. Admission: 400 dr. Open Apr.–Oct., Mon. and Wed.–Sat. 8–7, Sun. and holidays 8–6; Nov.–Mar., Wed.–Mon. 8–5.*

Dining and Lodging

For details and price category definitions, *see* Dining and Lodging in Staying in Greece.

Delphi
Dining

Taverna Pan. Decorated with local folk art and weavings, this taverna offers fixed-price meals as well as à la carte Greek specialties. *Isaia St., tel. 0265/82–473. Reservations not necessary. No credit cards. Inexpensive.*

Lodging **Vouzas.** The hotel sits on the edge of a gorge and has wonderful
★ views from every room. Friendly service may or may not compensate for the lack of air-conditioning. *Vas. Pavlou and Frederikis 1, tel. 0265/822–324. 58 rooms with bath. Facilities: restaurant. AE, DC, V. Expensive.*

Hermés. This small hotel is built on a hillside on a quiet part of the main street. It is perfectly adequate for a night's sleep and has good views from its top-story bedrooms. The lobby is decorated with local weavings. *Vas. Pavlou and Frederikis 29, tel. 0265/82–318. 24 rooms with bath. No credit cards. Closed Nov. –Feb. Inexpensive.*

Kalambaka **Planotos Taverna.** A great place for people watching, this
Dining taverna has a flower-covered archway entrance and a large patio overlooking the main square, serves simple meals of broiled meats and fresh vegetables. *Central Square, no telephone. Reservations not necessary. No credit cards. Inexpensive.*

Lodging **Motel Divani.** Below the Meteora is a hotel (in spite of its name)
★ that is more comfortable than you might expect to find so far off the beaten path. *Tel. 0432/22–5834. 165 rooms with bath. Facilities: restaurant, outdoor pool. AE, DC, MC, V. Expensive.*

Xenia. Looking across to the great rocks, this is a small, pleasant hotel, adequate for an overnight stay. Half-board is required. *Tel. 0432/22–327. 22 rooms with bath. Facilities: restaurant. No credit cards. Closed Nov.–Mar. Moderate.*

Thessaloniki **Cyprus Corner.** It is well worth making the trip outside town to
Dining this popular restaurant in the hilltop suburb of Panorama. Pink tablecloths, waiters in black tie, and a piano-and-sax duo lend an elegant and sophisticated air. A good variety of dishes— classical and Greek cuisine—is served with style and flair. *Komninon 16, Panorama, tel. 031/941–220. Reservations advised. DC, MC, V. Expensive.*

Ta Nissia. This very bright, clean restaurant, with tiled floor and wooden tables, is excellent for fresh seafood, especially mussels. The *mezedes* (hors d'oeuvres) are particularly unusual and tasty. *Koromila 13, tel. 031/285–991. Reservations advised. DC. Dinner only. Moderate.*

Lodging **Makedonia Palace.** This large, stylish hotel is beautifully positioned at the edge of a bay in a new residential section on reclaimed land, but it seems to be in the middle of nowhere; it is several kilometers into the center of town. Generally, this is a comfortable, luxurious hotel with all amenities, but totally lacking in charm. Ask for rooms overlooking the bay. *Megalou Alexandrou, tel. 031/837–521/9. 287 rooms with bath. Facilities: several restaurants, roof garden. AE, DC, MC, V. Very Expensive.*

★ **Elektra Palace.** This rather shabby but comfortable hotel is built in a neo-Byzantine style to match the other buildings on the square. It's conveniently located in the center of town. *Platia Aristotelous 5, tel. 031/23–221/30. 131 rooms with bath. Facilities: restaurant. AE, DC, MC, V. Expensive.*

Capsis. Near the railroad station, this is the largest hotel in Thessaloniki, popular with tour groups. The area around the station is very noisy and the lounge of the hotel can, on a busy day, be too much like the station itself, with all the comings and goings of tour groups. Otherwise, this hotel has all the expected facilities. *Monastiriou 28 and Prometheos, tel. 031/265– 421. 428 rooms with bath. Facilities: restaurant, roof garden with pool, disco, air-conditioning. AE, DC, MC, V. Moderate.*

The Greek Islands

The islands of the Aegean have colorful legends of their own—
the Minotaur in Crete; the lost continent of Atlantis, which
some believe was Santorini; and the Colossus of Rhodes, to
name a few. Each island has its own personality. Mykono has
windmills, dazzling whitewashed buildings, hundreds of tiny
churches and chapels on golden hillsides, and small fishing harbors. Visitors to volcanic Santorini sail into what was once a
vast volcanic crater and anchor near the island's forbidding
cliffs. Crete, with its jagged mountain peaks, olive orchards,
and vineyards, has the remains of the Minoan civilization. In
Rhodes, a bustling modern town surrounds a walled town with
a medieval castle.

Getting Around

The simplest way to visit the Aegean Islands is on a cruise,
lasting from one to 10 days. Visitors should consider a three-
day cruise, to the four most popular islands—Mykonos,
Rhodes, Crete, and Santorini. Car and passenger ferries sail to
these main destinations from Piraeus, the port of Athens.
There is also frequent air service from Athens. In summer, it's
important to book services well in advance. (*See* also Getting
Around By Boat at the beginning of this chapter.)

Guided Tours

Aegean Cruises From April through October there are many cruises to the
Greek Islands from Piraeus. Blue Aegean Sea Line, Cycladic
Cruises, Epirotiki, Hellenic Cruises, Hellenic Mediterranean,
K Lines, Oceanic Sun Line, and Saronic Cruises all offer one-
to-seven-day cruises. Contact **K Lines-Hellenic Cruises:** in the
United States, Olympic Tower, 645 Fifth Ave., New York, NY
10022, tel. 212/751-2435; in the United Kingdom, 50 Pall Mall,
London SW1, tel. 01/930-7610.

Tourist Information

There are **Greek National Tourist Organization** offices on **Crete,**
at Kriari 40, Hania (tel. 0821/26-426) and at Xanthoudidou 1,
Iraklio (tel. 081/222-487); on **Rhodes,** at Archbishop Makarios
and Papagou 5, Rhodes (tel. 0241/23-655).

Exploring the Greek Islands

Cruise ships and car ferries to Mykonos leave from Piraeus, the
port of Athens. As you sail to Mykonos, you will be able to see
one of the great sights of Greece: the Temple of Poseidon looming on a hilltop at the edge of Cape Sounion, about two hours
from shore.

Mykonos is the name of the island and also of its chief village—a
colorful place with narrow, paved streets lined with whitewashed houses, many with bright blue doors and shutters. Every morning, women scrub the sidewalks and streets in front of
their homes, undaunted by the many donkeys that pass by each
day. In the 1960s, the bohemian jet set discovered Mykonos and
most of the old houses along the waterfront are now restau-

The Greek Islands

rants, nightclubs, bars, and discos, all blaring loud music until the early morning; a quiet café or taverna is hard to find. Incidentally, although the jet set has moved on to other, more deserted retreats, the island is still *the* holiday destination for the young, lively, and liberated. Mykonos is, however, blessed with enough sandy beaches and tiny coves, ideal for swimming and snorkeling, to allow you to find your own quiet spot.

A half-hour by boat from Mykonos and its 20th-century holiday pleasures is the ancient isle of **Delos,** the legendary sanctuary of Apollo. Its **Terrace of the Lions,** a remarkable group of five large sculptures from the 7th century BC, is a must. Worth seeing, too, are some of the houses of the Roman period, with their fine floor mosaics. The best of these mosaics are in a museum, the **House of Dionysos.** *Tel. 0289/22–259. Admission: 500 dr. Open Mon. and Wed.–Sat. 8:45–3, Sun. and holidays 9:30–2:30.*

The large island of **Rhodes,** southeast of Mykonos, is 11.2 kilometers (7 miles) off the coast of Turkey. The northern end of the island is one of Greece's major vacation centers, and Rhodes town is full of the trappings of tourism, mainly evident in the pubs and bars catering to the large Western European market. The island as a whole is not particularly beautiful—most of the pine and cedar woods that covered its hilly center were destroyed by fire in 1987 and 1988. But it has fine beaches and an excellent climate. The town of Rhodes has an attractive harbor with fortifications; the gigantic bronze statue of the Colossus of Rhodes is supposed to have straddled the entrance. The old walled city, near the harbor, was built by crusaders, the

Knights Hospitaller of St. John, who ruled the island from 1310 until they were defeated by the Turks in 1522. Within its fine medieval walls, on the Street of the Knights, stands the **Knights' Hospital,** now a museum. *Tel. 0241/27–657. Admission: 300 dr. Open Apr.–Oct., Mon. and Wed.–Sat. 8–7, Sun. and holidays 8–6. Nov.–Mar., Mon. and Wed.–Sun. 8–5.*

Another museum that deserves your attention is the restored and moated medieval **Palace of the Grand Masters.** It is especially noted for its splendid Roman and early Christian floor mosaics. *Tel. 0241/27–657. Admission: 300 dr. Open Apr.–Oct., Mon. and Wed.–Sat. 8–7, Sun. and holidays 8–6. Nov.–Mar., Mon. and Wed.–Sun. 8–5.*

To get the best overall view of the walled city, including the surviving Turkish buildings, go to one of the flower-filled parks that surround it. Try to see the Son et Lumière (sound and light show)—English-language performances are held on Sunday evening.

Many attractive souvenir and handicraft shops in the old town sell decorative Rhodian pottery, local embroidery, and relatively inexpensive jewelry.

From the town of Rhodes, drive about 56 kilometers (35 miles) down the east coast to the enchanting village of **Lindos.** Take a donkey from the village center and ride, or put on your comfortable shoes and walk, up the steep hill to the ruins of the ancient **Acropolis of Lindos,** circled by a medieval castle. The sight of its beautiful colonnade with the sea far below is unforgettable. Look for little St. Paul's Harbor, far below the cliffs of the acropolis; seen from above it appears to be a lake, as the tiny entrance from the sea is obscured by the rocks. *Tel. 0241/27–674. Admission: 400 dr. Open Apr.–Oct., Mon.–Sat. 8–7, Sun. and holidays 8–6; Nov.–Mar., daily 8–5.*

Rhodes is also a good base for visiting other islands of the Dodecanese, the 12 islands near the Turkish coast, with their mixture of Aegean and Turkish architecture.

Crete, situated in the south Aegean and Greece's largest island, was the center of Europe's earliest civilization, the Minoan, which flourished from about 2000 BC to 1200 BC. It was struck a mortal blow by a devastating volcanic eruption on the neighboring island of Santorini (Thera) in about 1450 BC.

The most important Minoan remains are to be seen in the **Archaeological Museum of Heraklion** in Iraklio, Crete's largest city. The museum houses many Minoan treasures, including some highly sophisticated frescoes and elegant ceramics depicting Minoan life. *Xanthoudidou St., tel. 081/226–092. Admission: 500 dr. Open Apr.–Oct., Tues.–Sat. 8–7, Sun. and holidays 8–6; Nov.–Mar., Tues.–Sun. 8–5.*

Not far from Iraklio is the partly reconstructed **Palace of Knossos,** which will also give you a feeling for the Minoan world. Note the simple throne room, which contains the oldest throne in Europe, and the bathrooms with their efficient plumbing. The palace was the setting for the legend of the Minotaur, a monstrous offspring of Queen Pasiphae and a bull confined to the Labyrinth under the palace. *Tel. 081/231–940. Admission: 500 dr. Open Apr.–Oct., Mon.–Sat. 8–7, Sun. and holidays 8–6; Nov.–Mar., daily 8–5.*

Crete belonged to Venice from 1210 to 1669, at which time it was conquered by the Turks. The island did not become part of Greece until early in this century. The **Venetian ramparts** that withstood a 24-year Turkish siege still surround Iraklio. In addition to archaeological treasures, Crete can boast beautiful mountain scenery and a large number of beach resorts along the north coast. The most attractive is **Mallia**, which contains the remains of another Minoan palace. Two other beach resorts, **Agios Nikolaos** and the nearby **Elounda**, are east of Iraklio. The south coast offers good, quieter beaches for getting away from it all.

The best way to approach **Santorini** is to sail into its harbor, once the vast crater of its volcano, and dock beneath its black and red cliffs. In some parts, the cliffs rise nearly 310 meters (1,000 feet) above the sea. The play of light across them can produce strange color effects. The white houses and churches of the main town, Thira, cling to the rim in dazzling white contrast to the somber cliffs.

Most passenger ferries now use the new port, Athinos, where visitors are met by buses, taxis, and a gaggle of small-hotel owners hawking rooms. The bus ride into Thira takes about half an hour, and from there you can make connections to other towns on the island. Despite being packed with visitors in the summer, the tiny town is charming, with spectacular views. It has the usual souvenir and handicrafts shops and several reasonably priced jewelry shops. Be sure to try the local white wine—the volcanic soil gives it a light, distinctive taste.

The island's volcano erupted in the 15th century BC, destroying its Minoan civilization. At **Acrotiri**, on the southern end of Santorini, the remains of a Minoan city buried by lava were recently excavated. The site, believed by some to be part of the legendary Atlantis, is open to the public. *Tel. 0286/81–366. Admission: 500 dr. Open Apr.–Oct., Mon.–Sat. 8–7, Sun. and holidays 9:30–2:30; Nov.–Mar., Mon.–Sat. 8:45–3, Sun. and holidays 9:30–2:30.*

For an enjoyable but slightly unnerving excursion, take the short boat trip to the island's still active small offshore volcanoes called the **Kamenes** or Burnt Islands. You can descend into a small crater, hot and smelling of sulfur, and swim in the nearby water that has been warmed by the volcano.

Dining and Lodging

For details and price category definitions, *see* Dining and Lodging in Staying in Greece.

Crete Iraklio has many moderately priced open-air restaurants in the
Dining central area around Platia Venizelou and Platia Paedalou. The island is known for its fine local wine, fresh seafood, and fresh local produce, which is available year-round.
Minos Taverna. This is one of the many outdoor restaurants near the Venetian fountain. Lamb, fresh seafood, and yogurt dishes make this one of the island's most popular restaurants. Service is prompt and attentive. *10 Daedelou St., tel. 081/281–263. Reservations not necessary. No credit cards. Moderate.*

Lodging **Taverna Faros.** This is an excellent, inexpensive choice for a Greek fish supper, near the new port in Iraklio. The distinct fisherman's ambience is created by fishnet drapes, conch shells, and razor clams on the walls. *Tel. 081/423–233. Reservations not necessary. No credit cards. Inexpensive.*

Elounda Beach. Located 3 miles north of Agios Nicolaos, this is probably the best seaside resort complex on Crete. It is spacious, attractive, and spotlessly maintained. It's set in beautiful grounds—the pool is cleverly landscaped among carob trees—and has a private beach. *Tel. 0841/41–412/3. 301 rooms with bath. Facilities: restaurants, outdoor pool, miniature golf, tennis, nightclub. AE. Closed Nov.–Mar. Very Expensive.*

Irakos Village. This hotel complex, near Mallia on Crete's north coast, was created by a German company and fits the image of a typical Greek village. It's on the beach, about 32 kilometers (20 miles) east of Iraklio, and near the ruins of a Minoan palace. *Malia Pediados, tel. 0897/31–267/9. 179 rooms with bath. Facilities: restaurant, outdoor pool, tennis, private beach. AE. Closed Nov.–Mar. Expensive.*

★ **Mediterranean.** This is another comfortable hotel in the center of Iraklio and 4.8 kilometers (3 miles) from the beach. It's priced at the top of its category. *Smyrnis 1, tel. 081/228–003. 55 rooms with bath. Facilities: restaurant, roof garden, air-conditioning. AE, MC, V. Moderate.*

Mykonos
Dining

Nikos Taverna. This large restaurant near the port offers a wide selection of Greek and international dishes. The food is usually good. *Harborfront, no telephone. Reservations not necessary. AE, MC, V. Expensive.*

Philippi. A favorite with locals as well as tourists, this is where you can enjoy Continental cuisine and curries outdoors among the olive trees, beneath whitewashed walls, or in the elegant dining room. *Kalogeras St., tel. 0289/22–294. Reservations advised. AE, MC, V. Dinner only. Expensive.*

Lodging
★

Cavo Tagoo. Within walking distance of the center of town, this small, charming hotel sits above a beach. It has an attractively designed saltwater pool in the garden and is well worth the high rates. *Tagoo Beach, tel. 0289/23–692/4. 24 rooms with bath. Facilities: restaurant, outdoor pool. AE, MC, V. Closed Nov.–Mar. Expensive.*

Mykonos Beach. This is a charming group of bungalows on the edge of town, with superb views over the beach. *Kiklades St., tel. 0289/22–572/3. 27 bungalows. Facilities: nightclub. AE, MC, V. Closed Nov.–Mar. Moderate.*

Rhodes
Dining

Casa Castelana. Set in a 15th-century Inn of the Knights, this restaurant has a wonderful medieval atmosphere indoors; outdoors, there's an elegant but comfortable garden area for dining. The food is unusual and delicious, featuring a combination of Rhodian specialties and non-Greek dishes, including *trahanas*, an island village soup, and *stifado*, a pot-au-feu-style lamb dish. *Aristotelous 35, tel. 0241/28–803. Reservations advised. AE, DC, V. Expensive.*

The Plaka Taverna. This restaurant on the first floor, overlooking the fountain in the square, offers one of the prettiest settings in the town. The specialty here is fresh seafood, grilled or fried to order; the red mullet is particularly tasty. *Ippocratous Sq., tel. 0241/22–477. Reservations not necessary. AE, DC. Expensive.*

Kabo n' Toro Taverna. You can't go wrong at this tiny restaurant, which is one of the best in the town of Rhodes and possibly on the entire island. *Omilou and Parado Sts., tel. 0241/36–182. Reservations not necessary. No credit cards. Moderate.*

Lodging **Grand Hotel Astir Palace.** This beachfront establishment in Rhodes town has one of Greece's three casinos, as well as two restaurants and cocktail bars, an English-style pub, and the Isabella nightclub. Although the beach is ordinary, the situation is a great asset. Some rooms with verandas face the gardens and pools; others, slightly more expensive, face the sea. *Vass. Konstantinou St., tel. 0241/26–284/9. 378 rooms with bath. Facilities: restaurants, 1 indoor and 2 outdoor pools, private beach, tennis, casino. AE, DC, MC, V. Very Expensive.*

Steps of Lindos. This hotel, 4.8 kilometers (3 miles) out of the village of Lindos, is built on a sloping hillside above a long, good beach. The steps—and there are lots of them—link the white-washed buildings to the pool and beach. The service is friendly and efficient and food is plentiful, although variable. *Vlyha Lindos, tel. 0244/24–371/2. 156 rooms with bath. Facilities: restaurant, outdoor pool, tennis, beach. AE. Closed Nov.–Mar. Expensive.*

Spartalis. Many rooms have balconies overlooking the bay in this simple but lively hotel near the city's port. It does not have a restaurant. *Plastira 2, tel. 0241/24–371/2. 70 rooms with bath. AE, DC, MC. Moderate.*

Santorini **Camille Stefani.** This is one of the island's best restaurants,
Dining where you can enjoy seafood, Greek and Continental cuisine, and the local wines. A taste of the mellow Santorini Lava red wine, a product of the volcanic ash, is a must! *Main St., Thira, tel. 0286/22–265. Reservations advised. AE, MC, V. Moderate.*

Lodging **Atlantis.** Located in the main village, this is the island's best hotel. It has a magnificent view. *Thera, tel. 0286/22–232. 27 rooms with bath. Facilities: restaurant. AE, DC, MC, V. Closed Nov.–Mar. Expensive.*

Kamari Hotel. This pleasant resort hotel is on a black-sand beach on the side away from the cliffs. *Tel. 0286/312–1243. 55 rooms with bath. Facilities: restaurant, roof garden, outdoor pool, tennis, disco. AE, DC, MC, V. Closed Nov.–Mar. Moderate.*

15 Holland

Introduction

The tourist posters of Holland feature windmills, tulips, canals, and girls wearing lacy caps and clogs. All these picturesque images are to be found, certainly, but there is more to this tiny country than just these clichés.

Holland, known widely and more correctly as The Netherlands, is one of Europe's smallest countries. It has a population of around 14 million, occupying a land area that is less than half the size of Maine—40,145 square kilometers (15,500 square miles), almost half of which has been reclaimed by the industrious Dutch from the North Sea. The nation's history has been dominated by continuous resistance to two forces of invasion: the sea and successive foreign armies. Over the centuries, the Romans, Franks, Burgundians, Austrians, Spanish, English, French, and Germans have all tried to win and hold Holland, but none have succeeded for long. These endless struggles against nature and enemies have made the Dutch into a determined and independent nation, yet a remarkably tolerant one, often at the forefront of many liberal social reforms and attitudes. Religious and political freedom are an essential part of Dutch life.

Holland's eventful history and the great cultural energy of its people have created an abundance of ancient towns and buildings and filled its many museums with great works of art. The Dutch revere their past and have gone to great lengths to preserve their heritage. They have sensitively converted many of the gabled houses into hotels, restaurants, and exhibition halls. They also have a progressive approach to the creation of new design and architecture, as well as to the development of efficient services, railroads, roads, and excellent amenities for the traveler. Amsterdam's ancient Nieuwe Kerk, both a church and a cultural center, embodies the Dutch spirit of practicality and social responsibility.

This venture is also a sign of Amsterdam's cultural prominence. The city is now as famous for its jazz, modern art, and ballet as it is for its magnificent Rembrandts and van Goghs. Holland's most misunderstood painter, van Gogh, has a posthumous chance to put the record straight in 1990: The centennial of his death is marked by exhibitions of his work all over Holland. His genius, both tormented and celebratory, can be seen in exhibitions in Amsterdam, Dordrecht, Groningen, Rotterdam, and Den Haag (The Hague). The Hague, sedate and refined, presents a contrast to Amsterdam's vitality and progressiveness. Diplomacy and ceremony color the lives of all residents, from Queen Beatrix, ambassadors, and parliamentarians downward. Even the local herring seller will have a view on the role of the monarchy, probably favorable.

Speaking of herrings, traditional Dutch seafood can be found side by side with exotic Indonesian dishes from the former Dutch colonies. In landscape as in food, Holland is not as flat as it seems. Certainly low-lying Zeeland lives with the sea and on the sea—its oysters and mussels are world famous. But versatile northern Holland is not restricted to sand dunes and melancholy seascapes. Just inland from Bergen-aan-Zee, deep woods and moorland encircle the artists' village of Bergen. In

Holland

North Sea

Schiermonnikoog

Ameland

Terschelling

Delfzijl

Dokkum

Groningen

Winschoten

Vlieland

Leeuwarden

Franeker

Assen

Emmen

Harlingen

Sneek

Bolsward

Waddenzee

Heerenveen

Hoogeveen

Texel

Meppel

Den Helder

Ijsselmeer

Zwolle

Almelo

Alkmaar

Hoorn

Enschede

Zaanstad

Amsterdam

Apeldoorn

Winterswijk

Haarlem

Amersfoort

Arnhem

Doetinchem

Utrecht

WEST GERMANY

Leiden

Nijmegen

Rhine

The Hague (Den Haag)

R. Tiel

Delft

Rijn

Rotterdam

Oss

Waal

's Hertogenbosch

Dordrecht

Maas

Veghel

Haringvliet

Breda

Grevelingen

Overflakkee

Tilburg

Eindhoven

Schouwen/Duiveland

Steenbergen

Weert

Roermond

Oosterschelde

Tholen

Bergen op Zoom

Goes

Walcheren

Beveland

Sittard

Middelburg

Schelde

Wester Schelde

Terneuzen

Breskens

Maastricht

Vaals

BELGIUM

| 0 | | 50 miles |
| 0 | | 75 km |

southern Holland, bulb fields and windmills abound but so do nature reserves, inland lakes, lush lowland, and rolling hills.

The Dutch themselves reflect a number of contrasts. They are hospitable to visiting strangers, yet fiercely independent if their values are challenged by outsiders. They are dedicated to democracy, yet enjoy being one of the world's few remaining popular monarchies. Their ideals of social behavior are, perhaps, best described by their own two words *deftig* (dignified, respectable, and decorous) and *gezellig* (cozy, comfortable, and enjoying oneself).

Before You Go

When to Go The prime tourist season in Holland runs from mid-April through mid-October and peaks during school vacation periods (Easter, July, and August), when hotels may impose a 20% surcharge. Dutch bulb fields bloom from early April to mid-May— not surprisingly, the hotels tend to fill up then, too. June is the ideal time to catch the warm weather and miss the crowds, but every region of the Netherlands has its season. Delft is luminous after a winter storm, and fall in the Utrecht countryside can be as dramatic as in New England.

Climate Summers are generally warm, but beware of sudden rains and sharp coastal winds. Winters are cold and wet but are not without clear days. After a cloudburst, notice the watery quality of light that inspired Vermeer and other great Dutch painters.

The following are the average daily maximum and minimum temperatures for Amsterdam.

Jan.	40F	4C	May	61F	16C	Sept.	65F	18C
	34	1		50	10		56	13
Feb.	41F	5C	June	65F	18C	Oct.	56F	13C
	34	1		56	13		49	9
Mar.	47F	8C	July	70F	21C	Nov.	47F	8C
	38	3		59	15		41	5
Apr.	52F	11C	Aug.	68F	20C	Dec.	41F	5C
	43	6		59	15		36	2

Currency The unit of currency in Holland is the *guilder* (or florin), written as Fl., which is divided into 100 cents. Bills are in denominations of 1,000, 250, 100, 50, 25, 10, and 5 guilders. Coins are 2.5 and 1 guilder and 25, 10, and 5 cents. Be careful not to confuse the 2.5 and 1 guilder coins. Bills have a code of raised dots that can be identified by touch; this is for the blind.

At press time (spring 1989), the exchange rate for the guilder was Fl. 1.95 to the U.S. dollar and Fl. 3.54 to the pound sterling.

Most major credit cards are accepted in hotels, restaurants, and shops, but check first; not all establishments accept all cards.

What It Will Cost Holland is a prosperous country with a high standard of living, so overall costs are similar to those in other northern European countries. Prices for hotels and other services in major cities are 10%–20% above those in rural areas. Amsterdam and The Hague are the most expensive. Hotel and restaurant service charges and the 18.5% value-added tax (VAT) are usually included in the prices quoted.

The cost of eating varies widely in Holland, from a snack in a bar or a restaurant "tourist menu" at around Fl. 20 to the considerable expense of gourmet cuisine. A substantial breakfast is usually included in the overnight hotel price.

One cost advantage of Holland over other European countries is that, because it is so small, traveling around is inexpensive, especially if you use the many price-saving transportation deals available. The **Leisure Card,** for example, is a comprehensive discount card which provides significant reductions on rail travel, car rental, hotels, tours, entertainment, and shopping. Valid for a year, it costs Fl. 25, and is available from the Netherlands Board of Tourism (NBT) or main train stations and VVV offices.

Sample Prices Half a liter of wine, Fl. 12; bottle of beer, Fl. 2.50; cup of coffee, Fl. 2.50; cheese sandwich, Fl. 5; 1-mile taxi ride, Fl. 15.

Museums The **Museumkaart,** which can be purchased either from local information offices (VVV) or from museums, provides a year's free or reduced admission to 350 museums. It costs Fl. 30, or Fl. 15 if you're under 26. A photo and passport are required for purchase.

Customs on Arrival There are three levels of duty-free allowance for visitors to Holland. For travelers arriving from outside Europe the allowances are (1) 400 cigarettes or 100 cigars or 500 grams of tobacco, (2) one liter of spirits more than 22% by volume or two liters of alcohol less than 22% by volume or two liters of liqueur wine and two liters of wine, (3) 50 grams of perfume, (4) other goods to the value of Fl. 500.

For travelers arriving from a country that is not a member of the European Economic Community (EEC) or those coming from an EEC country who have bought goods in a duty-free shop, the allowances are (1) 200 cigarettes or 50 cigars or 100 cigarillos or 250 grams of tobacco, (2) one liter of alcohol more than 22% by volume or two liters of liqueur wine and two liters of wine, (3) 50 grams of perfume, (4) other goods to the value of Fl. 125.

For travelers arriving from an EEC country, the allowances for goods, provided they were not bought in a duty-free shop, are (1) 300 cigarettes or 75 cigars or 400 grams of tobacco; (2) 1½ liters of alcohol more than 22% by volume or three liters of alcohol less than 22% by volume or three liters of sparkling wine or three liters of liqueur wine and five liters of nonsparkling wine, (3) 75 grams of perfume and 37.5 centiliters of toilet water, (4) other goods to the value of Fl. 890.

All personal items are considered duty free, provided you take them with you when you leave Holland. Tobacco and alcohol allowances are for those 17 and older. There are no restrictions on the import and export of Dutch currency.

Language Dutch is a difficult language for foreigners, but luckily the Dutch are fine linguists, so almost everyone speaks at least some English, especially in larger cities and tourist centers.

Getting Around

By Car Holland has one of the best road systems in Europe, and even *Road Conditions* the longest trips between cities take only a few hours. Multilane expressways (toll-free) link major cities, but the smaller roads and country lanes provide more varied views of Holland. In towns, many of the streets are narrow, and you'll have to contend with complex one-way systems and cycle lanes.

Rules of the Road The speed limit on expressways is 120 kph (75 mph); on major roads it is 80 kph (50 mph); on city streets and in residential areas it is 50 kph (30 mph) or less, according to the signs. Driving is on the right, as in the United States.

Parking Parking in the larger towns is difficult and expensive, so consider parking on the outskirts of a town and using public transportation to get to the center.

Gasoline Gas, *benzin* in Dutch, costs around Fl. 1.55 per liter.

Breakdowns Experienced, uniformed mechanics of the **Wegenwacht** patrol the highways in yellow cars and will help if you have car trouble.

By Train Fast, frequent, and comfortable trains operate throughout the country. All trains have first- and second-class compartments, and many have buffet or dining-car services. Intercity trains run every 30 minutes and regular trains run at least once an hour to the smaller towns. Often one train contains two separate sections that divide during the trip, so be sure you are in the correct section for your destination.

Fares The best value in the Netherlands network (NS) is the **Rail Rover,** a ticket for unlimited train travel; you can buy one for one, three, or seven days, with no reductions for children. A second-class day pass costs Fl. 52.50; a three-day Rover costs Fl. 79.50; a seven-day Rover costs Fl. 115.50 (the three–day ticket may well be withdrawn in mid–1990). If you buy a Rail Rover, for a small extra charge you can also get a **Link Rover,** which is good for unlimited travel on all public transportation within the major cities. Your passport may be needed when you purchase Rover tickets.

If you are also traveling through Belgium and Luxembourg, the five-day **Benelux Tourrail** card is the best bet. It allows for unlimited travel and is valid for any five days within a period of 17 consecutive days. It costs Fl. 140, or Fl. 99 if you're under 26. **Dagtochtkaartjes** are special combined tickets covering train, boat, and bus trips, and an exhibition. Using the Leisure Card (*see* What it Will Cost) is another option. Ask about these fares at railway information bureaus or local tourist offices. **The Netherlands Board of Tourism's** (NBT) offices abroad have information on train services, as do overseas offices of Netherlands Railways (*see* Before You Go, Chapter 1).

By Plane KLM (Royal Dutch Airlines), under the banner of the NLM City Hopper, operates several domestic services connecting major cities. In this small country, however, it is probably as fast to travel by car or train.

By Bus Holland has an excellent bus network between and within towns. Bus excursions can be booked on the spot and at local VVV offices. In major cities, the best buy is a **strippenkaart** ticket (Fl. 8.85), which can be used for all bus, tram, and metro services. Each card has 15 strips, which are canceled by the driver as you enter the vehicle. More than one person can travel on a strippenkaart—it just gets used up more quickly. A strippenkaart with 45 strips is available for Fl. 25.35. You can buy a strippenkaart at train stations, post offices, and some

VVV offices. A one-day **dagkaart,** a travel-anywhere ticket, covers all urban bus/streetcar routes and costs Fl. 17.30. The NS train timetable also shows the areas served by the various bus companies. For details, write to **Streekvervoer ESO,** Postbus 19222, 3501 Utrecht.

By Bicycle Holland is a "cyclist-friendly" country with specially desig-nated cycle paths, signs, and picnic areas. Bikes can be rented in most cities and towns, often near train stations. Rental costs around Fl. 6.50 per day or from Fl. 28 per week, plus a deposit of Fl. 100–Fl. 200. Advice on rentals and routes is available at local VVV offices; cycling packages can be booked at the larger offices. For a brochure detailing more than 60 cycling routes, write to **NRTU** (Postbus 326, 3900AH Veendaal).

Staying in Holland

Telephones The telephone system in Holland is excellent and reliable. All
Local Calls towns and cities have area codes that are to be used only when you are calling from outside the area. Pay phones take 25¢ and Fl. 2.50 coins. Local calls cost 25¢.

International Calls Direct-dial international calls can be made from post offices and public booths (have plenty of coins ready). Read the instruc-tions in the phone booth carefully, as there are several different systems. Lower rates are charged from 6 PM to 8 AM weekdays, and from 6 PM Friday to 8 AM Monday. The average cost per min-ute to the U.S. is Fl. 4. Think twice about making international calls from your hotel room, because high service charges can tre-ble the cost.

Operators and Dial 0010 for international operators, all of whom speak En-
Information glish (this service is not available through coin-operated booths).

Mail The Dutch post office is as efficient as the telephone network.
Postal Rates Airmail letters to the United States cost Fl. 1.50 for the first 10 grams; postcards cost 75¢; aerograms cost Fl. 1. Airmail let-ters to the United Kingdom cost 75¢ for the first 20 grams; postcards cost 55¢; aerograms cost 60¢.

Receiving Mail If you're uncertain where you'll be staying, have mail sent to Poste Restante, GPO, in major cities along your route, or to American Express offices, where a small charge will be made on collection.

Shopping Purchases of many goods leaving Holland qualify for a value-
VAT Refunds added tax (VAT) refund of 18.5% which can be claimed at the airport or main border crossing when you leave, or by mail. Ask the salesperson for a VAT refund form when buying anything that may qualify.

Bargaining Prices are fixed in most shops, but you can try to bargain for items in any of the open-air markets.

Opening and **Banks.** Banks are open weekdays from 9 to 5. You can also
Closing Times change money at GWK bureaux de change, which are open Monday–Saturday 8–8, and Sunday 10–4. GWK offices in ma-jor cities or at border checkpoints are open 24 hours.

Museums. Most major museums now close on Monday, but not all, so check with local VVV offices. In rural areas, some muse-ums close or operate shorter hours during winter. Usual hours are 10–5.

Shops. In general, shops are open weekdays from 8:30 or 9 to 5:30 or 6, but some close for lunch. Department stores and most shops, especially in shopping plazas (in The Hague and Amsterdam) do not open until 1 PM on Monday, and many other shops close on Wednesday afternoon. Late-night shopping usually can be done until 9 PM Thursday or Friday.

National Holidays January 1 (New Year's Day); April 13, 16 (Easter); April 30 (Queen's Day; shops are open unless it falls on Sunday); May 5 (Liberation); May 24 (Ascension); June 4 (Pentecost Monday); December 24–26 (Christmas).

Dining Of the many earthly pleasures for the Dutch, eating probably heads the list. There is a wide variety of cuisines from traditional Dutch to Indonesian—the influence of the former Dutch colony.

Breakfasts tend to be hearty and substantial—several varieties of bread, butter, jam, ham, cheese, boiled eggs, and steaming coffee or tea. Dutch specialties for later meals include *erwtensoep*, a rich, thick pea soup with pieces of tangy sausage or pigs' knuckles, and *hutspot*, a meat, carrot, and potato stew; both are usually served in winter. *Haring* (herring) is particularly popular, especially the "new herring" caught between May and September and served in brine, garnished with onions. *Rodekool met rolpens* is red cabbage and rolled spiced meat with sliced apple. If Dutch food begins to pall, try an Indonesian restaurant, where the chief dish is *rijsttafel*, a huge bowl of steaming rice with 20 or more side dishes.

The indigenous Dutch liquor is potent and warming *jenever* (gin). Also popular are Dutch liqueurs and beers.

Eating places range from snack bars, fast-food outlets, and modest local cafés to gourmet restaurants of international repute. Of special note are the "brown cafés," traditional pub-style places of great character that normally offer substantial snack meals.

Mealtimes The Dutch tend to eat dinner early, normally around 6 or 7 PM, so many restaurants close at about 10 PM and accept last orders at 9. In larger cities some "foreign" restaurants stay open until midnight.

Dress Jacket and tie are suggested for restaurants in the Very Expensive and Expensive categories. Elsewhere, casual dress is acceptable. In general, Holland is a somewhat formal country, so when in doubt, it's better to dress up.

Ratings Prices are per person including two courses, dessert, service, and sales tax but not drinks. For budget travelers, many restaurants offer a tourist menu at an officially controlled price, currently Fl. 20. Best bets are indicated by a star ★. At press time (spring 1989), there were Fl. 1.95 to the dollar.

Category	Amsterdam	Other Areas
Very Expensive	over Fl. 130	over Fl. 100
Expensive	Fl. 100–Fl. 130	Fl. 80–Fl. 100
Moderate	Fl. 50–Fl. 100	Fl. 40–Fl. 80
Inexpensive	under Fl. 50	under Fl. 40

Credit Cards The following credit card abbreviations are used: AE, American Express; DC, Diners Club; MC, MasterCard; V, Visa.

Lodging Holland offers a wide range of accommodations, from the luxurious Golden Tulip hotel chain to traditional, small-town hotels and family-run guest houses. For young or adventurous travelers, the provinces abound with modest hostels, camping grounds, and rural bungalows. Budget travelers may prefer to stay in friendly bed-and-breakfast establishments; these are in short supply and need to be booked on the spot at local VVV offices.

Hotels Dutch hotels are generally spotless, no matter how modest their facilities, and service is normally courteous and efficient. There are many moderate and inexpensive hotels, most of which are relatively small. In the provinces, the range of accommodations is more limited, but there are pleasant, inexpensive family-run hotels that are usually centrally located and offer a friendly atmosphere. Most have good—if modest—dining facilities. English is spoken or understood by desk clerks almost everywhere. Hotels usually quote room prices for double occupancy, and rates include breakfast, service charges, and VAT.

To book hotels in advance, you can use the free **National Reservation Center,** (PO Box 404, 2260KA Leidschendam, tel. 070/202500). Alternatively, for a small fee, VVV offices can usually make reservations at short notice. Bookings must be made in person, however.

Ratings Prices are for two people sharing a double room. Best bets are indicated by a star ★. At press time (spring 1989), there were Fl. 1.95 to the dollar.

Category	Amsterdam	Other Areas
Very Expensive	Fl. 450–Fl. 600	over Fl. 350
Expensive	Fl. 300–Fl. 450	Fl. 250–Fl. 350
Moderate	Fl. 200–Fl. 300	Fl. 150–Fl. 250
Inexpensive	under Fl. 200	under Fl. 150

Credit Cards The following credit card abbreviations are used: AE, American Express; DC, Diners Club; MC, MasterCard; V, Visa.

Tipping Hotels and restaurants almost always include 15% service and VAT in their charges. Give a doorman 50¢ to Fl. 1 for calling a cab. Bellhops in first-class hotels should be tipped Fl. 1 for each bag they carry. The official minimum for porters in train stations is Fl. 2.50 a bag. Hat-check attendants expect at least 25¢, and washroom attendants get 50¢. Taxis in almost every town have a tip included in the meter charge, but you are expected to make up the fare to the nearest guilder nevertheless.

Amsterdam

Arriving and Departing

By Plane Most international flights arrive at Amsterdam's Schiphol Airport, one of Europe's finest. Immigration and customs formalities on arrival are relaxed, with no forms to be completed.

Between the Airport and Downtown The best transportation between the airport and the city center is the direct rail link, with three stops en route to the central station, where you can get a taxi or streetcar to your hotel. The train runs every 10 to 15 minutes throughout the day and takes about half an hour. Second-class fare is Fl. 4.40.

Taxis from the airport to central hotels cost about Fl. 50.

By Train The city has excellent rail connections with the rest of Europe. Fast services link it to Paris, Brussels, Luxembourg, and Cologne. The central station is conveniently located in the center of town.

Getting Around

By Bus, Streetcar, and Metro A zonal fare system is used. Tickets (starting at Fl. 1.95) are bought from automatic dispensers on the metro or from the drivers on streetcars and buses; or buy a money-saving **strippenkaart** (*see* Getting Around, By Bus). Even simpler is the one-day **dagkaart,** which covers all city routes for Fl. 8.85 (a two-day card costs Fl. 11.80). These can be obtained from the main VVV office, along with route maps of the public transportation system.

By Taxi Taxis are expensive: A short, 3-mile ride costs around Fl. 15. Taxis are not usually hailed on the street but are picked up at stands near stations and other key points. Alternatively, you can dial 777777.

By Car Thanks to its network of concentric canals, one-way systems, and lack of parking facilities, it is not easy to drive in Amsterdam. It's best to put your car in one of the parking lots on the edge of the old center and abandon it for the rest of your stay. Expensive hotels often have private parking lots.

By Bicycle Rental bikes are readily available for around Fl. 6.50 per day with a Fl. 100–Fl. 200 deposit. Bikes are an excellent and inexpensive way to explore the city. Several rental companies are close to the central station, or ask at the VVV offices for details.

On Foot Amsterdam is a small, congested city of narrow streets, which makes it ideal for exploring on foot. The VVV issues seven excellent guides which detail walking tours around the center. The best are "The Jordaan," a stroll through the lively canalside district, and "Jewish Amsterdam," a walk past the symbolic remains of old Jewish housing and lone synagogues.

Important Addresses and Numbers

Tourist Information There are two VVV offices: one outside the central station in the Old Dutch Coffee House (Stationsplein 10, tel. 020/266444), and the other at Leidsestraat 106. The VVV reserves for accommodations, tours, and entertainment, but reservations must be made in person. The Stationsplein office is open Easter–September, daily 9 AM–11 PM; October–Easter, daily 9–6.

Consulates	**U.S.:** Museumsplein 19, tel. 020/790321. **Canadian:** 7 Sophialaan, The Hague, tel. 070/614111. **U.K.:** Koningslaan 44, tel. 020/764343.
Emergencies	**Police:** tel. 020/2222; **Ambulance:** tel. 020/5555555; **Doctor: Academisch Medisch Centrum,** Meibergdreef 9, tel. 020/5669111. **Central Medical Service,** tel. 020/642111, will give you names of pharmacists and dentists as well as doctors.
English Bookstores	**American Discount Book Center:** Kalverstraat 158, 020/2555537. **Athenaeum Boekhandel:** Spui 14, tel. 020/233933.
Travel Agencies	**American Express:** Damrak 66, tel. 020/262042; **Holland International:** Rokin 54, tel. 020/264466; **Key Tours** (Wagon Lits/Cooks): Dam 19, tel. 020/247310; **De Vries & Co.:** Damrak 6, tel. 020/248174.

Guided Tours

Boat Tours   The most enjoyable way to get to know Amsterdam is by taking a boat trip along the canals. Several operators run trips, usually in glass-topped boats. There are frequent departures from points opposite the central station, by Smits Koffiehuis, beside the Damrak and along the Rokin and Stadhouderskade (near the Rijksmuseum). For a tour lasting about 1½ hours, costs range from Fl. 8 to Fl. 12, but the student guides expect a small tip for their multilingual commentary. On summer evenings, longer romantic cruises include wine and cheese snacks or a full buffet dinner. A few tours feature increasingly drunken stops for wine tastings in canalside bars. Costs range from Fl. 30 for wine and cheese tours to Fl. 60 for a candle-lit dinner. Trips can be booked through the VVV.

Alternatively, you may want to rent a pedal-boat and make your own canal tour. At **Canal-Bike,** prices begin at Fl. 18 per hour; for details, tel. 020/265574.

The **Museum Boat** capitalizes on the fact that the 12 major museums lie beside the canals. From April to September, a special boat ferries eager passengers between cultural landmarks. Tickets cost Fl. 8 for adults, Fl. 6 for children, and include a discount on museum admission. Details and bookings are available from the VVV.

Bus Tours   Guided bus tours around the city are also available and provide an excellent introduction to Amsterdam. Lindbergh's combined bus and boat tour includes the inevitable trip to a diamond factory. Costing Fl. 25, the comprehensive three-hour tour can be booked through **Lindbergh** (26 Damrak).

Exploring Amsterdam

Amsterdam is a gem of a city for the tourist. Small and densely packed with fine buildings, many dating from the 17th century or earlier, it is easily explored on foot or by bike. The old heart of the city consists of canals, with narrow streets radiating out like spokes of a wheel. The hub of this wheel and the most convenient point to begin sightseeing is the central station. Across the street, in the Old Dutch Coffee House, is a VVV office, offering helpful tourist information.

Amsterdam's key points of interest can be covered in two or three days, with each walking itinerary taking in one or two of the important museums and galleries. The following exploration of the city center can be broken up into several sessions.

Around the Dam *Numbers in the margin correspond with points of interest on the Amsterdam map.*

❶ Start at the **central station.** Just to the right, at Haalemmerstraat 75 (now an orphanage), a plaque commemorates the occasion in 1623 when the directors of the Dutch West India Company planned the founding of Nieuw Amsterdam on the southernmost tip of the island of Manhattan. In 1664, this colony was seized by the English and renamed New York.

❷ The street directly across from the station is Prins Hendrikkade. To the left is **St. Nicolaaskerk** (Church of St. Nicholas) consecrated in 1306. The church is notable for its organ, stained-glass windows (dating from 1555 but extensively restored, 1761–63), and a lovely carillon. During the summer, organ concerts are held on Tuesday, Wednesday, Friday, and Saturday evenings.

❸ Beside the St. Nicolaaskerk is the **Schreierstoren** (Weeping or Criers' Tower), where seafarers used to say goodbye to their women before setting off to sea. The tower was erected in 1487, and a tablet marks the point from which Henrik Hudson set sail on the *Half Moon* on April 4, 1609, on a voyage that took him to what is now New York and the river that still bears his name. Today the Weeping Tower is used as a combined reception and exhibition center and Old World tavern. It also houses the world's first diamond museum.

❹ Close to the Schreierstoren is the **Amstelkring Museum,** whose facade carries the inscription "Ons Lieve Heer Op Solder," or "Our Dear Lord in the Attic." In 1578, Amsterdam embraced Protestantism and outlawed the church of Rome. So great was the tolerance of the municipal authorities, however, that secret Catholic chapels were allowed to exist; at one time there were 62 in Amsterdam alone. One such chapel was established in the attics of these three neighboring canalside houses, built around 1661. The lower floors were used as ordinary dwellings, while services were held in the attics regularly until 1887, the year when St. Nicolaaskerk was consecrated for Catholic worship. *Oude Zijds Voorburgwal 40, tel. 020/246604. Admission: Fl. 4. Open Mon.–Sat. 10–5, Sun. 1–5.*

❺ To the right of the museum you can see the **Oude Kerk,** the city's oldest church. Built in the 14th century but badly damaged by iconoclasts after the Reformation, the church still maintains its original bell tower and a few remarkable stained-glass windows. From the tower, there is a typical view of old Amsterdam stretching from St. Nicolaaskerk to medieval gables and, if your eyesight is good, to glimpses of negotiations between a prostitute and a prospective client immediately below! *Admission: free. Open May–Oct., Mon.–Sat. 11:30–4:30; Nov.–Apr., Mon.–Sat. 11–3. Tower open June–Sept., Mon. and Thurs. 2–5, Tues. and Wed. 11–2.*

This area, bordered by Amsterdam's two oldest canals (Oude Zijds Voorburgwal and Oude Zijds Achterburgwal), is the heart of the *rosse buurt*, the red-light district. In the windows at canal level, lumpish women in sheer lingerie slouch, stare, or do their nails. Drawn red curtains above suggest a brisker trade. Although the area can be shocking, with its sex shops

Amsterdam

Het Ij

Central Station

de Ruijterkade

Ofen

Haven

Prins Hendrikkade

Nieuwendik

Front

Singelgracht

Spuistr.

Nieuwendijk

Damrak

Oudebrugsteeg

Geldersekade

Oosterdokskade

Oosterdokskade

Prins

Hendrikkade

Oosterdok

Damrak

Beursstraat

Warmoesstraat

Bantam

Binnen

Waals

kant

eilandsgracht

Oude waal

N

Nieuwezijdsvoorburgwal

Dam

Rokin

Nieuwe Markt

Zijds Voorburgwal

Achter

burgwal

Recht Boomssloot

Koning

Krom Boomsloot str.

straat

Schans

Rapenburg

Damstraat

Oude

Zijds

Hoogstr.

Oude

Antoniesbreestr.

Nieuwe Hoogstr.

Oude

Nieuwe Uilenburgerstraat

Uilenburgergracht

Nieuwe Uilenburgerstraat

Valkenburgerstraat

Rapenburgerstraat

Anne Frankstr.

Kalverstraat

Zijds

Hoogstr.

Klovaniersburgwal

Raamgr.

nenburgwal

Jodenbreestraat

gracht

Spui

Rokin

Nieuwe

Doelenstr.

Staalstraat

Groen

Zuid

burgwal

Waterloo plein

Muiderstraat

Wertheim Park

plantage parklaan

Plantage Middenlaan

Singel

Amstel

Amstel

Blaauwbrug

Heren

Nieuwe

Regulierbreestraat

Rembrandts plein

Amstelstr.

Nieuwe

Nieuwe

Keizersgracht

Weesperstraat

Kerkstraat

Vijzelstraat

Heren

gracht

Utrechtstraat

Amstel

Nieuwe

Prinsengracht

Keizersgracht

Regulters

Kerkstraat

Magere Brug

Nieuwe

Nieuwe Achter

gr.

Vijzelgracht

Prinsengracht

Noorderstr.

gracht

Utrechtse

dwarstraat

Valckenierstraat

Sarphatistraat

dwarstr.

Nieuwe Looiersstr.

Frederiks plein

Mauritskade

Wetering Pl.

Wetering Schans

Sarphatistraat

Wiboautstraat

str.

F. Bol Straat

Stadhouderskade

Stadhoudersbrug

Amstel

0   220 yards

0   200 m eters

and porn shows, it is generally safe, but midnight walks down dark side streets are not advised. The timid can view the area by boat, since most of the cruises pass this way. If you do decide to explore the area, take care; purse snatching is common.

6 Return to the Damrak and continue up to the **Dam,** the broadest square in the old section of the town. It was here that the fishermen used to come to sell their catch; today it is jammed with shops, people, and traffic; it is also a popular youth center for outdoor concerts. To the left, you will notice a simple monument to the Dutch victims of World War II. Eleven urns contain soil from the 11 provinces of Holland, while a 12th contains soil from the former Dutch East Indies, now Indonesia.

7 To the right of the square is the **Nieuwe Kerk** (New Church). A huge Gothic church, it was gradually expanded until 1540, when it reached its present size. Gutted by fire in 1645, it was reconstructed in an imposing Renaissance style, as interpreted by strict Calvinists. The superb oak pulpit, the 14th-century nave, the stained-glass windows, and the great organ (1645) are all shown to great effect on national holidays, when the church is bedecked with flowers. As befits Holland's national church, the Nieuwe Kerk is the site of all coronations, including the crowning of Queen Beatrix in 1980. But in democratic Dutch spirit, the church is also used as a meeting place and is the home of a lively café, temporary exhibitions, and concerts. Built into the north porch of the church are two of the smallest shops in Europe: One customer enters and the shop is full. *Open Mon.–Sat. 11–4, Sun. Noon–3.*

Time Out **De Drie Fleshjes** (The Three Bottles). Situated in a bell-gabled house is a crooked, medieval street behind the Nieuwe Kerk, this is one of the most typical 17th-century *proeflokalen* (wine- and spirit-tasting houses). The tone is set by the burnished wood interior, the candle-lit bar, and the profusion of kegs and taps. Quirky service complements a fairly eccentric clientele made up of radical students and walrus-mustached seafarers. Although the main emphasis is on drink, light snacks are also available. *Gravenstraat 16. Open Mon.–Sat. noon–8.*

8 Glance at the **Koninklijk Paleis** (Royal Palace), or **Dam Palace,** a vast, well-proportioned structure on Dam Square that was completed in 1655. It is built on 13,659 piles, sunk into the marshy soil. The great pedimental sculptures are an allegorical representation of Amsterdam surrounded by Neptune and mythological sea creatures.

Directly behind the palace is the main post office. From here, Raadhuisstraat leads west across three canals to the **9** **Westermarkt** and the **Westerkerk** (West Church), built in 1631. Its 85-meter (275-foot) tower is the highest in the city. It also features an outstanding carillon. Rembrandt and his son Titus are buried in the church. During the summer, you can climb to the top of the tower for a fine view over the city.

Opposite, at Westermarkt 6, is the house where Descartes, the great 17th-century French philosopher ("Cogito, ergo sum"— "I think, therefore I am") lived in 1634. Another more famous **10** house lies farther down the same street. This is the **Anne Frank Huis** (Anne Frank House), immortalized by the poignant diary kept by the young Jewish girl from 1942–1944, when she and her family hid here from the German occupying forces. A small exhibition on the Holocaust can also be seen in the house. *Prinsengracht 263, tel. 020/264533. Admission: Fl. 6. Open June–Aug., Mon.–Sat. 9–7, Sun. 10–7; Sept.–May, Mon.–Sat. 9–5, Sun. 10–5.*

⓫ Continuing right up the Prinsengracht, you reach the **Noorderkerk,** built 1623. In the square in front of the church, the Noorderplein, a bird market, is held every Saturday.

Time Out   Follow the Lelie Canal back to Dam Square. Hidden in a little alley off the square is **Wijnand Fockink,** a traditional tasting house. Pass under a naked Bacchus and the date 1679 on the door to the small bar with its mind-boggling list of drinks. The barman will gladly explain (in any of his six languages) how Dutch liqueurs should be drunk. The correct protocol is to bend over the glass, hands clasped behind one's back for balance. Don't walk too close to the canals if you have had the mysterious *half–en–halfje* liqueur in its special cone-shaped glass. *31 Pijlsteeg, tel. 020/243989. Closes 8 PM.*

South of the Dam   Turn down Kalverstraat, an attractive shopping street leading south from the Royal Palace. You will notice a striking Renaissance gate (1581) which guards a series of tranquil inner courtyards. In medieval times, this area was an island devoted to piety. Today the bordering canals are filled in.

⓬ The medieval doorway just around the corner in St. Luciensteeg leads to the former Burgerweeshuis (City Orphanage), once a nunnery but now the **Historisch Museum** (Museum of History). The museum traces the city's history from its origins as a fishing village through the 17th-century Golden Age of material and artistic wealth to the decline of the trading empire in the 18th century. The engrossing trail unfolds through a display of old maps, documents, and paintings, often aided by a commentary in English. *Kalverstraat 92. Admission: Fl. 5. Open daily 11–5.*

⓭ A small passageway and courtyard link the museum with the **Begijnhof,** an enchanting, enclosed square of almshouses founded in 1346. The *beguines* were women who chose to lead a form of convent life, often taking the vow of chastity. The last beguine died in 1974 and her house, no. 26, has been preserved as she left it. No. 34, dating from the 15th century, is the oldest and the only one to keep its wooden Gothic facade. But most of the brick gabled houses retain their beamed ceilings and stone tablets engraved with biblical scenes. Inside, copperware utensils glow against the dull beams, and new residents can be seen moving deferentially, as if aware of the sacredness of the spot. *(One house is occasionally open to the public. Tel. 020/235554.)*

In the center of the square is a church given to Amsterdam's English and Scottish Presbyterians over 300 years ago. On the church wall and also in the chancel are tributes to the Pilgrim Fathers who sailed from Delfthaven to New York in 1620. Opposite the church is another of the city's secret Catholic chapels, built in 1671.

Once back in Kalverstraat, you soon come to Spui, a lively square in the heart of the university area. It was a center for student rallies in revolutionary 1968. Now it is a center for boat trips and bars, including the cozy "brown cafés."

A right turn here would bring you to the Singel Canal and, following the tram tracks, to Leidsestraat, an important shopping
⓮ street that terminates in the **Leidseplein.** On the Singel's left
bank, just past the lock at Open Haven, is what is erroneously
called the smallest house in Amsterdam. In fact, it is just a door
opening onto a small alley. The real narrowest house is the art
gallery **Den Gulden Fonteyn,** at Singel 166.

If you continue straight along Kalverstraat instead of turning,
⓯ you soon reach the **Muntplein,** with its **Munttoren** (Mint Tower,
built in 1620), a graceful structure whose clock and bells still
seem to mirror the Golden Age. West from the Muntplein is the
⓰ floating **flower market** on the Singel Canal. *Open Mon.–Sat.
9–5.*

From the Singel, take Leidsestraat to the Herengracht, the
city's most prestigious "Gentlemen's Canal." The stretch of ca-
⓱ nal from here to Huidenstraat is named **The Golden Bend** for its
sumptuous patrician houses with double staircases and grand
entrances. Seventeenth-century merchants moved here from
the Amstel River to escape the disadvantageous byproducts of
their wealth: the noisy warehouses, the unpleasant smells from
the breweries, and the risk of fire in the sugar refineries. These
houses display the full range of Amsterdam facades: from neck,
bell, and step gables to grander Louis XIV-style houses with
elaborate cornices, and frescoed ceilings. In particular, look at
nos. 364–370 as well as no. 380, with its sculpted angels and
Louis XIV facade; nos. 390 and 392 display neck-shaped gables
surmounted by statues of a couple in matching 17th-century
dress. These houses are best seen from the east side of the canal. For more gables, turn left down Wolvenstraat into the
Keizersgracht, the Emperor's Canal. Walk northward toward
Westerkerk and the Anne Frank Huis.

Time Out   On the corner of Keizersgracht and Reestraat is the well-
restored **Pulitzer Hotel** and restaurant complex. Inside, you
can wander around quiet inner courtyards and a modern art
gallery before sitting down in the Pulitzer Coffeeshop for a
well-deserved apple tart or pastry. *Reestraat 2. Open 11–5.*

Along Herengracht, parallel to the Westerkerk, is the
⓲ **Nederlands Theater Instituut.** This theater museum is a dynamic find in such a genteel canal. Two frescoed Louis XIV-style
merchants' houses form the backdrop for a history of the circus,
opera, musicals, and drama. Miniature theaters and videos of
stage productions are just two entertaining features. In summer, the large garden is open for buffet lunches. *168–170
Herengracht. Admission: Fl. 3. Open Tues.–Sun. 11–5.*

Jewish Amsterdam   Take the Museumboat or the metro to Waterlooplein and walk
east to Jodenbreestraat. This is the heart of **Jodenbuurt,** the old
Jewish district, an important area to all Amsterdammers. The
original settlers here were wealthy Sephardic Jews from Spain
and Portugal, later followed by poorer Ashkenazic refugees
from Germany and Poland. At the turn of the century, this was
a thriving community of Jewish diamond polishers, dyers, and
merchants. During World War II, the corner of Jodenbreestraat marked the end of the *Joodse wick*, by then an imposed ghetto. Although the character of the street was largely
destroyed by partial demolition in 1965, neighboring Muiderstraat has retained much of the original atmosphere. Notice
the gateways decorated with pelicans, symbolizing great love;

according to legend, the pelican will feed her starving young with her own blood.

From 1639 to 1658, Rembrandt lived at Jodenbreestraat no. 4, now the **Museum Het Rembrandthuis** (Rembrandt's House). For over 20 years the ground floor was used by the artist as living quarters; the sunny upper floor was his studio. It is fascinating to visit, both as a record of life in 17th-century Amsterdam and as a sketch of Holland's most illustrious artist. It contains a superb collection of his etchings and engravings. From St. Antonies Sluis bridge, just by the house, there is a canal view little changed since Rembrandt's time. *Jodenbreestraat 4–6, tel. 020/249486. Admission: Fl. 4. Open Mon.–Sat. 10–5; Sun. 1–5.*

Visserplein is a square linking Jodenbreestraat with Muiderstraat. In the center is a burly statue of the **Dokwerker** (Docker), a profession that has played a significant part in the city's history. The statue commemorates the 1942 strike by which Amsterdam dockworkers expressed their solidarity with persecuted Jews. A memorial march is held every year on February 25.

Facing the Dokwerker is the 17th-century **Portuguese Synagogue.** As one of Amsterdam's four neighboring synagogues, it was part of the largest Jewish religious complex in Europe. The austere interior is still intact, even if the building itself is marooned on a traffic island. *Open Apr.–Oct., Sun.–Fri. 10–4.*

On the other side of the street is the intriguing **Joods Historisch Museum** (Jewish History Museum), set in a complex of three ancient synagogues. These synagogues once served a population of 100,000 Jews, shrunk to under 10,000 after 1945. The new museum, founded by American and Dutch Jews, displays religious treasures in a clear cultural and historical context. Since the synagogues lost most of their treasures in the war, their architecture and history are more compelling than the individual exhibits. *Jonas Daniel Meijerplein 204, tel. 020/269945. Admission: Fl. 8. Open daily 11–5.*

Time Out **Cafeteria Kosher.** Situated within the oldest part of the museum, the cafeteria is built above the former kosher meat halls that later became ritual baths. It still looks like part of a clandestine Catholic church, the original model for the synagogue. Jewish delicacies on offer include fish cakes, cheese tarts, bagels, and spicy cakes with gingerbread and almond cream filling. *Open daily 11–5.*

Instead of returning on foot, you can catch the Museumboat from Blauwbrug on Waterlooplein to the central station or to a destination near your hotel. If you feel like a breath of fresh air, stroll along Nieuwe Herengracht, once known as the "Jewish Gentlemen's Canal." In Rembrandt's day, there were views of distant windjammers sailing into port, but today the canal is oddly deserted.

The Museum Quarter On the southernmost edge of the outer Singel Canal, a few minutes' walk from Leidseplein, you'll find three of the most distinguished museums in Holland—the Rijksmuseum, the Stedelijk Museum, and the Rijksmuseum Vincent van Gogh. Of the three, the **Rijksmuseum,** easily recognized by its cluster of towers, is the most important, so be sure to allow adequate time to explore it. It was founded by Louis Bonaparte in 1808, but the current, rather lavish, building dates from 1885. The museum contains significant collections of furniture, textiles, ceramics, sculpture, and prints, as well as Italian, Flemish, and Spanish paintings, many of the highest quality. But the museum's fame rests on its unrivaled collection of 16th- and 17th-century Dutch masters. Of Rembrandt's masterpieces, make a point to see *The Nightwatch,* concealed during World War II in caves in Maastricht. The painting was misnamed because of its dull layers of varnish: In reality it depicts the Civil Guard in daylight. Also worth searching out are Jan Steen's family portraits, Frans Hals' drunken scenes, van Ruysdael's romantic but menacing landscapes, and Vermeer's glimpses of everyday life bathed in his usual pale light. *Stadhouderskade 42, tel. 020/ 732121. Admission: Fl. 7. Open Tues.–Sat. 10–5, Sun. 1–5.*

㉔ A few blocks down the road is the **Rijksmuseum Vincent van Gogh.** This museum contains the world's largest collection of the artist's works—200 paintings and 500 drawings—as well as works by some 50 other painters of the period. To mark the centennial of van Gogh's tragic death in 1890, there will be special exhibitions of his work here, and all over Holland. *Paulus Potterstraat 7, tel. 020/764881. Admission: Fl. 7. Open Tues.– Sat. 10–5, Sun. 1–5.*

㉕ Next door is the **Stedelijk Museum** (Municipal Museum), its austere neoclassical facade designed to counterbalance the Rijksmuseum's neo-Gothic turrets. The museum has a stimulating collection of modern art and ever-changing displays of contemporary art. Before viewing the works of Cézanne, Chagall, Kandinsky, and Mondrian, check the list of temporary exhibitions in Room 1. Museum policy is to trace the development of the artist rather than merely to show a few masterpieces. Don't forget the museum's artsy restaurant overlooking a garden filled with modern sculptures. *Paulus Potterstraat 13, tel. 020/5732911. Admission: Fl. 8. Open Mon. –Sat. 11–5, Sun. 1–5.*

Diagonally opposite the Stedelijk Museum, at the end of the broad Museumplein, is the **Concertgebouw,** home of the two ㉖ major national orchestras, the Amsterdam Philharmonisch and the Concertgebouworkest. Many visiting orchestras also perform here. The building has two auditoriums, the smaller of which is used for chamber music and recitals. A block or two in the opposite direction is **Vondelpark,** an elongated rectangle of paths, lakes, and pleasant shady trees. A monument honors the 17th-century epic poet Joost van den Vondel, for whom the park is named. From Wednesday to Sunday in summer, free concerts and plays are performed in the park.

The Jordaan One old part of Amsterdam that is certainly worth exploring is ㉗ the **Jordaan,** the area between Prinsengracht and Lijnbaansgracht. The canals and side streets here are all named for flowers and plants. Indeed, at one time, when this was the French quarter of the city, the area was known as *le jardin* (the garden), a name that over the years has become Jordaan. The best time to explore this area is on a Sunday morning, when there are few cars and people about, or in the evening. This part of the town has attracted many artists and is sort of a bohemian quarter, where rundown buildings are being renovated and converted into restaurants, antique shops, boutiques, and galleries.

Time Out The Jordaan is the best part of Amsterdam for relaxing in a brown café, so named because of the rich wood furnishings and —some say—because of the centuries-old pipe tobacco stains on the ceilings. You can while away a rainy afternoon chatting to friendly strangers over homemade meatballs or apple tart. Spend an hour or three over a beer or coffee at either **Doktorje** (Rozenboomsteegweg 4) or **De Egelantier** (Egelantierstraat 72).

Off the Beaten Track

Theater and ballet fans can go on a tour of the **Muziektheater,** the city's new opera and ballet center. A guided tour takes you around the dressing rooms, dance studios, and even the wig department. *Amfter 3. Tel. 020/551803. Cost: Fl. 8.50. Guided tours every Wed. and Sat. at 4.*

An otherwise unremarkable building at **Singel 460** (near Herengracht) has special significance for Americans. In this building—today used as an auction house—John Adams raised the first foreign loan ($2 million) for the United States from the banking house of van Staphorst in 1782. Additional loans from this and other banks soon followed, for a total of $30 million—a gesture of Dutch confidence in the future of America.

Beer lovers—or anyone with an interest in the production of a world-class product—will want to take time to visit the **Heineken Brewery.** There are two half-hour tours each morning (at 9 and 11), after which you may judge the product with some free samples. You even get a free beer stein if it's your birthday. *Van der Helstraat. Admission: Fl. 2.*

Shopping

Serious shoppers should buy the VVV's four excellent shopping guides to markets, art and antique shops, boutiques, and department stores (Fl. 10).

Gift Ideas **Diamonds.** Since the 17th century, "Amsterdam cut" has been synonymous with perfection in the quality of diamonds. You can see this craftsmanship at any of the diamond-cutting houses. The cutters explain how the diamond's value depends on the four c's—carat, cut, clarity, and color—before encouraging you to buy. There is a cluster of diamond houses on the Rokin. Alternatively, try **Van Moppes Diamonds** (Albert Cuypstraat 2–6, tel. 020/761242; open Mon.–Sat. 9–5).

Porcelain. The Dutch have been producing Delft, Makkum, and other fine porcelain for centuries. **Focke and Meltzer** stores have been selling it since 1823. The price range varies from affordable, newly painted tiles (Fl. 8) to expensive Delft blue-and-white pitchers. One store is situated near the Rijksmuseum (65–67 P. C. Hoofstraat, tel. 020/231944).

Shopping Districts Amsterdam's chief shopping districts, which have largely been turned into pedestrianized areas, are the **Leidsestraat, Kalverstraat,** and **de Nieuwendijk,** on the other side of Dam Square. **Rokin,** somber and sedate, houses a cluster of renowned antique shops selling 18th- and 19th-century furniture, antique jewelry, Art Deco lamps, and statuettes. By contrast, the **Nieuwe Spiegelstraat**'s old curiosity shops sell a more inexpensive range. For trendy small boutiques and unusual crafts shops favored by locals, try **P. C. Hoofstraat**. When leaving Holland, remember that Schipol Airport is Europe's best tax–free shopping center.

Department Stores **De Bijenkorf** (Damrak) is the city's number-one department store and excellent for contemporary fashions and furnishings. Running a close second is **Vroom and Dreesman** (Kalverstraat 201) with well-stocked departments carrying all manner of goods. The restaurants and cafeterias in these department stores are also worth trying.

Markets There is a lively open-air **flea market** on Waterlooplein around the Musiektheater (Mon.–Sat. 11–4). The **floating flower market** on the Singel is popular with locals and visitors alike. (Open Mon.–Sat. 10–5). An unusual Saturday **bird market** is held in the Noordmarkt. Philatelists will not want to miss the **stamp market** at Nieuwezijds Voorburgwal (Wed. and Sat. afternoons). If you are interested in old books, head for the **book market** at Oudemanhuispoort (Mon.–Sat.). For antiques, especially silver and toys, visit the Sunday **Nieuwe Markt** (New Market) in summer. You can also try the **Antiekmarkt de Looier** (Blandsgracht 109. Open Sat.–Thurs. 11–5). In summer, art lovers can buy etchings, drawings, and watercolors at the Sunday **art market** on Thorbeckeplein.

Dining

Amsterdammers are less creatures of habit than are the Dutch in general. Even so, set menus and early dinners are preferred by these health-conscious citizens. For travelers on a diet or budget, the blue-and-white "Tourist Menu" sign guarantees an economical (Fl. 20) yet imaginative set menu created by the head chef. For traditionalists, the "Nederlands Dis" soup tureen sign is a promise of regional recipes and seasonal ingredients. "You can eat in any language" is the city's proud boast, so when the Dutch restaurants are closed, Indonesian, Chinese, and Turkish restaurants are often open. Between meals, you can follow your nose to the nearest herring cart or drop into a cozy brown café for coffee and an apple tart. For details and price category definitions, *see* Dining in Staying in Holland.

Very Expensive **Excelsior.** Hôtel de l'Europe's renowned restaurant offers a varied menu of French cuisine that is based on local ingredients; try the sea bass in curry sauce and the smoked eel. The service is discreet and impeccable. *Nieuwe Doelenstraat 2–4, tel. 020/234836. Reservations required. AE, DC, MC, V. Closed Sat. lunch.*

★ **La Rive.** Set in the prestigious Amstel Intercontinental hotel, this intimate canalside restaurant basks in its reputation for creative French cuisine in a clubby atmosphere. In summer, tables spill out onto the terrace. Adventurous diners choose the chef's thematic menus, while others select the vegetarian menu. The Sunday brunch of fresh salmon and champagne is often attended by famous faces. *Professor Tulpplein 1, tel. 020/226060. Reservations required. AE, DC, MC, V. Dinner only.*

Seven Seas. This restaurant is in two restored 17th-century mansions, close to the Holiday Inn Crowne Plaza hotel. Its reputation is based on its excellent fish. Traditional Amsterdam recipes for herring and eel are worth trying, but the seafood also gets nouvelle and Oriental treatment. *Nieuwe Voorburgwal 5, tel. 020/200500. Reservations required. AE, DC, MC, V.*

Expensive   **Edo.** The Grand Hotel Krasnapolsky is home to a Dutch notion of Japanese cuisine. Artistic portions of raw fish and deep-fried tempura vegetables are served against a background of polished pine and equally polished service. You'll marvel at the way Dutch seafood lends itself to sushi preparation. *Sashimi* (raw fish) is prepared before your eyes. *Dam 9, tel. 020/ 5546096. Reservations required. AE, DC, MC, V.*

De Kersentuin. This superb restaurant, in the Garden Hotel de Kersentuin, is known as one of the best in Holland. The dining room is elegant—you eat amid the greenery of a covered garden—and the menu has the flair of nouvelle cuisine originality. Try the salmon specialties. *Dijsselhofplantsoen 7, tel. 020/ 642121. Reservations required. AE, DC, MC, V. Closed Sun. lunch.*

Les Quatre Canetons. Pleasantly informal, this canalside restaurant is popular with local businesspeople. It serves mainly nouvelle cuisine and freshwater trout. *Prinsengracht 111, tel. 020/246307. Reservations required. AE, DC, MC, V.*

★ **'t Swarte Schaep.** The Black Sheep is named after a proverbial 17th-century sheep which once roamed the area. With its creaking boards and array of copper pots, the interior is reminiscent of a somber ship's cabin. The Dutch chef uses seasonal ingredients to create classical French dishes with regional flourishes and a touch of nouvelle cuisine. Take advantage of the set lunch at only Fl. 50. Dinner orders are accepted until 11 PM—unusually late even for Amsterdam. *Korte Leidsewarsstraat, tel. 020/223021. Reservations required. AE, DC, MC, V.*

★ **d'Vliff Vlieghen.** Take a trip back in time to a warren of 17th-century charm. Each of the seven dining rooms is decorated in a different Renaissance style. The menu has a touch of nouvelle cuisine, more in presentation than in proportion; the game specialties are attractive but substantial. As befits an ex-tavern, the candle-lit atmosphere is warm and relaxed. *Spuistraat 294, tel. 020/248369. Reservations advised. AE, DC, MC, V.*

Moderate   **Bali.** Bali is a popular Indonesian restaurant in the heart of the
★ Leidseplein bustle. A safe choice is always the rijsttafel. Other popular dishes are *nasi goreng*, a spicy rice-based dish, and the pasta-based *bami goreng*. Even winter ice skaters from the nearby rink find Bali's portions generous enough! *Leidsestraat 89, tel. 020/227878. Reservations advised. AE, DC, MC, V. Closed Sun.*

Oesterbar. As its name suggests, the Oyster Bar specializes in seafood, some of which eyes you fishisly from the tank. The downstairs bistro offers relatively inexpensive dining, while upstairs, presentation and price are somewhat higher. Salmon and trout are the specialties, and the oysters themselves make a good, if expensive, first course. *Leidseplein 10, tel. 020/ 362463. Reservations advised. AE, DC.*

De Roode Leeuw. As a Nederlands Dis restaurant, the Red Lion guarantees traditional Dutch cuisine at its best. Depending on the season, you can sample smoked eel, Zeeland mussels, asparagus wrapped in ham, and varied regional dishes. The reasonable wine list, attentive service, and friendly atmosphere live up to the Nederlands Dis traditionla. *Damrak 93–4,* *tel. 020/249683 and 020/240396. Reservations advised. AE, DC, MC, V.*

Sea Palace. The Sea Palace is an appropriate establishment for a city built on canals—it's a huge, floating Chinese restaurant. The Cantonese menu is only of modest quality, but the surroundings make up for it. A special children's menu is also available. *Oosterdokskade (near the central station), tel. 020/264777. Reservations not necessary. No credit cards.*

Inexpensive   **Oud Holland.** This restaurant is in a convenient location for a night on the town: not far from the Leidseplein, yet just far enough from the red-light district. Oud Holland is one of the few Amsterdam restaurants to offer a tourist menu. A typical three-course meal is a game paté followed by pork in cream sherry sauce, and an apple pancake for dessert. A children's menu is also available. *NZ Voorburgwal 105, tel. 020/246848. Reservations not necessary. No credit cards.*

Pancake Bakery. Here is a chance to try a traditionally Dutch way of keeping costs down. The name of the game is pancakes—for every course including dessert, for which the topping can be ice cream, fruit, or liqueur. The Pancake Bakery is not far from Anne Frank Huis. *Prinsengracht 191, tel. 020/251233. No reservations. No credit cards.*

★ **Speciaal.** Although set in the Jordaan area, this Indonesian restaurant is slightly off the beaten track. From the outside, the Speciaal looks very unspecial, but once inside, the soothing Indonesian prints, raffia work, and bamboo curtains create an intimate atmosphere. Along with the usual rijsttafel, chicken, fish, and egg dishes provide tasty variants on a sweet-and-sour theme. *Nieuwe Leliestraat 142, tel. 020/249706. Reservations not necessary.*

Lodging

Accommodation is tight from Easter to summer, so early booking is advisable to secure a popular hotel. The other snag is parking: Amsterdam is a pedestrian's paradise but a driver's nightmare. Since few hotels have parking lots, cars are best abandoned in a multistory parking ramp for the duration of your stay. Most tourists prefer to stay inside the concentric ring of canals. This area, the quiet museum quarter, is a convenient choice for the Rijksmuseum, yet near enough to the Vondelpark for light jogging. More atmospheric lodgings can be found in the historic canalside neighborhood with its gabled merchants' houses. For details and price category definitions, *see* Lodging in Staying in Holland.

Very Expensive   **Amstel Intercontinental.** The Amstel has long been the city's
★ most exclusive hotel, noted for its grand entrance, romantic terrace, and majestic views over the Amstel River. The smoothness of the service and the profusion of cut flowers compensate for the slightly cramped bedrooms. A champagne brunch in the glittering Spiegelzaal (Hall of Mirrors) is a wonderful excuse to visit this refined 19th-century palace. *Professor Tulpplein 1, tel. 020/226060. 111 rooms with bath. Facilities: restaurant, terraces. AE, DC, MC, V.*

Amsterdam Hilton. One of the first international chain hotels to open in Amsterdam, the Hilton is still one of the most gracious. In the southern part of the city, it overlooks the attractive Noorder Amstelkanal. There is a delightful glassed-in floral garden that is heated in winter. All the rooms are luxuriously appointed. *Apollolaan 138, tel. 020/780780. 274 rooms with bath. Facilities: casino. AE, DC, MC, V.*

Hôtel de l'Europe. The hotel hides its modern facilities behind a Victorian facade. It has larger than average rooms, often decorated with old prints and Empire furniture. Apart from its international Excelsior restaurant, the Europe houses a sophisticated leisure complex and the city's only hotel swimming pool. *Nieuwe Doelenstraat 2–4, tel. 020/234836. 100 rooms with bath. Facilities: restaurant, pool, leisure complex. AE, DC, MC, V.*

★ **Sonesta.** Situated in the old port area, the Sonesta incorporates a striking domed church. The sumptuous hotel houses a good steak restaurant, but what really singles it out is the huge collection of modern art: Contemporary pictures and sculpture are scattered throughout the bars and bedrooms. *Kattengat 1, tel. 020/212223. 425 rooms with bath. Facilities: restaurant, bar, health club, shopping complex. AE, DC, MC, V.*

Expensive **Golden Tulip Pulitzer.** The Pulitzer succeeds in making living in
★ the past a positive pleasure. This is one of Europe's most ambitious hotel restorations, using the shells of a row of 17th-century merchants' houses. Inside, the refined atmosphere is sustained by the modern art gallery, the lovingly restored brickwork, oak beams, and split-level rooms—no two are alike. The tranquil inner courtyards are equally adapted to contemplation and outdoor concerts. *Prinsengracht 315–331, tel. 020/228333. 250 rooms with bath. Facilities: restaurant, bar. AE, DC, MC, V.*

★ **Grand Hotel Krasnapolsky.** This is one of the fine, Old World hotels in Amsterdam, dominated by its Winter Gardens, once a restaurant and now used for music recitals most Sundays. The cosmopolitan atmosphere carries through all the rooms, with decor ranging from Victorian to Art Deco. Each room is well equipped, and there is a choice of restaurants—Edo (*see* Dining) and the Reflet d'Or. *Dam 9, tel. 020/5549111. 370 rooms with bath. Facilities: parking. AE, DC, MC, V.*

Moderate **Ambassade.** With its beautiful canalside location, its Louis XV
★ style decoration, and its Oriental carpets, the Ambassade seems more like a stately home than a hotel. Service is attentive; although there is no restaurant, the neighborhood has a good choice for eating out. *Herengracht 341, tel. 020/262333. 11 rooms with bath. AE, MC, V.*

Atlas Hotel. Renowned for its friendly atmosphere, this small hotel has moderate-size rooms decorated in Art Nouveau style. It's also very handy for Museumsplein, whose major museums are within easy walking distance. Ask for a room facing Vondelpark. *Van Eegheerstraat 64, tel. 020/766336. 24 rooms with bath. Facilities: bar, restaurant. AE, DC, MC, V.*

Het Canal House. This is yet another canalside hotel that prefers to put antiques rather than televisions in the rooms. The American owners greet new guests with a drink at the curious Victorian bar. Spacious rooms overlook the canal or the illuminated garden. *Keizergracht 148, tel. 020/225182. 20 rooms with bath or shower. AE.*

Inexpensive **Agora.** Set beside the Singel flower market, this small hotel re-
★ flects the cheerful bustle. The rooms are light and spacious, some decorated with period furniture; the best overlook the canal or the university. Recently refurbished, this 18th-century house has a summery dining room. Considerate staff and a re-

laxed neighborhood ensure the hotel's popularity. Book well in advance to avoid disappointment. *Singel 462, tel. 020/272200. 14 rooms with bath or shower. Facilities: dining room. No credit cards.*

★ **De Gouden Kettingh.** This 17th-century merchant's house is called the Golden Necklace because an early mistress of the house accused a servant of stealing one; when it was found in the attic, the servant was hanged in Dam Square. Naturally, her ghost is supposed to haunt the upper reaches of the house, but guests are too busy enjoying a hearty breakfast to notice. *Keizersgracht 270, tel. 020/248287. 24 rooms, 20 with bath; 3 deluxe rooms. AE, DC, MC, V.*

Weichmann. Situated on the edge of the lively Jordaan area, the Weichmann is popular for its quiet warmth and reasonable prices. Although the modest bedrooms are modern, the old entrance hall and dining room are home to a shiny cannon and a suit of armor. Family rooms are also available. Book out of season or well in advance. *Prinsengracht 328–330, tel. 020/263321. 35 rooms, most with bath or shower. Facilities: dining room. No credit cards.*

The Arts

The arts flourish in tolerant and cosmopolitan Amsterdam. The best sources of information about performances are the monthly publication *What's On* (in English) and the weekly *Amsterdam This Week;* both can be obtained free from the VVV office, which also can help in obtaining tickets for the more popular events. Tickets must be booked in person from 10 to 4. You can also book at the **Amsterdam Uit Buro,** Stadsschouburg, Leidseplein 26, tel. 020/2112111.

Classical Music Classical music is featured at the **Concertgebouw** (Baerlestraat 98), home of two of Europe's finest orchestras. A smaller auditorium in the same building is used for chamber music, recitals, and even jam sessions. While ticket prices for international orchestras are fairly high, most concerts are good value and the Wednesday lunchtime concerts are free. The box office is open from 9:30 to 7; you can make telephone bookings (020/718345) from 10 to 3.

Opera and Ballet The Dutch national companies are housed in the new **Muziektheater** on Waterlooplein. Guest companies from foreign countries perform there during the three-week Holland Festival in June.

Theater The **Art Theater** (Kerkstraat 4, tel. 020/259495) performs contemporary American plays in English. For experimental theater and colorful cabaret in Dutch, try the **Shaffeytheater** (Keizersgracht 324, tel. 020/231311).

Film The largest concentration of movie theaters is on Leidseplein and Reguliersbreestraat. Most foreign films are subtitled rather than dubbed, but to be sure—and to find out times—see *Amsterdam This Week.*

Entertainment and Nightlife

Amsterdam has a wide variety of nightclubs, bars, and cabarets, including some that surpass even the "hot spots" of cities such as Hamburg; none, however, have the elegance of Paris.

Apart from the very expensive live shows around Rembrandtsplein, Leidseplein, and Thorbeckeplein, there are plenty of respectable, though earthy, nightclubs and an equally large number of less tasteful striptease shows. Names and locations change from year to year, but most bars and clubs are open every night from 5 PM to 2 AM or 4 AM. It is wise to steer clear of the area around the central station at night. Except on weekends, very few of the nightclubs charge admission, though the more lively ones sometimes ask for a "club membership" fee of Fl. 20 or more. Drink prices are normally not exorbitant.

Cabaret If you are looking for a floor show, the **Carousel** (Thorbeckeplein 20) is popular with Amsterdam's socialites. It is an informal spot, with topless waitresses, and you'll be welcomed as a player if you bring your own instrument.

Bars The **Bamboo Bar** (Lange Leidsewarsstraat) is informal, expensive, relaxing, and typically international. It boasts good jazz and blues around the longest bar in Amsterdam.

Jazz Clubs Set in a converted warehouse, the **BIMhuis** is currently the most fashionable jazz club. Ticket holders can sit in the adjoining BIMcafé and enjoy a magical view across Oude Schans to the port (Oude Schans 173–7, tel. 020/233373. Open Thurs.–Sat. from 9 PM). For jazz and vocals, try the discreet **Cab Kaye's Jazz Piano Bar** (Beulingstraat 9, tel. 020/233594. Open Tues.–Sat. until 3 AM). If you long for good Dixieland jazz, go to **Joseph Lam Jazz Club** (Van Diemenstraat 8, tel. 020/228086); it's only open on weekends.

Rock Clubs **Be-Bop** (Amstelstraat 24) caters to the slightly older-than-teenage crowd. A very trendy scene for teenagers and college-age music fans is **De Bios** (Leidseplein 12); it's open from 10 PM, and entrance is free.

Discos Mostly hidden in cellars around the Leidseplein, the discos only fill up after midnight. **Club La Mer** (Korte Leidsedwarstraat 73, tel. 020/242910) draws a trendy, young crowd into this stuffy cellar to dance to Motown and soul. **Zorba The Buddha** (OZ Voorburgwal 216, tel. 020/259642) is run by the religious Baghwan sect in the heart of the red-light district; despite or because of this, the young only seem interested in dancing. **Mazzo** (Rozengracht 114, tel. 020/267500) uses dramatic lighting and slick videos to attract student poseurs, would-be musicians, and artists.

Historic Holland

This circular itinerary can be followed either clockwise or counterclockwise, but whichever way you decide to follow it, you'll be sure to see some of Holland's most characteristic sights. There are the historic towns of Leiden and Utrecht and the major museums in Haarlem; in between these towns, you'll see the best of Holland's windmill-dotted landscape and pass through centers of tulip growing and cheese production.

Getting Around

The most convenient way to cover the following itinerary would be by rented car out of Amsterdam. If you want someone else to do the navigating, then all the towns listed below can be reached by bus or train. From Amsterdam, there are two trains per hour to Alkmaar, Gouda, Hoorn, and Maastricht, and three direct trains per hour to Haarlem, Leiden, and Utrecht. Check with the VVV office in Amsterdam for help in planning your trip.

Guided Tours

Alternatively, these towns are covered, in various permutations, by organized bus tours out of Amsterdam. Brochures for tour operators are available from the VVV offices in Amsterdam, either from Stationplein 10, tel. 020/266444, or from Leidsestraat 106.

The VVV organizes several excursions from Utrecht: a boat trip along the canals; a sightseeing flight over the city. There are also day trips to country estates and castles, often enclosed by Dutch Baroque gardens.

Tourist Information

Amersfoort. Stationsplein 28, tel. 033/635151.
Apeldoorn. Stationsplein 6, tel. 055/788421.
Gouda. Markt 27, tel. 01820/13666.
Haarlem. Stationsplein 1, tel. 023/319059.
Leiden. Stationsplein 210, tel. 071/146846.
Lisse. Grachtweg 53a, tel. 02521/14262.
Utrecht. Vredenburg 90, tel. 030/314132.

Exploring Historic Holland

Apeldoorn Traveling southeast from Amsterdam, 90 kilometers (56 miles) along highway A1, you will first visit Apeldoorn, but if you have time, stop off at **Amersfoort** en route. Although today it is a major industrial town, Amersfoort still manages to retain much of its medieval character and charm. Starting at the **Koopelport,** the imposing water gate across the Eem, dating from 1400, walk down Kleine Spui. On the right is **St. Pieters-en-Bloklands Gasthuis,** a hospice founded in 1390. Close by is the **Museum Flehite,** with its unusual medieval collections that give a fascinating insight into the history of the town. *Westsingel 50. Admission: Fl. 2. Open Tues.–Fri. 10–5, weekends 2–5.*

Continuing along Breestraat, you'll come to the graceful, 102-meter- (330-foot-) high **Onze Lieve Vrouwetorn** (Tower of Our Lady). The musical chimes of this Gothic church can be heard every Friday between 10 and 11 AM. Turning left down Langstraat, past the Gothic **St. Joriskerk,** you come to the **Kamperbinnenpoort,** the turreted land gate dating from the 15th century. Making your way left down Muurhuizen, you come to a short canal, the **Hovik,** which was once the old harbor. Just across from the Hovik you're back at the Museum Flehite.

The main attraction at **Apeldoorn** is the **Rijksmuseum Paleis Het Loo.** This former royal palace was built in the late 17th century for Willem III and has been beautifully restored to illustrate the domestic surroundings enjoyed by the House of Orange for more than three centuries. The museum, which is housed in the stables, has a fascinating collection of royal memorabilia, including cars and carriages, furniture and

Historic Holland

Ijsselmeer

Den Helder

Noordoost Polder

N

Alkmaar

Hoorn

Markerwaard

Castricum

Zaandam

O Vollendam

Oostelijk Flevoland

Monnikendam

Haarlem

Amsterdam

Zuidelijk Flevoland

Zaandvoort

Apeldoorn

Lisse

Leiden

Amersfoort

Utrecht

Arnhem

Gouda

Rotterdam

Lek

Thiel

photographs, silver and ceramics. The formal gardens and the surrounding parkland offer attractive walks. *Tel. 055/212244. Admission Fl. 5. Open Tues.–Sun. 10–5.*

Utrecht   West from Apeldoorn, 72 kilometers (44 miles), is the city of **Utrecht,** considered the center of Holland by the Dutch. With so much to see, you may decide to spend a couple of days here. Along with Maastricht, Utrecht is Holland's oldest city. The high gabled houses, the canals with their water gates, the 13th century wharves and storage cellars, and the superb churches and museums are just some of the key attractions, most of which are situated around the main cathedral square. The **Domkerk** is a late-Gothic cathedral containing many monumental tombs and a series of fine stained-glass windows. The Domtoren (bell tower) opposite the building was connected to the cathedral until a hurricane in 1674 rent the two asunder. The bell tower is the tallest in the country and it has 456 steep steps which lead to a magnificent view. A guide is essential if you are not to get lost in the labyrinth of steps and passageways, a medieval device to confuse pursuing enemies! *Domplein. Admission: free to cathedral; Fl. 1.50 to Domtoren. Open May–Sept., daily 10–5; Oct.–Apr., daily 11–4.*

Close by the cathedral are two contrasting museums. **The Nationaal Museum van Speelklok tot Pierement** (Musical Clocks Museum) is devoted to music machines—from music boxes to street organs and even musical chairs. During the guided tour, music students play some of the instruments. The museum is housed in Utrecht's oldest parish church. *Buurkerkhof 10. Admission: Fl. 6. Open Tues.–Sat. 11–5, Sun. 1–5.*

The other museum, the **Hedendaagse Kunst,** houses a contemporary art collection. *Achter de Dom 14. Admission: Fl. 2.50. Open Tues.–Sat. 10–5.*

Behind the museums is **Pieterskerk,** the country's oldest Romanesque church, built in 1048. Among the city's other Romanesque churches are Jacobikerk, Buurkerk, Nicolaikerk, and Janskerk. The grandeur of the city's churches reflects the fact that Utrecht was northern Holland's religious center in the Middle Ages. Most churches are open in summer and are staffed by helpful guides. Since Utrecht is as musical as it is religious, there is a church concert most days. In September the town hosts a festival of ancient music. For details contact Postbus 734, tel. 030/340981.

Walk south out of Domplein, down Lange Nieuwstraat. Halfway down to your left is St. Catharijnekerk, on the left. At different times a nunnery, a hospital, and a barracks, it now houses the **Rijksmuseum Het Catharijneconvent.** In addition to its collection of holy relics and vestments, this museum contains the country's largest display of religious art and history. *Nieuwe Gracht 63. Admission: Fl. 3.50. Open Tues.–Fri. 10–5, weekends 11–5.*

There are also some peaceful almshouses in this area: the **Bruntenhofje,** on Lepelenburg, for women, and the **Bartholomei Gasthuis,** on Langesmee, for men. Continue walking down Lange Nieuwstraat past the **Butcher's Guildhall,** dating from 1673; and the **Cracknel House** in Keistraat, with its extraordinary decorations. A little farther on, you'll notice a huge rock, dragged there by an 18th-century eccentric as a result of a bet.

There are more museums to be explored on Agnientenstraat, which runs across Lange Nieuwstraat. The **Centraal Museum** houses a confusing but rich collection of pictures and exhibits of the city. Amid the clutter is an original Viking ship (discovered in 1930) and a 17th-century dolls' house complete with period furniture, porcelain, and miniature Old Masters. *Agnietenstraat 1. Admission: Fl. 2.50. Open Tues.–Sat. 10–5, Sun. 2–5.*

Leave some time to drift around the canals and appreciate the unique two-tiered effect created by the quays at canal level and the terraced streets above. The Oudegracht (Old Canal) snakes past converted warehouses, houses decorated with ancient signs, and walls embellished with local modern sculpture. Bustling Nieuwegracht (New Canal) displays elegant facades built onto medieval canalside houses. By contrast, the quiet Kromme Niewengracht is as much a backwater as it was when the Rhine silted up.

Gouda West of Utrecht, 36 kilometers (22 miles) along the A12, you come to **Gouda,** famous for its cheese. Try to be there on a Thursday morning in July or August, when the cheese market, centered around the **Waag,** or Weigh House, is held. Brightly colored farm wagons are loaded high with orange cheeses. While the bargaining goes on, you can sample the cheese by stepping into the back of the **Stadhuis** (Town Hall), where a film explains how the cheese is made. Take a good look at the Stadhuis; it's one of Holland's quaintest, with parts dating back to 1449. (Admission: Fl. 1. Open weekdays 10–4.) After trying all five types of Gouda cheese, leave some space for syrup waffles, Gouda's other specialty.

By the side of the market square is **Sint Janskerk** (Church of St. John); what you see today was built in the 16th century. It has the longest nave in the country, and 70 glorious stained-glass windows, the oldest of which dates from 1555. Around the corner from the cathedral is the Cathorina Gasthuis, now the **Stedelijk Museum Het Catharina Gasthuis,** the municipal museum that houses many unusual exhibits, including a fearsome medieval torture chamber and an equally horrific operating room. *Oosthaven 10. Admission: Fl. 3. Open Mon.–Sat. 10–5, Sun. 1–5.*

If you're tired of cheese, museums, and towns, you can escape for a day's sailing on the nearby Reeuwijk lakes. Remember, too, that Gouda is in polder country: Just outside town, the dikes meander into the clear distance of lush meadows, working windmills, and lugubrious Dutch cows. The VVV will suggest itineraries.

Leiden Heading due north on A4, you come to the ancient city of **Leiden,** once renowned for its spirit of religious and intellectual tolerance. Today it is better known for its university and royal connections. Start at the **Lakenhal,** built in 1639 for the city's cloth merchants and now an art gallery, cloth, and antiques museum. Pride of place in the collection goes to the 16th- and 17th-century Dutch paintings, with works by Steen, Dou, Rembrandt, and, above all, Lucas van Leyden's *Last Judgment—* the first great Renaissance painting. Other rooms are devoted to furniture and to the history of Leiden's medieval guilds: the drapers, tailors, and brewers. *Oude Singel 28. Admission: Fl. 3. Open Tues.–Sat. 10–5, Sun. 1–5.*

Near the Lakenhal are other museums, including the **Molenmuseum** (Windmill Museum), housed in an original windmill, built in 1747, which was worked by 10 generations of millers until 1964. The seven floors still contain the original workings, an old forge, washrooms, and living quarters. In summer, the mill turns—but for pleasure, not business. The visit may inspire you to explore Holland's thousands of windmills and water mills. A flag above the mill means that visitors are welcome. *Binnenvesstgracht 2. Admission: Fl. 3. Open Tues.–Sat. 10–5, Sun. 1–5.*

The **Museum Boerhaave** (National Science Museum) is a fascinating place containing many historic Dutch scientific instruments, such as the two globes that belonged to the cartographer Blaeu, microscopes made by Van Leeuwenhoek, thermometers made by Fahrenheit, an early planetarium, and much more. *Steenstraat 1. Admission: Fl. 3.50. Open Tues.–Sat. 10–5, Sun. 1–5.*

Crossing the canal and walking into narrow, bustling Breestraat, you'll come to the imposing **St. Pieterskerk,** with its memories of the Pilgrim Fathers who worshiped here and of their spiritual leader, John Robinson, who is buried here. A narrow street by the **Persijnhofje** almhouse, dating from 1683, takes you downhill, across the pretty Rapenburg Canal to the **academie** (university) and the **Hortus Botanicus** gardens. The university was founded by William the Silent as a reward to Leiden for its victory against the Spanish in the 1573–74 siege. During the war, the dikes were opened and the countryside flooded so that the rescuing navy could sail right up to the city walls. Members of the royal family generally attend Leiden's university, a tradition maintained by the present crown prince. After failing to meet the studious young prince in the quiet courtyard, visit the adjoining botanical gardens. Founded in 1587, these are among the oldest in the world. The highlights are a faithful reconstruction of a 16th-century garden, the herb garden, the colorful orangery, and the ancient trees. *Rapenburg 28. Admission: Fl. 4. Open Tues.–Sat. 10–5, Sun. 1–3.*

Follow Keiserstraat out of Rapenburg and turn left into Boisotkade. On your left is the **Pilgrim Fathers Documentatie Centrum.** This tiny museum contains photocopies of documents and maps related to the Pilgrims during their stay in Leiden, before going to Delftshaven on the first stage of their arduous voyage to the New World. *Vliet 45. Admission: free. Open weekdays 9:30–4:30.*

Before leaving Leiden, retrace your steps to the patrician Rapenburg, the city's most prestigious canal. In Leiden, as in most old Dutch towns, the aristocracy continues to live in the center. The tree-lined canal is crossed by triple-arched bridges and bordered by stately 18th-century houses, including the prince's current home. The stretch of houses from no. 19 to no. 31 is the city's finest example of such architecture, but many visitors fail to pass by no. 2 without entering De Doelen, the canal's most intimate restaurant (*see* Dining).

Haarlem Continue north along the A12 for 32 kilometers (20 miles) to Haarlem, stopping off at **Lisse** if you have time, to visit the 283-square kilometer (70-acre) Keukenhof Gardens. Set in a park intersected by canals and lakes, the world's largest flower show draws huge spring crowds to its regimental lines of tulips, hyacinths, and daffodils. (A lazier way of seeing the flowers is from the windows of the Leiden–Haarlem train.) *Admission: Fl. 13. Open late Mar.–late May, daily 8–7:30.*

With its secret inner courtyards and pointed gables **Haarlem** can resemble a 17th-century canvas, even one painted by Frans Hals, the city's greatest painter. The area around the **Grote Markt,** the market square, provides an architectural stroll through the 17th and 18th centuries. Some of the facades are adorned with such homilies as "The body's sickness is a cure for the soul." Haarlem's religious faith can also be sensed in any of its 20 almshouses. The **Stadhuis** (Town Hall) was once a hunting lodge, and the site dates from the 13th century, though there have been many changes since then. Nearby is the **Vleeshal,** or meat market, which has an especially fine gabled front. This dates from the early 1600s and is now used as an art gallery and museum of local history. *Lepelstraat. Admission: free. Open Mon.–Sat. 10–5, Sun. 1–5.*

Across from the Vleeshal is the **Grote Kerk,** dedicated to St. Bavo. The church, built between 1400 and 1550, houses one of Europe's most famous organs. This massive instrument has 5,000 pipes and both Mozart and Handel played on it. It is still used for concerts, and an annual organ festival is held here in July. Make your way down Damstraat, behind the Grote Kerk, and turn left at the **Waag** (Weigh House). On the left is the **Teylers Museum,** which claims to be the oldest museum in the country. It was founded by a wealthy merchant in 1778 as a museum of science and the arts; it now houses a fine collection of the Hague school of painting as well as a collection of drawings and sketches by Michelangelo, Raphael, and other non-Dutch masters. Since the canvases in this building are lit by natural light, try to see the museum on a sunny day. *Spaarne 16. Admission: Fl. 3. Open Tues.–Sat. 11–5, Sun. 1–5.*

Follow the Binnen Spaarn and turn right into Kampervest and then Gasthuisvest. On your right, in Groot Heligland, you'll find the **Frans Hals Museum.** This museum, in what used to be a 17th-century hospice, contains a marvelous collection of the artist's work; his paintings of the guilds of Haarlem are particularly noteworthy. The museum also has works by Hals's contemporaries. *Groot Heligland 62. Admission: Fl. 4. Open Mon.–Sat. 11–5, Sun. 1–5.*

Time Out As a summer break from Haarlem's daunting museums, **Zandvoort**'s sandy beaches can be very alluring. Adventurous visitors prefer the casino or the two-mile-long nudist beach. There are regular bus services to Zandvoort in the summer. For information, contact the VVV, tel. 02507/17947.

Dining and Lodging

In towns such as Apeldoorn and Lisse, with few good hotels, bed-and-breakfast accommodations, booked through the VVV, make a more interesting choice. Hotels in Utrecht are in short supply, so book in advance or immediately upon arrival. For details and price category definitions, *see* Dining and Lodging in Staying in Holland.

Apeldoorn **De Echoput.** This delightful restaurant is a member of the Alli-
Dining ance Gastronomique Nederlandaise, a guarantee of an expensive meal of local and gourmet specialties. There is an attractive terrace, overlooking fountains and greenery, for summer dining. *Amersfoortseweg 86, tel. 05769/248. Reservations essential. AE, DC, MC, V. Closed Sat. lunch, Mon. Expensive.*

Lodging **Motel Apeldoorn.** This comfortable hotel is set in the woods bordering the royal palace. Welcoming service and tranquillity make up for a modest restaurant and facilities. It is an ideal location for a leisurely exploration of local farmsteads and the Veluwe National Park. *JC Wilslaan 2000, tel. 055/550855. 32 rooms with bath. AE, DC, MC, V. Moderate.*

Gouda **D'Ouwe Stee.** If the weather permits, dine on the waterside ter-
Dining race; if not, the antique Dutch interior is just as charming. Though about 4 miles out of town, the trip is worth it for the fresh seafood; try the *maatjes haring* (raw herring). *'s-Gravenbroekseweg 80, tel. 01829/4008. Reservations advised. AE, DC, MC. Closed Tues. Expensive.*

Haarlem **De Coninckshoek.** The restaurant is situated in an atmospheric
Dining wine house dating from the 1650s. The building has been lov-
★ ingly restored and decorated in period style. Sitting beside a vast fireplace, diners can sample fish caught earlier that day. The choice covers everything from a snack to classic French or nouvelle cuisine. Last orders are taken at 11 PM. *Koningsstraat 1–5, tel. 023/314001. Reservations not necessary. AE, DC, V. Closed Sun. Expensive.*

Lodging **Golden Tulip Lion d'Or.** Situated just five minutes from the old city center, this comfortable but unprepossessing hotel offers all the small luxuries associated with a Golden Tulip hotel. Special weekend deals include reduced room prices, gourmet evening meals, free cocktails, and a round of golf at the local golf club. *Kruisweg 34–36, tel. 023/321750. 38 rooms with bath. Facilities: restaurant, conference rooms. AE, DC, MC, V. Expensive.*

Leiden **Oudt Leiden.** This Old Dutch restaurant is in fact two contrast-
Dining ing restaurants run by the same management. One is the renowned Rotisserie, famous for its roast meats and seafood specialties; the other is a hearty pancake house, serving *pannekochen* (pancakes) on huge plates. *Steenstraat 51, tel. 071/13344. Reservations advised. AE, DC, MC. Closed Sat. lunch and Sun. Moderate–Expensive.*

Dining and Lodging **Hotel Restaurant De Doelen.** This small hotel is situated in a characteristic patrician house which overlooks the royal family's Leiden residence. The spartan decor is in keeping with the character of the 15th-century house but the nine rooms are comfortable and much sought after. The French menu is innovative in its adaptation of French style to Dutch ingredients and portions. Specialties include duck's liver in a truffle sauce, duck in blackcurrants, and poached sole in watercress sauce. *Rapenburg 2, tel. 071/120527. 9 rooms with bath. Facilities: restaurant (evening reservations required). AE, DC, MC, V. Moderate.*

★ **Nieuw Minerva.** This family-run hotel is a conversion of eight 15th-century buildings. While the original part of the hotel is decorated in Old Dutch style, the newer part is better equipped but has slightly less character. Many of the rooms overlook a quiet tributary of the Rhine. The restaurant caters for most tastes and pockets. The excellent three-course tourist menu (Fl. 20) always offers separate fish, meat, and vegetarian menus. At the other end of the scale, there is a gastronomic menu (Fl. 80). Specialties include *châteaubriand de limousine* (rabbit drenched in Armagnac); Zeeland mussels in Noilly Prat sauce; and *assiette norvégienne* (smoked salmon, eel, and Dutch shrimp). All these delicacies are also found on the à la carte menu. *Boommarkt 22–29, tel. 071/126358. 40 rooms, 30 with bath. Restaurant reservations advised. AE, DC, MC, V. Closed Sun. lunch. Moderate.*

Lisse **De Nachtegaal van Lisse.** The hotel's location just outside town
Lodging makes it ideal for visitors to the Keukenhof Gardens. Convenience, comfort, and excellent sports facilities compensate for an impersonal atmosphere. The restaurant serves international cuisine. *Heereweg 10, tel. 02521/14447. 148 rooms with bath. Facilities: restaurant, swimming pool, tennis. AE, DC, MC, V. Expensive.*

Utrecht **Het Draeckje.** This typical Dutch restaurant is set in a vaulted
Dining cellar on Utrecht's loveliest canal. As a member of the Nederlands Dis chain of traditional restaurants, it offers a seasonal menu at a reasonable price. Coffee is accompanied by the local spicy biscuits. *Oude Gracht 114–120, tel. 030/321999. Reservations advised on weekends. AE, DC, MC. Closed Sun. Moderate.*

Lodging **Malie.** The recently renovated Malie hotel is on a quiet leafy street, five minutes' walk from the old center. This small, friendly hotel has an attractive dining room (breakfast only) overlooking the garden and terrace. It offers special reduced weekend rates. *Maliestraat 2–4, tel. 030/316424. 30 rooms with bath or shower. AE, DC, MC, V. Moderate.*

The Hague, Scheveningen, and Delft

Within this itinerary you can visit the Netherlands's most dignified and spacious city: the royal, diplomatic, and governmental seat of Den Haag (in English, better known as The Hague); its close neighbor, the leading North Sea beach resort of Scheveningen; and nearby Delft, an historic city with many canals and ancient buildings.

Getting Around

The Hague and Delft are 60 kilometers (37.5 miles) southwest of Amsterdam and can be reached in less than an hour by fast and frequent trains. The hearts of both towns are compact enough to be explored on foot. Scheveningen is reached from The Hague's center by bus or tram. Travelers will find public transportation more convenient than driving because of severe parking problems at the resort. If the weather is bad or walking becomes tiring, taxis are readily available.

Guided Tours

Boat Trips From The Hague, various boat companies run short day trips and longer candle-lit dinner cruises. These can be booked at The Hague VVV or through **Rondvaartbadrijf RVH** (Spui 279, near the central station, tel. 070/3462437). Scheveningen offers fishing-boat tours around the Dutch coast. Contact **Sportsviscentrum** (Scheveningen, tel. 070/3541122). In Delft, the VVV organizes boat tours along the unspoiled canal system.

Orientation Tours City sightseeing tours of The Hague can be arranged by or through the main VVV office next to the central station. The size and diversity of the city make a bus tour a logical choice. The "Royal Bus Tour" leaves from outside the VVV office at 1:30 every day. The trip includes background on the royal family and visits to Queen Beatrix's residences. Book in advance at the VVV; cost: Fl. 20 for a three-hour tour. The Hague **Museum Bus** operates on the same principal as the Amsterdam Museum Boat: A special VVV shuttle bus takes visitors from one museum to another. The cost is Fl. 2; get details from the VVV.

Scheveningen and Delft are best seen on foot. Delft VVV organizes tours while Scheveningen VVV will advise on coastal strolls.

Tourist Information

Delft. Markt 85, tel. 015/126100. Open Mon.–Sat. 9–6, Sun. 11–3. When the VVV office is closed, the latest hotel information is posted in the window.

The Hague. Babylon Center, tel. 070/3546200. Open Apr.–mid-Sept., Mon.–Sat. 9–8, Sun. 10–5; mid-Sept.–Mar., Mon.–Sat. 9–6, Sun. 10–5.

Scheveningen. Gevers Deynootweg 126 (corner of Scheveningseslag), tel. 070/542402. Open Apr.–mid-Sept., Mon.–Sat. 9–8, Sun. 10–5; mid-Sept.–Mar., Mon.–Sat. 9–5, Sun. 10–5.

If you're staying a few days in The Hague, ask for the *VVV Info* brochure on city events and entertainment. Tickets can be reserved in person at the main VVV office.

Exploring The Hague, Scheveningen, and Delft

In the 17th century, The Hague was known as "The Whispering Gallery of Europe" because it was thought to be the secret manipulator of European politics. Although the Golden Age is over, The Hague remains a dignified diplomatic capital, quietly boastful of its royal connections.

Its heart is the **Ridderzaal** (Knight's Hall), the center of a government complex, which is located by the peaceful Vijver lake. Inside are vast beams spanning a width of 18 meters (59 feet), flags, and stained-glass windows. A sense of history pervades the 13th-century great hall. It is now mainly used for ceremonies: Every year the queen's gilded coach brings her here to open Parliament. The two government chambers sit separately in buildings on either side of the Ridderzaal and can be visited by guided tour only when Parliament is not in session. *Binnenhof 8a. Open Mon.–Sat. 10–4. Cost: Fl. 4.50. For a guided tour in English, book in advance, tel. 070/3646144.*

Keeping the Ridderzaal on your right, pass through two narrow archways and emerge on the far side of the **Binnenhof,** the inner court of the former castle. The small, well-proportioned Dutch Renaissance building immediately on your left, its back bordering Vijver lake, is the **Mauritshuis,** one of the greatest small art museums in the world. This superb 17th-century palace contains a feast of art from the same period, including 15 Rembrandts; of these the most powerful is *The Anatomy Lesson of Dr. Tulp*, a theatrical work depicting a gruesome dissection of the lower arm. Also featured are Vermeer's celebrated *Girl Wearing a Turban*, and his masterpiece, the glistening *View of Delft*, moodily emerging from a cloudburst. *Korte Vijverberg 8. Admission: Fl. 6.50. Open Tues.–Sat. 10–5, Sun. 11–5.*

Outside the Mauritshuis, follow the Korte Vijverberg past Vijver Lake. The lake is bordered by patrician houses with revamped 18th- and 19th-century facades, a sign of the area's continuing popularity with the local aristocracy. Only the presence of huge ducks ruffles the surface of this stately lake.

Turn right at Lange Vijverberg and walk until you come to Lange Voorhout, a large L-shaped avenue. In the last century, horse-drawn trams clattered along its cobbles and deposited dignitaries outside the various palaces. Apart from the trams, not much has changed: Diplomats still eat in the historic Hotel des Indes; Queen Beatrix and her staff work in the 16th-century Noordeinde Palace. No. 34 once belonged to William I, the first king of the Netherlands, but later it became the royal library; it is now the **Supreme Court.** With its clumsy skewed

The Hague, Scheveningen, and Delft

0   5 miles   Noordwijk-Binnen

0   5 km   Katwijk aan Zee

North Sea

Wassenaar   **Leiden**

Scheveningen

The Hague   Voorberg
(Den Haag)   Zoetermeer

Rijkswijk

Monster   Poeldijk

Hoek van   **Delft**
Holland

Naaldwijk   A13

Europoort   *Niewe*   A20

Maassluis   *Maas*   **Rotterdam**

A15

N

gable, the headquarters of the Dutch Red Cross at no. 6 seems out of place on this stately avenue. A few doors down, at the corner of Parkstraat, is The Hague's oldest church, the **Kloosterkerk,** built in 1400, and once used by the Black Friars. In spring, the adjoining square is covered with yellow and purple croci; on Thursdays in summer, it is covered with a colorful antique market.

If a less reverential detour is required, follow any of the small streets leading off Lange Voorhout to the northeast. This area, bounded by Denneweg, Hooikade, and Maliestraat, was a busy canal network until it was filled in during the last century. It is now the city's trendiest neighborhood, an appealing mixture of coffee bars, restaurants, and boutiques. The few remaining canals are surprisingly peaceful. It is just the place to grab a quick bowl of Dutch pea soup, a pancake, or an Indonesian snack. The locals often prefer the herring cart in Maliestraat.

Once back in Lange Voorhout, take the Kneuterdijk road south toward the inner court and lake. After pausing at the Plaats Square to admire the greedy Hague ducks, look at the **Gevangenpoort,** the 14th-century prison gate. For many centuries a prison, it is today a museum of instruments of torture. *Buitenhof 33. Admission: Fl. 4. Open Apr.–Sept., weekdays 10–5, weekends 1–5.*

As you leave the prison gate, a right turn brings you to the **Buitenhof** (Outer Court), opposite the entrance to the Ridderzaal, where this tour began.

A second route is farther out but within walking distance of the center. North of Lange Voorhout is the **Panorama Mesdag,** a huge painting-in-the-round which shows Scheveningen as it looked in 1880. Housed in a specially designed building, the painting encompasses you in its 124-meter (400-foot) circumference. Hendrik Mesdag was a late-19th-century marine painter, and his calming seascape is painted in the typically melancholic colors of the Hague School. However, Mesdag was helped by his wife, who painted much of the fishing village, and by a friend who painted the sky and dunes. *Zeestraat 65b. Admission: Fl. 3. Open Tues.–Sat. 10–5, Sun. noon–5.*

Just around the corner in Laan van Meerdervoort is the painter's home, now transformed into the **Rijksmuseum H. W. Mesdag.** Paintings by Mesdag and members of the Hague School are hung beside those of Corot, Courbet, and Rousseau. These delicate landscapes represent one of the finest collections of Impressionists outside France. *Laan van Meerdervoort 7f. Admission: Fl. 4. Open Tues.–Sat. 10–5, Sun. 1–5.*

The **Vredespaleis** (Peace Palace), just behind Laan van Meerdervoort, is a monument to an unrealized ideal. Following the first peace conference at The Hague in 1899, the American millionaire Andrew Carnegie donated $1.5 million for the construction of a building to house a proposed Court of Arbitration. The Dutch government donated the grounds, and other nations offered furnishings and decorations. Although it still looks like a dull multinational bank, it has been improved by such gifts as Japanese wall hangings, a Danish fountain, and a grand staircase presented by The Hague. Today, the **International Court of Justice,** consisting of 15 jurists, has its seat here. There are guided tours daily when the court is not in session; tel. 070/3469680 for details.

The adjacent **Haags Gemeentemuseum** (Municipal Art Museum) is the home of the largest collection of Mondrians in the world and a fascinating building in itself. It was built in 1935 and is an example of the International Movement in modern architecture. *Stadhouderslaan 41. Admission: Fl. 3. Open Tues.–Fri. 10–5, weekends noon–5.*

The Hague is a city of parks, the biggest of which is the **Zorgvliet,** separating city from countryside. Opposite the park is the **Omniversum,** described as Europe's first space theater. It is housed in a cylindrical building with a 75-foot dome that acts as a screen for the projection of dramatic presentations of outer space and oceanic voyages. *President Kennedylaan 5, tel. 070/3545454. Admission: Fl. 10 adults, Fl. 7 children. Open Tues.–Thurs. 11–4, Fri.–Sun. 11–9.*

Between The Hague and Scheveningen is **Madurodam,** a miniature city where everything is scaled to 1/52 of what its life-size counterpart would be. None of the details of a real city have been forgotten, from the harbor, with its lighthouse and quayside cranes, to the hand-carved furniture in the gabled houses. Son et lumière (sound and light) shows are planned for the summer months. *Haringkade 17, tel. 070/3553900. Admission: Fl. 8–Fl. 22. Open Mar.–June, 9 AM–10 PM; June–Aug., 9 AM–10:30 PM; Sept., 9–9; Oct.–Jan. 9–6.*

Scheveningen **Scheveningen** is adjacent to The Hague, to the north. A fishing village since the 14th century, it became popular as a beach resort during the last century, when the Kurhaus Hotel was built. After years of decline, the resort has become popular again and has been revitalized, with a casino, restaurants, and nightlife.

The beach itself, protected from tidal erosion by stone jetties, slopes gently into the North Sea in front of a high promenade whose function is to protect the boulevard and everything behind it from the fury of the winter storms. The surface of the beach is fine sand, and you can bicycle or walk for miles to the north.

The Pier, completed in 1962, stretches 372 meters (1,200 feet) into the sea. Its four circular end buildings provide a sun terrace and restaurant, a 43-meter- (141-foot-) high observation tower, an amusement center with children's play area, and an underwater panorama. Part of the new design around the Kurhaus area includes the Golfbad, a surf pool complete with artificial waves. At 11 on summer evenings, the Pier is the scene of dramatic fireworks displays.

Thirteen kilometers (8 miles) along the A13 from The Hague, you enter **Delft.** There is probably no spot in The Netherlands that is more intimate, more attractive, or more traditional than this little town, whose famous blue-and-white earthenware is so popular throughout the world. Compact and easy to explore, despite its web of canals, Delft is best discovered on foot, although water taxis are available in summer, when, on Tuesday, Wednesday, Friday, and Saturday, you also can enjoy a ride on a horse-drawn bus that leaves from the marketplace. Every street is lined with attractive medieval Gothic and Renaissance houses that bear such names as Wijnhaus (Wine House) and Boter Brug (Butter Bridge).

In the marketplace, the only lively spot in this tranquil town, is the **Nieuwe Kerk** (New Church), built in the 14th century, with its piercing Gothic spire 93 meters (300 feet) high, a magnificent carillon of 48 bells, and the tomb of William the Silent. Beneath this grotesque black marble sarcophagus is a crypt containing the remains of members of the Orange-Nassau line, including all members of the royal family since King William I ascended the throne in the mid-16th century. *Admission: Fl. 2. Open Apr.–Sept., Mon.–Sat. 9–5; Oct.–Mar., Mon.–Sat. 10– noon and 1:30–3.*

While in Delft, you will certainly want to see the famous local specialty—Delftware. Decorated porcelain was brought to Holland from China on East India Company ships and was so much in demand that Dutch potters of the time felt their livelihood was being threatened, so they set about the creation of pottery to rival Chinese porcelain. There are only two manufacturers which still make hand-painted Delftware: **De Delftse Pauw** and the more famous "Royal" **De Porceleyne Fleys.** Original Delft is sold here in the market in the De Backer shop, but to see it being made, visit the De Porceleyne Fleys workshops. *Rotterdamsweg 136, tel. 015/560234. Admission: free. Open Mar.–Oct., Mon.–Sat. 9–5, Sun. 10–4; Nov.–Feb., weekdays 9–5, Sat. 10–4.*

On the other side of the marketplace is the town hall, with a collection of paintings by Delft artists. Or walk around the right side of the Nieuwe Kerk, then left at the back and along the Vrouwenregt canal for a few steps before taking another left turn into Voldergracht. To the left, the backs of the houses rise straight from the water as you stroll to the end of the street, which is marked by the sculptured animal heads and outdoor stairs of the old **Meat Market** on the right. Cross the Wijnhaven and turn left along its far side to the Koornmarkt, a stately canal spanned by a high arching bridge that is one of the hallmarks of Delft.

At no. 67 is the **Paul Tetar van Elven Museum,** an artist's house with a Louis XIV–style room and an upstairs studio that seems to have been asleep since the time of Vermeer. *Koornmarkt 67. Admission: Fl. 3. Open mid–Apr.–mid.–Oct., Tues.–Sat. 11–5.*

Just before the end of the Koornmarkt is the **Wapenhuis van Holland** (arsenal), completed in 1692. Turn right to the **Oude Delft canal,** the city's oldest waterway. A few blocks farther along the canal, you will come upon the incredible Gothic facade of the **Gemeenlandshuis,** built as a private residence in 1520, with a flamboyant display of painted coats of arms from 1652. A few doors on is the **Prinsenhof,** formerly the Convent of St. Agatha, founded in 1400. The chapel inside dates from 1471; its interior is remarkable for the wooden statues under the vaulting ribs. Today, the Prinsenhof is a museum that tells the story of the liberation of the Netherlands after 80 years of Spanish occupation (1568–1648). For Dutch royalists, the spot is significant for the assassination of Prince William of Orange in 1584; the bullet holes can still be seen in the wall. *St. Agathaplein 1. Admission: Fl. 4.50. Open Tues.–Sat. 10–5, Sun. 1–5.*

Across the Oude Delft canal is the **Oude Kerk** (Old Church), a vast Gothic monument of the 13th century. Its beautiful tower, surmounted by a brick spire, leans somewhat alarmingly. *Admission: Fl. 2. Open Apr.–Sept. noon–4.*

Beyond the Prinsenhof on the same side of the Oude Delft canal is the **Lambert van Meerten Museum,** a mansion whose timbered rooms are filled with the country's most complete collection of old Dutch tiles as well as Delft pottery. *Oude Delft 199. Admission: Fl. 4. Open Tues.–Sat. 10–5, Sun. 1–5.*

Dining and Lodging

For details and price category definitions, *see* Dining and Lodging in Staying in Holland.

Delft
Dining
De Bark. A small, family-run restaurant in the old Hotel De Ark, De Bark's motto is "Sunday Meals the Whole Week 'Round," an excuse for rich, substantial dishes such as steak in red wine. The specialty is *wiener ark*, wiener schnitzel coated in asparagus and cheese. There is a small but pricy wine list. *Koornmarkt 59–65, tel. 015/140552. Reservations recommended. AE, MC, V. Expensive.*

Exprezzo. For a light meal in a trendy Italian designer café, Exprezzo is the place. In this bright black-and-white marble interior, fashion-conscious students eat pancakes or fresh pasta. Designed as an art gallery, the restaurant has plants, paintings, and geometric furniture—all as much fun as the food. *Oude Delft 135, tel. 015/123108. No reservations. No credit cards. Closed Mon. Inexpensive.*

Lodging
★
Hotel De Ark. This pleasant hotel is set in a small but perfectly formed 16th-century gentleman's house. When the present

owners renovated it, they discovered medieval latrines, pieces of Delftware, and an ancient walking stick—treasures now proudly displayed. The Richardus family has a light touch: service is gracious, personal, and gently ironic. The hotel's location on one of Delft's finest canals is convenient for the Delftware museum and for boat trips. *Koornmarkt 59–65, tel. 015/140552. 15 rooms with bath; 8 luxury apartments. Facilities: restaurant. Expensive.*

The Hague
Dining

Villa Rosenrust. The Villa Rosenrust is a converted 18th-century mansion in Leidschendam, 4.8 kilometers (3 miles) from The Hague. There is a summer terrace for outdoor dining; inside, there are numerous plants and an elegant atmosphere. As a member of the Alliance Gastronomique, the Villa promises a diverse menu of seasonal items and a superb wine list. The excellent French and Italian menu is supervised by the Italian owner. Keep an eye peeled for truffles. *Veursestraatweg 104, tel. 070/3600772. Reservations essential. AE, DC, MC, V. Closed Sat. lunch, Sun. Very Expensive.*

Dining and Lodging
★

Hotel des Indes. For over 100 years, des Indes has offered impeccable service to diplomats and kings, dancers and spies. Memories of famous guests remain in the form of Emperor Haile Selassie's gold chair and the ballerina Pavlova's silver candlesticks. Pavlova and the spy Mata Hari both have suites named for them. In the elegant Le Restaurant, Pavlova Meringue is as light as you would expect. A Menu Gastronomique offers a taste of everything (Fl. 100). The Menu des Gourmets includes such delicacies as pigeon soup followed by pheasant with wild mushroom, and goose liver salad followed by a steak in mustard sauce. *Lange Voorhout 54, tel. 070/3469553. 77 rooms with bath. Restaurant reservations advised. AE, DC, MC, V. Closed Mon. Expensive.*

Scheveningen
Dining

Seinpost. Located near historic Seinpostdune, where Hendrik Mesdag painted his famous panorama, Seinpost has wonderful sea views. The menu, which changes daily, is excellent; try the oysters, the new herring, or just about any of the seafood specialties. The restaurant is a member of the Alliance Gastronomique. *Zeekant 60. tel. 070/3555250. Reservations essential. AE, DC, MC, V. Closed Sat. lunch, Sun. Mon. and part of July and Aug.*

Lodging
★

Steigenberger Kurhaus. At the turn of the century, this was a fashionable and aristocratic resort hotel. After a long time in decline, it was restored and reopened, having added a casino among its new attractions. Many of the rooms have balconies that overlook the sea, creating a comfortable, spacious effect. The restaurant, Kandinsky, is well known for its classic French cuisine as well as its decor, which includes signed Kandinsky prints. *Gevers Deynootplein 30, tel. 070/3520052. 250 rooms with bath. AE, DC, MC, V. Very Expensive.*

16 Hungary

Introduction

Hungary sits at the crossroads of central Europe, having retained its own identity by absorbing countless invasions and foreign occupations. Its industrious, resilient people have a history of brave but unfortunate uprisings: against the Turks in the 17th century, the Habsburgs in 1848, and the Soviet Union in 1959. Each has resulted in a period of readjustment, a return to politics as the art of the possible.

Because it is a small, agriculturally oriented country, visitors are often surprised by its grandeur and Old World charm. Even though Hungarians complain about their current economic problems, high inflation, and stagnant wages, they spare visitors much of the bureaucratic hassle associated with the rest of eastern Europe. Westerners are allowed to travel freely and are not forced to exchange currency daily.

The interior of the country is bisected by two rivers: The famous Duna (Danube) flows from the west through Budapest on its way to the southern frontier, while the smaller Tisza flows from the northeast across the Nagyalföld (Great Plain). What Hungary lacks in size, it makes up for in beauty and charm. Western Hungary is dominated by the splendor of the largest lake in central Europe, Lake Balaton. Its shores are lined with Baroque villages, internationally known spas, magnificent vineyards, and inexpensive restaurants serving up the catch of the day. In eastern Hungary, the Nagyalföld offers visitors a chance to explore the folklore and customs of the Magyars (the Hungarians' name for themselves and their language). It is an area of spicy food, strong wine, and the proud Csikos (horsemen). The unspoiled towns of the provinicial areas are rich in history and culture.

However, it is Budapest, a city with over two million people, which draws travelers from all over the world. The hills of Buda shoot up from the banks of the Danube, while the Pest side is an endless array of cafés and restaurants. Throughout Hungary, comfortable accommodations–including an impressive network of inexpensive guest homes–and superb food and wine are coupled with modest prices.

Hungarians are a hospitable people who welcome and take an interest in foreigners. (Many young people now speak some English.) You'll find them expansive and amusing on the subject of their country and its tumultuous history but also justly proud of their rich and varied cuisine and delicious wines. Particularly attractive to music lovers, Hungary offers a feast of musical events throughout the year, from Budapest's spring and fall festivals to the lone violinist who accompanies your evening meal.

Before You Go

When to Go Many of Hungary's major fairs and festivals take place in the spring and fall. During July and August, Budapest can be hot and the resorts at Lake Balaton crowded, so late spring (May) and the end of summer (September) are the ideal times to visit.

Climate The following are average daily maximum and minimum temperatures for Budapest.

Hungary

SOVIET UNION

ROMANIA

CZECHOSLOVAKIA

YUGOSLAVIA

AUSTRIA

YUGOSLAVIA

50 miles
75 km

N

Kisvárda
Vásárosnamény
Mátészalka
Sárospatak
Sátoraljaújhely
Tokaj
Nyírbátor
Debrecen
Hajdú-
böszörmény
Hajdúszoboszló
Agtelek
Kazinbarcika
Leninváros
Nyíregyháza
Ózd
Miskolc
Mezőkövesd
Tiszafüred
Hortobágy
Karcag
Berettyó
Salgótarján
Eger
Gyöngyös
Heves
Kiskőrei
Reservoir
Kisújszállás
Túrkeve
Békés
Békéscsaba
Gyula
Jholy
Balassa-
gyarmat
Hatvan
Jászberény
Törökszentmiklós
Szolnok
Nagykőrös
Körös
Szarvas
Szentes
Orosháza
Hódmezővásárhely
Makó
Vác
Gödöllő
Budapest
Cegléd
Kecskemét
Csongrád
Tisza
Szeged
Ipoly
Esztergom
Dorog
Szentendre
Lake Velencei
Dunaújváros
Kiskun-
félegyháza
Kiskőrös
Kiskunhalas
Komárom
Tatabánya
Székesfehérvár
Dunaföldvár
Kalocsa
Danube
Mosonmagyaróvár
Zirc
Várpalota
Veszprém
Paks
Szekszárd
Baja
Győr
Pápa
Siófok
Sió
Dombóvár
Bátaszék
Mohács
Rába
Ajka
Balatonfüred
Tapolca
Lake Balaton
Tamási
Kapos
Komló
Pécs
Mórai
Kapuvár
Marcali
Nagykanizsa
Kaposvár
Nagyatád
Szigetvár
Barcs
Sopron
Szombathely
Sárvár
Vasvár
Zala
Keszthely
Boglárlelle
Dráva
Köszeg
Körmend
Zalaegerszeg
Lenti
Nensiedler
See

Danube
Tisza

Jan.	34F	1C	May	72F	22C	Sept.	73F	23C
	25	−4		52	11		54	12
Feb.	39F	4C	June	79F	26C	Oct.	61F	16C
	28	−2		59	15		45	7
Mar.	50F	10C	July	82F	28C	Nov.	46F	8C
	36	2		61	16		37	3
Apr.	63F	17C	Aug.	81F	27C	Dec.	39F	4C
	45	7		61	16		30	−1

Currency   The unit of currency is the forint (Ft.), divided into 100 fillérs (f.). There are bills of 50, 100, 500, and 1,000; and coins of 10, 20, and 50 fillérs and of 1,2,5,10, and 20 forints. The tourist exchange rate was 60 Ft. to the dollar and 100 Ft. to the pound sterling at press time (spring 1989), but these rates are likely to alter both before and during 1990. Note that official exchange rates are adjusted every Tuesday.

Hungary, unlike other Eastern European countries, does not require you to change a certain sum of money for each day of your stay. Exchange money as you need it at banks, hotels, or travel offices, but take care not to change too much because, although in theory you can change back 50% (up to $100) of the original sum when you leave, it may prove difficult in practice.

Most credit cards are accepted, though don't rely on them in smaller towns or less expensive accommodations and restaurants. Eurocheque holders can cash personal checks in all banks and in most hotels.

There is a black market in currency but you will not gain much and could lose a good deal by taking advantage of it. It is illegal to give or sell hard currency to a Hungarian. While you may bring in any amount of foreign currency, you may only bring in up to 100 Ft. in coins (no bills) of Hungarian currency.

What It Will Cost   Although first-class hotels chains in Budapest charge standard international prices, quality hotels are still modest by Western standards. Even though the introduction of value-added tax (VAT) in 1988 has increased many of the prices in the service industry by up to 25%, and the annual inflation rate of 15% keeps creeping higher, enjoyable vacations with all the trimmings still remain relatively inexpensive.

Sample Prices   Cup of coffee, 20–45 Ft.; bottle of beer, 50–75 Ft.; soft drinks, 20–50 Ft.; ham sandwich, 100 Ft.; 1-mile taxi ride, 40 Ft.; museum admission, 10 Ft.

Visas   American, Canadian, and British citizens need both a valid passport and a visa to visit Hungary. If you arrive by plane or car, you can obtain a visa on arrival, but it is advisable to arrange one in advance in order to avoid tiresome delays and an additional charge. If you are traveling by bus or train, you *must* get your visa in advance. Apply to the Hungarian consulate in your own country or to an accredited travel agent. For a 30-day visa, send your valid passport and two passport-size photos to: **Hungarian Consulate** (8 E. 75th St., New York, NY 10021, tel. 212/879–4126); **Hungarian Embassy** (3910 Shoemaker St., NW, Washington, DC 20008, tel. 202/362–6730); **Hungarian Embassy** (7 Delaware Ave., Ottawa K2P 0Z2, Ontario, Canada, tel. 613/234–8316); or **Hungarian Consulate** (35b Eaton Place, London SW1, tel. 01/491–2952). Visas are no longer required for groups staying less than 48 hours. At press time (spring 1989), the fee for obtaining a visa was U.S. $15 or U.K. £10. Call to confirm this before sending your passport through the mail.

Visitors must register with the police within 48 hours of arrival —this is taken care of automatically if you are staying in a hotel or in private accommodations arranged for you through a tourist office. If you are staying with relatives or friends, a form, which costs 10 Ft., must be bought from the post office and taken with your passport to the local police station. Your visa can be extended for a further 30 days at a cost of 300 Ft. (in stamps available from the post office) on application to the local police station.

Customs
On Arrival Objects for personal use may be imported freely. If you are over 16, you may also bring in 250 grams of tobacco, plus two liters of wine, one liter of spirits, and 250 grams of perfume. A 30% customs charge is made on gifts valued in Hungary at more than 10,000 Ft.

On Departure Take care when you leave Hungary that you have the right documentation for exporting goods. Keep receipts of any items bought from Konsumtourist, Intertourist, or Kepcsarnok Vallalat. A special permit is needed for works of art valued at more than 1,000 Ft.

Language Hungarian (Magyar) tends to look and sound intimidating to everyone at first because it is a non–Indo-European language. Generally, older people speak some German and many younger people speak at least rudimentary English. However, anyone in the tourist trade will speak at least one of the two languages.

Getting Around

By Car
Documentation To drive in Hungary, U.S. and Canadian visitors need an International Driver's License, and U.K. visitors need a domestic driving license.

Road Conditions There are three classes of road: highways (designated by the letter M and a single digit); secondary roads (designated by a two-digit number), and minor roads (three digits). Highways and secondary roads are generally excellent. The condition of minor roads varies considerably. There are no toll charges on highways.

Rules of the Road Hungarians drive on the right and observe the usual Continental rules of the road. The speed limit in developed areas is 60 kph (37 mph), on main roads 80 kph (50 mph), and on highways 120 kph (75 mph). Seat belts are compulsory and drinking strictly prohibited—the penalties are very severe. At press time a road toll affecting all motorists was being considered— contact Budapest Tourist (*see* Important Addresses and Numbers in Budapest) for the latest information.

Gasoline Gas stations are not as plentiful in Hungary as in Western Europe, so fill up whenever possible and check on tourist maps for exact locations of stations throughout the country. A gallon of gasoline *(benzin)* costs about $2. Unleaded gasoline, only slightly more expensive, is available at stations in Budapest, on all the major routes from the city, and at more and more stations in the provinces. Interag Shell and Afor stations at busy traffic centers stay open all night; elsewhere, from 6 AM to 8 PM. Diesel oil can be bought only with coupons from IBUSZ travel offices at the border or from hotels. They are nonrefundable, so try to calculate how many you will need.

Breakdowns The **Hungarian Automobile Club** runs a 24-hour "Yellow Angels" breakdown service from Budapest XIV, Fráncia Út 38/A, tel. 1/691–831 or 1/693–714. There are repair stations in all the major towns and emergency telephones on the main highways.

By Train Travel by train from Budapest to other large cities or to Lake Balaton is cheap and efficient. Remember to take *gyorsvonat* (express trains) and not *személyvonát* (locals), which are extremely slow. A *platzkarte* (seat reservation), which costs 16 Ft. and is sold up to 60 days in advance, is advisable for all express trains, especially during weekend travel in summer. It is also worth paying a little extra for first-class tickets.

Fares Unlimited travel tickets for seven or 10 days are inexpensive, 700 Ft. and 1,200 Ft. respectively (subject to change). All students with a valid I.D. receive 50% off. InterRail cards are valid for those under 26, and the Rail Europe Senior Travel Pass entitles senior citizens to a 30% reduction on all trains. Snacks and drinks are available on all express trains, but the supply often runs out quickly, especially in summer, so pack a lunch just in case. For more information about rail travel, contact or visit **MAV Passenger Service**, B.P. VI Népköztársaság útju 35, Budapest (tel. 1/228–049).

By Bus Long-distance buses link Budapest with many main cities in Eastern and Western Europe. Services to the eastern part of the country leave from Népstadion station (tel. 1/187–052). Buses to the west and south, to Austria and Yugoslavia, leave from the main Volán bus station at Engels Tér in the Inner City (tel. 1/172–511). Although cheap, they tend to be crowded, so reserve your seat.

By Boat Hungary is well equipped with nautical transport, and Budapest is situated on a major international waterway—the Danube. Vienna (five hours away) and many Hungarian resorts are accessible by hydrofoil or boat. For information about excursions or pleasure cruises, contact **MAHART Landing Stage** (1 Vigadó Tér, V, Budapest, tel. 1/181–223), or **IBUSZ** (Hungarian Travel Bureau) (Tanács Körút 3/C, V11, Budapest, tel. 1/423–140).

By Bicycle A land of rolling hills and flat plains, Hungary lends itself to the bicyclist. The larger train stations around Lake Balaton have bicycles for rent at about 50 Ft. a day. For information about renting bicycles in Budapest, contact **Tourinform** (Sütő Utca 2, tel. 1/179–800). **HUNTOURS** provides full service for guided bicycle tours (Retek Utca 34, tel. 1/152–403).

Staying in Hungary

Telephones Pay phones use 2 Ft. coins—the cost of a three-minute local
Local Calls call. Most towns in Hungary can be dialed directly—dial 06 and wait for the buzzing tone; then dial the local number.

International Calls Direct calls to foreign countries can be made from Budapest and all major provincial towns only by using the red push-button telephones, or from hotels and post offices, and by dialing 00 and waiting for the international dialing tone.

Operators International calls can be made through the operator by dialing

09; for operator-assisted calls within Hungary, dial 01. The entire system is currently being updated.

Information Dial 172–200 for information in English.

Mail Stamps can be bought from tobacco shops as well as post offices. The post offices at the Keleti (East) and Nyugati (West) train stations are open 24 hours.

Postal Rates An airmail postcard to the United States costs 12 Ft., and an airmail letter costs from 17 Ft. Postcards to the United Kingdom and the rest of Western Europe cost 10 Ft., letters 15 Ft.

Receiving Mail A poste restante service is available in Budapest. The address is Magyar Posta, H-1052 Budapest, Petőfi Sándor Utca 17–19.

Opening and **Banks.** Banks are open weekdays 8–1.
Closing Times **Museums.** Most museums are open daily from 10 to 6, and closed Mondays.
Shops. Shops are open weekdays 10–6, Saturday 9–1. Many shops stay open until 8 on Thursday.

National Holidays January 1 (New Year's Day); March 15 (Anniversary of 1848 revolution); April 4 (Liberation Day); April 15–16 (Easter); May 1 (Labor Day); August 20 (St. Stephen's and Constitution Day); December 25 and 26.

Dining There is no shortage of good, affordably priced restaurants offering a variety of Hungarian dishes. Meats, rich sauces, and creamy desserts are the dominant themes, but the more health- and figure-conscious will also find salads, even out of season. There are also self-service restaurants *(önkiszolgáló étterem)*, snack bars *(bistró* or *étel bár)*, buffets *(büfé)*, cafés *(eszpresszó)*, and bars *(drink-bár)*. The pastry shops *(cuk-rászda)* are also worth a try.

In almost all restaurants, an inexpensive fixed-price lunch, called a "menu," is available, usually for as little as 75 Ft. It includes soup or salad, an entrée, and a dessert.

Mealtimes Hungarians eat early—you risk off-hand service and cold food after 9 PM. Lunch—for many the main meal—is served noon–2. It is hard to find a sit-down meal between 2:30 and 4:30.

Dress Jacket and tie are appropriate for restaurants in the top price categories. At other restaurants, casual but neat dress is acceptable.

Ratings Prices are per person and include a first course, main course, and dessert, but no wine or tip. Prices in Budapest could be up to 30% higher. Best bets are indicated by a star ★. At press time (spring 1989), there were 60 Ft. to the dollar.

Category	All Areas
Expensive	over 750 Ft.
Moderate	450–750 Ft.
Inexpensive	under 450 Ft.

Credit Cards The following credit card abbreviations are used: AE, American Express; DC, Diners Club; MC, MasterCard; V, Visa.

Lodging There are no Very Expensive and few Expensive hotels outside
Hotels Budapest, but the Moderate hotels are generally comfortable

and well-run, although single rooms with baths are scarce. Establishments in the Inexpensive category seldom have private baths, but plumbing is satisfactory almost everywhere. Reservations should be made as far in advance as possible, especially with the less expensive establishments, which are still in short supply.

Rentals Apartments in Budapest and cottages at Lake Balaton are available. Rates and reservations can be obtained from tourist offices in Hungary and abroad. A Budapest apartment might cost 5,000 Ft. a week, while a luxury cottage for two on the Balaton costs around 23,000 Ft. a week. Bookings can be made in Budapest at the **IBUSZ** on Petőfi Tér 3 (tel. 1/185–707), which is open 24 hours a day, or through IBUSZ offices in the U.S. and U.K. (*See* Before You Go, Chapter 1).

Guest Houses Also called pensions, these offer simple accommodations in rooms with four beds. They are well suited to younger people on a budget, and there are separate bathrooms for men and women on each floor. Some offer simple breakfast facilities. Arrangements can be made through local tourist offices or travel agents abroad.

In the provinces it is safe to accept rooms that you are offered directly. "Szoba kiadó" means "Room to Rent." The rate per night for a double room in Budapest or at Lake Balaton is around 750 Ft., which includes the use of a bathroom but not breakfast. If you prefer, reservations can also be made through any tourist office.

Camping The 140 campsites in Hungary are open from May through September. Rates are 150–250 Ft. a day. There's a small charge for hot water and electricity plus an accommodations fee of 25–75 Ft. per person per night. Children get a 50% reduction. Camping is forbidden except in appointed areas. Reservations can be made through travel agencies or through the **Hungarian Camping and Caravanning Club** (Budapest IX, Kálvin tér 9, tel. 1/177–208).

Ratings The following price categories are for a double room with bath and breakfast during the peak season. For single rooms with bath, count on about 1,300–2,600 Ft. extra per night. Best bets are indicated by a star ★. At press time, there were 60 Ft. to the dollar.

Category	Budapest	Balaton	Provinces
Very Expensive	8,000–11,000	—	—
Expensive	5,500–8,000	5,200–6,500	3,400–5,000
Moderate	3,700–5,500	3,400–5,200	2,500–3,400
Inexpensive	1,500–3,750	1,000–3,400	800–2,500

During the peak season (June through August) full board may be compulsory at the Lake Balaton hotels. During the off-season (in Budapest, September through March; at Lake Balaton, May and September), rates are considerably lower than those given above.

Credit Cards The following credit card abbreviations are used: AE, American Express; DC, Diners Club; MC, MasterCard; V, Visa.

Tipping Being a socialist state has not altered the Hungarian habit of tipping generously. Cloakroom and gas-pump attendants, hairdressers, waiters, and taxi drivers all expect a tip. Although hotel bills contain a service charge, you should also tip the elevator operator, chambermaid, and head porter; together, they should get 10% of the bill. At least an extra 10% should be added to a restaurant bill or taxi fare. If a gypsy band plays for your table exclusively, you can leave 100 Ft. in a plate discreetly provided for that purpose.

Budapest

Arriving and Departing

By Plane Hungary's international airport, and the only commercial airport in the country, is about 22 kilometers (14 miles) southeast of the city. All **Malév** flights (except Paris flights) operate from the new terminal 2 (tel. 1/577–831); all other airlines use terminal 1 (tel. 1/572–122). For same-day flight information, tel. 1/577–155.

Between the Airport and Downtown Bus service to and from Engels Tér station, platform 1, leaves every half hour from 5 AM to 1 PM. The trip takes 30–40, minutes and costs either 20 Ft. or 30 Ft., depending on which terminal you use. A taxi ride to the center of Budapest should cost no more than 300 Ft. Avoid taxi drivers who offer their services before you are out of the arrivals lounge.

By Train There are three main train stations in Budapest: Keleti (East), Nyugati (West) and Déli (South). Trains from Vienna usually operate from the Keleti station, while those to the Balaton depart from the Déli.

By Bus Most buses to Budapest from the western region of Hungary, including the one from Vienna, arrive at **Engels Tér** station.

By Car The main routes into Budapest are the M1 from Vienna (via Györ) and the M7 from the Balaton.

Getting Around

Budapest is best explored on foot. The maps provided by tourist offices are not very detailed, so arm yourself with one from any of the bookshops in Váci Utca or from downtown stationery shops.

By Public Transportation The public transportation system—a metro (subway), buses, streetcars, and trolley buses—is cheap, efficient, and simple to use but closes down at around 11 PM. However, certain trams and buses run on a limited schedule all night. A day ticket *(napjegy)* costs 48 Ft. and allows unlimited travel on all services within the city limits. You can also buy tickets for single rides—blue for buses, costing 6 Ft., and yellow for streetcars, metro, and trolley buses, costing 5 Ft., from metro stations or tobacco shops; you can travel any distance on these tickets but you can't change lines.

Bus, streetcar, and trolley bus tickets must be canceled on board—watch how other passengers do it. Don't get caught without a ticket: Spot checks are frequent, especially at the beginning of the month, and you can be fined 200 Ft.

By Taxi Taxis are plentiful and a good value, but make sure that they have a meter that is working. The initial charge is 20 Ft., plus 10 Ft. per kilometer plus 3 Ft. per minute of waiting time. Note that these prices are only for **Volántaxi** and **Fötaxi** (run by the government). Private taxi services are more expensive. To call a taxi, tel. 1/222–222 or 666–666; to order one in advance, tel. 188–188.

By Boat In summer a regular boat service links the north and south of the city, stopping at points on both banks, including Margit-sziget (Margaret Island). From May to September boats leave from the quay at Vigadó Tér on 1½-hour cruises between the Árpád and Petöfi bridges. The trip, organized by IBUSZ, runs three times a day and costs around 60 Ft. (tel. 1/181–223).

Important Addresses and Numbers

Tourist Information **Tourinform:** Süto Utca 2 (Metro: Deák Tér), tel. 1/179–800. Open daily 8–8. **IBUSZ Accommodation Office:** Petöfi Tér 3, tel. 1/185–707. Open 24 hours. **Budapest Tourist:** Roosevelt Tér 5, tel. 1/173–555.

Embassies **U.S.:** Budapest V, Szabadság Tér 12, tel. 1/126–450. **Canadian:** Budapest II, Budakeszi Út 32, tel. 1/767–711. **U.K.:** Budapest V, Harmincad Utca 6, tel. 1/182–888.

Emergencies **Police:** tel. 07; **Ambulance:** tel. 04; **Doctor:** Ask your hotel or embassy to recommend one. U.S. and Canadian visitors are advised to take out full medical insurance. U.K. visitors are covered for emergencies and essential treatment.

English Bookstores Foreign publications—including those in English—can be bought at the reception desks of major hotels and at newsstands at major traffic centers.

Guided Tours

Orientation Tours Three-hour bus tours of the city operate all year and cost about 600 Ft. Starting from Engels Tér, they take in parts of both Buda and Pest and offer a good introduction for further exploring on foot. Contact IBUSZ *(see* Important Addresses and Numbers).

Special-Interest Tours and Excursions IBUSZ and Budapest Tourist organize a number of unusual tours, featuring trips to the Buda Hills or goulash parties, as well as visits to the National Gallery and Parliament and some of the other more traditional sights. These tour companies will provide personal guides on request.

Excursions further afield include day-long trips to the Puszta (the Great Plain), the Danube Bend, and Lake Balaton.

Exploring Budapest

Budapest, situated on the two banks of the Danube, joins the colorful hills of Buda and the wide boulevards of Pest. Though it was the site of a Roman outpost in the 1st century, the actual creation of the city did not occur until 1873, when the towns of Obuda, Pest, and Buda were united. The cultural, political, intellectual, and commercial heart of the nation beats here in Budapest; for the 20% of the nation's population who live in the capital, anywhere else is simply "the country."

So much of Budapest's real charm lies in unexpected glimpses into shadowy courtyards and in long vistas down sunlit cobbled streets. Although some 30,000 buildings were destroyed in World War II and in 1956, you'll find that a flavor of the past lingers on in the often crumbling architectural details of the structures, and in the memories and lifestyles of the citizens.

The principal sights of the city fall roughly into three areas, which can be comfortably covered on foot. The hills of Budapest are best explored by public transportation.

Numbers in the margin correspond with points of interest on the Budapest map.

1 2 Take a taxi or bus (no. 16 from **Engels Tér**) to **Dísz Tér**, at the foot of **Várhegy Castle Hill** where the painstaking work of reconstruction has been in progress since the last war. Having made their final stand in the Royal Palace itself, the Nazis left behind them a blackened wasteland. Under the rubble, archaeologists discovered the medieval foundations of the palace of King Matthias Corvinus, who, in the 15th century, presided over one of the most splendid courts in Europe.

3 The **Várpalota** (Palace), now a vast museum complex and cultural center, can be reached on foot from Dísz Tér, or by funicular railway *(Sikló)* from Clark Adám Tér. The northern wing of the building is devoted to the **Magyar Munkás osztály Mozgalom Múzeum** (Museum of the Hungarian Working Class Movement) (open Tues.–Sun. 10–6). The central block houses the **Nemzeti Galléria** (National Gallery) (open Tues. 12–6, Wed. 12–8, Thurs.–Sun. 10–6), exhibiting a wide range of Hungarian fine art, from medieval paintings to modern sculpture. Names to look for are Munkácsy, a 19th-century Romantic painter, and Csontváry, a Surrealist whom Picasso much admired. The southern block contains the **Budapesti Történeti Múzeum** (Budapest History Museum) (open Tues.–Sun. 10–6), with its permanent exhibition entitled "1,000 Years of Our Capital." Down in the cellars are the original medieval vaults of the palace, portraits of King Matthias and his second wife, Beatrice of Aragon, and many late-14th-century statues that probably adorned the Renaissance palace. *Palace Museums, 17 Dísz tér 1. Admission: 10 Ft., free on Sat.*

4 The **Mátyás templom** (Matthias Church), northeast of Dísz Tér, with its distinctive patterned roof, dates back to the 13th century. The former mosque built by the occupying Turks was destroyed and reconstructed in the 19th century, only to be bombed in WWII. Only the south porch is from the original structure. The Habsburg emperors were crowned kings of Hungary here, including Charles IV, in 1916. High mass is celebrated every Sunday at 10 AM with an orchestra and choir.

5 The turn-of-the-century **Halászbástya** (Fishermen's Bastion) is on your left as you leave the church. It was built as a lookout tower to protect what was once a thriving fishing settlement. Its neo-Romanesque columns and arches provide frames for views over the city and river. Near the church, in Hess András Tér, are the remains of the oldest church on Castle Hill, built by the Dominican friars in the 13th century. These have now been integrated into the modern structure of the Hilton hotel.

The town houses lining the streets of the Castle District are mostly occupied by offices, restaurants, and diplomatic resi-

dences, but the house where Beethoven stayed in 1800 is now
⑥ the **Zene Történeti Múzeum** (Museum of Music History).
*Táncsics Mihály Utca 7. Admission: 10 Ft. Open Wed.–Sun.
10–6, Mon. 4–9.*

⑦ The remains of a **medieval synagogue** are also in the neighborhood and are open to the public. On display are a number of
objects relating to the Jewish community including religious
inscriptions, frescoes, and tombstones dating back to the 15th
century. *Táncsics Mihály Utca 26. Admission: 10 Ft. Open
Apr.–Oct., Tues.–Fri. 10–4; weekends 10–6.*

⑧ The **Hadtörténeti Múzeum** (War History Museum) is at the far
end of Castle Hill. The collection includes uniforms and regalia,
many belonging to the Hungarian generals who took part in the
abortive uprising against Austrian rule in 1848. Other exhibits
trace the military history of Hungary from the original Magyar
conquest in the 9th century through the period of Ottoman rule
and right to the middle of this century. *Tóth Árpád Sétány 40.
Admission: 10 Ft. Open Tues.–Sat. 9–5, Sun. 10–6.*

Nearby stands a monument to Abdurrahman, the last Pasha of
Buda, commander of the Turkish troops in Hungary, who died,
sword in hand in 1686. For a good view of the Vérmezö (Blood
Meadow) and the surrounding Buda hills, stroll the length of
Tóth Árpád Sétány, along the rampart that defended Castle
Hill to the west.

The Heart of Cross the **Széchenyi lánchid** (Chain Bridge) from Clark Adám
the City Tér to reach **Roosevelt Tér** in Pest, with the 19th-century
⑨ neo-classical Academy of Sciences on your left. Pest fans out
from the **Belváros** (Inner City), which is bounded by the
Kiskörút (Little Circular Road). The **Nagykörút** (Grand Circular Road) describes a wider semicircle from the Margit Bridge
to Petőfi Bridge. To your right, an elegant promenade, the
Korzó, runs south along the river.

Time Out The **Bécsi Kávéház** (Vienna Coffeehouse) in the Forum Hotel
serves the best coffee and cream pastries in town. *Apáczai
Csere János Utca 12–14. Moderate.*

⑩ A square called **Vigadó Tér** is bordered by the Vigadó concert
hall, built in the Romantic style, where Liszt, Brahms, and
Bartók performed. Completely destroyed in World War II, it
⑪ has been rebuilt in its original style. Another square, **Március
15 Tér,** commemorates the 1848 struggle for independence from
the Habsburgs with a statue of the poet Petőfi Sándor, who
died later in the uprising. Every March 15, the square is packed
with patriotic Hungarians. Behind the square is the
⑫ 12th-century **Belvárosi plébánia templom** (Inner City Parish
Church), the oldest in Pest. The church has been redone in a
variety of western architectural styles; even Turkish influences, such as the Muslim prayer niche, remain. Liszt, who
lived only a few yards away, often played the organ here.

Parallel with the Korzó, in the Inner City, lies Budapest's most
⑬ upscale shopping street, **Váci Utca. Vörösmarty Tér,** a pleasant
and spacious square, is a welcome place to sit and relax in the
heart of the Inner City. Street musicians and sidewalk cafés
make it one of the liveliest places in Budapest.

Budapest

Time Out **Gerbeaud,** an elegant pastry shop, was founded in 1857 and retains the old imperial style; it's a fashionable meeting place. Try the chestnut purée with whipped cream while sitting on the terrace overlooking the square. *Vörösmarty Tér 7. Inexpensive.*

⑭ North of Vörösmarty Tér is the imposing neo-Gothic **Parliament** (open for tours only), the city's most famous landmark. To its left sits an expressive statue of József Attila (1905–37), who, in spite of his early death, became one of Hungary's greatest poets.

⑮ Across from the Parliament is the **Néprájzi Múzeum** (Museum of Ethnography), with exhibits relating to folk traditions and social customs including Hungarian costume and folklore. There is a particularly interesting collection from Oceania. *Kossuth Lajos Tér 12. Admission: 10 Ft. Open Tues.–Sun. 10–6.*

⑯ Dark and massive, the 19th-century **Szt. István Bazilica** (St. Stephen's Basilica) is one of the chief landmarks of Pest. It was planned early in the 19th century as a neo-classical building, but was in the neo-Renaissance style by the time it was completed more than 50 years later. During World War II, the most precious documents from the Municipal Archives were placed in the cellar of the Basilica—one of the few available bombproof sites.

⑰ Népköztársaság Útja runs 3.2 kilometers (two miles) from the Basilica to Hősök Tere (Heroes' Square). On the left is the **State Opera House,** with its statues of the Muses in the second floor corner niches. Completed in 1884, it was the crowning achievement of architect Miklós Ybl. It has been restored to its original ornate glory—particularly inside—and has been fortunate enough to be spared any attempts to modernize it.

Városliget Park In the center of Heroes' Square stands the 36.5 meter (118-foot)
⑱ **Millennium Monument,** begun in 1896 to commemorate the 1,000th anniversary of the Magyar Conquest. Prince Árpád and six other founders of the Magyar nation occupy the base of the monument, while between the columns on either side are Hungary's greatest rulers and princes.

⑲ The **Szépmuvészeti Múzeum** (Fine Arts Museum) stands on one side of the square. Egyptian, Greek, and Roman artifacts dominate a whole section of the museum, with an emphasis on rare ceramics. The works by the greatest of European painters have been chosen with great care, and few artists of renown are unrepresented. *Admission: 10 Ft. Open Tues.–Sun. 10–6.*

⑳ The **Műcsarnok** (Art Gallery), on the other side of the square, is the site of visiting exhibitions of fine arts, applied arts, and photography. *Admission: 10 Ft. Open Tues.–Sat. 10–6, Sun. 10–8.*

㉑ The **Városliget** (City Park) extends beyond the square; on the left as you enter it are the zoo, state circus, amusement park, and outdoor swimming pool of the Széchenyi mineral baths. On the right is the **Mezőgazdasági Múzeum** (Agricultural Museum), housed in a number of buildings representing different styles of Hungarian architecture—again a part of the Millennium Exhibition of 1896. *Széchenyi Sziget, Varosliget XIV. Admission: 10 Ft. Open Tues.–Sat. 10–5, Sun. 10–6.*

On the shores of the artificial lake stands the statue of George Washington, erected in 1906 from donations by Hungarians living in the United States. The recently renamed **Olaf Palme Sétány** (Walk) is a pleasant route through the park.

Off the Beaten Track

A chair lift *(libegő)* will take you to the highest point in Budapest, **Janoshégy** (Janos Hill), where you can climb a lookout tower for the best view of the city. *Take bus no. 158 from Moszkva Tér to the last stop, Zugligeti Ut. Admission: 20 Ft. Open May 15–Sept. 15, daily 9–5.*

For a more strenuous route to another good view, climb the staircase up the steep cliff overlooking the Danube at the Buda end of the Szabadság Bridge. This will lead you to **Gellért-hegy** (Gellert Hill), named for an 11th-century bishop who was hurled to his death here by some pagan Magyars. During the Middle Ages the hill was associated with witches; nowadays there is a memorial to the liberation of Budapest by the Red Army.

Shopping

You'll find plenty of folk art and souvenir shops, foreign-language bookshops, and classical record shops in or around **Váci Utca,** but a visit to some of the smaller, more typically Hungarian shops on **Lenin Kórút,** and to the new **Skála-Coop** department store near the Nyugati train station may prove more interesting.

The **central market hall** at **IX Tolbuhin Körút 1–3** and the **flea market** *(ecseri piac)* some way out on **Nagykörösi Utca 156** (take bus no. 58 from Boráros Tér) are well worth a visit.

Dining

Eating out in Budapest can be a real treat and should provide you with some of the best value for money of any European capital. There is a good selection of restaurants, from the grander establishments that echo the imperial past of the Habsburg era to the less expensive spots more favored by locals. For details and price category definitions, *see* Dining in Staying in Hungary.

Expensive **Alabardos.** Castle Hill is the setting for this small, intimate restaurant with a reputation for top-quality food and wine and outstanding service. The setting is medieval, and lute music helps to establish the Old World atmosphere. *I Országház Utca 12, tel. 1/160–828. Reservations essential. AE, DC, MC, V. Closed for lunch.*

Arany Hordó. True to its name (which means the Golden Barrel), this 14th-century building has a beer house on the ground floor. The cellar has a wine tavern, but the real attraction is the first-class restaurant on the second floor. The local specialty is *fogas,* a fish from Lake Balaton. There is gypsy music in the evening. *I Tárnok Utca 16, tel. 1/566–765. Reservations advised for restaurant. AE, DC, MC, V.*

★ **Fortuna.** Three medieval houses were reconstructed as a wood-furnished restaurant, nightclub, and café. The atmosphere, a key point, is matched by the range of food and the distinguished wine list. There is gypsy music in the evening. *I Hess András Tér 4, tel. 1/756–857. Reservations advised for dinner. AE, DC, MC, V.*

★ **Gundel.** Gundel is a famous restaurant in the City Park, where traditional meals are served with an almost stiff formality. *Gundel palacsinta* (pancakes, with chocolate, nuts, and cream) are the specialty. There are outdoor tables in the summer and gypsy music in the evenings. It has a moderate section, the Bagolyvár. *XIV Állatkerti Körút 2, tel. 1/221–002. Reservations accepted. AE, DC, MC, V.*

Moderate **Kisbuda.** A small restaurant near the Buda end of the Margaret Bridge, Kisbuda serves meat and fish specialties and a delicious variety of salads. In warm weather there are tables outside in a courtyard. A piano and violin duet play in the evening. *II Frankel L. Utca 34, tel. 1/152–244. Dress: casual. Reservations advised in evenings. No credit cards. Closed Sun. dinner.*

Tábani Kakas. Situated just below Castle Hill, Tábani Kakas is a popular restaurant with a friendly atmosphere. It specializes in large helpings of poultry dishes, particularly goose. A pianist plays and sings in the evening. *I Attila Út 27, tel. 1/757–165. No reservations. No credit cards.*

Szeged. This is a traditional fish restaurant near the Szabadság Bridge and Gellért Hill. Folk art covers the walls, and there is gypsy music in the evening. The fish soup is fiery. *XI Bartók Béla Út 1, tel. 1/251–268. Reservations accepted. No credit cards.*

Inexpensive **Halászkert.** There is plenty of fun to be had in the noisy and ★ lively Halászkert, one of the most typical of the old-style Budapest fish restaurants. Virtuoso gypsy musicians will attempt any tune. *II Lajos Utca 6, tel. 1/686–480. Dress: informal. No reservations. No credit cards. Closed Sun.*

Márvány Menyasszony. Summer is the best time to appreciate this spacious restaurant in a back street near the Déli train station. It is popular with groups, probably because its long wooden tables and benches give way to space for dancing to gypsy music. *I Márvány Utca 6, tel. 1/756–165. Reservations accepted. No credit cards.*

Lodging

If you arrive in Budapest without a reservation, go to the IBUSZ travel office (open 24 hours) at Petöfi Tér (tel. 1/185–707), or to one of the tourist offices at any of the train stations or at the airport. For details and price category definitions, *see* Lodging in Staying in Hungary.

Very Expensive **Atrium Hyatt.** This large luxury hotel in the Inner City has a ★ good view over the Danube. Its range of facilities has made it a popular stop for businesspeople and those who don't mind being pampered. *V Roosevelt Tér 2, tel. 1/383–000. 356 rooms with bath. Facilities: 2 restaurants, bar, indoor pool, sauna, gym, conference room, and ballroom. AE, DC, MC, V.*

Duna Intercontinental. The Duna makes the best of its location with a terrace café overlooking the river from the Danube Quay. Ask for a room facing west, across the river toward Gellért Hill in Buda. *V Apáczai Csere János Utca 4, tel. 1/175–122. 340 rooms with bath. Facilities: 3 restaurants, penthouse bar, nightclub, pool, squash. AE, DC, MC, V.*

Hilton. On Castle Hill in Buda, the Hilton has an excellent view over the city. It incorporates the tower and other remains of a 13th-century church. Try your luck at the casino *I Hess András Tér 1–3, tel. 1/751–000. 323 rooms with bath. Facilities: 3 restaurants, nightclub, casino. AE, DC, MC, V.*

Expensive **Béke Radisson.** This traditional hotel near Nyugati train station has undergone a facelift to give it modern comforts and easy access. Its nightclub Orfeus draws crowds. *VI Lenin Körút 97, tel. 1/323–300. 246 rooms with bath. Facilities: 2 restaurants, 2 bars, nightclub. AE, DC, MC, V.*

Buda-Penta. A new hotel, the Buda-Penta is located on a busy street near Déli train station, close to Castle Hill and most of the sights in Buda. It houses the fashionable Horoszkop nightclub. *I Krisztina Körút 41–43, tel. 1/566–333. 399 rooms with bath. Facilities: indoor pool, sauna, gym. AE, DC, MC, V.*

Gellért. This well-maintained old building overlooks the Danube near the Buda end of Szabadság Bridge. Rooms are all comfortable and many have a good view of the historic Gellért district. *XI Gellért Tér 1, tel. 1/852–200. 235 rooms with bath. Facilities: thermal pools, terrace restaurant. AE, DC, MC, V.*

Grand Hotel Hungaria. Though Budapest's largest hotel is directly across from the Keleti station and near the metro, noise is kept firmly at bay with the triple-glazed windows in all rooms. *VII Rákóczi Út 90, tel. 1/229–050. 528 rooms with bath. Facilities: 3 restaurants, nightclub, sauna, gym. AE, DC, MC, V.*

Moderate **Astoria.** This hotel reflects the atmosphere of the turn of the century. Located at a busy Pest intersection, it has been renovated and soundproofed. *V. Kossuth Lajos Utca 19, tel. 1/173–411. 198 rooms with bath or shower. Facilities: nightclub, café, sauna, gym. AE, DC, MC, V.*

Erzsébet. This well-known hotel with a long tradition of good service has recently been refurbished and modernized. It is located in the center of the Inner City and has a popular beer hall (Janos Pince) among its attractions. *V Károly Mihály Utca 11–15, tel. 1/382–111. 123 rooms, mostly doubles with shower. Facilities: restaurant, beerhall. AE, DC, MC, V.*

Nemzeti. Another hotel which reflects the grand mood of the turn of the century, Nemzeti was completely restored in 1987 and now offers all the modern comforts. It's cozy, with a central location in Pest. *VIII József Krt. 4, tel. 339–160. 76 rooms, mostly doubles with bath. Facilities: restaurant, brasserie. AE, DC, MC, V.*

★ **Vörös Csillag.** Perched 310 meters (1,000 feet) above the Danube near the upper terminus of the cog-wheel railroad, Vórós Csillag resembles a hunting lodge. Unless you have vertigo, you will admire the view of the whole city from the terrace. *XII Rege Út 21, tel. 1/750–522. 40 rooms with bath, 54 self-catering bungalows. Facilities: restaurant, bar terrace, pool, sauna. AE, DC, MC, V.*

Inexpensive **Citadella.** Comparatively basic, with four beds in some rooms and showers down the hall, the Citadella is nevertheless very popular, particularly with young people, who enjoy the lively communal atmosphere and the location—right inside the fortress. *XI Gellért Hegy, tel. 1/665–794. 40 rooms, none with bath. Facilities: restaurant, beerhall, nightclub. No credit cards.*

Wien. The Wien is located in the southwestern outskirts of the city, near the junction of the highways to Vienna and Balaton, making it popular and convenient for drivers. *XI Budaörsi Út 88, tel. 1/665–400. 110 rooms, most with bath. Facilities: restaurant, café, gas station, car repairs. AE, DC, MC, V.*

The Arts

Hotels and tourist offices will provide you with a copy of the monthly publication *Programme*, which contains details of all cultural events in the city. Tickets are available from your hotel desk, the **Central Booking Agency** (Vörösmarty Tér, tel. 1/176–222), or from **Budapest Tourist** (Roosevelt Tér 5, tel. 173/555).

There are two opera houses, for which dress is casual. Concerts are given all year at the **Academy of Music** on Liszt F. Tér, the **Vigadó** on Vigadó Tér and at the **Old Academy of Music** on Vörösmarty Út. Displays of Hungarian folk dancing are held at the **Cultural Center** on Corvin Tér.

Entertainment and Nightlife

Budapest is a fun and lively city at night. Places stay open late and Western European-style *drink-bárs* have sprung up all over the city.

Nightclubs
Many of the nightclubs are attached to the luxury hotels. Beware of the inflated costs. Admission starts at 100 Ft. Drinks cost from 200 Ft. to 500 Ft.

Casanova offers music and dancing in an attractive building a few yards from the riverbank on the Buda side. *II Batthyány Tér 4, tel. 1/338–320. Open 10 PM–4 AM.*

Duna-bár Boat sails up and down the river with dancing and disco music on board. *Board at Quay 3, opposite the Forum Hotel, on the Pest side. Tel. 1/170–803. Open 10 PM–3 AM.*

Pierrot is an elegant night spot in the Castle District with live piano music and good cocktails. *I Fortuna Utca 14, tel. 1/756–971. Open 5 PM–1 AM.*

Cabarets
Horoszkóp, in the Buda-Penta Hotel, is currently the favorite among Budapest's younger set. Floor shows begin at 11 PM. *I Krisztina Körút 41–43, tel. 1/566–333. Open 10 PM–4 AM.*

Maxim's, in the Hotel Emke, currently offers three variety shows daily plus a "Crazy Cabaret" show. *VII Akácfa Utca 3, tel. 1/227–858. Open 8 PM–3 AM.*

Fortuna, opposite the Matthias Church on Castle Hill, is one of the city's most elegant night spots. It is located in the medieval hall of a 14th-century building. The program starts at 12:30 AM. *I Hess András Tér, tel. 1/557–451. Open 10 PM–4 AM.*

Discos
The university colleges organize the best discos in town. Try the **ELTE Club** (Eötvös Loránd) in the Inner City, on the corner of Károly Mihály Utca and Irányi Utca. Admission and the price of drinks are reasonable. Bring some student I.D.

The Danube Bend

About 40 kilometers (25 miles) north of Budapest, the Danube abandons its eastward course and turns abruptly south toward the capital, cutting through the Börzsöny and Visegrád hills. This area is called the Danube Bend and includes the Baroque town of Szentendre, the hilltop castle ruins and town of Visegrád, and the cathedral town of Esztergom. The attractive combination of hillside and river should dispel any notions of Hungary as being one vast, boring plain.

Here, in the heartland, are the traces of the country's history —the remains of the Roman Empire's frontiers, the battle-fields of the Middle Ages, and the relics of the Hungarian Renaissance. Although the area can be covered by car in a day —the round-trip from Budapest is only 124 kilometers (78 miles)—two days, with a night in Visegrád or Esztergom, would be a better way to savor the charms of the area.

Getting Around

The most pleasant way to get around is by boat or hydrofoil on the Danube. The three main centers—Szentendre, Esz-tergom, and Visegrá—all have connections with each other and with Budapest. There is also regular bus service connect-ing all three with each other and with Budapest. Szentendre can also be reached by HÉV commuter rail, departing from the Batthyány Tér metro (fare 20 Ft.).

Guided Tours

IBUSZ organizes day trips from Budapest along the Danube from May through October, costing about 2,200 Ft. with lunch. Boat trips run on Wednesdays and Saturdays; buses go on Tuesdays, Fridays, and Saturdays. There is also a special bus trip to Szentendre on Thursdays.

Tourist Information

Esztergom. IBUSZ Office, Széchenyi Tér, tel. 1/484.
Szentendre. Dunatours, Bacsó Part 6 (on the quay), tel. 26/11–311.
Visegrád. Dunatours, Fő Utca 3/A, tel. 26/28–330.

Exploring the Danube Bend

Heading north from Budapest toward Szentendre, 19 kilome-ters (12 miles) by car on Road 11, or by train, on your right look for the reconstructed remains of **Aquincum,** capital of the Ro-man province of Pannonia. Careful excavations have unearthed a varied selection of artifacts and mosaics, giving a tantalizing feel for what life was like on the northern fringes of the Roman Empire.

Szentendre, nowadays a flourishing artists' colony with a lively Mediterranean atmosphere, was first settled by Serbians and Greeks fleeing from the advancing Turks in the 14th and 17th centuries. There is a Greek Orthodox church in the main square and a Serbian Orthodox cathedral on the hill. The narrow cob-bled streets are lined with cheerfully painted houses. Part of the town's artistic reputation can be traced to the life and work of the ceramic artist Margit Kovács, whose work blended Hun-garian folk art traditions with motifs from modern art. A **museum** devoted to her work is housed in a small 18th-century merchant's house with an attractive courtyard. *Margit Kovács Pottery Museum, Vastag György Utca 1. Admission: 10 Ft. Open daily 9–7.*

The Danube Bend

A short drive up Szabadság Forrás Út, or a bus ride from the train station, will take you to the **Szabadtéri Néprajzi Múzeum** (Open-Air Ethnographical Museum), where a collection of buildings has been designed to show Hungarian peasant life and folk architecture in the 19th century. *Admission: 10 Ft. Open Apr.–Oct., daily 10–5.*

Visegrád, 23 kilometers (14 miles) from Szentendre, was the seat of the kings of Hungary in the 14th century. Although the ruins of the Palace of King Matthias in the main street have been excavated and reconstructed and there are jousting tournaments in June, Visegrád is not the vibrant city it once was. Still, its historical treasures and scenic location make up for its lack of size.

Esztergom, 21 kilometers (13 miles) farther upriver, stands on the site of a Roman fortress. St. Stephen, the first Christian king of Hungary, was crowned here in the year 1000. The kings are long gone, but Esztergom is still the home of the Archbishop of Esztergom, the Cardinal Primate, head of the Catholic Church in Hungary.

The **cathedral,** the largest in Hungary, stands on a hill overlooking the town; it houses a valuable collection of ecclesiastical art. Below it are the streets of Viziváros (Watertown), lined with Baroque buildings. The **Keresztény Múzeum** (Museum of Christian Art) is situated in the Primate's Palace. It is the finest art gallery in Hungary, with a large collection of early Hungarian and Italian paintings. The Italian collection of 14th- and 15th-century works is unusually large for a museum out-

side Italy. This collection, coupled with the extensive number
of early Renaissance paintings from Flanders and the Lower
Rhine, provide insights into the transition of European sensi-
bilities from medieval Gothic to the humanistic Renaissance.
*Primate's Palace, Berényi U.2. Admission: 10 Ft. Open
Tues.–Sun. 10–6.*

To the north of the cathedral, on **Szt. Tamás Hill,** is a small
church dedicated to St. Thomas à Becket of Canterbury. From
here you can look down on the town and see how the Danube
temporarily divides, forming an island that locals use as a base
for water skiing and swimming. The Danube forms the frontier
with Czechoslovakia.

Dining and Lodging

For details and price category definitions, *see* Dining and Lodging in Staying in Hungary.

Esztergom **Kispipa.** A lively and popular establishment, not far from the
Dining town center, the Kispipa is memorable for its good choice of
wines. *Kossuth Lajos Utca 19. No telephone. No reservations.
No credit cards. Moderate.*
Halászcsárda. Eating here also allows you to explore the small
island formed by the temporary branching of the Danube. The
Halászcsárda is small, friendly, and informal, and reinforces its
riverside atmosphere with a good selection of fish specialties.
*Szabad Majus Sétány 14. No telephone. No reservations. No
credit cards. Inexpensive.*

Lodging **Fürdő.** This large hotel, near the center of town, has tennis
courts and is attached to the local spa, which has an open-air
swimming pool for those who like a good workout. *Bajcsy-
Zsilinszky Utca 14, tel. 1/292. 85 rooms with bath. Facilities:
restaurant, bar. No credit cards. Moderate.*
Vadvirág. A small guest house on the outskirts of town,
Vadvirág offers simple accommodations, a restaurant, and tennis courts. *Bánomi üdülő, tel. 1/174. 28 rooms, some with bath.
No credit cards. Closed Oct.–Apr. Inexpensive.*

Szentendre **Arany Sárkány.** This popular restaurant in the old town center
Dining is a must for anyone visiting Szentendre. The cooking is of high
★ quality, and the surroundings are pleasantly informal—long
tables with checked tablecloths. *Vörös Hadsereg Utca 2. Reservations essential. AE, DC, MC, V. Closed Feb. Moderate.*
Régi Módi. This attractive upstairs restaurant is approached
through a courtyard across from the Kovács Margit Múzeum.
The bright decor and wine and game specialties make up for the
slow service. *Futó Utca 3, tel. 26/11–105. Reservations advised. No credit cards. Moderate.*

Lodging **Danubius.** This quiet, cozy hotel is north of town on the riverbank. Guests can rent bicycles and other sports equipment.
*Ady Endre Utca 28, tel. 26/12–511. 50 rooms, mostly doubles
with bath. No credit cards. Moderate.*
Silvanus. Located on the top of a hill, Visegrád Hegy, this hotel
offers spectacular views. It's recommended for motorists and
offers a tennis court and linking trails in the forest for the more
active. *Fekete-hegy, tel. 26/136–063. 79 rooms, most with bath.
Facilities: restaurant, brasserie, terrace café. AE, DC, MC, V.
Moderate.*

Visegrád
Lodging

Vár. Situated at the foot of a steep hill beside the Danube, this is a good choice for those whose priorities include scenery and the great outdoors. There are excellent water sports facilities nearby, but the level of accommodations is very simple. *Fó Utca 9–11, tel. 26/28–264. 15 double rooms, all with hot water but no bath. No credit cards. Inexpensive.*

Lake Balaton

Lake Balaton, the largest lake in central Europe, stretches of 80 kilometers (50 miles) across western Hungary. It is within easy reach of Budapest by any means of transportation. Sometimes known as the nation's playground, it goes some way toward making up for Hungary's much lamented lack of coastline. On its hilly northern shore, ideal for growing grapes, is Balatonfüred, the country's oldest and most famous spa town. The national park on the Tihany Peninsula is just to the south, and regular boat service links Tihany and Balatonfüred with Siófok on the southern shore.

This shore is not as attractive as the northern one—being flatter and more crowded—with resorts, cottages, and trade union rest houses. Still, it is worth visiting because of its shallower, warmer waters, which make it a better choice for swimming.

A circular tour taking in Veszprém, Balatonfüred, and Tihany could be managed in a day, but two days, with a night in Tihany or Balatonfüred, would be more relaxed and allow for detours to Herend and its porcelain factory, or to the castle at Nagyvázsony.

Getting Around

Trains from Budapest serve all the resorts on the northern shore; a separate line links the resorts of the southern shore. Road 71 runs along the northern shore; M7 covers the southern. Bus services link most resorts. Regular ferries link the major resorts. Traffic can be heavy during summer weekends, and driving can be slow around the lake. Make sure that bus and train tickets are booked ahead of time.

Guided Tours

IBUSZ has several tours to Balaton from Budapest; inquire at the head office in Budapest *(see* Important Addresses and Numbers in Budapest). Other tours more easily organized from hotels in the Balaton area include boat trips to vineyards, folk music evenings, and overnight trips to local inns.

Tourist Information

Balatonfüred. Balatontourist, Blaha L. Utca 5, tel. 80/42–822.
Nagyvázsony. Balatontourist, Kinizsi Vár, tel. 80/31–015.
Tihany. Balatontourist, Kossuth Utca 20, tel. 80/44–052.
Veszprém. Balatontourist, Münnich F. Utca 3, tel. 80/13–750.

Exploring Lake Balaton

Hilly **Veszprém,** in the northeast corner of the lake, is the center of cultural life in the Balaton region. **Várhegy** (Castle Hill) is

Lake Balaton

the most attractive part of town, north of Szabadság Tér. **Hősök Kapuja** (Heroes' Gate), at the entrance to the Castle, houses a small exhibit on Hungary's history (Admission: 10 Ft. Open May–Oct., Tues.–Sun. 10–6). Just past the gate and down a little alley to the left, is the **Tűztorony** (Fire Tower); note that the lower level is medieval while the upper stories are Baroque. There is a good view of the town and surrounding area from the balcony.

Tolbuhin Út, the only street in the castle area, leads to a small square in front of the **Bishop's Palace** and **Cathedral;** outdoor concerts are held here in the summer. Tolbuhin Út continues past the square up to a terrace erected on the north staircase of the castle. Stand beside the modern statues of St. Stephen and his queen, Gizella, for a far-reaching view of the old quarter of town.

If you are traveling by car, go 5 kilometers (3 miles) west to the village of **Nemesvámos**, where you can slake your thirst or conquer your hunger at **Vámosi Csárda** (Highwayman's Inn). This 18th-century Baroque building takes its name from an infamous 19th-century highwayman who claimed it as one of his bases. Go down to the cellar to see the tables and seats made from tree trunks—a local architectural feature.

Herend, 16 kilometers (10 miles) northwest of Veszprém on Road 8, is a little town known internationally for its beautifully designed porcelain. The factory, founded in 1839, displays many valuable pieces in its **museum.** *Admission: 10 Ft. Open Tues.–Sun. 10–6.*

From Veszprém, take Road 73 about 15 kilometers (9 miles) to **Balatonfüred**, a spa and resort with good beaches. It is also one of the finest wine-growing areas of Hungary. Above the main square, where medicinal waters bubble up under a colonnaded pavilion, the hillsides are thick with vines.

A seven-minute boat trip takes you from Balatonfüred to the **Tihany Peninsula**, a national park rich in rare flora and fauna, and an ideal place to walk. From the ferry port, follow green markers to the springs (Oroszkút), or red ones to the top of **Csúcs-hegy,** a hill from which there is a good view of the lake.

The village of Tihany, with its famous **abbey,** is on the eastern shore. The abbey building houses a **museum** with exhibits relating to the Balaton area (Admission: 10 Ft. Open Tues.–Sun. 10–6). Also worth a look are the pink angels floating on the ceiling of the abbey church, and the abbey organ, on which recitals are given in summer. Consider a special detour to the Rege pastry shop at Batthyány Út 38, not far from the abbey.

The castle of **Nagyvázsony,** about 20 kilometers (12 miles) northwest of Balatonfüred, dates to the early 15th century. The 92-foot-high keep is the oldest part, and its upper rooms now house the **Castle Museum** (Admission: 10 Ft. Open Tues.– Sun. 10–6). Try to get to the highest balcony in late afternoon for the best view. The surrounding buildings, preserved in their original style, date from the period when post horses were changed here.

Dining and Lodging

For details and price category definitions, *see* Dining and Lodging in Staying in Hungary.

Balatonfüred
Dining

Baricska. A popular restaurant set among the vineyards on the outskirts of town, Baricska is conveniently located across from the hotels Marina and Margaréta. A good selection of local wines helps keep the atmosphere informal, and the food is of high quality. *Baricska dülő. Reservations not needed. No credit cards. Closed Nov.–Mar. Moderate.*

Lodging

Annabella. This is a large, modern hotel by the lakeside, offering excellent swimming and water sports facilities. It is just around the corner from the main square in town. *Beloiannisz Utca 25, tel. 86/42–222. 384 rooms; all double rooms have bath. No credit cards. Closed mid-Oct.–mid-Apr. Expensive.*

Hotel Margaréta. The Margaréta is right on the waterfront and is smaller and more intimate than some of its neighbors. Its restaurant is popular locally. *Szechenyi Utca 29, tel. 86/43–824. 52 rooms with bath. Facilities: restaurant, beach, fishing. No credit cards. Expensive.*

★ **Arany Csillag.** This is the choice if you've had enough of Hungary's more modern accommodations. The Arany Csillag is a simple and pleasantly old-fashioned hotel in the center of town, across from the park. *Zsigmond Utca 1, tel. 86/43–466. 79 rooms, none with bath. Facilities: restaurant. No credit cards. Inexpensive.*

Tihany
Dining

Fogas. The restaurant is named after a type of perch native to Lake Balaton; it specializes in this and other fish dishes. It is right at the northern end of Tihany village. *Kossuth Utca 1. No telephone. No reservations. No credit cards. Moderate.*

Halásztánya. The relaxed atmosphere and gypsy music in the evening help contribute to the popularity of the Halásztánya, which specializes in fish. *Visszhang Utca 11. No telepone. Dress: casual. No reservations. Closed Nov.–Mar. Moderate.*

Lodging

★ **Club Tihany Complex.** This complex, comprising the modern Tihany Hotel and Tihany Holiday Village, is near the pier where the ferries arrive from the south side of the lake. The top-quality facilities include cottages, restaurants, and sports of all sorts. *Rév Utca 3, 86/48–088. Facilities: restaurants, pools, squash, tennis, miniature golf. No credit cards. Closed Nov.–mid-Mar. Expensive.*

Veszprém
Dining

Bakony. An elegant restaurant in the center of town, Bakony specializes in fish dishes and has a wide-ranging menu. *Lenin*

Tér 2, tel. 80/12–215. No reservations. No credit cards. Moderate.

★ **Vadásztanya.** The Vadásztanya is just a little southwest of the town center, but worth the trip if you want to experience the old-fashioned charm of a small provincial Hungarian restaurant. The decor is what could be called "cozy traditional," and the fish and game specialties are perennial favorites. *József Attila Utca 22. No telephone. No reservations. No credit cards. Moderate.*

Lodging **Veszprém.** A modern and comfortable hotel in the center of town. *Budapesti Utca 6, tel. 80/12–345. Facilities: restaurant. No credit cards. Moderate.*

17 Iceland

Introduction

Iceland is anything but icy. The country is actually 90% ice-free, with warm summer afternoon temperatures and a winter climate milder than New York's. The coastal farms lie in sweet green meadows, where cows, sheep, and ponies graze among raging streams. Wildflowers grow among the quaking grasses and the sheep-colored rocks. Distant waterfalls drop from heath-covered mountains with great spiked ridges and snow-capped peaks.

Iceland's name can be blamed on Hrafna-Floki, a 9th-century Norse settler who failed to plant enough crops to see his live-stock through their first winter. Leaving in a huff, he passed a northern fjord filled with pack ice, and cursed the country with a name that's kept tourism in cold storage for 1,100 years.

The second-largest island of Europe, Iceland is in the middle of the North Atlantic, where the warm Gulf Stream from the south confronts the cold currents from the north. Beneath some of the country's glaciers are burning fires that become visible during volcanic eruptions—fires that heat the hot springs and geysers that are all over the country. The springs, in turn, heat the homes, hospitals, and public swimming pools in Reykjavik, keeping the nation's capital smokeless and smogless. But the costs of transporting imported goods on an isolated island raise the cost of living, which is, by any standard, high.

The first permanent settlers arrived from Norway in 874, though some Irish monks had arrived a century earlier. The country came under Danish control in 1380 and did not win complete independence until 1944. Today nearly two-fifths of the country's 245,000 people live in Reykjavik and its suburbs.

Iceland, as far from Washington as from Moscow, is advantageously placed in a political climate of improved relations between East and West. Having played host to the memorable Fischer-Spassky chess match in 1972, it moved onto the political chessboard in 1986, with the Reykjavik summit meeting of President Ronald Reagan and Soviet leader Mikhail Gorbachev.

Before You Go

When to Go The best time to visit is from May through November. The months of June and July are highly recommended because during that time there is perpetual daylight. In Reykjavik the sun disappears behind the mountains for only a couple of hours, and in the northern part of the island it barely sets at all. Although the weather is unpredictable, June through August is usually warm and sunny, mixed with a few short periods of rain showers. The winters are far from pleasant, on the other hand. It can rain a lot and snow a lot and it can be cold and windy. During December the sun shines for only three hours a day, but on a clear and cold evening you can see the Northern Lights dancing between the stars.

Climate Iceland enjoys a temperate ocean climate with cool summers and surprisingly mild winters. In the northern part of the country, the weather is more stable than in the south, with less

Iceland

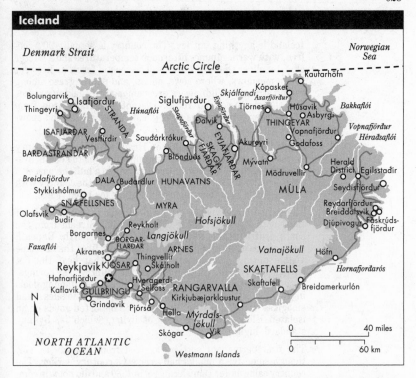

wind and rain. When there is rain and drizzle in the south, the skies are usually clear in the north, and vice versa.

The following are the average daily maximum and minimum temperatures for Reykjavik.

Jan.	35F	2C	May	50F	10C	Sept.	52F	11C
	28	−2		39	4		43	6
Feb.	37F	3C	June	54F	12C	Oct.	45F	7C
	28	−2		34	7		38	3
Mar.	39F	4C	July	57F	14C	Nov.	39F	4C
	30	−1		48	9		32	0
Apr.	43F	6C	Aug.	56F	14C	Dec.	36F	2C
	33	1		47	8		29	−2

Currency The Icelandic monetary unit is the krona (plural kronur), which is equal to 100 aurar. Coins are the IKR 50 and 50 aurar. There are kronur bills in denominations of 10 and 50 (both are rare) and 500, 1,000, and 5,000. At press time (spring 1989), the rate of exchange was IKR 52 to the dollar and IKR 90 to the pound sterling. You are not permitted to bring more than IKR 8,000 into the country, but you may bring any amount of foreign currency, which is easily cashed into kronur at the Icelandic banks. Major credit cards, especially MasterCard and Visa, are widely accepted in the capital but to a far lesser extent in the countryside.

What It Will Cost Iceland is expensive. Since the late 1970s, it has had the greatest rate of inflation of any West European country. Hotels and restaurants cost about 20% more in Reykjavik than elsewhere in the country. The airport departure tax is about IKR 850.

Sample Prices A cup of coffee or soft drink are about IKR 40 each; a bottle of imported beer costs IKR 150; a sandwich, about IKR 90; and a 2-mile taxi ride, about IKR 300.

Customs on Arrival Tourists can bring in one liter of drinks with 21% alcohol content; six liters of imported beer; one liter of liquor with up to 47% alcohol content, and 200 cigarettes.

Language The official language is Icelandic, a highly inflected Germanic tongue, brought to the country by early Norse settlers, that has changed little over the centuries. English is widely understood and spoken, particularly by the younger people.

Getting Around

By Car The Ring Road, which encircles the island, still has stretches that are unpaved, although improvements are made every year. Apart from this, there are asphalt roads connecting the major coastal towns and long stretches of paved highway from the capital to Keflavík and Selfoss. Except on these highways, driving can be a very bumpy experience, often along lava track or dirt and gravel surfaces. But the superb scenery more than makes up for it. Although service stations and garages are few and far between, the main roads are patrolled and fellow motorists are friendly and helpful. If you are traveling off the beaten path, you'll need a four-wheel-drive vehicle. An international driver's license is required—you can apply for one at the local police station if you are at least 20 years old and in possession of a valid driver's license from home.

By Plane **Icelandair** and **Arnarflug** (Eagle Air) have domestic flights to some 50 towns and villages.

By Bus A comprehensive network of buses compensates for the lack of any train network. A good buy, if you want to explore extensively, is the **Omnibus Passport,** which permits you to travel on all scheduled bus routes for one to four weeks. It costs IKR 9,000–IKR 18,000. Another choice is the **Full Circle Passport,** which costs IKR 8,000 and is valid for a circular trip around Iceland on the Ring Road. It will take you to some of the most popular attractions, but if you want to see more, there are scheduled bus tours for which you will have to pay extra. An **Air/Bus Rover Ticket** entitles the bearer to special discounts on certain Central Highland tours, camping grounds, youth hostels, and ferries.

Staying In Iceland

Telephones
Local Calls Pay phones take IKR 5 and IKR 10 coins and are found in hotels, shops, bus stations, and post offices. There are not many outdoor telephone booths in the towns and villages.

International Calls You can dial direct to almost anywhere in Europe and the United States. Hotels in Iceland, as elsewhere, add hefty service charges to international calls, so ask about the charges in advance before you place a call from your room.

Operators and Information For collect calls and assistance on overseas calls, dial 09; for local calls, dial 02; for information, dial 03.

Mail
Postal Rates

Airmail letters to the United States cost IKR 34; letters to Europe, IKR 24.

Receiving Mail

You can have your mail sent to the post office in any town or village in Iceland. In Reykjavik, have mail sent to the downtown post office (R/O Posthusstr[ae]ti, 101 Reykjavik).

Opening and Closing Times

Banks. Banks are open weekdays 9:15–4; they also open from 5 to 6 on Thursdays.

Museums. Museums are usually open 1–4:30, but some open as early as 10 and others stay open until 7.

Shops. Shops are open weekdays 9–6 and Saturdays 9–noon.

National Holidays

January 1 (New Year's Day); April 12–16 (Easter); April 19 (first day of summer); May 1 (Labor Day); May 5 (Ascension Day); June 4–5 (Pentecost); June 17 (National Day); August 1 (public holiday); December 25–26 (Christmas).

Dining

Seafood and lamb are the local specialties and they are recommended. The restaurants are small and varied—Oriental, French, Italian classical, and trendy. They are often located in old wooden houses, which give them distinctive, though not always attractive, character. The service is always inviting but sometimes amateurish. Street vendors sell tasty hot dogs with fried onion.

Mealtimes

Dinner, served between 6 and 9, is the main meal; a light lunch is usually served between noon and 2. Most restaurants are open from mid-morning until midnight.

Dress

Casual dress is acceptable in all but the most formal restaurants, where a jacket and tie are recommended.

Ratings

The following ratings are for a three-course meal for one person. Prices include taxes and service charges but not wine or cocktails. Best bets are indicated by a star ★ . At press time, there were IKR 52 to the dollar.

Category	Reykjavik	Other Areas
Expensive	over IKR 2,100	over IKR 2,000
Moderate	IKR 1,200–	IKR 1,000–
	IKR 2,100	IKR 2,000
Inexpensive	under IKR 1,200	under IKR 1,000

Credit Cards

The following credit card abbreviations are used: AE, American Express; DC, Diners Club; MC, MasterCard; V, Visa.

Lodging

There is a wide range of accommodations in Iceland designed to meet the demands of foreign visitors. The hotels are modern, without luxuries, but with a quiet and friendly atmosphere. Reykjavik and most villages have a number of basic and simple guest houses, and more sophisticated rooms are also easily available. Hostels are few and functional. Lodging in farmhouses in the countryside is highly recommended. The **Iceland Tourist Board** (tel. 91/25855) offers information on where to stay. Most hotels in Reykjavik include breakfast in the price and have rooms with private baths.

Ratings

Prices are for two people sharing a double room. Best bets are indicated by a star ★ . At press time there were IKR 52 to the dollar.

Category	Reykjavik	Other Areas
Expensive	over IKR 5,100	over IKR 4,500
Moderate	IKR 4,200–	IKR 3,000–
	IKR 5,100	IKR 4,500
Inexpensive	under IKR 4,200	under IKR 3,000

Credit Cards The following credit card abbreviations are used: AE, American Express; DC, Diners Club; MC, MasterCard; V, Visa.

Tipping Tipping is not customary in Iceland.

Reykjavik

Arriving and Departing

By Plane Flights from the United States and Europe arrive at Keflavík Airport, 50 kilometers (30 miles) from Reykjavik. Flights from Greenland arrive at Reykjavik City Airport. For information on arrivals and departures at Keflavík Airport, call 91/690100.

Between the Airport and Downtown Buses connect with all flights to and from Keflavík. The drive takes 45 minutes and costs IKR 250. Taxis are also available but they cost no less than IKR 4,000.

By Boat During the summer, the North Atlantic ferry **Norrona** sails from the Faroe Islands, Shetland Islands, Denmark, and Norway to Seydisfjördur, magnificent fjords on the east side of Iceland, 720 kilometers (450 miles) from Reykjavik. From Seydisfjördur, Reykjavik is a one-hour flight or a 10-hour drive. For information, contact **Smyril Line Passenger Department,** Box 370, 3800 Torshavn, Faroes, or c/o Úrval Travel, Pósthússtræti 9, Reykjavik.

Getting Around

The best way to see Reykjavik is on foot. Most of the interesting sites are in the city center, within easy walking distance of one another. Sightseeing tours are also a good way to familiarize yourself with the city. There is no subway system.

By Bus Buses run from 6 AM to midnight. The flat fare for Reykjavik and suburbs is IKR 40 for adults, IKR 11 for children. Ten- and 20-fare ticket sheets are available with a 10% reduction.

By Taxi Rates start at about IKR 150. Because Reykjavik is small, most taxi rides do not exceed IKR 350. The best taxis to call are: **Hreyfill** (tel. 685522), **BSR** (tel. 11720), and **Bæjarleidir** (tel. 33500).

Important Addresses and Numbers

Tourist Information The tourist information center, Ingólfsstræti 5 (tel. 91/623045), is near Bankastræti/Lanfávegur, the main shopping district. It's open weekdays 10–4, weekends, 10–2.

Embassies U.S.: Laufásvegur 21, tel. 91/21900. U.K.: Laufásvegur 49, tel. 91/15883. **Canadian Consulate:** Laufásvegur 77, 91/13721.

Emergencies Police: tel. 11166. Ambulance: tel. 11100. Doctors and dentists: weekdays 8 AM–5 PM, tel. 91/696600; weekdays 5 PM–* AM and weekends, tel. 91/21230. **Pharmacies** operate on a rotating basis during nights and weekends. Those that are open overnight will post the information in their windows. At any given time, at least one of the following will be open: **Ingolfs Apotek,** tel. 91/29300, and **Laugavegs Apotek,** tel. 91/24045.

English Bookstores **Bókaverslun Snæbjarnar:** Hafnarstræti 4, tel. 91/14281. **Sigfús Eymudsson:** Austurstræti, tel. 91/27077. **Mál og menning:** Laugavegur 18, 91/24240.

Travel Agencies **American Express:** Útsýn Travel, Austurstræti 17, tel. 91/26611. **Diners Club:** Atlantic Travel, Hallveigarstigur 2, tel. 91/28388. **Reykjavik Travel Bureau:** Adalstr[ae]ti 16, tel. 91/621490. **Samvinn-Travel:** Austurstræti 12, tel. 91/27077. **Úrval Travel:** Pósthússtræti 9, tel. 91/13491. **Iceland Tourist Bureau:** Skógarhlid 6, tel. 91/25855.

Guided Tours

Tour operators use clean, comfortable buses that hold from 16 to 45 people. For information, call the tourist information center, (tel. 91/623045).

Orientation Tours **Reykjavik Excursions** (tel. 91/621011 or 688922) offers "Reykjavik City-Sightseeing," a daily tour that takes about 2½ hours and includes commercial centers, folk museums, and art centers.

Excursions **Reykjavik Excursions** (*see* above) has many different types of tours. Perhaps the most interesting are the daily "Gullfoss/Geysir" tours: an eight-hour visit to volcanic craters, geysers, and waterfalls; three-hour pony-trekking trips; and, during the whaling season, a four-hour trip to the only whaling station in the North Atlantic, just outside Reykjavik. For trout fishing excursions, contact **Úrval Travel** (tel. 91/28522).

Personal Guides Many travel agencies offer English-speaking personal guides for tours of the city and outlying areas. For more extensive excursions, contact the **Touring Club of Iceland,** Öldugata 3, tel. 91/19533 or 11798, or **Outdoor Life Tours,** Grófin 1, 91/14606.

Exploring Reykjavik

Numbers in the margin correspond with points of interest on the Reykjavik map.

❶ The heart of Reykjavik is **Austurvöllur,** a small square in the center of the city. **Althingi** (the Parliament building), a 19th-century house, one of the oldest stone houses in Iceland, faces the square. In the center of the square is a statue of Jón Sigurdsson (1811–79), the national hero who led Iceland's fight for independence, which it fully achieved in 1944.

❷ Next to Althingi is the **cathedral,** a small, charming wooden church. Behind it is Tjörnin, a pond which is the ice-skating center of the city during the winter. One corner of the pond does not freeze; here thermal springs feed warm water, making it an attraction for birds year-round and a popular area for bird lovers.

❸ Head back along Lækjargata, beyond Austurvöllur to **Lækjartorg** Square. On the right is the **Bernhöftstorfa** district, a small hill with colorful, two-story wooden houses from the mid-19th century. No attempts have been made to modernize

Reykjavik

Arber Museum, **5**

Asgrims Museum, **5**

Asmundur Sveinsson
Gallery, **6**

Austurvöllur, **1**

Cathedral, **2**

Einar Jónsson
Gallery, **14**

Hallgrimskirkja, **13**

High Court, **10**

Icelandic Opera, **12**

Ingólfur Arnarson
statue, **9**

Kjavarlsstadir, **16**

Laekjartorg, **3**

Menntaskólinn i
Reykjavik, **4**

Museum of Natural
History, **7**

National Museum, **18**

National Theater, **11**

Nordic House, **17**

Offices of President
and Prime Minister, **8**

the area, and it keeps the spirit of the past. For a century and a half, the biggest building has housed the oldest educational institution in the country, **Menntaskólinn í Reykjavík**, a college whose graduates have from the early days dominated political and social life in Iceland. On the north side of Lækjartorg is one of the two city bus centers. During summer this square is lively, with an outdoor market, shops, and cafés.

Time Out **Café Hressó** is one of the oldest coffee shops in Reykjavik. The sweets are delicious, though other places are better for meals. An attractive back garden is open in the summertime. *Austurstræti 20, tel. 91/14353. Moderate.*

Leading west out of the square is Austurstræti, a pedestrian shopping street with the main post office on the right. From here, you can take bus no. 11 from the bus station for a 20-minute ride to the **Arbær** Open-Air Municipal Museum. It is actually a "village" of 18th- and 19th-century houses that portray the old way of living. *Tel. 91/84094. Admission: IKR 200 adults, IKR 100 children under 12. Open July–Aug., Tues.–Sat. 10–6; Sept., weekends 10–6; Oct.–June, call for hours.*

You can also take bus no. 4 from the square to the **Asmundur Sveinsson Gallery**. Sveinsson was a social-realist sculptor who started his career in the 1920s. Some of his originals are in the surrounding garden, which is accessible at all times free of charge. *v/Sigton. Admission: IKR 200. Open June–Sept, daily 10–4; Oct.–May, Tues., Thurs. and weekends 1–4.*

Both bus no. 11 and no. 4 pass the **Museum of Natural History**, located on Hlemmtorg Square along with the city's main bus station. The exhibits here vary from stuffed peacocks to giant sea turtles. *Tel. 91/29822. Admission: free. Open Tues. and Thurs.–Sun. 1:30–4:30.*

Leading east out of the square is Bankastræti, which is the busiest shopping street in the city. On the left-hand side is an 18th-century white mansion. Initially it was a prison building, but it now houses the **offices of Iceland's president and prime minister**.

Walk left toward Arnarhóll Hill. On top of the hill is a **statue** of the first settler in Iceland, Ingólfur Arnarson, a Viking who arrived in 874 and lived in Reykjavik. Nearby is the Bank of Iceland, a modern building which still aggravates residents because it narrows the view from the hill. Across the hill is a 19th-century building which is now the **High Court**. Behind it is the **National Theater**, built in the 1950s. Most of the other buildings in the area house government ministries.

From Arnarhóll Hill you can view the confusing architectural and cultural style of Reykjavik city center: 18th-century stone houses, 19th-century small wooden houses, office blocks from the '30s and '50s, and the brand-new futuristic bank building. Despite this mixture, the city has a warm and spacious feel.

Walk along Ingólfsstræti. To the right is the **Icelandic Opera** building, which housed the first Icelandic cinema for over half a century until it was closed in the early '80s. A bit farther up, across Bankastræti, is the tourist information center. Turn left along Bankastræti. If you walk straight ahead you can enjoy the various shops of what used to be the greatest shopping street in Iceland, Laugavegur.

Time Out **Café Laugavegur 22.** This is where the young and innovative pop and rock artists in Reykjavik gather for lunches, dinners, and coffee. The food and prices are reasonable, but the atmosphere can be outrageous. *Tel. 91/13628. Closed Fri. eve. and Sat. Inexpensive.*

To continue the tour from Bankastræti, turn right onto Skólavördustígur. At the end of that street towers ⑬ **Hallgrímskirkja,** a church with a 65-meter (210-foot) gray stone tower that dominates the city's skyline in the same way that its 17th-century namesake, Hallgrímur Pétursson, has dominated Icelandic theological poetry with his *Psalms of Passion,* which have been translated in over 50 languages. During the day the church, which took more than 50 years to build and was completed late in the '70s, is open to the public. The **church tower** offers a panoramic view of the city. There you will have a spectacular angle on the colorful city center, and its compactness will surprise you. You can also see how the spacious suburbs have spread out since World War II in order to accommodate a more than tenfold increase in population. *Tel. 91/10745. Admission to tower: IKR 100 adults, IKR 50 children under 12. Open daily 10–6.*

Art lovers will want to visit the neighboring **gallery of Einar** ⑭ **Jónsson,** who was Iceland's leading sculptor early in this century. His sculptures are made of metal, and the human being is always his subject. *v/Skólavörduholt. Admission: IKR 100. Open weekends only, 1:30–4.*

⑮ Nearby is the **Ásgrimss Museum,** which features the works of the popular neo-Impressionist painter Asgrimur Jónsson (1870 –1968). *Bergstadastræti 74. Admission: free. Open weekdays 4 –10, weekends 2–10.*

⑯ **Kjarvalsstadir,** a municipal art gallery named in honor of Jóhannes Kjarval (1889–1972), the nation's best-loved painter, is a 10-minute walk away from Hallgrimskirkja. It is nicely situated in the **Miklagardur,** one of two spacious parks in Reykjavik. *v/Flókagötu, tel. 91/26131. Admission: free, except for private exhibitions. Open daily 2–8.*

Return to the starting point of this tour and take another interesting route from the cathedral, along Tjaranagata and Bjarkag streets toward the pond and the city's other major park, Hljómskólagardur. South of the park, across Miklabraut, ⑰ is **Nordic House,** a cultural center with exhibitions, lectures, and concerts. *Call for information, tel. 91/17030. Open daily 2–7.*

On your right when you walk toward the Nordic House is the campus of the **University of Iceland** (founded 1911). On the cam- ⑱ pus grounds is the **National Museum,** and a visit here is compulsory for anyone interested in Icelandic culture. It has on display some Viking artifacts, national costumes, weaving, wood carving, and silver works. *v/Sudurgata/Miklabraut, tel. 91/13264. Admission: free. Open June–Sept., daily 1:30–4; Oct.–May, Tues., Thurs., and weekends 1:30–4.*

From the National Museum, it is a 10-minute walk back to the pond and the city center.

Shopping

The most attractive shops, selling Icelandic woolen goods and arts and crafts, are downtown on Adalstræti, Hafnarstræti, and Vesturgata streets. Some stores to look for include **Icelandic Handcrafts Center** (Falcon House, Hafnarstræti 3, tel. 91/11784); the **Handknitting Association of Iceland**, a cooperative (Skolavoroustigur 19, tel. 91/21890 or 21912); and **Hilda Ltd.** (Borgartun 22, tel. 91/24590).

Dining

Most Reykjavik restaurants feature excellent seafood dishes, cooked in a wide variety of ways. Many serve European cuisine, as well as local fish and lamb specialties. Reservations are vital on weekends in the better restaurants. Jacket and tie are appreciated but rarely required. Most are open from noon to midnight, and most take major credit cards. For details and price category definitions, *see* Dining in Staying in Iceland.

Expensive **Alex.** A wide range of fish and meat dishes is served here in an atmosphere that is bright, modern, and relaxed. *Laugavegur 126, tel. 91/24631. Reservations advised. AE, DC, MC, V.*

Arnarhóll. This formal restaurant is divided into small, intimate dining rooms and has exceptional service. Try the duck à l'orange. *Hverfisgata 8–10, tel. 91/18833. Reservations advised. AE, DC, MC, V.*

Hótel Holt. This restaurant, in the hotel of the same name, has for many years enjoyed the reputation of having one of the best kitchens in Iceland. Paintings by some of the country's finest artists hang on the walls. *Bergstadastræti 37, tel. 91/25700. Reservations advised. AE, DC, MC, V.*

★ **Vid Tjörnina.** This restaurant has a homey atmosphere, what the locals call a "grandmother ambience." The chef is a pioneer of Icelandic seafood cuisine; his marinated codgills are not to be missed. *Templarasund 3, tel. 91/18555. Reservations advised. AE, MC, V.*

Moderate **Hornió.** Try the Icelandic mountain lamb in this rather small and friendly resturant, which has a cosmopolitan flair and ambience. *Hafnarstræti 15, tel. 91/20366. AE, MC, V.*

Potturinn og Pannan. This small restaurant on the edge of the downtown area has service that is brisk and efficient without being impersonal. Lamb and fish dishes and American-style salads are the specialties. *Brautarholt 22, tel. 91/11690. Reservations advised. AE, MC, V.*

Torfan. This restaurant, in a 19th-century town house, is the best place for tasting authentic, traditional Icelandic seafood. *Amtmannsstígur 1, tel. 91/13303. Reservations advised. AE, DC, MC, V.*

Inexpensive **Café Hressó.** This is the place for a quick snack and some local color; it's as close to a French café as you'll find in Iceland. Alcohol is not served. *Austurstræti 20, tel. 91/14353. Reservations not necessary. MC, V.*

Múlakaffi. The fresh clean air of Reykjavik should give you the hearty appetite you'll need for this working-class café, especially popular for lunch. *Hallamúlli, tel. 91/37737. Reservations not necessary. MC, V.*

El Sombrero. Near the main square, this is another good spot for a snack and people watching. Spanish food and pizzas are served. *Laugavegur 73, tel. 91/23866. Reservations not neces-sary. AE, MC, V.*

Lodging

For details and price category definitions, *see* Lodging in Stay-ing in Iceland.

Expensive **Esja.** This recently renovated hotel is a little way out of town, in the business area near the outdoor thermal swimming pool and sports hall. All rooms have been attractively decorated. There are fine views of the bay and Mount Esja from the Penthouse Cocktail Bar. *Sudurlandsbraut 2, tel. 91/82200. 134 rooms with bath or shower. Facilities: restaurant and lounge. AE, DC, MC, V.*

★ **Holt.** One of Reykjavik's finest hotels, the Holt is in a quiet resi-dential suburb. Many of the rooms are furnished with Icelandic works of art. The restaurant (*see* Dining) is especially good. *Bergstadastræti 37, tel. 91/25700. 50 rooms with bath or show-er. Facilities: restaurant and lounge. AE, DC, MC, V.*

Loftleider. The largest hotel in Iceland, the Loftleider accom-modates both tourists and those attending meetings and conventions. Located near the airport, it's 15 minutes from the center of town. *Reykjavik Airport, tel. 91/22322. 218 rooms with bath. Facilities: indoor pool, sauna, solarium, restau-rant, cafeteria, and several lounges. AE, DC, MC, V.*

★ **Safa.** In a class of its own, this hotel is very popular with Ameri-can businesspeople. All rooms are above the fourth level and have spectacular views of the city and beyond. It's within walk-ing distance of most museums, shops, and restaurants. *Hagatory, tel. 91/29900. 162 rooms with bath. Facilities: res-taurant with live music and dancing, rooftop grill, 6 bars, sauna, in-room video. AE, DC, MC, V.*

Moderate **Borg.** Near the parliament and the cathedral, the Borg makes an ideal base for sightseeing. It's a traditional, comfortable ho-tel. *Pósthusstræti 11, tel. 91/11440. 46 rooms, most with bath. Facilities: restaurant and lounge, rooftop terrace. AE, DC, MC, V.*

Inexpensive **Gardur.** This establishment is owned by the university and is only open during the summer when the students are on vaca-tion. It has basic but comfortable rooms, adequate for travelers on a tight budget. It's within easy reach of the National Muse-um and other attractions. *Hringbraut, tel. 91/15656. 44 rooms without bath. No credit cards. Closed in winter.*

Guest house. These accommodations are basic but clean, and the rooms have basins in them. The main bus station is close by. No breakfast is served. *Snorrabraut 52, tel. 91/16522. 18 rooms. No credit cards.*

Salvation Army Guest house. Double bedrooms are available, but most lodgings are in halls where you have a bedframe for your sleeping bag.

The Icelandic Countryside

The real beauty of Iceland is in the countryside: The fjords of the east, the stark mountains of the north, the sands of the south, the rough coastline of the west, and the lava fields of the interior. Spend at least an hour pouring over the literature at the tourist bureau in Reykjavik before deciding where to go first.

Getting Around

There are daily flights to most of the large towns. Although flights are expensive, special family fares and vacation tickets are available. The longest domestic flight takes just over an hour. There are car rental agencies in Reykjavik and in many towns around the country. The ferries mainly go to the Westmann Islands in the south, and boat service is limited along the western coast. If you do not have your own car, your best bet is to buy one of the special bus tickets that cover scheduled routes throughout the country (*see* Getting Around in Staying in Iceland).

Guided Tours

Because of the remoteness of the countryside and the hassles of driving on roads that are often not in good condition, many people prefer an organized bus tour from Reykjavik. Such tours are excellent ways to relax and enjoy Iceland's spectacular scenery. Most tours operate between June and September and cost from IKR 25,000 to IKR 90,000 per person, including overnight accommodations and three meals a day. On some tours you'll stay in hotels; on others you'll camp out or sleep in tents. Tours are available from three days to 19 days and can be booked from the United States or the United Kingdom through **Icelandair** or travel agencies. Tours include:

Around Iceland. This is a nine- or 12-day tour that covers some of the most attractive scenery in Iceland. Hotel accommodations are included.
Iceland Interior. A six- or eight-day tour across the island, this takes you through the remote and wild but often beautiful interior. Hotel accommodations are included.
Glaciers, Geysers, and Waterfalls. Lakes, mountains, volcanoes, and waterfalls are the attractions on this five-day tour through the south of Iceland. Overnight accommodations are in hotels.
Trekking in the Interior. This 12-day tour is not difficult for those used to walking, but you will need to be in good shape. You will sleep in tents overnight. (For details of the above four tours, contact the **Iceland Tourist Bureau,** Skógarhlíd 6, 101 Reykjavik, tel. 91/25855.)
Grand Safari. This 19-day trip along the coastlines and into the interior includes camping at night. (**Olfar Jacobsen Travel,** Austurstræti 9, 101 Reykjavik, tel. 91/13499.)
Birdwatchers' Paradise. This is a 12-day trip by both air and land to the great bird colonies. You'll stay in hotels or guest houses. (**Samvinn Travel,** Austurstræti 12, 101 Reykjavik, tel. 91/27077.)
Riding in Landmannalauger. Here's a six-day tour by Icelandic pony, mostly around the interior. You'll stay overnight in mountain huts. (**Iceland Tourist Board,** Laugavegur 3, Reykjavik, tel. 91/27488.)
Meet the People. This is a six-day bus tour around the southwest of the country, visiting homes in the villages and on the farms. Lodging is in hotels. (**Útsýn Travel Agency,** Austurstræti 17, 101 Reykjavik, tel. 91/26611.)

Local Tours One-day tours are available in all the major towns in Iceland

and can be arranged through agencies in Reykjavik (*see* Important Addresses and Numbers).

From Akureyri there are several excursions:

Tours to **Lake Mývatn** take about 10 hours and cost about IKR 2,700 per person. On the "Midnight Sun Tour," you drive along Eyjafjördur and watch the sun reach its lowest point and then rise again. This is a four-hour tour and costs about IKR 1,900 per person. There's also a "Midnight Sun Flight" to Grimsey, which takes about one and a half hours and costs about IKR 4,800. Tours around the north of Iceland are also available from Lake Mývatn and Húsavik.

From Egilsstadir there's a tour to Mjóifjödur across the rough mountain passes—a strenuous eight-hour tour costing about IKR 1,800 per person. From Höfn in Hornafjördur you can go by bus on a "Glacier Tour." It's a 10-hour tour costing about IKR 3,900 per person. One-day tours are also available from Borgarnes and Flökalunder in the western part of the country. There are also bus and boat tours available from Vestmannæyjar.

Tourist Information

Akureyri. Tourist Center, Hafnarstræti 82, tel. 96/24442.
Egilsstadir. Kaupvangur 6, tel. 97/11510.
Höfn. Hótel Höfn, Hornafjordur, tel. 97/81240.
Lake Mývatn. Hótel Reynihlid, Myvatnssveit, tel. 96/44170.
Olafsvik. Hótel Nes, Olafsbraut 19, tel. 93/61300.
Seydisfjördur. Farfuglaheimili, tel. 97/21410.
Snæfellsnes. Hótel Búdir, tel. 93/8111.
Vestfirdir. Tourist Bureau, v/Hafnarstræti, tel. 94/3357.

Exploring Iceland

See the Iceland map for the location of towns on this tour.

The South Iceland is not a crowded place. Between tourist accommodations there can be up to 80 kilometers (50 miles), so you must be prepared for some considerable traveling every day. Start your tour around Iceland from Reykjavik, heading east on the main ring road around the country (road no. 1), which you will follow for most of your tour.

In **Hveragerdi,** some 40 kilometers (25 miles) away, are some interesting hot springs and botanic greenhouses where Icelandic bananas are grown. When you have passed **Selfoss,** 8 kilometers (5 miles) farther on, you are in the heartland of Icelandic farming, and soon you will cross the biggest river in the country, Thjórsá. For an overnight stop in this area, the Edda hotels in **Skógar,** 120 kilometers (75 miles) east of Selfoss, and **Kirkjubæjarklaustur,** 80 kilometers (50 miles) farther east on road 205, are recommended (see Dining and Lodging).

The landscape around Kirkjubæjarklaustur is shaped by 200-year-old lava deposits. When the volcano Laka erupted in 1972, it produced the greatest amount of lava from a single eruption in recorded history.

Traveling the route along the south coast on a clear day, you'll see that the landscape is the area's only true tourist attraction. Don't miss the **Skaftafell National Park.** There you can put down your tent for IKR 300 a night. The park is at the root of the glacier Svinafellsjökull, and farther up is the highest mountain in Iceland, Hvannadalshnjúkur, rising to 1,953 meters (6,300 feet). In the park you can walk for an hour or a day through a rare combination of green forest, clear waters, waterfalls, sands, mountains, and glaciers. About 32 kilometers (20 miles) east of the park is the adventure world of **Breidamerkurlón.** The white and blue icebergs on the water have been featured as exotic backdrops in James Bond films. Boat tours can be arranged on arrival for IKR 700; information is available at Skaftafell National Park.

One-day downhill skiing tours to **Vatnajökull** are scheduled from June through September from **Höfn** in Hornafjördur, road 99. These tours are a once-in-a-lifetime opportunity, as the trip takes you through some great nature spots. Details and general tourist information are available from the Hótel Höfn (tel. 97/81240).

The East From Höfn the journey goes on to Djúpivogur, road 98, and by then you have reached the east coast, where one fjord lies beside another. From **Breiddalsvik** there are two alternative routes. One is to continue along the coastline to visit the fishing villages of **Stödvarfjördur, Fáskrúdsfjördur,** and **Reydarfjördur,** which can be reached via roads 97, 96, and 92 respectively. These villages and others of their kind have been responsible for the economic growth in Iceland during the last two decades. The wealth from fishing and fish products amounts to 80% of the national income.

From Reydarfjördur the ring road continues for 32 kilometers (20 miles) to **Egilsstadir.** If you decide not to follow the coastline from Breiddalsvik, you'll reach Egilsstadir across Breiddalsheidi, which, at approximately 775-meters (2,500 feet), is the highest mountain road in Iceland. The road up the hill is excitingly steep. In Egilsstadir you are about 768 kilometers (480 miles) from Reykjavik, or halfway around the island, so you can either turn back the way you came or continue north. There is a tourist information center where you can get some traveling tips at Kaupvangur 6 (tel. 97/11510).

Some 24 kilometers (15 miles) south of Egilsstadir on road 931 is the national park of **Hallormsstadarskógur,** which comprises the largest forest in Iceland. There you can stop for the night at an Edda hotel, or pitch a tent by the Lögur lagoon. Perhaps you'll spot the Icelandic relative of the Loch Ness monster, which, according to myth, lives in the lagoon. This area is one of the most accessible paradises in Iceland and is strongly recommended.

From there you can travel around the **Hérad district** and to **Seydisfjördur,** 48 kilometers (30 miles) from Egilsstadir on road 93. Check with the tourist office there for information on activities such as boat trips and pony trekking.

From Egilsstadir the ring road continues for more than 160 kilometers (100 miles) across remote highlands to **Lake Mývatn.** It is a day-long journey through some of the most remote places in Iceland. You will pass by the highest inhabited farm in the country, Mödruvellir, approximately 418 meters (1,350 feet) above sea level. Lake Mývatn is a place for bird lovers. There is, for instance, the greatest variety of ducks in the world here. Few people live in the area, but there are two good hotels with restaurants (*see* Dining and Lodging, below). Information about bike rentals, fishing, and other activities is available in the Hótel Reynihlid (tel. 96/44170).

From Lake Mývatn there are two possible routes. One is to go directly along road 1 to Akureyri, the capital of the north, a journey of 96 kilometers (60 miles). An astonishing attraction on this route is **Godafoss**, a graceful but forceful waterfall.

The other alternative is to go for a day or so to **Húsavik** (road 87) and **Tjörnes** (road 85), a detour of over 160 kilometers (100 miles). The major attractions in this area are the waterfall **Dettifoss** (road 864), and the canyon of **Asbyrgi**, which legend says is a giant horseshoe of Sleipnir, the horse of the ancient pagan god, Odin.

The North and the West
In **Akureyri** there are many interesting sights. It is a well-situated town, and full of natural charm. Late–19th-century wooden houses give the city center a sense of history, as well as architectural variety. There is an **Arctic Botanic Gardens** with some rare arctic plants. *Admission: free. Open daily 8 AM–11 PM.*

From Akureyri you can go for an evening tour north along the coast of **Eyjafjördur** (road 82), to see the midnight sun; June and July are the brightest months. Information for traveling in the north of the country is available at the Akureyri tourist center.

Driving from Akureyri to Reykjavik, a journey of 400 kilometers (250 miles) takes an entire day, so if there is time to spare, a stay in **Saudárkrókur** (roads 75 and 76), **Blönduós**, or **Borgarnes** can be both pleasant and peaceful. Holders of the Omnibus Passport (*see* Getting Around) should not miss the 320-kilometer (200-mile) detour to **Snæfellsnes**, via roads 54 and 57, for a couple of days, at least. A night in the presence of the glacier Snæfellsjokull, where Jules Verne's *Journey to the Center of the Earth* begins, is recommended.

From **Olafsvik**, tours to the top of the glacier with a snowmobile can be arranged. The trip costs IKR 2,000 per person; information is available from the Hótel Nes (tel. 93/61300).

Another interesting detour, which can take up to a week, is to **Vestfirdir** (roads 68, 69, and 61). From Isafördur, trips to the inhabitable parts of Strandarsysla may be of interest to those keen on walking and mountaineering. Information is available at the Vestfirdir Tourist Bureau.

Dining and Lodging

If you tour Iceland on your own, whether by public transportation or by car, you can arrange to stay in farmhouses that have registered with the **Iceland Tourist Board** (tel. 91/27488). Its brochure, *Farm Holidays in Iceland*, lists 42 farms that take visitors. In addition, the **Icelandic Touring Club** operates a number of huts in the remote parts of the country that are clean, warm, and comfortable, but only available on a first-come, first-served basis.

Most restaurants outside Reykjavik are in hotels, and the following list is largely a selection of hotel/restaurants. The cost of lodging in the countryside is less than in Reykjavik, but the meals cost about the same. Most hotels are moderately priced, around IKR 3,500 for a double room with breakfast. Youth hostels and farmhouse lodging are also available around the country, ranging from IKR 600 to IKR 1,600 per person. For details and price category definitions, *see* Dining and Lodging in Staying in Iceland.

Akureyri
★ **Hótel KEA.** You'll receive first-class hotel service, and the price is a surprise—real value for the money. There is an excellent kitchen, and moderately priced food is available in the cafeteria. *Hafnarstræti 89, tel. 96/2200. 30 rooms with shower. AE, MC, V. Expensive.*

Hótel Akureyri. This hotel is well situated in the center of town. It has no restaurant. *Hafnarstræti 98, tel. 96/22525. 10 rooms without bath. AE, MC, V. Moderate.*

Hótel Edda. There is good service here, and a cafeteria. *Menntaskólinn, tel. 96/24055. 77 rooms without bath. Facilities: swimming pool. AE, MC, V. Moderate.*

Lónsá Youth Hostel. It's lodging only, but there are kitchen facilities available. *Glæsibæjarhreppur, tel. 96/25037. 11 rooms without bath. AE, MC, V. Inexpensive.*

Blönduós
Hótel Blönduós. This small hotel, located in the center of town, has a restaurant. *Adalgata 6, tel. 95/4126. 11 rooms without bath. AE, MC, V. Inexpensive.*

Borgarnes
Hótel Borgarnes. One of the biggest and most popular hotels on the west coast, this establishment offers both a cafeteria and an elegant restaurant. *Egilsgata 14–16, tel. 93/12012. 22 rooms with shower. AE, DC, MC, V. Expensive.*

Breiddalsvik
Hótel Bláfell. This is a newly built hotel, but it has no dining facilities. *Sólvellir 14, tel. 97/56770. 8 rooms without bath. AE, MC, V. Inexpensive.*

Búdir
Hótel Búdir. Under the magical glacier Snæfellsjökull and close to a golden beach, this hotel also has an excellent restaurant. *Snæfellsnes, tel. 93/56700. 10 rooms without bath. AE, DC, MC, V. Moderate.*

Djúpivogur
Hótel Pramtid. This small hotel by the harbor has a dining room where home-style food is served in a friendly atmosphere. *Tel. 97/88887. 10 rooms without bath. AE, MC, V. Moderate.*

Berunes Youth Hostel. This small hostel offers lodging for 15 people only. *Beruneshr., tel. 97/88988. Inexpensive.*

Egilsstadir
Hótel Valaskjálf. This hotel is large and practical, with a restaurant and a cafeteria. There is dancing on the weekends. *v/ Skógarströnd, tel. 97/11500. 66 rooms with shower. AE, MC, V. Moderate.*

Hótel Egilsstadir. This is a charming farmhouse hotel. *Tel. 97/11114. 10 rooms without bath. Inexpensive.*

Húsey Youth Hostel. A ways out of town, this hostel offers lodging only. *Hróarstunga, tel. 97/13010. Inexpensive.*

Hallormsstadur
Hótel Edda. The hotel is fair, but the harmony of forest, lake, and quiet bays is unique. It has a good restaurant. *Hallormsstad, tel. 97/11705. 17 rooms without bath. AE, DC, V. Closed Oct.–Apr. Moderate.*

Hornafjördur
Hótel Höfn. This clean and comfortable hotel has a restaurant with good food and service. Try the excellent almond trout. Fast food is also available at the grill, and there is dancing on the weekends. *Tel. 97/81240. 40 rooms, half with shower. AE, MC, V. Moderate.*

Hveragerdi Hótel Örk. Newly built with many facilities, the Örk has expensive rooms, but meals in the ground-floor restaurant are reasonable. *Breidamörk 1, tel. 99/4100. 60 rooms with shower. AE, MC, V. Expensive.*
Ból Youth Hostel. *Hveramörk 14, tel. 99/4588. No dining facilities. Inexpensive.*

Isafjördur Hótel Isafjördur. This is a good family hotel. The restaurant offers a great variety of tasty seafood. *Silfurtorgi 2, tel. 94/4111. 20 rooms with shower. AE, MC, V. Moderate.*

Kirkjubæjarklaustur Hótel Edda. This is an ordinary hotel with a restaurant. *Tel. 99/7799. 45 rooms with shower. Facilities: swimming pool. AE, MC, V. Closed Oct.–Apr. Moderate.*

Mývatn Hótel Húsavik. This highly reputable hotel is popular as a ski hotel during winter. It has a good restaurant and a practical cafeteria. *Ketilsbraut 22, tel. 96/41220. 21 rooms with shower. AE, DC, MC, V. Expensive.*
Hótel Reynihlid. This popular hotel offers a good general information service for tourists, and a restaurant. *Myvatnssveit, tel. 96/44170. 20 rooms with shower. AE, DC, MC, V. Expensive.*
Hótel Reykjahlid. This small hotel has an exclusive location by the lake, and a restaurant. *Myvatnssveit, tel. 96/44142. 7 rooms without bath. AE, MC, V. Closed Oct.–Apr. Moderate.*

Olafsvik Hótel Nes. This functional hotel is close to the harbor. Its cafeteria offers good food at moderate prices. *Olafsbraut 19, tel. 93/61300. 38 rooms without bath. Moderate.*

Saudarkrókur Hótel Mælifell. This attractive hotel has a restaurant and dancing on the weekends. *Adalgata 7, tel. 95/5265. 20 rooms with shower. AE, MC, V. Moderate.*

Seydisfjördur Hótel Snæfell. This is a new hotel in an old wooden house. Its ★ glassed-in restaurant, by a picturesque pond, serves good food. *Austurvegur 3, tel. 97/21460. 9 rooms with shower. AE, MC, V. Moderate.*

Skógar Hótel Edda. Close to the waterfall Skógarfoss, this hotel is beautifully located with views to the sea and to the mountains and glaciers. It has a restaurant. *Skógum, tel. 99/8187. 30 rooms without bath. AE, MC, V. Closed Oct.–Apr. Moderate.*

18 Ireland

Introduction

Ireland, the most westerly country in Europe, is a small island on which you are never more than an hour's drive from the sea. It's actually two countries in one. The northeast corner of the island, Northern Ireland, remains a part of the United Kingdom, while the Republic, with a population of only 3½ million, has been independent since 1921.

The Republic of Ireland is virtually free from the "troubles" that dominate the news from Northern Ireland. Over the past few years, millions of pounds have been spent on upgrading tourist facilities, but the attractions of Ireland as a vacation destination remain the same as ever: those of a small, friendly country with a mild climate and a relaxed pace of life, where simple pleasures are to be found in its scenery, its historical heritage, its sporting opportunities, and the informal hospitality of its loquacious inhabitants.

Dublin, the capital, is a thriving modern city. It's a strikingly elegant city, too, a fact of which the Dubliners are well aware. Trinity College, Dublin Castle, and the magnificent public buildings and distinctive Georgian squares of the city have all been restored, allowing the elegance of 18th-century Dublin to emerge again after centuries of neglect. You will find, too, that the courtesy and charm of the Dubliners themselves make an important contribution to your visit, introducing you to a city with an atmosphere that belongs to an older, less frenetic age.

The Irish way of life is unpretentious and informal. Pubs play an important part in it. The Irish will be found at their most convivial when seated in front of a pint of their famous black beer, Guinness, consumed here in vast quantities. Even if you do not usually frequent bars, a visit to an Irish pub or two will add greatly to the enjoyment of your visit.

The pace of life outside Dublin is even more relaxed. When a local was asked for the Irish-language equivalent of *mañana*, the reply came that there is no word in Irish to convey quite the same sense of urgency. An exaggeration, of course, but the farther you travel from the metropolis, the more you will be inclined to linger. Apart from such sporting attractions as championship golf, horse racing, deep-sea fishing, and angling, the thing to do in Ireland is to take it easy, and look around you. The Lakes of Killarney—romantic, boulder-strewn mountains, strung with a chain of deep-blue lakes—are justifiably the country's most famous beauty spot. The Ring of Kerry provides the motorist with a day-long tour through lush coastal vegetation. By contrast, you will have to explore the eerie limestone desert called The Burren, in County Clare, on foot in order to find its rare Alpine and Mediterranean flowers. Likewise, if you want to stand on the summit of the Cliffs of Moher to watch the Atlantic breakers pounding on the rocks 217 meters (700 feet) below you, you'll have to walk a bit first. The blue hills of Connemara remain the inspiration for many paintings. The history buff will delight in the Shannon region, peppered with numerous castles, some of which have been meticulously restored. Throughout the country, there are prehistoric and early-Christian remains to be discovered. You can also seek out the places made famous by James Joyce, William Butler Yeats,

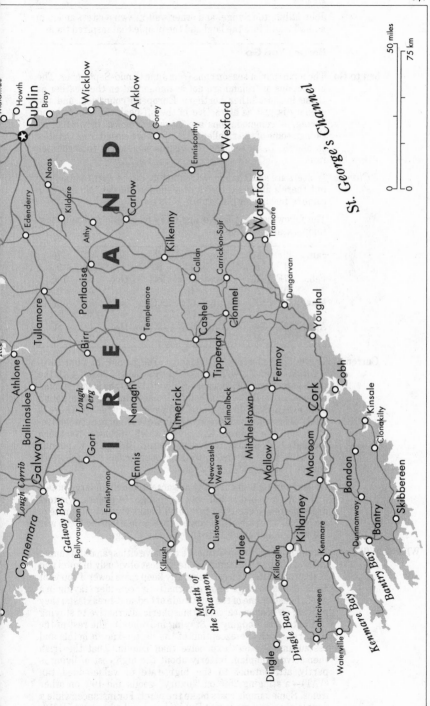

John Millington Synge, and other well-known writers and gain a new insight into the land and the people that inspired them.

Before You Go

When to Go The main tourist season runs from June to mid-September. The attractions of Ireland are not as dependent on the weather as those in most other northern European countries, and the scenery is just as attractive in the off-peak times of fall and spring. Accommodations are more economical in winter, although some of the smaller attractions are closed from October to March. In all seasons the visitor can expect to encounter rain.

Climate Winters are mild though wet; summers can be warm and sunny, but there's always the risk of a sudden shower. No one ever came to Ireland for a suntan.

The following are the average daily maximum and minimum temperatures for Dublin.

Jan.	46F	8C	May	60F	15C	Sept.	63F	17C
	34	1		43	6		48	9
Feb.	47F	8C	June	65F	18C	Oct.	57F	14C
	35	2		48	9		43	6
Mar.	51F	10C	July	67F	20C	Nov.	51F	10C
	37	3		52	11		39	4
Apr.	55F	13C	Aug.	67F	19C	Dec.	47F	8C
	39	4		51	11		37	3

Currency The unit of currency in Ireland is the pound, or punt (pronounced "poont"), written as IR£ to avoid confusion with the pound sterling. The currency is divided into the same denominations as in Britain (although Ireland doesn't have pound coins) with IR£1 divided into 100 pence (written *p*). There is likely to be some variance in the rates of exchange between Ireland and the United Kingdom (which includes Northern Ireland). This usually favors the visitor. Change U.K. pounds at a bank when you get to Ireland (pound coins not accepted); change Irish pounds before you leave.

Dollars and British currency are accepted only in large hotels and shops licensed as bureaux de change. In general, visitors are expected to use Irish currency. Banks give the best rate of exchange. The rate of exchange at press time (spring 1989) was .69 to the dollar and 1.18 to the pound sterling.

What It Will Cost Dublin is one of Europe's most expensive cities, an unfortunate state of affairs that manifests itself most obviously in hotel and restaurant rates. You can generally keep costs lower if you visit Ireland on a package tour. Alternatively, consider staying in a guest house or one of the multitude of bed-and-breakfasts; they provide an economical and atmospheric alternative to staying in a hotel (*see* Lodging in Staying in Ireland). The rest of the country—with the exception of the better-known hotels and restaurants—is less expensive than Dublin. That the Irish themselves complain bitterly about the high cost of living is partly attributable to the high rate of value-added tax (VAT)—a stinging 25% on "luxury" goods and 10% on other items. Some sample costs make the point. For instance, while a double room in a moderate Dublin hotel will cost about IR£50, with breakfast sometimes another IR£7 per person, the current rate for a country B&B is around IR£10 per person. A modest small-town hotel will charge around IR£12.50 per person.

Sample Prices Cup of coffee, 50p; pint of beer IR£1.45; Coca-Cola, 60p; ham sandwich, IR£1.20; one-mile taxi ride, IR£2.50.

Customs on Arrival Customs regulations for travelers entering Ireland are complex. There are three levels of duty-free allowance: one for residents of non-European countries; another for passengers arriving from other EEC countries bringing in goods that have *not* been bought in a duty-free shop; and a third for residents of European countries not in the EEC and for passengers arriving from other EEC countries with goods that *have* been bought in a duty-free shop.

In the first category you may import duty-free: 400 cigarettes or 200 cigarillos or 100 cigars or 500 grams of tobacco; plus one liter of alcoholic beverage of more than 22% volume or a total of two liters of alcoholic beverage of not more than 22% volume or sparkling or fortified wine, plus two liters of other wine; plus 50 grams of perfume and a quarter of a liter of toilet water; plus other goods to a value of IR£31 per person (IR£16 for children under 15).

In the second category you may import duty-free: 300 cigarettes or 400 grams of tobacco or 150 cigarillos or 75 cigars; plus 1½ liters of alcoholic beverage of more than 22% volume or a total of three liters of alcoholic beverage of not more than 22% volume or sparkling or fortified wines plus four liters of other wine; plus 75 grams of perfume and three-eighths of a liter of toilet water; plus, other goods to a value of IR£145 per person (IR£41 for children under 15).

In the third category you may import duty-free: 200 cigarettes or 100 cigarillos or 50 cigars or 250 grams of tobacco; plus one liter of alcoholic beverage of more than 22% volume or a total of two liters of alcoholic beverage of not more than 22% volume or sparkling or fortified wine plus two liters of other wine; plus 50 grams of perfume and a quarter of a liter of toilet water; plus, other goods to a value of IR£31 per person (IR£16 for children under 15).

Note that in all three categories the tobacco and alcohol allowances apply only to those aged 17 and older. If you have nothing more than the duty-free allowance when you arrive, walk straight through the green "nothing to declare" channel. If you have more than your duty-free allowance, however, you must go into the red channel and declare the goods you are bringing in.

Visitors may import any quantity of currency, whether foreign or Irish, and nonresidents may export any amount of foreign currency, provided it was declared on arrival. Otherwise, you may export no more than IR£100, in denominations no larger than IR£20, and no more than the equivalent of IR£500 in foreign currency.

Language Officially, the Irish language is the first language of the Republic, but the everyday language of the majority of Irish people is English. Except for the northwest, most signs are written in Irish with an English translation underneath. There is one important exception to this rule, with which all visitors should familiarize themselves: *Fir* and *mna* translate respectively into *men* and *women*. The *Gaeltacht*—areas in which Irish *is* the everyday language of most people—comprises only 6% of the land, and all its inhabitants are, in any case, bilingual.

Getting Around

By Car
Road Conditions

Ireland is one country where a car is more or less essential for successful travel. Despite improvements in public transportation, both the train and bus networks are limited, and many of the most intriguing areas are accessible only by car. Roads are reasonable, though the absence of turnpikes means that trip times can be long; on the other hand, you'll soon find that driving past an everchanging and often dramatic series of unspoiled landscapes can be very much part of the fun. There's a bonus in the fact that traffic is normally light, though you can easily find yourself crawling down country lanes behind an ancient tractor or a flock of sheep. This is not a country for those with a taste for life in the fast lane.

All principal roads are designated by the letter N, meaning National Primary Road. Thus, the main highway north from Dublin is N1, the main highway northwest is N2, and so on. Road signs are normally in both Irish and English; in the northwest, most are in Irish only, so make sure you have a good road map. Distances on the new green signposts are in kilometers; the old white signposts give distances in miles.

Rules of the Road

Driving is on the left. There is a general speed limit of 88 kph (55 mph) on most roads; in towns, the limit is 48 kph (30 mph). In some areas, the limit is 64 kph (40 mph); this will always be clearly posted. At junctions, traffic from the right takes priority.

Seat belts must be worn by the driver and front-seat passengers. Children under 12 must ride in the back. Drunk-driving laws are strict.

Parking

Despite the relative lack of traffic, parking in towns is a real problem. Signs with the letter P indicate parking lots, but if there's a stroke through the P, keep away or you'll collect a stiff fine, normally around IR£20. After 6 PM, restrictions are lifted. Give lot attendants about 20p when you leave.

Frontier Posts

There are 20 approved routes for crossing the border between the Republic of Ireland and Northern Ireland. If you plan to drive into Northern Ireland in a rented car, be sure the rental company furnishes the necessary papers. Formalities of crossing the border are minimal, though you may find additional checks just north of the border. *Don't* drive on roads near the border marked "Unapproved Road."

By Train

Iarnód Eaireann (Irish Rail) and **Bus Eireann** (Irish Bus) are independent components of the state-owned public transportation company **Coras Iompair Eireann** (CIE). The rail network, although much cut back in the past 25 years, is still extensive, with main routes radiating from Dublin to Cork, Galway, Limerick, Tralee, Killarney, Westport, and Sligo; there is also a line for the north and Belfast. All trains are diesel; cars on principal expresses have air-conditioning. There are two classes on many trains—Super Standard (first class), and Standard (second class). Dining cars are carried on main expresses. There are no sleeping cars.

Speeds are slow in comparison with those of other European trains. Dublin, however, now has a modern commuter train—

the DART—running south from the suburb of Howth through the city to Bray on the Wicklow coast, with various stops along the way.

Fares For the strictly independent traveler, the 15-day **Rambler** ticket gives unlimited travel by train and bus and is an excellent value at IR£95. It can be purchased from any city bus terminal or train station ticket office. Train-only and bus-only tickets are available for IR£77. There is an eight-day **Rambler** ticket (rail and bus) for IR£66. The train-only and bus-only tickets cost IR£52. One- and four-day round-trip train tickets are also available at discounted rates. The **Overlander** ticket includes travel in Norther Ireland via rail, bus, and Ulsterbus; it costs IR£109 for 15 days.

By Plane Distances are not great in Ireland, so air travel plays only a small role in internal travel. **Aer Lingus** has flights from Dublin to Shannon and Cork, with flying time around 30 minutes. There is frequent service to the Aran Islands, off Galway Bay, from Carnmore Airport, Galway. The flight takes 15–25 minutes.

By Bus The provincial bus system operated by Bus Eireann is widespread—more so than the train system—although service can be infrequent in remote areas. But the routes cover the whole country and are often linked to the train services; *see* By Train for details of combined train and bus discount tickets.

By Boat Exploring Ireland's lakes, rivers, and canals is a delightful offbeat way to get to know the country. Motor cruisers can be chartered on the Shannon, the longest river in the British Isles. The Irish Tourist Board has details of the wide choice of trips and operators.

For drifting through the historic Midlands on the Grand Canal and river Barrow, contact **Celtic Canal Cruisers,** Tullamore, County Offaly, tel. 0506/21861.

By Bicycle Biking can be a great way to get around Ireland. Details of bicycle rentals are available from the Irish Tourist Board. Rates average IR£4.50 per day or IR£22 per week. You must pay a IR£30 deposit. Be sure to make reservations, especially in July and August. If you rent a bike in the Republic, you may *not* take it into Northern Ireland; nor may you take a bike rented in Northern Ireland into the Republic.

Staying in Ireland

Telephones There are pay phones in all post offices and most hotels and
Local Calls bars, as well as in street booths. Local calls cost 20p for three minutes, calls within Ireland cost about 50p for three minutes, and calls to Britain cost about IR£1.75 for three minutes. Rates go down by about a third after 6 PM and all day Saturday and Sunday.

International Calls For calls to the USA and Canada, dial 161 followed by the area code. For calls to the United Kingdom, dial 031 for London followed by the number, and 03 for the rest of the country. Don't make international calls from your hotel room unless absolutely necessary. Most hotels add 200–300% to calls.

Mail Airmail rates to USA, Canada, and the Commonwealth are 46p
Postal Rates for the first 10 grams, air letters 40p, and postcards 30p. Letters to Britain and continental Europe cost 28p, postcards 24p.

Receiving Mail A general delivery service is operated free of charge from Dublin's General Post Office O'Connell St., Dublin 1, tel. 01/728888.

Shopping
VAT Refunds Visitors from outside Europe can take advantage of the "cash-back" system on value-added tax (VAT) if their purchases total more than IR£50. A cash-back voucher must be filled out by the retailer at the point of sale. The visitor pays the total gross price, including VAT, and receives green and yellow copies of the invoice; both must be retained. These are presented to—and stamped by—customs, as you leave the country. Take the stamped form along to the cashier and you will be refunded the VAT.

Opening and
Closing Times **Banks.** Banks are open weekdays 10–12:30 and 1:30–3, and until 5 on selected days.

Museums. Museums are usually open weekdays 10–5, Saturday 10–1, Sunday 2–5. Always make a point of checking, however, as hours can change unexpectedly.

Shops. Shops are open Monday–Saturday 9–5:30, closing earlier on Wednesday, Thursday, or Saturday, depending on the locality.

National Holidays January 1; March 17 (St. Patrick's Day); April 13 (Good Friday); April 16 (Easter Monday); June 4; August 6; October 29; December 25, 26 (Christmas). If you're planning a visit at Easter, remember that theaters and cinemas are closed for the last three days of the preceding week.

Dining When it comes to food, Ireland has some of the best raw materials in the world: prime beef, locally raised lamb and pork, free-range poultry, game in season, abundant fresh seafood, and locally grown seasonal vegetables. Despite the near legendary awfulness of much Irish cooking in the recent past, times are definitely changing, and a new generation of chefs is beginning to take greater advantage of this abundance of magnificent produce. In almost all corners of the country, you'll find a substantial choice of restaurants, many in hotels, serving fresh local food imaginatively prepared and served.

If your tastes run toward traditional Irish dishes, there are still a few old-fashioned restaurants serving substantial portions of excellent, if plain, home cooking. Look for boiled bacon and cabbage, Irish stew, and *colcannon* (cooked potatoes diced and fried in butter with onions and either cabbage or leeks and covered in thick cream just before serving). The best bet for daytime meals is "pub grub"—a choice of soup and soda bread, two or three hot dishes of the day, salad platters, or sandwiches. Most bars serve food, and a growing number offer coffee and tea as an alternative to alcohol. Guinness, a dark beer or "stout," brewed with malt, is the Irish national drink, consumed in vast quantities. Even if you never go out for a drink at home, you should visit at least one or two pubs in Ireland. The pub is one of the pillars of Irish society, worth visiting as much for entertainment and conversation as for drinking.

Mealtimes Breakfast is served between 8 and 10—earlier by special request only—and is a substantial meal of cereal, bacon, eggs, sausage, and toast. Lunch is eaten between 12:30 and 2. Having enjoyed a hearty breakfast, however, most visitors tend to have a light lunch and to eat their main meal in the evening. The old tradition of "high tea" taken around 5, followed by a light snack before bed, is still encountered in many Irish homes, including many bed-and-breakfasts. Elsewhere, however, it is generally assumed that you'll be eating between 7 and 9:30, and that this will be your main meal of the day.

Dress A jacket and tie or upscale casual dress are suggested for expensive restaurants. Otherwise, casual dress is acceptable.

Ratings Prices are per person and include a first course, main course, and dessert, but no wine or tip. Sales tax at 10% is included in all Irish restaurant bills. Some places, usually the more expensive establishments, add a 12% or 15% service charge, in which case no tip is necessary; elsewhere a tip of 10% is adequate. The most highly recommended restaurants are indicated by a star ★. At press time, there were .69 Irish pounds to the dollar.

Category	Cost
Expensive	over IR£25
Moderate	IR£15–IR£25
Inexpensive	under IR£15

Credit Cards The following credit card abbreviations are used: AE, American Express; DC, Diners Club; MC, MasterCard; V, Visa.

Lodging Accommodations in Ireland range all the way from deluxe castles and renovated stately homes to thatched cottages and farmhouses to humble B&Bs. Standards everywhere are high and are continuing to rise all the time. Pressure on hotel space reaches a peak between June and September, but it's a good idea to make reservations in advance at any time of year, particularly at the more expensive spots. Rooms can be reserved directly from the USA; ask your travel agent for details. The Irish Tourist Board's Central Reservations Service (14 Upper O'Connell St., Dublin 1, tel. 01/747733) can make reservations, as can local tourist board offices.

The Irish Tourist Board (ITB) has an official grading system and publishes a detailed price list of all approved accommodations, including hotels, guest houses, farmhouses, B&Bs, and hostels. No hotel may exceed this price without special authorization from the ITB; prices must also be displayed in every room. Don't hesitate to complain either to the manager or the ITB, or both, if prices exceed this maximum.

In general, hotels charge per person. In most cases (but not all, especially in more expensive places), the price includes a full breakfast. VAT is included, but some hotels—again, usually the more expensive ones—add a 10–15% service charge. This should be mentioned in their price list. In moderate and inexpensive hotels, be sure to specify if you want a private bath or shower; the latter is cheaper. Off-season (October–May) prices are reduced by as much as 25%.

Guest Houses Some smaller hotels are graded as guest houses. To qualify, they must have at least five bedrooms. A few may have restaurants; those that do not will often provide evening meals by arrangement. Few will have a bar. Otherwise, their rooms can be as comfortable as those of a regular hotel, and in major cities they offer very good value for money compared with the inexpensive hotels.

Bed-and-Breakfast Bed-and-breakfast means just that. The bed can vary from a four-poster in the wing of a castle to a feather bed in a white-washed farmhouse or the spare bedroom of a modern cottage. Rates are generally around IR£10 per person, though these can vary significantly. Although many larger B&Bs offer rooms with bath or shower, in the majority you'll have to use the bathroom in the hall and, in many cases, to pay 50p–IR£1 extra for the privilege.

Rentals In nearly 30 locations around Ireland, there are clusters of cottages for rent. The majority are built in traditional styles but have central heating and all other conveniences. The average rent for a three-bedroom cottage equipped for six adults is around IR£230 in mid-season; be sure to make reservations well in advance. The ITB's booklet *Self Catering* (IR£2) has full details.

Camping There are a variety of beautifully sited campgrounds and trailer parks, but be prepared for wet weather! The ITB publishes a useful booklet *Caravan and Camping Guide* (IR£1.50).

Ratings Prices are for two people in a double room, based on high season (June to September) rates. Best bets are indicated by a star ★. At press time, there were .69 Irish pounds to the dollar.

Category	Cost
Very Expensive	IR£100 and up
Expensive	IR£70–IR£100
Moderate	IR£50–IR£70
Inexpensive	under IR£50

Credit Cards The following credit card abbreviations are used: AE, American Express; DC, Diners Club; MC, MasterCard; V, Visa.

Tipping Other than in upscale hotels and restaurants, the Irish are not really used to being tipped. Some hotels and restaurants will add a service charge of about 12% to your bill, so tipping is not necessary unless you have received particularly good service.

Tip taxi drivers about 10% of the fare if the taxi has been using its meter. For longer journeys, where the fare is agreed in advance, a tip will not be expected, unless some kind of commentary (solicited or not) has been provided. In luxury hotels, porters and bellhops will expect IR£1; elsewhere, 50p is adequate. Hairdressers normally expect a tip of about IR£1. You don't tip in pubs, but if there is waiter service in a bar or hotel lounge, leave about 20p.

Dublin

Arriving and Departing

By Plane All flights arrive at Dublin's Collinstown Airport, 10 kilometers (six miles) north of town. For information on arrival and departure times, call individual airlines.

Between the Airport and Downtown Buses leave every 20 minutes from outside the Arrivals door for the central bus station in downtown Dublin. The ride takes about 30 minutes, depending on the traffic, and the fare is

IR£2.50. A taxi ride into town will cost from IR£5 to IR£10, depending on the location of your hotel.

By Train There are three main stations. Heuston Station (at Kingsbridge) is the departure point for the south and southwest; Connolly Station (at Amiens Street), for Belfast, the east coast, and the west; Pearse Station, (on Westland Row), for Bray and connections via Dun Laoghaire to the Liverpool/Holyhead ferries. Tel. 01/366222 for information.

By Bus The central bus station, Busaras, is at Store Street near the Custom House. Some buses terminate near Connolly Bridge. tel. 01/734222 for information on city services (Dublin Bus); tel. 01/366111 for express buses and provincial services (Bus Eireann).

By Car The main access route from the north is N1; from the west, N4; from the south and southwest, N7; from the east coast, N11. On all routes there are clearly marked signs indicating the center of the city: "An Lar."

Getting Around

Dublin is small as capital cities go—the downtown area is positively compact—and the best way to see the city and soak in the full flavor is on foot.

By Train An electric train commuter service, DART (Dublin Area Rapid Transport), serves the suburbs out to Howth, on the north side of the city, and to Bray, County Wicklow, on the south side. Fares are about the same as for buses. Street direction signs to DART stations read "Staisiun/Station." The **Irish Rail** office is at 35 Lower Abbey Street; for rail inquiries, tel. 01/787777.

By Bus Most city buses originate in or pass through the area of O'Connell Street and O'Connell Bridge. If the destination board indicates "An Lar," that means that the bus is going to the city's central area. Timetables (45p) are available from the **Dublin Bus** office, 59 Upper O'Connell St., tel. 01/720000) and give details of all routes, times of operation, and price codes. The minimum fare is 45p.

By Taxi Taxis do not cruise, but are located beside the central bus station, at train stations, at O'Connell Bridge, at St. Stephen's Green, and near major hotels. They are not of uniform type or color. Make sure the meter is on. The initial charge is IR£1.80; the fare is displayed in the cab. A one-mile trip in city traffic costs about IR£2.50.

Important Addresses and Numbers

Tourist Information There is a tourist information office in the entrance hall of the **Irish Tourist Board** headquarters, Baggot Street Bridge, tel. 01/765871; open weekdays 9–5. More conveniently located is the office at 14 Upper O'Connell St., tel. 01/747733; open weekdays 9–5, Saturday 9–1. There is also an office at the Airport, tel. 01/376387. From mid-June to September, there is an office at the Ferryport, Dun Laoghaire.

Embassies U.S.: 42 Elgin Rd., Ballsbridge, tel. 01/806984. **Canadian:** 65 St. Stephen's Green, tel. 01/781988. **U.K.:** 33 Merrion Rd., tel. 01/695211.

Emergencies Police: tel. 999; **Ambulance:** tel. 999; **Doctor:** tel. 01/537951 or

01/767273; **Dentist:** tel. 01/978435; **Pharmacy:** Hamilton Long, 5 Upper O'Connell St., tel. 01/748456.

Travel Agencies   **American Express:** 116 Grafton St., tel. 01/772874. **Thomas Cook:** 118 Grafton St., tel. 01/771721.

Guided Tours

Orientation Tours   Both **Bus Eireann** (tel. 01/366111) and **Gray Line Sightseeing** (tel. 01/744466; 01/612325 low season) offer bus tours of Dublin and its surrounding areas. **Gogan Tours** (tel. 01/796022) has a series of afternoon and evening bus tours, with author and historian Eamonn MacThomais as guide, which guarantee a real taste of Dublin wit.

Special-Interest Tours   **Bus Eireann** has a "Traditional Irish Music Night" tour. **Elegant Ireland** (tel. 01/751665) organizes tours for groups interested in architecture and the fine arts; these include visits with the owners of some of Ireland's stately homes and castles.

Walking Tours   **Tour Guides Ireland** (tel. 01/794291) offers a selection of walking tours, including "Literary Dublin", "Georgian Dublin", and "Pub Tours." The **Irish Tourist Board** has a "Tourist Trail" walk, which takes in the main sites of central Dublin and can be completed in about three hours. An accompanying booklet (75p) can be obtained from the office at 14 Upper O'Connell Street. Guided walking tours of Old Dublin leave from the main entrance to Christ Church Cathedral, Monday–Saturday at 10:30 and 2, and Sunday at 2. Tours last about two hours. Contact Joe Byrne (tel. 01/532407) for winter schedule.

Excursions   **Bus Eireann** (tel. 01/366111) and **Gray Line Sightseeing** (tel. 01/744466) offer day-long tours into the surrounding countryside, and longer tours elsewhere; price includes accommodations, breakfast, and admission costs. **CIE Tours International** offers vacations lasting from one to 10 days that include touring by train or bus, accommodations, and main meals. Costs range from around IR£176 (IR£269 including round-trip airfare from London) to IR£286 (IR£412 from London) for an eight-day tour in July and August.

Exploring Dublin

Numbers in the margin correspond with points of interest on the Dublin map.

Dublin is a small city with a population of just over one million. For all that, it has a distinctly cosmopolitan air, one that complements happily the individuality of the city and the courtesy and friendliness of its inhabitants. Originally a Viking settlement, Dublin is situated on the banks of the river Liffey. The Liffey divides the city north and south, with the more lively and fashionable spots, like the Grafton Street shopping area, to be found on the south side. Most of the city's historically interesting buildings date from the 18th century and, although many of its finer Georgian buildings disappeared in the over-enthusiastic redevelopment of the '70s, enough remain, mainly south of the river, to recall the elegant Dublin of the past. The slums romanticized by writers Sean O'Casey and Brendan Behan have virtually been eradicated, but literary Dublin can still be recaptured by those who want to follow the footsteps of Leopold Bloom's progress, as described in James Joyce's *Ulysses*. And

Trinity College, alma mater of Oliver Goldsmith, Jonathan Swift, and Samuel Beckett, among others, still provides a haven of tranquility.

Dubliners are talkative, self-confident people, eager to have visitors enjoy the pleasures of their city. You can meet a lively cross section of people in the city's numerous bars, probably the best places to sample the famous wit of the only city to have produced three winners of the Nobel Prize for Literature: William Butler Yeats, George Bernard Shaw, and Samuel Beckett.

O'Connell Begin your tour of Dublin at **O'Connell Bridge,** the city's most
Street central landmark. Look closely and you will notice a strange
❶ feature: The bridge is wider than it is long. The north side of O'Connell Bridge is dominated by an elaborate memorial to Daniel O'Connell, "The Liberator," erected as a tribute to the great 19th-century orator's achievement in securing Catholic Emancipation in 1829. Today, **O'Connell Street** is the city's main shopping area, though it seems decidedly parochial to anyone accustomed to Fifth Avenue or Rodeo Drive. Turn left just before the General Post Office and take a look at Henry Street. This pedestrians-only shopping area leads to the colorful **Moore Street Market,** where street vendors recall their most famous ancestor, Molly Malone, by singing their wares— mainly flowers—in the traditional Dublin style.

❷ The **General Post Office,** known as the GPO, occupies a special place in Irish history. It was from the portico of its handsome classical facade that Padraig Pearse read the Proclamation of the Republic on Easter Monday, 1916. You can still see the scars of bullets on its pillars from the fighting that ensued. The GPO remains the focal point for political rallies and demonstrations even today and is used as a viewing stand for VIPs during the annual St. Patrick's Day Parade.

❸ **The Gresham Hotel,** opposite the GPO, has played a part in Dublin's history since 1817; although, along with the whole O'Connell Street area, it is less fashionable now than in the last century. Just below the Gresham is the Irish Tourist Board information office; drop in for a free street map, shopping guides, and information on all aspects of Dublin tourism. Opposite is the main office of Bus Eireann, which can supply bus timetables and information on excursions.

❹ At the top of O'Connell Street is the **Rotunda,** the first maternity hospital in Europe, opened in 1755. Not much remains of the once-elegant Rotunda Assembly Rooms, a famous haunt of fashionable Dubliners until the middle of the last century. The **Gate Theater,** housed in an extension of the Rotunda Assembly Rooms, however, continues to attract crowds to its fine repertoire of classic Irish and European drama. The theater was founded by the late Micheál MacLiammoir in 1928.

❺ Beyond the Rotunda, you will have a fine vista of **Parnell Square,** one of Dublin's earliest Georgian squares. You will notice immediately that the first-floor windows of these elegant brick-face buildings are much larger than the others and that it is easy to look in from street level. This is more than simply the result of the architect's desire to achieve perfect proportions on the facades: These rooms were designed as reception rooms, and fashionable hostesses liked passersby o be able to peer in and admire the distinguished guests at their luxurious, candle-lit receptions.

Abbey Theater, **8**
Archbishop Marsh's Library, **22**
Brown Thomas, **19**
Christ Church Cathedral, **24**
City Hall, **26**
Civic Museum, **21**
Custom House, **33**
Dublin Castle, **25**
Four Courts, **32**
Genealogical Office, **17**
General Post Office, **2**
Gresham Hotel, **3**
Guinness Brewery, **28**
Halfpenny Bridge, **34**
Hugh Lane Municipal Gallery of Modern Art, **6**
Irish Whiskey Corner, **31**
Kilkenny Design Workshops, **11**
Leinster House, **14**
Merrion Square, **12**
National Gallery, **13**
National Library, **16**
National Museum, **15**
O'Connell Bridge, **1**
Parliament House, **9**
Parnell Square, **5**
Phoenix Park, **29**
Powerscourt Town House, **20**
Rotunda, **4**
Royal Hospital Kilmainham, **35**
Royal Irish Academy, **18**
St. Mary's Pro Cathedral, **7**
St. Michan's, **30**
St. Patrick's Cathedral, **23**
Temple Bar, **27**
Trinity College, **10**

Dublin

Charlemont House, whose impressive Palladian facade dominates the top of Parnell Square, now houses the **Hugh Lane Municipal Gallery of Modern Art.** Sir Hugh Lane, a nephew of Lady Gregory, who was Yeats's curious, high-minded aristocratic patron, was a keen collector of Impressionist paintings. The gallery also contains some interesting works by Irish artists, including Yeats's brother Jack. *Parnell Sq. Admission: free. Open Tues.–Sat. 9:30–6, Sun. 11–5.*

The area surrounding Parnell Square is rich in literary associations and features in the work of Sean O'Casey, James Joyce, and Brendan Behan. Only devout literary pilgrims will care for the detour to Mountjoy Square, since this badly run-down area is in the middle of a rebuilding program.

Return back down to O'Connell Street where a sign on the left will lead you to **St. Mary's Pro Cathedral,** the main Catholic church of Dublin. Try to catch the famous Palestrina Choir on Sunday at 11 AM. John McCormack is one of many famous voices to have sung with this exquisite ensemble. The **Abbey Theatre,** a new brick building dating from 1966, is a boxy disappointment from the outside but has some noteworthy portraits and mementoes in the foyer. Seats are usually available at about IR£7.50, and with luck you may just have a wonderful evening. The luck element, unfortunately, must be stressed, since the Abbey has had both financial and artistic problems lately.

Time Out On Westmoreland Street is **Bewley's Coffee House** (there's another one nearby on Grafton Street), an institution that has been supplying Dubliners with coffee and buns since 1842. The aroma of coffee is irresistible, and the dark interior, with marble-topped tables, original wood fittings, and stained-glass windows, evokes a more leisurely Dublin of the past. *12 Westmoreland St. and 78 Grafton St. Open Mon.–Sat. 9–5:30.*

Trinity and Stephen's Green It is only a short walk across O'Connell Bridge to **Parliament House.** Today, this stately early 18th-century building is no more than a branch of the Bank of Ireland; originally, however, it housed the Irish Parliament. The original House of Lords, with its fine coffered ceiling and 1,233-piece Waterford glass chandelier, is open to the public during banking hours (weekdays 10–12:30 and 1:30–3). It's worth taking a look at the main banking hall, too, whose judicial character—it was previously the Court of Requests—has been sensitively maintained.

Across the road is the facade of **Trinity College,** whose memorably atmospheric campus is a must for every visitor. Trinity College, Dublin (familiarly known as TCD) was founded by Elizabeth I in 1591 and offered a free education to Catholics—provided that they accepted the Protestant faith. As a legacy of this condition, right up until 1966, Catholics who wished to study at Trinity had to obtain a dispensation from their bishop or face excommunication. Today more than 70% of Trinity's students are Catholics, a clear indication of how far away those days seem to today's generation.

The facade, built between 1755 and 1759, consists of a magnificent portico with Corinthian columns. The design is repeated on the interior, so the view from outside the gates and from the quadrangle inside is the same. On the sweeping lawn in front of the facade are statues of two of the university's illustrious alumni—statesman Edward Burke and poet Oliver Goldsmith. Other famous students include the philosopher George Berkeley, who gave his name to the San Francisco area campus of the University of California; Jonathan Swift; Thomas Moore; Oscar Wilde; John Millington Synge; Henry Grattan; Wolfe Tone; Robert Emmet; Bram Stoker; Edward Carson; Douglas Hyde; and Samuel Beckett.

The 18th-century building on the left, just inside the entrance, is the chapel. There's an identical building opposite, the Examination Hall. The oldest buildings are the library in the far right-hand corner and a row of red-brick buildings known as the Rubrics, which contain student apartments; both date from 1712.

Ireland's largest collection of books and manuscripts is housed in **Trinity College Library.** There are more than 2½ million volumes gathering dust here; about half a mile of new shelving has to be added every year to keep pace with acquisitions. The library is entered through the library shop. Its principal treasure is the **Book of Kells,** a beautifully illuminated manuscript of the Gospels dating from the 8th century. Because of the beauty and the fame of the Book of Kells, at peak hours you may have to wait in line to enter the library; it's less busy early in the day. Apart from the many treasures it contains, the aptly named Long Room is impressive in itself, stretching as it does for 65 meters (209 feet). Originally it had a flat plaster ceiling, but the perennial need for more shelving resulted in a decision to raise the level of the roof and add the barrel-vaulted ceiling and the gallery bookcases. *Admission: IR£1.50. Open weekdays 9:30–4:45, Sat. 9:30–12:45.*

A breath of fresh air will be welcome after the library, so, when you're done admiring the award-winning modern architecture of the New Library and the Arts Building, pass through the gate to the sports grounds—rugby fields on your left, cricket on your right. Leave Trinity by the Lincoln Place Gate—a handy "back door."

Shoppers will find a detour along Nassau Street in order here. As well as being well-endowed with bookstores, it contains the
⑪ Kilkenny Design Workshops, which, besides selling the best in contemporary Irish design for the home, also holds regular exhibits of exciting new work by Irish craftsmen. *Open Mon.–Sat. 9–5.*

Time Out The **Kilkenny Kitchen,** a self-service restaurant on the first floor of the Kilkenny Design Workshops, overlooking the playing fields of Trinity, is an excellent spot for a quick, inexpensive lunch in modern, design-conscious surroundings. The emphasis is on natural fresh foods and home baking. *Nassau St. Open Mon.–Sat. 9–5.*

---

⑫ Nassau Street will lead you into **Merrion Square,** past a distinctive corner house that was the home of Oscar Wilde's parents. Merrion Square is one of the most pleasant in Dublin. Its flower gardens are well worth a visit in the summer months. Note the brightly colored front doors and the intricate fan lights above them—a distinctive feature of Dublin's domestic architecture.

⑬ The **National Gallery** is the first of a series of important buildings on the west side of the square. It is one of Europe's most agreeable and compact galleries, with more than 2,000 works

on view, including a major collection of Irish landscape paint-
ing, 17th-century French works, paintings from the Italian and
Spanish schools, and a collection of Dutch masters. *Merrion Sq.
Admission: free. Open weekdays 10–5, Sat. 10–1, Sun. 2–5.*

⓮ Next door is **Leinster House,** seat of the Irish parliament. This
imposing, 18th-century building has two facades: Its Merrion
Square facade is designed in the style of a country house, while
the other facade, in Kildare Street, is in the style of a town
house. Visitors may be shown the house when the Dail (pronounced "Doyle"), the Irish parliament, is not in session.

Time Out A half-block detour to your left, between Merrion Square and
Stephen's Green, will bring you to the door of **Doheny &
Nesbitt's,** an old Victorian-style bar whose traditional "snugs"—
individual, wood-paneled booths—are popular any time. Usually noisy and smoky, but always friendly, it is one of the few
authentic pubs left in the city.

Stephen's Green, as it is always called by Dubliners, suffered
more from the planning blight of the philistine '60s than did its
neighbor, Merrion Square. An exception is the magnificent
Shelbourne Hotel, which dominates the north side of the green.
It is still as fashionable—and as expensive—as ever.

Time Out Budget-conscious visitors should put on their finery and try afternoon tea in the elegant splendor of the Shelbourne's **Lord
Mayor's Room.** You can experience its old-fashioned luxury for
around IR£5 (including sandwiches and cakes) per head.

Around the corner on Kildare Street, the town-house fa-
⓯ cadeof Leinster House is flanked by the **National Museum** and
⓰ the **National Library,** each featuring a massive colonnaded rotunda entrance built in 1890. The museum (Admission: free.
Open Tues.–Sat. 10–5, Sun. 2–5) houses a remarkable collection of Irish treasures from 6000 BC to the present day, including
the Tara Brooch, the Ardagh Chalice, and the Cross of Cong. Every major figure in modern Irish literature, from James Joyce
onward, studied in the National Library at some point. In addition to a comprehensive collection of Irish authors, it contains
extensive newspaper archives. *Kildare St. Open Mon.–Thurs.
10–10, Fri. 10–5, Sat. 10–1.*

⓱ The **Genealogical Office**—the starting point for ancestor-
tracing—also incorporates the **Heraldic Museum,** which features displays of flags, coins, stamps, silver, and family crests
that highlight the uses and development of heraldry in Ireland.
*2 Kildare St. Genealogical Office. Open weekdays 10–5. Heral-
dic Museum. Admission: free. Open weekdays 10–12:30 and
2:30–4. Guided tours Mar.–Oct., cost IR£1.*

⓲ The **Royal Irish Academy,** on Dawson Street, is the country's
leading learned society and has many important manuscripts in
its unmodernized 18th-century library (open Mon.–Fri. 9:30–
5:15). Just below the academy is **Mansion House,** the official
residence of the Lord Mayor of Dublin. Its Round Room was the
location of the first assembly of the Dail Eireann—the Irish
parliament—in January 1919. It is now used mainly for exhibitions.

Grafton Street, which runs between Stephen's Green and
⓳ Trinity College, is a magnet for shoppers. Check out **Brown**

Thomas, Ireland's most elegant and old-fashioned department store; it has an extremely good selection of sporting goods and Waterford crystal—an odd combination. Many of the more stylish boutiques are just off the main pedestrians-only areas, so be sure to poke around likely corners. Don't miss the **Powerscourt**

㉒ **Town House,** an imaginative shopping arcade installed in and around the covered courtyard of an impressive 18th-century

㉑ building. Nearby is the **Civic Museum** containing drawings, models, maps of Dublin, and other civic memorabilia. *58 S. William St. Admission: free. Open Tues.–Sat. 10–6, Sun. 11–4.*

A short walk from Stephen's Green will bring you to one of the

㉒ smaller and more unusual gems of old Dublin, **Archbishop Marsh's Library.** It was built in 1701, and access is through a tiny but charming cottage garden. Its interior has been unchanged for more than 300 years and still contains "cages" into which scholars who wanted to peruse rare books were locked. (The cages were to discourage students who, often impecunious, may have been tempted to make the books their own.) *St. Patrick's Close. Open Wed.–Fri. 10:30–12:30 and 2–4, Mon. 2–4, Sat. 10:30–12:30.*

㉓ Opposite, on Patrick Street, is **St. Patrick's Cathedral.** Legend has it that St. Patrick baptized many converts at a well on the site of the cathedral in the 5th century. The building dates from 1190 and is mainly early English in style. At 93 meters (300 feet), it is the longest church in the country. Its history has not always been happy. In the 17th century, Oliver Cromwell, dour ruler of England and no friend of the Irish, had his troops stable their horses in the cathedral. It wasn't until the 19th century that restoration work to repair the damage was put in hand. St. Patrick's is the national cathedral of the Protestant Church of Ireland and has had many illustrious deans. The most famous was Jonathan Swift, author of *Gulliver's Travels,* who held office from 1713 to 1745. Swift's tomb is in the south aisle, and Dean Swift's corner at the top of the north transept contains his pulpit, his writing table and chair, his portrait, and his death mask. Memorials to many other celebrated figures from Ireland's past line the walls of St. Patrick's.

St. Patrick's originally stood outside the walls of Dublin. Its

㉔ close neighbor, **Christ Church Cathedral** (Christ Church Rd.), on the other hand, stood just within the walls and belonged to the See of Dublin. It is for this reason that the city has two cathedrals so close to one another. Christ Church was founded by Strongbow, a Norman baron and conqueror of Dublin for the English crown, in 1172, and it took 50 years to build. Strongbow himself is buried in the cathedral beneath an impressive effigy. The vast and sturdy **crypt** is Dublin's oldest surviving structure, and should not be missed.

㉕ Signs in the Christ Church area will lead you to **Dublin Castle.** Guided tours of the lavishly furnished state apartments are offered every half hour and provide one of the most enjoyable sightseeing experiences in town. Only fragments of the original 13th-century building survive; the elegant castle you see today is essentially an 18th-century building. The state apartments were formerly the residence of the English viceroys— the monarch's representative in Ireland—and are now used by the president of Ireland to entertain visiting heads of state. The state apartments are closed when in official use, so phone first to check. *Off Lord Edward St., tel. 01/777129. Admission: IR£2.50. Open weekdays 10–12:15 and 2–5, weekends 2–5.*

㉖ Step into the **City Hall** on Dame Street to admire the combination of grand classical ornament and understated Georgian simplicity in its circular main hall. It also contains a good example of the kind of gently curving Georgian staircase that is a typical feature of most large town houses in Dublin.

Time Out A mosaic stag's head in the pavement of Dame Street marks the entrance to a narrow alley and a beautiful pub, **The Stag's Head,** (1 Dame Court), dating from the early 19th century. Amid tall mirrors, stained-glass skylights, and mounted stags' heads, of course, you can enjoy a typical selection of lunchtime pub grub —smoked salmon sandwiches, hot meat dishes—and a pint of anything.

㉗ Between Dame Street and the river Liffey is a new semi-pedestrianized area known as **Temple Bar,** which should interest anyone wanting to discover "young Dublin." The area is chock-full of small, imaginative shops, innovative art galleries, and inexpensive restaurants.

㉘ The **Guinness Brewery,** founded by Arthur Guinness in 1759, dominates the area to the west of Christ Church, covering 60 acres. Guinness is proud of its brewery and invites visitors to attend a 30-minute film shown in a converted hops store next door to the brewery itself. After the film, you can sample the famous black beverage. *Guinness Museum and Visitors' Center, James's St. Admission: free. Open weekdays 10–3.*

Phoenix Park Across the Liffey is **Phoenix Park,** 7,122 square kilometers
and the Liffey (1,760 acres) of green open space. Though the park is open to
㉙ all, it has only two residents: the president of Ireland and the American ambassador. The park is dominated by a 64 meter-high (205-foot) obelisk, a tribute to the first duke of Wellington. Sunday is the best time to visit: A large open-air market is held from noon on the racecourse, while elsewhere games of cricket, soccer, polo, baseball, hurling—a combination of lacrosse, baseball, and field hockey—or Irish football will be in progress.

Returning to the city's central area along the north bank of the Liffey, you pass through a fairly run-down section that's scheduled for major redevelopment. A diversion up Church Street to
㉚ **St. Michan's** will be relished by those with a macabre turn of mind. Open coffins in the vaults beneath the church reveal mummified bodies, some more than 900 years old. The sexton, who can be found at the church gate on weekdays, will guide you around the church and crypt.

㉛ **Irish Whiskey Corner** is just behind St. Michan's. A 90-year-old warehouse has been converted into a museum to introduce visitors to the pleasures of Irish whiskey. There's an audiovisual show and free tasting. Reservations are necessary. *Bow St., tel. 01/725566. Admission: IR£2.*

The Liffey has two of Dublin's most famous landmarks, both of them the work of 18th-century architect James Gandon and
㉜ both among the city's finest buildings. The first is the **Four Courts,** surmounted by a massive copper-covered dome, giving it a distinctive profile. It is the seat of the High Court of Justice of Ireland. The building was completed between 1786 and 1802,

then gutted in the Civil War of the '20s; it has since been painstakingly restored. You will recognize the same architect's hand
③③ in the **Custom House,** farther down the Liffey. Its graceful
dome rises above a central portico, itself linked by arcades to
the pavilions at either end. Behind this useful and elegant landmark is an altogether more workaday structure, the central
bus station, known as Busaras.

Midway between Gandon's two masterpieces is the Metal
③④ Bridge, otherwise known as the **Halfpenny Bridge,** so-called
because, until early in this century, a toll of a half-penny was
charged to cross it. The poet W. B. Yeats was one among many
Dubliners who found this too high a price to pay—more a matter of principle than of finance—and so made the detour via
O'Connell Bridge. No such high-minded concern need prevent
you today from marching out to the middle of the bridge to admire the view up and down the Liffey as it wends its way
through the city.

③⑤ The **Royal Hospital Kilmainham** is a short ride by taxi or bus
from the center; it's well worth the trip. The hospital is considered the most important 17th-century building in Ireland and
has recently been renovated. It was completed in 1684 as a
hospice—the original meaning of the term "hospital"—for veteran soldiers. Note especially the chapel with its magnificent
Baroque ceiling. Although open year-round, it is also used as a
cultural center for conferences, concerts, and state functions,
and certain parts are sometimes closed to the general public.
*District of Kilmainham, tel. 01/718666. Guided tours: Sun.
noon–5 and holidays 2–5; cost £2. Exhibitions: open Tues.–
Sat. 2–5.*

Devotees of James Joyce may wish to take the DART train
south to **Sandycove,** about 8 kilometers (5 miles) out of the center. It was here, in a Martello tower (a circular fortification
built by the British as a defense against possible invasion by
Napoleon at the beginning of the 19th century), that the maverick Irish genius lived for some months in 1904. It now houses
the **Joyce Museum.** *Sandycove Coast. Admission: IR£1.10.
Open Apr.–Oct., Mon.–Sat. 10–1 and 2–5, Sun. 2:30–6.*

Off the Beaten Track

It is all too easy for the visitor to forget how close Dublin is to
the sea: Take advantage of fine weather and visit the fishing
village of **Howth**—it's easily reached on the DART train—and
watch the fishermen mending their nets on the pier. Or take
the DART in the opposite direction to **Sandycove,** where intrepid all-weather swimmers brave the waves at the men-only
Forty Foot bathing beach.

Everyone has heard of Waterford glass, but what about Dublin
crystal? The **Dublin Crystal Glass Co.** is open year-round, and
visitors are welcome to watch skilled crystal cutters at work
and to purchase crystal—seconds are available, too—at a discount. Phone for an appointment. *Carysfort Ave., Blackrock,
tel. 01/887932.*

The **Irish Jewish Museum** was opened in 1985 by Chaim Herzog,
the president of Israel and an ex-Dubliner himself, and displays
memorabilia of the Irish-Jewish community covering approximately 120 years of history. *3–4 Walworth Rd., tel. 01/832703.*

Shopping

Although the rest of the country is well-supplied with craft shops, Dublin is the place to seek out more specialized items—antiques, traditional sportswear, haute couture, designer ceramics, books and prints, silverware and jewelry, and designer handknits.

Shopping Districts The most sophisticated shopping area is around **Grafton Street:** Its delis stock Irish whiskey marmalade, Irish lakeside wholegrain mustard, whole handmade cheeses, and sides of smoked salmon or trout. The new **St. Stephen's Green Center** contains 70 stores, large and small, in a vast Moorish-style glass-roof building on the Grafton Street corner. **Molesworth** and **Dawson Streets** are the places to browse for antiques; **Nassau** and **Dawson Streets,** for books; the smaller cross side streets for jewelry, art galleries, and old prints.

Department Stores The shops north of the river tend to be less expensive and less design conscious; chain stores and lackluster department stores make up the bulk of them. The **ILAC Shopping Center,** on Henry Street, is worth a look, however. **Switzers** and **Brown Thomas** are Grafton Street's main department stores; the latter is an old-fashioned establishment noted for traditional sporting clothes and accessories and its food department. **Arnotts,** on Henry Street, is Dublin's largest department store and has a good range of cut crystal. Visit **Kilkenny Design Workshops** on Nassau Street for the best selection of Irish designs for the home. Nearby, the **House of Ireland** has an abundance of traditional gifts and souvenirs.

Tweeds and Woolens Ready-made tweeds for men can be found at **Kevin and Howlin,** on Nassau Street, and at **Cleo Ltd.,** on Kildare Street. **Westbury Designs,** at the Westbury Center, has an interesting range of high-fashion tweed and linen clothing for women. The **Woolen Mills,** at Halfpenny Bridge, has a good selection of handknits and other woolen sweaters at competitive prices.

Dining

The restaurant scene in Dublin has improved beyond recognition in recent years. Though no one is ever likely to confuse the place with, say, Paris, the days of chewy boiled meats and soggy, tasteless vegetables are long gone. Food still tends to be substantial rather than subtle, but more and more restaurants are at last taking advantage of the magnificent livestock and fish that Ireland has in such abundance. For details and price category definitions, *see* Dining in Staying in Ireland.

Expensive **Ernie's.** This luxurious place is built around a small floodlit courtyard shaded by an imposing mulberry tree. The rustic interior's granite walls and wood beams are adorned by paintings of Kerry, where, for generations, owner-chef Ernie Evans's family ran the famous Glenbeigh Hotel. Ernie serves generous portions of the very best seafood—try scallops Mornay or prawns in garlic butter—and steaks. *Mulberry Gardens, Donnybrook, tel. 01/693300. Reservations advised. AE, DC, MC, V. Dinner only. Closed Sun., Mon.*

Gallery 22. In a small basement room, with an open fire, modish pink-and-gray decor, and delicate bentwood chairs, Gallery 22 is *the* place for the style conscious. It is noted for rack of lamb with fresh rosemary and port-wine sauce, or try one of the imaginative seasonal combinations of meat and fruit: lamb with strawberries, for example, or chicken with lemon sauce. *22 St. Stephen's Green, tel. 01/616669. Reservations advised, especially at lunch. AE, DC, MC, V. Closed Sun., Mon. dinner.*

★ **King Sitric.** This quayside restaurant in the fishing village-cum-suburb of Howth is a 20-minute ride north of Dublin by DART or cab. It's worth the journey to taste the succulent selection of locally caught seafood; try wild Irish salmon steaks with Hollandaise sauce, or *goujons* of turbot with saffron. You eat in the quietly elegant Georgian dining room of the former harbormaster's house under the supervision of owner-chef Aidan MacManus. *East Pier, Howth, tel. 01/325235. Reservations advised. AE, DC, MC, V. Closed Sun., Sat. lunch, holidays, Dec. 24–Jan. 1, and the week preceding Easter.*

★ **Le Coq Hardi.** Award-winning owner-chef John Howard is noted for his wine cellar and specialties like Coq Hardi smokies—smoked haddock baked in tomato, cream, and cheese—and (in season) roast loin of venison with fresh cranberries and port wine. The seriousness of the cooking is complemented by the polished wood and brass and the gleaming mirrors of the sumptuous interior. *35 Pembroke Rd., Ballsbridge, tel. 01/689070. Reservations essential. AE, DC, MC, V. Closed Sun., Sat. lunch, and holidays.*

Patrick Guilbaud. This is an authentic, rather formal, French restaurant with a consistently good reputation, decked out in a refreshing combination of pink, white, and green with hanging plants. The emphasis is firmly on traditional bourgeois cuisine; the Gallic connection is reinforced by the all-French staff. *46 James Pl., tel. 01/764192. Reservations advised. AE, DC, MC, V. Closed Sun. and holidays.*

Whites on the Green. A sophisticated spot with soothing cream-and-white decor, this place will appeal to those who appreciate delicate and subtle nouvelle cuisine. Typical dishes include medallions of veal gratiné with a parsley mousse and roast mallard with honey and juniper berries. *119 St. Stephen's Green, tel. 01/751975. Reservations essential. AE, DC, MC, V. Closed Sun., Sat. lunch.*

Moderate ★ **Beefeaters.** The clientele here has long been loyal to this restaurant's type of hearty meat dishes. Specialties are fillets, sirloins, and T-bones of prime Irish beef, prepared in 15 different ways. Try Gaelic steak, with a sauce of Irish whiskey, onions, mushrooms, and cream, or Surf 'n' Turf, an eight-ounce fillet accompanied by Dublin Bay prawns. The restaurant is located in the labyrinthine basement of two Georgian town houses and is furnished with wood-top tables and burgundy drapes and carpets. *99–100 Lower Baggot St., tel. 01/760784. Reservations advised. AE, DC, MC, V. Closed Sun., Sat. lunch.*

Dobbin's Wine Bistro. Though Dobbin's aims at a French identity, with its red-and-white gingham tablecloths and sawdust-strewn slate floor, the cooking here is international and imaginative, with an emphasis on fresh Irish produce. Specialties are phyllo pastry with pepper and seafood filling, paupiettes of salmon and sole with spinach and dill sauce, and Szechuan boned crispy duckling with fresh peaches. *Stephen's La., tel. 01/764670. Reservations advised. AE, DC, MC, V. Closed Sun.*

Rudyard's. The three small floors that make up Rudyard's have an austere air: much dark unpolished wood, simple wooden tables with bentwood chairs, paper napkins, and a hint of art nouveau elegance in the mirrors and framed posters. The food, by contrast, is light; typical dishes include smoked-salmon eclairs, and canneloni with spinach and cream cheese stuffing. There's a quiet wine bar on the top floor. *15–16 Crown Alley, tel. 01/ 710846. Reservations for parties over 6 only. AE, DC, MC, V. Closed Sun.*

Inexpensive **Captain America.** The collection of outrageous Americana strewn throughout is dominated by a replica of the Statue of Liberty that visibly shudders at the loud rock music. A wide selection of specialty hamburgers graces the menu, plus beef tacos, burritos, enchiladas, and chili. *Grafton Court, Grafton St., tel. 01/715266. Reservations not accepted. AE, DC, MC, V.*

★ **Casper & Giumbini's Food Emporium.** This is a combination pub-restaurant near Trinity College where live piano music keeps the joint jumping, especially at weekend brunch. Charcoal-grilled steak, seafood, burgers, and pizza are served either at the bar or at your own table, with a choice of more than a dozen imported beers. *Wicklow St., tel. 01/794347. Reservations advised, especially weekends. AE, DC, MC, V.*

Flanagan's. Flanagan's, located half a block north of the General Post Office, is two restaurants in one: a reliable steak house on the ground floor, divided by velour-covered banquettes, and an excellent pizzeria in the basement, much patronized by Dublin's Italian community. *61 Upper O'Connell St., tel. 01/731388. Reservations advised on weekends. MC, V. Closed Sun.*

Pasta Pasta. This small, bright, and unpretentiously pretty Italian eatery serves combinations of pasta shapes and sauces plus a few Italian specials—medallions of pork *à la funghi, escalope milanesa*—against a background of muted jazz-rock. It's an excellent value. *27 Exchequer St., tel. 01/792565. Reservations advised for groups over 6 and on weekends. MC, V. Closed Sun.*

Pub Food All the pubs listed here serve food at lunchtime; some also have food in the early evening. They form an important part of the dining scene in Dublin and make a pleasant and informal alternative to a restaurant meal. In general, a one-course meal should not cost much more than IR£4–IR£5, but a full meal will put you in the lower range of the Moderate category. In general, credit cards are not accepted.

Barry Fitzgerald's. Salads and a freshly cooked house special are available in the upstairs bar at lunch on weekdays. Pretheater dinners are served in the early evening. *90 Marlboro St.*

Davy Byrne's. James Joyce immortalized Davy Byrne's in his sprawling novel *Ulysses.* Nowadays it's more akin to a cocktail bar than a Dublin pub, but it's good for fresh and smoked salmon, salads, and a hot daily special. Food is available at lunchtime and in the early evening. *21 Duke St.*

Kitty O'Shea's. Kitty O'Shea's cleverly, if a little artificially, re-creates the atmosphere of old Dublin. *23–25 Grand Canal St., tel. 01/609965. Reservations accepted for lunch and Sun. brunch.*

Lord Edward Bar. With its Old World ambience, the Lord Edward Bar serves a wide range of salads and a hot dish of the day at lunchtime only. *23 Christ Church Pl.*

Old Stand. Located conveniently close to Grafton Street, the Old Stand offers grilled food, including steaks. *37 Exchequer St.*

Lodging

Although no major hotels have opened in Dublin in the past few years, considerable investment in redevelopment, updating of facilities, and refurbishing of some of the older establishments is taking place. As in most major cities, there is a shortage of mid-range accommodations. For value-for-money, try one of the registered guest houses; in most respects they are indistinguishable from small hotels. Most economical of all is the bed-and-breakfast. Both guest houses and B&Bs tend to be located in suburban areas—generally a 10-minute bus ride from the center of the city. This is not in itself a great drawback, and savings can be significant.

The Irish Tourist Board (14 Upper O'Connell St.) publishes a comprehensive booklet *Guest Accommodation* (IR£2), which covers all approved possibilities in Dublin and the rest of the country, from the grandest hotel to the humblest B&B. The office can usually help if you find yourself without reservations.

There is a VAT of 10% on hotel charges, which should be included in the quoted price. A service charge of 12–15% is also included and listed separately in the bills of top-grade hotels; elsewhere, check to see if the service is included. If it's not, a tip of between 10% and 15% is customary—if you think the service is worth it. For details and price-category definitions, *see* Lodging in Staying in Ireland.

Very Expensive **Berkeley Court.** The most quietly elegant of Dublin's large modern hotels, Berkeley Court is located in Ballsbridge—a leafy suburb about a 10-minute cab ride from the center of town. Its new conservatory gives freshness and spaciousness to the atmosphere of the public rooms; among the other new features are five luxury suites, each with its own Jacuzzi. *Lansdowne Rd., Ballsbridge, Dublin 4, tel. 01/601711. 220 rooms with bath. Facilities: parking. AE, DC, MC, V.*

★ **Shelbourne.** The Shelbourne is one of Europe's grand old hotels whose guestbook contains names ranging from the Dalai Lama and Princess Grace to Laurel and Hardy, Richard Burton, and Peter O'Toole. The blazing open fire in its bustling marble lobby, flanked by two huge rose brocade sofas, is proof that the Shelbourne has not lost the sense of grandeur of its past. Between 1986 and 1988, IR£7 million was lavished on major refurbishment, which included restoring many original Georgian features and emphasizing them with luxurious drapes and a prominently displayed collection of fine antiques and heirlooms. A supplement is charged for rooms overlooking the leafy but busy green; the back bedrooms without views are far quieter, however. *27 Stephen's Green, tel. 01/766471. 170 rooms with bath. Facilities: bar, restaurant, coffee shop, sporting facilities available by arrangement. AE, DC, MC, V.*

Westbury. The Westbury overlooks the shopper's mecca of the Grafton Street area. A relative newcomer (1984), it is still regarded with suspicion by some for its ostentatious display of pastel-and-gilt luxury; others praise its restful atmosphere and central location. *Grafton St., tel. 01/791122. 150 rooms with bath. Facilities: gourmet restaurants, seafood bar, parking. AE, DC, MC, V.*

Expensive **Burlington.** Dublin's largest hotel is popular with American tour groups and Irish and European business travelers. It is about five minutes by car from the city's central area. At night its disco and Irish cabaret turn the Burlington into a lively spot for overseas visitors. Bedrooms are the usual modern plush in neutral tones. *Upper Leeson St., tel. 01/605222. 500 rooms with bath. Facilities: restaurants, bars, disco, and cabaret. AE, DC, MC, V.*

Buswell's. You'll either love or hate Buswell's. The hotel is located just across the street from the Dail, and its bars and conference rooms are dominated by the frantic bustle of politicians and lobbyists. Curiously, Buswell's also has a loyal provincial clientele, who seem blissfully blind to the clashing patterns of carpets, drapes, and wallpaper; the smallness of the bedrooms; and the grim food. The central location (between Stephen's Green and Grafton Street) and charming Georgian facade are a potent attraction for many independent American travelers, too. *Molesworth St., tel. 01/764013. 67 rooms with bath. AE, DC, MC, V.*

★ **Gresham.** With a prime central location opposite the historic General Post Office, this place has played a part in Dublin's history since 1817. The interior has a predominantly '30s character, with an emphasis on comfort rather than upscale chic. Bedrooms are reached via long windowless corridors, and the monumentally solid plumbing arrangements give character to the bland modern-repro style of the newly decorated rooms. The hotel feels much bigger than it actually is, and the lobby, decked out with "Gresham (royal) Blue" carpet and gold brocade armchairs, exudes a sense of history. *Higher O'Connell St., tel. 01/746881. 179 rooms with bath. AE, DC, MC, V.*

Jury's. This lively and fashionable spot has more atmosphere than most comparable modern hotels. It's a short cab ride from the center of town. Bedrooms are relatively spacious, standard modern plush, and each comes with a picture-window view of town. Head for the Dubliner Bar—all polished mahogany and brass fittings— between 5 and 7 PM to observe the stylish media set. *Ballsbridge, Dublin 4, tel. 01/605000. 300 rooms with bath. Facilities: indoor/outdoor pool, Jacuzzi, 2 bars, 3 restaurants, cabaret May–Oct. AE, DC, MC, V.*

Moderate **Ariel Guest House.** This red-brick Victorian town house lies only 50 paces from Lansdowne train station, a five-minute ride from the center of Dublin. The lobby, lounge, and restaurant are cozied-up with Victoriana and lace curtains, Irish style. The bedrooms, by contrast, are standard hotel-modern, most in a new extension at the back. *52 Lansdowne Rd., tel. 01/685512. 15 rooms with bath. Facilities: restaurant, lounge. AE, MC, V. Closed Dec. 21–Jan. 31.*

Ashling. This family-run hotel sits on the edge of the river Liffey, close to Heuston Station. Some may find that the Ashling's relentlessly bright modern decor verges on the garish. It has a faithful following, however, not least because of its proximity to Phoenix Park and its friendly staff. The center of town is a brisk 10–15 minute walk away, taking in many famed landmarks en route. *Parkgate St., Kingsbridge, tel. 01/772324. 56 rooms with bath. AE, DC, MC, V.*

Clarence. You'll find the Clarence either charmingly old-fashioned or just plain dowdy; it's all a matter of taste. Most of its Edwardian interior is dominated by oak-paneled walls and solid leather sofas and chairs. The restaurant and lobby have been prettified by fake art deco drapes and cane chairs. Bedrooms are small and functional: no frills here. Its central

Liffey-side location is relentlessly urban. Beware of early-morning traffic noise in the front bedrooms. It remains an excellent place to meet a cross section of Dubliners and mildly eccentric provincials. *6–7 Wellington Quay, tel. 01/776178. 67 rooms with bath. Facilities: restaurant. AE, DC, MC, V.*

Montrose. This well-designed modern hotel is located in Donnybrook—nowadays a staid suburb 10 minutes by car from central Dublin. It is next door to the Irish TV and radio studios (RTE), and across the road from University College's Belfield campus. Bedrooms are relatively spacious, if impersonal. *Stillorgan Rd., Donnybrook, tel. 01/693311. 190 rooms with bath. Facilities: health center. AE, DC, MC, V.*

Inexpensive **Abrae Court Guest House.** This is a typical, large early-Victorian house in the highly respectable suburb of Rathgar. It's a 10-minute bus ride to the center of Dublin. There are six bedrooms in the main house; the rest are in a carefully designed period-style annex with ornate stucco ceilings. All are furnished with Irish carpets and handcrafted Irish furniture. The restaurant is open for evening meals but cannot serve alcohol. *9 Zion Rd., Rathgar, tel. 01/979944. 20 rooms with bath. Facilities: restaurant. AE, DC, MC, V.*

Egan's Guest House. A large Edwardian house, Egan's is a friendly, family-run establishment just a 10-minute drive from the city's central area, six minutes from the car ferry, and 15 minutes from the airport. Bedrooms are small but well-equipped, The guest house is located in a leafy, if unexciting, suburb close to the Botanic Gardens, with good bus service to central Dublin. *7–10 Iona Park, Glasnevin, tel. 01/303611. 25 rooms with bath. Closed Dec. 20–Jan. 1.*

★ **Maples House.** According to the ITB's complex grading system, Maples House is a guest house; to the rest of the world, however, it is definitely a small hotel. The lobby of this Edwardian house is decked out with oil paintings, Waterford crystal chandeliers, and a discreetly modern carpet and is dominated by a vast mirror-topped Victorian rococo sideboard that sets the tone for the ornate decor of the public rooms. The bedrooms are small but adequate, lacking the rococo splendor of the rest of the building. *Iona Rd., Glasnevin, tel. 01/303049. 21 rooms with bath. Facilities: grill restaurant and bar. AE, DC, MC, V. Closed Dec. 25, 26.*

Mount Herbert Guest House. Located close to the swank luxury hotels in the tree-lined inner suburb of Ballsbridge, a 10-minute bus ride from Dublin's center of town, the Mount Herbert is popular with budget-minded American visitors in the high season. Bedrooms are small, but all have 10-channel TV and hair dryers. The restaurant has a wine license; there is no bar on the premises, but there are plenty to choose from nearby. *7 Herbert Rd., Ballsbridge, tel. 01/684321. 88 rooms, 77 with bath. Facilities: restaurant. AE, DC, MC, V.*

The Arts

The fortnightly magazine *In Dublin* contains comprehensive details of upcoming events, including ticket availability. In peak season, consult the free ITB leaflet *Events of the Week.*

Theaters Ireland has a rich theatrical tradition. The **Abbey Theatre,** Marlborough Street, is the home of Ireland's national theater company, its name forever associated with J. M. Synge, W. B. Yeats, and Sean O'Casey. The **Peacock Theatre** is the Abbey's

more experimental small stage. The **Gate Theatre,** Parnell
Square, is an intimate spot for modern drama and plays by
Irish writers. The **Gaiety Theatre,** South King Street, features
musical comedy, opera, drama, and revues. The **Olympia Theatre,** Dame Street, has seasons of comedy, vaudeville, and
ballet. The **Project Arts Centre,** East Essex Street, is an established fringe theater. The new **National Concert Hall,** in
Earlsfort Terrace, just off Stephen's Green, is the place to go
for classical concerts.

Entertainment and Nightlife

Dublin does not have sophisticated nightclubs in the international sense. Instead, there is a choice of discos (often billed as
nightclubs) and cabarets, catering mainly to visitors. There is
also a very animated bar-pub scene—some places with live music and folksinging. No visit to this genial city will be complete
without spending at least one evening exploring them.

Discos **New Annabels** (Mespil Rd., tel. 01/605222) is a popular late-
evening spot; so is **Raffles** (Morehampton Rd., tel. 01/680995).

Cabarets The following all offer Irish cabaret, designed to give visitors a
taste of Irish entertainment: **Braemor Rooms** (Churchtown,
tel. 01/988664); **Burlington Hotel** (Upper Leeson St., tel. 01/
605222, open Apr.–Oct.); **Jury's Hotel** (Ballsbridge, tel. 01/
605000, open Apr.–mid Oct.).

Pubs Check advertisements in evening papers for "sessions" of folk,
ballad, Irish traditional, or jazz music. The **Brazen Head** (20
Lower Bridge St., tel. 01/779549)—Dublin's oldest pub, dating
from 1688—and **O'Donoghue's** (15 Merrion Row, tel. 01/
607194) feature some form of musical entertainment on most
nights. Several of Dublin's centrally located pubs are noted for
their character and ambience; they're usually at their liveliest
from 5 to 7 PM and again from 10. The **Bailey** (2 Duke St.) is mentioned in *Ulysses* (under its original name, Burton's) and
retains something of its Edwardian character, while **William
Ryan's** (28 Parkgate St.) is a beautifully preserved Victorian
gem. **Henry Grattan** (47–48 Lower Baggot St.) is popular with
the business and sporting crowd; **O'Neill's Lounge Bar** (37
Pearse St.) is always busy with students and faculty from nearby Trinity College; and the **Palace Bar** (21 Fleet St.) is a
journalists' haunt. You can eavesdrop on Dublin's social elite
and their hangers-on at the expensive **Horseshoe Bar** in the
Shelbourne Hotel or bask in the theatrical atmosphere of
Neary's (Chatham St.)

For details on pubs serving food, *see* Dining.

Dublin to Cork

Ireland can be covered in three itineraries that, taken together, form a clockwise tour of the country, starting and ending in
Dublin. Distances in Ireland seem small—the total mileage of
the three itineraries combined is less than 960 kilometers (600
miles)—but roads are small and often twisty and hilly, and side
attractions are numerous, so you should aim for a daily mileage
of no more than 240 kilometers (150 miles). The consistently
dazzling scenery, intriguing ruins, and beguiling small villages
will lead to many impromptu stops and explorations along the

way. (We have tried to state full addresses for hotels, restaurants, and sights, though many of Ireland's villages and towns are so tiny they barely have street names, much less numbers. If in any doubt, just ask for directions.)

The first tour takes you southwest from Dublin to hilly Cork, the Republic's second largest city. On the way, you'll see the lush green fields of Ireland's famous stud farms and imposing Cashel, where Ireland built its reputation as the "Land of Saints and Scholars" while most of Europe was slipping into the Dark Ages.

Getting Around

By Train The terminus at Cork is Kent Station. There are direct services from Dublin and Tralee and a suburban line to Cobh. Tel. 021/504422 for information.

By Bus The main bus terminus in Cork is at Parnell Place, tel. 021/504422.

By Car All the main car rental firms have desks at Cork Airport. Be sure to get a map of Cork's complicated one-way system.

By Bicycle Bicycles can be rented from **D.M.D. Cycles,** 3 Washington St., Cork, tel. 021/271529.

Guided Tours

CIE operates a number of trips from Parnell Place in Cork; tel. 021/503399 for details.

Tourist Information

Tourist House, Grand Parade, Cork, tel. 021/273251.

Exploring Dublin to Cork

Leaving Dublin by N7 for **Naas**(pronounced "Nace"), you will pass through the area known as The Pale—that part of Ireland in which English law was formally acknowledged up to Elizabethan times. Beyond Naas, the road takes you to the center of the Irish racing world. **Goff's Kildare Paddocks** at Kill sells more than 50% of all Irish-bred horses. Naas has its own racecourse and lies just 4.8 kilometers (3 miles) from Punchestown, famous for its steeplechases. The **Curragh** begins just after Newbridge and is the biggest area of common land in Ireland, containing about 31 square kilometers (12 square miles). You will see the **Curragh Racecourse,** home of the Irish Derby, on your right-hand side; to the left is the training depot of the Irish army.

If you are interested in horses, **Kildare,** the traditional home of St. Brigid, is not to be missed. The main attraction is the **National Stud and Horse Museum** and its **Japanese Gardens.** *Tel. 045/261617. Open Easter–Oct., weekdays 10:30–5, Sat. 10:30–5:30, Sun. 2–5:30. Guided tours on request.*

Also in Kildare is a 6th-century round tower, next to the cathedral. It is open to the public.

At Portlaoise (pronounced "Portleash")—the location of Ireland's top-security prison—follow N8 to **Cashel.** Your first

Dublin to Cork

glimpse of the famous **Rock of Cashel** should be an unforgetta-
bly majestic sight: It rises imposingly to a height of 62 meters
(200 feet) above the plains and is crowned with a magnificent
group of gray stone ruins. The kings of Munster held it as their
seat for about seven centuries, and it is here that St. Patrick
reputedly plucked a shamrock from the ground, using it as a
symbol to explain the mystery of the Trinity, giving Ireland, in
the process, its universally recognized symbol. The central
building among the ruins is a 13th-century Gothic cathedral;
next to it is the Romanesque Cormac's chapel. There is also a
round tower and an impressive 12th-century cross. *Open Apr.–
Sept., daily 9–7:30; Oct.–Mar., Mon.–Sat., 10–5, Sun. 2–5.*

Cashel and the next town, **Cahir** (pronounced "Care"), are both
popular stopping places to break the Dublin–Cork journey. In
the center of Cahir, you will discover a formidable **medieval fortress** with a working portcullis, the gruesome barred gate that
was lowered to keep out attackers. An audiovisual display can
be seen in the castle complex. *Open mid-June–mid- Sept., daily 10–7:30; mid-Apr.–mid-June and mid- Sept.–Oct., Tues.–
Sat. 10–5, Sun. 2–5; Nov.–Mar., Tues.–Sat. 10–1 and 2–5.*

The road continues through Mitchelstown and Fermoy, both of
them busy market towns serving Cork's dairy farmers. A short
detour at Mitchelstown will allow you to visit President Reagan's ancestral home, **Ballyporeen,** a pretty little village with
wide streets built to accommodate the open-air cattle markets
held there until the '60s.

The road to **Cork City** passes through the beautiful wooded glen of Glanmire and along the banks of the river Lee. In the center of Cork, the Lee divides in two, giving the city a profusion of picturesque quays and bridges. The name Cork derives from the Irish *corcaigh*, meaning a marshy place. The city received its first charter in 1185 and grew rapidly in the 17th and 18th centuries with the expansion of its butter trade. It is the major metropolis of the south, and, with a population of about 135,000, the second-largest city in Ireland.

The main business and shopping center of Cork lies on the island created by the two diverging channels of the Lee, and most places of interest are within walking distance of the center. **Patrick Street** is the focal point of Cork. Here, you will find the city's most famous statue, that of **Father Theobald Mathew** (1790–1861), who led a nationwide temperance crusade, no small feat in a country as fond of a drink (or two) as this one. In the hilly area to the north of Patrick Street is the famous 120-foot **Shandon Steeple**, the bell tower of **St. Anne's Church**. It is shaped like a pepper pot and houses the bells immortalized in the song "The Bells of Shandon." Visitors can climb the tower, read the inscriptions on the bells, and, on request, have them rung over Cork.

Patrick Street is the main shopping area of Cork, and here you will find the city's two major department stores, **Roches** and **Cash's.** Cash's has a good selection of Waterford crystal. The liveliest place in town to shop is just off Patrick Street, to the west, near the city center parking lot, in the pedestrians-only **Paul Street** area. The **Stephen Pearce Shop** stocks the best in modern Irish design, including tableware, ceramics, knitwear, hand-woven tweeds, and high fashion. The **Donegal Shop** next-door specializes in made-to-order tweed suits and rain wear. At the top of Paul Street is the **Crawford Art Gallery**, which has an excellent collection of 18th- and 19th-century views of Cork and mounts adventurous exhibitions by modern artists. *Open weekdays 10–5, Sat. 9–1.*

One of Cork's most famous sons was William Penn (1644–1718), founder of the Pennsylvania colony. He is only one of thousands who sailed from Cork's port, the Cove of Cork on Great Island, 24 kilometers (15 miles) down the harbor. **Cobh,** as it is known nowadays, can be reached by train from Kent Station, and the trip provides excellent views of the magnificent harbor. Cobh is an attractive hilly town dominated by its 19th-century **cathedral.** It was the first and last European port of call for transatlantic liners, one of which was the ill-fated *Titanic*. Cobh has other associations with shipwrecks: It was from here that destroyers were sent out in May 1915 to search for survivors of the *Lusitania*, torpedoed by a German submarine with the loss of 1,198 lives. The tragedy is commemorated by a memorial on the quay. Many of the victims are buried at Cobh, and the **museum** has a display of contemporary photographs and reports of the disaster.

Fota Island, midway between Cork and Cobh, is a recent and very welcome addition to Cork's tourist attractions. The Royal Zoological Society has created a 238 square kilometer (70-acre) wildlife park here, and an enterprising Cork businessman has restored its **18th-century hunting lodge,** which is a splendid example of Irish Regency (early 19th-century) architecture, and has furnished its neoclassical interior in such a way as to give the impression that it is still lived in. *Open mid-Mar.–Sept., Tues.–Sat. 11–6, Sun. 1–6.*

Most visitors to Cork want to kiss the famous **Blarney Stone** in the hope of acquiring the "gift of gab." Blarney itself, 8 kilometers (5 miles) from Cork City, should not, however, be taken too seriously as an excursion. All that is left of **Blarney Castle** is its ruined central keep containing the celebrated stone. This is set in the battlements and to kiss it, you must lie on the walk within the walls, lean your head back and touch the stone with your lips. Nobody knows how the tradition originated, but Elizabeth I is credited with giving the word *blarney* to the language when, commenting on the unfulfilled promises of Cormac MacCarthy, Lord Blarney of the time, she remarked, "This is all Blarney; what he says, he never means." Adjoining the castle is a first-rate craft shop, and the outing provides a good opportunity to shop around for traditional Irish goods at competitive prices. *Open daily 10–5.*

Dining and Lodging

For details and price category definitions, *see* Dining and Lodging in Staying in Ireland.

Cahir
Lodging

Kilcoran Lodge Hotel. Set in its own grounds on the main road, Kilcoran Lodge Hotel is an ideal place to break the journey with coffee or a plainly cooked lunch. It occupies a bucolic country setting on the southern slope of the Galtees. *Just off N8, tel. 052/41288. 25 rooms, most with bath. AE, MC, V. Closed Dec. 26–30, Jan. 2–15. Expensive.*

Cashel
Lodging

Cashel Palace. This elegant Palladian mansion was once a bishop's palace. It has luxurious rooms and a beautiful garden. *Main St., tel. 062/61411. 20 rooms with bath. AE, MC, V. Closed Dec. 25–26. Very Expensive.*

Cork
Dining
★

Arbutus Lodge. One of Ireland's most highly acclaimed restaurants, the Arbutus Lodge is run by the Ryan family and is famous for its excellent wine list. There are 20 rooms as well. *Middle Glanmire Rd., Montenotte, tel. 021/501237. Reservations essential. AE, DC, MC, V. Closed Sun. and 1 week at Christmas. Expensive.*

★

Ballymaloe House. This country-house hotel is half an hour's drive from the city, but it's well worth the effort because the restaurant—run by Myrtle Allen, a world expert on Irish cookery—is outstanding. *Shanagarry, near Ballycotton, tel. 021/652531. Reservations advised. AE, DC, MC, V. Expensive.*

Glassialley's. Graced with marble-top tables and better-than-average food, this is a small, informal wine bar and restaurant near the Opera House. *17 Drawbridge St., tel. 021/272305. Reservations accepted. MC, V. Moderate.*

Oyster Tavern. This delightfully old-fashioned bar-restaurant has changed little in the past 30 years. *Market Lane, off Patrick St., tel. 021/272716. MC, V. Moderate.*

Bully's. This popular and busy wine bar does an excellent business serving pizza and pasta to visitors and locals. *Paul St. No credit cards. Inexpensive.*

The Gallery Café. If you can't make it out to Ballymaloe, you can sample their distinctive cooking style at the Crawford Gallery Café—the best inexpensive food in the city, served amid statues and prints from the municipal art collection. *Crawford Gallery, Emmet Pl. Open Mon., Tues., and Sat. 10:30–5:30; Wed.–Fri. 10:30–9:30. Inexpensive.*

Halpin's. This is a popular self-service restaurant at lunchtime; at night, the atmosphere is more intimate. It serves generous salads, curries, and pizzas. *Cook St., MC, V. Inexpensive.*

Lodging **Arbutus Lodge.** This exceptionally comfortable hotel has an
★ outstanding restaurant and panoramic views of the city and the river. *Montenotte. Middle Glanmire Rd., tel. 021/501237. 20 rooms with bath. AE, DC, MC, V. Closed 1 week at Christmas. Expensive.*

Jury's. This modern two-story hotel has a lively bar and occupies a riverside location just five minutes' walk from the downtown area. *Western Rd., tel. 021/966377. 140 rooms with bath. Facilities: restaurant, indoor and outdoor pools, health club, sauna. AE, DC, MC, V. Closed Dec. 25, 26. Expensive.*

Metropole. The Metropole is a well-established central hotel; Rooms in front can be noisy. *MacCurtain St., tel. 021/508122. 91 rooms with bath. AE, DC, MC, V. Moderate.*

Moore's. Good for its central location on a quiet part of the river bank, the hotel has a fine reputation for friendliness and personal attention. *Morrison's Island, tel. 021/271291. 39 rooms, most with bath. MC, V. Moderate.*

Glenvera House. A Victorian town house, the Glenvera is just three minutes from the bus and train stations. *Wellington Rd., tel. 021/502030. No credit cards. Inexpensive.*

★ **John Barleycorn Inn.** This converted 19th-century coaching inn retains much rustic charm. It's situated in its own grounds with a river and trees, 6½ kilometers (4 miles) off the main Dublin–Cork road. *Riverstown, Glanmire, tel. 021/821499. 17 rooms with bath. AE, DC, MC, V. Inexpensive.*

Newbridge **Red House Inn.** The Red House Inn is a cozy restaurant with
Dining open turf fires. Home-grown vegetables are a house specialty. *Tel. 045/31516. AE, DC, MC, V. Moderate.*

Cork to Galway

The trip from Cork to Galway is about 300 kilometers (188 miles) and includes stops in Killarney and Limerick. Killarney and the mysterious regions of the Burren are two very different areas of outstanding natural beauty. The Shannon region around Limerick is littered with castles, both ruined and restored.

Getting Around

By Train Trains run from Cork to Tralee, via Killarney, and from Cork to Limerick, changing at Limerick Junction.

By Bus Buses offer a more flexible service than trains; details are available from local tourist information offices.

By Car All major rental companies have facilities at Shannon Airport. **Killarney Autos Ltd.** (Park Rd., tel. 064/31355) is the major firm in Killarney. Taxis do not operate on meters; agree on the fare beforehand.

By Bicycle You can rent bicycles from: **O'Callaghan Bros.**, College St., Killarney, tel. 064/31465; **D. O'Neill**, Plunkett St., Killarney, tel.

064/315900; **Limerick Sports Store,** 10 William St., Limerick, tel. 061/45647.

Guided Tours

Bus Eireann offers day tours by bus from Killarney and Tralee train stations; check with the tourist office or rail station for details. **Shannon Castle Tours** (tel. 061/61788), and **Gray Line** (tel. 01/612325) also operate tours.

Tourist Information

All tourist information offices are open weekdays 9–6, Sat. 9–1.
Killarney. Town Hall, tel. 064/31633.
Limerick. The Granary, Michael St., tel. 061/317522.
Shannon Airport. tel. 061/61664.
Tralee. Godfrey Pl., tel. 066/21288.

Exploring Cork to Galway

Beyond Macroom, the main Cork–Killarney road passes through the west-Cork **Gaelteacht**—a predominantly Irish-speaking region—and begins its climb into the Derrynasaggart mountains. A detour to the left at Ballyvourney will take you to the lake of **Gougane Barra,** source of the river Lee and now a national park. The 6th-century monk St. Finbar, founder of Cork, had his cell on an island in the lake; this island can now be reached by causeway.

Killarney itself is an undistinguished market town, well-developed to handle the tourist trade that flourishes here in the peak season. To find the famous scenery, you must head out of town toward the lakes that lie in a valley running south between the mountains. Part of Killarney's lake district is within **Killarney National Park.** At the heart of the park is the 40,470-square kilometer (10,000-acre) **Muckross Estate.** (Open Easter–May and Sept.–Oct., daily 8–7; June–Aug., daily 9–5). Cars are not allowed in the estate, so if you don't want to walk, rent a bicycle in town or take a trip in a jaunting car—a small two-wheeled horse-drawn cart. At the center of the estate is **Muckross House,** a 19th-century manor that contains a folk museum and visitors' center. *Open Sept.–Oct., daily 10–7; Nov.–mid-Mar., Tues.–Sun. 11–5; July–Aug., daily 9–9.*

To get an idea of the splendor of the lakes and streams—of the massive glacial sandstone and limestone rocks and lush vegetation that characterize the Killarney district—take one of the day-long tours of the **Gap of Dunloe, the Upper Lake, Long Range, Middle and Lower Lakes,** and **Ross Castle.** The central section, the Gap of Dunloe, is not suitable for cars, but horses and jaunting cars are available at **Kate Kearney's Cottage,** which marks the entrance to the gap.

The **Ring of Kerry** will add about 176 kilometers (110 miles) to your trip, but in good weather it provides a pleasant experience. Leave Killarney by the Kenmare road. **Kenmare** is a small market town 34 kilometers (21 miles) from Killarney at the head of Kenmare Bay. Across the water, as you drive out along

Cork to Galway

the Iveragh Peninsula, will be views of the gray-blue mountain ranges of the Beara Peninsula. **Sneem,** on the estuary of the river Ardsheelaun, is one of the prettiest villages in Ireland, although its English-style central green makes it an exception among Irish villages. Beyond the next village, Caherdaniel, is **Derrynane House,** home of the 19th-century politician and patriot Daniel O'Connell, "The Liberator," and completed by him in 1825. It still contains much of its original furniture. *Open mid-June–Sept., daily 10–1 and 2–7; Oct.–mid-June, Tues.–Sat. 10–1, Sun. 2–5.*

The village of **Waterville** is famous as an angling center; it also has a fine sandy beach and a championship golf course. Offshore, protruding in conical shapes from the Atlantic, are the **Skellig Rocks,** which contain the cells of early-Christian monks. Beyond Cahirciveen, you are on the other side of the Ring, with views across Dingle Bay to the rugged peaks of the Dingle Peninsula. At the head of the bay is **Killorglin,** which has a three-day stint of unbridled merrymaking the first weekend in August, known as Puck Fair.

If time and the weather are on your side, turn off the main Killorglin–Tralee road and make a tour of the **Dingle Peninsula,** one of the wildest and least spoiled regions of Ireland, taking in the **Connor Pass, Mount Brandon, the Gallarus Oratory,** and stopping at **Dunquin** to hear some of Ireland's best traditional musicians. For an adventure off the beaten path, arrange for a boat ride to the **Blasket Islands** and spend a few blissful hours wandering along the cliffs.

Tralee is the commercial center of Kerry but has little to recommend it unless you happen to be visiting in September when the "Rose of Tralee" is selected from an international lineup of young women of Irish descent. Listowel is similarly transformed during its race week in October. From **Tarbert** (where a ferry provides a handy shortcut direct to County Clare and the Burren), the road skirts the estuary of the river Shannon. **Limerick** is the third-largest city in the Republic, with a population of 60,000; it's also arguably the least attractive city in Ireland. Its Newtown area, however, is dominated by pleasant Georgian buildings, one of which, the Granary, has been converted into the main tourist office.

Bunratty Castle is a famous landmark midway between Limerick and Shannon Airport. It is one of four castles in the area that offer nightly medieval banquets, which, though as fake as they come, at least offer some fairly uninhibited fun. The castle was the stronghold of the princes of Thomond and is the most complete and—despite its ye-olde-world banquets—authentic medieval castle in Ireland, restored in such a way as to give an idea of the 15th- and 16th-century way of life. The **Folk Park** on its grounds has farm buildings and craft shops typical of the 19th-century. *Open daily 9:30–5.*

Time Out Drop in to **Durty Nelly's,** beside Bunratty Castle—it's one of Ireland's most popular old-time bars.

There is an incredible number of castles—almost 900—in the Shannon area, ranging from fully restored ones like **Knappogue** at Quin, 14 kilometers (9 miles) from Bunratty, to the multitude of crumbling ruins that loom up all over the area.

Beyond Shannon Airport, you reach County Clare and its principal town, **Ennis,** the campaigning base of Eamon de Valera, the fearsome New York-born politician and demagogue whose character and views dominated the Republic in its early years. Just beyond Ennis, a detour to **Corofin** will take you to the **Clare Heritage Center,** which explains the traumatic story of Ireland in the 19th century, a story of famines and untold misery that resulted in the mass emigrations of the Irish to England and the USA.

Ennistymon or Lisdoonvarna, both quiet villages with an old-fashioned charm, make excellent bases for touring the Burren. **Lisdoonvarna** has developed something of a reputation over the years as a matchmaking center, with bachelor farmers and single women converging here each year around harvest time in order to get to know each other better. This strange, rocky, limestone district is a superb nature reserve, with a profusion of unique wildflowers that are at their best in late May. Huge colonies of puffins, kittiwakes, shags, guillemots, and razorbills nest along its coast. The **Burren Display Center** at **Kilfenora** explains the extraordinary geology and wildlife of the area in an audiovisual display. (Open mid-Mar.–Apr. and Sept.–Oct., daily 10–5:45; May–Aug., daily 10–6:45.)

The dramatic **Cliffs of Moher** are a must: They rise vertically out of the sea in a 8 kilometer (five-mile) wall that varies in height from 440 to 217 meters (700 feet) with **O'Brien's Tower** at their highest point. This contains a visitors' center. (Open Mar.–Oct. 10–6). On a clear day, the **Aran Islands** are visible from the cliffs, and in the summer there are regular day trips to them from **Doolin,** a small village popular with young travelers and noted for its spontaneous traditional music sessions.

At **Ailwee Cave** near Ballyvaughan, you can take a guided tour into the underworld of the Burren, where 1,041 meters (1,120 yards) of cave formed millions of years ago can be explored. *Open mid-Mar.–Sept., Sat. 10–5, Sun. 2–5; Oct.–mid-Mar. weekends and public holidays 10–3.*

The coast road continues into County Galway, through the pretty fishing village of Kinvara. Galway City itself is approached through **Clarinbridge,** the village that hosts Galway's annual Oyster Festival in September, featuring the superlative products of the village's oyster beds.

Dining and Lodging

For details and price category definitions, *see* Dining and Lodging in Staying in Ireland.

Ennis
Dining

Brogan's. Situated in the center of town, Brogan's offers a cheerful fire and cozy surroundings. *24 O'Connell St., tel. 065/ 29859. AE, DC, MC, V. Moderate.*
The Cloister. There is an Old World bar here, as well as a patio garden. *Abbey St., tel. 065/29521. DC, MC, V. Moderate.*

Lodging
★

Old Ground. A gracious, creeper-clad old building, Old Ground is carefully updated. *O'Connell St., tel. 065/28127. 60 rooms with bath. AE, DC, MC, V. Expensive.*
Queen's. This is a busy, unpretentious place in the center of town. *Tel. 065/28963. 30 rooms, some with bath. AE, DC, MC, V. Moderate.*

Ennistymon
Lodging
★

Falls Hotel. A Georgian manor house set in its own grounds just outside the village, close to two 18-hole golf courses. *Tel. 065/ 71004. 30 rooms with bath. AE, DC, MC, V. Inexpensive.*

Kenmare
Dining

Anchorage. Head here to enjoy the pleasant nautical atmosphere of the aptly named Anchorage. *Killaha E., tel. 064/ 41024. MC, V, Moderate.*
Jug's. This place specializes in seafood. *Gortamullen, tel. 064/ 41099. AE, DC, MC, V. Moderate.*

Lodging

Park. A guest feels truly pampered at this antique-laden hotel, widely considered one of Ireland's best. The French restaurant is superb. *Tel. 064/41200. 48 rooms with bath. Facilities: tennis, park land, garden. DC, MC, V. Closed mid-Nov.–Easter, except Christmas–New Years Day. Very Expensive.*

Killarney
Dining

★

Foley's. This popular eatery specializes in seafood, steaks, and Kerry mountain lamb. *23 High St., tel. 064/31217. AE, DC, MC, V. Moderate.*
Gaby's. For simple and fresh seafood, Gaby's can't be beat. *17 High St., tel. 064/32519. AE, DC, MC, V. Closed Sun. (except for dinner in July and Aug.), Mon. lunch, and Dec.–mid-Mar. Moderate.*

Lodging

Cahernane. This is a manor house-turned-hotel in a pretty setting. *Muckross Rd., tel. 064/31895. 52 rooms with bath. Facilities: 9-hole golf course. AE, DC, MC, V. Closed Nov.–Easter except Christmas–New Year's Day. Expensive.*
Great Southern. The Great Southern is housed in a vast 19th-century red-brick building set in large gardens. *Tel. 064/31262.*

180 rooms with bath. Facilities: heated indoor pool. AE, DC, MC, V. Closed Jan.–mid-Mar. Expensive.

Arbutus. Newly refurbished and centrally located, the Arbutus benefits from a lively bar and an Old World atmosphere. *College St., tel. 064/31037. 35 rooms with bath. AE, DC, MC, V. Moderate.*

Limerick   **Jury's.** This bright modern hotel is set in its own grounds over-
Lodging   looking the Shannon, about a three-minute walk from the town center. There is good French cuisine in the Copper Room restaurant and live music most nights in the bar. *Ennis Rd., tel. 061/55366. 96 rooms with bath. Facilities: restaurant, bar. AE, DC, MC, V. Moderate.*

Glentworth. This is a functional hotel just off Limerick's main street. *Glentworth St., tel. 061/43822. 55 rooms, most with bath. AE, DC, MC, V. Inexpensive.*

Lisdoonvarna   **Bruach na Haille.** This prettily converted cottage, 2 miles (3 ki-
Dining   lometers) from town, serves imaginative, country-style Irish meals. *V. Moderate.*

Lodging   **Hydro.** The Hydro is an old-fashioned spa-hotel that has undergone a recent facelift to make it perfectly adequate for the price. *Tel. 065/74027. 70 rooms with bath. V. Inexpensive.*

Sheedy's Spa View. A friendly, family-run establishment with open turf fires. *Sulphir Hill, tel. 065/74026. 11 rooms with bath. Facilities: restaurant, tennis. DC, MC, V. Closed Nov.–Mar. Inexpensive.*

The Northwest

This route from Galway to Sligo and then back to Dublin, via Kells, takes you through the rugged landscape of Connemara to the fabled Yeats country in the northwest and then skirts the borders of Northern Ireland before returning to Dublin. The whole trip is about 400 kilometers (250 miles) and passes through some of the wildest and loneliest parts of Ireland.

Getting Around

By Train   Trains to Galway, Westport, and Sligo operate from Dublin's Heuston or Connolly (Sligo) stations. There is no train service north of Sligo.

By Bus   Travel within the area is more flexible by bus; details are available from local tourist information offices.

By Car   In Galway, cars can be rented from **Avis,** tel. 091/68901; **Hertz,** tel. 091/66674; or **Murray's,** tel. 091/62222. Taxis do not operate on meters; agree on the fare beforehand.

By Bicycle   You can rent bikes from **Salthill Rentals,** Galway City, tel. 091/22085; **John Mannion,** Railway View, Clifden, tel. 095/21160; **Gerry Conway,** Wine St., Sligo, tel. 071/61240.

Guided Tours

CIE operates day tours of Connemara out of Galway City and bus tours into the Donegal highlands from Sligo train station; details are available from local tourist offices. **CIE** (tel. 01/302222 Bus Eireann) and **Gray Line** (tel. 01/612325) offer tours of the Boyne Valley and County Meath out of Dublin.

Tourist Information

All are open weekdays 9–6, Sat. 9–1.
Galway. Off Eyre Sq., tel. 091/63081.
Sligo. Temple St., tel. 071/61201.
Westport. The Mall, tel. 098/25711.

Exploring The Northwest

Galway City is the gateway to the ancient province of Connacht, the most westerly seaboard in Europe. Galway City was well established even before the Normans arrived in the 13th-century, rebuilding the city walls and turning the little town into a flourishing port. Later, its waterfront was frequented by Spanish grandees and traders. The salmon fishing in the river Corrib, which flows through the lower part of the town, is unsurpassed. In early summer, you can stand on the **Weir Bridge** beside the town's cathedral and watch thousands of salmon as they leap and twist through the narrow access to the inner lakes. **Lynch's Castle** in Shop Street, now a bank, is a good example of a 16th-century fortified house—fortified because the neighboring Irish tribes persistently raided Galway City, from whose commercial life they were excluded. Nowadays, the liveliest part of town is around the area between **Eyre Square** (the town's center) and **Spanish Arch.** Galway is a compact city, best explored on foot.

Time Out Drop in at **Noctan's** pub on the corner of Abbeygate Street for food at lunchtime and the latest news of what's on in town.

Galway has a lively and informal arts scene, particularly in mid-August during its annual Arts Festival. It is the home base of the **Druid Theatre;** if the group is performing, a visit to the tiny auditorium is highly recommended.

On the west bank of the Corrib estuary is the **Claddagh,** said to be the oldest fishing village in Ireland. **Salthill Promenade,** with its lively seaside amenities, is the traditional place "to sit and watch the moon rise over Claddagh, and see the sun go down on Galway Bay"—in the words of the city's most famous song.

Connemara is a land of romantic, underpopulated landscapes, and rugged craggy coastlines, where the Irish language is still used by many people. **Rossaveale,** a port on the coast road beyond Spiddal, is the handiest port for a trip to the Aran Islands, 48 kilometers (30 miles) off the coast, where J. M. Synge drew the inspiration for his play *Riders to the Sea.* The islands are still 100% Irish speaking and retain an atmosphere distinct from that of the mainland, which will be appreciated by those in search of the peace and quiet of a past century. **Inishmaan,** the middle island, is considered the most unspoiled of the three and will delight botanists, ornithologists, and walkers. *Sailings daily from Rossaveale and less frequently from Galway; round-trip fare about IR£12. Details from Galway Tourist Information Office. Also accessible by air from Galway City: daily flights, round-trip fare about IR£35.*

Oughterard is an important angling center on Lough Corrib. Boats can be rented for excursions to the lake's many wooded islands. The road to Clifden runs between the Maamturk and

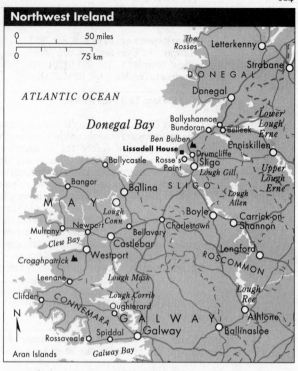

Northwest Ireland

ATLANTIC OCEAN

Donegal Bay

The Rosses

Letterkenny

Strabane

DONEGAL

Donegal

Lower Lough Erne

Ballyshannon
Bundoran
Belleek
Enniskillen

Ben Bulben
Lissadell House
Drumcliffe
Ballycastle
Rosse's
Point
Sligo

Upper Lough Erne

Lough Gill

SLIGO

Bangor
Ballina

Lough Allen

Lough Conn

Boyle
Carrick-on-Shannon

MAYO

Mulrany
Newport
Bellavary
Charlestown
Castlebar
Clew Bay
Westport
Croaghpatrick
Longford

ROSCOMMON

Leenane
Lough Mask

Clifden
Lough Corrib
Oughterard

Lough Ree

CONNEMARA
GALWAY
Athlone

N
Rossaveale
Spiddal
Galway
Ballinasloe

Aran Islands
Galway Bay

the Cloosh mountains beside a string of small lakes. **Clifden,** the principal town of Connemara, has an almost Alpine setting, nestling on the edge of the Atlantic with a spectacular mountain backdrop. Just beyond Clifden is the **Connemara National Park,** with its many nature trails offering views of sea, mountain, and lake. Its visitor center features an audiovisual presentation and has a collection of farm furniture. *Open Easter–Sept., daily 10–1 and 2–6.*

Westport is a quiet, mainly 18th-century town overlooking Clew Bay—a wide expanse of water studded with nearly 400 islands. The distinctive silhouette of **Croagpatrick,** a 775-meter (mountain, dominates the town. Today some 25,000 pilgrims climb it on the last Sunday in July in honor of St. Patrick, who is believed to have spent 40 days fasting on its summit in AD 441. Whether he did or not, the climb is an exhilarating experience and can be completed in about three hours; it should be attempted only in good weather, however.

County Sligo is noted for its seaside resorts, the famous golf course at Rosse's Point (just outside Sligo Town), and its links with Ireland's most famous 20th-century poet, William Butler Yeats, who is buried just north of **Sligo Town** at Drumcliffe. An important collection of paintings by the poet's brother, Jack B. Yeats, can be seen in the **Sligo Museum** (Stephen St., tel. 071/42212), which also has displays on the folk life of the area. Take a boat from Sligo up to **Lough Gill** and see the **Lake Isle of Innishfree** and other places immortalized in the poetry of W. B. Yeats. His grave is found beneath the slopes of Ben Bulben, just north of the town. Nearby is **Lissadell House,** a substantial mansion dating from 1830 that features prominently in his writings. It was the home of Constance Gore-Booth, later Countess Markeviecz, who took part in the 1916 uprising. *Admission: IR£1. Open May–Sept. Mon.–Sat. 2:25–5:15.*

Bundoran, the southernmost town of Donegal, is one of Ireland's major seaside resorts, with excellent sandy beaches. From **Donegal Town,** you can set off to tour the ever-changing landscape of Donegal's rugged coastline and highlands, visiting the "tweed villages" on the coast at the Rosses where the famous Donegal tweed is woven.

This route heads back to Dublin through **Belleek,** on the borders of Counties Donegal and Fermanagh, known for its fragile, lustrous china; a factory visit can be arranged (tel. 036565/501). For the remaining towns on this tour, *see* the Ireland country map. Belleek is a frontier post on an approved road that passes through Enniskillen in Northern Ireland and Newtown Butler, re-emerging in Clones, County Monaghan. (Tourists in private cars can cross the borders here with a minimum of formality.) At **Cootehill** (reached via Newbliss) is **Bellamont Forest,** a compact Palladian villa in its own park between two lakes, with fine plasterwork and statuary in the interior. (Open weekdays 2:30–5 and by appointment, tel. 049/32227.) This is one of many fine Irish country homes available for rent and overnight stays to small groups and individuals; details can be obtained from Elegant Ireland (tel. 01/751665).

The main N3 returns you to Dublin by way of **Kells,** in whose 8th-century abbey the Book of Kells was completed; a facsimile can be seen in **St. Columba's Church.** Among the remains of the abbey is a well-preserved round tower and a rare example of a stone-roof church dating from the 9th century. There are five richly sculptured stone crosses in Kells. Just south of **Navan** is the **Hill of Tara,** the religious and cultural capital of Ireland in ancient times. Its importance waned with the arrival of Christianity in the 5th century, and today its crest is, appropriately enough, crowned with a statue of the man who brought Christianity to Ireland—St. Patrick.

Dining and Lodging

For details and price category definitions, *see* Dining and Lodging in Staying in Ireland.

Cashel Bay
Dining and Lodging

Zetland. This hotel and restaurant offers excellent sea trout and salmon fishing amid the grandeur of Connemara. *Tel. 095/ 31011. 29 rooms with bath. AE, DC, MC, V. Closed mid-Oct.– mid-Apr. Expensive.*

Castlebar
Lodging

Breaffy House. This sturdy castellated stone mansion with a small modern extension is charmingly set in its own parkland. *Located 5 km (3 mi) southeast of town, on the N6, tel. 094/ 22033. 40 rooms with bath. Facilities: 18-hole golf course. AE, DC, MC, V. Moderate.*

Clifden
Lodging

Abbeyglen Castle. This comfortable hotel is quietly set a half-mile west of town, featuring panoramic views over the rolling green hillsides. The secluded garden is a haven for travel-weary souls. *Sky Rd., tel. 095/21201. 40 rooms with bath. Facilities: heated pool, tennis. AE, DC, MC, V. Closed Jan. 10–Feb. 1. Moderate.*

Rock Glen Manor House. Dating from 1815, this converted hunting lodge is 1½ kilometers (one mile) south of town in exceptionally peaceful surroundings. *Tel. 095/21035. 29 rooms with bath. AE, DC, MC, V. Moderate.*

Cong
Lodging
★
Ashford Castle. This imposing castle is set in its own park on the edge of Lough Corrib and has a superb restaurant, the Connaught Room. President Reagan stayed here in 1984. *Tel. 092/46003. 82 rooms with bath. Facilities: 9-hole golf course, tennis, fishing, garden. AE, DC, MC, V. Very Expensive.*

Galway City
Dining
Eyre House. Irish cuisine is served with a French accent. *Eyre Sq., tel. 091/62396. AE, MC, V. Moderate.*

Rabbitt's Bar and Restaurant. A well-established, family-run eating place. *Forster St., tel. 091/66490. DC, MC, V. Moderate.*

Lodging
Great Southern. Recently refurbished, this old-style town hotel enjoys a conveniently central location. *Eyre Sq., tel. 091/64041. 120 rooms with bath. Facilities: roof-top heated pool, sauna, health complex. AE, DC, MC, V. Closed Dec. 24–26. Expensive.*

Ardilaun House. This hotel is set in pleasant grounds midway between Galway City and the seaside suburb of Salthill. *Taylors Hill, tel. 091/21433. 91 rooms with bath. AE, DC, MC, V. Moderate.*

Moycullen
Dining
Drimcong House. The chef-owner prepares his award-winning meals in a 300-year-old lakeside house, 13 kilometers (8 miles) from Galway City. *1½ km (1 mi) northwest on N59, tel. 091/85115. AE, MC, V. Closed Sun. dinner, Mon., and Jan.–Feb. Moderate.*

Sligo Town
Dining
Knockmuldowney. This fine Georgian country-house inn is just outside town, near Strandhill, in four acres of parkland. It has 6 rooms, as well as a highly recommended restaurant. *Culleenamore, tel. 071/68122. AE, DC, MC, V. Closed Nov.–Feb. Expensive.*

Reflections. Located in the center of town, Reflections is a modern restaurant. *Gratten St., tel. 071/43828. MC, V. Moderate.*

Lodging
Ballincar House. Just outside of town, this converted country house with gardens serves excellent food. *Rosses Point Rd., tel. 071/45361. 20 rooms with bath. Facilities: squash, tennis, sauna, solarium. AE, DC, MC, V. Closed Dec. 23–Jan. 12. Moderate.*

Sligo Park. This is a modern two-story building, set in spacious grounds. *Pearse Rd., tel. 071/60291. 60 rooms with bath. AE, DC, MC, V. Moderate.*

Southern. This solid, four-story, 19th-century hotel is set in its own pretty gardens. *Lord Edward St., tel. 071/62101. 50 rooms, most with bath. AE, DC, MC, V. Inexpensive.*

Westport
Dining
Asgard. The Asgard is a pub with award-winning food in both its bar and second-floor restaurant. *The Quay, tel. 098/25319. AE. Moderate.*

Lodging
Westport Ryan. Woodlands surround this classy modern hotel beside a lake. *Louisburgh Rd., tel. 098/25811. 56 rooms with bath. AE, DC, MC, V. Dinner only. Expensive.*

Hotel Westport. Set in its own parkland, the modern, two-story Hotel Westport is five minutes from town. *The Demesne, tel. 098/25122. 49 rooms with bath. AE, DC, MC, V. Moderate.*

19 Italy

Introduction

Where else in Europe can you find the blend of great art, delicious food and wines, and sheer verve that awaits you in Italy? This Mediterranean country has profoundly contributed to the Western way of life, and has produced some of the world's greatest thinkers, writers, politicians, saints, and artists. Impressive traces of their lives and works can still be seen in the great buildings and lovely countryside.

The whole of Italy is one vast attraction, but the triangle of its most-visited cities—Rome, Florence, and Venice—gives a good idea of the great variety to be found here. In Rome and Florence, especially, you can feel the uninterrupted flow of the ages, from the Classical era of the ancient Romans to the bustle and throb of contemporary life carried on in centuries-old settings. Venice, by contrast, seems suspended in time, the same today as when it held sway over the eastern Mediterranean and the Orient. Each of these cities presents a different aspect of the Italian character: the Baroque exuberance of Rome, Florence's serene stylishness, and the dreamy sensuality of Venice.

The uninhibited Italian lifestyle can be entertaining or irritating, depending on how you look at it. Rarely do things run like clockwork here; it's more likely you will encounter unexplained delays and incomprehensible complications. Relax and try to see the bright side: There's usually something you can smile about even in the darkest circumstances.

For us as tourists, one of the current problems with visiting Italy is the country's rich artistic heritage. It draws hordes of visitors, all wanting to see the same thing at the same time. Especially from June, even May, through the middle of September, the Sistine Chapel, Michelangelo's *David*, St. Mark's Square, and other key sights are more often than not swamped by mobs of fellow tourists. Try to organize seeing the highlights at off-peak times in the day. If they are open during lunch—and many are not—that is often a good time. Special attractions for 1990 include the sight of Michelangelo's vibrant original colors on the half of the Sistine Chapel that has been cleaned so far, and the restored Masaccio frescoes in the Church of the Carmine in Florence. In Rome, the city is being spruced up to put its best face forward for the Soccer World Cup finals from early June to July, which will be a good time *not* to come to Italy unless you're a soccer fan yourself.

Recent regulations barring most automobile traffic from the centers of Rome and Florence (Firenze) have made those cities more pleasant to visit, and a lot less noisy.

Even in the major tourist cities, Italians generally take a friendly interest in their visitors. Only the most blasé waiters and salespeople will be less than courteous and helpful. However, the persistent attention Italian males pay to foreign females can be oppressive and annoying. If you're not interested, the best tactic is to ignore them. Security is important in Italy: Always be on guard against pickpockets and purse snatchers.

Making the most of your time in Italy doesn't mean rushing through it. To gain a rich appreciation for Italy, don't try to see everything all at once. Do what you really want to do, and if that means skipping a museum to sit at a pretty café, enjoying the sunshine and a cappuccino, you're getting into the Italian spirit. Art—and life—are to be enjoyed, and the Italians can show you how.

Before You Go

When to Go The main tourist season in Italy runs from mid-April to the end of September. The best months for sightseeing are April, May, June, September, and October, when the weather is generally pleasant and not too hot. Foreign tourists crowd the major cities at Easter, when Italians flock to resorts and the countryside. Avoid traveling in August, when the heat can be oppressive and when vacationing Italians cram roads, trains, and planes, as well as beach and mountain resorts. Especially around the August 15 holiday, cities such as Rome and Milan are deserted, and many restaurants and shops close. Except for year-round resorts such as Taormina, and a few on the Italian Riviera, coastal resorts close up tight from October or November to April. The best time for resorts is June and September, when everything is open but not crowded and the weather is usually fine.

The hottest months are July and August, when brief afternoon thunderstorms are common in inland areas. Winters are relatively mild in most places on the tourist circuit, but there are always some rainy spells.

Although low-season rates do not apply at hotels in Rome, Florence, and Milan, you can save on hotel accommodations in Venice (Venezia) and in resorts such as Sorrento and Capri during their low seasons—the winter, early-spring, and late-autumn months.

Climate The following are average daily maximum and minimum temperatures.

Rome									
Jan.	52F	11C	**May**	74F	23C	**Sept.**	79F	26C
	40	5		56	13		62	17
Feb.	55F	13C	**June**	82F	28C	**Oct.**	71F	22C
	42	15		63	17		55	13
Mar.	59F	15C	**July**	87F	30C	**Nov.**	61F	16C
	45	7		67	20		49	9
Apr.	66F	19C	**Aug.**	86F	30C	**Dec.**	55F	13C
	50	10		67	20		44	6

Milan									
Jan.	40F	5C	**May**	74F	23C	**Sept.**	75F	24C
	32	0		57	14		61	16
Feb.	46F	8C	**June**	80F	27C	**Oct.**	63F	17C
	35	2		63	17		52	11
Mar.	56F	13C	**July**	84F	29C	**Nov.**	51F	10C
	43	6		67	20		43	6
Apr.	65F	18C	**Aug.**	82F	28C	**Dec.**	43F	6C
	49	10		66	19		35	2

Currency The unit of currency in Italy is the lira (plural lire). There are bills of 1,000, 2,000, 5,000, 10,000, 50,000, and 100,000 lire; coins are worth 10, 20, 50, 100, 200, and 500 lire. At press time (spring 1989), the exchange rate was about 1,360 lire to the dollar and 2,340 lire to the pound sterling. Sooner or later the zeros will be lopped off the lire in order to simplify money deal-

Italy

ings and life in general. The long-heralded move has not yet been made, but seems imminent. If it does come to pass, 5,000 lire would become 5 lire, 50 lire would become 50 centesimi. When it does happen, both old and new values will be in effect until people become accustomed to the new system.

While the present system continues, and especially when your purchases run into hundreds of thousands of lire, beware of being short-changed, a dodge that is practiced at ticket windows and cashiers' desks as well as in shops and even banks. *Always count your change before you leave the counter.*

Always carry some smaller-denomination bills for sundry purchases; you're less likely to be short-changed, and you won't have to face the eye-rolling dismay of cashiers chronically short of change.

Credit cards are generally accepted in shops and hotels but may not be welcome in restaurants, so always look for those little signs in the window or ask, when you enter, to avoid embarrassing situations. When you wish to leave an extra tip beyond the 15% that is usually included with your bill, leave it in cash rather than add it to the credit card slip.

What It Will Cost Rome and Florence, and, especially, Milan and Venice, are the more expensive cities to visit. Taxes are usually included in hotel bills; a cover charge appears as a separate item in restaurant checks, as does the service charge, usually about 15%, if added. There is a 19% tax on car rentals.

Sample Prices A cup of espresso consumed while standing at a bar costs from 700 to 1,000 lire, triple that for table service. A bottle of beer costs from 1,600 to 3,000 lire, a soft drink costs 1,500 lire. A small sandwich *(tramezzino)* costs about 1,200 lire, a more substantial one about 2,000. You will pay about 6,000 lire for a short taxi ride in Rome, less in Florence, more in Milan. Admission to a major museum is about 5,000 lire; a three-hour sightseeing tour, about 30,000 lire.

Customs on Arrival Two still cameras and one movie camera can be brought in duty-free. Travelers arriving in Italy from an EEC country are allowed, duty-free, a total of 300 cigarettes (*or* 150 cigarillos *or* 75 cigars), 1½ liters plus 3 liters of still wine, and 99 milliliters of perfume if duty and taxes have been paid on them at the time of purchase. Visitors traveling directly from non-European countries are allowed 400 cigarettes and cigars or tobacco not exceeding 500 grams, 0.75 liter of spirits, 2 liters of still wine. Not more than 1 million lire in Italian bank notes may be taken into or out of the country.

Language Italy is accustomed to English-speaking tourists, and in major cities you will find that many people speak at least a little English. In smaller hotels and restaurants, a smattering of Italian comes in handy.

Getting Around

By Car The extensive network of *autostrade* (toll superhighways) con-
Road Conditions necting all major towns is complemented by equally well-maintained but nonpaying *superstrade* (highways), *strade di grande communicazione* (main trunk roads), *strade di interesse regionale* (regional highways), *strade importanti* (main roads), and *altre strade* (other roads). All are clearly

signposted and numbered. The ticket issued on entering an autostrada must be returned on leaving, along with the toll. On some shorter autostrade, mainly connections, the toll is payable on entering.

The Autostrada del Sole (A1, A2, and A3) crosses the country from north to south, connecting Milan to Reggio Calabria. A4 from west to east connects Turin to Trieste.

Rules of the Road Driving is on the right. At press time (spring 1989), the speed limit on an autostrada is 130 kph (81 mph) and 90 kph (56 mph) on other roads. Other regulations are largely as in the United States except that police have power to levy on-the-spot fines—even as high as $500!

Parking Check with your hotel as to the best place to park. Parking is greatly restricted in the center of most major Italian cities. Parking in "Zona Disco" is for limited periods.

Gasoline Gas costs about 1,300 lire per liter (more than $4 a gallon). Vouchers with tourist discounts of about 15%, together with five 2,000-lire autostrada vouchers and free breakdown service, are available as a package from the AA or RAC. Except on the autostrade, most gas stations are closed Sunday; they also close from 1 to 3 PM and at 7 PM for the night. Self-service pumps can be found in most cities and towns.

Breakdowns Dial 116 for towing and repairs, also for ambulance and highway police.

By Train The fastest service on the FS (Ferrovia dello State), the state-owned railroad, are the *intercity* trains, for which you pay a supplement and for which seat reservations may be required (and are always advisable). *Espresso* trains usually make more stops and are a little slower. *Diretto* and *locale* are slowest of all. You can buy tickets and make seat reservations at travel agencies displaying the FS symbol, avoiding long lines at station ticket windows. There is refreshment service on all long-distance trains. Tap water on trains is not drinkable. Carry compact bags for easy overhead storage. Trains are very crowded at holiday times; always reserve.

By Plane **Alitalia** and domestic affiliates **ATI** and **Aermed,** plus several privately owned companies, provide service throughout Italy. Alitalia offers several discount fares; inquire at travel agencies or at Alitalia agencies in major cities.

By Bus An extensive network of bus routes provides service throughout Italy. A timetable of routes of interest to tourists is published by **ANAC** Piazza Esquilino 29, Rome, tel. 06/463383.

By Boat Ferries connect the mainland with all the major islands. Car ferries operate to Sicily, Sardinia, Elba, Ponza, Capri (though cars are not advised), and Ischia, among others. Lake ferries connect the towns on the shores of the Italian lakes: Como, Maggiore, and Garda.

Staying in Italy

Telephones Pay phones take either 200-lire coins, two 100-lire coins, or a
Local Calls token *(gettone).* Some older phones take only tokens, which you insert in the slot before picking up the receiver; dial, and, when your party answers, push the little knob on the slot to release the token and complete the connection. Tokens can be pur-

chased from the token machine or from the nearest cashier. Local calls cost 200 lire for nine minutes. For *teleselezione* (long-distance direct dialing), have a handful of coins ready and place several in the slot; unused coins are returned when you push the large yellow knob.

International Calls Since hotels tend to add exorbitant service charges for long-distance and international calls, it's best to go to the "Telefoni" telephone exchange, where the operator assigns you a booth, can help place your call, and will collect payment when you have finished. Telefoni exchanges (usually marked *SIP)* are found in all cities.

Operators and Information For Europe and the Mediterranean area, dial 15; for intercontinental service, dial 170.

Mail The Italian mail system is notoriously erratic and often excruciatingly slow. Allow up to 21 days for mail to and from the United States and Canada, almost as much to and from the United Kingdom, and much more for postcards.

Postal Rates Airmail letters to the United States cost 1,050 lire for up to 20 grams; postcards with a short greeting and signature cost 750 lire but cost letter rate if the message is lengthy. Airmail letters to the United Kingdom cost 650 lire, postcards 550 lire.

Receiving Mail You can have mail sent to American Express offices or to Italian post offices, marked "Fermo Posta" and addressed to you c/o Palazzo delle Poste, with the name of the city in which you will pick it up. In either case you must show your passport and pay a small fee.

Shopping At Rome airport citizens of a non—EEC country can avail
Sales-Tax Refunds themselves of a sales-tax (IVA) refund of the tax paid on articles worth between 525,000 and 10 million lire purchased in shops displaying a Tax-Free System sign. The procedure: At time of purchase, ask for an invoice describing the article and price, and have the relevant data from your passport included on that invoice. At Fiumicino airport upon departure, show the article to the customs officer, who will put an exit stamp on the invoice. A teller at the exchange window in the transit area will refund the amount of the tax in cash. The catch is that you must spend more than 525,000 lire in one shop to be eligible for the refund.

Bargaining Most shops now have fixed prices *(prezzi fissi)*, but you may be able to get a discount on a large purchase. Always bargain with a street vendor or at a market (except for food).

Opening and **Banks.** Banks are open weekdays 8:30–1:30 and from 3 or 3:30
Closing Times to 4 or 4:30.
Churches. Churches are usually open from early morning to noon or 12:30, when they close for about two hours or more, opening again in the afternoon until about 7 PM.
Museums. National museums are usually open until 2 and close on Monday, but there are many exceptions. Other museums have entirely different hours, which may vary according to season. Archaeological sites are usually closed Monday. At all museums and sites, ticket offices close an hour or so before official closing time. Always check with the local tourist office for current hours.
Shops. Shops are open, with individual variations, from 9 to 1 and from 3:30 or 4 to 7 or 7:30. They are open from Monday through Saturday, but close a half-day during the week; for ex-

ample, in Rome most shops (except food shops) close Monday morning, or Saturday afternoon in July and August. Some tourist-oriented shops are open all day, every day, as in Venice.

National Holidays January 1 (New Year's Day), January 6 (Epiphany), April 15 and 16 (Easter Sunday and Monday), April 25 (Liberation Day), May 1, June 2, August 15 (the religious feast of the Assumption, known as Ferragosto, when cities are literally deserted and most restaurants and shops are closed), November 1, December 8, December 25 and 26.

Dining Generally speaking, a *ristorante* pays more attention to decor, service, and menu than does a *trattoria*, which is simpler and often family-run. An *osteria* used to be a lowly tavern, though now the term may be used to designate a chic and expensive eatery. A *tavola calda* offers hot dishes and snacks, with seating. A *rosticceria* has the same, to take out.

The menu is always posted in the window or just inside the door of an eating establishment. Check to see what is offered, and note the charges for *coperto* (cover) and *servizio* (service), which will increase your check. A *menu turistico* includes taxes and service, but beverages are extra.

Mealtimes Lunch hour in Rome lasts from 1 to 3, dinner from 8 to 10. Service begins and ends a half-hour earlier in Florence and Venice, later in the south. Practically all restaurants close one day a week; some close for winter or summer vacation.

Precautions Tap water is safe in large cities and almost everywhere else unless noted "Non Potabile." Bottled mineral water is available everywhere, *gassata* (with bubbles) or *non gassata* (without). If you prefer tap water, ask for *acqua semplice.*

Dress Except for restaurants in the Very Expensive and occasionally in the Expensive categories, where jacket and tie are advisable, casual attire is acceptable.

Ratings Prices are per person and include first course, main course, dessert or fruit, and house wine, where available. Best bets are indicated by a star ★. At press time (spring 1989), there were 1,360 lire to the dollar. Note that restaurant prices in Venice are slightly higher than those shown here.

Category	Rome	Other Areas
Very Expensive	over 100,000 lire	over 85,000 lire
Expensive	60,000–100,000 lire	60,000–85,000 lire
Moderate	30,000–60,000 lire	25,000–60,000 lire
Inexpensive	under 30,000 lire	under 25,000 lire

Credit Cards The following credit card abbreviations are used: AE, American Express; DC, Diners Club; MC, MasterCard; V, Visa.

Lodging Italy, and especially the main tourist capitals of Rome, Florence, and Venice, offers a good choice of accommodations. Room rates are on a par with other European capitals, and porters, room service, and in-house cleaning and laundering are disappearing in Moderate and Inexpensive hotels. Taxes and service are included in the room rate. Breakfast is an extra charge, and you can decline to take breakfast in the hotel, though the desk may not be happy about it; make this clear when booking or checking in. Air-conditioning also may be an extra charge. In older hotels, room quality may be uneven; if you don't like the room you're given, ask for another. This applies to noise, too; some front rooms are bigger and have views but get street noise. Specify if you care about having either a bath or shower, as not all rooms have both. In Moderate and Inexpensive places, showers may be the drain-in-the-floor type guaranteed to flood the bathroom. Major cities have hotel reservation service booths in the rail stations.

Hotels   Italian hotels are officially classified from five-star (deluxe) to one-star (guest houses and small inns). Prices are established officially and a rate card on the back of the door of your room or inside the closet door tells you exactly what you will pay for that particular room. Any variations should be cause for complaint and should be reported to the local tourist office. CIGA, Jolly, Space, Atahotels, and Italhotels are among the reliable chains or groups operating in Italy, with CIGA among the most luxurious. There are a few Relais et Châteaux member hotels which are noted for individual atmosphere, personal service, and luxury; they are also expensive. The AGIP chain is found mostly on main highways.

Pensions   Good-value accommodations can be found at one-star hotels and *locande* (inns). Rooms are usually spotlessly clean but basic, with shower and toilets down the hall.

Rentals   More and more people are discovering the attractions of renting a house, cottage, or apartment in the Italian countryside. These are ideal for families or for groups of up to eight people looking for a bargain—or just independence. Availability is subject to change, so it is best to ask your travel agent or the nearest branch of ENIT, the Italian tourist board, about rentals.

Camping   Italy has a wide selection of campgrounds, and the Italians themselves are taking to camping by the thousands, which means that beach or mountain sites will be crammed in July and August. It's best to avoid these peak months and to send for the (necessary) camping license from **Federazione Italiana del Campeggio,** Casella Postale 649, 50100 Firenze.

Ratings   The following price categories are determined by the cost of two people in a double room. Best bets are indicated by a ★. At press time, there were 1,360 lire to the dollar. As with restaurant prices, the cost of hotels in Venice is slightly more than those shown here.

Category	Rome	Other Areas
Very Expensive	over 400,000 lire	over 300,000 lire
Expensive	150,000–400,000 lire	140,000–300,000 lire
Moderate	90,000–150,000 lire	80,000–140,000 lire
Inexpensive	under 90,000 lire	under 80,000 lire

Credit Cards   The following credit card abbreviations are used: AE, American Express; DC, Diners Club; MC, MasterCard; V, Visa.

Tipping   In restaurants, a 15% service charge is usually added to the total, but it doesn't all go to the waiter. In large cities and resorts it is customary to give the waiter a 5% tip in addition to the service charge made on the check.

Charges for service are included in all hotel bills, but smaller tips to staff members are appreciated. In general, chambermaids should be given about 1,000 lire per day, 3,000–4,000 per week; bellhops, 1,000–2,000 lire; doormen, about 500 lire. Give the concierge about 15% of his bill for services. Tip a minimum of 1,000 lire for room service and valet service.

Taxi drivers expect 10%. Porters at railroad stations and airports charge a fixed rate per suitcase; tip an additional 500 lire per person, more if the porter is very helpful. Service station attendants are tipped a few hundred lire if they are especially helpful. Tip guides about 1,000 lire per person for a half-day tour, more if they are very good.

Rome

Arriving and Departing

By Plane Rome's principal airport is at Fiumicino 29 kilometers (18 miles) from the city. Though its official name is Leonardo da Vinci Airport, everybody calls it Fiumicino. For flight information, tel. 06/60121. The smaller military airport of Ciampino is on the edge of Rome and is used as an alternative by international and domestic lines, especially for charter flights.

Between the Airport and Downtown ACOTRAL buses connect Leonardo da Vinci Airport with the air terminal on Via Giolitti, on one side of the Termini railway station. They leave every 20 minutes or so, and the trip takes about 40 minutes, more if there's traffic at the city end. Fare is 5,000 lire; before boarding the bus, buy your ticket at booths inside the terminals. There's a taxi stand on Via Giolitti near the bus stop.

Train service between Leonardo da Vinci Airport and Ostiense station, with connections at the Piramide stop of Metro Line B, should begin sometime during 1990. Centrally located hotels are a fairly short taxi ride from Ostiense station.

A taxi to or from the airport at Fiumicino costs about 50,000 lire, including supplements. At a booth inside the terminal you can hire a car with driver for about the same amount. If you decide to take a taxi, use only yellow cabs, which must wait outside the terminal; make sure the meter is running. Gypsy drivers solicit your trade as you come out of customs; they're not reliable, and their rates may be rip-offs.

Ciampino is connected with the Subaugusta station of the Metro Line A by bus. A taxi to or from Ciampino costs about 30,000 lire.

By Train Termini station is Rome's main train terminal, while Tiburtina and Ostiense stations are used principally by commuters. For train information, try the English-speaking personnel at the Information Office in Termini, or at any travel agency. Tickets and seats can be reserved and purchased at travel agencies bearing the FS (Ferrovia dello Stato) emblem.

By Bus There is no central bus station in Rome; long-distance and suburban buses terminate either near Termini station or near strategically located metro stops.

By Car The main access routes from the north are the Autostrada del Sole (A1) from Milan and Florence, and the Aurelia highway (SS 1) from Genoa. The principal route to or from points south, such as Naples, is the southern leg of the Autostrada del Sole (A2). All highways connect with the GRA (Grande Raccordo Anulare), a beltway that encircles Rome and funnels traffic into the city. Markings on the GRA are confusing; take time in advance to study which route into the center best suits you.

Getting Around

The best way to see Rome is to choose an area or a sight that you particularly want to see, reach it by bus or Metro (subway), then explore the area on foot, following one of our itineraries or improvising one to suit your mood and interests. Wear comfortable, sturdy shoes, preferably with bouncy crepe soles to cushion you against the cobblestones. Heed our advice on security, and try to avoid the noise and polluted air of heavily trafficked streets, taking parallel byways wherever possible.

You can buy transportation route maps at newsstands and at ATAC information and ticket booths.

By Metro The subway, or Metro, provides the easiest and fastest way to get around. The Metro opens at 5:30 AM, and the last train leaves each terminal at 11:30 PM. The newer Line A runs from the eastern part of the city, with a stop at San Giovanni Laterano on the way, to Termini station and past Piazza di Spagna and Piazzale Flaminio to Ottaviano, near St. Peter's and the Vatican Museums. Fare is 700 lire. There are change booths and/or complicated ticket machines on station mezzanines; it's best to buy single tickets or books of five or 10 (latter only 6,000 lire) ahead of time at newsstands and tobacco shops. A daily tourist ticket known as a **BIG** is good on buses as well, costs 2,800 lire, and is sold at ATAC ticket booths.

By Bus Orange city buses (and two streetcar lines) run from about 6 AM to midnight, with skeleton *(notturno)* services on main lines throughout the night. The fare is 700 lire; you must buy your ticket before boarding. They are sold singly or in books of five or 10 (latter only 6,000 lire) at tobacco shops and newsstands. A **Biglietto Orario,** valid on all lines for a half-day (either 6 AM—2 PM or 2 PM—midnight) costs 1,000 lire. Weekly tourist tickets cost 10,000 lire and are sold at ATAC booths. When entering a bus, remember to board at the rear, exit at the middle.

By Taxi Taxis wait at stands and, for a small extra charge, can also be called by telephone. The meter starts at 2,800 lire; there are supplements for service after 10 PM, on Sundays and holidays, and for each piece of baggage. Use yellow cabs (with meters) only, and be very sure to check the meter. To call a cab, tel. 3570, 3875, 4994, or 8433.

By Bicycle Bikes provide a pleasant means of getting around when traffic isn't heavy. There are bike rental shops at Via del Pellegrino 89, near Campo dei Fiori, and at Piazza Navona 69, next to Bar Navona. Rental concessions are at the Metro stop of Piazza di Spagna, Piazza del Popolo, Largo San Silvestro, and Largo Argentina. There are also two in Villa Borghese, at Viale della Pineta and Viale del Bambino on the Pincio.

By Moped You can rent a moped or scooter and mandatory helmet at **Scoot-a-Long** (Via Cavour 302, tel. 06/678–0206) or **Scooters For Rent** (Via della Purificazione 66, tel. 06/465485).

Important Addresses and Numbers

Tourist Information The main **EPT** (Rome Provincial Tourist) office is at Via Parigi 5 (tel. 06/463748, open Mon.–Sat. 9–1:30 and 2–7). There also are EPT booths at Termini station and Leonardo da Vinci Airport. A booth on the main floor of the **ENIT** (National Tourist Board) building at Via Marghera 2 (tel. 06/4971222, open weekdays 9–1, Wed. also 4–6) can provide information on destinations in Italy outside Rome.

Consulates U.S.: Via Veneto 121, tel. 06/46741. **Canadian:** Via Zara 30, tel. 06/440–3028. **U.K.:** Via Venti Settembre 80a, tel. 06/475–5441.

Emergencies **Police:** tel. 06/4686; **Carabinieri:** tel. 06/112; **Ambulance:** tel. 06/5100 (Red Cross). **Doctor:** Call your consulate or the private **Salvator Mundi Hospital** (tel. 06/586041), which has an English-speaking staff, for a recommendation. **Pharmacies:** You will find American and British medicines, or their equivalents, and English-speaking personnel at **Farmacia Internazionale Capranica** (Piazza Capranica 96, tel. 06/679–4680), **Farmacia Internazionale Barberini** (Piazza Barberini 49, tel. 06/462996), and **Farmacia Doricchi** (Via Venti Settembre 47, tel. 06/474–1471), among others. They are open 8:30–1 and 4–8; some stay open all night.

English Bookstores You'll find English-language books and magazines at newsstands in the center of Rome, especially on Via Veneto. Also try the **Economy Book and Video Center** (Via Torino 136, tel. 06/474–6877); the **Anglo-American Bookstore** (Via della Vite 57, tel. 06/679–5222), or the **Lion Bookshop** (Via del Babuino 181, tel. 06/360–5837).

Travel Agencies **American Express:** Piazza di Spagna 35, tel. 06/67641. **CIT:** Piazza Repubblica 64, tel. 06/47941. **Wagons-Lits Travel:** Via Buoncompagni 25, tel. 06/481–7545.

Guided Tours

Orientation Tours **American Express** (tel. 06/67641), **CIT** (tel. 06/479–4372), and **Appian Line** (tel. 06/464151) offer three-hour tours in air-conditioned buses with English-speaking guides, covering Rome with four separate itineraries: "Ancient Rome" (including the Roman Forum and Colosseum), "Classic Rome" (including St. Peter's Basilica, Trevi Fountain, and the Janiculum Hill, with its panorama of the city), "Christian Rome" (some major churches and the Catacombs), and the "Vatican Museums and Sistine Chapel." Most tours cost about 30,000 lire, though the Vatican Museums tour is about 35,000 lire. American Express tours depart from Piazza di Spagna, CIT from Piazza della Repubblica, and Appian Line picks sightseers up at their hotel.

American Express can provide a car for up to three persons, limousine for up to seven, and minibus for up to nine, all with English-speaking driver. Guide service is extra. A minibus costs about 250,000 lire for three hours. Almost all operators offer "Rome by Night" tours, with or without dinner and entertainment. Reservations can be made through travel agents.

Special-Interest Tours	You can arrange to attend a public papal audience in the Vatican or at the Pope's summer residence at Castelgandolfo through **CIT** (tel. 06/479–4372), **Appian Line** (tel. 06/464151), or **Carrani** (tel. 06/460510).
Excursions	Most operators offer half-day excursions to Tivoli to see Villa D'Este's fountains and gardens; Appian Line's morning tour to Tivoli also includes Hadrian's Villa and its impressive ancient ruins. Most operators have all-day excursions to Assisi, to Pompeii and/or Capri, and to Florence. CIT also offers excursions to Anzio and Nettuno; its "Etruscan Tour" takes in some fascinating old towns and lovely countryside northwest of Rome.
Personal Guides	Visitors can arrange for a personal guide through **American Express** (tel. 06/67641), **CIT,** or the main **EPT** tourist office (tel. 06/463748).

Exploring Rome

Antiquity is taken for granted in Rome, where successive ages have piled the present on top of the past—building, layering, and overlapping their own particular segments of Rome's 2,500 years of history to form a remarkably varied urban complex. Most of the city's major sights are located in a fairly small area known as the *centro*. At its heart lies ancient Rome, where the Forum and Colosseum stand. It was around this core that the other sections of the city grew up through the ages: medieval Rome, which covered the horn of land that pushes the Tiber toward the Vatican and which extended across the river into Trastevere; and Renaissance Rome, which was erected upon medieval foundations and extended as far as the Vatican, creating beautiful villas on what was then the outskirts of the city.

The layout of the centro is highly irregular, but several landmarks serve as orientation points to identify the areas that visitors will most likely want to see: the Colosseum, the Pantheon and Piazza Navona, St. Peter's, the Spanish Steps, and Villa Borghese. You'll need a good map to find your way around; newsstands offer a wide choice. Energetic sightseers will walk a lot, a much more pleasant way to see the city now that most traffic has been barred from the centro during the day; others might choose to take taxis, buses, or the Metro. The important thing is to relax and enjoy Rome. Don't try to see everything, but do take time to savor its pleasures. If you are in Rome during a hot spell, do as the Romans do: Start out early in the morning, have a light lunch and a long siesta in the hottest hours, then resume sightseeing in the late afternoon and end your evening with a leisurely meal outdoors, refreshed by cold Frascati wine and the *ponentino*, the cool evening breeze.

Ancient Rome *Numbers in the margin correspond with points of interest on the Rome map.*

❶ Your first tour could very well start at the city's center, in **Piazza Venezia.** Behind the enormous marble monument honoring the first king of unified Italy, Victor Emmanuel II, stands the

❷ **Campidoglio** (Capitol Square) on the Capitoline Hill. The majestic ramp and beautifully proportioned piazza are Michelangelo's handiwork, as are the three palaces. **Palazzo Senatorio** at the center is still the ceremonial seat of Rome's city hall; it was built over the Tabularium, where ancient Rome's state archives were kept.

The palaces flanking Palazzo Senatorio contain the **Capitoline Museums.** On the left, the **Museo Capitolino** holds some fine classical sculptures, including the *Dying Gaul*, the *Capitoline Venus*, and a fascinating series of portrait busts of ancient philosophers and emperors. In the courtyard of the **Palazzo dei Conservatori** on the right of the piazza, you can use the mammoth fragments of a colossal statue of the emperor Constantine as amusing props for snapshots. Inside you will find splendidly frescoed salons, as well as sculptures and paintings. *Piazza del Campidoglio, tel. 06/678–2862. Admission: 4,500 lire (ticket valid for both museums). Open Tues.–Fri., 8–1:30 and 5–8, Sat. 8–1:30 and (May–Sept.) 8* PM–11 PM, Sun. 9–1; closed Mon.

The Campidoglio is also the site of the very old church of the **Aracoeli,** which you can reach by way of the stairs on the far side of the Museo Capitolino. Stop in to see the medieval pavement; the Renaissance gilded ceiling that commemorates the victory of Lepanto; some Pinturicchio frescoes; and a much-revered wooden statue of the Holy Child. The Campidoglio gardens offer some good views of the heart of ancient Rome, the Imperial Fora, built when the original Roman Forum became too small for the city's burgeoning needs.

In the valley below the Campidoglio, the **Roman Forum,** once only a marshy hollow, became the political, commercial, and social center of Rome, studded with public meeting halls, shops, and temples. As Rome declined, these monuments lost their importance and eventually were destroyed by fire or the invasions of barbarians. Rubble accumulated, much of it was carted off by medieval home-builders as construction material, and the site reverted to marshy pastureland; sporadic excavations began at the end of the 19th century.

You don't really have to try to make sense of the mass of marble fragments scattered over the area of the Roman Forum. Just consider that 2,000 years ago this was the center of the then-known world, and that much of the history you studied at school happened right here. Wander down the Via Sacra and climb the Palatine Hill, where the emperors had their palaces and where 16th-century cardinals strolled in elaborate Italian gardens. From the belvedere you have a good view of the Circus Maximus. *Entrances on Via dei Fori Imperiali, Piazza Santa Maria Nova and Via di San Gregorio, tel. 06/679–0333. Admission: 5,000 lire. Open Apr.–Sept., Wed.–Mon. 9–6; Oct.–Mar., Wed.–Mon. 9–3; closed Tues.*

Leave the Forum from the exit at Piazza Santa Maria Nova, near the Arch of Titus, and head for the **Colosseum,** inaugurated in AD 80 with a program of games and shows that lasted 100 days. On opening day alone 5,000 wild animals perished in the arena. The Colosseum could hold more than 50,000 spectators; it was faced with marble, decorated with stuccoes, and had an ingenious system of awnings to provide shade. Try to see it both in daytime and at night, when yellow floodlights make it a magical sight. The Colosseum, by the way, takes its name from a colossal, 36-meter (115-foot) statue of Nero that stood nearby. You must pay a fee to explore the upper levels, where you can also see a dusty scale model of the arena as it was in its heyday. *Piazza del Colosseo, tel. 06/735227. Admission: 3,000 lire to upper levels. Open Thurs.–Tues. 9–one hour before sunset, Wed. 9–1.*

Rome

Time Out Facing the Colosseum is **Il Gladiatore,** a handy place for a good, moderately priced lunch. *Piazza del Colosseo 15. Closed Wed.* For delicious ice cream try **Ristoro della Salute,** one of Rome's best *gelaterie. Piazza del Colosseo 2a.*

8 Stroll past the **Arch of Constantine.** The reliefs depict Constantine's victory over Maxentius at the Milvian Bridge. Just before this battle in AD 312 Constantine had a vision of a cross in the heavens and heard the words, "In this sign thou shalt conquer." The victory led not only to the construction of this majestic marble arch but, more importantly, was a turning point in the history of Christianity: Soon afterward a grateful Constantine decreed that it was a lawful religion and should be tolerated throughout the empire.

9 A fairly long but pleasant walk takes you to the **Baths of Caracalla,** which numbered among ancient Rome's most beautiful and luxurious, inaugurated by Caracalla in 217 and used up until the 6th century. An ancient version of a swanky athletic club, the baths were open to the public; citizens could bathe, socialize, and exercise in huge pools and richly decorated halls and libraries, now towering ruins. An open-air opera performance here can be an exciting experience, especially if the opera is *Aïda,* but dress warmly as the night air is very cool and damp. *Via delle Terme di Caracalla. Admission: 3,000 lire. Open Apr.–Sept., Tues.–Sat. 9–6, Sun. and Mon. 9–1; Oct.– Mar., Tues.–Sat. 9–3, Sun.–Mon. 9–1.*

Piazzas and Fountains **Piazza del Popolo** is one of Rome's most vast and airy squares, but for many years it was just an exceptionally beautiful parking lot with a 3,000-year-old obelisk in the middle. Now most **10** traffic and all parking has been barred, and the piazza is open to **11** strollers. The church of **Santa Maria del Popolo** over in the corner of the piazza near the arch is unobtrusive but rich in art, including two stunning Caravaggios in the chapel to the left of the main altar.

Time Out **Rosati** is a café that has never gone out of style, forever a rendezvous of literati, artists, and actors. Its sidewalk tables, tearoom, and new upstairs dining room can revive you with an espresso, snack, lunch, or dinner—all with a hefty price tag, of course! *Piazza del Popolo 4. Closed Tues.*

12 If you're interested in antiques, stroll along **Via del Babuino.** If trendy fashion and accessories suit your fancy, take Via del **13** Corso and turn into **Via Condotti,** Rome's most elegant and expensive shopping street. Here you can ogle fabulous jewelry and designer fashions and accessories in the windows of Buccellati, Ferragamo, Valentino, Gucci, and Bulgari.

Time Out The **Antico Caffè Greco** is a 200-year-old institution, haunt of writers, artists, and well-groomed ladies toting Gucci shopping bags. With its tiny, marble-topped tables and velour settees, it's a nostalgic sort of place—Goethe, Byron, and Liszt were regulars here, and even Buffalo Bill stopped in when his road show came to town. Table service is expensive. *Via Condotti 86. Closed Sun.*

Via Condotti gives you a head-on view of the Spanish Steps in **14** **Piazza di Spagna,** and of the church of **Trinità dei Monti.** In the

center of the piazza is Bernini's **Fountain of the Barcaccia** (Old
Boat) around which Romans and tourists cool themselves on
⑮ hot summer nights. The 200-year-old **Spanish Steps,** named for
the Spanish Embassy to the Holy See, opposite the American
Express office, is a popular rendezvous, especially for the
young people who throng this area. On weekend afternoons,
Via del Corso is packed with wall-to-wall teenagers, and
McDonald's, tucked away in a corner of Piazza di Spagna beyond the American Express office, is a mob scene. In contrast,
Babington's Tea Room, to the left of the Spanish Steps, is a
stylish institution catering to an upscale clientele.

Opposite, on the right of the steps, is the **Keats and Shelley Memorial House,** in which these Romantic poets lived; it's now a
quaint museum. *Piazza di Spagna 26, tel. 06/678–4235. Admission: 4,000 lire. Open Apr.–Sept., weekdays 9–1 and 3–6;
Oct.–Mar., weekdays 9–1 and 2:30–5:30.*

Time Out In a corner of Piazza Mignanelli behind the American Express
office, **La Rampa** is one of the best restaurants in this area. It's
usually crowded, however, and you may have to wait for a table.
Piazza Mignanelli 18. Closed Sun., Mon. lunch.

Head for Via Tritone and cross this heavily trafficked shopping
street into narrow Via della Stamperia, which leads to the
⑯ **Fountain of Trevi,** a spectacular fantasy of mythical sea creatures and cascades of splashing water. Legend has it that
visitors must toss a coin into the fountain to ensure their return
to Rome, but you'll have to force your way past crowds of tourists and aggressive souvenir vendors to do so. The fountain as
you see it was completed in the mid-1700s, but there had been a
drinking fountain on the site for centuries. Pope Urban VIII almost sparked a revolt when he slapped a tax on wine to cover
the expenses of having the fountain repaired. The most recent
restoration, begun in 1989, should be completed by the time
you see it.

⑰ At the top of Via del Tritone, **Piazza Barberini** boasts two fountains by Bernini: the jaunty **Triton** in the middle of the square,
and the **Fountain of the Bees** at the corner of Via Veneto. Decorated with the heraldic Barberini bees, this shell-shaped
fountain bears an inscription that was immediately regarded as
an unlucky omen by the superstitious Romans, for it erroneously stated that the fountain had been erected in the 22nd year
of the reign of Pope Urban VIII, who had commissioned it,
while in fact the 21st anniversary of his election was still some
weeks away. The wrong numeral was hurriedly erased, but to
no avail: Urban died eight days before the beginning of his 22nd
year as pontiff.

⑱ A few steps up Via Quattro Fontane is **Palazzo Barberini,**
Rome's most splendid 17th-century palace, now surrounded by
rather unkempt gardens and occupied in part by the **Galleria
Nazionale di Arte Antica.** Visit the latter to see Raphael's
Fornarina, many other good paintings, some lavishly frescoed
ceilings, and a charming suite of rooms decorated in 1782 on the
occasion of the marriage of a Barberini heiress. *Via Quattro
Fontane 13, tel. 06/475–4591. Admission: 3,000 lire. Open
Mon.–Tues. 9–2, Wed.–Sat. 9–7, Sun. 9–1.*

⑲ One of Rome's oddest sights is the **crypt** of the **Church of Santa
Maria della Concezione** on Via Veneto, just above the Fountain

of the Bees. In four chapels under the main church, the skeletons and scattered bones of some 4,000 dead Capuchin monks are arranged in decorative motifs, a macabre practice peculiar to the bizarre Baroque Age. *Via Veneto 27, tel. 06/462850. Admission: free, but a donation is encouraged. Open daily 9–noon and 3–6.*

The lower reaches of Via Veneto are quiet and sedate, but at the intersection with Via Bissolati, otherwise known as "Airline Row," the avenue comes to life. The big white palace on the right is the U.S. Embassy, and the even bigger white palace beyond it is the luxurious **Hotel Excelsior.** Together with Doney's next door and the Café de Paris across the street, the Excelsior was a landmark of La Dolce Vita, that effervescent period during the 1950s when movie stars, playboys, and exiled royalty played hide-and-seek with press agents and *paparazzi,* ducking in and out of nightclubs and hotel rooms along the Via Veneto. The atmosphere of Via Veneto is considerably more sober now, and its cafés cater more to tourists and expensive pickups than to barefoot cinema *contessas.*

Via Veneto ends at **Porta Pinciana,** a gate in the 12-mile stretch of defensive walls built by Emperor Aurelian in the 3rd century; 400 years later when the Goths got too close for comfort, Belisarius reinforced the gate with two massive towers. Beyond is **Villa Borghese,** most famous of Rome's parks, studded with tall pines that are gradually dying off as pollution and age take their toll. Inside the park, strike off to the right toward the **Galleria Borghese,** a pleasure palace created by Cardinal Scipione Borghese in 1613 as a showcase for his fabulous sculpture collection. In the throes of structural repairs for several years, the now-public gallery is, at press time, only partially open to visitors. It's still worth a visit to see the seductive reclining statue of Pauline Borghese by Canova, and some extraordinary works by Bernini, among them the unforgettable *Apollo and Daphne* in which marble is transformed into flesh and foliage. Until restorations have been completed you won't be able to see Titan's *Sacred and Profane Love* and a number of other fine works in the picture gallery upstairs. *During reconstruction the entrance is on Via Raimondi, reached from Via Pinciana. Via Pinciana (Piazzale Museo Borghese–Villa Borghese), tel. 06/858577. Admission: free for duration of renovations. Open Tues.–Sat. 9–7, Sun. 9–1, Mon. 9–2.*

Castel Sant'Angelo–St. Peter's–Vatican Museums **Ponte Sant'Angelo,** the ancient bridge across the Tiber in front of Castel Sant'Angelo, is decorated with lovely Baroque angels designed by Bernini and offers fine views of the castle and of St. Peter's in the distance. **Castel Sant'Angelo,** a formidable fortress, was originally built as the tomb of Emperor Hadrian in the 2nd century AD. It looked much like the **Augusteo,** or Tomb of Augustus, which still stands more or less in its original form across the river. Hadrian's Tomb was incorporated into the town walls and served as a military stronghold during the barbarian invasions. According to legend it got its present name in the 6th century, when Pope Gregory the Great, passing by in a religious procession, saw an angel with a sword appear above the ramparts to signal the end of the plague that was raging. Enlarged and fortified, the castle became a refuge for the popes, who fled to it along the **Passetto,** an arcaded passageway that links it with the Vatican. Inside the castle you see ancient corridors, medieval cells and Renaissance salons, a museum of antique weapons, courtyards piled with stone cannonballs, and terraces with great views of the city. There's a pleasant bar with outdoor tables on one level. The highest terrace of all, under the newly restored bronze statue of the legendary angel, is the one from which Puccini's heroine, Tosca, threw herself. *Lungotevere Castello 50, tel. 06/687–5036. Admission: 3,000 lire. Open Apr.–Sept., Mon. 3–8, Tues., Wed., Fri. 9–2, Thurs., Sat. 9–7, Sun. 9–1; Oct.–Mar., Tues.–Sat. 9–1, Sun. 9–noon, closed Mon.*

Via della Conciliazione, the broad avenue leading to St. Peter's Basilica, was created by Mussolini's architects by razing blocks of old houses. This opened up a vista of the basilica, giving the eye time to adjust to its mammoth dimensions, and thereby spoiling the effect Bernini sought when he enclosed his vast square (which is really oval) in the embrace of huge quadruple **㉒** colonnades. In **Piazza San Pietro** (St. Peter's Square), which has held up to 400,000 at one time, look for the stone disks in the pavement halfway between the fountains and the obelisk. From this point the colonnades seem to be formed of a single row of columns all the way around.

When you enter Piazza San Pietro (completed in 1667) you are entering Vatican territory. Since the Lateran Treaty of 1929, **Vatican City** has been an independent and sovereign state, which covers about 44 hectares (108 acres) and is surrounded by thick, high walls. Its gates are minded by the Swiss Guards, who still wear the colorful dress uniforms designed by Michelangelo. Sovereign of this little state is John Paul II, 264th Pope of the Roman Catholic Church. At noon on Sunday, the Pope **㉓** appears at his third-floor study window in the **Vatican Palace,** to the right of the basilica, to bless the crowd in the square. *Entry to St. Peter's and the Vatican Museums is barred to those wearing shorts, miniskirts, sleeveless T-shirts, and otherwise revealing clothing. Women should carry scarves to cover bare shoulders and upper arms or wear blouses that come to the elbow. Men should dress modestly, in slacks and shirts.*

㉔ **St. Peter's Basilica** is one of Rome's most impressive sights. It takes a while to absorb the sheer magnificence of it, however, and its rich decoration may not be to everyone's taste. Its size alone is overwhelming, and the basilica is best appreciated when providing the lustrous background for ecclesiastical ceremonies thronged with the faithful. (It is important to note that the Sistine Chapel is part of the Vatican Museums—not St. Peter's.) The original basilica was built in the early 4th century AD by the Emperor Constantine, over an earlier shrine that supposedly marked the burial place of St. Peter. After more than a thousand years, the old basilica was so decrepit it had to be torn down. The task of building a new, much larger one took almost 200 years and employed the architectural genius of Alberti, Bramante, Raphael, Peruzzi, Antonio Sangallo the Younger, and Michelangelo, who died before the dome he had planned had been completed. Finally, in 1626, St. Peter's Basilica was finished.

The basilica is full of extraordinary works of art. Among the most famous is Michelangelo's *Pietà* (1498), seen in the first chapel on the right just as you enter from the square. Michelangelo has four *Pietà*s to his credit. The most famous is entitled simply *Pietà*, and can be seen here. Two others—*Pietà (Deposition from the Cross)* and *Palestrina Pietà (Entombment)*—

are in Florence, and the fourth, the *Rondanini Pietà*, is in Milan.

At the end of the central aisle is the bronze statue of **St. Peter,** its foot worn by centuries of reverent kisses. The bronze throne above the altar in the apse was created by Bernini to contain a simple wood and ivory chair once believed to have belonged to St. Peter. Bernini's bronze *baldacchino* (canopy) over the papal altar was made with metal stripped from the portico of the Pantheon at the order of Pope Urban VIII, one of the powerful Roman Barberini family. His practice of plundering ancient monuments for material to implement his grandiose schemes inspired the famous quip, *"Quod non fecerunt barbari, fecerunt Barberini"* (What the barbarians didn't do, the Barberini did).

As you stroll up and down the aisles and transepts, observe the fine mosaic copies of famous paintings above the altars, the monumental tombs and statues, and the fine stucco work. Stop at the **Treasury** (Historical Museum), which contains some priceless liturgical objects, and take the elevator up to the roof of the basilica. From here you can climb a short interior staircase to the base of the dome for an overhead view of the interior of the basilica. Only if you are in good shape should you attempt the strenuous climb up the narrow, one-way stairs to the balcony of the lantern atop the dome, where the view embraces the Vatican Gardens as well as all of Rome.

The entrance to the **Crypt of St. Peter's** is in one of the huge piers at the crossing. It's best to leave this visit for last, as the crypt's only exit takes you outside the church. The crypt contains chapels and the tombs of many popes. It occupies the area of the original basilica, over the **grottoes,** where evidence of what may be St. Peter's burial place has been found. (Special permission is required to visit the grottoes.) *St. Peter's Basilica, tel. 06/6982. Open daily 7–7. Treasury (Museo Storico-Artistico): entrance in Sacristy. Admission: 2,000 lire. Open Apr.–Sept., daily 9–6; Oct.–Mar., daily 9–3. Roof and Dome: entrance between Gregorian Chapel and right transept. Admission: 3,000 lire, including use of elevator to roof, 2,000 lire if you climb the spiral ramp on foot. Open Apr.–Aug., daily 8–6; Sept.–Mar., daily 8–5. Crypt (Tombs of the Popes): entrance alternates among the piers at the crossing. Admission: free. Open Apr.–Sept., daily 7–6; Oct.–Mar., daily 7–5. Grottoes: Apply several days in advance to Ufficio Scavi, left beyond the Arco delle Campane entrance to the Vatican, left of the basilica, tel. 06/698–5318. Admission: 5,000 lire for 2-hour guided visit, 3,000 lire with tape cassette. Ufficio Scavi office hours: Mon.–Sat. 9–noon and 2–5; closed Sun. and religious holidays.*

For many visitors, a **papal audience** is the highlight of a trip to Rome. The Pope holds mass audiences on Wednesday morning; during the winter they take place in a modern audience hall (capacity 7,000) off the left-hand colonnade. From March to October they are held in **St. Peter's Square,** and sometimes at the papal residence at **Castel Gandolfo.** Since you have to apply for tickets in advance, you may find it easier to arrange for them through a travel agency. *For tickets, apply to the Papal Prefecture (Prefettura), which you reach through the Bronze Door in the right-hand colonnade, tel. 06/6982. Open Tues.*

9–1, Wed. 9–shortly before audience commences. Or arrange for tickets through a travel agent: Carrani Tours, Via V.E. Orlando 95, tel. 06/460510; Appian Line, Via Barberini 109, tel. 06/464151. Admission: about 30,000 lire if booked through an agent or hotel concierge.

25 Guided minibus tours through the **Vatican Gardens** show you some attractive landscaping, a few historical monuments, and the Vatican mosaic school, which produced the mosaics decorating St. Peter's. These tours give you a different perspective on the basilica itself. From March through October, you can choose a garden tour that includes the Sistine Chapel, which you would otherwise see as part of a tour of the Vatican Museums. Vatican Gardens. Tickets at information office, on the left side of St. Peter's Square, tel. 06/698–4466. Open Mon.–Sat. 8 AM–7 PM. Garden tour cost: 9,000 lire. Available Oct.–Mar., Tues., Fri., and Sat.; Nov.–Feb., Tues., Thurs., and Sat. Garden and Sistine Chapel tour cost: 18,000 lire. Available Oct.–Mar., Mon. and Thurs. All tours begin at 10 AM.

From St. Peter's Square information office you can take a shuttle bus (Cost: 1,000 lire) direct to the Vatican Museums. This operates every morning, except Wednesday and Sunday, and saves you the 15-minute walk that goes left from the square and continues along the Vatican walls.

26 The collections in the **Vatican Museums** cover nearly five miles (eight kilometers) of displays. If you have time, allow at least half a day for Castel Sant'Angelo and St. Peter's, and another half-day for the museums. Posters at the museum entrance plot out a choice of four color-coded itineraries; the shortest takes about 90 minutes, the longest more than four hours, depending on your rate of progress. All include the **Sistine Chapel.**

In 1508, Pope Julius II commissioned Michelangelo to fresco the more than 10,000 square feet (930 square meters) of the chapel's ceiling. For four years Michelangelo dedicated himself to painting over fresh plaster, and the result was his masterpiece. The cleaning operations, now completed, have revealed its original and surprisingly brilliant colors.

You can try to avoid the tour groups by going early or late, allowing yourself enough time before the closing hour. In peak season, the crowds definitely detract from your appreciation of this outstanding artistic achievement. Buy an illustrated guide or rent a taped commentary in order to make sense of the figures on the ceiling. A pair of binoculars helps.

The Vatican collections are so rich that unless you are an expert in art history, you will probably want only to skim the surface, concentrating on a few pieces that strike your fancy. If you really want to see the museums thoroughly, you will have to come back again and again. Some of the highlights that might be of interest on your first tour include the Laocoön, the Belvedere Torso, and the Apollo Belvedere, which inspired Michelangelo. The Raphael Rooms are decorated with masterful frescoes, and there are more Raphaels in the Picture Gallery (Pinacoteca). At the Quattro Cancelli, near the entrance to the Picture Gallery, a rather spartan cafeteria provides basic nonalcoholic refreshments. Viale Vaticano, tel. 06/698–3333. Admission: 8,000 lire, free on last Sun. of the month. Open Easter period and July–Sept., weekdays 8:45–4:45, Sat. 8:45–1:45; Oct.–

*June, Mon.–Sat. 8:45–1:45. Ticket office closes 45 minutes be-
fore museums close. Closed Sun., except last Sun. of the
month, and on religious holidays.*

Old Rome Take Via del Plebiscito from Piazza Venezia to the huge **Church
㉗ of the Gesù.** This paragon of Baroque style is the tangible symbol of the power of the Jesuits, who were a major force in the
Counter-Reformation in Europe. Encrusted with gold and precious marbles, the Gesù has a fantastically painted ceiling that
flows down over the pillars, merging with painted stucco figures to complete the three-dimensional illusion.

㉘ On your way to the Pantheon you will pass **Santa Maria Sopra
Minerva,** a Gothic church built over a Roman temple. Inside
there are some beautiful frescoes by Filippo Lippi; outside, a
charming elephant by Bernini with an obelisk on its back.

Originally built in 27 B.C. by Augustus's general Agrippa and re-
㉙ built by Hadrian in the 2nd century AD, the **Pantheon** is one of
Rome's most perfect, best-preserved, and perhaps least appreciated ancient monuments. Romans and tourists alike pay little
attention to it, and on summer evenings it serves mainly as a
backdrop for all the action in the square in front. It represents a
fantastic feat of construction, however. The huge columns of
the portico and the original bronze doors form the entrance to a
majestic hall covered by the largest dome of its kind ever built,
wider even than that of St. Peter's. In ancient times the entire
interior was encrusted with rich decorations of gilt bronze and
marble, plundered by later emperors and popes. *Piazza della
Rotonda. Open Mon.–Sat. 9–2, Sun. 9–1.*

Time Out There are two sidewalk cafés on the square in front of the Pantheon, both good places to nurse a cappuccino while you
observe the scene. On a nearby square is the **Bar
Sant'Eustachio** (Piazza Sant'Eustachio 82), famous for its coffee (which is served with plenty of sugar in it; if you prefer, tell
the counterman you want it without *(senza)* or with only a little
(poco) sugar *(zucchero)*. Serious coffee drinkers also like **Tazza
d'Oro** (Via degli Orfani 84), just off Piazza della Rotonda. And
for a huge variety of ice cream in natural flavors, **Giolitti** (Via
Uffizi del Vicario 40; closed Mon.) is generally considered by
gelati addicts as the best in Rome. It also has good snacks and a
quick-lunch counter.

㉚ Stop in at the church of **San Luigi dei Francesi** on Via della
Dogana Vecchia to see the three paintings by Caravaggio in the
last chapel on the left; have a few hundred-lire coins handy for
the light machine. The clergy of San Luigi considered the artist's roistering and unruly lifestyle scandalous enough, but his
realistic treatment of sacred subjects was just too much for
them. They rejected his first version of the altarpiece and
weren't particularly happy with the other two works either.
Thanks to the intercession of Caravaggio's patron, an influential cardinal, they were persuaded to keep them—a lucky
thing, since they are now recognized to be among the artist's
finest paintings.

㉛ Just beyond San Luigi is **Piazza Navona,** an elongated 17th-
century piazza that traces the oval form of the underlying Circus of Diocletian. At the center, Bernini's lively **Fountain of the
Four Rivers** is a showpiece. The four statues represent rivers in

the four corners of the world: the Nile, with its face covered in allusion to its then unknown source; the Ganges; the Danube; and the River Plate, with its hand raised. And here we have to give the lie to the legend that this was Bernini's mischievous dig at Borromini's design of the facade of the church of **Sant'Agnese in Agone,** from which the statue seems to be shrinking in horror. The fountain was created in 1651; work on the church's facade began some time later. The piazza dozes in the morning, when little groups of pensioners sun themselves on the stone benches and children pedal tricycles around the big fountain. In the late afternoon the sidewalk cafés fill up for the aperitif hour, and in the evening, especially in good weather, the piazza comes to life with a throng of street artists, vendors, tourists, and Romans out for their evening *passeggiata* (promenade).

Time Out   The sidewalk tables of the **Tre Scalini** café (Piazza Navona 30; closed Wed.) offer a grandstand view of this gorgeous piazza. Treat yourself to a *tartufo*, the chocolate ice cream specialty invented here. The restaurant is a pleasant place for a moderately priced lunch. For a more lavish meal, try **Mastrostefano** (Piazza Navona 94, tel. 06/654–1669; closed Mon.), a popular restaurant with a view of the piazza. Prices are at the top of the moderate range. There are a few café tables for those who want just coffee.

③ Across Corso Vittorio is **Campo dei Fiori** (Field of Flowers), the site of a crowded and colorful daily morning market. The hooded bronze figure brooding over the piazza is philosopher Giordano Bruno, who was burned at the stake here for heresy.

③ The adjacent **Piazza Farnese,** with fountains made of Egyptian granite basins from the Baths of Caracalla, is an airy setting for

③ **Palazzo Farnese,** now the French Embassy, one of the most beautiful of Rome's many Renaissance palaces. There are several others in the immediate area: **Palazzo Spada,** a Wedgwood kind of palace encrusted with stuccoes and statues; **Palazzo della Cancelleria,** a massive building that is now the Papal Chancellery, one of the many Vatican-owned buildings in Rome that enjoy extraterritorial privileges; and the fine old palaces along Via Giulia.

This is a section to wander through, getting the feel of daily life carried on in a centuries-old setting, and looking into the dozens of antique shops. Stroll along Via Arenula into a rather gloomy part of Rome bounded by Piazza Campitelli and Lungotevere Cenci, the ancient Jewish ghetto. Among the most interesting sights here are the pretty **Fountain of the Tartarughe** (Turtles) on Piazza Mattei, the **Via Portico d'Ottavia,** with medieval inscriptions and friezes on the old buildings, and the **Teatro di Marcello,** a theater built by Julius Caesar to hold 20,000 spectators.

③ A pleasant place to end your walk is on **Tiberina Island.** To get
③ there, walk across the ancient **Fabricio Bridge,** built in 62 BC, the oldest bridge in the city.

Off the Beaten Track

If the sky promises a gorgeous sunset, head for the **terrace of the Pincio** above Piazza del Popolo, a vantage point prized by Romans.

For a look at a real patrician palace, see the **Galleria Doria Pamphili**, still the residence of a princely family. You can visit the gallery housing the family's art collection and part of the magnificently furnished private apartments, as well. *Piazza del Collegio Romano 1/a, near Piazza Venezia, tel. 06/679–4365. Admission: 2,000 lire; additional 2,000 lire for guided visit of private rooms. Open Tues., Fri., Sat., Sun. 10–1; closed Mon., Wed., and Thurs.*

Make an excursion to **Ostia Antica,** the well-preserved Roman port city near the sea, as rewarding as an excursion to Pompeii, and much easier to get to from Rome. There's a regular train service from the Ostiense station (Piramide Metro stop). *Via dei Romagnoli, Ostia Antica, tel. 06/565–1405. Admission: 4,000 lire. Open daily 9–two hours before sunset.*

Delve into the world of the Etruscans, who inhabited Italy even in pre-Roman times and have left fascinating evidence of their relaxed, sensual lifestyle. Visit the **Museo Nazionale di Villa Giulia,** in a gorgeous Renaissance mansion with a full-scale Etruscan temple in the garden. You'll see a smile as enigmatic as that of the Mona Lisa on deities and other figures in terra cotta, bronze, and gold. Ask especially to see the **Castellani collection of ancient jewelry** hidden away on the upper floor. *Piazza di Villa Giulia 9, tel. 06/360–1951. Admission: 4,000 lire. Open Tues.–Sat. 9–7, Sun. 9–1; closed Mon.*

Shopping

Gift Ideas Shopping in Rome is part of the fun, no matter what your budget. The best buys are leather goods of all kinds, from gloves to handbags and wallets to jackets, silk goods, and quality knitwear. Shops are closed on Sunday and on Monday morning; in July and August, they close Saturday afternoon as well.

Antiques A well-trained eye will spot some worthy old prints and minor antiques in the city's fascinating little shops. For prints, browse among the stalls at **Piazza Fontanella Borghese;** at **Casali,** Piazza della Rotonda 81a, at the Pantheon; and **Tanca,** Salita de'Crescenzi 10, also near the Pantheon. For minor antiques, **Via dei Coronari** and other streets in the **Piazza Navona** area are good. The most prestigious antiques dealers are situated in **Via del Babuino** and its environs.

Boutiques Via Condotti, directly across from the Piazza di Spagna, and the streets running parallel to Via Condotti, as well as its cross streets, form the most elegant and expensive shopping area in Rome. Lower-price fashions may be found on display at shops on Via Frattina and Via del Corso.

Shopping Districts In addition to those mentioned, Romans themselves do much of their shopping along **Via Cola di Rienzo** and **Via Nazionale.**

Religious Articles These abound in the shops around St. Peter's, on **Via di Porta Angelica** and **Via della Conciliazione,** and in the souvenir shops tucked away on the roof and at the crypt exit in St. Peter's itself.

Department Stores You'll find a fairly broad selection of women's, men's, and children's fashions and accessories at the **Rinascente** stores on Piazza Colonna and at Piazza Fiume (the latter with a good housewares department in the basement), and at the **Coin** department store on Piazzale Appio near San Giovanni Laterno.

The **UPIM** and **Standa** chains have shops all over the city that offer medium-quality, low-price goods.

Food and Flea The open-air markets at **Piazza Vittorio** and **Campo dei Fiori**
Markets are colorful sights. The flea market held at **Porta Portese** on Sunday morning is stocked mainly with new or second-hand clothing. If you go, beware of pickpockets and purse snatchers.

Dining

There are plenty of fine restaurants in Rome serving various Italian regional cuisines and international specialties with a flourish of linen and silver, as well as a whopping *conto* (check) at the end. If you want family-style cooking and prices, try the *trattorias*, usually smallish and unassuming, often family-run places. Fast-food places and Chinese restaurants are proliferating in Rome; very few can be recommended. Fixed-price tourist menus can be scanty and unimaginative. The lunch hour in Rome lasts from about 1 to 3 PM, dinner from 8 or 8:30 to about 10:30, though some restaurants stay open much later. During August many restaurants close for vacation.

For details and price category definitions, *see* Dining in Staying in Italy.

Very Expensive **Le Restaurant.** The resplendent dining room of the Grand ho-
★ tel's restaurant is a model of 19th-century opulence, lavish with fine damasks and velvets, crystal chandeliers, and oil paintings. The menu varies with the seasons; there is always a daily recommended menu. Among the specialties are *carpaccio tiepido di pescatrice* (brill with thin slices of raw beef) and *medaglioni di vitello al marsala con tartufo* (veal medallions with marsala wine and truffles). The wine list offers some majestic vintages. *Via Vittorio Emanuele Orlando 3, tel. 06/4709. Reservations advised. DC, MC, V. Closed Aug.*

La Terrazza dell'Eden. The Eden Hotel's rooftop restaurant is a favorite haunt of Italian politicians and other powerbrokers drawn by the classic regional Italian cooking and breathtaking views. Entirely redecorated in soft colors and period furnishings, the dining room and adjacent bar have acquired new elegance and style. Terrace space has been doubled for outdoor dining and for gourmet buffet brunches on balmy weekends. As we go to press (spring 1989), a new brigade of chefs is drawing up a menu offering a wide range of fine Italian specialties and some strictly Roman dishes. The wine list promises to be exceptionally good. *Eden Hotel, Via Ludovisi 49; tel. 06/474–3551, ext. 437. Dinner reservations advised. AE, DC, MC, V.*

★ **El Toulà.** On a little byway off Piazza Nicosia in Old Rome, El Toulà has the warm, welcoming atmosphere of a 19th-century country house, with white walls, antique furniture in dark wood, heavy silver serving dishes, and spectacular arrangements of fruits and flowers. There's a cozy little bar off the entrance where you can sip a *prosecco*, the aperitif best suited to the chef's Venetian specialties, among them the classic *pasta e fagioli* (bean soup), risotto with radicchio, and *fegato alla veneziana* (liver with onions). *Via della Lupa 29/b, tel. 06/687–3750. Reservations required. AE, DC, MC, V. Closed Sat. lunch, Sun., Aug., and Dec. 24–26.*

Expensive **Alberto Ciarla.** Located on a large square in Trastevere, scene
★ of a busy morning food market, Alberto Ciarla is one of Rome's

best seafood restaurants. In contrast with its workaday location, the ambience is upscale, with red-and-black decor. Bubbling aquariums, a sure sign that the food is super-fresh, are set around the wall. Seafood salads are a specialty. Meat eaters will find succor in the house pâté and the lamb. *Piazza San Cosimato 40, tel. 06/581–8668. Reservations required. AE, DC, MC, V. Closed lunch, all day Sun., Aug. 5–25, and Christmas.*

★ **Andrea.** Ernest Hemingway and King Farouk used to eat here; FIAT motors supremo Gianni Agnelli and other Italian powerbrokers still do. A half-block off Via Veneto, Andrea offers classic Italian cooking in an intimate, clubby ambience in which snowy table linens gleam against a discreet background of dark green paneling. The menu features delicacies such as homemade *tagliolini* (thin noodles) with shrimp and spinach sauce, spaghetti with seafood and truffles, and mouthwatering *carciofi all'Andrea* (artichokes simmered in olive oil). *Via Sardegna 26, tel. 06/493707. Reservations advised. AE, DC, MC, V. Closed Sun. and most of Aug.*

Coriolano. The only tourists who find their way to this classic restaurant near Porta Pia are likely to be gourmets looking for quintessential Italian food—that means light homemade pastas, choice olive oil, and market-fresh ingredients, especially seafood. Although seafood dishes vary, *tagliolini all'aragosta* (thin noodles with lobster sauce) is usually on the menu, as are *porcini* mushrooms (in season) cooked to a secret recipe. The wine list is predominantly Italian but includes some French and California wines. *Via Ancona 14, tel. 06/861122. Reservations advised. No credit cards. Closed Sun. and Aug. 1–25.*

Piperno. Located in the old Jewish ghetto next to historic Palazzo Cenci, Piperno has been in business for more than a century. It is *the* place to go for Rome's extraordinary *carciofi alla giudia*, crispy-fried artichokes, Jewish-style. You eat in three small, wood-paneled dining rooms or, in fair weather, at one of a handful of tables outdoors. Try *filetti di baccala* (cod fillet fried in batter), *pasta e ceci* (a thick soup of pasta tubes and chickpeas), and *fiori di zucca* (stuffed zucchini flowers)—but don't miss the *carciofi. Monte dei Cenci 9, tel. 06/654–2772. Reservations advised. No credit cards. Closed Sun. dinner, Mon., Christmas, Easter, and Aug.*

★ **Ranieri.** On a quiet street off fashionable Via Condotti near the Spanish Steps, this historic restaurant was founded by a one-time chef of Queen Victoria. It remains a favorite with tourists for its traditional atmosphere and decor, with damask-covered walls, velvet banquettes, crystal chandeliers, and old paintings. Among the many specialties on the vast menu are *gnocchi alla parigina* (souffléed gnocchi with tomato and cheese sauce) and *mignonettes alla Regina Vittoria* (veal with pâté and cream). *Via Mario de' Fiori 26, tel. 06/679–1592. Reservations advised. AE, DC, MC, V. Closed Sun.*

Il Veliero. The attractive sailing ship decor of this top fish restaurant near Piazza Farnese sets the scene for seafood feasts accompanied by fresh-baked bread from a wood-burning oven. There are many types of pasta and risotto, with shellfish or squid to follow the splendid choice of seafood *antipasti.* For your main course, try grilled or baked fish, or succulent Mediterranean crayfish, scampi, or shrimp. Have the bluefish if it's on the menu. *Via Monserrato 32, tel. 06/654–2636. Reservations advised. AE, DC, V. Closed Mon.*

Moderate **Colline Emiliane.** Located near Piazza Barberini, the Colline Emiliane is an unassuming trattoria offering exceptionally good food. Behind an opaque glass facade, there are a couple of plain little dining rooms where you are served light homemade pastas, a very special chicken broth, and meats ranging from pot roast to *giambonetto di vitella* (roast veal) and *cotoletta alla bolognese* (veal cutlet with cheese and tomato sauce). *Via degli Avignonesi 22, tel. 06/475-7538. Reservations advised. No credit cards. Closed Fri.*

Pierluigi. Pierluigi, in the heart of Old Rome, is a longtime favorite: On busy evenings it's almost impossible to find a table, so make sure you reserve well in advance. Seafood predominates—if you fancy a splurge, try the lobster—but traditional Roman dishes are offered, too, such as *orecchiette con broccoli* (disk-shaped pasta with greens) or just simple spaghetti. In summer eat in the pretty piazza. *Piazza dei Ricci 144, tel. 06/686-1302. Reservations advised. AE. Closed Mon. and 2 weeks in Aug.*

★ **Quattro Mori.** Quattro Mori is probably the best Sardinian restaurant in town. The menu includes a tempting *antipasto* selection, then a choice between such Sardinian pastas as *malloreddus* (small shells made of semola), *culingiones* (vegetarian ravioli), and *spaghetti all'aragosta* (with lobster sauce). Second courses offer either meat or fish, including the Sardinian *maialino* (roast piglet) and the Roman *pajata* (baby lamb innards). For dessert, try *sebadas* (fried cheese-filled ravioli doused with honey). *Via Santa Maria delle Fornaci 8/a (near the Vatican , tel. 06/632609. Reservations advised. No credit cards. Closed Mon. and Aug. 10–Sept. 4.*

★ **Romolo.** Generations of Romans have enjoyed the romantic garden courtyard and historic dining room of this charming Trastevere haunt, the Fornarina, reputedly once home of Raphael's ladylove. In the evening, strolling musicians serenade diners. The cuisine is appropriately Roman; specialties include *mozzarella alla fornarina* (deep-fried mozzarella with ham and anchovies) and *braciolette d'abbachio scottadito 'a(grilled baby lamb chops)*. Alternatively, try one of the new vegetarian pastas featuring *darciofi* (artichokes) or *radicchio* (the fashionalbe reddish leaf). *Via di Porta Settimiana 8, tel. 06/581-8284. Reservations advised. AE, DC, V. Closed Mon. and Aug. 2–23.*

★ **Vecchia Roma.** The frescoed walls of this historic restaurant located in a one-time palace in Old Rome, and the specialties— among them *fettucine verdi* (spinach-flavored pasta with cream sauce) and *petti pollo con gamberi di fiume* (chicken breasts with freshwater shrimp)—have long made this a classic choice of resident foreigners and sophisticated travelers. In summer you dine under white umbrellas. *Piazza Campitelli 18, tel. 06/ 656-4604. Reservations advised. No credit cards. Closed Wed. and Aug.*

Inexpensive **Baffetto.** Rome's best-known inexpensive pizza restaurant is
★ plainly decorated and *very* popular: You'll probably have to wait in line outside on the *sampietrini*—the cobblestones. The interior is mostly given over to the ovens, the tiny cash desk, and the simple paper-covered tables. *Bruschetta* (toast) and *crostini* (mozzarella toast) are the only variations on the pizza them. Expect to share a table. *Via del Governo Vecchio 114, tel. 06/686-1617. Reservations not accepted. No credit cards. Closed lunch, Sun., and all of Aug.*

★ **L'Eau Vive.** This is an offbeat choice for an inexpensive lunch, but be aware that prices rise sharply in the evening. The restaurant is run by trainee Catholic missionaries, many from developing countries. The food is predominantly French. Order one of the fixed-price menus; they are among Rome's best-kept gastronomic secrets. You may have to hunt for the inconspicuous entrance, a little door hard by the entrance to Palazza Lante, just off Piazza Sant'Eustachio near the Pantheon. *Via Monterone 85, tel. 06/654–1095. Reservations advised. AE, DC, V. Closed Sun. and 2 weeks in Aug.*

Hostaria Farnese. This is a tiny trattoria between Campo dei Fiori and Piazza Farnese, in the heart of Old Rome. Papa serves, Mamma cooks and, depending on what they've picked up at the Campo dei Fiori market, you may find *rigatoni* with tuna and basil, spaghetti with vegetable sauce, *spezzatino*(stew), and other homey specialties. *Via dei Baullari 109, tel. 06/654–1595. Reservations advised. AE, V. Closed Thurs.*

Pollarola. Located near Piazza Navona and Campo dei Fiori, this typical Roman trattoria has (artificial) flowers on the tables and an antique Roman column embedded in the rear wall, evidence of its historic site. You can eat outdoors in fair weather. Try a pasta specialty such as *fettucine alla gorgonzola* (noodles with creamy gorgonzola sauce) and a mixed plate from the temptingly fresh array of antipastos. The house wine, white or red, is good. *Piazza della Pollarola 24 (Campo dei Fiori), tel. 06/6541654. Reservations advised for groups. AE, V. Closed Sun.*

Lodging

The list below covers mostly those hotels that are within walking distance of at least some sights, and which are handy to public transportation. Those in the Moderate and Inexpensive categories do not have restaurants but serve Continental breakfast. Rooms on street level can get traffic noise throughout the night, and few hotels in the lower categories have double glazing. Ask for a quiet room, or bring earplugs!

We strongly recommend that you always make reservations in advance. Should you find yourself in the city without reservations, however, contact one of the following EPT offices: at Fiumicino Airport (tel. 06/601–1255); Termini train station (tel. 06/475–0078); on the A1 autostrada at the Feronia service area (tel. 0765/255465); and on the A2 autostrada at the Roma-Sud Frascati service area (tel. 06/946–4341; summer only).

For details and price category definitions, *see* Lodging in Staying in Italy.

Very Expensive **Cavalieri Hilton.** Though it is outside the main part of Rome and a taxi ride to wherever you are going, this is a large elegant resort hotel set in its own park and with an excellent restaurant. *Via Cadlolo 101, tel. 06/31511. 387 rooms with bath. Facilities: restaurant, pool, terrace. AE, DC, V.*

Grand. This 100-year-old establishment, located between Termini station and Via Veneto, caters to an elite international clientele. The spacious guest rooms are decorated in Empire style, with smooth fabrics and thick carpets in blue and pale gold tones. Crystal chandeliers and marble baths add luxurious notes. Afternoon tea is served daily in the split-level main lounge. One of Italy's most beautiful dining rooms, Le Restaurant, is here as well (*see* Dining). *Via Vittorio Emanuele Orlando 3, tel. 06/4709. 170 rooms with bath. Facilities: 2 bars, 2 restaurants. AE, DC, MC, V.*

★ **Hassler-Villa Medici.** Guests can expect a cordial atmosphere and magnificent service at this hotel, just at the top of the Spanish Steps. The public rooms are memorable, especially the first-floor bar (a chic city rendezvous), and the glass-roof lounge, with gold marble walls and hand-painted tile floor. The elegant bedrooms are decorated in a variety of classic styles; some feature frescoed walls. *Piazza Trinità dei Monti 6, tel. 06/ 679–2651. 101 rooms with bath. Facilities: bar, restaurant. AE.*

Lord Byron. The most elegant hotel in Rome is the Lord Byron. Located in the diplomatic residential section of Rome away from its bustling center, the small villa has neat, fresh, and cheerful bedrooms that do, however, tend to be small. The staff offers the best service in any Rome hotel, and its dining room has extremely creative Italian cooking that has earned its two Michelin stars. *Via de Notaris 5, tel. 06/360–9541. 55 rooms with bath. Facilities: bar, restaurant, garden. AE, DC, V.*

Expensive **Eden.** Just off the Via Veneto, the Eden celebrated its centenary in 1989, having renovated three of its four floors. The uncluttered decor is a fun mix of antiques, Art Deco, and streamlined modern, augmented by mirrors and marbles. Rooms on the upper floors have terrific views (the best is from the penthouse bar and restaurant). *Via Ludovisi 49, tel. 06/ 474–3551. 93 rooms with bath. Facilities: bar and restaurant. AE.*

Forum. A centuries-old palace converted into a fine hotel, the Forum is on a quiet street within hailing distance of the Roman Forum and Piazza Venezia. The wood-paneled lobby and street-level bar are warm and welcoming, as are the smallish, pink-and-beige bedrooms. The view of the Colosseum from the rooftop restaurant is superb: Breakfast here—or a nightcap at the roof bar—can be memorable. *Via Tor dei Conti 25, tel. 06/ 6792446. 80 rooms with bath. Facilities: bar, restaurant. AE, DC, MC, V.*

★ **Valadier.** Once famous as an elite bordello, the Valadier will appeal to guests with a taste for understated luxury. Bedrooms feature textured fabrics in light blue and beige with black accents, while mirrored walls, indirect lighting, and sleek bathrooms heighten the effect. Suite 308 and room 201 are among the larger rooms in what is bound to become one of Rome's classiest little hotels. The 300-year-old building is a short walk from the Spanish Steps. *Via della Fontanella 15, tel. 06/361–0592. 46 rooms with bath. Facilities: bar, restaurant. AE, DC, MC, V.*

Victoria. Oriental rugs, oil paintings, welcoming armchairs, and fresh flowers add charm to the public rooms of this hotel, a favorite of American businessmen who prize the personalized service and restful atmosphere. Some upper rooms and the roof terrace overlook the Villa Borghese. *Via Campania 41, tel. 06/ 473931. 150 rooms with bath. Facilities: bar, restaurant. AE, DC, MC, V.*

Moderate **Gregoriana.** Bedroom decor at this former convent near the Spanish Steps is low-key enough, but the owners have gone wild in the public rooms: Two floors have leopard-skin wallpaper; the third has a splashy floral print; and the lobby is decked out in rattan. Reserve well in advance: The Gregoriana is popular with the high-fashion crowd. *Via Gregoriana 18, tel. 06/699 -4269. 19 rooms with bath. No credit cards.*

★ **Internazionale.** Within easy walking distance of many downtown sights, this has long been one of Rome's best midsize hotels. Decor throughout is in soothing pastel tones, with some antique pieces, mirrors, and chandeliers heightening the English country-house look. Guests relax in small, homey lounges downstairs and begin the day in the pretty breakfast room. *Via Sistina 79, tel. 06/679-3047. 40 rooms with bath. AE, DC, MC, V.*

Inexpensive **Ausonia.** This small pension has big advantages in its location
★ on Piazza di Spagna and in its helpful management and family atmosphere. Six rooms face the famous square (quieter now that most through traffic has been banished); all others face the inner courtyard. Furnishings are simple, but standards of cleanliness are high, and rates are low. The hotel has many American guests; make sure you make reservations well in advance. *Piazza di Spagna 35, tel. 06/679-5745. 10 rooms, none with bath. No credit cards.*

Suisse. The mood in the Suisse's public rooms may be old-fashioned—the check-in desk is distinctly drab—but bedrooms, while small, are cheerful enough, with bright bedspreads, framed prints, and some charming old furniture. Some rooms face the (fairly) quiet courtyard. There's an upstairs breakfast room, but no restaurant. *Via Gregoriana 56, tel. 06/678-3649. 28 rooms, half with bath. No credit cards.*

The Arts

Pick up a copy of the *Carnet di Roma* at EPT tourist offices; issued monthly, it's free and has an exhaustive listing of scheduled events and shows. The bi-weekly booklet *Un Ospite a Roma;* free from your hotel concierge, is another source of information. If you want to go to the opera, ballet, or to a concert, it's best to ask your concierge to get tickets for you. They are on sale at box offices only, just a few days before performances.

Opera The **Teatro dell'Opera** is on Via del Viminale (tel. 06/463641); the summer season at the **Baths of Caracalla** in July and August is famous for spectacular performances amid the Roman ruins. Tickets are on sale at the opera box office or at the box office at Caracalla (*see* Exploring).

Concerts The main concert hall is the **Accademia di Santa Cecilia** (Via della Conciliazione 4, tel. 06/654-1044). The Santa Cecilia Symphony Orchestra has a summer season of concerts in the splendid setting of **Piazza del Campidoglio.**

Film The only English-language movie theater in Rome is the **Pasquino** (Vicolo del Piede, just off Piazza Santa Maria in Trastevere, tel. 06/580-3622). The program is listed in Rome daily newspapers.

Entertainment and Nightlife

Rome's "in" nightspots change like the flavor of the month, and many fade into oblivion after a brief moment of glory. The best source for an up-to-date list is the weekly entertainment guide

"Trovaroma" published each Saturday in the Italian daily *La Repubblica*.

Bars Jacket and tie are in order in the elegant **Blue Bar** of the Hostaria dell'Orso (Via dei Soldati 25, tel. 06/656–4221), and in **Le Bar** of the Grand Hotel (Via Vittorio Emanuele Orlando 3, tel. 06/4709). **Harry's Bar** (Via Veneto 150, tel. 06/474–5832) is popular with American businessmen and journalists residing in Rome.

Young Romans favor **Calisé** (Piazza Mastai 7, tel. 06/5809404) in Trastevere, where sandwiches and salads, as well as drinks, are available until 3 AM. Current favorites around the Pantheon, a hub of after-dark activity, include **Le Cornacchie** (Piazza Rondanini 53, tel. 06/656–4485), where Roman yuppies hang out, and **Hemingway** (Piazza delle Coppelle 10, tel. 06/654–4135), which attracts a crowd from the movie, TV, and fashion world. Both are open evenings only, but until very late.

Discos and Nightclubs There's deafening disco music for an under-30s crowd at the **Acropolis** (entrance at Via Luciani 52, tel. 06/870504). Special events such as beauty pageants and theme parties are a feature, and there's a restaurant on the premises. **Jackie-O** (Via Boncompagni 11, tel. 06/461401) has long been a favorite of the wealthy, who party to disco music, dine in La Graticola restaurant, or sip drinks in the cocktail lounge. Sports personalities and other celebrities are attracted to **Veleno** (Via Sardegna 27, tel. 06/493583), one of the few places in Rome to offer black dance music, including disco, rap, funk, and soul.

Singles Scene Locals and foreigners of all nations and ages gather at Rome's cafés on **Piazza della Rotonda** in front of the Pantheon, at **Piazza Navona;** and **Piazza Santa Maria** in Trastevere. The cafés on **Via Veneto** and the bars of the big hotels draw tourists mainly and are good places to meet other travelers in the over-30 age group. In fair weather, under-30s will find crowds of contemporaries on the **Spanish Steps,** where it's easy to strike up a conversation.

Florence

Arriving and Departing

By Plane The nearest, medium-size airport is the Galileo Galilei Airport at Pisa (tel. 050/28088), connected with Florence by train direct from the airport to the Santa Maria Novella Station. Service is hourly through the day and takes about 60 minutes. Some domestic and a few European flights use Florence's Peretola Airport (tel. 055/3498), connected by bus to the downtown area.

By Train The main train station is Santa Maria Novella Station, abbreviated SMN on signs. There is an Azienda Transporti Autolinee Fiorentina (ATAF) city bus information booth in the station, as well as an Informazione Turistiche Alberghiere (ITA) hotel association booth, where you can get hotel information and bookings.

By Bus The bus terminal is near Santa Maria Novella train station.

By Car The north–south access route to Florence is the Autostrada del Sole (A1) from Milan or Rome. The Florence—Mare autostrada

(A11) links Florence with the Tyrrhenian coast, Pisa, and the A12 coastal autostrada.

Getting Around

On Foot You can see most of Florence's major sights on foot, as they are packed into a relatively small area in the city center. It's best not to plan to use a car in Florence; most of the center is off-limits and ATAF buses will take you where you want to go. Wear comfortable shoes and wander to your heart's content. It is easy to find your way around in Florence. There are so many landmarks that you cannot get lost for long. The system of street numbers is unusual, with commercial addresses written with a red "r" and residential addresses in blue (32/r might be next to or even a block away from 32 blue).

By Bus ATAF city buses run from about 5:15 AM to 1 AM. Buy tickets before you board the bus; they are on sale singly or in books of five at many tobacco shops and newsstands. Cost is 600 lire for one ride, 700 lire for a ticket good for 70 minutes on all lines. An all-day ticket (*giornaliero*) costs 2,500 lire.

By Taxi Taxis wait at stands. Use only authorized cabs, which are white with a yellow stripe or rectangle on the door. The meter starts at 2,000 lire. To call a taxi, tel. 055/4798 or 055/4390.

By Bicycle You can rent a bicycle at **Ciao e Basta**, on Via Alamanni, on the stairway side of the train station; at **Free Motor**, Via Santa Monaca 6/r, tel. 055/295102; and at Piazza Pitti and Fortezza da Basso.

By Moped For a moped, go to **Program**, Borgo Ognissanti 135/r, tel. 055/262724; or to Free Motor (*see* By Bicycle).

Important Addresses and Numbers

Tourist Information The municipal tourist office has a booth outside the railway station. The **Azienda Autonoma Turismo (AAT)** tourist board is at Via Tornabuoni 15 (tel. 055/216544; open Mon.–Sat. 9–1). The **Ente Provinciale per il Turismo (EPT)** provincial tourist board has an information office at Via Manzoni 16 (tel. 055/247–8141; open Mon.–Sat. 8:30–1:30).

Consulates U.S.: Lungarno Vespucci 38, tel. 055/298276. U.K.: Lungarno Corsini 2, tel. 055/284133.

Emergencies **Police:** tel. 113. **Ambulance:** (Red Cross) tel. 055/215381. **Doctor:** Call your consulate for recommendations, or call the **Tourist Medical Service** (tel. 055/475411), associated with IAMAT, for English-speaking medical assistance 24 hours a day. **Pharmacies:** There are 24-hour pharmacies at Via Calzaiuoli 7/r (tel. 055/263490); Piazza San Giovanni 20/4 (tel. 055/284013); and at the train station (tel. 055/263435).

English Bookstores You'll find English-language magazines and paperbacks on the newsstands in Piazza della Repubblica. **The Paperback Exchange** (Via Fiesolana 31/r, tel. 055/247–8154), in the Santa Croce area, has new and used paperbacks for sale. **The BM Bookshop** (Borgognissanti 4/r, tel. 055/294575) has a good selection of English-language books.

Travel Agencies **American Express:** Via Guicciardini 49/r, tel. 055/278751. **CIT:** Via Cavour 54/r, tel. 055/294306. **Wagons-Lits:** Via del Giglio 27/r, tel. 055/218851.

Guided Tours

Orientation Tours **American Express** (tel. 055/278751), **CIT** (tel. 055/294306), and **SITA** (tel. 055/214721) offer three-hour tours in air-conditioned buses. Two tours cover most of the important sights: The morning itinerary gives you a look at the outside of the cathedral, baptistry, and bell tower, takes you to the Accademia to see Michelangelo's *David*, to Piazzale Michelangelo for the view, and then to the Pitti Palace to visit the Palatine Gallery; the afternoon tour includes Piazza della Signoria, a visit to the Uffizi Gallery and to Santa Croce, and an excursion to Fiesole. Cost is about 30,000 lire for a three-hour tour, including entrance fees, and can be booked through travel agents.

The 45-minute "Florence Experience" program is a fine way to get oriented, at the **Edison Cinema** (Piazza della Repubblica). Admission is 8,000 lire and it is shown every hour on the hour, weekdays 9–5, weekends 9–3. During July and August it's shown daily 9 AM–10 PM.

Personal Guides **American Express** (tel. 055/278751) can arrange for limousine or minitours and personal guide services. **Europedrive** (Via Tartini 7, tel. 055/351025) will provide cars with English-speaking drivers.

Special-Interest Tours Inquire at travel agents or at **Agriturist** (Piazza San Firenze 3, tel. 055/287838) for visits to villa gardens around Florence from April to June, or for visits to farm estates during September and October.

Excursions Operators offer a half-day excursion to Pisa, usually in the afternoon, and a full-day excursion to Siena and San Gimignano, costing about 30,000 lire and 40,000 lire, respectively. Pick up a timetable at ATAF information offices in the train station, at Piazza Duomo 57/r (tel. 055/580528), or at the AAT Tourist Office (*see* Tourist Information in Important Addresses and Numbers).

Exploring Florence

Founded by Julius Caesar, Florence has the familiar grid pattern common to all Roman colonies. Except for the major monuments, which are appropriately imposing, the buildings are low and unpretentious. It is a small, compact city of ocher stone and pale plaster; its narrow streets open unexpectedly into spacious squares populated by strollers and pigeons. At its best, it has a gracious and elegant air, though it can at times be a nightmare of mass tourism. Plan, if you can, to visit Florence in late fall, early spring, or even in winter, to avoid the crowds.

A visit to Florence is a visit to the living museum of Italian Renaissance. The Renaissance began right here in Florence, and the city bears witness to the proud spirit and unparalleled genius of its artists and artisans. In fact, there is so much to see that it is best to savor a small part rather than attempt to absorb it all in a muddled vision.

Numbers in the margin correspond with points of interest on the Florence map.

Piazza del Duomo and the Piazza della Signoria

❶ The best place to begin a tour of Florence is **Piazza del Duomo,** where the cathedral, bell tower and baptistry stand in the rather cramped square. The lofty **cathedral of Santa Maria del Fiore** is one of the longest in the world. Begun by master sculptor and architect Arnolfo di Cambio in 1296, its construction took 140 years to complete. Gothic architecture predominates; the facade was added in the 1870s but is based on Tuscan Gothic models. Inside, the church is cool and austere, a fine example of the architecture of the period. Among the sparse decorations, you should take a good look at the frescoes of equestrian monuments on the left wall; that on the right is by Paolo Uccello, the one on the left is by Andrea del Castagno. The dome frescoes by Vasari have been hidden by the scaffolding put up some years ago in order to study a plan for restoring the dome itself, Brunelleschi's greatest architectural and technical achievement. It was also the inspiration of such later domes as Michelangelo's dome for St. Peter's in Rome and even the Capitol in Washington. You can climb to the cupola gallery, 463 fatiguing steps up between the two skins of the double dome for a fine view of Florence and the surrounding hills. *Dome entrance is in the left aisle of cathedral. Admission: 3,000 lire. Open Mon.–Sat. 10–5. Cathedral open Mon.–Sat. 10–5, Sun. 2:30–5.*

❷ Next to the cathedral is Giotto's 14th-century **bell tower,** richly decorated with colored marble and fine sculptures (the originals are in the Museo dell'Opera del Duomo). The 414-step climb to the top is less strenuous than that to the cupola. *Piazza del Duomo. Admission: 3,000 lire. Open Apr.–Sept., daily 9–7; Oct.–Mar., daily 9–5.*

❸ In front of the cathedral is the **baptistry,** one of the city's oldest and most beloved edifices, where, since the 11th century, Florentines have baptized their children. Pollution is threatening the bronze reliefs on the baptistry's three portals, and had so badly affected those by Ghiberti's on the doors facing the cathedral (dubbed "The Gate of Paradise" by Michelangelo), they **❹** are being restored and relocated to the **Museo dell'Opera del Duomo** (Cathedral Museum). The museum contains some superb sculptures by Donatello and Luca della Robbia—especially their *cantorie,* or choir decorations—as well as an unfinished *Pietà* by Michelangelo, which he intended for his own tomb. *Piazza del Duomo 9, tel. 055/213229. Admission: 3,000 lire. Open Mar.–Sept., Mon.–Sat. 9–6; Oct.–Feb., Mon. –Sat. 9–8, Sun. 9–1.*

❺ Stroll down fashionable Via Calzaiuoli to the church of **Orsanmichele,** for centuries an odd combination of first-floor church and second-floor wheat granary. The statues in the niches on the exterior constitute an anthology of the work of eminent Renaissance sculptors, including Donatello, Ghiberti, and Verrocchio, while the tabernacle inside is an extraordinary piece by Andrea Orcagna. In 1990 parts of the building may still be under wraps for restoration.

Continuing another two blocks along Via Calzaiuoli you come upon **Piazza della Signoria,** the heart of Florence, and the city's largest square. It's now being torn up in patches to be repaved. In the process, well-preserved remnants of Roman and medieval Florence have come to light, and there's talk of creating an underground museum so that these can still be seen after the square has been repaved. In the center of the square a slab

marks the spot where in 1497 Savonarola—the Ayatollah Khomeini of the Middle Ages—induced the Florentines to burn their pictures, books, musical instruments, and other worldly objects—and where a year later he was hanged and then burned at the stake as a heretic. The square, the **Neptune Fountain** by Ammanati, and the surrounding cafés are popular gathering places for Florentines and for tourists who come to admire the massive **Palazzo della Signoria,** better known as the
❻ **Palazzo Vecchio,** the copy of Michelangelo's *David* on its steps, and the frescoes and art works in its impressive salons. *Piazza della Signoria, tel. 055/27681. Admission: 4,000 lire; Sun. free. Open weekdays 9–7, Sun. 8–1; closed Sat.*

Time Out Stop in at **Riviore,** a Florentine institution, for some of its delectable ice cream and/or chocolate goodies. *Piazza della Signoria 5/r.*

If you'd like to do a little shopping, make a brief detour off Piazza della Signoria to the **Loggia del Mercato Nuovo** on Via
❼ Calimala. It's crammed with souvenirs and straw and leather goods at reasonable prices; bargaining is acceptable here. *Open Mon.–Sat. 8–7 (closed Mon. AM).*

❽ If time is limited, this is your chance to visit the **Uffizi Gallery,** which houses Italy's most important collection of paintings. (Try to see it at a more leisurely pace, though—it's too good to rush through!) The Uffizi Palace was built to house the administrative offices of the Medics, one-time rulers of the city. Later, their fabulous art collection was arranged in the Uffizi Gallery on the top floor, which was opened to the public in the 17th century—making this the world's first public gallery of modern times. The emphasis is on Italian, especially Italian Gothic or Renaissance art. Make sure you see the works by Giotto, and look for the Botticellis in Rooms X–XIV, Michelangelo's *Holy Family* in Room XXV, and the works by Raphael next door. In addition to its art treasures, the gallery offers a magnificent close-up view of Palazzo Vecchio's tower from the little coffee bar at the end of the corridor. *Loggiato Uffizi 6, tel. 055/218341. Admission: 5,000 lire. Open Tues.– Sat. 9–7, Sun. 9–1.*

Accademia, San Marco, San Lorenzo, Santa Maria Novella
❾ Start at the **Accademia Gallery,** and try to be first in line at opening time so you can get the full impact of Michelangelo's *David* without having to fight your way through the crowds. Skip the works in the exhibition halls leading to the *David;* they are of minor importance and you'll gain a length on the tour groups. Michelangelo's statue is a tour de force of artistic conception and technical ability, for he was using a piece of stone that had already been worked on by a lesser sculptor. Take time to see the forceful *Slaves,* also by Michelangelo; the rough-hewn, unfinished surfaces contrast dramatically with the highly polished, meticulously carved *David.* Michelangelo left the *Slaves* "unfinished" for the aesthetic power that accentuates their trying to escape the bondage of stone. *Via Ricasoli 60, tel. 055/214375. Admission: 4,000 lire. Open Tues.–Sat. 9–2, Sun. 9–1.*

You can make a detour down Via Cesare Battisti to Piazza Santissima Annunziata to see the arcade of the **Ospedale degli Innocenti** (Hospital of the Innocents) by Brunelleschi, with
❿ charming roundels by Andrea della Robbia, and the **Museo**

724

Archeologico (Archaeological Museum) on Via della Colonna, under the arch. It has some fine Etruscan and Roman antiquities, and a pretty garden. *Via della Colonna 36, tel. 055/247–8641. Admission: 3,000 lire. Open Tues.–Sat. 9–2, Sun. 9–1.*

⑪ Retrace your steps to Piazza San Marco and the **Museo di San Marco,** housed in a 15th-century Dominican monastery. The unfortunate Savonarola meditated on the sins of the Florentines here, and Fra Angelico decorated many of the austere cells and corridors with his brilliantly colored frescoes of religious subjects. (Look for his masterpiece, *The Annunciation.*) Together with many of his paintings arranged on the ground floor, just off the little cloister, they form an interesting collection. *Piazza San Marco 1, tel. 055/210741. Admission: 3,000 lire. Open Tues.–Sat. 9–2, Sun. 9–1.*

⑫ Lined with shops, Via Cavour leads to **Palazzo Medici Riccardi,** a massive Renaissance mansion (*see* Off the Beaten Track).
⑬ Turn left here to the elegant **Church of San Lorenzo,** with its Old Sacristy designed by Brunelleschi, and two pulpits by Donatello. Rounding the left flank of the church, you'll find yourself in the midst of the sprawling **San Lorenzo Market,** dealing in everything and anything, including some interesting leather items. *Piazza San Lorenzo, Via dell'Ariento. Open Tues.–Sat. 8–7.*

Time Out On Via Sant'Antonio near the big covered food market, **Palla d'Oro** is a favorite with market workers for a quick sandwich or plate of pasta, which they usually eat standing at the counter. You can sit at the tables in the back for an extra charge. It's impossibly crowded between 1 and 1:30. *Via Sant'Antonino 45/r. Closed Sun.*

⑭ Enter the **Medici Chapels** from Piazza Madonna degli Aldobrandini, behind San Lorenzo. These remarkable chapels contain the tombs of practically every member of the Medici family, and there were a lot of them, for they guided Florence's destiny from the 15th century to 1737. Cosimo I, a Medici whose acumen made him the richest man in Europe, is buried in the crypt of the Chapel of the Princes, and Donatello's tomb is next to that of his patron. The chapel upstairs is decorated in an eye-dazzling array of colored marble. In Michelangelo's New Sacristy, his tombs of Giuliano and Lorenzo Medici bear the justly famed statues of *Dawn* and *Dusk*, and *Night* and *Day*. *Piazza Madonna degli Aldobrandini, tel. 055/213206. Admission: 4,350 lire. Open Tues.–Sat. 9–2, Sun. 9–1.*

Time Out **Baldini** is an unpretentious trattoria, low on atmosphere but offering a good range of antipasti and delicious *fazzoletti*, pasta filled with ricotta and spinach. *Via Panzani 57. Closed Wed.*

You can take either Via Panzani or Via del Melarancio to the
⑮ large square next to the massive church of **Santa Maria Novella,** a handsome building in the Tuscan version of Gothic style. See it from the other end of Piazza Santa Maria Novella for the best view of its facade. Inside are some famous paintings, especially Masaccio's *Trinity*, a Giotto crucifix in the sacristy, and Ghirlandaio's frescoes in the apse. *Piazza Santa Maria Novella, tel. 055/210113. Open Mon.–Sat. 7–11:30 and 3:30–6, Sun. 7–11:30 and 3:30–5.*

Next door to the church is the entrance to the **cloisters,** worth a visit for their serene atmosphere and the restored Paolo Uccello frescoes. *Piazza Santa Maria Novella 19, tel. 055/282187. Admission: 3,000 lire. Open Mon.–Thurs., Sat. 9–2, Sun. 8–1.*

Only a few blocks behind Piazza della Signoria is the **Bargello,** a fortresslike palace that served as residence of Florence's chief magistrate in medieval times, and later as a prison. Don't be put off by its grim look, for it now houses Florence's **Museo Nazionale** (National Museum), a treasure house of Italian Renaissance sculpture. In a historically and visually interesting setting, it displays masterpieces by Donatello, Verrochio, and Michelangelo, and many other major sculptors. This museum is on a par with the Uffizi, so don't shortchange yourself on time. *Via del Proconsolo 4, tel. 055/210801. Admission: 3,000 lire. Open Tues.–Sat. 9–2, Sun. 9–1.*

Time Out From Piazza San Firenze follow Via degli Anguillara or Borgo dei Greci toward Piazza Santa Croce. Don't miss the chance to taste what's held by many to be the best ice cream in Florence at **Vivoli,** on a little side street, the second left off Via degli Anguillara as you head toward Santa Croce. *Via Isole delle Stinche 7/r. Closed Mon.*

The mighty church of **Santa Croce** was begun in 1294; inside, Giotto's frescoes brighten two chapels and monumental tombs of Michelangelo, Galileo, Machiavelli, and other Renaissance luminaries line the walls. In the adjacent museum, you can see what remains of a Giotto crucifix, irreparably damaged by a flood in 1966, when water rose to 16 feet in parts of the church. The **Pazzi Chapel** in the cloister is an architectural gem by Brunelleschi. *Piazza Santa Croce, tel. 055/244619. Church open Mon.–Sat. 7–12:30 and 3–6:30, Sun. 3–6. Opera di Santa Croce (Museum and Pazzi Chapel), tel. 055/244619. Admission: 2,000 lire. Open Mar.–Sept., Thurs.–Tues. 10–12:30 and 2:30–6:30; Oct.–Feb., Thurs.–Tues. 10–12:30 and 3–5.*

The monastery of Santa Croce harbors a leather-working school and showroom, with entrances at Via San Giuseppe 5/r and Piazza Santa Croce 16. The entire Santa Croce area is known for its leather factories and inconspicuous shops selling gold and silver jewelry at prices much lower than those of the elegant jewelers near Ponte Vecchio.

Time Out You have several eating options here. For ice cream, the **bar** on Piazza Santa Croce has a tempting selection. If it's a snack you're after, the **Fiaschetteria** (Via dei Neri 17/r) makes sandwiches to order and has a choice of antipasti and a hot dish or two. **Da Marco,** between Santa Croce and the Arno, is a typical trattoria, where you can either eat downstairs or outdoors. (Via dei Benci 13/r. Closed Mon.)

Now head for **Ponte Vecchio,** Florence's oldest bridge. It seems to be just another street lined with goldsmiths' shops until you get to the middle and catch a glimpse of the Arno flowing below. Spared during World War II by the retreating Germans (who blew up every other bridge in the city), it also survived the 1966 flood. It leads into the **Oltrarno district,** which has its own charm and still preserves much of the atmosphere of oldtime Florence, full of fascinating craft workshops.

But for the moment you should head straight down Via
⑲ Guicciardini to **Palazzo Pitti**, a 15th-century extravaganza that
the Medicis acquired from the Pitti family shortly after the latter had gone deeply into debt to build it. Its long facade on the
immense piazza was designed by Brunelleschi: Solid and severe, it looks like a Roman aqueduct turned into a palace. The
palace houses several museums: One displays the fabulous
Medici collection of objects in silver and gold; another is the
Gallery of Modern Art. The most famous museum, though, is
the **Palatine Gallery,** with an extraordinary collection of paintings, many hung frame-to-frame in a clear case of artistic
overkill. Some are high up in dark corners, so try to go on a
bright day. *Piazza Pitti, tel. 055/210323. Gallery of Modern
Art. Admission: 4,000 lire. Palatine Gallery. Admission:
3,000 lire (includes state apartments). Silver Museum. Admission: 3,000 lire. Porcelain Museum. Admission: 3,000 lire.
Historical Costume Gallery. Admission 3,000 lire. All open
Tues.–Sat. 9–2, Sun. 9–1.*

⑳ Take time for a refreshing stroll in the **Boboli Gardens** behind
Palazzo Pitti, a typical Italian garden laid out in 1550 for
Cosimo Medici's wife, Eleanor of Toledo. *Piazza dei Pitti, tel.
213440. Admission: free. Open May–Sept., daily 9–6:30; Oct.
and Mar.–Apr., 9–5:30; Nov.–Feb., 9–4:30.*

In the far corner of Piazza dei Pitti, poets Elizabeth Barrett
㉑ and Robert Browning lived at no. 9 **Casa Guidi,** facing the smaller Piazza San Felice.

Time Out From Piazza San Felice it's not far to the **Caffè Notte,** a wine
and sandwich shop featuring a different salad every day (corner
of Via della Caldaia and Via della Chiesa). For more substantial
sustenance, go to the **Cantinone del Gallo Nero,** an
atmosphereic wine cellar where Chianti is king and locals lunch
on soups, pastas, and salads (Via Santo Spirito 6/r. Closed
Mon.). The street directly opposite Palazzo Pitti's main entrance leads into Via Michelozzi, where **La Casalinga** is a
favorite neighborhood trattoria (Via Michelozzi 9/r. Closed
Sun.).

㉒ The church of **Santo Spirito** is important as one of
Brunelleschi's finest architectural creations, and it contains
some superb paintings, including a Filippino Lippi *Madonna.*
Santo Spirito is the hub of a colorful neighborhood of artisans
and intellectuals. An **outdoor market** enlivens the square every
morning except Sunday; in the afternoon, pigeons, pet owners,
and pensioners take over. The area is definitely on an upward
trend, with new cafés, restaurants, and upscale shops opening
every day.

Walk down Via Sant'Agostino and Via Santa Monaca to the
㉓ church of **Santa Maria del Carmine,** of no architectural interest
but of immense significance in the history of Renaissance art.
It contains the celebrated frescoes painted by Masaccio in the
Brancacci Chapel, unveiled not long ago after a lengthy and meticulous restoration. The chapel was a classroom for such
artistic giants as Botticelli, Leonardo da Vinci, Michelangelo,
and Raphael, since they all came to study Masaccio's realistic
use of light and perspective, and his creation of space and
depth. *Piazza del Carmine. Church open Mon.–Sat. 9–noon
and 4–5, Sun. 4–5.*

Time Out The small trattoria on the square has a friendly atmosphere and is a delightful spot where you can eat outdoors and enjoy the view. *Piazza del Carmine 18/r. Closed Sat. evening and Sun.*

Off the Beaten Track

Few tourists get to see one of Florence's most precious works of art, Benozzo Gozzoli's glorious frescoes in the tiny chapel on the second floor of **Palazzo Medici Riccardi**, representing the Journey of the Magi as a spectacular cavalcade with Lorenzo the Magnificent on a charger. *Via Cavour 1, tel. 055/27601. Admission: free. Open Mon.–Tues., Thurs.–Sat. 9–12:30 and 3–5, Sun. 9–noon.*

One of Europe's oldest **botanical gardens,** founded in 1545, is a pleasant place for a pause; gardening hobbyists will enjoy the **Botanical Museum** next door, although it may be closed for restoration in 1990. *Via Micheli 3, tel. 055/284696. Admission: free. Open Mon., Wed., Fri. 9–noon.*

The **English Cemetery** is on a cypress-studded knoll in the middle of heavily trafficked Piazza Donatello, not far from the botanical garden. Here you can walk with the shades of Elizabeth Barrett Browning, Algernon Swinburne, and other poets. You will need to ask the custodian to let you into the cemetery. It is kept locked. *Piazza Donatello. Ring bell at entrance for admission.*

Take afternoon tea with the Florentines at **Giacosa,** an elegant café at Via Tornabuoni 83/r, or in the plush salon of the **Hotel Excelsior** on Piazza Ognissanti.

Take the no. 13 bus from the train station or cathedral up to Piazzale Michelangelo, then walk along Viale dei Colli and climb to **San Miniato al Monte,** a charming green-and-white marble Romanesque church full of artistic riches.

Visit the **synagogue** on Via Farini and the **Jewish Museum** next door, which contains antique scrolls and ritual objects. *Via Farini 4; tel. 055/245252. Admission: free. To visit, telephone for an appointment.*

Shopping

Gift Ideas Florence offers top quality for your money in leather goods, linens and upholstery fabrics, gold and silver jewelry, and cameos. Straw goods, gilded wooden trays and frames, hand-printed paper desk accessories, and ceramic objects make good inexpensive gifts. Many shops offer fine old prints.

Shopping Districts The most fashionable streets in Florence are **Via Tornabuoni** and **Via della Vigna Nuova.** Goldsmiths and jewelry shops can be found on and around **Ponte Vecchio** and in the **Santa Croce area,** where there is also a high concentration of leather shops.

Antiques Most of Florence's many antiques dealers are located in **Borgo San Jacopo** and **Borgo Ognissanti,** but you'll find plenty of small shops throughout the center of town.

Department Stores **Principe,** in Piazza Strozzi, is a quality apparel store incorporating several designer boutiques. At the other end of the price range, **UPIM**, in Piazza della Repubblica and various other locations, has inexpensive goods of all types.

Markets The big food market at **Piazza del Mercato Centrale** is open in the morning (Mon.–Sat.) and is worth a visit. The **San Lorenzo market** on Piazza San Lorenzo and Via dell'Ariento is a fine place to browse for buys in leather goods and souvenirs (open Tues. and Sat. 8–7; also Sun. in summer). The **Mercato del Porcellino,** Piazza del Mercato Nuovo, takes its name from the famous bronze statue of a boar at one side, and is packed with stalls selling souvenirs and straw goods (open Tues.–Sat. 8–7; closed Sun. and Mon. morning in winter). There's a colorful neighborhood market at **Sant'Ambrogio,** Piazza Ghiberti (open Mon.–Sat. morning), and a permanent flea market at **Piazza Ciompi** (open Mon.–Sat. 9–1 and 4–7, Sun. 9–1 in summer).

Dining

Mealtimes in Florence are 12:30–2 and 7:30–9 or later. Many Moderate and Inexpensive places are small and you may have to share a table. Reservations are always advisable; to find a table at inexpensive places, get there early.

For details and price category definitions, *see* Dining in Staying in Italy.

Very Expensive **Cestello.** The restaurant of the hotel Excelsior has a lovely setting, whether you dine on the rooftop terrace overlooking the Arno in the summer, or in a ritzy salon with coffered ceiling, pink linen tablecloths, and antique paintings in the winter. The menu features such deliciously visual delights as *linguine con rughetta e scampi* (flat spaghetti with chicory and shrimps) and *tagliata di manzo con mosaico di insalatine* (sliced beef on a bed of salad greens arranged in a mosaic pattern). *Piazza Ognissanti 3, tel. 055/294301. Reservations advised in summer. AE, DC, MC, V.*

★ **Enoteca Pinchiorri.** In the beautiful Renaissance palace and its charming garden courtyard that was home to Giovanni da Verrazzano (a 15th-century Florentine navigator), husband-and-wife team Giorgio Pinchiorri and Annie Feolde have created an exceptional restaurant that ranks as one of Italy's best. Guests can enjoy Annie's rediscoveries of traditional Tuscan dishes, or her own brand of imaginatively creative nouvelle cuisine, while Giorgio oversees the extraordinary wine cellar. There is a moderately priced luncheon menu. *Via Ghibellina 87, tel. 055/242777. Reservations well in advance are advised at all times. AE, DC, V. Closed Sun., Mon. lunch, Aug.*

★ **Terrazza Brunelleschi.** The rooftop restaurant of the hotel Baglioni has the best view in town. The dining room, in creamy tones and with a floral carpet, has big picture windows; the summer-dining terrace is charming, with tables under arbors, and turrets for guests to climb to get an even better view. The menu offers traditional Tuscan dishes such as *minestra di fagioli* (bean soup), and other more innovative choices, such as a pâté of peppers and tomato. *Hotel Baglioni, Piazza Unità Italiana 6, tel. 055/215642. Reservations advised, especially in summer. AE, DC, MC, V.*

Expensive **Cammillo.** This is a classic Florentine eating place, with terracotta tiles on the floor and several brick-vaulted rooms where guests enjoy regional and international specialties such as chicken livers with sage and beans, or curried scampi. The menu usually features truffled dishes as well. The excellent house wine and olive oil are made by the owners. *Borgo San Jacopo 57/r, tel. 055/212427. Reservations advised; required for dinner Easter–Oct. AE, DC, MC, V. Closed Wed., Thurs.; 3 weeks in Aug.; 3 weeks in Dec.–Jan.*

★ **Da Noi.** Located near Santa Croce, Da Noi has a reputation as one of Florence's best for creative cuisine and a relaxed atmosphere. It's small, seating only 28 in a dining room whose dark antique sideboards contrast with rustic white walls. The cooking reflects French influences; among the specialties are crêpes with a sauce of peppers, and warm squab salad. *Via Fiesolana 46/r, tel. 055/242917. Reservations required; call 3 days ahead. No credit cards. Closed Sun., Mon., Aug.*

★ **Sabatini.** One of Florence's finest for many years, Sabatini upholds the tradition very well. Classic Florentine decor, with dark wood-paneled walls, terra-cotta floors, and white linen tablecloths, is brightened by the paintings on the walls and by a cordial welcome. Specialties on the menu, which offers both Tuscan and international cuisine, are *panzerotti alla Sabatini* (creamy, cheese-filled crêpes) and baked spinach with a chicken liver sauce. *Via Panzani 9/a, tel. 055/211559. Reservations advised. AE, DC, MC, V. Closed Mon.*

Moderate **Buca Mario.** Visitors can expect to share a table at this characteristically unadorned *buca* (downstairs trattoria), whose menu includes such hearty down-to-earth Tuscan food as homemade *pappardelle* (noodles) and *stracotto* (beef stew with beans). It's near Santa Maria Novella Station. *Piazza Ottaviani 16/r, tel. 055/214179. Reservations not accepted. AE, V. Closed, Wed., Thurs. lunch, and Aug.*

Il Fagioli. This typical Florentine trattoria near Santa Croce has a simple decor and a menu in which local dishes such as *ribollita* (a sort of minestrone) and *arista* (roast pork) predominate. The antipasti are always tempting here. *Corso Tintori 47/r, tel. 055/244285. Dress: informal. Reservations advised. No credit cards. Closed Sun., also Sat. in summer, Aug.*

Leo. Located in the Santa Croce area, Leo serves tourists (especially at lunch) and locals in an attractive setting of vaulted ceilings and dark Tuscan-style wooden chairs. Order the daily specials here and the *crostini Pier Capponi* (toast rounds with a savory topping) and *Lombatina alla Leo* (veal chop with mushrooms, asparagus, and truffle). *Via Torta 7/r, tel. 055/210829. Dinner reservations advised. AE, DC, MC, V. Closed Mon. and mid-July–mid-Aug.*

Mario da Ganino. Highly informal, rustic, and cheerful, this trattoria greets you with a taste of mortadella, and offers homemade pastas and *gnudoni* (ravioli without pasta), plus a heavenly cheesecake for dessert. There are plenty of other taste-tempters on the menu. It's tiny, seating only 35, double that in summer at outdoor tables. *Piazza dei Cimatori 4/r, tel. 055/214125. Reservations advised. AE, DC. Closed Sun. and Aug. 15–25.*

Inexpensive **Angiolino.** You won't regret taking a meal at this bustling little
★ trattoria, which has a real charcoal grill and an old woodburning stove to keep its customers warm on nippy days. Glowing with authentic atmosphere, Angiolino offers Tuscan specialties such as *ribollita* (minestrone) and juicy *bistecca alla fiorentina* (T-bone steak basted in olive oil and black pepper).

The bistecca will push the bill up into the Moderate range. *Via Santo Spirito 36/r, tel. 055/298976. Reservations advised in the evening. No credit cards. Closed Sun. dinner, Mon., and last 3 weeks in July.*

Caminetto. Try the *maccheroni alla Maremmana* (pasta with sausages, tomato, and black olive) or *pappa al pomodoro* (tomato and bread soup) in the typically rustic setting of Caminetto. It's very handy for a quick lunch before or after visiting the cathedral. *Via dello Studio 34/r, tel. 055/296274. Dinner reservations advised. No credit cards. Closed Tues., Wed., and July.*

Lodging

What with mass tourism and trade fairs, rooms are at a premium in Florence for most of the year. Make reservations well in advance. If you arrive without a reservation, the ITA office in the railway station (open 8:20–9) can help you, but there may be a long line. Now that most traffic is banned in the downtown area, hotel rooms are quieter. Local traffic and motorcycles can still be bothersome, however, so check the decibel level before you settle in.

For details and price category definitions, *see* Lodging in Staying in Italy.

Very Expensive **Excelsior.** One of the flagships of the CIGA chain, the Excelsior
★ provides consistently superlative service and is lavishly appointed with old prints, bouquets of flowers, pink marble, and carpets so deep you could lose a shoe in them. The hotel occupies a former patrician palace on the Arno, and many rooms have river views (some with Tuscan antiques scattered around as well). The Cestello restaurant (*see* Dining) is excellent. *Piazza Ognissanti 3, tel. 055/264201. 205 rooms with bath. Facilities: garage. AE, DC, MC, V.*

Regency. One of the Ottaviani family's small, select hotels, the Regency has the intimate and highly refined atmosphere of a private villa, luxuriously furnished with antiques and decorated with great style. Just outside the historic center of the city, it has a charming garden and the pleasant Le Jardin restaurant. *Piazza Massimo d'Azeglio 3, tel. 055/245247. 31 rooms with bath. Facilities: garage. AE, DC, MC, V.*

Villa Cora. Located in a residential area on a hill overlooking the Oltrano section of Florence and across the Arno to the Duomo and Bell Tower, the Villa Cora is a converted private villa. Furnishings are exquisite and the atmosphere is quietly elegant. There are gardens in which to stroll, a pool in which to wallow, and a formal but charming restaurant in which to dine. There is a Mercedes shuttle service between the hotel and the center of Florence. *Viale Machiavelli 18, tel. 055/229–8451. 48 rooms with bath. AE, DC, V.*

Expensive **Baglioni.** Spacious, elegant, and very grand, Baglioni has well-
★ proportioned rooms tastefully decorated in antique Florentine style. Many rooms have leaded glass windows, and some have views of Santa Maria Novella. The hotel also has a charming roof terrace, and the splendid Terrazza Brunelleschi restaurant (*see* Dining), which has the best view in all Florence (the food is memorable, too). *Piazza Unità d'Italia 6, tel. 055/218441. 195 rooms with bath. Facilities: garage. AE, DC, MC, V.*

Bernini Palace. The atmosphere here is one of austere yet elegant simplicity: Rooms are unostentatious but well-furnished in pastel fabrics and mahogany furniture. Entirely air-conditioned and double-glazed, the Bernini has a quiet, tranquil feel, yet is only a few steps from the frenetically busy Piazza della Signoria. There is no restaurant, but breakfast is served in a historic salon. *Piazza San Firenze 29, tel. 055/ 278621. 86 rooms with bath. AE, DC, MC, V.*

Grand Hotel Minerva. A modern building just around the corner from the train station, the Minerva will suit travelers who care more for efficiency than atmosphere. The nicest rooms overlook the garden, and the rooftop pool provides a refreshing diversion. *Piazza Santa Maria Novella 16, tel. 055/284555. 111 rooms with bath. Facilities: pool. AE, DC, MC, V.*

★ **Monna Lisa.** This place is the closest you may come to living in an aristocratic palace in the heart of Florence. American visitors in particular are fond of its smallish but homey bedrooms, and sumptuously comfortable sitting rooms. Ask for a room on the quiet 17th-century courtyard, especially the one with a delightful balcony. A lavish buffet breakfast is included in the price. Make reservations months in advance to be assured of a room at this very special pension. *Borgo Pinti 27, tel. 055/247–9751. 20 rooms with bath. Facilities: garden, bar. AE, DC, MC, V.*

Moderate **Calzaiuoli.** While there's an elegant entrance on the pedestrians-only shopping street connecting the cathedral with Piazza della Signoria, don't expect distinctive decor once you're inside (it's actually anemic modern). Still, you couldn't ask for anything more central. *Via dei Calzaiuoli 6, tel. 055/ 212456. 37 rooms with bath. Facilities: bar. AE, DC.*

★ **Loggiato dei Serviti.** You'll find the Loggiato dei Serviti tucked under an arcade in one of the city's quietest and most attractive squares. Vaulted ceilings and tasteful furnishings (some of them antiques) go far to make this hotel a real find for those who want to get the genuine Florentine feel and who will appreciate the 19th-century town house surroundings while enjoying modern creature comforts. There is no restaurant. *Piazza Santissima Annunziata 3, tel. 055/219165. 20 rooms with bath. No credit cards.*

Porta Rossa. This period piece is only a few steps from the Porcellino straw market and the city's major sights. The authentic Art Nouveau lobby gives a clue to the age of this establishment, as do the worn carpets and creaky plumbing. But it exudes atmosphere; most of the rooms are spacious and comfortable in an old-fashioned way, and a lot of discerning people love it. There is no restaurant. *Via di Porta Rossa 19, tel. 055/287551. 71 rooms, half with bath. AE, DC, MC, V.*

Inexpensive **Liana.** Located in a residential neighborhood, this small hotel is within walking distance of most sights. It's a dignified 19th-century town house with pleasant rooms on the garden. *Via Vittorio Alfieri 18, tel. 055/245785. 20 rooms, 16 with bath. Facilities: parking lot, garden. No credit cards.*

Palazzo Vecchio. The Vecchio presents a fine example of minimal decor in an otherwise attractive 19th-century building. It's close to the train station, and the proprietor owns a restaurant a block or two away. *Via Cennini 4, tel. 055/212182. 18 rooms, 16 with bath. Facilities: parking lot. AE, DC, MC, V.*

The Arts

For a list of events, pick up a *Florence Concierge Information* booklet from your hotel desk, or the monthly information bulletin published by the **Comune Aperto** city information office (available at the booth in front of the train station).

Music and Ballet Most major musical events are staged at the **Teatro Comunale** (Corso Italia 16, tel. 055/277–9236). The box office (closed Monday) is open from 9 to 1, and a half-hour before performances. It's best to order your tickets by mail, however, as they're difficult to come by at the last minute. You can also order concert and ballet tickets through **Universalturismo** (Via degli Speziali 7/r, tel. 055/217241). **Amici della Musica** (Friends of Music) puts on a series of concerts at the **Teatro della Pergola** (box office, Via della Pergola 10a/r, tel. 055/247–9651). For program information, contact the Amici della Musica directly at Via Sirtori 49 (tel. 055/608420).

Film English-language films are shown at the **Cinema Astro**, on Piazza San Simone near Santa Croce. There are two shows every evening, Tuesday through Sunday. It closes in July.

Entertainment and Nightlife

Piano Bars Many of the top hotels have piano bars; that of the **Plaza Lucchesi** (Lungarno della Zecca Vecchia 38, tel. 055/264141) is particularly spacious and pleasant. The terrace of the hotel **Baglioni** (*see* Lodging) has no music but has one of the best views in Florence, candlelit tables, and a wonderful atmosphere. **Loggia Tornaquinci** (Via Tornabuoni 6, tel. 055/219148) is a sophisticated cocktail lounge with yet another soul-stirring view.

Nightclubs **The River Club** (Lungarno Corsini 8, tel. 055/282465) has winter-garden decor and a large dance floor (closed Sunday). **Central Park** (Via Fosso Macinante 13, tel. 055/356723), in the Cascine park, is the sophisticated summer premises of the Yab Yum disco (*see* below), open from May to September.

Discos **Jackie O** (Via dell'Erta Canina 24a, tel. 055/234–2443) is a glittering Art Deco disco with cream leather upholstery, lots of mirrors and marble, and a trendy clientele (closed Wed.). **Space Electronic** (Via Palazzuolo 37, tel. 055/293082) is exactly what its name implies: ultramodern and psychedelic (closed Mon.). **Yab Yum** (Via Sassetti 5/r, tel. 055/282018) is another futuristic-style disco popular with the young international set. It's closed Monday and May through September, when it moves to the Cascine (*see* above).

Tuscany

Tuscany is a blend of rugged hills, fertile valleys, and long stretches of sandy beaches that curve along the west coast of central Italy and fringe the pine-forested coastal plain of the Maremma. The gentle, cypress-studded green hills may seem familiar: Leonardo and Raphael often painted them in the backgrounds of their masterpieces. The cities and towns of Tuscany house the centuries-old heritage of culture and art that produced magnificent medieval cathedrals and the marvels of the

Renaissance. Come to Tuscany to enjoy its unchanged and gracious atmosphere of good living, and, above all, its unparalleled artistic treasures, many still in their original settings in tiny old churches and patrician palaces.

Getting Around

By Train The main train network connects Florence with Arezzo and Prato. Another main line runs to Pisa, while a secondary line goes via Lucca.

By Bus The entire region is crisscrossed by bus lines, good alternatives to trains, especially for reaching Siena. Use local buses to tour the many pretty hill towns around Siena such as San Gimignano, and then take a train or LFI bus from Siena to Arezzo, where you can get back onto the main Rome-Florence train line.

By Car The main autostrade run parallel to the train routes. Roads throughout Tuscany are in good condition, though often narrow.

Guided Tours

American Express (Via Guicciardini 49/r, tel. 055/278751) operates one-day excursions to Siena and San Gimignano out of Florence, and can arrange for cars, drivers, and guides for special-interest tours in Tuscany. **CIT** (Via Cavour 56, tel. 055/294306) has a three-day Carosello bus tour from Rome to Florence, Siena, and San Gimignano, as well as a five-day tour that also takes in Venice.

Tourist Information

Arezzo. Piazza Risorgimento 116, tel. 0575/20839.
Cortona. Via Nazionale 72, tel. 0575/603056.
Lucca. Via Vittorio Veneto 40, tel. 0583/43639; Vecchia Porta San Donat (Piazzale Verdi), tel. 0583/53592.
Pisa. Piazza del Duomo, tel. 050/560–4641.
Pistoia. Piazza del Duomo, tel. 0573/21622.
Prato. Via Cairoli 48, tel. 0574/24112.
Siena. Via Montanini 92, tel. 0577/47051; Piazza del Campo 56, tel. 0577/280551.

Exploring Tuscany

Prato Since the Middle Ages, **Prato** has been Italy's major textile-producing center: It now supplies the country's knitwear and fashion industries. Ignore the drab industrial outskirts and devote some time to the fine old buildings in the downtown area, crammed with artworks commissioned by Prato's wealthy merchants during the Renaissance. The **Duomo** (cathedral), erected in the Middle Ages, was decorated with paintings and sculptures by some of the most illustrious figures of Tuscan art, among them Fra Filippo Lippi, who took 12 years to complete the frescoes in the apse (perhaps because in the meantime he was being tried for fraud, as well as wooing the nun with whom he then eloped). Look in particular for his passionate portrayals of *Herod's Feast* and *Salome's Dance. Piazza del Duomo.*

Tuscany

In the former bishop's palace, now the **Museo dell'Opera del Duomo,** you can see the original reliefs by Donatello for the Pulpit of the Holy Girdle (Mary's belt, supposedly given to Doubting Thomas as evidence of her assumption; the relic is kept in a chapel of the cathedral). *Piazza del Duomo 49, tel. 0574/26234. Admission: free. Open Tues.–Sat. 9–noon and 3–6:30, Sun. 9–noon.*

Architects and architecture buffs rhapsodize over the church of **Santa Maria delle Carceri,** off Via Cairoli. Built by Giuliano Sangallo in the 1490s, it was a landmark of Renaissance architecture. Next to it, the formidable **castle** built for Frederick II of Hohenstaufen is another impressive sight, the only castle of its type to be seen outside southern Italy. *Piazza Santa Maria dell Carceri. Admission: free. Open Tues.–Sat. 9–noon and 3–6, Sun. 9–noon.*

Pistoia   **Pistoia** lies about 14 kilometers (10 miles) northwest of Prato. A floricultural capital of Europe, it's surrounded by greenhouses and plant nurseries. Flowers aside, Pistoia's main sights are all in the downtown area, so you can easily see them on the way to Lucca. The Romanesque **Duomo** (cathedral) is flanked by a 13th-century bell tower, while in a side chapel dedicated to San Jacopo (St. James) there's a massive **silver altar** that alone is worth the stopover in Pistoia. Two hundred years in the making, it's an incredible piece of workmanship, begun in 1287. *Piazza del Duomo.*

Follow Via delle Pappe to the church of **Sant'Andrea** (Via Sant'Andrea) to see Pistoia's greatest art treasure, Giovanni

Pisano's powerfully sculpted 13th-century **pulpit,** before heading back toward the train station and bus terminal, stopping on the way to take in the green and white marble church of **San Giovanni Fuorcivitas** (Via Francesco Crispi, off Via Cavour). Highlights here include a *Visitation* by Luca della Robbia, a painting by Taddeo Gaddi, and a holy water font by Giovanni Pisano.

Lucca Your next destination is **Lucca,** Puccini's hometown and a city well-loved by sightseers who appreciate the careful upkeep of its medieval look. Though it hasn't the number of hotels and other tourist trappings that, say, Pisa does, for that very reason it's a pleasant alternative. You can easily make an excursion to Pisa from here—it's only 22 kilometers (14 miles) away. Enjoy first the views of the city and countryside from the tree-planted 16th-century ramparts that encircle Lucca. Then explore the city's marvelously elaborate Romanesque churches, fronted with tiers and rows of columns, and looking suspiciously like oversize marble wedding cakes.

From vast **Piazza Napoleone,** a swing around the Old Town will take you past the 11th-century **Duomo** (cathedral) on Piazza San Martino, with its 15th-century tomb of Ilaria del Carretto by Jacopo della Quercia. Don't neglect a ramble through the **Piazza del Mercato,** which preserves the oval form of the Roman amphitheater over which it was built, or the three surrounding streets that are filled with atmosphere: **Via Battisti, Via Fillungo,** and **Via Guinigi.** In addition to the Duomo, Lucca has two other fine churches. **San Frediano** (Piazza San Frediano) is graced with an austere facade ornamented by 13th-century mosaic decoration. Inside, check out the exquisite reliefs by Jacopo della Quercia in the last chapel on the left. **San Michele in Foro** (Piazza San Michele) is an exceptional example of the Pisan Romanesque style and decorative flair peculiar to Lucca: Note its facade, a marriage of arches and columns crowned by a statue of St. Michael.

The **Villa Reale** is 8 kilometers (5 miles) outside town, at Marlia. Gardening buffs, especially, will appreciate this handsome villa, surrounded by attractive parkland and gardens laid out in the 17th century. *Marlia, tel. 0583/30108. Admission: July–Oct. 4,000 lire, Nov.–June 3,500 lire. Guided visits on the hour, July–Sept., Tues.–Thurs. and Sun. 10, 11, 4, 5, and 6; Oct.–June, Tues.–Sun. 10, 11, 3, 4, 5, and 6.*

Pisa As you drive southwest, the next Tuscan town of note you'll come to is **Pisa,** a dull, overcommercialized place, though even skeptics have to admit the **Torre Pendente** (Leaning Tower) really is one of the world's more amazing sights. Theories vary as to whether the now famous list is due to shifting foundations or an amazing architectural feat by Bonanno Pisano (the first of three architects to work on the tower). A 294-step staircase spirals its way up the tower, providing a marvelous view from the top; a visit to Pisa wouldn't be the same without a trip up those worn steps. If you want a two-foot marble imitation of the Leaning Tower, perhaps even illuminated from within, this is your chance to grab one! *Piazza dei Miracoli. Admission: 4,000 lire. Open daily from 9 to an hour before sunset.*

Pisa has two other fine buildings, and, conveniently enough, they're near the Leaning Tower. The **Baptistery** was begun in

1153 but not completed until 1400, the Pisano family doing most of its decoration. Test out the excellent acoustics (occasionally the guard will slam shut the great doors and then sing a few notes—the resulting echo is very impressive, and costly, too, since he'll expect a tip). *Piazza del Duomo, in the Campo dei Miracoli. Open daily 9–1 and 3–7.*

Pisa's **Duomo** (cathedral) is elegantly simple, its facade decorated with geometric and animal shapes. The cavernous interior is supported by a series of 68 columns, while the pulpit is a fine example of Giovanni Pisano's work. Be sure to note the suspended lamp that hangs across from the pulpit; known as Galileo's Lamp, it's said to have inspired his theories on pendular motion. *Piazza del Duomo. Open daily 9–1 and 3–7.*

Visitors may find it more convenient to take a train back to Florence and get a bus or train there for the 85-minute trip to Siena, but for a more leisurely look at the Tuscan countryside, investigate the possibility of taking local trains from Pisa to Siena, passing through **Certaldo,** a pretty hill town that's the birthplace of Biovanni Boccaccio, 14th-century author of the *Decameron.*

Siena   **Siena** is one of Italy's best-preserved medieval towns, rich both in works of art and in expensive antique shops. The famous **Palio** is held here, a breakneck, 90-second horse race that takes place twice each year in the Piazza del Campo, on July 2 and August 16. Built on three hills, Siena is not an easy town to explore, for everything you'll want to see is either up or down a steep hill or stairway. But it is worth every ounce of effort. Siena really gives you the chance of seeing and feeling what the Middle Ages must have been like: dark stone palaces, low dwellings, and narrow streets opening out into airy squares.

Siena was a center of learning and art in the Middle Ages, and almost all the public buildings and churches in the town have enough artistic or historical merit to be worth visiting. Unlike most churches, Siena's **Duomo** has a mixture of religious and civic symbols ornamenting both its interior and exterior. The cathedral museum in the unfinished transept contains some fine works of art, notably a celebrated *Maestà* by Duccio di Buoninsegna. The animated frescoes of papal history in the Piccolomini Library (with an entrance off the left aisle of the cathedral) are credited to Pinturicchio, and are worth seeking out. *Piazza del Duomo. Library. Admission: 1,000 lire. Open Apr.–Oct., daily 9:30–1 and 2:30–6; Nov.–Mar., daily 10–1 and 2:30–5. Cathedral Museum. Admission: 4,000 lire. Open mid-Mar.–Oct., daily 9–7:30; Nov.–mid-Mar., daily 9–1:30.*

Nearby, the fan-shaped **Piazza del Campo** is Siena's main center of activity, with 11 streets leading into it. Farsighted planning has preserved it as a medieval showpiece, containing the 13th-century **Palazzo Pubblico** (City Hall) and the **Torre del Mangia** (Bell Tower). Try to visit both these buildings, the former for Lorenzetti's frescoes on the effects of good and bad government, the latter for the wonderful view (you'll have to climb 503 steps to reach it, however). *Piazza del Campo, tel. 0577/292111. Bell Tower. Admission: 2,500 lire. Open Apr.–Sept., Mon.–Sat. 9:30–7:30; Oct.–Mar., Mon.–Sat. 9:30–1:30, Sun. 9:30–1. Palazzo Pubblico (Civic Museum). Admission: 5,000 lire. Open Apr.–Oct., Mon.–Sat. 9:30–7:30, Sun. 9:30–1:30; Nov.–Mar., daily 9:30–1:30.*

Time Out **Al Mangia** is a good outdoor café-cum-restaurant where you can enjoy a Tartufo ice cream and a cup of coffee, imagining the noise and excitement generated by the Palio riders careening around the corners of the piazza during the 90-second race.

From Siena make an excursion to **San Gimignano,** perhaps the most delightful of the Tuscan medieval hill towns with their timeless charm. There were once 79 tall towers here, symbols of power for the wealthy families of the Middle Ages. Thirteen are still standing, giving the town its unique skyline. The bus stops just outside the town gates, from which you can stroll down the main street to the picturesque Piazza della Cisterna.

Just around the corner is the church of the **Collegiata.** Its walls, and those of its chapel dedicated to Santa Fina, are decorated with radiant frescoes. From the steps of the church you can observe the town's countless crows as they circle the tall towers. In the pretty courtyard on the right as you descend the church stairs, there's a shop selling Tuscan and Deruta ceramics, which you'll also find in other shops along the Via San Giovanni. The excellent San Gimignano wine could be another souvenir of your visit; it's sold in gift cartons from just about every shop in town.

Arezzo A local bus or train takes you from Siena to **Arezzo** about 48 kilometers (30 miles) east, over thickly wooded hills, past vineyards and wheat fields, and the broad ribbon of the Autostrada del Sole in the fertile Chiana valley, known for its pale beef cattle that provide the classic *bistecca Fiorentina.* Arezzo is not a beautiful town, nor is it quaint. What makes Arezzo worth a visit, however, is its fine array of Tuscan art treasures, including frescoes, stained glass, and ancient Etruscan statues.

The **Museo Archeologico** (Archaeological Museum) is near the train station, next to what's left of an ancient **Roman amphitheater.** The museum has a rich collection of Etruscan art, artifacts, and pottery, copied by Arezzo's contemporary artisans and sold in the local ceramic shops of the town. *Via Margaritone 10, tel. 0575/20882. Admission: 3,000 lire. Open Tues.–Sat. 9–2, Sun. 9–1.*

Via Guido Monaco, named after the 11th-century originator of the musical scale, leads to the church of **San Francesco,** where one of the town's main attractions, the frescoes by Piero della Francesca, are currently due for restoration and will probably be at least partially hidden through 1990. Faded as they are, they still rank among the outstanding examples of Italian painting, and art lovers are looking forward to seeing them in renewed splendor. *Via Cavour.*

Now you enter the old part of Arezzo, where the poet Petrarch (1304–74), the artist Vasari (1511–74), and the satirical author Pietro Aretino (1492–1556) all lived. Climb Via Cesalpino uphill to the fine Gothic **cathedral** (Piazza del Duomo), then stroll past **Petrarch's House** to **Piazza Grande,** an attractive, sloping square where an extensive open-air fair of antiques and old bric-a-brac is held the first weekend of every month. The shops around the piazza also specialize in antiques, with prices lower than those you will encounter in Florence. The colonnaded apse and bell tower of the Romanesque church of **Santa Maria della Pieve** grace one end of this pleasant piazza.

Cortona A full day may be enough for you to get the feel of Arezzo, but you may wish to stay overnight, especially during the antique fair, or if you want to use the town as a base for an excursion to **Cortona,** about 30 kilometers (18 miles) south. This medieval town is known for its excellent small art gallery and a number of fine antiques shops, as well as for its colony of foreign residents. Cortona has the advantage of being on the main train network, though you will have to take a local bus from the station up into the town, passing the Renaissance church of **Santa Maria del Calcinaio** on the way.

The heart of Cortona is formed by **Piazza della Repubblica** and the adjacent **Piazza Signorelli.** Wander into the courtyard of the picturesque **Palazzo Pretorio,** and, if you want to see a representative collection of Etruscan bronzes, climb its centuries-old stone staircase to the **Museo dell'Accademia Etrusca** (Gallery of Etruscan Art). *Piazza Signorelli 9, tel. 0575/62534. Admission: 2,000 lire. Open June–Sept., Tues.–Sun. 10–1 and 4–7; Oct.–May, Tues.–Sun. 9–1 and 3–5.*

The nearby **Museo Diocesano** (Diocesan Museum) houses an impressive number of large and splendid paintings by native son Luca Signorelli, as well as a beautiful *Annunciation* by Fra Angelico, a delightful surprise to find in this small, eclectic town. *Piazza del Duomo 1, tel. 0575/62830. Admission: 2,000 lire. Open June–Sept., Tues.–Sun. 9–1 and 3–6:30; Oct.–May, Tues.–Sun. 9–1 and 3–5.*

Dining and Lodging

For details and price category definitions, *see* Dining and Lodging in Staying in Italy.

Arezzo **Buca di San Francesco.** Travelers and passing celebrities come
Dining to this rustic and historic cellar restaurant for the 13th-century
★ cantina atmosphere, but locals love it for the food, especially *ribollita* (minestrone) and *sformato di spinaci con cibreo* (spinach with giblet sauce). *Piazza San Francesco 1, tel. 0575/23271. Dinner reservations advised. AE, DC, MC, V. Closed Mon. dinner, Tues., and July. Moderate.*

Tastevin. Arezzo's purveyor of creative *nuova cucina* serves traditional Tuscan dishes as well, in three attractive, elegantly rustic rooms, with a Belle Epoque café doubling as a piano bar. Specialties are *risotto Tastevin*, with cream of truffles, and seafood or meat *carpaccio* (sliced raw). *Via de'Cenci 9, tel. 0575/28304. Dinner reservations advised. AE, MC, V. Closed Mon. (Sun. in summer). Moderate.*

Spiedo d'Oro. Cheery red-and-white tablecloths add a colorful touch to this large, reliable trattoria near the Archaeological Museum. The menu offers Tuscan home-style specialties like *zuppa di pane* (bread soup), *pappardelle oll'ocio* (noodles with duck sauce), and *ossobuco aretina* (sautéed veal shank). *Via Crispi 12, tel. 0575/22873. Reservations not needed. No credit cards. Closed Thurs. and first 2 weeks in July. Inexpensive.*

Lodging **Minerva.** This six-story 1960s construction is on a main road in the newer part of town (you'll have to take a taxi or bus to the downtown area). The expanses of plate glass and dull brown furnishings may leave you cold, but it's one of the best in Arezzo, and it has a good restaurant. *Via Fiorentina 6, tel. 0575/27891. 118 rooms with bath. AE, DC, V. Moderate.*

Continental. The circa-1950 Continental has fairly spacious rooms decorated in white and bright yellow, gleaming bathrooms, and the advantage of a central location within walking distance of all major sights. *Piazza Guido Monaco 7, tel. 0575/ 20251. 74 rooms with bath. Facilities: restaurant. AE, DC, MC, V. Inexpensive.*

Cortona
Dining
★

Tonino. This is the place to eat in Cortona, known for its delicious *antipastissimo*, and for succulent steaks of Chiana valley beef. It's best on weekdays, when it's quieter. The big dining room has a window-wall overlooking the valley. The restaurant is crowded and noisy on weekends. *Piazza Garibaldi, tel. 0575/ 603100. Weekends reservations advised. AE, DC, MC, V. Closed Mon. dinner and Tues. Moderate.*

Lucca
Dining
★

Buca di Sant'Antonio. A Lucca favorite, located near the church of San Michele, Buca di Sant'Antonio was around more than a century ago, and it has retained something of its rustic look. It specializes in traditional local dishes, some unfamiliar but well worth trying, among them *tacconi al sugo* (fresh pasta in rabbit or mushroom sauce), and kid or lamb roasted with herbs. *Via della Cervia 1, tel. 0583/55881. Dinner reservations advised. AE, DC, MC, V. Closed Sun. dinner, Mon., and July 9–24. Moderate.*

Il Giglio. Off vast Piazza Napoleone, Il Giglio has a quiet, turn-of-the-century charm and a dignified atmosphere. In the summer the tables outdoors have a less formal air. The menu is classic: *crostini* (savory Tuscan chicken liver, anchovy and caper paste on small pieces of toast), *stracotto* (braised beef with mushrooms), and seafood, as well. *Piazza del Giglio 2, tel. 0583/ 44058. Dinner reservations advised. AE, DC, MC, V. Closed Tues. dinner and Wed. Moderate.*

★ **La Mora.** You'll need a car or a taxi to take you to this charming old way station 10 kilometers (6 miles) outside Lucca, but its authentic local cooking is worth every effort. It is widely considered to be one of the best regional restaurants in Italy. *Via Sesto di Moriano 1143, Ponte a Moriano, tel. 0583/57109. Reservations advised. AE, DC, MC, V. Closed Wed. dinner, Thurs., June 26–July 7. Moderate.*

Lodging
★

Villa La Principessa. This pretty 19th-century country mansion, 3½ kilometers (2 miles) outside Lucca, is an exclusive hotel whose rooms feature original beamed ceilings. All rooms are individually, and tastefully, decorated. Antique floors, furniture, and portraits set the tone, and the restaurant is known for its fine Tuscan dishes. *Massa Pisana, tel. 0583/370037. 44 rooms with bath. Facilities: park, pool, restaurant. AE, DC, MC, V. Closed Jan. 8–Feb. 18. Expensive.*

★ **Universo.** There's plenty of genteel, Old World charm here to please those looking for the atmosphere of times past. In the spacious, high-ceilinged rooms, even huge 1920s wardrobes look small, and you have to climb two steps to open the tall windows. Bathrooms are on the same scale. Furnishings are old but comfortable, and the plumbing works! *Piazza del Giglio 1, tel. 0583/43678. 60 rooms, half with bath. AE, DC, MC, V. Moderate.*

Ilaria. This small, family-run hotel sits in a pretty location on a minuscule canal within easy walking distance of the main sights. Renovated in 1987, rooms are smallish but fresh and functional. *Via del Fosso 20, tel. 0583/47558. 17 rooms, most with bath. AE, DC, MC, V. Inexpensive.*

Pisa
Dining

Bruno. Checked curtains, wood paneling, and soft lights make Bruno a pleasant place to lunch on classic Tuscan dishes, from *crostini*—toast topped with a creamy mixture of chicken livers, capers, and anchovy—to *coniglio* (rabbit). It's just outside the old city walls and only a short walk from the bell tower and cathedral. *Via Luigi Bianchi 12, tel. 050/550964. Dinner reservations advised. AE, DC, MC, V. Closed Mon. dinner, Tues., Aug. 1–20. Moderate.*

Spartaco. Centrally located on the station square, Spartaco has the solid look of the well-established trattoria that it is, with contemporary white chairs contrasting with terra-cotta-tiled walls and some fine antique pieces. It's large, and seating doubles in the summer when tables are set out on the square. Specialties include a cocktail of ravioli in different colors, and grilled fish, along with the usual Tuscan dishes. *Piazza Vittorio Emanuele 22, tel. 050/23335. Reservations not required. AE, DC, MC, V. Closed Sun. Moderate.*

Pistoia
Dining

Cucciolo della Montagna. Just a block or two from the cathedral and the church of San Giovanni Fuorcivitas, Cucciolo della Montagna is popular with businesspeople and does a big lunch trade, so get there early or reserve ahead. The specialties are Tuscan in flavor: pasta with duck sauce, and grilled duck. *Via Panciatichi 2, tel. 0573/29733. Reservations advised. AE, DC, MC, V. Closed Mon. and Aug. 1–25. Moderate.*

Il Duomo. This unpretentious trattoria is practically on Piazza del Duomo, and locals as well as tourists enjoy its typical Tuscan *ribollita* (minestrone) and *carne in umido* (stewed meats) at very reasonable prices. *Via Bracciolini 5, tel. 0573/31948. Reservations not required. No credit cards. Closed Sun. Moderate.*

Prato
Dining

Da Bruno. Decor at this upscale little restaurant near the castle is simple, with wood-paneled walls and yellow and white accents. The menu offers traditional dishes with creative touches, such as *farinata*, made of cornmeal, red cabbage and tomato, or the duck breast in a sauce of balsamic vinegar and sweet peppers. *Via Verdi 12, tel. 0574/23810. Reservations advised. AE, DC, MC, V. Closed Thurs. dinner, Sun., and Aug. Moderate.*

Stefano. At the lower end of the moderate price range, this trattoria is popular with the locals. A simple place, it serves regional dishes such as *ribollita* (minestrone), *fagioli* (beans) laced with local olive oil, and grilled meat. *Via Pomeria 23, tel. 0574/34665. Reservations not accepted. No credit cards. Closed Sun. Moderate.*

San Gimignano
Dining
★

Le Terrazze. You'll find this one tucked under the eaves of the Hotel Cisterna on the town's prettiest square. Under low, beamed ceilings, windows give you a panoramic view of red-tiled rooftops and the surrounding countryside. Cooking is appropriately Tuscan, from ribollita that's heated in the oven to make it even thicker, to *fritto misto* (fried meats and vegetables). *Piazza della Cisterna, tel. 0577/940328. Reservations advised. AE, DC, MC, V. Closed Tues., Wed. lunch. Moderate.*

Bel Soggiorno. A slightly simpler version of Le Terrazze, Bel Soggiorno, too, is attached to a small hotel. It has a homey, familiar atmosphere and slightly lower prices. Specialties are *morsello di San Gimignano* (a hearty vegetable soup) and a spicy fillet of pork. *Via San Giovanni 89, tel. 0577/940375. Res-*

ervations advised. AE, DC, MC, V. Closed Mon. and Mar. Moderate.

Siena **Ai Marsili.** Located in a medieval palace near the Duomo, Ai
Dining Marsili is a spacious, brick-vaulted wine cellar with refectory
★ tables and excellent Tuscan cuisine; it's a place for a leisurely
meal accompanied by classic Chianti wines. Specialties include
ceci (chick-peas with garlic and rosemary) and *faraona* (guinea
hen). *Via del Castoro 3, tel. 0577/47154. Reservations advised.
AE, DC, MC, V. Closed Mon. Moderate.*

Osteria Le Logge. Just off Piazza del Campo, this is a fine choice
for an informal but memorable meal. Get there early to claim a
table. Among the specialties are *pennette all'Osteria* (spicy
pasta) and *terra di Siena*, a piquant roast beef. *Via del
Porrione 33, tel. 0577/48013. Reservations advised. No credit
cards. Closed Sun. and mid-Nov.–mid-Dec. Moderate.*

Le Tre Campane. Boasting a convenient location between Piazza del Campo and the Duomo, this small trattoria expands into
the little square in fair weather. Popular with the locals, it specializes in seafood, as well as the standard Tuscan *crostini.
Piazzetta Bonelli, tel. 0577/286091. Reservations advised. No
credit cards. Closed Tues. and Jan.–Feb. Moderate.*

Lodging **Certosa di Maggiano.** An easy and attractive walk (less than a
mile) southeast of Siena takes you to this old Carthusian monastery, which has been converted into a sophisticated oasis
furnished in impeccable style. The bedrooms have every comfort, and the atmosphere is that of an aristocratic family villa.
*Strada di Certosa 82, tel. 0577/288180. 14 rooms with bath. Fa-
cilities: pool, tennis. AE, DC, MC, V. Closed Dec.–Feb. Very
Expensive.*

★ **Park Hotel.** Just outside the walls of the old city, Park Hotel is a
handsome 15th-century villa on its own grounds. Furnished in
classic Tuscan style, with antiques and luxuriant plants in
gleaming copper planters on highly polished terra-cotta floors,
it has a simple but sophisticated ambience, in which you can
pretend you're a house guest of the Medicis. There's a fine restaurant and garden terrace. *Via di Marciano 18, tel. 0577/
44803. 69 rooms with bath. Facilities: pool, tennis. AE, DC,
MC, V. Very Expensive.*

Palazzo Ravizza. Set just within the town walls, these accommodations are not far from the cathedral (though it's an uphill
walk). The hotel is a converted 17th-century building with garden, and it's furnished as a private residence, with comfortable
bedrooms, some small. Half-board is required in summer (Mar.
–Nov.). *Piano del Mantellini 34, tel. 0577/280462. 28 rooms,
most with bath. AE, DC, MC, V. Moderate.*

★ **Santa Caterina.** This newcomer to the Siena hotel scene opened
in 1986 in a totally renovated and air-conditioned town house, a
few steps from Porta Romana and a 10-minute walk from the
cathedral. It's decorated in classic Tuscan style, with light
walls and dark wood furniture. Bedrooms are cheery, with floral prints, and two have the original frescoed ceilings. The
hotel has a pretty garden and a small parking area. *Via
Piccolomini 7, tel. 0577/221105. 19 rooms with bath. AE, DC,
MC, V. Closed mid-Nov.–Feb. Moderate.*

Milan

Arriving and Departing

As Lombardy's capital and the most important financial and commercial center in northern Italy, Milan is well connected with Rome and Florence by fast and frequent rail and air service, though the latter is often delayed in winter by heavy fog.

By Plane Linate Airport 11 kilometers (7 miles) outside Milan, handles mainly domestic and European flights (tel. 02/7485–2200). Malpensa, 50 kilometers (30 miles) from the city, handles intercontinental flights (tel. 02/7485–2200).

Between the Airport and Downtown Buses connect both airports with Milan, stopping at the central station and at the Porta Garibaldi station. Fare from Linate is 2,200 lire on the special airport bus or 800 lire on municipal bus no. 73 (to Piazza San Babila); from Malpensa 7,000 lire. A taxi from Linate to the center of Milan costs about 35,000 lire, from Malpensa about 100,000 lire.

By Train The main train terminal is the central station in Piazzale Duca d'Aosta (tel. 02/67500). Several smaller stations handle commuter trains. There are several fast Intercity trains between Rome and Milan, stopping in Florence. A nonstop Intercity leaves from Rome or Milan morning and evening, taking about four hours to go between the two cities.

By Car From Rome and Florence, take the A1 Autostrada. From Venice, take the A4. With bans on parking throughout the center of Milan, it's easier to park on the outskirts and use public transportation.

Getting Around

By Subway Milan's subway network, the Metropolitana, is modern, fast, and easy to use. "MM" signs mark Metropolitana stations. There are at present two lines, with another scheduled to open soon. The ATM (city transport authority) has an information office on the mezzanine of the Duomo Metro station (tel. 02/875494). Tickets are sold at newsstands at every stop, and in ticket machines *for exact change only*. The fare is 800 lire, and the subway runs from 6:20 AM to midnight.

By Bus and Streetcar There is an extensive network. Buy tickets at newsstands, tobacco shops, and bars. Fare is 800 lire. One ticket is valid for 75 minutes on all surface lines, and one subway trip. Daily tickets valid for 24 hours on all public transportation lines are on sale at the Duomo Metro station ATM Information Office, and at Stazione Centrale Metro station.

By Taxi Use yellow cabs only. They wait at stands or can be telephoned in advance (tel. 6767, 8585, or 8388).

Guided Tours

City Tours Three-hour morning or afternoon sightseeing tours depart from Piazzetta Reale, next to the Duomo; cost is about 37,000 lire and can be purchased at some travel agencies or aboard the bus.

Excursions CIT (Galleria Vittorio Emanuele, tel. 02/866661, or central station, tel. 02/220224) offers an all-day tour of Lake Maggiore, including a boat trip to the Borromean Islands and lunch. There is a brief stop at Lake Como. Cost is about 80,000 lire.

Personalized Tours Arrange for guide service and interpreters through the **Centro Guide Turistiche** (Via Marconi 1, tel. 02/863210).

Tourist Information

APT information offices are located at the following addresses: Via Marconi 1, tel. 02/870016; Central Station, tel. 02/669-0432. There's a **Municipal Information Office** at Galleria Vittorio Emanuele at the corner of Piazza della Scala, tel. 02/870545.

Exploring Milan

Numbers in the margin correspond with points of interest on the Milan map.

The center of Milan is the Piazza del Duomo. The massive
① **Duomo** (cathedral) is one of the largest churches in the world, a mountain of marble fretted with statues, spires, and flying buttresses. The interior is a more solemn Italian Gothic. Take the elevator or walk up 158 steps to the roof, from where—if it's a clear day—you can see over the city to the Lombard plain and the Alps beyond, all through an amazing array of spires and statues. The **Madonnina,** a gleaming gilt statue on the highest spire, is a Milan landmark. *Entrance to elevator and stairway outside the cathedral, to the right. Admission: 3,500 lire. Open Mar.–Oct., daily 9–5:45; Nov.–Feb. 9–4:15.*

Outside the cathedral to the right is the elegant, glass-roofed
② **Galleria,** where the Milanesi and visitors stroll, window-shop, and sip pricey cappuccinos at trendy cafés. At the other end of
③ the Galleria is **Piazza della Scala,** with Milan's city hall on one
④ side and **Teatro alla Scala,** the world-famous opera house, opposite.

Via Verdi, flanking the opera house, leads to Via Brera, where
⑤ the **Pinacoteca di Brera** houses one of Italy's great collections of paintings. Most are of a religious nature, confiscated in the 19th century when many religious orders were suppressed and their churches closed. *Via Brera 28, tel. 02/808387. Admission: 4,000 lire. Open Tues., Wed., Thurs. 9–5:30, Fri.–Sat. 9–1:20, Sun. 9–12:30.*

Time Out A pleasant café with tables outdoors in fair weather is open to Brera visitors, just inside the entrance to the gallery.

After an eyeful of artworks by Mantegna, Raphael, and many other Italian masters, explore the Brera neighborhood, dotted with art galleries, chic little restaurants, and offbeat cafés such
⑥ as the **Jamaica** (Via Brera 26), once a bohemian hangout. Take Via dei Fiori Chiari in front of the Brera and keep going in the
⑦ same direction to the moated **Castello Sforzesco,** a somewhat sinister 19th-century reconstruction of the imposing 15th-century fortress built by the Sforzas, who succeeded the Viscontis as lords of Milan in the 15th century. It now houses wide-ranging collections of sculptures, antiques, and ceramics, including Michelangelo's *Rondanini Pietà,* his last work, left

Milan

0   440 yards

400 meters

unfinished at his death. *Piazza Castello, tel. 02/6236 ext. 3947. Admission: free. Open Tues.–Sun. 9:30–12:15 and 2:30–5:15.*

From the vast residence of the Sforzas it's not far to the church
⑧ of **Santa Maria delle Grazie.** Although portions of the church were designed by Bramante, it plays second fiddle to the **Refectory** next door, where, over a three-year period, Leonardo da Vinci painted his mega-famous fresco, *The Last Supper.* The fresco has suffered more than its share of disaster, beginning with the experiments of the artist, who used untested pigments that soon began to deteriorate. *The Last Supper* is now a mere shadow of its former self, despite meticulous restoration that proceeds at a snail's pace. To save what is left, visitors are limited in time and number, and you may have to wait in line to get a glimpse of this world-famous work. *Piazza Santa Maria delle Grazie 2, tel. 02/498–7588. Admission: 4,000 lire. Open Tues.–Sat. 9–1:15 and 2–6:15, Sun.–Mon. 9–1:15.*

If you are interested in medieval architecture, go to see the
⑨ medieval church of **Sant'Ambrogio** (Piazza Sant'Ambrogio). Consecrated by St. Ambrose in AD 387, it's the model for all Lombard Romanesque churches, and contains some ancient works of art, including a remarkable 9th-century altar in precious metals and enamels, and some 5th-century mosaics. On December 7, the feast day of St. Ambrose, the streets around the church are the scene of a lively flea market. Another noteworthy church
⑩ is **San Lorenzo Maggiore** (Corso di Porta Ticinese), with 16 ancient Roman columns in front and some 4th-century mosaics in the Chapel of St. Aquilinus. Closer to Piazza del Duomo on Via
⑪ Torino, the church of **San Satiro** is another architectural gem in which Bramante's perfect command of proportion and perspective, a characteristic of the Renaissance, made a small interior seem extraordinarily spacious and airy.

Time Out Stop in at the **Peck** shops a few steps from San Satiro. One is a gourmet delicatessen, the other has a tempting array of snacks to eat on the premises. *Via Spadari 9; Via Cantù 3.*

---

⑫
⑬ ⑭ ⑮ Now head for Milan's most elegant shopping streets: **Via Monte Napoleone, Via Manzoni, Via Spiga,** and **Via Sant'Andrea.** The **Café Cova** (Monte Napoleone 8) is famous for its pastries; Hemingway loved them. And the **Sant'Ambroeus,** not far away, is the epitome of a genteel tearoom (Corso Matteotti 7). If the chic goods of this area are a shock to your purse, make your way to
⑯ **Corso Buenos Aires,** near the central station, which has hundreds more shops and accessible prices, too.

Dining

For details and price category definitions, *see* Dining in Staying in Italy.

Expensive **Biffi Scala.** The elegant Biffi Scala caters mainly to the after-opera crowd that pours in around midnight. Built in 1861, it features a high ceiling and polished wood walls. Specialties include *crespelle alle erbette* (pancakes stuffed with wild mushrooms and other vegetables) and *carpaccio alla biffi scala* (thin slices of cured raw beef with a tangy sauce). *Piazza della Scala, tel. 02/876332. Dinner reservations required, especially after the opera. AE, DC, MC, V. Closed Sun., Aug.*

★ **Boeucc.** Milan's oldest restaurant is situated not far from La Scala, and is subtly lit, with fluted columns, chandeliers, thick carpet, and a garden for warm-weather dining. In addition to the typical Milanese foods, it also serves such exotica as *penne al branzino e zucchine* (pasta with sea bass and zucchini sauce) and *gelato di castagne con zabaglione caldo* (chestnut ice cream with hot zabaglione). *Piazza Belgioioso 2, tel. 02/790224. Reservations required. AE. Closed Sat., Sun. lunch, and Aug.*

Don Lisander. This 17th-century chapel has been drastically redecorated, and now features designer lighting, abstract prints, and a modern terra-cotta tile floor, creating an uncompromisingly contemporary effect. Try the *terrina di brasato alle verdure* (terrine of braised beef with vegetables), or else go for the *branzino al timo* (sea bass with thyme). *Via Manzoni 12A, tel. 02/90130. Reservations required. AE, DC, MC, V. Closed Sat. dinner, Sun., 2 weeks in mid-Aug., and 2 weeks at Christmas.*

Giannino's. You'll find great character and style at this roomy, old-fashioned restaurant, with oak beams, stained-glass windows, and a huge lobster aquarium. If it's on the menu, be daring and try the *dadolata di capriolo* (venison in cream sauce) or *quaglie con risotto* (quails with rice). *Via A. Sciesa 8, tel. 02/545-2948. Dinner reservations required. AE, DC, MC, V. Closed Sun., Aug.*

Gualtiero Marchesi. Owner Gualtiero Marchesi has written several books on nuova cucina (nouvelle cuisine). Your eye, as well as your taste buds, should relish his *raviolo aperto* (pasta, scallops, and a ginger sauce) or the *costata di manzo bollita alle piccole verdure* (thinly sliced boiled pork with steamed vegetables). Portions are minuscule. *Via Bonvesin de la Riva 9, tel. 02/741246. Reservations advised. AE, DC, MC, V. Closed Sun., Mon. lunch, and Aug.*

★ **Savini.** Red carpets and cut-glass chandeliers characterize the classy Savini, a typical, Old World Milanese restaurant whose dining rooms spread over three floors. There's also a "winter garden" from which patrons can people-watch shoppers in the Galleria. The *risotto al salto* (rice cooked as a pancake, tossed in the pan, a Milanese specialty) is excellent here, as is the *costoletta di vitello* (fried veal cutlets). *Galleria Vittorio Emanuele, tel. 02/805-8343. Dinner reservations advised. AE, DC, MC, V. Closed Mon., 3 weeks in Aug.*

Moderate
★ **Antica Brasera Meneghina.** A huge fireplace, ornate mirrors, black-and-white tiled floor, and bentwood chairs lend this restaurant a 17th-century air, while the long garden, shaded by a 450-year-old wisteria and featuring fig trees, fountains, and frescoes, make it absolutely delightful in the summer. The menu features typical Milanese dishes such as *rustin negàa* (veal cooked in white wine with ham, bacon, sage, and rosemary) and *cassoeula* (casserole of pork, sausage, and cabbage). *Via Circo 10, tel. 02/808108. Winter reservations advised. No credit cards. Closed Mon., Aug.*

Al Buon Convento. The granite columns and oak beams here date back to the 15th century, when a bevy of nuns occupied the premises. Expect genuine, home-style cooking served up in an intimate, candlelit ambience. Don't miss the *spaghetti alla lucana* (spaghetti with a tomato and chili sauce). *Corso Italia 26, tel. 02/805-0623. Reservations advised. V. Closed Sun., Aug.*

Opera Prima. If you've always imagined yourself dining by candlelight, from silver plates, and with strains of classical music lilting in the background—well, then, Opera Prima is the place you've been searching for. The *crespelle alla vaniglia e al cioccolato* (vanilla and chocolate pancakes) are sinfully good, the *tagliolini opera prima* (pasta with chicken, vegetables, and a cream and chili sauce) is a good way to start off your meal. *Via Rovello 3, tel. 02/865235. Reservations advised. AE, DC, MC, V. Closed Sun., middle 2 weeks in Aug.*

★ **Tencitt.** This chic, ultra-1980s restaurant is decorated in stark black and white, with suffused wall lighting and a striped tent effect on the ceiling. Dishes that sit well with the professional/academic clientele (it's near the university) are the *risotto con zucche e scampi* (rice with squash and scampi) and the *storione all'erba e cipolline* (sturgeon with herbs and spring onions). *Via Laghetto 2, tel. 02/795560. Reservations required. AE, DC, MC, V. Closed Sat. lunch, Sun., Aug.*

Inexpensive   **La Bruschetta.** A winning partnership of Tuscans and Neapolitans run this tiny, busy, and first-class pizzeria near the Duomo. It features the obligatory wood-burning stove, so you can watch your pizza being cooked, though there are plenty of other dishes to choose from as well—try the *spaghetti alle cozze e vongole* (spaghetti with clams and mussels). *Piazza Beccaria 12, tel. 02/802494. Reservations are handy, but service is so fast you don't have to wait long. No credit cards. Closed Mon., 3 weeks in Aug.*

Al Cantinone. Opera goers still come to the Cantinone bar for a drink after the final curtain, just as they did a century ago. Decor is basic, the atmosphere lively, the service fast, and the food reliable. The proprietor stocks 240 different wines. Try the *costolette al Cantinone* (veal cutlets with mushrooms, olives, and a cream and tomato sauce). *Via Agnello 19, tel. 02/807666. Reservations advised. AE, MC, V. Closed Sat. lunch, Sun., 3 weeks in Aug.*

13 (Tredici) Giugno. Gino Sant'Ercole, the proprietor, is an ex-pop star, and his restaurant features live music in the evenings. Enjoy *lasagne con le noci e prosciutto di praga* (lasagne with walnuts and ham sauce) in the garden in summer, or in the Art Deco dining room in winter. *Via Giulio Uberto 5 (corner of Via Goldoni), tel. 02/719654. Dinner reservations advised. AE, MC, V. Closed Sat. lunch, Sun., Aug.*

Lodging

Make reservations well in advance, particularly when trade fairs are on, which can be most of the year except for August (when many hotels close) and mid-December to mid-January. March and October are months with the highest concentration of fairs, and it's virtually impossible to find a room at this time. Should you arrive without reservations, there's a booking service at Via Palestro 24 (tel. 02/706095).

For details and price category definitions, *see* Lodging in Staying in Italy.

Very Expensive   **Duomo.** Just 20 yards from the cathedral, this hotel's first-, third-, and fourth-floor rooms all look out onto the church's Gothic gargoyles and pinnacles. Rooms are spacious, snappily furnished in gold, cream, and brown. *Via San Raffaele 1, tel.*

02/8833. 160 rooms with bath. Facilities: restaurant, bar. MC, V. Closed Aug.

Galileo. In spite of its location on busy Corso Europa, this hotel is surprisingly quiet. Rooms have chic designer lighting, tartan carpets, and original modern prints on the walls. Bathrooms are particularly grand, with two basins each. *Corso Europa 9, tel. 02/7743. 76 rooms with bath. Facilities: piano bar, restaurant. AE, DC, MC, V.*

★ **Pierre.** No expense was spared to furnish each room of Milan's newest luxury hotel in a different style, using the most elegant fabrics and an assortment of modern and antique furniture. Electronic gadgetry is rife: You can open the curtains, turn off the lights, and who knows what else, merely by pressing buttons on a remote-control dial. The Pierre is located near the medieval church of Sant'Ambrogio. *Via De Amicis 32, tel. 02/ 805–6220. 47 rooms with bath. Facilities: restaurant, bar. AE, DC, MC, V.*

Principe di Savoia. The most fashionable and glitzy hotel in Milan is the Principe di Savoia. This is where fashion buyers and expense account businesspeople stay and, if you want all the amenities of an international hotel, you may want to stay here. *Piazza della Repubblica 17, tel. 02/6230. 280 rooms with bath. Facilities: restaurant, bar. AE, DC, V.*

Expensive **Carlton-Senato.** Visitors who intend to spend lots of time shopping in nearby high-fashion streets (Via della Spiga, Via Sant'Andrea, and Via Monte Napoleone) will find this place ideally located. The atmosphere is very light and airy, and there are lots of little touches (such as complimentary chocolates and liqueurs in the rooms) to make up for the rather functional room furnishings. *Via Senato 5, tel. 02/798583. 79 rooms with bath. Facilities: restaurant, bar, private parking. AE, MC, V. Closed Aug.*

Excelsior Gallia. This vast, circa-1930 mock-Victorian hotel is located near the central station. Rooms are opulently decorated in a variety of 1930s, '40s, and '80s styles, and bathrooms are big enough to hold a party in. Rooms overlooking the station are more attractive, but noisier. *Piazza Duca d'Aosta 9, tel. 02/6277. 266 rooms with bath. Facilities: sauna, Turkish bath, health club, restaurant. AE, DC, MC, V.*

★ **Grand Hotel et de Milan.** With its marble fireplace, bronze statues, and palms in the lobby, and antique furniture and tapestry curtain pelmets in the bedrooms, the Grand is definitely Milan's most atmospheric hotel, even if the parquet floors do creak and some of the curtains are faded. It's just down from La Scala. *Via Manzoni 29, tel. 02/870757. 89 rooms with bath. Facilities: bar. AE, DC, MC, V.*

Moderate **Centro.** The fragments of a Roman column and bust in the entrance lead you to expect something more old-fashioned and classier than is the case: Rooms are decorated in 1960s modern, with floral wallpaper and bare wood floors. Avoid rooms on the Via Broletto side—cars rumbling over cobblestones sound like thunder. *Via Broletto 46, tel. 02/875232. Facilities: bar, coffee shop. AE, DC, MC, V.*

Gritti. This bright, clean hotel has a cheerful atmosphere. Rooms are adequate, with picturesque views from the upper floors over the tiled roofs to the gilt Madonnina on top of the Duomo, only a few hundred yards away. *Piazza Santa Maria Beltrade (north end of Via Torino), tel. 02/801056. 48 rooms with bath. AE, DC, MC, V.*

King. Within easy walking distance of Leonardo's *Last Supper* at Santa Maria delle Grazie, the King has high ceilings and an imposing mock–Louis XV lobby. Built in 1966, it was restored in 1986 in pseudo-antique style, with aptly regal red rugs, armchairs, and bedsteads. *Corso Magenta 19, tel. 02/874432. 48 rooms, 44 with bath. AE, MC, V.*

Inexpensive **Antica Locanda Solferino.** Make reservations well in advance for this one: Rooms are few, and provide excellent value. The building is 19th-century, but rooms were all recently redecorated with delightful peasant-print bedspreads, low bedside lights draped with lace-edge cloths, attractive dried-flower arrangements on the tables, and 19th-century prints on the walls. *Via Castelfidardo 2, tel. 02/659–9886. 11 rooms with bath. V. Closed 10 days mid-Aug., and another 10 days at Christmas.*

Pensione Rovello. Accommodations here are simple and spanking clean, with warm terra-cotta tile floors and plain white walls. It's a favorite with younger travelers and American fashion models. Expect to pay in advance. *Via Rovello 18A, tel. 02/873956. 12 rooms, 3 with bath. No credit cards.*

The Arts

The most famous spectacle in Milan is **La Scala Opera,** which presents some of the world's most impressive operatic productions. The house is invariably sold out in advance; ask at your hotel if tickets can be found for you. You can also book tickets at CIT travel agencies elsewhere in Italy and in foreign countries, but no more than 10 days before the performance. The opera season begins early in December and ends in May. The concert season runs from May to the end of June and from September through November. There is a brief ballet season in September. Programs are available at principal travel agencies and tourist information offices in Italy and abroad. *Box Office, Teatro alla Scala, Piazza della Scala, tel. 02/809126. Open Tues.–Sun. 10–1 and 3:30–5:30. Tickets for same evening's performance on sale from 5:30.*

Venice

Arriving and Departing

By Plane Marco Polo International Airport is situated about 10 kilometers (6 miles) northeast of the city on the mainland. For flight information, tel. 041/661262.

Between the Airport and Downtown ATVO and ACTV (Venice City Transit) buses make the 25-minute trip in to Piazzale Roma, going through the city's unappealing outlying regions; the cost is around 4,000 lire. From Piazzale Roma visitors will most likely have to take a *vaporetto* (water bus) to their hotel. The Cooperative San Marco motor launch is only slightly more costly (11,000 lire), and presents a far more attractive introduction to the city; it drops passengers directly across the lagoon at Piazza San Marco. (It works on a limited schedule in winter.) Land taxis are available, running the same route as do the buses; cost is about 40,000 lire. Water taxis (slick high-power motorboats) are a real rip-off: Negotiate the fare in advance, usually upward of 100,000 lire.

By Train Make sure your train goes all the way to Santa Lucia train station in Venice's northeast corner; some trains leave passengers at the Mestre station on the mainland, from where you must connect with a local to Santa Lucia. The EPT-AAST information booth (open daily 8–8) and the baggage depot in the station are usually festooned with long lines of tourists. If you need a hotel room, go to the AVA hotel association desk (open daily 9–9); there are others at the airport and at the city garage at Piazzale Roma. The 20,000-lire deposit is discounted on your hotel bill. Vaporetto landing stages are directly outside the station. *Make sure you know how to get to your hotel before you arrive.* Don't take water taxis, as they are expensive and probably can't take you right to the door of your hotel. By water taxi or vaporetto you'll have to walk some distance anyway. For this reason, try to obtain a map of Venice before you arrive—and take a luggage cart, as porters are hard to find.

By Car You will have to leave your car in the Piazzale Roma garage, on the Tronchetto parking island, or even on the mainland. Some visitors park in Padua or Mestre and then take the train into Venice. From Tronchetto take ACTV bus no. 17 to Piazzale Roma, where you can get a vaporetto, or take Line 34 water bus direct to St. Mark's.

Getting Around

First-time visitors find that getting around Venice presents some unusual problems: the complexity of its layout (the city is made up of more than 100 islands, all linked by bridges); the bewildering unfamiliarity of waterborne transportation; the illogical house numbering system and duplication of street names in its six districts; and the necessity of walking whether you enjoy it or not. It's essential you have a good map showing all street names and water bus routes; buy one at any newsstand.

By Vaporetto ACTV water buses run the length of the Grand Canal and circle the city. There are several lines, some of which connect Venice with the major and minor islands in the lagoon; Line 1 is the Grand Canal local. Timetables are posted on all landing stages, where ticket booths are located (open early morning–9 PM). Buy single tickets or books of 10, and count your change carefully; shortchanging is a nasty habit in these parts. Fare is 1,500 lire on most lines, 2,000 lire for the Line 2 express between the train station, Rialto, San Marco, and the Lido. Stamp your ticket in the machine on the landing stage. A daily tourist ticket costs 8,000 lire. Vaporetti run every 10 minutes or so during the day; Lines 1, 2, and 5 run every hour between midnight and dawn. Landing stages are clearly marked with name and line number and serve boats going in both directions.

By Water Taxi Known as *motoscafi*, or *taxi*, these are excessively expensive, and the fare system is as complex as Venice's layout. A minimum fare of about 35,000 lire gets you nowhere, and you'll pay three times as much to get from one end of the Grand Canal to the other. *Always agree on the fare before starting out.* To avoid arguments, overcharging, and rip-offs, avoid them altogether.

By Traghetto Few tourists know about the two-man gondolas that ferry people across the Grand Canal at various fixed points. It's the cheapest and shortest gondola ride in Venice, and can save a lot of walking. Fare is 350 lire, which you hand to one of the gondoliers when you get on. Look for "Traghetto" signs.

By Gondola Don't leave Venice without treating yourself to a gondola ride, preferably in the quiet of the evening, when the churning traffic on the canals has died down, the palace windows are illuminated, and the only sounds are the muted splashes of the gondolier's oar. Make sure he understands you want to see the *rii*, or smaller canals, as well as the Grand Canal. They're supposed to charge a fixed minimum rate of about 50,000 lire for 50 minutes, but in practice they ask for 80,000–100,000 lire for a 30- to 40-minute ride. Come to terms with your gondolier *before* stepping into his boat.

On Foot This is the only way of reaching many parts of Venice, so wear comfortable shoes. Invest in a good map naming all streets, and count on getting lost more than once.

Important Addresses and Numbers

Tourist Information The main Venice **AAST Tourist Office** (tel. 041/522–6356) is at Calle Ascensione 71C, just off Piazza San Marco, under the arcade in the far left corner opposite the basilica. Open Mon.–Sat., Nov.–Mar., 8:30–1:30; Apr.–Oct., 8:30–7:30. There are EPT-AAST information booths at the Santa Lucia station (tel. 041/715016); in the bus terminal at Piazzale Roma (tel. 041/522–7402), open summer only; at Marco Polo airport; and at Tronchetto parking lot.

Consulates **U.K.:** Campo Santa Maria della Carità 1051, Dorsoduro, tel. 041/522–7207. **U.S.:** The nearest U.S. Consulate is in Milan, at Largo Donegani 1, tel. 02/652841.

Emergencies **Police:** tel. 113. **Ambulance:** tel. 041/523–0000. **Doctor:** Try the emergency room at Venice's hospital (tel. 041/523–0000), or call the British Consulate (*see* above) and ask for recommendations. **Pharmacies: Farmacia Italo-Inglese** Calle della Mandola (tel. 041/522–4837). **International Pharmacy** Calle Lunga San Marco (tel. 041/522–2311). Pharmacies are open weekdays 9–12:30 and 4–7:45; Saturday 9–12:45; Sunday and night service by turns.

Travel Agencies **American Express:** San Moise 1471, tel. 041/520–0844. **CIT:** Piazza San Marco 4850, tel. 041/528–5480. **Wagons-Lits/Travel:** Piazzetta dei Leoncini 289, tel. 041/522–3405.

Guided Tours

Orientation Tours **American Express** (tel. 041/520–0844) and **CIT** (tel. 041/528–5480) offer two-hour walking tours of the San Marco area, taking in the basilica and the Doge's Palace. The cost is about 30,000 lire. American Express also has an afternoon walking tour from April to October that ends with a gondola ride and glass-blowing demonstration. The cost is about 35,000 lire. "The Venice Experience" is a 45-minute multivision show about the history of the city, shown daily at **Cinema Centrale** (Piscina di Frezzeria, tel. 041/522–8201). Admission is 8,000 lire.

Special-Interest Tours **American Express, CIT,** and other operators offer group gondola rides with serenade. Cost is about 25,000 lire. During July and August free guided tours of St. Mark's basilica are offered by the Patriarchate of Venice; information is available at a desk in the atrium of the church (tel. 041/520–0333). Some tours are in English, and there are several daily, except Sunday.

Excursions Don't take organized tours to the islands of Murano, Burano, and/or Torcello. These tours are annoyingly commercial and emphasize glass factory showrooms, pressuring you to buy. You can easily do these islands on your own. **American Express** offers a bus trip to the Venetian Villas and Padua. The cost is about 50,000 lire, and they run from April to October on Tuesday, Thursday, and weekends. **CIT** runs an excursion on the Burchiello motor launch along the Brenta Canal, with return by bus.

Personal Guides **American Express** and **CIT** can provide guides for walking or gondola tours of Venice, or cars with driver and guide for excursions on the mainland. Pick up a list of licensed guides and their rates from the **AAST** Information Office in Piazza San Marco (tel. 041/522–6356).

Exploring Venice

Venice—La Serenissima, the Most Serene—is disorienting in its complexity, an extraordinary labyrinth of narrow streets and waterways, opening now and again onto some airy square or broad canal. The majority of its magnificent palazzos are slowly crumbling; though this sounds like a recipe for a down-at-the-heels slum, somehow in Venice the shabby, derelict effect is magically transformed into one of supreme beauty and charm rather than horrible urban decay. The place reeks with atmosphere, especially at night when the lights from the vaporetti and the stars overhead pick out the gargoyles and arches of the centuries-old facades. For hundreds of years Venice was the unrivaled mi tress of trade between Europe and the Orient, and the staunch bulwark of Christendom against the tide of Turkish expansion. Though the power and glory of its days as a wealthy city-republic are gone, the art and exotic aura remain.

To really enjoy the city, you will have to come to terms with the crowds, which take over from May through September. Hot and sultry in the summer, Venice is much more welcoming in early spring and late fall. Romantics like it in the winter when prices are much lower, the streets are deserted (well, nearly), and the sea mists impart a haunting melancholy to the *campi* (squares) and canals. Piazza San Marco (St. Mark's Square) is the pulse of Venice, crowded with people and pigeons no matter what time of year. But after joining with the crowds to visit the Basilica di San Marco and the Doge's Palace, strike out on your own and just follow where your feet take you—you won't be disappointed.

Numbers in the margin correspond with points of interest on the Venice map.

Piazza San Marco and the Accademia ❶ Even the pigeons have to fight for space on **Piazza San Marco,** and pedestrian traffic jams clog the surrounding byways. Despite the crowds and because it is the most famous piazza in Venice, San Marco is the logical starting place of each of our various itineraries. Pick up pamphlets and a copy of *A Guest in Venice,* a free information booklet, at the **AAST Information Office** in the far left corner of Piazza San Marco, opposite the basilica. The information office is in the wing built by order of

Napoleon to complete the much earlier palaces on either side of the square, enclosing it to form what he called "the most beautiful drawing room in all of Europe." Upstairs is the **Museo Correr,** with eclectic collections of historical objects and a picture gallery of fine 15th-century paintings. *Piazza San Marco, Ala Napoleonica, tel. 041/522-5625. Admission: 3,000 lire. Open Mon., Wed.-Sat. 10-4, Sun. 9-12:30.*

③ The **Basilica di San Marco** (St. Mark's Cathedral) was begun in the 11th century to hold the relics of St. Mark the Evangelist, the city's patron saint, and its richly decorated facade is surmounted by copies of the four famous gilded bronze horses (the originals are in the basilica's upstairs museum). Inside, golden mosaics sheathe walls and domes, lending an extraordinarily exotic aura, half Christian church, half Middle Eastern *souk.* Be sure to see the **Pala d'Oro,** an eye-filling 10th-century altarpiece in gold and silver, studded with precious gems and enamels. From the atrium, climb the steep stairway to the museum: The bronze horses alone are worth the effort. *The Basilica is open from early morning, but tourist visits are allowed Mon.-Sat. 9:30-5:30, Sun. 2:30-5:30. No admission to those wearing shorts or other revealing clothing. Pala d'Oro and Treasury. Admission: 500 lire. Open Apr.-Sept., Mon.-Sat. 9:30-5:30, Sun. 2-5:30. Oct.-Mar., Mon.-Sat. 10-5, Sun. 2-5. Gallery and Museum. Admission: 500 lire. Open Apr.-Sept., daily 9:30-5:30; Oct.-Mar., daily 10-5.*

④ Next to St. Mark's is the **Palazzo Ducale** (Doge's Palace), which, during Venice's prime, was the epicenter of the Serene Republic's great empire. More than just a palace, it was a combination White House, Senate, Supreme Court, torture chamber, and prison rolled into one. The exterior is striking: The lower stories consist of two rows of fragile-seeming, almost flimsy, arches, while above rests a massive pink-and-white marble wall, whose solidity is barely interrupted by its six great Gothic windows. The interior is a maze of vast halls, monumental staircases, secret corridors, state apartments, and the sinister prison cells and torture chamber. The palace is filled with frescoes, paintings, carvings, and a few examples of statuary by some of the Renaissance's greatest artists. Don't miss the famous view from the balcony, overlooking the piazza and St. Mark's Basin, and the church of San Giorgio Maggiore across the lagoon. *Piazzetta San Marco, tel. 041/522-4951. Admission: 5,000 lire. Open daily 8:30-7.*

⑤ For a pigeon's-eye view of Venice take the elevator up to the top of the **Campanile di San Marco** (St. Mark's bell tower) in Piazza San Marco, a reconstruction of the 1,000-year-old tower that collapsed one morning in 1912, practically without warning. Fifteenth-century clerics found guilty of immoral acts were suspended in wooden cages from the tower, sometimes to live on bread and water for as long as a year, sometimes to die of starvation and exposure. (Look for them in Carpaccio's paintings of the square that hang in the Accademia.) *Piazza San Marco, tel. 041/522-4064. Admission: 1,500 lire. Open Apr.-Oct., daily 9:30-7:30; Nov.-Mar. 10-4.*

Time Out **Caffè Florian** is a Venetian landmark, a great place to while away an hour or so nursing a Campari or a cappuccino. The pleasure of relaxing amid so much history does not come cheap. A pot of hot chocolate indoors runs about $10, and outside on

Venice

San Michele

0   440 yards
0   400 meters

Sacca
della
Misericordia

Canale delle Navi

Racchetta
Fondamenta
Rio S. Caterina
Gesuiti Nuovo
R.d.

Strada
Nuova

Rio d. Santi Apostoli
Rio della Panada
C.d Squero
dei Mendicanti

Campo d.
Pescheria

Erberia

C.d Testa
C.d Pistor

Campo Santi
Giovanni e Paolo

R.d S. Giustina

dal Vin

del Carbon

⑭

Rio d. S. Marina

R. Barbaria delle Tole

⑫

⑬

R.d. Fava

Sot. di S. Lio

Ruga
Giuffa

R.d. S. Severo

R.d. S. Lorenzo

⑪

R.d S. Francesco

Canale d. Galeazze

Campo
Manin

C.d. Bande

R. d. Palazzo

C. Lion
Furlani

C.d. Scudi

R.d Gorne

Fond. Osmarin

R.d Greci

R.d Pietà

Fabbri

Frezzeria

①

②

⑤

③

④

Darsena
Grande

Rio d. Vergini

di S. Pietro

Rio d. S. Daniele

Mola

Riva degli

Schiavoni

S. Moisè

R. d.

⑥

⑦

Piazza
San Marco

R.d. Arsenale

Rio della Tana

V. Garibaldi

Rio d. S. Anna

Can.

Canale di S. Marco

Riva dei Sette Martiri

R.d S. Giuseppe

Isola di
S. Giorgio
Maggiore

Viale Trieste

Rio dei Giardini

Ci

Fond.
delle Zitelle

Calle
Michelangelo

the piazza, which is really where you want to sit, prices are even higher, and there's an extra charge if you're served when the orchestra is playing.

6 Armed with a street map, head west out of San Marco (in the opposite direction to the basilica), making your way past **San Moisè**'s elaborate Baroque facade and by the American Express office, on to Calle Lunga 22 Marzo, where the inconspicuous **Caravella** restaurant of the hotel Saturnia (*see* both Dining and Lodging) is one of the city's best. Continue on **7** to the church of **Santa Maria del Giglio,** behind the **Gritti Palace hotel** (also considered tops). Across the bridge behind the church, **Piazzesi** on Campiello Feltrina is famous for its handprinted paper and desk accessories. In the next little square, **Norelene** (Campo San Maurizio 2606) has stunning handprinted fabrics in opulent Fortuny designs.

Time Out You must cross yet another bridge to get to Campo Santa Stefano, also known as Campo Morosini, where you can indulge yourself with some of the best ice cream you've ever eaten, at **Paolin,** a tiny bar whose outdoor tables occupy a good chunk of the vast campo.

8 Join the stream of pedestrians crossing the Grand Canal on the wooden **Accademia Bridge,** and head straight on for the **Galleria dell'Accademia** (Academy of Fine Arts), Venice's most important picture gallery and a must for art lovers. Try to spend at least an hour viewing this remarkable collection of Venetian art, which is attractively displayed and well lit. Works range from 14th-century Gothic and Bellini's 15th-century oils to the Golden Age of the 16th century, represented by Titian, including his last work, the *Pietà;* Tintoretto, including his *Virgin of the Treasures* and *Miracles of St. Mark;* and Veronese. *Campo della Carità, tel. 041/522-2247. Admission: 4,000 lire. Open Mon.–Sat. 9–2, Sun. 9–1.*

Once again consulting your map, make your way through Calle Contarini, Calle Toeletta, and Campo San Barnaba to Rio Terra Canal, where **Mondonovo** ranks as one of the city's most interesting mask shops (Venetians love masks of all kinds, from gilded lions to painted sun faces and sinister death's heads). Just around the corner is Campo Santa Margherita, which has a homey feel.

Time Out **Antico Capon** is a good, simple trattoria whose tables spill out onto the square in fair weather. Stop in for a pizza, or just relax outside with a glass of beer. *Campo Santa Margherita.*

9 Continue past Campo San Pantalon to Campo San Rocco, just beside the immense church of the Frari. The **Scuola di San Rocco** was embellished with more than 50 canvases by Tintoretto in the 1500s; they are an impressive sight, dark paintings aglow with figures hurtling dramatically through space amid flashes of light and color. *The Crucifixion* in the Albergo (the room just off the great hall) is held to be his masterpiece. *Campo di San Rocco. Admission: 5,000 lire. Open daily 10–1 and 3:30–6:30.*

10 The church of Santa Maria Gloriosa dei Frari (known simply as the **Frari**) is one of Venice's most important churches, a vast soaring Gothic building of brick. As it is the principal church of the Franciscans, its design is suitably austere to reflect that order's vows of poverty, though paradoxically it contains a number of the most sumptuous pictures in any Venetian church. Chief among these are the magnificent Titian altarpieces, notably the immense *Assumption of the Virgin* over the main altar. Titian was buried here at the ripe old age of 88, the only one of 70,000 plague victims to be given a personal church burial. *Campo dei Frari. Admission: 500-lire donation "for lighting expenses."*

San Zanipolo and the Rialto Backtracking once again to the Piazza San Marco, go to the arch under the Torre dell'Orologio (Clock Tower) and head off northeast into the **Merceria,** one of Venice's busiest streets and, with the **Frezzeria** and **Calle Fabbri,** part of the shopping area that extends across the Grand Canal into the **Rialto district.** At Campo San Zulian, turn right into Calle Guerra and Calle delle Bande to the graceful white marble church of **Santa Maria Formosa;** it's situated right on a lively square (of the same name) with a few sidewalk cafés and a small vegetable market on weekday mornings. **⑪**

Use your map to follow Calle Borgoloco into Campo San Marina, where you turn right, crossing the little canal, and take Calle Castelli to **Santa Maria dei Miracoli** (Calle Castelli). Perfectly proportioned and sheathed in marble, this late-15th-century building embodies all the classical serenity of the early Renaissance. The interior is decorated with marble reliefs by the church's architect, Pietro Lombardo, and his son Tullio. **⑫**

Retrace your steps along Calle Castelli and cross the bridge into Calle delle Erbe, following signs for "SS. Giovanni e Paolo." The massive Dominican church of Santi Giovanni e Paolo—**San Zanipolo,** as it's known in the slurred Venetian dialect—is the twin (and rival) of the Franciscan Frari. The church is a kind of pantheon of the doges (25 are buried here), and contains a wealth of artworks. Outside in the campo stands Verrocchio's equestrian statue of Colleoni, who fought for the Venetian cause in the mid-1400s. **⑬**

Cross the canal in front of the church (keeping an eye out to the left for the pop-eyed, tongue-lolling gargoyle at head height), and continue along Calle Larga, crossing a pair of bridges to Campiello Santa Maria Nova. Take Salita San Canciano to Salita San Giovanni Crisostomo to find yourself once again in the mainstream of pedestrians winding their way to the **Rialto Bridge.** Street stalls hung with scarves and gondolier's hats signal that you are entering the heart of Venice's shopping district. Cross over the bridge, and you'll find yourself in the market district. Try to visit the Rialto market when it's in full swing, with fruit and vegetable vendors hawking their wares in a colorful and noisy jumble of sights and sounds. Not far beyond is the fish market, where you'll probably find sea creatures you've never seen before (and possibly won't want to see again). A left turn into Ruga San Giovanni and Ruga del Ravano will bring you face to face with scores of shops: At **La Scialuppa** (Calle Saoneri 2695) you'll find hand-carved wooden models of gondolas and their graceful oar locks known as *forcole.* **⑭**

The Grand Canal Just off the Piazzetta di San Marco (the little square that abuts St. Mark's) you can catch Vaporetto Line 1 at either the San Marco or San Zaccaria landing stages (on Riva degli Schiavoni), to set off on a boat tour along the **Grand Canal.** Serving as Venice's main thoroughfare, the canal winds in the shape of an "S" for more than 3½ kilometers (2 miles) through the heart of the city, past some 200 Gothic-Renaissance palaces. This is the route taken by vaporetti, gondolas, water taxis, mail boats, police boats, fire boats, ambulance boats, barges carrying provisions and building materials, bridal boats, and funeral boats. See it both when traffic is at a peak (preferably from a vantage point such as the Rialto Bridge), and again when it's calm and quiet. Your vaporetto tour will give you an idea of the opulent beauty of its palaces, and a peek into the side streets and tiny canals where the Venetians go about their daily business. *Vaporetto Line 1. Cost: 1,500 lire.*

Here are some of the key buildings that this tour passes. The **Gallerie dell'Accademia,** with its fine collection of 14th- to 18th-century Venetian paintings, that were visited earlier. The **⓯ Ca'Rezzonico** was built in 1680 and is now a museum with Vene- **⓰** tian paintings and furniture. **Ca'Foscari** is a 15th-century Gothic building that was once the home of Doge Foscari, who was unwillingly deposed and died the following day! Today it's **⓱** part of Venice's university. The **Fondaco dei Turchi** was an original Byzantium "house-warehouse" of a rich Venetian merchant, but the building has suffered some remodeling in the last **⓲** 100 years. **Ca'd'Oro** is the most flowery palace on the canal; it **⓳** now houses the Galleria Francheti. The **Palazzo Vendramin Calergi** is a Renaissance building where Wagner died in 1883. It's also the winter home of the municipal casino. Last but not **⓴** least, there is the **Peggy Guggenheim Museum,** which usually has excellent exhibitions (*see* Off the Beaten Track).

Off the Beaten Track

Explore the **Ghetto,** where Venice's Jewish community lived in cramped quarters for many centuries, and visit the **Museo Ebraico** (Jewish Museum, Campo del Ghetto, tel. 041/521–5359) and the Ghetto's several synagogues. In the same area, go to view the Tintorettos in the Gothic church of the **Madonna dell'Orto** (just off the Strada Nuova).

Visit late heiress Peggy Guggenheim's house and collection of modern art, **Palazzo Venier dei Leoni** on the Grand Canal. *Entrance: Calle San Cristo, tel. 041/520–6288. Admission: 5,000 lire, free on Sat. Open Apr.–Oct., Sun., Mon., Wed.–Fri. noon–6, Sat. 6–9 PM.*

Have an ice cream at one of the cafés on the Zattere and watch the big ships steam slowly down the Giudecca Canal.

Explore the island of San Pietro di Castello, at the end of Via Garibaldi. The Renaissance church of **San Pietro** and its tipsy bell tower stand on a grassy square surrounded by workaday canals and boatyards. San Pietro was Venice's cathedral for centuries (St. Mark's was the Doges' ceremonial chapel).

Take Vaporetto Line 20 from Riva degli Schiavoni to visit the Armenian monastery on the island of San Lazzaro degli Armeni, near the Lido. *Tel. 041/526–0104. Donation welcome. Open Thurs.–Tues. 3:30–5:10.*

Shopping

Glass   Venetian glass is as famous as the city's gondolas, and almost every shop window displays it. There's a lot of cheap glass for sale; if you want something better, among the top showrooms are **Venini** (Piazzetta dei Leoncini 314), **Pauly** (Calle dell'Ascensione 72, opposite the AAST information office), **Salviati** (Piazza San Marco 78 and 110), **Cenedese** (Piazza San Marco 139), and **Isola** (Campo San Moisè and Mercerie 723). On the island of Murano, where prices are generally no lower than in Venice, **Domus** (Fondamenta dei Vetrai) has a good selection.

Shopping District   The main shopping area extends from the Piazza San Marco through the Mercerie and Calle Fabbri toward the Rialto.

Department Stores   The **Coin** store (Campo San Bartolomeo) specializes in fashion and accessories. **Standa** has stores on Campo San Luca and Strada Nuova, where you can pick up medium-price goods of all kinds.

Dining

Venetian restaurants are more expensive than those in Florence or Rome; figure on spending about 15,000 to 20,000 lire more for the same sort of meal. Beware of the tourist traps around the Piazza San Marco: prices here are higher than most, and the food isn't up to par. City specialties include *pasta e fagioli*, a thick bean soup; risotto and all kinds of seafood; and the delicious *fegato alla veneziana*, thin strips of liver cooked with onions, served with grilled *polenta*, cornmeal cakes.

For details and price category definitions, *see* Dining in Staying in Italy.

Very Expensive   **Danieli Terrace.** Seafood is the star here: Try the *branzino al*
★   *forno* (baked sea bass) if it's on the menu, otherwise the scampi is almost as good as that at the Gritti. Desserts such as *zabaglione* (a fluffy confection combining egg yolk, sugar, and dry marsala) are fabulous—it's worth bearing this in mind as you order the main meal. Fair weather sees patrons dining on the candlelit terrace; otherwise you'll be seated in the opulent pastel-toned dining room—either way you'll be treated to a view of San Giorgio and the lagoon. *Hotel Danieli, Riva degli Schiavoni 4196, tel. 041/522-6480. Reservations advised. AE, DC, MC, V.*

Gritti. The dining room of the Gritti Palace hotel is one of Venice's most elegant eating spots. Its flower-filled terrace overlooking the Grand Canal is magical in the evening when the traffic dies down and the white dome of Santa Maria della Salute gleams in the distance. The *risotto con scampi* is delicious as prepared by the Gritti's talented chef, and the sole is well worth trying, too. *Hotel Gritti, Campo Santa Maria del Giglio 2467, tel. 041/522-6044. Reservations advised. AE, DC, MC, V.*

Expensive   **Antico Martini.** This Venetian institution is both chic and discreet, and its menu is made up mostly of Venetian specialties, though there are a few concessions to international palates. The seafood cocktail is first-class, the creamy *tiramesù* (a coffee-flavored sponge cake with soured cream cheese) an admirable end to any meal. There are outdoor tables in the summer, and a softly lit wood-paneled winter dining room.

Campo San Fantin 1983, tel. 041/522-4121. Reservations advised. AE, DC, MC, V. Closed Tues., Wed. lunch, Dec., and Feb.

★ **La Caravella.** Tiny and intimate, La Caravella is decorated like the dining saloon of an old Venetian sailing ship, with lots of authentic touches. The menu is huge and slightly intimidating, though the highly competent maître d' will advise you well. The *granseola* (crab) is marvelous in any of several versions. *Calle Larga XXII Marzo 2397, tel. 041/520-8901. Reservations essential. AE, DC, MC, V. Closed Wed. from Nov.-Apr.*

Moderate **Da Arturo.** The tiny Da Arturo makes a refreshing change from the numerous seafood restaurants Venetians are so fond of. The cordial proprietor prefers, instead, to offer spaghetti with seasonal vegetables, and meat dishes like the excellent *braciolona di maiale* (pork chop in vinegar). *Calle degli Assassini, tel. 041/528-6974. Reservations essential. No credit cards. Closed Sun., Aug., and the week after Christmas.*

★ **Fiaschetteria Toscana.** This is one of the city's best Moderate restaurants, which is why you'll see so many Venetians in the pleasant upstairs dining room or under the arbor in the square out front. Courteous, cheerful waiters serve such specialties as *rombo* (turbot) with capers, and an exceptionally good *spaghetti con frutti di mare* (pasta with shellfish). Some seafood dishes can be expensive. *Campo San Giovanni Crisostomo, tel. 041/ 528-5281. Reservations advised. AE, DC, MC, V. Closed Tues. and first 2 weeks in July.*

Locanda Montin. Though unlikely to win any gastronomic awards, Montin is friendly and fun, and enjoys a considerable reputation. You'll find all sorts of patrons sharing white linen-clothed tables, from the neighborhood locals to Viscount Linley, nephew of England's Queen Elizabeth. The garden out back is used as a flower-filled extension during summer months. At any time of year, try the *fegato alla veneziana* (liver and onions) or the delicious veal escalope. *Fondamenta Eremite 1147, tel. 041/522-7151. Reservations advised. No credit cards. Closed Tues. eve. and Wed.*

Inexpensive **Ai Coristi.** This family-run restaurant near the Teatro La
★ Fenice has a wood-beamed indoor dining room and an attractive summer terrace across the narrow street, candlelit on summer evenings. Among the specialties are *papardelle alla buranea* (noodles with scallops), and grilled meat or fish. The salads are excellent. *Calle della Chiesa, tel. 041/522677. Reservations advised. No credit cards. Closed Wed.*

Da Ignazio. A smiling waiter will welcome you to this attractive little trattoria in the Rialto district, where you'll find a tempting display of fruits and vegetables fresh from the nearby market. Specialties include *pasta e fagioli* (bean soup) and *seppie* (squid) Venetian-style. *Calle dei Saoneri, near San Polo, tel. 041/523-4852. Dinner reservations advised. No credit cards. Closed Sat.*

Osteria ai Schiavoni. If it's authentic Venetian atmosphere and cooking you're after, this is the place. A few steps off Riva degli Schiavoni near Campo Bandiera e Moro, the Schiavoni has a few tables outdoors and a dark-paneled dining room. Seafood is the specialty; try *sardine in saor* (marinated sardines) or fish risotto, but don't expect large portions. *Calle del Dose 3743, tel. 041/522-6763. Dinner reservations advised. AE, DC, MC, V. Closed Wed. and last week in Nov.*

Lodging

Venice is made up almost entirely of time-worn buildings, so it stands to reason that the majority of hotels are in renovated palaces. Top hotels may still contain palatial trappings, though some Cinderella-type rooms may be small and dowdy. Rooms in Moderate and Inexpensive hotels are often cramped and spartanly decorated, with thin walls, and little or no lounging space. Air-conditioning is essential for survival in summer heat; many hotels charge a hefty supplement for it. The main tourist season runs from mid-March through October, December 20 to New Year's Day, and the two-week Carnival period in mid-February. Make reservations well in advance at all times, but especially so for these periods.

Hotel rates are higher than those in Rome or Florence, but you can save considerably on low-season rates. For details and price category definitions, *see* Lodging in Staying in Italy.

Very Expensive **Cipriani.** A sybaritic oasis of stunningly decorated rooms and suites, the Cipriani is located across St. Mark's Basin on the island of Giudecca (pronounced jew-dekka), offering a panorama of romantic views of San Giorgio Maggiore and the entire lagoon. The hotel launch whisks guests back and forth to the Piazza San Marco at any hour of day or night. Cooking courses and fitness programs are offered as special programs to occupy the guests. Then, for sheer dining pleasure, there is the excellent Cipriani restaurant. Some rooms have pretty garden patios. *Guidecca 10, tel. 041/520–7744. 98 rooms with bath. Facilities: pool, gardens, tennis, health club. AE, DC, MC, V. Closed Nov. 11–Feb. 26.*

Danieli. A 15th-century palazzo is the hub of this exceptionally gracious and opulent hotel, surrounded by a cluster of modern, balconied wings. Sumptuous Venetian decor and atmosphere predominates, though some lower-price rooms can be drab. Celebrities love the Danieli, and it's an especial favorite of English-speaking visitors. The restaurant (*see* Dining) and bar are unashamedly swanky; and the terrace has a fantastic view of St. Mark's Basin. *Riva degli Schiavoni 4196, tel. 041/522–6480. 230 rooms with bath. AE, DC, MC, V.*

★ **Gritti Palace.** The atmosphere of an aristocratic private home is what the management is after here, and they succeed beautifully. Fresh-cut flowers, fine antiques, sumptuous appointments, and Old World service make this a terrific choice for anyone who wants to be totally pampered. The dining terrace overlooking the Grand Canal is best in the evening when boat traffic dies down. *Campo Santa Maria del Giglio 2467, tel. 041/794611. 98 rooms with bath. AE, DC, MC, V.*

Expensive **Londra Palace.** You get the obligatory view of San Giorgio and St. Mark's Basin at this distinguished hotel whose rooms are decorated in dark paisley prints, with sophisticated touches such as canopied beds. Do Leoni restaurant serves creative cuisine (try the avocado with scampi), the piano bar is open late, and a jogging map thoughtfully provided by the management will help you work off the previous night's excesses. *Riva degli Schiavoni 4171, tel. 041/520–0533. 69 rooms with bath. Facilities: terrace solarium. AE, DC, MC, V.*

★ **Metropole.** With a wonderful decadence, guests can step from their water taxi or gondola into the lobby of this small hotel just five minutes from the Piazza San Marco. Many rooms have a view of the lagoon and all rooms are furnished with style. Ask for one of the quiet spacious rooms on the garden (room 141 is the nicest). *Riva degli Schiavoni 4149, tel. 041/520–5044. 65 rooms with bath. Facilities: restaurant, bar and grill room. AE, DC, MC, V.*

Saturnia Internazionale. Beamed ceilings, damask-hung walls, and authentic Venetian decor impart real character and charm to the solid comfort of the Saturnia's rooms and salons. Many rooms, among them nos. 80, 82, and 84, have been redecorated in chic style and endowed with glamorous bathrooms. The historic palace-hotel is centrally located near Piazza San Marco. *Calle Larga XXII Marzo 2398, tel. 041/520–8377. 97 rooms with bath. Facilities: 2 restaurants, bar. AE, DC, MC, V.*

★ **Accademia.** There's plenty of atmosphere and a touch of the romantic in this delightful hotel in a 17th-century villa. Rooms are comfortable and brightly furnished, as are the sitting rooms on the ground floor. Many rooms overlook the pretty gardens, where you can sit in warm weather. Lots of regulars come back year after year. *Fondamenta Bollani 1058, Dorsoduro, tel. 041/523–7846. 27 rooms, most with bath. Facilities: gardens, bar. AE, DC, MC, V.*

Moderate **La Residenza.** A Gothic palace makes a delightful setting for this charming hotel, conveniently close to both San Marco and the San Zaccaria landing stage. The comfortable breakfast room is furnished with some antique touches, and rooms on the lower floor are especially good. Make reservations well in advance. *Campo Bandiera e Moro 3608, tel. 041/528–5315. 19 rooms, some with bath. AE, DC, MC, V. Closed 2nd week Jan–mid-Feb, mid-Nov.–2nd week Dec.*

Scandinavia. Despite its curiously un-Italian name, this hotel indulges heavily in traditional—and somewhat overpowering—Venetian decor, with cut-glass chandeliers and dizzying combinations of damask patterns on walls, floor, sofas, and chairs. The entrance is at the top of a very steep staircase, just off the lively Campo Santa Maria Formosa (near the San Zaccaria landing stage). *Campo Santa Maria Formosa 5240, tel. 041/522–3507. 27 rooms, 17 with bath. AE, V.*

Inexpensive **Alboretti.** Redecorated in 1986, this small hotel is simply but at-
★ tractively furnished. Despite its size and central location, the Alboretti has a little garden courtyard off the breakfast room and a lounge upstairs from the tiny lobby and bar area. There is no restaurant and no elevator. Although rates are slightly high for this category, the Alboretti offers good value. *Rio Terra Sant'Agnese 882, tel. 041/523–0058. 19 rooms with bath. AE, MC, V. Closed Nov. 14–Dec. 15.*

Galleria. Guests won't find much in the way of luxury here, but low prices, friendly staff (definitely no English spoken, but lots of smiles and nods), and a fine location hard by the Accademia Bridge make this a strong favorite. Ask for a room overlooking the Grand Canal—the view is one of the best in Venice. *Accademia 878–A, Dorsoduro, tel. 041/704–4172. 10 rooms, most with bath. No credit cards.*

★ **San Stefano.** This is a hotel in miniature, from the tiny reception area to the minuscule courtyard and breakfast room; even the elevator is skinny. Rooms are well-furnished in Venetian style, with optional air-conditioning and TV. All in all, it's an excellent value, and centrally located, too. *Campo San Stefano*

2957, tel. 041/520–0166. 14 rooms, most with bath. No credit cards.

The Arts

For a program of events, pick up the free *Guest in Venice* booklet at the AAST tourist office in Piazza San Marco, or at most hotel desks. Your hotel may also be able to get you tickets for some events.

Concerts A **Vivaldi Festival** is held in September, and concerts are held year-round in the city's churches; contact the **Kele e Teo Agency** (Piazza San Marco 4930, tel. 041/520–8722), which supplies tickets for many of the city's musical events.

Opera The opera season at **Teatro La Fenice** (Campo San Fantin, tel. 041/521–0161) runs from December to May. The box office is open September to July, daily 9:30–12:30 and 4–6.

Entertainment and Nightlife

You won't find much in the way of organized nightlife in this city. The **Martini Scala Club** (Calle delle Veste, near Teatro La Fenice, tel. 041/522–4121) is an elegant piano bar with late-night restaurant. The bars of the top hotels stay open as long as their customers keep on drinking. **El Souk** disco (Calle Contrarini 1056, near the Accademia, tel. 041/520–0371) draws a fairly sophisticated young crowd.

Campania

Campania (made up of Naples and its environs) is where most people's preconceived ideas of Italy become a reality. You'll find lots of sun, good food that relies heavily on tomatoes and mozzarella, acres of classical ruins, and gorgeous scenery. The exuberance of the locals doesn't leave much room for efficient organization, however, and you may have to revise your concept of real time; here minutes dilate into hours at the drop of a hat.

Once a city that rivaled Paris as a brilliant and refined cultural capital, Naples is afflicted by acute urban decay and chronic delinquency. You need patience, stamina, and a healthy dose of caution to visit Naples on your own, but it's worth it for those who have a sense of adventure and the capacity to discern the enormous riches the city has accumulated in its 2,000-year existence.

On the other hand, if you want the fun without the hassle, head for Sorrento, Capri, and the Amalfi coast, legendary haunts of the sirens who tried to lure Odysseus off course. Sorrento is touristy but has some fine old hotels and beautiful views; it's a good base for a leisurely excursion to Pompeii. Capri is a pintsize paradise, though sometimes too crowded for comfort, while the Amalfi coast has some enchanting towns and spectacular scenery.

Getting Around

By Plane There are several daily flights between Rome and Naples's Capodichino Airport (tel. 081/780–5763, 7 kilometers (4 miles) north of the downtown area. During the summer months there's a direct helicopter service between Capodichino and Capri; for information tel. 081/837–0644.

By Train A great number of trains run between Rome and Naples every day; Intercity trains make the journey in less than two hours. There are several stations in Naples, and a network of suburban trains connects the city with several points of interest in Campania. The central station is at Piazza Garibaldi (tel. 081/264644). Naples has a Metropolitana (subway), but it's old, and trains are infrequent; the fare is 600 lire.

By Bus For bus information, call **SITA** (tel. 081/552–2176) or the Naples Transport Board (tel. 081/554–0507).

By Car The Naples–Pompeii–Salerno toll road has exits at Ercolano (Herculaneum) and Pompeii, and connects with the tortuous coastal road to Sorrento and the Amalfi coast at the Castellamare exit. Driving within Naples is not recommended: Window smashing and robbery are not uncommon.

By Boat Boats and hydrofoils for the islands, the Sorrento peninsula, and the Amalfi coast leave from the Molo Beverello, in Naples's Piazza Municipio. **Caremar** (tel. 081/551–3882) has frequent passenger and car ferry service, and operates hydrofoils as well. **Alilauro** (tel. 081/684288) and **SNAV** (tel. 081/660444) provide hydrofoil service.

Guided Tours

Aside from the one-, two-, or three-day guided tours of the area departing from Rome, offered by **American Express** (tel. 06/67641), **CIT** (tel. 06/47941), **Appian Line** (tel. 06/464151) and other operators, **CIT** in Naples (Piazza Municipio 70, tel. 081/552546) has a wide range of half-day and all-day tours on the mainland and to the islands. Similar tours are offered by **Cima Tours** (Piazza Garibaldi 114, tel. 081/554–0646), **Tourcar** (Piazza Matteotti 1, tel. 081/323310), and **Aritur** (Piazza Trieste e Trento 7, tel. 081/400487).

Tourist Information

Capri. Piazza Umberto I 19, tel. 081/837–0686.
Naples. EPT Information Offices at Via Partenope 10, tel. 081/406289; central station, tel. 081/268779; Mergellina station, tel. 081/7612102; and Capodichino Airport, tel. 081/780–5761. AAST Information Office, Piazza del Gesù, tel. 081/552–3328.
Sorrento. Via De Maio 35, tel. 081/878–2104.

Exploring Campania

Naples Founded by the Greeks, **Naples** became a playground of the Romans, and was ruled thereafter by a succession of foreign dynasties, all of which left traces of their cultures in the city and its environs. The most splendid of these rulers were the Bourbons, who were responsible for much of what you will want to see in Naples, starting with the 17th-century **Palazzo Reale** (Royal Palace), still furnished in the lavish Baroque style that suited them so well. *Piazza Plebiscito, tel. 081/413888. Admission: 3,000 lire. Open Mon.–Sat. 9–2, Sun. 9–1.*

Across the way is the massive stone **Castel Nuovo,** which was built by the city's Aragon rulers in the 13th century; it's not

Campania

open to the public. Walk up Via Toledo, keeping an eye on the antics of the Neapolitans, whose daily lives are fraught with theatrical gestures and fiery speeches: They all seem to be unselfconscious actors in their own human comedy.

Time Out Stop in at **Caflish,** a historic café that has recently added a good fast-food counter, and try a *sfogliatella,* a delicious, clam-shaped Neapolitan pastry. *Via Toledo 253.*

Continue along Via Toledo, whose name changes to Via Roma, and make a detour to the right to see the oddly faceted stone facade and elaborate Baroque interior of the church of the **Gesù** (Via Benedetto Croce) and, directly opposite, the church of **Santa Chiara,** built in the early 1300s in Provençal Gothic style. A favorite Neapolitan song celebrates the quiet beauty of its cloister, decorated in delicate floral tiles.

Time Out For an authentic Neapolitan pizza in a 100% genuine pizzeria, stop in at **Lombardi,** where you can have a classic pizza made in a wood-fired brick oven or a full meal in a tiny, crowded setting with no frills and lots of atmosphere. *Via Benedetto Croce 59.*

Another detour off Via Roma, to the left this time, takes you from **Piazza Dante** to the Montesanto funicular, which ascends to the Vomero hill, where you can see the bastions of **Castel Sant'Elmo** and visit the museum in the **Certosa di San Martino,** a Carthusian monastery restored in the 17th century. It contains an eclectic collection of Neapolitan landscape paintings, royal carriages, and *presepi* (Christmas crèches). Check out the view from the balcony off room no. 25. *Certosa di San Martino, tel. 081/377005. Admission: 3,000 lire. Open Tues.– Sat. 9–2, Sun. 9–1.*

Return to Piazza Dante and follow Via Pessina to (an extension of Via Roma) the **Museo Archeologico Nazionale.** Dusty and unkempt, the museum undergoes perpetual renovations, but it holds one of the world's great collections of antiquities. Greek and Roman sculptures, vividly colored mosaics, countless objects from Pompeii and Herculaneum, and an equestrian statue of Nerva are all worth seeing. *Piazza Museo, tel. 081/440166. Admission: 4,000 lire. Open Mon.–Sat. 9–2, Sun. 9–1.*

About a mile north on the same road (take a bus or a taxi), you'll come to the **Museo di Capodimonte,** housed in an 18th-century palace built by Bourbon king Charles III, and surrounded by a vast park that must have been lovely when it was better cared for. In the picture gallery are some fine Renaissance paintings; climb the stairs to the terrace for a magnificent view of Naples and the bay. Downstairs you can visit the State Apartments and see the extensive collection of porcelain, much of it produced in the Bourbons' own factory right here on the grounds. *Parco di Capodimonte, tel. 081/741–0881. Admission: 4,000 lire. Tues.–Sat. 9–2, Sun. 9–1.*

Herculaneum   **Herculaneum** (Ercolano) lies 14 kilometers (9 miles) southeast of Naples. Reputed to have been founded by the legendary Hercules, the elite Roman resort was devastated by the same volcanic eruption that deluged Pompeii in AD 79. Recent excavations have revealed that many died on the shore in an attempt to escape, as a slow-moving mud slide embalmed the entire town by covering it with a 11-meter (35-foot), deep blanket of volcanic ash and ooze. While that may have been unfortunate for Herculaneum's home owners, it was fortunate for us. Herculaneum has been marvelously preserved for nearly two millennia! *Corso Ercolano, tel. 081/739–0963. Admission: 4,000 lire. Open daily 9–one hour before sunset.*

Pompeii   **Pompeii,** a larger community 8 kilometers (5 miles) farther to the east, lost even more residents. An estimated 2,000 of them perished on that fateful August day. The ancient city of Pompeii was much larger than Herculaneum, and excavations have progressed to a much greater extent (though the remains are not as well preserved, due to some 18th-century scavenging for museum-quality artworks, most of which you are able to see at Naples's Museo Archeologico Nazionale). This prosperous Roman city had an extensive forum, lavish baths and temples, and patrician villas richly decorated with frescoes. It's worth buying a detailed guide of the site in order to give meaning and understanding to the ruins and their importance. Be sure to see the **Villa dei Misteri,** whose frescoes are in mint condition. Perhaps that is a slight exaggeration, but the paintings are so rich with detail and depth of color that one finds it difficult to believe that they are 1,900 years old. Look at how the women in the frescoes impose sensuality, how the depictions of sacrifices give spirit, how the scenes of flagellation give torment, how the wedding of Dionysus and Ariadne gives ribald joy, and how the dressing of the bride inspires anticipation. Have lots of small change handy to tip the guards at the more important houses so they will unlock the gates for you. *Pompeii Scavi, tel. 081/862–1181. Admission: 5,000 lire. Open daily 9–one hour before sunset.*

Sorrento Another 28 kilometers (18 miles) southwest is **Sorrento,** in the not-too-distant past a small, genteel resort for a fashionable elite. Now the town has spread out along the crest of its fabled cliffs. Once this was an area full of secret haunts for the few tourists who came for the beauty of this coastline. Now, it has been "discovered" and the secret haunts are the playground for package tours. In Sorrento's case, however, the change is not as grim as it sounds, since nothing can dim the delights of the marvelous climate and view of the Bay of Naples. For the best views go to the **Villa Comunale,** near the old church of **San Francesco** (in itself worth a visit), or to the terrace behind the **Museo Correale.** The museum, an attractive 18th-century villa, houses an interesting collection of decorative arts (furniture, china, and so on), and paintings of the Neapolitan school. *Via Capasso, tel. 081/878–0000. Open Oct.–Jan. and Mar., Mon., Wed.–Sat. 9:30–12:30 and 3–5, Sun. 9:30–12:30; Apr.–Sept., Mon., Wed.–Sat. 9:30–12:30 and 4–7, Sun. 9:30–12:30; closed Tues. and Feb.*

Capri Sorrento makes a convenient jumping-off spot for a boat trip to **Capri.** No matter how many day-trippers crowd onto the island, no matter how touristy certain sections have become, Capri remains one of Italy's loveliest places. Incoming visitors disembark at Marina Grande, from where you can take some time out for an excursion to the **Grotta Azzurra** (Blue Grotto). Be warned that this must rank as one of the country's all-time great rip-offs: Motorboat, rowboat, and grotto admissions are charged separately, and if there's a line of boats waiting, you'll have little time to enjoy the grotto's marvelous colors. At Marina Grande you can also embark on an excursion boat around the island.

A cog railway or bus service takes you up to the town of Capri, where you can stroll through the **Piazzetta,** a choice place to watch the action and window-shop expensive boutiques on your way to the **Gardens of Augustus,** which have gorgeous views. The town of Capri is deliberately commercial and self-consciously picturesque. To get away from the crowds, hike to **Villa Jovis,** one of the many villas that Roman emperor Tiberius built on the island, at the end of a lane that climbs steeply uphill. The walk takes about 45 minutes, with pretty views all the way and a final spectacular vista of the entire Bay of Naples and part of the Gulf of Salerno. *Via Tiberio. Admission: 2,000 lire. Open daily 9–one hour before sunset.*

Or take the bus or a jaunty open taxi to **Anacapri** and look for the little church of **San Michele,** off Via Orlandi, where a magnificent handpainted majolica tile floor shows you an 18th-century vision of the Garden of Eden.

From Piazza della Vittoria, picturesque Via Capodimonte leads to **Villa San Michele,** charming former home of Swedish scientist-author Axel Munthe, now open to the public. *Via Axel Munthe. Admission: 3,000 lire. Open daily 9–one hour before sunset.*

Amalfi and Positano From Sorrento, the coastal drive down to the resort town of Amalfi provides some of the most dramatic and beautiful scenery you'll find in all Italy. Midway along, **Positano**'s jumble of pastel houses, topped by whitewashed cupolas, cling to the mountainside above the sea. The town—the prettiest along this stretch of coast—attracts a sophisticated group of visitors and summer residents who find that its relaxed and friendly atmosphere more than compensates for the sheer effort of moving about this exhaustingly vertical town, most of whose streets are stairways. This former fishing village has now opted for the more regular and lucrative rewards of tourism and commercialized fashion. Practically every other shop is a boutique displaying locally made casual wear. The beach is the town's main focal point, with a little promenade and a multitude of café-restaurants.

Amalfi itself is a charming maze of covered alleys and narrow byways straggling up the steep mountainside. The piazza just below the cathedral forms the town's heart—a colorful assortment of pottery stalls, cafés, and postcard shops grouped around a venerable old fountain. The cathedral's exterior is its most impressive feature, so there's no need to climb all those stairs unless you really want to.

Ravello   Do not miss **Ravello,** 16 kilometers (10 miles) north of Amalfi. Ravello is not actually on the coast, but on a high mountain bluff overlooking the sea. The road up to the village is a series of switchbacks, and the village itself clings precariously on the mountain spur. The village flourished in the 13th century and then fell into tranquility, unchanging for the past six centuries. The center of the town is **Piazza Vescovado,** with its cathedral, founded in 1087 and recently restored. Note its fine bronze 12th-century door, and, just inside on the left, the pulpit with mosaics telling the story of Jonah and the whale. Look to the right as well and you will see another pulpit with fantastic carved animals.

To the right of the cathedral is the entrance to the 11th-century **Villa Rufolo.** The composer Richard Wagner once stayed in Ravello, and there is a Wagner festival every summer on the villa's garden terrace. There is a moorish cloister with interlacing pointed arches, beautiful gardens, an 11th-century tower, and a belvedere with a fine view of the coast.

Across the square from the cathedral is a lovely walk leading to the Villa Cimbrone. At the entrance to the villa complex is a small cloister that looks medieval but was actually built in 1917, with two bas-reliefs: one representing nine Norman warriors, the other illustrating the seven deadly sins. Then, the long avenue leads through peaceful gardens scattered with grottoes, small temples, and statues emphasizing a contemplative silence to a belvedere and terrace where, on a clear day, the view stretches out over the Mediterranean Sea.

Dining and Lodging

For details and price category definitions, *see* Dining and Lodging in Staying in Italy.

Amalfi   **La Caravella.** Tucked away under some arches lining the coast
Dining   road, the Caravella has a nondescript entrance but pleasant interior decorated in a medley of colors and paintings of old Amalfi. It's small and intimate, and proprietor Antonio describes the cuisine as *"sfiziosa"* (taste-tempting). Specialties

include *scialatelli* (homemade pasta with shellfish sauce) and *pesce al limone* (fresh fish with lemon sauce). *Via M. Camera 12, tel. 089/871029. Reservations advised. AE, MC, V. Closed Tues. and Feb. 11–28. Moderate.*

Lodging **Santa Caterina.** A large mansion perched above terraced and
★ flowered hillsides on the coast road just outside Amalfi proper, the Santa Caterina is one of the best hotels on the entire coast. Rooms are tastefully decorated, and most have small terraces or balconies with great views. There are lounges and terraces for relaxing, and an elevator whisks guests down to the seaside saltwater pool, bar, and swimming area. Amid lemon and orange groves, there are two romantic villa annexes. Some rooms and suites are in the Very Expensive category. *Strada Amalfitana, tel. 089/871012. 54 rooms with bath. Facilities: restaurant, bar, pool, swimming pool, swimming area, and beach bar. AE, DC, MC, V. Expensive.*

Capri **La Capannina.** Only a few steps away from Capri's social cen-
Dining ter, the Piazzetta, La Capannina has a delightful vine-hung courtyard for summer dining, and a reputation as one of the island's best eating places. Antipasto features fried ravioli and eggplant stuffed with ricotta, and house specialties include chicken, scaloppine, and a refreshing, homemade lemon liqueur. *Via Botteghe 14, tel. 081/837-0732. Reservations advised. AE, V. Closed Wed. (except during Aug.), and Nov.–mid-Mar. Moderate.*

Da Gemma. One of Capri's favorite places for a homey atmosphere and a good meal, Da Gemma features spaghetti *con cozze* or *vongole* (with mussels or clams) and *fritto misto* (mixed fish fry). If you're budgeting, don't order fish that you pay for by weight; it's always expensive. You can have pizza as a starter in the evening. *Via Madre Serafina 6, tel. 081/837-0461. Reservations advised. AE, DC, MC, V. Closed Mon. and Nov.–Dec. 10. Moderate.*

★ **Al Grottino.** This small family-run restaurant, with a handy location near the Piazzetta, sports autographed photographs of celebrity customers. House specialties are *gnocchi* (dumplings) with mozzarella and *linguine con gamberini* (pasta with shrimp sauce). *Via Longano 27, tel. 081/937-0584. Dinner reservations advised. AE, DC, MC, V. Closed Tues. and Nov. 3–Mar. 20. Moderate.*

Lodging **Quisisana.** One of Italy's poshest hotels is sited right in the center of the town of Capri. Rooms are spacious, and many have arcaded balconies with views of the sea; decor is traditional or contemporary, with some antique accents. From the small terrace at the entrance you can watch all of Capri go by, but the enclosed garden and pool in the back are perfect for getting away from it all. The bar and restaurant are casual in a terribly elegant way. *Via Camerelle 2, tel. 081/837-0788. 143 rooms with bath. Facilities: restaurant, pool. AE, DC, MC, V. Closed Nov.–Feb. Very Expensive.*

★ **Scalinatella.** *Scalinatella* means "little stairway," and that's how this hotel is built, on terraces overlooking its own gardens and pool, the Certosa's pretty little domes, and the sea. Bedrooms are intimate, with alcoves and fresh, bright colors. This small hotel has an ambience of sophisticated luxury at rates that are not astronomical. *Via Tragara 8, tel. 081/837-0633. 28 rooms with bath. Facilities: pool, bar. No credit cards. Closed Nov.–mid-Mar. Expensive.*

Flora. This one has the look of a genteel resort hotel, with pretty garden furniture, potted plants, and terraces. It's decorated in the sparse but sparkling local style. *Via Serena 26, tel. 081/ 837–0211. 25 rooms with bath. AE, DC, MC, V. Closed Nov.– Mar. Moderate.*

Naples
Dining

La Sacrestia. This lovely restaurant is in an elevated position, above Mergellina, with a fine view and a delightful summer terrace. The menu offers traditional Neapolitan cuisine; among the specialties are *vermicelli al sughetto di gamberi* (pasta with shrimp sauce) and *spigola* (sea bass), either steamed or baked. *Via Orazio 116, tel. 081/664186. Reservations required. AE, V. Closed Wed. (Sept.–June), Sun. (in July), and Aug. Expensive.*

La Bersagliera. This restaurant has been making tourists happy for years, with a great location on the Santa Lucia waterfront, cheerful waiters, mandolin music, and good spaghetti *alla disgraziata* (with tomatoes, capers, and black olives) and *mozzarella in carrozza* (cheese fried in batter). *Borgo Marinaro 10, tel. 081/415692. Reservations advised. No credit cards. Closed Tues. Moderate.*

★ **Ciro a Santa Brigida.** Centrally located off Via Toledo near the Castel Nuovo, this no-frills place is a favorite with businessmen, artists, and journalists. Tables are arranged on two levels, and the decor is classic trattoria. This is the place to try traditional Neapolitan *sartù di riso* (a rich rice dish with meat and peas) and *melanzane* (eggplant) *alla parmigiana* or *scaloppe alla Ciro*, with prosciutto and mozzarella. There's pizza, too. *Via Santa Brigida 71, tel. 081/324072. Reservations advised. No credit cards. Closed Sun. and Aug. Moderate.*

Lodging

Excelsior. Splendidly located on the shore drive, the Excelsior has views of the bay from its front rooms. The spacious bedrooms are well-furnished in informal floral prints and Oriental carpets, and have a comfortable, traditional air. The salons are more formal, with chandeliers and wall paintings, and the excellent Casanova restaurant is elegant. *Via Partenope 48, tel. 081/417111. 138 rooms with bath. Facilities: restaurant, bar, sauna. AE, DC, MC, V. Very Expensive.*

★ **Jolly Ambassador.** This hotel is the only skyscraper on the downtown skyline, and its rooms and roof restaurant have wonderful views of Naples and the bay. It's furnished in dark brown, beige, and white in the functional, modern style typical of this reliable chain, which promises comfort and efficiency in a city where these are scarce commodities. *Via Medina 70, tel. 081/416000. 251 rooms with bath. Facilities: restaurant. AE, DC, MC, V. Expensive.*

Cavour. Located in the rundown Stazione Centrale area, on the square in front of the main train station, it's handy for anyone wanting to use Naples as a touring base. The hotel is gradually being renovated and can offer clean, comfortable rooms. Those on the courtyard are quieter. *Piazza Garibaldi 32, tel. 081/ 283122. 92 rooms, most with bath. Facilities: restaurant. AE, DC, MC, V. Moderate.*

Positano
Dining

Capurale. Among all the popular restaurants on the beach promenade, Capurale (just around the corner) has the best food and lowest prices. Tables are set under vines on a breezy sidewalk in the summer, upstairs and indoors in winter. *Spaghetti con melanzane* (with eggplant) and *crèpes al formaggio* (cheese-filled crèpes) are good choices here. *Via Marina, tel.*

*089/875374. Reservations advised for outdoor tables. No credit
cards. Closed mid-Dec.–Mar. Moderate.*

Lodging **Il San Pietro di Positano.** Situated on the side of a cliff, this is
quite possibly one of the world's most attractive hotels. The
views over the Mediterranean are magnificent. The decor of
the hotel is eclectic with unusual antiques and, everywhere,
hanging bougainvillea. The furnishings are perfectly arranged
to give an openness and to create an easy elegance. The guest
rooms are decorated with an eye to detail, and even the smallest
rooms are a delight. Strewn with flowers, the light open dining
room offers some of the best Italian cuisine on the Amalfi coast.
The only limitation to San Pietro is its small, pebbly beach. *Via
Laurito 2, tel. 089/875454. 55 rooms with bath. Facilities: restaurant, pool, tennis. AE, DC, MC, V. Closed Nov.–Mar.
Very Expensive.*

Le Sireneuse. The most conservative, fashionable hotel in
Positano is this converted 18th-century villa that has been in
the same family for eight generations. The hotel rambles alongside the hill about 200 feet above Positano's harbor. Most of the
bedrooms face the sea—these are the best. Because of the hotel's location, the dining room is like a long, closed-in terrace
overlooking the village of Positano—a magnificent view. Cuisine varies from acceptable to excellent. *Via C. Colombo 30,
tel. 089/875454. 65 rooms with bath. Facilities: restaurant,
pool, sauna. AE, DC, MC, V. Very Expensive.*

Palazzo Murat. The location is perfect, in the heart of town,
near the beachside promenade, but set within a walled garden.
The old wing is a historic palazzo, with tall windows and
wrought-iron balconies; the newer wing is a whitewashed Mediterranean building with arches and terraces. Guests can relax
in antique-strewn lounges, or on the charming vine-draped patio. *Via dei Mulini, tel. 089/875177. 28 rooms with bath.
Facilities: bar, garden. No credit cards. Closed mid-Oct.–Mar.
Moderate.*

Ravello **Hotel Palumbo.** Of all the hotels on the Amalfi coast, the Hotel
Lodging Palumbo is the most genteel—a refined 12th-century retreat.
Some of the bedrooms do tend to be small, but they are beautifully furnished and full of character. Also, the rooms facing the
sea are the choice ones—and the more expensive. The lounge
area is filled with the owner's antiques and, with the greatest
of ease, guests quickly come to view the Hotel Palumbo as their
private palazzo. *Via Toro 28, tel. 089/857244. 20 rooms with
bath. Facilities: restaurant, bar, garden. No credit cards. Very
Expensive.*

Sorrento **Kursaal.** Occupying a 19th-century villa perched on the edge of
Dining the vine-covered gorge of the Mulini, Kursaal is an elegant ve-
randa restaurant. Try the *spaghetti del vallone* (with a tangy
sauce) or the *pesce al cartoccio* (fish baked in parchment). *Via
Fuorimura 7, tel. 081/878–1216. Reservations advised. AE,
DC, MC, V. Closed Mon. Moderate.*

★ **Parrucchiano.** One of the town's best and oldest, Parrucchiano
features greenhouse-type dining rooms dripping with vines
and dotted with plants. Among the antipasti, try the
panzarotti (pastry crust filled with mozzarella and tomato); as
a main course, a good choice would be *scalloppe alla
sorrentina*, again with mozzarella and tomato. *Corso Italia 71,
tel. 081/878216. Reservations advised. AE, V. Closed Wed.
from Nov. to May. Moderate.*

Zi'Ntonio. Zi'Ntonio is a cheerful sort of place, with a fresh, country-inn look. The specialties of the house are a classic *spaghetti al pomodoro* (with fresh tomato sauce and basil), fish (which can be pricey), and *melanzane* (eggplant) *alla parmigiana. Via de Maio 11, tel. 081/878-1623. Reservations advised. AE, DC, MC, V. Closed Thurs. Moderate.*

Lodging **Cocumella.** In a lovely cliffside garden in a quiet residential area just outside Sorrento, this historic old villa (it features a 17th-century chapel) has been totally renovated for comfort. Furnishings are a tasteful blend of antique and modern: There are vaulted ceilings and archways, a dining veranda, and stunning tiled floors. Cocumella has an exclusive, elegant atmosphere, without being stuffy. *Via Cocumella 7, tel. 081/878216. 60 rooms with bath. Facilities: pool, tennis, restaurant. AE, DC, MC. Expensive.*

Excelsior Vittoria. In the heart of Sorrento, but removed from the main square by an arbored walk, the Excelsior Vittoria is right on the cliff and has old-fashioned, Art Nouveau furnishings, some very grand, though faded. Tenor Enrico Caruso's bedroom is preserved as a relic; guest bedrooms are spacious and elegant in a turn-of-the-century way. It overlooks the bay, and is recommended for those who like a lot of atmosphere with their views. *Piazza Tasso 34, tel. 081/878-1900. 125 rooms with bath. Facilities: pool. AE, DC, MC, V. Expensive.*

★ **Bellevue Syrene.** A palatial villa in a garden overlooking the sea, the Syrene features solid, old-fashioned comforts and plenty of charm, with nooks and crannies and antique paintings. *Piazza della Vittoria 5, tel. 081/878-1024. 50 rooms, most with bath. AE, DC, MC, V. Moderate.*

Eden. Eden occupies a fairly quiet but central location, with a garden. Bedrooms are bright but undistinguished; the lounge and lobby have more character. It's an unpretentious but friendly hotel, with some smaller rooms in the Inexpensive category. *Via Correale 25, tel. 081/878-1909. 60 rooms with bath. Facilities: pool. AE, V. Closed Nov.-Feb. Moderate.*

20 Luxembourg

Introduction

Luxembourg, one of the smallest countries in the United Nations, measures only 2,587 square kilometers (999 square miles) which is less than the size of Rhode Island.

Nestled in the heart of Europe between Belgium, West Germany, and France, Luxembourg was shaped by the tides of European history. The capital city has been a fortified citadel since Siegfried, a descendant of Charlemagne, built a castle on the Bock promontory at the end of the 10th century. When allowed to mind its own business, Luxembourg was what it is today: an independent duchy. But those times were rare. Successive invaders—the Burgundians, the Hapsburgs, the French, the Spanish, the Dutch, and the Austrians—came, added to the defenses, and left.

Surprisingly, the massive fortifications were finally destroyed by peace, not war; in expectation of a more peaceful age, the European powers guaranteed Luxembourg's neutrality in the Treaty of London, signed in 1867. One of its conditions was the systematic destruction of the fortress. This took 16 years to accomplish, and what is left today, although impressive, is only a reminder of what was one of the most fortified sites in Europe. Since then, Luxembourg has passed through two more periods of war and only in the last 40 years has it found a less precarious way to live out its destiny. The headquarters of many European institutions are now here, and Luxembourg prefers to see itself as the heart, rather than as the crossroads, of modern Europe.

Outside the capital, fairy-tale castles still abound, the legacy of the country's warlike past. In the north is a hilly, wooded region of the Ardennes known as La Petite Suisse (Little Switzerland). Along the eastern boundary lies the Moselle Valley, renowned for its crisp, white wines.

Before You Go

When to Go   The main tourist season in Luxembourg is the same as in Belgium—early May to late September. But temperatures in Luxembourg tend to be cooler than those in Belgium, particularly in the hilly north, where there is frequent snow in winter.

Climate   In general, temperatures in Luxembourg are moderate. It does drizzle frequently, however, so be sure to bring a raincoat.

The following are the average daily maximum and minimum temperatures for Luxembourg.

Jan.	37F	3C	May	65F	18C	Sept.	66F	19C
	29	-1		46	8		50	10
Feb.	40F	4C	June	70F	21C	Oct.	56F	13C
	31	-1		52	11		43	6
Mar.	49F	10C	July	73F	23C	Nov.	44F	7C
	35	1		55	13		37	3
Apr.	57F	14C	Aug.	71F	22C	Dec.	39F	4C
	40	4		54	12		33	0

Currency   In Luxembourg, as in Belgium, the unit of currency is the franc. Luxembourg issues its own currency in bills of 100, 500, 1,000, and 5,000 francs and coins of 1, 5, 10, 20, and 50 francs.

Luxembourg

Belgian currency can be used freely in Luxembourg and the two currencies have exactly the same value. However, Luxembourg currency is not valid in Belgium. At press time (spring 1989), the exchange rate was 38 fr.L. to the dollar and 65 fr.L. to the pound sterling.

What It Will Cost Luxembourg is a developed and sophisticated country with a high standard and cost of living. Luxembourg City is an international banking center and a number of European institutions are based there, a fact which tends to push prices slightly higher in the capital than in the countryside.

Sample Prices Cup of coffee, 35 fr.L.; glass of beer, 35 fr.L.; movie ticket, 150 fr.L.; 3-mile taxi ride, 300 fr.L.

Customs on Arrival For information on customs regulations, *see* Customs on Arrival in Belgium.

Language Native Luxembourgers speak three languages fluently: Luxembourgish (best described as a dialect of German), German, and French. Most also speak English.

Staying in Luxembourg

Telephones You can find public phones both on the street and in city post offices. A local call costs about 5 fr.L. (slightly more from restaurants and gas stations). The cheapest way to make an international call is to dial direct from a public phone. For operator-assisted calls, dial 0010.

Mail
Postal Rates

Airmail postcards and letters weighing less than 20 grams cost 20 fr.L. to the United States. Letters to the United Kingdom cost 12 fr.L., postcards (maximum five words!) 9 fr.L.

Receiving Mail

If you are uncertain of where you'll be staying, have your mail sent care of American Express (6/8 rue Origer, 2269 Luxembourg).

Shopping
Sales Tax Refunds

Purchases of goods for export may qualify for a sales tax (TVA) refund of 12%. Ask the shop to fill out a refund form. You must then have the form stamped by customs officers on leaving either Luxembourg, Belgium, or Holland.

Opening and Closing Times

Banks. Banks generally are open weekdays 9–noon and 2–4:30.
Museums. Opening hours vary, so check individual listings. Many close on Monday, and most also close for lunch between noon and 2.
Shops. Large city department stores and shops are generally open weekdays, except Monday morning, and Saturday 9–noon and 2–6. Many stay open one evening a week. Small family businesses are open Sunday morning from 8 to noon.

National Holidays

January 1 (New Year's Day); February 26 (Carnival); April 16 (Easter Monday); May 1 (May Day); May 24 (Ascension); June 4 (Pentecost Monday); June 23 (National Day); August 15 (Assumption); November 1 (All Saints' Day); November 2 (All Souls' Day); December 25, 26 (Christmas).

Dining

Restaurants in Luxembourg are generally excellent. The cuisine combines French finesse with German portions. Local dishes—they tend to be fairly heavy—include *treipen* (blood sausage) with mashed potatoes; smoked pork with broad beans; Ardennes ham; jellied suckling pig; and *quenelles* (calf's liver dumplings) with sauerkraut and boiled potatoes. You can also find excellent fresh fish from the country's many rivers.

Mealtimes

Most hotels serve breakfast until 10. Lunch hours are noon–2, sometimes extending until 3. Luxembourgers eat their main meal in the evening between 7 and 10.

Lodging
Hotels

Most hotels in the capital are relatively modern and vary from the international style, mainly near the airport, to family-run establishments in town. Outside Luxembourg City, many hotels are housed in more picturesque buildings, often in beautiful countryside settings. Prices vary considerably between town and country, but as Luxembourg City is an important business center, many of its hotels offer reduced rates at weekends, particularly out of season.

Youth Hostels

Inexpensive youth hostels are plentiful in Luxembourg. They are often set in ancient fortresses and castles. For information, contact **Centrale des Auberges de Jeunesse** (18 pl. d'Armes, Luxembourg, tel. 25588).

Camping

The Grand Duchy is probably the best organized country in Europe for camping. It offers some 120 sites, all with full amenities and most with scenic views. Information is available from the **Fédération Luxembourgeoise de Camping et de Caravaning** (174 rue de Soleuvre, Belvaux). You can also get a list at the National Tourist Office.

Tipping

In Luxembourg hotels and restaurants, taxes and service charges are included in the overall bill and it is not necessary to leave more. If you wish to, then round off the sum to the nearest 50 fr.L. or 100 fr.L. Bellhops and doormen should receive between 50 fr.L. and 100 fr.L., depending on the grade of the hotel. At the movies, tip the usher 20 fr.L. In theaters, tip about 50 fr.L. for checking your coat, and the same to the program seller. In public washrooms the attendant will usually expect between 5 fr.L. and 10 fr.L. Taxi drivers expect a tip; add about 15% to the amount on the meter.

Luxembourg City

Arriving and Departing

By Plane All international flights arrive at Luxembourg's Findel Airport, 6 kilometers (4 miles) from the city.

Between the Airport and Downtown Bus No. 9 leaves the airport at regular intervals for Luxembourg's main bus depot, located just beside the train station. Buses 2, 4, 11, and 12 go to the city center. Individual tickets cost 25 fr.L. A taxi will cost you about 450 fr.L. If you are driving, follow the signs for the city center (Centre Ville).

Getting Around

One of the best transportation options in Luxembourg is the 5-Day Travel Card, good for unlimited transportation on trains and buses throughout the country. Cards are on sale, for 658 fr.L., at Gare Centrale (the main train station) in Luxembourg City.

By Bus Luxembourg City has a highly efficient bus service. The blue-and-yellow buses outside the city train station will take you all around the city and also to some of the outlying areas. Get details about services at the information counter in the station arrivals hall. Fares are low, but the best bet is to buy a 10-ride ticket, available from banks or from the bus station in the Aldringen Center. Other buses, connecting Luxembourg City with towns throughout the country, leave from Gare Centrale.

By Train Luxembourg is served by frequent direct trains from Paris and Brussels. From Paris, travel time is about four hours; from Brussels, just under three hours. From Amsterdam, the journey is via Brussels and takes about six hours. There are connections from most German cities via Koblenz. Outside Luxembourg City, three major train routes extend north, south, and west into the Moselle Valley. For all train information, phone 492424. All service is from Gare Centrale in place de la Gare.

By Car You can easily see most of the country in a day or two, and you might want to rent a car for this purpose. Major highways and smaller roads are excellent, and they are usually fairly uncrowded. Speed limits are 120 kph (70 mph) on highways, 90 kph (55 mph) on major roads, and 60 kph (35 mph) in built-up areas.

Street parking in Luxembourg City is difficult. Make use of one of the underground parking lots, or park at the fairgrounds on the outskirts of town.

By Bicycle Bicycling is a popular sport in Luxembourg, and it is an excellent way to see the city and outlying regions. In Luxembourg City, you can rent bikes from **Velo Francis Hansen** (16 rue Beaumont, tel. 29654). To rent a bike for about half the price, travel 48 kilometers (30 miles) outside the city to **Syndicat**

D'Initiative (Station, Reisdorf, tel. 86778 or 86698). Maps are available from the tourist office.

By Taxi There are taxi stands near Gare Centrale and the main post office. It is almost impossible to stop one in the streets, and there are few taxi stands available. To call a taxi, phone 480058 or 482233.

Important Addresses and Numbers

Tourist The main **Office Nationale du Tourisme** (ONT) in Luxembourg
Information City is located at the Air Terminal, place de la Gare, tel. 481199, open daily 9–noon and 2–6:30 (July–mid-Sept., 9–7:30). The Luxembourg City tourist office is located on the place d'Armes, tel. 22809; open mid-Sept.–mid-June, weekdays 9–1 and 2–6; mid-June–mid-Sept., weekdays 9–7, Sat. 9–1 and 2–7, Sun. 10–noon and 2–6.

Embassies **U.S.:** 22 blvd. Emmanuel Servais, tel. 460123. **U.K.:** 14 blvd. F. D. Roosevelt, tel. 026791. **Canada:** The Brussels embassy at ave. de Tervoren 2, 1040 Brussels, tel. 00(32)2/7356040, covers Luxembourg.

Emergencies **Police, Ambulance, Doctor, Dentist:** tel. 012. **Pharmacies** in Luxembourg stay open nights on a rotation system. Signs listing late-night facilities are posted outside each pharmacy.

English Bookstores **Magasin Anglais** (13 allée Scheffer, tel. 024925).

Travel Agencies **American Express:** 6/8 rue Origer, tel. 496041. **C.I.T.:** pl. de la Gare, tel. 485102. **Keiser Tours:** 34 rue Philippe II, tel. 472717. **Wagons Lits/Cook:** 6 rue Aldringen, tel. 460315. **Emile Weitzel:** 15 rue Notre-Dame, tel. 22931.

Guided Tours

Orientation Tours **H. Sales** offers tours of the city every morning during the peak tourist season and several days a week in winter. The tours leave from the bus station, next to the railway station, platform 5, and visit the historic sights of the center, the new European area, and some of the villas on the city outskirts, together with the military cemeteries: General Patton is buried in the American one. Tours cost 240 fr.L. For information and bookings, contact H. Sales, pl. du Bruxelles, tel. 352/501050. Other tours go to the Ardennes, the Moselle, and the Petite Suisse.

Walking Tours Information on weekend walking tours can be obtained from the tourist office or from the **Fédération Luxembourgeoise des Marches Populaires,** 176 rue de Rollingergrund.

Excursions Pick up the booklet *Circuits Auto-Pedestres,* available at newsstands and bookstores, for information on combination driving-walking tours outside the city.

Exploring Luxembourg City

Numbers in the margin correspond with points of interest on the Luxembourg City map.

This walk takes you through Luxembourg City's maze of ancient military fortifications, now transformed into peaceful paths. Begin at Gare Centrale, in the southern section of the city. As you head from the station toward the city center, you will pass through a bustling shopping district.

❶ Take the **Passerelle Viaduct,** a 19th-century road bridge that links the station with the valley of the Petrusse. The Petrusse is more of a stream than a river and is now contained by concrete, but the valley has become a singularly beautiful park. From here you'll see the city perched on the rocky edges which are partly natural, partly man-made.

❷ At the town end of the Passarelle, on the right, is the **Monument de la Solidarité Nationale** (National Monument to Luxembourg Unity). Despite its modern design, the monument doesn't look out of place: It appears to be just another broken tower on top of the rocks.

Follow the road to the left along the remains of the old city fortifications, known as the **Citadelle du St-Ésprit** (Citadel of the ❸ Holy Spirit). This 17th-century citadel was built by Vauban, the French military engineer, on the site of a former monastery. Ahead of you are the three spires of the cathedral.

❹ In **place de la Constitution** is the entrance to the ancient military tunnels, carved into the rocky **Bock** fortifications. During the many phases of the fortress's construction, the rock itself was hollowed out to form a honeycomb of passages running for nearly 24 kilometers (15 miles) below the town. These were used both for storage and as a place of refuge when the city was under attack. Two sections of the passages, known as the **Casemates,** are open to the public. These sections contain former barracks, cavernous abattoirs, bakeries, and a deep well. Amid the gloom, openings in the rock suddenly reveal glimpses of tumbledown towers stretching into the distance. *Admission: 40 fr.L. adults, 20 fr.L. children. Open Easter, Pentecost, and July–mid-Sept.; check times locally.*

During the summer, plays are performed inside the Casemates. The productions are usually in German, but the atmosphere inside the excavated tunnels provides a unique experience. *Théâtre des Casemates, tel. 460832.*

Take rue de l'ancien Athénée alongside the former Jesuit college, now the National Library. In rue Notre-Dame is the main ❺ entrance to the **Cathédrale Notre-Dame,** originally the 17th-century Jesuit church, with its Baroque organ gallery and crypt. The original church was rebuilt after a fire in 1985. *Open daily 8–noon and 2–7; crypt open 9–noon and 2–6.*

Opposite the cathedral lies the place Guillaume, known locally as the Knuedler, a name derived from the girdle worn by Franciscan monks who once had a monastery on the site. The same monastery was later used as a powder storehouse and exploded in 1554, taking large parts of the original town and castle with it. On market days the square is noisy and colorful.

Time Out   The place Guillaume is an excellent spot to sit in an outdoor café and enjoy the passing scene. You might also walk one block north to the smaller place d'Armes and have lunch at the fashionable **Le Rabelais** (4 pl. d'Armes, tel. 22202) or the traditional and reasonably priced **l'Académie** (11 pl. d'Armes, tel. 27131).

The lively place d'Armes, with its cafés and restaurants, lies just beyond the place Guillaume. Open-air concerts are held every evening in summer. The town tourist office is located on the ❻ square, and on rue du Curé there is a small museum, **Maquette,** which houses models of the fortress at various stages of its con-

Luxembourg City

Bock, **10**
Cathédrale
Notre-Dame, **5**
Chapel of
St.-Quirin, **11**
Citadelle du
St. Esprit, **3**

Grand Ducal Palace, **7**
J.P. Pescatore Art
Museum, **12**
Maquette, **6**
Musées de l'Etat, **8**
Monument de la
Solidarité Nationale, **2**
Passerelle Viaduct, **1**

Place de la
Constitution, **4**
Pont Grande Duchesse
Charlotte, **13**
Trois Tours, **9**

struction: It provides a fascinating glimpse of the historical city. *Admission: 40 fr.L. adults, 20 fr.L. children. Open July–Aug. only, 10–12:30 and 2–6.*

7 From place Guillaume, rue de la Reine leads to the **Grand Ducal Palace,** open to curious visitors only when the monarch takes his vacation. The decor is tastefully elegant: Chandeliers hang from richly decorated ceilings, and Gobelin tapestries adorn the walls. If you are visiting in July or August, check with the tourist office for dates and times. The palace has been the dukes' residence since 1815, but the left wing of the building dates back to 1572, when it formed the *Hôtel de ville* (town hall).

Behind the palace is the oldest part of town, the Marché-aux-Poissons, site of the old fish market and originally the crossing point of two Roman roads. Although now a quiet square, it comes alive on Easter Monday with the quaint, if obscure, Emals'chen Festival in which lovers exchange terra-cotta birds amid dancing and merriment.

8 On the left is the **Musées de l'Etat** (State Museum), set in an attractive row of 16th-century houses. The museum contains an eclectic collection of exhibits from the Stone Age to the Space Age, encompassing humble village crafts and fine arts. Dramatic views over the ramparts compensate for the slightly confusing museum route. Like that of the grand duchy itself, the secret of the museum's success is variety in miniature. *Admission: free. Open Tues.–Fri. 10–noon and 1–5, Sat. 2–6, Sun. 10–noon and 2–6.*

Time Out   In the rue Wiltheim is the **Welle Man,** the museum bar. Sit on the terrace and enjoy the magnificent view along the Alzette Valley. Sip a glass of Elbling or Rivaner, the finest white wines, or try a local kir, made from black-currant liqueur and white wine. Toasted *kachkes,* a strongly flavored cheese, is often available. The locals like this snack drenched in mustard, so be warned! *No credit cards. Closed Mon. Inexpensive.*

9 At the bottom of rue Wiltheim is the gate of the **Trois Tours** (Three Towers), the oldest of which was built around 1050. During the French republic, the guillotine was set up in these towers. From here you can clearly see the source of Luxembourg's strength as a fortress.

10 To the left is the **Bock** promontory, the site of the earliest castle and always the duchy's most fortified point. From the Bock, steep cliffs plunge downward to the Alzette Valley. The Bock also has a series of passages similar to the Petrusse Casemates. *Admission: 40 fr.L. adults, 20 fr.L. children. Open Mar.–Oct., daily 10–5.*

The scenic ramparts of the Bock's **Corniche** provide a view over the lower town, known as the Grund. Many of the houses on your right were refuges, used in times of danger by nobles and churchmen from the surrounding area. The massive towers on the far side of the valley date back to the Wenceslas fortifications, which, in 1390, extended the protected area, while the blocklike *casernes* (barracks) were built in the 17th century by the French.

At the ruined fortifications of the Citadelle du St-Ésprit, take the elevator down to the Grund and follow the Petrusse Valley

⓫ below the cliffs. The little **chapel of St-Quirin** is built into the rock near the Passerelle Viaduct. At Pont Adolphe, walk back up to city level and you are suddenly face-to-face with the 20th century. The boulevard Royal, once the main moat of the fortress, is now Luxembourg's Wall Street, packed with the famous names of the international banking scene.

From here you can either take avenue de la Liberté, an important shopping street, toward the station or head back into town, perhaps to the Grand-Rue shopping area. Or if you want
⓬ to extend your tour, take avenue Émile Reuter to the **J. P. Pescatore Art Museum,** housed in Villa Vauban in the municipal park and containing Dutch and Flemish paintings of the 17th and 18th centuries. *Admission: 20 fr.L. adults, 10 fr.L. children. Open June 23–Sept. 25, Mon. and Wed.–Fri. 1–6, weekends 9–noon and 3–7.*

⓭ Walk through the park to the **Pont Grande Duchesse Charlotte.** From this bridge, a view across the valley reveals the starkly modern "European" area, built to house the European Court of Justice and various European Economic Community buildings. The centerpiece is the 23-story **Centre Européen,** where the European Council meets three times a year. Luxembourgers jealously guard their share of European institutions from predatory Brussels and Strasbourg bureaucrats. Still, the excellent French restaurants in the European area keep resident Eurocrats happy and may even safeguard Luxembourg's slice of the "Euro-cake."

Off the Beaten Track

Le Musée des Instruments de la Musique (Museum of Musical Instruments) is a collection of musical instruments situated in a striking modern building, the new Conservatoire de Musique (Music Conservatory). Many of the instruments are old or are connected with the music of well-known musicians. If you can, persuade one of the music students to play an instrument for you! The custodian will tell you that Luxembourg's tradition of music is maintained by the RTL, the country's famous national orchestra, which performs every Thursday. (Consult the tourist office for details). To reach the Conservatoire catch bus no. 11 from Gare Centrale. *33 rue Charles Martel, tel. 47962951. Admission: free. Open Mon., Wed., and Fri. 3–8; Tues., Thurs., Sat., and Sun. 2–7.*

Shopping

Luxembourg City has two main shopping areas: the **Grand-Rue** and the **avenue de la Gare.** Jewelry and designer fashions are particularly well represented in the Grand-Rue. There are a few small department stores near the train station, but most of the stores in this area are specialist shops: Hi-fi equipment is considerably cheaper here than in neighboring countries.

Excursions from Luxembourg City

It would be a shame to leave Luxembourg without having explored some of the areas around the capital. To see the Ardennes, take Route N7 to **Diekirch,** where there is an ancient church dating from the 7th to the 9th centuries. There are traces here of older occupation: the **Devil's Altar,** a Celtic dolmen, and some 4th-century Roman mosaics from nearby villas.

Another rewarding drive is northeast on Route E29 to **Echternach,** where St. Willibrord, a 7th-century English missionary, founded a Benedictine abbey. Many of the abbey buildings are now schools, but each year on the Tuesday after Pentecost, 15,000 pilgrims flock to the basilica, built on the site of the original chapel. In the crypt are frescoes dating back to the 11th century.

The scenic route through the **Valley of the Eisch** is known as the Valley of the Seven Castles. Take Route N6 west from the capital to Steinfort, the capital of the valley. The road continues through Koerich to **Septfontaines,** situated below a cliff where there is a ruined **Castle of the Knights Templar.** The road goes north, passing the former monastic settlement of Marienthal, and **Hollenfells,** where there is a 9th-century castle tower. Eventually you reach the castle town of Mersch, the geographical center of Luxembourg: From here, you can take Route N7 back to Luxembourg City.

Dining

It is easy to find excellent French cuisine in Luxembourg, but the country's immigrant populations have also ensured a wide variety of Italian and Chinese restaurants, together with a few that feature Spanish, Japanese, Greek, and North African cuisine. A number of restaurants serve Luxembourg dishes, best described as "substantial." Many restaurants offer a fixed-price menu that is usually good value. Your bill will include service charges.

Menus in the better restaurants usually provide English and German translations of French dishes. International hotels hold "Gastronomic Festivals," which are opportunities to sample local wines, liqueurs, and seasonal or regional dishes.

Dress Stylish, casual dress is generally acceptable in most restaurants but, if in doubt, err on the formal side. In expensive French restaurants, formal dress is taken for granted.

Ratings Prices quoted here are per person and include a first course, main course, and dessert, but not wine. Best bets are indicated by a star ★. At press time (spring 1989), there were 38 fr.L. to the dollar.

Category	All Areas
Very Expensive	over 3,000 fr.L.
Expensive	1,500fr.L.–3,000fr.L.
Moderate	900 fr.L.–1,500 fr.L.
Inexpensive	under 900 fr.L.

Credit Cards The following credit card abbreviations are used: AE, American Express; DC, Diners Club; MC, MasterCard; V, Visa.

Very Expensive **St-Michel.** Located in a 16th-century building behind the ducal palace, St-Michel offers a wide variety of seafood specialties and an exhaustive wine list. Try the turbot, trout, or the *cuisses de grenouille à la luxembourgeoise* (frogs' legs cooked in a creamy sauce). Although this is an Expensive restaurant, there is always at least one filling *plat bourgeois* on the menu at around 600 fr. L. *32 rue Eau, tel. 23215. Reservations required. AE, DC, MC, V. Closed weekends, Aug., and Christmas holidays.*

Expensive   **Bouzonvilliers.** This restaurant offers imaginative cuisine in a parkland setting. The wild game is particularly good and pigeons from the nearby Alzette Valley often find their way to the table. Try the *pigeonneau en feuillete au beurre de cresson,* a young pigeon and cress specialty. Situated a short distance out of town, this restaurant is well worth the trip, for both the food and the view. *138 rue Albert Unden, tel. 472259. Reservations required. AE, DC, MC, V. Closed weekends.*

Clairfontaine. This elegant restaurant, situated near the Foreign Ministry, specializes in nouvelle cuisine and seafood. The excellent wines are matured in the restaurant's own cellars. Try the *saumon fumé* (smoked salmon) followed by *turbotin aux langoustines et pistou* (turbot with lobster and pine kernels). For dessert, there is an assortment of freshly baked pastries. *9 rue de Clairefontaine, tel. 462211. Reservations required. AE, DC, MC, V. Closed Sat. lunch, Sun., and Aug. 1–14.*

Moderate   **Bacchus.** For an excellent and varied Italian menu in elegant surroundings, this restaurant offers interesting pasta dishes, pizzas, and main courses. *32 rue Marché-aux-Herbes, tel. 471397. Reservations advised. AE, DC, MC, V.*

★ **Osteria del Téatro.** Conveniently located just beside the Foire (fairground), Osteria del Téatro specializes in authentic Italian cuisine. It also offers an attractive bar and terrace. *21–25 allée Scheffer, tel. 28811. Reservations advised. AE, DC, MC, V. Closed Thurs.*

La Poêle d'Or. On the first floor of a former chapel, looking out onto the ducal palace, this classic French restaurant provides few surprises but excels in regional classics. Try the *lotte aux poivrons doux* (monkfish in sweet peppers). *20 rue Marché-aux-Herbes, tel. 460813. Reservations advised. AE, DC, MC, V. Closed Mon. and Jan.*

Inexpensive   **Ancre d'Or.** This friendly brasserie just off the place Guillaume serves a wide variety of dishes, including Luxembourg specialties such as Eslecker ham (Ardennes ham) and *judd mat gardebohn'en* (pork with beans) throughout the day and evening. *23 rue du Fossé, tel. 472973. Reservations not required. MC, V. Closed Sun.*

Kamakura. If Luxembourg cuisine palls, take the elevator to the Grund and try this Japanese restaurant. The Kamakura offers a number of fixed-price menus in a relaxed atmosphere. A la carte specialties include *sushi* (raw fish) and *tempura* (deep-fried) vegetables. *2–4 rue Munster, tel. 470604. Reservations not required. AE, MC, V.*

★ **Um Bock.** This lively restaurant in the oldest part of town features an Italian menu with an interesting mixture of French dishes. You can choose from several fixed-price menus. *4 rue de la Loge, tel. 475308. Reservations advised. AE, DC, MC, V.*

Lodging

Hotels in Luxembourg City are mainly in three areas: the town center, the station area, and the area close to the airport. By far the largest number are around the station. Most hotels are modern, but a warm welcome and high standards compensate for the relative lack of character.

Price categories are determined by the cost of a double room. Best bets are indicated by a star ★ . At press time (spring 1989), there were 38 fr. L. to the dollar.

Category	Cost
Very Expensive	over 3,800 fr. L.
Expensive	2,800–3,800 fr. L.
Moderate	2,000–2,800 fr. L.
Inexpensive	under 2,000 fr. L.

Credit Cards The following credit card abbreviations are used: AE, American Express; DC, Diners Club; MC, MasterCard; V, Visa.

Very Expensive **Intercontinental.** Located in parkland on the outskirts of town, near to the airport and "European" area, this modern luxury hotel has two outstanding restaurants and numerous amenities. Despite its size, it manages to achieve a personal touch. *12 rue Jean Engling, tel. 43781. 344 rooms with bath. Facilities: meeting rooms, pool, health club, free transportation to city center. AE, DC, MC, V.*

Royal. The city's newest and probably most expensive hotel, the Royal is located on Luxembourg's "Wall Street," close to parks and tourist sites. It offers three restaurants, a nightclub, and a piano bar. *12 blvd. Royal, tel. 41616. 170 rooms with bath. Facilities: indoor pool, sauna, solarium, terrace. AE, DC, MC, V.*

Expensive **Nobilis.** Situated between the station and the Old Town, this modern, extremely comfortable hotel also features a good restaurant. *47 ave. de la Gare, tel. 494971. 43 rooms with bath. Facilities: restaurant, bar. AE, DC, MC, V.*

Moderate **Français.** Located on the central square, the Français is close to all sights and shops. The restaurant offers French cuisine and summer dining on a terrace overlooking the square. *14 pl. d'Armes, tel. 474534. 26 rooms with bath. Facilities: restaurant. AE, DC, MC, V.*

International. The International is a comfortable, centrally located hotel offering a fine French restaurant and easy access to all the downtown sights. *20-22 pl. de la Gare, tel. 485911. 60 rooms, most with bath. Facilities: meeting rooms, restaurant, sidewalk café, bar. AE, DC, MC, V.*

Italia. This comfortable, modern hotel is friendly and family operated. Although it is close to the station, the Italia is set on a quiet side street. Its excellent restaurant serves Italian specialties. *15-17 rue d'Anvers, tel. 486626 or 486627. 20 rooms with bath. Facilities: bar, restaurant with outdoor terrace. AE, DC, MC, V.*

Inexpensive **Chemin de Fer.** This modest but friendly hotel is located on a small street close to the station. It has a good, reasonably priced restaurant. *4 rue Joseph Junck, tel. 493528. 25 rooms some with bath. Facilities: restaurant. AE, DC, MC, V.*

Dauphin. Centrally located, yet only 4.8 kilometers (3 miles) from the airport, the Dauphin is a small, modest hotel, particularly suited to youth groups. It offers simple, modern furnishings. Only breakfast is served. *42 ave. de la Gare, tel. 485252. 37 rooms, most with bath. AE, MC, V.*

Walsheim. This modern hotel is conveniently situated opposite the train station. It has a friendly atmosphere and a reasonably priced restaurant with a varied menu. *28 pl. de la Gare, tel. 484798. 19 rooms with bath. Facilities: restaurant. AE, DC, MC, V.*

21 Malta

Introduction

The Mediterranean island of Malta, and its two sister islands of Gozo and Comino, enjoy a mild sunny climate and attractive bays and beaches—a felicitous setting for such a festive and hospitable people.

For those interested in history and archaeology, tiny Malta—with only 17 miles between its two farthest points—displays the remains of a long and eventful history. Among the most fascinating ruins are Neolithic temples and huge stone megaliths left by prehistoric inhabitants. In AD 60, St. Paul, shipwrecked here, converted the people to Christianity. Other, less welcome visitors, attracted by Malta's strategic position, conquered and ruled. These included the Phoenicians, Carthaginians, and Romans. The Knights of the Order of St. John of Jerusalem arrived here in 1530 after they had been driven from their stronghold on the island of Rhodes by the Ottoman emperor Suleiman the Magnificent. In 1565, with only a handful of men, the Knights held Malta against the Ottoman Turks in a dramatic and bloody siege. They ruled the islands until Napoleon arrived on the scene in 1798 and left massive fortifications, rich architecture, and the city of Valletta, Malta's capital. The British drove the French out in 1800 and gave the island the distinctive British feel that it retains to this day. In 1942, during World War II, King George VI awarded the Maltese people the George Medal for their courage in withstanding repeated German and Italian attacks, especially from the air. Malta gained independence from Britain in 1964.

Before You Go

When to Go   The archipelago is a year-round delight, but May through October is the time of the main tourist season. April and May are the months for spring freshness; the summer months can be very hot, though tempered by sea breezes. If you visit in the winter, you'll find the climate pleasant and mild, but you may encounter sudden rainstorms.

Climate   The following are the average daily maximum and minimum temperatures for Valletta.

Jan.	58F	14C	**May**	71F	22C	**Sept.**	81F	27C
	50	10		61	16		71	22
Feb.	59F	15C	**June**	79F	26C	**Oct.**	75F	24C
	51	10		67	19		66	19
Mar.	61F	16C	**July**	84F	29C	**Nov.**	67F	20C
	52	11		72	22		60	16
Apr.	65F	18C	**Aug.**	85F	29C	**Dec.**	61F	16C
	56	13		73	23		54	12

Currency   The unit of currency is the Maltese lira (LM), also sometimes referred to as the pound. It's divided into 100 cents, and the cents are divided into 10 mils. There are 10 LM, 5 LM, and 1 LM bills; coins—1¢, 2¢, 5¢, 10¢ and 50¢—are bronze and silver. At press time (spring 1989), the exchange rate was .34 LM to the dollar and .58 LM to the pound.

What It Will Cost   Malta is one of the cheapest holiday destinations in Europe, though with the rapid tourist development, prices are inevitably rising. Prices tend to be uniform across the island, except in Valletta, the capital, where they are slightly higher.

Malta

Mediterranean Sea

N

0   5 miles

0   5 km

Sample Prices   Cup of coffee, 40¢ (Maltese); bottle of beer, 25¢; Coca-Cola, 25¢.

Customs on Arrival   You may bring into Malta, duty-free, 200 cigarettes, one bottle of liquor, one bottle of wine, and perfume not exceeding 2 LM in value. You may bring in up to 50 LM.

Language   The spelling of many Maltese words can be bewildering. Both English and Maltese are the official languages on the island, so you shouldn't experience any problems.

Getting Around

By Car   The roads around Valletta can get busy at times, but road conditions are generally good, and driving around the island is pleasant. Driving is on the left-hand side of the road. Speed limits are 40 kph (25 mph) in towns, 80 kph (50 mph) elsewhere. International and British driving licenses are acceptable.

By Bus   Most routes throughout the island are via Valletta, which facilitates travel out of the capital, but makes cross-country trips longer, though not impossible. Buses are remarkably inexpensive; you can cover the whole island for about 12¢. The old green buses sometimes have difficulty keeping to the timetable, however, and are often filled to capacity.

By Boat   Daily ferries operate year-round from Marfa to Mġarr on Gozo and Comino. Telephone 603964 for details. The crossing from Marfa to Mġarr on Gozo lasts 20 minutes, with sailings every 45 minutes. The round-trip fare is 1 LM adults, 50¢ children.

There is also one service daily from Sliema to Gozo, leaving at 9:30 AM and taking an hour and 15 minutes each way. Fare is 50¢ each way.

By Taxi There are plenty of metered taxis available and fares are reasonable compared with those in other European countries. Be sure the meter is switched on when your trip starts. Tip the driver 10%.

Staying in Malta

Telephones There is direct dialing to most parts of the world from Malta. The best place to make calls is either from your hotel or from the Overseas Telephone Division of Telemalta at St. George's, Qawra, Buggiba, and Valletta. Calls from hotels generally are much more expensive.

Mail Airmail letters to the United States cost 14¢, postcards cost 10¢. Airmail letters to the United Kingdom cost 9¢, postcards 8¢.

Opening and Closing Times **Banks.** Banks are open weekdays 8:30–noon, Saturday 8:30–11:30.

Museums. Most museums run by the Museums Department are open mid-June through September, daily, 8–2; October through mid-June daily, 8:30–5; closed holidays. Other museums' hours may vary slightly, so check locally.

Shops. Shops are open weekdays 9–7, Saturday 9–1, 4–8.

National Holidays January 1 (New Year's Day); February 10 (St. Paul's shipwreck); March 31 (National Freedom Day); April 13, 15, 16 (Easter); May 1 (Workers' Day); August 15 (Assumption); September 21 (Independence Day); December 13 (Republic Day); December 25.

Dining There is a good choice of restaurants, ranging from expensive hotel restaurants to fast-food hamburger joints. Fish is a staple on the Maltese menu. Local specialties include *lampuki* (fish pie), *dentici* (sea bream), tuna, and lobster. *Minestra* is the local variant of minestrone soup, and the *timpana* (baked macaroni and meat) is filling. Rabbit and chicken also appear on the menu quite often. Accompany your meal with the locally produced wine: *Marsonvin* comes in red, white, or rosé; *lachryma vitis*, in red or white. Maltese beers are good, too.

Precautions The water on Malta is safe to drink, with the only drawback being its bitter salty taste: You've probably never tasted water quite like it. You may prefer bottled mineral water.

Dress A jacket and tie are suggested for higher-priced restaurants. Otherwise, casual dress is acceptable.

Ratings Prices are for a three-course meal, not including wine or tip. Best bets are indicated by a star ★. At press time, there were .34 Maltese lire (LM) to the dollar.

Category	Cost
Expensive	over 6 LM
Moderate	2 LM–6 LM
Inexpensive	under 2 LM

Credit Cards The following credit card abbreviations are used: AE, American Express; DC, Diners Club; MC, MasterCard; V, Visa.

Lodging Malta has a variety of lodgings, from deluxe modern hotels to modest guest houses. Since Malta is primarily a coastal resort, most accommodations are to be found along the beaches. There are also self-contained complexes geared mainly to package tours. Generally, most places will be clean and comfortable. Breakfast is usually included in the price of your room.

Ratings Prices are for two people sharing a double room. At press time, there were .34 Maltese lire (LM) to the dollar.

Category	Cost
Very Expensive	over 35 LM
Expensive	20 LM–25 LM
Moderate	12 LM–20 LM
Inexpensive	8 LM–12 LM

Credit Cards The following credit card abbreviations are used: AE, American Express; DC, Diners Card; MC, MasterCard; V, Visa.

Tipping A tip of 10% is expected when a service charge is not included.

Valletta

Arriving and Departing

By Plane There are no direct flights from the United States, but several airlines, including **Air Malta,** fly from London, Paris, Frankfurt, Milan, and Rome to Luqa Airport, 6 kilometers (4 miles) south of Valletta.

Between the Airport and Downtown There is a local bus service from the airport to Valletta. It operates every 10 or 15 minutes from 6 AM to 11 PM; the trip takes about 20 minutes, and the fare is about 5¢.

Taxis are also available and prices are reasonable.

By Boat The **Gozo Channel Co.** (tel. 603964) operates weekly car and passenger ferries from Syracuse, Sicily, during the summer. The **Tirrenia Line** (U.K. agents: **Serena Holidays,** 40–42 Kenway Rd., London SW5 ORA, tel. 01/248–8422), operates ferries year-round, three times a week from Syracuse, Catania, and Reggio Calabria, and a weekly ferry service from Naples.

Important Addresses and Numbers

Tourist Information Gozo. Mgarr Harbor, tel. 553343.
St. Juliens Bay. Balluta Bay, tel. 342671 or 342672.
Sliema. Bisazza St., tel. 313409.
Valletta. 1 City Gate Arcade, tel. 227747; Luqa Airport, tel. 229915.

Embassies U.S. Development House, St. Anne St., Floriana, tel. 620424. **British High Commission:** 7 St. Anne St., Floriana, tel. 233134.

Emergencies Hospital: St. Luke's, Gwardamanga, Valletta, tel. 621251. **Police:** tel. 991. **Ambulance:** tel. 996. **Fire Brigade:** tel. 999.

Travel Agencies   **Thomas Cook:** 20 Republic St., Valletta, tel. 620538. **American Express** (representative), Brockdorff, 14 Zachary St., Valletta, tel. 232141.

Guided Tours

Orientation   Sightseeing tours are arranged by local travel agents and the large hotels. There are half-day, full-day, and "Malta by Night" taxi tours; rates vary according to the sights covered and whether or not meals are included. Contact the tourist offices above for details.

One-hour boat trips of the harbor of Valletta leave regularly from Sliema jetty. Prices vary; buy tickets at most travel agencies.

Personal Guides   Licensed guides can be hired through the tourist information office at the City Gate Arcade in Valletta.

Exploring Valletta

The mini-city of Valletta, with ornate palaces and museums protected by massive honey-colored walls, was built by the Knights of the Order of St. John who occupied the island from 1530.

The main entrance to the city is through the arched **City Gate** (where all bus routes end), which leads onto Republic Street, the spine of the city and the main shopping street. From Republic Street, other streets are laid out on a grid pattern, many sloping precipitously to the harbors on either side. Some streets are stepped. Houses along the narrow streets have overhanging wooden balconies so close to each other they nearly touch.

Valletta's small size makes it ideal to explore on foot. Before setting out along Republic Street, stop at the tourist information office for maps, brochures, and a copy of *What's On.* On your left is the Auberge de Provence (the hostel of the knights from Provence), which now houses the **National Museum of Archaeology.** Its collection includes finds from Malta's many prehistoric sites—Taxien, Hagar Qim, and the Hypogeum of Hal Saflini. You'll see pottery, statuettes, temple carvings, and, on the upper floor, finds from Punic and Roman tombs. *Republic St., tel. 225577. Admission: 15¢. Open mid-June–Sept., daily 8–2; Oct.–mid-June, daily 8:30–5; closed holidays.*

From Republic Street, turn right to St. John's Square. Dominating the square (where an open-air market is held) is **St. John's Co-Cathedral.** This was the Order of St. John's own church, completed in 1578. It became a co-cathedral with that of Mdina in 1822 when it was placed under the authority of the Bishops of Mdina for the first time. A side chapel was given to each national group of knights, who decorated it in their own distinctive way. The cathedral **museum** includes the oratory in which hangs *The Beheading of St. John,* the masterpiece painted by Caravaggio when he was staying on Malta in 1608. In the museum, you'll find a rich collection of Flemish tapestries based on drawings by Poussin and Rubens, antique embroidered vestments, and illuminated manuscripts. Keep your ticket, since you can use it to get into the cathedral at

Mdina. *St. John's Sq. Admission: 50¢. Open weekdays 9:30–noon and 3–5:30.*

While in St. John's Square, visit the **Government Craft Center,** which has a wide range of traditional, handmade goods. *Open weekdays 9–7, Sat. 9–1 and 4–8.*

Continue along Republic Street to the **Magisterial Palace,** where Malta's parliament sits. You can walk through the shady courtyards. Inside, friezes in the sumptuously decorated state apartments depict scenes from the history of the Knights. There is also a gallery with Gobelin tapestries. At the back of the building is the **Armoury of the Knights,** with displays of arms and armor down through the ages. *Republic St. Admission: 15¢. Open mid-June–Sept., daily 8–2; Oct.–mid-June, 8:30–5; closed holidays.*

Another building from the days of the Knights of Malta is the order's library, now the **Royal Malta Library,** which stands on Republic Square. There are some outdoor cafés here, where you can dine beneath a statue of Queen Victoria. On Old Theatre Street, you can see the elegant **Manoel Theatre.** Built in 1731, it is said to be Europe's oldest theater still in operation.

Return to Republic Street and continue to Fort St. Elmo and the War Museum. **Fort St. Elmo** was built by the Knights to defend the harbor. Though completely destroyed during the siege of 1565, it was rebuilt by succeeding military leaders. Today, part of the fort houses the **War Museum,** with its collection of armaments largely related to Malta's role in World War II. Here you can see an Italian E-boat and the Gladiator *Faith,* one of three Gloster Gladiator biplanes that defended the island. The other two, *Hope* and *Charity,* were shot down in the air battles of 1942–44. aircraft that defended the island. *St. Elmo. Admission: 15¢. Open mid-June–Sept., daily 8–2; Oct.–mid-June, daily 8:30–5; closed holidays.*

Continue along the seawall to the **Hospital of the Order** at the end of Merchants Street. This gracious building has been converted into the Mediterranean Conference Center. For an excellent introduction to the island, see the "Malta Experience," a multimedia presentation on the history of Malta that is given here six times a day. *Admission: $2.*

Continue along the seawall and climb up to the **Upper Barracca Gardens.** Once part of the city's defenses, they're now a pleasant area from which to watch the comings and goings in the Grand Harbour.

Next, cut along South Street, across Republic Street, to the **National Museum of Fine Art.** The former 18th-century palace has paintings from the 16th century to the present day, including works by Tintoretto, Preti, and Tiepolo, as well as local artists. *South St., tel. 225769. Admission: 15¢. Open mid-June–Sept., daily 8–2; Oct.–mid-June, daily 8:30–5; closed holidays.*

Dining

For details and price category definitions, see Dining in Staying in Malta.

Expensive **Bologna.** On the main shopping street in Valletta, this is an excellent place for typical Maltese food or well-cooked international cuisine, both presented with imagination and flair. *59 Republic St., tel. 626149. Reservations advised. AE, DC, MC, V.*

Moderate
★ **Pappagallo.** This is an "in" place in Valletta, and it's popular with locals and visitors alike. Traditional Maltese food is featured, and the bustling atmosphere is warm and friendly. *Melitte St., tel. 226195. Reservations advised. AE, DC, MC, V. Closed Mar.*

Scalini. An attractive cellar restaurant with walls of Malta's golden limestone, it features seafood and Italian-style pastas. The prix fixe menu is a good value. *32 South St., tel. 606221. Dress: casual. Reservations advised. AE, DC, MC, V.*

Inexpensive **The Midland.** Come here for good, filling Maltese fare at excellent prices. The fish dishes are all worth a try. This is a good place for a quick lunch during a busy sightseeing day. *25 St. Ursula St. (no phone). Reservations not necessary. No credit cards.*

Pizzeria Bologna. A street-level annex of the good restaurant upstairs, it serves delicious pizzas with an interesting choice of ingredients. *59 Republic St., tel. 218014. Open until 9 in the evening.*

Lodging

For details and price category definitions, *see* Lodging in Staying in Malta.

Very Expensive **Grand Hotel Excelsior.** Admire the view of Ta' Xbiex Marina and Lazaretto Creek from this elegantly modern hotel. The rooms are beautifully and comfortably furnished, all with balconies. There's an excellent restaurant as well as a poolside bar-restaurant. *Great Siege Rd., Floriana, tel. 623661. 188 rooms with bath. Facilities: pool, children's pool, water sports, tennis courts. AE, DC, MC, V.*

Phoenicia. The best-known hotel in Valletta is a typically grand hotel, with comfort and service second to none. The rooms are large and elegantly classical; the ambience is just right for a truly luxurious vacation. There is a choice of restaurants and bars. The Phoenicia is set in eight acres of landscaped gardens and is only a few minutes from the center of Valletta. *The Mall, tel. 22541. 110 rooms with bath. Facilities: pool, children's pool, shops, hairdresser, restaurants, bars. AE, DC, MC, V.*

Expensive **Fortina Hotel.** At Sliema seafront, the Fortina has excellent views of Valletta's dramatic fortifications. The atmosphere here is relaxed and informal; the service, attentive. *Tigne Seafront, tel. 30449. 98 rooms with bath. Facilities: game room, waterfront lido with pool and snack bar, sunroof, regular entertainment. AE, DC, MC, V.*

Moderate **British.** If you want to be at the center of things, stay at the British, within Valletta's city walls. There are pleasant views across the harbor. *267 St. Ursula St., tel. 226019. 42 rooms with bath. Facilities: restaurant, bar. MC, V.*

Castille. For a touch of old Malta, stay at the Castille in what used to be a 16th-century palazzo. This is a gracious, comfortable, Old World hotel with a friendly, relaxed ambience. It has an ideal central location, close to the museums and the bus terminus. There's a good rooftop restaurant with a very good prix fixe menu offering several choices. A pianist plays most evenings during dinner, and the views across the harbor are stunning. *St. Paul's St., tel. 623677. 26 rooms with bath. Facilities: coffee shop-bar, sun terrace. AE.*

Inexpensive **Regina.** This is one of many inexpensive hotels that line the Sliema seafront. Offering excellent value, the Regina has its own restaurant and a pleasant garden. The rooms, though modest, are clean and comfortable, and the staff is helpful and friendly. *Tower Rd., tel. 330721. 14 rooms, most with bath. Facilities: restaurant, garden. AE, DC, MC, V.*

Beyond Valletta

It is impractical to attempt a tour of Malta and Gozo in one day. Allow at least two days for the main island—three to include Valletta—and one full day for Gozo.

The rest of Malta has much to offer, ranging from strange prehistoric sites to richly decorated churches.

Leaving Valletta, head first for the **Hypogeum of Hal Saflieni** at **Paola,** 6 kilometers (3½ miles) south of the capital. This massive area of underground chambers was used for burials more than 4,000 years ago. Built on three levels, the chambers extend up to 40 feet beneath the ground, and there are examples of fine carving to be seen. *Admission: 15¢. Open mid-June–Sept., daily 8–2; Oct.–mid-June, daily 8:30–5; closed holidays.*

Nearby is **Tarxien,** an ordinary suburban town with extraordinary megalithic monuments. The **Tarxien Temples** are three interconnecting temples with curious carvings, oracular chambers, and altars, all dating from about 2000 BC. *Admission: 15¢. Open mid-June–Sept., daily 8–2; Oct.–mid-June, daily 8:30–5; closed holidays.*

Now make your way south to **Ghar Dalam.** A cave here, dating from the late stone age, was found to contain the semi-fossilized remains of long-extinct species of dwarf elephants and hippopotamuses that roamed the island. You can visit the cave and see the fossils on display in the small museum. *Admission: 15¢. Open mid-June–Sept., daily 8–2; Oct.–mid-June, daily 8:30–5; closed holidays.*

Follow the coast northwest to the **Blue Grotto,** near Wiedzi-Zurrieq. This is part of a group of water-filled caves made vivid by the phosphorescent marine life that color the water a distinctive and magical blue. You can reach the grotto only by sea. Local fishermen will take you there for about $1.50.

Continue northwest to Rabat and Mdina via the colorful **Buskett Gardens,** best in the spring when the orange and lemon trees are in blossom. In **Rabat,** visit the beautiful **St. Paul's Church,** built next to a grotto where St. Paul is said to have taken refuge when he was shipwrecked on Malta in AD 60. Also of interest are the 4th-century **catacombs** of St. Paul and St. Agatha, unusual for their rock "agape" tables where mourners would hold celebratory meals for the dead. *Admission: 15¢. Open mid-June–Sept., daily 8–2; Oct.–mid-June, daily 8:30–5; closed holidays.*

A visit to the **Crafts Village** at Ta' Qala, just outside Rabat, is a must. Here, in this converted World War II aerodrome, you can see filigree silver, gold jewelry, and hand-blown Mdina glass being made by age-old methods. There are also leather workshops and pottery shops selling gaily colored items. And, of course, you'll be invited to buy. Some of the seconds in the glass workshops are good buys; the faults are often noticeable only to those with a trained eye.

Adjoining Rabat is **Mdina,** Malta's ancient walled capital. Also called the Silent City, it certainly lives up to its sobriquet: There's no traffic here, and the noise of the busy world outside somehow doesn't penetrate the thick, golden walls. Wandering through the peaceful streets is like entering an earlier age. Visit the serene Baroque cathedral of **St. Peter and St. Paul** for a look at Preti's 17th-century fresco *The Shipwreck of St. Paul.* In the museum (you can use the ticket from the cathedral museum of St. John in Valletta), see the Dürer woodcuts and illuminated manuscripts. *Admission: 50¢. Open Mon.–Sat. 9–1 and 2–5.*

You have two choices. The first is to make your way back to Valletta by way of **Mosta** to see the **Church of St. Mary.** The Rotunda, as it is also known, has the third largest unsupported dome in Europe, after the Pantheon and St. Peter's, both in Rome. You can also see the bomb (now rendered harmless) that crashed through the dome during a service in 1942 and fell to the ground without exploding—a miraculous escape for those in the crowded church.

The second choice is to head for the northwest tip of the island and take a ferry to **Gozo,** Malta's lusher, quieter sister island. The capital, Victoria, has a charming old town with attractive cafés and bars around the main square, and the hilltop citadel of **Gran Castello,** with an impressive Roman-Baroque cathedral. The museum here offers displays of ceremonial silver and manuscripts. *Admission: 15¢. Open mid-June–Sept., daily 8–2; Oct.–mid-June, daily 8:30–5; closed holidays.*

The town also has a recent **Folklore Museum** (Milite Bernardo St.) and an impressive archaeological collection in the **Gozo Museum** (Cathedral Square). *Admission to each: 15¢. Open mid-June–Sept., daily 8–2; Oct.–mid-June, daily 8:30–5; closed holidays.*

On Xaghra Plateau stands the extraordinary pair of **Ggantija Prehistoric Temples.** *Admission: 15¢. Open mid-June–Sept., daily 8–2; Oct.–mid-June, daily 8:30–5; closed holidays.*

In the town of **Xaghra** itself, there are two underground alabaster caves with delicately colored stalagmites and stalactites. In the cliffs nearby is the cave where the sea nymph Calypso, mentioned in Homer's *Odyssey,* is said to have lived; with such stunning views, it's easy to imagine that the myth might be true.

Dining and Lodging

For details and price category definitions, *see* Dining and Lodging in Staying in Malta.

Gozo
Lodging

Calypso. There's so much to do at this modern hotel that you don't even need to relax. The choice of dining spots includes a Chinese restaurant. Rooms are comfortably furnished and have balconies, most with sea views. *Marsalforn, tel. 556131.*

92 rooms with bath. Facilities: restaurants, nightclub, squash courts, lighted tennis courts, game room, rooftop splash pool, boutique, bank. AE, DC, MC, V. Moderate.

Cornucopia. For pleasant, personal service and a restful vacation, try this lovingly restored farmhouse near the village of Xaghra—it's an ideal base for exploring the island, and the sea is just a short drive away. There's a good restaurant and barbecues in the summer. *10 Grien Imrik St., Xaghra, tel. 556486. 16 rooms with bath. Facilities: pool. AE, DC, MC, V. Moderate.*

Mdina
Dining
Mdina Restaurant. There's a tempting choice of Maltese dishes or well-presented international cuisine. The decor is attractive and restful, and the service, attentive and professional. *Holy Cross St., tel. 674004. Reservations advised. AE, DC, MC, V. Expensive.*

Lodging
Xara Palace. Staying at the romantic Xara Palace is like taking a step back in time. It's situated in the 16th-century palace of one of Malta's old noble families, and it retains much of a dusty, aristocratic feel, with high-ceiling rooms, antique furnishings, and grand oil paintings. There isn't much in the way of modern-day facilities, but this is more than made up for by the charm and character of the place. *St. Paul's Sq., tel. 674002. 19 rooms with bath. V. Inexpensive.*

Tarxien
Dining
Il Kastell. If you're into healthy eating, try this restaurant attached to the Malta Health Farm. Dishes are imaginative and wholesome, particularly the flambé specialties. *62 Main St., tel. 823581. Reservations advised. AE, DC, MC, V. Moderate.*

Lodging
Malta Health Farm. Your stay in this converted hunting lodge will include an individually planned diet, supervised gym sessions, and a daily steam bath and massage. Then relax in the garden in the glorious Maltese sunshine. *62 Main St., tel. 786477. Facilities: tennis courts, health and fitness center, pool, disco. AE, DC, MC, V. Moderate.*

22 Norway

Introduction

Norway has some of the most remote and dramatic scenery in Europe. Along the west coast, deep fjords knife into steep mountain ranges. Inland, cross-country ski trails follow frozen trout streams, and downhill trails career through forests whose floors teem with wildflowers and berries in the summer. In older villages, wooden houses spill down toward docks where Viking ships—and later, whaling vessels—once were moored. Today the maritime horizon is dominated by tankers and derricks, for oil is now Norway's economic lifeblood. Fishing and timber, however, still provide many Norwegians with a staple income.

Inhabited since 1700 BC, Norway is today considered a peaceful nation. This was hardly so during the Viking period (the 9th and 10th centuries AD), when, apart from vicious infighting at home, the Vikings were marauding as far afield as Seville and Iceland. This fierce fighting spirit remained, despite Norway's subsequent centuries of subjugation by the Danes and Swedes. Independence came early this century, but was put to the test during World War II, when the Germans occupied the country. Norwegian Resistance fighters rose to the challenge, eventually squashing Nazi efforts to develop atomic weapons.

The foundations for modern Norwegian culture were laid in the 19th century, during the period of union with Sweden, which lasted until 1905. Oslo blossomed at this time, and Norway produced its three greatest men of arts and letters: composer Edvard Grieg (1843–1907), dramatist Henrik Ibsen (1828–1906), and painter Edvard Munch (1863–1944). The polar explorers Roald Amundsen and Fridtjof Nansen also lived during this period.

All other facts aside, Norway is most famous for its fjords, which were formed during an ice age a million years ago. The ice cap burrowed deep into existing mountain-bound riverbeds, creating enormous pressure. The pressure was less along the coast, so the entrances to most fjords are shallow, about 155 meters (500 feet), while inland depths reach 1,240 meters (4,000 feet). Although Norway is riddled with them from bottom to top (Oslo is at the head of a fjord), the most dramatic fall within "fjord country," where crooked fingers of the sea indent the high coastal terrain between Stavanger and Trondheim.

Oil-prosperous or fisherman-poor, friendly or taciturn, Norwegians remain outdoor fanatics firmly in the grips of their own country's natural beauty. Norway's fantastically high prices and its vastness (it is over 3,200 difficult road-kilometers [2,000 miles] long) are the only reasons the country isn't overrun with tourists. Even other Scandinavians find Norway expensive, and oppressive when it comes to the official attitude toward alcohol. There are, however, discount schemes and travel strategies to appease the cost of traveling here *(see* What It Will Cost).

Before You Go

When to Go Cross-country skiing was born in Norway, and it remains an important winter sports center. While much of the country is dark and impassable through the winter, you can cross-country or downhill ski within Oslo's city limits. February and early

Norway

0 ————————— 200 miles
0 ————————— 300 km

North Cape

Vardø
Vadsø
Kirkenes
Hammerfest
Alta
Masi
Tromsø

FINLAND

Bardu
Narvik

ATLANTIC
OCEAN

Vestfjorden

Bodø
Fauske
Saltdal

Arctic Circle

Mo-i-Rana
Umbukta
Sandnessjøen
Mosjøen
Brønnøysund

SWEDEN

Gulf of Bothnia

Vikna
Namsos
Steinkjer
Trondheim
Meråker
Støren

Kristiansund
Oppdal
Røros
Ålesund
Tynset
Dombås
Otta
Nord fjord
Florø
Jostedalsbreen
Koppang
Lillehammer
Rena
Sognefjord
Voss
Lake Mjøsa
Hamar
Bergen
Eidsvoll
Hardangerfjord
Hønefoss
Haugesund
Kongsberg
Drammen
Larvik
Stavanger
Sandnes
Porsgrunn
Evje
Arendal
Grimstad
Mandal
Kristiansand

Oslo
Oslofjord
Sarpsborg
Fredrikstad

Baltic Sea

Skagerrak
Kattegat

N

March are good skiing months, and hotel rooms are plentiful then. Avoid late March and April, when sleet, rain, and countless thaws and refreezings ruin the good skiing snow and leave the roads—and spirits—in bad shape. Hotels are heavily booked at Easter, when the Norwegians take their vacations, so if you plan to visit at this time, reserve well in advance.

Summers are generally mild. Then there's the famous midnight sun: Even in the "southern" city of Oslo, night seems more like twilight around midnight, and dawn comes by 2 AM. The weather can be fickle, however, and raingear and sturdy waterproof shoes are recommended even in summer. The best times to avoid crowds in museums and on ferries are May and September; Norwegians themselves are on vacation in July and August. Bear in mind that the country virtually closes down for the five-day Easter holidays, when Norwegians make their annual migration to the mountains. Hotels are more crowded and expensive during this period, but some offer discounts in the two weeks before Easter—which is a good time for skiing.

Climate   The following are the average daily maximum and minimum temperatures for Oslo.

Jan.	28F	−2C	May	61F	16C	Sept.	60F	16C
	19	−7		43	6		46	8
Feb.	30F	−1C	June	68F	20C	Oct.	48F	9C
	19	−7		50	10		38	3
Mar.	39F	4C	July	72F	22C	Nov.	38F	3C
	25	−4		55	13		31	−1
Apr.	50F	10C	Aug.	70F	21C	Dec.	32F	0C
	34	1		53	12		25	−4

Currency   The unit of currency in Norway is the krone, also known as kr., but officially written as NOK. It is divided into 100 øre. Bills of 10, 50, 100, 500, and 1,000 NOK are in general use. Coins are 1, 5, 10, 50, and 100 øre. Credit cards are accepted in most hotels, stores, restaurants, and many gas stations and garages, but generally not in smaller shops and inns in rural areas. Banks charge per transaction, so it is more economical to change larger amounts of money or traveler's checks. The exchange rate at press time (spring 1989) was NOK 6.7 to the dollar and NOK 11.7 to the pound sterling.

What It Will Cost   Norway has a high standard—and cost—of living, but there are ways of saving money by taking advantage of some special offers for accommodations and travel during the tourist season and on weekends throughout the year.

The **Oslo Card**—valid for one, two, or three days—entitles you to free admission to museums and galleries and unlimited travel on transportation operated by the Oslo Transport system and the Norwegian Railways commuter trains within the city limits. Adults get a 50% discount on trains to and from Oslo, free parking, and discounts on car rentals and at restaurants, stores, and sports centers. You can get the card at Oslo's tourist information offices (*see* Important Addresses and Numbers). A one-day card costs NOK 75 adults, NOK 35 children; two days, NOK 110 adults, NOK 50 children; three days, NOK 140 adults, NOK 65 children.

Hotels in larger towns have special weekend and summer rates from late June to early August. Discounts in rural hotels are offered to guests staying several days; meals are then included in the rate. Meals are generally expensive, so take hotel breakfast when it's offered. Alcohol is very expensive, and is sold only during short, strictly regulated hours.

Sample Prices Cup of coffee, NOK 8–NOK 10; bottle of beer, NOK 35; soft drink, NOK 15; ham sandwich, NOK 35; one-mile taxi ride, NOK 40.

Customs on Arrival Residents of non-European countries may import duty-free into Norway 400 cigarettes or 50 grams of cigars or tobacco, two liters of alcohol (not stronger than 60% content) or two liters of wine and two liters of beer, 50 grams of perfume and 0.5 liter of eau-de-cologne, plus other goods to the value of NOK 3,500.

Residents of European countries may import 200 cigarettes or 250 grams of tobacco or cigars, one liter of liquor and one liter of fortified wine or two liters of fortified wine or two liters of table wine and two liters of beer, a small amount of perfume or eau-de-cologne, and goods to the value of NOK 700.

Language In larger cities, on public transportation, and in most commercial establishments people speak English. Younger Norwegians generally speak it well; English is the main foreign language taught in schools, and movies and cable TV reinforce its popularity.

There are two official forms of the Norwegian language plus many dialects, so don't be disappointed if you've studied it but then can't understand everyone. Typical of Scandinavian languages, Norwegian's additional vowels—æ, ø, and å—come at the end of the alphabet. Remember this when you're using alphabetical listings.

Getting Around

By Car Roads are narrow and winding, so never expect to cover more
Road Conditions than 240 kilometers (150 miles) in a day. The climate plays havoc with the roads: Even the best suffer from frost, and the only Bergen–Oslo route to remain open all year is via the Telemark. Make sure you have snow tires or chains; if renting, choose a smaller model with front-wheel drive.

Rules of the Road Driving is on the right. The speed limit is 90 kph (55 mph) on highways, 80 kph (50 mph) on main roads, 50 kph (30 mph) in towns, and 30–40 kph (20–25 mph) in residential areas. From September through April, low-beam headlights are mandatory at all times. Drivers of British automobiles must adjust beams so that they sweep right. The **Norges Automobil Forbund (NAF)** —the Norwegian Automobile Association—can assist. Contact them at Storgate 2–6, Oslo 1, tel. 02/337080. Also remember that at intersections, cars approaching from the right have the right of way. Passing areas on narrow roads are marked with a white M (for *Møtepas*) on a blue background. Do not drink and drive: There are spot checks, and you can face a jail sentence, the loss of your license, and a heavy fine.

Parking Street parking in cities and towns is clearly marked. There are also municipal parking lots. You cannot park on main roads or on bends. Details can be found in the leaflet *Parking in Oslo*, available free from tourist offices and gas stations.

Gasoline Gas costs about NOK 5.30 per liter.

Breakdowns The Norwegian Automobile Association (NAF) patrols main roads and has emergency telephones on mountain roads. For NAF 24-hour service, dial 02/429400.

By Train Norwegian trains are punctual and comfortable, and most routes are scenic. They fan out from Oslo and leave the coasts (except in the south) to buses and ferries. Some express trains have observation cars, and all have dining or buffet cars. (Reservations are required on all express *(ekspresstog)* and some fast *(hurtigtog)* services.) The Oslo–Bergen route is superbly scenic, while the Oslo–Trondheim–Bodø route takes you within the Arctic Circle. Most trains leave Oslo from Sentralstasjon (Oslo S or Central Station) Jernbanetorget (at the end of Karl Johansgate). But do check, because some trains leave from Vestbanestasjon, west of Rådhusplassen.

Fares Apart from the Europe-wide passes (EuRailpass and Inter-Rail), a special Scandinavian pass called **Nordturist** allows unlimited travel in Norway, Sweden, Denmark, and Finland for 21 days. Cost is NOK 1, 433, and the ticket is available through the **Norwegian State Railway** (21–24 Lockspur St., London SW1Y 5DA, tel. 01/930–6666); there is no U.S. branch, so U.S. tourists should write or call the London office. Credit card payments are accepted. A 21-day **Youth Pass** is also available for 12–26 year olds, at a cost of NOK 1,075.

By Plane The remoteness of so much of Norway means that air travel is a necessity for many inhabitants. The main Scandinavian airline, **SAS,** operates a network, along with **Braathens SAFE** and **Widerøes.** Fares are high, but the time saved makes it attractive if you are in a hurry. For longer distances, flying can be cheaper than driving a rented car and paying for gas and incidentals. Inquire about "Visit Norway" passes, which give you relatively cheap domestic flight coupons (usually only good for summer travel). Norwegian airlines can be contacted at the following addresses: **SAS** (SAS Building, Ruseløkkveien 6, Oslo 2, tel. 02/429970); **Braathens SAFE AS** (Ruseløkkveien 26, Oslo 2, tel. 02/411020); and **Widerøes Flyveselskap AS** (Mustadsveien 1, Oslo 2, tel. 02/555960).

By Bus The Norwegian bus network makes up for some of the limitations of the country's train system, and several of the routes are particularly scenic. For example, the north Norway bus service, starting at Fauske (on the train line to Bodø), goes right up to Kirkenes on the Russian-Norwegian border, covering the 625 miles (1,000 kilometers) in four days. Long-distance bus routes also connect Norway with all its Scandinavian neighbors. Most buses leave from Grønlands Torg, one subway stop or about one-half a kilometer's (one-third of a mile's) walk from Oslo S-train station.

By Ferry Norway's long, fjord-indented coastline is served by an intricate and essential network of ferries and passenger ships. A wide choice of services is available, from simple hops across fjords (saving many miles of traveling) and excursions among the thousands of islands, to luxury cruises and long journeys the entire length of the coast. Most ferries carry cars. Reservations are required on ferry journeys of more than one day but are not needed for simple fjord crossings. Fares and exact times of departures depend on season and ship availability. The main Norwegian tourist office (*see* Important Addresses and Numbers) has the most accurate information.

One of the world's great sea voyages is a mail and passenger service called the **Hurtigrute,** which runs up the Norwegian coast from Bergen to Kirkenes, well above the Arctic Circle.

The **Landslaget for Reiselivet i Norge** (Norwegian Travel Association) Langkai 1, Oslo 1, tel. 02/427044) will answer your queries about long-distance travel.

Staying in Norway

Telephones Norway's phone system is one of the world's most expensive, so try to make calls when rates are reduced (5 PM–8 AM weekdays, and all day on weekends). Also, avoid using room phones in hotels unless you're willing to pay a hefty service charge. In public booths, place coins in the phone before dialing. Unused coins are returned. The largest coins accepted are NOK 5, so make sure you have enough small change.

Local Calls Costs of calls within Norway vary according to distance: Within Oslo, the cost goes up according to the amount of time used after the three-minute flat fee. Pages 1–9 of the Oslo phone book have full details on charges. Oslo's code is 02, needed only when dialing from outside Oslo.

International Calls To call North America, dial 095–1, then the area code and number. For the United Kingdom, dial 095–44, then the area code (minus the first 0) and number.

Operators and Information Dial 093 for an English-speaking operator. For local information, dial 0180. For international information, dial 0181.

Mail
Postal Rates Letters and postcards to the USA cost NOK 4.80 for the first 20 grams. For the United Kingdom, the rate is NOK 3.80 for the first 50 grams.

Receiving Mail Have letters marked "poste restante" after the name of the town, with the last name underlined. The service is free, and letters are directed to the nearest main post office.

Shopping
VAT Refunds Most department stores have good selections.
Much of the 20% Norwegian value-added tax (VAT) will be refunded to visitors spending more than NOK 300 in any one store. Ask for a special tax-free check and show your passport. All purchases must be presented together with the tax-free check at the tax-free counter at ports, on ferries destined for abroad, airports, and border posts. The VAT will be refunded, minus a 4.5% service charge. General information about the tax-free system is available on tel. 02/592650.

Opening and Closing Times **Banks.** Banks are open weekdays 8:30–3:30.
Museums. Museums are usually open Monday–Saturday 10–6 and are either closed or have shorter hours on Sunday.
Shops. Though times vary enormously, most shops are open weekdays 8:30–4:30 or 5, and Saturday 8:30–1. Many stay open one day a week until 7.

National Holidays January 1; April 12–16 (Easter); May 1 (May Day); May 17 (Constitution Day); May 24 (Ascension Day); June 3, 4 (Pentecost); December 25, 26 (Christmas).

Dining The Norwegians depend on protein and carbohydrates to outlast the fierce winters. Breakfast is usually a large buffet of smoked fish, cheeses, sausage, cold meats, and cereal, washed down with tea, good coffee, or milk. Lunch is often a lighter version of breakfast, or the famous *smörbröd* open sandwich. Dinners are wholesome three- or four-course meals, starting with cold hors d'oeuvres and soup and often ending with delicious fresh fruit and berries. The main course may be salmon, summer trout, or other fish; alternatives can include lamb or pork, reindeer, or even ptarmigan. Remember that the most expensive part of eating is drinking (*see* What It Will Cost) and that alcohol is not served on Sunday in most areas. One consolation is the quality of the water, which is still among the purest in the world despite the growing problem of acid rain.

Mealtimes Lunch is from noon to 3. Dinner has traditionally been early, but in hotels and major restaurants it is now more often from 6 to 10. Some rural places still serve dinner from 4 to 7.

Dress Jacket and tie are recommended for all restaurants in the Very Expensive and Expensive categories and even in some Moderate ones. If in doubt, assume jacket and tie. Casual dress is acceptable elsewhere.

Ratings Prices are per person and include a first course, main course, and dessert, without wine or tip. Best bets are indicated by a star ★. At press time (spring 1989), there were NOK 6.7 to the dollar.

Category	All Areas
Very Expensive	over NOK 300
Expensive	NOK 200–NOK 300
Moderate	NOK 100–NOK 200
Inexpensive	under NOK 100

Credit Cards The following credit card abbreviations are used: AE, American Express; DC, Diners Club; MC, MasterCard; V, Visa.

Lodging Accommodations in Norway are usually spotless and smaller
Hotels establishments are often family run. Service is thoughtful and considerate, right down to blackout curtains to block out the midnight sun. Passes are available for discounts in hotels. The **Scandinavia Bonus Pass,** costing approximately $20 and also valid in Denmark, Sweden, and Finland, gives discounts of 15% to 40% in many hotels in the summer (June 15–August 20). In addition, children under 15 stay in their parents' room at no extra charge. For full details, write to **Inter Nor Hotels** (Kronsprinsensgt 5, Oslo 2, Norway). **Nordturist** passes (*see* Getting Around By Train) also offer discounts of about 40% in nearly 100 top hotels.

Camping Camping is a popular way of keeping down the cost of a stay in Norway. There are more than 1,400 authorized campsites in the country, many set in spectacular surroundings. Prices vary according to the facilities provided: A family with a car and tent can expect to pay about NOK 100 per night. Some campsites have log cabins available for less than NOK 200 per night. A *Camping Norway* guide is available from tourist offices, or go to NAF (the Automobile Association), Storgaten 2, Oslo, tel. 02/337080.

Youth Hostels There are about 80 youth hostels in Norway; some are schools or farms doing extra summer duty. You must be a member of the Youth Hostel Association (YHA) to stay in the hostels. For a full list, write to **Norske Ungdom-Sherberger (NUH)** (Dronningens-gata 2b, N Oslo 1).

International YHA guides are available to members in the UK and North America. (Despite the name, there are no age restrictions for YHA membership.) In the USA, contact **American Youth Hostels Inc.** (National Offices, Box 37613, Washington, DC 20013-7613, tel. 202/783-6161). In Canada, contact **Canadian Hostelling Association** (333 River Rd., 3rd Floor, Tower A, Vanier, Ottawa, Ont. K1L 8H9, tel. 613/748-5638).

Rentals Norwegians escape to mountain cabins whenever they have a chance. Stay in one for a week or two and you'll see why—magnificent scenery, pure air, fresh fruits and berries, and the chance to hike, fish, or cross-country ski. For full details of this most popular of Norwegian vacations, write to Norske Hytte Formidlingen (Kierschowsgt 7, 0405 Oslo 4 tel. 02/356710). The brochure *Norsk Hytteferiel* can be requested from tourist offices. Farm accommodations are also available. An unusual alternative is to rent a *rorbu* (primitive wooden dwelling) in the northerly Lofoten Islands.

Ratings Prices are for two people in a double room with bath and include breakfast, service, and all taxes. Best bets are indicated by a star ★. At press time (spring 1989), there were NOK 6.7 to the dollar.

Category	Oslo	Other Areas
Very Expensive	over NOK 850	over NOK 650
Expensive	NOK 600–NOK 850	NOK 400–NOK 650
Moderate	NOK 400–NOK 600	NOK 200–NOK 400
Inexpensive	under NOK 400	under NOK 200

Credit Cards The following credit card abbreviations are used: AE, American Express; DC, Diners Club; MC, MasterCard; V, Visa.

Tipping In Norway, a 10% service charge is generally added to bills at hotels and restaurants. If you have had exceptional service, then give an additional tip. It is not the custom to tip taxi drivers unless they act as tourist guides; tip porters at airports NOK 5 per bag. If a doorman hails a taxi for you, you can give NOK 5. If 10% has not been added to the check at a restaurant or café (ask if in doubt), then leave this amount and round it off to the nearest krone. On sightseeing tours, tip the guide if you are satisfied; NOK 5 is the usual tip for all services.

Oslo

Arriving and Departing

By Plane Most international flights go to Fornebu Airport on the edge of the fjord, about 20 minutes west of Oslo. Charter flights usually go to Gardemoen Airport, about 50 minutes north of Oslo.

Between the Airport and Downtown Buses from Fornebu to Oslo Central Station leave every 15 minutes (7:30 AM–11:30 PM) and run every half hour on weekends; the fare is NOK 20. Buses meet flights to Gardemoen and take passengers to the Central Station; the fare is NOK 50. Taxis from either airport to downtown cost between NOK 80 and NOK 100.

By Train Trains from all international routes arrive at Central Station. West Station is used by trains from the south of Norway.

Getting Around

By Public Transportation Far and away the best way to get around Oslo is by using the **Oslo Card** (*see* What It Will Cost), which offers unlimited travel for one, two, or three days on all Oslo's public transportation—bus, T-bane (the subway), streetcar, and even local ferries. You can buy the Oslo Card at the tourist office, (Rådhuset [City Hall], Rådhusplassen, Oslo 1 tel. 02/427170), or from hotels, travel agents in Oslo, larger stores, and downtown branches of ABC Bank.

If you are using public transportation only occasionally, you can get tickets (NOK 12—flat fare) at bus and subway stops. For NOK 30, the **Tourist Ticket** gives 24 hours' unlimited travel on any means of public transportation, including the summer ferries to Bygdøy. The **Minikort** gives you bus or streetcar rides for NOK 40, including transfers, while the **Maxikort** offers 14 rides for NOK 120.

By Taxi A taxi is available if its roof light is on. There are taxi stands at Central Station and West Station; or call 02/388090, but be prepared to wait for up to an hour.

Important Addresses and Numbers

Tourist Information Ground floor of Rådhuset (harbor side), Rådhusplassen, tel. 02/427170. Open May 15–Sept. 15, Mon.–Sat. 8:30–7, Sun. 9–5; Sept. 16–May 14, Mon.–Fri. 8:30–4, Sat. 8:30–2:30, closed Sun.

Embassies U.S.: Drammensvn. 18, tel. 02/448550. **Canadian:** Oscarsgate 20, tel. 02/466955. **U.K.:** Thos. Heftyesgate 8, tel. 02/563890.

Emergencies Police: Gronlandsleiret 44, tel. 02/669050 (24-hour service—02/669966). **Ambulance:** 24-hour service, tel. 02/201090. **Dentist:** (emergencies), Oslo Kommunal Tannlegevakt, Toyen Center, Kolstadsgate 18, Oslo 6, tel. 02/674846. Emergency treatment, weekdays 8 PM–11 PM, weekends and holidays 11 AM–2 PM. **Pharmacy: Jernbanetorgets Apotek,** Jernbanetorget 4B, tel. 02/412482. Open 24 hours.

Post Office The main post office is located at Dronningensgate 15. The **Telegraph Office** is at Kongensgate 21.

English Bookstores **Tanum:** Karl Johansgate 43, tel. 02/429310. **Ovist:** Drammensvn. 16, tel. 02/440326 (beside the U.S. Embassy).

Travel Agencies **Winge** (agent for American Express): Karl Johansgate 33–35, tel. 02/429150; **Bennett:** Karl Johansgate 3, tel. 02/209090; **Berg-Hansen** (agent for Thomas Cook): Arbiensgate 3, tel. 02/391901.

Guided Tours

Orientation Tours **H. M. Kristiansen** provides three tours, all lasting three hours, and all starting from the Rådhusex (harbor side). Tickets are available on the bus or from the Oslo tourist information office (*see* Important Addresses and Numbers). The "Oslo Highlights" morning tour goes to the Vigeland Sculpture Park, Holmenkollen Ski Jump, the Viking Ship Museum, and the *Kon-Tiki. Admission: NOK 100 adults, NOK 50 children. Open May–Sept., daily at 10 AM.*

The "Morning Sightseeing" tour visits Akershus Castle, Vigeland Sculpture Park, the Munch Museum, and Holmenkollen Ski Jump. *Admission: NOK 100 adults, NOK 50 children. Open Apr.–Oct., daily at 10 AM.*

The "Afternoon Tour" goes to the Norwegian Folk Museum, Viking Ships, *Kon-Tiki*, and the polar ship *Fram. Admission: NOK 120. Open Apr.–Oct., daily at 2:30.*

Walking Tours The *Oslo Guide* brochure (free from the tourist office) has several walking tours on its map. Some go farther afield and link up with public transportation.

Personal Guides Taxis also give sightseeing tours in English for NOK 200 per hour. Call 02/388090 or 02/388000 to reserve a personal tour.

Exploring Oslo

Oslo is a small capital city, with a population of just less than half a million. The downtown area is compact, but the geographic limits of Oslo spread out to include forests, fjords, and mountains, which give the city a pristine airiness that complements its urban amenities. Oslo has an excellent public transportation network. Explore downtown on foot, enjoying its jazz clubs and museums, then venture beyond via bus, streetcar, or train.

Numbers in the margin correspond with points of interest on the Oslo map.

Oslo's main street, an avenue called **Karl Johansgate,** runs right through the center of town, from Central Station uphill to the Royal Palace. Half its length is closed to traffic, and it is in this section that you will find most of the city's shops, outdoor cafés, and markets.

① Start at the **Slottet** (Royal Palace), the king's residence (there is no visiting inside). The palace was built in the early 19th-century Classical style and is as sober, sturdy, and unpretentious as the Norwegian character. The surrounding park is open to the public. Time your visit to coincide with the changing of the guard (daily at 1:30). When the king is in residence, the Royal Guard strikes up the band.

② Walk down Karl Johansgate to the **universitet** (university) on your left. A small park in front of the building, which is open except on official occasions, has a collection of **runic stones,** some dating back to the 5th century. The main hall of the university is decorated with murals by Edvard Munch (1863–1944), Norway's most famous artist. The hall *(aula)* is only open during July, on weekdays 12–2 (admission: free). The Nobel Peace Prize is presented at the universitet each year on December 10.

③ Behind the university is the **Nasjonalgalleriet** (National Gallery), Norway's largest public gallery. It has a small but high-quality selection of paintings by European artists from Rembrandt to Picasso. Of particular interest is the collection of works by Norwegian artists. Edvard Munch is represented here, but most of his work is in the Munch Museum (see below) east of the center. *Universitetgaten 13. Admission: free. Open weekdays 10–4, Sat. 10–3, Sun. noon–3.*

④ The **Historisk Museum** (Historical Museum) is just across from the National Gallery. It features displays of daily life and art from the Viking period, including treasures recovered from Viking ships. The Ethnographic Section houses a collection related to the great polar explorer Roald Amundsen, the first man to reach the South Pole. *Frederiksgate 2. Admission: free. Open Tues.–Sun. 11–3.*

⑤ Return to Karl Johansgate and cross over for a closer look at the neoclassical **Nationalteatret,** watched over by the statues of Bjørnstjerne Bjørnson and Henrik Ibsen. Bjørnson was the nationalist poet who wrote Norway's anthem. Internationally lauded playwright Ibsen wrote *Peer Gynt* (he personally requested Edvard Grieg's musical accompaniment), *A Doll's House,* and *Hedda Gabler,* among others. He worried that his plays, packed with allegory, myth, and sociological and emotional angst, might not have appeal outside Norway. Instead, they were universally recognized and changed the face of modern theater.

Time Out Stop for a snack or a drink at one of the open-air cafés in the gardens surrounding **Studenterlunden** pond, which is the setting for band concerts, election rallies, and other special events.

---

⑥ At the far (eastern) end of the gardens is the **Storting** (Parliament), a bow-windowed, yellow-brick building stretched across the block. It is open to visitors when Parliament is not in session (mid-June through August): A guided tour takes visitors around the frescoed interior and into the debating chamber. *Karl Johansgate, tel. 02/313050. Admission: free. Open mid-June–Aug., Mon.–Sat. Guided tours noon–2.*

⑦ Karl Johansgate is closed to traffic near the staid, bronze-doored **Domkirken** (Cathedral). The much-renovated cathedral, consecrated in 1697, is modest by the standards of some European capital cities, but the interior is rich with treasures, such as the Baroque carved wooden altarpiece and pulpit. The ceiling frescoes by Hugo Lous Mohr were done after World War II.

⑧ Behind the cathedral is an area of arcades, small restaurants, and street musicians. Or, facing away from the cathedral, you can turn left and walk along Storgata, past the flower market to **Youngstorvet,** the fruit and vegetable market and the best place to buy the makings of a picnic lunch.

⑨ Head back toward the cathedral until you reach Kirkegate and turn left. Three blocks down, turn right onto Rådhusgate and then almost immediately left onto Kongensgate. This takes you to **Akershus Castle** on the harbor. The castle was built in the Middle Ages but restored in 1527 by Christian IV of Denmark —Denmark then ruled Norway—after fire damage; he then laid out the present city of Oslo (naming it Christiana after himself) around his new residence. Oslo's street plan still follows his design. Some rooms are open for guided tours, and the grounds form a park around the castle. The grounds also house

Oslo

Akershus Castle, **9**
Domkirken, **7**
Framhuset, **15**
Harbor, **10**
Historisk Museum, **4**
Kon-Tiki Museum, **14**
Maritime Museum, **16**

Nasjonalgalleriet, **3**
Nationalteatret, **5**
Norsk
Folkemuseum, **13**
Rådhuset, **11**
Slottet, **1**
Storting, **6**
Toyen, **17**
Universitet, **2**
Vikingskiphuset, **12**
Youngstorvet, **8**

the **Norsk Hjemmefrontsmuseum** (Norwegian Defense and Resistance Museums). Both will give you a feel for the Norwegian fighting spirit from the time of the Vikings to the time of the German occupation, when the Nazis set up headquarters there and had a number of patriots executed within its walls. *Akershus Castle and Museums. Entrance from Festingpl., tel. 02/412521. Admission: NOK 5. Guided tours of the castle, May –Sept., Mon.–Sat. 11–4, Sun. 12:30–4. Museums open Tues., Thurs. 10–8, Wed., Fri. 10–3, Sat. 10–4, Sun. 11–4.*

⑩ Continue along the waterfront toward the central **harbor**—the heart of Oslo and head of the fjord. Shops and cafés stay open later here, and you can buy seafood snacks, sit amid the fountains and statues, and watch the portside activities.

⑪ The large red-brick **Rådhuset** (City Hall) is here: Go inside (admission: free) and see murals depicting daily life in Norway, myths, and Resistance activities. To some, however, the Rådhuset is ugly and pretentiously civic-minded. You can set your watch by the astronomical clock in the inner courtyard.

The **Oslo Tourist Office** is on the harbor side of the Rådhuset. From nearby Pipervika Bay, you can board a ferry for the seven-minute crossing of the fjord to the **Bygdøy**, peninsula, where there is a complex of seafaring museums.

⑫ There are two museums at the first ferry stop. The **Vikingskiphuset** (Viking Ship Museum) contains 9th-century ships recovered from the fjord, where they had been ritually sunk while carrying the mortal remains of Viking kings and queens to the next world in Valhalla. Also on display are the treasure and jewelry that accompanied the royal bodies on their last voyage. The ornate craftsmanship evident in the ships and jewelry dispels any notion that the Vikings were skilled only in looting and pillaging. *Admission: NOK 10 adults, NOK 5 children. Open Nov.–Mar., daily 11–3; Apr. and Oct., daily 11–4; May–Aug., daily 10–6; Sept., daily 11–5.*

⑬ It's a few minutes' walk up a well-marked road to the **Norsk Folkemuseum** (Folk Museum), a large park where historic farmhouses, some of them centuries old, have been collected from all over the country and reassembled intact. A whole section of 19th-century Oslo was moved here, as was a 12th-century wood stave church. There are displays of weaving and sheepshearing on Sunday, and throughout the park there are guides in period costume. *Admission: NOK 15. Open Mon.–Sat. 10–6, Sun. 11–6.*

Reboard the ferry or follow signs for the 10-minute walk to the **⑭** **Kon-Tiki Museum,** where the *Kon-Tiki* raft and the reed boat *RA II* are on view. Thor Heyerdahl made no concessions to the modern world when he used these boats to cross the Pacific *(Kon-Tiki)* and the Atlantic *(RA II). Admission: NOK 10 adults, NOK 5 children. Open Nov.–Mar., daily 10:30–4; Apr.– May 15 and Sept.–Oct., daily 10:30–5; May 16–Aug., daily 10–6.*

Directly across from the Kon-Tiki Museum is a large triangular **⑮** building, the **Framhuset.** This museum is devoted to the polar ship *Fram*, the sturdy wooden vessel that belonged to bipolar explorer Fridtjof Nansen. (It was also used by Amundsen.) In 1893 Nansen led an expedition that reached latitude 86°14′ N, the most northerly latitude to have been reached at that time.

The book *Farthest North* tells his story. (Active in Russian famine-relief work, Nansen received a Nobel peace Prize in 1922.) You can board the ship and imagine yourself in one of the tiny berths, while outside a force-nine gale is blowing and the temperature is dozens of degrees below freezing. *Admission: NOK 7 adults, NOK 3 children. Open Apr. 15–30, daily 11–2:45; May 1–15, daily 11–4:45; May 16–Aug., daily 10–6; Sept., daily 11–4:45; Oct., daily 11–2:45; Nov., Sun. 11–2:45.*

⑯ The **Maritime Museum** next door focuses not on an individual ship but on the entire history of Norwegian seamanship. Attractions include a slide show, demonstrations, and a fascinating model of a Norwegian shipyard. *Admission: NOK 7 adults, NOK 3 children. Open Apr. 15–Sept., daily 10–8; Oct., Dec.–Apr. 14, 10:30–4, Tues. and Thurs. 10:30–8; Nov. 10:30–4, Tues. and Thurs. 10:30–7.*

Time Out | Before catching the ferry back to the center of Oslo, consider a meal or snack at the **Najaden** restaurant and cafeteria on the top floor of the Maritime Museum. In summer, you can sit on the terrace, which commands a view of the whole harbor.

⑰ Back at city hall, board bus 29 to **Toyen,** the area northeast of Oslo where you'll find the **Munch-Musset** (Munch Museum). In 1940, four years before his death, Munch bequeathed much of his work to the city of Oslo; the museum opened in 1963, the centennial of his birth. Although only a fraction of its 22,000 items—books, paintings, drawings, prints, sculptures, and letters—are on display, you can still get a sense of the tortured expressionism that was to have such an effect on European painting. *Toyengaten 53. Admission: NOK 10 (free mid-Sept.–mid-May). Open Tues.–Sat. 10–8, Sun. noon–8.*

Off the Beaten Track

Head east on streetcar 9 (from Nationaltheatret or Jernbanetorget) to the Sjømannsskolen stop to see 5,000-year-old carvings on the runic stones in **Ekebergseletta (park). Ekeberg Hall** is a major sports complex with miniature golf and a miniature zoo. Walk through the park and take Oslogate and then Bispegata to the **Ladegarden,** which has scale models of old Oslo on the site of the 13th-century Bispegard (Bishop's Palace). *Admission: free. Open May–Sept., Wed. 6–7 and Sun. 1–2.*

Continue up to St. Halvard's plass to the Gamlebyen (Old Town) excavations.

The jury is still out on the question of the artistic merit of Gustav Vigeland's magnum opus *The Wheel of Life,* but few would deny the perseverance involved in its creation. More than 15 meters (50 feet) high and covered with more than 100 linked human forms, this sculpture is the focal point of **Frogner Park,** which is north of the Bygdø Peninsula. Open-air restaurants, tennis courts, and swimming pools provide additional diversions. To get there, take streetcar 2; look for the word "Frogner" on the front. *Free. Park open 24 hours.*

The **Holmenkollen ski jump,** at 62 meters (200 feet) above ground level, is one of the world's highest and the site of an international contest each March. At the base of the jump is a ski museum carved into the rock face. To get there, board any

Frognerseter/Holmenkollen suburban train from Nationalteatret; get off at Holmenkollen. The half-hour ride sweeps
from down underground up to 403 meters (1,300 feet) above sea
level.

The forests within Oslo's vast city limits include 11 sports chalets, geared to exercise and the outdoor life. **Skullerudstua** and
Skistua are recommended for their walking and skiing trails.
Contact Oslo Kommune (Forestry Services), Skogvesenet, tel.
02/227560. Or, for winter or summer "safaris" through the forest by Land Rover, contact the main tourist information office
(*see* Important Addresses and Numbers).

Beyond Oslo, trips might include a visit to **Lillehammer.** Designated as the site of the 1994 Winter Olympics. Lillehammer is
at the top of the long finger of **Lake Mjøsa,** and is reached by
train from Oslo (Sentralstasjon) in about two hours or less.
Apart from the world-class ski resort, there is the nearby
Sandvig Collection, a tremendous outdoor museum where you
can participate in demonstrations of a number of traditional
crafts. A paddle steamer travels the length of Lake Mjøsa (six
hours each way) in the summer, making several stops. At the
southern tip of the lake is **Eidsvoll,** where the Norwegians
announced their new constitution in 1814, marking the end to
centuries of domination by Denmark. There are limitless possibilities for outdoor activities in the Lake Mjøsa region, all of it
within easy reach of Oslo.

Shopping

Gift Ideas   Since prices are controlled, Oslo is the obvious place to buy, as
the selection is widest: Pewter, silver, enamelware, sheepskin,
leather, and knitwear are all appealing samples of Norwegian
craftsmanship.

Shopping Districts   Many of the larger stores are located in the area **between the
Storting and the cathedral;** much of this area is for pedestrians
only. Oslo's newest shopping area is **Aker Brygge** (meaning
"quayside"). Right on the waterfront, it is a complex of stalls,
offices, and gardens. The **Basarhallene,** on the Johansgate side
of the Domkirken, is an art and handicraft boutique center.
Shops stay open until 8, compared with the city's normal shopping hours of 9–5 (Thurs. to 7).

Department Stores   Oslo's best department stores, **Steen & Strøm** and **Glas-
magasin,** are both in the shopping district near the cathedral.

**Food and Flea
Markets**   **Youngstorvet,** on Storgata near the cathedral, is the best place
for fresh fruit and vegetables. **Stortovet** is the flower market.

Dining

For details and price category definitions, *see* Dining in Staying
in Norway.

Very Expensive
★   **Annen Etage.** Top-quality food is prepared with an international flavor at this restaurant in the Continental Hotel. Inside it's
all elegant rococo decor with red damask and gilt-edged furnishings. Annen Etage attracts the lion's share of international
visitors, and caters for state banquets in Akershus Castle.
*Continental Hotel, Stortingsgate 24/26, tel. 02/419060. Reser-
vations essential. AE, DC, MC, V.*

De Fem Stuer. The tab is high, but you're still getting good value in this 19th-century building next to the famous ski jump in Holmenkollen. Gourmet entrées include a wide variety of game. *Holmenkollen Park Hotel, Kongevn. 26, tel. 02/146090. Reservations essential. AE, DC, MC, V.*

Expensive

★ **Blom.** The coats of arms and mottoes lining Blom's paneled walls belong to the many artists who have dined here over nearly a century. A lunch buffet helps keep prices within reason, as does the Fru Blom wine and food bar next door, serving pâté and quiche. *Karl Johansgate 41, tel. 02/427300. Reservations essential. MC, V.*

Etoile. Fresh Norwegian fish and shellfish are given classic and nouvelle treatment in this restaurant on the roof of the Grand Hotel, with panoramic views of the city. *Grand Hotel, Karl Johansgate 31, tel. 02/429390. Reservations essential. AE, DC, MC, V.*

Frognerseteren. Located next to the Holmenkollen ski jump, this restaurant looks down on the whole city. Come for the view, for the Norwegian specialties, or for a decor dominated by traditional old timbers and an open hearth. *Voksenkollen, tel. 02/143736. Reservations essential. DC, MC, V.*

★ **Mølla.** This charmingly renovated spinning mill on the Aker River has a unique atmosphere enhanced by candle-lit vaults, live music, cabaret, and dancing. The menu features fresh fish and game. *Sagvn 21, tel. 02/375450. Reservations advised. AE, DC, V.*

Moderate

La Brochette. Choose your own steak in this intimate French-style, Italian-run restaurant next door to the Concert Hall. The atmosphere is subdued, and there's much attention to detail. *Dronning Maudsgate 1–3, tel. 02/416733. Reservations advised. AE, MC, V.*

Gamle Rådhus. The "old city hall," Oslo's oldest restaurant, is located in a building dating from 1640. Specialties include mussels and fresh shrimp. *Nedre Slottsgate 1, tel. 02/420107. Reservations advised. No credit cards. Closed Sun.*

Grand Café. Ibsen was the most famous of the café's turn-of-the-century clientele, and his favorite chair and table are here to prove it. A luxuriant decor and formal china add extra atmosphere. Norwegian specialties—whale meat, stingray, and big-game meat—are served for dinner, but light meals and salads are also available. *Karl Johansgate 31, tel. 02/334870. Reservations advised. AE, DC, MC, V.*

Mamma Rosa. Under the same management as La Brochette, this Italian restaurant is located on the second floor of a building looking down on Karl Johansgate. The atmosphere is informal, with guitar music in the evening. Pasta and pizza are at the lower end of a menu featuring mainly Italian specialties. *Øvre Slotsgate 12, tel. 02/420130. Reservations advised. AE, MC, V.*

Peking House. Crisp white damask table linen, dark mahogany furniture, and friendly service create an attractive atmosphere for this Chinese restaurant near the center of town. *St. Olavsgate, tel. 02/114878. Reservations accepted. AE, DC, MC, V.*

Inexpensive

★ **Albin Upp.** A real find for people who like the unusual, this intimate wine and snack bar is in a farmer's renovated cottage, right in the heart of town. It's directly behind a stop for streetcar 1. Contemporary Norwegian arts and crafts are on display inside. *Briskebyvn. 42, tel. 02/564448. No reservations. No credit cards.*

Café Frohlich. Oslo's only café with music is furnished in Old Viennese style. Entertainment—jazz, classical, and even rock —is provided by music students or any guest competent enough to play the instruments, one of which is a grand piano. The menu features light meals and ice-cream specials. *Drammensvn. 20, tel. 02/443737. No reservations. No credit cards.*

Vegeta. Next to the bus and streetcar Nationalteatret station, this is a popular spot for hot and cold vegetarian meals and salads. It is a nonsmoking restaurant. The all-you-can-eat specials offer top value. *Munkedamsvn. 36, tel. 02/428557. No reservations. No credit cards.*

Lodging

The tourist office's accommodations bureaus (open daily 8 AM–11 PM) in Central Station can help you find rooms in hotels, pensions, and private homes. You must apply in person and pay a fee of NOK 10 (NOK 5, children) plus 10% of the room rate, which will be refunded when you check in. For details and price category definitions, *see* Lodging in Staying in Norway.

Very Expensive **Bristol.** Quietly located on a side street, the Bristol offers plush comfort and tranquility as well as a central location. Rooms are spacious and airy, and the hotel features two good restaurants: the excellent international-style Bristol Grill, and El Toro, a Spanish restaurant with dancing and floor shows. *Kristian IV Gate, tel. 02/415840. 220 rooms with bath. Facilities: 2 bars, nightclub, disco. AE, DC, MC, V.*

★ **Grand.** It's hard to beat the Grand's location on Oslo's main street, opposite the Parliament and city park. The hotel has all the comforts and history to match its name: Ibsen had a permanent table in its Grand Café, a famous Oslo rendezvous. It has four other restaurants, ranging from the Palmen, a sandwich bar, to the gourmet French Etoile and the exclusive Speilen. *Karl Johansgate 31, tel. 02/429390. 350 rooms with bath or shower. Facilities: indoor pool, sauna, solarium. AE, DC, MC, V.*

★ **Holmenkollen Park.** Located near the ski jump, this hotel is an imposing Norse-style building with a luxurious annex. Rooms are bright, and most have balconies with excellent views of the city below. The hotel runs a shuttle bus for its guests. It's probably the best place for anyone hoping to do some skiing. *Kongeveien 26, tel. 02/146090. 200 rooms with bath. Facilities: ski trails, bar, nightclub, whirlpool, sauna, squash, indoor pool, curling rink. AE, DC, MC, V.*

SAS Hotel Scandinavia. Norway's largest hotel and tallest building is more like a small town under one roof. The hotel is comfortable and has impeccable service, while its gourmet grill, the Café Royal, offers a spectacular *smørgasbord* for lunch. Summit 21 is the rooftop lunch bar, with commanding views of the whole city. Downstairs you'll find a shopping center and the city air terminal. *Holbersgate 30, tel. 02/113000. 476 rooms with bath. Facilities: 2 bars, indoor pool, tennis, disco. AE, DC, MC, V.*

Expensive **Gabelshus Hotel.** Only five minutes from the center of town, the Gabelshus is a moderate-sized hotel on an attractive side street. Rooms are spacious and airy, and the hotel has more of the feel of a large country house. Its restaurant is recommended. *Gabelsgate 16, tel. 02/552260. 45 rooms with bath. No credit cards.*

KNA. The Royal Norwegian Auto Club runs this comfortable hotel in a quiet street just west of the downtown area, so you can capitalize on some expert advice on touring options and road conditions. All rooms are clean and comfortable, and there is an intimate restaurant and bar as well as a lively bistro. *Parkvein 68, tel. 02/562690. 226 rooms with bath or shower. AE, DC, MC, V.*

SAS Park Royal Hotel. Ten minutes from the center of Oslo, this hotel is clean, efficient, and convenient for Fornebu Airport. Rooms are large, and the top-class facilities are well suited for business stays. *Fornebu Park, Lysaker, tel. 02/120220. 350 rooms and 10 suites with bath. Facilities: restaurant, sauna, fitness room, tennis, direct airport check-in, executive office space. AE, DC, MC, V.*

Moderate   **Europa.** This centrally located modern hotel is a more moderately priced alternative to its next-door neighbor, the SAS Hotel Scandinavia. Rooms are comfortable (all have color TV), and there are special reductions for children. *St. Olavsgate 31, tel. 02/209990. 150 rooms with bath. DC, MC, V.*

Stefan. Service is cheerful and accommodating in this hotel in the center of Oslo. One of its main attractions is the popular restaurant Eighth Floor (no alcohol is served); the excellent buffet includes *rommegrot*, a traditional sour cream porridge eaten with smoked meats. *Rosenkrantzgate 1, tel. 02/336290. 140 rooms with bath or shower. AE, MC, V.*

Inexpensive   **Anker Stiftelsen Yrkesskolens Hybelhus.** These centrally located accommodations are rather basic student residences open during the summer vacation (May to September), but they do have cooking facilities, a supermarket, cafeteria, and restaurant. Some rooms are like dormitories, with four beds to the room, but it's clean and friendly. *Storgate 55, tel. 02/114005. 426 beds, a few rooms with shower. AE, MC, V.*

Ritz. A little less grand than some of the others that share its name, this Ritz is still an attractive place on a quiet street, about seven minutes from downtown by streetcar. It also has a restaurant. *Fr. Stansgate, tel. 02/443960. 42 rooms, some with bath. AE, DC, MC, V.*

The Arts

For a small city, Oslo has a surprising amount of artistic life. Consult the *Oslo Guide* or *Oslo This Week* for details. Winter is *the* cultural season, with the **Nationalteatret** featuring modern plays, classics, and a good sampling of Ibsen. Its experimental stage, called the **Amphitheater,** is more intimate and goes in for avant-garde productions. The **Dukketeatret** in the City Museum (Frognerveien 67) is a puppet theater that is popular with families.

Oslo's modern **Konserthuset** (Concert Hall), at Ruseløkkveien, is the home of the Oslo Philharmonic, famous for its recordings of Tchaikovsky's symphonies. A smaller hall in the same building is the setting for performances of chamber music and—in summer only—folk dancing. There are also musical and ballet performances at the **Henie-Onstad Kunstsenter (Art Center)** at Høvikodden. This center specializes in 20th-century art and was a gift from the Olympic Norwegian skater Sonje Henie and her husband, rower Niels Onstad.

Nightlife

The deadly combination of prices and puritanism used to put a damper on spirits in Oslo, but now, with the influx of free-spending oil men and the generally high standard of living, things have begun to loosen. For those who like discos, the best are in the luxury hotels *(see* Lodging). Jazz is a bit more established; a few of the recommended spots include:

Amalienborg Jazzhouse (Arbeidergate 2, tel. 02/423024); **Ben Joseph** (La Petite Cuisine); (Solligate 2, tel. 02/444575); **Jazz Alive** (Observatoriegate 2, tel. 02/440745); **Stortovets Gjæastiveri** (Grensel 1, tel. 02/428863); and **Storyville** (Universitetsgaten 26, tel. 02/423596).

The Coast Road to Stavanger

This tour follows the Sørland coast south of Oslo toward the busy port Kristiansand and then west to Stavanger. It is an area where whaling has given way to canneries, lumber, paper production and petrochemicals. Yet the beauty of this 608-kilometer (380-mile) route has not been greatly marred, and you'll find seaside towns, rocky headlands, and stretches of forest (fjord country does not begin until north of Stavanger).

The route outlined here edges round the coast, but it is also possible to reach Stavanger via an inland route through the Telemark region.

Getting Around

By Car Driving is recommended because it gives visitors the chance to stop at coastal villages that are either not served by trains or have only sporadic service. The route is simple: E18 as far as Flekkefjord, and then E44 to Stavanger. When driving in even this relatively populated part of Norway, make sure to keep your tank full because gas stations can be a rarity on some rural roads.

By Train The best train service is the Sørland line, which leaves West Station in Oslo and goes all the way to Stavanger. The Oslo-Drammen stretch is an engineering feat and features Norway's longest tunnel, an 11-kilometer (7-mile) construction through sheer rock.

By Bus Local buses cover the entire route. For details on fares and schedules, check with the tourist offices listed below or the main one in Oslo *(see* Important Addresses and Numbers).

Guided Tours

In summer, there is a daily boat excursion from Oslo to the coastal resorts of Kragerø, Jomfruland, and Risør southwest of the capital in the direction of Stavanger. Sightseers return the same day, and refreshments are served on board. The excursion is organized by the Oslo tourist information office (*see* Important Addresses and Numbers).

Tourist Information

Arendal. Box 344, tel. 041/22193.
Drammen. Rådhuset, tel. 03/834094.
Flekkefjord. tel. 043/24254.
Kristiansand. Henrik Wergelandsgate. 17, tel. 042/26065.
Larvik. Storgaten 20, tel. 034/82623.
Stavanger. Tourist Pavilion, tel. 04/528437.
Tønsberg. Storgate 55, tel. 033/14819.

Exploring the Coast Road to Stavanger

From Oslo, take highway E18 west for about 40 kilometers (25 miles) to the bustling port of **Drammen.** Located at the mouth of a large timber-floating river, Drammen operates as a processing and shipping center for lumber and paper products. Take a short detour west of town on E76, turn right on Kongsgate, and climb the mile-long "Corkscrew Road," a series of spiraling tunnels leading to the top of **Bragernes Hill.** In the '50s, locals decided against any further quarrying of building stone and turned instead to tunneling for it. The result is this scenic and dramatic road with panoramic views of **Drammensfjord** and the larger **Oslo Fjord** beyond.

Return to E18 and continue to the coastal town of **Åsgård-strand,** an unspoiled summer resort where Edvard Munch painted many of his best works. His small white frame house is open to visitors during the summer (admission: NOK 10). Farther along is **Tønsberg,** which inhabitants claim is Norway's oldest town, founded in AD 870. The steep hill beside the train station leads to the ruins of **Tønsberghus,** an extensive fortress and abbey. The outlook tower, built in 1870 to commemorate the town's millennium, has a good view of the coast. The rise of Oslo as Norway's capital led to the decline of Tønsberg, although it developed as a whaling port in the 18th century.

Attractive **Sandefjord,** 15 kilometers (9 miles) down E18, is a port that served as the base for the Norwegian whaling fleet until after World War II, when large-scale competition from the Soviet Union and Japan made the operation uneconomical. The port remains busy as a depot for timber shipping.

Just beyond Sandefjord, E18 crosses the important lumbering river Lågen and then follows it to the port of **Larvik,** which is the terminus for ferries to Frederikshavn in Denmark. Like Tønsberg and Sandefjord, Larvik once looked to whaling for its livelihood, but it, too, has turned to lumber and ferrying for employment.

Larvik is the birthplace of Thor Heyerdahl, so it is fitting that pride of place should go to the **Maritime Museum** (admission charges and opening times vary; check with the tourist office). Located in the former customs house, it chronicles Larvik's seafaring history and gives special emphasis to Heyerdahl's voyages, with models of *Kon-Tiki* and *RA II.*

After Larvik, progress is faster, as E18 cuts across some of the narrower peninsulas on its way south. Side roads offer the

The Coast Road to Stavanger

chance to explore the smaller coastal village of **Kragerø,** where Edvard Munch spent many summers painting, and its neighboring islands, **Risør,** with its patrician 19th-century harborfront homes, and **Tvedestrand,** with its crooked streets. **Arendal,** 120 kilometers (70 miles) beyond Larvik, was once called Little Venice, but its canals have now been turned into wide streets. The atmosphere of bygone whaling prosperity in this and other Sørland ports is like that of Nantucket, with tidy cottages and grandiose captains' houses all within shouting distance of the docks. Explore Arendal's **Tyholmen quarter** for a glimpse into this 19th-century world.

Kristiansand is another 50 kilometers (30 miles) along the coast from Arendal. With a population of 60,000, it's the largest town in Sørland and has important air, sea, road, and rail links. It was laid out in the 17th century in a grid pattern, with the imposing **Christiansholm Fort** guarding the eastern harbor approach. (Exhibitions are sometimes held inside the fort in summer.) Just to the northeast of Kristiansand is the open-air **Agder County Museum,** with 28 old buildings and farms rebuilt in the local style of the 18th and 19th centuries. There are also displays of folklore and costumes. *Admission: NOK 15. Open 10–6, Sun. noon–6.*

Continue along E18 for another 30 kilometers (20 miles) to **Mandal,** Norway's most southerly town, famous for its beach, salmon, and 18th- and 19th-century houses. For the next 30 kilometers (20 miles), the road climbs and weaves its way through steep, wooded valleys and then descends to the fishing port of

Flekkefjord, with its charming **Hollenderbyen,** or Dutch Quarter.

E18 heads inland here to Stavanger, but it is more rewarding to follow the coast road (E44) past the fishing port of **Egershund,** 40 kilometers (25 miles) ahead, and a little farther to **Ogna,** with its good, sandy beach. For the last hour or so before Stavanger, you will be in the region known as the **Jæren.** Flat and stony, it is the largest expanse of level terrain in this mountainous country. The mild climate and the absence of good harbors meant that the population here turned to agriculture, and the miles of stone walls are a testament to their labor.

Stavanger, at the end of the tour, is a former trading town that in the past 15 years has become a champion (some environmentalists say victim) of the oil boom. The population has gone from 10,000 to nearly 100,000, and drilling platforms and oil tankers take the place of fishing boats in the harbor. In contrast to the new high-rise complexes is an old quarter with narrow cobbled lanes and clapboard houses at odd angles. The town is believed to date from the 8th century; its Anglo-Norman **St. Svithens Cathedral,** next to the central market, was established in 1125 by the Bishop of Winchester in England. (Trading and ecclesiastical links between Norway and England were strong throughout the Middle Ages.)

Ledaal is a fine patrician mansion where the king resides when he's visiting Stavanger, and which is part of the **Stavanger Museum.** It houses relics from the area and a special maritime display. An ultramodern concert hall and arts center opened in Stavanger in the mid-1980s. Also of interest is **Viste Cave** outside the city. It is said to be 6,000 years old. And **Ullandhaug** is a reconstructed Iron Age farm.

The **Ryfylke fjords** north and east of Stavanger form the southern end of the Fjord Country. The city is a good base for exploring this region, since its "white fleet" of low-slung seabuses makes daily excursions into even the most distant fjords of Ryfylke. The Lysefjord excursion is superb.

Dining and Lodging

For details and price category definitions, *see* Dining and Lodging in Staying in Norway.

Arendal   **Grand Restaurant.** Norwegian seafood specialties are featured
Dining   in this traditional restaurant in attractive Arendal. *Langbryggen 19, tel. 041/25160. Reservations advised. AE, DC, MC, V. Moderate.*

Lodging   **Phønix.** Despite being the hub of Arendal's nightlife—with its restaurant, bar, and disco—the Phønix has rooms that are quiet and comfortable. *Tyholmen, tel. 041/25160. 80 rooms with bath or shower. DC, MC, V. Expensive.*

Drammen   **Skansen.** At the top of the spiraling "Corkscrew Road" that
Dining   tunnels its way up from town, the Skansen offers excellent views as well as freshly prepared fish and game specialties. *Bragernessen (no tel.). No reservations. No credit cards. Moderate.*

Lodging   **Park.** This comfortable and centrally located hotel has well-equipped rooms and a good restaurant. *Gamle Kirkeplass 3,* *tel. 03/838280. 120 rooms with bath or shower. MC, V. Moderate.*

Kristiansand
Dining

Bowlers Steakhouse. Good portions of steak and roasts are served here with fresh salads. Try the fruit desserts in summer. *Kirkegate 7, tel. 042/29009. No reservations. No credit cards. Expensive.*

Bøgen Grill. Local soups and game are featured in this attractive waterfront restaurant in the eastern part of central Kristiansand. *Elvegate 1, tel. 042/25838. Reservations advised. No credit cards. Moderate.*

Lodging

Rica Fregatten. You're right in the center of town in this medium-size hotel, a stone's throw from the Town Hall and Cathedral. Rooms are comfortable and well appointed, and there is a good restaurant. *Droningensgate 66, tel. 042/21500. 70 rooms, most with bath. AE, DC, MC, V. Moderate.*

Savoy. The clean and comfortable rooms in this pension and inn are quite adequate for an inexpensive overnight stay. *Kr. Ivsgate 1, tel. 042/24175. 14 rooms, none with bath. No credit cards. Inexpensive.*

Larvik
Lodging

Grand. The rooms are spotless and service is attentive in this large hotel overlooking the fjord. There is a choice of restaurants to sample the local fish soup and smoked meat platters, which are particularly good at lunchtime. *Storgaten 38–40, tel. 034/83800. 117 rooms, most with bath. AE, MC, V. Moderate.*

Sandefjord
Lodging
★

Park. Overlooking Sandefjord's attractive harbor, the imposing Park is considered one of the best hotels in Norway. The rooms are large and comfortable, with excellent views over the water. The service is flawless. *Strandprom 9, tel. 034/65550. 160 rooms with bath or shower. Facilities: restaurant, bar, pool, saunas. AE, DC, MC, V. Expensive.*

Stavanger
Dining

La Gondola. Freshly caught local seafood in spicy fish soups with risotto add some variety to the palates of oilmen jaded from a surfeit of cafeteria meals. La Gondola is located right by the market. *Nytorget 8, tel. 04/534235. Reservations advised. No credit cards. Moderate.*

Viking. Don't be put off by a name that suggests a tourist comeon. Game and seafood are served here in healthy portions and with no gimmicks. *Jernbaven 15, tel. 04/588747. Reservations advised. No credit cards. Moderate.*

Lodging

SAS Royal. Like its counterparts in Oslo (Park Hotel and Scandinavia), the Royal is modern, clean, and efficient, but still has a pleasant, informal atmosphere. The rooms are large and comfortable, and the hotel is capable of dealing, with equal ease, with a gathering of business tycoons demanding conference space or with a party of fly fishermen. *Løkkevn. 26. 210 rooms with bath. Facilities: pool, sauna, airport check-in, business service center. AE, DC, MC, V. Very Expensive.*

Commandør. The Commandør is much smaller and considerably more basic than the Royal, but it offers clean and comfortable accommodations. *Valbergsgate 9, tel. 04/528000. 48 rooms with bath. AE, DC, MC, V. Moderate.*

Through Telemark to Bergen

The Telemark region lies between Oslo and Bergen, and is characterized by steep valleys, pine forests, lakes, and fast-flowing rivers full of trout. The destination of this itinerary, Bergen, is Norway's second largest city and is in the heart of Fjord Country. The last leg of this westward route includes Hardangerfjord, the source of inspiration of many a Norwegian artist and outdoorsman. The area is renowned for its skiing—especially the Morgedal Valley—and as the former stronghold of Norway's Resistance fighters. Today it is a peaceful region, where flowers sprout from the turf roofs of old wooden houses in some of the sleepier villages.

Fjord Tours Fjord transportation is good, as crossing fjords is a necessary as well as a scenic way to travel in Norway. Hardangerfjord (below Bergen) and Sognefjord and Nordfjord (both below Bergen) are three of the deepest and most popular fjords. Local tourist offices will be able to recommend excursions and travel routes.

Guided Tours

Bergen is the center for many excursions, covering most of the last half of this tour as well as the fjords farther north. Contact the tourist information office (see below) for details of these constantly changing tours.

Tourist Information

Bergen. Slottsgate 1, tel. 05/313680.
Drammen. Rdhuset, tel. 03/834094.
Kinsarvik. tel. 054/63450.
Kongsberg. tel. 03/731526.
Røldal. tel. 054/47289.

Exploring Through Telemark to Bergen

Take E18 west from Oslo to nearby **Drammen** (*see* Exploring The Coast Road to Stavanger). Following E76 west out of Drammen, you pass Kongsgate Street on the right. This leads to the "Corkscrew Road" up to the top of **Bragernes Hill.** The brief detour pays dividends, with a good view back toward Oslo Fjord.

Return to E76 and continue west for about 40 kilometers (25 miles) to **Kongsberg,** on the fast-flowing Lager River. Kongsberg was founded in 1624 as a silver-mining town. Although there is no more mining, the town is still the seat of the Royal Norwegian Mint. In the center of town is an 18th-century Rococo church that's the size of some cathedrals. It reflects the town's former wealth from silver.

Kongsberg is one of the gateways to Telemark, which you'll know you've reached once the road climbs past Meheia on the county border. Forests give way to rocky peaks and desolate spaces farther into the plateau. **Heddal** is the first town you encounter in Telemark. Norway's largest stave church is here.

Through Telemark to Bergen

Stave churches, built with wooden planks staked vertically into the ground or base, and found almost exclusively in southern Norway, were medieval forerunners of modern high-rise buildings. The Heddal church is typical in having richly carved ornamentation on the doors and around the aisle.

E76 climbs up from Heddal and skirts the large Telemark plateau. You'll see its highest peak, **Lifjell,** 6,720 kilometers (4,200 feet), on the left before descending toward **Seljord,** on the lake of the same name. The countryside down by the lake is richer than up on the plateau; meadows and pastureland run down to the lakefront. The attractive village of Seljord has richly ornamented wooden houses and a medieval church.

Continue south from Seljord, making sure to stay right (on E76) at the Brunkeberg crossroads, while the other road continues south to Kristiansand. You are now entering the steep valley of **Morgedal.** It was here in the last century that Sondre Nordheim developed the slalom method of skiing—*sla lom* means "make turns." You can get the full story on the development of skiing at the **Olav Bjaland's Museum,** named for the south polar explorer and ski hero. *Admission NOK 10. Open July–Aug. 20, Tues.–Sun. 10–3.*

Turn left at Hoydalsmo for a scenic diversion to mountainbound **Dalen.** At Dalen is **Tokke I,** one of Europe's largest hydroelectric power stations. From here, it's an 8-kilometer (5 mile) drive to **Eidsborg,** where there is a stave church and a dramatic view back down to the Dalen Valley.

From Dalen, you can also drive up to one of Telemark's wonders, the **Ravnejuvet ravine,** a 310-meter (1,000-foot) sheer drop into the Tokke Valley. Throw paper into the ravine and a peculiar updraft returns it to you. But experiment with waste paper rather than money!

Take E38 from Dalen along the Tokke Valley to **Åmot.** The 93-meter (300-foot) Hyllandfoss Falls were destroyed by the hydroelectric project, but the drive through the valley is still spectacular.

Rejoin E76 at Åmot. At the next crossroads (Haukeigrend), E76 begins really to climb, and you'll see why the Norwegians are so proud of keeping this Telemark route open all year. Before leaving Telemark, you'll pass through the 6-kilometer (3 ½-mile) Haukeli Tunnel and then begin a long descent to **Røldal,** another lakefront town with a hydroelectric plant.

Turn north on Route 47 a few miles after Røldal, and drive to the **Skr Fjord** at Odda. Continue along the fjord to the attractive town of **Kinsarvik.** For the best view of the junction of the Sør and mighty Hardanger fjords, take the ferry across the Sør to Utne. On the dramatic 30-minute ferry crossing from Utne to Kyvanndal, you will understand how this area was such a rich source of inspiration for Romantic composer Edvard Grieg.

At Kyvanndal, turn left on E68. The road follows the fjord west, then veers right to **Nordheimsund.** After climbing over another coastal mountain spur, it winds through the wild **Tokagjel Gorge** and across the mountains of **Kramskogen,** and then descends in a series of twists and tunnels into Bergen, capital of the fjords.

Bergen is Norway's second largest city, with a population of 200,000. It is the most international of Norway's cities, having been an important trading and military center when Oslo was an obscure village. Bergen was a member of the medieval Hanseatic League, benefiting from its ice-free harbor and convenient trading location on the west coast. Natives of Bergen still think of Oslo as a dour provincial town in the grip of a dreary climate. Today, Bergen is an active base for travelers to the fjord country.

Despite numerous fires in its past, much of medieval Bergen has remained. Seven surrounding mountains set off the weathered wooden houses, cobbled streets, and Hanseatic-era warehouses of the **Bryggen** (harbor area). Founded in 1070, the town was first named Vågen (harbor), and its center was where the Torget (fish market) is today.

The best way to get a feel for Bergen's medieval trading heyday is to visit the **Hanseatic Museum** on the Bryggen. One of the oldest and best-preserved of Bergen's wooden buildings, it is furnished in 16th-century style. The guided tour is excellent. *Admission: NOK 10 adults, NOK 5 children. Open June–Aug., daily 10–4; May, Sept., daily 10–2; Oct.–Apr., 11–2, closed Tues., Thurs., Sat.*

On the western end of the Vågen is the Rosenkrantz Tower, part of the **Bergenhus,** the 13th-century fortress guarding the harbor entrance. The tower and fortress were destroyed in World War II but restored meticulously in the '60s, and are now rich with furnishings and household items from the 16th century. *Admission: NOK 10. Open mid-May–mid-Sept., daily 10–4.*

Across the Vågen is the **Nordness Peninsula,** where you can look back toward the city and the mountainous backdrop. Save time to meander through the winding back streets, intersected by broad *almenninger* (wide avenues built as protection against fires). For the best view of Bergen and its surroundings, take the funicular from the corner of Lille Øvregate and Vetrlidsalmenning. It climbs 310 meters (1,000 feet) to the top of Fløyen, one of the seven mountains guarding this ancient port.

Trodlhaugen manor on Nordås Lake, once home to Edvard Grieg, is now a museum and includes a new chamber music hall. Recitals are held each Wednesday and Sunday at 8 PM from late June through early August. *Hopsvegen, Bergen, tel. 02/135438.*

Admission: NOK 10 adults, NOK 5 children. Open May–Sept., daily 10:30–1:30 and 2:30–5:30.

Another outstanding site is the nearby **Fantoft Stave Church,** built in the 12th century. It is a 10-minute walk beyond Trodlhaugen and can be reached on city buses. *Fantoft Stavkirke, tel. 05/280710. Admission: NOK 5 adults, children free. Open May 15–Sept. 15, daily 10:30–1:30 and 2:30–5:30.*

Excursions from Bergen

Lysøen Island Ole Bull was one of Norway's favorite musicians and he passed many a violin-playing hour on **Lysøen Island,** the site of what was his villa. It is now a national monument, donated to the nation by his American granddaughter. Apart from Ole Bull memorabilia, there are 13 kilometers (8 miles) of nature trails. Ferries to Lysøen leave Bergen from Buena pier (Sorestraumen), 26 kilometers (16 miles) south of the center. *Tel. 05/309077. Roundtrip fare is NOK 25 adults, NOK 10 children. Open May 18–Sept. 4, Mon.–Sat. 12–4; May 18–Oct. 2, Sun. 11–5.*

Bergen is the start of fjord cruises of all descriptions; details on these can be obtained from Bergen's information center at Torgalmenning, tel. 05/321480.

Dining and Lodging

For details and price category definitions, *see* Dining and Lodging in Staying in Norway.

Bergen **Bellevue.** It's hard to imagine a more imposing or dramatic setting for a restaurant than the Bellevue's, high up on a hillside looking down on Bergen and the Hardanger Fjord. The restaurant itself is a 17th-century manor house. Fine crystal and silverware accompany the excellent food. Not surprisingly, the Bellevue puts emphasis on fresh seafood. The service is attentive and polished. *Bellevuebakken 9, tel. 05/310240. Reservations essential. AE, DC, MC, V. Expensive.*
Dining
★

Bryggen Tracteursted. Set among the medieval Hanseatic warehouses, this is the place to try the freshest ingredients from the adjacent fish market. *Bryggestredet, tel. 05/314046. DC. Moderate.*

Wesselstuen. In some respects, you'll find this more of a café than a restaurant: Notice particularly how Bergeners wander in and out throughout the day, seeming to sense when the latest catch of fresh fish has arrived. The atmosphere is bustling and friendly. *Engen 14, tel. 05/322900. No reservations. No credit cards. Moderate.*

Lodging **SAS Royal.** Located right at the harbor, the SAS Royal was opened in 1982 on the site of old warehouses ravaged by a series of nine fires since 1170. The houses were rebuilt each time in the same style, which SAS has incorporated into this well-equipped hotel. *Bryggen, tel. 05/318000. 265 rooms with bath. Facilities: pool, sauna, Hanseatic exhibition. AE, DC, MC, V. Very Expensive.*

Scandic. Located just outside town near Bergen's Flesland airport, Scandic is comfortable and well equipped, making it a convenient stop if you are driving or flying into Bergen. *Kokstadflaten 2, Kokstad, tel. 05/227150. 175 rooms with bath.*

Facilities: tavern, restaurant, indoor pool, sauna. DC, MC, V. Moderate.

Strand. Facing the harbor in the center of Bergen, the Strand is a moderate-size, efficient hotel. Most rooms have a view of the harbor. *Strandkaien 2–4, tel. 05/310815. 60 rooms, most with bath. AE, DC, MC, V. Moderate.*

Kinsarvik
Lodging

Kinsarvik Fjord Hotel. There are good views of Hardanger Fjord and the glacier above it from this handsome hotel near the busy ferry port. The rooms are bright and spacious. *Kinsarvik, tel. 054/63100. 70 rooms with bath or shower. AE, MC, V. Moderate.*

Kongsberg
Dining

Ernst's Kafeteria. Good, fresh food is well presented in this inexpensive cafeteria in the center of town. x3Drammensvn. 87, tel. 03/733530. No reservations. No credit cards. Inexpensive.

Utne
Dining and Lodging

Utne Hotel. The white frame house dates from 1722 and the hotel, the oldest in Norway, has been run by the same family since 1787. The Utne has all the cared-for atmosphere of an old home. The dining room is wood paneled and hand painted, decorated with copper pans, old china, and paintings. Old furniture also fills the rooms, many of which have good views of the ferry port and Hardanger Fjord. The Utne makes a good base for hiking or cycling in the region. *Utne, tel. 054/66983. 28 rooms with bath or shower. AE, DC, MC. Moderate.*

Above Bergen: The Far North

The fjords continue northward from Bergen all the way to Kirkenes, at Norway's border with the Soviet Union. Norway's north is for anyone eager to hike, climb, fish, birdwatch (seabirds), see Lappland, or experience—in June and July—the unending days of the midnight sun. The Lofoten Islands present the grand face of the "Lofoten Wall"—a rocky, 96-kilometer (60-mile)–long massif surrounded by the sea and broken into six pieces. Svolvær, the most populated island, has a thriving summer artists' colony. It's also known for winter cod fishing.

Getting Around

By Ship
One of the best ways to travel in northern Norway is the **Hurtigrute** or coastal steamer, which begins in Bergen and turns around 2,000 nautical kilometers (1,250 miles) later at Kirkenes. Many steamers run this route, so you can put in at any of the ports for any length of time and pick up the next one coming through: Schedules and reservations through from Major tourist offices. Have the schedules, and you can make reservations there. Most ferries in Norway take cars.

By Car
Drivers have no choice of route but E6 and its feeder roads after Trondheim, where the country dramatically narrows.

By Train
Major train routes are Oslo–Bergen and Oslo–Trondheim–Bodø (the Trondheim–Bodø leg lasts one day). From Bodø there are tours to the Lofoten and Vesterålen Islands, and the Vaeren Islands, two tiny, remote islands at the tail of the Lofoten chain. You can get to Svolvær, the Lofotens' main port, via

ferry from Skutvik. Train rides from Trondheim to Bodø take about a day.

To get all the way to Nordkapp (the North Cape and northern-most mainland point in Norway and Europe) and the Land of the Midnight Sun, there is the "Polar Express" train trip from Fauske (near Bodø) via the Nordland railroad to Kirkenes. It takes four days and you are guaranteed modest accommodations at every overnight stop.

Guided Tours

The major towns north of Bergen are Ålesund, Trondheim, Narvik, Tromsø, Bodø, Hammerfest, and Kirkenes. The area covered is enormous, so use the local tourist offices *(see* below) for tour information, area maps, and arranging travel. Special tours are included below in Exploring, where each town is individually described. Cheaper accomodations are the rule in the north, whether you stay in a fell hut (in the mountains—free of charge), campsite, guest house, or *rorbu*—fishermen's huts in the islands that are available to rent outside the January–April fishing season.

Tourist Information

Ålesund. Rådhuset (City Hall), tel. 071/21202.
Bodø. Tollbugata 10, tel. 081/21240.
Hammerfest. Sjøgata, tel. 084/12185.
Kirkenes. Off the E6 in wooden hut behind Rica Hotel (on Pasvikveien), tel. 085/91751.
Narvik. Kongensgate 66, tel. 082/43309.
Tromsø. Grunnegata 48, tel. 083/84776.
Trondheim. Kongensgate 7 (entrance form Torvet, the market-place), tel. 071/527201.

Exploring The Far North

See the Norway country map for the location of towns on this tour.

The steamer is probably the best route to Ålesund and then Trondheim, as no main road connects them directly. **Ålesund,** a much-overlooked coastal city flanked by fjords, is perhaps the only example you'll find of true architectural eccentricity in Norway. After a fire here in the early 1900s, anyone who had any aspirations to architecture designed his or her own new home, and the result is a rich, playful mixture of styles ranging from austere to Art Nouveau. There are excellent tours of the Romsdal, Geiranger and Hjorund fjords. Pick up the free *Ålesund Guide* and *On Foot in Ålesund* from the tourist office *(see* above).

Trondheim sits at the southern end of Norway's widest fjord, Trondheimfjord. This waterbound city is the third largest in the country, and is also the traditional coronation place of Norwegian royalty. Scandinavia's largest medieval building, **Nidaros cathedral,** built in 1320, is here. For centuries it served as a goal for religious pilgrims. There is an historic fish market which is worth seeing—and participating in (some restaura-

teurs will cook the fish you bring them from the market).
Scandinavia's two largest wooden buildings are in Trondheim.
One is the Rococo **Stiftsgarden,** a royal palace built in 1774, and
the other is a student hostel.

After Trondheim the country thins into a vertebral cord of land
hugging the border with Sweden and hunching over the top of
Finland. **Bodø** is the first "city" in many hundreds of miles after
leaving Trondheim. As the northern terminus of the Nordland
railway, Bodø is bathed in midnight sun from early June to mid-
July. For those who want boat excursions to **coastal bird colonies** (the Vaeren Islands), Bodø is the best base. The city was
bombed by the Germans in 1940. The stunning, contemporary
Bodø Cathedral, its spire separated from the main building,
was built after the war. Inside are rich, modern tapestries; outside is a war memorial. The **Nordland County Museum** depicts
the life of the *Same* (Lapps) and of the ancestors of the Nord-
landers, or north country people. *Prinsengate 116, tel. 081/
26128. Admission: NOK 10 adults, NOK 2 children. Open weekdays 9–3, Sat. 10–3, Sun. 12–3.*

If you've never seen a real **maelstrom**—a furious natural whirlpool—inquire at the tourist office *(see* above) about **Salt-
straumen.** Bodø is considered a gateway to the Lofoten and
Vesterålen islands; the tourist office will make arrangements.

Narvik is a rebuilt city, an "ice-free" seaport, and a major shipping center for iron ore. An excellent railway connects it to the
mines over the Swedish border. Its old outline was erased by
war damage. The **Krigsminne War Museum** has gripping displays on wartime intrigues and suffering. *Kongensgate, near
main square. Admission: NOK 10. Open Mar.–Sept., daily
10–2; Jun.–Aug., daily 10AM–10 PM.*

Tours of the busy **Narvik docks** start from the LKAB building.
For panoramic views, hop the *gondolbaner* (cable car) up **Fager-
nesfjellet's** 682-meter (2,200-foot) cliffs (fare: NOK 35). Hiking
it takes at least two hours. Also try to see the **Brennholtet rock
carvings.** Note that the tourist office *(see* above) rents rooms in
private homes, as Narvik's hotels are very pricey. Narvik is a
good base for mountain excursions.

Tromsø dubs itself "the Paris of the North" for the nightlife inspired by the midnight sun. Looming over this remote Arctic
university town are 1,860-meter (6,000-foot) peaks with permanent snowcaps. Tromsø trails off into the islands: Half the
town lives "offshore." Its population is about 50,000, slightly
swelled by oil-rig workers. Make sure to see the spectacular
Arctic Church across the long stretch of **Tromsø bridge**
(Scandinavia's longest suspension bridge). Coated in alumi-
num, its triangular peaks make a bizarre mirror for the
midnight sun. One wall (the eastern) is made entirely of stained
glass.

Make sure to walk around old Tromsø (along the waterfront)
and to visit the **Tromsø Museum,** which concentrates on science, the Same people, and northern churches. *Strandveien via
no. 21 bus. Admission: NOK 5 adults, NOK 2 children. Open
Sept.–May, weekdays 9–3 (Wed. also 7–10), Sat. noon– 3,
Sun. 10–3.*

Hammerfest is the world's northernmost town. It is surrounded by Same settlements, and is home to the **Royal and Ancient Polar Bear Society.** Don't go if you don't like real stuffed
bears. *Town Hall basement. Admission free. Open weekdays
8–6, weekends 10–3.*

Hammerfest is an elegant, festive-looking port town despite
having been razed twice. The first time, in the late 19th century, a fire leveled the town; the second, defeated German troops
rampaged through on their retreat so as not to leave anything
to the Russians. The town's **quayside** is lined with stores and
eating places. Hammerfest claims it was the first European
city with electric street lamps.

Kirkenes is not much more than a terminus for the long, long
road from Oslo—the country's end station. It was one of the
most heavily war-damaged places in all Europe. Iron-ore mining keeps it alive today. The surrounding area is worth
exploring, though, once you've come this far; consult the tourist office *(see* above) for how to get to St. Georg's chapel in
Neiden and the Bygdetunet Bjørkland farm at Svanvik.
Kirkenes enjoys the light of the midnight sun for two full
months each summer, from late May until late July.

Dining and Lodging

For details and price category definitions, *see* Dining and Lodging in Staying in Norway.

Ålesund **Fjellstua.** This mountaintop restaurant has tremendous views
Dining over the surrounding peaks, islands, and fjords. There are several different eating facilities here, but the main restaurant
serves excellent fresh seafood, meat dishes, and homemade
desserts. *Fjellstua, tel. 071/26582. Reservations recommended. V. Expensive (lunch Moderate). Closed Christmas week–
Mar. 1.*
Skateflue Kafeteria. You have views of the ferry docks and
wheeling seagulls from this quayside lunch and sandwich restaurant. *Skaregt 1, tel. 071/24259. No reservations. No credit
cards. Inexpensive. Closed dinner.*

Lodging **Noreg.** This large hotel features good views of Ålesund and the
harbor. The decor is modern, and an orchestra plays in the hotel's sky-lit restaurant. *Kongensgate 27, tel. 071/22938. 44
rooms with bath. Facilities: salt-water pool, restaurant. AE,
DC, MC, V. Expensive.*
Havly Pension. Its exterior is austere, but once inside you'll get
unspoiled views of the mountains and fjords. Clean and ultramodern, this hotel underwent a 1986 renovation; it's centrally
located, too. *Rasmus Rønnebergsgate 4, tel. 071/24960. 45 rooms
with bath or shower. DC, MC. Inexpensive.*

Bodø **Marlene Restaurant.** Set within the SAS Royal hotel, the
Dining Marlene offers a superb seafood buffet throughout the summer. Make sure to try one of the salmon dishes. *Storgata 2, tel.
081/24100. Reservations recommended. AE, DC, MC, V. Moderate–Expensive.*
Turisthytta. This mountaintop lodge (accessible by taxi) is a
fine place to eat if you want to bask in the midnight sun. From
snacks and open-faced sandwiches to fresh fish, there is a good
range of dishes. *Turisthytta, tel. 081/217131. Reservations rec-*

ommended. *No credit cards. Moderate. Closed Sept.–mid-June.*

Lodging   **SAS Royal.** This hotel, apart from being grandly appointed, is throbbing with life. A bar, food and wine "cabinette," and dancing at the Marlene Night Club (open late) can keep you entertained virtually around the clock. *Storgata 2, tel. 081/24100. 184 rooms with bath or shower. Facilities: sauna. AE, DC, MC, V. Expensive.*

SAS Norrona. This bed-and-breakfast-style establishment is run by the SAS chain. Furnishings are comfortable, with the location just as grand as that of the SAS Royal next door. *Storgata 4, tel. 081/24100. 150 rooms, most with bath or shower. AE, DC. Moderate.*

Hammerfest   **Finnmarksbø Gjesthaus.** Sited on the pleasant Rådhusplassen
Dining and Lodging   (Town Hall Square), this guest house provides handsome, harbor-view rooms for relatively tolerable prices in a town where hotels are notoriously expensive. The restaurant and cafeteria serve a healthy range of local fare and the service is good. *Strandgate 2–4, tel. 084/11622. 40 rooms, some with bath or shower. No credit cards. Expensive.*

Kirkenes   **Kirkenes Rica Hotel.** This hotel has made every effort to pro-
Dining and Lodging   vide diversion for guests in this spectacularly remote outpost. The facilities are modern and spacious. To the obvious outdoor activities (hiking and more hiking), the hotel has added tennis and badminton. Its stained-glass windows and tapestries provide stark contrast to the rocky hinterlands around it. *Pasvikveien 63, tel. 085/91491. 64 rooms with bath or shower. Facilities: bar, restaurant, sauna. AE, DC, MC, V. Expensive.*

Narvik   **Grand Royal Hotel.** This is a classy, handsome hotel, enhanced
Dining and Lodging   by a staff that is eager to please. The location, right by the train station, is a plus, and there are many chances to try the skiing and fishing nearby. The Grand Royal was renovated in 1987 and rooms are well equipped. *Kongensgate 64, tel. 082/41500. 112 rooms with bath. Facilities: gym, sauna, 2 restaurants. AE, DC, MC, V. Expensive.*

Nordkalotten Ungdomsherberge. The basic but modern facilities of this popular youth hostel consist of dormitory-style rooms, with a few singles. There is also a decent, inexpensive restaurant. *Havnegaten 3, tel. 082/42598. 60 rooms, none with bath. No credit cards. Inexpensive.*

Tromsø   **SAS Royal.** Each room in this beautifully set hotel gives splen-
Dining and Lodging   did views over Tromsø's shoreline, although the location is in the heart of town. The Caravelle restaurant serves Scandinavian and Continental cuisine, and the Charly Bar is a focal point of Tromsø nightlife. *Sjøgate 10, tel. 083/56000. 192 rooms with bath. Facilities: 3 bars, restaurant. AE, DC, MC, V. Expensive.*

Saga. Sited on a pretty town square, the Saga combines its central location with the staff's expertise in advising you on the outdoor pursuits just outside of town. The Satagun restaurant has affordable, hearty meals, and the rooms—although somewhat basic—are quiet and comfortable. *Richard Withs Plass 2, tel. 083/81180. 52 rooms with bath. Facilities: restaurant, cafeteria, fishing. AE, DC, MC, V. Moderate.*

Trondheim   **Bryggen.** This popular restaurant, set near the Gamle Bybrø
Dining   (Old Town Bridge), serves a feast of Norwegian gourmet spe-

cialties with a Gallic flourish. With a choice of creperie, wine and cheese room, and bistro serving French cuisine, you can't go wrong. *Gamle Bybrø, tel. 07/534055. Reservations recommended. No credit cards. Expensive (lunch Moderate).*

Coq d'Or. Part of the elegant Prinsen Hotel complex, this sophisticated restaurant serves fine Continental cuisine. If you want something a bit less exclusive, there is also a wine lodge, beer garden, bistro cafeteria, and theater grill. *Kongensgate 30, tel. 07/530650. Reservations recommended. AE, DC, MC, V. Expensive (lunch Moderate).*

Braseriet Pizzeria. This pizzeria, featuring a good selection of toppings, is popular with the young crowd locally. More substantial fare is available from the grill menu. *Nordregate 11, tel. 07/524730. No reservations. No credit cards. Moderate.*

Lodging **Ambassadeur.** Take in the panoramic view from the roof terrace of this first-rate modern hotel, located about 93 meters (100 yards) from the market square. The deep blue waters of the Trondheimsfjord reflect the dramatic and irregular coastline. Most rooms in the Ambassadeur have fireplaces and some have balconies. *Elvegate 18, tel. 07/527050. 34 rooms with bath. Facilities: bar, restaurant. AE, DC, MC, V. Expensive.*

Royal Garden Hotel. This five-year-old hotel has excellent facilities for sports and fitness, as well as many features to help handicapped guests. It's built in three wings, which are connected by glassed walkways. *Kjøpmannsgate 73, tel. 07/521100. 297 rooms with bath. Facilities: bar, 3 restaurants, sauna, solarium, indoor pool, gymnasium. AE, DC, MC, V. Expensive.*

Norrøna Misjonshospits. This mission-owned hotel provides good, clean value for your money. The restaurant is ideal if you're on a budget. *Thomas Angellsgate 20, tel. 07/532020. 14 rooms, some with bath. Facilities: restaurant. No credit cards. Moderate.*

23 Poland

Introduction

Poland is a land rich in natural beauty and contrasts. Its landscape varies from rolling plains with slow-moving rivers, broad fields, and scattered villages to lakes, forests, and marshes in the north and jagged mountains in the south. This makes for a wide variety of outdoor activities, from hunting to hiking, sailing, and skiing.

Every one of the major cities, with the exception of Cracow, had to be rebuilt after the destruction of World War II. Particularly fine restoration work has been done on Warsaw's Old Town and in Gdańsk on the Baltic coast.

Poland does not fit into preconceptions of a Communist country. After more than 40 years of Communist rule, a majority of the people remain devoutly Catholic. In the countryside especially, the people are religious and conservative. Both rural and urban life remain centered on the home and family, where old traditions are diligently upheld. Four-fifths of the country's farmland is privately owned, while, in the towns, the number of private boutiques and restaurants is increasing.

Poland's geographical position between Germany and Russia has determined its history of almost continual war and struggle for independence since the late 18th century. After "liberation" by the Red Army in 1945, a Communist government was imposed. Although the country recovered economically and experienced rapid industrialization, 40 years of such government have today left Poland in prolonged economic crisis. The hopes and aspirations of the postwar generations have remained unfulfilled.

Social discontent erupted in 1980 with strikes and the formation of Solidarity, the first free trade union in the Communist bloc. After a year, martial law was imposed and Solidarity was banned. Though martial law has since been lifted, and talks between Solidarity and the government have become regular events, life for the average Pole remains hard, and no one has simple answers to the country's complicated political and economic problems. In spite of all this, the Polish people continue to be resilient, resourceful, and not without hope.

Poles openly welcome visitors; their uninhibited sense of hospitality makes them eager to please their guests. It is easy to make friends here and to exchange views with strangers on trains and buses. Poles have a passionate interest in all things Western, from current affairs to the arts, clothes, and music.

Before You Go

When to Go The official tourist season runs from May through September. The best times for sightseeing are in late spring and early fall. Major cultural events usually take place in the cities during the fall. The early spring is often wet and windy.

The following are the average daily maximum and minimum temperatures for Warsaw.

Poland

Bornholm
(Denmark)

Baltic Sea

SOVIET
UNION

Kołobrzeg

Słupsk
Lebork
Gdynia
Gdańsk

Swinoujscie

Koszalin

Baligrod

Tczew
Starogard
Elbląg
Malbork

Szczenek

*Masurian
Lakes*

Suwałki

Szczecin

Stargard

Chojnice

Kwidzyń
Ostróda
Olsztyn
Nidzica

Ełk

Piła

Chełmno
Grudziądz

Bydgoszcz
Toruń

Mława

Łomza
Ostrolecka
Biaystok

Inowrocław

Ciéchanow

Poznań
Gniezno

Włocławek
Plonsk

Ostrów-
Mazowiecka

Gorzów
Wielkopolski

Płock

Koscian
Konin
Kutno

Zielona
Góra

Ozorków
Łowicz
★ Warsaw

Siedlce

Głogów

Zgierz
Skierniewice
Otwock

Miedrzec
Biała
Podlaska

Lubin
Ostrów
Łódź

Bolesławiec

Legnica

Wieluń

Tomaszów
Mazowiecki
Deblin

Jelenia
Góra
Wrocław

Radomsko

Radom

Lublin

Świdnica
Walbrzych
Częstochowa

Kielce
Ostowiec

Chełm

Nysa
Prudnik
Tarnowski
Gory
Zawiercie

Zamość

Zabrze
Sosnowiec

Katowice
Cracow

Rzeszów
Jarosław

Bielsko Biała

Krosno
Przemyśl

Nowy Sącz

EAST GERMANY

Odra

Nessa

Vistula

Bug

Vistula

E7

E22

CZECHOSLOVAKIA

N

0   100 miles
0   150 km

Jan.	32F	0C	May	67F	20C	Sept.	66F	19C
	22	−6		48	9		49	10
Feb.	32F	0C	June	73F	23C	Oct.	55F	13C
	21	−6		54	12		41	5
Mar.	42F	6C	July	75F	24C	Nov.	42F	6C
	28	−2		58	16		33	1
Apr.	53F	12C	Aug.	73F	23C	Dec.	35F	2C
	37	3		56	14		28	−3

Currency The monetary unit in Poland is the złoty (Zł), which is divided into 100 groszy (rarely seen). There are notes of 10, 20, 50, 100, 200, 500, 1,000, 2,000, 5,000, and 10,000 złoty and coins of 1, 2, 5, 10, and 20 złoty. At press time (spring 1989), the exchange rate for the złoty was 500 to the U.S. dollar and 920 to the pound sterling. There is a black market rate that offers at least four times the official rate, but this is illegal. You will find that Polish taxi drivers, waitresses, and porters are only too happy to be paid in dollars or any other Western currency, so have some currency in small denominations ($1 or $5 bills are preferred). Money exchanged into złoty can be reconverted upon presentation of official exchange receipts when leaving the country.

Credit Cards American Express, Diners Club, MasterCard, and Visa are accepted in all Orbis hotels, in the better restaurants and nightclubs, and for other Orbis services. In small cafés and shops, credit cards may not be accepted.

What It Will Cost All visitors must exchange foreign currency to the value of $15 a day. Exceptions are persons under 21 years of age, students, and persons whose Polish descent has been recognized by the appropriate Polish consular office: They must exchange $7 daily (including arrival day but excluding day of departure). Exempt altogether from obligatory currency exchange are children under 16, visitors in transit to neighboring countries, and visitors who have prepaid their stay through vouchers or package bookings. Vouchers may be used toward hotel costs and must be paid at the official exchange rate.

Poland is one of the least expensive countries of Eastern Europe. Although inflation is high—about 60%—the złoty is devalued against Western currencies about three times a year. This offsets rising costs and keeps expenses down. Don't buy more złoty than you need or you will have to go to the trouble of changing them back at the end of your trip. If you have to change money, go to a bank—the exchange rate is much better than in hotels. Prices are highest in the big cities, especially in Warsaw. The more you stray off the tourist track, the cheaper your vacation becomes. The cost difference can sometimes be enormous. What you save in money, however, you may lose in quality of service.

Sample Prices A cup of coffee, 200–400 Zł; a bottle of beer, 300–500 Zł; a soft drink, 400–800 Zł; a ham sandwich, 700 Zł; one-mile taxi ride, 1,200 Zł.

Museums Admission to museums and other attractions changes rapidly, in line with inflation. But entrance fees are low, and you can expect to pay about $1 or less.

Visas Visas are required and cost $20. Apply at any Orbis office (the official Polish tourist agency), an affiliated travel agent, or from the Polish Consulate General in any country. Each visitor must complete three visa application forms and provide two photographs. Allow about two weeks for processing. Visas are issued for a specific length of time but can be extended in Poland, if necessary, either through the local county police headquarters or through Orbis.

You can contact the **Polish Consulate General** at the following addresses: **In the United States:** 233 Madison Ave., New York, NY 10016 (tel. 212/391–0844); 1530 North Lake Shore Dr., Chicago, IL 60610 (tel. 312/337–8166); 2224 Wyoming Ave., Washington DC 20008 (tel. 202/234–2501).
In Canada: 1500 Pine Ave., Montreal, Quebec H3G (tel. 514/937–9481); 2603 Lakeshore Blvd. W., Toronto, Ont. M8V 1G5 (tel. 416/252–5471).
In the United Kingdom: 73 New Cavendish St., London W1 (tel. 01/636–4533).

Customs on Arrival Persons over 17 may bring in duty-free: personal belongings, up to 250 cigarettes or 50 cigars, musical instruments, typewriter, radio, two cameras with 24 rolls of film, one liter each of wine and spirits, and goods to the value of 25,000 Zł. Any amount of foreign currency may be brought in but must be declared on arrival.

Language German is spoken by older people, and English by younger. In the big cities, you will find people who speak English, especially in hotels, but you may have difficulties in the provinces and countryside.

Getting Around

By Car
Road Conditions Despite the extensive road network, driving conditions, even on main roads, have deteriorated in the past few years. Minor roads tend to be narrow and cluttered with horse-drawn carts and farm animals. Drivers in a hurry should stick to roads marked E or T.

Rules of the Road Driving is on the right, as in the United States. The speed limit on highways is 110 kph (68 mph) and on roads in built-up areas, 60 kph (37 mph). A built-up area is marked by a white rectangular sign with the name of the town on it.

Gasoline Foreigners can obtain gas only by presenting prepurchased coupons at gas stations. Coupons can be bought prior to departure at Orbis travel agencies, at the Polish frontier, or at Orbis offices in Poland. The price of gas is about $5.80 for 10 liters of high octane. Filling stations are located every 30 kilometers (20 miles) or so and are usually open 6 AM–10 PM; there are some 24-hour stations.

Breakdowns Poland's **Motoring Association** (BTM PZMot) offers breakdown, repair, and towing services to members of various international insurance organizations. For names of affiliated organizations, check with Orbis before you leave home. Carry a spare parts kit. For emergency road help, call 981 or 954.

Car Rentals You can rent cars from Avis or Hertz at international airports or through Orbis offices. Rates vary according to season, car model, and mileage. Fly/drive vacations are also available through Orbis.

By Train Poland's PKP railway network is extensive and cheap. Most trains have first- and second-class accommodations, but most foreign visitors prefer to travel first class. Arrive at the station at least one hour before departure time. The fastest trains are intercity and express trains, which require reservations. Some Orbis offices furnish information, reservations, and tickets. Overnight trains have first- and second-class sleeping cars and second-class couchettes. All long-distance trains carry buffets, but the quality of the food is variable and you may want to bring your own.

Fares For convenience buy a **Polrailpass,** which offers unlimited first-class travel for one ($72), two ($84), three ($96), or four ($108) weeks, but it is much cheaper to simply buy your tickets with złotys in Poland.

By Plane **LOT,** Poland's national airline, operates daily flights linking 11 main cities. Fares begin at about $100 round-trip. Tickets and information are available from LOT or Orbis offices. All flights booked through Orbis in the United Kingdom carry a discount. In Poland, flights must be paid for in foreign currency. Be sure to book well in advance, especially for the summer season.

By Bus Express bus services link all main cities as well as smaller towns and villages off the rail network. Buses are inexpensive but crowded. PKS bus stations are usually located near railway stations. Tickets and information are best obtained from Orbis. A two-week unlimited travel ticket costs less than $4. from Warsaw's central bus terminal on aleje Jerozolimskie.

Staying in Poland

Telephones Public phone booths (for local as well as long-distance calls)
Local Calls take 5, 10, and 20 Zł coins. Place a 5 Zł coin in the groove on the side or top of the phone, lift the receiver, and dial the number. Push the coin into the machine when the call is answered.

International Calls Post offices and first-class hotels have assigned booths, at which you pay after the completion of your call. To place an international call, dial 901; for domestic long-distance calls, dial 900. There's a heavy surcharge on calls made from hotel rooms.

Information For general information (including international codes), tel. 913.

Mail Airmail letters to the United States cost 200 Zł, postcards, 100
Postal Rates Zł. Letters to the United Kingdom or Europe cost 150 Zł, postcards, 80 Zł. Post offices are open 8 AM–8 PM (except weekends). At least one post office is open 24 hours in every major city. In Warsaw, it is located on ulica Swietokrzyska 31.

Opening and **Banks.** Banks are open weekdays 8 AM–1 PM.
Closing Times **Museums.** Museums are open Tuesday–Sunday 9–5.
Shops. Food shops are open 7 AM–7PM; other stores are open 11–7, closed Sunday.

National Holidays January 1 (New Year's Day); April 15, 16 (Easter); May 1 (Labor Day); June 2 (Corpus Christi); July 22 (National Day); November 1 (Remembrance); December 25, 26.

Dining Polish food and drink are basically Slavic with Baltic overtones. There is a heavy emphasis on soups and meat (especially pork) as well as freshwater fish. Much use is made of cream, and pastries are rich and often delectable.

The most popular soup is *barszcz* (known to many Americans as borscht), a clear beet soup often served with such Polish favorites as sausage, cabbage, potatoes, sour cream, coarse rye bread, and beer. Other dishes: *pierogi* (a kind of ravioli), which may be stuffed with savory or sweet fillings: *gołąbki*, cabbage leaves stuffed with minced meat; *bigos*, sauerkraut with meat and mushrooms; *flaki*, a select dish of tripe, served boiled or fried. Polish beer is good; vodka is a specialty and is often downed before, with, and after meals.

There is a wide selection of eating places, but as a result of continuing food shortages, the quality of the cuisine may vary from one day to the next. The more expensive hotels and restaurants offer the most consistently high-quality dining.

Roadside inns *(Zajazdy)*, which are less expensive than regular restaurants, serve more traditional food. More economical yet, and ideal for snacks, are the milk bars *(Bary Mleczne)* selling dairy and vegetable dishes. As elsewhere in central Europe, cafés are a way of life in Poland and are often stocked with delicious pastries and ice creams.

Mealtimes At home, Poles eat late lunches and late suppers; the latter is their main meal. Many restaurants, however, close around 9 PM. Most hotel restaurants serve the evening meal until 10:30.

Precautions Tap water is unsafe, so ask for mineral water. Beware of meat dishes served in cheap snack bars. Avoid the food on trains.

Dress In Warsaw and Cracow, formal dress is customary at Very Expensive and Expensive restaurants. Casual dress is appropriate elsewhere.

Ratings Prices are for one person and include three courses and service but no drinks. Best bets are indicated by a star ★. At press time, there were 500 złoty to the dollar.

Category	Warsaw	Other Areas
Very Expensive	over 13,000 Zł	over 10,000 Zł
Expensive	8,000–13,000 Zł	7,000–10,000 Zł
Moderate	4,000–8,000 Zł	3,000–7,000 Zł
Inexpensive	under 4,000 Zł	under 3,000 Zł

Credit Cards The following credit card abbreviations are used: AE, American Express; DC, Diners Club; MC, MasterCard; V, Visa.

Lodging
Hotels The government rates hotel accommodations on the basis of one to five stars. Orbis hotels are the only ones that can guarantee a reasonable standard of cleanliness and service, and you are strongly advised to stick to them in order to avoid unpleasant surprises. Almost all Orbis hotels are of four- or five-star quality. Orbis hotels include a number of foreign-built luxury hotels such as Intercontinental and Holiday Inn. Prices range from Moderate to Very Expensive. *Payment must be in foreign currency,* but you can pay in złoty if you have a receipt proving that they were exchanged officially.

Municipal Hotels and Dom Turysty hotels are run by local authorities or the Polish Tourist Association. They are frequently rather old and limited in bath and shower facilities. Prices are inexpensive.

Hostels The Polish Youth Hostels Association operates hostels at a very inexpensive 100–300 Zł per night; in addition, hostels are open to people of all ages. Information is available from your local branch of the International Youth Hostel Association.

Roadside Inns A number of roadside inns *(Zajazdy)*, often very attractive, offer inexpensive food and a few guest rooms at moderate rates.

Private Rooms can be arranged either in advance through Orbis or on
Accommodations the spot at the local tourist information office. Villas, lodges, rooms, or houses are more personal than hotels, and the prices are often negotiable. Rates vary from about $6 to over $150.

Ratings The following chart is based on a rate for two people in a double room, with bath or shower and breakfast. These prices are in U.S. dollars. Best bets are indicated by a star ★.

Category	Warsaw	Other Areas
Very Expensive	over $150	–
Expensive	$80–$150	$70–$80
Moderate	$50–$80	$40–$70
Inexpensive	under $45	under $45

Credit Cards The following credit card abbreviations are used: AE, American Express; DC, Diners Club; MC, MasterCard; V, Visa.

Tipping Waiters get a standard 10% of the bill. Hotel porters and doormen should get about 100–200 Zł. In Warsaw and other big towns frequented by foreign tourists, waiters also often expect a tip to help find you a table. If you choose to tip in foreign currency (readily accepted), remember that on the black market $1 is worth an average day's wage.

Warsaw

Arriving and Departing

By Plane All international flights arrive at Warsaw's Okecie Airport just southwest of the city. Another airport nearby, also called Okecie, serves all domestic flights. For flight information, contact the airlines, or call the airport at tel. 22/46–96–70 or 22/46–11–43.

Between the LOT operates a regular bus service into Warsaw. Orbis cars or
Airport and minivans also transport visitors to their hotels. Otherwise, the
Downtown 175 bus leaves every 10 minutes from the international terminal. The trip takes about 15 minutes and the fare is 15 Zł; after 11 PM, 30Zł. Getting a taxi may be difficult.

By Train Trains to and from Western Europe arrive at Dworzec Centralny on aleje Jerozolimskie in the center of town. For tickets and information, contact Orbis.

By Car There are seven main access routes to Warsaw, all leading to the city center. Drivers heading to or from the West will use the E8 or E12 highways.

Getting Around

By Tram and Bus These are often crowded, but they are the cheapest ways of getting around. Trams and buses cost 15 Zł; express buses cost

30 Zł. The bus fare goes up to 90 Zł between 11 PM and 5:30 AM. Tickets must be bought in advance from **Ruch** newsstands. You must cancel your own ticket in a machine on the tram or bus when you get on; watch others do it.

By Taxi Consider yourself lucky if you catch a taxi in less than 15 minutes. Taxis are a relatively cheap ride—about 500 Zł for a 1.6 kilometer (one-mile) ride—and you can either hail them or line up at a stand. The best places to find one are in front of the Victoria Hotel or the Forum Hotel.

By Buggy Horse-drawn carriages can be rented at a negotiated price from the Old Town Market Square.

Important Addresses and Numbers

Tourist Information The **Center for Tourist Information** is open 24 hours; it is located at ulica Krucza 16, tel. 22/27–00–00. There are two **Orbis** offices in Warsaw: ulica Brackna 16, tel. 22/26–02–71; and ulica Marszałkowska 142, tel. 22/27–80–31 or 22/27–36–73.

Embassies U.S.: aleje Ujazdowskie 29–31, tel. 22/28–30–40; **Canadian:** ulica Matejki 1/5, tel. 22/29–80–51; **U.K.:** aleje. Róż 1, tel. 22/25–80–31.

Emergencies Police: tel. 997; **Ambulance:** tel. 998; **Doctor:** tel. 998 or call your embassy.

Travel Agencies Polish Motoring Association (PZMot): aleje Jerozolimskie 63, tel. 22/29–45–30.

Guided Tours

Bus tours of the city depart in the morning and afternoon from the major hotels. **Orbis** also has half-day excursions into the surrounding countryside. These usually include a meal and some form of traditional entertainment. Check for details with your hotel, the Orbis office, or tourist information office.

Exploring Warsaw

At the end of World War II, Warsaw lay in ruin, a victim of systematic Nazi destruction. Only one-third of its prewar population survived the horrors of German occupation. The experience has left its mark on the city and is visible everywhere in the memorial plaques describing mass executions of civilians and in the bullet holes on the facades of buildings.

Against all the odds, Warsaw's survivors have rebuilt their historic city. The old districts have been painstakingly reconstructed according to old prints and paintings, including those of Belotto and Canaletto from the 18th century. The result, a city of warm pastel colors, is remarkable.

Surrounding the old districts, however, is the modern Warsaw, built since the war in functionalist Socialist-Realist style. Whether you like it or not is your business, but it is worth noting as testimony to one approach to urban life. The sights of Warsaw are all relatively close to each other, making most attractions accessible by foot.

Numbers in the margin correspond with points of interest on the Warsaw map.

Warsaw

PRAGA

Skaryszewski Park

Francuska

Lipska

Waleczných

Obrankow

Wal

Al. Zieleniecka

Jana Zamoyskiego

Markowska

Brzeska

Zadkowska

Białostocka

Kijowska

Al. J. Poniatowskiego

Most J. Poniatowskiego

Wybrzeże Szczecińskie

Targowa

Jagiellonska

S. Okrzei

Szczecińskie

Wybrzeże Szczecińskie

Kościuszkowskie

Solec

Targowa

Al. Gen. Świerczewskiego

Sokola

Most Śląsko-Dąbrowski

Wybrzeże Kościuszkowskie

Wybrzeże

Most Śląsko-Dąbrowski

Jerozolimskie

Ratuszowa

Al. Stalingradzka

Wybrzeże Helskie

Vistula

Ul. Tamka

Solec

Zoological Gardens

Vistula

Wybrzeże Gdańskie

Dobra

Dobra

Topiel

19

Nowy Świat

Browarna

Rynek

Marensztat

Bednarska

Karowa

Karowa

8

9

Ul. Dziekania

Świętojańska

Ul. Piwna

13

Bagat

3

Ul.

2

Pl.

1

Krakowskie Przedmieście

Mazowiecka

Rybaki

4

Długa

Zamkowa

Pl. Miodowa

Ul. Freta

18

Rynek Nowomiejski

6

5

Rynek Starego Miasta

Długa

12

Pl. Teatralny

20

Wierzbowe

17

Saxon Gardens

Marszałkowska

Konwiktorska

Bonifraterska

Franciszkańska

Świętojerska

Długa

Senatorska

Królewska

Świętokrzyska

Miedzyparkowa

Wołowa

Elektoralna

Marcelego Nowotki

MURANÓW

Nowolipki

Karmelicka

Juliana Marchlewskiego

Pereca

Mariana Buczka

Stawki

Stanisława Dubois

Ul. Zamenhofa

16

Al. Gen. K. Świerczewskiego

Nowolipki

Al. Gen. Anielewicza

Grzybowska

Grzybowska

Zelazna

Major Attractions
Barbican, **5**
Belvedere Palace, **7**
Cathedral of
St. John, **3**
Church of the Holy
Cross, **8**
Lazienki Palace, **10**
Marie Curie-
Sklodowska
Museum, **6**
Old Market Square
(Rynek), **4**

Plac Zamkowy, **1**
Royal Castle, **2**
Warsaw University, **9**
Wilanów, **11**

Other Attractions
Church of the Blessed
Sacrament Sisters, **18**
Frederick Chopin
Society, **19**
Grand Theater of
Opera and Ballet, **20**

Monument to the
Heroes of the
Ghetto, **16**
Monument to the
Heroes of Warsaw, **12**

Museum of
Literature, **13**
National Museum, **15**
Palace of Culture and
Science, **14**
Tomb of the Unknown
Soldier, **17**

The Old Town A walking tour of the old historic district takes about two
1 hours. Begin in the heart of the city at **Plac Zamkowy,** where
you will see a slender column supporting the statue of
Zygmund III Vasa, the king who made Warsaw his capital in
1586. It is the city's oldest monument and, symbolically, the
first to be rebuilt after the wartime devastation. Dominating
2 the square is the **Royal Castle.** Restoring the interior was a her-
culean task, requiring workers to relearn traditional skills,
match ancient woods and fabrics, even reopen abandoned quar-
ries to find just the right kind of stone. A visit is worthwhile,
despite the crowds. *Open Tues., Thurs. 10–2:45; Wed., Fri.,
Sat. noon–5:30; Sun. 10–6.*

Enter the narrow streets of the **Old Town,** with its colorful
medieval houses, cobblestone alleys, uneven roofs, and
wrought-iron grillwork. On your right as you proceed along
3 Świętojanska Street is the **Cathedral of St. John,** the oldest
church in Warsaw, dating back to the 14th century. Several Polish kings were crowned here. Soon you will reach the **Old Mar-
4** **ket Square,** the charming and intimate center of the old town.
The old Town Hall, which once stood in the middle, was pulled
down in the 19th century. It was not replaced, and today the
square is full of open-air cafés, tubs of flowering plants, and the
inevitable artists displaying their talents for the tourists. At
night, the brightly lighted Rynek (marketplace) is the place to
go if you want good food and atmosphere.

Continue along Nowomiejska Street until you get to the impos-
5 ing red brick **Barbican,** a fine example of a 16th-century defensive fortification. From here, you can see the partially restored
town wall that was built to enclose the Old Town; enjoy a splendid view of the Vistula River, with the district of Praga on its
east bank.

Follow the street called ulica Freta to Warsaw's **New Town,**
which was founded at the turn of the 15th century. Rebuilt after the war in 18th-century style, this district has a more
elegant and spacious feeling about it. Of interest here is the
6 **Marie Curie-Skłodowska Museum,** where the Polish discoverer
of radium and polonium was born. *Ul. Freta 16. Open Tues.–
Sun. 10–5.*

Time Out Before retracing your steps, stop for refreshments at the **Café
Bombonierka,** good for ice cream, pastries, and people-watch-
ing both inside the café and out on the square. *Rynek Starego
Miasta 13.*

The Royal Way All towns with kings had their Royal Routes; the one in Warsaw
stretched south from Castle Square down Krakowskie Prz-
edmieście, curving through Nowy Świat and on along aleje
7 Ujazdowskie to the **Belvedere Palace** and Łazienki Park. Some
of Warsaw's finest churches and palaces are found along this
route, as well as the names of famous Poles. The **Church of the
8** **Holy Cross** contains a pillar in which the heart of the great Polish composer Frédéric Chopin is entombed. Farther down, on
9 your left, is **Warsaw University,** founded in 1818. As you pass
the statue of Nicolaus Copernicus, Poland's most famous as-
tronomer, you enter the busy Nowy Świat thoroughfare.
Crossing aleje Jerozolimskie, on your left is the Polish Communist Party headquarters, a large solid gray building typical of
the Socialist-Realist architectural style.

Aleje Ujazdowskie is considered by many locals to be Warsaw's finest street. It is lined with some magnificent buildings and has something of a French flavor to it. A hundred years ago, this fashionable *corso* (avenue) was thronged with fancy carriages and riders eager to see and be seen. It is now a favorite with Sunday strollers. Down at its southern end, before the name inexplicably changes to Belwederska, the French-style landscaped **Łazienki Park,** with pavilions and a royal palace, stands in refreshing contrast to the bustling streets. The **10** **Łazienki Palace,** a gem of Polish neo-Classicism, was the private residence of Stanisław August Poniatowski, last king of Poland. It stands on a lake stocked with huge carp. At the impressionistic Chopin monument nearby, you can stop for a well-deserved rest and, on summer Sundays, listen to an open-air concert.

11 The Royal Route extends along aleje Belwederskie to **Wilanów,** 10 kilometers (6 miles) from the town center. This charming Baroque palace was the summer residence of King Jan III Sobieski, who, in 1683, stopped the Ottoman advance on Europe at the Battle of Vienna. The palace interior is open and houses antique furniture and a fine poster museum. *Al. Belwederskie. Open Mon., Wed., Fri.–Sun. 10–2:30.*

Off the Beaten Track

The Jewish contribution to Polish culture, tradition, and achievement cannot be overstated. Some three million Polish Jews were put to death by the Nazis during World War II. A simple monument to the **Heroes of the Warsaw Ghetto,** a slab of dark granite with a bronze bas relief, stands on ulica Zamhofa in the Muranów district, the historic heart of the old prewar Warsaw ghetto. The armed revolt that broke out in April 1943 was put down with unbelievable ferocity, and the Muranów district was flattened. Now there are only bleak gray apartment blocks here.

With ironic humor, Warsaw locals tell you that the best vantage point from which to admire their city is atop the 37-story **Palace of Culture and Science.** Why? Because it is the only point from which you can't see the Palace of Culture and Science. This wedding cake-style skyscraper was a personal gift from Stalin. Although it is disliked by Poles as a symbol of Soviet domination, it does afford a panoramic view and is the best example of 1950s "Socialist Gothic" architecture. *Plac Defilad. Open daily 9–5.*

Shopping

Nowy Świat, Krakowskie Przedmieście, and ulica Rutkowskiego are lined with boutiques selling good-quality leather goods, clothing, and trinkets. Try **Cepelia** stores (Marszałkowska 99 and Nowy Świat 35) for a wide range of handicrafts, such as glass, enamelware, amber, and handwoven woolen rugs. **Orno** shops (Marszałkowska 83 and Nowy Świat 52) offer handmade jewelry and silverware. **Desa** stores (Marszałkowska 34) specialize in ornaments and objets d'art. Foreign currency shops called **Pewex** and **Baltona** can be found all over the city (try the Victoria hotel). These sell imported items, especially spirits, clothing, and chocolates, at competitive prices. You can also buy film and cigarettes. State-owned department stores, **Junior** and **Dom Centralny,** which sell standardized goods of questionable quality, are on ulica Marszałkowska opposite the Palace of Culture and Science.

For the more adventurous, there is a flea market, **Bazar Różyckiego,** on ulica Targowa 55, where you can find almost anything. Another market is open at the Skra Warszawa sports stadium on Sunday.

Dining

Current difficulties with food supplies mean that only hotels and the very best restaurants can guarantee a full menu and quality meals. If you want to avoid eating at hotels, your best bet is the Old Town and its atmospheric Market Square. The area is brightly lighted at night and makes for a pleasant walk before or after dinner. Reservations for dinner can be made by telephone (by your hotel receptionist if you don't speak Polish), but if you decide to go to a restaurant on the spur of the moment, a table (for Westerners) will always be found. For details and price category definitions, *see* Dining in Staying in Poland.

Expensive **Bazyliszek.** Dimly lit and elegant, the Bazyliszek excels in such game as boar, venison, and duck. A good café and snack bar are located downstairs. *Rynek Starego Miasta 7/9. No reservations. AE, DC, MC, V.*

Canaletto. Located in the Victoria Intercontinental hotel, this is probably the best restaurant in town and serves Polish specialties with a good selection of European wines. The two paintings of old Warsaw on the walls are by Canaletto himself. *Plac Zwycięstwa, tel. 22/27–92–91. Reservations advised. AE, DC, MC, V.*

Forum. Another good hotel restaurant, the Forum's menu offers traditional Polish mixed with conventional central European (meat dishes). Like Canaletto, it is frequented by Western businesspeople and tourists. *Ul. Nowogrodzka 24, tel. 22/ 21–01–19. Reservations advised. AE, DC, MC, V.*

Moderate **Kamienne Schodki.** This intimate, candlelit restaurant is located in one of the Market Square's medieval houses. Try the duck and the pastries. *Rynek Starego Miasta 26. No reservations. No credit cards.*

Pod Sansonem. This small restaurant, decorated in wood, has a smoke-filled Warsaw atmosphere and friendly waitresses. The fish and *pierogi* (ravioli) are good, when available. *Ul. Freta 4. No reservations. No credit cards.*

Staropolska. Fish dishes and old-fashioned Polish cuisine are the specialties. Portions are on the small side. *Krakowskie Przedmieście 8. No reservations. No credit cards. Open until 11 PM.*

Lodging

Orbis hotels are recommended for convenience and high standards. Rooms are comfortable though standardized, with functional, nondescript carpeting and furniture. Some are beginning to show signs of wear. Private accommodations are cheap and hospitable and are available through Orbis or through the Center for Tourist Information. There is no off-season for tourism. For details and price category definitions, *see* Lodging in Staying in Poland.

Very Expensive **Warsaw Marriott.** Warsaw's only five-star hotel is brand new— completed in late 1989—and at 40 storeys tall (20 make up the hotel, the rest are set aside for office and retail shopping space) is also the city's tallest building. Luxuries include 11 restaurants, 24-hour room service, and color TV in every room. *Al. Jerozolimskie 65, tel. 22-28-34-44. 525 rooms with bath. Facilities: restaurants and bars, casino, healthclub, swimming pool, sauna, shopping arcade. AE, DC, MC, V.*

Victoria Intercontinental. Frequented by Western businesspeople, this is a large 1970s hotel in an ideal location in the center of town. It has a variety of facilities, including a fine restaurant and nightclub. Try to get a room facing Victory Square. *Ul. Królewska 11, tel. 22/27-92-91. 370 rooms, most with bath or shower. Facilities: restaurant, nightclub, sauna, indoor pool. AE, DC, MC, V.*

Expensive **Hotel Europejski.** Warsaw's finest old hotel is located in the heart of the city. It was built in the 19th century in neo-Renaissance style, and its decor is elegant and refined. Rooms are spacious and attractive; some have hosted kings, presidents, and diplomats. The hotel takes pride in its restaurant. *Ul. Krakowskie Przedmieście 13, tel. 22/25-50-51. 279 rooms, most with bath or shower. Facilities: restaurant. AE, DC, MC, V.*

Hotel Forum. The Swedes built this Intercontinental chain hotel in the '70s. Frequented by businesspeople and the Arab community, it has a good restaurant. A room higher up will give you a view of the city. *Ul. Nowogródzka 24, tel. 22/21-01-19. 750 rooms, some with bath or shower. Facilities: restaurant, nightclub, hairdresser. AE, DC, MC, V.*

Moderate **Hotel Solec.** This comfortable, modest, '70s hotel is down by the river in a residential area of the central town. Food and service are good, but the hotel tends to be inundated with tour groups. *Ul. Zagórna 1, tel. 22/25-92-41. 150 rooms with bath. AE, DC, MC, V.*

Novotel. This small member of the French Novotel chain is ideal for visitors with a car and is well situated near Warsaw's airport. *Ul. 1 Sierpnia 1, tel. 22/46-40-51. Facilities: restaurant, café, outdoor pool. AE, DC, MC, V.*

Orbis Grand. Conveniently located in the center of the city, this large hotel was built in the 1950s and is a prime example of the Socialist-Realist architecture of the period. It houses a rooftop restaurant-café and offers live jazz, dancing, or cabaret in the evening. *Ul. Krucza 28, tel. 22/29-40-51. 415 rooms, some with shower. Facilities: restaurant, nightclub, indoor pool, hairdresser, Pewex shop. AE, DC, MC, V.*

Zajazd Karczma Napoleonska. This small, privately owned inn has an excellent restaurant and deluxe facilities. Napoleon reputedly stayed here when his Grand Army passed through Warsaw on its way to Russia. Book well in advance. It is situated about 12.8 kilometers (8 miles) outside of town. *Ul. Płowiecka 83. No telephone. Facilities: restaurant. AE, DC, MC, V.*

Inexpensive **Hotel Vera.** All the modern conveniences are available at this medium-size functionalist-style hotel, but it lacks character. Built in 1980, it is situated in the western part of town. *Ul. Wery Kostrzewy 16, tel. 22/22-74-21. AE, DC, MC, V.*

The Arts

For information, buy the newspaper *Życie Warszawy* or the weekly *Stolica* at Ruch newsstands. Tickets can be ordered by your Orbis hotel receptionist, through the tourist information center (ul. Kurcza 16, tel. 22/27–00–00), or at the ticket office on aleje Marszałkowska 104.

Theaters There are 17 theaters in Warsaw, attesting to the popularity of this art form, but none offers English performances. **Teatr Narodowy**, opened in 1764 and the oldest in Poland, is on Plac Teatralny. **Teatr Polski** (Foksal 16) has a small stage and is thus more intimate. **Współczesny** (Mokotowska 13) shows contemporary works.

Concerts **The National Philharmonic** puts on the best concerts. The hall is on ulica Sienkiewicza 12. In the summer, free Chopin concerts take place both at the Chopin monument in **Łazienki Park** and, each Sunday at **Żelazowa Wola,** the composer's birthplace, 58 kilometers (36 miles) outside Warsaw.

Opera **Teatr Wielki** (Plac Teatralny) hosts the Grand Theater of Opera and Ballet. It has a superb operatic stage—one of the largest in Europe.

Film Many non-Polish films are shown in their original versions, but check before you buy your tickets. Of interest on a rainy day, is the nonstop cinema of short films on ulica Rutkowskiego 33.

Entertainment and Nightlife

Cabaret The Victoria, Forum, Grand, and Europejski hotels all have nightclubs that are popular with Westerners. The acts vary, so check listings in the weekly *Stolica*. These clubs also present striptease and jazz. The most famous cabaret is **Pod Egidą** on Nowy Świat, renowned for its risqué political satire.

Bars **Fukier** (Rynek Starego Miasta 27) is a crowded, noisy wine barcafé in medieval style. **Gwiazdeczka** (Piwna 42) is a noisy, hip, upscale joint, popular with chic young Warsovians.

Jazz Clubs **Akwarium** (ul. Emilii Platter) and **Wanda Warska's Modern Music Club** (Stare Miasto) are popular jazz clubs. Jazz musicians are booked frequently at the major hotels, too.

Discos Apart from the hotels, the most popular discos are **Hybrydy** (ul. Koniewskiego 7) and **Stodoła** (ul. Batorego 2).

Cafés Warsaw is filled with cafés *(kawiarnie)*, which move outdoors in the summer. They are popular meeting places and usually serve delicious coffee and pastries in the best central European style.

Antyczna is an elegant 19th-century-style café with a fine assortment of cakes. *Plac Trzech Krzyży 10.*
Bombonierka is in the New Town Square. It is elegant, spacious, and tranquil. *Rynek Nowego Miasta 1.*
Le Petit Trianon is a tiny, intimate 18th-century French-style restaurant and café. It is difficult to find a seat, but worth it once you do. *Ul. Piwna 40.*
Telimena is a small corner café with outdoor tables in summer. *Krakowskie Przedmiéscie 27.*

Trou Madame has a secluded setting in Łazienki Park.
Ujazdowska is elegant and spacious in a 19th-century French-style house. *Al. Ujazdowska 47.*

Cracow and its Environs

Cracow, seat of Poland's oldest university and once the capital of the country (before losing the honor to Warsaw in 1611), is the only major Polish city to escape devastation in the last war. Hitler's armies were driven out before they had a chance to destroy it. Today its fine ramparts, towers, facades, and churches, illustrating seven centuries of Polish architecture, make Cracow a major attraction for visitors. Its location—about 270 kilometers (160 miles) south of Warsaw—also makes it a good base for hiking and skiing trips in the mountainous south of Poland.

Also within exploring range from Cracow are the famous Polish shrine to the Virgin Mary at Częstochowa, and, at Auschwitz, the grim reminder of man's capacity for inhumanity.

Getting Around

Cracow is reached by major highways—E7 direct from Warsaw and E82 from Częstochowa. Trains link Cracow with most major destinations in Poland; the station is in the central city on ulica Pawia. The bus station is nearby.

Guided Tours

Bus or walking tours of Cracow and its environs are provided by **Orbis.** Horse-drawn carriages can be rented at the main market square for a negotiated price.

Tourist Information

Cracow. Ulica Pawia 8, tel. 12/204–71.
Częstochowa. II al., tel. 12/40–42.

Exploring Cracow

Numbers in the margin correspond with points of interest on the Cracow map.

Cracow's old city is ringed by a park called the **Planty.** The park replaced the old walls of the town, which were torn down in the mid-19th century. Begin your tour at **St. Florian's Gate,** which leads to the old town. The gate is guarded by an imposing 15th-century fortress called the **Barbican.** Enter the city, passing along Florianska Street, the beginning of the Royal Route through the town.

Time Out Don't pass up the chance to stop for refreshments at Cracow's most famous café, **Jama Michalikowa,** now with a non-smoking area. It serves good coffee and excellent ice cream. *Ul. Florianska 8.*

Ulica Florianska leads to the **Main Market,** one of the largest and finest Renaissance squares in Europe. The calm of this spacious square, with its pigeons and flower stalls, is interrupted

Cracow

| 0 | 440 yards |
| 0 | 400 meters |

Major Attractions:
Church of the Virgin Mary, **3**
Jagiellonian University, **5**
Main Market, **2**
St. Florian's Gate, **1**
Sukiennice, **4**
Wawel Castle and Cathedral, **6**

Other Attractions:
Barbican, **15**
Central Station, **8**
Czartoryski Museum, **14**
Ethnographic Museum, **14**
Helena Modrzejewska Stary Theater, **10**
Jagiellonian University Museum, **9**

K. Szymanowski State Philharmonic Hall, **11**
Lenin Museum, **12**
National Museum, **13**
St. Adalbert Romanesque Church, **7**

every hour by four short bugle calls drifting down from the spire of the Church of the Virgin Mary. The plaintive notes recall a centuries-old tradition in memory of a trumpeter whose throat was pierced by a well-aimed enemy arrow as he was warning his fellow citizens of an impending Tartar attack. The **③** square Gothic **Church of the Virgin Mary** contains a 15th-century wooden altarpiece—the largest in the world—carved by Wit Stwosz. The faces of the saints are reputedly those of Cracovian burghers. In the center of the square stands **④** a covered market called **Sukiennice** (Cloth Hall), built in the 14th century but remodeled during the Renaissance. The ground floor is still in business, selling trinkets and folk art souvenirs.

From the Main Market, turn down ulica Sw. Anny to no. 8, the **⑤** **Collegium Maius,** the oldest building of the famous **Jagiellonian University** (founded 1364). Its pride is the Italian-style arcaded courtyard. Inside is a museum where you can see the Copernicus globe, the first on which the American continent was shown, as well as astronomy instruments belonging to Cracow's most famous graduate.

⑥ Backtracking on ulica Grodzka will lead you to the **Wawel Castle and Cathedral.** This impressive complex of Gothic and Renaissance buildings stands on fortifications dating as far back as the 8th century. Inside the castle is a museum with an exotic collection of Oriental tents that were captured from the Turks at the battle of Vienna in 1683 and rare 16th-century Flemish tapestries. Wawel Cathedral is where, until the 18th century, Polish kings were crowned and buried. Up to 1978, the cathedral was the see of Archbishop Carol Wojtyla, now known as Pope John Paul II. *Ul. Grodzka. Open 9–5.*

About 50 kilometers (30 miles) west of Cracow is the Nazi concentration camp of Oswiecim, better known by its German name, **Auschwitz.** Here four million victims (mostly Jews) from 29 countries were executed by the Nazis during World War II. The camp has been left just as it was found in 1945 by the Soviet army, and crematoria and barracks now house dramatic displays of Nazi atrocities. Oswiecim itself is an industrial town with good connections from Cracow; buses and trains leave Cracow approximately every hour, and signs in Oswiecim direct visitors to the camp. *Admission free. Open Mar. and Nov., Tues.–Sun. 8–4; Apr. and Oct., Tues.–Sun. 8–5; May and Sept., daily 8–6; June–Aug., daily 8–7; Dec.–Feb., Tues.–Sun. 8–3.*

Wieliczka, about 8 kilometers (5 miles) southeast of Cracow, is the oldest salt mine in Europe, in operation since the end of the 13th century. It is famous for its magnificent underground chapel hewn in crystal rock, the **Chapel of the Blessed Kings.** *Wieliczka Mines. Admission: 250 Zł. Open Apr.–Oct. 8–6; Nov.–Mar. 8–4. Guided tours only.*

Częstochowa, 120 kilometers (70 miles) from Cracow and reached by regular trains and buses, is the home of the holiest shrine in a country that is more than 90% Catholic. Inside the 14th-century **Pauline monastery** on Jasna Góra (Light Hill) is the famous *Black Madonna* a painting of Our Lady of Częstochowa attributed by legend to St. Luke. It was here that an invading Swedish army was halted in 1655 and finally driven out of the

country. Between Częstochowa and Cracow is the little town of
Wadowice, birthplace of Pope John Paul II.

Dining and Lodging

For details and price category definitions, *see* Dining and Lodging in Staying in Poland.

Cracow
Dining

Staropolska. Traditional Polish cuisine is served in a medieval setting. Try the pork, duck, or veal. *Ul. Sienna 4. No reservations. AE, DC, MC, V. Expensive.*

Wierzynek. One of the best restaurants in the country, Wierzynek serves traditional Polish specialties and excels in soups and game. It was here in 1364, after a historic meeting, that the king of Poland wined and dined the German Emperor Charles IV, five kings, and a score of princes. *Rynek Główny 15, tel. 12/210–25. Reservations advised. AE, DC, MC, V. Expensive.*

Lodging

Cracovia. This large, Orbis-run, five-story hotel boasts one of the best restaurants in town. There is also a lively nightclub where Western tourists like to meet. *Al. Puszkina 1, tel. 12/22–86–66. 427 rooms with bath. Facilities: restaurant, nightclub. AE, DC, MC, V. Expensive.*

Holiday Inn. This was the first Holiday Inn in Eastern Europe. Rather bland but comfortable with a fine restaurant, this high-rise establishment is pleasantly located near Cracow's Green Meadows. *Ul. Koniewa 7, tel. 12/37–50–44. 310 rooms with bath. Facilities: restaurant, solarium, sauna, indoor pool. AE, DC, MC, V. Expensive.*

Europejski. This small, older hotel overlooking the Planty park has seen better days, so make sure you see your room before you accept it. *Ul. Lubicz 5, tel. 12/209–11. 55 rooms, some with bath. No credit cards. Moderate.*

Francuski. This small hotel is just inside the old town's walls, within walking distance of all the main sites. Built at the turn of the century, it offers an intimate atmosphere and friendly service. Rooms are elegant but a little tacky in a homey, East European way. The excellent restaurant is tranquil and plush and has a café with dancing. *Ul. Pijarska 13, tel. 12/22–51–22. 59 rooms, most with bath or shower. Facilities: restaurant, café. No credit cards. Moderate.*

Częstochowa
Lodging

Centralny. The Centralny makes a good base for exploring Poland's holiest shrine, and since most of the other guests are pilgrims, the atmosphere is an interesting mixture of piety and good fun. *Ul. Świerczewkiego, tel. 12/440–67. 62 rooms, most with bath or shower. No credit cards. Moderate.*

Gdańsk and the North

In contrast to Cracow and the south, Poland north of Warsaw is the land of medieval castles and chateaux, dense forests and lakes, and sandswept beaches along the Baltic coast. If you haven't got a car, consider going straight to Gdańsk and making excursions from there. The alternative is to travel by car along the course of the Vistula River through majestic countryside.

Getting Around

Gdańsk is a major transportation hub, with an airport just outside town (and good bus connections to downtown) and major road and rail connections with the rest of the country.

Guided Tours

Orbis arranges an eight-day tour of Warsaw, Toruń, Gdańsk, and Poznań. It also handles group and individual tours of Toruń, Gdańsk, and the surrounding areas.

Tourist Information

Elbąg. Ul. Maja 1, tel. 222–75; Orbis, ul. Hetmańska 23, tel. 223–64.
Gdańsk. Ul. Heweliusza 8, tel. 31–03–38; Orbis, pl. Górskiego 1, tel. 31–49–44.
Ostróda. Orbis, ul. Czdrnieckiego 10, tel. 35–57.
Płock. Ul. Tuńska 4, tel. 226–00; Orbis, al. Jachowa 47, tel. 229–89.
Toruń. Ul. Kopernika 27, tel. 272–99; Orbis, ul. Żeglarska 31, tel. 261–30.

Exploring Gdańsk and the North

From Warsaw, follow routes E81 and 107 through **Płock.** Once you get through Płock's industrial area, you'll find a lovely medieval city that was, for a short time, capital of Poland. Worth seeing are the 12th-century cathedral, where two Polish kings are buried, and the dramatic 14th-century Teutonic castle. Continue through Włocławek to Toruń, where an overnight stay is recommended.

Toruń, birthplace of Nicolaus Copernicus, is an interesting medieval city that made its fortune from its location on the north-south trading route along the Vistula. Its old town district is a remarkably successful blend of Gothic buildings—churches, town hall, and burghers' homes—with Renaissance and Baroque patricians' houses. The Town Hall's Tower (1274) is the oldest town in Poland. Don't leave without trying some of Toruńs famous gingerbread and honey cakes.

The route leading north from Toruń to Gdańsk passes through some of the oldest towns in Poland. Along the way are many medieval castles, chateaux, and churches that testify to the wealth and strategic importance of the area. Two short detours are a must: one is to **Kwidzyń** to see the original 14th-century castle and cathedral complex. The other is to **Malbork.** This huge castle, 58 kilometers (36 miles) from Gdańsk, was one of the most powerful strongholds in medieval Europe. From 1308 to 1457, it was the residence of the Grand Masters of the Teutonic Order. The Teutonic Knights were a thorn in Poland's side until their defeat at the battle of Grunwald in 1410. Inside Malbork castle is a museum with beautiful examples of amber —including lumps as large as melons and pieces containing perfect specimens of prehistoric insects.

Gdańsk, formerly the free city of Danzig, is another of Poland's beautifully restored towns, displaying a rich heritage of Goth-

Gdańsk and the North

Słupsk · Lebork · Gdynia · *Gulf of Danzig* · Sopot · Gdańsk · Nowy Dwar Gdański · Braniewo · Elbląg · Tczew · Starogard · Malbork · Lidzbark · Chojnice · Kwidzyń · Olsztyn · Ostróda · Świecie · Chełmno · Grudziądz · Olsztynek · Wyrzysk · Chełmża · Bydgoszcz · Toruń · Brodnica · Mława · Inowrocław · *Vistula* · Sierpc · Gniezno · Włocławek · Płock · Września · Koło

40 miles

60 km

ic, Renaissance, and Mannerist architecture. This is where the first shots of World War II were fired and where the free trade union Solidarity was born after strikes in 1980. The city's old town has a wonderful collection of historic town houses and narrow streets. The splendid Długa and Długi Targ streets (best for shopping) form the axis of the town and are a good starting point for walks into other parts of the city. The evocative **Solidarity Monument** stands outside the Lenin shipyards—erected in honor of workers killed by the regime during strikes in 1970. The nearby town of **Sopot** is Poland's most popular seaside resort.

For a different route back to Warsaw, follow highway E81 southeast through Poland's scenic forest and lake district. The area is rich in nature and wildlife attractions as well as places of historical interest. Recommended is a diversion (or night stop) 42 kilometers (26 miles) east of Ostróda to the medieval town of **Olsztyn.** The old town was once administered and fortified by Copernicus.

About 30 kilometers (19 miles) farther south on E81 is **Olsztynek,** where the **Museum of Folk Buildings** holds a collection of timber buildings from different parts of the country. They include a small Mazurian thatch-roofed church, an inn, a mill, a forge, old windmills, and thatched cottages, some of which have been furnished period-style.

Time Out Located on E81, the **Mazurski** is a good place to stop for a meal. The food varies but is generally tasty. *Moderate.*

Another diversion, 17 kilometers (10½ miles) west of Olsztynek, is the **site of the battle of Grunwald,** possibly the greatest battle of the Middle Ages. Here on July 15, 1410, Władysław Jagiełło and his Polish Lithuanian army annihilated the Grand Master of the Teutonic Order, Ulrich von Jungingen, and thousands of his knights. A small museum on the site (open summer only, 10–10) graphically explains the course of the battle.

Dining and Lodging

For details and price category definitions, *see* Dining and Lodging in Staying in Poland.

Elbąg   **Karczma Słupska.** This is the best restaurant in town. It's usu-
Dining   ally crowded and specializes in fresh fish. *Ul. Krótka 1. No. reservations. No credit cards. Moderate.*

Gdańsk   The best restaurants—here as elsewhere in Poland—are in the
Dining   more expensive Orbis hotels. Other good places, however, can be recommended.
Pod Łososiem. The name of this restaurant refers to salmon, which, if available on the day you visit, is highly recommended. You can't go wrong with any fish dishes, however. *Ul. Szeroka 51. No telephone. No reservations. AE, DC, MC, V. Expensive.*
Pod Wiezą. This restaurant has a reputation for good meat dishes and generous portions. *Piwna 51. No telephone. No reservations. AE, DC, MC, V. Expensive.*
Kashubska. The specialties here come from Kahubia, a hilly and wooded lakeland region near the coast. Smoked fish dishes are highly recommended. *Ul. Kartuska 1. No telephone. No reservations. AE, DC, MC, V. Moderate.*

Lodging   **Hewelius.** This large, modern, highrise hotel is situated in the center of the city, within walking distance of the old town. Rooms are standard, spacious, blandly furnished, with all the modern conveniences. The hotel has a good restaurant and one of the best nightclub-discos in town. *Ul. Heweliusza 22, tel. 31–56–31. 250 rooms, most with bath. Facilities: restaurant, nightclub. AE, DC, MC, V. Expensive.*
Marina. Built in 1982, this large high rise, popular with Western businesspeople, is one of the newest hotels in Poland and probably the best in town. Upper floors have splendid views. *Ul. Jelitkowska 20, tel. 53–12–46. 193 rooms with bath or shower. Facilities: restaurant, nightclub, indoor pool, tennis courts, bowling alley. AE, DC, MC, V. Expensive.*
Posejdon. Though this modern, functional hotel is a bit out of town, it is well equipped with leisure facilities. *Ul. Kapliczna 30, tel. 53–02–27. 140 rooms with bath or shower. Facilities: solarium, sauna, indoor pool, disco. AE, DC, MC, V. Moderate.*

Olsztyn   **Orbis Novotel.** This standard 1970s hotel is typical of the kind
Lodging   found in Poland. It is, however, the most comfortable lodging in the area and is located in beautiful surroundings on the shores of lake Ukiel. It has a good restaurant (reservations recommended in summer). *Ul. Sielska 3a, tel. 240–81. 98 rooms. Facilities: restaurant, pool. Expensive.*

Ostróda   This town is not visited by many foreign tourists and is lacking
Lodging   in good-quality facilities. The undistinguished *Panorama Hotel* is the best, unless Orbis can find you private lodging. *ul. Krasickiego 23, tel. 22–27.*

Toruń
Dining

The best restaurants are in the expensive Orbis hotels. Others are listed below.

Pod Kurantem. Regional cuisine is featured in this attractive old wine cellar. Slow service is the penalty for popularity. *Rynek Staromiejski 28. No telephone. No reservations. No credit cards. Expensive.*

Polonia. Try the Polonia for the excellent meat dishes and soups such as *barszcz (beet soup). Pl. Armii Czerwonej 5. No telephone. No reservations. No credit cards. Moderate.*

Wodnik. This large café along the banks of the Vistula is very popular with locals. *Blvd. Filadelfijski. No telephone. No credit cards. Inexpensive.*

Lodging

Helios. This friendly, medium-size hotel is situated in the city center and offers a good restaurant (albeit with slow service). *Ul. Kraszewskiego 1, tel. 250–33. 140 rooms, most with bath or shower. Facilities: restaurant, sauna, nightclub, beauty parlor. AE, DC, MC, V. Moderate.*

Kosmos. A functional 1960s hotel, Kosmos is beginning to show signs of wear and tear. It is situated near the river, in the city center. *Ul. Portowa 2, tel. 298–00. 180 rooms, most with bath or shower. AE, DC, MC, V. Moderate.*

24 Portugal

Introduction

Given its long Atlantic coastline, it isn't surprising that Portugal has been a maritime nation for most of its history. The valor of its seamen is well known; from the charting of the Azores archipelago in 1427 to the discovery of Japan in 1542, Portuguese explorers unlocked the major sea routes to southern Africa, India, and Far East, and the Americas. To commemorate this great era of exploration, a period which reached its height in the 15th century under the influence of Prince Henry the Navigator, the years 1988 to 2000 have been set aside for various celebrations throughout the country.

Despite its sailors' worldly adventures, Portugal itself has remained relatively undiscovered. Although it shares the Iberian Peninsula with Spain, it attracts far fewer visitors—a strange fact, because Portugal has much to recommend it to tourists: fine beaches, beautiful castles, charming fishing villages, well-maintained hotels and *pousadas* (government-owned inns), excellent restaurants, and colorful folk traditions.

About the size of Maine, Portugal is small enough so that its main attractions can be seen during a short visit; at the country's widest point the distance between the Atlantic and Spain is a mere 240 kilometers (150 miles). Short distances don't mean monotony, however, for this narrow coastal strip of land has more geographic and climatic variations than virtually any other nation in Western Europe.

Portugal is divided into six provinces. Most visitors head for the low-lying plains of the southern Algarve or the region around the Lisbon/Estoril coast, but as traditional tourist destinations become more crowded, adventurous travelers are venturing in other directions. The northern and central provinces—Minho, Beira, and Trás-os-Montes—are largely unspoiled, full of tiny villages and splendid scenery. The major drawbacks here are inefficient communication and poor roads: In the far north, the zigzag tracks are unsuited to fast or heavy traffic. The south has its own traffic problems, however: There are few turnpikes and the Portuguese are count d among the world's most reckless drivers.

Observant visitors are likely to notice other differences between Portugal's northern and southern regions and people. The northern character is decidedly more Celtic, while in the south, Moorish ancestry is apparent. But throughout the country, the Portuguese people are welcoming wherever you meet them.

For the purposes of this guide, we have concentrated on the southern part of the country—the section most frequented by foreign visitors—including Lisbon, Portugal's sophisticated capital, and the Algarve.

Before You Go

When to Go The tourist season runs from spring through autumn, but some parts of the country—especially the Algarve, which boasts some 3,000 hours of sunshine annually—are balmy even in winter. Hotel prices are greatly reduced between November and February.

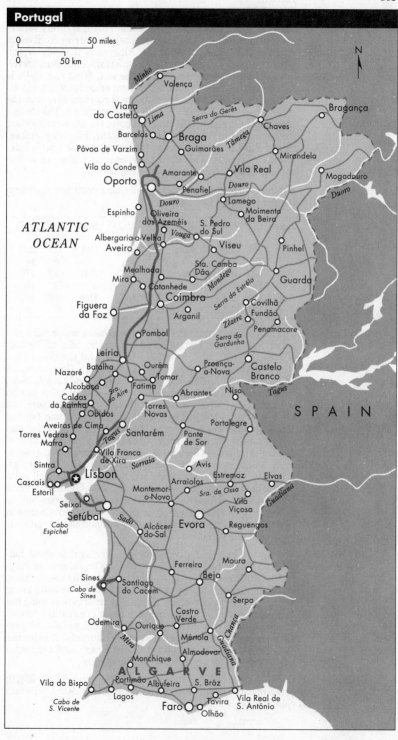

Portugal

0 — 50 miles
0 — 50 km

N

ATLANTIC OCEAN

Minho
Valença
Viana do Castelo
Lima
Serra do Gerês
Braga
Barcelos
Guimarães
Póvoa de Varzim
Vila do Conde
Amarante
Oporto
Penafiel
Espinho
Douro
Oliveira dos Azeméis
Albergaria-a-Velha
Vouga
Aveiro
S. Pedro do Sul
Viseu
Mealhada
Sta. Comba Dão
Mira
Mondego
Catanhede
Coimbra
Figuera da Foz
Arganil
Serra da Estrêla
Pombal
Zêzere
Leiria
Serra da Gardunha
Nazaré
Batalha
Ourém
Proença-a-Nova
Alcobaça
Sra. do Aire
Tomar
Caldas da Rainha
Fatima
Castelo Branco
Obidos
Torres Novas
Abrantes
Nisa
Tagus
Aveiras de Cima
Tagus
Santarém
Torres Vedras
Mafra
Ponte de Sor
Portalegre
Vila Franca de Xira
Sorraia
Sintra
Avis
Cascais
Lisbon
Arraiolos
Estremoz
Elvas
Estoril
Montemor-o-Novo
Sra. de Ossa
Guadiana
Seixal
Setúbal
Sado
Vila Viçosa
Cabo Espichel
Alcácer-do-Sal
Evora
Reguengos
Ferreira
Moura
Sines
Cabo de Sines
Santiago do Cacem
Beja
Serpa
Odemira
Castro Verde
Ourique
Mira
Mértola
Almodovar
Chança
Guadiana
Monchique
A L G A R V E
Vila do Bispo
Portimão
Albufeira
S. Bráz
Cabo de S. Vicente
Lagos
Faro
Tavira
Vila Real de S. António
Olhão

Valença
Chaves
Bragança
Mirandela
Vila Real
Mogadouro
Douro
Lamego
Moimenta da Beira
Duero
Pinhel
Guarda
Covilhã
Fundão
Penamacore

S P A I N

Climate   Since Portugal's entire coast is on the Atlantic Ocean, the country's climate is temperate year-round. Portugal rarely suffers the extremes of heat that Mediterranean countries do. Even in August, the hottest month, the Algarve is the only region where the midday heat may be uncomfortable, but most travelers go there to swim and soak up the sun. What rain there is falls from November to March; December and January can be chilly outside the Algarve, but there is no snow except in the mountains of the Serra da Estrêla in the northeast. The almond blossoms and vivid wildflowers that cover the countryside start to bloom early in February. The dry months, June–September, can turn much of the landscape the tawny color of a lion's hide, but there is always a breeze in the evening in Lisbon, as well as along the Estoril coast west of the capital.

The following are the average daily maximum and minimum temperatures for Lisbon.

Jan.	57F	14C	May	71F	21C	Sept.	79F	26C
	46	8		55	13		62	17
Feb.	59F	15C	June	77F	25C	Oct.	72F	22C
	47	8		60	15		58	14
Mar.	63F	17C	July	81F	27C	Nov.	63F	17C
	50	10		63	17		52	11
Apr.	67F	20C	Aug.	82F	28C	Dec.	58F	15C
	53	12		63	17		47	9

Currency   The unit of currency in Portugal is the *escudo*, which can be divided into 100 centavos. Escudos come in bills of 100$00, 500$00, 1,000$00, and 5,000$00. (In Portugal the dollar sign stands between the escudo and the centavo). Coins come in 1$00, 2$50, 5$00, 10$00, 20$00, 25$00, 50$00, and 100$00. Newly minted 1$00, 5$00, and 10$00 yellow-colored coins can be confused for older coins still in circulation, so make sure you know exactly what you're spending. At press time (spring 1989), the exchange rate was 143$00 to the U.S. dollar and 263$00 to the pound sterling. Owing to the complications of dealing in millions of escudos, 1,000$00 is always called a *conto*, so 10,000$00 is referred to as 10 contos. Credit cards are accepted in all the larger shops and restaurants, as well as in hotels; however, better exchange rates are obtained in banks and *cambios* (exchange offices). Short-changing is rare but, as in every country, restaurant bills should be checked. Change in post offices and railway booking offices should also be counted. Shops are usually honest.

What It Will Cost   The cost of hotels and restaurants in Portugal is about half what it is in the rest of Europe. Produce is fresh, and few luxury foodstuffs are imported, so dining is generally inexpensive, except in the very top restaurants. The most expensive areas are Lisbon, the Algarve, and the tourist resort areas along the Tagus estuary. The least expensive areas are country towns, which all have reasonably priced hotels and *pensão*, or pensions, as well as numerous café-type restaurants. A sales tax (VAT) of 17% is imposed on hotel, restaurant, and car rental bills, as well as for services such as car repairs.

Sample Prices   Cup of coffee, 60$00; bottle of beer, 90$00; soft drink, 80$00; bottle of house wine, 250$00; ham sandwich, 140$00; 1-mile taxi ride, 170$00.

Customs on Arrival Visitors over age 17 are allowed to bring the following items into Portugal duty-free: 200 cigarettes or 250 grams of tobacco, one liter of liquor (22% volume), two bottles of wine, 100 ml of perfume, and a reasonable amount of personal effects (camera, binoculars, etc). No more than 30,000$00 may be brought into Portugal, and you may not leave with more foreign currency than you declared on arrival. Computerized customs services make random and often thorough checks on arrival.

Language Portuguese is easy to read by anyone with even slight knowledge of a Latin language, but it is difficult to pronounce and understand (most people speak quickly and eliptically). However, you will find that in the larger cities and major resorts many people, especially the young, speak English. In the country, people are so friendly and eager to be helpful that visitors can usually make themselves understood in sign language.

Getting Around

By Car
Road Conditions Apart from the few turnpikes (moderate tolls) and the major highways between Lisbon and the Algarve, Oporto, and Guincho beyond Cascais alongside the river Tagus, road conditions in Portugal are poor, with lots of winding roads and unpredictable surfaces.

Motorists going north from Lisbon will find that the recently built autoroute from Leiria up to Oporto is well designed, making fast driving easy. From Lisbon to Leiria, there is a turnpike through Vila Franca de Xira up to Aveiras de Cima that will be extended sometime in the future. The current road from Aveiras de Cima to Leiria is often congested. New highways are under construction which will link Portugal with the European network of main roads via eastern border points at Vilar Formosa and Caia, and the far northeastern point of Quintanhila.

Driving to the Algarve from Lisbon is a pleasure except for the section between Setúbal and Alcacer do Sal, the entire route is via highway. South of Alcacer all the towns are bypassed by a new highway built down to Messines, inland from Albufeira. At Messines, the old roads, now widened, go west to Portimão, Lagos, and Sagres, south for Albufeira, and east for Faro and the frontier with Spain at Vila Real de Santo Antonio.

There are no highways from Lisbon to the nearest frontier post with Spain at Caia, outside Elvas, but the route through Setúbal (turnpike from Lisbon), over the Tagus bridge to Montemor-o-Novo, Arraiolos, and Estremoz, is good and fast.

Rules of the Road Driving is on the right. At the junction of two roads of equal size, traffic coming from the right has priority. Vehicles already in a traffic circle have priority over those entering it from any point. Traffic in the country is light, but local people are apt to walk in the road and occasional horse- or donkey-drawn carts may hold things up. Seat belts are obligatory. Horns should not be used in built-up areas, and a red warning triangle, for use in a breakdown, must be carried. The speed limit on turnpikes is 120 kph (72 mph); on other roads it is 90 kph (54 mph), and in built-up areas, 50–60 kph (30–36 mph). Speed bumps are sometimes placed across the road entering a village. Side roads usually have stop signs at the intersections.

Parking A few towns and cities are experimenting with parking meters, although these are still rare. Parking lots and underground garages proliferate in major cities, but those in Lisbon and Oporto are no longer cheap. Parking in side streets is usually chaotic. In the country, parking is unlimited, but on narrow roads it is wise to draw in as much as possible and avoid curves.

Gasoline Gas prices are among the highest in Europe: 119$00 per liter for super and 112$00 for regular. Unleaded gas is now available for 119$00. Many gas stations around the country are self-service. Credit cards are widely accepted.

Breakdowns All large garages in and around towns have breakdown services. Special emergency (SOS) telephones are located at intervals on turnpikes and highways. Motorists in Portugal are very helpful; if your car breaks down, aid from a passing driver is usually forthcoming within a short time. The national automobile organization, **Automóvel Club de Portugal** (Rua Rosa, Araujo 49-A, Lisbon) provides reciprocal membership with other European automobile associations, provided the membership is up-to-date. For a list of associations, tel. 01/553558.

By Train The Portuguese railway system is surprisingly extensive for so small a country. Trains are clean and leave on time, but there are few express runs except between Lisbon and Oporto. These take under three hours for the 210-mile journey. Several of the Oporto/Lisbon trains take cars, as does one train a day between Lisbon–Castelo Branco–Regua–Guarda and some Lisbon–Algarve trains during the summer. Cars must be at the station an hour before departure; prices are reasonable, and tickets can be bought then or in advance. Most trains have first- and second-class compartments; suburban lines around Lisbon have a single class. Tickets should be bought, and seats reserved if desired, at the stations or through travel agents, two or three days in advance. Timetables are the same on Saturday and Sunday as on weekdays, except on suburban lines. **Wasteels–Expresso** (Ave. Antonio Augusto Aguiar 88, 1000 Lisbon, tel. 01/579180) is reliable for all local and international train tickets and reservations.

Special **tourist passes** can be obtained through travel agents or at main train stations. These are valid for periods of seven, 14, or 21 days for first- and second-class travel on any domestic train service; mileage is unlimited. At press time (spring 1989), the cost was 11,475$00 for seven days; 18,300$00 for 14 days; and 26,140$00 for 21 days.

International trains to Madrid, Paris, and other parts of Europe depart from the Santa Apolonia Station in Lisbon and Campanhã in Oporto.

By Plane The internal air services of **Air Portugal** (TAP) are good. Lisbon is linked at least four times daily with Oporto and Faro; daily with Funchal (Madeira), more at peak periods; weekly with Porto Santo, an island some way off Madeira; and several times a week with the archipelago of the Azores. Flights to Viseu, Vila Real, and Bragança are all run by TAP, Praça Marques Pombal 3, 1200 Lisbon, tel. 01/575020.

By Bus The nationalized bus company, **Rodoviaria Nacional,** has passenger terminals in Lisbon at Ave. Casal Ribeiro 18, tel. 01/545826 or 545863, with regular bus services throughout Portugal. Most long-distance buses have toilet facilities, and the fares are cheaper than for trains, which usually are faster and more restful.

By Boat Ferries across the river Tagus leave from Praça do Comércio, Cais do Sodré, and Belém. From April to October, a two-hour boat excursion leaves the ferry station at Praça do Comércio in Lisbon daily at 2:30 PM for Paço d'Arcos. The price is 1,500$00.

Boat trips on the river Douro (Oporto) are organized from May to October by **Porto Ferreira**, Rua da Cavalhosa, 19, Vila Nova de Gaia, Oporto. They leave every day on the hour, except Saturday afternoon and Sunday.

Six-day canoe trips down the Guadiana River, departing from Lisbon and ending in Faro (including full accommodation and side trips), are available from **Turalgarve** (Rua Luciano Cordeiro 6, Lisbon, tel. 01/577064). The cost is 60,000$00.

By Bicycle **Tip Tours.** (Ave. Costa Pinto 91-A, 2750 Cascais, tel. 01/283821) rents out bicycles by the day or half day. **Cycle Portugal** (Box 877, San Antonio, FL 34266, USA, tel. 800/2828932 or, in Portugal, tel. 01/2687754) offers bicycle tours throughout the country with accommodations in first-class hotels. Each tour is accompanied by a guide, a mechanic, and a van for luggage.

Staying in Portugal

Telephones Pay phones take 2$50, 5$00, and 25$00 coins; 7$50 is the minimum payment for short local calls (some pay phones may not accept the newly minted yellow-colored coins). Some specially marked pay phones will accept plastic phone cards, which can be purchased at most tobacconist shops. Long-distance calls cost less from 8 PM to 8 AM. All telephone calls are more expensive when made from a hotel, so it is wise to make international calls from a post office, where you will be assigned a private booth. Collect calls can also be made from post offices, and some telephone booths accept international calls.

Mail Postal rates, both domestic and foreign, increase twice a year. Country post offices close for lunch and at 6 PM weekdays; they are not open on weekends. Main post offices in towns are open weekdays 8:30 to 6 with no midday closings. In Lisbon, the post office in the Praça dos Restauradores is open 24 hours.

Receiving Mail Mail can be sent in care of American Express Star (Ave. Sidonio Pais 4, 1000 Lisbon); there is no service charge. Main post offices also accept poste restante letters.

Shopping Bargaining is not common in city stores or shops, but it is possible in flea markets, antique shops, and outdoor markets that sell fruit, vegetables, and household goods. The **Centro de Turismo Artesanato** (Rua Castilho 61, 1200 Lisbon) will ship goods abroad even if they were not bought in Portugal. By air to the United States, parcels take about three weeks; by sea, two months.

VAT Refunds Value-added tax (VAT) is included in the price of goods, but the tax on items over a certain value can be reclaimed, although the methods are time-consuming. For Americans and other non-EEC residents, the tax paid on individual items costing more than 10,000$00 can be reclaimed on presentation of receipts to special departments in airports (in Lisbon, near Gate 23). For British citizens and other EEC visitors, a more complicated procedure must be followed, which involves claiming the tax refund from customs officials when returning home; tax may be reclaimed on items worth more than 53,000$00. Shops specializing in VAT-refund purchases are clearly marked throughout the country, and shop assistants can help with the forms.

Opening and Closing Times

Banks. Banks are open weekdays 8:30–11:45 and 1–2:45. Some private banks are open through lunch. There is also an automatic currency exchange machine in the Praça dos Restauradores.

Museums. Museums are usually open 10–5; some close for lunch and on Monday. At palaces, closing days vary.

Shops. Shops are open weekdays 9–1 and 3–7, Saturdays 9–1. Shopping malls in Lisbon and other cities remain open until 10 PM or midnight and are often open on Sunday.

National Holidays

January 1 (New Year's Day); February 27 (Carnival, Shrove Tuesday); April 13 (Good Friday); April 25 (Anniversary of the Revolution); May 1 (Labor Day); June 14 (Corpus Christi); June 10 (National Day); August 15 (Assumption); October 5 (Day of the Republic); November 1 (All Saints); December 1 (Independence Day); December 8 (Immaculate Conception); December 25 (Christmas Day).

Dining

Eating is taken quite seriously in Portugal, and, not surprisingly, seafood is a staple. Freshly caught lobster, crab, shrimp, tuna, sole, and squid are prepared in innumerable ways, but if you want to sample a little bit of everything, try *caldeirada*, a piquant stew made with whatever is freshest from the sea. In the Algarve, *cataplana* is a must—a mouth-watering mixture of clams, ham, tomatoes, onions, garlic, and herbs named for the dish in which it is cooked. There are some excellent local wines, and even in modest restaurants the *vinho da casa* (house wine) is usually very good. Water is generally safe, but visitors may want to drink bottled water—*sem gas* for still, *com gas* for fizzy—from one of the many excellent Portuguese spas.

Mealtimes

Lunch usually begins around 1 PM; dinner is served at about 8 PM.

Dress

Jacket and tie are generally advised for restaurants in the Expensive category. Otherwise, casual dress is acceptable.

Ratings

Prices are per person, without alcohol. Taxes and service are usually included, but a tip of 5–10% is always appreciated. All restaurants must post a menu with current prices in a window facing the street. Best bets are indicated by a star ★. At press time (spring 1989), there were 143$00 to the dollar.

Category	All Areas
Expensive	over 4,000$00
Moderate	2,000$00–4,000$00
Inexpensive	under 2,000$00

Credit Cards

The following credit card abbreviations are used: AE, American Express; DC, Diners Club; MC, MasterCard; V, Visa.

Lodging

Visitors have a wide choice of lodging in Portugal, which offers the lowest rates in Europe for accommodations. Hotels are graded from one up to five stars, as are the smaller inns called *estalagems*, which usually provide breakfast only. *Pensions* go up to four stars and often include meals. The state-subsidized *pousadas*, most of which are situated in castles, old monasteries, or have been built where there is a particularly fine view, are five-star luxury properties. *Residencias* (between a pension and a hotel) are located in most towns and larger villages; most rooms have private baths or showers, and breakfast is usually included in the charge. They are extremely good value, under 2,000$00 a night.

A recent innovation is **Turismo de Habitacão** (Country House Tourism), in which private homeowners all over the country, but mostly in the north, offer visitors a room and breakfast (and sometimes provide dinner on request). This is an excellent way to experience life on a country estate. Details are available from Ave. Antonio Augusto Aguiar 86, 1000 Lisbon, tel. 01/575883.

Tourist offices can help visitors with hotel or other reservations, and will provide lists of the local hostelries without charge. Few international chains have hotels in Portugal. Almost all bathrooms have showers over the tubs.

Aparthotels, with double rooms, bath, and kitchenette, are to be found in the main resorts and are good value. Villas can be rented by the week or longer in the Algarve from various agents. One of the best-run complexes is Luz Bay Club, at Praia da Luz near Lagos, where all the well-designed villas have daily maid service.

Camping Camping has become increasingly popular in Portugal in recent years, and there are now more than 100 campsites throughout the country offering a wide range of facilities. The best-equipped have markets, swimming pools, and tennis courts. For further information, contact: **Federacão Portuguesa de Campsimo** (Ave. 5 Outubro 15, 3, 1000 Lisbon, tel. 01/523308).

Ratings Prices are for two people in a double room, based on high-season rates. Best bets are indicated by a star ★. At press time (spring 1989), there were 143$00 to the dollar.

Category	All Areas
Very Expensive	over 25,000$00
Expensive	17,000$00–25,000$00
Moderate	10,000$00–17,000$00
Inexpensive	under 10,000$00

Credit Cards The following credit card abbreviations are used: AE, American Express; DC, Diners Club; MC, MasterCard; V, Visa.

Tipping In Portugal, modest tips are usually expected by those who render services. Service is included in bills at hotels and most restaurants. In luxury hotels, give the porter who carries your luggage 200$00; in less expensive establishments, 100$00. If the maid brings your breakfast, give her 100$00 a day or 500$00 for a stay of a week or two. If you regularly dine in the hotel, give between 500$00 and 1,000$00 to your waiter at the end of your stay, somewhat less to the wine waiter if you order wine with every meal. Otherwise, tip 5–10% on restaurant bills, except at inexpensive establishments, where you may just leave any coins given in change. Taxi drivers get 10%; cinema and theater ushers who seat you, 20$00 to 50$00; train and airport porters, 100$00 per bag; service station attendants, 25$00–50$00 for gas, 20$00–25$00 for checking tires and cleaning windshields; hairdressers, around 10%.

Lisbon

Arriving and Departing

By Plane Lisbon's Portela Airport is only about 20 minutes from the city by car or taxi. The airport is small, but has been recently modernized; for information, tel. 01/802060.

Between the Airport and Downtown There is a special bus service from the airport into the city center called the *Linha Verde* (Green Line), but taxis are so much cheaper than in other European capitals that visitors would be wise to take a taxi straight to their destination. The cost into Lisbon is about 500$00, and to Estoril or Sintra, 3,000$00. There are no trains or subways between the airport and the city. Car rental firms at the airport will provide free maps.

By Train International trains from Paris and Madrid arrive at Santa Apolonia Station (tel. 01/876025), in the center of the city. There is a tourist office at the station and plenty of taxis and porters, but car-rental firms do not have offices there.

Getting Around

Lisbon is a hilly city, and the sidewalks are paved with cobblestones, so walking can be tiring, even when wearing comfortable shoes. Fortunately, Lisbon's tram service is one of the best in Europe and buses go all over the city. A **Tourist Pass** for unlimited rides on the tram or bus costs 1,245$00 for a week or 900$00 for four days; it can be purchased at the Cais do Sodré Station and other terminals. Books of 20 half-price tickets also are available.

By Tram and Bus Buses and trams operate from 4 AM to 2 AM. Try tram routes 13, 24, 28, 29, and 30 for an inexpensive tour of the city; buses nos. 52, 53, and 54 cross the Tagus bridge. Many of the buses are double-deckers, affording an exceptional view of the city's architecture, which includes a remarkable number of Art Nouveau buildings.

By Subway Avoid the subway, called the Metropolitano, which operates from 6:30 AM to 1 AM; it isn't extensive and has become a favorite haunt of pickpockets.

By Taxi Taxis are easily recognizable by a lighted sign on green roofs. There are ranks in the main squares, but it is easy to hail a cruising vehicle. Taxis take up to four passengers at no extra charge. Rates start at 80$00.

Important Addresses and Numbers

Tourist Information The main Lisbon tourist office (tel. 01/363314) is located in the Palacio Foz, Praça dos Restauradores, at the Baixa end of the Avenida da Liberdade, the main artery of the city; open Mon.–Sat. 9–8, Sun. 10–6. The tourist office at Lisbon airport (tel. 01/885974 or 01/893689) is open daily 9 AM–midnight, and the office at Avenida António Augusto Aguiar 86 (tel. 01/575091) is open daily 9–6.

Embassies U.S.: Avenida Forças Armadas, tel. 01/726600. **Canadian:** Rua Rosa Araujo é, tel. 01/563821. **U.K.:** Rua S. Domingos à Lapa 37, tel. 01/661191.

Emergencies SOS **Emergencies:** tel. 115. **Police:** tel. 01/366141. **Ambulance:** tel. 01/617777. **Fire Brigade:** tel. 01/322222. **Doctor:** British Hospital, Rua Saraiva de Carvalho 49, tel. 01/602020; night: 01/603785. You can also contact native English-speaking doctors at tel. 01/531315, (Lisbon) and tel. 01/2845317 (Cascais). **Pharmacies:** open weekdays 9–1, 3–7, Saturday 9–1; consult notice on door for nearest one open on weekends or after hours.

Travel Agencies **American Express Star:** Avenida Sidonio Pais 4, tel. 01/539871. **Wagons-Lits/Thomas Cook:** Avenida da Liberdade 103, tel. 01/361521. **Viagens Rawes:** Rua Bernardino Costa 47, tel. 01/370231/9.

Guided Tours

Orientation Tours and Excursions Various companies organize half-day tours of Lisbon and environs and also full-day trips to more distant places of interest. Those listed below are reliable and offer similar trips and prices. Reservations can be made through any travel agent or hotel. A half-day tour of Lisbon will cost about 2,900$00. A full-day trip north to Obidos, Nazaré, and Fatima will run about 7,900$00. A full day east on the "Roman Route" to Evora and Monsaraz will cost about 7,900$00. Companies are: **Grey Line Tours** (Ave. Fontes Pereira de Melo 14–12, tel. 01/577523); **Capristanos** (Ave. Duque de Loulé 47, tel.01/542973); **Citirama** (Ave. Praia da Vitoria, 12–b, tel. 01/575564); and **Tip Tours** (Ave. Costa Pinto 91–A, 2750 Cascais, tel. 01/283821).

Personal Guides You can arrange to have the services of a personal guide by contacting the main Lisbon tourist office (*see* Important Addresses and Numbers). Beware of unauthorized guides who will approach you at some of the most popular attractions. These people usually are more concerned with "guiding" you to a particular shop or restaurant.

Exploring Lisbon

North of the river Tagus estuary, spread out over a string of hills, Portugal's capital presents unending treats for the eye. Its wide boulevards are bordered by black and white mosaic sidewalks made up of tiny cobblestones. Modern, pastel-colored apartment blocks vie for attention with Art Nouveau houses faced with decorative tiles. Winding, hilly streets provide scores of *miradouros*, natural vantage points which offer spectacular views of the bay.

Lisbon is not a city easily explored on foot, however. The steep inclines of many streets present a tough challenge to the casual tourist, and visitors are often surprised to find that, because of the hills, places that appear to be close to one another on a map are actually on different levels. Yet the effort is worthwhile—judicious use of cable cars and the majestic city-center elevator makes walking tours a treat, even on the hottest summer's day.

With a population of under 2 million, Lisbon is a small capital by European standards. Its center stretches north from the spacious Praça do Comércio, one of the largest riverside squares in Europe, to the Rossio, a smaller square lined by shops and sidewalk cafés. This district is known as the Baixa (Low District), and it is one of the earliest examples of town planning on a large scale. The grid of parallel streets between the two squares was built after an earthquake and tidal wave destroyed much of the city in 1755.

The Alfama, the old Moorish quarter which survived the earthquake, lies just to the east of the Baixa, while Belém, where many of the royal palaces and museums are situated, is about 3.2 kilometers (2 miles) to the west.

Numbers in the margin correspond with points of interest on the Lisbon map.

Castelo de São Jorge and the Alfama The Moors, who imposed their rule on most of the southern Iberian Peninsula during the 8th century, left their mark on Lisbon in many ways. The most visible examples are undoubtedly the imposing castle, set on one of the city's highest hills, and the Alfama, a district of narrow, twisting streets that wind their way up toward the castle. The best way to tour this area of Lisbon is to take a taxi—they're plentiful and cheap—to the castle and walk down; otherwise, you'll have little energy left for sightseeing.

❶ Although the **Castelo de São Jorge** (St. George's Castle) is Moorish in construction, it stands on the site of a fortification used by the Visigoths in the 5th century. Today, its idyllic atmosphere is shattered only by the shrieks of the many peacocks which strut through the grounds, a well-tended area that is also home to swans, turkeys, ducks, ravens, and other birds. The castle walls enclose an Arabian palace which formed the residence of the kings of Portugal until the 16th century; there is also a small row of houses used by artists and craftspeople. Panoramic views of Lisbon can be seen from the castle walls, but visitors should take care, as the uneven, slippery surfaces have barely been touched for centuries. *Admission: free. Open daily 8:30–6.*

❷ After leaving the castle by its impressive gate, wander down through the warren of streets that make up the **Alfama.** This jumble of whitewashed houses, with their flower-laden balconies and red-tiled roofs, managed to survive devastating earthquakes because they rest on foundations of dense bedrock.

❸ The Alfama district is a notorious place for getting lost, but if you can find your way to the Largo Rodrigues de Freitas, a street to the east of the castle, then take a look at the **Museu Marionetta** (Puppet Museum) at no. 20 (Admission: 150$00. Open Tues.–Sun. 10–5). From there, head south along the Rua de São Tome to the Largo das Portas do Sol, where you'll find ❹ the **Museu de Artes Decorativas** (Museum of Decorative Arts) in the Fundaçaõ Ricardo Espirito Santo (Admission: 150$00. Open Mon.–Sat. 10–1). Both make interesting diversions out of the noonday sun.

❺ Head southwest past the Largo de Santa Luzia along the Rua do Limoeiro, which eventually becomes the Rua Augusto Rosa. This route takes you past the **Sé** (cathedral), which is also worth a visit. Built in the 12th century, the Sé has an austere Romanesque interior; its extremely thick walls bear witness to the fact that it also served as a fortress. *Sé. Largo da Sé. Open daily 8:30–6.*

Lisbon

Alfama, **2**	Ingreja de Carmo, **13**	Parque Eduardo VII, **7**
Ascensor de Santa Justa, **14**	Igreja de São Roque, **11**	Rossio Square, **6**
Castelo de São Jorge, **1**	Institute do Vinho do Porto, **10**	Sé, **5**
Elevador da Gloria, **9**	Largo do Chiado, **12**	
Gulbenkian Foundation, **8**	Museu de Artes Decorativas, **4**	
	Museu Marionetta, **3**	

Continue northwest from the cathedral along the Rua de Santo António da Sé, turn left along the Rua da Conceiçao, then right and north up the Rua Augusta. A 10-minute stroll along this street takes you through the **Baixa** and one of Lisbon's main shopping and banking districts. Semipedestrianized, this old-fashioned area boasts a small crafts market, some of the best shoe shops in Europe, and a host of delicatessens selling anything from game birds to *queijo da serra*—a delicious mountain cheese from the Estrela range north of Lisbon.

Avenida da Liberdade
6

Rua Augusta leads into the **Rossio,** Lisbon's principal square, which in turn opens on its northwestern end into the Praça dos Restauradores. This can be considered the beginning of modern Lisbon, for here the broad, tree-lined **Avenida da Liberdade** (sometimes known as the Portuguese Champs-Élysées) begins its northwesterly ascent, ending more than 1.6 kilometers (one mile) away at the **Parque Eduardo VII** (Edward VII Park).

7

A leisurely stroll from the Praça dos Restauradores to the park takes about 45 minutes. As you make your way up the Liberdade, you'll find several cafés at its southern end serving coffee and cool drinks, notably the open-air *esplanada* (café) which faces the main post office on the right. You'll also pass through a pleasant mixture of ornate 19th-century architecture and Art Deco buildings from the '30s—a marked contrast to the cool, green atmosphere of the park itself. Rare flowers, trees, and shrubs thrive in the *estufa fria* (cold greenhouse) and the *estufa quente* (hot greenhouse). *Parque Eduardo VII. Admission: 48$00. Open daily 9–5.*

8

Turn right from the park and head north along the Avenida António Augusto de Aguiar. A 15-minute walk will bring you to the busy Praça de Espanha, to the right of which, in the Parque de Palhava, is the renowned **Gulbenkian Foundation,** a cultural trust. The foundation's art center houses treasures which were collected by Armenian oil magnate Calouste Gulbenkian and donated to the people of Portugal. The collection includes superb examples of Greek and Roman coins, Persian carpets, Chinese porcelain, and paintings by such Old Masters as Rembrandt and Rubens. *Museu de Calouste Gulbenkian. Admission: 50$00. Open Tues., Thurs., Fri., and Sun. 10–5; Wed. and Sat. 2–7:30.*

The complex also houses two concert halls where music and ballet festivals are held during the winter and spring. Modestly priced tickets at the box office (tel. 01/774167) are available thanks to subsidies from the Gulbenkian Foundation.

Bairro Alto
9

Lisbon's **Bairro Alto** (High District) is largely made up of 18th- and 19th-century buildings which house an intriguing mixture of restaurants, theaters, nightclubs, churches, bars, and antique shops. The best way to start a tour of this area is via the **Elevador da Gloria** (funicular railway), located on Avenida da Liberdade a few hundred yards from Praça dos Restauradores. The trip takes about a minute and drops passengers at the São Pedro de Alcāntara miradouro, a viewpoint which looks toward the castle and the Alfama (Cost: 22$50. Open 5 AM–midnight).

10

Across the street from the miradouro is the **Instituto do Vinho do Porto** (Port Wine Institute), where, in its cozy, clublike lounge, visitors can sample from more than 100 brands of Portugal's most famous beverage—from the extra-dry white varieties to the older, ruby-red vintages. *Rua S. Pedro de*

Alcântara 45, tel. 01/323307. Admission: free. Prices of tastings vary. Open Mon.–Sat. 9–6.

From the institute, turn right and walk down Rua da Misericórdia. On your left is the Largo Trinidade Coelho, site of the **⑪** highly decorative **Igreja de São Roque** (Church of São Roque). The church (open daily 8:30–6) is best known for the flamboyant 15th-century **Capel de São João Baptista** (Chapel of St. John the Baptist), but it is nonetheless a showpiece in its own right. The precious stones which adorn its walls were imported from Italy. Adjoining the church is the **Museu de Arte Sacra** (Museum of Sacred Art). *Admission: 25$00. Open Tues.–Sun. 10–5.*

Continue south down Rua da Misericórdia until you reach the **⑫** **Largo do Chiado** on your left. The Chiado, once Lisbon's chic shopping district, was badly damaged by a fire in August 1988, but it still houses some of the city's most fashionable department stores.

Time Out The Chiado's wood-paneled coffee shops attract tourists and local bohemian-types alike; the most popular of these is the **Brasileira,** which features a life-size statue of Fernando Pessoa, Portugal's national poet, at one of the sidewalk tables. *Rua Garrett 120, tel. 01/369541. Closed Sun. Inexpensive.*

North of the Chiado, on the Largo do Carmo, lies the partially **⑬** ruined **Ingreja de Carmo** (Carmo Church), one of the few older structures in the area to have survived the 1755 earthquake. Today, open-air orchestral concerts are held beneath its majestic archways during the summer, and its sacristy houses an **archaeological museum.** *Museu Arqueologico. Largo do Carmo. Admission: 150$00. Open Mon.–Sat. 10–1 and 2–5.*

Return directly to the Praça dos Restauradores via the nearby **⑭** **Ascensor de Santa Justa** (the Santa Justa elevator), which is enclosed in a Gothic tower created by Raul Mesnier, the Portuguese protégé of Gustave Eiffel. (Cost: 22$50. Open 5 AM–midnight.)

An alternative, though somewhat macabre, route can be taken through the fire ruins. A temporary covered walkway has been built through parts of Rua Garrett and Rua do Carmo, and here visitors can see the disastrous effects of the 1988 fire on what was once the heart of sophisticated Lisbon.

Belém *Numbers in the margin correspond with points of interest on the Belém map.*

To see the best examples of that uniquely Portuguese, late-Gothic architecture known as Manueline, head for Belém at the far southwestern edge of Lisbon. If traveling in a group of three or four, taxis are the cheapest means of transportation; otherwise, take a no. 15, 16, or 77 tram from the Praça do Comércio for a more scenic, if bumpier, journey.

⑮ Trams nos. 15 and 16 stop directly outside the **Mosteiro dos Jerónimos,** Belém's Hieronymite monastery, located in the Praça do Império. This impressive structure was conceived and planned by King Manuel I at the beginning of the 16th century to honor the discoveries of Portugal's great explorers such as Vasco da Gama, who is buried here. Construction of the monastery began in 1502, largely financed by treasures brought back from the so-called *descobrimentos*—the "discoveries" made by

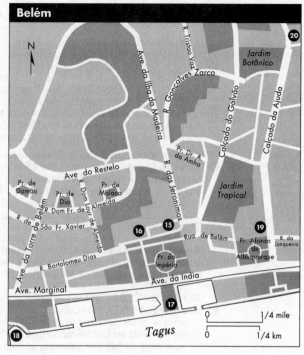

Belém

the Portuguese in Africa, Asia, and South America. Don't miss the stunning double cloister with its arches and pillars heavily sculpted with marine motifs. *Admission: 150$00. Open Oct.–Apr., daily 10–5; May.–Sept., daily 10–6:30.*

16 The **Museu de Marinha** (Maritime Museum) is partially located in the monastery, with one modern wing stretching across a small square. Its huge collection reflects Portugal's long seafaring tradition, and exhibitions range from early maps and navigational instruments to entire ships, including the sleek caravels that took Portuguese explorers and traders around the globe. *Admission: 150$00, free Wed. Open Tues.–Sun. 10–5.*

Time Out There are a number of small shops and cafés close to the monastery on Rua de Belém. Stop for coffee at the **Fabrica dos Pasteis de Belém** (the Belém Pastry Factory) to sample the delicious custard pastries served hot with cinammon and powdered sugar.

Across from the monastery at the water's edge stands the **17** **Monumento dos Descobrimentos** (Monument to the Discoveries). Built in 1960, this modern tribute to the seafaring explorers stands on what was the departure point of many of their voyages. An interesting mosaic lies at the foot of the monument, surrounded by an intricate wave pattern composed of black and white cobblestones. *Admission: 150$00. Open Tues.–Sun. 10–5.*

⑱ A 15-minute walk west of the monument brings you to the **Torre de Belém** (the Belém Tower), another fine example of Manueline architecture with openwork balconies, loggia, and domed turrets. Although it was built in the 16th century on an island in the middle of the river Tagus, today the tower stands near the north bank—the river's course has changed over the centuries. *Torre de Belém. Ave. de India. Admission: 150$00. Open Tues.–Sun., 10–6:30.*

⑲ Away from the Tagus and southeast of the monastery, on the Praça Afonso de Albuquerque, is the **Museu Nacional do Coches** (National Coach Museum), which houses one of the largest collections of coaches in the world. The oldest vehicle on display was made for Philip II of Spain in the late 16th century, but the most stunning exhibits are three golden Baroque coaches, created in Rome for King John V in 1716. *Admission: 250$00. Open daily 10–1 and 2:30–5:30.*

⑳ Head north of the coach museum on Calçada da Ajuda to the **Palácio da Ajuda** (Ajuda Palace). Once a royal residence, this pink-walled building now contains a collection of 18th-century paintings, furniture, and tapestries. *Admission: 150$00. Guided tours arranged on request. Open Tues.–Sun. 10–5.*

Off the Beaten Track

North of the city in the suburb of São Domingos de Benfica is one of the most beautiful private houses in the capital. The **Palácio da Fronteira** was built in the late 17th century and contains splendid reception rooms with 18th-century figurative tiles, contemporary furniture, and paintings, but it is the gardens that are unique. A long rectangular water tank is backed by 17th-century tiled panels of heroic-size knights on prancing horses. Stone steps at either side lead to a terraced walk above, between pyramid pavilions roofed with copper-colored tiles. Surrounding this beautiful conceit is a topiary garden, statuary, fountains, and terraces. *Admission: 1,000$00. Open Sat. 1–5; Mon. 10–12 and 2:30–5; first Sunday of every month 2:30–5.*

Portuguese **bullfighting** is a treat on a summer evening—particularly since the bull is not killed but wrestled to the ground by a group of *forcados* in their traditional red-and-green costumes. The bull, its horns padded, is also fought from horseback in what is a first-class display of the remarkable Portuguese riding skills. The ornate Campo Pequeno (Avenida da República) hosts weekly bullfights from Easter to September, on Sunday afternoons and Thursday evenings. Prices range from 1,500$00 to 6,000$00 for the best seats.

Shopping

Gift Ideas
Leather Goods
Fine leather handbags and luggage are sold at **Galeão**, Rua Augusto 190, and at **Casa Canada**, 232 Rua Augusto. Shoe stores abound in Lisbon, but they may have a limited selection of large sizes (the Portuguese have relatively small feet); however, the better shops can make shoes to measure on short notice. Leather gloves can be purchased at a variety of specialty shops on Rua do Carmo and Rua do Ouro.

Handicrafts **Vivuva Lamego,** Largo do Intendente 25, has the largest selection of tiles and pottery, while **Fabrica Sant'Anna,** Rua do Alecrim 95, Chiado, sells wonderful handpainted ceramics and tiles based on antique patterns. For embroidered goods and baskets, try **Casa Regional da Ilha Verde,** Rua Paiva de Andrade 4, or **Tito Cunha** at Rua do Ouro, 179 and 246. **Casa Quintão,** Rua Ivens 30, probably has the largest selection of *arraiolos* rugs, the traditional, hand-woven Portuguese rugs, in town. For fine porcelain, visit **Vista Alegre** in the Largo do Chiado.

Jewelry and **Antonio da Silva,** Praça Luis de Camoes 40, at the top of the
Antiques Chiado, specializes in antique silver jewelry. The best costume jewelry in the city can be found at **Casa Batalha,** Rua Nova de Almada 75, at the bottom of the Chiado. Most of the antique shops are along the Rua Escola Politecnica, the Rua de São Bento, and the Rua de Santa Marta.

Look for characteristic Portuguese gold- and silver-filigree work at **Sarmento,** Rua do Ouro 251.

Shopping Districts Fire destroyed much of Lisbon's chicest shopping street in 1988, and it will be years before this part of the **Chiado,** as it is called, will reopen. Another important shopping area is in the **Baixa** quarter between the Rossio and the Tagus River. The blue-and-pink towers of the **Amoreiras,** a huge modern shopping center located on Avenida Gugenheiro Duarte Paceco, dominate the Lisbon skyline.

Flea Markets A **Feira da Ladra** (flea market) is held on Tuesday and Saturday in the Largo de Santa Clara behind the Church of São Vicente, near the Alfama district.

Dining

For details and price category definitions, *see* Dining in Staying in Portugal.

Expensive **António Clara.** Housed in an attractive Art Nouveau building, this restaurant serves French and international dishes with a flourish in an elegant room with a decorated ceiling, heavy draperies, and huge chandelier. *Ave. República 38, tel. 01/ 766380. Reservations advised. AE, DC, MC, V. Closed Sun.*

★ **Aviz.** One of the best and classiest restaurants in Lisbon, Aviz has a Belle Époque decor—even the rest rooms are impressive—and an excellent French and international menu. *Serpa Pinto 12, tel. 01/328991. Reservations required. AE, DC, MC, V. Closed Sat. lunch and Sun.*

Casa da Comida. Imaginative French and Portuguese fare is served in a former private house surrounding a flower-filled patio. *Travessa das Amoreiras 1, tel. 01/685376. Reservations advised. AE, DC, MC, V. Closed Sat. lunch and Sun.*

Gambrinus. One of Lisbon's older restaurants, Gambrinus is noted for its fish and shellfish. Entered through an inconspicuous door on a busy street, the restaurant has numerous small dining rooms. *Rua Portas S. Antão 23, tel. 01/321466. Reservations advised. AE, DC, MC, V.*

Michel's. Innovative French cooking is served in an intimate atmosphere in this attractive restaurant just inside the walls of St. George's Castle. *Largo S. Cruz do Castelo 5, tel. 01/867763. AE, DC, MC, V. Closed Sat. lunch, Sun.*

O Terraco. On the top of the Tivoli hotel, The Terrace offers a panoramic view of Lisbon. The food is excellent, especially from the grill, and the service is quietly attentive. *Ave. da Liberdade 185, tel. 01/530181. AE, DC, MC, V.*

★ **Tavares.** Superb food, an excellent wine list, and a handsome Edwardian dining room have made this one of Lisbon's most famous restaurants. *Rua Misericórdia 35, tel. 01/321112. Reservations advised. AE, DC, MC, V. Closed Sat. and Sun. lunch.*

Moderate **Comida de Santo.** The Brazilian-style food is excellent, and is served in an attractive, bohemian atmosphere. Lively Brazilian music ensures that this restaurant is packed during later hours. *Rua Engenheiro Miguel Pais 39, tel. 01/663339. Reservations not necessary. AE, DC, MC, V. Closed Mon.*

Forno da Brites. The food is practical, the red and white decor is cheery, and the staff is helpful to tourists. *Rua Tomas Ribeiro 73, tel. 01/542724. No credit cards.*

O Paco. Good steaks, regional food, and folkloric decor attract a literary crowd to this restaurant opposite the Gulbenkian Foundation. *Ave. Berna 44, tel. 01/770642. AE, DC, MC, V. Closed Mon.*

Pap' Acorda. This very popular restaurant in the Bairro Alto is housed in a converted bakery. It offers good food and service in a pleasant garden atmosphere. *Rua da Atalaia 57, tel. 01/364811. Reservations advised. AE, DC, MC, V. Closed Sun.*

Petit Folie. French and Portuguese dishes are the specialties at this pleasant restaurant near Parque Eduardo VII. *Ave. António Augusto Aguiar 74, tel. 01/521948. AE, DC, MC, V.*

Solmar. This restaurant near the Rossio, Lisbon's main square, is best known for its seafood and shellfish, but try the wild boar or venison in season. *Rua Portas de S. Antão 106, tel. 01/323371. AE, DC, MC, V.*

Inexpensive **A Quinta.** A menu of Portuguese, Russian, and Hungarian dishes is available at this country-style restaurant overlooking the Baixa and the Tagus from next to the top of the Santa Justa elevator. *Carmo Sq., tel. 01/265588. AE, DC, MC, V. Closed Sat. and Sun. dinner.*

Bonjardim. Known locally as *Rei dos Frango* (the King of Chickens), the Bonjardim specializes in the spit-roasted variety. Just off the Restauradores, it gets very crowded at peak hours. *Travesssa S. Antão 11, tel. 01/324389. AE, DC, MC, V.*

Cervejaria Trindade. You get good value for your money at this large restaurant which has a garden and a cave-style wine cellar. *Rua Nova da Trindade 20, tel. 01/323506. AE, DC, MC, V.*

Frascati. An attractive, Italian family restaurant near Parque Eduardo VII. The service here is friendly and efficient. The pizzas, flat and rolled up, are especially good. *Rua Padre António Vieira 12, tel. 01/682282. Closed Sat. eve. and Sun.*

Lodging

Lisbon has a good array of hotels in all price categories, from major international chain hotels to charming little family-run establishments. During peak season, however, reservations should be made well in advance. For details and price category definitions, *see* Lodging in Staying in Portugal.

Very Expensive **Meridian Lisboa.** The rooms in Lisbon's newest luxury hotel are a bit on the small side, but they are soundproofed and attractively decorated; the front ones overlook the park. *Rua Castilho 149, tel. 01/690900. 331 rooms with bath. Facilities: health club with sauna, shops, garage. AE, DC, MC, V.*

★ **Ritz Lisboa.** One of the finest hotels in Europe, this Intercontinental is renowned for its excellent service. The large, handsomely decorated guest rooms all have terraces, and the elegantly appointed public rooms feature tapestries, antique reproductions, and fine paintings. The best rooms are in the front overlooking Parque Eduardo VII. *Rua Rodrigo da Fonseca 88, tel. 01/692020. 304 rooms with bath. Facilities: shops, garage. AE, DC, MC, V.*

Expensive   **Lisboa Sheraton.** This is a typical Sheraton hotel with a huge reception area and medium-size rooms. The deluxe rooms in the Towers section, which has a separate reception desk in the lobby and a private lounge, are about the same size but are more luxuriously appointed. The hotel is centrally located and is just across the street from a large shopping center. *Rua Latino Coelho 1, tel. 01/575757. 388 rooms with bath. AE, DC, MC, V. Facilities: outdoor pool, health club and sauna. AE, DC, MC, V.*

★ **Tivoli Lisboa.** Located on a main thoroughfare, this comfortable, well-run establishment has a large public area furnished with inviting armchairs and sofas. The guest rooms are all pleasant, but the ones in the rear are quieter. There's also a good restaurant, and the grill on the top floor has wonderful views of the city and the Tagus. *Ave. da Liberdade 185, tel. 013/ 530181. 344 rooms with bath. Facilities: outdoor pool, tennis courts, shops, garage. AE, DC, MC, V.*

Moderate   **Florida.** This centrally located hotel has a pleasant atmosphere and is popular with Americans. *Rua Duque de Palmela 32, tel. 01/576245. 112 rooms with bath. AE, DC, MC, V.*

Lisboa Penta. The city's largest hotel, the Penta is located about midway between the airport and the city center, next to the U.S. Embassy and close to the Gulbenkian Foundation (shuttle-bus service to the center of the city is available). The rooms are rather small, but each one has a terrace. *Ave. dos Combatantes, tel. 01/7264054. 592 rooms with bath. Facilities: outdoor pool, health club and solarium, squash courts, shops, garage. AE, DC, MC, V.*

★ **Novotel Lisboa.** There's an attentive staff and a quiet, welcoming atmosphere at this pleasant, modern hotel near the U.S. Embassy. The public rooms are spacious and the guest rooms attractive. *Ave. Jose Malhoa, tel. 01/7266022. 246 rooms with bath. Facilities: pool, garage. AE, MC, V.*

York House. A former convent, this pension is set in a shady garden, up a long flight of steps, near the **Museu de Arte Contemporânea** (Museum of Ancient Art). It has a good restaurant, and full or half board is available. Book well in advance: This atmospheric place is small and has a loyal following. *Rua das Janelas Verdes 32, tel. 01/662544. 59 rooms with bath. AE, DC, MC, V.*

Inexpensive   **Eduardo VII.** An elegant old hotel, the Eduardo is well situated
★ in the center of the city. The best rooms are in the front overlooking Parque Eduardo VII, but the ones in the rear are quieter. The top-floor restaurant has a marvelous view of the city and the Tagus. *Ave. Fontes Pereira de Melo 5, tel. 01/ 530141. 110 rooms with bath. AE, DC, MC, V.*

Fenix. Located at the top of Avenida da Liberdade, this hotel has largish guest rooms and a pleasant first-floor lounge. Its restaurant serves good Portuguese food. *Praça Marques de Pombal 8, tel. 01/535121. 113 rooms with bath. AE, DC, MC, V.*

Flamingo. Another good value near the top of the Avenida da Liberdade, this hotel has a friendly staff and pleasant guest rooms, though the ones in the front tend to be noisy. There's a pay parking lot right next door, which is a bonus in this busy area. *Rua Castilho 41, tel. 01/532191. 39 rooms with bath. AE, DC, MC, V.*

★ **Senhora do Monte.** The rooms in this unpretentious little hotel, located in the oldest part of town near St. George's Castle, have terraces that offer some of the loveliest views of Lisbon, especially at night when the castle and Carmo ruins in the middle distance are softly illuminated. The top-floor grill has a picture window. The surrounding neighborhood is quiet, and parking is available. *Calçada do Monte 39, tel. 01/862846. 27 rooms with bath. AE, DC, MC, V.*

The Arts

Two local supplements provide listings of music, theater, ballet, film, and other entertainment in Lisbon: *Sete*, published on Wednesdays, and *Sabado*, published Fridays.

Plays are performed in Portuguese at the **Teatro Nacional de D. Maria II** (Praça Dom Pedro IV, tel. 01/372246) year-round except in July, and there are revues at small theaters in the Parque Mayer. Classical music, opera, and ballet are presented in the beautiful **Teatro Nacional de Opera de São Carlos** (Rua Serpa Pinto 9, tel. 01/327172). The season runs from mid-December to May. Classical music and ballet seasons are also staged from autumn to summer by the **Fundação Calouste Gulbenkian** (Ave. Berna 45, tel. 01/774167). Of particular interest is the annual Early Music and Baroque Festival held in churches and museums around Lisbon every spring; for details contact the Gulbenkian Foundation. The **Nova Filarmonica,** a recently established national orchestra, performs concerts around the country throughout the year; consult local papers for details.

Nightlife

The most popular night spots in Lisbon are the **adegas tipicas** (wine cellars), where customers dine on Portuguese specialties, drink wine, and listen to *fado*, those haunting songs unique to Portugal. Most of these establishments are scattered throughout the Alfama and Bairro Alto districts. Try the **Senhor Vinho,** Rua Meio a Lapa 18, tel. 01/672681 (closed Sun.), **Lisboa à Noite,** Rua das Gaveas 69, tel. 01/368557 (closed Sun.); **Machado,** Rua do Norte 91, tel. 01/360095 (closed Mon.) The singing starts at 10 PM, and reservations are advised.

Discos New discos open and close with frequency in Lisbon, and many have high cover charges. Among the more respectable ones are **Ad Lib,** Rua Barata Salgueiro 28–7, tel. 01/561717; **Banana Power,** Rua Cascais 51, tel. 01/631815; **Stones,** Rua do Olival 1, tel. 01/664545; **Plateau,** Escadinas da Praia 3, tel. 01/665116; and **Alcantara-Mar,** Rua da Cozinha Económica 11, tel. 01/636432.

The Portuguese Riviera

Just 32 kilometers (20 miles) west of Lisbon lies a stretch of coastline known as the Portuguese Riviera. Over the years, the fashionable beaches and casinos of Cascais and Estoril have provided playgrounds for the wealthy as well as homes for expatriates and exiled crown heads of Europe. Both towns form one side of an irregular quadrangle on a day tour which also takes in the lush, green mountains of Sintra and the historic town of Queluz, dominated by its 18th-century Rococo palace and formal gardens. Whether you stick to the coast or head for the mountains, the entire area is heavily populated, with highly varied scenery and attractions.

The villas, chateaus, and luxury *quintas* (small holdings) of Sintra contrast notably with Cascais and Estoril, where life revolves around the sea. Beaches here differ both in quality and cleanliness. Some display the blue Council of Europe flag, which signals a high standard of unpolluted water and sands, but others leave much to be desired—be guided by your nose. The waters off Cascais and Estoril are calmer, but show the polluted results of being near the meeting of the sea and Lisbon's Tagus estuary. To the north, around Guincho's rocky promontory and the Praia de Maças coast, the ocean is often windswept and rough, but provides good surfing, windsurfing, and scuba diving. The entire region offers comprehensive sports facilities: golf courses, horseback riding, fishing, tennis, squash, swimming, water sports, grand prix racing, mountain climbing, and country walking.

Getting Around

The area is served by two main roads—the winding and often congested four-lane coastal road, the Marginal, and the N117–N24. A commuter train leaves regularly from Cais do Sodré Station in Lisbon for the 45-minute trip to Cascais. The line affords splendid sea views as it hugs the seashore.

Guided Tours

Cater Incoming Portugal (Largo da Academia Nacional de Belas Artes 12, 1200 Lisbon, tel. 01/368916) offers a seven-hour excursion which takes in principal sites; it costs 6,900$00 and includes lunch. **Citirama Viagens e Turismo SA** (Ave. Praia de Vitoria 12-B, tel. 01/575564) offers a similar tour at the same price. Both tours have daily departures.

Tourist Information

Cascais. Ave. Marginal, tel. 01/2868204.
Estoril. Arcadas de Parque, tel. 01/2680113 or 01/2687044.
Queluz. Praça do Restauradores, Lisbon, 01/363624.
Sintra. Casa de Republica 3, tel. 01/9231157 or 01/9233919.

Exploring the Portuguese Riviera

Leave Lisbon by car via the Marginal highway (following signs for Cascais/Estoril) and take the curving coastal route to Estoril. Both Estoril and Cascais are favored residential areas;

The Portuguese Riviera

ATLANTIC OCEAN

São Pedro de Sintra

Monserrate

Penedo

Sintra

Capuchin Monastery

Castelo dos Mouros

Palácio Nacional de Pena

Cabo da Roca

N375

N249

N117

SERRA DE SINTRA

Queluz

Oeiras

Barcarena

Barcarena

Guincho

N247

Marginal

Estoril

Cascais

Boca de Inferno

Oeiras

Tagus

N

0   50 miles
0   75 km

thanks to their special microclimate, they boast milder winters than does nearby Lisbon.

Estoril is filled with grand homes and gardens, and many of its large mansions date from the last century when the resort was a favorite with the European aristocracy. Portugal's jet-set resort is expensive, with little in the way of sights. People-watching is always a satisfying pastime, and one of the best places for it is on the **Tamariz esplanade,** especially from an alfresco restaurant. A palm-studded coastline, plush accommodations, sports facilities, and restaurants are among Estoril's other attractions, but it is perhaps best known for its **casino,** an excellent gambling hall and night spot which includes a restaurant, bar, cinema, and art gallery. A major handicrafts and ceramics fair is held each summer (July–September), and many of the Costa do Sol summer music festival concerts are staged here (a schedule is available at the tourist office).

Time Out The luxurious **Hotel Palácio** is worth a visit simply to take tea in one of its ample salons. During World War II, it was an espionage center where the Germans and Allies kept watch on each other in neutral Portugal, and where exiled European courts waited out the war. *Parque do Estoril.*

Cascais lies less than 3.2 kilometers (2 miles) west of Estoril. A pretty but heavily developed tourist resort, it is packed with shopping centers, restaurants, cinemas, and hotels. Its beach is small and crowded, and in summer, parking is a real headache. Even so, there are still some sights worth seeing, including the **Igreja de Nossa Senhora da Assunção** (Church of Our Lady of the Assumption), which contains paintings by Portuguese artist Josefa de Obidos. *Largo de Igreja. Admission: free. Open during evening masses.*

Out of the town center in the direction of Guincho beach lies the notorious **Boca de Inferno,** or Hell's Mouth. This rugged section of coastline is made up of numerous grottoes; visitors are able to see the full impact of the sea as it pounds into the walkways and viewing platforms. A path leads down to a secluded beach.

Not far from the grottoes is the **Museu Conde de Castro Guimaraes,** (Museum of the Count of Castro Guimaraes), a large, stately home set in vast grounds on the road to Guincho. It houses some good paintings, ceramics, furniture, and other items. *Estrada de Boca de Inferno. Admission: 150$00. Open Tues.–Sun. 11–12:30 and 2–5.*

The **Parque do Marachel Carmona,** which contains a lake and a modest zoo, can be found in the same area. It is located alongside the Cascais football stadium, where a jazz festival takes place every summer. *Open Tues.–Sun. 11–12:30 and 2–5.*

Towering above central Cascais is a large pink tourist complex called the **Parque do Gandarinha** (Gandarinha Park). Inside, you'll find the new **Museu do Mar** (Museum of the Sea), which opened in 1988. *Park open daily 9-7, closed Mon. morning.*

From Cascais, take the scenic drive along the Guincho coast road toward **Sintra,** a fairy-tale region with centuries-old ties to a host of eccentric and famous Englishmen, among them the poet Lord Byron. Pass the rocky surfing beach at Guincho and follow the curving cliffs until you come to **Cabo da Roca** (Cape of the Rocks). Stop here at the lighthouse for a look at continental Europe's westernmost landfall.

Back on the Marginal, turn into the hills on N375. This is the beginning of the **Serra de Sintra** (Sintra Mountains), and here, at **Capuchos,** you can visit the **Convento Santa Cruz,** built in 1560 by Franciscan monks. The 12 diminutive cells, hacked out of solid rock, are lined with cork for warmth and insulation—hence the nickname the "Cork Convent." *Admission: free. Open Tues.–Sun. 10–12:30 and 2:30–5.*

Return to the main road and follow its winding course through the village of **Penedo,** which offers terrific views of the sea and the surrounding mountains, until you reach the world-renowned gardens of **Monserrate,** 5½ kilometers (3 miles) from **Seteais.** This botanical wonderland was laid out by Scottish gardeners in the mid-1800s, and is the site of an exotic and architecturally extravagant domed Moorish palace (closed to visitors). In addition to a dazzling array of tree and plant species, the gardens house one ⌐f the largest collections of fern varieties in the world. *Admission: free. Open daily 9–6.*

Time Out Follow the signs to Seteais and stop for a meal at the **Palácio de Seteais** (Seteais Palace), built by Dutchmen in the 18th century. Now a luxury hotel (*see* Dining and Lodging), the Seteais has an excellent restaurant, and its stately rooms are decorated with vast, delicate wall and roof frescoes. *Rua Barbosa do Bocage 8, tel. 01/9233200. AE, DC, MC, V. Expensive.*

From here, the main road gently winds down toward **Sintra,** where Portuguese kings and aristocrats formerly had their summer residences. One of Portugal's oldest towns, Sintra is full of art, history, and architecture. At the center of the **Old Town** near the Hotel Tivoli stands the 14th-century **Palácio Nacional de Sintra** (Sintra Palace). This twin-chimneyed building, a combination of Moorish and Gothic architectural styles, was once the summer residence of the House of Avis, Portugal's royal lineage. Today it's a museum that houses some fine examples of mozarabic *azulejos* (handpainted tiles). *Admission: 150$00. Open Mon., Tue., and Thurs.–Sun. 10–12:30 and 2:30–5.*

If you stand on the steps of the palace and look up toward the Sintra Mountains, you can spot the 8th-century ruins of the **Castelo dos Mouros** (Moors' Castle), which defied hundreds of invaders until it was finally conquered by Dom Afonso Henriques in 1147. For a closer look, follow the steep, partially cobbled road that leads up to the ruins; or, if you're a romantic, rent one of the horse and carriages outside the palace for the trip. From the castle's serrated walls, you can see why its Moorish architects chose the site: the panoramic views falling away on all sides are breathtaking. *Estrada da Pena*, tel. 01/9230137. Admission: 50$00. Open daily 10–5.

Farther up the same road you'll reach the **Palácio Nacional de Pena** (the Pena Palace), a Wagnerian-style extravaganza built by the reputedly mad Ferdinand Saxe-Coburg in 1840. It is a cauldron of clashing styles, from Arabian to Victorian, and was home to the final kings of Portugal, the last of whom went into exile in 1910 after a republican revolt. The nucleus of the palace is a convent commissioned by Dom Fernando I, consort to Queen Dona Maria II. The palace is surrounded by a splendid park filled with a lush variety of trees and flowers brought from every corner of the Portuguese empire by Dom Fernando II in the 1840s. *Admission (for guided tour): 200$00. Open Tues.–Sun. 10–12:30 and 2:30–5.*

Back in downtown Sintra, the **Museu do Brinquedo** (Toy Museum) houses an enjoyable collection of dolls and traditional toys from this region of Portugal. *Largo Latino Coelho 9, tel. 01/9232875, ext. 280. Admission: 150$00. Open Tues.–Sun. 10–12:30 and 2:30–5.*

If you're in the area on the second or fourth Sunday of each month, visit the **Feira de Sintra** (Sintra Fair) in the nearby village of **São Pedro de Sintra.** This is one of the best known fairs in the country.

From the fairgrounds, drive on to the traffic circle (there's a gas station in the middle of it) and take N117 back toward Lisbon, keeping an eye out for the left turnoff to **Queluz.** As soon as you swing off the main road, you'll be confronted by the magnificent **Palácio Nacional de Queluz** (Queluz Palace). Partially inspired by Versailles, this salmon-pink Rococo palace was begun by Dom Pedro III in 1747 and took 40 years to complete. The formal landscaping and waterways which surround it are the work of the French designer Jean-Baptiste Robillon. Restored after a disastrous fire in 1934, the palace is used today for formal banquets, music festivals, and as accommodations for visiting heads of state. In summer, a month-long medieval festival, the **Noites de Queluz** (Queluz Nights), is staged in the gardens, complete with costumed cast and orchestra. Visitors may walk through the impressive state rooms, including the Music Salon, the Hall of the Ambassadors, and the mirrored Throne Room with its crystal chandeliers and gilt trimmings. The 14-kilometer (8½-mile) drive back to Lisbon takes about 15 minutes. *Admission: 200$00. Open Mon. and Wed.–Sun. 10–12:30 and 2:30–5.*

Dining and Lodging

For details and price category definitions, *see* Dining and Lodging in Staying in Portugal.

Cascais **Restaurante Baluarte.** This restaurant offers good regional
Dining food, a pleasant atmosphere, and panoramic views over the coast. *Ave. Dom Carlos I, tel. 01/2865471. Reservations advised. AE, DC, MC, V. Closed Mon. Expensive.*

Restaurante/Estralagem Muchaxo. The sound of the sea accompanies your meal at this restaurant nestled on the rocks overlooking Guincho beach. It is one of Cascais's oldest and best-known eating places, and the Portuguese and fish specialties here are beautifully cooked and presented. There are also 24 rooms available for guests. *Praia do Guincho, tel. 01/2850342. Reservations advised. AE, DC, MC, V. Moderate (inn), Expensive (restaurant).*

Lodging **Hotel Albatroz.** Situated on a rocky outcrop, this attractive old house is the most luxurious of Cascais's hotels, converted from an aristocrat's summer residence. Though it's been extended and modernized, it has retained its character, with charming bedrooms and a pleasant terrace bar. The restaurant boasts superior views of the sea and over the coast toward Lisbon; it specializes in fish dishes. *Rua Frederico Arouca 100, tel. 01/282821. 40 rooms with bath. Facilities: bar, restaurant, pool, garage. Restaurant reservations essential. AE, DC, MC, V. Expensive.*

Estoril **A Choupana.** Just outside of town, toward Lisbon, this restau-
Dining rant overlooks the beach. You can sample high-quality fresh fish, seafood, and other local dishes and dance to a live band until 2 AM. *Estrada Marginal, São João de Estoril, tel. 01/2683099. Reservations advised. AE, DC, MC, V. Closed Mon. Expensive.*
Restaurante Furusato. Customers come here for good-quality Japanese food, a pleasant atmosphere, and attentive service on the Estoril beachfront. *Praia do Tamariz, tel. 01/2683512 or 2683677. Reservations advised. AE, DC, MC, V. Closed Mon. Expensive.*
The English Bar. This mock-Tudor-style establishment serves good Portuguese cuisine in friendly, comfortable surroundings. There are good views over the beach to Cascais. *Ave. Saboia 9, Monte Estoril, tel. 01/2681254. Reservations advised. AE, DC, MC, V. Closed Sun. Moderate.*
Restaurante Frolic. The Frolic is a friendly restaurant/bar which also features nightly dancing. *Arcadas do Parque, tel. 01/2681219. No credit cards. Closed Sun. Inexpensive.*

Lodging **Hotel Estoril Eden.** This is a comfortable, modest hotel with tastefully decorated rooms and superb views over the sweeping Estoril coast. It is one minute off the beach via an underpass. *Ave. Saboia, tel. 01/2670958. 62 rooms with bath and cooking* *facilities. Facilities: pool, gym, restaurant. AE, DC, MC, V. Expensive.*

Hotel Palácio. During World War II, exiled European courts came to wait out the war at this luxurious hotel. The pastel rooms are decorated in Regency style. It contains one of Portugal's most famous restaurants, the elegant Restaurant Grill Four Seasons, which serves buffets around the garden pool in summer. It's a two-minute walk from the beach and golfers can tee off using the hotel's membership in the Estoril golf course. *Parque do Estoril, tel. 01/2680400. 200 rooms with bath. Facilities: outdoor pool, restaurant. Restaurant reservations advised. AE, DC, MC, V. Expensive.*

Sintra
Dining

Tacho Real. The Tacho Real serves high-quality local and international food in a luxurious setting. *Rua do Ferraria 4, tel. 01/9235277. Reservations advised. AE, DC, MC, V. Closed Wed. Expensive.*

Solar São Pedro. Highly recommended by its habitués, this restaurant specializes in French cooking. Its English-speaking host adds to the warm and friendly atmosphere. *Praça Dom Fernando II, tel. 01/9231860. Reservations advised. AE, DC, MC, V. Closed Wed. Moderate.*

Lodging

Palácio de Seteais. This luxurious former palace (*see* Exploring) houses a splendid restaurant. *Rua Barbosa do Bocage 8, tel. 01/9233200. 18 rooms with bath. Facilities: restaurant. AE, DC, MC, V. Expensive.*

Tivoli Sintra. The Tivoli has excellent views over the valleys and has its own welcoming restaurant, the Monserrate. *Praça da República, tel. 01/9233505. 75 rooms with bath. Facilities: restaurant. AE, DC, MC, V. Expensive.*

Queluz
Dining

Restaurante de Cozinha Velha. This restaurant was formerly the great kitchens of the adjoining Queluz Palace, and is magnificently decorated with an open fireplace which dominates the room. There are some fine wines in the cellar to go with the traditional Portuguese cooking. *Palácio Nacional de Queluz, tel. 01/4350232. Reservations advised. AE, DC, MC, V. Expensive.*

The Algarve

The Algarve, Portugal's southernmost holiday resort, encompasses some 240 kilometers (150 miles) of sun-drenched coast below the Monchique Mountains and the Caldeirão Hills. It is the top destination for foreign visitors to Portugal. During the past two decades, this area, indelibly marked by centuries of Arab occupation, has been heavily developed in an effort to create a playground for international sun worshipers. Well-known by Europeans as a holiday center of clean, sandy beaches, championship golf courses, and local color, this most southerly section of Portugal is only now being discovered by Americans. Although some parts of the coastline have been seriously overbuilt, there are still plenty of picturesque fishing villages and secluded beaches to leaven the concentration of hotels, casinos, disco nightclubs, and sports facilities.

This itinerary takes you to some of the most interesting and typical towns and villages in the Algarve, starting near the Portuguese border with Spain in the east and ending at the most southwesterly point of the European continent.

Getting Around

Faro, the capital of the Algarve, is only 45 minutes from Lisbon by air. **TAP Air Portugal** has daily service from Lisbon, and there are frequent international flights to Faro from London, Frankfurt, and Brussels. There is also daily bus and rail service between Lisbon and several towns in the Algarve. The drive from Lisbon to Faro or Portimão takes about 5 to 5½ hours.

The main east-west highway in the Algarve is the two-lane N125, which extends 165 kilometers (100 miles) from Vila Real de Santo António, on the Spanish border, to a point above Cabo de São Vicente. This road does not run right along the coast, but turnoffs to beachside destinations mentioned here are posted along the route. Local rail and bus services link most of the villages and towns in the Algarve, and organized guided bus tours of some of the more noteworthy villages and towns depart from Faro, Quarteira, Vilamoura, and Albufeira.

Tourist Information

Albufeira. Rua 5 de Outubro, tel. 089/52144 or /55428.
Armação de Pêrá. Ave. Marginal, tel. 082/32145.
Faro. Airport, tel. /22582; Rua da Misericorida 8/12, tel. 089/25404; Rua Afaide de Oliveira 100, tel. 089/24067.
Lagos. Largo Marquês de Pombal, tel. 082/63031.
Loulé. Edifico do Castelo, tel. 089/03900.
Olhão. Largo da Lagoa, tel. 089/73936.
Portimão. Largo 1° de Dezembro, tel. 082/22065 or 23695.
Praia da Rocha. Ave. Tomás Cabreira, tel. 082/22290.
Quarteira. Ave. Infante de Sagres, tel. 082/32217.
Sagres. Promontory, tel. 082/64125.
Silves. Rua 25 de Abril, tel. 082/42255.
Tavira. Praça da República, tel. 081/22511.
Vila Real de Santo António. Praça Marquês de Pombal, tel. 081/44495; Frontier Tourist Post, tel. 081/43272.

Exploring the Algarve

To reach the Algarve from Lisbon, cross the 25 Abril bridge and take the A2 toll road to Setúbal. Turn off at the signs for Alcácer-do-Sal, and Grandola Ourique, reaching the coast near Albufeira. The road has recently been improved and is the fastest route to the Algarve; the trip takes about 3½ hours.

Visitors coming to the Algarve from Spain by car can take a ferry from Ayamonte, the Spanish frontier town, across the River Guadiana to **Vila Real de Santo António.** This showcase of 18th-century Portuguese town planning is set out on a grid pattern, similar to the Baixa section of Lisbon. A few miles west of this border town, pine woods and orchards break up the flat landscape around **Praia de Monte Gordo,** a town of brightly colored houses and extensive tourist facilities, including hotels, a casino, nightclubs, and discos. The long, flat stretch of beach here is steeply sloped, and swimmers quickly find themselves in deep water.

Tavira   Continuing west past the excellent **Manta Rota** beach, you come to **Tavira,** which many people call the prettiest town in the Algarve. Situated at the mouth of the River Gilão, it is famous

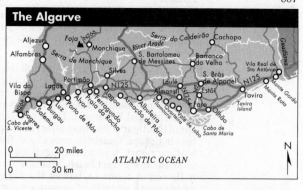

The Algarve

Aljezur Foja Monchique Serra do Caldeirão Cachopo
Alfambras Serra de Monchique River Arade S. Bartolomeu de Messines Barranco do Velho Vila Real de Sto António
Silves S. Brás de Alportel
Vila do Bispo Portimão N125 Loulé N125 Monte Gordo
Lagos Lagoa Almansil Estôi Manta Rota
Alvor Ferragudo Armação de Pêra Quarteira Tavira
Luz Porto de Mós Praia da Rocha Albufeira Vale de Lobo Faro Olhão Tavira Island
Burgau Salema Cabo de S. Vicente Cabo de Santa Maria

0 — 20 miles
0 — 30 km

ATLANTIC OCEAN

N

for its figs, arcaded streets, a seven-arched Roman bridge, old Moorish defense walls, and interesting churches. There are good sand beaches on nearby Tavira Island. Another 22 kilometers (14 miles) west lies the fishing port and market town of **Olhão.** Founded in the 18th century, Olhão is most notable for its North African–style architecture—cube-shaped whitewashed buildings, many with outside staircases.

Faro From Olhão, it's just 9 kilometers (6 miles) to **Faro,** the provincial capital of the Algarve, located roughly at the center of the coast. When this city was finally taken by Afonso III in 1249, it ended the Arab domination of Portugal, and remnants of the medieval walls and gates that surrounded the city then can still be seen in the older district. One of the gates, the **Arco da Vila,** with a white marble statue of St. Thomas Aquinas in a niche at the top, leads to the Largo de Sé. The **Gothic cathedral** here has a stunning interior decorated with 17th-century tiles. There are also several fascinating museums in Faro, notably the **Museu do Etnografia Regional** (Algarve Ethnographic Museum) on Rua do Pedacruz, with good historical and folkloric displays (Admission: 110$00. Open weekdays 9–noon and 2–5); and the **Museu Maritimo** (Maritime Museum) on Avenida República near the yacht basin (Admission: free. Open weekdays 9–noon and 2–5, Sat. 9–3). The **Museu Municipalo** (Municipal Museum) on Largo Afonso II has a section dedicated to the Roman remains found at Milreu (Admission: 110$00. Open weekdays 9–noon and 2–5). There's a large sand beach on Faro Island, which is connected to land by road.

About 9 kilometers (6 miles) north of Faro, a road branches east from N2 to the village of **Estôi,** which has an 18th-century **palace** with a formal park and fountains. The palace itself is closed to the public, but the caretaker will let passing visitors in to stroll around the gardens (a tip of 100$00 or more is always welcome). Close by are the 1st-century **Roman ruins** at **Milreu** (Admission: free. Open Tues.–Sun. 9–noon and 2–5). Another worthwhile excursion from Faro is to **Loulé.** Take N1245—4 northwest from N125 about 8 kilometers (5 miles) west of Faro. This little market town in the hills was once a Moorish stronghold and is now best known for its crafts—you can usually see coppersmiths and leather craftsmen toiling in their workshops along the narrow streets—and the highly decorative white chimney stacks on its houses. You can also visit the ruins of a medieval Saracen **castle** and a 12th-century church, the **Igreja Nossa Senhora da Concepcão** (the Church of Our Lady of the

Conception), decorated with handsome tiles and wood carvings that features an unusual wrought-iron pulpit. *Rua Dom Paeo Peres Correia. Admission: free. Castle open daily 9–12:30 and 2:30–5; church open daily until 5:30.*

Back on N125, in the town of **Almansil** stop at the 18th-century Baroque chapel of **São Lourenco,** with its blue-and-white tile panels and intricate gilt work. As you continue west, look for turnoffs to the south for the beach resort areas of Vale de Lobo, Quarteira, and Vilamoura. The tennis center at **Vale de Lobo,** one of the Algarve's earliest resort developments, is among the best in Europe. **Quarteira,** once a quiet fishing village, is now a bustling resort, with a casino, golf courses, and tennis courts as well as an excellent beach. **Vilamoura** is one of the most highly developed resort centers in the Algarve: There's a large yacht marina, several golf courses, a major tennis center, one of Europe's largest shooting centers, and other sports facilities, as well as modern luxury hotels.

Albufeira Continuing on N125, you arrive at **Albufeira**. At one time an attractive fishing village, it has long since mushroomed into the Algarve's largest and busiest resort, too brash for many. Even the dried-up riverbed has been turned into a parking lot. With its steep, narrow streets and hundreds of whitewashed houses snuggled on the slopes of nearby hills, the old town has a distinctly Moorish flavor. Its attractions include the lively fish market (held daily); interesting rock formations, caves, and grottoes along the beach; and plenty of night life. Just west of Albufeira, about 14 kilometers (8 miles), is the fishing village of **Amarção de Pêra,** which has the largest beach in the Algarve and local boats that take sightseers on cruises to the caves and grottoes along the shore.

At **Lagoa,** a market town known for its wine, turn north to **Silves.** Once the Moorish capital of the Algarve, it lost its importance after it was almost completely destroyed by the 1755 earthquake. The 12th-century sandstone **fortress,** together with its impressive parapets, was restored in 1835 and still dominates the town. Beside the fortress stands the 12th–13th-century **Santa Maria Sé** (Cathedral of Saint Mary), which contains the remains of a Moorish mosque behind the altar. (Admission: free. Both open daily until 5:30.) The **Cruz de Portugal,** a 16th-century limestone cross, stands on the road to Messines.

Portimão Return to N125 and continue to **Portimão,** the most important fishing port in the Algarve. There was a settlement here at the mouth of the river Arade even before the Romans arrived. This is the main terminal point for trains from Lisbon and a good center for shopping. In the morning you can watch fishermen unload the day's catch from t eir colorful boats in the dock area; the open-air wood shacks here are a good place to sample the local specialty, grilled sardines. Across the bridge, in the fishing hamlet of **Ferragudo,** are the ruins of a 16th-century castle, and less than a mile south of town is **Praia da Rocha.** This was the first resort area developed in the Algarve; it has an excellent beach, made all the more interesting by a series of huge, colored rocks that have been worn by sea and wind into strange shapes.

For an entirely different aspect of the Algarve, you can drive north from Portimão on routes 2 and 266 about 24 kilometers

(15 miles) into the hills of the Serra de Monchique to the spa town of **Monchique.** Besides its attractive 17th-century buildings, in a shady wood, there's a theraputic spa that dates from Roman times. The cool breezes here can provide a welcome respite from the heat of the coast during the height of summer.

Return to N125 to continue your route west through **Lagos,** a busy fishing port with an attractive harbor. The 18th-century Baroque **Ingreja do Santo António** (Church of Santo António), off the Rua Henrique C. Silva, is renowned for its gilt, carved wood, and exuberant decoration (open until 5:30). Lagos is the western terminus of the coastal railway that runs from Vila Real de Santo António.

Sagres　After Lagos, the terrain becomes more rugged as you approach the windy headland at **Sagres,** where Prince Henry established his famous school of navigation in the 15th century. Take N268 south from N125 at Vila do Bispo to the promontory hundreds of feet above the sea. From here, a small road leads through the tunnel-like entrance to the **Forteleza do Sangres** (Sangres Fortress), which was rebuilt in the 17th century. The **Compass Rose** of stone and earth in the courtyard was uncovered in this century, but is believed to have been used by Prince Henry in his calculations. The **Graça Chapel** is also located inside the fortress (which is always open), as are Henry's house and his school of navigation—the first of its kind. Both are now used as a youth hostel.

There are spectacular views from here and from **Cape São Vicente** to the west. This point, where the tip of the continent juts into the rough waters of the Atlantic, is sometimes called *O Fim do Mundo,* the end of the world. Admiral Nelson defeated the French off this cape in 1797. The lighthouse at Cape São Vincente is said to have the strongest reflectors in Europe, casting a beam 96 kilometers (60 miles) out to sea; it is open to the public. From this breathtaking spot, where Christopher Columbus, Vasco da Gama, Ferdinand Magellan, and other great explorers learned their craft 500 years ago, you can return to the sybaritic diversions of the modern Algarve along N125.

Dining and Lodging

For details and price category definitions, *see* Dining and Lodging in Staying in Portugal.

Albufeira　**A Ruina.** A big, rustic restaurant on the beach, built on several
Dining　levels, this is the place for charcoal-grilled seafood. *Off Praça da Republica, tel. 089/52094. DC, MC. Moderate.*
Cabaz da Praia. This long-established restaurant has a spectacular view of the main beach as well as a cliffside terrace for alfresco dining. Try the soufflé omelets (served at lunchtime only). *Praça Miguel Bombarda 7, tel. 089/52137. No credit cards. Inexpensive.*

Lodging　**Hotel du Balaia.** This modern clifftop hotel 3.2 kilometers (2 miles) east of Albufeira is well laid out; each of the spacious rooms has its own balcony. *Praia Maria Luisa, tel. 089/52681. 193 rooms with bath. Facilities: 2 pools, water sports, tennis courts, practice golf. AE, DC, MC. Expensive.*
Hotel-Apartamente Auramar. This pleasant beachside complex offers well-appointed self-service apartments. *Just outside of*

town at Areias de S. João, tel. 089/53337. 287 units. Closed Nov.–Mar. DC, MC. Moderate.

Alvor
Lodging

Penina Golf. This impressive golf hotel, on 360 well-maintained acres off the main road between Portimão and Lagos, has spacious, elegant public rooms, pleasant guest rooms, and offers attentive service. Most of the guest rooms have balconies; those in the back of the hotel face the Monchique Mountains and have the best views. The excellent golf courses were designed by Henry Cotton. There's a special bus to the beach. *Montes de Alvor, tel. 082/22051. 202 rooms with bath. Facilities: 18-hole championship golf course plus two 9- hole courses, tennis, pool, small private airport, sauna, billiard room, shops. AE, DC, MC, V. Very Expensive.*

Apartamentos Torralta. This large complex offering good-size rooms, fully equipped kitchens, and daily maid service is a very good value and has exceptionally low winter rates. *Praia de Alvor, tel. 082/20211. 644 units. Facilities: pools, horseback riding, restaurants, discos, tennis, shop. AE, DC, MC, V. Moderate.*

Armacão de Pera
Dining

Santola. This well-established, delightful restaurant overlooking the beach is probably the best in town. There is a varied menu, but the seafood is especially good. Try the excellent cataplana. *Largo 25 Abril, tel. 082/32332. AE, MC, V. Moderate.*

Lodging

Hotel Viking. About half a mile west of town, the Viking stands near the coast, with its swimming pools, tennis courts, and bars situated between the main building and the cliff top. The hotel isn't far from the beach, where you can bargain with the local fishermen for a sail around the grottoes. *Praia da Senhora da Rocha, tel. 082/32336. 184 rooms with bath. Facilities: pool, tennis courts, disco. AE, DC, MC, V. Moderate.*

Faro
Dining

Cidade Velha. Located in an 18th-century house within the walls of the Old City, this small, intimate restaurant serves excellent international cuisine. *Larguarda Se 19, tel. 089/27145. AE, DC, MC. Expensive.*

Alfagher. Portuguese dishes are served in this pleasant bar which was once a bishop's palace. *Rua Tenente Valadim 30, tel. 089/23740. DC, MC. Moderate.*

Lodging

Hotel Eva. This well-appointed modern hotel block is located on the main square overlooking the yacht basin. The best rooms overlook the sea. There's a courtesy bus to the beach. *Ave. da República, tel. 089/24054. 146 rooms. Facilities: pool, restaurant, disco. AE, DC, MC, V. Moderate.*

Casa de Lumena. Originally the home of a Faro businessman, the Casa de Lumena has been tastefully converted. Each room has its own individual ambience. *Praça Alexandre Herculaho 27, tel. 089/22028. 11 rooms with bath. Facilities: restaurant. AE, DC, MC, V. Inexpensive.*

Lagos
Dining

Alpendre. This is one of the oldest and best restaurants in the Algarve. The service is leisurely and the food excellent. The specialty of the house is mouth-watering flambés. *Rua António Barbosa Viana 17, tel. 082/62705. Reservations advised. MC, V. Expensive.*

Dom Sebastião. Portuguese cooking and charcoal-grilled specials and fish are the main attractions at this cheerful restaurant. It has a wide range of Portuguese aged wines. *Rua 25 de*

Abril 20, tel. 082/62795. AE, DC, MC. Closed Sun. in winter. Expensive.

Lodging **Hotel de Lagos.** This modern hotel is right in town and is attractively laid out in a spacious manner. The rooms are large and the restaurant is good. There is a regular courtesy bus to the beach, where the hotel has outstanding club facilities. *Rua Nova Aldria, tel. 082/62011. 273 rooms with bath. Facilities: pool, volleyball, windsurfing, tennis, billiards. AE, DC, MC, V. Expensive.*

Monchique **Estralagem Abrigo da Montanha.** This pleasant inn, noted for
Dining its garden of magnolias and camelias, serves excellent regional dishes. It also has six bedrooms. *Estrada da Foia, tel. 0882/92131. AE, DC, MC, V. Moderate.*

Restaurant Terezinha. Simply decorated, this modest restaurant serves good country cooking. The terrace overlooks a lovely valley and the coastline. *Estrada da Foia. No telephone. Closed Mon. Inexpensive.*

Monte Gordo **Mota.** The Mota is a lively, unpretentious restaurant located
Dining right on the sand. Noted for its seafood and regional cuisine, it has live music in the evenings. *Tel. 081/42650. No credit cards. Inexpensive.*

Lodging **Alcazar.** This is one of the most attractive hotels in town, with unusual architecture and interior design. *Rua de Ceuta, tel. 081/42184. 95 rooms with bath. Facilities: pool. AE, DC, MC, V. Moderate.*

Vasco da Gama. This long, relatively low-lying hotel occupies a choice position on the extensive, sandy beach. The staff is friendly and helpful. *Ave. Infante Dom Henrique, tel. 081/42321. 165 rooms with bath. Facilities: pool, tennis, bowling, disco, water sports. AE, DC, MC, V. Moderate.*

Portimão **Laterna.** This well-run restaurant is located just over the
Dining bridge at Ferragudo. Its specialty is seafood; try the exceptional fish soup. *Tel. 082/23948. MC. Closed Sun. Moderate.*

Praia da Luz **Luz Bay Club.** You can rent well-appointed, self-service villas
Lodging (with daily maid service) here for short or long stays. One of the best villa complexes in the Algarve, the Luz Bay is located near the beach. *Rua da Praia, tel. 089/69640. Facilities: 3 pools, tennis courts, windsurfing, 3 restaurants, various sports. AE, DC, MC, V. Expensive.*

Praia da Rocha **Safari.** This lively Portuguese restaurant has a distinctly Afri-
Dining can flavor. Seafood and delicious Angolan recipes are the specialties. *Rua António Feu, tel. 082/23540. Moderate.*

Lodging **Algarve.** This modern, luxurious hotel is perched on a cliff top. Decorated in Moorish style, it has good-sized rooms and a large, attentive staff. There is an exciting disco set into the cliffs, with windows looking out between the rocks. *Ave. Tomás Cabraira, tel. 082/24001. 219 rooms with bath. Facilities: pool, disco. AE, DC, MC, V. Very Expensive.*

Solar Penguin. English-owned and run, this charming old house has a terrace and steps leading down to the beach. Winter rates are particularly reasonable. *Ave. António Féu, tel. 082/24308. 14 rooms with bath. No credit cards. Inexpensive.*

Vale do Lobo **Dona Filipa.** One of the best hotels in the Algarve, the Dona
Lodging Filipa has a lavish and striking interior, pleasant rooms, and first-rate service. Set in extensive, beautifully landscaped

grounds near the beach, the hotel houses a chic restaurant which offers an excellent international menu. *Vale do Lobo/ Almansil, tel. 089/94141. 135 rooms with bath. Facilities: golf, pool, tennis center. AE, DC, MC, V. Very Expensive.*

Vilamoura
Lodging

Hotel Dom Pedro. Situated in the heart of this highly successful vacation complex, the Dom Pedro is close to the casino and not far from the beach. Each room is attractively furnished and has its own balcony. *Tel. 089/35450. 260 rooms with bath. AE, DC, MC, V. Moderate.*

Vila Real de Santo António
Dining

Caves do Guadiana. Located in a large, old-fashioned building facing the fishing docks, this restaurant is well known for its seafood and Portuguese specialties. *Ave. República 90, tel. 081/44498. Closed Thurs. DC, MC. Inexpensive.*

25 Romania

Introduction

Romania, the least visited but perhaps the most beautiful of the countries of Eastern Europe, welcomes many visitors from the West each year, principally to the summer resorts on the Black Sea coast, to the excellent ski resorts in the Carpathian mountains, and to its numerous spas and health resorts.

Comparable in size to the state of Oregon, Romania is made up of the provinces of Wallachia, Moldavia, and Transylvania and borders the Soviet Union, Bulgaria, Yugoslavia, and Hungary. With a population of 22 million, Romania is a "Latin Island" in a sea of Slavs and Magyars. Her people are the descendants of the Dacian tribe and of the Roman soldiers who garrisoned this easternmost province of the Roman Empire. Romanians speak a language which is derived from vernacular Latin and is similar to French, Italian, and Spanish. In the south, they have the dark, romantic looks of a Mediterranean race, and boast a tradition and temperament to match. Barbaric invasions, struggles against the Turks, the Austro-Hungarian domination of Transylvania, and a strong French cultural influence have endowed them with a rich heritage to add to a folk culture that survives to this day.

Bucharest, with its wide, tree-lined avenues, Arc de Triomph, and lively café life was once known as the Paris of the East. Transylvania, a region wrapped in myth, is home to a sizable minority of Hungarians, with their own folk traditions and distinctive building styles. This area has long been a favorite with tourists because of the real and fictional sites associated with Dracula. The dark forested mountains and craggy peaks, particularly around Braşov, are evocative of the legend. Many enchanting Orthodox monasteries, including some of medieval origin that sport colorful frescoes on their outside walls, characterize the remote and mountainous region of Moldavia. To the south of Bucharest lies the Danube Delta, a watery wilderness populated by fishermen (many of Ukrainian origin) and visited by hundreds of rare bird species. The Carpathian mountain ranges, which form a crown in the center of the country, offer the double pleasure of skiing in winter and hiking in summer. Unattractive effects of industrialization are generally confined to the cities; life in the countryside remains picturesquely simple. Horse and cart is a popular means of transportation, horse-drawn plows a common sight, and folk costume everyday wear in the northern regions of Maramures and Bukovina. In an attempt to modernize many of the more rural areas, large numbers of villages are being systematically destroyed and replaced by high-rise blocks. Similarly, collectivization of agriculture is being ruthlessly enforced. Both policies have been condemned around the world, though the Romanian government has taken little notice.

The state imposes few "official" restrictions on the independent traveler's freedom of movement within Romania, but it must be stressed that the individual is at a serious disadvantage when compared with the package tourist. The independent traveler will encounter varying standards of service, a scarcity of tourist amenities, overpriced hotels, and undersupplied restaurants. If you are traveling independently, it is best to take food supplies with you. Shops contain old stock that is best avoided, peasant markets sell fresh produce, though not meat

Romania

or fish, and only one or two types of cheese. Mineral water is hard to find in the shops and erratically available in restaurants. Tap water is safe, but tastes chlorinated. Drinking-water fountains in most towns provide natural spring water. Visas, obligatory money exchange, accommodations, and meals work out to be a great deal more expensive than the very reasonably priced seaside, skiing, and spa holidays or the flexible fly-and-drive arrangements with vouchers for accommodations.

Romania enjoyed a period of comparative prosperity in the 1970s but is currently the poorest country in Europe after Albania. The present leadership, under President Ceauşescu, has decided to repay quickly a substantial foreign debt incurred by his country's development from a mainly agricultural economy into an industrial one. Most of Romania's farm produce is now being exported for hard currency, while imports are kept to a minimum. As an important source of foreign currency, tourists are given priority, but, outside the main resorts, it is difficult to escape or ignore the effects of nationwide food and fuel shortages. Many of the most basic commodities are scarce, waiting lines are long, and street lighting is inadequate. Inevitably, there is a thriving black market in practically everything—from lipstick and toothpaste to food and gasoline. While other Eastern European countries are blossoming under the benign influence of *glasnost*, Romania remains firmly wedded to Stalinist ethics and practices.

Romania is likely to remain underexplored until these serious economic difficulties are resolved, but, in the meantime, the package tourist is still assured a good bargain, while the intrepid independent traveler will experience that rare sensation of having stepped back in time to a world that, for the most part, exists only in the memories of another generation.

Before You Go

When to Go Bucharest, like Paris, is at its best in the spring. The Black Sea resorts open in mid-to-late May and close at the end of September. Winter ski resorts in the Carpathians are now well developed and increasingly popular, while the best time for touring the interior is late spring to fall.

Climate The Romanian climate is temperate and generally free of extremes, but snow as late as April is not unknown, and the lowlands can be very ho in midsummer.

The following are the average daily maximum and minimum temperatures for Bucharest.

Jan.	34F	1C	May	74F	23C	Sept.	78F	25C
	19	−7		51	10		52	11
Feb.	38F	4C	June	81F	27C	Oct.	65F	18C
	23	−5		57	14		43	6
Mar.	50F	10C	July	86F	30C	Nov.	49F	10C
	30	−1		60	16		35	2
Apr.	64F	18C	Aug.	85F	30C	Dec.	39F	4C
	41	5		59	15		26	−3

Currency Unless you have booked on a prepaid tour, you must exchange $10 or its equivalent per day in any hard currency for the number of days for which you have requested your visa. Children under 14 are exempt from this requirement. If you keep all your exchange slips, it is possible to change surplus *lei* back into hard currency at the end of your stay, but only if you have changed more than the required amount of $10 a day. It is essential to keep all exchange slips. You will need to show them when paying for tourist amenities such as accommodation in hotels and camping sites; otherwise, you will have to pay in Western currency. The import and export of Romanian currency is not allowed, but you may bring in any amount of hard currency and exchange it at currency desks in hotels, banks, and border stations.

The unit of currency is the *leu* (plural *lei*), divided into 100 *bani*. There are coins of 15 and 25 bani, and 1, 3, and 5 lei. Banknotes come in denominations of 10, 25, 50, and 100 lei. The tourist exchange rate was 8.6 lei to the dollar and 14.8 lei to the pound sterling at press time (spring 1989). Despite the disadvantageous exchange rates, tourists are advised to follow currency regulations, since dabbling in the extensive currency black market is illegal. However, packs of Kent cigarettes, packets of coffee, and soap bars are practically an alternative currency and work wonders in speeding up service and generally achieving the impossible; they are also useful barter in more remote areas of the country. The lack of consumer goods also means that people appreciate such items as coffee, sweets and chocolate, and pocket calculators.

Credit Cards Major credit cards are welcome in the major hotels and their restaurants but are not accepted in shops and independent restaurants.

What It Will Cost Prices of hotels and restaurants are as expensive as those in Western Europe as far as the independent traveler is concerned. Those with prepaid arrangements enjoy reductions of up to 30% and more.

Sample Prices Museum admission costs 4–12 lei; a bottle of beer in a restaurant around 25 lei; a bottle of good wine in a top restaurant around 150 lei. A one-mile taxi ride will cost around 10 lei.

Visas All visitors to Romania must have a visa, obtainable from Romanian embassies abroad or on arrival at any entry point by whatever means of transport. Long delays may be avoided by getting a visa in advance, but only visitors born in Romania are obliged to do so. For those with prepaid arrangements, the cost of the visa (USA, $16; Canada, $16; UK, £20) is included and substantially reduced. Send the price of the visa, a letter explaining your reasons for wanting to go to Romania, a stamped, self-addressed envelope, and your passport to the relevant consulate: in the **United States,** Romanian Consulate, 1067 23rd Street NW, Washington DC 20008; in **Canada,** Romanian Consulate, 655 Rideau Street, Ottawa, Ontario; in the **United Kingdom,** Consular Section of the Romanian Embassy, 4 Palace Green, London W8.

Customs on Arrival Personal belongings: two cameras, 20 rolls of film, one small movie camera, two rolls of movie film, a typewriter, binoculars, a radio/tape recorder, 200 cigarettes, two liters of liquor and four of wine, as well as gifts up to the value of 2,000 lei are permitted; camping and sports equipment may be imported freely.

Language Romanian sounds appealingly familiar to anyone with a smattering of French, Italian, or Spanish. French is widely spoken and understood. Romanians involved with the tourist industry, in all hotels and major resorts, speak English.

Getting Around

By Car
Road Conditions A good network of main roads covers the country, though the great majority are still a single lane wide in each direction. Smaller roads connecting villages are not asphalted. Progress may be impeded by convoys of farm machinery on the move, by horses and carts, or herds of animals. Night driving can be dangerous: Roads and vehicles are lighted either poorly or not at all.

Rules of the Road Driving is on the right, as in the United States. Speed limits are 60 kph (37 mph) in built-up areas and 80–100 kph (50–62 mph) on all other roads. Driving under the influence of alcohol is prohibited. Police are empowered to levy on-the-spot fines of 250 lei for speeding. Radar checks are very frequent; keep an eye out for the police force's black cables stretched across the road.

Gasoline Gas must be purchased with coupons paid for in hard currency which enable you to go straight to the front of the long petrol lines; these are obtainable from hotel reception desks, border crossing points, and tourist offices. Gas is expensive (around 36 lei a gallon) and gas stations scarce, usually cropping up on the outskirts of towns. The Automobil Club Roman *(see* Breakdowns) and tourist offices can provide visitors with a useful Tourist and Motor Car Map, pinpointing the location of each gas station. Stations should have two pumps marked "Comturist," reserved for foreign tourists. Keep your tank filled and be sure to carry a spare-parts kit.

Breakdowns **Automobil Club Roman** (ACR, Strada Cihoschi 2, Bucharest 1, tel. 40/123456 in Bucharest and tel. 12345 elsewhere) offers mechanical assistance in case of breakdown and medical and legal assistance at fixed rates in case of accident.

By Train Romanian Railways (CPR), operates "accelerat", "rapide", and "personal" trains; avoid, if possible, the "personal" trains because they are very slow. Trains are inexpensive but are very crowded; you may find yourself having to step over farm animals such as geese and hens in the corridors! It is always advisable to make reservations in advance (up to six hours before departure). If you're in Bucharest, go to the Advance Reserve Office, Strada Brezoianu 10, tel. 40/132644, just behind the Bucureşti Hotel. Allow plenty of time, since lines are usually long. It will charge you a small commission fee but it is a less time-consuming process than buying your ticket at the railway station (upstairs at the central reservations office, Strada Brezoianu 10).

By Plane **Tarom** (upstairs at the central reservations office, Strada Brezoianu 10) operates daily flights to 15 major cities from Bucharest's Baneasa Airport. In summer, additional flights link Constanţa with major cities, including Cluj and Iaşi. Fares are low, but be prepared for delays.

By Bus Bus stations, or *autogara*, are usually located near train stations. Buses are generally crowded and far from luxurious. Tickets are sold at the stations up to two hours before departure.

By Boat Regular passenger services operate on various sections of the Danube; tickets are available at the ports. Often included in package tours to the Black Sea coast is a trip by pleasure boat via the middle or southern arms of the Danube Delta.

Staying in Romania

Telephones The Romanian telephone system is erratic, but calls can be made from hotels or post offices. Be warned that international calls are outrageously expensive—three minutes to Western Europe cost 98 lei. Calls to the United States are even more costly—nearly $100 (payable in hard currency) for three minutes. Even at these rates, it is less expensive to telephone from the post office than from hotels. Post offices have a waiting system whereby you order your call and pay at the counter. When your call is ready, the name of the town or country you are phoning is announced, together with the number of the cabin you should proceed to for your call. There are no cheap rates for phoning at certain times.

Try to use phone books instead of searching in vain for the number for Information—it is different at each exchange.

Mail The central post office in Bucuresti is at Calea Victoriei 37 and is open Monday through Saturday from 7 AM to 8 PM. The telephone section is open at the same times on Sunday as well.

Postal Rates A letter to the United States costs 16 lei, a postcard 13 lei. Letters to Western Europe, including the United Kingdom, cost 11 lei, postcards 8 lei.

Opening and Closing Times **Banks.** Open weekdays 9 to noon and 1 to 3, Saturday 9 to noon. **Museums.** Museums and art galleries are usually open from 10 to 6, but it's best to check with local tourist offices. Most museums are closed on Monday.
Shops. Shops are generally open Mon.–Sat. from 9 or 10 AM to 6 or 8 PM, and shut between 1 and 3, though some food shops open earlier.

National Holidays January 1 (New Year's Day); January 2; May 1 (Labor Day); May 2; August 23 (Liberation); August 24.

Dining Chronic food shortages and problems of distribution mean that the range and quality of food, even in the deluxe hotels in Bucharest, remain low by international standards. Traditional Romanian cuisine is not easy to come by; instead, french fries and meat coated in thick sauces predominate. Outside the capital your choice may be limited to one dish. Where no menu is provided, you should check the price in advance. In most resorts, package tour guests are given a choice of dishes from which to make their selection for the following day's meals.

Mealtimes Plan to dine early. Outside the Black Sea and Carpathian resorts, restaurants close at 10 PM, when the lights are turned off, and you'll find it difficult to get served anywhere after 9 PM (though a packet of Kent cigarettes will sometimes do the trick!).

Precautions The far less expensive *bufet expres, lacto vegetarian* snack bars, and *autoservire* cannot be recommended, but excellent creamy cakes are available at the better *cofetarie* (coffee shops), such as the Cofetarie Hotel Bucuresti, side entrance of the Hotel Bucuresti, Calea Victorei. If you cannot survive without a heavy intake of coffee, you should bring your own.

Dress   In Bucharest, jacket and tie is customary at Expensive restaurants outside the hotels. Casual dress is appropriate elsewhere.

Ratings   Prices are per person and include first course, main course, and dessert, plus wine and tip. Best bets are indicated by a star ★. At press time, there were 8.6 lei to the dollar.

Category	Cost
Very Expensive	over 200 lei
Expensive	150–200 lei
Moderate	80–150 lei
Inexpensive	under 80 lei

Credit Cards   The following credit card abbreviations are used: AE, American Express; DC, Diners Club; MC, MasterCard; V, Visa.

Lodging   Prepaid arrangements with reductions and advance reservations are highly recommended, but it is possible to book hotels, campsites, and self-contained cottages through the local national tourist office (ONT) or directly with a hotel. In each case you must have proof of official money exchange if you want to pay in lei. Inexpensive accommodations outside the capital, in the form of pensions and hostels, are almost nonexistent. However, the better campsites (Braşov, Cluj, Sibiu, and Suceava) have wooden cabins which are worth considering for those on a budget.

Hotels   The star system of hotel classification does not operate in Romania. Instead, you will encounter Deluxe categories A and B, First-class categories A and B, and so on. Deluxe A is equivalent to five-star or Very Expensive, Deluxe B to four-star or Expensive, first-class A to three-star or Moderate, and first-class B to two-star or Inexpensive. Plumbing may be erratic in the Moderate and Inexpensive categories, and cost-cutting measures have meant that in some areas hot water is available only at certain hours of the day; these hours will always be clearly posted in the reception area. In principle, at least, all hotels leave a certain quota of rooms unoccupied until 8 PM, for unexpected foreign visitors.

Rentals   A few delightfully rustic cottages may be rented at such skiing resorts as Sinaia and Predeal. Details are available from Romanian tourist offices abroad *(see* Important Addresses and Numbers).

Hostels   There are a number of student hostels in major towns, though they are open only in July and August. Bookings can be made through the ONT office on arrival in Bucharest, but availability is limited.

Camping   There are more than 100 campsites in Romania; they provide an inexpensive way of exploring the country, but standards vary. The best ones are at Braşov, Cluj, Sibiu, and Suceava. They all have clean toilets and showers with hot water at least some of the time. The worst ones—Hunedoară, Iaşi, Moldoviţă—have no running water apart from a natural spring and very unpleasant toilets. Rates start from 100 lei or 150 lei with bathroom per day. They are clean and comfortable but are only for use in the summer. A few offer bungalow accommodations. Details are available from Romanian tourist offices abroad.

Ratings The following hotel price categories are for two people in a double room. Supplements for single rooms range from 90 to 180 lei per night. Best bets are indicated by a star ★. At press time, there were 8.6 lei to the dollar.

Category	Bucharest	Black Sea Coast
Very Expensive	over 900 lei	over 540 lei
Expensive	675–900 lei	400–540 lei
Moderate	360–675 lei	270–400 lei
Inexpensive	under 360 lei	under 270 lei

Credit Cards The following credit card abbreviations are used: AE, American Express; DC, Diners Club; MC, MasterCard; V, Visa.

Tipping A 12% service charge is added to meals at most restaurants. Elsewhere, tipping is discouraged; the practice persists, however, though nowhere is it obligatory. You may want to leave about 10% if service is exceptional. Give porters and taxi drivers about 5–10 lei.

Bucharest

Arriving and Departing

By Plane All international flights to Romania operate from Bucharest's Otopeni Airport (tel. 40/333137), 16 kilometers (9 miles) north of the city.

Between the Airport and Downtown Buses leave every one to two hours from outside the airport and stop outside the TAROM office, Strada Brezoianu 10; tickets cost 15 lei. Your hotel can arrange transport by car from the airport for around 90 lei. Taxis are in short supply, and the fare is about 100 lei.

By Train There are five main stations in Bucharest, though international lines operate from Gara de Nord (tel. 052). For tickets and information, go to the Advance Booking Office (Str. Brezoianu 10, tel. 40/132644).

By Car There are two main access routes into the city—E70 west from the Hungarian border and E60 north via Braşov.

Getting Around

Bucharest is spacious and sprawling. Though the old heart of the city and the two main arteries running the length of it are best explored on foot, long, wide avenues and vast squares make some form of transportation necessary. Hotels and the ONT office will supply maps of the downtown area, but no map is absolutely up to date because of the intensive redevelopment which has been going on for the last five years, particularly around Piaţa Unirii and Bulevardul Nicolae Bălcescu.

Public transportation is efficient but best avoided during rush hours. Tickets can be bought at the small kiosks found near the tram and bus stops, and at tobacconists. Note that the system shuts up at 11:30 PM.

By Subway	Thirty kilometers (18 miles) of the city's projected 56 kilometers (34 miles) are now in operation. Tickets cost 2 lei for any distance.
By Tram, Bus, and Trolley Bus	Trams cost 1 lei, buses 1.75 lei, and trolley buses 1.50 lei for any distance.
By Taxi and Maxi-taxi	Inexpensive but in short supply, taxis can be ordered by phoning 053. All have meters, but some drivers will not use them. Prices should start at around 6 lei, plus 6 lei per kilometer; around 20 lei should take you anywhere in the city. Maxi-taxis are blue-and-white minibuses that stop as requested along a given route; tickets cost 5 lei.

Important Addresses and Numbers

Tourist Information The main **Romanian National Tourist Office (ONT)** is located at 7 Boulevard General Magheru, tel. 40/145160, and deals with all inquiries related to tourism (open weekdays 8–4). There are ONT offices at Otopeni Airport, open 24 hours, and at the Gara de Nord, open 7:30 AM–3:30 PM. ONT offices in major hotels close at 3:30 PM. There are also county offices, known as **UJT**, in most Romanian towns and resorts.

For information before your trip, write or call **in the United States:** 573 Third Avenue, New York, NY 10016, tel. 212/697–6971; **in the United Kingdom:** 29 Thurloe Place, London, SW7 2HP, tel. 01/584–8090.

Guided Tours

For detailed information on guided tours, contact the ONT office (*see* Tourist Information).

Orientation Tours ONT offices organize sightseeing tours of the city by car, bus, or minibus, depending on the size of the group. A four-hour tour by car will cost 135 lei.

Special-Interest Tours The ONT office arranges tours of Romanian folk art, museums, and the city's churches.

Excursions Day and weekend excursions outside Bucharest cover the ski resorts, the Danube Delta, and the monasteries of Bukovina. A half-day tour by car to monasteries nearer Bucharest costs 270 lei.

Exploring Bucharest

The old story goes that a simple peasant named Bucur settled on the site upon which the city now stands. True or not, the name Bucurest was officially used first only in 1459, by none other than Vlad Ţepeş, the real-life Dracula (sometimes known as Vlad the Impaler for his bloodthirsty habit of impaling unfortunate victims on wooden stakes). Two centuries later, this citadel on the Dimboviţa (the river that flows through Bucharest) became the capital of Wallachia, and after another 200 years, it was named the capital of Romania. The city developed along the old trading route, now Boulevard 1848, Boulevard North Bălcescu, Boulevard General Magheru, and Boulevard Ana Ipătescu. The first Princely Court was built just west of the lower stretch of these boulevards. The bustling trading area nearby, known as the Lipscani District, links the old trading route with another main street, Calea Victoriei, where many of the city's historical buildings, elegant shops, and hotels are found.

Like Paris, Bucharest is at its best in the spring. However, though once a gracious city characterized by pretty villas set in leafy courtyards and elegant neo-Classical 19th-century buildings, Bucharest is rapidly being transformed into a modern capital of high-rise buildings. The impetus for the rebuilding has been supplied almost entirely by President Ceauşescu, eager to seize the opportunity for self-aggrandizement that this vast project offers. It is a policy that those who knew the old, elegant Bucharest can only mourn. The speed of the transformation has been such that no up-to-date map yet exists for the Romanians, much less for tourists. Parts of the city look like they have undergone a blitz: The bewildered inhabitants seem to be waiting patiently for this man-made earthquake to stop, which it is scheduled to do in 1990. The replanning of Bucharest and the completion of the new Metro system appear to be just as urgent as the repayment of the foreign debt. For a preview of the Bucharest of the 21st century, don't miss the impressive and almost completed civic center to the southeast of the Piaţa Unirii.

Against a backdrop of such dramatic upheaval, Bucharest has acquired a new and peculiarly subtle aura, unlike that of anywhere else in Europe. Though the population looks well nourished enough, grocery stores are stocked with little else but champagne and canned tomatoes; there are many more flowers than there is food in the markets. The roads seem far wider and grander than is warranted by the number of cars that use them. In even the most expensive restaurants, supplies of food often run out by 9 PM, and, as if recalling those days at summer camp, it's lights out at 10 PM.

Numbers in the margin correspond with points of interest on the Bucharest map.

Historic Bucharest A tour of this city should start at its core, the **Curtea Veche** (old
❶ Princely Court) and the Lipscani District. The Princely Court now houses **Muzeul Curtea Veche-Palatul Voievodal,** a museum exhibiting the remains of the palace built by Vlad Ţepeş in the 15th century. One section of the cellar wall presents the palace's history from the 15th century onward. You can see the rounded river stones used in the early construction, later alternating with red brick, and later still in plain brick. Prisoners were once kept in these cellars, which extend far into the surrounding city; a pair of ancient skulls belonging to two young *boyars* (aristocrats), decapitated at the end of the 17th century, will interest some. In the 18th century, the palace was auctioned off in sections, and during the last century, the lower levels of the complex were used as the cellars of merchants' premises and craftsmen's workshops. *Str. 30 Decembrie 31. Admission: 5 lei. Open Tues.–Sun. 10–6.*

❷ The **Biserica din Curtea Veche** (Curtea Veche Church), beside the Princely Court, was founded in the 16th century and remains
❸ an important center of worship in the city. Nearby, **Hanul Manuc** (Manuc's Inn), a renovated 19th-century inn arranged in the traditional Romanian fashion around a courtyard, now houses a hotel and restaurant which is packed in the summer afternoons and evenings. Manuc was a wealthy Armenian merchant who died in Russia by poisoning—at the hand of a famous

Bucharest

N

Barbu Momuleanu

Str. Iconei

Str. Orientului

Str. Galați

Str. Maria Rosetti

Str. Tunari

Str. Aurel Vlaicu

Eminescu

B-dul Dacia

Piața Al. Sahia

Str. Iconei

Str. Polonă

Str. Mihail

Str. Dionisie Lupu

Str. Pictor Verona

A. Rosetti

C. Dorobanților

Piața Cosmonauților

B-dul G-ral Magheru

i

9

Str. Roma

Str. Căderea Bastiliei

Piața Romană

Piața Gheorghiu Dej

Str. Londra

Str. Grigore Alexandrescu

Str. Biserica Amzei

Piața Amzei

C. Victoriei

B-dul Ilie Pintilie

B-dul Ana Ipătescu

Calea   Victorei

B-dul Aviatorilor

Piața Victoriei

Str. Occidentului

C. Griviței

Șos. Kiseleff

10

11 **12**

B-dul 1 Mai

Șos. Nicolae Titulescu

Str. Buzești

Piața Ilie Pintilie

Str. Ștefan Furtună

Str. Nuferilor

B-dul Alex Ioan Cuza

Str. Berzei

Arc de Triomph, **11**
Ateneul Român, **9**
Biserica din Curtea
Veche, **2**
Biserica Ortodoxă, **4**

Columna Traiană, **6**
Crețulescu Church, **7**
Curtea Veche, **1**
Hanul Manuc, **3**
Muzeul de Artă al
R.S.R., **8**

Muzeul de Istorie
Naturală, **10**
Muzeul de Istorie al
R.S.R., **5**
Muzeul Satului, **12**

French fortuneteller who, having forecast Manuc's death on a certain day, could not risk ruining her reputation. The 1812 Russian-Turkish Peace Treaty was signed here.

Nearby, Lipscani is a bustling area of narrow streets, open stalls, and small artisans' shops, which combine to create the atmosphere of a bazaar. At Strada Selari 11–13, you'll find glassblowers hard at work; glassware is sold next-door. On **④** Strada Stavreopolos, a small but exquisite circa 1724 **Biserica Ortodoxă** (Orthodox church) combines late Renaissance and Byzantine styles with elements of the Romanian folk-art style. Go inside to look at the superb wood and stone carving and a richly ornate iconostasis, the painted screen that partitions off the altar. Boxes on either side of the entrance contain votive candles—for the living on the left, for the "sleeping" on the right.

Time Out | Down the road, at Strada Stavreopolos 3, is the **Carul cu Bere,** serving half-liter tankards of beer, appetizers, and Turkish coffee.

⑤ At the end of the street is the **Muzeul de Istorie al R.S.R.** (Romanian History Museum), which contains a vast collection of exhibits from neolithic to modern times. The Treasury, which can be visited and paid for separately, has a startling collection of objects in gold and precious stones—royal crowns, weapons, plates, and jewelry—dating from the 4th millennium BC through the 20th century. Opposite the Treasury is a full-size **⑥** replica of **Columna Traiană** (Trajan's Column) (the original is in Rome), commemorating a Roman victory over Dacia in AD 2. *Calea Victoriei 12. Admission: 5 lei. Open Tues.–Sun. 10–6.*

Turning north along the Calea Victoriei, you pass a military **⑦** club and academy before reaching the pretty little **Crețulescu Church** on your left. Built in 1722, the church and some of its original frescoes were restored during the 1930s. Immediately north is a massive building, once the royal palace and **⑧** now the Palace of the Republic. The **Muzeul de Artă al R.S.R.** (National Art Museum) is housed here, with its fine collection of Romanian art, including works by the world-famous sculptor Brâncuși. The foreign section has many fine examples of European, Eastern, and Far Eastern art. *Str. Stribei Voda 1. Admission: 5 lei. Open Tues.–Sun. 10–6.*

Opposite the palace, in Piața Gheorghiu-Dej, is the **headquarters of the Romanian Communist Party;** you are forbidden to walk in front of it, and God forbid you should try to photo-**⑨** graph it. The **Ateneul Român** (Romanian Athenaeum Concert Hall) is impressive, with its Baroque dome and Greek columns. Built in 1888, the building has an ornate art nouveau entrance hall that is well worth a look. The George Enescu Philharmonic Orchestra is based here.

Time Out | The cafeteria of the **Athenée Palace Hotel,** opposite the concert hall, has excellent cream cakes and a terrace.

Follow Calea Victoriei as far as the Piața Victoriei. Opposite is **⑩** the Grigore Antipe **Muzeul de Istorie Naturală** (Natural History Museum) with its exceptional butterfly collection and the skeleton of *Dinotherium gigantissimum. (Șoseaua Kiseleff 1. Admission: 10 lei. Open Tues.–Sun. 10–6).*

Şoseaua Kiseleff, a pleasant tree-lined avenue, brings you
(11) to the **Arc de Triomph,** built in 1922 to commemorate the Allied
victory in World War I. Originally constructed of wood and
stucco, it was rebuilt in the 1930s and carved by some of
Romania's most talented sculptors.

Still farther north lies Herăstrău Park, accommodating the fas-
(12) cinating **Muzeul Satului** (Village Museum) as well as Herăstrău
Lake itself. The museum is outstanding, with more than 300
authentic, fully furnished peasant houses, with folk styles tak-
en from all over Romania. *Şoseaua Kiseleff 28–30. Admission:
5 lei. Open daily 10–5.*

Shopping

Gifts and   There are Comturist branches in all the main hotels, but stroll
Souvenirs   down Calea Victoriei and you'll find glassware at **Stirex,** handicrafts at **Arta Populara,** woolens at **Electa,** records and musical
instruments at **Muzica,** and jewelry at **Bijuteria. Horizont,** almost directly opposite the Intercontinental on Boulevard
North Balcescu, specializes in high-quality arts and crafts.

Antiques   **Bazarul Hanul cu tei,** a picturesque, restored inn in the old district, is now a complex of small, specialized shops. **Consignaţia,**
on the second floor, is a vast warehouse of antique and secondhand items, with a particularly fine selection of carpets.

Market   The main food market is in Piaţa Unirii, open seven days a week
and best visited in the morning. It sells a limited variety of
fresh fruit and vegetables, as well as flowers and handicraft.

Dining

The restaurants of the Athenée Palace, Minerva, Bucureşti,
and Intercontinental hotels are all recommended for a reasonable meal in pleasant surroundings. Depending on your choice
of menu, you can eat moderately in most expensive restaurants
and inexpensively in most moderate restaurants. Generally low
standards of cuisine, owing to food shortages, are often combined with loud live music, to make eating out in Bucharest an
interesting but frequently disappointing experience. For details and price category definitions, *see* Dining in Staying in
Romania.

Very Expensive   **Athenée Palace Hotel.** This is the city's most glamourous night
spot, and its restaurant is frequented mainly by foreign diplo-
mats and celebrities. Though it offers the most sumptuous
surroundings in Bucharest, the food is your average steak,
fries, and salad fare. *Str. Episcopei 1–3, tel. 40/140899. Reservations advised. AE, DC, MC. V.*
Hotel Bucureşti. The restaurant in this modern hotel sometimes has a loud band playing in the evenings, but the air-
conditioning makes it comfortable, and it is one of the few
places where you can enjoy good, genuine Romanian cuisine.
*Calea Victoriei 63–81, tel. 40/154580. Reservations not neces-
sary. AE, DC, MC, V.*
Rapsodia. Located in the modern Hotel Intercontinental, this
is a quiet, elegant restaurant with a pianist in the evenings.
There is a wide choice of authentic Romanian and international
dishes. *Bulevardul Nicolae Bălcescu 4–6, tel. 40/140400. Reservations not necessary. AE, DC, MC, V.*

Expensive **Capşa.** Elegant in the Belle Epoque style, Capşa was founded in 1842 and has a tradition of haute cuisine that it is struggling to maintain. Recommendations from the headwaiter are useful. The restaurant also has some excellent vintage wines, and the creamy desserts are delicious. *Calea Victoriei 34, tel. 40/ 134482. Reservations required for lunch. No credit cards.*

Hanul Manuc. Downtown opposite the Princely Court, this renovated 19th-century inn now houses the city's most appealing hotel and restaurant. Courtyard and gallery tables make for a lively atmosphere and the *pastrame* ham and sweet pastries are good bets. *Str. 30 Decembrie 62, tel. 40/131415. Weekend reservations advised. No credit cards.*

Pescarus. This modern, wooden hunting lodge-style restaurant, on the edge of Herăstrău Park by the lake, offers an evening folklore show on the terrace. A relaxed and convivial atmosphere makes it one of the city's most popular restaurants. Try the *frigarui*—meat and onion on a skewer. *Herăstrău Park, tel. 40/794640. Evening reservations advised. No credit cards.*

Moderate **Cina.** Alongside the Athenaeum and centrally located with its garden café, Cina is popular with the locals. Stained-glass windows, neoclassical decor, dim lighting, and soulful live music lend a pleasantly romantic atmosphere. The house specialty is *cotelet Valdostana*, a hearty veal dish. Service may be slow. *Str. C. A. Rossetti 1, tel. 40/130217. Reservations advised. No credit cards.*

Carul cu Bere. This beautifully restored old beer house is situated near the Museum of Romanian History. Once a meeting place for artists and writers, it retains an Old World feel. Guests are served with tankards of delicious cold beer to wash down *cîrnati*, a tasty spiced sausage. *Str. Stavreopolos 3, tel. 40/163793. No credit cards.*

La Doi Cocosi. "The Two Cockerels" specializes in chicken; supplies are unreliable, though, so you may want to check beforehand. Located about nine miles (14 kilometers) out of town, it is an excellent choice for large parties, with its informal and pleasant outdoor terrace. *Şoseaua Strauteşti 6, tel. 40/671998. Reservations required. No credit cards.*

Doina. Located on one of the main boulevards heading out of town, Doina was once much frequented by elegant promenaders. It has a pretty garden terrace and an attractive wine cellar; make it a point to sample wines from the vineyards inscribed over the door. There's music and dancing in the evenings. *Şoseaua Kiseleff 4, tel. 40/176715. Reservations required. No credit cards.*

Inexpensive **Beijin.** This is Bucharest's one and only Chinese eatery. It's located in the Hotel Minerva and gives excellent value for the
★ money. *Str. Lt. Lemnea 2–4, tel. 40/506010. Reservations advised. AE, DC, MC, V.*

Lodging

Hotels in Bucharest are often heavily booked during the tourist season. If you don't have reservations, the ONT office will be of help in suggesting available alternatives. For details and price category definitions, *see* Lodging in Staying in Romania.

Very Expensive **Athenée Palace.** The old-fashioned Athenée Palace is one of the
★ city's most famous hotels, still comfortable despite ongoing

renovation. The restaurant is the most elegant the city can offer, and there is also a popular nightclub with a floor show. *Str. Episcopiei 1–3, tel. 40/140899. 300 rooms with bath. Facilities: pool, health club, sauna. AE, DC, MC, V.*

Bucureşti. The city's largest hotel has an excellent central location and spacious, pleasantly furnished rooms. Its modern ambience is complemented by the vast range of facilities. *Calea Victoriei 63–81, tel. 40/154580. 442 rooms with bath. Facilities: 2 pools, health club, sauna, cafeteria, restaurant. AE, DC, MC, V.*

Flora. The modern Flora, situated on the outskirts of the city near Herăstrău Park, offers its cosmopolitan clientele top facilities for geriatric (anti-aging) treatment. The sun terraces are havens of relaxation. Most guests stay in this quiet, restful hotel for at least two weeks. *Blvd. Poligrafiei 1, tel. 40/184640. 155 rooms with bath. Facilities: pool, spa care unit, health club, sauna, restaurant. AE, DC, MC, V.*

★ **Intercontinental.** The Intercontinental is a good landmark to set your bearings by, since it's the city's tallest building. Every room is air-conditioned, and all come complete with balcony. *Blvd. N. Bălcescu 4-6, tel. 40/140400/137040. 423 rooms with bath. Facilities: fitness center, sun terrace, mini casino, 7 bars and restaurants. AE, DC, MC, V.*

Expensive **Ambassador.** The 13-story Ambassador was built in 1937 and enjoys a fine central location. Its rooms are comfortably furnished if somewhat spartan in decoration. *Blvd. General Magheru 6–8, tel. 40/110440. 233 rooms with bath. Facilities: restaurant, pool, health club. AE, DC, MC, V.*

Bulevard. This old-style hotel is conveniently situated near the main tourist attractions. Small and intimate and benefiting from attractive *fin de siècle* furnishings, it exudes a charming Old World feel. Category B rooms are less expensive since their windows don't look out onto the busy Boulevard Georghiu-Dej (this means they can be quieter, however). *Blvd. Georghiu-Dej 1, tel. 40/153300. 89 rooms with bath. AE, DC, MC, V.*

Dorobanţi. The modern and busy Dorobanţi has 18 floors of colorfully—one could say garishly—furnished rooms; they will not appeal to everyone! On the bright side, however, the restaurant offers dancing in the evenings, and the Video Discotheque Club is open until 1 AM. *Calea Dorobanţi 1, tel. 40/110860. 298 rooms with bath. Facilities: restaurant, nightclub. AE, DC, MC, V.*

★ **Hanul Manuc.** This restored 19th-century inn near the busy Lipscani District houses a fine hotel as well as a good restaurant *(see Dining, above).* Rooms are comfortable, whether decorated with pale Biedermeier furniture or in folk-art style; however, some rooms are noisy. *Str. 30 Decembrie 62, tel. 40/131415. 30 rooms with bath. Facilities: restaurant. No credit cards.*

Moderate **Capitol.** The circa 1907 Capitol is situated in a lively part of town near the Cişmigiu Gardens. In days gone by, it was the stamping ground of Bucharest's mainstream artists and writers. Today the Capitol is fully modernized and offers comfortable rooms and a large restaurant—though the literati have long since moved on. *Calea Victoriei 29, tel. 40/140926. 70 rooms with bath. Facilities: restaurant. No credit cards.*

Parc. Located near the Herăstrău Park and the Flora Hotel, the Parc is modern and within easy reach of the airport; many guests stay here before moving on to the Black Sea resorts. There's a good restaurant that provides music each evening. *Blvd. Poligrafiei 3, tel. 40/506081. 314 rooms with bath. Facilities: restaurant, pool, sauna, tennis. AE, DC, MC, V.*

The Arts

You can enjoy Bucharest's lively theater and music life at prices way below those in the West. Tickets can be obtained directly from the theater or hall, or from your hotel (for a commission fee). Performances usually begin at 7 PM. **Opera Română** (The Opera House), Blvd. Georghiu-Dej 70, and the **Teatrul de Operetă** (Operetta House), Piața Natiunile 1, regularly present excellent productions. Theater performances range from serious drama at the **Teatrul Național** (Caragiale National Theater), Blvd. N. Bălcescu 2, to lighter entertainment at the **Teatrul de Comedie** (Comedy Theater), Str. Mandinesti; despite the language barrier, there is often enough spectacle to ensure a very good evening's entertainment. **Teatrul Tăndărică** (The Tandarica Puppet Theater), Calea Victoriei 50, has an international reputation, and the **Teatrul Evreesc de Stat** (State Jewish Theater), Str. Barasch 15, stages Yiddish-language performances. Don't miss the fine folkloric show at the **Rapsodia Română Artistic Ensemble,** Str. Lipscani 53. Bucharest has many movie theaters; some run old, undubbed American and English films.

Entertainment and Nightlife

Strict economy measures, such as unlit restaurants after 10 PM and dark streets, mean that the city's nightlife is very limited.

Nightclubs The **Athenée Palace** and **Intercontinental** hotels have nightclubs with floor shows. Several other hotels in the Expensive category run video shows.

Cafés Cafés with outdoor terraces remain a feature of the city. The **Gradinița, Casata,** and **Turist** on Boulevard General Magheru are all lively in summer.

The Black Sea Coast and Danube Delta

The southeastern Dobruja region, only 45 minutes by air from Bucharest, 265 kilometers (165 miles) by road, is one of the major focal points of Romania's rich history. Within a clearly defined area are the historic port of Constanța; the Romanian Riviera pleasure coast; the renowned Murfatlar vineyards; Roman, Greek, and earlier ruins; and the Danube Delta, one of Europe's leading wildlife sanctuaries. The rapid development of the Black Sea resorts and increasing interest in the delta region mean that tourist amenities (such as hotels and restaurants) and train, bus, and plane connections are good.

Getting Around

By Bus Bus trips from the Black Sea resorts and Constanța to the Danube Delta, the Murfatlar vineyards, Istria, and Adamclisi are arranged by ONT offices *(see* Tourist Information).

By Car Rental cars can be arranged through local ONT offices.

By Boat Regular passenger and sightseeing boats operate along the middle and southern arms of the delta. If money is no object, there are motorboats for rent in the Danube Delta—or rent one of the more restful fishermen's boats.

Guided Tours

ONT Litoral offers trips to the Danube Delta; the two-day trip is a particularly good value at 450 lei a head. Transportation to Tulcea by bus is followed by a visit to the Danube Delta museum and a hydrobus ride down the center channel of the delta to Crişan, with accommodation at the Lebeda Hotel. A boat tour of the delta's channels, topped off by a meal of locally caught fish, completes the trip. Daily bus trips from Mamaia and Constanţa connect in Tulcea, with pleasure boats plying the middle arm of the river.

Tourist Information

Constanţa. UJT, 69 Blvd. Tomis, tel. 16/4162.
Mamaia. ONT Litoral, Hotel Bucureşti, tel. 18/31780.
Tulcea. UJT, Strada Garii Faleza 2, tel. 15/14720.

Exploring the Black Sea Coast

Tulcea, the main town of the Danube Delta, is the gateway to the splendors of the region. Built, like Rome, on seven hills, this former Oriental-style market town is now an important sea and river port and the center of the Romanian fish industry. The **Muzeul Deltei Dunării** (Danube Delta Museum) provides a good introduction to the flora, fauna, and way of life of the communities in the area. *Str. Progresului 32. Admission: 5 lei. Open 10–6.*

The **Delta Dunării** (Danube Delta) is Europe's largest nature reserve, covering 2,681 square kilometers (1,676 square miles), with a sprawling, watery wilderness that stretches from the Soviet border to a series of lakes north of the Black Sea resorts. It is Europe's youngest land; more than 43.7 square meters (47 square yards) are added each year by normal silting action. As it approaches the delta, the great Danube divides into three. The northernmost branch forms the border with the Soviet Union, the middle arm leads to the busy port of Sulina, and the southernmost arm meanders gently toward the little port of Sf întu Gheorghe. From these channels, countless canals widen into tree-fringed lakes, reed islands, and pools covered with water lilies; there are sand dunes and pockets of lush forest. More than 80% of the delta area is water. Over 300 bird species visit the area; 70 of them come from as far away as China and India. The delta is a natural stopover for migratory birds, but the most characteristic bird is the common pelican, the featured star of this bird-watchers' paradise. Fishing provides most of the area's inhabitants, many of whom are of Ukrainian origin, with a livelihood. Common sights are the long lines of fishing boats strung together to be towed by motorboats to remote fishing grounds. Smaller communities, such as Independenţa on the southern arm and Crişan on the middle arm, rent out the services of a fisherman and his boat to for-

The Black Sea Coast

SOVIET UNION

Galați

Danube

Brăila

Tulcea

Danube Delta

Sulina

Dunavatu

Sfîntu Gheorghe

Babadag

Lake Razelm

Giurgeni

Hîrșova

Crișan

Lake Sinoe

Istria

Slobozia

Fetești

Cernavodă

Mamaia

Black Sea

Danube

Medgidia

Constanța

Călărași

Techirgiol

Eforie

N

Mangalia

BULGARIA

0   20 miles

0   30 km

eigners. The waters here are particularly rich in caviar-bearing sturgeon, catfish, perch, and carp.

There are good roads to the Black Sea resorts from Tulcea, which take you via the strange, eroded Macin hills to **Babadag**. It was here, according to local legend, that Jason and his Argonauts cast anchor in their search for the mythical golden fleece. Farther south is **Istria**, an impressive archeological site founded in 6 BC by Greek merchants from Miletus. Its name derives from *Istros*, the Greek word for the Danube; these early merchants mistakenly thought they had reached one of the mouths of the great river. Once sited on a sea bay, over the centuries it has become closed off by the vast quantities of silt carried down the Danube. The Romans and Byzantines followed the Greeks, and the town thrived until the 6th century AD, defending itself successfully from barbarian attacks. Defensive walls, hastily constructed in any material found near at hand, are still visible today. Early settlers overcame the problem of a freshwater supply by constructing sophisticated pipelines to transport it from the hills over 14.4 kilometers (nine miles) away; sections of these pipes survive, too. There are traces of early Christian churches and baths and even residential, commercial, and industrial districts. A useful English-language booklet, available on the spot, will help make sense of the remains of a number of cultures.

Istria is a popular excursion from the Black Sea resorts and lies only 60 kilometers (37 miles) from **Mamaia**, the largest. The resort is 6.4 kilometers (4 miles) long—a strip of land bordered by the Black Sea and fine beaches on one side, and the fresh waters of the Mamaia lake on the other. Like all the resorts along this stretch of the coast, facilities include high-rise modern apartments, villas, restaurants, nightclubs, and discos. Now that all the hotels have been built, all resources are being channeled into improving the quality of services and expanding the range of entertainment, sports facilities, and excursions. There are cruises down the coast to Mangalia and along the new channel now linking the Danube with the Black Sea near Constanța. Sea-fishing expeditions can also be arranged for early risers, with all equipment provided. These resorts are completely self-contained communities, offering everything necessary for a vacation by the sea.

Constanța is Romania's second-largest city, only a short ride by trolley bus from Mamaia. With the polyglot flavor characteristic of so many seaports, Constanța is also steeped in history. Founded by Greeks in the 6th century BC, Constanța was known as Tomis until the 4th century AD, when it was renamed after Constantine the Great. The famous Roman poet Ovid was exiled here from Rome in AD 8, probably for his part in court scandals and for the amorality of his poem *Ars Amandis (The Art of Making Love)*. He became desperately homesick and appears to have spent much of his time writing letters of complaint back to Rome. A city square has been named in his honor and provides a fine backdrop for a statue of him by sculptor Ettore Ferrari. Behind the statue, in the former town hall, is one of the best museums in Europe, the **Muzeul de Istorie Nationala Arheologie** (National History and Geographical Museum). Of special interest here are the unique *Glykon Serpent* and the *Goddess of Fortune*, protector of the city of Tomis, both surviving from the 2nd and 3rd centuries AD. Two other items not to be missed are the statuettes of the *The Thinker* and *The Seated Woman*, from the neolithic Hamangian culture (4000 to 3000 BC). Collections from the Greek, Roman, and Daco-Roman cultures are generally outstanding. *Piata Ovidiu 12. Admission: 5 lei. Open Tues.–Sun. 10–6.*

Near the museum is **Edificiu Roma cu Mozaic,** a Roman complex of warehouses and shops from the 4th century AD, including a magnificent mosaic floor measuring over 6,510 square meters (21,000 square feet) (Piata Ovidiu 1). Not far away are the remains of the Roman Thermae from the same period. The **Parcul Arheologic** (Archaeology Park) on Boulevard Republicii contains items dating from the 3rd and 4th centuries AD and from a tower erected by the butchers' guild in the 6th century. Modern-day attractions include an **Acvariul,** or aquarium (Str. Februarie 16), and **Delfinariul,** the dolphinarium (Blvd. Lenin 265), which offers aquatic displays by trained dolphins.

A whole string of seaside resorts lie just south of Constanța. **Eforie Nord** is an up-to-date thermal treatment center. A series of resorts built in the 1960s are named for the coast's Greco-Roman past—**Neptune, Jupiter, Venus,** and **Saturn.** Not in any way typically Romanian, these resorts offer good amenities for relaxed, seaside vacations. The old port of **Mangalia** is the southernmost resort.

Most of the old Greek city of **Callatis** lies under water now, but a section of the walls and the remains of a Roman villa are still visible.

ONT offices organize regular excursions from the seaside resorts to the **Columna Traiană** (replica of Trajan's Column), the
Podgoriile Murfatlar (Murfatlar vineyards) for wine tastings,
and the ruins of the Roman town at **Tropaeum Trajani.**

Dining and Lodging

For details and price category definitions, *see* Dining and Lodging in Staying in Romania.

Constanţa **Casino.** A turn-of-the-century former casino situated close to
Dining the aquarium, the Casino is decorated in an ornate 20th-
century style; there's an adjoining bar by the sea. Seafood
dishes are the house specialties. *Str. Februarie 16. No telephone. No credit cards. Moderate.*

Lodging **Palas.** Located near the city's historic center, the large and
gracious old Palas has been renovated recently. It has a good
restaurant and a terrace overlooking the sea and the tourist
port of Tomis. *Str. Opreanu 5–7, tel. 916/14696. 132 rooms. Facilities: restaurant. Expensive.*

Continental. Older, slightly less luxurious, but larger than the
Palas, the Continental is conveniently situated near the open-
air archaeological museum in the downtown area. *Blvd.
Republicii 20, tel. 916/15660. 140 rooms. Moderate.*

Crişan **Lebeda.** This is a comfortable hotel from which to make fishing
Lodging trips into the more remote parts of the delta. *Tel. 915/14720. 74
rooms. Facilities: restaurant, currency exchange. Moderate.*

Mamaia **Insula Ovidiu.** This is a reed-thatched complex of rustic-style
Dining buildings with lively music every evening. A relaxed, informal
atmosphere provides a good setting for delicious seafood
dishes. *Lake Siurghiol. No telephone. Moderate.*

Satul de Vacanţa. This holiday village is an attractive complex
of traditional Romanian buildings, built in styles from all over
Romania and featuring many small restaurants serving local
specialties.

Lodging **International.** One of King Carol's former residences, this is the
largest and grandest of all the hotels in Mamaia. An outdoor
swimming pool, an excellent restaurant, a bar, and a cafeteria
are among its facilities. *Tel. 918/31592 or 31520. 102 rooms.
Very Expensive.*

Ambassador, Lido, and **Savoy.** Among the many modern hotels,
these three are all newly built and moderately priced. They are
grouped in a horseshoe around open-air pools near the beach at
the north of the resort. All *Moderate.*

Tulcea **Delta.** A large, modern hotel on the banks of the Danube, the
Lodging Delta currently enjoys a mixed reputation. Amenities include a
restaurant, bar, and cafeteria. *Str. Isaacei 2, tel. 915/14720.
117 rooms. Moderate.*

26 Spain

Introduction

Spain has long had a rather schizophrenic reputation as a vacation destination among English-speaking tourists. On the one hand, as Europe's premier package-vacation destination, the country is almost instinctively associated in many minds with the worst excesses of the cheap-holiday-in-the-sun, an image conjured up by the vast numbers of faceless hotels along the Mediterranean coasts. The other half of the equation is infinitely more appealing. For Spain is also the land of the fountain-singing courtyards of Moorish Granada and Córdoba, dusty plains where Don Quixote fought imaginary enemies, and of timeless hilltop towns.

Still, if it's beaches you're after, there is the jet-set Costa del Sol in the south, or San Sebastián in the Basque country, formerly the summer capital of Spain. Farther west is the resort city of Santander and La Coruña, a long-standing favorite of British visitors. In the east is the Costa Brava, while to the south, around Alicante, is the Costa Blanca, with its most popular tourist center at Benidorm. When you tire of roasting in the sun, rent a car and head for one of the thousands of castles, ruins, or museums. Perhaps the number-one tourist attraction is the Alhambra, in Granada. Following close behind it come the Mosque of Córdoba, and the Alcázar and cathedral of Seville. Avila is a historic walled town and Segovia boasts a Roman aqueduct and proud Alcázar. Madrid, the capital, contains some of the greatest art collections in the world, while Toledo, home of El Greco, and boasting a cathedral, synagogues, and startling views, is one of Spain's greatest treasures. Finally, Barcelona, capital of Catalonia, has a charm and vitality quite its own.

Before You Go

When to Go The tourist season runs from Easter to mid-October. The best months for sightseeing are May, June, September, and early October, when the weather is usually pleasant and sunny without being unbearably hot. During July and August try to avoid Madrid or the inland cities of Andalusia, where the heat can be stifling and many places close down at 1 PM. If you visit Spain in high summer, the best bet is to head for the coastal resorts or to mountain regions such as the Pyrenees or Picos de Europa. The one exception to Spain's high summer temperatures is the north coast, where the climate is similar to that of northern Europe.

As for crowds, Easter is always a busy time, especially in Madrid, Barcelona, and the main Andalusian cities of Seville, Córdoba, Granada, Málaga, and the Costa del Sol resorts. July and August, when most Spaniards and other Europeans take their annual vacation, see the heaviest crowds, particularly in coastal resorts. Holiday weekends are naturally busy, and major fiestas such as Seville's April Fair or Pamplona's bull runnings make advance booking essential and cause prices to soar. Off-season travel offers fewer crowds and lower rates in many hotels.

Climate The following are the average daily maximum and minimum temperatures for Madrid.

Jan.	47F	9C	May	70F	21C	Sept.	77F	25C
	35	2		50	10		57	14
Feb.	52F	11C	June	80F	27C	Oct.	65F	19C
	36	2		58	15		49	10
Mar.	59F	15C	July	87F	31C	Nov.	55F	13C
	41	5		63	17		42	5
Apr.	65F	18C	Aug.	85F	30C	Dec.	48F	9C
	45	7		63	17		36	2

Currency The unit of currency in Spain is the peseta. There are bills of 500, 1,000, 2,000, 5,000, and 10,000 ptas. Coins are 1 pta., 5, 25, 50, 100, 200, and 500 ptas. The 2- and 10-ptas. coins and the old 100-ptas. bills are rare but still legal tender. At press time (spring 1989), the exchange rate was about 115 ptas. to the U.S. dollar and 200 ptas. to the pound sterling.

Credit Cards Most hotels, restaurants, and stores (though not gas stations) accept payment by credit card. Visa is the most widely accepted piece of plastic, followed by MasterCard (called EuroCard in Spain). More expensive establishments may also take American Express and Diners Club.

Changing Money The word to look for is "Cambio" (exchange). Most Spanish banks take a 1½% commission, though some less scrupulous places charge more; always check, as rates can vary greatly. To change money in a bank, you need your passport and a lot of patience, because filling out the forms takes time. Hotels offer rates lower than banks, but they rarely make a commission, so you may well break even. Restaurants and stores, other than those catering to the tour bus trade, usually will not accept payment by dollars or traveler's checks.

Currency Regulations Visitors may take any amount of foreign currency in bills or traveler's checks into Spain as well as any amount of pesetas. When leaving Spain you may take out only 100,000 ptas. per person in Spanish bank notes and foreign currency up to the equivalent of 500,000 ptas. Unless you can prove you declared the excess at customs on entering the country.

What It Will Cost Prices rose fast in the first decade of Spain's democracy, and Spain's inflation rate was one of the highest in Europe. By the end of 1988, however, inflation had been curbed and was running at around 5%. Generally speaking, the cost of living in Spain is now on a par with that of most other European countries, and the days when Spain was the bargain basement of Europe are truly over. Hotel rates compare favorably with those of France or Britain, restaurants are fairly expensive but offer value-for-money, snacks in cafés and bars are expensive by American or British standards, and alcohol is generally reasonable, except for cocktails in hotel bars. Trains and long-distance buses are inexpensive, and car rental rates are lower than in many other countries. City buses and subways are good value, and cab fares are bargains compared with rates in the United States.

Taxes A value-added tax known as IVA was introduced in 1986 when Spain joined the European Economic Community (EEC). IVA is levied at 6% on most goods and services, but a luxury rate of 12% applies to five-star hotels and to car rental. IVA is always included in the purchase price of goods in stores, but for hotels and car rentals, the tax will be added to your bill. Many restau-

Spain

Bay of
Biscay

El Ferrol
La Coruña
Villalba
Ribadeo
Luarca
Gijón
Santander

Santiago de
Compostela
Lugo
Oviedo
Mieres
Reinosa
Bilbao

CANTABRIAN MTS.

León

Pontevedra
Orense
Ponferrada
Palencia
Burgos

Vigo
Túy
Benavente
Valladolid

Duero

PORTUGAL

Tordesillas
Zamora

Salamanca
Arévalo
Segovia
Guadalajara

Ciudad
Rodrigo
Avila
El Escorial
Madrid

Plasencia
Toledo
Tarancón
Aranjuez

Tajo
Talavera
de la Reina
Alcázar

Cáceres
Trujillo

Miajadas
Guadiana
Ciudad
Real

Mérida
Piedrabuena
Valdepeñas

Badajaz
Zafra
Puebla de
Don Rodrigo

Jerez de los
Caballeros
Bailén
Linares

Fregenal
de la Sierra
Córdoba
Jaén
Cazorla

Aroche
Guadalquivir

Seville
Ejica
Lucena
Guadix

Carmona
Loja
Granada

Huelva
Antequera
Nerja

Gulf of
Cadiz
Sanlúcar de
Barrameda
Ronda
Torremolinos
Málaga
Motril

Cádiz
Jerez de
la Frontera
Marbella
COSTA DEL SOL

ATLANTIC
OCEAN
Algeciras
Gibraltar

Strait of Gibraltar

rants include IVA in their menu prices, but plenty do not. Large stores such as the Corte Inglés and Galerías Preciados operate a tax refund plan for foreign visitors who are not EEC nationals; but to qualify for this refund, you need to spend at least 48,000 ptas. in any one store, and, in theory, on any one item. There is no airport tax in Spain.

Sample Prices A cup of coffee will cost around 100 ptas., a Coca-Cola 120 ptas., bottled beer 140 ptas., a small draught beer 90 ptas., a glass of wine in a bar 60–80 ptas., an American-style cocktail 300–400 ptas., a ham sandwich 220 ptas., an ice cream cone about 100 ptas., a local bus or subway ride 70–90 ptas., and a one-mile taxi ride about 350 ptas.

Language In major cities and coastal resorts you should have no trouble finding people who speak English. In such places, reception staff in hotels of three stars and up are required to speak English. Don't expect the man in the street or the bus driver to speak English, although you may be pleasantly surprised.

Getting Around

By Car
Road Conditions Roads marked A *(autopista)* are toll roads. N stands for national or main roads, and C for country roads. A huge road improvement scheme is currently under way, but many N roads are still single lane and the going can be slow. Tolls vary but are high; for example, Bilbao–Zaragoza 2,930 ptas., Salou–Valencia 2,065 ptas., Seville–Jerez 585 ptas.

Rules of the Road Driving is on the right, and horns and high-beam headlights may not be used in cities. The wearing of front seat belts is compulsory on the highway but not in cities (except the M30 Madrid ring road). Children may not ride in front seats. At traffic circles give way to traffic coming from the right unless your road has priority. Your home driving license is essential and must be carried with you at all times, along with your car insurance and vehicle registration document. You will also need an International Driving License and a Green Card if you are bringing your own car into Spain. Speed limits are 120 kph (74 mph) on autopistas, 100 kph (62 mph) on N roads, 90 kph (56 mph) on C roads and 60 kph (37 mph) in cities unless otherwise signed.

Parking Parking restrictions should be checked locally. A red-and-white-striped line on the curb means no parking. Never leave *anything* on view inside a parked car. Thefts are common and it is safer to leave your car in one of the many paying parking lots; charges are reasonable.

Gasoline At press time, gas costs 74 ptas. a liter for super and 69 ptas. a liter for regular. Unleaded gas *(sin plombo)* is now available at a few pumps. Outside cities, gas stations are few and far between, so don't run low on gas. There is attendant service at most pumps, but there's no need to tip for just a fill-up. Few gas stations accept payment by credit card.

By Train The Spanish railroad system, known usually by its initials RENFE, has greatly improved in recent years. Air-conditioned trains are now widespread but by no means universal. Most overnight trains have first- and second-class sleeping cars and second-class *literas* (couchettes). Dining, buffet, and refreshment services are available on most long-distance trains. There are various types of trains—*Talgo*, ELT (electric unit expresses), TER (diesel rail cars) and ordinary *expresos* and *rápidos*. Fares are determined by the kind of train you travel on and not just by the distance traveled. Talgos are by far the quickest and most comfortable and expensive train; *expresos* and *rápidos* are the slowest and cheapest of the long-distance services. A few lines, such as the FEVE routes along the north coast from San Sebastián to El Ferrol and on the Costa Blanca around Alicante, do not belong to the national RENFE network, and international rail passes are not valid on these lines.

Ticket Purchase and Seat Reservation Tickets can be bought from any station (whether or not it is your point of departure), and from downtown RENFE offices and travel agents displaying the blue and yellow RENFE sign. The latter are often best in the busy holiday season. At stations, buy your advance tickets from the window marked "Largo Recorrido, Venta Anticipada" (Long Distance, Advance Sales). Seat reservation can be made up to 60 days in advance and is obligatory on all the better long-distance services.

Fare Savers The **RENFE Tourist Card** is an unlimited-kilometers pass, valid for eight, 15, or 22 days' travel and can be bought by anyone who lives outside Spain. It is available for first- or second-class travel and can be purchased from RENFE's General Representative in Europe, 3 Ave Marceau, 75116 Paris, France; from selected travel agencies and main railroad stations abroad; and within Spain, at RENFE travel offices and the stations of Madrid, Barcelona, Port Bou, and Irún. At press time the second-class pass cost 10,000 ptas. for eight days, 16,000 ptas. for 15 days, and 21,000 ptas. for 22 days. RENFE has no representative in the United States or Great Britain.

Blue Days *(Días Azules)* leaflets are available from RENFE offices and stations and show those days of the year (approximately 270) when you can travel at reduced rates. Be warned, though, that some of these bargains may apply only to Spaniards or to foreigners officially resident in Spain.

By Plane **Iberia** and its subsidiary **Aviaco** operate a wide network of domestic flights, linking all the main cities and the Balearic Islands. Distances are great and internal airfares are low by European standards, so plane travel around Spain is well worth considering. Flights from the mainland to the Balearics are heavily booked in summer, and the Madrid–Málaga route is frequently overbooked at Easter and in high season. A frequent shuttle service operates between Madrid and Barcelona. Iberia has its own offices in most major Spanish cities and acts as agent for Aviaco. In Madrid, Iberia headquarters are at Velázquez 130 (tel. 91/411–1011 for domestic flights; 91/411–2011 for international flights). Flights can also be booked at most travel agencies.

By Bus Spain has an excellent bus network, but there is no national or nationwide bus company. The network simply consists of numerous private regional bus companies *(empresas)* and there are therefore no comprehensive bus passes. Some of the buses on major routes are now quite luxurious, although this is not always the case in some of the more rural areas. Buses tend to be more frequent than trains, they are sometimes cheaper, and often let you see more of the countryside. On major routes and at holiday times it is advisable to buy your ticket a day or two in advance. Some cities have central bus stations but in many, including Madrid and Barcelona, buses leave from various boarding points. Always check with the local tourist office. Bus stations, unlike train stations, usually provide luggage storage facilities.

Staying in Spain

Telephones
Local Calls

Pay phones work with coins of 5, 25, and either 50 or 100 ptas. Ten ptas. is the minimum for short local calls. In the older gray phones, place several coins in the slot, or in the groove on top of the phone, lift the receiver, and dial the number. Coins then fall into the machine as needed. In the newer green phones, place several coins in the slot, watch the display unit and feed as needed. These phones take 100-ptas. coins. Area codes always begin with a 9 and are different for each province. In Madrid province, the code is 91; in Málaga province, it's 952.

International Calls

Calling abroad can be done from any pay phone marked "Teléfono Internacional." Though good for short European calls, pay phones are not really feasible for transatlantic calls. Use 50 ptas. (or 100 if the phone takes them) coins initially, then coins of any denomination to prolong your call. Dial 07 for international, wait for the tone to change, then 1 for the USA, or 44 for England, followed by the area code and number. For calls to England, omit the initial 0 from the area code. For lengthy international calls, go to the *telefónica*, a telephone office found in all sizable towns, where an operator assigns you a private booth and collects payment at the end of the call; this is the least expensive way of phoning abroad. The cost of calls made from your hotel room includes a service charge, even for collect calls.

Operators and Information

For the operator and information for the city you are in, dial 003; for information for the rest of Spain, 009. If you're in Madrid, dial 008 for Europe; 005 for the rest of the world. From anywhere else in Spain, dial 9198 for Europe, and 9191 for the rest of the world.

Mail
Postal Rates

To the United States, airmail letters up to 15 grams cost 70 ptas., postcards 65 ptas., to the United Kingdom and other EEC countries, letters up to 20 grams cost 45 ptas., postcards 40 ptas. Letters to non-EEC European countries cost 48 ptas. Within Spain, letters cost 19 ptas., postcards 14 ptas. Rates may well change by 1990. Mailboxes are yellow with red stripes, and the slot marked "Extranjero" is the one for mail going abroad. Buy your stamps *(sellos)* at a post office *(correos)* or in a tobacco shop *(estanco)*.

Receiving Mail

If you're uncertain where you'll be staying, have mail sent to American Express or to the Poste Restante *(Lista de Correos)* of the local post office. To claim your mail, you'll need to show your passport. American Express has a $2 service charge per letter, for non-cardholders. The Spanish mail is notoriously slow and not always very efficient.

Shopping
Sales Tax Refunds

If you purchase goods up to a value of 48,000 ptas. or more in any one store (and in theory this should be on only *one* item), you are entitled to a refund of the IVA tax paid (usually 6% but more in the case of certain luxury goods), provided you leave Spain within three months. You will be given two copies of the sales invoice, which you must present at customs together with the goods as you leave Spain. Once the invoice has been stamped by customs, mail the blue copy back to the store, which will then mail your tax refund to you. If you are leaving via the airports of Madrid, Barcelona, Málaga or Palma de Mallorca, you can get your tax refund immediately from the Banco Exterior de España in the airport. The above does not apply to residents of EEC countries, who must claim their IVA refund through customs in their own country. The Corte Inglés and Galerías Preciados department stores operate the above system, but don't be surprised if other stores are unfamiliar with the tax refund procedure and do not have the necessary forms.

Bargaining   Prices in city stores and produce markets are fixed; bargaining is possible only in flea markets, some antiques stores, and with gypsy vendors, with whom it is *essential*, though you'd do best to turn them down flat as their goods are almost always fake and grossly overpriced.

Opening and   **Banks.** Banks are open weekdays 8:30–2, Saturdays 8:30–1 (of-
Closing Times   ten noon in summer). At press time, the situation regarding Saturday banking hours was uncertain, with some banks opening Saturday mornings while others were closed. Be sure to check.

Museums and churches. Opening times vary. Most are open in the morning, and most museums close one day a week, often Monday.

Post offices. These are usually open weekdays 9–2, but this can vary; check locally.

Stores. Stores are open weekdays from 9 or 10 until 1:30 or 2, then again in the afternoon from around 4–7 in winter, and 5–8 in summer. In some cities, especially in summer, stores close on Saturday afternoon. The Corte Inglés and Galerías Preciados department stores in major cities are open continuously from 10–8, and some stores in tourist resorts also stay open through the siesta.

National Holidays   January (New Year's Day); January 6 (Epiphany); March 19 (St. Joseph); April 12 (Holy Thursday); April 13 (Good Friday); May 1 (May Day); June 14 (Corpus Christi); July 25 (St. James); August 15 (Assumption); October 12 (National Day); November 1 (All Saints); December 6 (Constitution); December 8 (Immaculate Conception); December 25 (Christmas Day). Other holidays include May 2 (in the province of Madrid) and June 24 (St. John). Not all these holidays are celebrated in every region; always check locally.

Dining   Visitors have a choice of restaurants, tapas bars, and cafés. Restaurants are strictly for lunch and dinner; they do not serve breakfast. Tapas bars are ideal for a glass of wine or beer accompanied by an array of savory tidbits *(tapas)*. Cafés, called *cafeterías*, are basically coffee houses serving snacks, light meals, tapas, pastries, and coffee, tea, and alcoholic drinks. They also serve breakfast, and are perfect for afternoon tea.

Mealtimes   Mealtimes in Spain are much later than in any other European country. Lunch begins between 1 and 3:30, with 2 being the usual time, and 3 more normal on Sunday. Dinner is usually available from 8:30 onward, but 10 PM is the usual time. An important point to remember is that lunch is the main meal, not dinner. Tapas bars are busiest between noon and 2 and from 8 PM on. Cafés are usually open from around 8 AM to midnight.

Precautions Tap water is said to be safe to drink in all but the remotest villages. However, most Spaniards drink bottled mineral water; ask for either *agua sin gas* (without bubbles) or *agua con gas* (with). A good paella should be served only at lunchtime and should be prepared to order (usually 30 minutes); beware the all-too-cheap version.

Typical Dishes Paella—a mixture of saffron-flavored rice with seafood, chicken, and vegetables—is Spain's national dish. Gazpacho, a cold soup made of crushed garlic, tomatoes, and olive oil and garnished with diced vegetables, is a traditional Andalusian dish and is served mainly in summer. The Basque Country and Galicia are the gourmet regions of Spain, and both serve outstanding fish and seafood. Asturias is famous for its *fabadas* (bean stews), cider, and dairy products; Extremadura for its hams and sausages, and Castile for its roasts, especially *cochinillo* (suckling pig), *cordero asado* (roast lamb), and *perdiz* (partridge). The best wines are those from the Rioja and Penedés regions. Valdepeñas is a pleasant table wine, and most places serve a perfectly acceptable house wine called *vino de la casa*. Sherries from Jerez de la Frontera make fine aperitifs; ask for a *fino* or a *manzanilla;* both are dry. In summer you can try *horchata*, a sweet white drink made from ground nuts, or *granizados de limón* or *de café*, lemon juice or coffee served over crushed ice. *Un café solo* is a small, black, strong coffee, and *café con leche* is coffee with cream, cappuccino-style; weak black American-style coffee is hard to come by.

Dress In Very Expensive and Expensive restaurants, jacket and tie are the norm. Elsewhere, casual dress is appropriate.

Ratings Spanish restaurants are officially classified from five forks down to one fork, with most places falling into the two- or three-fork category. In our rating system, prices are per person and include a first course, main course, and dessert, but not wine or tip. Sales tax (IVA) is often included in the menu price; check the menu for *IVA incluído* or *IVA no incluído*. When it's not included, a further 6% will be added to your bill. Most restaurants offer a fixed-price menu called a *menú del día*. This is usually the cheapest way of eating; *à la carte* dining is more expensive. Service charges are never added to your bill; leave around 10%, less in inexpensive restaurants and bars. Major centers such as Madrid, Barcelona, Marbella, and to a lesser extent Seville, tend to be a bit more expensive. Best bets are indicated by a star ★. At press time, there were 115 pesetas to the dollar.

Category	All Areas
Very Expensive	over 6,000 ptas.
Expensive	4,000 ptas.–6,000 ptas.
Moderate	2,000 ptas.–4,000 ptas.
Inexpensive	800 ptas.–2,000 ptas.

Credit Cards The following credit card abbreviations are used: AE, American Express; DC, Diners Club; MC, MasterCard; V, Visa. Visa is the most widely accepted credit card.

Lodging Spain has a wide range of accommodations, including luxury palaces, medieval monasteries, converted 19th-century houses, modern hotels, high rises on the coasts, and inexpensive hostels in family homes. All hotels and hostels are listed with their rates in the annual *Guía de Hoteles* available from bookstores for around 500 ptas., or you can see a copy in local tourist offices. Rates are always quoted per room, and not per person. Single occupancy of a double room costs 80% of the normal price. Breakfast is rarely included in the quoted room rate; always check. The quality of rooms, particularly in older properties, can be uneven; always ask to see your room *before* you sign the acceptance slip. If you want a private bathroom, state your preference for shower or bathtub; the latter usually costs more though many hotels have both. Local tourist offices will provide you with a list of accommodations in their region, but they are not allowed to make reservations for you. In Madrid and Barcelona, hotel booking agencies are found at the airports and railroad stations.

Hotels and Hostels Hotels are officially classified from five stars (the highest) to one star, hostels from three stars to one star. Hostels are usually a family home converted to provide accommodations that often occupy only part of a building. If an R appears on the blue hotel or hostel plaque, the hotel is classified as a *Residencia*, and full dining services are not provided, though breakfast and cafeteria facilities may be available. A three-star hostel usually equates with a two-star hotel; two- and one-star hostels offer simple, basic accommodations. The main hotel chains are Husa, Iberotel Melia, Sol, and Tryp, and the state-run *paradores* (tourist hotels). Holiday Inn, Inter Continental and Trusthouse Forte also own some of the best hotels in Madrid, Barcelona, and Seville; only these and the paradores have any special character. The others mostly provide clean, comfortable accommodation in the two- to four-star range.

In many hotels rates vary according to the time of year. The hotel year is divided into *estación alta, media,* and *baja* (high, mid, and low season); high season covers the summer and usually Easter and Christmas periods, plus the major fiestas. IVA is rarely included in the quoted room rates, so be prepared for a further 6%, or, in the case of a luxury five-star hotel, 12%, to be added to your bill. Service charges are never included.

Paradores There are about 80 state-owned-and-run paradores, many of which are located in magnificent medieval castles or convents or in places of great natural beauty. Most of these fall into the four-star category and are priced accordingly. All have restaurants that specialize in local regional cuisine and serve a full breakfast. The most popular paradores (Granada's San Francisco parador, for example) are booked far in advance, and many close for a month or two in winter (January or February) for renovations.

Villas Villas are plentiful all along the Mediterranean coast, and cottages in Cantabria and Asturias on the north coast are available from a few agencies. Several agencies in both the United States and United Kingdom specialize in renting property; check with the Spanish National Tourist Office.

Camping There are approximately 530 campsites in Spain, with the highest concentration along the Mediterranean coast. The season runs from April to October, though some sites are open all year-round. Sites are listed in the annual publication *Guía de Campings* available from bookstores or local tourist offices, and further details are available from the Spanish National Tourist Office. Reservations for the most popular seaside sites can be made either directly with the site or through camping reservations at: Federación Española de Empresarios de Campings (Príncipe de Vergara 85, 2°-dcha, 28006 Madrid, tel. 91/262–9994).

Ratings   Prices are for two people in a double room and do not include breakfast. Best bets are indicated by a star ★. At press time, there were 115 pesetas to the dollar.

Category	Major City	Other Areas
Very Expensive	over 17,500 ptas.	15,000–22,000 ptas.
Expensive	11,000–17,000 ptas.	8,500–13,500 ptas.
Moderate	6,500–11,000 ptas.	5,500–8,500 ptas.
Inexpensive	4,000–6,500 ptas.	3,500–5,500 ptas.

Credit Cards   The following credit card abbreviations are used: AE, American Express; DC, Diners Club; MC, MasterCard; V, Visa.

Tipping   Spaniards appreciate being tipped, though the practice is becoming less widespread. Restaurants and hotels are by law not allowed to add a service charge to your bill, though confusingly your bill in both will most likely say *servicios e impuestos incluídos* (service and tax included). Ignore this unhelpful piece of advice, and leave 10% in most restaurants where you have had a full meal; in humbler eating places, bars, and cafés, 5% is often enough, or you can round out the bill to the nearest 100 ptas. A cocktail waiter in a hotel will expect at least 25 ptas. a drink, maybe 50 ptas. in a luxury establishment. Tip taxi drivers 10% when they use the meter, otherwise *nothing*— they'll have seen to it themselves. Gas station attendants get no tip for pumping gas, and about 50 ptas. for checking tires and oil and cleaning windshields. Train and airport porters usually operate on a fixed rate of about 60 ptas. a bag. Coat-check attendants get 25 ptas., and rest room attendants 5 ptas., or 10 ptas. in smarter establishments. In top hotels doormen get 100 ptas. for carrying bags to the check-in counter or for hailing taxis, and bellhops get 50 ptas. for room service or for each bag they carry to your room. In moderate hotels 35–50 ptas. is adequate for the same services. Leave your chambermaid about 300 ptas. for a week's stay. There's no need to tip for just a couple of nights. The waiter in your hotel dining room will appreciate 500 ptas. a week.

Madrid

Arriving and Departing

By Plane   All international and domestic flights arrive at Madrid's Barajas Airport (tel. 91/205–4372), 16 kilometers (10 miles) northeast of town just off the N-II Barcelona highway. For information on arrival and departure times, call **Inforiberia** (tel. 91/411–2545) or the airline concerned.

Between the Airport and Downtown   Buses leave the national and international terminals every 15 minutes from 5:15 AM to 12:45 AM for the downtown terminal at

Plaza de Colón just off the Paseo de la Castellana. The ride takes about 20 minutes and the fare at press time was 200 ptas. Most city hotels are then only a short ride away. The fastest and most expensive route into town (about 1,200 ptas. plus tip) is by taxi. Pay what is on the meter plus 150 ptas. surcharge and 25 ptas. for each suitcase. By car, take the N-II into town, which becomes Avda. de América, then head straight into Calle María de Molina, and left on either Calle Serrano or the Castellana.

By Train Madrid has three main railroad stations. Chamartín, in the northern suburbs beyond the Plaza de Castilla, is the main station, with trains to France, the north and northeast (including Barcelona). Many trains to Valencia, Alicante, and Andalusia now leave from here, too. Atocha, off the Glorieta del Emperador Carlos V, at the southern end of Paseo del Prado, has trains for Toledo, Seville, Granada, Extramdura, and Lisbon; also some services to Valencia and Alicante. Norte (or Príncipe Pío), on Paseo de la Florida, in the west of town below the Plaza de España, is the departure point for Salamanca, Santiago, La Coruña and all destinations in Galicia.

Trains to nearby places like Alcalá, Avila, Segovia, and El Escorial, but *not* Toledo, leave from the suburban stations of Mediodía and Chamartín Cercanías; you can board at either station.

For all train information, tel. 91/552–0518 or 91/429–0518, or go to the RENFE office on Calle de Alcalá 44, open weekdays 9–3 and 5–7. There's another RENFE office at Barajas Airport in the International Arrivals Hall, or you can purchase tickets at any of the three main stations, or from travel agents displaying the blue and yellow RENFE sign.

By Bus Madrid has no central bus station. The two main bus stations are the Estación del Sur (Canarias 17, tel. 91/468–4200), nearest metro Palos de la Frontera, for buses to Toledo, La Mancha, Alicante, and Andalusia (and due to move shortly, so double-check its location); and Auto Res (Plaza Conde de Casal 6, tel. 91/251–6644), nearest metro Conde de Casal, for buses to Extremadura, Cuenca, Salamanca, Valladolid, Valencia, and Zamora. Auto Res has a central ticket and information office at Salud 19 near the Hotel Arosa, just off Gran Vía. Buses to other destinations leave from various points, so check with the tourist office. For Avila, Segovia, and La Granja, Empresa La Sepulvedana (tel. 91/247–5261) leaves from Paseo de la Florida 11, metro Norte; and to El Escorial and Valley of the Fallen, Empresa Herranz (tel. 91/243–8167) leaves from Isaac Peral 10, metro Moncloa.

By Car The main roads are north–south, the Paseo de la Castellana and Paseo del Prado; and east–west, Calle de Alcalá, Gran Vía, and Calle de la Princesa. The M30 ring road circles Madrid to the east and south. For Burgos and France, drive north up the Castellana and follow the signs for the N-I. For Barcelona, head up the Castellana to Plaza Dr. Marañón, then right onto María de Molina and the N-II; for Andalusia and Toledo, head south down Paseo del Prado, then follow the signs to the N-IV and N401, respectively. For Segovia, Avila, and El Escorial, head west along Princesa to Avenida Puerta de Hierro and onto the N-VI La Coruña road.

Getting Around

Madrid is a fairly compact city and most of the main sights are close enough together to be visited on foot. But if you're staying in one of the modern hotels in the north of town off the Castellana, you may well need to use the bus or subway (metro). As a rough guide, the walk from the Prado to the Royal Palace at a comfortable sightseeing pace but without stopping, takes around 30 minutes; from Plaza del Callao on Gran Vía to the Plaza Mayor takes about 15 minutes.

By Metro The subway offers the simplest and quickest means of transport and is open from 6 AM to 1:30 AM. Metro maps are available from ticket offices, hotels, and tourist offices. Fares are 65 ptas. a ride. Savings can be made by buying a *taco* of 10 tickets for 410 ptas., or a tourist card called **Metrotour** that is good for unlimited travel for three or five days. Keep some change (5, 25, and 50 ptas.) handy for the ticket machines, especially after 10 PM.

By Bus City buses are red and run from 6 AM to midnight (though check, as some stop earlier). Again there is a flat fare system, with each ride costing 65 ptas. The smaller, yellow microbuses also cost 65 ptas. and are slightly faster. Route plans are displayed at bus stops *(paradas)*, and a map of the entire system is available from EMT (Empresa Municipal de Transportes) booths on Plaza de la Cibeles, Callao, or Puerta del Sol. Savings can be made by buying a **Bonobus,** good for 10 rides, from EMT booths or any branch of the Caja de Ahorros de Madrid.

By Taxi Madrid has more than 18,000 taxis, and fares are low by New York or London standards. The meter starts at 100 ptas. and each additional kilometer costs 42 ptas. The average city ride costs 300–400 ptas. Cabs available for hire display a "Libre" sign during the day and a green light at night. They hold four passengers. Make sure the driver puts his meter on when you start your ride, and tip 10% of the fare.

Important Addresses and Numbers

Tourist Information The main Madrid tourist office (tel. 91/241–2325) is on the ground floor of the Torre de Madrid in Plaza de España, near the beginning of Calle Princesa and is open weekdays 9–7, Saturdays 10–2. The municipal tourist office is at Plaza Mayor 3 (tel. 91/226–5477) and is open weekdays 10–1:30 and 4–7, Saturdays 10–1:30. A third office is in the International Arrivals Hall of Barajas Airport (tel. 91/205–8656) and is open weekdays 8–8; Saturdays 8–1.

Embassies U.S.: Serrano 75, tel. 91/276–3600; **Canadian:** Núñez de Balboa 35, tel. 91/431–4300; **U.K.:** Fernando el Santo 16, tel. 91/419–1528.

Emergencies Police: National Police, tel. 091; Municipal Police, tel. 092; Main Police (Policía Nacional) Station, Puerta del Sol 7, tel. 91/221–6516. To report lost passports, go to Los Madrazos 9 (tel. 91/221–9350) just off the top of Paseo del Prado. **Ambulance:** Municipal Ambulance Service, tel. 91/230–7145; Red Cross, tel. 91/734–4794. **Doctor:** Your hotel reception will contact the nearest doctor for you. Emergency clinics: **Clínica San Carlos,** Ciudad Universitaria, tel. 91/244–1500; **La Paz Ciudad Sanitaria,** Paseo de la Castellana 261, tel. 91/734–2600. **Bel-San** (Princesa 10, 4th floor, tel. 91/542–6068/6301) is a small clinic with English-speaking doctors and dentists. **Pharmacies:** A list of pharmacies open 24 hours *(farmacias de guardia)* is published daily in *El País*. Hotel receptions usually have a copy. **Company** Puerta del Sol 14, has English-speaking pharmacists. It does not stock American medicines but will recognize many American brand names.

English Bookstores   **Booksellers S.A.:** José Abascal 48, tel. 91/442–7959; **Turner's English Bookshop:** Génova 3, tel. 91/410–2915.

Travel Agencies   **American Express:** Plaza de las Cortes 2, tel. 91/429–7943; **Marsans:** Gran Vía 59, tel. 91/241–5584; **Wagons-Lits/Cook:** Alcalá 23, tel. 91/231–5940.

Airlines   **Iberia:** Velázquez 130, tel. 91/261–9100 and Plaza Cánovas del Castillo 5, tel. 91/429–7443; **British Airways:** Avda. Palma de Mallorca 43, 1st floor, tel. 91/431–7575 and Princesa 1 in the Torre de Madrid, tel. 91/248–7544/9574/2065; **TWA:** Plaza de Colón 2, tel. 91/410–6012/6512.

Guided Tours

Orientation Tours   City sightseeing tours are run by **Juliá Tours**, Gran Vía 68 (tel. 91/270–4600), **Pullmantur**, Plaza de Oriente 8 (tel. 91/241–1805), and **Trapsatur**, San Bernardo 23 (tel. 91/266–9900). All three run the same tours, mostly in 48-seat buses and conducted in Spanish and English. Book tours directly with the offices above, through any travel agent, or through your hotel. Departure points are from the addresses above, though in many cases you can be picked up at your hotel. "Madrid Artístico" is a morning tour of the city with visits to the Royal Palace and Prado Museum, entrances included. The "Madrid Panorámico" tour includes the University City, Casa del Campo park, and the northern reaches of the Castellana. This is a half-day tour, usually in the afternoon, and makes an ideal orientation for the first-time visitor. Also offered are "Madrid de Noche," a night tour combining a drive round the illuminations, dinner in a restaurant, flamenco show, and cabaret at La Scala nightclub; and "Panorámica y Toros," on bullfight days only (usually Sunday), a panoramic drive and visit to a bullfight.

Walking and Special-Interest Tours   Spanish-speaking people can take advantage of a hugely popular selection of tours recently launched by the **Ayuntamiento** (city hall) under the title "Conozcamos Madrid." Walking tours are held most mornings and afternoons in spring and summer, and visit many of the capital's hidden corners, as well as the major sights. Special-interest tours include "Madrid's Railroads," "Medicine in Madrid," "Goya's Madrid," and "Commerce and Finance in Madrid." Some tours are by bus, others on foot. Schedules are listed in the "Conozcamos Madrid" leaflet available from the municipal tourist office.

Excursions   **Juliá Tours, Pullmantur,** and **Trapsatur** run full- or half-day trips to El Escorial, Avila, Segovia, Toledo, and Aranjuez, and in summer to Cuenca and Salamanca; for further details, *see* Madrid Environs. The "Tren de la Fresa" (Strawberry Train) is a popular excursion on summer weekends; a 19th-century train carries passengers from the old Delicias Station to Aranjuez and back. Tickets can be obtained from RENFE offices, travel agents, and the Delicias Station, Paseo de las Delicias 61. Other one- or two-day excursions by train to places such as Avila, Cuenca, or Salamanca are available on weekends in summer. Details from RENFE.

Personal Guides Contact any of the tourist offices, or the Association of Madrid Guides, Duque de Medinaceli 2 (tel. 91/429–4951). A most knowledgeable English-speaking guide is Conchita de los Reyes (Alcalde Sainz de Baranda 63-8°-B, tel. 91/273–7620). She can arrange private transport and is qualified to take tours of Madrid and all surrounding cities.

Exploring Madrid

Numbers in the margin correspond with points of interest on the Madrid map.

You can walk the following route in a day, or even half a day if you stop only to visit the Prado and Royal Palace. Two days should give you time for browsing. Begin in the Plaza Atocha, more properly known as the Glorieta del Emperador Carlos V, at the bottom of the Paseo del Prado, and check out what's showing in the **Reina Sofía Arts Center** opened by Queen Sofía in 1986. This converted hospital, home of art and sculpture exhibitions and symbol of Madrid's new cultural pride, aims to become one of Europe's most dynamic venues—a Madrileño rival to Paris's Pompidou Center. The main entrance is on Calle de Santa Isabel 52. *Admission: 400 ptas. Open daily except Tues. 10 AM–9 PM.*

Walk up Paseo del Prado to Madrid's number-one sight, the famous **Prado Museum,** one of the world's most important art galleries. Plan on spending at least one and a half hours here, though to view its treasures properly will take at least two full days. Brace yourself for the crowds. The greatest treasures— the Velázquez, Murillo, Zurbarán, El Greco, and Goya galleries —are all on the upstairs floor. Two of the best works are Velázquez's *Surrender of Breda* and his most famous work, *Las Meninas*, which occupies a privileged position in a room of its own. The Goya galleries contain the artist's none-too-flattering royal portraits—Goya believed in painting the truth—his exquisitely beautiful *Marquesa de Santa Cruz*, and his famous *Naked Maja* and *Clothed Maja*, for which the 13th Duchess of Alba was said to have posed. Goya's most moving works, the *2nd of May* and the *Fusillade of Moncloa* or *3rd of May*, vividly depict the sufferings of Madrid patriots at the hands of Napoleon's invading troops in 1808. Before you leave, feast your eyes on the fantastic flights of fancy of Hieronymus Bosch's *Garden of Earthly Delights* and his triptych *The Hay Wagon*, both downstairs on the ground floor. *Admission: 400 ptas. Open Tues.–Sat. 9–7, Sun. 9–2.*

Time Out Downstairs is a pleasant cafeteria, ideal for a light lunch.

Across the street is the **Ritz,** the grand old lady of Madrid's hotels, built in 1910 by Alfonso XIII when he realized that his capital had no hotels elegant enough to accommodate the guests at his wedding in 1906. The Ritz garden is a delightfully aristocratic place to lunch in summer—men always need ties.

In the **Casón del Buen Retiro,** entrance on Calle Alfonso XII, Picasso's *Guernica* hangs behind bulletproof glass, a haunting expression of the artist's anguish and outrage at the German bombing of this small Basque town in April 1937. *Open same hours as Prado and visited on same ticket.*

⑤ The **Retiro,** once a royal retreat, is today Madrid's prettiest park. Visit the beautiful rose garden, **La Rosaleda,** and enjoy the many statues and fountains. You can hire a carriage, row a boat on **El Estanque,** gaze up at the monumental **statue to Alfonso XII,** one of Spain's least notable kings though you wouldn't think so to judge by its size, or wonder at the **Monument to the Fallen Angel**—Madrid claims the dubious privilege of being the only capital to have a statue dedicated to the Devil. The **Palacio de Velázquez** and the beautiful steel and glass **Palacio de Cristal,** built as a tropical plant house in the 19th century, now host art exhibits.

⑥ Leaving the Retiro via its northwest corner, you come to the Plaza de la Independencia, dominated by the **Puerta de Alcalá,** a grandiose gateway built in 1779 for Charles III. A customs post once stood beside the gate, as did the old bullring until it was moved to its present site at Ventas in the 1920s. At the turn of the century, the Puerta de Alcalá more or less marked the eastern limits of Madrid.

Time Out The **Café Lyon,** Alcalá 57, with its marble-topped tables and charming old world air, is an ideal place for some light refreshment.

⑦ Continue to the **Plaza de la Cibeles,** one of the great landmarks of the city, at the intersection of its two main arteries, the Castellana and Calle de Alcalá. If you can see it through the roar and fumes of the thundering traffic, the square's center is the **Cibeles Fountain,** the unofficial emblem of Madrid. Cybele, the Greek goddess of fertility, languidly rides her lion-drawn chariot, overlooked by the mighty **Palacio de Comunicaciones,** a splendidly pompous cathedral-like building often jokingly dubbed Our Lady of Communications. In fact, it's the main post office, erected in 1918. The famous goddess looks her best at night when she's illuminated by floodlights.

⑧ Now head down the long and busy Calle de Alcalá toward the Puerta del Sol, resisting the temptation to turn right up the Gran Vía, which beckons temptingly with its mile of stores and cafés. Before you reach the Puerta del Sol, art lovers may want to step inside the **Real Academia de Bellas Artes** at Alcalá 13. This recently refurbished fine arts gallery boasts an art collection second only to the Prado's and features all the great Spanish masters: Velázquez, El Greco, Murillo, Zurbarán, Ribera, and Goya. *Open Tues.–Sat. 9–7, Sun. and Mon. 9–2.*

Time Out A small detour down Sevilla, then right down San Jerónimo, brings you to two atmospheric places for a drink or light lunch. **Lhardy,** San Jerónimo 8 (tel. 91/222–2207), is a veritable old Madrid institution that opened as a pastry shop in 1839. Today it combines the roles of expensive restaurant and delicatessen. *Closed Sun. evening and in Aug.*

Next door, at no. 6, on the corner of Espoz y Mina, is the more moderately priced **Museo de Jamón,** a relative newcomer on the Madrid scene, with hundreds of hams hanging from its ceilings. It's ideal for a beer or glass of wine and a generous plate of cheese or ham.

Major Attractions

Other Attractions

⑨ The **Puerta del Sol** is at the very heart of Madrid. Its name means Gate of the Sun, though the old gate disappeared long ago. It's easy to feel you're at the heart of things here—indeed, of all of Spain—for the kilometer distances for the whole nation are measured from the zero marker in front of the Police Headquarters. The square was expertly revamped in 1986 and now accommodates both a copy of **La Mariblanca** (a statue that 250 years ago adorned a fountain here) and, at the bottom of Calle Carmen, the much loved statue of the **bear and *madroño*** (strawberry tree). The Puerta del Sol is inextricably linked with the history of Madrid and of the nation. Here, half a century ago, a generation of literati gathered in the long-gone cafés to thrash out the burning issues of the day; and if you can cast your thoughts back almost 200 years, you can conjure up the heroic deeds of the patriots' uprising immortalized by Goya in the *2nd of May*.

This is a good place to break the tour if you've had enough sightseeing for one day. Head north up Preciados or Montera for some of the busiest and best shopping streets in the city, or southeast toward Plaza Santa Ana, for tavern-hopping in Old Madrid.

Time Out If it's teatime (6–7 PM), don't miss **La Mallorquina,** an old pastry shop between Calle Mayor and Arenal. Delicious pastries are sold at the downstairs counter; the old-fashioned upstairs tea salon offers an age-old tea ritual and unbeatable views over the Puerta del Sol.

⑩ Art lovers will want to make a detour to the **Convento de las Descalzas Reales** on Plaza Descalzas Reales just above Arenal. It was founded by Juana de Austria, daughter of Charles V, and is still inhabited by nuns. Over the centuries the nuns, daughters of the royal and noble, endowed the convent with an enormous wealth of jewels, religious ornaments, superb Flemish tapestries, and the works of great masters like Titian and Rubens. A bit off the main tourist track, it's one of Madrid's better kept secrets. Your ticket includes admission to the nearby, but less interesting, **Convento de la Encarnación.** *Admission: 200 ptas. Guided tours only. Open Tues.–Thurs., Sat. 10:30–12:30 and 4–5:15; Fri. 10:30–12:30; Sun. 11–1:15.*

Walk up **Calle Mayor,** the Main Street of Old Madrid, past the shops full of religious statues and satins for bishops' robes, to **⑪** the **Plaza Mayor,** the capital's greatest architectural showpiece. It was built in 1617–19 for Philip III—that's Philip on the horse in the middle. The plaza has witnessed the canonization of saints, burning of heretics, fireworks and bullfights, and is still one of the great gathering places of Madrid.

Time Out In summer you can relax over a drink in any of the delightful sidewalk cafés that adorn the square; in winter, head for the **Mesón del Corregidor** at no. 8, near the Cuchilleros arch. This colorful tavern restaurant has typical dishes and tapas.

If you're here in the morning, take a look inside the 19th-century steel and glass San Miguel market, a colorful provi- **⑫** sions market, before continuing down Calle Mayor to the **Plaza de la Villa.** The square's notable cluster of buildings includes some of the oldest houses in Madrid. The **Casa de la Villa,** the

Madrid city hall, was built in 1644 and has also served as the city prison and the mayor's home. Its sumptuous salons are now open to the public on Mondays at 5 PM. The free guided visits are usually in Spanish, but English tours can be arranged with advance notice. An archway joins the Casa de la Villa to the **Casa Cisneros,** a palace built in 1537 for the nephew of Cardinal Cisneros, primate of Spain and infamous inquisitor general. Across the square, the **Torre de Lujanes** is one of the oldest buildings in Madrid. It once imprisoned Francis I of France, archenemy of the Emperor Charles V.

Time Out If it's lunchtime, close by is a moderately priced restaurant that is a long-standing Madrid tradition: **Casa Ciriaco** on Calle Mayor 84.

13 The last stop on the tour, but Madrid's second most important sight, is the **Royal Palace.** This magnificent granite and limestone residence was begun by Philip V, the first Bourbon king of Spain, who was always homesick for his beloved Versailles, the opulence and splendor of which he did his best to emulate. His efforts were successful, to judge by the 2,800 rooms with their lavish Rococo decorations, precious carpets, porcelain, time pieces, mirrors, and chandeliers. From 1764, when Charles III first moved in, till the coming of the Second Republic and the abdication of Alfonso XIII in 1931, the Royal Palace proved a very stylish abode for Spanish monarchs. Today King Juan Carlos, who lives in the far less ostentatious Zarzuela Palace outside Madrid, uses it only for official state functions. The Palace can be visited only on guided tours, available in English. Allow 1½–2 hours for a visit. A *visita completa* (full visit), including the Royal Carriage Museum (below), costs 500 ptas.; most visitors opt for the *Salones Oficiales* (State Rooms) ticket at 300 ptas. *Open Mon.–Sat. 9:30–12:45 and 4–6 (3:30–5:15 in winter), Sun. 9:30–1. Closed during official functions.*

14 The **Royal Carriage Museum,** which belongs to the palace but has a separate entrance on Paseo Vírgen del Puerto, can be visited on an all-inclusive or separate ticket. One of its highlights is the wedding carriage of Alfonso XIII and his English bride, Victoria Eugenia, granddaughter of Queen Victoria, which was damaged by a bomb thrown at it in the Calle Mayor during their wedding procession in 1906; another is the chair that carried the gout-stricken old Emperor Charles V to his retirement at the remote monastery of Yuste. *Admission: 150 ptas., or 500 ptas. joint ticket to Royal Palace. Open Mon.–Sat. 9:30–12:45 and 4–6 (3:30–5:15 in winter), Sun. 9:30–1 only. Closed during official functions.*

Off the Beaten Track

Stroll around the narrow streets of the **Chueca** between Hortaleza and Paseo de Recoletos. Look for the architectural features of the old houses, the dark, atmospheric bars and restaurants well known to discerning Madrileños, and the small stores with their wooden counters and brass fittings, many of which have been run by the same family for generations. Calle Infantas has some real gems: the **Bolsa de los Licores** at no. 13 selling wines and liqueurs from every corner of Europe; the splendid silver shop at no. 25; the Old World grocery store **Casa Jerez** at no. 32. And don't miss the **Tienda de Vinos** restaurant in

Augusto Figueroa, affectionately nicknamed "El Comunista" and long famed for its rock-bottom prices. The whole quarter seems to come straight from the pages of a 19th-century novel.

The old **Lavapiés** quarter, between Calle Atocha and Embajadores, is another area with plenty of atmosphere. Traditionally one of the poorest parts of Old Madrid, it is now the home of artists and actors, writers and musicians. Health-food restaurants—a novelty in Spain generally—have flourished. You can get a good cheap lunch at **La Biótica,** Amor de Diós 3, or **El Granero de Lavapiés,** Argumosa 10. In summer you can eat in the courtyard of the old tenement building **La Corrala,** Mesón de Paredes 32, and watch a *zarzuela* performance on its ancient balconies.

Casa Mingo (Paseo de la Florida 2, tel. 91/247–7918), is a tiny Asturian tavern behind Norte Station. A real Madrid institution, it's long been famous for its Asturian cider, goat cheese, and succulent chicken at amazingly low prices.

Shopping

Gift Ideas   There are no special regional crafts associated with Madrid itself, but traditional Spanish goods are on sale in many stores. The **Corte Inglés** and **Galerías Preciados** department stores both stock good displays of Lladró porcelain, as do several specialist shops on the Gran Vía and behind the Plaza hotel on Plaza de España. Department stores stock good displays of fans, but for really superb examples, try the long-established **Casa Diego** in Puerta del Sol. Two stores opposite the Prado on Plaza Cánovas del Castillo, **Artesanía Toledana** and **El Escudo de Toledo,** have a wide selection of souvenirs, especially Toledo swords, inlaid marquetry ware, and pottery.

Antiques   The main areas to see are the Plaza de las Cortes, the Carrera San Jerónimo, and the Rastro flea market, along the Ribera de Curtidores and the courtyards just off it.

Boutiques   Calle Serrano has the largest collection of smart boutiques and designer fashions. Another up-and-coming area is around Calle Argensola, just south of Calle Génova. **Loewe,** Spain's most prestigious leather store, has boutiques on Serrano 26 and Gran Vía 8. Adolfo Domínguez, one of Spain's top designers, has several boutiques in Salamanca, and another on Calle Orense in the north of town.

Shopping Districts   The main shopping area in the heart of Madrid is around the pedestrian streets of **Preciados** and **Montera,** between Puerta del Sol and Plaza Callao on Gran Vía. The smartest and most expensive district is the **Barrio de Salamanca** northeast of Cibeles, centered around Serrano, Velázquez, and Goya. **Calle Mayor** and the streets to the east of **Plaza Mayor** are lined with fascinating old-fashioned stores straight out of the 19th century.

Department Stores   **El Corte Inglés** is the biggest, brightest, and most successful Spanish chain store. Its main branch is on Preciados, just off the Puerta del Sol. **Galerías Preciados** is its main rival, with branches on Plaza Callao right off Gran Vía, Calle Arapiles, Goya corner of Conde de Peñalver, Serrano and Ortega y Gasset, and its newest branch at La Vaguada. Both stores are open Monday–Saturday 10–8, and neither closes for the siesta.

Food and Flea Markets The Rastro, Madrid's most famous flea market, operates on Sundays from 9 to 2 around the Plaza del Cascorro and the Ribera de Curtidores. A **stamp and coin** market is held on Sunday mornings in the Plaza Mayor, and there's a **secondhand book** market most days on the Cuesta Claudio Moyano near Atocha Station.

Bullfighting

The Madrid bullfighting season runs from March to October. Fights are held on Sunday, and sometimes also on Thursday; starting times vary between 4:30 and 7 PM. There are two bullrings: The main one is Ventas, Alcalá 237 (metro Ventas); the other is Vista Alegre, Avenida Plaza de Toros in Carabanchel, south of the Manzanares River. Buy your tickets at the rings or from the official "Despacho" (ticket office) on Calle Victoria 9 (tel. 91/221–4870), just off Carrera San Jerónimo and Puerta del Sol. The best fights are held during the San Isidro festivals in mid-May.

Dining

For details and price category definitions, *see* Dining in Staying in Spain.

Very Expensive **Irízar Jatetxea.** Owned by the famous Basque restaurateur Luis Irízar, this is one of Madrid's most luxurious and renowned restaurants. It's opposite the Teatro Zarzuela (next to Armstrong's) and the cuisine is Basque, but much influenced by nouvelle cuisine from France and Navarre. Definitely a place for a treat. *Jovellanos 3, tel. 91/231–4569. Reservations essential. AE, DC, V. Closed Sat. lunch, Sun. dinner.*

★ **Zalacaín.** This private villa with elegant decor, top-notch cuisine, and personalized service is the highest-rated restaurant in Spain. Located just off the Castellana and María de Molina, it is the only Spanish restaurant awarded three Michelin stars. *Alvarez de Baena 4, tel. 91/261–4840. Reservations essential. AE, DC. Closed Sat. lunch, Sun., Holy Week, Aug.*

Expensive ★ **El Cenador del Prado.** This elegant and stylish restaurant just off Plaza Santa Ana offers beautiful decor and an imaginative menu with more than a hint of nouvelle cuisine. The chef learned his trade in New York, and specialties include *caracoles con setas en hojaldre* (snails and mushrooms en croute) and *salmón marinado a la pimienta verde* (salmon marinated in green peppers). *Calle del Prado 4, tel. 91/429–1549. Reservations advised. AE, DC, MC, V. Closed Sat. lunch, Sun., two weeks in Aug.*

La Dorada. One of Madrid's most outstanding fish restaurants, the seafood here is flown in daily in the owner's private plane from the Costa del Sol. Its sister restaurants in Barcelona and Seville are equally esteemed. It's located in the modern north of town, near the Azca Center and Holiday Inn. *Orense 64, tel. 91/270–2004. Reservations essential. AE, DC, V. Closed Sun., Aug.*

New Yorker. This fashionable restaurant, popular with business-people, opened in 1985. The ambience is elegant, and contemporary Spanish paintings adorn the walls. The menu offers international specialties and service that's highly professional. *Amador de los Ríos 1, to the west of the Castellana* *just above the Plaza Colón, tel. 91/410–1522. Reservations essential. AE, V. Closed Sat. lunch, Sun.*

Solchaga. Here you can choose between several dining rooms, each with its own distinctive character. Pot-bellied stoves and ornate gilt mirrors help convey the atmosphere of an old-fashioned private house rather than a restaurant; a charming find. *Plaza de Alonso Martínez 2, tel. 91/447–1496. Reservations advised. AE, DC, MC, V. Closed Sat. lunch, Sun.*

Moderate **Armstrong's.** This charming English-owned restaurant opposite the Teatro Zarzuela is bright and modern with refreshing pink decor and is quite a change from the usual Madrid scene. Its imaginative menu mixes French and Spanish nouvelle cuisine with English and American favorites, and there's a good choice of salads, brunch on weekends, and a special teatime menu. It even opens for dinner at 6 PM! *Jovellanos 5, tel. 91/522 –4230. Reservations advised but not essential. AE, DC, MC, V. Closed Sun. evening and Mon.*

La Barraca. A Valencian restaurant with cheerful blue and white decor, colorful windowboxes, and ceramic tiles, this is the place to go for a wonderful choice of paellas. Located just off Gran Vía (Alcalá end), behind Loewe, it's popular with businesspeople and foreign visitors. Try the *paella reina* or the *paella de mariscos. Reina 29, tel. 91/232–7154. Reservations advised. AE, DC, MC, V.*

Botín. Madrid's oldest and most famous, restaurant, just off the Plaza Mayor, has been catering to diners since 1725. Its decor and food are traditionally Castilian. *Cochinillo* (suckling pig) and *cordero asado* (roast lamb) are its specialties. It was a favorite with Hemingway; today it's very touristy and a bit overrated, but fun. Insist on the *cueva* or upstairs dining room. *Cuchilleros 17, tel. 91/266–4217. Reservations, especially at night. AE, DC, MC. V. Two sittings for dinner, at 8 and 10:30.*

★ **Carmencita.** Dating back to 1850, this charming restaurant is small and intimate, with ceramic wall tiles, brass hat racks, and photos of bullfighters. The menu recounts the famous who have dined here and their life stories. The cuisine is part traditional, part nouvelle with an emphasis on *pasteles* (a kind of mousse) both savory and sweet. *Libertad 16, on the corner of San Marcos in the Chueca area above Gran Vía; tel. 91/231–6612. Reservations not essential. V. Closed Sun.*

Casa Ciriaco. In this atmospheric old standby only a few paces from the Plaza Mayor and city hall, the Madrid of 50 years ago lives on. You won't find many foreigners here—just businesspeople and locals, enjoying traditional Spanish cooking and delicious *fresones* (strawberries) for dessert. *Mayor 84, tel. 91/ 248–0620. Reservations usually unnecessary. No credit cards. Closed Wed., and Aug.*

★ **Fuente Real.** Dining here is like eating in a turn-of-the-century home. Tucked away between Mayor and Arenal, it's brimming with personal mementoes such as antique dolls, Indian figures, and Mexican Christmas decorations. The cuisine is French and Spanish with an emphasis on quality meats and crêpes. Try the *pastel de espinacas* (spinach mousse) or *crêpes de puerros* (leeks). *Fuentes 1, tel. 91/248–6613. Reservations not needed. AE, MC, V. Closed Sun. PM and Mon.*

Inexpensive **El Cuchi.** "Hemingway *never* ate here" is the sign that will lure
★ you inside this colorful tavern at the bottom of the Cuchilleros steps off the Plaza Mayor. A fun-packed experience awaits.

The ceilings are plastered with photos of Mexican revolutionaries, huge blackboards announce the menu and list the calories in the irresistible desserts, and home-baked rolls are lowered in baskets from the ceiling to your table. Salads are on the house. This is a place you shouldn't miss. *Cuchilleros 3, tel. 91/ 266-4424. Reservations advised. AE, DC, MC, V. Never closes.*

El Luarqués. One of many budget restaurants on this street, El Luarqués is decorated with photos of the port of Luarca on Spain's north coast, and it's always packed with Madrileños who recognize its good value. *Fabada asturiana* (bean and meat stew) and *arroz con leche* (rice pudding) are two of its Asturian specialties. *Ventura de la Vega 16, tel. 91/429-6174). Reservations not accepted. No credit cards. Closed Sun. evening, Mon., and Aug.*

Lodging

Hotels around the center in the midst of all the sights and shops are mostly located in old 19th-century houses; many of these are currently undergoing restoration to bring them up to standard. Most of the newer hotels that conform to American standards of comfort are located in the northern part of town on either side of the Castellana and are a short metro or bus ride from the center. There are hotel reservation desks in the national and international terminals of the airport, and at Chamartín station. Or you can contact **La Brújula** (tel. 91/248-9705) on the sixth floor of the Torre de Madrid in Plaza de España, which is open 9–9. It has English-speaking staff and can book hotels all over Spain.

For details and price category definitions, *see* Lodging in Staying in Spain.

Very Expensive **Fénix.** Located just off the Castellana near the Plaza Colón and convenient for the Salamanca shopping district, this is fast becoming Madrid's leading four-star hotel. It's a favorite with influential businesspeople and conveys a feeling of style and luxury. Its bar and cafeteria are popular meeting places. *Hermosilla 2, tel. 91/431-6700. 216 rooms. AE, DC, MC, V.*

Palace. This dignified turn-of-the-century hotel opposite parliament and the Prado is a slightly less dazzling step-sister of the nearby Ritz but full of charm and style. Long a favorite of politicians and journalists, its Belle Epoque decor—especially the glass dome over the lounge—is superb. *Plaza de las Cortes 7, tel. 91/429-7551. 518 rooms. AE, V.*

★ **Ritz.** Spain's most exclusive hotel is elegant and aristocratic with beautiful rooms, spacious suites, and sumptuous public salons furnished with antiques and handwoven carpets. Its palatial restaurant is justly famous and its garden terrace is the perfect setting for summer dining. Features are brunches with harp music on weekends and tea or supper chamber concerts from February through May. Close to the Retiro Park and overlooking the famous Prado Museum, it offers pure unadulterated luxury. It is substantially more expensive than most other hotels in this category. *Plaza Lealtad 5, tel. 91/521-2857. 156 rooms. AE, DC, MC, V.*

Villa Magna. Second in luxury only to the Ritz, a modern facade belies a palatial interior exquisitely furnished with 18th-century antiques. Set in a delightful garden, it offers all the facilities one would expect in a hotel of international repute. It is substantially more expensive than most other hotels in this category. *Paseo de la Castellana 22, tel. 91/261–4900. 194 rooms. AE, DC.*

Expensive **Alcalá.** Close to the Retiro Park and Goya shopping area, this ★ comfortable hotel has long been recognized for high standards. Bedrooms are well furnished, each with TV and minibar, and the cafeteria serves a good lunch menu for around 900 ptas. The hotel restaurant, Le Basque (closed Sun. and Mon. lunch), is owned by Luis Irízar of the famous Irízar Jatetxea restaurant, and its Basque culinary delights are well known to Madrileños. *Alcalá 66, tel. 91/435–1060. 153 rooms. AE, DC, MC, V.*

Emperador. This older hotel on the corner of San Bernardo has been renovated throughout, and storm windows now help to shut out the roar of Gran Vía traffic. All the rooms have TV and VCR, and a special feature is the rooftop pool and terrace with superb views. *Gran Vía 53, tel. 91/247–2800. 231 rooms. AE, DC, MC, V.*

★ **Plaza.** This elegant hotel at the bottom of Gran Vía has long been a favorite with American visitors. New storm windows cut down the traffic noise, security safes have been installed in each room, and the mattresses have all been changed for harder ones more suited to American tastes. The view from its legendary rooftop pool is a favorite with Spanish and foreign photographers. *Plaza de España, tel. 91/247–1200. 306 rooms. AE, DC, MC, V.*

Sanvy. Backing onto the Fénix, the Sanvy, located just off the Plaza Colón on the edge of the Salamanca district, is a comfortable, well-renovated hotel with a swimming pool on the top floor. Its **Belagua Restaurant** is gaining prestige. *Goya 3, tel. 91/276–0800. 141 rooms. AE, DC, MC, V.*

Moderate **Capitol.** If you like being right in the center of things, then this hotel on the Plaza Callao is for you. It's an older hotel, of which four floors have been renovated, and these rooms are comfortable indeed. There's a well-decorated reception area and a pleasant cafeteria for breakfast. *Gran Vía 41, tel. 91/521–8391. 145 rooms. AE, DC, V.*

Mayorazgo. An older hotel that has yet to be renovated, but comfortable as long as you're not seeking all the conveniences of home. Advantages are its friendly old-fashioned service and its prime location right in the heart of town, yet it's tucked away in a quiet back street off Gran Vía leading down to Plaza de España. *Flor Baja 3, tel. 91/247–2600. AE, DC, MC, V.*

Rex. This is a sister hotel to the Capitol next door, and both belong to the Tryp chain. It's located on the corner of Silva just down from Callao, and the lobby, bar, restaurant, and two floors have so far been completely refurbished. The unrenovated rooms are considerably cheaper, but you'll be much more comfortable in one of the newer ones. *Gran Vía 43, tel. 91/247–4800. 147 rooms. AE, DC, V.*

Inexpensive **Cliper.** This simple hotel offers good value for the cost-conscious traveler. It's tucked away in a side street off the central part of Gran Vía between Callao and Red San Luis. *Chinchilla 6, tel. 91/231–1700. 52 rooms. AE, MC, V.*

★ **Inglés.** The exterior may seem shabby but don't be deterred. The Inglés is a long-standing budget favorite. Its rooms are comfortable, with good facilities, and the location is a real bonus: You're a short walk from the Puerta del Sol one way, and from the Prado the other; inexpensive restaurants and atmospheric bars are right at hand. *Echegaray 10, tel. 91/429-6551, 58 rooms. AE, DC, MC, V.*

Paris. Overlooking the Puerta del Sol, the Paris is a stylish hotel full of old-fashioned appeal. It has an impressive turn-of-the-century lobby and a restaurant where you can dine for around 1500 ptas. Currently being refurbished, it's to be hoped that the renovations do nothing to detract from the charm. *Alcalá 2, tel. 91/521-6496). 114 rooms. MC, V.*

Bars and Cafés

Bars **The Mesones.** The most traditional and colorful taverns are on Cuchilleros and Cava San Miguel just west of Plaza Mayor, where you'll find a whole array of mesones with names like **Tortilla, Champiñón,** and **Huevo.**

Old Madrid. Wander the narrow streets between Puerta del Sol and Plaza Santa Ana, which are packed with traditional tapas bars. Favorites here are the **Cervecería Alemana,** Plaza Santa Ana 6, a beer hall founded more than 100 years ago by Germans and patronized, inevitably, by Hemingway; **Los Gabrieles,** Echegaray 17, with magnificent ceramic decor; **La Trucha,** Manuel Fernández y González 3, with loads of atmosphere; and **Viva Madrid,** Fernández y González 7, a lovely old bar.

Calle Huertas. Fashionable wine bars with turn-of-the-century decor and chamber or guitar music, often live, line this street. **La Fídula** at no. 57 and **El Elhecho** at no. 56 are two of the best.

Plaza Santa Barbara. This area just off Alonso Martínez is packed with fashionable bars and beer halls. Stroll along Santa Teresa, Orellana, Campoamor, or Fernando VI and take your pick. The **Cervecería Santa Barbara** in the plaza itself is one of the most colorful, a popular beer hall with a good range of tapas.

Cafés If you like cafés with old-fashioned atmosphere, dark wooden counters, brass pumps and marble-topped tables, try any of the following: **Café Comercial,** Glorieta de Bilbao 7; **Café Gijón,** Paseo de Recoletos 21, a former literary hangout and the most famous of the cafés of old, now one of the many café-terraces that line the Castellana; **Café Lyon,** Alcalá 57, just up from Cibeles; **Café Roma** on Serrano; and **El Espejo,** Paseo de Recoletos 31, with art-nouveau decor and an outdoor terrace in summer. And don't forget **La Mallorquina** tearooms on Puerta del Sol (*see* Exploring).

The Arts

Details of all cultural events are listed in the daily newspaper *El País* or in the weekly *Guía del Ocio.*

Concerts and The main concert hall is the new **Auditorio Nacional de Madrid,**
Opera Príncipe de Vergara 136 (metro, Prosperidad), which opened at the end of 1988. The old **Teatro Real** on the Plaza de Oriente opposite the Royal Palace is being converted into Madrid's long-needed opera house.

Zarzuela and Zarzuela, a combination of light opera and dance ideal for non-
Dance Spanish speakers, is held at the **Teatro Nacional Lírico de la Zarzuela,** Jovellanos 4, tel. 91/429-8216. Another zarzuela ven-

ue is the **Teatro Apolo,** Plaza Tirso de Molina 1, tel. 91/227–3816. The season runs from October to July.

Theater   If language is no problem, check out the fringe theaters in Lavapiés (*see* Off the Beaten Track) and the **Centro Cultural de la Villa** (tel. 91/275–6080) beneath the Plaza Colón, and the open-air events in the Retiro Park. Other leading theaters—you'll also need reasonable Spanish—include the **Círculo de Bellas Artes,** Marqués de Casa Riera 2, just off Alcalá 42 (tel. 91/231–8507); the **Teatro Español,** Príncipe 25 on Plaza Sta. Ana (tel. 91/429–6297) for Spanish classics; and the **Teatro María Guerrero,** Tamayo y Baus 4 (tel. 91/419–4769), the home of the Centro Dramático Nacional, often puts on plays by García Lorca. Most theaters have two curtains, at 7 and 10:30 PM, and close on Mondays. Tickets are inexpensive and often easy to come by on the night of performance.

Films   Foreign films are mostly dubbed into Spanish but movies in English are listed in *El País* or *Guía del Ocio* under "V.O.," meaning *versión original.* Good places to try for films in English are: **Alphaville** and **Cines Renoir,** both in Martín de los Heros, and the **Filmoteca Española** at Cine Torre, Princesa 1. All are just off Plaza España.

Nightlife and Entertainment

Cabaret   **Florida Park** (tel. 91/273–7804), in the Retiro Park, offers dinner and a show that often features ballet, Spanish dance, or flamenco and is open Monday to Saturday from 9:30 PM with shows at 11 PM. **Lola** (Costanilla de San Pedro 11, tel. 91/265–8801) opens at 9:30 PM for a dinner that is good by most cabaret standards, followed by a show and dancing until 4 AM. **La Scala** (Rosario Pino 7, tel. 91/450–4500), in the Meliá Castilla hotel, is Madrid's top nightclub, with dinner, dancing, and cabaret at 8:30, and a second, less expensive show around midnight. This is the one visited by most night tours.

Flamenco   Madrid offers the widest choice of flamenco shows in Spain; some are good, but many are aimed at the tourist trade. Dinner tends to be mediocre and overpriced, but it ensures the best seats; otherwise, opt for the show and a drink *(consumición)* only, usually starting around 11 PM and costing 2,000–2,500 ptas. **Arco de Cuchilleros** (Cuchilleros 7, tel. 91/266–5867), behind the Plaza Mayor, is one of the better, cheaper ones. **Café de Chinitas** (Torija 7, tel. 91/248–5135) and **Corral de la Morería** (Morería 17, tel. 91/265–8446) are two of the more authentic places where well-known troupes perform. **Venta del Gato** (Avda de Burgos 214, tel. 91/202–3427) is authentic, too, but it's to the north. **Zambra** (Velázquez 8, tel. 91/435–5164), in the Hotel Wellington, is one of the smartest (jacket and tie essential), with a good show and dinner served into the small hours.

Jazz   **Whisky Jazz Club** (Diego de León, tel. 91/261–1165) is the leading old-timer. Other venues with live jazz are **Café Berlín** (Jacometrezo 4, tel. 91/231–0810) just off Callao; **Clamores** (Albuquerque 14, tel. 91/445–7938); **El Despertar** (Torrecilla del Leal 18, tel. 230–8095) in Lavapiés, open Thursday to Sunday 8:30–11; and **Hamilton Jazz Club** (Alberto Aguilera 54, tel. 91/241–1695), open Tuesday to Saturday 11 PM–3 AM.

Casino   Madrid's Casino (tel. 91/859–0312) is 28 kilometers (17 miles) out at Torrelodones on the N-VI road to La Coruña. *Open 5 PM–4 AM. Free transportation service from Plaza de España 6.*

Madrid Environs

The beauty of the historic cities surrounding Madrid and the role they have played in their country's history rank them among Spain's most worthwhile sights. Ancient Toledo, the former capital, the great palace-monastery of El Escorial, the sturdy medieval walls of Avila, Segovia's Roman aqueduct and fairy-tale Alcázar, and the magnificent Plaza Mayor of the old university town of Salamanca, all lie within an hour or so from the capital.

All the towns below, with the possible exception of Salamanca, can easily be visited on day-trips from Madrid. But if you've had your fill of the hustle and bustle of Spain's booming capital, you'll find it far more rewarding to tour from one place to another, spending a day or two in one or more of these fascinating locales. Then, long after the day-trippers have gone home, you can enjoy the real charm of these small provincial towns and wander at leisure through their medieval streets.

Getting There from Madrid

Trains to Toledo leave from Madrid's Atocha Station; to Salamanca, from Norte Station; and to El Escorial, Avila, and Segovia, from either Mediodía or Chamartín Cercanías.

Getting Around

There's a direct train line between El Escorial, Avila, and Salamanca; otherwise, train connections are poor and you'll do better to go by bus. All places are linked by bus services and the local tourist offices will advise on schedules. Toledo's bus station is on the Ronda de Castilla la Mancha (tel. 925/215850) just off the road from Madrid. Avila's bus station is on Avda de Madrid (tel. 918/220154); Segovia's is on Paseo Ezequiel González (tel. 911/427725); and Salamanca's is on Filiberto Villalobos 73 (tel. 923/236717). The N403 from Toledo to Avila passes through spectacular scenery in the Sierra de Gredos mountains, as does the C505 Avila-El Escorial route. From El Escorial to Segovia, both the Puerto de León and Puerto de Navacerrada mountain passes offer magnificent views. The N501 from Avila to Salamanca will take you across the tawny plain of Castile.

Guided Tours

Juliá Tours, Pullmantur, and Trapsatur run day tours from Madrid. Details are available from any travel agent.

Tourist Information

Avila. Plaza de la Catedral 4, tel. 918/211387; open weekdays 8–3 and 4–6 (5–7 in summer), Saturday 9–1:30 only.
El Escorial. Floridablanca 10, tel. 91/890–1554; open weekdays 9:45–2:15 and 3–6, Saturday 9:45–1:15.

Salamanca. Gran Vía (C. España) 39, tel. 923/243730; open weekdays 9:30–2 and 4:30–8, Saturday 9:30–2. There's also an information booth on the Plaza Mayor (market side).
Segovia. Plaza Mayor 10, tel. 911/430328; open Monday–Sat. 9–2; also weekdays 4–6 in summer only.
Toledo. Puerta Nueva de Bisagra tel. 925/220843; open weekdays 9–2 and 4–6, Saturday 9:30–1:30.

Exploring the Madrid Environs

The following tour goes from Toledo to El Escorial, the Valley of the Fallen, La Granja, Segovia, Riofrio, Avila, Alba de Tormes, and Salamanca.

Head south from Madrid on the road to Toledo. About 20 minutes from the capital look left for a prominent rounded hill topped by a statue of Christ. This is the **Hill of the Angels**, which marks the geographical center of the Iberian Peninsula. After 90 minutes of drab, industrial scenery, the unforgettable silhouette of **Toledo** suddenly rises before you, the imposing bulk of the Alcazar and the slender spire of the cathedral dominating the skyline. This former capital, where Moors, Jews, and Christians once lived in harmony, is now a living national monument, depicting all the elements of Spanish civilization in hand-carved, sun-mellowed stone. For a stunning view and to capture the beauty of Toledo as El Greco knew it, begin with a panoramic drive around the Carretera de Circunvalación, crossing over the Alcántara bridge and returning by way of the bridge of San Martín. As you gaze at the city rising like an island in its own bend of the Tagus, reflect how little the city skyline has changed in the four centuries since El Greco painted *Storm Over Toledo.*

Toledo is a small city steeped in history and full of magnificent buildings. It was the capital of Spain under both Moors and Christians until some whim caused Philip II to move his capital to Madrid in 1561. Begin your visit with a drink in one of the many terrace cafés on the central **Plaza Zocodover,** study a map, and try to get your bearings, for a veritable labyrinth confronts you as you try to find your way to Toledo's great treasures. While here, search the square's pastry shops for the typical marzipan candies *(mazapanes)* of Toledo.

Begin your tour with a visit to the 13th-century **Cathedral,** seat of the Cardinal Primate of Spain, and one of the great cathedrals of Spain. Somber but elaborate, it blazes with jeweled chalices, gorgeous ecclesiastical vestments, historic tapestries, some 750 stained-glass windows, and paintings by Tintoretto, Titian, Murillo, El Greco, Velázquez, and Goya. The cathedral has two surprises: a **Mozarabic chapel,** where Mass is still celebrated on Sundays according to an ancient Mozarabic rite handed down from the days of the Visigoths (AD 419–711); and its unique **Transparente,** an extravagent Baroque roof that gives a theatrical glimpse into heaven as the sunlight pours down through a mass of figures and clouds. *Admission: 250 ptas. Open 10:30–1 and 3:30–6 (7 in summer).*

En route to the real jewel of Toledo, the **Chapel of Santo Tomé,** you'll pass a host of souvenir shops on Calle Santo Tomé, bursting with damascene knives and swords, blue and yellow pottery from nearby Talavera, and El Greco reproductions. In the tiny

Madrid Environs

chapel that houses El Greco's masterpiece, *The Burial of the Count of Orgaz,* you can capture the true spirit of the Greek painter who adopted Spain, and in particular Toledo, as his home. Do you recognize the sixth man from the left among the painting's earthly contingent? Or the young boy in the left-hand corner? The first is El Greco himself, the second his son Jorge Manuel—see 1578, the year of his birth, embroidered on his handkerchief. *Admission: 85 ptas. Open 10–1:45 and 3:30–5:45 (6:45 in summer).*

Not far away is **El Greco's House,** a replica containing copies of his works. *Admission: 200 ptas. Open 10–1:45 and 3:30–5:45 (4–6:45 in summer); closed Sun. PM and Mon.*

The splendid **Sinagoga del Tránsito** stands on the corner of Samuel Levi and Reyes Católicos. Commissioned in 1366 by Samuel Levi, chancellor to Pedro the Cruel, the synagogue shows Christian and Moorish as well as Jewish influences in its architecture and decoration—look at the stars of David interspersed with the arms of Castile and León. There's also a small **Sephardic Museum** chronicling the life of Toledo's former Jewish community. *Admission: 200 ptas. Open 10–2 and 3:30–6 (4–7 in summer); closed Sun. PM and Mon.*

Another synagogue, the incongruously named **Santa María la Blanca** (it was given as a church to the Knights of Calatrava in 1405), is just along the street. Its history may have been Jewish and Christian, but its architecture is definitely Moorish, for it resembles a mosque with five naves, horseshoe arches, and capitals decorated with texts from the Koran. *Closed at press*

*time due to archeological excavations but could be open by
1990.*

Across the road is **San Juan de los Reyes,** a beautiful Gothic
church begun by Ferdinand and Isabella in 1476. Wander
around its fine cloisters and don't miss the iron manacles on the
outer walls; they were placed there by Christians freed by the
Moors. The Catholic Kings originally intended to be buried
here, but then their great triumph at Granada in 1492 changed
their plans. *Admission: 75 ptas. Open 10–2 and 3:30–6 (7 in
summer).*

Walk down the hill through the ancient **Cambrón Gate** and your
visit of Toledo is over. Should you have more time, however,
head for the **Museum of Santa Cruz,** just off the Zocodover,
with its splendid El Grecos. *Admission: 200 ptas. Open Tues.–
Sat. 10–6:30, Sun. 10–2.*

Also consider a visit to the **Hospital de Tavera,** outside the
walls, where you can see Ribera's amazing *Bearded Woman.*
Admission: 150 ptas. Open 10:30–1:30 and 3:30–6.

In the foothills of the Guadarrama Mountains, 50 kilometers
(31 miles) from Madrid, and 120 kilometers (74 miles) from Toledo, lies **San Lorenzo de El Escorial,** burial place of Spanish
kings and queens. The **Monastery,** built by the religious fanatic
Philip II as a memorial to his father, Charles V, is a vast rectangular edifice, conceived and executed with a monotonous
magnificence worthy of the Spanish royal necropolis. It was designed by Juan de Herrera, Spain's greatest Renaissance
architect. The **Royal Pantheon** contains the tombs of monarchs
from Charles V to Alfonso XIII, grandfather of Juan Carlos,
and those of their consorts. Only two kings are missing, Philip
V, who chose to be buried in his beloved La Granja, and Ferdinand VI, buried in Madrid. In the **Pantheon of the Infantes** rest
the 60 royal children who died in infancy, and those queens who
bore no heirs. The lavishly bejewelled tomb here belongs to
Don Juan, bastard son of Charles V and half-brother of Philip
II, dashing hero and victor of the Battle of Lepanto. The
monastery's other highlights are the magnificent **Library of
Philip II,** with 40,000 rare volumes and 2,700 illuminated manuscripts, including the diary of Santa Teresa; and the **Royal
Apartments.** Contrast the spartan private apartment of Philip
II and the simple bedroom in which he died in 1598, with the
beautiful carpets, porcelain, and tapestries with which his less
austere successors embellished the rest of his somber
monastery-palace. *Admission: 300 ptas. for a partial visit
(Pantheon, Royal Apartments, Basilica, and Library), or 500
ptas. for whole complex, including Casita del Príncipe. Open
Tues.–Sun. 10–1 and 3:30–5:30 (6:30 in summer); closed Mon.
Last entry is 45 mins. before closing time.*

Eight kilometers (5 miles) along the road to Segovia, the
mighty cross of the **Valley of the Fallen** looms up on your left.
This vast basilica hewn out of sheer granite was built by Gener-
al Franco between 1940 and 1959 as a monument to the dead of
Spain's Civil War of 1936–39. Buried here are 43,000 war dead,
José Antonio Primo de Rivera, founder of the Falangists and
early martyr of the war, and Franco himself, who died in 1975.
Admission: 200 ptas. Open daily 10–7 (6 in winter).

A spectacular drive lies ahead, from the resort of Navacerrada
up through the Guadarrama Mountains by way of the

Navacerrada pass at 1,860 meters (6,000 feet). The steep descent through fragrant pine forests via the hairpin bends of the Siete Revueltas (Seven Curves) brings you straight into La Granja.

The **Palace of La Granja,** with its splendid formal gardens and fountains, was built between 1719 and 1739 by the homesick Philip V, first Bourbon king of Spain and grandson of France's Louis XIV, to remind him of his beloved Versailles. The whole place is like an exquisite piece of France in a Spanish wood, and it's small wonder that Philip chose to be buried here in the splendor of his own creation rather than in the austerity of El Escorial. The splendid gardens are open until dusk and you can stroll around them for free except when the fountains are playing. *Admission: 300 ptas. Palace open Tues.–Sat. 10–1:30 and 3–5, Sun. 10–2; closed Mon. Fountains play on Thurs. and weekend afternoons in summer (but check).*

From La Granja, a 10-minute drive will bring you to the golden-stone market town of **Segovia.** In front of you rises the majestic Roman aqueduct, its huge granite blocks held together without mortar. At its foot is a small bronze statue of Romulus and the wolf, presented by Rome in 1974 to commemorate the 2,000-year history of Spain's most complete Roman monument.

Drive around the base of the rock on which Segovia stands. The Ronda de Santa Lucía leads to the most romantic view of the Alcázar, perched high on its rock like the prow of a mighty ship. Return via the Carretera de los Hoyos for yet another magical view, this time of the venerable cathedral rising from the ramparts. Next, fend off the pestering gypsies around the aqueduct, and make for the **Calle Real,** the main shopping street. As you climb, you'll pass the Romanesque church of **San Martín,** with its porticoed outer gallery. Continue to the picturesque **Plaza Mayor** with its colorful ceramic stalls (good bargains) and pleasant cafés set against the backdrop of ancient arcaded houses and one of the loveliest, externally, at least, Gothic cathedrals in Spain.

Segovia **cathedral** was the last Gothic cathedral to be built in Spain (the one in Avila was the first). Begun in 1525 by order of Charles V, its interior is sadly disappointing, as many of its treasures were carried off by Napoleon's troops in the Peninsular War of the early 1800s. Its museum has the first book printed in Spain (1472). You should also seek out the tomb of Don Pedro, two-year-old son of Henry IV who slipped from his nurse's arms and tumbled to his death over the battlements of the Alcázar (his distraught nurse cast herself over after him). *Admission: 150 ptas. Open daily in summer, 9–7; in winter, weekdays 9:30–1 and 3–6, weekends 9:30–6.*

The turreted **Alcázar** with its *esgrafiado* facade—an architectural peculiarity of Segovia whereby houses were embellished with small pieces of coke—is largely a fanciful re-creation of the 1880s, the original 13th-century castle having been destroyed by fire in 1862. The view from its ramparts—and, even better, from its tower if you can manage the 156 steps—is breathtaking. The Alcázar served as a major residence of the Catholic Kings. Here Isabella met Ferdinand, and from here she set out to be crowned Queen of Castile. The interior successfully re-creates the era of this dual monarchy that established Spain's Golden Age. *Admission: 150 ptas. Open 10–6 in winter, 10–7 in summer.*

The **Palace of Riofrio,** 8 kilometers (5 miles) south of Segovia, off the road to San Rafael, was bought by Isabel Farnese, widow of Philip V, with the idea of turning it into a splendid dwelling along the lines of Madrid's Royal Palace. Her dream was never fulfilled and the palace, which houses a small **Hunting Museum,** is now of minor importance. Far more attractive is its surrounding **parkland,** where deer will come right up to your car. *Admission: 300 ptas. Palace open 10–1:30 and 3–5, Sun. 10–2; closed Tues.*

Avila, almost 1,240 meters (4,000 feet) above sea level, is the highest provincial capital in Spain. Alfonso VI and his son-in-law, Count Raimundo de Borgoña, rebuilt the town and walls in 1090, bringing it permanently under Christian control. It is these walls, the most complete military installations of their kind in Spain, that give Avila its special medieval quality. Thick and solid, with 88 towers tufted with numerous untidy storks' nests, they stretch for 2½ kilometers (1½ miles) around the entire city, and make an ideal focus for the start of your visit. For a superb overall view and photo spot, drive out to the **Cuatro Postes,** three-quarters of a kilometer (half a mile) out on the road to Salamanca.

The personality of Santa Teresa the Mystic, to whom the city is dedicated, lives today as vividly as it did in the 16th century. Several religious institutions associated with the life of the saint are open to visitors, the most popular of which is the **Convent of Santa Teresa,** which stands on the site of her birthplace. There's an ornate Baroque chapel, a small gift shop, and a museum with some of her relics: her rosary, books, walking stick, a sole of her sandal, and her finger wearing her wedding ring. *Free. Located at Plaza de la Santa, just inside the southern gate. Open 9–1:30 and 3:30–7.*

Avila's other ecclesiastical monuments are far older and more rewarding than those that commemorate the saint. The impregnable hulk of the **cathedral** is in many ways more akin to a fortress than a house of God. Though of Romanesque origin— the Romanesque sections are recognizable by their red and white brickwork—it is usually claimed as Spain's first Gothic cathedral. Inside, the ornate alabaster tomb of Cardinal Alonso de Madrigal, a 15th-century bishop whose swarthy complexion earned him the nickname of "El Tostado" (the toasted one) is thought to be the work of Domenico Fancelli, who also sculpted the tomb of Prince Juan in Santo Tomás and the sepulchers of the Catholic Kings in Granada's Royal Chapel. *Admission free. Cathedral open 8–1 and 3–7 (5 in winter). Cathedral Museum open 10–1 and 3–7 (5 in winter). Admission: 75 ptas.*

The **Basilica of San Vicente,** just outside the walls, is one of Avila's finest Romanesque churches, standing on the spot where St. Vincent and his sisters Sabina and Cristeta were martyred in AD 306. Here, too, Santa Teresa is said to have experienced the vision that told her to reform the Carmelite order. *Admission: 25 ptas. Open 10–1 and 4–6; Sun. 10:30–2.*

Before continuing to the **Monastery of Santo Tomás,** you can relax in the pleasant **Plaza de Santa Teresa** with its outdoor cafés and statue of the saint erected for Pope John Paul's visit in 1982. Built between 1482 and 1493 by Ferdinand and Isabella, who used it as a summer palace, it houses the tomb of their only son, Prince Juan—who died at the age of 19 while a student at Salamanca—as well as the tomb of that far less lovable character, the notorious Inquisitor General Tomás de Torquemada. *Admission: monastery free, cloisters 50 ptas., Museum of Oriental Art 50 ptas. Open 10–12:30 and 4–7.*

From Avila it's straight sailing all the way to Salamanca unless you're a devotee of Santa Teresa and choose to take a small detour to the old ducal town of **Alba de Tormes** to visit the **Carmelite Convent** (open 9–2 and 4–8) where the saint is buried.

Salamanca is an ancient city, and your first glimpse of it is bound to be unforgettable. Beside the road flows the Tormes River and beyond it rise the old houses of the city and the golden walls, turrets, and domes of the Plateresque cathedrals. "Plateresque" comes from *plata* (silver) and implies that the stone is chiseled and engraved as intricately as that delicate metal. A superb example of this style is the facade of the Dominican **Monastery of San Esteban** (50 ptas.; open 9–1 and 4–7), which you'll pass on your way to the cathedrals. The **old cathedral** far outshines its younger sister, the **new cathedral,** in beauty. (The new cathedral's funds ran out during construction—1513–1733—leaving a rather bare interior.) Inside the sturdy Romanesque walls of the old cathedral, built between 1102 and 1160, your attention will be drawn to Nicolás Florentino's stunning altarpiece with 53 brightly painted panels. Don't miss the splendid **cloisters** which now house a worthwhile collection of religious art, and the **Degree Chapel,** where anxious students sought inspiration on the night before their final exams. *New cathedral free; old cathedral and cloisters 50 ptas. Open Oct.–June, 9:30–1:30 and 3:30–6; July–Sept., 10–2 and 4–8.*

Founded by Alfonso IX in 1218, **Salamanca University** is to Spain what Oxford University is to England. On its famous **doorway** in the Patio de las Escuelas, a profusion of Plateresque carving surrounds the medallions of Ferdinand and Isabella. See if you can find the famous frog and skull, said to bring good luck to students in their examinations. Inside, the **lecture room** of Fray Luis de León has remained untouched since the days of the great scholar, and the prestigious **Library** boasts some 50,000 parchment and leather-bound volumes. *Admission: 100 ptas. Open 9:30–1:30 and 4–6, Sat. 9:30–1:30 only, Sun. 11–1. Slightly longer hours July–Sept.*

Now make for Salamanca's greatest jewel, the elegant 18th-century **Plaza Mayor.** Here you can browse in stores offering typical *charro* jewelry (silver and black flowerheads), head down the steps to the market in search of colorful tapas bars, or simply relax in an outdoor café. In this, the city's crowning glory, and the most exquisite square in Spain, you've found the perfect place to end your tour of Salamanca and Castile.

Dining and Lodging

For details and price category definitions, *see* Dining and Lodging in Staying in Spain.

Avila **El Fogón de Santa Teresa.** Traditional Castilian roasts, lamb
Dining chops, and trout feature on the menu of this attractive restau-

rant in the vaults of the Palacio de Valderrábanos. *Alemania 3, tel. 918/211023. AE, DC, MC, V. Moderate.*

★ **El Rastro.** This ancient inn tucked into the city walls is Avila's most atmospheric place to dine. Local specialties include Avila's famous veal *(ternera)* and *yemas de Santa Teresa*, a rather sickly dessert made from candied egg yolks. *Plaza del Rastro 1, tel. 918/211219. AE, DC, MC, V. Moderate.*

El Torreón. Castilian specialties are served in this typical mesón situated in the basement of the old Velada Palace, opposite the cathedral. *Tostado 1, tel. 918/213171. AE, MC, V. Moderate.*

Lodging **Palacio de Valderrábanos.** Avila's best hotel is located in a 15th-century mansion opposite the cathedral. It was once the residence of the first bishop of Avila. *Plaza Catedral 9, tel. 918/211023. 73 rooms. AE, DC, MC, V. Expensive.*

★ **Parador Raimundo de Borgoña.** The location of this parador in a 15th-century palace just inside the northern walls of the city is superb. The rooms are decorated in traditional Castilian style and have spacious, well-equipped bathrooms. Some rooms also have four-poster beds and a view of the city walls. Its dining room is atmospheric and serves local Avilan dishes, including the inevitable *yemas*, and the parador garden offers the only access to the walls. *Marqués de Canales y Chozas 16, tel. 918/211340. 62 rooms. AE, DC, MC, V. Expensive.*

Don Carmelo. This functional, modern, and comfortable hotel close to the station is Avila's best moderate bet. *Paseo Don Carmelo 30, tel. 918/228050. 60 rooms. V. Moderate.*

El Escorial **Charolés.** This elegant restaurant has a terrace above the
Dining street for summer dining. Its meat dishes are famous through-
★ out the region. Try the *Charolés a la pimienta* (pepper steak). Fresh fish is brought in daily from Spain's north coast. *Floridablanca 24, tel. 91/890–5975. Reservations essential most weekends. AE, DC, MC, V. Expensive.*

Mesón de la Cueva. Founded in 1768, this atmospheric mesón has several small, rustic dining rooms. This inn is a must for ambience, and the food is good, too. *San Antón 4, tel. 91/890–1516. Reservations advised on weekends. AE, DC, MC, V. Expensive to Moderate.*

El Candil. One of the best of the many middle-range restaurants in El Escorial, El Candil is situated above a bar on the corner of Plaza San Lorenzo on the village's main street. In summer you can dine outdoors in the square, a delightful spot. *Reina Victoria 12, tel. 91/896–0111. AE, DC, MC, V. Moderate.*

Lodging **Victoria Palace.** The rooms at the back of this grand old-world hotel close to the monastery have balconies and a splendid view toward Madrid; there's a garden and pool, too. *Juan de Toledo 4, tel. 91/890–1511. 89 rooms. AE, DC, MC, V. Expensive.*

Miranda Suizo. Rooms are comfortable in this charming old hotel on the main street, and the hotel café, with its dark wood fittings and marble tables, is right out of the 19th century. *Floridablanca 20, tel. 91/890–4711. 47 rooms. AE, DC, MC, V. Moderate.*

Salamanca **Chez Victor.** Salamanca's best restaurant ranks among the top
Dining in Spain. There's a distinctly French touch to the cuisine.
★ *Espoz y Mina 26, tel. 923/213123. Reservations advised. Closed Sun. evening, Mon., and Aug. AE, V. Expensive.*

Nuevo Candil. The two Candil restaurants are a long-standing tradition in Salamanca, offering high standards of cuisine. This, the more formal of the two, is a restaurant only; its twin on Ruíz Aguilera 10 is also a colorful tapas bar. *Plaza de la Reina 1, tel. 923/219027. AE, DC, MC, V. Expensive but with a moderate set menu.*

El Mesón. There's plenty of colorful atmosphere and good traditional Castilian food in this typical mesón just off the Plaza Mayor, beside the Gran Hotel. *Plaza Poeta Iglesias 10, tel. 923/ 217222. AE, MC, V. Moderate.*

Río de la Plata. This small, atmospheric restaurant close to El Mesón and the Gran Hotel, serves superb *farinato* sausage; it's a great find. *Plaza del Peso 1, tel. 923/219005. No credit cards. Closed Mon., July. Moderate.*

Lodging **Monterrey.** A pleasant older hotel that offers the best accommodation in the center of town, the Monterrey was renovated a few years ago, and its El Fogón restaurant has a good reputation. *Azafranal 21, tel. 923/214400. 89 rooms. AE, DC, MC, V. Expensive.*

★ **Parador.** One of Spain's newest paradores stands across the river with superb views of the city's skyline. Its rooms are spacious and comfortable and there's a pool, but it's a bit far from the center. *Teso de la Feria 2, tel. 923/228700. 110 rooms. AE, DC, MC, V. Expensive.*

Castellano III. Overlooking the Alamedilla Park just a few minutes' walk from the center, this comfortable, modern hotel is considered the best medium-price hotel in town. *San Francisco Javier 2, tel. 923/251611. 73 rooms. MC, V. Moderate.*

Condal. A functional but comfortable hotel in a central location just off Calle Azafranal, two minutes from the Plaza Mayor. *Santa Eulalia 2, tel. 923/218400. 70 rooms. AE, DC, MC, V. Inexpensive.*

Segovia **Casa Duque.** Located at the end of the main shopping street,
Dining this restaurant has several floors of beautifully decorated traditional dining rooms and is the main rival to the famous **Cándido.** There's plenty of local atmosphere, and the food is pure Castilian—try the *ponche segoviano* for dessert. *Cervantes 12, tel. 911/430537. Reservations advised on weekends. AE, DC, V. Expensive to Moderate.*

★ **Mesón de Candido.** Segovia's most prestigious restaurant has seven dining rooms pulsating with atmosphere and decorated with bullfighting memorabilia and photos of the dignitaries who have dined here over the years. Specialties are *cochinillo* (suckling pig) and *cordero asado* (roast lamb). *Plaza Azoguejo 5, tel. 911/428102. Reservations advised for Sun. lunch. AE, DC, MC, V. Expensive to Moderate.*

César. This agreeable restaurant near the aqueduct specializes in fish dishes and fresh vegetables—a refreshing change in this mecca of traditional Castilian roasts. *Ruíz de Alda 10, tel. 911/ 428101. AE, DC, Closed Wed., Nov. Moderate.*

La Oficina. Traditional Castilian dishes are served in two delightful dining rooms that date back to 1893. It's just off Plaza Mayor. *Cronista Lecea 10, tel. 911/431643. AE, DC, MC, V. Moderate.*

Lodging **Los Linajes.** The advantages of this pleasant, modern hotel, built in Castilian style, are its central location and its superb views. *Dr. Velasco 9, tel. 911/431201. 55 rooms. AE, DC, MC, V. Expensive.*

★ **Parador.** To the north of town is this modern parador offering comfortable, spacious rooms and a pool. The views of the city, especially when illuminated, are magnificent. *Off the N601 toward Valladolid, tel. 911/430362. 80 rooms. AE, DC, MC, V. Expensive.*

Acueducto. Ask for a room at the front in this comfortable older hotel with balconies overlooking the famous aqueduct. Well renovated, it's Segovia's best medium-range bet. *Padre Claret 10, tel. 911/424800. 73 rooms. AE, DC, MC, V. Moderate.*

Toledo **Hostal del Cardenal.** Toledo's best restaurant is set in the 17th-
Dining century palace of Cardinal Lorenzana, up against the city ram-
★ parts, and boasts five dining rooms and a delightful garden for summer dining. Both food and service are excellent (try the roast suckling pig). *Paseo Recaredo 24, tel. 925/220862. Reservations advised in high season. AE, DC, V. Expensive to Moderate.*

Asador Adolfo. This restaurant is situated near the cathedral and is well known for its good food (try the superb roast meat) and service. *La Granada 6, tel. 925/227321. AE, DC, MC, V. Moderate.*

La Bótica. Enjoy your aperitif in a café on the main square, then make for this stylish French restaurant nearby. *Plaza Zocodover 13, tel. 925/225557. AE, DC, V. Moderate.*

Casa Aurelio. There are two branches of this popular restaurant, both around the corner from the cathedral. Try the partridge or quail. *Sinagoga 6, tel. 925/222097, and Sinagoga 1, tel. 925/221392. AE, DC, MC, V. Closed Wed. Moderate.*

Los Cuatro Tiempos. The picturesque downstairs bar, decorated with ceramic tiles, is an ideal place for a *fino* and tapas before you head upstairs for a traditional Toledo meal. *Sixto Ramón Parro 7, tel. 925/223782. MC, V. Moderate to Inexpensive.*

Los Arcos. Located off Toledo de Ohio, this attractive modern restaurant offers good value *menus del día* as well as inexpensive main courses such as roast partridge, and is fast gaining in popularity. *Cordonerías 11, tel. 925/210051. AE, DC, MC, V. Inexpensive.*

Lodging **Parador Conde de Orgaz.** This is one of Spain's most popular
★ paradores, and the best and most expensive hotel in Toledo (a 15-minute drive from city center). It's a modern parador built in traditional Toledo style and stands on a hill across the river, commanding magnificent views of the city. Book far ahead. *Paseo de los Cigarrales, tel. 925/221850. 77 rooms, pool. AE, DC, MC, V. Expensive.*

Alfonso VI. This pleasant modern hotel has Castilian-style decor and is conveniently located in the center of town by the Alcázar. *Gen. Moscardó 2, tel. 925/222600. 80 rooms. AE, DC, MC, V. Moderate.*

María Cristina. You'll pass this comfortable new hotel on your way from Madrid. Located beside the bullring, it opened in 1986 and provides excellent facilities. Its El Abside restaurant is fast gaining in prestige. *Marqués de Mendigorría 1, tel. 925/213202. 43 rooms. AE, V. Moderate.*

Maravilla. This simple but very central old-world hotel just off Plaza Zocodover has a good, old-fashioned restaurant. *Barrio Rey 7, tel. 925/223304. 18 rooms. AE, DC, MC, V. Inexpensive.*

Barcelona

Arriving and Departing

By Plane
All international and domestic flights arrive at El Prat de Llobregat airport, 14 kilometers (8½ miles) south of Barcelona just off the main highway to Castelldefels and Sitges. For information on arrival and departure times, call the airport (tel. 93/370–1011) or Iberia information (tel. 93/301–3993).

Between the Airport and Downtown
The airport–city train leaves every 30 minutes between 6:30 AM and 11 PM and reaches the Barcelona Central (Sants) Station in 15 minutes. Taxis will then take you to your hotel. RENFE provides a bus service to the Central Station during the night hours. A cab from the airport to your hotel, including airport and luggage surcharges, will cost about 1,500 ptas.

By Train
The main railroad station is Barcelona Central (or Sants) on the Plaça Països Catalans (tel. 93/322–4141). Almost all long-distance trains arrive and depart from here. Many also stop at the Passeig de Gràcia underground station at the junction of Aragó. This station is closer to the Plaça de Catalunya and Ramblas area than Central (Sants), but though tickets and information are available here, luggage carts and taxi ranks are not. The old Terminal (or França) Station on Avda. Marquès de l'Argentera is little used now except for local trains to the Costa Brava and Gerona. For RENFE information call 93/322–4142 (24 hours).

By Bus
Barcelona has no central bus station, but many buses operate from the old Estació Vilanova (or Norte) at the end of Avenida Vilanova. **Juliá**, Ronda Universitat 5, runs buses to Zaragoza and Montserrat; and **Alsina Graëlls**, Ronda Universitat 4, to Lérida and Andorra.

Getting Around

Modern Barcelona above the Plaça de Catalunya is mostly built on a grid system, though there's no helpful numbering system as in the United States. The Old Town from the Plaça de Catalunya to the port is a warren of narrow streets, however, and you'll need a good street map to get around. Most sightseeing can be done on foot—you won't have any other choice in the Gothic Quarter—but you'll need to use the metro or buses to link sightseeing areas.

By Metro
The subway is the fastest way of getting around, as well as the easiest to use. You pay a flat fare, no matter how far you travel, or purchase a **targeta multiviatge,** good for 10 rides. Plans of the system are available from main metro stations or from branches of the Caixa savings bank.

By Bus
City buses run from about 5:30 or 6 AM to 10:30 PM, though some stop earlier. Again, there's a flat-fare system though tickets cost a little more on weekends. Plans of the routes followed are displayed at bus stops. A reduced-rate targeta multiviatge, good for 10 rides, can be purchased at the transport kiosk on Plaça Catalunya.

By Taxi
Taxis are black and yellow, and when available for hire show a "Libre" sign in the daytime and a green light at night. The me-

ter starts at 200 ptas., and there are small supplements for luggage, night travel (10 PM–6 AM), Sundays and fiestas, rides from a station or the port, and for going to or from the bullring or a soccer match. The supplement to the airport is 150 ptas. There are cab stands all over town; cabs may also be flagged down on the street. Make sure the driver puts on his meter.

By Cable Car and Funicular Montjuïc Funicular is a cog railroad that runs from the junction of Avenida Paral-lel and Nou de la Rambla to the Miramar Amusement Park on Montjuïc. It runs only when the amusement park is open (weekends from noon–9:15 PM, more often in summer). A cable car (*teleferic*) then runs from the amusement park up to Montjuïc Castle; same hours.

A **Transbordador Aeri** Harbor Cable Car runs from Miramar on Montjuïc across the harbor to the Torre de Jaume I on Barcelona *moll* (jetty), and on to the Torre de Sant Sebastià at the end of Passeig Nacional in Barceloneta. You can board at either stage. The cable car runs from 11:30 AM to 9:30 PM in summer, and only on Sunday in winter.

To reach Tibidabo summit, take either bus 58 or the Ferrocarrils de la Generalitat train from Plaça Catalunya to Avenida Tibidabo, then the *tramvía blau* (blue tram) to Peu del Funicular, and the Tibidabo Funicular from there to the Tibidabo Fairground. The funicular runs every half hour from 7:15 AM to 9:45 PM.

By Boat **Golondrinas** harbor boats operate short harbor trips from the Portal de la Pau near the Columbus Monument between 9 AM and 9:30 PM in summer, and on Sundays in winter.

Important Addresses and Numbers

Tourist Information Tourist offices are located at the **Airport; Central Station,** tel. 93/250–2594; **Terminal Station,** tel. 93/319–2791; **Gran Vía Corts Catalanes 658,** tel. 93/301–7443; the **Columbus Monument** in Plaça Portal de la Pau at the bottom of Ramblas, tel. 93/302–5234; and in the **Ajuntament** in Plaça Sant Jaume, tel. 93/318–2525.

American Visitors' Bureau, Gran Vía 591 between Rambla de Catalunya and Balmes, 3rd floor, tel. 93/301–0150/0032.

Consulates **U.S.:** Vía Laietana 33, tel. 93/319–9550; **Canadian:** Vía Augusta 125, tel. 93/209–0634; **U.K.:** Diagonal 477, tel. 93/322–2151.

Emergencies **Police:** National Police, tel. 091; Municipal Police, tel. 092; Main Police (Policía Nacional) Station, Vía Laietana 43, tel. 93/301–6666. **Ambulance:** tel. 93/300–0422. **Doctor: Hospital Clínic,** Casanova 143, tel. 93/323–1414; **Hospital Evangélico,** Alegre de Dalt 87, tel. 93/219–7100.

English Bookstores Several bookstalls on the Ramblas sell English guide books and novels. Also try **Librería Laie,** Pau Claris 85, or **Librería Francesca,** Passeig de Gràcia 91.

Travel Agencies **American Express:** Rosselló 257, on the corner of Passeig de Gràcia, tel. 93/217–0070; **Wagons-Lits/Cook:** Passeig de Gràcia 8, tel. 93/317–5500.

Guided Tours

Orientation Tours City sightseeing tours are run by **Juliá Tours,** Ronda Universitat 5 (tel. 317–6454) and **Pullmantur,** Gran Vía Corts

Catalanes 635 (tel. 318–0241). Tours leave from the above terminals, though it may be possible to be picked up at your hotel. The content and price of tours are the same with both agencies. A morning sightseeing tour visits the Gothic Quarter and Montjuïc; an afternoon tour concentrates on Gaudí and the Picasso Museum. "Panorámica y Toros" (usually on Sundays only) takes in a bullfight and city drive; and various night tours include a flamenco show, dinner in a restaurant, and cabaret at La Scala.

Special-Interest and Walking Tours Consult any tourist office for details. Serious Gaudí enthusiasts should contact **Friends of Gaudí,** (Avda. Pedralbes 7, tel. 204–5250) well ahead of their visit.

Excursions These are run by **Juliá Tours** and **Pullmantur** and are booked as above. Principal trips are a half-day tour to **Montserrat** to visit the monastery and shrine of the famous Black Virgin; a full-day trip to the **Costa Brava** resorts, including a boat cruise to Lloret de Mar; and a full-day trip to **Andorra** for tax-free shopping.

Personal Guides Ask at any tourist office, or contact the Barcelona Tourist Guide Association (tel. 93/345–4221).

Exploring Barcelona

Numbers in the margin correspond with points of interest on the Barcelona map.

Barcelona, capital of Catalonia and Spain's second-largest city, thrives on its business acumen and industrial muscle. Its hardworking citizens are almost militant in their use of their own language—with street names, museum exhibits, newspapers, radio programs, and movies all in Catalan. Their latest cause for rejoicing is the realization of their long-cherished goal to host the Olympic Games, and the city is currently in the throes of a massive building program in anticipation of the big event of 1992. This thriving metropolis also has a rich history and an abundance of sights. Few places can rival the narrow alleys of its Gothic Quarter for medieval atmosphere, the elegance and distinction of its Modernista Eixample area, or the fantasies of Gaudí's whimsical imagination.

It should take you two full days of sightseeing to complete the following tour. The first part covers the Gothic Quarter, the Picasso Museum, and the Ramblas. The second part takes you to Passeig de Gràcia, the Sagrada Familia, and Montjuïc.

❶ Start on Plaça de la Seu, where on Sunday morning the citizens of Barcelona gather to dance the *Sardana*, a symbol of Catalan pride. Step inside the magnificent Gothic **Cathedral** built between 1298 and 1450, though the spire and Gothic facade were not added until 1892. Highlights are the beautifully carved **choir stalls,** Santa Eulalia's tomb in the crypt, the battle-scarred crucifix from Don Juan's galley in the **Lepanto Chapel,** and the cloisters. *Open 7:30–1:30 and 4–7:30.*

❷ Around the corner at Comtes de Barcelona 10 is the **Frederic Marès Museum,** where you can browse for hours among the miscellany of sculptor-collector Frederic Marès. On display is everything from polychrome crucifixes to hat pins, pipes, and walking sticks. *Admission: free. Open Mon.–Sat. 9–2 and 4–7, Sun. 9–2.*

Barcelona

❸ The neighboring **Plaça del Rei** embodies the very ess⟨
Gothic Quarter. Legend has it that after Columbus's ⟨
age to America, the Catholic Kings received him in th⟨
Tinell, a magnificent banqueting hall built in 1362. Ot⟨
cient buildings around the square are the **Lieutenant's P**⟨
the 14th-century **Chapel of St. Agatha,** built right into the ⟨
man city wall; and the **Padellás Palace,** which houses the C⟨
History Museum.

Cross Vía Laietana, walk down Princesa, and turn right into
Montcada, where you come to one of Barcelona's most popular
❹ attractions, the **Picasso Museum.** Two 15th-century palaces
provide a striking setting for the collections donated in 1963
and 1970, first by Picasso's secretary, then by the artist himself. The collection ranges from early childhood sketches done
in Málaga to exhibition posters done in Paris shortly before his
death. Of particular interest are his Blue Period pictures and
his variations on Velázquez's *Las Meninas. Admission: free.
Open Tues.–Sun. 10–7.*

Time Out   At the bottom of Montcada, on the left, is **La Pizza Nostra** (Arc
de Sant Vicens 2, tel. 93/319–9058), an ideal spot for a cup of
coffee, a slice of cheesecake, or a pizza and a glass of wine.

---

❺ **Santa María del Mar** is one of the loveliest Gothic churches in
Barcelona. It was built between 1329 and 1383 in fulfillment of a
vow made a century earlier by Jaume I to build a church for the
Virgin of the Sailors. Its simple beauty is enhanced by a stunning rose window and magnificent soaring columns. *Open 8–1
and 4–7:30.*

Continue up Carrer Argentería, cross Vía Laietana, and walk
❻ along Jaume I till you come to **Plaça Sant Jaume,** an impressive
square built in the 1840s in the heart of the Gothic Quarter. The
two imposing buildings facing each other across the square are
very much older. The 15th-century **Ajuntament,** or City Hall,
has an impressive black and gold mural (1928) by Josep María
Sert (who also painted the murals for New York's Waldorf
Astoria), and the famous **Saló de Cent** from where the Council
of One Hundred ruled the city from 1372 to 1714. The **Palau de
la Generalitat,** seat of the Catalan Regional Government, is a
15th-century palace open to the public on Sunday mornings
only.

Time Out   Among the best lunch spots in this area are **Agut d'Avignon** and
La Cuineta (*see* Dining), and **Tinell** (Frenería 8, tel. 93/315–
4604).

Continue along the Carrer Ferrán, with its attractive 19th-
❼ century shops and numerous Modernista touches, to the **Plaça
Reial.** Here in this splendid, if rather dilapidated, 19th-century
square arcaded houses overlook the wrought-iron **Fountain of
the Three Graces,** and lampposts designed by a young Gaudí in
1879. Watch out for drug pushers here; the safest and most colorful time to come is on a Sunday morning when crowds gather
at the stamp and coin stalls and listen to soap-box orators.

Time Out   Nearby are two atmospheric restaurants, **Los Caracoles** and
Can Culleretes.

---

8 Head to the bottom of Ramblas and take an elevator to the top of the **Columbus Monument** for a breathtaking view over the city. *The monument is open Mon.–Sat. 9:30–1:30 and 4:30–8:30, Sun. 11:30–7:30.* Columbus faces out to sea, overlooking a replica of his own boat, the **Santa María.** Nearby you can board the cable car that crosses the harbor to Montjuïc.

9 Our next stop is the **Maritime Museum** (Plaça Portal de la Pau 1) housed in the 13th-century Atarazanas Reales, the old Royal Dockyards. The museum is packed with ships, figureheads, nautical paraphernalia, and several early navigation charts, including a map by Amerigo Vespucci, and the 1439 chart of Gabriel de Valseca from Mallorca, the oldest chart in Europe. *Admission: 150 ptas. Open Tues.–Sat. 10–2 and 4–7, Sun. 10–2.*

10 Turn back up the Ramblas to Nou de la Rambla. At no. 3 is Gaudí's **Palau Güell,** which houses the **Museum of Scenic Arts.** Gaudí built this mansion between 1885 and 1890 for his patron Count Eusebi de Güell, and it's the only one of his houses readily open to the public. It makes an intriguing setting for the museum's collection of theatrical memorabilia. *Admission: 100 ptas. Open Mon.–Sat. 10–1 and 5–7.*

11 Back to the Ramblas and our next landmark, the **Gran Teatre del Liceu,** on the corner of Sant Pau. Built between 1845 and 1847, the Liceu claims to be the world's oldest opera house and is the only one in Spain. A fairly mundane facade conceals an exquisite interior with ornamental gilt and plush red velvet fittings. Anna Pavlova danced here in 1930 and Maria Callas sang here in 1959. *Admission: 100 ptas. Open for guided visits (some in English) Mon., Wed., Fri. at 11:30 and 12:15.*

12 This next stretch of the **Ramblas** is the most fascinating. The colorful paving stones on the Placa de la Boquería were designed by Joan Miró. Glance up at the swirling Modernista dragon and the Art Nouveau street lamps. Then take a look inside the bustling **Boquería Food Market** and the **Casa Antigua Figueras,** an old grocery store on the corner of Petxina, with a splendid mosaic facade.

13 The **Palau de la Virreina** (corner of Carme and Rambla de las Flores 99, tel. 93/301–7775) was built by a viceroy from Peru in 1778. It's recently been converted into a major exhibition center, and you should check to see what's showing while you're in town. *Open Tues.–Sat. 10–2 and 4:30–9, Sun. 10–2, Mon. 4:30–9. Last entrance 30 mins. before closing.* On the next block is the 18th-century **Church of Betlem** (Bethlehem) and, opposite, the handsome ocher Baroque **Palau de Moja,** built in 1702.

14 The final stretch of the Ramblas brings us out onto the busy **Plaça de Catalunya,** the frantic business center and transport hub of the modern city. The first stage of the tour ends here. You may want to head for the Corte Inglés department store across the square or for any of the stores on the nearby **Porta de l'Angel.** Alternatively, you can relax on the terrace of the ancient **Café Zurich** on the corner of Pelai, or stop at the colorful beer hall, the **Cervecería,** opposite the Hostal Continental.

Above the Plaça de Catalunya you come into modern Barcelona and an elegant area known as the **Eixample,** which was laid out in the late 19th century as part of the city's expansion scheme.

Much of the building here was done at the height of the **Modernista** movement, a Spanish and mainly Barcelonian off-shoot of Art Nouveau, whose leading exponents were the architects Antoní Gaudí, Domènech i Montaner, and Puig i Cadafalch. The principal thoroughfares of the Eixample are the Rambla de Catalunya and the Passeig de Gràcia, where some of the city's most elegant shops and cafés are found. Modernista houses are one of Barcelona's special drawing cards, so walk up **Passeig de Gràcia** until you come to the **⑮ Manzana de la Discordía,** or Block of Discord, between Consell de Cent and Aragó. Its name is a pun on the word *manzana,* which means both "block" and "apple." The houses here are quite fantastic: The floral **Casa Lleó Morera** at no. 35 is by Domènech i Montaner. The pseudo-Gothic **Casa Amatller** at no. 41 is by Puig i Cadafalch. At no. 43 is Gaudí's **Casa Batlló.** Far-ther along the street on the right, on the corner of Provença, is **⑯** Gaudí's **Casa Milà,** more often known as **La Pedrera.** Its re-markable curving stone facade with ornamental balconies actually ripples its way around the corner of the block.

Time Out You can ponder the vagaries of Gaudí's work over a drink in **Amarcord,** a terrace café in the Pedrera building. If you're feel-ing a bit homesick, sip a cocktail or munch a deep-pan pizza in the **Chicago Pizza Pie Factory** at Provença 300. For a more se-date, old-world tearoom, head for the **Salón de Té Mauri** on the corner of Rambla de Catalunya and Provença.

Now take the metro at Diagonal directly to Barcelona's most **⑰** eccentric landmark, Gaudí's **Church of the Sagrada Familia** (Holy Family). Far from finished at his untimely death in 1926 —the absentminded Gaudí was run over by a tram and died in a pauper's hospital—this striking creation will cause consterna-tion or wonder, shrieks of protest or cries of rapture. In 1936 during the Civil War the citizens of Barcelona loved their crazy temple enough to spare it from the flames that engulfed all their other churches except the cathedral. An elevator takes visitors to the top of one of the towers for a magnificent view of the city. Gaudí is buried in the crypt. *Admission: 250 ptas. Open daily 9–8.*

Way across town to the south, the hill of **Montjuïc** was named for the Jewish community that once lived on its slopes. Montjuïc is home to a castle, an amusement park, several de-lightful gardens, a model Spanish village, an illuminated fountain, the recently rebuilt Mies van der Rohe Pavilion, and a cluster of museums—all of which could keep you busy for a day or more. The extensive construction here is in preparation for the 1992 Olympics—Montjuïc is to be the principal venue.

⑱ One of the leading attractions here is the **Museum of Catalan Art** in the Palau Nacional atop a long flight of steps. The collec-tion of Romanesque and Gothic art treasures—medieval frescoes and altarpieces, mostly from small churches and chap-els in the Pyrenees—is simply staggering. *Admission free. Open Tues.–Sun. 9–2. Visits restricted at press time due to res-toration.* The **Ceramics Museum** is in the same building (same hours and ticket).

⑲ Nearby is the **Miró Foundation,** a gift from the artist Joan Miró to his native city. One of Barcelona's most exciting contempo-rary galleries, it has several exhibition areas, many of them

devoted to Miró's works. Miró himself now rests in the cemetery on the southern slopes of *Montjuïc. Admission: 300 ptas.
Open Tues.–Sat. 11–7 (9:30 on Thurs.), Sun. 10:30–2:30.*

Off the Beaten Track

If you're hooked on **Modernista** architecture, you can follow a
walking trail around the **Dreta de l'Eixample,** the area to the
right of Rambla de Catalunya. Ask at a tourist office for a Gaudí
or Modernismo trail brochure for the Eixample. Attend a concert at Domènech i Montaner's fantastic **Palau de la Música.**
Make a trip to the **Parc Güell,** Gaudí's magical but uncompleted
attempt at creating a garden city. *Open daily 8:30–7:30.
Metro: Lesseps. Bus: 24.*

Explore the **Major de Gràcia** area, above the Diagonal. It's a
small, almost independent village within a large city, a warren
of narrow streets, changing name at every corner, and filled
with tiny shops where you'll find everything from old-fashioned
tin lanterns to feather dusters.

Take a stroll around **Barceloneta,** the old fishermen's quarter
built in 1755 below Terminal Station and the Ciutadela Park.
Along its narrow streets are atmospheric taverns (try C.
Maquinista). There are no-frills fish restaurants on the Passeig
Nacional and beach restaurants along the Passeig Marítim that
are well known to locals and worth experiencing.

Hunt out the tiny **Shoe Museum** in Plaça Sant Felip Neri, in a
hidden corner of the Gothic Quarter, between the cathedral
and Bishop's Palace. The collection includes clowns' shoes and a
pair worn by Pablo Casals. *Admission free. Open weekends
11–4.*

Shopping

Gift Ideas There are no special handicrafts associated with Barcelona, but
you'll have no trouble finding typical Spanish goods anywhere
in town. If you're into fashion and jewelry, then you've come to
the right place, as Barcelona makes all the headlines on Spain's
booming fashion front. **Xavier Roca i Coll,** Sant Pere mes Baix
24, just off Laietana, specializes in silver models of Barcelona's
buildings.

Antiques Carrer de la Palla and Banys Nous in the Gothic Quarter are
lined with antiques shops where you'll find old maps, books,
paintings, and furniture. An **antiques market** is held every
Thursday morning in Plaça Nova in front of the cathedral. The
Centre d'Antiquaris, Passeig de Gràcia 57, has some 75 antiques
stores. **Gothsland,** Consell de Cent 331, specializes in
Modernista designs.

Boutiques The most fashionable boutiques are in the **Galerías** on Passeig
de Gràcia and Rambla de Catalunya. Others are on Gran Vía be-
tween Balmes and Pau Claris; and on the Diagonal between
Ganduxer and Passeig de Gràcia. **Adolfo Domínguez,** Spain's
top designer, is at Passeig de Gràcia 89 and Valencia 245;
Loewe, Spain's top leather store, is at Passeig de Gràcia 35 and
Diagonal 570; **Joaquín Berao,** a top jewelry designer, is at
Rosselló 277.

Shopping Districts Elegant shopping districts are the Passeig de Gràcia, Rambla de Catalunya, and the Diagonal. For more affordable, more old-fashioned and typically Spanish-style shops, explore the area between Ramblas and Vía Laietana, especially around C. Ferran. The area around Plaça del Pi from Boquería to Portaferrisa and Canuda is recommended for young fashion stores and imaginative gift shops.

Department Stores El Corte Inglés is on the Plaça de Catalunya 14 (tel. 93/302–1212); and at Diagonal 617 (tel. 93/259–1449) near María Cristina metro. Galerías Preciados is at Porta de l'Angel 19 just off the Plaça de Catalunya; Diagonal 471 on the Plaça Francesc Macià; and Avenida Meridiana 352. All are open Monday to Saturday 10–8.

Food and Flea Markets The Boquería or Sant Josep Market on the Ramblas between Carme and Hospital is a superb, colorful food market, held every day except Sunday. Els Encants, Barcelona's fascinating Flea Market, is held every Monday, Wednesday, Friday, and Saturday at the end of Dos de Maig on the Plaça Glòries Catalanes. Sant Antoní Market, at the end of Ronda Sant Antoní, is an old-fashioned food and clothes market, best on Sundays when there's a secondhand book market with old postcards, press cuttings, lithographs, and prints. There's a stamp and coin market in the Plaça Reial on Sunday mornings, and an artists' market in the Placeta del Pi just off Ramblas and Boquería on Saturday mornings.

Bullfighting

Barcelona has two bullrings, the Arènes Monumental on Gran Vía and Carles I, and the smaller, rarely used, Arènes las Arenas on the Plaça d'Espanya. Bullfights are held on Sundays between March and October; check the newspaper for details. The official ticket office, where there is no markup on tickets, is at Muntaner 24 (tel. 93/253–3821) near Gran Vía. There's a Bullfighting Museum at the Monumental ring, open daily 10–1 and 5:30–7; closed Nov.–Feb.

Bars and Cafés

Cafés and Tearooms Zurich, Plaça Catalunya 35, on the corner of Pelai, is one of the oldest and most traditional cafés, perfect for watching the world go by. The Croissant Show, Santa Anna 10 just off Ramblas, is a small coffee and pastry shop, ideal for a quick mid-morning or afternoon break. Salón de Té Mauri, on the corner of Rambla de Catalunya and Provença, and Salón de Té Llibre i Serra, Ronda Sant Pere 3, are both traditional tearooms with a good selection of pastries.

Tapas Bars You'll find these all over town, but two of the most colorful are Alt Heidelberg, Ronda Universitat 5, with German beer on tap and German sausages; and the Cervecería at the top of Ramblas, opposite the Hostal Continental.

Cocktail Bars These places are both popular and plentiful everywhere, but the two best areas are the Passeig del Born, which is near the Picasso Museum and very fashionable with the affluent young; and the Eixample, near Passeig de Gràcia. A bar called Dry Martini, at Aribau 162, has more than 80 different gins; Ideal Cocktail Bar, on Aribau 89, has some good malt whiskeys. El Paraigua, on Plaça Sant Miquel, in the Gothic Quarter behind the city hall, serves cocktails in a stylish setting with classical music. **Boadas,** Tallers 1, on the corner of Ramblas, has been going strong for over 50 years.

Champagne Bars *Xampanyerías*, serving sparkling Catalan *cava*, are popular all over town and are something of a Barcelona specialty. Try **Brut,** Trompetas 3, in the Picasso Museum area; **La Cava del Palau,** Verdaguer i Callis 10, near the Palau de la Música; **La Folie,** Bailén 169, one of the best; or **La Xampanyería,** Provença 236, on the corner of Enric Granados.

Special Cafés **Els Quatre Gats,** Montsiò 5, off Porta de l'Angel, is a reconstruction of the original café that opened in 1897, and a real Barcelona institution. Literary discussions, jazz, and classical music recitals take place in this café where Picasso held his first show, Albéniz and Granados played their piano compositions, and Ramón Casas painted two of its original murals. **Café de l'Opera,** Ramblas 74, right opposite the Liceu, is a long-standing Barcelona tradition, ideal for a coffee or drink at any time of day.

Dining

For details and price category definitions, *see* Dining in Staying in Spain.

Very Expensive **El Dorado Petit.** In 1984 Luis Cruañas moved to Barcelona from
★ the Costa Brava and opened this restaurant, which rapidly became known as the best in Barcelona and one of the top restaurants in Spain. The setting—a private villa with a delightful garden for summer dining—is simply beautiful, and so is the cuisine. *Dolors Monserdá 51, tel. 93/204–5153. Reservations essential. AE, MC, V. Closed Sun. and two weeks in Aug.*

Expensive **Agut d'Avignon.** This venerable Barcelona institution takes a bit of finding; it's near the junction of Ferran and Avinyó in the Gothic Quarter. The ambience is rustic and it's a favorite with businesspeople and politicians from over the road in the Generalitat. The cuisine is traditional Catalan and game specialties are recommended in season. *Trinidad 3, tel. 93/302–6034. Reservations essential. AE, DC, MC, V. Closed Sun., Holy Week.*

★ **Azulete.** This is one of Barcelona's most beautiful restaurants —its dining room an old conservatory filled with flowers and plants. The highly imaginative cuisine is a mixture of Catalan, French, and Italian with an interesting blend of traditional and new dishes. *Vía Augusta 281, tel. 93/203–5943. Reservations essential. AE, DC, MC, V. Closed Sat. lunch, Sun., and first two weeks of Aug.*

La Cuineta. This small intimate restaurant in a 17th-century house just off Plaça Sant Jaume specializes in Catalan *nouvelle cuisine*. The decor is smart but charming, the service professional; and it's popular with businesspeople at lunchtime. *Paradis 4, tel. 93/315–0111. Reservations not essential. AE, DC, MC, V. Closed Mon.*

Quo Vadis. Located just off the Ramblas, near the Boquería Market and Betlem Church, is an unimpressive facade camouflaging one of Barcelona's most respected restaurants. Its much-praised cuisine includes delicacies like *pot pourri de setas* (mushrooms), *lubina al hinojo* (sea bass in fennel) and *hígado de ganso con ciruelas* (goose liver with cherries).

Carme 7, tel. 93/317–7447. Reservations advised. AE, DC, MC, V. Closed Sun.

Moderate **Can Culleretes.** This picturesque old restaurant began life as a pastry shop in 1786, and it is one of the most atmospheric and reasonable finds in Barcelona. Located on an alleyway between Ferran and Boquería, its three dining rooms are decorated with photos of visiting celebrities. It serves real Catalan cooking and is very much a family concern; don't be put off by the prostitutes outside! *Quintana 5, tel. 93/317–6485. Reservations not necessary. No credit cards. Closed Sun. evening and Mon.*

Los Caracoles. Just below the Plaça Reial is Barcelona's most famous restaurant, which caters to tourists but has real atmosphere. Its walls are hung thick with photos of bullfighters and visiting celebrities; its specialties are mussels, paella and, of course, snails (*caracoles*). Don't miss it, it's fun. *Escudellers 14, tel. 93/301–2041. Reservations not essential. AE, DC, MC, V.*

★ **Sete Portes.** With plenty of old-world charm, this delightful restaurant near the waterfront has been going strong since 1836. The cooking is Catalan, the portions enormous, and specialties are *paella de pescado* and *zarzuela sete portes* (seafood casserole). *Passeig Isabel II 14, tel. 93/319–3033. Reservations advised at weekends. AE, DC, MC, V. Open 1 PM–1 AM.*

★ **Sopeta Una.** Dining in this delightful small restaurant with old-fashioned decor and intimate atmosphere is more like eating in a private home. The menu is in Catalan, all the dishes are Catalan, and the atmosphere is very genteel and middle class. For dessert, try the traditional Catalan *música*—a plate of raisins, almonds, and dried fruit served with a glass of muscatel. It's near the Palau de la Música; don't be put off by the narrow street. *Verdaguer i Callis 6, tel. 93/319–6131. Reservations not essential. V. Closed Sun., and Mon. AM.*

Inexpensive **Agut.** Simple, hearty Catalan fare awaits you in this unpretentious restaurant in the lower reaches of the Gothic Quarter. Founded in 1924, its popularity has never waned. There's plenty of wine to wash down the traditional home cooking, but you won't find frills like coffee or liqueurs. *Gignàs 16, tel. 93/315–1709. Reservations not necessary. No credit cards. Closed Sun. evening, Mon., and July.*

★ **Egipte.** This small, friendly restaurant hidden away in a very convenient location behind the Boquería Market—though it's far better known to locals than to visitors—is a real find. Its traditional Catalan home cooking, huge desserts, and swift personable service all contribute to its popularity and good value. *Jerusalem 12, tel. 93/317–7480. No reservations. No credit cards.*

Lodging

For a city of its size and importance, Barcelona has long been underendowed with hotels, but with the coming of the Olympics in 1992, the city's hotel industry is having to think afresh. New hotels are going up fast, international chains are vying for business, and existing hotels are undergoing extensive renovations. Hotels in the Ramblas and Gothic Quarter have plenty of old-world charm, but are less strong on creature comforts; those in the Eixample are mostly '50s or '60s buildings, often recently renovated; and the newest hotels are found out along the Diagonal or beyond, in the residential district of Sarriá.

There are hotel reservation desks at the airport and Sants Central Station.

For details and price category definitions, *see* Lodging in Staying in Spain.

Very Expensive **Avenida Palace.** Right in the center of town, between the Rambla de Catalunya and Passeig de Gràcia, this hotel dates from 1952 but conveys a feeling of elegance and old-world style. Some rooms are rather plain, but most have been recently renovated and there's a superbly ornate lobby. *Gran Vía 605, tel. 93/301–9600. 211 rooms. AE, DC, MC, V.*

★ **Ritz.** Founded in 1919 by Caesar Ritz, this is still the grand old lady of Barcelona hotels. Extensive refurbishment has now restored it to its former splendor. The entrance lobby is awe-inspiring, the rooms spacious, and the service impeccable. *Gran Vía 668, tel. 93/318–5200. 314 rooms. AE, DC, MC, V.*

Sarriá Gran Hotel. This is a bit far out off the Diagonal, but if you like modern, luxurious hotels, this is the one for you. It's been dramatically refurbished with a spectacular waterfall and special executive floor ideal for businesspeople. *Avda Sarriá 50, tel. 93/239–1109. 314 rooms. AE, DC, V.*

Expensive **Colón.** This cozy, older hotel has a unique charm and intimacy
★ reminiscent of an English country hotel. It's in an ideal location right in the heart of the Gothic Quarter, and the rooms on the front overlook the cathedral. It was a great favorite of Joan Miró. *Avda Catedral 7, tel. 93/301–1404. 161 rooms. AE, DC, MC, V.*

★ **Condes de Barcelona.** Situated in the Old Batlló House with plenty of Modernista character, this is one of Barcelona's most popular hotels, and rooms need to be booked well in advance. The decor is stunning, with marble floors and columns, an impressive staircase, and an outstanding bar area. *Passeig de Gràcia 75, tel. 93/215–0616. 100 rooms. AE, DC, MC, V.*

Regente. This smallish hotel on the corner of Valencia has a rooftop pool, plenty of style and charm, and a wonderful Modernista lobby. *Rambla de Catalunya 76, tel. 93/215–2570. 78 rooms. AE, DC, MC, V.*

Moderate **Gran Vía.** Architectural features are the special charm of this 19th-century mansion, close to the main tourist office. The original chapel has been preserved, you can have breakfast in a hall of mirrors, climb its Modernista staircase, and call from elaborate Belle Epoque phone booths. *Gran Vía 642, tel. 93/318 –1900. 48 rooms. AE, DC, MC, V.*

★ **Oriente.** Barcelona's oldest hotel opened in 1843. Its public rooms are a delight—the ballroom and dining rooms have lost none of their 19th-century magnificence—though the bedrooms have undergone rather featureless renovation. It's located just below the Liceu and its terrace café is the perfect place for a drink. *Ramblas 45, tel. 93/302–2558. 142 rooms. AE, DC, MC, V.*

Rialto. In the heart of the Gothic Quarter, just two paces down from the Plaça Sant Jaume, this old 19th-century house has been renovated to high standards of comfort while preserving its charm. Here you're surrounded by sights, shops, and some of Barcelona's best restaurants. *Ferran 40, tel. 93/318–5212. 112 rooms. AE, DC, MC, V.*

Inexpensive **Continental.** Something of a legend among cost-conscious travelers, this comfortable hostel with canopied balconies stands at the top of Ramblas, just below Plaça Catalunya. The rooms are homey and comfortable, the staff is friendly, and the location's ideal. Buffet breakfasts are a plus. *Ramblas 136, tel. 93/301–2508. 30 rooms. V.*

★ **Urbis.** This family-run hostel on Barcelona's central parade is popular with businesspeople and Spanish families. Though generally comfortable, room standards can vary, so it's best to check first. Its location close to stores and only a short walk from most major sights is an advantage. *Passeig de Gràcia 23, tel. 93/317–2766. 61 rooms. AE, DC, MC, V.*

The Arts

To find out what's on in town, look in the daily papers or in the weekly *Guía del Ocio,* available from newsstands all over town. *Actes a la Ciutat* is a weekly list of cultural events published by the Ajuntament and available from its information office on Plaça Sant Jaume.

Concerts Catalans are great music lovers, and their main concert hall is **Palau de la Música** (Amadeo Vives 1, tel. 93/301–1104). The ticket office is open Monday to Friday 11–1 and 5–8; and Saturday 5–8 only. Its Sunday morning concerts are a popular tradition. Tickets are reasonable and can usually be purchased just before the concert.

Opera The **Gran Teatre del Liceu** is one of the world's finest opera houses, considered by some second only to Milan's La Scala. The box office for advance bookings is on Sant Pau 1 (tel. 93/318–9277), open Monday to Friday 8–3, Saturday 9–1. Tickets for same-day performances are on sale in the Ramblas entrance (tel. 93/301–6787) 11–1:30 and 4 PM onward. Tickets are inexpensive by New York or London standards.

Dance You can watch the traditional Catalan Sardana danced in front of the cathedral on Sunday mornings and often on Wednesday evenings, too.

Theater Most theater performances are in Catalan but look out for mime shows, especially if Els Joglars or La Claca, two famous Catalan troupes, are appearing.

Film Most foreign movies are dubbed into Spanish. Try the **Filmoteca** on Travessera de Gràcia 63, on the corner of Tusset, for original English-language films.

Nightlife

Cabaret **Belle Epoque** (Muntaner 246, tel. 93/209–7385) is a beautifully decorated music hall with the most sophisticated shows. **El Mediévolo** (Gran Vía 459, tel. 93/325–3480) has medieval feasts and entertainment; it's all geared to tourists but fun. **Scala Barcelona** (Passeig Sant Joan 47, tel. 93/232–6363) is the city's leading nightclub, with two shows nightly, the first with dinner.

Jazz Clubs Try **Abraxas Jazz Auditorium,** Gelabert 26; **La Cova del Drac,** Tuset 30, just off the Diagonal; and **Zeleste,** Almogávares 122.

Rock Check out **Zeleste,** Almogávares 122. Major concerts are usually held in sports stadiums; keep an eye out for posters.

Flamenco The best place is **El Patio Andaluz** (Aribau 242, tel. 93/209–3524). Also check out **La Venta Andaluza** (Obradors 11, in the heart of the Gothic Quarter) but after dark take a cab there and back. **El Cordobés** (Ramblas 35, tel. 93/317–6653) is aimed at tour groups but can be fun.

Casino The **Gran Casino de Barcelona** (tel. 93/893–3666), 42 kilometers (26 miles) south in Sant Pere de Ribes, near Sitges, also has a dance hall and some excellent international shows in a 19th-century atmosphere. Jacket and tie essential.

Moorish Spain

Stretching from the dark mountains of the Sierra Morena in the north, west to the plains of the Guadalquivir valley, and south to the mighty snowcapped Sierra Nevada, Andalusia rings with echoes of the Moors. In the kingdom they called Al-Andalus, these Muslim invaders from North Africa dwelt for almost 800 years, from their first conquest of Spanish soil (Gibraltar) in 711 to their expulsion from Granada in 1492. And to this day the cities and landscapes of Andalusia are rich in their legacy. The great Mosque of Córdoba, the magical Alhambra Palace in Granada, and the Giralda tower, landmark of Seville, were the inspired creations of Moorish architects and craftsmen working at the behest of Al-Andalus's Arab emirs. The brilliant white villages with narrow streets and sturdy-walled houses clustered round cool inner patios, the white-washed facades with heavily grilled windows, and the deep wailing song of Andalusia's flamenco, so reminiscent of the muezzin's call to prayer, all stem from centuries of Moorish occupation.

Getting There from Madrid

Seville, Córdoba, and Granada all lie on direct train routes from Madrid, and Seville and Córdoba are on the same line. Two fast *talgos* (express trains) leave Atocha Station during the day and take 4½ hours to reach Córdoba, and 5½–6 hours to reach Seville. Or you can opt for a slower (8½ hour) overnight sleeper to Seville that arrives at 7 AM. Some trains to Córdoba also leave from Chamartín Station. To Granada you have the choice of a talgo that leaves Atocha at 3 PM and arrives Granada at 9 PM, or an overnight sleeper leaving Atocha at 11:30PM and arriving in Granada at 8 AM. Major bus services also run from Madrid (usually Estación del Sur) to all three cities. Check details at tourist offices. By car, it's plain sailing down the N-IV by way of La Mancha (shades of Don Quixote) and the Despeñaperros Pass into Andalusia. Then the N-IV follows the course of the Guadalquivir to Córdoba, and on to Seville. For Granada, you leave the N-IV at Bailén and head down the N323 through endless olive groves to Jaén and Granada. Both routes offer dramatic scenery.

Getting Around

From Seville to Córdoba, there's a direct train line or bus services by way of Carmona and Ecija. If you're driving, head out of Seville by way of Avenida de Kansas, or Carretera de Carmona, past the airport and onto the N-IV; this will take you through Carmona and Ecija, too. Elsewhere in this area, it's best to travel by bus or car as train services between Córdoba and Granada tend to be slow and tortuous and often involve

Moorish Spain

changing trains at Andalusia's infamous Bobadilla junction. Buses from Córdoba to Granada go by way of Jaén or Baena. If you're driving, it's faster via Jaén, but even more picturesque by way of either the poorly surfaced N432 through Baena, or the N331 to Lucena then C334 through Iznájar to Loja. Seville's Bus Station (tel. 954/417111) is on José María Osborne and Manuel Vázquez Sagastizabal not far from the San Bernardo train station. Córdoba has no central bus depot, so check at the tourist office for departure points. Granada's main bus station is *Alsina Graells* (Camino de Ronda 97, tel. 958/251358) though departure points vary according to destination.

Guided Tours

Guided tours of Seville, Córdoba, Granada, and Ronda are run by **Juliá Tours, Pullmantur,** and **Trapsatur,** both from Madrid, and resorts of the Costa del Sol; check with travel agents. Local excursions may be available from Seville to the sherry bodegas and equestrian museum of Jerez de la Frontera. From Granada, there's a once-weekly day trip to the villages of the Alpujarras; check details with tourist offices. In Córdoba, **Viajes Vincit** (Alonso de Burgos 1, tel. 957/470890) runs daily sightseeing tours of the city.

Tourist Information

Córdoba. Palacio de Congresos y Exposiciones, Torrijos 10, tel. Plaza Judas Levi, tel. 957/290740.

Granada. Casa de los Tiros, Pavaneras 19, tel. 958/221022, a short walk from Plaza Isabel la Católica.

Seville. Avenida Constitución 24, tel. 954/225653 or 221094, not far from the cathedral and Archives of the Indies.

Exploring Moorish Spain

Our tour begins in Seville and continues to Carmona, Ecija, Córdoba, Baena, Granada, Sierra Nevada, Lanjarón, Orgiva and Alpujarras.

The downside to a visit here, especially to Seville, is that petty crime, much of it directed against tourists, is rife. Purse snatching and thefts from cars, frequently when drivers are in them, are depressingly familiar. *Always* keep your car doors *and* trunk locked. *Never* leave any valuables in your car. Leave your passport, traveler's checks, and credit cards in your hotel's safe, *never* in your room. Don't carry expensive cameras or wear jewelry. Take only the minimum amount of cash with you. There comes a point, however—if, your windshield is smashed or your bag is snatched, for example—when all the precautions in the world will prove inadequate. If you're unlucky, it's an equally depressing fact that the police, again especially in Seville, have adopted a distinctly casual attitude to such thefts, and often combine indifference to beleaguered tourists with rudeness in about equal measure. Frankly, there's little you can do except remain calm.

Numbers in the margin correspond with points of interest on the Seville map.

Seville 957/471235, right beside the mosque. Municipal Tourist Office, Lying on the banks of the Guadalquivir, **Seville**—Spain's fourth-largest city and capital of Andalusia—is one of the most beautiful and romantic cities in Europe. Here in this city of the sensuous Carmen and the amorous Don Juan, famed for the spectacle of its Holy Week processions and April Fair, you'll come close to the spiritual heart of Moorish Andalusia. Begin ❶ your visit in the **Cathedral,** begun in 1402, a century and a half after St. Ferdinand delivered Seville from the Moors. This great Gothic edifice, which took just over a century to build, is traditionally described in superlatives. It's the biggest and highest cathedral in Spain, the largest Gothic building in the world, and the world's third-largest church after St. Peter's in Rome and St. Paul's in London. And it boasts the world's largest carved wooden altarpiece. Despite such impressive statistics, the inside can be dark and gloomy with too many overly ornate Baroque trappings. But seek out the beautiful Virgins by Murillo and Zurbarán, and reflect on the history enshrined in these walls. In a silver urn before the high altar rest the precious relics of Seville's liberator, St. Ferdinand, said to have died from excessive fasting, and down in the crypt are the tombs of his descendants Pedro the Cruel, founder of the Alcázar, and his mistress María de Padilla. But above all, you'll want to pay your respects to Christopher Columbus, whose mortal vestiges are enshrined in a flamboyant mausoleum in the south aisle. Borne aloft by statues representing the four medieval kingdoms of Spain, it's to be hoped the great voyager has found peace at last after the transatlantic quarrels that carried his body from Valladolid to Santo Domingo, and from Havana to

Seville

Major Attractions

Alcázar, **3**

Barrio Santa Cruz, **5**

Calle Betis, **9**

Cathedral, **1**

Giralda, **2**

Golden Tower, **10**

Maestranza
Bullring, **11**

María Luisa Park, **6**

Patio de las
Banderas, **4**

Plaza de America, **8**

Plaza de España, **7**

Other Attractions

Museo Arte
Comtemporaneo, **12**

San Telmo Palace, **13**

Tobacco Factory
(University), **14**

Seville. *Admission: 200 ptas. Open in summer 10:30–1:30 and 4:30–6:30; in winter 10:30–1 and 4–6; closed Sun. PM*

Every day the bell that summons the faithful to prayer rings out from a Moorish minaret, relic of the Arab mosque whose admirable tower of Abu Yakoub the Sevillians could not bring themselves to destroy. Topped in 1565–68 by a bell tower and weather vane and called the **Giralda,** this splendid example of Moorish art is one of the marvels of Seville. In place of steps, a gently sloping ramp climbs to the viewing platform 71 meters (230 feet) above Seville's rooftops. St. Ferdinand is said to have ridden his horse to the top to admire the view of the city he had conquered. Seven centuries later your view of the Golden Tower and shimmering Guadalquivir will be equally breathtaking. Try, too, to see the Giralda at night when the floodlights cast a new magic on this gem of Islamic art. *Open same hours as Cathedral and visited on same ticket. Admission to Giralda only: 50 ptas.*

❸ The high fortified walls of the **Alcázar** belie the exquisite delicacy of the palace's interior. It was built by Pedro the Cruel—so known because he murdered his stepmother and four of his half-brothers—who lived here with his mistress María de Padilla from 1350 to 1369. Don't mistake this for a genuine Moorish palace as it was built more than 100 years after the reconquest of Seville; rather its style is Mudéjar—built by Moorish craftsmen working under orders of a Christian king. The Catholic Kings (Ferdinand and Isabella), whose only son, Prince Juan, was born in the Alcázar in 1478, added a wing to serve as administration center for their New World empire, and Charles V enlarged it further for his marriage celebrations in 1526. Pedro's Mudéjar palace centers around the beautiful **Patio de las Doncellas** (Court of the Damsels) whose name pays tribute to the annual gift of 100 virgins to the Moorish sultans whose palace once stood on the site. Resplendent with the most delicate of lacelike stucco and gleaming azulejo decorations, it is immediately reminiscent of Granada's Alhambra, and is in fact the work of Granada craftsmen. Opening off this are the apartments of María de Padilla whose hold over her lover, and seemingly her courtiers, too, was so great that they apparently vied with one another to drink her bath water!

The **Alcázar Gardens** are fragrant with jasmine and myrtle, an orange tree said to have been planted by Pedro the Cruel, and a lily pond well stocked with fat, contented goldfish. The end of your visit brings you to the **Patio de las Banderas** for an unrivaled view of the Giralda. *Admission: 150 ptas., free on Sat. Open daily 9–12:45 and 3–5:45.*

❺ The **Barrio Santa Cruz,** with its twisting alleyways, cobbled squares, and whitewashed houses, is a perfect setting for an operetta. Once the home of Seville's Jews, it was much favored by 17th-century noblemen and today boasts some of the most expensive properties in Seville. All the romantic images you've ever had of Spain will come to life here: Every house gleams white or deep ochre yellow; wrought-iron grilles adorn the windows, and every balcony and patio is bedecked with geraniums and petunias. You'll find the most beautiful patio at Callejón del Agua 12. Ancient bars nestle side by side with antiques shops. Don't miss the famous **Casa Román** bar in Plaza de los Venerables Sacerdotes with its ceilings hung thick with some of the best hams in Seville, or the **Hostería del Laurel** next door, where in summer you can dine in one of the loveliest squares in the city. Souvenir and excellent ceramic shops surround the **Plaza Doña Elvira,** where the young of Seville gather to play guitars around the fountain and azulejo benches. And in the **Plaza Alianza,** with its well-stocked antiques shops and **John Fulton gallery** (Fulton is the only American ever to qualify as a full-fledged bullfighter), stop a moment and admire the simplicity of the crucifix on the wall, framed in a profusion of bougainvillea.

❻ Take a cab, or better still, hire a horse carriage from the Plaza Virgen de los Reyes, below the Giralda, and visit **María Luisa park,** whose gardens are a delightful blend of formal design and wild vegetation, shady walkways and sequestered nooks. In the 1920s the park was redesigned to form the site of the 1929 Hispanic-American exhibition, and the impressive villas you see here today are the fair's remaining pavilions. Visit the mon-

❼ umental **Plaza de España,** whose grandiose pavilion of Spain was the centerpiece of the exhibition. At the opposite end of the park you can feed the hundreds of white doves that gather

❽ round the fountains of the lovely **Plaza de America;** it's a magical spot to while away the sleepy hours of the siesta.

❾ An early evening stroll along the **Calle Betis** on the far side of the Guadalquivir is a delight few foreigners know about. Between the San Telmo and Isabel II bridges, the vista of the sparkling water, the palm-lined banks, and the silhouette of

❿ ⓫ the **Golden Tower** (built 1220) and the **Maestranza Bullring** (built 1760–63), one of Spain's oldest, is simply stunning.

Thirty kilometers (19 miles) from Seville, the N-IV brings you to **Carmona.** This unspoiled Andalusian town of Roman and Moorish origin is worth a visit, either to stay at the parador or to enjoy its wealth of Mudéjar and Renaissance churches, and its streets of whitewashed houses of clear Moorish influence. Most worthwhile is the **Church of San Pedro** begun in 1466, whose extraordinary interior is an unbroken mass of sculptures and gilded surfaces, and whose tower, erected in 1704, is an unabashed imitation of Seville's famous Giralda. Carmona's most moving monument is its splendid **Roman Necropolis,** where in huge underground chambers some 900 family tombs dating from the 2nd to the 4th centuries AD have been chiseled out of the rock. *Open Tues.–Sat. 10–2 and 4–6.*

A little farther along the N-IV brings you to **Ecija,** a dazzling white cluster reputed to be the hottest town in Spain—its nickname is *sarten de Andalucía,* "Andalusia's frying pan." With its history going back to Greek and Roman times, you'll find plenty of Renaissance and Baroque palaces here and a bewildering array of churches whose towers and turrets rise before you as you approach along the main road.

Numbers in the margin correspond with points of interest on the Córdoba map.

Córdoba Ancient **Córdoba,** city of the caliphs, is one of Spain's oldest cities and the greatest embodiment of Moorish heritage in all Andalusia. From the 8th to the 11th centuries, the Moorish emirs and Caliphs of the West held court here and it became one of the Western world's greatest centers of art, culture, and learning. Moors, Christians, and Jews lived together in harmony within its walls. Two of Córdoba's most famous native sons were Averröes, the great Arab scientist, and Maimónides, the notable Jewish doctor and philosopher. But above all it is for its

❶ famous **Mosque** (or Mezquita), one of the finest built by the Moors, that Córdoba is known first and foremost. Its founder was Abd ar-Rahman I (756–788), and it was completed by Al Mansur (976–1002) around the year 987. As you step inside you'll come face to face with a forest of gleaming pillars of precious marble, jasper, and onyx, rising to a roof of red and white horseshoe arches, one of the most characteristic traits of Moorish architecture. Not even the heavy Baroque cathedral that Charles V so mistakenly built in its midst—and later regretted —can detract from the overpowering impact and mystery wrought by the art of these Moorish craftsmen of a thousand years ago. It was indeed a fitting setting for the original copy of the Koran and a bone from the arm of the Prophet Mohammed, holy relics once housed in the Mezquita which were responsible for bringing thousands of pilgrims to its doors in the great years before St. Ferdinand reconquered Córdoba for the Christians in 1236. In Moorish times, the mosque opened onto the **Orange Tree Courtyard,** where the faithful performed their ablutions before worshiping, and the bell tower, which you can climb for a magnificent view of the city, served as the mosque's minaret. *Admission: 250 ptas. Open daily 10:30–1:30 and 3:30–5:30 (4–7 in summer).*

Near the mosque, the streets of Torrijos, Cardenal Herrero, and Deanes are lined with tempting souvenir shops specializing in local handicrafts, especially the filigree silver and embossed leather for which Córdoba is famous. In her niche on Cardenal

❷ Herrero, the **Virgin of Lanterns** stands demurely behind a lantern-hung grille, rather like a lovely lady awaiting a serenade. In a narrow alleyway off to your left is the **Callejón de las Flores,** its houses decked with hanging flower baskets. Now

❸ make your way westward to the old **Judería,** or Jewish quarter.

❹ On the **Plaza Judás Levi** you'll find the municipal tourist office. A few paces down, on Calle Manríquez, is another outstanding patio open to visitors.

❺ Overlooking the Plaza Maimónides (or Bulas) is the **Museum of Bullfighting,** housed in two delightful old mansions. You'll see a well-displayed collection of memorabilia, paintings, and posters by early 20th-century Córdoban artists, and rooms dedicated to great Córdoban *toreros*—even the hide of the bull that killed the legendary Manolete in 1947. *Admission: 100 ptas. Open Tues.–Sat. 9:30–1:30 and 5–8 (4–7 in winter); Sun. 9:30–noon.*

❻ A moving statue of the great Jewish philosopher **Maimónides** stands in the Plaza Tiberiades. A few paces along Judíos, you

❼ come to the only **synagogue** in Andalusia to have survived the expulsion of the Jews in 1492. It's one of only three remaining synagogues in Spain—the other two you saw in Toledo—and it boasts some fine Hebrew and Mudéjar stucco tracery and a women's gallery. *Admission: 50 ptas. Open Tues.–Sat. 10–2 and 5–7; Sun. 10–noon.* Across the way is the courtyard of El Zoco, a former Arab souk, with some pleasant shops and stalls, and sometimes a bar open in summer.

As you leave Córdoba and head for Granada, the N432 climbs from the Guadalquivir valley up into the mountains of central

Córdoba

Major Attractions
Judería, **3**
Maimónides Statue, **6**
Mosque, **1**
Museum of Bullfighting, **5**
Plaza Judás Levi, **4**
Synagogue, **7**
Virgin of Lanterns, **2**

Other Attractions
Alcázar, **8**
Cristo de los Faroles, **11**
Museo Arqueológico, **9**
Museo de Bellas Artes, **10**

Andalusia. It is 63 kilometers (39 miles) to **Baena,** a picturesque Andalusian town of white houses clustered on the hillside, where you may want to stop for a drink and wander the narrow streets and squares as yet largely untouched by tourism. Mountain views line the route as the road twists toward its highest point, the 931-meter (3,000-foot) Puerto del Castillo, before dropping down onto the *vega* (fertile plain) of Granada. At Pinos Puente, you can take a short detour to the village of **Fuente Vaqueros** where Federico García Lorca was born on June 5, 1898. In 1986, to commemorate the 50th anniversary of his assassination in Granada at the outbreak of the Civil War, his birthplace was restored as a museum. The nearby village of Valderrubio inspired his *Libro de Poemas* and *La Casa de Bernarda Alba. Museo de Lorca, open 10–1 and 6–8 with tours every hour on the hour.*

Numbers in the margin correspond with points of interest on the Granada map.

Granada The city of **Granada** rises majestically on three hills dwarfed by the mighty snowcapped peaks of the Sierra Nevada, which boasts the highest roads in Europe. Atop one of these hills the pink-gold palace of the Alhambra, at once splendidly imposing yet infinitely delicate, gazes out across the rooftops and gypsy caves of the Sacromonte to the fertile *vega* rich in orchards, tobacco fields, and poplar groves. Granada, the last stronghold of the Moors and the most treasured of all their cities, fell finally to the Catholic Kings in January 1492. For Ferdinand and Isabella their conquest of Granada was the fulfillment of a long cherished dream to rid Spain of the Infidel, and here they built

❶ the flamboyant **Royal Chapel** where they have lain side by side since 1521, later joined by their daughter Juana la Loca. Begin your tour in the nearby Plaza de Bib-Rambla, a pleasant square with flower stalls and outdoor cafés in summer, then pay a

❷ quick visit to the huge Renaissance **Cathedral** commissioned in 1521 by Charles V who thought the Royal Chapel "too small for so much glory" and determined to house his illustrious grandparents somewhere more worthy. But his ambitions came to little, for Granada Cathedral is a grandiose and gloomy monument, not completed until 1714, and is far surpassed in beauty and historic value by the neighboring Royal Chapel, which, despite the great emperor's plans, still houses the tombs of his grandparents and less fortunate mother. *Admission to both: 75 ptas., Sun. AM free. Cathedral and Royal Chapel open 11–1 and 3–6 in winter (4–7 in summer).*

❸ The adjacent streets of the **Alcaicería,** the old Arab silk exchange, will prove a haven for souvenir hunters. Here you can find any number of local handicrafts inspired by Granada's Moorish heritage: brass and copperware, green and blue Fajalauza pottery, wooden boxes, tables and chess sets inlaid with mother of pearl, and woven goods from the villages of the Alpujarras in which the colors green, red, and black predominate. Across the Gran Vía de Colón, Granada's main shopping street, the narrow streets begin to wind up the slopes of the

❹ **Albaicín,** the old Moorish quarter, which is now a fascinating mixture of dilapidated white houses and beautiful *cármenes,* luxurious villas with fragrant gardens. Few visitors find their

❺ way to the balcony of **San Nicolás church,** which affords an unforgettable view of the Alhambra, particularly when it is floodlit at night.

Granada

Major Attractions
Alabaicín, **4**
Alcaicería, **3**
Alhambra, **8**
Alhambra Precincts, **6**
Cathedral, **2**
Puerta de la Justicía, **7**
Generalife, **9**
San Nicolás Church, **5**
Royal Chapel, **1**

Other Attractions
Casa de los Tiros, **12**
Casa Museo de
Falla, **10**
Corral del Carbón, **14**
Museo
Arqueológico, **11**
San Jerónimo, **15**
San Juan de Diós, **16**
Santo Domingo, **13**

❻ The Cuesta de Gomérez climbs steeply to the **Alhambra precincts** where the Duke of Wellington planted shady elms, and Washington Irving tarried among the gypsies from whom he learned the Moorish legends so evocatively recounted in his **❼** *Tales of the Alhambra.* Above the **Puerta de la Justicía** the hand of Fatima, her fingers evoking the five laws of the Koran, beckons you inside the mystical Alhambra, the most imposing and infinitely beautiful of all Andalusia's Moorish monuments. The **❽** history of the **Alhambra** is woven through the centuries. Once inside its famous courts the legends of the Patio of the Lions, the Hall of the Two Sisters, and the murder of the Abencerrajes spring to life in a profusion of lacy walls, frothy stucco, gleaming tiles, and ornate domed ceilings. Here in this realm of myrtles and fountains, festooned arches and mysterious inscriptions, every corner holds its secret. Here the emirs installed their harems, accorded their favorites the most lavish of courts and bathed in marble baths. In the midst of so much that is delicate the Baroque palace of Charles V seems an intrusion, heavy and incongruous, were it not for the splendid acoustics that make it a perfect setting for Granada's summer music festival.

❾ Wysteria, jasmine, and roses line your route to the **Generalife,** the nearby summer palace of the caliphs, where crystal drops shower from slender fountains against a background of stately cypresses. The view of the white, clustered houses of the Albaicín, the Sacromonte riddled with gypsy caves, and the imposing bulk of the Alhambra towering above the tiled roofs of the city will etch on your memory an indelible image of this most beautiful of settings and greatest of Moorish legacies. *Admission to Alhambra and Generalife, 425 ptas.; Generalife only, 100 ptas. Free Sun. after 3 PM. Open Mon.–Sat. 9:30–8:30, Sun. 9:30–6; also Wed.–Sat. 10 PM–midnight for illuminations. (Ticket office closes 45 mins. before closing times above.) Shorter opening hours in winter.*

If you have a day to spare, you can drive to the mountains of the nearby **Sierra Nevada.** The ski resort itself, where you can ski from December to May, is truly unmemorable, but the surrounding scenery viewed from the highest mountain route in Europe makes for a memorable day out. A bus leaves Granada daily from the Hotel Zaida on the Acera de Darro and returns at around 6 PM. Above the resort the road climbs to the Pico de Veleta, Spain's second-highest mountain at 3,100 meters (10,000 feet), and the view across the Alpujarra range to the sea at Motril is simply stunning. Away to the left rises the mighty Mulhacén, at 3,558 meters (11,477 feet), Spain's highest peak.

If you opt instead for a trip to the villages of the high **Alpujarras,** leave Granada on the N323 toward Motril, then branch east to **Lanjarón** a delightful old spa town with an air of faded gentility. From **Orgiva,** the main town of the Alpujarras, the highest road in Europe ascends to picturesque villages like **Bubión, Capileira** beneath the summit of the Veleta, and **Trevélez,** Europe's highest village, on the slopes of Mulhacén. These ancient villages, only recently brushed by modern tourism, became the final refuge of the Moors as they fled the Conquest of Granada, and here they remained until their expulsion from Spain in 1609. With their squat, square houses and flat roofs so reminiscent of the land across the Straits of Gibraltar, they are the last vestige of Andalusia's great Moorish past.

Dining and Lodging and Entertainment

For details and price category definitions, *see* Dining and Lodging in Staying in Spain.

Carmona
Lodging
★

Parador del Rey Don Pedro. The beauty of this modern parador is its splendid, peaceful setting in the ruins of the old Moorish alcázar on top of the hill above Carmona, and its magnificent views across the vast fertile plain below. *Tel. 954/141010. 59 rooms. Facilities: pool. AE, DC, MC, V. Expensive.*

Córdoba
Dining
★

El Caballo Rojo. The Red Horse, located close to the mosque, is Córdoba's most outstanding restaurant, famous throughout Andalusia and all of Spain. The decor resembles a cool Andalusian patio, and the menu features traditional specialties such as *rabo de toro* (bull's tail); *salmorejo*, a local version of gazpacho with chunks of ham and egg; and other exotic creations inspired by Córdoba's Moorish heritage. *Cardenal Herrero 28, tel. 957/475375. Reservations advised. AE, DC, MC, V. Expensive.*

La Almudaina. This attractive restaurant is located in a 15th-century house and former school that overlooks the Alcázar at the entrance to the Judería. It has an Andalusian patio, and the decor and cooking are both typical of Córdoba. *Campo Santo de los Mártires 1, tel. 957/474342. AE, DC, MC, V. Closed Sun. evening. Moderate.*

El Blasón. Under the same management as El Caballo Rojo, this charming restaurant is fast gaining a name for fine food and unbeatable ambience. Located in an old inn with a pleasant tapas patio and a whole array of restaurants upstairs, its specialties include *salmón con naranjas* (salmon in orange) and *ternera con salsa de alcaparrones* (roast veal in caper sauce). *José Zorrilla 11, tel. 957/480625. AE, DC, MC, V. Closed Sun. evening in summer. Moderate.*

El Cardenal. Close to the mosque, beside the Marisa hotel, this restaurant in the heart of Córdoba's tourist center offers a stylish setting for lunch or dinner. A marble staircase with Oriental carpets leads up to the second-floor dining room. Good food and professional service complement the cool, agreeable atmosphere. *Cardenal Herrero 14, tel. 957/480346. AE, DC, MC, V. Closed Sun. evening and Mon. Moderate.*

★ **El Churrasco.** Ranking second only to El Caballo Rojo, this atmospheric restaurant with a patio is famous for its grilled meat dishes. Specialties are, of course, *churrasco*, a pork dish in pepper sauce, and an excellent *salmorejo*. *Romero 16, tel. 957/290819. AE, DC, MC, V. Closed Thurs. and Aug. Moderate.*

Lodging
★

Adarve. This delightful contemporary hotel on the east side of the mosque is built in Andalusian Moorish style with a charming patio and ceramic decor. The hotel itself has no restaurant, but guests can dine in the attractive Mesón del Bandolero in Calle Torrijos on the opposite side of the mosque. *Magistral González Francés 15, tel. 957/481102. 103 rooms, pool. AE, DC, MC, V. Expensive.*

El Califa. This is a small, modern hotel in a reasonably quiet, central location in the heart of the old city. It accepts no tour groups, only individual guests, and is a comfortable place to stay, with the sights and shops close at hand. *Lope de Hoces 14, tel. 957/299400. 46 rooms. V. Moderate.*

Maimónides. Its location is convenient, right beside the mosque, with restaurants and souvenir shops outside the door.

The lobby is impressive; rooms are functional but comfortable. *Torrijos 4, tel. 957/471500. 61 rooms. AE, DC, MC, V. Moderate.*

Marisa. A charming old Andalusian house whose location in the heart of the old town overlooking the mosque's Patio de los Naranjos is its prime virtue. You'll find the decor quaint and charming, and the rates reasonable. *Cardenal Herrero 6, tel. 957/473142. 28 rooms. AE, DC, V. Inexpensive.*

Granada
Dining
★

Baroca. Located one block above the Camino de Ronda, the locals consider this Granada's best restaurant. The menu favors international cuisine; desserts are especially good. Service is professional and the ambience agreeable. *Pedro Antonio de Alarcón 34, tel. 958/265051. Reservations advised. AE, DC, MC, V. Closed Sun. and Aug. Expensive.*

Cunini. Located in the center of town, close to the cathedral, Cunini has long been famous for the quality of its seafood. *Pescadería 9 or Capuchina 14, tel. 958/263701. Reservations advised. AE, DC, MC, V. Closed Sun. evening. Expensive.*

Carmen de San Miguel. This is a restaurant to visit for its superb setting in a villa with an outdoor terrace and magnificent views over Granada. Located on the Alhambra hill beside the Alhambra Palace hotel, the setting is unbeatable, the food rather more average. *Paseo Torres Bermejas 3, tel. 958/226723. V. Closed Sun. Moderate.*

Sevilla. This is a very atmospheric, colorful restaurant located in the Alcaicería beside the cathedral. There's a superb tapas bar at the entrance, and the dining room is picturesque but rather small and crowded. The menu can be rather tourist-oriented. *Oficios 12, tel. 958/221223. AE, DC, MC, V. Closed Sun. evening. Moderate.*

Los Manueles. This old inn is one of Granada's long-standing traditions. The walls are decorated with ceramic tiles, and the ceiling is hung with hams. There's lots of atmosphere, good old-fashioned service, and plenty of traditional Granada cooking. *Zaragoza 2, tel. 958/223415. No credit cards. Inexpensive.*

Lodging

Parador de San Francisco. Magnificently located in an old convent right within the Alhambra precincts, the parador was where Queen Isabella was entombed before the completion of the Royal Chapel. It's one of Spain's most popular hotels, and you need to book at least six months in advance. *Alhambra, tel. 958/221440. 39 rooms. AE, DC, MC, V. Very expensive.*

★ **Alhambra Palace.** This flamboyant ochre-red Moorish-style palace was built about 1910, and sits halfway up the hill to the Alhambra. The mood is more harried than at the more isolated parador. Though recently renovated, it remains a conversation piece with rich carpets, tapestries, and Moorish tiles. Rooms overlooking the town are preferable. The terrace is the perfect place for an early evening drink as the sun sets over the Sierra Nevada mountains. *Peña Partida 2, tel. 958/221468. 121 rooms. AE, DC, MC, V. Expensive.*

América. A simple but charming hostel in a magnificent location, within the Alhambra precincts, this is very popular, and you should book months ahead. *Real de la Alhambra 53, tel. 958/227471. 14 rooms. No credit cards. Open March–Oct. only. Moderate.*

Juan Miguel. This comfortable, modern hotel right in the center of town opened in 1987. The rooms are well equipped, service is professional, and there's a good restaurant. *Acera del*

Darro 24, tel. 958/258912. 66 rooms. AE, DC, MC, V. Moderate.

Inglaterra. Set in a period house just two blocks above the Gran Vía de Colón in the heart of town, this is a hotel that will appeal to those who prefer old-world charm to creature comforts, though accommodations are perfectly adequate for the reasonable rates. *Cetti Meriem 6, tel. 958/221559. 40 rooms. V. Inexpensive.*

★ **Kenia.** A distinctive hotel set in a personalized villa in a quiet residential section of town. Service is attentive, and there's a large leafy garden, a blessing in summer. Accommodations are simple, but the Kenia has a charm not found in functional business hotels. *Molinos 65, tel. 958/227506. 16 rooms. No credit cards. Inexpensive.*

Flamenco There are several "impromptu" flamenco shows in the caves of the Sacromonte, but these can be dismally bad and little more than tourist rip-offs. Go only if accompanied by a Spanish friend who knows his way around. There are also two regular flamenco clubs that cater largely to tourists and tour groups: **Jardines Neptuno** and **Reina Mora.** Both can be booked through your hotel.

Seville **La Albahaca.** Set in an attractive old house in the heart of the
Dining Barrio Santa Cruz, the Albahaca offers plenty of style and atmosphere and original, imaginative cuisine. Specialties of the chef, who was formerly in the Hotel Alfonso XIII, are *ajo blanco con pasas de Corinto* (garlic with raisins) and *filetitos de ciervo con ciruelas* (venison and cherries). *Plaza Santa Cruz 12, tel. 954/220714. Reservations advised. AE, DC, MC, V. Closed Sun. Expensive.*

★ **Egaña Oriza.** This is currently one of Seville's most fashionable restaurants. Basque specialties include *merluza con almejas en salsa verde* (white fish in clam sauce) and *solomillo con foie en salsa de trufas* (steak with goose liver pâté in truffle sauce). It's opposite the old tobacco factory, now Seville University. *San Fernando 41, tel. 954/227211. Reservations essential. AE, DC, MC, V. Closed Sun. and Aug. Expensive.*

Enrique Becerra. This small intimate restaurant in an old Andalusian house just off the Plaza Nueva is well known for its Andalusian cuisine. *Gamazo 2, tel. 954/213049. Reservations advised. AE, V. Closed Sun. Expensive to Moderate.*

San Francisco. An old convent on the central square is the setting for this restaurant. The decor is nothing special but the food is excellent and the wine list is exceptional. The cuisine is predominantly French. Try *puding de puerros con langostinos* (leek and crayfish mousse) or *redondilla de ternera* (veal cutlets). For a view of the splendid Plateresque City Hall, book table number 1. *Plaza San Francisco 10, tel. 954/222056. MC, V. Closed Sun. evenings, Mon. and Aug. Expensive to Moderate.*

El Bacalao. This popular fish restaurant, opposite the church of Santa Catalina, is in an Andalusian house decorated with ceramic tiles. As its name suggests, the house specialty is *bacalao* (cod); try the *bacalao con arroz* or the *bacalao al pilpil*. *Plaza Ponce de León 15, tel. 954/216670. Reservations advised. AE, DC, V. Closed Sun. and Aug. Moderate.*

La Isla. Located in the center of town between the cathedral and the Convent of La Caridad, La Isla has long been famous for its superb seafood and paella. *Arfe 25, tel. 954/215376. AE, DC, MC, V. Closed Aug. Moderate.*

★ **La Judería.** This bright, modern restaurant near the Hotel Fernando III is fast gaining recognition for the quality of its Andalusian and international cuisine and reasonable prices. Fish dishes from the north of Spain, and meat from Avila are specialties. Try *cordero lechal* (roast baby lamb) or *urta a la roteña* (a fish dish unique to Rota). *Cano y Cueto 13, tel. 954/ 412052. Reservations essential. AE, DC, MC, V. Closed Tues. Moderate.*

★ **Mesón Don Raimundo.** Located in an old convent close to the cathedral, the atmosphere and decor are deliberately Sevillian. Its bar is the perfect place to sample a *fino* and some splendid tapas, and the restaurant, when not catering to tour groups, is one of Seville's most delightful. *Argote de Molina 26, tel. 954/ 223355. Reservations advised. AE, DC, MC, V. Closed Sun. evening. Moderate.*

Mesón Castellano. This old Sevillian house opposite the church of San José is an ideal place for lunch after a morning's shopping on Calle Sierpes. Specialties are Castilian meat dishes, at reasonable prices. *Jovellanos 6, tel. 954/214128. Open for lunch only. AE, DC, V. Closed Sun. Inexpensive.*

Lodging **Alfonso XIII.** This ornate Mudéjar-style palace was built for Alfonso XIII's visit to the 1929 exhibition. It is worth a visit for its splendid Moorish decor, despite the fact that parts of the hotel are faded and fall short of five-star expectations. Rooms are spacious. The restaurant is elegant but falls short of expectations, too. *San Fernando 2, tel. 954/222850. 128 rooms and 21 suites, pool. AE, DC, MC, V. Very expensive.*

Colón. This classic Seville hotel reopened at the end of 1988 after several years of renovation. Its 204 rooms and 14 suites have been modernized to a high degree of comfort while retaining much of their style. It's located right in the heart of town, close to the main shopping center. You can dine in the elegant El Burladero restaurant or in the more typical La Tasca. *Canalejas 1, tel. 954/222900. AE, DC, MC, V. Very expensive.*

★ **Doña María.** Close to the cathedral, this is one of Seville's most charming hotels. Some rooms are small and plain; others are tastefully furnished with antiques. Room 310 has a four-poster double bed, and 305 two single four-posters; both have spacious bathrooms. There's no restaurant, but there's a rooftop pool with a good view of the Giralda. *Don Remondo 19, tel. 954/ 224990. 61 rooms. AE, DC, MC, V. Expensive.*

Inglaterra. A modern, comfortable hotel right on the main square, it was renovated throughout in 1988. Rooms on the fifth floor have the best view, and the restaurant is well known for its good food and professional service. *Plaza Nueva 7, tel. 954/224970. 120 rooms. AE, DC, MC, V. Expensive.*

★ **Sevilla Sol.** This new hotel behind the Plaza de España opened in 1988. Rooms are comfortable and spacious, with views over the city, wide beds, and large bathrooms. The best rooms are on the eighth and ninth floors. *Avenida de la Borbolla 3, tel. 954/422611. AE, DC, MC, V. Expensive.*

Bécquer. This functional, modern hotel with attentive service is convenient for the shopping center and offers comfortable if unexciting accommodations. It's one of the best moderate bets. *Reyes Católicos 4, tel. 954/228900. 126 rooms. AE, DC, MC, V. Moderate.*

Giralda. Recently modernized and extensively renovated, this is a comfortable, functional hotel with spacious, light rooms decorated in typical Castilian style. Located in a cul-de-sac off

Avenida Menéndez Pelayo, it lies on the edge of the old city; rooms on the fifth floor are best. *Sierra Nevada 3, tel. 954/416661. 107 rooms, garage. AE, DC, MC, V. Moderate.*

Internacional. Well maintained and charming, this old-world hotel lies in the narrow streets of the old town near Casa Pilatos. *Aguilas 17, tel. 954/213207. 26 rooms. Inexpensive.*

Murillo. This picturesque hotel in the heart of the Barrio Santa Cruz was redecorated in 1987. Rooms are simple and small, but the setting is a virtue. You can't reach the hotel by car, but porters with trolleys will fetch your luggage from your taxi. *Lope de Rueda 7, tel. 954/216095. 61 rooms, 30 with bath, 31 with shower. AE, DC, MC, V. Inexpensive.*

La Rábida. With lots of delightful 19th-century touches, this is a charming old-fashioned hotel in the center of town. *Castelar 24, tel. 954/220960. 87 rooms and a restaurant. Inexpensive.*

Flamenco   Regular flamenco clubs cater largely to tourists, but their shows are colorful and offer a good introduction for the uninitiated. Try any of the following: **El Arenal** (Rodo 7, tel. 954/216492); **Los Gallos** (Plaza Santa Cruz 11, tel. 954/216981), a small intimate club in the heart of the Barrio Santa Cruz offering fairly pure flamenco; and **El Patio Sevillano** (Paseo de Colón, tel. 954/214120), which caters largely to tour groups.

Bullfights   Corridas take place at the Maestranza bullring on Paseo de Colón, usually on Sunday from Easter to October. The best are during the April Fair. Tickets can be bought in advance from the windows at the ring (one of the oldest and most picturesque in Spain) or from the kiosks in Calle Sierpes (these charge a commission).

Costa del Sol

What were impoverished fishing villages in the 1950s are now retirement villages and package-tour meccas for northern Europeans and Americans. Despite the abuses of this naturally lovely area during the boom years of the 1960s and '70s, and the continuing brashness of the resorts that cater to the package-tour trade, the Costa del Sol has managed to preserve at least some semblance of charm. Behind the hideous concrete monsters—some of which are now being demolished—you'll come across old cottages and villas set in gardens that blossom with jasmine and bougainvillea. The sun still sets over miles of beaches and the lights of small fishing craft still twinkle in the distance. Most of your time should be devoted to indolence—sunbathing and swimming (though not in the polluted Mediterranean; all hotels have pools for this reason). When you need something to do, you can head inland to the historic town of Ronda and the perched white villages of Andalusia. You can also make a day trip to Gibraltar or Tangier.

Getting There

Daily flights on Iberia or Aviaco from Madrid to Málaga take about one hour; from Barcelona, 1½ hours. Iberia has direct flights from New York or London to Málaga. Málaga Airport (tel. 952/322000) is 12 kilometers (7 miles) west of Málaga. There's bus and train service from the airport to Málaga, and a train to Torremolinos and Fuengirola. A fast train runs from Madrid to Málaga; there's also a comfortable overnight sleeper that arrives in Málaga around 7:30 AM. The best way to reach Málaga from Seville or Granada is by bus. Córdoba has good train and bus connections to Málaga.

Getting Around

Buses are the main means of transport on the Costa del Sol. Contact **Portillo** (Córdoba 7, Málaga, tel. 952/227300) or Portillo bus stations in Torremolinos, Fuengirola, and Marbella. Portillo also serves Mijas, Ronda and Gibraltar. For bus services to Granada, Córdoba, Seville, and Nerja contact **Alsina Graells** (Plaza de Toros Vieja, Málaga, tel. 952/310400. There's also a useful suburban train service between Málaga, the airport, Torremolinos, and Fuengirola and all intermittent resorts. It runs every half hour between 6 AM and 10:30 PM, and its terminus is Málaga's Guadalmedina station just over the river opposite the Corte Inglés. In Fuengirola the train terminus is close to the bus station, where you can make connections for Mijas, Ronda, and Marbella.

Guided Tours

Organized one- and two-day excursions to places such as Seville, Granada, Córdoba, Ronda, Gibraltar, and Tangier are run by **Juliá Tours** and **Pullmantur** and numerous smaller companies from all the Costa del Sol resorts and can be booked through your hotel desk or any travel agent.

Tourist Information

Estepona. Paseo Marítimo Pedro Manrique, tel. 952/800913.
Fuengirola. Plaza de España, in the park, tel. 952/476166.
Gibraltar. On Cathedral Square, the Piazza, and John Mackintosh Square, tel. 9567/76400.
Málaga. Larios 5, tel. 952/213445, and at the airport in both national and international terminals.
Marbella. Miguel Cano 1, tel. 952/771442.
Nerja. Puerta del Mar 4, tel. 952/521531.
Ronda. Plaza de España 1, tel. 952/871272.
Torremolinos. La Nogalera 517, tel. 952/381578.

Exploring the Costa del Sol

Our tour of the Costa del Sol begins in Nerja, some 50 kilometers (30 miles) to the east of Málaga, and takes us along the coast as far as Gibraltar, with a detour inland to the picturesque town of Ronda set high in the mountains.

Nerja is a small but expanding resort that so far has escaped the worst excesses of the property developers. Its growth to date has been largely confined to villages such as El Capistrano, one of the showpieces of the Costa del Sol. There's pleasant bathing here, though the sand is gray and gritty. The **Balcón de Europa** is a fantastic lookout, high above the sea. The famous **Cuevas de Nerja** (a series of stalacite caves) are off the road to Almuñecar and Almería. A kind of vast underground cathedral, they contain the world's largest known stalactite (62 meters [200 feet] long). *Admission: 175 ptas. Open May–Sept., daily 9:30–9; Oct.–Apr., 10–1:30 and 4–7.*

Costa del Sol

Málaga is a busy port city with ancient streets and lovely villas set among exotic foliage, but it has little to commend itself to the overnight visitor. The central Plaza de la Marina, overlooking the port, is a pleasant place for a drink. The main shops are along the Calle Marqués de Larios.

The **Alcazaba** is a fortress begun in the 8th century when Málaga was the most important port of the Moorish kingdom. The ruins of the Roman amphitheater at its entrance were uncovered when the fort was restored. The inner palace dates from the 11th century when, for a short period after the breakup of the Caliphate of the West in Córdoba, it became the residence of the Moorish emirs. Today you'll find the **Archaeological Museum** here and a good collection of Moorish art. *Admission: 50 ptas. Open Mon.–Sat. 10–1 and 4–7 (5–8 in summer).*

Energetic souls can climb through the Alcazaba gardens to the summit of **Gibralfaro.** Others can drive by way of Calle Victoria or take the parador minibus that leaves roughly every 1½ hours from near the cathedral on Molina Lario. The Gibralfaro fortifications were built for Yusuf I in the 14th century. The Moors called it Jebelfaro meaning "rock of the lighthouse" after the beacon that stood here to guide ships into the harbor and warn of invasions by pirates. Today the beacon has gone, but there's a small parador that makes a delightful place for a drink or a meal, and some stunning views.

As you approach **Torremolinos** through an ocean of concrete blocks, it's hard to grasp that as recently as the early 1960s this was an inconsequential fishing village. Today, this grossly overdeveloped resort is a prime example of 20th-century tourism run riot. The town center, with its brash Nogalera Plaza, is full of overpriced bars and restaurants. Much more attractive is the district of La Carihuela, farther west, below the Avenida Carlota Alexandra. You'll find some old fishermen's cottages here, a few excellent seafood restaurants, and a traffic-free esplanade for an enjoyable stroll on a summer evening.

Head west from Torremolinos, toward the similar but more staid resorts of **Benalmádena** and **Fuengirola,** both retirement havens for British and American senior citizens. A short drive from Fuengirola up into the mountains takes you to the picturesque village of **Mijas.** Though the vast tourist-oriented main square may seem like an extension of the Costa's tawdry bazaar, there are hillside streets of whitewashed houses where you'll discover an authentic village atmosphere that has changed little since the days before the tourist boom of the 1960s. Visit the bullring, the nearby church, and the chapel of Mijas's patroness, the Virgen de la Peña (to the side of the main square), and enjoy shopping for quality gifts and souvenirs.

Marbella is the most fashionable and sedate resort area along the coast. It does have a certain Florida land boom feel to it, but development has been controlled, and Marbella will, let's hope, never turn into another Torremolinos. There is a town with both a charming old Moorish quarter and a modern, T-shirt-and-fudge section along the main drag; but when people speak of Marbella they refer both to the town and to the resorts—some more exclusive than others—stretching 16 kilometers (10 miles) or so on either side of town, between the highway and the beach. If you're vacationing in southern Spain, this is the place to stay. There's championship golf and tennis, fashionable waterfront cafés, and trendy boutiques in the charming, medieval quarter of town.

A short drive up into the hills behind Marbella brings you to the village of **Ojén.** Its typical streets are a far cry from the promenades of the coastal resorts. Look out for the traditional pottery sold here, and for the picturesque cemetery with its rows of burial-urn chambers.

Back on the coastal highway, Marbella's Golden Mile, with its mosque, Arab banks, and residence of King Fahd of Saudi Arabia, proclaims the ever-growing influence of wealthy Arabs in this playground of the rich. In **Puerto Banús,** Marbella's plush marina, with its flashy yachts, fashionable people, and expensive restaurants, the glittering parade outshines even St. Tropez in ritzy glamour.

Ronda is reached via a spectacular mountain road from San Pedro de Alcántara. One of the oldest towns in Spain, and last stronghold of the legendary Andalusian bandits, Ronda's most dramatic feature is its ravine, known as **El Tajo,** which is 279 meters (900 feet) across and divides the old Moorish town from the "new town" of El Mercadillo. Spanning the gorge is the **Puente Nuevo,** an amazing architectural feat built between 1755 and 1793, whose parapet offers dizzying views of the River Guadalevin way below. Countless people have plunged to their death from this bridge, including its own architect, who accidentally fell over while inspecting his work, and numerous victims of the Civil War of 1936–39 who were hurled into the ravine—an episode recounted in Hemingway's *For Whom the Bell Tolls.* Ronda is visited more for its setting, breathtaking views, and ancient houses than for any particular monument. Stroll the old streets of **La Ciudad;** drop in at the historic **Reina Victoria** hotel, built by the English from Gibraltar as a fashionable resting place on their Algeciras to Bobadilla railroad line; and visit the **bullring,** one of the earliest rings in Spain. Here Ronda's most famous native son, Pedro Romero (1754–1839), father of modern bullfighting, is said to have killed 5,600 bulls during his 30-year career; and in the **Bullfighting Museum** you can see posters dating back to the very first fights held in the ring in May 1785. Above all, don't miss the cliff-top walk and the gardens of the **Alameda del Tajo,** where you can contemplate one of the most dramatic views in all of Andalusia.

Returning to the coast road, the next town is **Estepona,** which until recently marked the end of the urban sprawl of the Costa del Sol. Estepona lacks the hideous high rises of Torremolinos and Fuengirola, and set back from the main highway, it's not hard to make out the old fishing village this once was. Wander the streets of the Moorish village, around the central food market and the **Church of San Francisco,** and you'll find a pleasant contrast to the excesses higher up the coast.

Twenty kilometers (12 miles) northwest of Estepona, the mountain village of **Casares** lies high in the Sierra Bermeja. Streets of ancient white houses perch on the slopes beneath a ruined Moorish castle. Admire the view of the Mediterranean and check out the village's thriving ceramics industry.

Between Estepona and Gibraltar, the highway is flanked by prosperous vacation developments known as *urbanizaciones.* These have mushroomed since the border between Spain and Gibraltar was reopened in 1985. The architecture here is much more in keeping with traditional Andalusian style than the concrete blocks of earlier developments. The new **Puerto de Sotogrande** near Manilva is one of the showpieces of the area.

Gibraltar

To enter **Gibraltar,** simply walk or drive across the border at La Línea and show your passport. In theory car drivers need an International Driver's License, insurance certificate, and registration book; in practice, these regulations are usually waived. It is also possible to fly into Gibraltar on daily flights from London but, as yet, there are no flights from Spanish airports. There are, however, plenty of bus tours from Spain. **Juliá Tours, Pullmantur,** and many smaller agencies, run daily tours (not Sunday) to Gibraltar from most Costa del Sol resorts. Alternatively, you can take the regular **Portillo** bus to La Línea and walk across the border. In summer, **Portillo** runs an inexpensive daily tour to Gibraltar from Torremolinos bus station. Once you reach Gibraltar the official language is English and the currency is the British pound sterling.

The Rock of Gibraltar acquired its name in AD 711 when it was captured by the Moorish chieftain Tarik at the start of the Arab invasion of Spain. It became known as Gib el Tarik (Rock of Tarik), later corrupted to Gibraltar. After successive periods of Moorish and Spanish domination, Gibraltar was captured by an Anglo-Dutch fleet in 1704 and ceded to the British by the Treaty of Utrecht in 1713. This tiny British colony, whose impressive silhouette dominates the straits between Spain and Morocco, is a rock just 6½ kilometers (four miles) long, three-quarter kilometers (half a mile) wide and 425 meters (1,369 feet) high.

On entering Gibraltar by road you have to cross the airport runway on the narrow strip of land that links the Rock with La Línea in Spain. Here you have a choice. You can either plunge straight into exploring Gibraltar town, or opt for a tour around the Rock. Several minibus tours are readily available at this point of entry.

Numbers in the margin correspond with points of interest on the Gibraltar map.

The tour around the Rock is best begun on the eastern side. As you enter Gibraltar, turn left down Devil's Tower Road, and
1 drive as far as **Catalan Bay,** a small fishing village founded by Genoese settlers in the 18th century, and now one of the Rock's most picturesque resorts. The road continues on beneath water catchments that supply the colony's drinking water, to another
2 resort, **Sandy Bay,** and then plunges through the Dudley Ward Tunnel to bring you out at the Rock's most southerly tip,
3 **Europa Point.** Stop here to admire the view across the Straits to the coast of Morocco, 22½ kilometers (14 miles) away. You are standing on what was called in ancient times one of the two Pillars of Hercules. Across the water in Morocco, a mountain between the cities of Ceuta and Tangier formed the second pillar. The Europa Point lighthouse has stood above the meeting point of the Atlantic and the Mediterranean since 1841. Plaques explain the history of the gun installations here, and,
4 nearby on Europa Flats, you can see the **Nuns Well,** an ancient
5 Moorish cistern, and the shrine of **Our Lady of Europe,** venerated by sailors since 1462.

Europa Road winds its way high on the western slopes above
6 **Rosia Bay,** to which Nelson's flagship, HMS *Victory,* was towed after the Battle of Trafalgar in 1805. Aboard were the dead of the battle, who are now buried in Trafalgar Cemetery on the southern edge of town, and the body of Admiral Nelson himself, preserved in a barrel of rum. He was then taken to London for burial.

7 Continue on Europa Road as far as the **casino** above the Alame-
8 da Gardens. Make a sharp right here up Engineer Road to **Jews Gate,** an unbeatable lookout point over the docks and Bay of Gi-
9 braltar to Algeciras in Spain. Queens Road leads to **St. Michael's Cave,** a series of underground chambers adorned with stalactites and stalagmites, which provides an admirable setting for concerts, ballet, and drama. Sound-and-light shows are held here most days at 11 AM and 4 PM. A skull of Neanderthal Woman (now in the British Museum in London) was found in the caves some eight years *before* the world-famous discovery in Germany's Neander Valley in 1856. *Admission: £1.20. Open daily 10–7 (5:30 in winter).*

10 Drive down Old Queens Road to the **Apes' Den** near the **Wall of Charles V.** The famous Barbary Apes are a breed of cinnamon-colored, tailless monkeys, natives of the Atlas Mountains in Morocco. Legend holds that as long as the apes remain, the British will continue to hold the Rock. Winston Churchill himself issued orders for the maintenance of the ape colony when

Gibraltar

its numbers began to dwindle during World War II. Today the apes are the responsibility of the British Army, and a special Officer in Charge of Apes is assigned to feed them twice daily at 8 AM and 4 PM.

Passing beneath the cable car that runs to the Rock's summit, drive up to the **Upper Galleries** at the northern end of the Rock. These huge galleries were carved out during the Great Siege of 1779–1783. Here, in 1878, the Governor, Lord Napier of Magdala, entertained ex-President Ulysses S. Grant at a banquet in **St. George's Hall.** From here, the **Holyland Tunnel** leads out to the east side of the Rock above Catalan Bay. *Admission: 80 pence. Open daily 10–7 (5:30 in winter).*

The last stop before the town is at the **Moorish Castle** on Willis Road. Built by the successors of the Moorish invader Tarik, the ⑫ present **Tower of Hommage** was rebuilt by the Moors in 1333. Admiral Rooke hoisted the British flag from its top when he captured the Rock in 1704, and here it has flown ever since. *Admission: 30 pence. Open daily 10–7 (5:30 in winter).*

Willis Road leads steeply down to the colorful, congested town of Gibraltar where the dignified Regency architecture of Britain blends with the shutters, balconies, and patios of southern Spain. Apart from the attraction of shops, restaurants, and pubs on Main Street, you'll want to visit some of the following: ⑬ the **Governor's Residence,** where the ceremonial Changing of ⑭ the Guard takes place each Tuesday at 11 AM; the **Law Courts,** where the famous case of the *Mary Celeste* sailing ship was ⑮ heard in 1872; the Anglican **Cathedral of the Holy Trinity;** the ⑯ ⑰ Catholic **Cathedral of St. Mary the Crowned;** and the **Gibraltar Museum,** whose exhibits recall the history of the Rock throughout the ages. *Gibraltar Museum, Bomb House La., Admission: 60 pence. Open Mon.–Sat. 10–6.*

⑱ Finally, the **Nefusot Yehudada Synagogue** on Line Wall Road is worth a look for its inspired architecture, and, if you're inter-⑲ ested in guns, the **Koehler Gun** in **Casemates Square** at the northern end of Main Street, is an impressive example of the type of gun developed during the Great Siege.

Dining and Lodging

For details and price category definitions, *see* Dining and Lodging in Staying in Spain.

Estepona   **El Libro Amarillo.** Also known by its English name, The Yellow
Dining   Book, and located 4½ kilometers (3 miles) out on the road to
★   Málaga, this is one of the Costa del Sol's most outstanding restaurants. The menu changes frequently. The service is excellent, and the decor is tasteful with attractive potted plants. Meat dishes are a specialty; try the *cordero asado* (roast lamb) or *pintado a la crema* (guinea fowl in cream sauce). *Rte. N340, km. 161, tel. 952/800484. Open for dinner only, 8 PM–midnight. Closed Sun. and Jan. Reservations essential; book well ahead. AE, MC, V. Expensive.*

★   **La Pulga que Tose.** Don't let the name (the Coughing Flea) put you off! This charming Belgian-owned restaurant is located in a beautiful old Andalusian house right in the center of town. The food is delicious, offering nouvelle cuisine specialties alongside classic dishes, and the atmosphere is delightful. *Pozo Pila 25, tel. 952/802749. Reservations strongly advised. MC, V. Open for dinner only. Closed Sun. Expensive to Moderate.*

Lodging   **Santa Marta.** This is a small, quiet hotel with just 37 rooms in chalet bungalows set in a large, peaceful garden. Some rooms are a little faded after 30 years, but the tranquil setting is a plus. Good lunches are served by the pool. *Rte. N340, km. 173, tel. 952/780716. AE, MC, V. Open Apr.-Sept. only. Moderate.*

Gibraltar   **La Bayuca.** This is one of the Rock's longest established restau-
Dining   rants. Prince Charles and Prince Andrew have dined here when on naval service. It is especially renowned for its onion soup and Mediterranean dishes. *21 Turnbull's La., tel. 9567/*

75119. Reservations advised. AE, DC, MC, V. Closed Tues. and Sun. lunch. Expensive.

Country Cottage. Opposite the Catholic cathedral, this is the place to go for a taste of Old England. Enjoy steak and kidney pie, Angus steak, and roast beef, by candlelight. *13 Giro's Passage, tel. 9567/70084. Reservations advised. AE, MC, V. Closed Sun. Moderate to Expensive.*

Wood's. One of three good restaurants at the Marina, Wood's menu includes crab roulade, noisettes of lamb, pork Dijonnaise, and Angus steak; fresh fish is available daily. *Marina Bay, tel. 9567/79241. Reservations advised but not essential. AE, DC, MC, V. Closed Sat. and Sun. lunch. Moderate.*

Lodging **Rock.** The Rock has undergone a massive refurbishment pro-
★ gram with the aim of bolstering its reputation as Gibraltar's supreme luxury hotel. You'll find a comfortable, old-fashioned English atmosphere, along with a pool, sun terrace, and gardens. Located on Gibraltar's western slopes, the hotel overlooks the town and harbor. *3 Europa Rd., tel. 9567/73000. 160 rooms with bath. AE, DC. Expensive.*

Bristol. This colonial-style hotel is just off Gibraltar's main street, right in the heart of town. Rooms are large and comfortable, and the tropical garden is a real haven for those guests who want to relax in peaceful isolation. *10 Cathedral Sq., tel. 9567/76800. 60 rooms with bath. AE, DC, MC, V. Moderate.*

Málaga **Café de Paris.** The owner of this stylish restaurant in the Paseo
Dining Marítimo area is a former chef of Maxim's in Paris, and La Hacienda in Marbella. The *menú degustación* lets you try a little of everything. Specialties include *rodaballo con espinacas* (sea bass and spinach). *Vélez Málaga, tel. 952/225043. Reservations advised. AE, DC, MC, V. Closed Tues. and last 2 weeks of Sept. Expensive.*

★ **La Alegría.**This old-fashioned restaurant in the heart of town has long been famous for its fresh seafood dishes, though meat entrées are served, too. It's one of the classic restaurants of Málaga. *Martín García 18, tel. 952/224143. Reservations not essential. AE, DC, MC, V. Closed Sat. Expensive to Moderate.*

Antonio Martín. This is another old Málaga standby, with a splendid terrace overlooking the ocean, at the beginning of the Paseo Marítimo. It's long been famous for its fresh seafood and paella. Try the local *fritura malagueña. Paseo Marítimo 4, tel. 952/222113. Reservations advised. AE, DC, MC, V. Closed Sun. evening. Moderate.*

Guerola. This is one of the best of the many restaurants in the pedestrian shopping streets between Calle Larios and Calle Nueva. Its menu is more original than most. In summer, there are tables outside on the sidewalk. *Esparteros 8, tel. 952/223121. Reservations not needed. V. Moderate.*

La Cancela. This is a colorful restaurant in the center of town, just off Calle Granada. Dine indoors or alfresco. *Denís Belgrano 3, tel. 952/223125. Reservations not necessary. V. Inexpensive.*

Lodging **Los Naranjos.** This small hotel owned by the Luz chain is situated on a pleasant avenue in a residential district a little to the east of the city center. There's a small garden in front, but rooms overlooking the street can be noisy. *Paseo de Sancha 35, tel. 952/224317. 41 rooms. AE, DC, V. Expensive.*

★ **Parador de Gibralfaro.** Located in a small wood on top of Gibralfaro mountain 3½ kilometers (2 miles) above the city, this tiny parador has recently been renovated and offers spectacular views over the city and bay. Its accommodations are the best in Málaga, and it's a good place to dine even if you're not staying here. A bus service runs between the parador and cathedral. *Gibralfaro, tel. 952/221902. 12 rooms. Reservations essential, long in advance. AE, DC, MC, V. Expensive.*

Las Vegas. In a pleasant part of town, just east of the center, this hotel has a dining room overlooking the Paseo Marítimo, an outdoor pool, and a large leafy garden. Rooms at the back enjoy a good view of the ocean. *Paseo de Sancha 22, tel. 952/217712. 73 rooms. AE, DC, V. Moderate.*

Victoria. This small, recently renovated hostel in an old house just off Calle Larios, offers excellent budget accommodations in a convenient central location. *Sancha de Lara 3, tel. 952/224223. 13 rooms. Inexpensive.*

Marbella
Dining
★

La Fonda. In a beautiful 18th-century house with antique furniture and located in one of the loveliest old squares in Marbella, La Fonda is owned by one of Madrid's leading restaurateurs. Its cuisine combines the best of Spanish, French, and Austrian influences, and it has been awarded the National Gastronomic Prize. A delightful patio filled with potted plants makes a perfect setting for summer dining. *Plaza del Santo Cristo 9, tel. 952/772512. Reservations essential. AE, DC, V. Open for dinner only, 8 PM–midnight. Closed Sun. Very Expensive.*

★ **La Hacienda.** This restaurant, owned by Belgian chef-proprietor Paul Schiff, belongs to the Relais Gourmand group, and is one of the highest rated in Spain. The menu reflects the influence of both Paul Schiff's native Belgium and his adopted Andalusia. The *menú degustación* at around 5,500 ptas. will enable you to sample the very best creations of this famous European chef. *Las Chapas, Rte. N340, km. 193, 12 km (7 mi) east on the road to Málaga; tel. 952/831267. Reservations essential. AE, DC, MC, V. Closed Mon., Tues.; also, mid-Nov.–mid-Dec. Very Expensive.*

La Meridiana. Another of Marbella's most outstanding restaurants and a favorite with the local jet set, La Meridiana is located just west of town, toward Puerto Banús, and is famous for its original Bauhaus-type architecture and the superb quality and freshness of the ingredients. *Camino de la Cruz, tel. 952/776190. Reservations essential. Open for lunch Wed.–Sun. in winter only; open daily for dinner. AE, DC, MC. Very Expensive.*

Mena. One of the best of the many colorful restaurants in the delightful main square of Marbella, Mena offers indoor dining in beautifully decorated dining rooms or on a terrace. Food and service are good, and the atmosphere, charming. *Plaza de los Naranjos 10, tel. 952/771597. Reservations not essential. AE, V. Expensive to Moderate.*

El Refugio. Located 3½ kilometers (2 miles) from Marbella on the road to Ojén, El Refugio is in a charming Andalusian house with a garden and a terrace offering splendid views of the coast. Food and service are both outstanding. *Rte. de Ojén, km. 3, tel. 952/771848. Reservations advised. AE, V. Closed Sun., Mon., and Feb.–mid-Mar. Expensive to Moderate.*

Lodging
The only reason to stay in town is if you're on a tight budget and have no car. Students can stay in small, family-run hotels in the old quarter of Marbella for as little as $15 a night. There are a few reasonably priced, package-tour-type high-rise hotels only

a block from the busy town beach. For most visitors, air-conditioning in summer is a must. The ocean is uninviting at times, thanks to improper pollution controls, so a hotel pool is a plus. Most visitors prefer to stay at one of the sparkling white resorts strung along the beach on either side of town. Finding the right one is critical.

★ **Los Monteros.** Situated 2½ kilometers (1½ miles) east of Marbella, on the road to Málaga, this deluxe hotel offers all the facilities of a top hotel, including an 18-hole golf course, seven tennis courts, three pools, horseback riding, and gourmet dining in its famous El Corzo Grill restaurant. This is the third most expensive hotel in Spain, after the Ritz and Villa Magna in Madrid. Eighty percent of the guests are British, which may explain the somewhat starched formality of the rooms. *Urb. Los Monteros, tel. 952/771700. 171 rooms. AE, DC, MC, V. Very Expensive.*

Marbella Club. The grande dame of Marbella tends to attract an older clientele, who request the same room year after year. The bungalow-style rooms run from cramped to spacious, and the decor varies considerably; specify the type you prefer, but ask for a room that's been recently renovated. The grounds are exquisite. Breakfast is served on a patio where songbirds flit through the vegetation. *Rte. N340, km. 178, tel. 952/771300. 77 rooms with bath. Facilities: Restaurant, bar, gym, sauna, nightclub, hairdresser, tennis. AE, DC, MC, V. Very Expensive.*

Puente Romano. A spectacular, modern hotel and apartment complex of low, white stucco buildings located 2 miles west of Marbella on the road to Puerto Banús. The "village" has a Roman bridge in its beautifully landscaped grounds as well as two pools, a tennis club, and a disco run by Régine. *Rte. N340, km. 184, tel. 952/770100. 171 rooms. AE, DC, V. Very Expensive.*

El Fuerte. This is the best of the few hotels in the center of Marbella, with simple, adequate rooms. It's located in a 1950s-type building in the midst of a large garden with an outdoor pool. *Avenida El Fuerte, tel. 952/771500. 146 rooms. AE, DC, V. Moderate.*

Alfil. If you're looking for inexpensive accommodations right in the heart of town, then this recently renovated hotel on the main street will meet your needs. Rooms at the back are quieter. *Avenida Ricardo Soriano 19, tel. 952/772350. 41 rooms. V. Inexpensive.*

Mijas
Dining

Valparaíso. *Pato a la naranja* (duck in an orange sauce) is one of the specialties served in a pleasant villa with garden and terrace on the road leading from Fuengirola to Mijas. And it's all set to live piano music. *Tel. 952/485996. AE, DC, MC, V. Dinner only. Closed Sun. Expensive.*

Mirlo Blanco. Here in the "White Blackbird," set in an old village house just below the bullring, you can sample Basque specialties such as *txangurro* (crab) and *merluza a la vasca* (hake with asparagus, eggs, and clam sauce). *Plaza Constitución 13, tel. 952/485700. Reservations not needed. AE, DC, V. Moderate.*

La Reja. This charming restaurant has two dining rooms overlooking the main square of Plaza Virgen de la Peña. There's an atmospheric bar and an inexpensive pizzeria, too. *Caños 9, tel. 952/485068. Reservations not needed. AE, DC, MC, V. Closed Mon. Moderate.*

Lodging ★ **Byblos Andaluz.** In this new, luxury hotel set in a huge garden of palms, cypresses, and fountains, you'll find every comfort for a pampered vacation. Facilities include pools, saunas, tennis, and an 18-hole golf course. The hotel is known for its water cures. Its Le Nailhac restaurant is famous for its French cuisine; special low-calorie meals are also available. *Urbano Mijas-Golf, tel. 952/473050. 135 rooms. AE, DC, MC, V. Very Expensive.*

★ **Hotel Mijas.** You'll find this beautifully situated hotel at the entrance to Mijas village. The hotel is modern and peaceful, with a delightful rose garden, terrace, and afternoon tea. *Urbano Tamisa, tel. 952/485800. 106 rooms, pool. AE, DC, MC, V. Expensive.*

Nerja **Casa Luque.** This is one of the most authentically Spanish of
Dining Nerja's restaurants, located in a charming old Andalusian house behind the Balcón de Europa church. The menu is small and often includes pasta dishes. *Plaza Cavana 2, tel. 952/521004. Reservations not essential. AE, V. Closed Mon. and Feb. Moderate.*

Cortijo. This small, family-run restaurant in a 200-year-old house is owned by a father and his two sons, who act as host, chef, and waiter. Andalusian dishes share the menu with international favorites. *Barrio 26, no phone. DC, MC, V. Inexpensive.*

Lodging **Monica.** Nerja's newest beach hotel opened in 1986. It's spacious and luxurious, with Moorish-style architecture. Facilities include tennis, pool, nightclub, and disco. *Playa Torrecilla, tel. 952/521100. 234 rooms. AE, DC, MC, V. Expensive.*

★ **Parador.** All the rooms in this small parador a little to the east of the center of Nerja have balconies overlooking the sea. There's a pleasant leafy garden and outdoor pool, and an elevator takes you down to the beach. The restaurant is well known for its fish dishes. *El Tablazo, tel. 952/520050. 73 rooms. AE, DC, MC, V. Expensive.*

Ronda **Don Miguel.** Located by the bridge over the Tajo gorge, the
Dining restaurant's terrace offers spectacular views of the ravine. Lamb is a specialty; try *pierna de cordero lechal Don Miguel* (leg of baby lamb). *Villanueva 4, tel. 952/871090. Reservations advised. Closed Tues. evening and all day Sun. June–Sept.; closed Tues. evening and all day Wed. Oct.–May. AE, DC, MC, V. Expensive.*

Pedro Romero. Located opposite the bullring, with the inevitable bullring decor. Try the *sopa de mesón*—the soup of the house. *Virgen de la Paz 18, tel. 952/871061. AE, DC, MC, V. Moderate.*

Mesón Santiago. This typical Andalusian mesón with colorful decor opens for lunch only and has a pleasant outdoor patio. It serves hearty portions of home-cooked food—but be prepared for long waits. *Marina 3, tel. 952/871559. MC, V. Open 1–4 PM only. Inexpensive.*

Lodging **Reina Victoria.** A spectacularly situated old-world hotel with a distinctly British air, the Reina Victoria sits atop the very rim of the gorge. Views and style are tops but, unfortunately, it's very much patronized by tour groups. *Jerez 25, tel. 952/871240. 89 rooms. AE, DC, MC, V. Moderate to Expensive.*

Polo. A cozy, old-fashioned hotel in the center of town, Polo sports a reasonably priced restaurant. The staff is friendly and the rooms simple but comfortable. *Mariano Soubiron 8, tel. 952/872447. 33 rooms. AE, DC, V. Moderate.*

Torremolinos **El Atrio.** This small, stylish restaurant is located in the Pueblo
Dining Blanco. Its cuisine is predominantly French. In summer, you can dine on the terrace. *Off Calle Casablanca, no phone. AE, V. Open 8 PM–midnight. Closed Sun. and Dec. Moderate.*

El Cangrejo. This is one of several classic seafood restaurants in La Carihuela. You can succumb to a full dinner in the restaurant or enjoy succulent seafood tapas in the entrance bar. *Bulto 25, tel. 952/380479. Reservations not needed. MC, V. Moderate.*

La Primavera. Set in one of the old Torremolinos villas just below Calle Casablanca, its patio offers delightful outdoor dining amid foliage, and its indoor restaurant is attractively decorated with paintings and ceramic plates. Service is good, food attractively presented, but the cuisine only average—go for the setting rather than the food. *Guetaria, tel. 952/380909. Reservations not needed. AE, DC, MC, V. Moderate.*

El Roqueo. Owned by a former fisherman, this is one of the locals' favorite Carihuela fish restaurants. Ingredients are always fresh and the prices very reasonable. *Carmen 35, tel. 952/384946. AE, V. Closed Tues. and Nov. Moderate.*

Lodging **Cervantes.** This busy cosmopolitan hotel in the heart of town has comfortable rooms, good service, and a well-known dining room on its top floor; this is one of Torremolinos's consistently good hotels. *Las Mercedes, tel. 952/384033. 393 rooms. AE, DC, MC, V. Expensive.*

Meliá Torremolinos. Torremolinos's only five-star hotel is located west of town, off the main highway toward Benalmádena. It overlooks the sea and offers all the facilities of a luxury hotel, but standards are not always up to par. *Avenida Carlota Alessandri 109, tel. 952/380500. 282 rooms. AE, DC, MC, V. Expensive.*

Tropicana. Located on the beach at the far end of the Carihuela in one of the pleasantest areas of Torremolinos, this is a comfortable, relaxing resort hotel with several good restaurants nearby. *Trópico 6, tel. 952/386600. 86 rooms. Facilities: pool. AE, DC, MC, V. Moderate.*

★ **Miami.** Set in an old Andalusian villa in a shady garden to the west of the Carihuela, this is something of a find amid the ocean of concrete blocks. It's small, friendly, and intimate, and very popular with Spaniards, so book ahead. *Aladino 14, tel. 952/385255. 26 rooms. Inexpensive.*

27 Sweden

Introduction

Sweden's 277,968 square kilometers (173,730 square miles) contain only 8.4 million people, so its population density ranks among Europe's lowest, and its vast open spaces and good, uncrowded roads make it a country where you can easily escape the frantic pace of modern life. But the long, narrow shape of the country means that on a typical visit it is possible to explore only a relatively small area, and it is unwise to be overly ambitious when planning your trip. The distances are considerable, especially by European standards—almost 1,600 kilometers (1,000 miles) as the crow flies, from north to south. The 2,128-kilometer (1,330-mile) train journey from Trelleborg, in the far south, through endless birch forests to Riksgränsen, in the Arctic north, is claimed to be the world's longest stretch of continuously electrified railroad.

This chapter concentrates on the more densely populated southern part of the country—essentially the area dominated by the two largest cities, Stockholm and Gothenburg—although it also suggests an itinerary through the celebrated Folklore District, where the most distinctly Swedish cultural traditions are faithfully maintained.

The Swedish Tourist Board would be the first to admit that it faces something of an uphill task in marketing the country to the overseas visitor, if only because it does not have such a long-established tourist industry as neighboring Norway or traditional favorites such as France, Italy, and Switzerland. But those who do visit Sweden usually return home raving about its exceptionally high standards of lodging and dining. Even the most modest establishment is always spotlessly clean, and you will be given a warm welcome (almost certainly in excellent English, too).

Sweden may not have scenic attractions as spectacular as the Norwegian fjords across the border, but it offers a more varied landscape, with more than 96,000 lakes and a jagged coastline with countless archipelagoes, forests, mountains, and rushing rivers. And there is a fascinating contrast in lifestyles between the bustling, sophisticated cities and the isolated, rural communities where the leisurely pace of life has changed little with the passing centuries.

Each of Sweden's major cities has its own special atmosphere. Stockholm, with its spectacular lakeside setting, has an exhilarating quality. Gothenburg, on the other hand, is a comfortable city of wide avenues and verdant parks. Malmö, 45 minutes by hovercraft from Denmark, combines a cosmopolitan flavor with small-town friendliness.

Before You Go

When to Go The main tourist season runs from June through August, and Sweden needs to extend the season to encourage visitors from abroad. It's disappointing to note how many visitor attractions do not start operating until mid-June and then suddenly restrict their opening times or close down altogether in mid-August, when the Swedes' own vacation season ends and the children return to school. The weather can be magnificent in the spring and fall, and there are plenty of tourists who would

Sweden

N

Norwegian
Sea

Kiruna

Laleälven

Jokkmokk

Tärnaby   Arjeplog   Kalix   Tornio

Arvidsjaur

Sorsele   Luleå

Storuman   Piteå

Lycksele   Skellefteå

Strömsund   Åsele   Umeälven   Umeå

Åre

Östersund

FINLAND

Tännäs

Sundsvall   Gulf
of
Bothnia

Ljungan

Idre

Hudiksvall

Bollnäs

Mora   Söderhamn

Falun

Klarälven

Borlänge   Avesta

Fagersta

Karlstad   Västerås   Uppsala

Lake
Mälaren   Stockholm

Mellerud   Örebro   Gulf of Finland

Strömstad   Lake
Vänern

Uddevalla   Trollhättan   Norrköping   Gotska
Sandön

Lake
Vättern   Linköping   Baltic
Sea

Gothenburg   Jönköping   Gulf of
Riga

Borås   Nässjö   Visby

Falkenberg   Värnamo   Gotland

Halmstad   Växjö   Oskarshamn   SOVIET
UNION

Kalmar

Öland

Helsingborg   Karlskrona

Malmö   Kristianstad

DEN.   Trelleborg   Ystad

NORWAY

0   50 miles
0   75 km

like to do some sightseeing when there are fewer people around. Sweden virtually shuts up shop for the entire month of July, so avoid planning a business trip at that time. The concentrated nature of the Swedes' own vacation period can make it difficult to get hotel reservations during July and early August. On the other hand, the big city hotels, which cater mainly to business travelers, reduce their rates drastically in the summer, when their ordinary clients are on vacation. Ask your travel agent about special discount schemes offered by the major hotel groups.

Climate As in the rest of northern Europe, Sweden's summer weather is unpredictable but, as a general rule, it is more likely to be rainy on the west coast than in the east. When the sun shines, the climate is usually agreeable; it is rarely unbearably hot. In Stockholm, it never really gets dark in mid-summer, while in the far north, above the Arctic Circle, the sun doesn't set between the end of May and the middle of July.

The following are the average daily maximum and minimum temperatures for Stockholm.

Jan.	30F	−1C	May	58F	14C	Sept.	60F	15C
	23	−5		43	6		49	9
Feb.	30F	−1C	June	67F	19C	Oct.	49F	9C
	22	−5		51	11		41	5
Mar.	37F	3C	July	71F	22C	Nov.	40F	5C
	26	−4		57	14		34	1
Apr.	47F	8C	Aug.	68F	20C	Dec.	35F	3C

Currency The unit of currency in Sweden is the krona (plural kronor), which is divided into 100 öre and is written as SEK or kr. Coins come in values of 10 or 50 öre and 1 or 5 kronor, while bills come in denominations of 10, 50, 100, 500, 1,000, and 10,000 SEK. Traveler's checks and foreign currency can be exchanged at banks all over Sweden and at post offices bearing the "PK Exchange" sign. At press time (spring 1989), the exchange rate was 6.12 kronor to the dollar and 11.10 kronor to the pound.

What It Will Cost Sweden has a not-altogether-justified reputation as an expensive country. Hotel prices are marginally above the European average, probably about the same as in the United Kingdom, but higher than in France. As in most countries, the most expensive hotels are found in major cities such as Stockholm and Gothenburg. Restaurant prices are generally fairly high, but there are plenty of bargains to be had: Look for the *dagens rätt* (dish of the day) in many city restaurants. This costs about SEK 40–SEK 45 and includes a main dish, salad, soft drink, bread and butter, and coffee.

Many hotels have special low summer rates and cut costs during weekends in winter. But because of heavy taxes and excise duties, liquor prices are among the highest in Europe. It pays to take in your maximum duty-free allowance. Value-added tax (known as *Moms* in Swedish) is imposed on all goods and services at a flat rate of 19% and is included in all prices. You can avoid most of this tax if you take advantage of the tax-free shopping service offered at some 19,000 stores throughout the country (*see* Shopping).

Sample Prices Cup of coffee, SEK 10–SEK 15; bottle of beer, SEK 30–SEK 40; Coca-Cola, SEK 10–12; ham sandwich, SEK 25–SEK 35; one-mile taxi ride, SEK 50.

Customs on Arrival You may bring duty-free into Sweden 400 cigarettes or 200 cigarillos or 100 cigars or 500 grams of tobacco. You may also import one liter of spirits and one liter of wine *or* two liters of beer, plus a reasonable amount of perfume and other goods to the value of SEK 600. Residents over the age of 15 of other European countries may bring duty-free into Sweden 200 cigarettes or 100 cigarillos, or 50 cigars or 250 grams of tobacco; visitors aged 20 or more may import one liter of spirits, one liter of wine, and two liters of beer, plus a reasonable amount of perfume, and other goods to the value of SEK 600. You can take up to SEK 6,000 in and out of Sweden, and there is no limit on the amount of foreign currency that can be imported.

Language Virtually all Swedes you are likely to meet will speak English, for it is a mandatory subject in all schools and is the main foreign language that Swedish children learn. Some of the older people you meet in the rural areas may not be quite so familiar with English, but you'll soon find someone who can help out. Swedish is one of the Germanic languages and is similar to Danish and Norwegian. Grammatically it is easier than German, although pronunciation can pose some problems. Also, the letters Å, Ä, and Ö rank as separate letters in the Swedish alphabet and come at the end after *Z*. So if you're looking up a Mr. Angelholm in a Swedish telephone book, you'll find him near the end. Few Swedish place-names have anglicized spellings, with the notable exception of Göteborg (Gothenburg).

Getting Around

By Car
Road Conditions Sweden has an excellent highway network of more than 80,000 kilometers (50,000 miles). The fastest routes are those with numbers prefixed with an E (for "European"), some of which are the equivalent of American superhighways or British motorways—for part of the way, at least. Road E4, for instance, covers the whole of the distance from Malmö, in the south, to Stockholm, and on to Sundsvall and Umeå, in the north, finishing at Haparanda, on the frontier with Finland. All main and secondary roads are well surfaced, but some minor roads, particularly in the north, are graveled. No tolls are levied on Swedish highways.

Rules of the Road You drive on the right and must always yield to traffic coming from the right, unless signs indicate otherwise. You must also yield to traffic already in a traffic circle. No matter where you sit in a car, you must wear a seat belt, and cars must have low-beam headlights on at all times. Signs indicate five basic speed limits, ranging from 30 kph (18 mph) in school or playground areas to 110 kph (68 mph) on E roads. For vehicles towing a trailer, the limit is 70 kph (43 mph) if the towed unit has brakes; otherwise, 40 kph (25 mph). Drunk-driving laws are strictly enforced.

Parking Vehicles must always be parked on the right-hand side of the road, but if you want to park overnight, particularly in suburban areas, be sure not to do so on the night the street is being cleaned; signs should indicate when this occurs. Parking meters are available for use in larger towns, usually between 8 AM and 6 PM. The fee varies from about SEK 6 to SEK 15 per hour. A circular sign with a red cross on a blue background with a red border means parking is prohibited. A yellow plate with a red border below it means restricted parking.

Gasoline Gas costs the equivalent of about $2.85 per US gallon, depending on grade. Lead-free gasoline is readily available. Most gas stations are self-service places, indicated by the sign "Tanka Själv." Many have automatic pumps, which accept SEK 10 or SEK 100 bills, and where you can fill up at any time, night or day.

Breakdowns The **Larmtjänst** organization, run by a confederation of Swedish insurance companies, provides a 24-hour breakdown service. Its phone numbers are listed in all telephone books. A toll-free emergency number, tel. 90000, is also available.

By Train Sweden's rail network, mostly electrified, is highly efficient, and trains operate frequently, particularly on the main routes linking Stockholm with Gothenburg and Malmö, on which there is a frequent service. First- and second-class cars are provided on all main routes, and sleeping cars are available in both classes on overnight trains. On virtually all long-distance trains, there is a buffet or dining car. Seat reservations are always advisable, and on some trains—indicated with R or IC in the timetable—they are compulsory. Reservations can be made right up to departure time at a cost of SEK 15 per seat.

Fares The Swedish rail-fare structure was radically changed during 1989. Normal full fares now apply throughout the week, not just on Friday and Sunday, as previously. However, on certain trains, listed as "Low price" or "Red" departures, fares are reduced by 50%, so careful planning is necessary to take advantage of the lower prices. Passengers paying low fares cannot make stopovers and the tickets are valid for only 36 hours. There is a flat-rate maximum fare for all journeys of 900 kilometers (560 miles) or more.

By Plane Sweden's domestic air network is highly developed. Most major cities are served by **SAS** (Scandinavian Airlines) or its domestic partner **Linjeflyg**. From Stockholm, there are services to about 30 points around the country. SAS and Linjeflyg offer cut-rate roundtrip "mini-fares" every day of the week on selected flights, and these fares are available on most services during the peak tourist season, from late June to mid-August. Some even more favorable offers on domestic flights are frequently available from the end of June through early August.

By Bus Sweden has an excellent network of express bus services that provides an inexpensive and relatively speedy way of getting around the country. **GDG** offers daily express services from Gothenburg to many parts of Sweden; **SJ** (Swedish State Railways) is another major bus operator. A number of other private companies operate weekend-only services on additional routes. In the far north of Sweden, post buses delivering mail to remote areas also carry passengers, and provide an offbeat and inexpensive way of seeing the countryside.

By Boat The classic boat trip in Sweden is the four-day journey along the Göta Canal between Gothenburg and Stockholm, operated by **Göta Kanal**, Gothenburg, tel. 031/177615. A new tourist route is the 480-kilometer (300-mile) coastal cruise between Öregrund, northeast of Stockholm, and Oskarshamn, on the mainland opposite the island of Öland. It's operated by **KustLinjen,** tel. 08/240970.

By Bicycle Cycling is a popular activity in Sweden, and the country's uncongested roads make it ideal for extended bike tours. Bicycles can be rented throughout the country; inquire at the local tourist information office. Rental costs average around SEK 50 per day or SEK 200 per week. The **Swedish Touring Club** (STF) in Stockholm (tel. 08/227200) can give you information about cycling packages that include bike rental, overnight accommodations, and meals. **Cykelfrämjandet** (tel. 08/751–6204) has an English-language guide to cycling trips.

Staying in Sweden

Telephones Sweden has plenty of pay phones, although they are not found
Local Calls (as in many other European countries) in post offices. There are, however, special offices marked "Tele" or "Telebutik" from which you can make calls. There are two types of pay phones in Sweden: One accepts only SEK 1 coins, while the other takes 50 öre, SEK 1, and SEK 5 coins. For a local call, you need a SEK 1 coin.

International Calls These can be made from any pay phone. For calls to the USA and Canada, dial 009, then 1 (the country code), then wait for a second dial tone before dialing the area code and number. When dialing the United Kingdom, omit the initial zero on area codes (for London you would dial 009 followed by 44, then 1 and the local number). Making calls from your hotel room is convenient, but can be expensive, so check with the front desk about rates first. You pay the normal rate at Telebutik offices.

Operators and There is no single number to dial for an English-speaking oper-
Information ator. Check the telephone book for the service you require.

Mail Airmail letters to the USA and Canada weighing less than 20
Postal Rates grams cost SEK 3.60; airmail postcards, SEK 3.10. Postcards and letters within Europe cost SEK 2.50 and 3.10, respectively.

Receiving Mail If you're uncertain where you will be staying, have your mail sent to Poste Restante, S-101 10 Stockholm. The address for collection is Vasagatan 28–32. A Poste Restante service is also offered by American Express (*see* Important Addresses and Numbers in Stockholm).

Shopping Swedish goods have earned an international reputation for elegance and quality, and any visitor to the country should spend some time exploring the many impressive shops and department stores. The midsummer tourist season is as good a time as any to go shopping, for that is when many stores have their annual sales. The best buys are to be found in glassware, stainless steel, pottery and ceramics, leather goods, and textiles. You will find a wide selection of goods available in major stores such as **NK, Åhléns, Tempo,** and **Domus,** which have branches all over the country.

High-quality furniture is a Swedish specialty, and it is worthwhile visiting one of the many branches of **IKEA,** a shop usually located on the outskirts of major towns. IKEA's prices are extremely competitive, and the company also operates an export service. For glassware at bargain prices, head for the "Kingdom of Glass" (*see* The West Coast and The Glass Country). All the major glassworks, including **Orrefors** and **Kosta Boda,** have large factory outlets where you can pick up "seconds" (normally indistinguishable from the perfect product) at only a fraction of the normal retail price. For clothing, the best center is Borås, not far from Gothenburg. Here you can find bargains from the leading mail-order companies. In country areas, look for the local **Hemslöjd** craft centers, featuring high-quality clothing and needlework items at low prices.

VAT Refunds   About 19,000 Swedish shops—1,000 in Stockholm alone—participate in the tax-free shopping service for visitors, enabling you to claim a refund on most of the value-added tax (*Moms*) that you have paid. Shops taking part in the scheme display a distinctive black, blue, and yellow sticker in the window. (Some stores offer the service only on purchases worth more than SEK 200.) Whenever you make a purchase in a participating store, you are given a "tax-free shopping check" equivalent to the tax paid, less a handling charge. This check can be cashed when you leave Sweden, either at the airport or aboard ferries. Goods that you have bought using the tax-free shopping service will be sealed, and the seal must not be broken until you have left the country. You should have your passport with you when you make your purchase and when you claim your refund.

Opening and   **Banks.** Banks are open weekdays from 9:30–3, but some stay
Closing Times   open until 6 in some larger cities. Banks at Stockholm's Arlanda Airport and Gothenburg's Landvetter Airport open every day, with extended hours.

Museums. Hours vary widely, but museums are typically open weekdays 10–4 or 10–5. Many are also open weekends, but may close Monday.

Shops. Shops are generally open weekdays from 9 or 9:30 to 6 and Saturday 9–1 or 9–4. Some large department stores stay open until 8 or 10 on certain evenings, and some also open on Sunday.

National Holidays   January 1 (New Year's Day); April 13 (Good Friday); April 16 (Easter Monday); May 1 (Labor Day); May 4 (Ascension Day); June 4 (Pentecost Monday); June 22, 23 (Midsummer's Eve and Day); November 3 (All Saints' Day); December 25 (Christmas); December 26 (St. Stephen's Day).

Dining   Swedish cuisine used to be considered somewhat uninteresting, but lately it has become much more cosmopolitan. The inevitable fast-food outlets, such as McDonald's and Wimpy, have come on the scene, as well as Clock, the homegrown version. But there is also a good range of more conventional restaurants, ranging from the usual top-class establishments to inexpensive places where you can pick up a bargain-price lunch or snack.

High-class cafés and cafeterias are increasingly popular, and in larger cities some stay open during the night, serving open-face sandwiches, salads, and snacks. Many restaurants all over the country specialize in *Husmanskost*—literally "home cooking"—which is based on traditional Swedish recipes.

Sweden is best known for its *smörgåsbord*, a word whose correct pronunciation defeats non-Swedes. It consists of a tempting buffet of hot and cold dishes, with usually a strong emphasis on seafood, notably herring, prepared in a wide variety of ways. Authentic smörgåsbord can be enjoyed all over the country, but the best is found in the many inns in Skåne, where you can eat as much as you want for about SEK 180. Virtually all Swedish hotels now serve a lavish smörgåsbord-style breakfast, often included in the room price. Do justice to your breakfast and you'll probably want to skip lunch!

Mealtimes The Swedes tend to eat early. Restaurants start serving lunch at about 11 AM, and outside the main cities you may find that they close quite early in the evening (often by 9) or may not even open at all. Don't wait too late to look for someplace to have a meal.

Dress Except for the most formal restaurants, where a jacket and tie are advisable, casual—or casual chic—attire is perfectly acceptable for restaurants in all price categories.

Ratings Prices are per person and include a first course, main course (Swedes tend to skip desserts), and service charge, but no drinks. A service charge of 13–15% is added to meal prices, so there is no need to tip. If you want to leave something extra, round the total to the nearest SEK 5 or so. Best bets are indicated by a star ★. At press time, there were 6.12 kronor (SEK) to the dollar.

Category	Cost
Very Expensive	over SEK 350
Expensive	SEK 200–SEK 350
Moderate	SEK 100–SEK 200
Inexpensive	under SEK 100

Credit Cards The following credit card abbreviations are used: AE, American Express; DC, Diners Club; MC, MasterCard; V, Visa.

Lodging Sweden offers a wide range of accommodations, from simple village rooms and campsites to top-class hotels of the highest international standard. Except at the major hotels in the larger cities, catering mainly to business clientele, rates are fairly reasonable. Prices are normally on a per-room basis and include all taxes and service and usually breakfast. Apart from the more modest inns and the cheapest budget establishments, private baths and showers are now standard features, although it is just as well to double-check when making your reservation. Whatever their size, virtually all Swedish hotels provide scrupulously clean accommodations and courteous service. In Stockholm, there is a hotel reservation office—**Hotellcentralen**—at the central train station. In other areas, local tourist offices will help you with hotel reservations.

Hotels There is no official star-rating system in Sweden, but you can get a good idea of the facilities and prices at a particular hotel by consulting the official annual guide, *Hotels in Sweden*, obtainable free of charge from the Swedish National Tourist Office. There is a good selection of hotels in all price categories in every town and city, though major international chains such as Sheraton have made only small inroads in Sweden thus far. The main homegrown chains are SARA, Scandic, and RESO. The Sweden Hotels group has about 100 independently owned hotels and offers a central reservation office. The group also has its own star-rating system—from one to four stars—A, B, or C—based on the facilities available at each establishment. Chain hotels in Sweden, as elsewhere, tend to be rather standardized, but there are many attractive, privately owned country hotels, some of which are modernized farmhouses and manors dating back many centuries.

House-Rental Vacations In Sweden, these are popular among other Europeans, particularly the British and Germans. There are about 250 chalet villages with amenities, such as grocery stores, restaurants, saunas, and tennis courts. You can often arrange such accommodations on the spot at local tourist information offices. An alternative is a package, such as the one offered by **Longship Holidays** (run by Scandinavian Seaways), which combines a ferry trip from Britain across the North Sea with a stay in a chalet village. Longship is based in the United Kingdom at Parkeston Quay, Harwich, Essex (tel. 0255/241234).

Camping Camping is also popular in Sweden. There are about 750 officially approved sites throughout the country, most located next to the sea or a lake and offering activities such as windsurfing, riding, and tennis. They are generally open between June 1 and September 1, though some are available year round. The Swedish Tourist Board publishes, in English, an abbreviated list of sites.

Ratings Prices are for two people in a double room, based on high-season rates. Best bets are indicated by a star ★. At press time, there were 6.12 kronor (SEK) to the dollar.

Category	Cost
Very Expensive	over SEK 1,000
Expensive	SEK 800–SEK 1,000
Moderate	SEK 600–SEK 800
Inexpensive	under SEK 600

Credit Cards The following credit card abbreviations are used: AE, American Express; DC, Diners Club; MC, MasterCard; V, Visa.

Tipping Unlike some countries, Sweden cannot be described as "the land of the outstretched palm"—probably because earnings are relatively high anyway, and hotel and restaurant staff do not depend on their tips for their existence. In hotels, the only extra tip you need to give is to the porter who carries your bags (about SEK 5 per case). Taxi drivers expect a tip of about 10%, and it is quite safe to ask them to add this on themselves. Checkroom attendants should receive about SEK 7 per coat.

Stockholm

Arriving and Departing

By Plane All international flights arrive at Arlanda Airport, 40 kilometers (25 miles) north of the city. The airport is linked to Stockholm by a fast freeway. For information on arrival and departure times, call the individual airlines.

Between the Airport and Downtown Buses leave both the international and domestic terminals every 10–15 minutes, from 7:10 AM to 10:30 PM, and run to the city terminal at Klarabergsgatan next to the central train station. A taxi from the airport will cost at least SEK 350, but a useful and flexible alternative is the SAS (Scandinavian Airlines) limousine service to any point in Greater Stockholm. It operates as a shared taxi at between SEK 185 and SEK 280, depending on the distance. If two or three people travel together in a limousine to the same address, only one pays the full rate; all others pay half price.

By Train All major domestic and international services arrive at Stockholm Central Station on Vasagatan, in the heart of the city. This is also the terminus for local commuter services. For 24-hour train information, tel. 08/225060. At the station, there is a ticket and information office, where you can make seat or sleeping-car reservations. An automatic ticket-issuing machine is also available. If you buy your ticket from the conductor on the train, you must pay a surcharge of SEK 12, plus a seat reservation fee of SEK 15, if applicable.

By Bus Long-distance buses, from such places as Härnösand and Sundsvall, arrive at Norra Bantorget, a few blocks north of the central station, and all others at Klarabergsviadukten, just beside it. Bus tickets can also be bought at the railroad reservations office.

By Car There are two main access routes from the west and south: the E3 main highway from Gothenburg and E4 from Malmö, which continues as the main route to Sundsvall, the far north, and Finland. All routes to the city center are well marked.

Getting Around

The most cost-effective way of getting around Stockholm is to use a **Stockholmskortet** (Key to Stockholm) card. Besides giving unlimited transportation on city subway, bus, and rail services, it offers free admission to 50 museums and several sightseeing trips. The card, valid for up to four days, costs from SEK 70 to SEK 280, depending on the time allotted. It is available from the tourist center at Sweden House, at Kungsträdgården, and the Hotellcentralen accommodations bureau at the central station.

Maps and timetables for all city transportation networks are available from the SL information desks at Norrmalmstorg or Sergels Torg. You can also obtain information by phone (tel. 08/236000).

By Bus and Subway The Stockholm Transit Authority (SL) operates both the bus and subway systems. Tickets for the two networks are interchangeable.

The subway system, known as "T-banan" (the *T* stands for tunnel), is the easiest and fastest way of getting around the city. Some of the stations offer permanent art exhibitions. Station entrances are marked with a blue T on a white background. The T-banan has about 100 stations and covers more than 60 route-miles. Trains run frequently between 5 AM and 2 AM, although some services cease at midnight.

Individual tickets are available at ticket counters, but it is cheaper to buy a special discount coupon that gives a savings of SEK 18 compared with buying separate tickets each time you travel. The coupons are available at Pressbyrån newsstands. A one-day ticket for the city center alone, valid on both bus and subway, costs SEK 22. A ticket covering the entire Greater Stockholm area costs SEK 40 for 24 hours or SEK 76 for 72 hours.

The Stockholm bus network is one of the world's largest. Services run not only within the central area but also to out-of-town points of interest, such as Waxholm, with its historic fortress, and Gustavsberg, with its well-known porcelain factory. Within Greater Stockholm, buses run throughout the night.

By Train SL operates conventional train services from Stockholm Central Station to a number of nearby points, including Nynäshamn, a departure point for ferries to the island of Gotland. Trains also run from the Slussen station to the fashionable beach resort of Saltsjöbaden.

By Taxi Taxis are difficult to come by on the street (although you may find one at an official taxi stand), so they usually have to be ordered. Telephone 08/150000 or 08/150400 if you need to reserve one well in advance. It costs between SEK 10 and SEK 20 just for the taxi to get to you. You will pay up to SEK 100 for a trip of 10 kilometers (6 miles), depending on the number of people in the taxi and the time of day; there is an additional charge if you book the taxi in advance.

Important Addresses and Numbers

Tourist Information The main tourist center is at **Sweden House,** Kungsträdgärden, tel. 08/789–2000; weekends, 08/789–2417. During the peak tourist season (mid-June to mid-August), it is open weekdays 8:30–6; weekends 8–5. Off-season the hours are 9–5 and 9–2, respectively. Besides providing information, it is the main ticket center for sightseeing excursions. There are also information centers at the central station, in the City Hall (summer only), and in the Kaknäs TV tower.

Embassies U.S.: Strandvägen 101, tel. 08/783–5300. **Canadian:** Tegelbacken 4, tel. 08/237920. **U.K.:** Skarpögatan 6–8, tel. 08/667–0140.

Emergencies **Police:** tel. 08/769–3000 (emergencies only: 08/90000); **Ambulance:** tel. 08/90000; **Doctor** (Medical Care Information): tel. 08/449200—tourists can get hospital attention in the district where they are staying or can contact the private clinic, **City Akuten,** tel. 08/117177; **Dentist:** tel. 08/235845; **Pharmacy:** C. W. Scheele, tel. 08/248280 (all are indicated by the sign "Apotek").

English Bookstores Most bookstores have a good selection of English books. **Hedengrens Bokhandel,** Kungsgatan 4 (tel. 08/212107) offers dictionaries and maps in all languages.

Travel Agencies **American Express:** Birger Jarlsgatan 1, tel. 08/235330. **Wagon Lits/Thomas Cook:** Vasagatan 22, tel. 08/762–5827.

Guided Tours

Orientation Tours A guided sightseeing tour lasting 2½ hours departs from Karl XII Torg every morning. Multilingual commentary is provided. The tour covers the central city area, the Old Town (Gamla Stan), the Cathedral, and the Royal Palace. An afternoon tour leaving at 2 takes in the Djurgården leisure area and the Wasa

Museum, as well as the City Hall. A convenient budget-price tour by boat and/or bus is SL's "Tourist Route" (Turistlinjen). The tour departs every 15 minutes during peak vacation periods and every half hour at other times; you can get on and off at any one of the 14 stops.

Boat Tours You'll find a bewildering variety of tours available at Stockholm's quaysides. The **Waxholm Steamship Company** (tel. 08/140–8300) operates scheduled services to many of the islands in the archipelago on its famous white steamers. Trips range from one to three hours each way. Popular one-day excursions include Waxholm, Utö, Sandhamn, and Möja. Conventional sightseeing tours include a one-hour circular city tour operated by the **Strömma Canal Company** (tel. 08/233375). It leaves from the Nybroplan quay every hour between 10 and 5 during the summer.

Special-Interest Tours A new Stimulating Stockholm program offers a range of unusual and offbeat excursions. These include free trips to the Gustavsberg Ceramics Center, the Stockholm auction chambers, and the Association of Friends of Textile Art (Handarbetets Vänner). Information on the full range of excursions is available at the "Stimulating Stockholm" desk at the tourist center.

Excursions Not to be missed is the boat trip to the Palace of Drottningholm, the 17th-century private residence of the Royal Family and a smaller version of Versailles. It departs from the City Hall Bridge (Stadshusbron) every half hour between 9:30 and 4:30 during the summer. Another popular trip goes from Stadshusbron to the ancient towns of Sigtuna and Skokloster, and then to Uppsala, where you can catch a train back to Stockholm. Information is available from the **Strömma Canal Company** (tel. 08/233375) or the tourist center at Sweden House.

Personal Guides Contact the **Guide Center** at **Stockholm Information Service**, tel. 08/789–2000.

Exploring Stockholm

Numbers in the margin correspond with points of interest on the Stockholm map.

Because Stockholm's main attractions are concentrated in a relatively small area, the city itself can be explored in several days. But if you want to take advantage of some of the full-day excursions offered, it is worthwhile to devote a full week to your visit.

The city of Stockholm, built on 14 small islands among open bays and narrow channels, has been dubbed the "Venice of the North" by advertising copywriters. It is a handsome, civilized city, full of parks, squares, and airy boulevards, and a bustling, modern metropolis. Glass-and-steel skyscrapers abound, yet you are never more than five minutes' walk from twisting, medieval streets and waterside walks.

The first written mention of Stockholm dates from 1252, when a powerful regent named Birger Jarl is said to have built a fortified castle and city here. And it must have been this strategic position, where the calm, fresh waters of Lake Mälaren meet the salty Baltic Sea, that prompted King Gustav Vasa to take

Stockholm

Major Attractions
City Hall, **1**
Gröna Lund Tivoli, **6**
Kungsträdgården, **4**
Museum of National
Antiquities, **9**
Nordic Museum, **8**
Riddarholm Church, **2**
Royal Palace, **3**
Skansen, **7**
Wasamuseet, **5**

Other Attractions
Cathedral, **22**
Concert Hall, **12**
House of Nobles, **20**
Kaknäs Tower, **15**
Museum of Far
Eastern Antiquities, **18**
Museum of Modern
Art, **14**
National Museum, **16**
Parliament, **21**

Royal Dramatic
Theter, **11**
Royal Library, **13**
Royal Opera House, **17**
Supreme Court, **19**
Stock Exchange, **10**

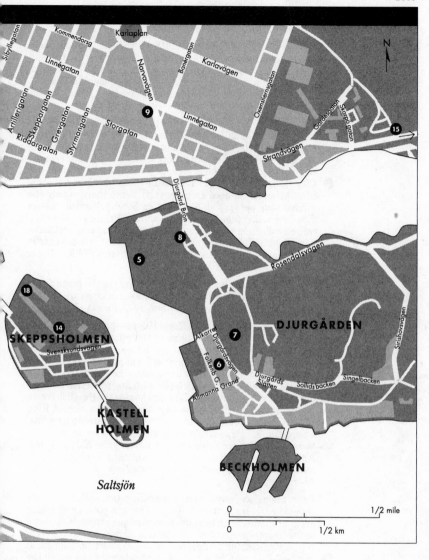

over the city in 1523, and King Gustavus Adolphus to make it the heart of an empire a century later.

During the Thirty Years' War (1618–48), Sweden gained importance as a Baltic trading state, and Stockholm grew commensurately. But by the beginning of the 18th century, Swedish influence was waning, and Stockholm's development had slowed. It did not revive until the Industrial Revolution, when the hub of the city moved north from the Old Town area.

City Hall and Old Town Anyone in Stockholm with limited time should give priority to a tour of the **Gamla Stan** (Old Town), a labyrinth of narrow, medieval streets, alleys, and quiet squares just south of the city center. Ideally, you should devote a whole day to this section. But before crossing the bridge, pay a visit to the modern-day **❶ City Hall,** constructed in 1923 and now one of the symbols of Stockholm. You'll need an early start, since there is only one guided tour per day at 10 AM, 12 on Sunday. Lavish mosaics grace the walls of the **Golden Hall,** and the **Prince's Gallery** features a collection of large murals by Prince Eugene, brother of King Gustav V. Take the elevator to the top of the 348-foot tower for a magnificent view of the city. *Admission: SEK 5. Tower open May–Sept., daily 11–3.*

❷ Crossing into the Old Town, you come first to the magnificent **Riddarholm Church,** where a host of Swedish kings are buried. *Admission: SEK 5. Open Mon.–Sat. 10–3, Sun. 1–3.*

❸ From there, proceed to the **Royal Palace**—preferably by noon—to see the colorful changing-of-the-guard ceremony. The smartly dressed guards seem superfluous, since tourists wander at will into the castle courtyard and around the grounds. Several separate attractions are open to the public. Be sure to visit the **Royal Armory,** with its outstanding collection of weaponry and royal regalia. The **Treasury** houses the Swedish crown jewels, including the regalia used for the coronation of King Erik XIV in 1561. You can also visit the **State Apartments,** where the king swears in each successive government. *Admission: SEK 7 for Treasury and Armory; SEK 10 for State Apartments. Treasury and Armory open weekdays 10–4, weekends 11–4. State Apartments open Tues.–Fri. 10–3, Sun. 12–3.*

❹ From the palace, stroll down **Västerlånggatan,** one of two main shopping streets in the Old Town. This is a popular shopping area, brimming with boutiques and antique shops. Walk down to the Skeppsbron waterfront, then head back toward the center over the Ström bridge, where anglers cast for salmon. If you feel like a rest, stop off at **Kungsträdgården** and watch the world go by. Originally built as a royal kitchen garden, the property was turned into a public park in 1562. During the summer, entertainments and activities abound, and you can catch a glimpse of local people playing open-air chess with giant chessmen.

Djurgården Be sure to spend at least a day visiting the many attractions on the large island of **Djurgården.** Although it's only a short walk from the city center, the most pleasant way to approach it is by ferry from Skeppsbron, in the Old Town. The ferries drop you off near two of Stockholm's best-known attractions, the Wasa Museum and Gröna Lund Tivoli. The *Wasa,* a restored 17th-century warship, is the oldest preserved war vessel in the world, and has become Sweden's most popular tourist sight.

She sank ignominiously in Stockholm harbor on her maiden voyage in 1628, reportedly because she was not carrying sufficient ballast. Recovered in 1961, she has been restored to her original appearance and has now been moved into a new museum, the **Wasamuseet,** scheduled to open in June 1990, which will feature films, tours, and new exhibitions. *Galarvarvsvagen 14, tel. 08/666–4900. Admission: SEK 15 adults, SEK 5 children. Open June 16–mid-Aug., daily 9:30–7; mid-Aug.–mid-June, daily 10–5.*

6 **Gröna Lund Tivoli,** Stockholm's version of the famous Copenhagen amusement park, is a favorite family attraction, featuring hair-raising roller coasters as well as tamer delights. *Tel. 08/ 660–3000. Admission: SEK 20 adults, SEK 10 children. Open June 27–Aug. 19, Mon.–Sat. 1–midnight, Sun. 1–10; Apr. 21– June 26 and Aug. 20–Sept. 17, hours vary (check locally).*

7 Just across the road is **Skansen,** a large, open-air folk museum consisting of 150 reconstructed traditional buildings from Sweden's different regions. Here you can see a variety of handcraft displays and demonstrations. There is also an attractive open-air zoo—with many native Scandinavian species, such as lynxes, wolves, and brown bears—as well as an excellent aquarium. *Tel. 08/663–0500. Admission: May–Aug., SEK 22 adults, SEK 7 children; Sept.–Apr., SEK 15 adults, SEK 5 children. Open Jan.–Apr. and Sept.–Dec., daily 9–5; May– Aug., daily 9 AM–10 PM.*

8 From the zoo, head back toward the city center. Just before the Djurgård bridge, you come to the **Nordic Museum,** which, like Skansen, provides an insight into the ways Swedish people have lived over the past 500 years. The collection includes displays of peasant costumes, folk art, and Lapp culture. *Admission: SEK 10. Open Mon.–Sat. 10–4, Sun. noon–5.*

9 Once you're back on the "mainland," drop into the **Museum of National Antiquities.** Though its name is uninspiring, it houses some remarkable Viking gold and silver treasures. **The Royal Cabinet of Coin,** located in the same building, boasts the world's largest coin. *Narvavägen 13–17. Admission: SEK 20. Open Tues.–Sun. 11–4.*

Time Out For a snack with a view, try the **Solliden Restaurant** at Skansen. Skansen also offers a selection of open-air snack bars and cafés; Gröna Lund itself has four different restaurants.

Stockholm Environs

The region surrounding Stockholm offers many attractions that can easily be seen on day trips out of the capital.

One "must" is the trip to the majestic 16th-century **Gripsholm Castle,** at Mariefred, on the southern side of Lake Mälaren and about 64 kilometers (40 miles) from Stockholm. Gripsholm, with its drawbridge and four massive round towers, is one of Sweden's most romantic castles. There had been a castle on the site as far back as the 1380s, but this was destroyed, and King Gustav Vasa had the present building erected in 1577. The castle is known best today for housing the Swedish state collection of portraits and is one of the largest portrait galleries in the world, with some 3,400 paintings.

Stockholm Environs

The most pleasant way of traveling to Gripsholm from Stockholm is on the vintage steamer *Mariefred*, the last coal-fired ship on Lake Mälaren. Departures, between mid-June and late August, are from Klara Mälarstrand, near the city hall, daily except Monday at 10 AM, returning from Mariefred at 4:30. The journey takes 3½ hours each way, and there is a restaurant on board. *Roundtrip fare: SEK 90. Tel. 08/698850. Admission to castle: SEK 10. Open daily 10–4.*

Another popular boat trip goes to **Skokloster Palace,** about 70 kilometers (43 miles) from Stockholm. Departures are from the city hall bridge (Stadshusbron) daily, except Monday and Friday, between early June and mid-August. The route follows the narrow inlets of Lake Mälaren along the "Royal Waterway" and calls at **Sigtuna,** the ancient capital of Sweden. You can get off the boat here, visit the town, which has medieval ruins and an 18th-century town hall, and catch the boat again on the return journey. But it is worthwhile, too, to stay on board and continue to Skokloster, an impressive palace dating from the 1650s. Built by the Swedish field marshal Carl Gustav Wrangel, it contains many of his trophies from the Thirty Years' War. Other attractions include what is reckoned to be the largest private collection of arms in the world, as well as some magnificent Gobelin tapestries. Next door to the palace is a motor museum that houses Sweden's largest collection of vintage cars and motorcycles. The roundtrip boat fare is SEK 90, and there is a restaurant and cafeteria on board. *Admission to Skokloster Palace: SEK 18 (free with Key to Stockholm card). Open daily*

11–4. Admission to motor museum: SEK 15 (free with Key to Stockholm card). Open May–Sept., daily 10–5; Oct.–Apr., daily 11–4.

A popular day excursion by tour bus from Stockholm takes you to **Kolmården Zoo** and **Safari Park,** on the shores of Bråviken, a large bay in the Baltic near Norrköping. It is claimed to be one of Europe's largest zoos in terms of area, and one of the most popular attractions is the dolphinarium, where the dolphins can be seen performing daily. The bus takes you through the safari park, where lions, zebras, wolves, and other animals roam freely. *Departures from Sweden House, late June–mid-Aug., every Saturday at 9 AM, arriving back at about 6:15. Fare: SEK 200, includes admission to the zoo. Information and reservations are available at the tourist center.*

Lovers of the sea could easily spend a whole week cruising among the 24,000 islands in the **Stockholm archipelago.** The **Båtluffarkortet** (Inter-Islands Card), available from early June to mid-August, gives you 16 days' unlimited travel on the Waxholm Steamship Company boats, which operate scheduled services throughout the archipelago. The card is on sale in the Excursion Shop at the Sweden House Tourist Center and at the Waxholm Steamship Company terminal at Strömkajen. It costs SEK 130. If your time is more limited, the "Sandhamn Package" is a good idea for an offbeat trip. Sandhamn is Stockholm's main marine outpost and pilot station, but today it is best known as a sailing center.

The Sandhamn Package price includes the round-trip boat fare plus one night's lodging and breakfast at the comfortable Sandhamns Hotel, where most of the rooms overlook the water. The package price is about SEK 250 per person, plus SEK 170 for an additional night. The Sandhamn Package should be booked in advance at the Excursion Shop in the tourist center.

Off the Beaten Track

Just over 155 meters (500 feet) tall, the **Kaknäs TV Tower** at Djurgården is the highest structure in Scandinavia. From the top you can catch a magnificent view of the city and surrounding archipelago. Facilities include a cafeteria, restaurant, and souvenir shop. *Djurgården, tel. 08/678030.*

You can see the world's largest variety of water lily at the **Bergius Botanical Garden,** just north of the city center. Its leaves are more than 2.17 kilometers (seven feet) in diameter. *Frescati, tel. 08/153912.*

Fjäderholmarna (the Feather Islets), the collective name for a group of four secluded islands in the Stockholm archipelago, have only recently been opened to the public after 50 years as a military zone. An archipelago museum and fish farm are under construction. Boats leave from Slussen and Strömkajen, in downtown Stockholm.

Shopping

Gift Ideas Stockholm is an ideal place to find items that reflect the best in Swedish design and elegance, particularly glass, porcelain, furs, handcrafts, home furnishings, and leather goods. The quality is uniformly high, and you can take advantage of the tax-free shopping service in most stores (*see* Essential Information). Film, cameras, and hi-fi equipment are generally cheaper here than in most other European countries.

Department Stores The largest is **NK**, on Hamngatan, where you can find just about anything. Other major stores are **PUB**, on Hötorget, and **Åhléns City**, on Klarabergsgatan. All three are open on Sunday.

Shopping Districts The center of Stockholm's shopping activity has shifted from Kungsgatan to Hamngatan, a wide boulevard along which a huge, covered shopping complex, named **Gallerian**, has been built. The **Old Town** area is best for handcrafts, antiquarian bookshops, and art shops.

Food and Flea Markets The biggest flea market in northern Europe is located in **Skärholmen** shopping center, a 20-minute subway ride from the downtown area. Market hours are weekdays 11–6, Sat. 9–3, Sun. 10–3. Superior food markets selling such Swedish specialties as marinated salmon and reindeer can be found on **Östermalmstorg** and **Hötorget**.

Glassware For the best buys, try **Nordiska Kristall**, on Kungsgatan, or **Rosenthal Studio-Haus**, on Birger Jarlsgatan. The latter operates its own shipping service. The **Crystal Showrooms**, on Drottninggatan and Norrmalmstorg, cater mainly to American visitors, and all prices—claimed to be 30–50% lower than their advertised U.S. prices—are in U.S. dollars. Shipping and insurance are included, and these shops even send a limousine to pick you up at your hotel!

Handicrafts A good center for all kinds of Swedish handicrafts in wood and metal is **Svensk Hemslöjd**, on Sveavägen. It also sells embroidery kits and many types of weaving and knitting yarn. For reindeer purses and wooden craft items, try **Brinkens Konsthantverk** on Storkyrkobrinken, in the Old Town. **Länshemslöjden**, on Drottninggatan, has a wide selection of Swedish folk costumes and handicraft souvenirs from different parts of Sweden.

Dining

Prices quoted here are per person and include a first course, main course, tax, and service, but not wine. Best bets are indicated by a star ★.

For details and price category descriptions, *see* Dining in Staying in Sweden.

Very Expensive **Erik's.** The authentic marine atmosphere owes much to its location: a restored barge moored in Stockholm harbor. The cuisine is principally French, with an accent on seafood—especially salmon. During the summer, guests enjoy deck-side dining and a pleasant harbor view. *Strandvägskajen 17, tel. 08/660–6060. Reservations advised. AE, DC, MC, V. Closed Sun., Christmas, New Year's, and Midsummer Night (June 22).*

★ **Operakällaren.** Located in part of the elegant Opera House building, this is one of Stockholm's best-known traditional restaurants. Royal chef Werner Vogli prepares both Scandinavian and Continental cuisine; the specialty is Turbot Karl XII. The restaurant faces Kungsträdgården, the waterfront, and the

Royal Palace. *Operahuset, tel. 08/111125. Reservations advised. AE, DC, MC, V. Closed July.*

Teatergrillen. Small, friendly, and centrally located, Teatergrillen is a favorite among local businesspeople. The cuisine is international, but steaks are a specialty. *Nybrogatan 3, tel. 08/107044. Reservations advised. AE, DC, MC, V. Dinner only weekends. Closed Christmas and June 22.*

Expensive

Aurora. Located in a 300-year-old building complete with authentic cellar vaults, Aurora is one of the best-known restaurants in the Old Town. The cuisine is both Swedish and international. Try the house specialty, the three-course "Queen's Menu". *Munkbron 11, tel. 08/219359. Reservations advised. AE, DC, MC, V. Dinner only. Closed Sun.*

La Brochette. This popular, French-style restaurant specializes in charcoal-broiled steak served on skewers. *Storgatan 27, tel. 08/662–2000. Dress: casual. Reservations advised. AE, DC, MC, V. Closed Sat. lunch, Sun.*

Clas på Hörnet. Located just outside the city center, Clas på Hörnet is a small, intimate establishment occupying the ground floor of a restored 200-year-old town house, now a hotel (*see* Lodging). It offers a choice of international or Swedish cuisine. *Surbrunnsgatan 20, tel. 08/165136. Reservations advised. AE, DC, MC, V. Closed Christmas.*

Fem Små Hus. "Five small houses" is a well-known Old Town restaurant. The menu features both Swedish and French dishes. The chef's specialty is fillet of veal "Anna Lindberg." *Nygränd 10, tel. 08/100482. Reservations advised. AE, DC, MC, V.*

Gourmet. The accent is on French cuisine, but Swiss and Swedish specialties are also available. Seafood figures prominently. Try the house specialty, Sea Crayfish in Love. *Tegnérgatan 10, tel. 08/314398. Reservations advised. AE, DC, MC, V. Closed weekends for lunch, July.*

Quarter Deck. Located on the Old Town waterfront near the Royal Palace, the Quarter Deck, part of the Hotel Reisen, offers a superb harbor view. The cuisine is both Swedish and French, and a moderate fixed-price weekend menu is available. *Skeppsbron 12–14, tel. 08/223260. Reservations advised. AE, DC, MC, V.*

★ **Stallmästaregården.** An historic old inn with an attractive courtyard and garden, Stallmästaregården is near the Haga Air Terminal, some distance from the city center. But the fine French and Swedish cuisine is well worth the journey. After-dinner coffee is served in the courtyard overlooking Brunnsviken Lake. During the weekends and throughout the summer, a lower, fixed-price menu is available. *Norrtull, near Haga, tel. 08/243910. Reservations advised. AE, DC, MC, V.*

Moderate

★ **Glada Laxen.** Since the name means "Happy Salmon," it is not surprising that salmon in various guises, from smoked to mousse, is the star attraction here. Centrally located in the Gallerian shopping center near the Sweden House Tourist Center, this is a popular spot. *Regeringsgatan 23, tel. 08/211290. Reservations advised, especially for lunch. AE, DC, MC, V. Closed Sun. Dinner finishes at 8 PM.*

Gondolen. Suspended under the gangway of the *Katarina* elevator at Slussen, Gondolen offers a magnificent view over the harbor, Lake Mälaren, and the Baltic Sea. The cuisine is international, and a range of fixed-price menus is available. *Slussen, tel. 08/402021. Reservations advised. AE, DC, MC, V.*

Markurell's. The two separate restaurants, the Wärdshuset and the Bistro, are conveniently located opposite the central station. It's a busy establishment serving international cuisine. *Mäster Samuelsgatan 73, tel. 08/211012. Reservations advised. AE, DC, MC, V.*

Sturehof. Centrally located, with an unpretentious, nautical ambience, Sturehof's specialty is its seafood. It also boasts an English-style pub. *Stureplan 2, tel. 08/142750. Reservations advised. AE, DC, MC, V. Closed Sat. lunch, Sun., Christmas, New Year's, and June 22.*

Inexpensive **Annorlunda.** This is a small, self-service restaurant specializing in light meals and salads. The daily "Annorlunda Special" features a main course, dessert, and coffee for SEK 95. *Malmskillnadsgatan 50, tel. 08/219569. AE, DC, MC, V. Closed Sun.*

Cassi. This centrally located restaurant specializes in French cuisine at reasonable prices. *Narvavägen 30, tel. 08/661–7461. Reservations advised. MC. Closed Sat.*

★ **Open Gate Yet.** Located near the Slussen locks, on the south side of Stockholm harbor, this is a popular, trendy Art Deco Italian-style trattoria. Pasta dishes are the house specialty. *Högbergsgatan 40, tel. 08/439776. No reservations. AE, DC, MC, V. Dinner only.*

Lodging

Stockholm has plenty of hotels in most price brackets, although relatively few are in the Inexpensive category. Many hotels cut their rates in high season, however, when business travelers are on vacation, so that during the summer even a hotel classified as Very Expensive can become affordable. The major hotel chains also have a number of bargain schemes available on weekends throughout the year and daily during the summer.

More than 40 hotels offer the "Stockholm Package," providing accommodations for one night, costing between SEK 220 and SEK 440 per person, including breakfast and a Key to Stockholm card *(see* Getting Around). Details of the Stockholm Package can be obtained from the **Stockholm Information Service,** Excursion Shop, Box 7542, S-103 93 Stockholm. Also, you can call **The Hotel Center** (tel. 08/240880) or reserve the package through travel agents.

If you arrive in Stockholm without a hotel reservation, the **Hotellcentralen** in the central station will arrange accommodations for you. The office is open daily 8 AM–9 PM, June–September; weekdays 8:30–5 the rest of the year. There's a small fee for each reservation. Or phone one of the central reservations offices run by the major hotel groups: RESO (tel. 08/235700); SARA (tel. 08/753–7350); Scandic (tel. 08/343–5550); Sweden Hotels (tel. 08/204311), or Best Western (tel. 08/300420).

Ratings Prices quoted here are for two people in a double room. Best bets are indicated by a star ★ . For details and price category definitions, *see* Lodging in Staying in Sweden.

Very Expensive **Amaranten.** Only five minutes' walk from the central station, Amaranten is a large, modern hotel, built in 1969 and refurbished in 1988. The "executive tower" offers a roof garden and 52 rooms. Guests enjoy a gourmet restaurant and brasserie, nightclub, and piano bar. *Kungsholmsgatan 31, tel. 08/541060.*

415 rooms with bath. Facilities: sauna, pool, restaurants, nightclub, piano bar, and solarium. AE, DC, MC, V.

★ **Continental.** Located in the city center across from the central station, the Continental is popular with American guests. It was first opened about 25 years ago and is now undergoing renovation that's scheduled for completion in 1992. It offers three restaurants in different price brackets—an international gourmet restaurant, a French-style bistro, and a café that's popular for lunch and quick meals. *Klara Vattugränd 4, tel. 08/244020. 250 rooms, with bath. Facilities: 3 restaurants. AE, DC, MC, V.*

★ **Diplomat.** This is an elegant hotel located within easy walking distance of Djurgården Park and Skansen, and offers magnificent views over Stockholm harbor. The building itself is a turn-of-the-century town house that was converted into a hotel in 1966. The teahouse is a popular spot for light meals. *Strandvägen 7C, tel. 08/663–5800. 130 rooms with bath. AE, DC, MC, V. Closed Christmas and New Year's.*

Grand. Located on the waterfront in the center of town, the Grand is a large, gracious, Old World-style hotel dating back to 1874. It faces the Royal Palace. The two restaurants—French and Swedish—offer harbor views; there is also a café for light snacks. *S. Blasieholmshamnen 8, tel. 08/221020. 330 rooms with bath, most with waterfront views. Facilities: sauna, restaurant, beauty salon. AE, DC, MC, V. Closed Christmas and New Year's.*

★ **Lady Hamilton.** Considered one of Stockholm's most desirable hotels, the Lady Hamilton, in the Old Town, was built as a private home in 1470 and has been a hotel only since 1980. It houses an extensive collection of antiques, including one of George Romney's portraits of Lady Hamilton. *Storkyrkobrinken 5, tel. 08/234680. 35 rooms with bath. Facilities: sauna, pool, cafeteria. AE, DC, MC, V. Closed Christmas and New Year's.*

Reisen. The building dates from 1819, although it was refurbished several years ago. It's situated in a waterfront sector of the Old Town and offers a fine restaurant, a grill, and what is reputed to be the best piano bar in town. The swimming pool is built under medieval arches. *Skeppsbron 12–14, tel. 08/223260. 113 rooms with bath. Facilities: sauna, pool, library. AE, DC, MC, V. Closed Christmas and New Year's.*

SAS Royal Viking. This is a large, modern, somewhat impersonal hotel adjoining the central station. Rooms are on the small side for a hotel in this price category. *Vasagatan 1, tel. 08/141000. 340 rooms with bath. Facilities: sauna, pool, rooms for disabled guests. AE, DC, MC, V.*

SAS Strand. Acquired in 1986 by the SAS group, this is a gracious, Old World hotel. It was built in 1912 but fully modernized in 1982–83. No two rooms are the same; many are furnished with antiques. An SAS check-in counter adjoins the main reception area. The principal restaurant specializes in seafood dishes and offers a superb selection of wines. Lighter meals are served in the Piazza. *Nybrokajen 9, tel. 08/222900. 137 rooms with bath. Facilities: sauna, cafeteria, function rooms. AE, DC, MC, V.*

Sergel Plaza. Opened in 1984, the modern Sergel Plaza incorporates part of an older building located in the city center. Its distinctive feature is its glass-roof lobby, complete with trees and waterfall. The young staff provides attentive service.

Brunkebergstorg 9, tel. 08/226600. 407 rooms with bath. Facilities: restaurant, café, sauna, health club. AE, DC, MC, V.

Expensive **Birger Jarl.** A short subway ride from the city center, Birger Jarl is a modern, characteristically Scandinavian hotel that opened in 1974. There is no full-service restaurant. *Tulegatan 8, tel. 08/151020. 252 rooms with bath. Facilities: sauna, pool, coffee shop. AE, DC, MC, V. Closed Christmas and New Year's.*

★ **Clas på Hörnet.** An 18th-century inn converted into a small hotel in 1982, Clas på Hörnet is just outside the city center. Its rooms, furnished with antiques of the period, go quickly. If you can't manage to reserve one, at least have a meal in the gourmet restaurant *(see* Dining*). Surbrunnsgatan 20, tel. 08/165130. 10 rooms with bath. AE, DC, MC, V.*

Karelia. A turn-of-the-century building on one of the main shopping streets, Karelia has a Finnish atmosphere with its saunas and Finnish bands. The restaurant specializes in Russian cooking. *Birger Jarlsgatan 35, tel. 08/247660. 103 rooms with bath. AE, DC, MC, V. Closed Christmas and New Year's.*

Lord Nelson. This companion hotel to the Lady Hamilton was built in much the same style. Its location on a busy pedestrian street in the Old Town makes it rather noisy at night. The atmosphere throughout is distinctly nautical—even down to the cabin-size rooms. There is no restaurant, but light snacks are available. *Västerlånggatan 22, tel. 08/232390. 31 rooms with bath. AE, DC, MC, V. Closed Christmas and New Year's.*

Mornington. Although it is not particularly imposing from the outside, Mornington is a comfortable, quiet hotel, situated near the indoor market at Östermalmstorg and within walking distance of the city center. It has an excellent fish restaurant. *Nybrogatan 53, tel. 08/663–1240. 141 rooms with bath. AE, DC, MC, V. Closed Christmas and New Year's.*

Moderate **Alfa.** About 20 minutes from the city center, Alfa is a medium-size, medium-class hotel. Opened in 1972, it has recently been refurbished. *Marknadsvägen 6, tel. 08/810600. 104 rooms with bath. Facilities: sauna, restaurant. AE, DC, MC, V. Closed Christmas and New Year's.*

City. A large, modern-style hotel built in the 1940s but modernized in 1982–83, City is located near the city center and the Hötorget market. It is owned by the Salvation Army, so alcohol is not served in either the restaurant or café. *Slöjdgatan 7, tel. 08/222240. 300 rooms with bath. Facilities: restaurant, café, rooms for disabled guests. AE, DC, MC, V.*

Stockholm. This hotel has an unusual location—the upper floors of a downtown office building. The mainly modern decor is offset by traditional Swedish furnishings that help create its family atmosphere. Breakfast is the only meal served. *Norrmalmstorg 1, tel. 08/221320. 92 rooms with bath. AE, DC, MC, V. Closed Christmas and New Year's.*

Inexpensive **Alexandra.** Although it is in the Södermalm area, to the south of the Old Town, the Alexandra is only five minutes by subway from the city center. It is a small, modern hotel, opened 13 years ago and renovated in 1988. Only breakfast is served. *Magnus Ladulåsgatan 42, tel. 08/840320. 90 rooms with bath. Facilities: sauna, solarium. AE, DC, MC, V. Closed Christmas and New Year's.*

Gustav af Klint. A "hotel ship" moored at Stadsgården quay, near Slussen subway station, the Gustav af Klint is better described as a youth hostel—albeit with its own sauna. It was refurbished in 1989. *Stadsgårdskajen 153, tel. 08/404077. 28 cabins, none with bath. No credit cards. Closed Christmas and New Year's.*

Zinken. The Zinken complex consists of a number of pavilions near Zinkensdam subway station, five minutes from the city center. It is a popular spot for travelers on a budget. There is an adjacent youth hostel. *Zinkensväg 20, tel. 08/585011. 28 rooms, none with bath. Facilities: sauna, solarium, Jacuzzi, garden, children's play area, access to washing machine and kitchen. AE, DC, MC, V. Closed Christmas and New Year's.*

The Arts

Stockholm's main theater and concert season runs from September through May or June, so there are not many major performances during the height of the tourist season. But for a list of events, pick up the free booklet *Stockholm This Week*, available from hotels and tourist information offices. You can get last-minute tickets to theaters and shows at the cut-price ticket booth on Norrmalmstorg Square. Tickets sold here are priced 25% below box office rates. The booth is open Monday noon–5 and Tuesday–Saturday noon–7. There is also a **central reservation office** for regular-price tickets (tel. 08/108800).

Concerts The city's main concert hall is the **Concert House** (Konserthuset) at Hötorget 8, home of the Stockholm Philharmonic Orchestra. The main season runs from mid-September to mid-May. In addition to full-scale evening concerts, there are "coffee break" or lunchtime concerts some days. During the summer, free concerts are given in many city parks. For information, phone 08/221800.

Opera The season at the **Royal Opera House,** just across the bridge from the Royal Palace, runs from mid-August to early June and offers performances at top-class international standards (tel. 08/248240). And from early June to early September, there are performances of opera, ballet, and orchestral music at the exquisite **Drottningholm Court Theater,** which was the setting for Ingmar Bergman's film *The Magic Flute*. The original 18th-century stage machinery is still used in these productions. You can get to Drottningholm by subway or special theater-bus (leaving from the Grand Hotel or Vasagatan, opposite the central station) or by boat *(see* Getting Around Stockholm). For tickets, tel. 08/660–8285 or 08/660–8281.

Theater Stockholm has about 20 top-rank theaters, but dramatic productions are unlikely to interest those who don't understand Swedish. A better option is to go to a musical; several city theaters hold regular performances. Plays in English are featured at the **Regina Theater,** Drottninggatan 71A (tel. 08/207000).

Film English and American films predominate, and they are screened with the original soundtrack and Swedish subtitles. Programs are listed in the local evening newspapers, which usually give titles in both Swedish and English. Movie buffs should visit **Filmstaden** (Film City), Mäster Samuelsgatan 25 (tel. 08/225420), where 11 cinemas under one roof show a variety of films from noon until midnight.

Entertainment and Nightlife

Cabaret   Stockholm's biggest nightclub, **Börsen** (Jakobsgatan 6, tel. 08/
249210), offers high-quality international cabaret shows. Another popular spot is the **Cabaret Club,** Barnhusgatan 12 (tel.
08/110608). Although it can accommodate 450 guests, reservations are advised.

Bars and   **Alexandra** (Birger Jarlsgatan 29, tel. 08/104646) is one of
Nightclubs   Stockholm's most famous night spots, renovated in 1989. Reservations are advised. Piano bars are also an important part of
the Stockholm scene. Try the **Anglais Bar** at the Hotel Anglais
(tel. 08/249900) or the **Clipper Club** at the Hotel Reisen,
Skeppsbron (tel. 08/223260).

Jazz Clubs   **Fasching** (Kungsgatan 63, tel. 08/216267) is Stockholm's largest, but another popular spot is **Stampen** (Grämunkegränd 7,
tel. 08/205793). Get here in good time if you want a seat, and
phone first to be sure the establishment hasn't been reserved
for a private party.

Discos   **Café Opera** (tel. 08/110026), adjoining the Opera House, is one
of the most popular night spots and there is always a long line to
get in. Others are **Downtown** (Norrlandsgatan 5A, tel. 08/
119488) and **Karlsson** (Kungsgatan 65, tel. 08/119298).

Uppsala
and the Folklore District

The area of Sweden referred to as the "Folklore District"—
essentially the provinces of Dalarna and Värmland—has the
merit of being both easily accessible from Stockholm and the
best region in which to see something of the country's enduring
folk traditions. This itinerary takes you to Dalarna through the
ancient city of Uppsala and returns to Stockholm through the
Bergslagen region, the heart of the centuries-old Swedish iron
industry.

Getting Around

The route can be covered entirely by train. The ride from
Stockholm to Uppsala takes only 45 minutes, and the service is
fairly frequent. A car, however, will give you the flexibility to
explore some of the attractions that are not so accessible by
public transportation.

Guided Tours

While Uppsala is compact enough to explore on foot, guided
sightseeing tours are available each day. Check with the tourist information office.

Tourist Information

Falun. Stora Torget, tel. 023/83637.
Ludvika. Sporthallen, tel. 0240/86050.
Mora. Ångbåtskajen, tel. 0250/26550.
Örebro. Drottninggatan 9, tel. 019/211080.
Rättvik. Torget, tel. 0248/10910.
Uppsala. Gamla Torget, tel. 018/117500.

Uppsala and the Folklore District

Uppsala is really the cradle of Swedish civilization, so it is well worth spending a day or two exploring it. If you opt for a guided tour, you'll be taken first to **Gamla Uppsala** (Old Uppsala), the site of an ancient pagan temple just outside of town. The temple consists of three huge burial mounds, sometimes called the **Pyramids of Scandinavia.** During the 5th century AD, Aun, Egil, and Edils, the first Swedish kings, were buried here. Adjoining the burial mounds is the Odinsborg restaurant, where you can sample local mead, brewed from a 14th-century recipe.

Back in **Uppsala** itself, your first stop should be the enormous **cathedral,** with its twin towers dominating the city skyline. The cathedral has been the seat of the archbishop of the Swedish church for 700 years, although its present appearance owes much to major restoration work completed in the late 19th century. Make a point of visiting the **Cathedral Museum** in the north tower, which boasts one of Europe's finest collections of ecclesiastical textiles. *Admission: free. Open weekdays 8–8, weekends 8–6.*

Nearby, in a strategic position atop a hill, is **Uppsala Castle.** This prepossessing structure was built in the 1540s by King Gustav Vasa. Having broken his ties with the Vatican, the king was eager to show who was actually running the country. He arranged to have the cannons aimed directly at the archbishop's palace. *Admission: SEK 5 for main hall, SEK 10 for museum and ruins. Open mid-May–Sept. Check times with the local tourist office.*

Uppsala is the site of Scandinavia's oldest university, founded in 1477. Be sure to visit one of its most venerable old buildings, the **Gustavianum,** located near the cathedral. Just below the cupola is the anatomical theater, where public dissections of executed convicts were a popular 17th-century tourist attraction. *Admission: SEK 3. Open daily noon–3.*

Also, try to fit in a visit to the university library, called **Carolina Rediviva,** for a look at the **Codex Argenteus** (Silver Bible), a priceless relic dating from the 6th century. *Admission: SEK 2 on weekends, free weekdays. Open weekdays 9–7, Sat. 9–6, Sun. 1–3:30.*

One of Uppsala's most famous sons was Carl von Linné, known as Linnaeus. A professor of botany at the university during the 1740s, he developed a system of plant and animal classification that is still used today. You can visit the **gardens** he designed, as well as his former residence, now a **museum.** *Admission: SEK 5. Open 1–4; closed Mon.*

From Uppsala, the route heads northwest through a pleasant agricultural landscape into the province of Dalarna, passing through **Säter,** one of the best-preserved wooden villages in Sweden. This is a pleasant spot just to wander around. For an overnight stop it is best to head for Falun, Dalarna's provincial capital.

Falun is best known for a huge hole in the ground, referred to as the **"Great Pit."** The hole has been there since 1687, when an abandoned copper mine collapsed. Other mines on the site are still working today. You can take a guided tour down into some of the old shafts and hear the gruesome story of 17th-

Uppsala and the Folklore District

century miner Fat Mats, whose body was perfectly preserved in brine for 40 years following a cave-in. There is also a museum that tells the story of this important local industry. *Admission: SEK 20. Open May–mid-June, daily 10–4:30; mid-June–Aug., daily 9–7; Sept.–mid-Nov., weekends only 10–4:30.*

Just outside Falun, at **Sundborn,** is the former home of Swedish artist Carl Larsson. Here, in an idyllic, lakeside setting, you can see a selection of his paintings, which owe much to local folk-art traditions. His grandchildren and great-grandchildren are on hand to show you around. *Admission: SEK 25. Open May–Sept., Mon.–Sat. 10–5, Sun. 1–5.*

But the real center of Dalarna folklore is the area around **Lake Siljan,** by far the largest of the 6,000 lakes in the province. A good base from which to begin your tour is the attractive lakeside village of **Tällberg,** or **Mora,** toward the north end of the lake. In the neighboring village of **Rättvik,** hundreds of people wearing traditional costumes arrive in longboats to attend Midsummer church services. Mora itself is best known as the home of the artist Anders Zorn. His house and **studio** are open to the public. *Admission: SEK 10. Open Mon.–Sat. 9–5, Sun. 11–5; closed Mon. in winter.*

Near Mora is the village of **Nusnäs.** This is the village where the famous, brightly colored **Dalarna wooden horses** are produced. You can visit either of the two workshops where they are made.

Heading south again you come to **Ludvika,** an important center of the old Bergslagen mining region. This region stretches from the forests of Värmland in the west to the coastal forges in the east. Ludvika has a notable open-air mining museum, **Gammelgården.** *Admission: SEK 7. Open May 15–Aug., daily 11–5.*

Another local attraction is **Luosa Cottage.** The poet Dan Andersson lived here during the early part of the century so he could experience for himself the rigorous life of the local charcoal burners. *Admission: SEK 10. Open daily 11–4.*

"Safaris" from Ludvika into the local outback can be arranged for visitors eager to try their hands at gold panning, canoeing, fishing, shooting, and wildlife watching. Information about these trips is available from the local tourist office.

Continuing south from Ludvika, you come to **Örebro,** a sizable town at the western edge of **Lake Hjälmaren,** which is connected to Lake Mälaren and the sea by the Hjålmare Canal. Örebro received its charter in the 13th century and developed as a trading center for the farmers and miners of the Bergslagen region. Rising from a small island in the Svartån River, right in the center of town, is an imposing **castle,** parts of which date back to the 13th century. The castle is now the residence of the regional governor. Guided tours run from mid-June to mid-August at 11, 12, 1, and 3 each day. Check with the Örebro tourist office for further information. An added attraction is the excellent restaurant in the castle tower.

To get a feel for the Örebro of bygone days, wander around the **Wadköping** district, where a number of old houses and craftsmen's workshops have been painstakingly preserved. At the north end of town is **Svampen** (The Mushroom), a water tower rising 59 meters (190 feet) into the air. If you climb to the top, you can catch a magnificent view of the surrounding countryside. There is also a cafeteria and tourist office there. The tower is open daily from May through Sept.

Direct train service from Örebro back to Stockholm operates at two-hour intervals, and the journey takes just under three hours. You can also take the hourly train to Hallsberg and change there to the frequent Gothenburg–Stockholm service.

Dining and Lodging

For details and price category definitions, *see* Dining and Lodging in Staying in Sweden.

Falun
Lodging

Bergmästaren Falun. Situated in the town center, Bergmästaren Falun is a small, cozy hotel built in traditional Dalarna style and filled with antique furnishings. It was completely refurbished in 1985. The restaurant serves breakfast only. *Bergskolegränd 7, tel. 023/63600. 89 rooms, most with bath. Facilities: sauna, solarium. AE, DC, MC, V. Closed Christmas. Expensive.*

Sara Hotel Grand. Centrally located and close to the train station, the Sara Hotel Grand is a large, modern hotel. Part of the building dates from the turn of the century, though it underwent a complete modernization in 1987. The restaurant serves international cuisine. *Trotzgatan 9–11, tel. 023/18700. 183* rooms with bath. *Facilities: disco, restaurant, swimming pool, solarium. AE, DC, MC, V. Expensive.*

Ludvika
Lodging

Grand. A medium-size, modern-style hotel, the Grand is located in the town center. It was built 12 years ago and refurbished in 1986. *Eriksgatan 6, tel. 0240/18220. 103 rooms with bath. Facilities: sauna, disco, 2 restaurants. AE, DC, MC, V. Moderate.*

Rex. The Rex is a fairly basic but modern hotel conveniently located near the city center. It was built in 1960. Its restaurant serves breakfast only. *Engelbrektsgatan 9, tel. 0240/13690. 27 rooms with bath. AE, DC, MC, V. Closed Christmas and one week in summer. Inexpensive.*

Mora
Lodging
★

Siljan. Taking its name from the nearby lake, the largest in Dalarna, the Siljan is a popular, small but modern-style hotel. Opened 65 years ago, it was renovated in 1983. *Moragatan 6, tel. 0250/13000. 46 rooms with bath. Facilities: sauna, disco, restaurant. AE, DC, MC, V. Inexpensive.*

Örebro
Dining and Lodging

RESO Grand. Located in the heart of town, the Grand is the city's largest hotel. Though it was built 85 years ago, it has been refurbished periodically and offers all the modern comforts. *Fabriksgatan 23, tel. 019/150200. 228 rooms with bath. Facilities: sauna, Jacuzzi, à la carte restaurant, VIP rooms. AE, DC, MC, V. Expensive.*

City. Opened only within the past several years, City is a modern, centrally located hotel. It offers special facilities for disabled guests and those suffering from allergies. The restaurant serves "home cooking" at lunchtime and more elaborate, à la carte fare in the evening. *Kungsgatan 24, tel. 019/100200. 113 rooms with bath. Facilities: restaurant. AE, DC, MC, V. Moderate.*

Tällberg
Lodging
★

Åkerblads. Located near the shores of Lake Siljan, Åkerblads is a real rural Swedish experience. The hotel occupies a typical Dalarna farmstead, parts of which date back to the 16th century. It is run by the 14th and 15th generations of the Åkerblad family. A hotel since 1910, it was modernized in 1987. The restaurant serves table d'hôte meals only. *793 03 Tällberg, tel. 0247/50800. 64 rooms, most with bath. Facilities: sauna, Jacuzzi, restaurant, pub-style bar. AE, DC, MC, V. Closed Christmas. Expensive.*

Uppsala
Dining
★

Domtrappkällaren. One of the city's most popular restaurants, Domtrappkällaren is located in a 14th-century cellar near the cathedral. The cuisine is a mixture of French and Swedish. *St. Eriksgränd 15, tel. 018/130955. Reservations essential. AE, DC, MC, V. Moderate.*

Lodging

Sara Gillet. A centrally located, medium-size, modern hotel, the Sara Gillet was opened 18 years ago and has been modernized recently. *Dragarbrunnsgatan 23, tel. 018/155360. 169 rooms with bath. AE, DC, MC, V. Closed Christmas. Expensive.*

Grand Hotel Hörnan. An Old World, medium-size hotel, the Grand Hotel Hörnan is in the city center near the train station. Opened in 1906, it has been refurbished during the past several years. The restaurant serves breakfast only. *Bangårdsgatan 1, tel. 018/139380. 37 rooms with bath. AE, MC. Closed July 15–31. Moderate.*

The West Coast and the Glass Country

For many visitors traveling to Sweden by ferry, Gothenburg (or Göteborg) is the port of arrival. But those who arrive in Stockholm should not miss making a side trip to this great shipping city and Sweden's scenic western coast. This itinerary combines a western trip with a route through the Glass Country to the medieval fortress town of Kalmar, on the east coast.

Getting Around

As with the previous itinerary, the route can be followed by both train and car. Trains for Gothenburg depart from Stockholm's central station about every hour, and normal travel time is about 4½ hours. There are also four daily City Express trains that make faster time, but these require a supplementary fare of SEK 110 in first class (this includes breakfast on morning trains) or SEK 30 in second class. Seat reservations are compulsory on most trains to Gothenburg. There are also hourly flights to Gothenburg from Stockholm's Arlanda Airport between 7 AM and 9 PM on weekdays, slightly less frequently on weekends. The trip by air takes 55 minutes.

For getting around the city of Gothenburg itself, the best transportation option for the visitor is the **Göteborgskortet** (Key to Gothenburg) card, similar to the Key to Stockholm card. This entitles the user to free travel on all public transportation, free parking, and free admission to the Liseberg amusement park and all city museums. Prices for the card range from SEK 70 for one day to SEK 200 for four days.

Guided Tours

Free 50-minute sightseeing tours of Gothenburg leave regularly from Kungsportsplatsen, just beside the city tourist office. They must be reserved at the office in advance.

Tourist Information

Gothenburg. Basargatan 10, tel. 031/100740.
Jönköping. Djurläkartorget, tel. 036/105050.
Kalmar. Larmgatan 6, tel. 0480/15350.
Växjö. Kronobergsgatan 8, tel. 0470/41410.

Exploring the West Coast and the Glass Country

Visitors arriving in **Gothenburg** by car often drive straight through the city in their haste to reach their coastal vacation spots, but it is well worth spending a day or two exploring this attractive harbor city. A quayside jungle of cranes and warehouses attests to the city's industrial might, yet within 10 minutes' walk of the waterfront is an elegant, modern city of broad avenues, green parks, and gardens. It is an easy city to explore: Most of the major attractions are within walking dis-

The West Coast and the Glass Country

Uddevalla
Trollhättan
Falköping
Lake Vättern
Norrköping
Linköping
Gothenburg
Borås
Jönköping
Huskvarna
Nässjö
Västervik
Riddersberg
Falkenberg
Varberg
Värnamo
Oskarshamn
Kattegat
Alvesta
Halmstad
Växjö
Nybro
Kalmar
Laholm
Öland
Helsingborg
Hässleholm
Karlshamn
Karlskrona
Ronneby
DEN.
Landskrona
Kristianstad
Malmö
Baltic Sea
N
0   40 miles
0   60 km
Trelleborg
Ystad

tance of each other, and there is an excellent streetcar network. In the summer, you can even take a sightseeing trip on a vintage open-air streetcar.

Gothenburg's development was pioneered mainly by British merchants in the 19th century, when it acquired the nickname "Little London." But a more accurate name would have been "Little Amsterdam," for the city was designed in the 17th century by Dutch architects, who gave it its extensive network of straight streets divided by canals. There is only one major canal today, but you can explore it on one of the popular "Paddan" sightseeing boats. The boats got their nickname, Swedish for toad, because of their short, squat shape, necessary for negotiating the city's 20 low bridges. You embark at the **Paddan terminal** at Kungsportsplatsen in the city center. *Fare: SEK 33. Departures: May 1–mid-Sept., daily 10–5. (10–6 in July).*

The hub of Gothenburg is **Kungsportsavenyn,** better known as "The Avenue." It is a broad, tree-lined boulevard flanked with elegant shops, restaurants, and sidewalk cafés. During the summer, it has a distinctively Parisian air. The avenue ends at **Götaplatsen Square,** home of the municipal theater, concert hall, and library (where there's an excellent selection of English-language newspapers). Just off the avenue is **Trädgårdsföreningen,** an attractive park with a magnificent Palm House that was built in 1878 and recently restored. *Admission to park: SEK 3 May–Aug., free Sept.–Apr. Admission*

to Palm House: SEK 10. Open May–Aug, daily 7 AM–9 PM;
Sept.–Apr., daily 7 AM–6 PM.

If you're interested in shopping, the best place to go is
Nordstan, a covered complex of shops near the central train station. Many of its businesses participate in the tax-free
shopping service. In the harbor near the Nordstan shopping
complex, you will find the new **Maritime Center.** The center
houses a historic collection of ships, including a destroyer, a
lightship, a trawler, and tugboats. *Admission: SEK 45. Open
June 5–Aug. 28, daily 10–6; May 1–June 4 and Aug. 29–Sept.
25,weekends only 10–6.*

To reach **Jönköping,** the next stop on the journey, take the train
from Gothenburg's central station and change at Falköping.
Jönköping is an attractive town on the southern shores of **Lake
Vättern,** Sweden's largest lake.

Jönköping, which celebrated its 700th anniversary in 1984, is
known as the "matchstick town." For it was here, in the 19th
century, that the match-manufacturing industry got its start.
The **Matchstick Museum,** built on the site of the first factory,
has an exhibition on the development and manufacture of
matches. *Admission: SEK 5. Open May 19–Sept. 12, weekdays
9–7, Sat. 10–noon, and Sun. 3–5. Limited opening times the
rest of the year.*

A few miles from Jönköping is **Riddersberg,** home of the famous
wood sculptor Calle Örnemark. You can get here on the no. 30
bus from the Jönköping train station. **Örnemark's home** boasts
an impressive selection of his works, among them *The Indian
Rope-trick,* at 105 meters (338 feet) the world's tallest sculpture, and *Mutiny on the Bounty,* a re-creation of Captain
Bligh's famous vessel. If you are lucky, the artist himself may
show you around. *Admission: free. Open daily.*

To the southeast of Jönköping lies **Växjö,** Kronoberg County's
main town and the best center for exploring Sweden's Glass
Country. It is also an important sightseeing destination for
hundreds of American visitors each year, for it was from this
area that their Swedish ancestors set sail in the 19th century.
The **Emigrants' House,** located in the town center, tells the story of the migration, during which close to a million Swedes—
one quarter of the entire population—departed for the promised land. The museum exhibits provide a vivid sense of the
rigorous journey, and an archive room and research center allow American visitors to trace their ancestry. On the second
Sunday in August, Växjö celebrates "Minnesota Day." Swedes
and Swedish-Americans come together to commemorate their
common heritage with fun and festivities.

Many of Sweden's most famous glassworks are within easy
reach of Växjö, and it is usually possible to take an organized
sightseeing tour of the facilities. Inquire at the tourist office
for information. The manufacture of Swedish glass dates back
to 1556, when Venetian glassblowers were first invited to the
Swedish court. But it was another 200 years before glass manu-
facturing became a real Swedish industry. The area between
Växjö and Kalmar was chosen for its dense forest, which offered
limitless wood supplies for heating the furnaces. All the major
Swedish glass companies, including **Orrefors** and **Kosta Boda,**
still have their works in this area, and most of them are open to
the public. Most also have factory outlets where you can pick up

near-perfect seconds at bargain prices. *Open Mon.–Sat. 8–3, Sun. 11–4.*

An attractive coastal town, **Kalmar** is dominated by its imposing seaside castle. The town was once known as the "lock and key" of Sweden, for it is situated on the southern frontier of the kingdom, and thus open to constant enemy invasion. The castle's history goes back 800 years, although the present building dates only from the 16th century, when it was rebuilt by King Gustav Vasa. Among other treasures, its museum contains a selection of relics from the royal battleship *Kronan*, which sank off the nearby island of Öland in 1676 during a battle with a combined Danish and Dutch fleet. The wreck, unearthed in 1980, has already yielded some rich archaeological finds, including a cask of 300-year-old brandy. *Admission: SEK 10. Open May–Sept., Mon.–Sat. 10–4, Sun. 1–4. Tours begin once an hour, mid-June–mid-Aug.*

To return to Stockholm from Kalmar, catch the train to Alvesta (the service runs every two hours) and change there for the Stockholm service. Two trains–one day service and one night service–run direct to Stockholm each day. The journey takes about 6½ hours. **Linjeflyg** operates several flights a day to Stockholm from the Kalmar airport, located 5 kilometers (3 miles) from the town center. The trip takes about 50 minutes. For information, phone 0480/58800 or 0480/58811.

Dining and Lodging

For details and price category definitions, *see* Dining and Lodging in Staying in Sweden.

Gothenburg
Dining
★

Johanna. This must rate among Sweden's most celebrated restaurants. It is presided over by its distinguished owner-chef, Crister Svanteson, trained at the famous Paris Tour d'Argent. The entrance is unpretentious, but the interior suggests a London club. It features nouvelle cuisine, with an accent on seafood. *Södra Hamngatan 47, tel. 031/112250. Reservations advised. AE, DC, MC, V. Closed lunchtime, Sun., July, Christmas, and New Year's. Expensive.*

★

Räkan. An informal and popular restaurant, Räkan makes the most of an unusual gimmick. The tables are arranged around a long tank, and if you order shrimp, the house specialty, they arrive at your table in radio-controlled boats you navigate yourself. *Lorensbergsgatan 16, tel. 031/169839. Reservations essential. AE, DC, MC, V. Closed lunchtime on weekends, Christmas, New Year's, and June 22. Expensive (with moderate fixed-price menus also available).*

Bräutigams. Near the tourist office, Bräutigams is an elegant café, ideal for a snack or light meal in a turn-of-the-century atmosphere. The restaurant specializes in homemade cakes and coffee, but light lunches—open-faced sandwiches and salads— are also available. *Östra Hamngatan 50B, tel. 031/136046. AE, DC, MC, V. Closed Christmas Eve. Moderate.*

Lodging
★

Sheraton Hotel and Towers. Opened in 1986, the Sheraton Hotel and Towers is Gothenburg's most modern and spectacular international-style hotel. It features an American atrium-style lobby. There are several restaurants with varying prices, including a popular Italian-style café, open at lunchtime, and a gourmet restaurant. *Södra Hamngatan 59–65, tel. 031/101600. 343 rooms with bath. Facilities: restaurants, health* *club, nightclub, 16 rooms especially equipped for disabled guests. AE, DC, MC, V. Closed Christmas. Very Expensive.*

★ **Eggers.** Dating back to 1859, Eggers has probably more Old World character than any other hotel in the city. It is located near the train station and was probably the last port of call in Sweden for many emigrants to the United States. The rooms feature antique furnishings, and there is a popular brasserie-style restaurant. *Drottningtorget, tel. 031/171570. 77 rooms with bath. AE, DC, MC, V. Closed Christmas. Expensive.*

Liseberg Heden. Not far from the famous Liseberg amusement park, Liseberg Heden is a popular, modern family hotel. It offers a sauna and gourmet restaurant. *Sten Sturegatan, tel. 031/200280. 160 rooms with bath. AE, DC, MC, V. Closed Christmas and New Year's. Moderate.*

Royal. Located in the city center near the train station, the Royal is a small and fairly basic traditional-style hotel. It was built in 1854 and refurbished in the mid-1980s. Only breakfast is served. *Drottninggatan 67, tel. 031/806100. 80 rooms, 55 with shower. AE, DC, MC, V. Closed Christmas and New Year's. Inexpensive.*

Jönköping **Stora Hotellet.** Translated to mean "The Big Hotel," Stora
Lodging Hotellet is an old-fashioned establishment opened in 1861 but recently modernized. It is centrally located, only 93 meters (100 yards) from the train station. Its restaurant serves international cuisine. *Hotellplan, tel. 036/119300. 111 rooms with shower. Facilities: restaurant, sauna, tennis courts. AE, DC, MC, V. Expensive.*

City. City is a medium-size hotel located in the city center. Rooms offer a view of Lake Vättern. Built in the late 1960s, the hotel was recently renovated. *Västra Storgatan 23–25, tel. 036/119280. 70 rooms with bath. Facilities: sauna, car rental, restaurant. AE, DC, MC, V. Closed Christmas. Moderate.*

Dining **Mäster Gudmunds Källare.** Nestled in cozy, 16th-century cellar
★ vaults and only two minutes from the train station, Mäster Gudmunds Källare is a particularly inviting restaurant. Though the cuisine is international, there is one typically Swedish specialty: plank steak. *Kapellgatan 2, tel. 036/112633. Reservations advised. AE, DC, MC, V. Closed Sun. dinner, Christmas, New Year's, June 22. Moderate.*

Kalmar **Stadshotellet.** Located in the city center, Stadshotellet is a fair-
Lodging ly large, Old World hotel. The main building dates from the 19th century. It features a fine restaurant. *Storgatan 14, tel. 0480/15180. 140 rooms with bath. Facilities: restaurant, Jacuzzi, disco. AE, DC, MC, V. Closed Christmas and New Years. Expensive.*

Slottshotellet. Situated in a gracious old town house on a quiet street, Slottshotellet bears no resemblance to a hotel from the outside. But inside, it offers a host of modern facilities. Only breakfast is served. *Slottsvägen 7, tel. 0480/88260. 35 rooms with shower. AE, DC, MC, V. Closed Christmas. Expensive.*

Continental. Located about 93 meters (100 yards) from the train station, the Continental is a fairly basic but comfortable family hotel. Only breakfast is served. *Larmgatan 10, tel. 0480/15140. 40 rooms, most with bath. AE, MC, V. Closed Christmas. Inexpensive.*

Växjö **Sara Statt.** A conveniently located, traditional-style hotel, Sara
Lodging Statt is popular with tour groups. The building dates from the early 19th century, but the rooms themselves are modern, and

the hotel has a resident piano bar and à la carte restaurant. *Kungsgatan 6, tel. 0470/13400. 130 rooms with bath. AE, DC, MC, V. Closed Christmas and Midsummer. Expensive.*

Esplanad. Centrally located, Esplanad is a small, family hotel offering basic amenities; it has been recently renovated. Only breakfast is served. *Norra Esplanaden 21A, tel. 0470/22580. 30 rooms, most with shower. MC, V. Closed Christmas and New Year's. Inexpensive.*

28 Switzerland

Introduction

In Switzerland you'll find coziness under strict control: An electric eye beams open a sliding glass door into a room lined with carved wood, copper, and old-fashioned rafters. That is the paradox of the Swiss, whose two primary aesthetics pitch high-tech urban efficiency against rustic Alpine comfort. Fiercely Protestant, rigorously clean, prompt as their world-renowned watches, the Swiss are a people who drink their eau de vie in firelit *stübli* (cellars)—but rarely on Sunday. Liquors here are measured with scientific precision into glasses marked for one deciliter or two, and the local wines come in sized carafes reminiscent of laboratory beakers. And as for passion—well, the "double" beds have separate mattresses and sheets that tuck firmly down the middle. (Foreigners may request a French—that is, a standard double—bed.) Switzerland is a country of contrasts: While cowbells tinkle on the slopes of Klewenalp, the hum of commerce in Zürich isn't far away. As befurred and bejeweled beauties shop in Geneva, across the country in Appenzell the fight for women's right to vote presses on.

But the trains run on time. In fact, all Swiss public transportation is chillingly precise: Step up to a tram stop, check the posted arrival time, and watch your second hand sweep toward the 12 as the streetcar pulls into view. Sleek, swift national trains may be the best in the world, while the roads and autoroutes are direct, scenic, and pothole-free.

Switzerland comprises most of the attractions of its larger European neighbors—Alpine grandeur, urban sophistication, ancient villages, scintillating ski slopes, and all around artistic excellence. It's the heart of the Reformation, the homeland of William Tell; its cities are full of historic landmarks, its countryside strewn with castles. The varied cuisine reflects an ethnic mix, with three distinct cultures dominating: French in the southwest, Italian in the southeast, and German—a 70% majority—in the north and east.

All these assets have combined to create a major center of tourism, and the Swiss are happy to pave the way. A welcoming if reserved people, most of them well versed in English, they have earned their age-old reputation as fine hosts. Their hotels and inns are famous for cleanliness and efficiency, and the notorious high prices are justified, for the most part, by standards unrivaled in the world.

Before You Go

When to Go There's always something happening—it just depends on what you want. Winter sports begin around Christmas and last usually until mid-April, depending on the state of the snow. The countryside is a delight in spring when the wild flowers are in bloom, and the fall colors rival those in New England. In the Ticino (the Italian-speaking area) and around Lake Geneva (Lac Léman), summer stays late. There is often sparkling weather in September and October, and the popular resorts are less crowded then.

Climate Summer in Switzerland is generally warm and sunny, though the higher you go, of course, the cooler it gets, especially at

Switzerland

1033

night. Winter is cold everywhere: In low-lying areas the weather is frequently damp and overcast, while in the Alps there are often brilliantly clear days, but it is guaranteed to be cold and snowy.

Summer or winter, some areas of Switzerland are prone to an Alpine wind that blows from the south and is known as the Föhn. This gives rise to clear but rather oppressive weather, which the Swiss claim causes headaches. The only exception to the general weather patterns is the Ticino. Here, protected by the Alps, the weather is positively Mediterranean; even in winter, it is significantly warmer than elsewhere.

The following are the average daily maximum and minimum temperatures for Zürich.

Jan.	36F	2C	May	67F	19C	Sept.	69F	20C
	26	−3		47	8		51	11
Feb.	41F	5C	June	73F	23C	Oct.	57F	14C
	28	−2		53	12		43	6
Mar.	51F	10C	July	76F	25C	Nov.	45F	7C
	34	1		56	14		35	2
Apr.	59F	15C	Aug.	75F	24C	Dec.	37F	3C
	40	4		56	13		29	−2

Currency The unit of currency is the Swiss franc (Fr.), divided into 100 rappen (known as centimes in French-speaking areas). There are coins of 5, 10, 20, and 50 rappen, and of 1, 2, and 5 francs. The bills are of 10, 20, 50, 100, 500, and 1,000 francs.

At press time (spring 1989), the Swiss franc stood at 1.58 to the dollar and 2.77 to the pound sterling.

All banks will change your money. Traveler's checks get a better exchange rate than cash. Main airports and train stations have exchange offices (bureaux de change) that are open longer hours than banks and often offer equally good rates of exchange. Most hotels and some restaurants will change money but usually at a far-less-favorable rate. Most major credit cards are generally, though not universally, accepted at hotels, restaurants, and shops.

What It Will Cost High standards of living mean that Switzerland is generally expensive: If it's luxury you're after, you'll pay more for it here than in almost any other European country. You'll find plenty of reasonably priced hotels and restaurants, however, if you look for them. Those who have visited Switzerland before will be surprised at how little prices have changed recently: Inflation has been less than 2% for years.

As in any other European country, the cities are more expensive than the smaller towns. Zürich and Geneva are the priciest; Basel, Bern, and Lugano are also quite expensive. Elsewhere, prices drop appreciably, particularly off the beaten track and in the northeast.

Sample Prices Cup of coffee, 2.20 Fr.; bottle of beer 2.50 Fr., Coca-Cola 2 Fr., ham sandwich 7 Fr.; a 1-mile taxi ride, 5 Fr. (except in Geneva or Zürich).

Customs on Arrival There are two levels of duty-free allowance for visitors to Switzerland. Residents of non-European countries may import 400 cigarettes or 100 cigars or 500 grams of tobacco, plus two liters of alcoholic beverage below 15% and one liter of alcoholic beverage in excess of 15%. Residents of European countries may import 200 cigarettes or 50 cigars or 250 grams of tobacco, plus two liters of alcoholic beverage below 15% and one liter of alcoholic beverage in excess of 15%. These allowances apply only to those aged 17 and above.

There are no restrictions on the import or export of any currency.

Language French is spoken in the southwest, around Lake Geneva, and in the cantons of Fribourg, Neuchâtel, Jura, and Vaud; Italian is spoken in the Ticino, and lilting dialects of German are spoken everywhere else—in more than 70% of the country, in fact. Enthusiasts are trying to revive the last gasps of a Latin dialect called Romansch, as well. English, however, is spoken everywhere. Most public signs are in English as well as in the regional language, and all hotels, restaurants, tourist offices, train stations, banks, and shops will have someone who can speak English fluently.

Getting Around

By Car
Road Conditions
Swiss roads are usually well surfaced but are mostly winding and often mountainous. It's not really possible to achieve high average speeds. When estimating likely travel times, look carefully at the map: There may be only 20 miles between one point and another, but there could also be a mountain pass along the way. There is a well-developed highway network, though some notable gaps still exist in the south along an east-west line, roughly between Lugano and Sion. Under some mountain passes, there are tunnels through which cars can be transported by train while passengers remain in the cars—a system recently improved and encouraged.

A combination of steep or winding routes and hazardous weather conditions means that some roads will be closed in winter. Dial 120 or 163 for bulletins and advance information on road conditions. For tourists, Swiss Radio 1 broadcasts information in English at around 7 PM.

Rules of the Road
Driving is on the right. In built-up areas, the speed limit is 50 kph (30 mph) and on main highways, it's 120 kph (75 mph). On other roads outside built-up areas, the limit is 80 kph (50 mph).

Children under 12 are not permitted to sit in the front seat. Driving with parking lights is prohibited, and lights are compulsory in heavy rain or poor visibility; you *must* use headlights in road tunnels. Always carry your car registration papers and your valid license.

To use the main highways, you must display a disk, which you can buy from the Swiss National Tourist Office before you leave: It costs 30 Fr. Cars rented within Switzerland already have these disks.

Traffic going up a mountain has priority except for postal buses coming down. A sign with a yellow posthorn on a blue background means that postal buses have priority.

In winter, snow chains are advisable—sometimes compulsory. They can be rented in all areas, and snow-chain service stations have signs marked "Service de Chaînes à Neige," or "Schneekettendienst."

If you have an accident, even a minor one, you must call the police.

Parking Parking areas are clearly marked. Parking in public lots normally costs between 0.5 Fr. and 1 Fr. per hour.

Gasoline Lead-free *(sans plomb* or *blei frei)* gas costs 0.89 Fr. per liter, and leaded premium costs 0.95 Fr. per liter. Leaded regular is no longer available.

Breakdowns Assistance is available through the telephone exchange: Ask for "Autohilfe." Roadside repairs and towage are free to holders of international touring documents. The Touring Club Suisse has a 24-hour breakdown service. Useful organizations are the **Automobile Club de Suisse** (ACS) (Wasserwerkegasse 39, Bern) and the **Touring Club Suisse** (TCS) rue Pierre Fatio 9, Geneva, both of which have branches throughout Switzerland.

By Train Switzerland's trains are among Europe's finest. Generally, they are swift (except through the mountains), immaculate, and unnervingly punctual. Don't linger between international connections: The Swiss don't wait for languorous travelers. If you plan to use the trains extensively, get the official timetable *(Offizieles Kursbuch)*, which costs 10 Fr.

Trains described as Inter-City or Express are the fastest, stopping only at principal towns. *Regionalzug* means a local train, often affording the most spectacular views. Meals, snacks, and drinks are provided on most main services. Seat reservations are useful in rush hours and high season, especially on international trains.

Fares There are numerous concessions for visitors. The **Swiss Pass** is the best value, offering unlimited travel on Swiss Federal Railways, postal buses, lake steamers, and the local bus and tram service of 24 cities. It also gives reductions on many privately owned railways, cable cars, and mountain railways. It's available from the Swiss National Tourist Office (SNTO) and from travel agents outside Switzerland. The card is valid for four days (cost 160 Fr.), eight days (195 Fr.), 15 days (235 Fr.), or one month (325 Fr.). Prices are for second-class travel; first-class travel costs about 40% more.

Within some popular tourist areas, **Regional Holiday Season Tickets,** issued for 15 days, give five days free travel by train, postal buses, steamers, and mountain railways, with half fare for the rest of the validity of the card. Central Switzerland offers a similar pass for seven days, with two days free travel. Prices vary widely (38–147 Fr.) depending on the region and period of validity, but they do assure you of savings over full fare. Increasingly popular with tourists is a **Swiss Half-Fare Travel Card,** which allows half-fare travel for 30 days (65 Fr.) or one year (100 Fr.).

The new **Swiss Card,** which can only be purchased outside Switzerland, is valid for 30 days and grants full round-trip travel from your arrival point to any destination in the country, plus a half-price reduction on any further excursions during your stay (125 Fr. first class, 100 Fr. second class). For more information about train travel in Switzerland, get the free *Discover Switzerland* brochure from the SNTO.

By Bus Switzerland's famous yellow postal buses link main cities with villages off the beaten track. Both postal and city buses follow posted schedules to the minute: You can set your watch by them. Free timetables can be picked up at any post office.

The **Swiss Pass** (*see* above) gives unlimited travel on the postal buses. The **Postal Coach Weekly Card** gives unlimited travel within certain regions and can be bought at local post offices.

The postal buses pay special attention to hikers. You can get a free booklet, *The Best River and Lakeside Walks,* from the SNTO. The booklet describes 28 walks you can enjoy by hopping on and off postal buses. Most walks take around three hours.

By Boat Drifting across a Swiss lake and stopping off here and there at picturesque villages nestling by the water makes a relaxing day's excursion, especially if you are lucky enough to catch one of the elegant old paddle steamers. Trips are scheduled on most of the lakes, with increased service in summer. Unlimited travel is free to holders of the **Swiss Pass** (*see* above). Most boats have refreshments, and several have restaurants with excellent food.

By Bicycle Bikes can be rented at all train stations and can be returned to any station. Rates are 14 Fr. per day, or 56 Fr. per week for a conventional bike; tandems cost 30 Fr. per day, 120 Fr. per week. Families, regardless of size, are entitled to a special rate of 36 Fr. per day and 144 Fr. per week for all bikes. Groups get reductions according to the number of bikes involved. Reservations are necessary by 6 PM the day before use by individuals and a week ahead for groups.

Staying in Switzerland

Telephones There is direct dialing to everywhere in Switzerland. For local
Local Calls and international codes, consult the pink pages at the front of the telephone book.

International Calls You can dial most international numbers direct from Switzerland, adding a 00 before the country code. If you want a number that cannot be reached directly, dial 114 for a connection. Dial 191 for international numbers and information. It's cheapest to use the booths in train stations and post offices: Calls made from your hotel cost a great deal more. Rates are lower between 5 PM and 7 PM, after 9 PM, and on weekends. Calls to the United States cost 2.70 Fr. per minute, to the United Kingdom 1.50 Fr. per minute.

Operators and All telephone operators speak English, and there are instruc-
Information tions printed in English in all telephone booths.

Mail All mail goes by air. Current rates to the United States are 1.40
Postal Rates Fr. for letters under 10 grams; 1.70 Fr. for letters under 20 grams; and 1.10 Fr. for postcards. Letters to the United Kingdom under 20 grams cost 0.90 Fr., postcards 0.80 Fr.

Receiving Mail If you're uncertain where you'll be staying, you can have your mail, marked Poste Restante or Postlagernd, sent to any post office in Switzerland. It needs the sender's name and address on the back, and you'll need proof of identity to collect it. You can also have your mail sent to American Express for a small fee, payable when you collect it.

Shopping A 6.2% value-added tax (VAT) on all goods is included in the
VAT Refunds price. Nonresidents may claim a VAT refund either at the time

of purchase, or the shop will send the refund to your home. In order to qualify for a refund, you must sign a form at the time of purchase and present it to Swiss customs on departure.

Bargaining Don't try bargaining: It just doesn't work. As with everything in Switzerland, prices are efficiently controlled.

Opening and Closing Times **Banks.** Banks are open weekdays 8:30–4:30 or 5.
Museums. Museum times vary considerably, though many close on Monday. Check locally.
Shops. Shops are generally open 8–noon and 1:30–6:30. Some will close at 4 on Saturday, and some are closed Monday morning. In cities, many large stores do not close for lunch.

National Holidays January 1, 2 (New Year's); April 13 (Good Friday); April 15, 16 (Easter); May 1* (Labor Day); May 24 (Ascension); June 4 (Pentecost); August 1* (National Day); December 25, 26.
*Not throughout the country.

Dining Options range from luxury establishments to modest cafés, *stübli* (cellars), and restaurants specializing in local cuisine.

Because the Swiss are so good at preparing everyone else's cuisine, it is sometimes said that they have none of their own, but there definitely is a distinct and characteristic Swiss cuisine. Switzerland is the home of great cheeses—Gruyère, Emmentaler, Appenzeller, and Vacherin—which form the basis of many dishes. *Raclette* is cheese fried over a fire; *rösti* are hash browns (fried potatoes) cooked in a fragrant herb cheese, and *fondue* is melted cheese, often flavored with kirsch, into which you dip chunks of bread. Other Swiss specialties to look for are *geschnetzeltes Kalbfleisch*, diced veal in cream sauce, and *stuffato alla luganese*, beef stewed in marsala. A wide variety of Swiss sausages make both filling and inexpensive meals, and in every region the breads are varied and superb.

Mealtimes At home, the main Swiss meal of the day is lunch, with a snack in the evening. Restaurants, however, are open at midday and in the evening; often limited menus are offered all day. Watch for *tagesteller* (fixed-price lunch menus), which enable you to experience the best restaurants without paying high à la carte rates.

Dress Jacket and tie are suggested for restaurants in the Very Expensive and Expensive categories; casual dress is acceptable elsewhere.

Ratings Prices are per person, without wine or coffee, but including tip and taxes. Best bets are indicated by a star ★. At press time, there were 1.58 Swiss francs to the dollar.

Category	Zürich/Geneva	Other Areas
Very Expensive	over 80 Fr.	over 70 Fr.
Expensive	50 Fr.–80 Fr.	40 Fr.–70 Fr.
Moderate	20 Fr.–50Fr.	20 Fr.–40 Fr.
Inexpensive	under 20 Fr.	under 20 Fr.

Credit Cards The following credit card abbreviations are used: AE, American Express; DC, Diners Club; MC, MasterCard; V, Visa.

Lodging Switzerland's accommodations cover a broad range, from the most luxurious hotels to the more economical rooms in private homes. Pick up the *Schweizer Hotelführer* (Swiss Hotel Guide) from the SNTO before you leave home. The guide is free and lists all the members of the Swiss Hotel Association (comprising nearly 90% of the nation's accommodations), and sets out everything you will want to know.

Switzerland is justly proud of its hotels because of their emphasis on fast, friendly service. If you have a complaint, the manager will want to hear it. Equally, if you have a word of praise, go to the top as well. Any special requests, such as one concerning diet, should be made known as soon as you arrive.

Most hotel rooms today have private bath and shower; those that don't are usually considerably cheaper. Single rooms are generally about two-thirds the price of doubles, but this can vary considerably. Remember that the no-nonsense Swiss sleep in separate beds or, at best, a double with separate bedding. If you prefer more sociable arrangements, ask for the rare "matrimonial" or "French" bed. Service charges and taxes are included in the price quoted and the bill you pay. Breakfast is included unless there is a clear notice to the contrary.

All major towns and train stations have hotel-finding services, which sometimes charge a small fee. Local tourist offices will also help.

Hotels Hotels are graded from one star (the lowest) to five stars. Always confirm what you are paying before you register, and check the posted price when you get to your room. Major credit cards are generally accepted, but, again, make sure beforehand.

Two important hotel chains are the Romantik Hotels and Restaurants and Relais & Châteaux, with premises that are generally either in historic houses or in houses that have some special character. Another chain with a good reputation is Ambassador Hotels. The Check-In E and G Hotels is a voluntary group of small hotels, boarding houses, and mountain lodges that offer accommodations at reasonable prices. Details are available from the SNTO, which also offers pamphlets recommending family hotels and a list of hotels and restaurants catering specifically to Jewish travelers.

Country Inns Country inns offer clean, comfortable, and hospitable accommodations, often in areas of great scenic beauty. Many are in the inexpensive category and are a good value.

Rentals Switzerland has literally thousands of furnished châlets. Off-season, per-day prices are around 50 Fr. per person for four sharing a châlet. In peak season, prices would be at least twice as expensive. Deluxe chalets cost much more. For more information, pick up an illustrated brochure from the **Swiss Touring Club** (Wasserwerkgasse 39, 3000 Bern 13) or from **Uto-Ring AG** (Beethovenstr. 24, 8022 Zürich). In the United States, write to **Interhome** (36 Carlos Dr., Fairfield, NJ 07006). In Britain, contact **Interhome** (383 Richmond Rd., Twickenham, Middlesex TW1 2EF).

Ratings Prices are for two people in a double room with bath or shower, including taxes, service charges, and breakfast. Best bets are indicated by a star ★. At press time, there were 1.58 Swiss francs to the dollar.

Category	Zürich/Geneva	Other Areas
Very Expensive	over 300 Fr.	over 250 Fr.
Expensive	200 Fr.–300 Fr.	150 Fr.–250 Fr.
Moderate	100 Fr.–200 Fr.	70 Fr.–150 Fr.
Inexpensive	under 100 Fr.	under 70 Fr.

Credit Cards The following credit card abbreviations are used: AE, American Express; DC, Diners Club; MC, MasterCard; V, Visa.

Tipping Generally speaking, there is no need to tip. With service charges of 15% and with taxes included in your hotel and restaurant bill, no one will expect or demand a tip, though if someone has been particularly helpful, a tip is appreciated. Nonetheless, waiters often leave blank the "tip" and "total" spaces on charge slips; the locals often simply round up to the nearest franc. Elsewhere, give bathroom attendants 1 Fr. and hotel maids 2 Fr. Tip station porters well, especially for excessively heavy luggage. Theater and opera house ushers get 2 Fr. for showing you to your seat and selling you a program.

Zürich

Arriving and Departing

By Plane Kloten (tel. 01/8164081) is Switzerland's most important airport and is among the most sophisticated in the world. Several airlines fly directly to Zürich from major cities in the United States, Canada, and the United Kingdom.

Between the Airport and Downtown Beneath the air terminals, there's a train station with an efficient, direct service into the Hauptbahnhof (main station) in the center of Zürich. Fast trains run every 20 minutes, and the trip takes about 10 minutes. The fare is 4.20 Fr. and the ticket office is in the airport. There are express trains to most Swiss cities at least every hour. Trains run from 6 AM to midnight.

Taxis are very expensive: about 40 Fr. into town. Some hotels provide their own bus service. Cars can be rented at the airport.

By Bus All bus services to Zürich will drop you at the Hauptbahnhof.

By Car There are direct highways from the border crossings with France, Germany, and Italy. The German frontier is the nearest.

Getting Around

Although Zürich is Switzerland's largest city, it has a population of 362,000 and is not large by European standards. That's one of its nicest features: You can explore it comfortably on foot. As in most cities, however, it's a good idea to take a guided bus tour first to get your bearings, then go alone at your leisure (*see* Guided Tours).

By Bus and Streetcar The city transit network is excellent. VBZ Züri-Line (Zürich Public Transport) buses run from 5:30 AM to midnight, every six minutes on all routes at peak hours, and about every 12 minutes at other times. Before you board the bus, you must buy your ticket from the automatic vending machines (instructions appear in English) found at every stop. A money-saving ticket for all travel for 24 hours is a good buy at 5 Fr. Free route plans are available from VBZ offices.

By Taxi Taxis are very expensive and should be avoided unless you have no other means of getting around.

Important Addresses and Numbers

Tourist Information The tourist office is located at Bahnhofplatz 15 (Main Station), tel. 01/2114000. Open Mar.–Oct., weekdays 8 AM–10 PM, weekends 8 AM–8:30 PM; Nov.–Feb., Mon.–Thurs. 8–8, Fri. 8 AM–10 PM, weekends 9–6.

Consulates U.S.: Zollickerstr. 141, tel. 01/552566. U.K.: Dufourstr. 56, tel. 01/471520.

Emergencies **Police:** tel. 117. **Ambulance:** tel. 01/3611661. **Doctor:** tel. 01/474700; poisoning cases, 01/2515151. **Dentist:** tel. 01/474700. **Pharmacy: Bellevue,** Theaterstr. 14, tel. 01/2424411, offers an all-night service.

English Bookstores **Payot:** Bahnhofstr. 9. **Travel Book Shop:** Rindermarkt 20.

Travel Agencies **American Express:** Bahnhofstr. 20, tel. 01/2118370. **Kuoni:** Bahnhofplatz 7, tel. 01/2213411. **Thomas Cook:** 22 Talacker, Sihlporteplatz, tel. 01/2118710.

Guided Tours

Orientation Tours There are four bus tours available. The daily "Sights of Zürich" tour (19 Fr. adults, 9.5 Fr. children) gives a good general idea of the city in two hours. "In and Around Zürich" goes farther and includes an aerial cableway trip to Felsenegg. This is also a daily tour that takes 2½ hours; it costs 25 Fr. adults, 12.50 Fr. children. "Goldtimer," a one-hour tour of the center of Zürich by an old tram, operates between May and October (14 Fr. adults, 10 Fr. students, 7 Fr. children). Another May-to-October tour is "Zürich by Night," which takes in everything from folklore to striptease in 3½ hours (55 Fr.). All tours start from the main station. Contact the tourist office for reservations.

Special-Interest Tours If you have a special interest, inquire at the tourist office for details about available tours.

Walking Tours From June to October, conducted walking tours (10 Fr.) start from the tourist office and take roughly 2½ hours. Check times at the tourist office.

Excursions There are many bus excursions to other areas, such as the Bernese Oberland, St. Gotthard, the Ticino, Lucerne, and Geneva. Since these depend on the season and weather, it's best to book them after you arrive and can check with the tourist office.

Exploring Zürich

Zürich is not at all what you'd expect. Stroll around on a fine spring day and you'll ask yourself if this can really be one of the great business centers of the world: The lake glistening and blue in the sun, the sidewalk cafés, swans gliding in to land on the river, the hushed and haunted old squares of medieval guildhouses, and elegant shops. There's not a gnome (a mocking nickname for a Swiss banker) in sight, not a worried business frown to be seen. The point is that for all its economic importance, Zürich is a place where people enjoy life. Hard-working, inventive, serious when need be, the Swiss love the good things in life, and they have the money to enjoy them.

Zürich started as a Roman customs post on the Lindenhof over-looking the river Limmat. That was in 15 BC. Its growth really began around the 10th century AD. It became a free imperial city in 1336, a center of the Reformation in 1519, then gradually as-sumed commercial importance in the 19th century. Today there is peace as well as prosperity here, and since Zürich is so compact, you can take in its variety in a morning's stroll.

Numbers in the margin correspond with points of interest on the Zürich map.

Collect your map (it's essential) from the tourist office (Bahnhofplatz 15), then start your walk from the nearby

❶ **Bahnhofstrasse,** famous for its shops and cafés and as the center of the banking network, though you'd be unlikely to guess it. Take Rennweg on your left, and then turn left again into the Fortunagasse, a quaint medieval street leading to the

❷ **Lindenhof,** a square where there are remains of Zürich's Ro-man origins. The fountain commemorates the ingenuity of the Zürich women who, when the city was besieged by the Hapsburgs in 1292, donned armor and marched around the walls. The invaders thought they were reinforcements and beat a hasty retreat.

An alley on the right leads to a picturesque square dating from

❸ the Middle Ages, with the **Peterskirche,** Zürich's oldest parish church (13th century), which also happens to have the largest clock face in Europe. Walk down to the river and follow it to the

❹ 13th century **Fraumünster** (church), which has modern stained-glass windows by Chagall. There are two handsome guildhalls nearby: the **Zunfthaus zur Waag** hall of the linen weavers (Münsterhof 8), built in 1637, and the **Zunfthaus zur Meise** (Münsterhof 20), built in the 18th century for the wine mer-chants.

Time Out Head away from the river to the Bahnhofstrasse, then to Paradeplatz to visit **Sprüngli,** the famous café/sweets shop where glossy Zürichers gather to see and be seen. The choco-late truffles are sinfully rich.

Continue along Bahnhofstrasse to Bürkliplatz and cross the **Quai Bridge** to take in the impressive views of the lake and town. Now, on the other side of the river, head left to the

❺ **Wasserkirche** (Water Church), dating from the 15th century, a lovely example of late-Gothic architecture. It is attached to the **Helmhaus,** originally an 18th-century cloth market.

❻ Now turn right toward the **Grossmünster** church, which dates from the 11th century. In the 3rd century AD, St. Felix and his sister Regula were martyred by the Romans. Legend declares that having been beheaded, they then walked up the hill carrying their heads and collapsed on the spot where the Grossmünster now stands. On the south tower you can see a statue of Charle-magne (768–814), emperor of the West. In the 16th century, the Zürich reformer Huldrych Zwingli preached sermons here that were so threatening in their promise of fire and brimstone that Martin Luther himself was scared.

Zürich

Main Attractions
Bahnhofstrasse, 1
Fraumünster, 4
Grossmünster, 6
Limmatquai, 7
Lindenhof, 2
Niederdorf, 9
Old Town, 8
Peterskirche, 3
Schweizerisches
Landesmuseum, 10
Wasserkirche, 5

Other Attractions
Centre Le
Corbusier, 18
Federal Institute of
Technology, 11
Opernhaus, 14
Rathaus, 16
Stadthaus, 17
University of
Zürich, 12
Wohnmuseum, 15
Zoo, 13

❼ Back at the river on the **Limmatquai** are some of Zürich's most enchanting old buildings. Today most of them are restaurants. In the **Haus zum Ruden,** a 13th-century noblemen's hall, you eat under a 300-year-old wooden ceiling. Other notable buildings here are the **Zunfthaus zur Saffran** (built in 1723 for haberdashers) and the **Zunfthaus zur Zimmerleuten** (built in 1708 for carpenters). The 17th-century baroque **Rathaus** (Town Hall) is nearby.

❽ Turn right into the **Old Town,** and you enter a maze of fascinating medieval streets where time seems to have stood still. The Rindermarkt, Napfplatz, and Kirchgasse all have their charming old houses. Just wander around at will.

❾ Head back to the river through **Niederdorf** (Zürich's nightlife district), and cross the bridge to the Hauptbahnhof. On the
❿ northern edge of the Hauptbahnhof, go to the **Schweizerisches Landesmuseum,** housed in a curious 19th-century building, for a look at Swiss history. There are fascinating pre-Romanesque and Romanesque church art, glass paintings from the 15th to 17th centuries, splendid ceramic stoves, gold and silver from Celtic times, and weapons from many ages. *Museumstr. 2, tel. 01/2211010. Admission: free. Open Tues.–Sun. 10–5.*

Off the Beaten Track

The scheduled services of the steamers from the Bürkliplatz stop at several attractive villages on the lake shore. **Rapperswil** has a romantic-looking castle dating from the 12th century and an attractive Gothic Rathaus (town hall). This village also has many good fish restaurants. The **Forchbahn** train line from Stadelhofen station takes you to Forch with long views and good walking. A round-trip ticket costs 6.40 Fr. A 25-minute ride on the Uetlibergbahn from Selnau station provides a panoramic view of the city, lake, and far-off Alps. A round-trip ticket costs 8 Fr.

Shopping

Gift Ideas Typical Swiss products, all of the highest quality, include watches (not as expensive as you'd expect), clocks, jewelry, music boxes, embroidered goods, wood carvings, and the famous multiblade Swiss army pocket knife.

Shopping Districts The **Bahnhofstrasse** is as fine a shopping street as you'd come upon in Paris. Here you'll find **Jelmoli** (Seidengasse 1), Switzerland's largest department store, carrying a wide range of tasteful Swiss goods. **Heimatwerk** (Bahnhofstr. 2) specializes in handmade Swiss crafts, all of excellent quality. For high fashion, go to **Madame** (Bahnhofstr. 63), and for the finest porcelain, glass, and silverware, visit **Sequin-Dormann** (Bahnhofstr. 69a). If you have a sweet tooth, stock up on truffles at **Sprüngli** (Paradeplatz).

In the **Old Town** and off the **Limmatquai,** you'll find boutiques, antiques shops, bookstores, and galleries in picturesque byways. The **Löwenstrasse** has such a diversity of shops it's been nicknamed "Shopville." The **Langstrasse** is another good shopping area and often has slightly lower prices.

Food and Flea Markets In many parts of town, there are lively markets where fruit, vegetables, and flowers are competitively priced. The best are at **Bürkliplatz, Helvetiaplatz, Milkbuckstrasse,** and **Marktplatz** (on the way to the airport). Get there early for the best buys. *Open Tues. 6 AM–11 AM.*

Bürklianlage is a flea market open May through October, and a curio market is held at **Rosenhof** every Thursday between April and Christmas.

Dining

You're likely to be served seconds in Zürich's generous restaurants, where the rest of your Rösti and *Geschnetzeltes KalbFleisch nach Zürcher Art* (veal pieces in mushroom-cream sauce) simmer in copper pans by your table while you relish the hefty first portion. This is a Germanic city, after all, though its status as a minor world capital means that most international cuisines are represented as well. But brace yourself: The cash register rings portentiously when the waiter places your order. For details and price category definitions, *see* Dining in Staying in Switzerland.

Very Expensive **Agnes Amberg.** Every meal is a dégustation, a parade of exquisitely presented nouvelle delights. Though the decor may seem excessive, the service is unpretentious and usually impeccable. *Hottingerstr. 5, tel. 01/252626. Reservations required. AE, DC, MC, V.*

★ **Chez Max.** Owner Max Kehl deserves his reputation as one of the leading chefs of Switzerland, combining French and Japanese techniques to create unique, imaginative nouvelle dishes. Just over three kilometers (two miles) out of the city on the road to Rapperswil, it's worth the trip. *Seestr. 53, Zollikon, tel. 01/3918877. Reservations required. AE, DC, MC, V. Closed three weeks in July–Aug.*

Piccola Accademia. This extraordinary restaurant serves world-class Italian cuisine to a loyal clientele of theater and arts personalities, whose photos and grateful testimonies line the walls. *Rotwandstr. 48, tel. 01/2416243. Reservations required. DC, MC, V.*

Expensive **Kronenhalle.** Owned by the Zumsteg family (silk barons and
★ patrons of the arts) for most of this century, this lively, genial old dining hall doubles as a gallery, its wainscoted walls crowded with personalized works by Picasso, Matisse, Bonnard, and Chagall. The hefty French cuisine with a local accent includes duck, trout, and lamb specialties. *Le tout* Zürich eats here, and drinks prize-winning cocktails hip-to-hip in the bar. *Raemistr. 4, tel. 01/2510256. Reservations required. AE, DC, MC, V.*

Zunfthaus zur Schmiden. Of Zürich's several grand old guildhouses converted to restaurants, this 570-year-old blacksmith's hall is the loveliest, all burnished wood and leaded glass. Its typical menu of veal dishes and Rösti is also the least expensive. *Marktgasse 20, tel. 01/2515287. Reservations advised. AE, DC, MC, V.*

Zunfthaus zur Waag. Another, airier guildhall, its woodwork whitewashed, its windows looking out to the Fraumünster, this one offers generous portions of fine Swiss specialties, though rather formally served. *Münsterhof 8, tel. 01/2110730. Reservations advised. AE, DC, MC, V.*

Moderate **Bierhalle Kropf.** Under the giant boar's head, businessmen,
★ workers, and shoppers crowd shared tables to feast on gener-

ous hot dishes and a great selection of sausages. The *Leber-knodli* (liver dumplings) are terrific. The florid murals and woodwork of this establishment (just 101 years old), have been recently restored. *Gassen 16, tel. 01/2211805. Reservations advised. AE, DC, MC, V.*

Zeughauskeller. Built as an arsenal in 1487, this enormous stone-and-beam hall offers hearty meat platters and a variety of beers and wines in comfortable and friendly chaos. It's great for families. *Bahnhofstr. 28a, off Paradeplatz, tel. 01/2112690. Reservations advised. No credit cards.*

Inexpensive **Haupbahnhof.** Three courses for under 20 Fr. are hard to find in this pricey city, but smart Zürichers with big appetites heap their plates at the cafeteria here—when they don't treat themselves at the slicker restaurants under the same enormous roof. *Hauptbahnhof, tel. 01/2111510. No reservations. AE, DC, MC, V.*

Migros. All across Zürich you'll find branches of this popular supermarket chain, their restaurants full of savvy locals in search of large portions and low prices. *No wine or liquor. No reservations. No credit cards.*

Lodging

Zürich has an enormous range of hotels, from some of the most chic and prestigious in the country to modest guest houses. Standards of cleanliness and comfort, even at the lowest end of the scale, are high. Because this is Switzerland, prices tend to be higher than anywhere else in Europe, but you can be sure that you will get what you pay for: Quality and good service are guaranteed. For details and price category definitions, *see* Lodging in Staying in Switzerland.

Very Expensive **Baur Au Lac.** Have a pedicure and borrow the Rolls at this most
★ magnificent of European luxury hotels, owned by the same family since 1844. The rooms are posh but discreet; the sumptuous lounges and restaurants teem with the rich and famous. The staff of 300 is courteous but rarely stuffy. It's steps from the Bahnhofstrasse and lake, with a private park and alpine views. *Talstrasse 1, tel. 01/2211650. 156 rooms with bath. Facilities: restaurants, grillroom, American bar, disco, summer restaurant and terrace bar, beauty shop, Rolls-Royce limo service, parking. AE, DC, MC, V.*

Dolder Grand. High on the wooded hill over Zürich, this sprawling Victorian fantasy-palace provides quarters for bodyguards, nannies, and harems. The public areas are splendid, the recently decorated rooms spacious, and the views magnificent, whether from the original structure or the sleek new wing. *Kurhausstr. 65, tel. 01/2516231. 207 rooms with bath. Facilities: swimming pool with wave machine, 9-hole golf course, tennis courts, ice-skating rink, French restaurant, terrace, bar, garage. AE, DC, MC, V.*

Expensive **Neues Schloss.** Step off the busy street and past the cold, modern exterior and you'll find a warm welcome. This fine establishment is run by the Seiler family, experienced Swiss hoteliers who specialize in comfort, discretion, and personal service. It's close to the main shopping district. *Stockerstr. 17, tel. 01/2016550. 59 rooms with bath. Facilities: restaurant. AE, DC, MC, V.*

★ **Zum Storchen.** In a stunning central location, tucked between

Fraumünster and St. Peter on the gull-studded banks of the Limmat, this airy 600-year-old structure houses an impeccable modern hotel. It has warmly appointed rooms, some with French windows that open over the water. *Weinplatz 2, tel. 01/2115510. 77 rooms with bath. Facilities: restaurant, terrace café, two bars. AE, DC, MC, V.*

Moderate **Chesa Rustica.** It's small and central, modern but warmed with dark wood and rustic antiques, and has an ideal, if noisy, location on the edge of the Old Town overlooking the Limmat. *Limmatquai 70, tel. 01/2519291. 23 rooms with bath. Facilities: restaurant, fondue keller, bar. AE, DC, MC, V.*

Limmathof. Austere and dormlike but ideally placed, it's minutes from the bahnhof on the edge of the Niederdorf nightlife district. Despite the no-frills decor, all rooms have tile baths. It's excellent value. *Limmatquai 142, tel. 01/474220. 65 rooms with ath. Facilities: restaurant. No credit cards.*

★ **Sonnenberg.** If you're traveling by car and want to avoid the urban rush, escape to this hillside refuge east of town. There are breathtaking views of the city, lake, and mountains, and the wood, stone, and beam decor encourage the resort atmosphere. Train travelers take tram no. 3 or no. 8 to Klusplatz, then walk 10 minutes uphill—or catch a cab. *Aurorastr. 98, tel. 01/470047. 35 rooms with bath. Facilities: restaurant, summer dining pavilion. AE, DC, MC, V.*

Inexpensive **Linde Oberstrasse.** Near the university, in a sterile residential area, this small hotel, built as a guildhouse in 1628, offers a handful of modest but agreeable rooms. The baths are down the hall, but you get sink, TV, and minibar to compensate. There's a tram to the city center that stops out front. *Universitaetsstr. 91, tel. 01/3262109. 10 rooms, none with bath. Restaurant. AE, DC, MC, V.*

Rothaus. It's a trade-off: You get a private shower at bargain rates, but there's a strip joint on the ground floor. (Avoid it by using the side entrance.) It's functional and tidy, with modern baths, and has a great Niederdorf location. Breakfast is extra. *Marktgasse 14, tel. 01/2521530. 50 rooms, some with bath/shower. Facilities: restaurant. AE, DC, MC, V.*

★ **Vorderer Sternen.** On the edge of the old town and near the lake, this plain but adequate establishment takes in the bustle (and noise) of the city. It's steps from the opera house, theaters, art galleries, cinemas, and a shopping area; it's also close to a tram junction. It serves breakfast, but there's no restaurant; with the money you save, treat yourself at the nearby Kronenhalle. *Theaterstr. 22, tel. 01/2514949. 15 rooms, none with bath. AE, DC, MC, V.*

The Arts

Pick up *Zürich News*, published each week by the tourist office, to check what's on. Ticket reservations can be made through the **Billetzentrale**. *Werdmühleplatz, tel. 01/2212283. Open weekdays 10–6:30, Sat. 10–2.*

The **Zürich Tonhalle Orchestra** (Gotthardstr. 5, tel. 01/2011580) ranks among Europe's best. The **Opernhaus** (Schillerstr., tel. 01/2516922) is renowned for its adventurous opera, operetta, and ballet productions. The **Schauspielhaus** (Ramistr. 34, tel. 01/2511111) is one of the finest German-speaking theaters in the world. Zurich has 40 movie theaters, with English-language films appearing regularly. The city boasts many art galleries of interest. Among them is **Sammlung E. G. Buhrle** (Zollikerstr. 172, tel. 01/550086), which specializes in 19th-century French masters. Take streetcar no. 2 or no. 4. Open Tues. and Fri. 2–5, and the first Fri. of each month, 2–8.

Entertainment and Nightlife

Zürich has a lively nightlife scene, mostly centered in the Niederdorf, parallel to the Limmat, across from the Hauptbahnhof. Many spots are short-lived, so check in advance. Informal dress is acceptable in most places, but again, check to make sure. The hotel porter is a good source of information.

Nightclubs Traditional nightclub atmosphere is to be found at the **Terrasse,** Limmatquai 3 (tel. 01/2511074); **Red House** (Marktgasse 17, tel. 01/2521110); **Le Privé,** Helvetiaplatz, tel. 01/2416487; **Moulin Rouge,** Mühlegasse 14 (tel. 01/690730); and **Bali-Hari** (Langstr. 20, tel. 01/2415985). All these nightclubs feature striptease shows.

Discos There's disco-dancing at the **Birdwatchers' Club** (Schutzengasse 16, tel. 01/2115058); **City 5 (Limmatstr. 195, tel. 01/422270); Club of Clubs** (Nova Park Hotel, Badenstr., tel. 01/4912222); **Evergreen** (Fraumünsterstr. 14, tel. 01/2115750); **Mascotte** (Bellevue/Theaterstr. 10, tel. 01/2524481); and **Le Petit Prince** (Bleicherweg 21, tel. 01/2011739).

Jazz For jazz, try the **Casa Bar** (Münstergasse 30, tel. 01/472020).

Excursion from Zürich: Liechtenstein

For an international day trip out of Zürich, you can just dip a toe into tiny Liechtenstein: There isn't room for much more. Just 80 kilometers (50 miles) southeast on the Austrian border, this miniature principality covers a scant 158 square kilometers (61 square miles). An independent nation since 1719, Liechtenstein is united with Switzerland in a customs union, which means they share trains, currency, and diplomats—but not stamps, which is why collectors prize the local releases. It's easiest to get there by car, as Liechtenstein is so small that Swiss trains pass through without stopping. If you're using a train pass, ride to Sargans or Buchs, and take a postbus across the border to the Liechtenstein capital of Vaduz.

Tourist Information

The principal tourist office in Liechtenstein is at Städtle 38, Box 139, FL 9490, Vaduz, tel. 075/21443. It's open weekdays 8–noon and 1:30–5.

Exploring Liechtenstein

Green and mountainous, lined with vineyards along the Rhine, greater Liechtenstein is best seen by car. But if you're on foot, you won't be stuck: The postbuses are prompt and take you everywhere at a scenic snail's pace.

In fairy-tale **Vaduz,** Prince Franz Josef II still lives in **Vaduz Castle,** a massive 16th-century fortress perched high on the cliff over the city. Only honored guests of the prince tour the interior, but its exterior and the views from the grounds are worth the climb. In the modern center of town, head for the tourist information office to have your passport stamped with the Liechtenstein crown. Upstairs, the **Prince's Art Gallery and the State Art Collection** feature Flemish masters. *Städtle 37, tel. 075/22341. Admission: 3 Fr. adults, 1.5 Fr. children. Open Apr.–Oct., daily 10:30–noon and 1:30–5:30; Nov.–Mar., daily 10–noon and 2–5:30.*

On the same floor, the **Postage Stamp Museum** attracts philatelists from all over the world to see the 300 frames of beautifully designed—and relatively rare—stamps. Place subscriptions here for future first-day covers. *Städtle 37, tel. 075/66259. Admission: free. Open daily 10–noon and 2–6.*

Next, move on to the **Liechtenstein National Museum,** which houses historical artifacts, church carvings, ancient coins, and arms from the prince's collection. *Städtle 43, tel. 075/22310. Admission: 2 Fr. Open May–Oct., daily 10–noon and 1:30–5:30; Nov.–Mar., Tues.–Sun. 2–5:30.*

In **Schaan,** just north of Vaduz, visit the Roman excavations and the parish church built on the foundations of a Roman fort. Or drive up to the chalets of picturesque **Triesen** for spectacular views of the Rhine Valley. Higher still, **Malbun** is a sun-drenched ski bowl with magnificent slopes and a comfortable family ambience.

Dining

For details and price category definitions, *see* Dining in Staying in Switzerland.

Very Expensive **Real.** Here you'll find rich, old-style Austrian-French cuisine in all its buttery glory, prepared by unpretentious chef/owner Felix Real and his son, Martin. There's game, seafood, soufflés, and an extraordinary wine list. *Städtle 21, Vaduz, tel. 075/22222. Reservations advised. AE, DC, MC, V.*

Inexpensive **Café Wolf.** For a hearty daily special, light sandwiches, enormous pastries, rich hot chocolate, and frothy Vienna-roast coffee, join the mobs of locals in this pleasant, pristine café. *Städtle 29, Vaduz, tel. 075/22818. AE, DC, MC, V.*

★ **Wirthschaft zum Lowen.** Though there's plenty of French, Swiss, and Austrian influence, Liechtenstein has a cuisine of its own, and this is the place to try it. In a wood-shingled farmhouse on the Austrian border, the friendly Biedermann family serves tender homemade *Schwartenmagen* (the pressed pork-mold unfortunately known as headcheese in English), pungent *Sauerkase* (sour cheese), and *Kaseknöpfli* (cheese dumplings), plus lovely meats and the local crusty, chewy bread. Try the local wines and the automatic snuff machine. *Schellenberg, tel. 075/31162. Reservations advised. V.*

Lodging

For details and price category definitions, *see* Lodging in Staying in Switzerland.

Expensive **Park-Hotel Sonnenhof.** A garden oasis commanding a superb view over the valley and mountains beyond, this hillside retreat offers discreet luxury minutes from downtown Vaduz. It has an excellent restaurant exclusive to guests. *Mareestr. 29, tel. 075/ 21192. 29 rooms with bath. Facilities: indoor pool, sauna. AE, DC, MC, V.*

Inexpensive **Alpenhotel.** Well above the mists of the Rhine in sunny Malbun, this 82-year-old chalet has been remodeled and a modern wing added. The old rooms are small and cozy; the higher-priced new rooms modern and spare. The Vögeli family's welcoming smiles and good food have made it a Liechtenstein institution. *Tel. 075/21181. 25 rooms with bath. Facilities: indoor pool. AE, DC.*

Geneva

Arriving and Departing

By Plane Cointrin (tel. 022/7993111), Geneva's airport, is served by several airlines that fly directly to the city from New York, Toronto, or London. Check with individual airlines for their schedules.

Between the Airport and Downtown Cointrin has a direct rail link with Cornavin, the city's main train station, which is located in the center of town. Trains run about every 10 minutes from 5:30 AM to midnight. The trip takes about six minutes, and the fare is 4.50 Fr.

There is regular bus service from the airport to the center of Geneva. The bus takes about 20 minutes, and the fare is 1.50 Fr. Some hotels have their own bus service.

Taxis, though plentiful, are very expensive, charging at least 20 Fr. to the city center.

By Train All services—domestic and international—use Cornavin Station in the center of the city. For information, dial 022/7316450.

By Bus Buses generally arrive at and depart from the bus station at place Dorcière, behind the English church, in the city center.

By Car Since Geneva sits on France's doorstep, entry from France, just a few minutes away, is the most accessible. Or enter from the north, via Lausanne.

Getting Around

By Bus and Streetcar There are scheduled services by local buses and trains every few minutes on all routes. Before you board, you must buy your ticket from the machines at the stops (they have English instructions). Save money and buy a ticket covering six trips for 8 Fr. If you have a **Swiss Pass,** you travel free (*see* Getting Around Switzerland By Train).

By Taxi Taxis are extremely expensive; use them only if there's no alternative. There is a 5 Fr. minimum charge per passenger just to get into the cab.

Guided Tours

Orientation Tours Bus tours around Geneva are operated by **Key Tours** (tel. 022/ 7314140). They leave from the bus station in place Dorcière, behind the English church, at 9:30, 10, 2, and 2:30. These tours last about two hours and cost 19 Fr.

Special-Interest Tours The United Nations organizes tours around the Palais des Nations. Enter by the Pregny Gate in the avenue de la Paix. Tours, lasting about an hour, are given regularly from September to June, 10–noon and 2–4; July and August, 9–noon and 2–6. They cost 5 Fr.

The tourist office will provide you with an audio-guided tour (in English) of the Old Town that covers 26 points of interest, complete with map, cassette, and player; rental: 7 Fr.

Excursions There are bus excursions from Geneva to Lausanne, Montreux, the Mont Blanc area, the Jura, and the Bernese Oberland. They vary considerably according to the weather and time of year, so inquire locally.

Boat excursions vary for the same reasons. When the weather is good, take one of the delightful day-long trips that stop at some of the waterside villages on the vineyard-fringed lake; some trips also pass by or stop at the 13th-century Château de Chillon, inspiration of Byron's *The Prisoner of Chillon*. Full details are available from **Mouettes Genevoises** (tel. 022/7322944); **Swiss Boat** (tel. 022/7324747); **Compagnie de Navigation** (tel. 022/212521); or from the tourist office. Boat trips vary in cost and duration, with some as low as 6 Fr. and lasting half an hour.

Tourist Information

Cornavin Station, tel. 022/455200. Open July–Sept., daily 8 AM –10 PM; Oct.–June, weekdays 8:15–7:30, Sat. 9–6.

Exploring Geneva

Draped at the foot of the Juras and the Alps on the westernmost tip of Lac Léman (as the natives know it), Geneva is the most cosmopolitan and graceful of Swiss cities and the stronghold of the French-speaking territory. Just a stone's throw from the French border and 160 kilometers (100 miles) or so from Lyon, its grand mansarded mansions stand guard beside the river Rhône, where yachts bob, gulls dive, and Rolls-Royces purr beside manicured promenades. The combination of Swiss efficiency and French savoir faire gives the city a chic polish, and the infusion of international blood from the United Nations adds a heterogeneity rare in a population of only 160,000.

Headquarters of the World Health Organization and the International Red Cross, Geneva has always been a city of humanity and enlightenment, offering refuge to writers Voltaire, Hugo, Dumas, Balzac, and Stendhal as well as religious reformers Calvin and Knox. Byron, Shelley, Wagner, and Liszt all fled from scandals to Geneva's sheltering arms.

A Roman seat for 500 years (from 120 BC), then home to early Burgundians, Geneva flourished under bishop-princes into the 11th century, fending off the greedy dukes of Savoy in conflicts that lasted into the 17th century. Under the guiding fervor of Calvin, Geneva shunned Catholicism for Protestant reforms. In 1798 it fell to the French, but joined the Swiss Confederation as a canton in 1815, shortly after Napoleon's defeat. The French accent remains nonetheless.

Numbers in the margin correspond with points of interest on the Geneva map.

① Start your walk from Gare de Cornavin (Cornavin Station) and head down the rue du Mont Blanc to the **Pont du Mont Blanc,** which spans the last gasp of the Rhône as it pours into the open waters of Lac Léman. From the middle of the bridge (if it's clear) you can see the snowy peak of Mont Blanc itself, and from March to October you'll have a fine view of the **Jet D'Eau,** Europe's highest fountain, gushing 132 meters (425 feet) into the air.

② Back at the foot of the bridge, turn right onto quai du Mont Blanc to reach the **Monument Brunswick,** the high-Victorian tomb of a duke of Brunswick who left his fortune to Geneva in 1873. Just north are the city's grandest hotels, overlooking a manicured garden walk and the embarkation points for excursion boats. If you continue north some distance through elegant parks and turn inland on the avenue de la Paix, you'll reach the **③** enormous **International Complex,** home of the United Nations. (You also can reach it by bus no. 8 or F from the train station. For guided tour information, *see* Special-Interest tours.)

Or turn left from the Pont du Mont Blanc and walk down the elegant quai des Bergues. In the center of the Rhône is **④** **Rousseau Island,** with a statue of the Swiss-born philosopher. **⑤** Turn left onto the **Pont de l'Ile,** where the tall Tour de l'Ile, once a medieval prison, houses the tourist office. Turn left again and cross the place Bel-Air, the center of the business and banking **⑥** district, and follow the rue de la Corraterie to the **place Neuve.** Here you see the **Grand Théâtre,** which hosts opera, ballet, and sometimes the Orchestre de la Suisse Romande (they also perform at nearby Victoria Hall), and the **Conservatoire de Musique.** Also at this address is the **Musée Rath,** with top-notch temporary exhibitions *Tel. 022/285616. Admission: 5 Fr. Open Tues.–Sun. 10–noon; also Wed. evening 8–10).*

⑦ Above the ancient ramparts on your left are some of the wealthiest old homes in Geneva. Enter the gated park before you, the promenade de Bastion, site of the university, and keep left until you see the famous **Reformation Monument,** which pays homage to such Protestant pioneers as Bèze, Calvin, Farel, and Knox. Take the park exit just beyond the monument and turn left on the rue St-Leger, winding up into the **Vieille Ville,** or Old Town.

⑧ When you reach the ancient place Bourg-de-Four, once a Roman forum, you can turn right on rue des Chaudronniers and head for the **Musée d'Art et Histoire,** with its fine collection of paintings, sculpture, and archeological relics. *2 rue Charles-Galland, tel. 022/290011. Admission: free. Open Tues.–Sun. 10–5.*

⑨ Just beyond are the spiraling cupolas of the **Russian church, ⑩** and the **Bauer Collection** of Oriental arts. *8 rue Munier-Romilly, tel. 461729. Admission: 3 Fr. Open Tues.–Sun. 2–6.*

⑪ Alternatively, from the place Bourg-de-Four, head left up any number of narrow streets and stairs toward the **Cathédrale St-Pierre,** with its schizophrenic mix of Classical and Gothic styles. Under its nave (entrance outside) is concealed one of the biggest archeological digs in Europe, a massive excavation of the cathedral's early Christian roots, now restored as a stunning maze of backlit walkways over mosaics, baptisteries, and ancient foundations. *Admission: 5 Fr. Open Tues.–Sun. 10–1 and 2–6.*

⑫ Opposite the cathedral is the 16th-century **Hôtel de Ville,** where in 1864, in the Alabama Hall, the Geneva Convention was signed by 16 countries, laying the foundations for the International Red Cross. In the same hall, in 1872, a court of arbitration settled lingering disputes between Great Britain and the United States over British support for Confederate ships in the American Civil War. *Individual visits by request. Guided group tours by advance arrangement, tel. 22/272209.*

The winding, cobbled streets leading from the cathedral down to the modern city are lined with antique shops, galleries, and unique but often expensive boutiques. The medieval Grand Rue is the oldest in Geneva; the rue Hôtel de Ville features lovely 17th-century homes; and the rue Calvin has noble mansions of the 18th century (no. 11 is on the site of Calvin's house). No. 6
⑬ on the rue du Puits-St-Pierre is the **Maison Tavel,** the oldest building in town and home of an intimate re-creation of daily life through urban history. *Admission: free. Open Tues.–Sun. 10–5.*

Down the hill, plunge back into the new city and one of the most luxurious shopping districts in Europe, which stretches temptingly between the quai Général-Guisan, rue du Rhône, rue du Croix d'Or, and rue du Marché. It's tough enough to resist top name *prêt-à-porter* (ready-to-wear clothing), dazzling jewelry and watches, luscious chocolates, and luxurious furs and leathers, but the glittering boutiques of the new three-story
⑭ **Confédération Centre**—where all of the above are concentrated with a vengeance—could melt the strongest resolve. Escape across the quai, head back toward the lake, and come to your
⑮ senses in the **Jardin Anglais,** where the famous floral clock tells you it's time to stop.

Dining

Perch fresh from Lac Léman, cream-sauced *omble chevalier* (a kind of salmon trout), Lyonnaise *cardon* (a celery-like vegetable often served in casseroles), and the famous cheese fondue are specialties of this most French of Swiss cities. For details and price category definitions, *see* Dining in Staying in Switzerland.

Very Expensive **Auberge d'Hermance.** On a sunny day, take a culinary excursion to Hermance, catching a boat from Mont Blanc, and dine in the garden under stunning mountain views. Good fish specials may include the local perch filets and omble chevalier. *12 rue du Midi, Hermance, tel. 022/511368. Reservations required. AE, DC, MC, V. Closed Dec.–Mar.*

Cheval Blanc. This is top-notch cuisine in the best Franco-Swiss tradition, served in comfortable but impeccable surroundings. The desserts are a specialty. *Route de Meinier 1, Vandoeuvres, tel. 022/501401. Reservations required. AE, MC, V. Closed Sun., Mon., and three weeks in July.*

Expensive **Brasserie Lipp.** Oddly out of context on the third floor of a glitzy
★ new shopping center, this clever variation on its Parisian counterpart serves upscale brasserie fare (oysters, foie gras) to mobs of glossy, lively internationals. The casual dress code is augmented by plenty of furs! There's a good list of open wines. *Confédération Centre, tel. 022/293122. Reservations advised. AE, DC, MC, V.*

Geneva

Lac Léman

Rue de Berne
Rue Rossi
Rue de Pâquis
Rue Ph. Plantamour
Rue des Alpes
Rue du Mont Blanc
Quai du Mont Blanc

Bergues
Pont des Bergues
Pont du Mont Blanc
Ile Rousseau

Promenade du Lac
Quai Gustav Ador
Rue du Lac
Rue Muzy
R. de la Scie

Pl. de la Fusterie
Rue du Rhône
Pl. du Port
Quai Général - Guisan
Rue Versonnex
Ave. Pictet de Rochemont
Rue des Eaux Vives

Pl. Longemalle
R. du Marché
Rue de la Croix d'Or
Rue d'Italie
Rue P. Fatio
Pl. des Eaux Vives

Rue de la Rôtisserie
Rue de Rive
Blvd. Helvétique
Pl. du Pre l'Eveque

Rue Calvin
Rue Verdaine
Rue Ferdinand Hodler
Rue de la Terrassière

Rue
Granges
Treille
Rue Puits St-Pierre
Rue Hôtel de Ville
Pl. Bourg-de-Four
Rue des Chaudronniers
R. d. Glacis-de-Rive
R. A. Lachenal
Rue de Villereuse

la Croix-Rouge

Blvd. Jaques-Dalcroze
R. Sturm
Route de
Malagnou

Rue St-Léger
R. de l'Athénée
Blvd. Helvétique
Rue Toepffer
Rue Ch. Galland
Blvd. des Tranchées

Cours des Bastions

Restaurant et Brasserie Lyrique. Across the place Neuve from the Grand Théâtre, this grand old bentwood-and-tile café and its plush, pillared dining hall share several menu items (you pay about 20% more for the full restaurant experience), including hot entrée salads and classic grilled meats. Last seating is after the opera. *12 blvd. du Théâtre, tel. 022/280095. Reservations required. AE, DC, MC, V.*

Moderate **Café des Banques.** In a comfortable setting of fresh pastels, you'll find bistro cuisine with a few nouvelle twists, and a chef who comes out to chat with regulars and newcomers alike. *Rue Hesse 6, tel. 022/214498. Reservations advised. No credit cards.*

★ **Cave Valaisanne et Chalet Suisse.** Try a variety of fondues, raclette and regional meats in the cozy chalet or its no-frills sister (as close as you'll come to a Geneva diner). Its friendly, even rowdy, with service past midnight. *Blvd. Georges-Favon 23 (place du Cirque), tel. 022/281236. Reservations advised. AE, DC, MC, V.*

Inexpensive **Buffet de la Gare.** It's the real thing, with wooden benches, mesh curtains, and locals dining and drinking at all hours. The noisy open kitchen, bustling waiters, and incongruous cocktail piano give a sausage, schnitzel, or omelet a festive touch. There are generous portions and daily wine specials. One isolated wing attracts young unsavory characters, so stick to the cheery main room off the "restaurant français." *Gare Cornavin, tel. 022/7324306. AE, DC, MC, V.*

★ **Le Café du Grutli.** A high-tech, high-styled student canteen in the postmodernized Maison Grutli, where Geneva offers creative space to its painters, sculptors, photographers, and filmmakers. The light nouvelle lunches and late snacks are as hip as the clientele. *Maison Grütli, rue Général-Dufour 16, tel: 022/294495. Reservations advised. No credit cards.*

Lodging

For details and price category definitions, *see* Lodging in Staying in Switzerland.

Very Expensive **Les Armures.** In the heart of the Vielle Ville, this archeological
★ treasure, restored to its 17th-century splendor, offsets its charming original stonework, frescoes, and stenciled beams with impeccable modern comforts. Its popular restaurant—the oldest in Geneva—serves Swiss specialties. *Rue du Puits-St.-Pierre 1, tel. 022/289172. 28 rooms with bath. Facilities: restaurant. AE, DC, MC, V.*

Beau Rivage. Hushed, genteel, and a trifle creaky, this grand old Victorian palace has had much of its original 1865 decor restored: it's all velvet, parquet, and frescoed splendor. Its highly rated restaurant, Le Chat Botté, has a terrace with magnificent views across the Rhône. *Quai du Mont-Blanc 13, tel. 022/7310221. 115 rooms with bath. Facilities: 2 restaurants, terrace bar. AE, DC, MC, V.*

Expensive **Metropole.** Once the home of Red Cross archives for prisoners
★ of war, and lovingly renovated by its management of 23 years, the Metropole has more riverside splendor than the *grand dames* on the Right Bank. There's a masculine ambience, with leather and hunting prints. The river-view rooms are noisier but worth that inconvenience. Here, you're seconds from the best shopping area. *Quai Général-Guisan 34, tel. 022/211344.*

140 rooms with bath. Facilities: restaurant, bar, café. AE, DC, MC, V.

La Cigogne. Offbeat and fantastical, every room here showcases varied decorative styles and sometimes questionable tastes. You can enjoy antiques, some working fireplaces, and lovely slate-roof-and-chimney views while being in the heart of the luxury shopping area. *Pl. Longmalle 17, tel. 022/214242. 50 rooms with bath. Facilities: restaurant, bar. AE, DC, MC, V.*

Moderate **Bernina.** This is a big-city hotel with a French flavor. You pay for the convenient location (across from the station) rather than the basic, sometimes shabby quarters, but it's considerably cheaper than its neighbors. Ask for a renovated room in the quiet back, and you'll get a new tile bath. *22 pl. Cornavin, tel 022/7314950. 80 rooms, some with bath. AE, DC, MC, V.*

★ **Touring-Balance.** The old wing is tired but gracious, with French doors and chic new paint; pay 20 Fr. more and you'll get to stay in the slick, solid, new wing in wood-warmed high-tech style. There are framed lithos everywhere. The single rooms without bath are the best deal in town at 80 Fr. It's in the same great location as La Cigogne. *Pl. Longmalle 13, tel. 022/ 287122. 64 rooms, 58 with bath. Facilities: restaurant, café. AE, DC, MC, V.*

Inexpensive **St. Gervais.** The term "inexpensive hotel" is a bit of a misnomer in Geneva, but you can play la bohème here and buy a Fendi bag with the savings. It's quaint, plain, and tidy on a historic block in the center of town, and the pleasant management will accommodate families. Ask for the big room with ancient beams. *Rue Corps Saints 20, tel. 022/7324572. 26 rooms, two with bath. AE, MC, V.*

Lugano

Arriving and Departing

By Plane There are short connecting flights by **Crossair**—the Swiss domestic network—to Lugano Airport (tel. 091/505001) from Zürich, Geneva, Basel, and Bern, as well as Paris, Nice, Rome, Florence, and Venice. The nearest intercontinental airport is at Milan, Italy, about 56 kilometers (35 miles) away.

Between the Airport and Downtown There is regular bus service (5 Fr.) between the local airport and central Lugano, 7 kilometers (4 miles) away. Taxis are available but are very expensive, about 25 Fr. to the center.

By Train There's a train from Zürich seven minutes past every hour, and the trip takes about three hours. If you're coming from Geneva, you can catch the Milan express at various times, changing at Domodossola and Bellinzona. There's a train 30 minutes past every (daytime) hour from Milan's Centrale Station: The trip takes about an hour and a half. Always keep passports handy and confirm times with the SNTO. For train information in Lugano, tel. 091/226502 or 237501.

By Car There are fast, direct highways from Milan and from Zürich. If you plan on coming from Geneva, check the weather conditions with the automobile associations beforehand.

Getting Around

By Bus Well-integrated services run regularly on all local routes. You must buy your ticket from the machine at the stop before you board. Remember that with a **Swiss Pass** you travel free (*see* Getting Around Switzerland By Train). If you don't have one of these cards, get a **Regional Holiday Season Ticket** for Lugano from the tourist office. This gives unlimited free travel for seven consecutive days on most routes from Easter to October and a 50% discount on longer trips. It costs 60 Fr. for adults and 30 Fr. for children 6–16.

By Taxi Though less expensive than in Zürich or Geneva, taxis are still not cheap, with a 10 Fr. minimum. If you find this is the only way to get to your destination, call 091/512121 or 091/547722.

Guided Tours

The tourist office is the best source of information about hiking tours into the mountains surrounding Lugano, offering several topographical maps and suggested itineraries. There are bus trips to Locarno, Ascona, Lake Como, Lake Maggiore, Milan, Venice, St-Moritz, Florence, the Alpine passes, and the Italian market in Como.

Tourist Information

Ente Turistico Lugano: riva Albertolli 5, tel. 091/214664. Open weekdays 8–noon and 2–6; also open Easter–Oct., Sat. 9–noon and 2–5.

Exploring Lugano

The largest city in the Ticino—the Italian-speaking corner of Switzerland—Lugano stands for sunshine, color, vitality, and warmth, which can be applied as much to the outgoing character of its people as to its weather. Its sparkling bay attracts windsurfers, boaters, and sun worshipers. The view from the waterfront is unforgettable, its boulevards are fashionable, and its old quarter is reminiscent of sleepy old towns in Italy.

The Etruscans and Romans left their mark, as did the medieval Italian conflicts into which the city was drawn. From its incorporation into the Swiss Confederation in the early 19th century, Lugano grew to its present prosperity: a city that somehow blends the natural Italian *brio* (vigor) with smooth Swiss efficiency.

Numbers in the margin correspond with points of interest on the Lugano map.

Start your walk under the broad porticos of the tourist office and cross over to the tree-lined promenade, where you can stroll along the waterfront and take in stunning mountain views. Palm trees, pollards, and funereal cypresses—the standard greenery of Italian lake resorts—are everywhere. Head ❶ left along the waterfront and into the **Parco Civico,** with its cacti, exotic shrubs, and more than 1,000 varieties of roses. There's an aviary, a tiny "deer zoo," and a fine view of the bay ❷ from its peninsula. The **Villa Ciani,** built in 1759 and reconstructed in 1821, contains the Milich Collection of paintings and

Lugano

Belvedere Gardens, **8**
Cathedral San Lorenzo, **6**
Church of Santa Maria degli Angioli, **7**
Lido, **4**
Museum of Natural History, **3**
Parco Civico, **1**
Parco Tassino, **9**
Parco degli Ulivi, **10**
Piazza della Riforma, **5**
Villa Ciani, **2**
Villa Favorita, **11**

sculpture, from Tintoretto to Giacometti. *Tel. 091/236162. Admission: 2 Fr. Open Tues.–Sun. 10–noon and 2–6.*

③ There's also the canton's **Museum of Natural History,** which contains exhibits on animals, plants, and mushrooms. *Viale Cattaneo 4, tel. 091/237827. Admission: free. Open Tues.–Sat. 9–noon and 2–5.*

④ If you continue left along the waterfront you'll find the **Lido,** with a stretch of sandy beach, several swimming pools, and a restaurant. *Entrance: 4 Fr., changing cabins 3 Fr.*

⑤ Or follow the promenade right until you reach the **statue of George Washington.** In fact, he never visited Lugano, though this statue of him was erected in 1859 by a grateful Swiss engineer who made his fortune in America. Press on to the **piazza della Riforma,** then turn inland onto the Via Luvini, the scene of Lugano's vigorous Italian life, where the modish locals wax sociable in outdoor cafés. From here, enter the **Old Town** and follow the steep, narrow streets lined with chic Italian clothing shops and small markets offering pungent local cheeses and porcini mushrooms. Swiss culture only asserts itself at lunch stands, where *panini* (small sandwiches) are made not only of prosciutto, tuna, or mozzarella, but of sauerkraut and sausage as well.

⑥ On the street of the same name, you'll find the **Cathedral San Lorenzo,** with its graceful Renaissance facade and noteworthy frescoes inside. Then shop your way down the Via Nassa until **⑦** you reach the **Church of Santa Maria degli Angioli** in Piazza Luini, started in 1455. Within, you'll find a splendid fresco of the *Passion and Crucifixion* by Bernardino Luini (1475–1532).

⑧ Across the street, the waterfront **Belvedere Gardens** frame 12 modern sculptures with palms, camelias, oleanders, and magnolias. At the far end there's public bathing, to your right (Admission: 2 Fr.).

⑨ If you want to see more of Lugano's luxurious parklands, take the funicular from the Old Town to the station: Behind, deer greet you as you enter the floral **Parco Tassino.** Or take bus no. **⑩** 2 east to the San Domenico stop in Castagnola to reach the **Parco degli Ulivi** (Olive Park), where you can climb the olive-lined slopes of Monte Brè for views of the surrounding mountains.

⑪ An even greater draw in Castagnola is the massive, coveted private art collection at the **Villa Favorita,** owned by the Baron Heinrich von Thyssen. A textbook sampler of masterpieces includes van Eyck's *Annunciation* and Dürer's *Jesus Among the Scribes. Strada Castagnola, tel. 091/521741. Admission: 12 Fr., supplements for special exhibits. Open Tues.–Sun. 10–5.*

Dining

The Ticinese were once poor mountain people, so their cuisine shares the earthy delights of the Piemontese: *polenta* (maize), and *gnocchi* (dumplings), game and mushrooms. But as in all prosperous resorts, the mink-and-Vuarnets set draws the best in upmarket international cooking. Fixed-price lunches are almost always cheaper, so dine as the Luganese do—before your siesta. That way you can sleep off the fruity local *merlot* wine before the requisite sunset stroll. For details and price category definitions, *see* Dining in Staying in Switzerland.

Very Expensive **Al Portone.** The settings are formal (silver and lace), the ambi-
★ ence strictly at ease. They call it *laschia fare Roberto* (let Roberto do it) when the chef/proprietor takes you on a personalized gastronomic adventure in *nuova cucina* (nouvelle cuisine). *Viale Cassarate 3, tel. 091/235995. Reservations required. AE, DC, MC, V.*

Santabbondio. Ancient stone and terracotta blend with pristine pastels in this upgraded grotto, where superb and imaginative new Franco-Italian dishes are served in a setting of rustic but impeccable elegance. It's a 12 Fr. cab ride from town, toward the airport, but worth the trip. *Via ai Grotti di Gentilino, Lugano/Sorengo, tel. 091/548535. Reservations advised. AE, DC, MC, V.*

Expensive **Galleria.** A charming and classic Italian experience, where family warmth and vigor peek through chinks in the formality. Sample homemade pastas, grilled meats, and seafood in a setting that combines old dark wood and very modern art. *Via Vegazzi, tel. 091/236288. Reservations advised. AE, DC, MC, V.*

★ **Locando del Boschetto.** The grill is the first thing you see in this no-nonsense restaurant, a specialist in simple but sensational seafood *alla griglia* (broiled). The decor combines linens and rustic wood and the low-key service is tops. *Via Boschetto 8, tel. 091/542493. Reservations advised. AE, DC, MC, V.*

Moderate **Al Barilotto.** Despite its generic pizzeria decor and American-
★ style salad bar, this restaurant draws local crowds for grilled meats, homemade pasta, and wood-oven pizza. Take bus no. 10 from the center. *Hôtel de la Paix, via Cattori 18, tel. 091/542331. Reservations advised. AE, DC, MC, V.*

Inexpensive **Sayonara.** There's nothing Japanese about it: This is a modern urban pizzeria where the old copper polenta machine stirs year-round. Enjoy homemade pastas and several polenta combinations, including mountain hare. *Via F. Soave 10, tel. 091/220170. Reservations not necessary. AE, DC, MC, V.*

★ **La Tinera.** This tiny taverna crowds loyal locals, tourists, and families onto wooden benches for authentic regional specialties, hearty meats, and pastas. Regional wine is served in traditional ceramic bowls. It's tucked down an alley off Via Pessina in the Old Town. *Via dei Gorini 2, tel. 091/235219. Reservations advised. AE, DC, MC, V.*

Lodging

There are few Moderate hotels in the downtown area, but a brief drive into the surrounding countryside increases your options. As this is a summer resort, many hotels close for the winter, so call ahead. For details and price category definitions, *see* Lodging in Staying in Switzerland.

Very Expensive **Grand Hotel Eden.** This is of shabby modern construction but it has a glitzy high-gloss decor, elaborate facilities, and a spectacular lakeside setting: Every room has a lake view. *Riva Paradiso 7, tel. 091/550121. 126 rooms with bath. Facilities: 2 restaurants, bar, freshwater and saltwater indoor pools, sauna, fitness room. AE, DC, MC, V.*

★ **Villa Principe Leopoldo.** In a price range all its own, but with Old World service and splendor to match, this sumptuously appointed garden mansion sits on a hillside high over the lake. There is free transportation to the airport and town. *Via Montalbano 5, tel. 091/558855. 24 suites with bath. Facilities: pool, indoor golf, gymnasium, hydromassage, solarium, tennis courts, covered parking. AE, DC, MC, V.*

Expensive **Du Lac-Seehof.** Here is more lakefront luxury, managed by the Kneschaurek family since 1920. All rooms face the lake, but the sixth floor is the quietest, with a warm, sleek new decor. *Riva Paradiso 3, tel. 091/541921. 53 rooms with bath. Facilities: terrace bar, restaurant, pool, private swimming area on lake, sauna, solarium, massage room. AE, DC, MC, V.*

★ **Romantik Ticino.** In this warmly appointed, 16th-century house in the heart of the Old Town, shuttered windows look out from every room onto a glassed-in garden and courtyard, and there are vaulted halls lined with art and antiques. It's steps away from the funicular to the station. The terrace restaurant serves Ticinese specialties. *Piazza Cioccaro 1, tel. 091/227772. 23 rooms with bath. Facilities: restaurant, parking. AE, DC, MC, V.*

Moderate **International au Lac.** This is a big, old-fashioned, friendly city hotel, half a block from the lake, with many lake-view rooms. It's next to Santa Maria degli Angioli, on the edge of the shopping district and the Old Town. *Via Nassa 68, tel. 091/227541. 86 rooms with bath. Facilities: restaurant, garden. AE, DC, MC, V.*

San Carlo. The San Carlo offers one of the better deals in a high-priced town: It's a small, clean, freshly furnished hotel on the main shopping street, a block from the waterfront. There are no frills, but it's friendly. *Via Nassa 28, tel. 091/227107. 22 rooms with bath. AE, DC, MC, V.*

Inexpensive **Rex.** These plain but roomy quarters hold the dubious honor of being the only accommodations in this price range in town. They're clean and serviceable, and located off the Parco Civico and near the private beaches. *Viale Cattaneo 11, tel. 091/227608. 25 rooms, some with bath and balcony. AE, DC, MC, V.*

Bern

Arriving and Departing

By Plane **Belpmoos** is a small airport 9 kilometers (6 miles) south of the city with flights from London, Paris, Nice, Venice, and Lugano. A bus from the airport to the train station costs 8 Fr., a taxi about 25 Fr.

By Train Bern is a major link between Geneva, Zürich, and Basel, with fast connections running usually every hour from the enormous central station. The high-speed French TGV gets to Paris in 4½ hours.

By Car The Geneva–Zürich expressway runs by Bern, with crossroads leading to Basel and Lugano as well.

Getting Around

By Bus and Tram Bern is a small, concentrated city and it's easy to get around on foot. There are 6½ kilometers (4 miles) of covered shopping arcades in the center. Bus and tram service is excellent, however, if you don't feel like walking. Fares range from 0.80 Fr. to 1.20 Fr. Buy individual tickets from the dispenser at the tram or bus stop; the posted map will tell you the cost. Tourist cards for unlimited rides are available at 3 Fr. for one day, 5 Fr. for two, and 7 Fr. for three. Buy them at the bahnhof tourist office or from the public-transportation ticket office in the subway leading down to the main station (take the escalator in front of Loeb's department store and turn right through the Christoffel Tower). A **Swiss Pass** lets you travel free.

By Taxi This cumbersome alternative to walking costs between 6 Fr. and 10 Fr. across town.

Important Addresses and Numbers

Tourist Information The tourist office is located at Bahnhofplatz (main station, tel. 031/221212); open May–Oct., Mon.–Sat. 8–8:30 and Sun. 9–8:30; Nov.–Apr., Mon.–Sat. 8–6:30 and Sun. 10–5.

Embassies U.S.: Jubiläumsstrasse 93, tel. 031/437011. **Canadian:** 88 Kirchenfeldstr., tel. 031/446381. **U.K.:** Thunstrasse 50, tel. 031/445021.

Emergencies Police: tel. 117. **Ambulance:** tel. 144. **Doctor/Dentist:** tel. 22-9211. All-Night **Pharmacy:** tel. 229211.

Travel Agencies Thomas Cook: von Werdt-Passage 3–5, tel. 031/223545.

Guided Tours

Walking Tours A two-hour tour around the Old Town, covering all the principal sights, is offered daily by the tourist office.

Excursions Bern prides itself on its central location, with easy access to Zürich and Geneva as well as the remote farmlands of the Bernese Mittelland, where you can visit the Emmental Valley. A popular outing is to the Jungfrau in the Alpine Bernese Oberland. Round-trip rail tickets cost 134 Fr. second-class and 154 Fr. first-class. The train passes through Interlaken, Lauterbrunnen, Wengen, and Kleine Scheidegg to the Jungfraujoch, which, at 3,513 meters (11,333 feet), has the highest rail station in Europe. Contact the tourist office for details.

Exploring Bern

No cosmopolitan nonsense here: The local specialties are fatback and sauerkraut, the annual fair features the humble onion, and the president takes the tram to work. Walking down broad, medieval streets past squares teeming with farmers' markets and cafés full of shirt-sleeved politicos, you might forget that Bern is the federal capital—indeed, the geographic and political hub—of a sophisticated, modern, and prosperous nation.

It earned its pivotal position through a history of power and influence that dates to the 12th century, when Berchtold V of the

Holy Roman Empire established a fortress on this gooseneck in the river Aare. By the 15th century the Bernese had overcome the Burgundians to expand their territories west to Geneva. Napoleon seized them, briefly, from 1798 until his defeat in 1815, but by 1848 Bern was back in charge, as the capital of the Swiss Confederation.

Today it's not the massive Bundeshaus (capitol building) that dominates the city but the perfectly preserved arcades, fountains, and thick, sturdy towers of the Middle Ages. They're the reason UNESCO granted Bern World Landmark status, ranking it with the Pyramids and the Taj Mahal.

Numbers in the margin correspond with points of interest on the Bern map.

1 Start on the busy **Bahnhofplatz** in front of the grand old Schweizerhof hotel, facing the station. To your left is the **2** **Heiliggeistkirche** (church of the Holy Spirit) finished in 1729 and at odds with both the modern and medieval in Bern. Walk down Spitalgasse outside the arcades to see some of the city's stunning architecture. Inside the sheltered walkways, you'll be seduced by modern shops and cafés.

3 Head for the **Bagpiper,** the first of the city's many signature **4** fountains erected between 1539 and 1546, and the **Käfigturm** (prison gate), which dates from the 13th and 14th centuries. There's a small museum of economic and cultural life inside. *Tel. 031/222306. Admission: free. Open Tues.–Sun. 10–1 and 2–6, also Thurs. 7–9.*

5 **6** Continue down Marktgasse past the **Anna Seiler** and **Marksman 7** **fountains** to the **Zytgloggeturm** (clock tower), built as a city gate in 1191 but transformed by the addition of an astronomical clock in 1530. At four minutes before every hour you can see the famous mechanical puppet bears perform their ancient dance. **8** To your right is the Theatreplatz, to your left the **Ogre fountain** and the Kornhausplatz. There you will see the imposing 18th- **9** century **Kornhaus** (granary), its magnificent vaulted cellar a popular beer hall today.

Pass the clock tower and continue down Kramgasse, past fine **10** **11** 18th-century houses and the **Zähringer** and **Samson fountains.** Turn left at the next small intersection and head for Ratha- **12** **13** usplatz, with its **Ensign fountain,** and the late-Gothic **Rathaus** (city hall), where the city and cantonal government meet.

Head back to the main route, here named Gerechtigkeitsgasse, **14** and continue past the **Justice fountain** and lovely patrician houses. Artisan shops, galleries, and antiquaries line this leg of the endless arcades. Turn left at the bottom and head down the steep Nydegg Stalden through one of the city's oldest sections, **15** past **Messenger fountain,** to the river Aare. Here the **Nydegg-kirche** church was built from 1341 to 1571 on the foundations of Berchtold V's ruined fortress.

Cross the river by the Untertorbrucke bridge, then turn right and climb up to the **Nydeggbrücke** bridge. Here you'll find the **16** **bear pits,** where Bern keeps its famous live mascots. According to legend, Berchtold named the town after the first animal he killed while hunting—a bear, as the woods were thick with them.

Bern

Anna Seiler
Fountain, **5**
Bagpiper, **3**
Bahnhofplatz, **1**
Bear Pits, **16**

Bernisches
Historisches
Museum, **18**
Bundeshaus, **22**
Ensign Fountain, **12**
Heiliggeistkirche, **2**

Justice Fountain, **14**
Käfigturm, **4**
Kornhaus, **9**
Kunsthalle, **21**
Marksman Fountain, **6**

Messenger
Fountain, **15**
Münster, **17**
Naturhistorisches
Museum, **19**
Ogre Fountain, **8**
Rathaus, **13**

Samson Fountain, **11**
Schweizerisches
Schützenmuseum, **20**
Zähringer
Fountain, **10**
Zytgloggeturm, **7**

17 Now cross the bridge and head back into town, turning left up Junkerngasse to the magnificent Gothic **Münster** (cathedral), begun in 1421. It features a fine portal (1490) depicting the *Last Judgment* and stunning stained-glass windows, both originals and period reproductions.

Arty boutiques line the Münstergasse, leading to the **Casino,** which houses a concert hall and restaurants, but no casino. If you head even farther south, (across the river yet again) you find Helvetiaplatz, a historic square surrounded by museums.

18 The **Bernisches Historisches Museum** has a prehistoric collection, 15th-century tapestries, and Bernese sculptures. *Helvetiaplatz 5, tel. 031/431811. Admission: 3 Fr. Open Tues.– Sun. 10–5.*

19 The **Naturhistorisches Museum** is one of Europe's major natural-history museums. It features enormous wildlife dioramas and a splendid collection of Alpine minerals. *Bernastr. 15, tel. 031/431839. Admission: 1 Fr. Open Mon.–Sat. 9–noon and 2–5, Sun. 10–noon and 2–5.*

20 The **Schweizerisches Schützenmuseum** traces the development of firearms from 1817, and celebrates Swiss marksmanship beyond the apple-splitting accuracy of William Tell. *Bernastr. 5, tel. 031/430127. Admission: free. Open Tues.–Sat. 2–4, Sun. 10–noon and 2–4.*

21 The **Kunsthalle** is full of modern and contemporary works of art, and specializes in temporary exhibitions of important international artists. *Helvetiaplatz 1, tel. 031/430031. Admission: 4 Fr. Open Tues. 10–9, Wed.–Sun. 10–5.*

22 Alternatively, head back from the casino on Kochergasse past the enormous domed **Bundeshaus** (capitol).

Dining

While Bern teeters between two cultures politically, Teutonic conquers Gallic when it comes to cuisine. Dining in Bern is usually a down-to-earth affair, with Italian home cooking running a close second to the local standard fare of meat and potatoes. Specialties include the famous *Bernerplatte* (sauerkraut with boiled beef, fatty pork, sausages, ham, and tongue), *Buurehamme* (hot smoked ham), and *Ratsherrentopf* (Rösti with roast veal, beef, liver, and sausage). Coffee and *Kuchen* (pastry) is the four-o'clock norm.

For details and price category definitions, *see* Dining in Staying in Switzerland.

Very Expensive
★
Schultheissenstube. This restaurant has the best reputation in Bern, offering Franco-Swiss haute cuisine in a formal but intimate setting of warm woods and leather. It's in the grand Schweizerhof hotel. *Scheizerhoflaube 11, tel. 031/224501. Reservations required. AE, DC, MC, V.*

Expensive
Casino. The largest in a complex of restaurants, the Casino offers old-style French standards, including Scotch lamb and seafood, and a lovely view over the Aare. The garden decor and tableside service are slightly stuffy, but the wine list is deep (excellent cellar-quality specials by the carafe) and the dessert cart heaped high. There's a limited menu served on a stunning terrace. *Herengasse 25, tel. 031/222027. Reservations advised. AE, DC, MC, V.*

★ **Della Casa.** You can stay downstairs in the steamy, rowdy *Stübli* (cellar), where necktied businessmen roll up their sleeves and play cards, or you can head up to the linen-and-silver restaurant, where they leave their jackets on. It's an unofficial Parliament headquarters, with generous local and Italian specialties—a good place to try the Bernerplatte. *Schauplatzgasse 16, tel. 031/222142. Reservations advised upstairs and down. DC, MC, V. No credit cards downstairs.*

Moderate **Lorenzini.** In a town where the cozy or stuffy hold sway, this
★ hip, bright spot stands apart. Delicious homemade pasta and Tuscan specialties are served with authentic, contemporary flair. *Marktgass-Passage 3, tel. 031/227850. DC, MC, V.*

Inexpensive **Klötzlikeller.** A cozy muraled wine cellar, this is more intimate
★ than the famous Kornhauskeller and just as lovely. There's a good, limited menu of meat specialties with Rösti and beer. *Gerechtigkeitgasse 62, tel. 031/227456. AE, MC, V.*

Kornhauskeller. This spectacular vaulted old wine cellar, under the Kornhaus granary, is now a popular beer hall with live music on weekends. Decent hot food is served as an afterthought. *Kornhausplatz 18, tel. 031/221133. AE, DC, MC, V.*

Lodging

For details and price category definitions, *see* Lodging in Staying in Switzerland.

Very Expensive **Bellevue Palace.** This is a palace indeed, with a view to boot. It
★ is 75 years old, with Art Nouveau details that include a spectacular stained-glass ceiling in the lobby. The room decor varies greatly but each one is deluxe. It's next to the Bundeshaus. *Kochergasse 3–5, tel. 031/224581. 155 rooms with bath. Facilities: 2 restaurants, grill, bar, summer terrace bar. AE, DC, MC, V.*

Schweizerhof. With roomy, luxuriously appointed quarters and antique trimmed halls, this grand, graceful landmark by the Bahnhof offers excellent service. One of its restaurants serves Japanese food. *Bahnhofplatz 11, tel. 031/224501. 94 rooms with bath. Facilities: 2 restaurants, café, deli, bar, nightclub. AE, DC, MC, V.*

Expensive **Bern.** Behind a spare and imposing neo-classic facade, this for-
★ mer theater and one-time modest hotel has been transformed into a sleek, modern gem, with an airshaft garden "courtyard" lighting the better rooms. *Zeughausgasse 9, tel. 031/211021. 96 rooms with bath. Facilities: 2 restaurants, piano bar. AE, DC, MC, V.*

Savoy. Discreetly modern in cool pastels, this convenient spot provides surprising peace and quiet for its central location, just steps from the Bahnhof. It serves breakfast only. *Neuengasse 26, tel. 031/224405. 56 rooms with bath. AE, DC, MC, V.*

Moderate **Goldener Schlüssel.** This is a bright, tidy spot with wood, crisp linens, and tiled baths. It's in the heart of the Old Town, so the rooms are quieter in the back. There are two good restaurants serving Swiss and international specialties. *Rathausgasse 72, tel. 031/220216. 29 rooms, some with shower. Facilities: 2 restaurants. DC, MC, V.*

Hospiz zur Heimat. The elegant 18th-century exterior belies the dormitory gloom inside, but baths are new and rooms immaculate. It's in an excellent Old Town location. *Gerech-*

tigkeitgasse 50, tel. 031/220436. 40 rooms, some with bath. Facilities: restaurant (no alcohol). AE, DC, MC, V.

★ **Krebs.** A classic, small, Swiss hotel, Krebs is impeccable and solid, with an eye for detail. The spare decor is warmed with wood and made comfortable by the personal, friendly service of the Buri family. *Genferstr. 8, tel. 031/224942. 44 rooms, 41 with shower. Facilities: restaurant. AE, DC, MC, V.*

Inexpensive **Marthahaus.** Take bus no. 20 over the river Aare to this spare, old-style pension, where rates are low and the service is friendly. Only breakfast is served. *Wyttenbachstr. 22a, tel. 031/424135. 40 rooms, none with bath. No credit cards.*

29 Turkey

Introduction

Turkey is one place to which the term "East meets West" really applies, both literally and figuratively. It is in Turkey's largest city, Istanbul, where the continents of Europe and Asia meet, separated only by the Bosphorus, which flows 29 kilometers (18 miles) from the Black Sea to the Sea of Marmara.

Although most of Turkey's land mass is in Asia, Turkey has faced West politically since 1923, when Mustapha Kemal, better known as Atatürk, founded the modern republic. He transformed the remnants of the shattered Ottoman Empire into a secular state with a Western outlook. So thorough was this changeover, culturally, politically, and economically, that in 1987, 49 years after Atatürk's death, Turkey applied for full membership to the European Economic Community (EEC). It has been a member of the North Atlantic Treaty Organization (NATO) since 1952.

For 16 centuries Istanbul, originally known as Byzantium, played a major part in world politics, first as capital of the Eastern Roman Empire, when it was known as Constantinople; then, as capital of the Ottoman Empire, the most powerful Islamic empire in the world, it was renamed Istanbul. Atatürk moved the capital to Ankara at the inception of the Turkish Republic.

The legacy of the Greeks, Romans, Ottomans, and numerous other civilizations has made the country a vast outdoor museum. The most spectacular of the reconstructed classical sites are along the western Aegean coast and the southwest Mediterranean coast, which are lined with magnificent sandy beaches and sleepy little fishing villages, as well as busy holiday spots with sophisticated tourism facilities.

For those with more time, an extra five to seven days, an excursion inland to central Anatolia and the eroded lunar valleys of the Cappadocia area will show some of the enormous diversity of the landscapes and people of Turkey.

Turkey remains solidly Islamic. Of its 52 million people, 99% are Muslim; primarily these are rural people whose lives are deeply rooted in tradition. You can drive through areas where peasants still pick cotton by hand or collect hay with a pitchfork, while smoke rises from a nearby campsite—scenes that have barely changed over the centuries.

Before You Go

When to Go The height of the tourist season runs from April through October. July and August are the busiest and warmest months. They are also the best time to visit central and eastern Anatolia in Asia Minor, which can be extremely cold in winter, with roads and mountain passes closed by snow. April through June and September and October are the best months to visit archaeological sites or Istanbul and the Marmara area because the days are cooler and the crowds are smaller. Istanbul is hot in the summer and cold in the winter.

Climate The Mediterranean and Aegean coasts have mild winters and hot summers. You can swim in the sea from late April through October. The Black Sea coast is mild and damp, with a rainfall

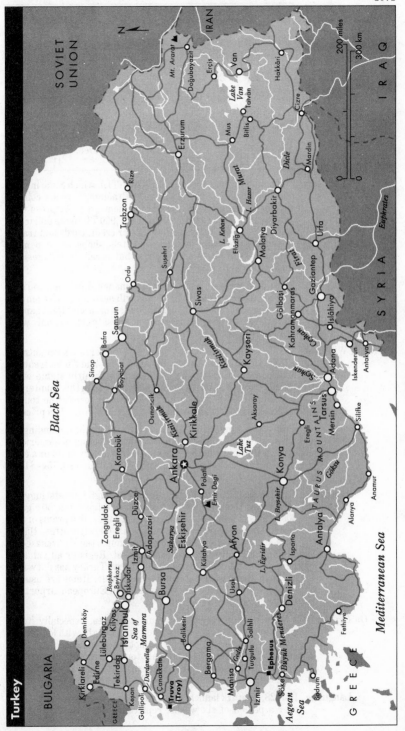

Turkey

of 228 centimeters (90 inches) a year. Summer brings hot and dry weather to eastern Anatolia, but evenings are cool.

The following are the average daily maximum and minimum temperatures for Istanbul.

Jan.	46F	8C	**May**	69F	21C	**Sept.**	76F	24C
	37	3		53	12		61	16
Feb.	47F	9C	**June**	77F	25C	**Oct.**	68F	20C
	36	2		60	16		55	13
Mar.	51F	11C	**July**	82F	28C	**Nov.**	59F	15C
	38	3		65	18		48	9
Apr.	60F	16C	**Aug.**	82F	28C	**Dec.**	51F	11C
	45	7		66	19		41	5

Currency The monetary unit is the Turkish lira (TL), which come in bank notes of 1,000, 10,000, and 20,000. Although there are coins of smaller denominations, they are seldom used. At press time (spring 1989), the exchange rate was 1,900 TL to the dollar and 3,300 TL to the pound sterling. Major credit cards and traveler's checks are widely accepted in hotels, shops, and expensive restaurants in cities and resorts, but rarely in villages and small shops and restaurants.

Be certain to retain your original exchange slips when you convert money into Turkish lira—you will need them to reconvert the money. Because the Turkish lira is worth a lot less than the dollar or most foreign currencies, it's best to convert only what you plan to spend.

What It Will Cost Turkey is the least expensive of the Mediterranean countries. Although inflation hovers between 50% and 70%, frequent small devaluations of the lira keep prices fairly stable when measured against foreign currencies. Prices in this chapter are quoted in dollars, which indicate the real cost to the tourist more accurately than do the constantly increasing lira prices.

Sample Prices Coffee can range from about 30¢ to $2 a cup, depending on whether it's the less expensive Turkish coffee or American-style coffee and whether it's served in a luxury hotel or a café; tea, 15¢ to 30¢ a glass; local beer, $1–$2; soft drinks, 75¢–$1.80; lamb shish kebab, $1.50–$7; taxi, $1 for 1 mile.

Customs
On Arrival Turkish customs officials rarely look through tourists' luggage on arrival. You are allowed to take in 400 cigarettes, 50 cigars, 200 grams of tobacco, 1.5 kilograms of coffee, 500 grams of tea, and 2.5 liters of alcohol. An additional 600 cigarettes, 100 cigars, or 500 grams of tobacco may be imported if purchased at the Turkish duty-free shops on arrival. Register all valuable personal items in your passport on entry. Turkey has duty-free shops in airports for international arrivals. Items are usually less expensive than in duty-free shops in European airports or than what's offered in-flight.

On Departure You must keep receipts of your purchases, especially items such as carpets, as proof that they were bought with legally exchanged currency. Also, it cannot be emphasized strongly enough that Turkey is extremely tough on anyone attempting to export antiques without authorization or on anyone caught with illegal drugs, regardless of the amount.

Language In 1928, Atatürk launched his sweeping language reforms that, over a period of six weeks, replaced Arabic script with the

Latin-based alphabet and eliminated many difficult and obtuse Arabic and Persian words from the Turkish language. The result has been dramatic: The literacy rate today is 75%, compared with 9% before the reforms.

English and German are widely spoken in hotels, restaurants, and shops in cities and resorts. In the villages or in remote areas, you'll have a hard time finding anyone who speaks anything but Turkish. Try learning a few basic Turkish words; the Turks will love you for it.

Getting Around

By Car
Road Conditions
Turkey has excellent roads—25,000 miles of well-maintained, paved highways—but signposts are few and marked poorly, lighting is scarce, and city traffic is chaotic. City streets and highways are jammed with vehicles operated by high-speed lunatics and drivers who constantly blast their horns. In Istanbul, it's safer and faster to drive on the modern highways. Avoid the many small one-way streets, since you never know when someone is going to barrel down one of them in the wrong direction. Better yet, leave your car in a garage and use public transportation or take taxis. Parking is a big problem in the cities and larger towns.

Rules of the Road
The best way to see Turkey is by car, but be warned that it has one of the highest accident rates in Europe. In general, Turkish driving conforms to Mediterranean customs, with driving on the right and passing on the left. But watch out for drivers passing on a curve or on the top of a hill. Other hazards are peasant carts, which are unlit at night, and motorcycles weaving in and out of traffic, even though they may be carrying an entire family.

Gasoline
Throughout the country Mobil, Shell, and British Petroleum, as well as two Turkish oil companies, have gas stations which are open 24 hours on the main highways. Others are open from 6 AM to 10 PM.

Breakdowns
Before you start out, check with your hotel or a tourist information office about how, in case of an emergency, to contact one of the road rescue services available on some highways. Turkish mechanics in the villages will usually manage to get you going again, at least until you reach a city for full repairs. In the cities, entire streets are given over to car repair shops—one repairs radiators; another, electrical fittings; another, steering wheels. Each shop is run by a team of experts. Prices are not high, but it's good to give a small tip to the person who does the actual repair work. If you're not in the shop during the repairs, take all the car documents with you.

By Train
Although there are express trains in Turkey, the term is usually a misnomer. These trains ply several long-distance routes, but they tend to be slow. The best trains are Mototren, Ekspres, and Mavi. Dining cars on some trains have waiter service and serve surprisingly good and inexpensive food. Overnight expresses have sleeping cars and bunk beds.

Fares
Train fares tend to be less expensive than bus fares. Seats on the best trains, as well as those with sleeping berths, should be booked in advance. Round-trip fares are cheaper than two one-way fares. There are 10% student discounts and 30% discounts for groups of 24 or more. In railroad stations, buy tickets at windows marked "Bilgisayar Giseleri."

By Bus Buses, which are run by private companies, are much faster than trains and provide excellent, inexpensive service. Buses are available, virtually around the clock, between all cities and towns. They are fairly comfortable and some are air-conditioned. Companies have their own fixed fares for different routes. Istanbul to Ankara, for instance, varies from $5.50 to $10; Istanbul to Izmir varies from $8 to $10.50. *Maden suyu* (bottled mineral water) is included in the fare. You can purchase tickets at stands in a town's *octogar* (central bus terminal). All seats are reserved. Fares don't vary much among the competing companies, but there's often a great deal of difference between the age of the buses and their comfort level. Whether you end up on a new bus or a rattling old one is simply a matter of luck. For very short trips, or getting around within a city, take minibuses or a *dolmuş* (shared taxi). Both are inexpensive and comfortable.

By Plane **Turkish Airlines (THY)** operates an extensive domestic network. There are nine flights daily on weekdays between Istanbul and Ankara. During the summer, many flights between the cities and coastal resorts are added. Try to arrive at the airport at least 45 minutes before your flight because security checks, which are rigidly enforced without exception, can be time-consuming. Checked luggage is placed on trolleys on the tarmac and must be identified by boarding passengers before it is put on the plane. Unidentified luggage is left behind and checked for bombs or firearms.

THY offers several discounts on domestic flights: 10% for family members, including spouses; 50% for children aged 12 and under; 90% for children under two; and 50% for sports groups of five or more. The THY sales office is at Sishane terminal, tel. 144–0296 or 145–4238; reservations by phone, 573–3515–40 (26 lines).

By Boat **Turkish Maritime Lines** operates car ferry and cruise services from Istanbul. Cruises are in great demand, so make your reservations well in advance, either through the head office in Istanbul (Rihtim Cad. 1, Karaköy, tel. 1/144–0207) or through **Sunquest Holidays Ltd.** in London (Aldine House, Aldine St., London W128AW, tel. 01/749–9933). One of its cruises is the 10-day Mediterranean Cruise from Istanbul to Alanya, with ports of call at resorts along the way. The cruises, from May through September, depart every 15 days. Round-trip fares are about $900, including all meals and land tours.

The **Black Sea Ferry** sails from May through September from Istanbul to Samsun and Trabzon and back, from Sirkeci Dock in Istanbul. One-way fares to Trabzon are about $15 for a reclining seat, $20 to $55 for cabins, and $35 for cars. The Istanbul to Izmir car ferry departs every Friday at 3 PM. Prices, including breakfast and meal, are $9.20 for a reclining seat, $23 for a cabin, and $21 for the car.

Staying in Turkey

Telephones Most pay phones are yellow, push-button models, although a few older, operator-controlled telephones are still in use. Multilingual directions are posted in phone booths.

Local Calls Public phones use *jetons* (tokens), which can be purchased for 150 TL at post offices and street booths. For a local call, deposit the token, wait until the light at the top of the phone goes off, then dial the number. If you need operator assistance for long-distance calls within Turkey, dial 031. For intercity automatic calls, dial 9, wait for a buzzing sound, then dial the city code and the number. Jetons are available for 750 TL and 2250 TL for long-distance calls.

International Calls For direct-dial calls to the United States and Canada, dial 99, the country code, the area code, and the number. For calls to the United Kingdom, dial 44 first. You can use the higher-price jetons for this, or reach an international operator by dialing 032.

If you must make a call abroad, you're better off calling from a phone booth and using jetons or a telephone credit card; hotels in Turkey, as elsewhere, have hefty service charges for international calls.

Mail Post offices are painted bright yellow and have PTT (Post, Telegraph, and Telephone) signs on the front. The major ones are open Monday–Saturday, from 8 AM to 9 PM, Sundays from 9 to 7. Smaller branches open Monday–Saturday 8:30–5.

Postal Rates Because rates change constantly to keep up with inflation, check with your hotel desk for the latest rates.

Receiving Mail If you're uncertain where you'll be staying, have mail sent to Post Restante, Merkez Postanesi (central post office) in the town of your choice.

Shopping The best part of shopping in Turkey is visiting the *bedestans*
Bargaining (bazaars), all brimming with copper and brassware items, hand-painted ceramics, alabaster and onyx goods, fabrics, and richly colored carpets. The key word for shopping in the bazaars is "bargain." You must be willing to bargain, and bargain hard. It's great fun once you get the hang of it. As a rule of thumb, offer 50% less after you're given the initial price and be prepared to go up by about 25% to 30% of the first asking price. It's both bad manners and bad business to grossly underbid or to start bargaining if you're not serious about buying. Outside the bazaars, prices are usually fixed, although in resort areas some shopkeepers may be willing to bargain if you ask for a "better price." Part of the fun of roaming through the bazaars is having a free glass of *cay* (tea), which vendors will offer you whether you're a serious shopper or just browsing. Beware of antiques. Chances are you will end up with an expensive fake, but even if you do find the genuine article, it's illegal to export antiques of any type.

VAT Refunds Value-added tax (VAT) is nearly always included in the price. You can claim back the VAT if you buy articles from shops authorized to refund VAT. The net total value of articles subject to VAT on your invoice must be over $26.31 (50,000 TL) and these articles must be exported within three months of purchase. The invoice must be stamped by customs. If the VAT to be refunded is less than 50,000 TL you can obtain it from a bank outside customs boundaries where the dealer has an account. Otherwise, mail back the stamped invoice to the dealer within one month of departure and the dealer will send back a check.

Opening and **Banks.** Banks are open weekdays, 8:30–noon and 1:30–5.
Closing Times **Mosques.** Most mosques are open to the public, except during prayer hours *(namaz)*, which are observed five times a day. These times are based on the position of the sun, so they vary

through the seasons between the following hours: sunrise (5–7); lunchtime (noon–1, when the sun is directly overhead); afternoon (3–4); sunset (5–7); bedtime (9–10). Prayers last 30–40 minutes.

Museums. Museums are generally open Tuesday–Sunday, 9:30–4:30, and closed Monday. Palaces, open the same hours, are closed Thursday.

Shops. Most shops are closed daily from 1 PM to 2 PM and all day Sunday. Generally they're open Monday–Saturday, 9:30–1 and 2–7. There are some exceptions in the resort areas, where shops stay open until 9 PM and are often open Sunday.

National Holidays January 1 (New Year's Day); April 23 (National Independence and Children's Day); April 24 (sunset) to April 27 (sunset): *Seker Bayrami* (sugar feast), three-day feast marking the end of Ramadan, a month-long Islamic observance that includes daytime fasting; Ramadan is based on the Muhammadan lunar calendar and varies yearly; May 19 (Atatürk's Commemoration, Youth and Sports Day); July 1 (sunset) to July 5 (sunset): *Kurban Bayrami* (sacrificial feast), Turkey's most important religious holiday, celebrates Abraham's willingness to sacrifice his son to God; the holiday varies yearly according to the lunar calendar; August 30 (Victory Day); October 29 (Republic Day).

Dining Turkish cuisine is one of the best in the world. The old cliché about it being hard to find a bad meal in Paris more aptly describes Istanbul, where the tiniest little hole-in-the-wall place serves delicious food. It's also an extremely healthful cuisine, full of fresh vegetables, yogurt, legumes, and grains, not to mention fresh seafood, roast lamb, and shish kebab made of lamb, beef, or chicken. Because Turkey is predominantly Muslim, pork is not readily available. But there's plenty of alcohol, including local beer and wine, which are excellent and inexpensive. Particularly good wines are Villa Doluca and Kavaklidere, available in *beyaz* (white) and *kirmizi* (red). The most popular local beer is Efes Pilsen. The national alcoholic drink, *raki*, is made from grapes and aniseed. Turks mix it with water or ice and sip it throughout their meal or serve it as an aperitif.

Hotel restaurants have English-language menus and usually serve a bland version of Continental cuisine. Far more adventurous and tasty are meals in *restorans* and in *lokantas* (Turkish restaurants). Most lokantas do not have menus because they serve only what's fresh and in season, which varies daily. At lokantas, you simply sit back and let the waiter bring food to your table, beginning with a tray of *mezas* (appetizers). You point to the dishes that look inviting and take as many as you want. Then you select your main course from fresh meat or fish—displayed in glass-covered refrigerated units—which is then cooked to order, or from a steam table laden with casseroles and stews. For lighter meals, there are *kebabcis*, tiny restaurants specializing in kebabs served with salad and yogurt, and *pidecis*, selling *pides*, a pizzalike snack on flat bread, topped with butter, cheese, egg, or ground lamb, and baked in a wood-fired oven.

Mealtimes Lunch is generally served from 1 to 2, and dinner from 8 to 9. In the cities, you can find restaurants or cafés open virtually any time of day or night, but in the villages, finding a restaurant open at odd hours can be a problem.

Dress Except for Very Expensive restaurants, where formal dress is appropriate, informal dress is acceptable at restaurants in all price categories.

Precautions Tap water is heavily chlorinated and supposedly safe to drink in cities and resorts. It's best to play it safe, however, and drink bottled mineral water *(maden suyu)* or bottled water *(sisye suyu)*, which is better tasting and inexpensive.

Ratings Prices are per person and include an appetizer, main course, and dessert. Wine and gratuities are not included. A service charge of 10%–15% is added to the bill; waiters expect another 10%. Best bets are indicated by a star ★.

Category	Major Cities	Other Areas
Very Expensive	over $20	$17
Expensive	$11–$20	$8–$17
Moderate	$5–$11	$3.50–$6.50
Inexpensive	under $5	under $3.50

Credit Cards The following credit card abbreviations are used: AE, American Express; DC, Diners Club; MC, MasterCard; V, Visa.

Lodging Hotels are officially classified in Turkey as HL (luxury), H1 to H5 (first- to fifth-class); motels, M1 to M2 (first- to second-class); and P, *pansiyons* (guest houses). The classification is misleading because the lack of a restaurant or a lounge automatically relegates the establishment to the bottom of the ratings. A lower-grade hotel may actually be far more charming and comfortable than one with a higher rating. There are also many local establishments that are licensed but not included in the official ratings list. You can obtain their names from local tourist offices.

Accommodations range from international luxury chains in Istanbul, Ankara, and Izmir to comfortable, family-run pansiyons. Plan ahead for the peak summer season, when resort hotels are often booked solid by tour companies. Turkey does not have central hotel reservations offices.

Rates vary from $7 to more than $240 a night for a double room. In the less expensive hotels, the plumbing and furnishings will probably leave much to be desired. You can find very acceptable, clean double rooms with bath for between $20 and $70, with breakfast included. Room rates are displayed in the reception area.

It is accepted practice in Turkey to ask to see the room in advance. Your room probably will be much more basic than the well-decorated reception area. Check for noise, especially if the room faces a street.

Ratings Prices are for two people in a double room, including VAT and service charge. Best bets are indicated by a star ★.

Category	Major Cities	Other Areas
Very Expensive	over $130	over $120
Expensive	$80–$130	$70–$120

Moderate	$50–$80	$50–$70
Inexpensive	under $50	under $50

Credit Cards The following credit card abbreviations are used: AE, American Express; DC, Diners Club; MC, MasterCard; V, Visa.

Tipping Except at inexpensive restaurants, a 10% to 15% charge is added to the bill. Since the money does not necessarily find its way to the waiter, leave an additional 10% on the table or hand it to the waiter. In the top restaurants, waiters expect tips of between 10% and 15%. Hotel porters expect between $2 and $5, and the chambermaid, about $2 a day. Taxi drivers don't expect tips, although they are becoming accustomed to foreigners giving them something. Round off the fare to the nearest 100 TL. At Turkish baths, the staff that attends you expects to share a tip of 30% to 35% of the bill. You won't miss them, they'll be lined up expectantly on your departure.

Istanbul

Arriving and Departing

By Plane All international and domestic flights arrive at Istanbul's Atatürk Airport. For information on times, call the individual airline or the airport's information desk (tel. 1/574–7300; 20 lines).

Between the Airport and Downtown Shuttle buses run between the airport's international and domestic terminals to the Turkish Airlines (THY) terminal in downtown Istanbul, at Meşrutiyet Caddesi, near the Galata Tower. Buses depart for the airport at the same address, every half hour from 5:30 AM to 10 AM, every hour from 10 AM to 2 PM, and every half hour from 2 PM to 11 PM. After that, departure time depends on the number of passengers. Allow at least 45 minutes for the bus ride. Plan to be at the airport two hours before your international flight because of the lengthy security and check-in procedures. The ride from the airport into town takes from 30 to 40 minutes, depending on traffic. Taxis charge about $8.

By Train Trains from the west arrive at Sirkeci station (tel. 1/527–5984) in Old Istanbul. Eastbound trains to Anatolia depart from Haydarpasa station (tel. 1/337–8724 or 336–4470) on the Asian side.

By Bus Buses arrive at Topkapi terminal (not to be confused with the area around the Topkapi Palace) just outside the city at the Cannon Gate. The smaller Trakya Otogari terminal is used for buses serving cities and villages on the European side of Turkey. The Anadolu Otogari serves Anatolian Turkey and European destinations. A few buses from Anatolia arrive at Harem terminal, on the eastern shore of the Bosphorus. Some bus companies have minibus services *(servis arabasi)* to the hotel areas of Taksim Square and Aksaray. There are local buses (no. 83 to Taksim and no. 84 to Eminönü from Topkapi terminal) as well as dolmuslar. If you arrive with baggage, it is much easier to take a taxi, which will cost about $4 to Taksim from the bus terminals and about $3 to Old Istanbul.

By Car If you drive in from the west, the busy and often hair-raising E5 highway, also called Londra Asfalti, leads from Edirne to Atatürk Airport and on through the city walls at Cannon Gate. E5 heading out of Istanbul leads into central Anatolia and on to Iran and Syria. An alternative to E5, when leaving the city, is to take one of the numerous car ferries that ply the Sea of Marmara and the Dardanelles from Kabatas Dock, or try the overnight ferry to İzmir, which leaves from Sirkeci.

Getting Around

The best way to get around all the magnificent monuments in Sultanahmet in Old Istanbul is to walk. They're all within easy distance of each other, along streets filled with peddlers, shoeshine boys, children playing, and craftsmen working. To get to other areas, you can take a bus or one of the many ferries that steam between the Asian and European continents. Dolmuşlar and taxis are plentiful, inexpensive, and more comfortable than city buses. There's no subway system, but there is the Tünellar, a tiny underground train that's handy for getting up the steep hill from Karaköy to the bottom of Istiklal Caddesi. It runs every 10 minutes and costs about 10¢.

By Bus Buy a ticket before boarding a bus. You can buy them individually or in books of 10, at ticket stands around the city. Shoeshine boys or men on the street will also sell them to you, for a few cents more. Fares are about 20¢ per ride.

By Dolmuş These are shared taxis that stop at one of the red, black, and white dolmuş signs. The destination is shown either on a roof sign or a card in the front window. Many of them are classic American cars from the '50s.

By Taxi Taxis are inexpensive. Since most drivers do not speak English and may not know the street names, write down the street you want, the nearby main streets, and the name of the area. Taxis are metered. Although tipping is not expected, you should round off the fare to the nearest 100 TL.

By Boat For a fun and inexpensive ride, take the *Anadolu Kavaği* boat along the Bosphorus to its mouth at the Black Sea. The boat leaves year-round from the Eminönü Docks, next to the Galata Bridge on the Old Istanbul side, at 10:30 AM and 1:30 PM, with two extra trips on weekdays and four extra trips on Sundays from April to September. The fare is $4. The trip takes two hours and 45 minutes one way. You can disembark at any of the stops and return by land if you wish. Regular ferries depart from Kabataş Dock, near Dolmabahçe Palace on the European side, to Üsküdar on the Asian side; and also from Eminönü Docks 1 and 2, near Sirkeci station.

Important Addresses and Numbers

Tourist Information Official tourist information offices are at **Atatürk Airport** (tel. 1/573–7399 or 1/573–4136); the **Hilton Hotel** (tel. 1/133–0592); **Yolcu Salonu,** International Maritime Passenger Terminal (tel. 1/149–5776); and in a pavilion in the Sultanamet district of **Old Istanbul** (Divan Yolu Cad. 3, tel. 1/522–4903).

Consulates U.S.: Meşrutiyet Caddesi 106, Tepebaşi, Beyoğlu, tel. 1/151–3602. **Canada:** Büyükdere Caddesi 10773, Bengün Han, tel. 1/172–5174. **U.K.:** Meşrutiyet Caddesi 34, Tepebaşi, Beyoğlu, tel. 1/144–7540.

Emergencies	**Tourism Police:** tel. 1/528–5369 or 1/527–4503. **Ambulance:** tel. 077. **Doctors:** For an English-speaking doctor, call the American Hospital (Güzelbahçe Sok. 20, Nişantaşi, tel. 1/131–4050) or Beyoğlu Hospital (Kuledibi, Karaköy, tel. 1/151–5900). You may also find English-speaking doctors at the French Hospital on Taksim Square, behind the Divan hotel (tel. 1/148–4756). **Pharmacies:** There is one on duty 24 hours in every neighborhood; tel. 011 for details. Consult the notice in the window of any pharmacy for the name and address of the nearest all-night shop. One that's centrally located is **Pamuk** in the Taksim district (Tak-i Zafer Cad. 1, tel. 1/149–2252).
English-Language Bookstores	The most complete is **Redhouse,** near the Grand Bazaar (Riza Paşa Yokuşu 50, Sultanhamam, tel. 1/527–8100). Others include **Haset Bookshop** (Istiklal Cad. 469, tel. 1/143–1343); **Tünel,** with several branches, including one in the Hilton and the Sheraton hotels; and **Net,** publishers of tourism guides (Yerebatan Cad. 15/3, Sultanahmet, tel. 1/520–8406).
Travel Agencies	Most are concentrated along Cumhuriyet Caddesi, off Taksim Square, in the hotel area. They include **American Express** (Hilton Hotel, Cumhuriyet Cad., Harbiye, tel. 1/140–3939); **Intra** (Halaskargazi Cad. 111, Harbiye, tel. 1/148–1406); **Orion Tur** (Halaskargazi Cad. 287/1 Osmanbey, tel. 1/148–8014 or 148–8437); **Setur** (Cumhuriyet Cad. 107, Harbiye, tel. 1/130–0336); and **Vitur** (Cumhuriyet Cad. 261, Harbiye, tel. 1/130–0895).

Guided Tours

There are guided tours for virtually every interest, from Islamic arts, religion, and architecture to nightclub tours that include the sound and light show at the Blue Mosque and full- or half-day tours that include lunch. You can also arrange for private tours with English-speaking guides.

Tours are arranged through travel agencies (*see* Travel Agencies, above). Choices include the "Classical Tour," either half- or full-day. The half-day tour costs $21 and includes St. Sophia, the Museum of Turkish and Islamic Arts, the Hippodrome, Yerebatan Sarayi, and the Blue Mosque; the full-day tour costs $42, and, in addition to the above sights, includes the Topkapi Palace, the Süleymaniye Mosque, the Covered or Egyptian Bazaar, and lunch. The "Bosphorus Tour" costs $21 for a half day or $42 for a full day, and includes lunch at Sariyer and visits to the Dolmabahçe and Beylerbeyi palaces. The "Night Tour" costs $47 and includes dinner and drinks at Kervansaray, where there is a show. The full-day guided "Classical Tour" by private car costs about $120 per person.

Exploring Istanbul

Istanbul is a noisy, chaotic, and exciting city, where Asia meets Europe and spires and domes of mosques and medieval palaces dominate the skyline. At dawn, when the call to muezzin's prayer rebounds from ancient minarets, many people are making their way home from the nightclubs and bars, while others are kneeling on their prayer rugs, facing Mecca.

Day and night, Istanbul has a schizophrenic air to it. Women in jeans, business suits, or elegant designer outfits pass women wearing the long skirts and head coverings that village women

have worn for generations. Donkey-drawn carts vie with old
Chevrolets and Pontiacs for dominance of the noisy, narrow
streets, and the world's most fascinating Oriental bazaar competes with Western boutiques for the time and attention of both
tourists and locals.

Ironically, Istanbul's Asian side is filled with Western-style
sprawling suburbs, while its European side contains Old Istanbul—an Oriental wonderland of mosques, opulent palaces, and
crowded bazaars. The Golden Horn, an inlet 6½ kilometers
(four miles) long, flows off the Bosphorus on the European side,
separating Old Istanbul from New Town. The center of New
Town is Beyoglu, a modern district filled with hotels, banks,
and shops grouped around Taksim Square. There are three
bridges spanning the Golden Horn: the Atatürk, the Galata,
and the Halic. The Galata Bridge is a central landmark and a
good place to get your bearings, although it will be replaced by
a new bridge due to be completed this year. From here, you can
see the city's layout and its seven hills. The bridge will also give
you a taste of Istanbul's frenetic street life. It's filled with peddlers selling everything from pistachio nuts and spices to curly-
toed slippers fancy enough for a sultan; fishermen meanwhile
grill their catch on coal braziers and sell them to passersby.
None of this sits well with motorists, who blast their horns constantly, usually to no avail. If you want to orient yourself in a
quieter way, take a boat trip from the docks on the Stamboul
side of the Galata Bridge up the Bosphorus.

Old Istanbul *Numbers in the margin correspond with points of interest on*
(Sultanahmet) *the Istanbul map.*

❶ The number one attraction in Istanbul is the **Topkapi Palace**
(Topkapi Saray), located on Seraglio Point in Old Istanbul,
known as Sultanahmet. The palace, which dates from the 15th
century, was the residence of a number of sultans and their harems until the mid-19th century. In order to avoid the crowds,
try to get there by 9:30, when the gates open. If you're arriving
by taxi, tell the driver you want the Topkapi *Saray* (palace) in
Sultanahmet, or you could end up at the Topkapi bus terminal
on the outskirts of town.

Sultan Mehmet II built the first palace in the 1450s, shortly after the Ottoman conquest of Constantinople. Over the centuries, sultan after sultan added ever more elaborate architectural fantasies, until the palace eventually ended up with more
than four courtyards and some 5,000 residents, many of them
concubines and eunuchs. Topkapi was the residence and center
of bloodshed and drama for the Ottoman rulers until the 1850s,
when Sultan Abdül Mecit moved with his harem to the European-style Dolmabahçe Palace farther up the Bosphorus coast.

❷ In Topkapi's outer courtyard is the **Church of St. Irene** (Aya
Irini), open only during festival days for concerts, and the
❸ **Court of the Janissaries** (Merasim Avlusu), members of the sultan's elite guard. Today, the area where the Janissaries once
prepared their meals in giant soup kettles is occupied by the
central ticket booth for entrance to the grounds, as well as a
parking lot for taxis and buses.

Adjacent to the ticket office is the **Bab-i-Selam** (Gate of Saluta-
tion), built in 1524 by Süleyman the Magnificent, who was the
only person allowed to pass through it. From the towers on either side, prisoners were kept until they were executed beside

Archaeological
Museum, **4**
Blue Mosque, **6**
Church of St. Irene, **2**
Cistern Basilica, **9**
Court of the
Janissaries, **3**
Dolmabahçe
Mosque, **16**
Dolmabahçe Palace, **17**
Egyptian Bazaar, **13**
Flower Market, **15**
Galata Tower, **14**
Grand Bazaar, **10**
Hippodrome, **7**
Museum of Turkish
and Islamic Arts, **8**
St. Sophia, **5**
Süleymaniye
Mosque, **12**
Topkapi Palace, **1**
University, **11**

Cad.

Kurtulus Cad.

Yenisehir-dere Caddesi

Caddesi

TEŞVIKIYE

Küçük
Çiflik
Park

Spor Cad.

Yıldız
Parkı

Bulvarı

BESIKTAŞ

Barbaros

Cirağan Cad.

Barbaros

YENESEHIR

Tarlabası Cad.

Taksim
Meydanı

Cumhuriyet Caddesi

Taşkısla Cad.

Mete Cad.

Gümüşsuyu Cad.

Kadiragalargecitti

Dolma bahçe Cad.

17

16

KABATAŞ

Caddesi

Bahriye Cad.

15
i

Saydam Cad.

Mesru iye Cad.

Refik

Yeni Çarşı Cad.

Istiklâl Caddesi

BEYOGLU

Sıraselviler Cad.

Deftardar
Yokutu

C.

Evliyaçelebi.
Cad.

Meclisimebusan

ol cuzade
Cad.

Kemeralti Cad.

14

Vayvoda Cad.

Tersane

Kemankes Cad.

KARAKÖY
Cad.

i

Galata Bridge

Boğaziçi   (Bosphorus)

ÜSKÜDAR

Cad.

EMINÖNÜ

13   **Sirkeci
Station**   Kennedy Caddesi

SIRKECI

CAGALOGLU

Gülhane
Park

4   **1**

10

2

ALEMDAR

9   **5**

3

Divanyolu Cad.

i

niçeriler Cad.

7   **6**

8   Alemdar

ani Cad.

Kennedy Caddesi

N

Sea of Marmara

**Haydarpasa
Station**

the fountain outside the gate in the first courtyard. In the second courtyard, amid the rose gardens, is the **Divan-i-Humayun,** the assembly room of the council of state, once presided over by the grand vizir (prime minister). The sultan would sit behind a latticed window, hidden by a curtain so no one would know when he was listening, although occasionally he would pull the curtain aside to comment.

One of the most popular tours in Topkapi is the **Harem,** a maze of nearly 400 halls, terraces, rooms, wings, and apartments grouped around the sultan's private quarters on the west side of the second courtyard. Forty rooms have been meticulously restored and are open to the public. Next to the entrance are the quarters of the eunuchs and about 200 of the lesser concubines, who were lodged in tiny cubicles, as cramped and uncomfortable as the main rooms of the Harem are large and opulent. Because only a limited number of visitors are allowed through the Harem each day, buy a ticket (50¢)—at the entrance to the Harem—as soon as you enter the palace grounds. Tours begin about every half hour.

In the third courtyard is the **Treasury,** (Hazine Dairesi), four rooms filled with jewels, including two uncut emeralds, each weighing 3½ kilograms (7.7 pounds), that once hung from the ceiling. Here, too, you will be dazzled by the emerald dagger used in the movie *Topkapi* and the 84-carat "Spoonmaker" diamond that, according to legend, was found by a pauper and traded for three wooden spoons.

Time Out | Just past the Treasury, on the right side of the courtyard, are steps leading to a 19th-century Rococo Mecidiye pavilion, now the **Konyali Restaurant** (tel. 1/513–9596), which serves excellent Turkish food and has a magnificent view of the *seraglio* (sultan's household, including harem) and the Golden Horn. On a terrace below is an outdoor café, with an even better view. Go early or reserve a table to beat the tour-group crush. The restaurant and café are open for lunch only.

In the fourth and last courtyard of the Topkapi Palace are small, elegant summer houses, mosques, fountains, and reflecting pools scattered amid the gardens on different levels. Here you will find the **Erivan Kiosk,** also known as the Revan Kiosk, built by Murat IV in 1636 to commemorate his capture of Rivan in Caucasus. In another kiosk in the gardens, called the **Golden Cage** (Iftariye), the closest relatives of the reigning sultan lived in strict confinement under what amounted to house arrest. The custom began in the 1800s after the old custom of murdering all possible rivals to the throne had been abandoned. The confinement of the heirs apparently helped keep the peace, but it deprived them of any chance to prepare themselves for the formidable task of ruling a great empire. *Topkapi Palace. Admission: $5.25, harem 50¢. Open Tues.–Sun. 9:30–5.*

❹ To the left as you enter the outer courtyard, a lane slopes downhill to three museums grouped together: the **Archaeological Museum** (Arkeoloji Müzesi), which houses a fine collection of Greek and Roman antiquities, including finds from Ephesus and Troy; the **Museum of the Ancient Orient** (Eski Şark Eserleri Müzesi), with Sumerian, Babylonian, and Hittite treasures; and the **Tiled Pavilion** (Çinili Köşkü), which houses ceramics from the early Seljuk and Osmanli empires. *Museums. Admission: $2.60. Open Tues.–Sun. 9:30–5.*

⑤ Just outside the walls of Topkapi Palace is **St. Sophia** (Ayasofya), one of the world's greatest examples of Byzantine architecture. Built in AD 532 under the supervision of Emperor Justinian, it took 10,000 men and six years to complete. St. Sophia is made of ivory from Asia, marble from Egypt, and columns from the ruins of Ephesus. The dome, one of the most magnificent in the world, was also the world's largest until the dome at St. Peter's Basilica was built in Rome 1,000 years later. St. Sophia was the cathedral of Constantinople for 900 years, surviving earthquakes and looting Crusaders until 1453, when it was converted into a mosque by Mehmet the Conqueror. Minarets were added by succeeding sultans. St. Sophia originally had many mosaics depicting Christian scenes, which were plastered over by Süleyman I, who felt they were inappropriate for a mosque. In 1935, Atatürk converted St. Sophia into a museum. Shortly after that, American archaeologists discovered the mosaics, which were restored and are now on display.

According to legend, the **Sacred Column,** in the north aisle of the mosque, "weeps water" that can work miracles. It's so popular that, over the centuries, believers have worn a hole through the marble and brass column. You can stick your finger in it and make a wish. *Ayasofya Meydani. Admission: $5.25. Open Tues.–Sun. 9:30–4:30.*

⑥ Across from St. Sophia is the **Blue Mosque** (Sultan Ahmet Camii), with its shimmering blue tiles, 260 stained-glass windows, and six minarets, as grand and beautiful a monument to Islam as St. Sophia was to Christiandom. Mehmet Aga, also known as Sedefkar (Worker of Mother of Pearl) built the mosque during the reign of Sultan Ahmet I in eight years, beginning in 1609, nearly 1,100 years after the completion of St. Sophia. His goal was to surpass Justinian's masterpiece, and many in the world believe he succeeded.

Turkey is one of the few Islamic countries that opens its mosques to tourists. If you hear the muezzin calling the faithful to prayer, wait about a half hour before entering as a courtesy to the worshippers.

Enter the mosque at the side entrance that faces St. Sophia. You must remove your shoes and leave them at the entrance. Immodest clothing is not allowed, but an attendant at the door will lend you a robe if he feels you are not appropriately dressed. *Blue Mosque. Admission: free. Open daily 9–5.*

The **Carpet and Kilim museums** (Hünkar Kasri) are in the mosque's stone-vaulted cellars and upstairs at the end of a stone ramp, where the sultans rested before and after their prayers. *Admission: Joint ticket 20¢. Open Apr.–Oct., Tues.– Sun. 9–4; Nov.–Mar., Tues.–Sat. 9–4.*

Historical pageants are held in the mosque on summer evenings. Check the outside bulletin boards for a schedule and to see which ones are presented in English.

⑦ The **Hippodrome** is a long park directly in front of the Blue Mosque. As a Roman stadium with 100,000 seats, it was once the focal point for public entertainment, including chariot races and circuses. It was also the site of many riots and public executions. What remains today are an **Egyptian Obelisk**

(Dikilitas), the **Column of Constantinos** (Örme Sütun), and the **Serpentine Column** (Yilanli Sütun) taken from the Temple of Apollo at Delphi in Greece. You'll also encounter thousands of peddlers selling postcards, nuts, and trinkets.

On the western side of the Hippodrome is **Ibrahim Paşa Palace,** the grandiose residence of the son-in-law and grand vizir of Süleyman the Magnificent. Ibrahim Paşa was executed when he became too powerful for Süleyman's liking. The palace now ⑧ houses the **Museum of Turkish and Islamic Arts,** which gives a superb insight into the lifestyles of Turks of every level of society, from the 8th century to the present. *Şifahane Sok, across from the Blue Mosque, in line with the Serpentine Column. Admission: $2.60. Open Tues.–Sun. 10–5.*

Walk back along the length of the Hippodrome and cross the busy main road, Divanyolu. Turn left onto Hilaliahmer ⑨ Caddesi. On your left is the **Cistern Basilica** (Yerebatan Sarayi). This is an underground network of waterways first excavated by Emperor Constantine in the 3rd century and then by Emperor Justinian in the 6th century. It has 336 marble columns rising 8 meters (26 feet) to support Byzantine arches and domes. The cistern was always kept full as a precaution against long sieges. *Hilaliahmer Cad. Admission: $1. Open daily 9–5.*

Time Out If you need some time out and want a real treat, spend an hour in a Turkish bath. One of the best is **Cägaloğlu Hamami,** near St. Sophia in a magnificent 18th-century building. *Hilaliahmer Cad. 34, tel. 1/522–2424. Admission: $2.60 for self-service bath, $8.40 for full service. Open daily 8:30 AM–6:30 PM for women; 7 AM–9 PM for men.*

⑩ The next grand attraction is the **Grand Bazaar** (Kapali Carsişi) about a quarter-mile northwest of the Hippodrome. You can walk to it in about 15 minutes or take a five-minute taxi ride. The Grand Bazaar, also called the Covered Bazaar, is a maze of 65 winding, covered streets, with 4,000 shops, tiny cafés, and restaurants. Originally built by Mehmet the Conqueror in the 1450s, it was ravaged by two modern-day fires, one in 1954 that virtually destroyed it, and a smaller one in 1974. In both cases, the bazaar was quickly rebuilt. It's a shopper's paradise, filled with thousands of different items, including fabrics, clothing, brass candalabra, furniture, and jewelry. It's extremely popular with locals as well as tourists. If you're thirsty or hungry, you can also shop for a place to eat, for there's an abundance of tea shops and small restaurants. The bazaar even has its own post office. *Yeniçeriler Cad. and Fautpasa Cad. Admission: free. Open Apr.–Oct., Mon.–Sat. 8:30–7; Nov.–Mar., Mon.–Sat. 8:30–6:30.*

When you leave the bazaar, cross Fuatpasa Caddesi and walk ⑪ around the grounds of the **university,** which has a magnificent gateway facing Beyazit Square. Follow Besim Ömer Paşa Caddesi, the western border of the university, to the right to the ⑫ 16th-century **Süleymaniye Mosque.** The mosque was designed by Sinan, the architectural genius who masterminded more than 350 buildings and monuments under the direction of Süleyman the Magnificent. This is Sinan's grandest and most famous monument, and the burial site of both himself and his patron, Süleyman. *Admission: free. Open daily outside prayer hours.*

The Grand Bazaar isn't the only bazaar in Istanbul. Another
⑬ one worth visiting is the **Egyptian Bazaar** (Misir Carsişi). You
reach it by walking down Çarşi Caddesi to Çakmakçilar Yokuşu
and Firincilar Sokak, and then into Sabunchani Sokak, where
you will see the back of the bazaar. It was built in the 17th century as a means of rental income for the upkeep of the Yeni
Mosque. The bazaar was once a vast pharmacy, filled with bur-
lap bags overflowing with herbs and spices for folk remedies.
Today, you're more likely to see bags full of fruit, nuts, Royal
Jelly from the beehives of the Aegean coast, and white sacks
spilling over with culinary spices. It's a lively, colorful scene.
Nearby are the fruit and fish markets, which are equally colorful. *Yeni Cami. Open Mon.–Sat. 8–7.*

Time Out **Pandelli.** Excellent food is served in this Ottoman-tiled, turn-
of-the-century restaurant, with its domed alcoves. It can be
reached up two flights of stairs over the arched gateway to the
Egyptian bazaar. *Misir Carsişi, Eminönü, tel. 1/522–5534.
AE, DC, MC, V. Lunch only. Closed Sun. Moderate.*

New Town New Town is the area on the northern shore of the Golden
Horn, the waterway that cuts through Istanbul and divides
Europe from Asia. The area's most prominent landmark is the
⑭ **Galata Tower,** built by the Genoese in 1349 as part of their forti-
fications. In this century, it served as a fire lookout until 1960.
Today it houses a restaurant and nightclub (*see* Entertainment
and Nightlife), and a daytime viewing tower. *Büyük Hendek
Cad. Admission: 75¢. Open daily 9–8.*

⑮ North of the tower is the **Flower Market** (Çiçek Pasaji), off
Istiklâl Caddesi, a lively blend of flower stalls, tiny restaurants,
bars, and street musicians. Here you can eat inexpensively in
scores of outdoor cafés and people-watch as you drink beer or
sip tea.

⑯ Next head for **Dolmabahçe Mosque** and Dolmabahçe Palace,
which are reached by following Istiklâl Caddesi to Taksim
Square and then taking Gümüssuyu Caddesi around the square
to a junction. You will see the Dolmabahçe Mosque on your
right and the clock tower and gateway to Dolmabahçe Palace on
your left. The mosque is a separate building from the palace. It
was founded by Valide Sultan Bezmialem, mother of Abdül
Mecit I, and was completed in 1853. *Admission: free. Open daily outside prayer hours.*

⑰ The **Dolmabahçe Palace** was also built in 1853 and, until the
declaration of the modern republic in 1923, was the residence of
the last sultans of the Ottoman Empire. It was also the residence of Atatürk, who died here in 1938. The palace, floodlit at
night, is an extraordinary mixture of Hindu, Turkish, and European styles of architecture and interior design. Queen Victoria's contribution to the lavishness was a chandelier weighing
4½ tons. Guided tours of the palace take about 80 minutes.
*Gümüssuyu Cad. Admission: $5.25. Open Apr.–Oct. 9–4;
Nov.–Mar. 9–3. Closed Mon. and Thurs.*

Off the Beaten Track

The views of the Istanbul skyline at sunset are enough to warrant a trip to this city. The best views are from **Çamlica,** the

highest hill on the Asian side of the city. The area has several pavilions where you can order tea and sit on cushions at low brass tables, and outdoor booths where you can buy such snacks as pancakes with honey or corn on the cob. At the Çamlica café, you can dine by candlelight after the sun has set and be served by waiters in traditional Turkish garb. *Sefatepsesi, tel. 1/335–3301. Reservations not necessary. No credit cards. Open Apr.–Oct., daily 9:30 AM–midnight; Nov.–Mar., daily 9:30 AM–10:30 PM. Moderate.*

Another great area for watching sunsets is **Salacak,** also on the Asian side, opposite Leander's Tower. You can reach it by ferry from Eminönü to Üsküdar; then it's a 10-minute walk along the waterfront. The area has open-air cafés and *yalis* (old wooden houses) at water's edge. In the cafés and restaurants along the waterfront, you can enjoy fish from the daily catch. A popular restaurant on the wharf, with an excellent view of the minaret-studded skyline, is **Huzur** (Iskele Cad. 20, tel. 1/333–3157).

Shopping

Gift Ideas The **Grand Bazaar** *(see* Exploring Istanbul) is a treasure trove of all things Turkish—carpets, brass, copper, jewelry, textiles, and leather goods.

Stores Stores and boutiques are located in New Town on streets such as **Istiklâl Caddesi,** which runs off Taksim Square, and **Rumeli, Halaskargezi,** and **Valikonagi Caddleri,** north of the Hilton Hotel. Two streets in the Kadikoy area where there's good shopping are **Bagdat and Bahariye Caddleri. Ataköy Shopping and Tourism Center** is a large shopping and leisure mall near the airport. It's a good place for children, too.

Markets **Balikpazari** (fish market) is in Beyoglu Caddesi, off Istiklal Caddesi. Despite its name, you will find anything connected with food at this market. A **flea market** is held in Beyazit Square, near the Grand Bazaar, every Sunday.

Dining

Istanbul has a wide range of eating establishments, with prices to match. Most of the major hotels have dining rooms serving rather bland international cuisine. It's far more rewarding to eat in Turkish restaurants. For details and price category definitions, *see* Dining in Staying in Turkey.

Very Expensive **Bebek Ambassadeurs.** Here you can dine on French and international cuisine while enjoying the views over the Bosphorus from the terrace. *Cevdet Paşa Cad. 113, Bebek, tel. 1/163–3002. Reservations advised. AE, DC, MC, V.*

Orient Express. This restaurant offers French cuisine amid decor styled after the famous train. *Etap Marmara Hotel, Taksim Square, tel. 1/151–4696. Reservations advised. AE, DC, MC, V.*

Restaurant 29. This popular restaurant serves French and Turkish cuisine. After midnight there is a discotheque upstairs until 2 AM. *Nispetiye Cad. 29, Etiler, tel. 1/163–5411. Reservations required. AE, DC, MC, V.*

Ziya. This restaurant features international cuisine amid elegant modern decor. *Mim Kemal Öke Cad. 21/1, Nişantaşi, tel. 1/140–7523. Reservations advised. AE, DC, MC, V.*

Expensive **Cemal Balik.** This is one of many excellent restaurants in the Kumkapi area that serves a wide variety of fish dishes. Try the fish kebabs or pickled fish. *Capariz Sok. 27, tel. 1/527–2288. Reservations not necessary. AE, DC, MC, V.*

Divan. You'll enjoy gourmet Turkish-French cuisine, elegant surroundings, and excellent service at this restaurant, located in the Divan hotel. *Cumhuriyet Cad. 2, Elmadağ, tel. 1/131–4100. Reservations advised. AE, DC, MC.*

Gelik. This restaurant, located in a two-story 19th-century villa, is usually packed, often with people who want to savor its specialty: all types of meat cooked in deep wells. *Sahil Yolu 68–70, tel. 1/572–0806. Reservations advised. AE, DC, MC, V.*

Moderate **Borsa.** This unpretentious restaurant serves some of the best
★ food in Turkey. The baked lamb in eggplant puree and the stuffed artichokes are not to be missed. *Lokantasi, Yaliköskü Cad. Yaliköskü Han 60–62, Eminönü, tel. 1/522–4173. Reservations not necessary. No credit cards. Lunch only. Closed Sun.*

Dört Mevsim. Located in a large Victorian building, Dört Mevsim is noted for its blend of Turkish and French cuisine and for its owners, Gay and Musa, an Anglo-Turkish couple who opened it in 1965. On any given day, you'll find them in the kitchen overseeing such delights as shrimp in cognac sauce and baked marinated lamb. *Istiklal Cad. 509, Beyoğlu, tel. 1/145–8941. Reservations advised. DC, MC, V. Closed Sun.*

Inexpensive **Hacibaba.** This is a large, cheerful-looking place, with a terrace overlooking the Greek Orthodox churchyard. Fish, meat, and a wide variety of vegetable dishes are on display for your selection. Before you choose your main course, you'll be offered a tray of appetizers that can be a meal in themselves. *Istiklal Cad. 49, Taksim, tel. 1/144–1886. Reservations advised. AE, DC, V.*

★ **Haci Salih.** A tiny, family-run restaurant, Haci Salih has only 10 tables, so you may have to line up and wait—but it's worth it. Traditional Turkish food is the fare here, with special emphasis on vegetable dishes and lamb. Alcohol is not served, but you can bring your own. *Anadolu Han 201, Alyon Sok, off Istiklal Cad., tel. 1/143–4528. Reservations sometimes accepted. No credit cards.*

Kaptan. An animated, crowded fish restaurant right on the shores of the Bosphorus. It's worth taking a taxi here. *Birinçi Cad. 53, Arnavutköy, tel. 1/165–8487. Reservations advised. No credit cards.*

Rejans. Founded by three Russian dancing girls fleeing the revolution, this restaurant offers grand East European decor and excellent Russian food and vodka, served by eccentric old waiters. *Istiklal Cad., Olivo Geçidi 15, Galatasaray, tel. 1/144–1610. Reservations required. V. Closed Sun.*

Lodging

The top hotels are located mainly around Taksim Square in New Town. Hotels generally include the 26.5% tax and service charge in the rate. Modern, middle-range hotels usually have a friendly staff, which compensates for the generally bland architecture and interiors. In Old Istanbul, the Aksaray, Laleli, Sultanahmet, and Beyazit areas have many conveniently located, inexpensive small hotels and family-run pansiyons.

Istanbul has a chronic shortage of beds, so plan ahead. For details and price category definitions, *see* Lodging in Staying in Turkey.

Very Expensive **The Hilton.** Lavishly decorated with Turkish rugs and large brass urns, this is one of the best Hiltons in the chain, and worth a visit even if you don't plan to stay. Ask for a room with a view of the Bosphorus. *Cumhuriyet Cad., Harbiye, tel. 1/131–4646. 410 rooms with bath. Facilities: Turkish baths, beauty and health spa, pool, rooftop bar and restaurant, tennis, squash, shopping arcade. AE, DC, MC, V.*

Pera Palace. A grand hotel with a genuinely Turkish feel, the Pera Palace was built in 1892 to accommodate guests arriving on the "Orient Express." Although it has been modernized, it has lost none of its original Victorian opulence. Ask to see the room where Atatürk used to stay—it's been maintained with some of his personal belongings and is a popular attraction. *Meşrutiyet Cad. 98, Tepebaşi, tel. 1/151–4560. 116 rooms with bath. Facilities: bar. DC, V.*

Ramada. The first international chain to open in Old Town, the Ramada is in a converted, four-story apartment block with courtyards leading into it. *Ordu Cad. 226, Laleli, tel. 1/519–4050. 275 rooms with bath. Facilities: restaurant, bar, pool, casino. AE, DC, MC, V.*

The Sheraton. Taksim Park provides a splendid setting for this hotel. All rooms have views of the Bosphorus or the square. For a night's spree, try the rooftop restaurant and nightclub. *Asker Ocaği Cad., Taksim, tel. 1/131–2121. 437 rooms with bath. Facilities: restaurant, bar, nightclub and disco, pool, health and beauty spa. AE, DC, MC, V.*

Expensive **Ayasofia Pansiyons.** These guest houses are part of an imaginative project undertaken by the Touring and Automobile Club to restore a little street of historic wooden houses along the outer wall of Topkapi Palace. One of the houses has been converted into a library and two into pansiyons, furnished in late Osmanli style, with excellent dining rooms. During the summer, tea and refreshments are served in the gardens to guests and nonguests alike. *Soğukçesme Sokak, Sultanahmet, tel. 1/513–3660. AE, DC, V.*

Divan. This is a quiet, small hotel with an excellent restaurant. *Cumhuriyet Cad. 2, Şisli, tel. 1/131–4100. 98 rooms with bath. Facilities: restaurant, bar, tea shop, beauty salon. AE, DC, MC.*

Yeşil Ev (Green House). This hotel is decorated in old-fashioned Ottoman style with lace curtains and latticed shutters. In the summer, you can dine on marble tables in a high-walled garden. *Kabasakal Sok. 5, Sultanahmet, tel. 1/511–1151. 20 rooms with bath. Facilities: restaurant and garden. V.*

Moderate **Barin.** Modern, clean, and comfortable, with good friendly service, the Barin caters to business travelers as well as tourists. *Fevziye Cad. 25, Sehzadebaşi, tel. 1/522–8426. 30 rooms with bath. No credit cards.*

Barut's Guesthouse. Quiet and secluded and in the heart of Old Istanbul, Barut's has a roof terrace overlooking the Sea of Marmara. The owners, Hikmet and Füsun Barut, run this friendly, pleasant establishment. The foyer has a modern art gallery. *Ishakpaşa Cad. 8, Sultanahmet, tel. 1/520–1227. 22 rooms with bath. No credit cards.*

Büyük Londra. This is another old Victorian hotel, similar to the Pera Palace, but not as grand, that has grown old gracefully. *Meşrutiyet Cad. 117, Tepebaşi, tel. 1/149–1025. 42 rooms with bath. AE, MC, V.*

Inexpensive **Berk Guest House.** Clean and exceptionally comfortable, this is run by an English-speaking couple, Gungor and Nevin Evrensel. Two rooms have balconies overlooking a garden. *Kutlugün Sok. 27, Cankurtaran, Sultanahmet, tel. 1/511–0737. 7 rooms with bath. No restaurant. No credit cards.*
Plaza. This is an older-style, well-run hotel overlooking the Bosphorus. *Siraselviler Cad. Arslanyatağı Sok. 19, Taksim, tel. 1/145–3273. 18 rooms with bath. No credit cards.*

The Arts

Entertainment in Istanbul ranges from the **Istanbul International Festival**—held late June through mid-July and attracting internationally renowned artists and performers—to local folklore and theatrical groups, some amateur, some professional. Because there is no central ticket agency, ask your hotel to help you. You can also pick up tickets at the box office or through a local tourist office.

For tickets to the Istanbul International Festival, apply to the **Istanbul Foundation for Culture and Arts** (Kültür ve Sanat Vakfi, Yildiz, Besiktas, tel. 1/160–4533 and 1/160–9072). Performances, which include modern and classical music, ballet, opera, and theater, are given throughout the city in historic buildings, such as St. Irene Church and Rumeli Castle. The highlight of the festival is the performance of Mozart's opera *Abduction from the Seraglio*, at Topkapi Palace, the site that inspired the opera.

Concerts Tickets for performances at the main concert hall, **Atatürk Kültür Merkezi**, are available from the box office at Taksim Square (tel. 1/143–5400). From October through May, the **Istanbul State Symphony** gives performances here. It's also the location for ballet and dance companies. The Touring and Automobile Association organizes chamber music performances at **Beyaz Kösk** and **Hidiv Kasri**, two 19th-century mini-palaces. For information, contact the **Touring and Automobile Association** (Halaskargazi Cad. 364, Şişli, tel. 1/131–4631).

Film Most cinemas show foreign films in the original language.

Entertainment and Nightlife

Bars and **Kulis** (Cumhuriyet Cad. 117, tel. 1/146–9345), an all-night
Nightclubs hangout for actors and writers, offers good piano music. Open daily 10 PM–5 AM. Local young professionals patronize **Zihni** (Bronz Sok. 21, Tesvikiye, Macka, tel. 1/146–9043) for lunch or evening cocktails. Open daily noon–3 and 6–10.

Bebek Bar (Bebek Ambassadeurs hotel, Cevdet Paşa Cad. 113, Bebek, tel. 1/163–3000) has views over the Bosphorus. Open daily until midnight.

A well-established nightclub, where you can dine, dance, and watch belly-dancing shows, is **Kervansaray** (Cumhuriyet Cad. 30, Elmadağ, tel. 1/147–1630). Open daily 8 PM–midnight. Two other good places for floor shows are **Balim** (Kemerhatun Mah. Hamalbaşi Cad. 8, Beyoğlu, tel. 1/149–5608), and **Olimpia**

(Acar Sok. Tomtom Mah., off Istiklal Cad., tel. 1/144–9456). **Galata Tower** (Kuledibi, tel. 1/145–1160) offers dinner between 8:30 and 10, with a Turkish show and dancing from 10 to 1 AM. *Reservations advised. AE, DC, MC, V.*

Jazz **Bilsak** (Soğanci Sok. 7, Siraselviler Cad., tel. 1/143–2899) is an easygoing restaurant and jazz bar, where local groups and singers sometimes perform.

Discos A popular disco with a lively atmosphere is **Hydromel** (Cumhuriyet Cad. 12, Elmadağ, tel. 1/140–5893). In the summer, it's open from 9 PM to 2 AM. **Club 29** (Iskele Cad. Fevit Tek Sok. 1, Moda., tel. 1/338–1088) is suitable for all ages and has a restaurant. **Regine** (Cumhuriyet Cad. 16, Elmadağ, tel. 1/146–7449) is an upscale disco-nightclub that is open from 10 PM to 4 AM.

The Aegean Coast

Some of the finest reconstructed Greek and Roman cities, including the fabled Pergamum, Ephesus, Aphrodisias, and Troy, are to be found in this region of Turkey. Bright yellow road signs pointing to historical sites or to those currently undergoing excavation are everywhere here. There are so many Greek and Roman ruins, in fact, that some haven't yet been excavated and others are going to seed.

Grand or small, all the sites are steeped in atmosphere and are best explored early in the morning or late in the afternoon, when there are fewer crowds. You can spend the heat of the day on one of the sandy beaches which line the coast.

Getting Around

The E24 from Çanakkale follows the coast until it turns inland at Kuşadasi to meet the Mediterranean again at Antalya. All the towns on the itinerary are served by direct bus routes, and there are connecting services to the ancient sites.

Guided Tours

The travel agencies in all the major towns offer organized tours of the historical sites. **Troy-Anzac Tours** (tel. 1961/1447 or 1961/1449), in central Çanakkale, has guided tours of the battlefields at Gallipoli. The tour takes about three hours and costs about $6 per person. Travel agencies along Teyyare Caddesi in Kuşadasi offer escorted tours to Ephesus; Priene, Miletus, and Didyma; and Aphrodisias and Pamukkale.

Tourist Information

Contact the tourist office in each town for names of travel agencies and licensed tour guides.

Ayvalik. Yat Limani Karisi, tel. 6631/2122.
Bergama. Zafer Mah. Izmir Cad. 54, tel. 5411/1862.
Bursa. Ahmet Hamdi Tanpinar Cad. Saydan iş Merkezi Knat 5, tel. 24/227513; Ulu Cami Parki, Atatürk Cad. 64, tel. 24/212359.
Çanakkale. Iskele Meyd. 67, tel. 1961/1187.
Çeşme. Iskele Meyd. 8, tel. 5492/6653.

İzmir. Atatürk Cad. 418, Alsancak, tel. 51/216841; Gazi Osman Paşa Bulvari, Büyuk Efes Oteli Alti, tel. 51/142147.
Kuşadasi. Iskele Meyd. tel. 6361/1103.

Exploring the Aegean Coast

Bursa **Bursa,** the first capital of the Ottoman Empire, is known as Yeşil (Green) Bursa, not only because of its many trees and parks but also because of its **Yeşil Cami** (Green Mosque) and **Yeşil Turbe** (Green Mausoleum). Both the mosque and mausoleum derive their names from the green tiles that line the interior of the buildings. They are located opposite each other on Yeşil Caddesi (Green Avenue). *Admission: free outside namaz (prayer) hours. Open daily.*

Bursa is also the site of **Ülüdag** (the Great Mountain), Turkey's most popular ski resort. To fully appreciate why the town is called Green Bursa, take a ride on the *teleferik* (cable car) from Namazgah Caddesi up the mountain for a panoramic view.

The town square is called **Heykel,** which means "statue," and is named for its statue of Atatürk. Off Heykel, along Atatürk Caddesi, is the **Ulu Cami** (Great Mosque) with its distinctive silhouette of 20 domes. *Admission: free outside namaz hours. Open daily.*

Next to Ulu Cami, by the park, is **Koza Han,** a restored silk market in a two-story caravansery located within the town's covered bazaar. *Atatürk Cad. Open Mon.–Sat. 8–8.*

A spa since Roman times, Bursa has thermal baths built on the slopes of Cekirge, a suburb with many hotels and guest houses that offer *celiks* (mineral baths) as part of the package.

Çanakkale, at the northernmost tip of the Aegean coast, is 5½ hours west of Bursa by bus. This is a good stopping-off point if you're heading for the battlefields of Gallipoli.

Troy The ruins of ancient **Troy** are 40 minutes southwest of Çanakkale. Long thought to be simply an imaginary city from Homer's *Iliad,* Troy was excavated in the 1870s by Heinrich Schliemann, a German amateur archaeologist. While others laughed at him, he poured his considerable wealth into the excavations and had the last laugh: He found the remains not only of the fabled Troy but also of nine successive civilizations, one on top of the other, dating back 5,000 years. Considering Troy's fame, the site is surprisingly small. It's best to take a guided tour to appreciate fully the significance of this discovery and the unwavering passion of the man who proved that Troy was not just another ancient myth. *Admission: $2.60. Open daily 8–7.*

The E24 highway leads around the **Gulf of Edremit,** a glorious area of olive groves, pine forests, and small seaside resorts patronized more by Turks than by foreign visitors. Colorful tea gardens sprawl along the shores, and good seafood restaurants abound, most of them serving plates heaped with oysters.

Some worthwhile nearby villages include **Behram Kale** (a short detour off E24 at Ayvacik), where you'll find the ruins of **Assos,** an ancient Greek town; **Akçay,** with its hot springs and thermal baths; and Ören, which has camping grounds nearby.

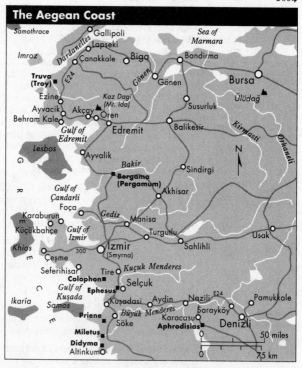

The Aegean Coast

Ayvalik, 5 kilometers (3 miles) off the main bus route, between Çanakkale and Izmir, is an ideal place to stay while visiting the ruins of ancient Pergamum, 40 kilometers (24 miles) away. From Ayvalik you can take boats to **Ali Bey Adasi**, a tiny island with pleasant waterfront restaurants, and to the Greek island of Lesbos.

Pergamum **Pergamum** is reached by driving southeast along E24 following the signs toward Bergama, the modern-day name of the ancient Greek-Roman site. If you're traveling by bus, be certain it is going all the way to Bergama, or you'll find yourself dropped off at the turn-in, 8 kilometers (5 miles) from the site.

Because the ruins of Pergamum are spread out over several miles, it's best to take a taxi from one site to the next. The most noteworthy places are the Asklepieion, the Ethnological Museum, the Red Hall, and the **Acropolis.** *Admission: $2.60. Open Apr.–Oct., daily 8:30–6:30; Nov.–Mar., daily 8:30–5.*

Pergamum's glory peaked during the Greek Attalid dynasty (241–133 BC), when it was one of the world's most magnificent architectural and artistic centers—especially so under the rule of Eumenes II, who lavished his great wealth on the city. Greek rule continued until 133 BC, when the mad Attalus III died, bequeathing the entire kingdom to Rome.

The most famous building at the acropolis is the **library,** which once contained a collection of 200,000 books, all on papyrus. The library's collection was second only to the one in Alexandria, Egypt. When the troops of Julius Caesar burned down the library in Alexandria, Mark Antony consoled Cleopatra by shipping the entire collection of books from Pergamum to Alexandria. These, too, went up in flames 400 years later, in wars between Muslims and Christians. *Admission: 20¢. Open daily 9–noon and 1–7.*

All that remains of the original **Altar of Zeus** (Zeus Sunagi) are its foundations. It was excavated by German archaeologists who sent every stone to the Pergamum Museum in what is now East Berlin.

On the opposite side of Pergamum is **Kizil Avlu** (Red Hall), a huge basilica made of red brick. Farther up the hill is the **Ethnological Museum,** where you can see local costumes and carpets, and archaeological displays. *Admission: $1 each. Both open daily 8:30–5:30.*

The **Asklepieion** was the temple of Asklepios, god of medicine, and was a cultural and healing center of ancient times. The snake and staff of Asklepios are accepted as the symbol of modern medicine. *Admission: $2.60. Open daily 8:30–5.*

Farther north are the scanty remains of a 50,000-seat **amphitheater,** which in ancient days was often partially flooded with river water so people could be entertained by watching battles between crocodiles and hippos.

İzmir The coastal area between Bergama and **İzmir,** 104 kilometers (64 miles), was once thick with ancient Greek settlements. Today only İzmir remains. Called Smyrna by the Greeks, it was a vital trading port that was often ravaged by wars and earthquakes. İzmir was completely destroyed by a fire in 1922 following Turkey's War of Independence against Greece. The war was a bloody battle to win back the Aegean coast, which had been given to the Greeks in the 1920 Treaty of Sèvres. Atatürk was in İzmir helping to celebrate the victory when celebrations soon turned to horror as the fire engulfed the city.

The city was quickly rebuilt, and it then became known by its Turkish name, İzmir. It's a beautiful, modern city filled with wide boulevards and apartment houses and office buildings. The center of the city is **Kültürpark,** a large green park that is the site of İzmir's industrial fair from late August to late September, a time when most hotels are full.

On top of İzmir's highest hill is the **Kadifekale** (Velvet Fortress), built in the 3rd century BC, the Hellenistic Age, by Lysimachos. It is easily reached by dolmuş and is one of the few ancient ruins that was not destroyed in the fire. At the foot of the hill is the restored **Agora,** the market of ancient Smyrna. The modern-day marketplace is in **Konak Square,** a maze of tiny streets filled with shops and covered stalls. *Open 8–8. Closed Sun.*

The road southwest of Konak Square leads to a coastal road and Route 300, lined with beaches and spas. Although the entire peninsula is filled with resorts, the area is too remote as a base for sightseeing.

Kuşadasi **Kuşadasi,** about 80 kilometers (50 miles) south of İzmir, has grown since the late 1970s from a fishing village into a sprawling, hyperactive town geared to serving thousands of tourists who visit the nearby ruins and beaches. Although it's packed with curio shops, Kuşadasi has managed to retain a pleasant atmosphere.

Ephesus	The major attraction near Kuşadasi is **Ephesus,** a city created by the Ionians in the 11th century BC and now one of the grandest reconstructed ancient sites in the world. It is the showpiece of Aegean archaeology. Ephesus was a powerful trading port and the sacred center for the cult of Artemis, Greek goddess of chastity, the moon, and hunting. The Ionians built a temple in her honor, one of the Seven Wonders of the Ancient World. During the Roman period, it became a shrine for the Roman goddess Diana. Today, waterlogged foundations are all that remain of the temple.

Allow yourself at least one full day to tour Ephesus. It's especially appealing out of season, when it can seem like a ghost town with its shimmering, long, white marble road grooved by chariot wheels. In the summer it's packed with tourists, many of them coming off the Greek ships that cruise the Aegean and call at Kuşadasi. Two of the ancient city's most famous visitors were Mark Antony and Cleopatra.

Some of the splendors you can see here include the two-story **Library of Celsus,** filled with rolls of papyrus; houses of noblemen, with their terraces and courtyards; a 25,000-seat **amphitheater,** still used today during the Selçuk Ephesus Festival of Culture and Art; remains of the municipal baths; and a brothel. *Admission: $5. Admission to the houses on the slopes: $1. Open Tues.–Sun. 8:30–6.*

Selçuk	On Ayasoluk Hill in **Selçuk,** 4 kilometers (2½ miles) from Ephesus, is the restored **Basilica of St. John,** (St. Jean Aniti), containing the tomb of the apostle. Near the entrance to the basilica is the **Ephesus Museum,** with two statues of Artemis. The museum also has marvelous frescoes and mosaics among its treasures. *Admission: $2.60. Basilica and museum open Tues.–Sun. 8:30–6.*

St. Paul and St. John preached in both Ephesus and Selçuk and changed the cult of Artemis into the cult of the Virgin Mary. **Meryemana,** 5 kilometers (3 miles) from Ephesus, has the **House of Mary,** thought to have been the place where St. John took the mother of Jesus after the crucifixion and where some believe she ascended to heaven. *Admission $1.25. Open daily 8:30–6.*

Priene and Miletus	Priene and Miletus, 40 kilometers (25 miles) from Kuşadasi, are sister cities, also founded by the Ionians in 11 BC. Nearby is **Didyma,** a holy sanctuary dedicated to Apollo.

Priene, on top of a steep hill, was an artistic and cultural center; Miletus, 8 kilometers (5 miles) from the sea, was a prosperous port city where commerce reigned supreme. You reach Priene by climbing up the hill and you go on from there to Miletus. Priene's main attraction is the **Temple of Athena,** a spectacular sight, with its five fluted columns and its backdrop of mountains and the fertile plains of the Meander River. You can also see the city's small amphitheater, gymnasium, council chambers, marketplace, and stadium. *Admission: $1. Open Tues.–Sun. 8:30–6.*

Prosperous **Miletus,** a short walk away, was the first Greek city to use coins for money. It also became an Ionian intellectual center and home to such philosophers as Thales, Anaximander, and Anaximenes, all of whom made contributions to mathematics and the natural sciences.

The city's most magnificent building is the **Great Theater,** a remarkably intact 25,000-seat amphitheater built by the Ionians and kept up by the Romans. Climb to the highest seats in the amphitheater for a view across the city to the bay. *Admission: ruins $1, museum $1. Open Tues.–Sun. 8:30–6.*

The temple of **Didyma** is reached by a 32-kilometer (20-mile) road called the **Sacred Way,** starting from Miletus at the bay. The temple's oracles were as revered as those of Delphi.

Under the courtyard is a network of corridors whose walls would throw the oracle's voice into deep and ghostly echoes. The messages would then be interpreted by the priests. Fragments of bas-relief include a gigantic head of Medusa and a small statue of Poseidon and his wife, Amphitrite. *Admission: $1. Open Tues.–Sun. 8:30–6.*

Pamukkale   East of Kuşadasi, 120 kilometers (75 miles), is **Pamukkale,** which first appears as an enormous chalky white cliff rising some 102 meters (330 feet) from the plains. Mineral-rich volcanic spring water cascades over basins and natural terraces, crystallizing into white stalactites, curtains of solidified water seemingly suspended in air. The hot springs in the area were popular with the ancient Romans, who believed they had curative powers. You can see the remains of Roman baths among the ruins of nearby **Hierapolis.**

The village of Pamukkale has many small hotels surrounding the hot springs, which are used today by people who still believe that they can cure a variety of problems, including rheumatism. Farther down in the village are inexpensive pansiyons, some also with hot springs.

It's best to stay overnight in Pamukkale before heading on to the ruins of **Aphrodisias,** a city of 60,000 dedicated to Aphrodite, the Greek goddess of love and fertility. It thrived from 1 BC to AD 5. Aphrodisias is reached via **Karacasu,** a good place to stop for lunch at one of its many restaurants, where fresh trout is the local specialty.

Aphrodisias is filled with marble baths, temples, and theaters, all overrun with wild blackberries and pomegranates. Across a field sprinkled with poppies and sunflowers is a well-preserved **stadium,** which was built for 30,000 spectators.

Dining and Lodging

For details and price category definitions, *see* Dining and Lodging in Staying in Turkey.

Ayvalik   **Buyuk Berk.** This is a modern hotel on Ayvalik's best beach,
Lodging   about 3½ kilometers (2 miles) from the center of town. *Sarimsakli Mev., tel. 661/2311. 97 rooms with bath. Facilities: outdoor pool, restaurant, disco. AE, DC, MC, V. Moderate.*
Ankara Oteli. Located on Sarimsakli beach, just a few feet from the surf, the Ankara Oteli gives excellent value for the money. *Sarimsakli Mev., tel. 661/1195. 57 rooms with bath. Facilities: café, bar, game room. No credit cards. Inexpensive.*

Bergama   **Tuscan Bergama Moteli.** On the main road leading into Berga-
Lodging   ma, the Tuscan has a pool fed by hot springs. The rooms are simple and clean. *İzmir Yolu, Cati Mev., tel. 5411/1173. 42 rooms with bath. Facilities: outdoor pool. No credit cards. Moderate.*

Bursa
Dining

Özkent. Located in Kültür Park, the Özkent serves excellent Turkish food in a quiet setting. *Kültür Park, tel. 241/67666. Reservations advised. AE, DC, MC, V. Moderate.*

Lodging

Celik Palace. The main attraction of this luxurious five-star hotel is a domed, Roman-style pool fed by hot springs. *Çekirage Cad. 79, tel. 241/61900. 173 rooms with bath. Facilities: restaurant, bar, pool. AE, DC, MC, V. Expensive.*

Ada Pala. Located near Kültür Park, this hotel has an inviting thermal pool. *Murat Cad. 21, tel. 241/61600. 11 rooms with bath. No credit cards. Moderate.*

Artic. In the center of town, the Artic is a good base for sightseeing. Ask for an inside room because the traffic noise can be fierce. *Fevzi Çakmak Cad. 123, tel. 241/19500. 63 rooms with bath. No credit cards. Inexpensive.*

Huzur Oteli. Clean and tidy, this hotel is near the Hüdavendigâr Mosque and a good base for sightseeing. Another plus is its friendly staff. *Birinçi Murat Camii Bitisgi, tel. 241/68021. No credit cards. Inexpensive.*

Çanakkale, Troy,
and Gallipoli
Lodging

Anafartalar. Located along the waterfront in Çanakkale, this is a quiet, pleasant hotel. *Kayserili A. Paşa Cad., tel. 1961/14451. 69 rooms with bath. Facilities: restaurant. No credit cards. Moderate.*

Truva. Near the center of Çanakkale, the Truva is an excellent base for sightseeing. *Yaliboyu, tel. 1961/1024. 66 rooms with bath. No credit cards. Moderate.*

Tusan-Truva. Surrounded by a pine forest on a beach at Intepe, north of Troy, the Tusan-Truva is one of the most popular hotels in the area. Be certain to reserve well in advance. *Intepe, E24, tel. 1961/1461. 64 rooms with bath. No credit cards. Closed Oct.–Feb. Moderate.*

Çeşme
Lodging

Çeşme Kervansaray. Built in 1528 during the reign of Sülleyman the Magnificent, the Kervansaray is decorated in traditional Turkish style. It has an excellent restaurant, with outdoor dining in an ancient courtyard. Adjacent to the hotel is a medieval castle. *Cumhuriyet Mey, tel. 5492/6490. 32 rooms with bath. AE, DC, MC, V. Expensive.*

İzmir
Lodging

Büyük Efes. Elegant but showing its age, this hotel is distinguished by a beautiful and relaxing enclosed garden. *Cumhuriyet Mey., tel. 51/144300. 296 rooms with bath. Facilities: restaurant, outdoor pool, disco. AE, DC, MC, V. Very expensive.*

Kismet. Tastefully decorated, the Kismet is a quiet, comfortable hotel with friendly service. *1377 Sok. 9, tel. 51/217050. 68 rooms with bath. Facilities: restaurant. AE, DC, MC, V. Moderate.*

Kuşadasi
Dining

Sultan Han. Full of atmosphere, with excellent food to boot, Sultan Han is an old house built around a courtyard, where the focal point is a gigantic tree. You can dine in the courtyard or upstairs in small rooms. One of the specialties is fresh seafood, which you select from platters piled high with fish and shellfish of every possible variety. Ask to have your after-dinner coffee served upstairs, where you can sit on cushions at low brass tables. *Bahar Sok. 8, tel. 6361/3849. Reservations necessary. No credit cards. Expensive.*

Lodging

Club Kervansaray. A refurbished, 300-year-old caravansery, this hotel is decorated in the Ottoman style and loaded with charm and atmosphere. It's in the center of town and features a restaurant with a floor show. There's dancing after dinner in the courtyard, where the camels were once kept. *Barbaros Cad., tel. 6361/4115. 38 rooms with bath. Facilities: restaurant, nightclub, bar. No credit cards. Expensive.*

Kismet. Although it's a small hotel, Kismet is run on a grand scale, surrounded by beautifully maintained gardens on a promontory overlooking the marina on one side and the Aegean on the other. Ask for rooms in the garden annex. Its popularity makes reservations a must. *Akyar Mev., tel. 6361/2005. 89 rooms with bath. Facilities: private beach, restaurant. MC, V. Closed Nov.–Mar. Expensive.*

Akman. One of the many reasonably priced, family-run pansiyons in and around Kuşadasi, Akman is well located on a beach a few minutes from town. *Istiklal Cad. 13, tel. 6361/1501. 46 rooms with bath. No credit cards. Moderate.*

Stella. Set atop a steep hillside outside town, Stella has a very pleasant bar and a beautiful roof terrace. *Bezirgan Sok. 44, tel. 6361/1632. 15 rooms with bath. No credit cards. Moderate.*

Aran. Although it's quite a climb up the steep hill to this hotel, it's worth it for the view from the roof terrace. *Kaya Aldogan Cad. 4, tel. 6361/1632. 22 rooms with bath. No credit cards. Inexpensive.*

Pammukale
Lodging

Tusan. The best feature of the Tusan is its pool, one of the most inviting in the area. The rooms are basic and comfortable. The one-story building is at the top of a steep hill. *Tel. 6218/1010. 47 rooms with bath. Facilities: restaurant, outdoor pool. AE, DC, MC, V. Moderate.*

Selçuk
Lodging

Hulya. This is a pleasant, family-run pansiyon, where one of the family members is a fisherman who brings in some of his daily catch. You can enjoy a delicious fish meal cooked to order. *Atatürk Cad., Ozgur Sok. 15, tel. 5451/2120. No credit cards. Inexpensive.*

Kale Han. Located in a refurbished stone inn, Kale Han is another pansiyon run by a warm, welcoming family. *Atatürk Cad. 49, tel. 5451/1154. 18 rooms with bath. No credit cards. Inexpensive.*

The Mediterranean Coast

Until the mid-1970s, Turkey's southwest coast was inaccessible to all but the most determined travelers—those intrepid souls in four-wheel-drive vehicles or on the backs of donkeys. Today, well-maintained highways wind through the area and jets full of tourists arrive at the new Dalaman Airport.

Thanks to strict developmental control, the area has not been glutted with high-rise hotels and condos, but has maintained its Turkish flavor, with low, whitewashed buildings and tiled roofs. The beaches are clean, and you can swim and snorkel in turquoise waters so clear that you can see fish 6 meters (20 feet) below. There are excellent outdoor cafés and seafood restaurants in which to dine, and you won't find a shortage of bars, discos, and nightclubs.

Getting Around

By Car Although the highways between towns are well maintained, the smaller roads are usually unpaved and very rough.

By Boat There are lots of coves and picnic areas accessible only by boat. For a small fee, local fishermen will take you to and from the coves; also, you can take one of the many water taxis. Or charter a small yacht, with or without skipper, at the marinas of Bodrum and Marmaris. Many people charter boats and join small flotillas that leave the marinas daily for sightseeing in the summer. One of the most enjoyable ways to see the coast is to take a one- or two-week **Blue Voyage** cruise on a *gulet*, a wooden craft with a full crew. There are also three-night mini Blue Voyage trips for scuba divers and snorkelers. For information, contact the following Blue Voyage agencies in the United Kingdom: **Turkish Delight,** 164B Heath Road, Twickenham, Middlesex, tel. 01/891–5901; **Simply Turkey,** 486 Chiswick High Road, London W4, tel. 01/747–1011; **Falcon Sailing,** 33 Notting Hill Gate, London W11, tel. 01/727–0232.

Guided Tours and Tourist Information

Local tourist offices list all the guided tours for the area and will also arrange for local guides.

Bodrum. Eylül Meyd. 12, tel. 6141/1091.
Dalaman. Dalaman Airport, tel. 6119/1220.
Datça. Iskele Mah. Belediye Binasi, tel. 6145/1163.
Fethiye. Iskele Meyd. 1, tel. 6151/1527.
Kaş. Cumhuriyet Meyd. 6, tel. 3226/1238.
Marmaris. Iskele Meyd. 39, tel. 6121/1035.

Exploring the Mediterranean Coast

Bodrum **Bodrum,** which sits between two crescent-shaped bays, has for years been the favorite haunt of the Turkish upper classes. Today, the elite are joined by thousands of foreign visitors, and the area is filling rapidly with hotels and guest houses, cafés, restaurants, and discos. Many compare it to St. Tropez on the French Riviera. Fortunately, it is still beautiful and unspoiled, with gleaming whitewashed buildings covered with bougainvillea and magnificent unfettered vistas of the bays.

People flock to Bodrum not for its beach, which is a disappointment, but for its fine dining and nightlife. You'll find beautiful beaches in the outlying villages on the peninsula—**Torba, Türkbükü, Yalikavak, Turgutreis, Akyarlar, Ortakent Bitez,** and **Gümbet.** Easy to reach by mini-bus or dolmuş, these villages are about an hour's drive away and have clean hotels and plenty of outdoor restaurants.

One of the outstanding sights in Bodrum is **Bodrum Castle,** known as the **Castle of St. Peter.** Located between the two bays, the castle was built by crusaders in the 11th century. It has beautiful gardens and a **Museum of Underwater Archaeology.** *Castle and museum. Admission: $2.60. Open Tues.–Sun. 8– noon and 1–5.*

The peninsula is downright littered with ancient Greek and Roman ruins, although getting to some of them involves driving over rough dirt roads. Five kilometers (3 miles) from Bodrum is **Halikarnas,** a well-preserved 10,000-seat Greek amphitheater, built in the 1st century BC and still used for town festivals. *Admission: free. Open daily 8:30–sunset.*

The Mediterranean Coast

Marmaris Another beach resort situated in the middle of two bays is **Marmaris,** which has some of the best sailing on the Mediterranean. It is 178 kilometers (111 miles) along Route 400 from Bodrum via Muğla. You'll climb steep, winding mountain passes, with cliffs that drop straight into the sea. The final 30 kilometers (19 miles) into Marmaris is a broad boulevard lined with eucalyptus trees.

Marmaris, like Bodrum, is a sophisticated resort with boutiques, elegant restaurants, and plenty of nightlife. Nearby are quiet villages, easy to reach by boat or taxi. One of these is **Knidos,** where you can see the ruins of Aphrodite's circular temple and an ancient theater. By road, Knidos is a very rough 108 kilometers (67 miles) from Marmaris. It's easier and quicker to take a boat. Another town is **Turunc,** worth a day's visit, especially for its beaches.

Time Out At the **Turunc Bay Yacht Club** you can dine on a small terrace built into a hill above a sandy cove, surrounded by mountains and pine forests. It's a five-minute walk on the road toward Kumlubuk Road. *No credit cards. Closed Nov.–mid-May. Expensive.*

Day-long boat excursions from Marmaris will take you to the **Dalyan delta,** breeding grounds of the loggerhead turtle. Smaller boats will take you farther upstream to the ruins of the acropolis at **Kaunus.** It's a steep climb to the top of the acropolis, but you can reward yourself with a soak in one of the local hot springs.

Freshwater **Lake Köyceğiz** is also reached by boat through the reed beds of the Dalyan delta, and this entire area is a wildlife preserve, filled with such birds as kingfishers, kestrals, egrets, and cranes. Köyceğiz and **Dalyan** villages, both 20 minutes' drive from Dalaman Airport, are good stopping-off places for exploring the area. It costs $16 to rent a boat with a boatsman to sail from Dalyan to the ruins and beach.

Fethiye   **Fethiye,** 130 kilometers (80 miles) from Bodrum and 167 kilometers (104 miles) from Marmaris, was rebuilt after the original town was destroyed in an earthquake in 1957. The town is especially appealing at night, when residents promenade along the lighted harbor or relax in their gardens sipping tea. Although modern in appearance, it's still an old-fashioned agricultural community, where goats and sheep are herded along the main roads on their way to market.

Ölü Deniz   One of Turkey's greatest natural wonders is **Ölü Deniz,** an azure lagoon flanked by long, white beaches. The area is about 15 kilometers (9 miles) from Fethiye and can be reached by ferry. There are a few wooden chalets in camping grounds and one beachfront hotel. Opposite the beach, you'll find small restaurants with rooftop bars, many with live music that goes on all night. One of the beachside restaurants, **Ada Kamp,** serves excellent lobsters and barbecued jumbo shrimp. The area around the lagoon is a national park.

Southeast of Fethiye, near Route 400, are several ancient sites, including the ruins of **Pinara,** one of the most important cities of the former Roman province of Lycia. It is 40 kilometers (24 miles) from Fethiye. Near Pinara, up a steep and strenuous dirt road, you'll find nearly 200 Roman tombs cut honeycomb-fashion into the face of the cliffs. *Admission: $1. Open daily 8:30–sunset.*

Xanthos   Return to Route 400 and head 18 kilometers (11 miles) south toward the village of Kinik. At Kinik leave the main highway and take a mile-long bumpy road to **Xanthos,** another major city of ancient Lycia. It was excavated in 1838 and much of what was found here is now in the British Museum in London. What's left is still well worth the bumpy ride: the acropolis, the Tomb of Harpies, some plastercast reliefs, and ruins of some Byzantine buildings. *Admission: $1. Open daily 8:30–sunset.*

Patara   Ten minutes from Xanthos is **Patara,** once the city's port. At
and Kalkan   Patara (Admission: $1), you'll find ruins scattered around the marshes and sand dunes. The area's long, wide beaches remain beautiful and unspoiled, despite the fact that they attract hundreds of Turkish families and tourists. You can find two small restaurants at the beach and some makeshift stalls with cold drinks for sale. The nearest place to stay is **Kalkan,** a fishing village 20 minutes away by minibus. Kalkan has plenty of small hotels, guest houses, and restaurants with roof terraces—ideal spots from which to watch sunsets across the bay. Its waterfront is lined with excellent seafood restaurants. From Kalkan, which has a small rocky beach, you can take a boat to nearby sandy coves and to the phosphorescent **Blue Caves,** where seals frolic.

Kaş   **Kaş,** 30 kilometers (18 miles) from Kalkan, is another fishing village that has become a popular resort, and is also developing into a major yachting center. Although luxury hotels have replaced many of the tiny houses on the hills, there are still plenty of old-fashioned pansiyons for those on a budget. One of the attractions here is the underwater city of **Kekova,** where you can look overboard and see ancient Roman and Greek columns that were once part of a thriving city before the area was flooded. Kekova is especially popular with scuba divers and snorkelers, but to scuba-dive or fish in this area, a permit must be obtained from the directorate of the harbor and from the directorate of the ministry of tourism. Motorboats leave daily at 9:30 and cost about $4.

Two interesting side trips from Kaş by boat include a visit to **Kale,** where you can roam through a Byzantine fortress at the top of a steep hill, and **Demre,** site of **St. Nicholas's Basilica,** built soon after the saint's death in the 4th century. His remains were stolen and taken to Bari, Italy, in 1087. St. Nicholas, the original Santa Claus, was a bishop of Myra in Asia Minor.

The 190-kilometer (119-mile) road from Kaş to Antalya is under reconstruction and the trip takes a good four hours by car and five hours by bus. You can visit Kale and Demre along the way.

For romantic ruins, it would be hard to beat **Phaselis.** The Roman agora, theater, aqueduct, and a necropolis with fine sarcophagi are scattered through the pine woods which surround the Temple of Athena. Overgrown streets descend to the translucent water, ideal for a swim.

Kemer is the center of intensive touristic development, with hotels and restaurants, well-equipped marina, and club-style holiday villages where you wouldn't know you're in Turkey. The remaining 35 kilometers (26 miles) are increasingly occupied by villas and motels along the smooth pebbles of Konyalti Beach, which stretches to the outskirts of Antalya.

Antalya The resort of **Antalya,** on the Mediterranean, is a good base for several worthwhile excursions. The city is on a beautifully restored harbor and filled with narrow streets lined with small houses, restaurants, and pansiyons. On the hilltop are tea gardens where you can enjoy tea made in an old-fashioned samovar and look across the bay to the Taurus Mountains, which parallel the coast. To the right of the port is the 13th-century **Fluted Minaret** (Yivli Minare). The Hisar Café, Tophane tea garden, and Mermerli tea garden all overlook Antalya's harbor.

Dining and Lodging

For details and price category definitions, *see* Dining and Lodging in Staying in Turkey.

Antalya **Talya.** This is a luxurious resort hotel with its own beach that
Lodging you reach by taking an elevator down the side of the cliff. From every angle there's a view of the sea. It has a five-star rating and gets booked up quickly in high season. *Fevzi Çakmak Cad., tel. 311/15600. 150 rooms with bath. Facilities: disco, restaurant, pool, game room. AE, DC, MC, V. Very Expensive.*
Turban Adalya. Built in 1869 as a bank, the Turban Adalya has been imaginatively transformed into a luxurious hotel overlooking the colorful fishing port. *Kaleiçi Yat Limani, tel. 311/18066. 23 rooms with bath. Facilities: restaurant. AE, DC. Expensive.*
Altun Pansiyon. Near the Fluted Minaret and minutes from the seaport, this is a recent addition to Antalya's hotels. The staff

is extremely helpful. It has a well-stocked bar and a pleasant courtyard. *Kaleiçi Mev., tel. 311/16624. 15 rooms, some with shower. No credit cards. Inexpensive.*

Bodrum **Club Pirinç.** This restaurant has a pleasant bar and swimming
Dining pool, and offers Turkish-French cuisine. *Akçabuk Mev., tel. 6141/2902. Expensive.*
Restaurant No. 7. Octopus casseroles are a specialty. *Eski Banka Sok. 7. Expensive.*
Balik Restaurant. Specialties include fish, meat, and chicken kebabs. *Yeniçarşi 28, tel. 6141/3018. No credit cards. Moderate.*
Korfez Restaurant. This is a seaside fish restaurant. *Cumhuriyet Cad. 18, tel. 6141/1169. No credit cards. Moderate.*

Lodging **Manzara Aparhotel.** On a hill looking across the bay toward Bodrum Castle, the Manzara is a group of 20 small apartments, each with living room, kitchen, and terrace. At peak times, you may have to pay half-board. *Kumbahce Mah. Meteoroloji Yani, tel. 6141/1719. Facilities: restaurant, outdoor pool. AE, DC, MC, V. Expensive.*
Merhaba Pansiyon. Here, on the waterfront, you'll find a beautiful roof terrace and simply furnished but clean rooms. *Akasya Sok. 5, tel. 6141/2115. No credit cards. Inexpensive.*

Dalyan **Yali Restaurant.** This is a waterside eatery reached by a short
Dining boatride from Dalyan. It's also a good stopping-off point if you're planning a walk to the Kaunus ruins. *Tel. 6116/1150. No credit cards. Inexpensive.*

Lodging **Hotel Turtle.** This is a quiet 10-room hotel tucked away in a bay of orchards on the lakeside. The hotel boat picks up guests from Dalyan. Vefa Ülkü, the owner, cooks excellent dishes served under a big plane tree. *Kücük Karaağac, Sultaniye Köyü, Köyceğiz, tel. 6114/1487. No credit cards. Moderate.*
Kaunos Hotel. Overlooking the river, some of the rooms have views. Good outdoor restaurant. *Posta Kodu 48810, Dalyan, tel. 6116/1057. Inexpensive.*

Fethiye **Ulgen.** Travelers on a budget will find the Ülgen a pleasant,
Lodging simply furnished pansiyon. *Cumhuriyet Mah. Pasptir Mev. 3, Merdivenli Yokusu, tel. 6151/3491. No credit cards. Inexpensive.*

Kalkan **Kalkan Han.** A rambling old house in the back part of the vil-
Lodging lage, the Kalkan Han has a special treat for visitors: a roof terrace with sweeping views of the bay, a perfect place to enjoy breakfast. *Koyici Mev., tel. 3215/151. 16 rooms with bath. No credit cards. Moderate. Closed Nov.–Apr.*

Kaş **Mercan.** On the eastern side of the harbor, the Mercan serves
Dining good, basic Turkish food in an attractive open-air setting. The water is so close you can actually hear fish jumping. *Hukumet Cad. Reservations not necessary. No credit cards. Moderate.*

Lodging **Kaş Oteli.** This hotel has wonderful views of the Greek island of Kastellorizo. There's good swimming off the rocks in front of the hotel, or you can laze in the sun with drinks and snacks from the bar or restaurant. *Hastana Cad. 15, tel. 3226/1271. No credit cards. Closed Nov.–Apr. Moderate.*
Mimosa. This is a new hotel conveniently located on a hill near the bus station, with plain but perfectly adequate rooms, all with balconies and views. *Elmali Cad., tel. 3226/1272. 20 rooms with bath. No credit cards. Moderate.*

Çan Otel. Turkish carpets and antiques grace this village house that's been lovingly restored and turned into a pansiyon. It's on a tiny side street near the harbor. *Off Hukumet Cad., tel. 3226/ 1441. No credit cards. Inexpensive.*

Köyceğiz **Hotel Özay.** This lakeside hotel is quiet, modern, and efficiently
Lodging run. *Kordon Boyu 11, Köyceğiz, tel. 6114/1300. Facilities: swimming pool. AE, DC, MC, V. Expensive.*
Hotel Deniz Feneri. The owner is an artist whose wood carvings hang in Golbasi Restaurant. The hotel is located in a picturesque square; the rooms are basic. *Atatürk Square, Köyceğiz, tel. 6114/1777. No credit cards. Inexpensive.*

Ölü Deniz **Beyaz Yunus.** Wicker chairs and wooden floors fill this domed
Dining restaurant, whose name means "white dolphin." The most elegant restaurant in the area, it's situated on a promontory near Padirali and serves Continental and Turkish cuisine, imaginatively prepared and presented. *No telephone. Reservations not necessary. No credit cards. Expensive.*
Kebapici Salonu. You can grill meat at your table in this outdoor restaurant, where tables and chairs are clustered around trees in a field. Meals are served with meze, salad, and wine. *Behind Han Camp, no telephone. Reservations not necessary. No credit cards. Inexpensive.*

Lodging **Meri Oteli.** Located on a steep incline above the lagoon, this is a series of bungalows, with rooms a bit down-at-the-heel but clean. These are the only accommodations at the lagoon. *Tel. 6151/1. 75 rooms with bath. Facilities: restaurant. AE, DC, MC, V. Moderate.*
Balikci Han. This delightful pansiyon is in a converted 19th-century inn, directly on the waterfront. *Tel. 3215/75. 7 rooms with bath. No credit cards. Inexpensive.*

Central Anatolia: Cappadocia

Cappadocia, an area filled with ruins of ancient civilizations, is in the eastern part of Anatolia. Cappadocia has changed little over the centuries. People travel between their farms and villages in horse-drawn carts, women drape their houses with strings of apricots and paprika for drying in the sun, and nomads pitch their black tents beside wheat and sunflower fields and cook on tiny fires that send smoke billowing through the tops of the tents. And in the distance, a minaret pierces the sky.

Getting Around

By Car There are good roads between Istanbul and the main cities of Anatolia—Ankara (the capital of Turkey), Konya, and Kayseri. The highways are generally well maintained and lead to all the major sites. Minor roads are full of potholes and are very rough. On narrow, winding roads, look out for oncoming trucks, whose drivers apparently don't believe in staying on their side of the road.

By Bus There is a good interlinking bus network between most towns and cities, and fares are reasonable.

By Train Though there are frequent trains between the main cities, they are almost nonexistent between small towns. It's much quicker to take a bus.

By Taxi Drivers are usually willing to take you to historical sites out of town, for reasonable fares.

Guided Tours

Since the Cappadocia area is so vast, you'll need at least two days to see the main sights. If you are driving, consider hiring a guide for about $13–$26 a day. Local tourist offices and hotels will be able to recommend guides and excursions.

Tourist Information

Check with local tourist offices for names of travel agencies and English-speaking guides.

Aksaray. Hükümet Konaği, tel. 481/12474.
Nevsehir. Devlet Hastanesi Yani, tel. 4851/3659.
Ürgüp. Kayseri Cad. 37, tel. 4868/1059.

Exploring Central Anatolia and Cappadocia

An hour's drive, 30 kilometers (19 miles) to the northwest of Antalya, is **Termessos,** which has an almost complete Roman amphitheater built on a mountainside, and the unexcavated remains of a Roman city on the other side of the mountain. There are organized tours to Termessos from Antalya. *Admission: free. Open daily 9–5:30.*

Perge, 19 kilometers (11 miles) east of Antalya, has many Roman ruins to explore. You can climb up a 22,000-seat amphitheater, walk down a restored colonnaded street, visit well-preserved thermal baths and a Roman basilica, and see the spot where St. Paul preached his first sermon in AD 45. *Admission: $2.60. Open daily 9–5:30.*

Nearby is **Aspendos,** 44 kilometers (23 miles) to the east of Antalya, which contains Turkey's best-preserved amphitheater. The acoustics are so fine that modern-day performers don't need microphones or amplifiers. *Admission: $2.60. Open daily 9–5:30.*

Konya, home of the Whirling Dervishes, is reached by driving 427 kilometers (267 miles) northeast of Antalya past **Lake Beyşehir.** There is also a longer and more difficult road via **Lake Eğridir.** The Whirling Dervishes belong to a religious order founded in the 13th century by Melvana, a Muslim mystic, who said, "There are many ways of knowing God. I choose the dance and music." You can see the dervishes whirl to the sounds of a flute at the annual commemorative rites held in Konya in early December. Tickets are available from travel agencies or **Konya Turizm Vakfi** (tel. 33/116255).

Sultan Han, 95 kilometers (59 miles) northeast of Konya, is Anatolia's largest and best-preserved caravansery, once a place of rest and shelter for travelers and their camels plying the ancient trade routes. Traditionally, caravanseries opened into vast courtyards from private and public rooms and had kitchens, a bathhouse, and a small mosque. Lodging was free because these were run by religious foundations funded by sul-

Central Anatolia and Cappadocia

Kızılırmak

Afyon · Lake Tuz · Avanos · Üçhisar · Kayseri · Nevşehir · Göreme · Ürgüp · Derinkuyu · Kaymakli

Akşehir · Aksaray · Sultan Han · Niğde

L. Eğridir · L. Beyşehir · Konya · **Çatalhuyuk** · Karapinar · Bor

Eğridir · Behşehir · Cumra · Ayranci · Eregli · Seyhan

Isparta · Bozkir · Kara Dağ · Karaman

Bucak · T A U R U S · M O U N T A I N S

Termessos · **Perge** · Gölsu · Tarsus · Mersin · Adana

Aspendos

Antalya · Manavgat · **Side** · Ermenek · Mut · Erdemli · Karates

Kemer · Alanya · Silifke

Gulf of Anatolia · Gazipasa · Ovacik · *Gulf of Alexandretta*

Anamur · Aydinik

Mediterranean Sea

NORTHERN PORTION OF CYPRUS
OCCUPIED BY TURKEY

0 — 50 miles
0 — 75 km

CYPRUS

N

tans. Caravanseries were built between 20 and 25 miles apart, a comfortable day's journey for a camel laden with goods.

Cappadocia roughly forms the triangular area between **Kayseri, Nevşehir,** and **Niğde.** Most of the main sights are within an even smaller triangular area linked by Urgup, Göreme, and Avanos. **Ürgup** is the center from which to explore the villages and the best place to shop, as well as to arrange tours.

The landscape is stark and lunarlike. It was formed by prehistoric volcanic eruptions that dumped layers of mud, ashes, and lava on the area. Eventually the ground turned to *tufa* (soft, porous rock). Rain, snow, and wind created a fantasyland of rock formations resembling chimneys, cones, needles, pillars, and pyramids, often topped by perfectly balanced gigantic slabs of rock. Then came earthquakes to add vast valleys, and oxidation to give the area the final artistic touch: rocks "painted" yellow, pink, red, russet, and gray-violet.

The softness of the rock in this area was ideal for hollowing out cave dwellings and forming defenses from invading armies. The Cappadocians carved out about 40 underground cities, with some structures as deep as 20 stories underground. The largest of these cities housed 20,000 people. Each had dormitories, dining halls, sewage disposal systems, ventilation chimneys, a cemetery, and a prison. Large millstones sealed off the entrances from enemies. Two of these cities are open to the public, one at **Derinkuyu,** 21 kilometers (13 miles) south of Nevşehir, and the other at **Kaymakli** 30 kilometers (10 miles) south of Nevşehir. *Admission: $2.60. Open daily 8–sunset.*

Lodging The Christians also hid in these underground cities when the Islamic forces swept through Cappadocia in the 7th century. Some of the earliest relics of Christianity are to be found in the **Göreme Valley,** a few miles east of Nevşehir. There are dozens of old churches and monasteries covered by frescoes. For a history of the area, visit the **Göreme Open-Air Museum,** 1 kilometer (.62 miles) outside of Göreme village on the Ürgüp road. *Admission: free. Open daily 8:30–5:30.*

Dining and Lodging

For details and price category definitions, *see* Dining and Lodging in Staying in Turkey.

Konya   **Ali Baba Kebapçisi.** This restaurant serves good kebabs, and is
Dining   famous for its Firin kebap, cooked over an open charcoal fire. *Eski Avukatlar Sokak 11/A, tel. 33/110307. No credit cards. Inexpensive.*

Bolu Restaurant. You can eat dishes here for which Konya is reknowned: *etli ekmek* (flat bread with ground lamb) and *tereyağli borek* (buttered pastries). *Pürküklü Mah. 31/c, tel. 33/124533. Inexpensive.*

Damla Restaurant. Damla is owned and run by a woman who is famous for her cooking, especially *piliç* (roast chicken) and *saç kavurma* (sauteed lamb). *Hükümet Alani, Şahin Oteli Alti, tel. 33/113705. Inexpensive.*

Meram Tavusbaba Cafeteria. This restaurant has a good view overlooking the city. Its most famous dish is *kuzu cevirme* (lamb). *In Meram Tavusbaba, tel. 33/179525. Inexpensive.*

Basak Palas. An older but charming small hotel, Basak Palas is also comfortable. *Hukumet Alani 3, tel. 331/11338. 40 rooms, most with bath. No credit cards. Moderate.*

Ürgüp   **Hanedan.** Located in the cellar of an old Greek house, the
Dining   Hanedan is on a hill a short distance from town. You can sit on the terrace and watch the sunset across the plains toward the mountains. The food is very good and presented with flair. *Nevsehir Yolu Uzen, tel. 4868/1266. Reservations not necessary. No credit cards. Moderate.*

Lodging **Buyuk.** Located in the center of town, this is a friendly hotel that features folk dancing in the evenings—you're encouraged to join in, but can just sit back and watch if you prefer. *Kayseri Cad., tel. 4868/1060. 49 rooms with bath. No credit cards. Moderate.*

Hitit. The family-run Hitit is a comfortable, small hotel with a restaurant serving basic but enjoyable food. *Dumlupinar Cad. 54, tel. 4868/1481. 15 rooms without bath. No credit cards. Inexpensive.*

Hotel Ozata. This is an ideal hotel if you're on a tight budget. It's a clean, family-run place, just outside the center of town. *Atatürk Bulvari 56, tel. 4868/1355. 32 rooms with bath. No credit cards. Inexpensive.*

30 Yugoslavia

Introduction

"Never the twain shall meet," declared Rudyard Kipling, referring, of course, to East and West. Had modern Yugoslavia existed at the time, he might just have changed his mind.

The line that divided the Roman Empire into Byzantine East and Papal West in the 4th and 5th centuries ran straight through present-day Yugoslavia. A thousand years later, roughly the same boundary divided the Turkish Ottoman Empire from the rest of Europe.

It was along the coast that graceful Venetian Gothic and Italian Renaissance flourished, while Central European Baroque left its greatest imprint on the plains. And deep in the south, glorious medieval Orthodox monasteries survive alongside the slender minarets and domed hamams of Islam. The Roman and Cyrillic alphabets spell out more or less the same words, according to whether you're in the north and west or the center and south. And music, customs, costume, and architecture reflect influences that kept two halves of the country poles apart for centuries.

Yugoslavia (land of the South Slavs) first made it onto the map of Europe with the demise of the Hapsburg Empire in 1918, initially as a kingdom, subsequently as a Socialist Federal Republic. The West regards it as communist rather than socialist but finds this particular brand of communism difficult to classify. Small-scale private business thrives; enterprises compete hotly with each other. They've even developed such Western economic ills as unemployment and inflation. These have recently grown to such proportions, along with ethnic unrest in parts of the country, that the situation is unpredictable as we go to press (spring 1989)—though main tourist areas are unaffected and prices tend more than ever to be in the visitor's favor.

It is a beautiful country, replete with mountain massifs, river gorges, a rugged coastline, hundreds of islands, and fertile plains. The freedom of your own four wheels is the best answer to Yugoslavia's staggering variety, but escorted bus tours radiate from most resorts, so you can see a lot with very little effort.

Since the tourist boom of the '60s and early '70s, when enthusiastic developers produced uninspired architecture, the Yugoslavs have graduated to much more attractive modern buildings. The plumbing can still be unreliable and the service a bit frenetic (especially in high season), but resort facilities and service have acquired a polish that would have been hard to predict in the '50s. That was when the country was still piecing itself together after a war that destroyed 10% of its population, along with most of its industry and communications.

One country, two alphabets, three religions, four languages, five nationalities, six republics, and seen frontiers: That's the easy way to sum it up. But our simple arithmetic merely hints at the reality.

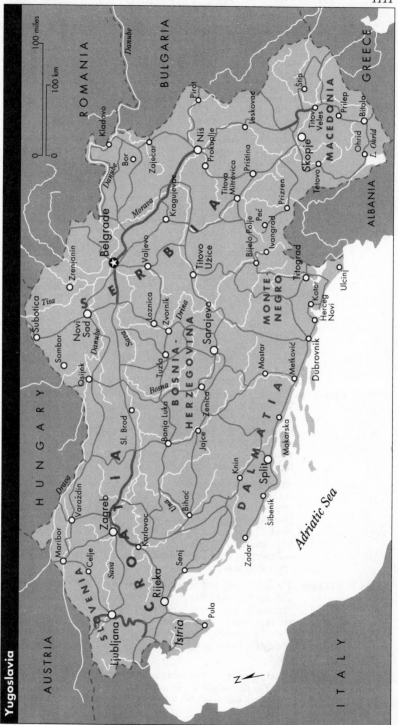

Yugoslavia

Before You Go

When to Go The tourist season runs from April or May through October. Outside this period, many resort hotels close, but you will find good bargains in those that don't. July and August are the hottest and most crowded months, to be avoided unless you've planned to attend one of the major festivals. Spring and fall have all the advantages of good weather and reduced rates for accommodations. If you must visit in summer, it's a good idea to split your stay between the coast and the mountains.

Climate Along the coast, winters are relatively mild, although rain can be heavy through April. Summers are hot. There can be strong winds: *bura* (dry, northerly, mainly in winter), *Yugo* (humid, southerly, mainly in winter), and *maestral* (steady, generally westerly, and the most frequent). Summer storms are fierce but brief. Inland, summers are extremely hot and the mountains are your best bet; in winter it gets very cold. The main winter sports season is January through March or April, depending on altitude.

The following are the average daily maximum and minimum temperatures for Belgrade.

Jan.	37F	3C	May	73F	23C	Sept.	76F	24C
	26	−3		54	12		56	13
Feb.	42F	5C	June	79F	26C	Oct.	64F	18C
	29	−2		59	15		47	8
Mar.	52F	11C	July	83F	28C	Nov.	51F	11C
	36	2		62	17		39	4
Apr.	64F	18C	Aug.	83F	28C	Dec.	42F	5C
	45	7		62	17		32	0

Currency The unit of currency is the dinar. Bills are in denominations of 50, 100, 500, 1,000, 5,000, 10,000, 20,000, and 50,000 dinars. Coins are 1, 2, 5, 10, 20, 50, and 100 dinars. Some of the newer coins are a different size and color from the older ones, which are gradually being phased out though they represent the same values—or lack of them! You are allowed to import or export up to 150,000 dinars.

At press time (spring 1989), the exchange rate was 6,000 dinars to the dollar and 10,000 dinars to the pound sterling, but this is constantly changing to match the ferocious rate of inflation. *Don't* exchange more than enough to meet your immediate needs. Traveler's checks can be exchanged at banks, exchange bureaus, travel agencies, and many hotels. Major credit cards —American Express, Diners Club, MasterCard, and Visa— are widely accepted.

What It Will Cost The rate of inflation was running at about 300% at press time and the rate of exchange was constantly changing, so the approximate equivalents in dollars are given. For visitors, prices are very reasonable, but you will notice big variations, in the cost of accommodations for different parts of the country (*see* Lodging). Costs generally drop as you progress inland and south.

Hotel taxes are included in the rates quoted. There is no sales tax. The departure tax at airports for international flights at press time was about $6, for domestic flights about $1.50.

Sample Prices Cup of coffee, 40¢; bottle of beer, 60¢; Coca-Cola, 40¢; ham sandwich, 80¢; one-mile taxi ride, $1.30.

Museums Because of the high rate of inflation, admission charges change frequently, along with the value of the dinar. But entrance fees are very modest—from 50¢ to $1.

Visas U.S. and Canadian citizens require both a valid passport to enter Yugoslavia and a visa. A visa can be obtained free at Yugoslav embassies or, for a small fee, at Yugoslav entry points.

All British citizens need a passport to enter Yugoslavia; visas are not required. The British Visitor's Passport is accepted, but if it has less than three months' validity, you must obtain a Tourist Pass, valid for 30 days, at entry points; these are issued free.

Customs
On Arrival Visitors are permitted to bring in personal effects and normal amounts of photographic, recording, and sports equipment. All travelers 16 and older may also bring in 200 cigarettes or their equivalent in tobacco, one liter of wine, one liter of liquor, a quarter liter of eau de cologne, and small quantities of perfume.

On Departure A special permit is needed only if you have purchased goods of historical or cultural value. If you have any questions on this point be sure to ask the seller when you make your purchase.

Language English is widely spoken among the young and those in the travel industry. Away from tourist areas, you're likely to have some communication problems, although German is understood by many of the older generation.

The main language is Serbo-Croat, an umbrella name for the similar Serbian and Croatian languages understood by most Yugoslavs. Slovene is spoken in Slovenia, Macedonian in Macedonia.

The Roman alphabet is used in the north, the west, and along the coast; the Cyrillic alphabet predominates in the center and south, though road signs and important notices are often in both alphabets. It's a good idea to get a working knowledge of Cyrillic, however, if only to recognize a PECTOPAH for the restaurant that it is.

Getting Around

By Car
Road Conditions Yugoslavia's network of major highways (*autopat*) is expanding, especially the network connecting Zagreb, Belgrade, Niš, and Skopje. A toll is charged on a few newer sections. Most main roads are good, but often twisting and narrow for the weight of traffic carried in summer. Take care because Yugoslavs are impetuous drivers, and so are many of their visitors. The dirt roads, marked in green on the free, annually revised map available from the Yugoslav National Tourist Office, are usually rough and often spectacular.

Rules of the Road Driving is on the right; at intersections, traffic from the right has priority, except on main highways or where otherwise indicated. The speed limit in cities and towns is 60 kph (37 mph); otherwise it's 80 kph (50 mph), 100 kph (62 mph), or 120 kph (75 mph) as indicated. Seat belts are compulsory. Penalties are severe for drunk driving.

Parking Drivers will have trouble finding parking spaces in summer resorts and larger towns. Facilities range from inexpensive meters, occasional multistory garages, and free areas. Cars parked illegally may be removed by a menacing machine known as the "spider," and retrieval is costly.

Gasoline The price of gasoline is about 40¢ per liter. At the border you can buy gas coupons that allow a 5% reduction, but it's not really worth the hassle.

Breakdowns The **Yugoslav Automobile Association (AMSJ)** runs a 24-hour breakdown service and a fleet of yellow patrol vehicles marked "Pomoć-Informacije." To summon help, phone 987. In case of accident, you're legally obliged to call the police (tel. 92) and, in case of injury, ambulance (tel. 94).

By Train Lateral routes link the major inland cities with the coast. With so many mountains, journeys are often slow but scenically rewarding. Car trains are on routes linking Ljubljana, Zagreb, and Belgrade; and Ljubljana and Zagreb with Rijeka, Split, and Sarajevo-Kardeljevo.

By Plane Yugoslavia's national airline **(JAT)** has domestic service with links to 18 centers; **Adria Airways**'s network links 12. In summer, you'll need to make reservations well in advance.

By Bus Express buses link main centers, slower ones serve the villages. Reserve a seat if you can (though this is possible only at main terminals) because buses are usually crowded.

By Boat **Jadrolinija** operates an extended network of express services, passenger and car ferries, and hydrofoils linking coastal and island centers. Try to take at least one boat trip during your stay. A hydrofoil trip on the Danube from Belgrade to the Iron Gates (gorge and dam) on the Yugoslav-Romanian border is a wonderful experience. Timetables are available from Yugoslav National Tourist Offices overseas and local travel agencies.

Staying in Yugoslavia

Telephones Pay phones work with 10, 50, and 100 dinar coins. Lift the re-
Local Calls ceiver, insert the coins, and dial: The money is returned if the connection is not made. Phone cards are available from post offices and some kiosks.

International Calls Direct dialing is in service to the United States and Britain, but during high season and in the south insufficient lines can cause long delays. The cheapest way is to call from a post office; you may do the dialing yourself or have the operator do it for you. Either way, you pay after your call. It can cost up to twice as much from your hotel.

Mail At press time (spring 1989), airmail letters to the United States
Postal Rates cost 6,500 dinars up to 20 grams; to the United Kingdom, 3,800 dinars. Prices will certainly have increased by 1990. Make sure you use an airmail label; there are lower rates for surface mail, but it's very slow.

Receiving Mail If you are uncertain about your itinerary, you can collect mail "kept waiting" (Poste Restante) at any post office. There is no charge. American Express (*see* Important Addresses) also offers a free clients' mail service and will hold mail up to one month.

Opening and Closing Times

Banks. Banks in major cities are open weekdays 7–7, Saturday 7–1.

Museums. Museums are normally open 9–1, sometimes 10–12; also 2–6 or 4–7; normally closed one day a week, usually Sunday or Monday. Always check before going.

Shops. Most stores are open weekdays, 8–8, Saturday 8–3. Some close for three or four hours in the middle of the day, and some are open Sunday morning. In tourist resorts small shops stay open until late in the evening. Markets usually operate in the morning, 5:30–12:30.

National Holidays

January 1 (New Year's Day); January 2; May 1 (Labor Day); May 2; July 4 (Veterans); November 29, 30 (Republic). In addition, in Serbia: July 7; in Macedonia: August 2, October 11; in Montenegro: July 13; in Slovenia: July 22, 23; and in Croatia and Bosnia-Herzegovina: July 27.

Dining

There is a wide selection of restaurants, many of them now privately owned. There are also inexpensive cafeterias, *kafana* (cafés), and ice cream parlors. If a restaurant name includes the word *riblji*, it specializes in fish. Charcoal-grilled dishes—you'll find them everywhere—are *čevapčiči* (small spiced ground beef or lamb rolls); *ražnjiči* (pieces of pork or veal on skewers); and *pleskavica* (a kind of hamburger with raw onions and red peppers). It is worth being adventurous. Yugoslavia's typically Balkan dishes include various vegetables or leaves (cabbage and grape) stuffed with spiced meats and rice. There are also a variety of *čorba* (savory stews) and extremely rich *paprikaš* (fish or chicken soups).

Coffee in Slovenia and Croatia is Italian-style espresso and cappuccino; farther south it's more likely to be *turksa kava*—thick black Turkish coffee. Ask for it *bez šećera* if you don't like it sweet. The beer is fairly tasteless, but there are very good wines.

Mealtimes

The main meal is lunch, usually from 1 to 3. Dinner is normally from 7 to 10.

Precautions

It is not necessary to be on your guard here, but if you're worried about the tap water, excellent *mineralni voda* (mineral waters) and *gusti sok* (fruit juices) are available.

Dress

Casual dress is appropriate for restaurants in all price categories.

Ratings

Prices are per person and include a first course, main course, and dessert, without wine and tip. The service charge is usually included in the bill, but you can add 5% to 7% if you're satisfied with the service. Best bets are indicated by a star ★. Due to the volatility of the dinar, prices are given in U.S. dollars.

Category	Belgrade and Major Resorts	Other Areas
Very Expensive	over $15	over $12
Expensive	$10–$15	$8–$12
Moderate	$5–$10	$4–$8
Inexpensive	under $5	under $4

Credit Cards	The following credit card abbreviations are used: AE, American Express; DC, Diners Club; MC, MasterCard; V, Visa.
Lodging	The Yugoslavs saw the error of their ways before the building boom of the '60s and '70s got out of hand and have avoided the worst excesses of other coastal resorts. There are still enough eyesores, but some of the newer hotels are tastefully designed, and in the older resorts the traditional grand or villa styles survive. Local travel agencies will make reservations for you, but you'll run into trouble along the coast in the peak season if you haven't made reservations in advance. Tourist complexes in some resorts can be several miles from the resort itself, so if you like to stroll out of your hotel and feel part of the local scene, make sure of its location.
Hotels	Yugoslavian hotels are officially classified Deluxe, A, B, C, or D—all Bs and up, and some Cs, will have all or some rooms with bath or shower. It's difficult to generalize about standards. In main resorts they are generally good, but elsewhere service doesn't always match the amenities, especially as you travel inland and south. Some of the newer B-classified hotels are better than some older establishments in the A category. Despite a constant program of renovation, plumbing and electric wiring are still quite variable in efficiency. Always take a standard bath plug or rubber drain cover with you.
Guest Houses	You'll find these mostly in Slovenia (*gostilna*) and Croatia (*gostionica*). They can be charming as well as inexpensive.
Private Homes	Thousands of private rooms are available through local tourist offices and travel agencies. The Yugoslav National Tourist Office publishes a free booklet detailing price ranges and facilities.
Farmhouses	Most of these are in Slovenia and offer deals where you have two or three meals, but a growing number are located in other areas. Local tourist offices will have details.
Apartments and Villas	A growing number of new complexes along the coast give you the option of renting, with supermarkets, restaurants, and recreational amenities nearby.
Camping	The Yugoslav National Tourist Office publishes an annually revised list of sites. These get packed in the summer, so start looking early.
Budget Accommodations	During summer months, student hostels become inexpensive lodging for tourists in most main towns. Local tourist offices can advise.
Ratings	Prices are for two people in a double room with bath; those at the low end of the scale are off-season rates. All prices include breakfast and tips. Best bets are indicated by a star ★. Due to the volatility of the dinar, prices are given in U.S. dollars.

Category	Belgrade and Major Resorts	Other Areas
Very Expensive	over $120	over $80
Expensive	$70–$120	$50–$80
Moderate	$45–$70	$30–$50
Inexpensive	under $45	under $30

Credit Cards The following credit card abbreviations are used: AE, American Express; DC, Diners Club; MC, MasterCard; V, Visa.

Tipping Yugoslavs don't take tips for granted, but appreciate being rewarded for good service. They'll especially appreciate hard currency, although it's not officially encouraged. *See* Dining, above, for hints on tipping in restaurants. For taxis, add 5%. Train and airport porters have a fixed charge, but check this in advance; you can add 50¢ per bag if they've been helpful. At top hotels, give doormen and bellhops 50¢ per bag; at moderate hotels 30¢. There is no need to tip theater ushers and service station attendants.

Belgrade

Arriving and Departing

By Plane All flights arrive at Belgrade airport at Surčin, 18 kilometers (11 miles) from the city along the highway. For information on arrivals and departures, tel. 011/675–992 or 011/601–424.

Between the Airport and Downtown Regular JAT buses run from the airport to Trg Sveti Marko (on Bulevar revolucije), the Jugoslavija hotel (New Belgrade), and the Slavija hotel. The trip by bus will cost about $1; by taxi, about $5.

By Train The main train station is Belgrade Central, Trg bratstva i jedinstva 2, tel. 011/645–822.

By Bus The main bus station is at Železnička 4, tel. 011/624–751 or 011/672–049.

By Car Downtown exits off the highway are clearly marked "Centar."

Getting Around

By Streetcar and Bus You can buy an economical day ticket giving unlimited travel from ticket offices marked "Duvan," near train and bus stops. A single ride costs about 20¢. Punch your ticket in a machine when you board the vehicle.

By Taxi Taxi meters start at 25¢, and rates are quite inexpensive. Taxis are easy to come by, but if you have any problems, tel. 011/444–3443 or 011/457–277.

Important Addresses and Numbers

Tourist Information The main tourist information center is in Terazije's underground pedestrian crossing, near the Albanija Palace (open daily 8–8, tel. 011/635–343 or 011/635–622). Tourist information offices are also at the central train station (open daily, 7 AM–9 PM, tel. 011/646–240) and at Belgrade airport (open daily, 7 AM–9 PM, tel. 011/602–326).

Embassies U.S.: Kneza Miloša 50, tel. 011/645–655; **Canadian:** Kneza Miloša 75, tel. 011/644–666; **U.K.:** Generala Ždanova 46, tel. 011/645–055.

Emergencies **Police:** tel. 92. **Ambulance:** tel. 94. **Doctor: Boris Kidrič Health Center,** Pasterova 1, tel. 011/683–755. **Dentist: Dental Polyclinic,** Ivana Milutinovića 15, tel. 011/444–3491. **Pharmacies:** The following are open 24 hours: **Prvi Maj,** Maršala Tita 9; **Savski venac,** Nemanjina 2; **Zemun,** Maršala Tita 34.

English Bookstores English-language publications are not always available. You are most likely to find newspapers at the Hotel Moskva and other main hotels, at booths at the train station, the pedestrian subway by the Beograd cinema, or in front of the Beograd department store. •

Travel Agencies **American Express:** Atlas Travel Agency, Moše Pijade 11, tel. 011/341–471. **Thomas Cook:** KSR, Moše Pijade 21, tel. 011/335–331.

Guided Tours

Orientation Tours One of the main agencies for sightseeing tours is **Putnik,** Dragoslava Jovanovića 1, tel. 011/320–697 or 011/332–591. It has a three-hour tour, covering the main sights, as well as a museum treasures tour, a tour of Belgrade by night, and a shopping tour. Check with the tourist information office for details.

Excursions **Putnik** also offers a range of day excursions and longer trips. A popular short one is to the hill of Avala (18 kilometers, 11 miles), with its lovely scenery and famous Memorial to the Unknown Soldier by Ivan Meštrović. Others are a long day–trip by hydrofoil down the Danube and tours to some of the magnificent medieval monasteries of Serbia.

Personal Guides Contact the **Association of Tourist Guides,** Studentski trg 21, tel. 011/629–811.

Exploring Belgrade

From the deck of a Danube passenger boat, British traveler Michael Quin described Belgrade as "a splendid collection of mosques, with their white tall minarets, palaces with their domes, gardens, cypresses, and shady groves." That was in the 1830s, with the end of Turkish rule just over the horizon. Today, you'll find just one mosque. The rest of the scene has been replaced by solid Central European architecture and the white high rises of New Belgrade, built on land that was still a swamp 40 years ago.

Poised at the meeting point of the rivers Danube and Sava, Belgrade—Beograd to the Yugoslavs—was destined for centuries to be on the edge of somebody's empire: Roman, Turkish, or Hapsburg. It has taken such an incredible battering over the past 2,000 years that its great age is far from obvious. Most of the more spectacular sights are in museums. But remember that this was also the first capital of a free South Slav state in modern times, the first to shake off both Ottoman Turk and Hapsburg rule and to struggle for its own identity.

Historic Belgrade *Numbers in the margin correspond with points of interest on the Belgrade map.*

When you've collected a map and the latest information from the tourist information center, head for one of the café terraces on nearby Trg Republike (Republic Square) where you can get your bearings over a Turkish coffee in this bustling hub of the city.

❶ **The National Museum** is right on the square, and its collections, from prehistory on, will keep history buffs happy for hours. Its main message is that some of Europe's earliest cultures—a

Belgrade

Fresco Gallery, **5**
Kalemegdan, **3**
Military Museum, **4**
National Museum, **1**
Orthodox Church Museum, **6**
Skadarlija, **2**
Tito Memorial Center, **7**
Zemun, **8**

number going back as far as 5000 BC—had their origins in these parts. Seek out the Bronze Age Duplja Chariot, borne by swamp birds and driven by an elegantly stylized charioteer, and the fine collection of gold jewelry from Greco-Roman times. *Open Tues., Wed., Fri., and Sat. 10–5, Thurs. 10–7, Sun. 10–2.*

② **Skadarlija** is to Belgrade what Montmartre is to Paris, though in this case it's the name of a small district centered on the narrow street of Skadarska. The Bohemian set made it theirs in the 19th and early 20th centuries, filling its cafés with smoke and hot debate. It's best to return here in the evening, for restoration has made it a favorite area for dining out (*see* Dining), as well as for street entertainment based on national poetry, drama, and music.

③ Along Knez Mihailova, which you pass on your way to **Kalemegdan,** you'll find some of the best shops in the city. The old fortifications of Kalemegdan are on the site of Belgrade's earliest roots. You'll understand why when you stand below Meštrović's Statue of Victory and look down on the meeting of the waters of the Sava and Danube, even less blue here than in Vienna! Until 1918, the opposite shores of both rivers were Hapsburg territory, from which the guns were turned on Belgrade for those first salvos of World War I. Nearly 2,000 years earlier, that same Danube had been the Romans' line of defense against invading barbarians. All in all, Kalemegdan Park is the **④** right place for the **Military Museum,** which is infinitely more interesting than it sounds. Its excellent displays show how Yugoslavia came to exist—and survive. *Open Tues.–Sun. 10–5.*

⑤ If you're not able to visit any of southern Yugoslavia's famous medieval monasteries, you'll find good reproductions of the best frescoes and sculptures in the **Fresco Gallery.** *Cara Uroša 20. Open Tues., Wed., and Fri., 10–5, Thurs. 10–7, Sun. 10–2.*

Time Out **Znak?**—"Café of the Question Mark"—offers respite and refreshment in one of Belgrade's oldest secular buildings. Its frame structure and bulging upper floor are typical of early 19th-century Balkan architecture. Znak? owes its name to the owner, who couldn't think of another after being admonished for "indecently" naming it Café of the Cathedral! Linger over a hearty soup or some strong coffee. *7 Jula 6.*

⑥ The **Orthodox Church Museum,** in the same block, has collections of paintings, manuscripts, vestments, and other ecclesiastic treasures. *Admission free. Open Sun. and Tues.–Fri. 8–1; Sat. 8–noon.*

The **Orthodox Cathedral** across the street, built around 1840, isn't really worth stopping to see unless your visit coincides with choral practice or one of the concerts often held there.

⑦ The late President Tito spent many hours at the **House of Flowers.** It has now become his mausoleum, his tomb surrounded by banks of flowers. This, together with his residence and other buildings dedicated to his life and times, make up the **Tito Memorial Center.** The peaceful park setting is south of the city center in the Dedinje District. *Bulevar oktobarske revolucije. Admission free. Open Tues.–Sun. 9–4.*

⑧ Join strollers and fishermen along the banks of the Danube from New Belgrade to its elderly neighbor **Zemun.** You can eat inexpensive *paprikaš* (rich fish or chicken soup) and other Dan-

ube specialties at one of the waterside restaurants and watch
the heavy traffic of barges and pleasure boats on Europe's most
famous river.

Off the Beaten Track

You'll find a restful oasis in **Topčider Park,** a favorite excursion
spot for Belgrade's citizens, about 45 minutes away by bus. A
number of early 19th-century buildings survive from the time
of Prince Miloš Obrenović, including his elegant "cottage."

Shopping

Shopping Districts Belgrade's main shopping districts are in and around Terazije
and Knez Mihailova. The city's largest department store is
Beogradjanka, located in the high-rise block of the Beograd
Palace on Maršala Tita. Another is **Beograd,** at Terazije 15–23,
with a 24-hour drugstore (*Dragstor*) in Nušićeva's pedestrian
subway.

Gift Ideas For exclusive (and expensive) fashions, look for the name
Jugoexport. For traditional handcrafts, head for the reliable
chain of **Narodna Radinost** stores. Don't forget about the major
museums as a source, especially for replicas and prints.
Zadruga Pravoslavnog Svestenstva, at Bulevar revolucije 24, is
excellent for reproduction icons and jewelry.

Food and Flea **Zeleni Venac,** in the city center, sells just about everything
Markets from just about every part of Yugoslavia—usually at the lowest
prices you're likely to come across. *Open 5 AM, including Sun.*

Dining

For details and price category definitions, *see* Dining in Staying
in Yugoslavia.

Very Expensive **Arhiv.** In the same building as the Metropol Hotel, Arhiv overlooks Tašmajdan Park. Its atmosphere is quiet and pleasant.
The menu includes Serbian specialties. *Bulevar revolucije 69,
tel. 011/330–910. Reservations accepted. AE, DC, V.*
Dva Jelena. This old favorite in the Skadarlija quarter spreads
over several rooms in different styles. Hors d'oeuvres and
grilled items are the specialties here, and there's music every
evening. *Skadarska 32, tel. 011/334–885. Reservations accepted. AE, DC, V.*
Ima Dana. Another favorite in Skadarlija, Ima Dana goes in for
steaks and other grilled meats. There is music each night in a
late 19th-century atmosphere. *Skadarska 38, tel. 011/334–422.
Reservations accepted. AE, DC, V.*
★ **Tri Šešira.** Diners here sometimes join in the nostalgic old
songs that make for a very bohemian atmosphere. Spicy pork
and lamb are the specialties. *Skadarska 29, tel. 011/347–501.
Reservations accepted. AE, DC, V.*

Expensive **Dunavski Cvet.** It is worth getting here early for a table with
fine views over the Danube. There are also performances of folk
and popular music, and the specialties include Balkan grills and
fresh fish. *Tadeuša Košćukog 63, tel. 011/186–823. Reservations accepted. AE.*
Zlatan Bokal. This is one of the less expensive Skadarlija establishments, matching the others for atmosphere and serving its

own special "Skadarlija Supper," a fixed-price menu featuring grilled lamb or fish and lots of spices. *Skadarska 26, tel. 011/ 334–834. Reservations accepted. AE, DC, MC, V.*

Zlatna Ladja. You'll find this excellent restaurant, serving mainly freshwater fish, right in the center of town. The decor is suitably nautical, with nets and a feeling that you're in a Danube barge. *Kolarčeva 9, tel. 011/334–018. Reservations accepted. AE, DC, V.*

Moderate **Ali Baba.** As its name suggests, this restaurant goes in for Oriental specialties, with Ottoman decor to match. It's in the old town of Zemun, about 25 minutes by bus from the center of Belgrade. *Cara Dušana 128, Zemun, tel. 011/102–302. Reservations accepted. No credit cards.*

Klub Književnika. The Pen Club is the translation of the name of this intriguing restaurant, with some of the best food in the city and an interesting clientele. Its animated atmosphere—journalists love the place—spreads over several small rooms. Don't be put off by the shabby entrance. Specials change often so ask for the day's recommended meal. *Francuska 7, tel. 011/ 627–931. Reservations advised. No credit cards.*

★ **Milošev Konak.** You'll find this popular restaurant in the pleasant setting of Topčider Park, about 45 minutes by bus from the center. The menu features Serbian specialties as well as more international fare. Be sure to include one of the hearty—and spicy—soups in your choice of meal. *Topčider 1, tel. 011/663–146. Reservations accepted. No credit cards.*

Inexpensive **Atina.** This popular pizzeria is good for a quick snack. It has a counter, opening onto the street, selling *piroški* (a kind of turnover). *Terazije 28. No reservations. No credit cards.*

Koloseum. Another express restaurant, Koloseum serves fast food and Serbian specialties. *Terazije 40. No reservations. No credit cards.*

Skala. One of the best restaurants for vegetarian meals, Skala is located out in the old town of Zemun, about 25 minutes by bus from the center of Belgrade. *Bežanijska 3, Zemun, tel. 011/ 196–605. Reservations accepted. No credit cards.*

Lodging

The hotels in the center of Belgrade are quite old, though most have been renovated. The best of the modern hotels are in New Belgrade, across the Sava River—less convenient but in a quieter location. For details and price category definitions, *see* Lodging in Staying in Yugoslavia.

Very Expensive **Beograd Intercontinental.** Built in 1979, the Intercontinental is
★ a high rise adjoining the glossy Sava Center, the main site for international conferences in New Belgrade. It's the most expensive—and best equipped—hotel in Belgrade, and the favorite among Americans. *Vladimira Popoviča 10, tel. 011/134–760, 011/138–708. 420 rooms with bath and shower. Facilities: saunas, pool, tennis, nightclub. AE, DC, MC, V.*

Jugoslavija. On the banks of the Danube in New Belgrade, the Jugoslavija is about a 15-minute cab ride from the center. Rooms on the top three floors have the best views of the city and the Danube. *Bulevar Edvarda Kardelja 3, tel. 011/600–222, 011/606–433. 600 rooms with bath and shower. Facilities: saunas, pool, nightclub, casino. AE, DC, MC, V.*

Expensive **Excelsior.** A town house dating from the '20s and renovated in 1988, the Excelsior is centrally located near Tašmajdan Park. The room decor ranges from traditional, with high windows and heavy curtains, to more modern, with better soundproofing and chrome. *Kneza Miloša 5, tel. 011/331–381. 81 rooms with bath. AE, DC, MC, V.*

★ **Metropol.** Looking out on Tašmajdan Park, the Metropol is sumptuous, if somewhat old-fashioned. Renovated in 1987, it attracts many Americans. *Bulevar revolucije 69, tel. 011/330–911–19. 218 rooms with bath. Facilities: nightclub, casino. AE, DC, MC, V.*

Slavija. This is a comfortable and modern hotel, but a little less central and more impersonal than the others in this price range. Rooms in the annex are less expensive. *Svetosavska 1–3, tel. 011/450–842. 536 rooms with bath or shower. AE, DC, MC, V.*

Moderate **Kasina.** This is a town house in the heart of the city. Some of the rooms can be noisy: It was last renovated in 1968 and the soundproofing needs some renewing. *Terazije 25, tel. 011/335–574. 96 rooms with bath. AE, DC, V.*

Splendid. Unlike most other Belgrade hotels, the Splendid has no restaurant, but it is in a quiet, central location near the Federal Assembly. This pre-World War II building was renovated in 1987 and the rooms are much brighter as a result. *Dragoslava Jovanoviča 5, tel. 011/335–443. 50 rooms with bath or shower. AE, DC, MC, V.*

Inexpensive **Taš.** Your money goes a long way at the quiet Taš, with its
★ pleasant location near the swimming stadium in Tašmajdan Park. The facilities—and the low cost—make it a favorite for families. *Borisa Kidriča 71, tel. 011/343–507. 19 rooms with bath. Facilities: saunas, pool, gymnasium. DC, V.*

The Arts

For listings of upcoming events, get the free magazine *Beogradscope* from a hotel or travel agency. Belgrade has no central ticket agency, so unless you have a guide or a helpful hotel reception clerk, you'll have to get your own tickets.

Concerts On summer evenings, the **Skadarlija** district is the scene of lively street entertainment, including national music. You'll also find open-air concerts in the parks, at **Kalemegdan,** and in the **Fresco Gallery.** Classical concerts are held in the **Zuzorić Art Pavilion,** Kalemegdan and, in winter, **Kolorac Hall,** Studentski trg.

Opera and Ballet The leading company is attached to the **National Theater;** the main season is in winter.

Folklore If the **Kolo Company** is in town, don't miss one of its performances at Kolorac Hall, Studentski trg.

Entertainment and Nightlife

Again, the bohemian quarter of Skadarlija is where most things happen.

Nightclubs In addition to the hotel nightclubs, try the **Lotos,** Zmaj jovina 4.

Discos Belgrade has no shortage of discos. Try **Amadeus,** Ćirila i Metodija 2A; **Disko-Videoteka,** Bezistan, Terazije 27; **Dom**

omladine (Youth Center), Makedonska 18; **Italijanski Bistro,** Masarikova 5.

Istria and the Julian Alps

On first impressions of scenery and architecture, Slovenia might be an extension of Austria or Italy, depending on the direction from which you approach it. And, historically, so it was. But listen closely and you'll hear the unmistakable Slav-ness of the Slovene language and become aware of countless differences in custom, dress, and food.

Most of Slovenia was ruled by the Austrian Hapsburgs until 1918. The Turks never got this far, and Hapsburg wealth, combined with Slovene intelligence and diligence, left a heritage that still makes it the most affluent part of Yugoslavia. The chalet-style houses of the mountains are neatly tended, as are the villas on the coast, their gardens bright with flowers. Indeed, the well-organized Slovenes believe that they contribute more than their fair share to the federal coffers, funds that, in turn, are distributed to their less favored compatriots in the south.

As you cross the invisible border into neighboring Croatia, the more volatile Croats might echo similar sentiments. But with accessible plains as well as mountains, the Croats have often been more active in both condoning and opposing oppression. The sinister pro-Nazi Ustaše movement, before and during World War II, was Croat, but, then, so were its fiercest and most dedicated opponent, Josip Broz Tito, and many of his partisan followers.

From Roman temples to Venetian Gothic to ornate Baroque, this is a region where you can pick your way through European cultural influences. This route is scenically glorious, too, and historically fascinating. A bonus is that some of the tourist amenities are as good as you'll find anywhere in Yugoslavia.

Getting Around

The whole of this itinerary is well served by bus, and this is the best way of seeing the countryside if you are not traveling by car. The main bus station in Ljubljana is by the railroad station at Trg osvobod fronte 4 (tel. 061/325–885). The final leg from Rijeka (near Opatija) to Zagreb takes about five hours by train.

Tourist Information

Bled. Kompas, Ljubljanska 7, tel. 064/77–245.
Ljubljana. Tourist Information Center, Titova 11, tel. 061/215–412, 061/224–222.
Opatija. Tourist Office Opatija, Maršala Tita 183, tel. 051/711–310.
Poreč. Adriatikturist, Trg Slobode 5, tel. 053/31–140.
Zagreb. Tourist Information Center, Trg Republike 11, tel. 041/278–910; Nikole Zrinjskog (Zrinjevac) 14, tel. 041/411–883, 041/441–880; Lotrščak Tower in the Upper Town.

Guided Tours

Many travel agencies run guided tours from Ljubljana and the major resorts. The main operators for this region are **Kompas,** in Ljubljana (tel. 061/331–444), and **Kvarner Express,** in Opatija (051/711–111).

Exploring Istria and the Julian Alps

The descent from the Würzen Pass drops you more or less into **Kranjska Gora,** a winter sports resort as well as a border town jammed with traffic in the main season.

Lakeside **Bled,** a few miles off the main road to Ljubljana, is the oldest and best equipped resort. All have a spectacular backdrop: the towering Julian Alps, which include Triglav, Yugoslavia's highest mountain at 2,912 meters (9,393 feet). Bled is full of self-confident style and was much favored by the Hapsburg aristocracy, not to mention the late President Tito, whose villa is now a hotel. Bled has a craggy castle on a cliff, a church on an islet, and Yugoslavia's only (and very good) golf course, yet it's basically a place for walking and climbing and just looking at stunning scenery. You can do this on a pleasant ride by *kočija* (horse-drawn carriage) to the **Vintgar Gorge,** 5 kilometers (3 miles) away.

Ljubljana sits astride the Ljubljanica river in the Ljubljana Gap, one of the few natural breaks in the mountains between inland Europe and the Mediterranean. That's why every empire builder passed this way and why the dominant building is the castle. The most interesting part of the city is at its feet, near the river around Mestni trg, medieval in origin but largely Baroque in decoration. Napoleon stayed in the Bishop's Palace, next to the cathedral, and must have looked out from those lovely arcaded balconies while he was busy re-creating the Roman province of Illyria, alas for him short-lived. You will come across traces of the Roman original (when Ljubljana was called Emona). Some can be found in the modern conference complex of Cankarjev in the downtown area west of the river. History buffs will get a fuller picture at the nearby **National Museum,** where treasures such as the magnificent bronze Vače urn predate the Romans by another half millenium. *Trg Herojev 1. Open Tues., Thurs., Sat., and Sun. 9–1, Wed. and Fri. 9–1 and 4–7.*

Even if caves usually leave you cold, don't miss the ones at **Postojna.** Dress warmly. Guided tours start with a 1½-mile train ride, followed by a walk through some of the labyrinthine passages that link caves into a series of glittering art galleries, created over many eons by the stalactites and stalagmites. *Postojna. Open 10–5, closed Mon.*

From Postojna take the main road in the direction of Koper and Portorož. To enjoy some lovely hill country that many of the sun seekers on the coast never see, take a left when you come upon signposts to **Buzet,** then head for the coast via Istarske Toplice. This was once border country between the territory of Venice and its Hapsburg rival, hence so many fortified hill villages. Buzet is one, **Motovun** another, and both are worth the detour.

Poreč is one of the largest resorts on the entire coast, but so widely scattered that you're unlikely to realize it. Most of the

Istria and the Julian Alps

accommodations are in well-planned, self-contained modern complexes up to several miles out of town, near beaches of rock or pebble. (Again, it's a good idea to check on a hotel's location before making reservations.) The town itself clusters on a headland and is packed in summer. Poreč attracts a lot of daytrippers just because it is so charming and has many note-worthy aspects dating back to Roman times. The most important sight is the **Basilica of Euphrasius,** built in the 6th century, with fabulous Byzantine mosaics in the apse. And ev-ery evening you can count on the waterfront to become an animated mini-bazaar for souvenirs and handcrafts, with street artists ready to immortalize you with a few swift strokes on paper.

There's a direct route across the Istrian Peninsula to Opatija, but it's worth the longer run via **Pula** to see its huge oval 1st-century AD amphitheater. Take in the hill villages of **Bale** and **Vodnjan** on the way.

In contrast to Poreč, **Opatija** is a much younger town but an older resort. It draws its Central European flavor from the no-bles and notables of the Austrian and Hungarian courts who came in droves during the 19th century to take advantage of its balmy winter climate. Visitors included Emperor Franz Josef, who entertained his mistress in neighboring Volosko. Opatija still attracts a winter clientele, but it's much more of a summer center nowadays and the closest thing to a French Riviera re-sort you'll find in Yugoslavia. A pleasant if extensive walk along the shore is the 12.8-kilometer (8-mile) meander from Volosko through Opatija to Lovran.

Neighboring **Rijeka** is Yugoslavia's biggest port; from here, it's a pleasant drive through the hills of Gorski Kotar to Karlovac, where you join the highway to **Zagreb.** The capital of Croatia, this large, unpretentious, straightforward city has the benefit of some of the country's best museums, theaters, and sports amenities. Stand in traffic-free **Trg Republike** and you're in the heart of the city, with most of the main sights within walking distance.

The first of these is the **cathedral.** It is remarkable not so much as a piece of architecture or house of worship but for the bustling humanity and varied wares on sale daily at Dolac Market, not far from its walls. This is the heart of Kaptol, the ecclesiastic community that for centuries developed separately from its secular neighbor, Gornji Grad, or Upper Town.

Gornji Grad is easily the most attractive part of Zagreb. If you're feeling lazy, take the venerable funicular up—the trip is less than a minute—from just off the main thoroughfare of Ilica. The cable railway will deposit you by **Lotrščak Tower,** where there's a tourist information center and small museum. But you would do better to climb up by steps through the narrow streets from Dolac to **Kamenita vrata** (Stone Gate). A devastating fire is said to have been miraculously halted here, and the gate now shelters a small shrine where those seeking solace have placed countless little plaques inscribed *hvala* (thank you), including one in English.

Gornji Grad is quite compact, so you can never really get lost. Browse through the old streets lined with the Baroque and neoclassical palaces replacing much older predecessors that were destroyed by earthquake or fire. Two churches here are worth seeing: **St. Catherine** and, especially, **St. Mark,** in which modern sculptures and frescoes blend well with the 14th-century Gothic sanctuary. The sculptures are by Ivan Meštrović, Yugoslavia's best known sculptor, who spent his last years in the United States. Not far away you'll find displays of his work in the **Meštrović Studio.** *Mletačka 8. Open Tues.–Sat. 10–6; Sun. 10–1.*

Also nearby is one of the finest buildings in Zagreb—the **Arts Center**—an old Jesuit monastery that has been beautifully restored to house world-class exhibits and is worth visiting for the building alone. *Jezuitski trg 4. Open Tues.–Sun. 10–8, Mon. 2–8.*

One more "must" is the **Mimara Museum** in the Lower Town, a fabulous one-man collection of art treasures from every major culture in the world. *Rooseveltova trg 4. Open Tues.–Sun. 10–8, Mon. 2–8.*

Finally, try to make time to visit **Sljeme,** high above Zagreb. Take the cable car from the Gračani district (or trams 14 and 21 from the center) or drive up. The views over Zagreb and its hilly hinterland of Zagorje are memorable.

Dining and Lodging

For details and price category definitions, *see* Dining and Lodging in Staying in Yugoslavia.

Bled
Dining

Golf Club Restaurant. This is attached to the splendid golf course about 3½ kilometers (2 miles) east of the resort. It's a glorious setting, and the food is good. Grilled pork and lamb are always tasty here. *Tel. 064/78–180. Reservations advised. AE, DC, MC, V. Closed Jan.–Feb. Very Expensive.*

Lodging

Grand Hotel Toplice. Built in the '30s and renovated in 1968, the Grand Hotel is a pretty, vine-covered building, very much in the old tradition. It's located by the lake and is a favorite among Americans. *Lakefront, tel. 064/77–222. 121 rooms with bath or shower. Facilities: saunas, pool, gymnasium. AE, DC, MC, V. Very Expensive.*

★ **Vila Bled.** Formerly a summer residence of President Tito, Villa Bled is an elegant villa set in gardens by the lake. It is a lovely location, even if the rates are high. *Cesta Svobode 26, tel. 064/77–436. 30 rooms with bath and shower. Facilities: lake beach, tennis, golf, boats for rent. AE, DC, MC, V. Closed Jan. 15–Mar. 15. Very Expensive.*

Jelovica. The Jelovica is modern, with gardens extending to the lake shore. Extensive improvements were completed in 1987 and rooms are comfortable. Jelovica also has the unusual facility of a bowling alley. *Cesta Svobode 5, tel. 064/77–316. 176 rooms with shower. AE, DC, MC. Closed Nov. 1–Dec. 15. Moderate.*

Ljubljana
Dining

Na Brinju. This small restaurant goes in for good home cooking. You can eat out in the pleasant small garden in summer, but either arrive early or make reservations for the best tables. Start any meal with the soup of the day, which is almost a meal in itself. *Vodovodna 44, tel. 061/342–783. Reservations advised. Closed weekends. Moderate.*

Pod Velbom. The in-house restaurant of the Hotel and Catering School, Pod Velbom is located in the old town. Try the Slovene specialties, which include *Dumaiski Zrezek* (a type of wiener schnitzel), or the Austrian-influenced sausages. *Stari trg 3, tel. 061/222–136. Reservations advised. MC, V. Closed Sun. Moderate.*

Lodging

Holiday Inn. Built in 1980, this is the best and most expensive hotel in Ljubljana. Most Americans who stay here are attracted by the location and services. This hotel is often busy with conferences, so it is best to make reservations. *Miklošičeva 3, tel. 061/211–434. 133 rooms with bath. Facilities: saunas, pool. AE, DC, MC, V. Very Expensive.*

Slon. Right in the heart of the city, the Slon has the benefits and drawbacks of a central location. Rooms overlooking the main street will be noisy. Its restaurant is good, specializing in national dishes: Try the *Štruklji*, a buckwheat and cheese pastry. *Titova 10, tel. 061/211–232. 185 rooms with bath or shower. AE, DC, MC, V. Moderate.*

Ilirja. A bit removed from it all on the city outskirts, Ilirja is worth considering if you're on a budget. This hotel is also a conference favorite, so try to make reservations. *Trg prekomorskih brigad 4, tel. 061/551–162. 136 rooms, 129 with bath. AE, DC, MC. Inexpensive.*

Opatija
Dining

Ariston. Spread over several rooms, the intimate Ariston restaurant features regional specialties such as *Skampa* (Adriatic shrimp). It's about a mile from the resort center and is very popular. *Maršala Tita 243, tel. 051/711–379. Reservations advised. AE, DC, MC, V. Expensive.*

Bevanda. Priding itself on its fish dishes, Bevanda has a coastal setting that is appropriately maritime—about 2½ kilometers (1½ miles) from the resort center toward Volosko. Try the grilled fish or *ostrige* (mussels cooked in wine). *Maršala Tita 62, tel. 051/712–036. Reservations advised. No credit cards. Closed Jan. 1–15, June 15–July 10. Expensive.*

Plavi Podrum. Seafood is the specialty at this restaurant, which is right by the water about 2 miles from the resort center. Try the *brodet* (fish soup), which has a variety of fresh ingredients and winds up tasting like the French *bouillabaisse. Obala F. Supila 4, tel. 051/713–629. Reservations advised. AE, MC, V. Moderate.*

Lodging **Ambassador.** A high rise, dating from the '60s, the Ambassador is on the sea by a rock-and-pebble beach near the resort center. It is one of the most popular local hotels with Americans and does service as an attractive conference center. *F. Peršića 1, tel. 051/712–211. 280 rooms with bath and shower. Facilities: pools, sauna. AE, DC, V. Expensive.*

Kristal. The Kristal is an old hotel that was attractively modernized in 1970. It is also right by the sea and has separate beaches for sunning and swimming. Off-season rates drop dramatically. *Maršala Tita 207, tel. 051/711–333. 136 rooms with bath or shower. Facilities: saunas, pool. AE, DC, V. Expensive.*

Kvarner. The grande dame of Opatija, the Kvarner was built in 1884 with spacious public rooms lit by glittering chandeliers. Even now, the atmosphere is reminiscent of the Hapsburg era and the heady days of the Orient Express. Rooms are comfortable and large, with good views of the hotel's rocky beach and the neighboring coastline. *Park 1 maja 4, tel. 051/711–211. 57 rooms with bath or shower. Facilities: saunas, pools. AE, DC, V. Expensive.*

Poreč **Parentium.** The main advantage of the Parentium is its quiet
Lodging location among gardens on a wooded headland, about 5 kilometers (3 miles) from the resort and just by a rock-and-pebble beach. Rooms are airy and bright, and the Taverna serves Istrian specialties. *Zelena Laguna, tel. 053/31–144. 362 rooms with bath or shower. Facilities: saunas, pools, casino, nightclub, and facilities of nearby Zelena Laguna sports center. AE, DC, MC, V. Expensive.*

Neptun. This is one of the few hotels located within the resort center. It is about a 10-minute walk from a beach but overlooks the old harbor and is therefore ideal for those who want to feel part of the local scene. *Poreč center, tel. 053/31–711. 143 rooms with bath or shower. AE, DC, MC, V. Moderate.*

Zagreb **Gradski Podrum.** On a corner of Republic Square, Gradski
Dining Podrum is one of Zagreb's best-known and most elegant eating places. It is probably the best place to try local specialties, such as *pohovano pile* (breaded chicken) and the flaky *štrudla* pastry. Wash it down with either *Zumberak* or *Moslavina:* Both are light local wines. *A. Cesarca 2, tel. 041/276–597. Reservations advised. AE, DC, MC, V. Very Expensive.*

Pod mirnim krovovima. The specialties here are *jagnje* (lamb-on-a-spit) and freshwater fish dishes. It's fairly central, in the direction of Maksimir Park, and almost always crowded. *Fijanova 7, tel. 041/216–269. Reservations advised. AE, DC, MC, V. Expensive.*

Starogradski podrum. Set in the cellars of the old city hall in the Upper Town, this restaurant has a great atmosphere. It features unusual specialties taken from an early 19th-century recipe book. *Ćirila i Metoda 5, tel. 041/423–646. Reservations advised. AE, DC, MC, V. Closed lunch. Expensive.*

Lodging
★
Esplanade. Opposite the main railroad station, this imposing turn-of-the-century town house was last renovated in the mid '80s. The service is good and the hotel is generally very comfortable, but rooms overlooking the terrace (with dancing) can be noisy in summer. It is the first choice of most American visitors. *Mihanovićeva 1, tel. 041/534–444. 236 rooms with bath or shower. Facilities: nightclub. AE, DC, MC, V. Very Expensive.*

Dvorac Brezovica. If you have a car, it is worth going about 9½ kilometers (6 miles) south of the city to this hotel in a quiet location. Once an old castle, it now offers cottage-style accommodations along with an elegant restaurant. *Brezovica center, tel. 041/521–880. 28 rooms with bath or shower. No credit cards. Moderate.*

Central Yugoslavia and the Dalmatian Coast

This route starts from Sarajevo and heads south, through Mostar, to Korčula and the coast, ending up at Dubrovnik. There's nothing restful about the scenery you'll see. It is mountainous all the way, some of them thick with forests, others rocky and arid. Most of them are rent by magnificent river gorges until you reach the Dalmatian Coast, when horizons open out to the island-studded Adriatic.

It would be difficult to find an itinerary with greater contrasts—scenically, culturally, even gastronomically. When Bosnia fell to the Turks in the 16th century, it became one of their most westerly provinces. Ivo Andrić's Nobel Prize-winning novel, *Bridge Over the Drina*, gives a gripping account of the uneasy and changing relationships between Muslim and Christian during those centuries. The story ends more than 400 years later, with Bosnia becoming a leading pawn in the chess game of Hapsburg power politics and eventually the scene of events leading to the horrors of World War I. As a result, few regions can boast a skyline shared by so many minarets, church domes, and spires, while plaintive Oriental music mingles with the latest pop blaring from modern apartment blocks a stone's throw from Oriental-style bazaars.

When you come to the coast, it's a totally different stage set. The medieval walled city of Dubrovnik never fell to anyone until Napoleon ended its status as independent republic in 1806. Farther south, the Montenegrins in the rugged fastness of their mountains were never wholly subjugated by the Turks. Their ferocious independence and bitter blood feuds had much in common with those of the Highland Scots! "Those are men who, when asked to pay tribute, offer stones," thundered British statesman William Gladstone in the House of Commons in the 19th century. "These are the men who dress cowards into women's clothes, and whose wives, when need requires, boldly get hold of the gun."

Getting Around

In order to see all the sights, you'll need a car. Otherwise, you have the choice of train or bus from Sarajevo to Kardeljevo on the coast. From Kardeljevo down to Dubrovnik and Budva, there are only buses. Alternatively, you can make use of the coastal services (*see* the section below about the stretch from Korčula to Dubrovnik). There are flights back to Belgrade from Tivat, Budva's nearest airport. For a much wider choice of flights (Belgrade, Zagreb, overseas), you will need to return to Dubrovnik.

Tourist Information

Budva. Montenegroturist, tel. 086/41–414.
Dubrovnik. Tourist Information Center, P. Miličevića 1, tel. 050/26–354, 050/26–355.
Korčula. Tourist Office Marko Polo, tel. 050/711–067.
Mostar. Tourist Information Center, Mala Tepe, tel. 088/36–878.
Sarajevo. Tourist Bureau, JNA 50, tel. 071/24–844, 071/25–151.

Guided Tours

The mainland route from Sarajevo to Dubrovnik is a well-traveled trail featured in many tours marketed overseas, as well as by Yugoslav agencies. If you're staying in Dubrovnik and other main coastal areas, you'll also find local agencies arranging excursions inland to Mostar and Sarajevo. Regular runs by bus or boat are available to see most of the sights, too. Among the main agencies in these regions are **Unis-Turist** in Sarajevo (tel. 071/23–140, and **Atlas** in Dubrovnik (tel. 050/27–333.

Exploring Central Yugoslavia and the Dalmatian Coast

Sarajevo, the capital of Bosnia-Herzegovina, is a city engulfed by mountains. To find the most interesting sections of Sarajevo, you'll have to wend past its high-rise suburbs and industrial complexes because nature forced this city to grow up rather than out. But you will reach the solid Hapsburg structures, built between 1878 and World War I, and finally the old Turkish core of what was originally called *Sarajovasi* (Plain around the Palace) at the head of a narrow valley.

The tourist office is only a short stroll from the hub of the old town that is known as **Baščaršija** (the old bazaar), which, despite a lot of tidying up, is still a maze of alleys. They thread their way past tiny shops with double-shuttered doors, behind which merchants often double as craftsmen. Whole streets are dedicated to any one of a dozen crafts: There are saddlers, weavers, blacksmiths, coppersmiths, and goldsmiths. Among them are eating places known as *aščinica*, serving spicy local specialties, as well as a growing number of café-discos.

A number of the most attention-getting buildings in this part of town date from the more enlightened rule of Gazi Husref-Bey in the 16th century, including the finest of the city's 73 mosques, **Begova Džamija** (Mosque of the Bey). Sightseers

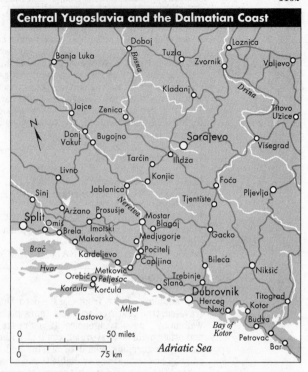

Central Yugoslavia and the Dalmatian Coast

Adriatic Sea

here often outnumber the faithful, and it's arranged so that you won't need to remove your shoes as in most other mosques. Other old buildings have been converted for more mundane purposes, like the *hamam* (public baths that are now a restaurant) and *bezistan* (a covered market that's now commercial premises).

Close to Baščaršija you will find the **Orthodox church** (Maršala Tita 83), crouching behind a high wall to conform with a Turkish law that restricted the height of Christian places of worship. The magnificent iconostasis, a screen on which icons are placed, dates from its restoration in the 18th century. On the same street, there is also a restored **synagogue** commemorating the large Jewish community that flourished here from 1500, following the expulsion of Sephardic Jews from Spain.

Several bridges span the little Miljacka river that flows through the city. On a street corner by **Princip Bridge,** you'll see two footsteps sunk into the sidewalk. They mark (more or less) the spot from which student Gavrilo Princip fired the fatal shots at Archduke Franz Ferdinand, the first of a series of sparks that exploded into World War I.

Pleasant excursions can be taken into the mountains of **Trebević, Jahorina,** and **Bjelašnica,** scene of the 1984 Winter Olympics. But your first choice should be an outing much closer to Sarajevo. Climb above the old town to the eastern slopes, scattered with ancient Jewish and Muslim cemeteries, and at one of the unpretentious cafés, sit over a Turkish coffee (Bosnians make the best) or *slivovica* (plum brandy). On a summer night, especially at soft twilight, the views from above the city are magical.

A few miles out of Sarajevo on your way to the coast, you pass the small spa of **Ilidža,** where Archduke Ferdinand spent the evening before his assassination. It is worth a short detour here, on foot or by horse and buggy, to see **Vrelo Bosne,** the source of the river Bosna as it peacefully bubbles out of the rock from several springs. Rivers are a major feature of Bosnia-Herzegovina's landscape; some now tamed into a series of lake-like reservoirs, such as those along the Neretva, which you'll follow for much of the way to Mostar. The mountain scenery changes dramatically as you pass from the deeply wooded ranges of Bosnia into the pale, arid limestone ridges of Herzegovina, which, despite its thirsty look, produces excellent wines, olives, almonds, and tobacco.

Mostar is Herzegovina's main town. It has grown beyond recognition since its days as a backwoods halt in a remote Turkish province, but it is the Turkish-era Old Town that everyone wants to see. Its center is the slender steep-arched **bridge** built in 1556 and flanked by two watch towers—one of Yugoslavia's most photographed sights. You'll probably find some of Mostar's youth trying to prove their manhood by diving from its highest point into the fast green waters of the Neretva below. The most interesting of the town's many mosques is that of **Karadjoz Beg,** a few hundred yards away. **Kajtaz House,** in Gaše Ilića street, is the place to go for an insight into how a Moslem and his harem once lived—a splendid 16th-century residence that has been adapted over the centuries.

Stay with the river Neretva all the way to the coast. Apart from lovely scenery, there are three particular curiosities along (or a little off) the way. One is **Blagaj,** where a 16th century monastery of the Dervishes overlooks the source of the Buna river, which gushes out from a sheer rock face. The second is probably Europe's newest place of pilgrimage, the village of **Medjugorje.** It was catapulted out of obscurity in 1981 when visions of the Virgin Mary appeared to local schoolchildren. Hordes of believers and sightseers now throng to this spot, about 30 kilometers (20 miles) southwest of Mostar.

The third is **Počitelj,** an attractive fortified village, restored in recent years and now an active artists' colony.

If you're not traveling by car, it will be more practical to visit the island and town of **Korčula** by regular boat from Dubrovnik (*see* below), which takes just over three hours. If you are driving, you should now head down the long, narrow, and mountainous Pelješac Peninsula to **Orebić** for the ferry. It carries you across the strait to the exquisite old walled town of Korčula in about 20 minutes.

Korčula is attractive and charming. Narrow, crooked streets suddenly open out onto little squares bordered by old churches and former palaces, all bearing the imprint of long periods of Venetian rule. One of them is known as Marco Polo's house, where this formidable Venetian traveler of medieval times is said to have been born. Was he born here? No one can say for sure, but Polos are still in residence in Korčula.

Korčula offers a long list of art and architectural treasures. The most important is the Cathedral of **Sveti Marko** (St. Mark), a blend of Romanesque, Gothic, and Baroque. But at almost every turn, there's some unheralded feature to be observed: a Renaissance balcony or Gothic window, a family crest or elaborate cornice. If you try the good, sometimes powerful, local wines, beware of the amber-colored Grk—it goes straight to your knees!

The next stop on the tour is **Dubrovnik,** though the best approach is from the south. You have to negotiate the harbor area of Gruž from the north, and that means missing the full visual impact of this walled city crowning a headland.

By means of sheer diplomatic guile, Dubrovnik survived until the 19th century as a tiny independent republic while every place around it fell to Turk, Venetian, or Hapsburg. (It was then called Ragusa, from which comes the word "argosy," meaning a great merchant ship.) The city also survived a number of earthquakes: The worst was in 1667, although the most recent, centered on Montenegro in 1979, also left its mark. Current restoration has led to new discoveries, but this is a long-term project and you may find a number of buildings still closed for restoration. The general effect of Gothic and Renaissance in pale Dalmatian stone is exquisite, however, and it will be very surprising if Dubrovnik disappoints you.

If you want to be within strolling distance of the old walled city, which is closed to traffic, choose your hotel carefully. Most of them are on the peninsula of **Lapad,** three to five kilometers (two or three miles) to the north, but the bus service is good.

The tourist information center is in the Old Town, near Pile (West) Gate. After collecting a map and the excellent free *Information Dubrovnik* booklet, get your bearings by following the main thoroughfare of **Placa** (also known as Stradun), which links Pile Gate with Ploče (East) Gate. You can climb up onto the **walls** (open summer 9–7) from either of these gates. The total circuit is about a mile (if you're short on time, at least do the landward side), and it's worth it for views of ancient tiled roofs, domes, and spires or glimpses into monastic courtyards and tiny rooftop gardens. In summer, you'll be accompanied by the tireless swoopings of swifts.

Allow time to wander up and down the maze of alleys and stairways that thread through the Old Town, which now has a large number of art studios, boutiques, and restaurants. In the course of your wanderings, you'll come across several small statues of Sveti Vlaho (St. Blaise), the city's patron saint, set into niches in the walls or adorning a church. The most famous is made of silver and shows the saint holding a model of the city: This is in the Baroque **church of Sveti Vlaho** at the eastern end of the Placa. Just around the corner in Pred Dvorom is one of the city's most beautiful buildings, the Rector's Palace. It houses the **Cultural and Historical Museum,** which tells of the life and times of the Ragusan Republic. It was from here that the rector ruled, a month at a time; during this period he was barred from leaving the confines of the palace for fear that he would be distracted from his duties. *Pred Dvorom. Open daily 9–1 and 2–6.*

For peace and quiet, seek out the lovely Gothic cloisters of the **Dominican Monastery,** near Ploče Gate. Try to make time for the short trip from the Old Town harbor to the green island of **Lokrum,** a protected nature reserve and favorite swimming place, from which you get wonderful views of the city.

The road from Dubrovnik to Budva features some of the finest coastal scenery in southern Europe. There are sweeping views back to Dubrovnik, while the magnificent Bay of Kotor in Montenegro is the closest you'll come to a Norwegian fjord this side of Oslo. Beneath towering mountains are a score of small communities, scattered along the shores of this contorted sea arm. Most share a seafaring history. The walled town of **Kotor** is the most attractive, although it is still being restored after major earthquake damage in 1979. The 12th-century cathedral is still closed, but the **Maritime Museum,** housed in the ancient Grgurin Palace, provides a fascinating picture of the region's seafaring tradition.

South of the Bay of Kotor, the old section of **Budva** sits appealingly on a headland that was once an island. The Greeks and Romans were here for a time, but the Turks didn't quite get this far. Most of the buildings in the old walled town (again restored after the 1979 earthquake) date from the nearly four centuries of Venetian rule. Budva, in such a lovely setting, has considerable charm—not to mention its many modern tourist amenities. Most hotels are near the coarse sand or pebble beaches of **Slovenska Plaža,** about a mile from the town center or a little farther away in **Bečići.** Budva is an excellent base for excursions along the coast or into the Montenegrin mountains.

Dining and Lodging

For details and price category definitions, *see* Dining and Lodging in Staying in Yugoslavia.

Budva
Lodging

Avala. The modern Avala, dating from the early '80s, is close to the Old Town and about 232 meters (250 yards) from a small beach of coarse sand. Rooms are bright, well equipped, and quiet. This hotel is particularly popular with young people—many of whom are German—eager to get involved with the water sports. *Budva center, tel. 086/41-022. 223 rooms with bath or shower. Facilities: pools, water skiing, boat rental, nightclub, casino. AE, DC, MC, V. Expensive.*

Slovenska Plaža. This is a major new complex built in the early '80s, surrounded by landscaped gardens and close to a long, pebbled beach of coarse sand, about a mile from the Old Town. Accommodations, reception area, restaurants, and other amenities are in separate units to create a "village" atmosphere. *Slovenska Plaža, Budva, tel. 086/41-044. 703 rooms with bath or shower, plus apartments. Facilities: pools, tennis, water skiing, wind surfing, table tennis, boat rental. AE, DC, MC, V. Closed Nov. 15–Mar. 15. Moderate to Expensive.*

Dubrovnik
Dining

Amfora. Located at Gruž Harbor, Amfora has a warm and casual atmosphere. Its wide-ranging menu features specialties using locally caught fish. Try the seafood risotto or any of the grilled fish specials. *Gruška obala 22, tel. 050/22-919. Reservations advised. V. Very Expensive.*

Dubravka. With an attractive location near Pile Gate, Dubravka has tables set under shady trees. The menu covers both local seafood specialties and more international fare. Squid and octopus—both regulars on the menu—are always good and fresh. *Brsalje 1, tel. 050/26-319. Reservations ad-*

vised. AE, DC, MC, V. Closed Nov. 15–Apr. Moderate to Expensive.

Lodging **Belvedere.** One of the best coastal hotels in Yugoslavia, the Belvedere opened in 1985 with top-class facilities and service in a good location about a mile from the Old Town (boat service across the bay in summer). It's near a rocky beach and has dining terraces looking out over the sea, and it's a favorite among Americans. *Frana Supila 28, tel. 050/28–655. 200 rooms with bath and shower, plus suites. Facilities: saunas, pools, table tennis, gymnasium, solarium, billiards, nightclub, several bars and restaurants. AE, DC, MC, V. Very Expensive.*

Dubrovnik President. Built in 1976 and renovated annually, the President is on the Lapad Peninsula, 4 kilometers (2½ miles) from the Old Town. It rises five stories on streamlined tiers above a pebbled beach. Every room has its own balcony with a seaview. *Dubrava-Babin Kuk, tel. 050/22–999, 050/20265. 163 rooms with bath, plus suites. Facilities: drugstore, pizzeria, saunas, pool, tennis, and sports facilities of nearby Dubrava Center. AE, DC, MC, V. Closed Jan. 4–Mar. Very Expensive.*

Dubrovnik Palace. In a quiet location on a wooded headland, 4 kilometers (2½ miles) from the Old Town in the Lapad district, the Dubrovnik Palace is popular with Americans. A modern hotel, renovated in 1985, it also has a rocky beach. Most of the well-equipped rooms have seaviews. *Masarykov put 18, tel. 050/28–556. 270 rooms with bath, 47 with shower. Facilities: saunas, swimming pool, tennis, table tennis, disco nearby. AE, DC, V. Closed Nov. Expensive.*

Korčula **Adio Mare.** The specialties here are old Korčula and Venetian
Dining dishes, served on the vine-covered terrace of a fine late Gothic-Renaissance building in the Old Town. Try the fish soup, which is more like a chowder or stew, and then either *jastog* (lobster) or *rak* (crayfish). *Korčula Old Town, tel. 050/711–253. Reservations advised. AE, V. Closed Oct. 15–Apr. Moderate.*

Planjak. This is the favorite with the locals, who are likely to burst into Dalmatian song while you enjoy the restaurant's good home cooking on its covered terrace by the sea. Follow their lead and accompany a meal of seafood with the locally produced *Grk* white wine. *Old Town, tel. 050/711–015. No reservations. AE, DC, MC, V. Moderate.*

Lodging **Liburna.** Located on a wooded promontory, Liburna is a short walk from the Old Town. It opened in 1985 and has the best facilities of any hotel in Korčula. It's by a rocky beach and has many choices for water sports fans. *Korčula, tel. 050/711–026, 050/711–006. 84 rooms, 25 apartments with bath or shower. Facilities: pool, tennis, miniature golf, windsurfing, boat and bicycle rental, table tennis, billiards. AE, DC, MC, V. Expensive.*

Korčula. Renovated in 1982 and a real favorite with regular visitors to Korčula, this hotel is by the sea in the heart of the Old Town. About 186 meters (200 yards) from a beach, the Korčula is ideal if you want to feel part of the local scene or if you prefer accommodations on a smaller scale. Ask for a room *not* facing the street if you want to be spared late-night noise. *Old Town, tel. 050/711–078. 24 rooms with bath. AE, DC, MC, V. Closed Nov.–Apr. Moderate.*

Mostar **Labirint.** The main attraction here is the setting in the Old
Dining Town, with a terrace overlooking the river and a fine view of the Old Bridge. It's somewhat over-geared for tourists. *Ku-*

jundžiluk 12, tel. 088/32–681. Reservations advised. AE. Closed Dec.–Mar. Expensive.

Ruža. This is Mostar's newest hotel, and it is well placed for the Old Bridge and Old Town. *Oneščukova bb, tel. 088/36–257. 70 rooms with bath or shower. AE, DC, MC, V. Expensive.*

Stari Most. This restaurant takes its name from the Old Bridge, which is nearby. Roast lamb is the specialty here. Reserve or come early for one of the best tables in the garden. *Oneščukova 18, tel. 088/37–215. Reservations advised. AE. Moderate.*

Lodging **Neretva.** One of the oldest hotels in Yugoslavia, Neretva was built in the 1890s. It was renovated in 1950, but is showing its age today. It will suit those with a taste for more traditional accommodations—which in some rooms means a bathroom down the hall. The Neretva has a good central location by the river. *Trg Republike 7, tel. 088/32–330, 088/21–454. 42 rooms, 28 with bath. AE, DC, MC, V. Moderate.*

Sarajevo **Aeroplan.** Decorated in typical Bosnian style and located in the
Dining city center, Aeroplan has Bosnian specialties to match. Among them is *Bosanski lonac*, the delicious and hearty local stew. *Sarači 3, tel. 071/216–719. Reservations advised. AE, DC, MC. Expensive.*

Daire. Daire has been charmingly converted from a complex of 17th-century storehouses. Again, the food and decor are typically Bosnian, reflecting the centuries of Turkish influence. Try the *musaka* or *sarma*, stuffed vine leaf. *Halači 5, tel. 071/537–614. Reservations advised. AE, DC, MC. Expensive.*

Lodging **Holiday Inn Sarajevo.** Given its trial by fire when it was the base for many journalists covering the 1984 Olympics, the Holiday Inn remains the hotel most frequented by Americans. It is a modern, businesslike hotel, built in 1983, near the railroad station. *Vojvode putnika 6a, tel. 071/215–688. 330 rooms with shower. Facilities: saunas, pool. AE, DC, MC. Expensive.*

Europa. Here is a hotel that has been accommodating travelers for more than 100 years; it was renovated and expanded in 1978. Service can be erratic, but it has style and is ideally placed in the Old Town. *JNA bb, tel. 071/532–722. 225 rooms with shower. AE, DC, MC. Moderate.*

National. Across the river from the center, the National is an older hotel, but worth considering if you're on a budget. It has fewer comforts than its more modern counterparts, but the dark carpets and old wood everywhere combine to give it more of an exotic feel. *Obala P. Komune 5, tel. 071/532–266. 75 rooms, 43 with bath. No credit cards. Inexpensive.*

Macedonia

It is quite a trek to reach Macedonia, Yugoslavia's landlocked southernmost republic. But it's worth it to experience one of the least spoiled corners of Europe. At one time, of course, Macedonia was the most powerful nation in the ancient world and was even Alexander the Great's launchpad for a vast empire. Today, the original territory of Macedonia is fragmented between Yugoslavia, Greece, and Bulgaria, although many Macedonians share an intense feeling of nationality that transcends any such boundaries.

It's not only the name that has survived centuries of Roman, Byzantine, and Turkish rule, along with the more recent games of power. The resemblance between some young Macedonians and the classical busts of their forefathers is really quite startling.

In addition to fine scenery—mountains, fertile plains, and river gorges—Macedonia has a number of lakes skirting its borders with Greece and Albania. These are good for the more typical tourist pursuits of swimming and sailing.

Continuing excavations at Heraclea Lyncestis (near Bitola), Lichnidos (Ohrid), Skupi (Skopje), and Stobi reveal ever more evidence of the sophisticated lifestyles enjoyed in Greco-Roman and Roman-Byzantine times. But above all, this was a stronghold of the Orthodox faith, and you'll see dozens of medieval monasteries—some of the earliest and finest examples of an architectural style that expressed a dynamism never before seen in the Byzantine period. Some art historians claim that this style foreshadowed the Renaissance of the 15th and 16th centuries, by which time Macedonia itself had been submerged under Ottoman rule.

Modern industrialization and tourism have imposed their own imprint, sometimes regrettable. But in the bazaars and marketplaces and in scores of small communities, a profusion of folklore is alive and well. The jet age still seems a world away.

Getting Around

Two or three flights a week are scheduled from Skopje to Ohrid, taking 30 minutes. To see all the sights mentioned, you need a car. Otherwise the main areas of the region are well served by bus. The bus terminus in Skopje is in the center of town, near the Stone Bridge (tel. 091/236–254.

Tourist Information

Ohrid. Turist bureau Biljana, Partizanska, tel. 096/22–494.
Skopje. Gradski zid, blok III, tel. 091/233–843; also at the entrance to Čaršija (Bazaar), near the Stone Bridge.

Guided Tours

Tours around Macedonia are arranged in the main season from Skopje by **Interimpex** (tel. 091/239–669 or 091/228–604). Sightseeing tours from either Skopje or Ohrid take in all the main historic sights and places of natural beauty in their respective localities. Much of this itinerary also is featured in monastery tours from Belgrade.

Exploring Macedonia

Skopje is in a beautiful setting at the foot of the mountain of Vodno, with views to the more distant range of Šar Planina. First impressions are of a thoroughly modern and fast-growing city. In fact, its roots are in prehistory. As the Roman town of Skupi, it prospered on a site about 8 kilometers (five miles) northwest of the present center.

An earthquake destroyed ancient Skupi in AD 518, and nearly 1,500 years later, a similar disaster caused Skopje's rebirth as a modern city. If you arrive by train, you'll see, next to the new rail-

Macedonia

road station, the restored remnants of the old one (now housing the **Skopje Town Museum**), with its clock stopped at 5:17. That was the time on the morning of July 26, 1963, when the first of a series of tremors rumbled beneath Skopje. The earthquake ultimately destroyed 80% of the buildings and took more than 1,000 lives. The building of the new Skopje and restoration of the old are the result of a massive national effort with international support.

The city is divided by the winding river Vardar. The remains of the original fortified town rise above the north bank. The core of the **Old Town,** developed over 500 years of Turkish rule, is below: It is a maze of narrow alleys threading through the Čaršija, or Bazaar. From the modern center, you reach it by crossing the fine old **Stone Bridge.** You soon come to the tourist information center, where you can get a map and the latest information. **Čaršija** is by far the most interesting quarter, with its workshops and boutiques offering slippers and other leather goods and items of gold and silver. You eventually come out into the lively marketplace near the largest of Skopje's several mosques.

Three main sights are not to be missed. The first is the little Orthodox church of **Sveti Spas** (St. Savior) on Samoilava Street. Its iconostasis—a magnificent carved screen separating nave from chancel—was completed in 1824. On the far right panel, you'll find self-portraits of the artists as they wield their tools at a workbench.

Kuršumli han is the second stop, a fine inn from the 16th century, now restored and housing the imposing archaeological exhibits of the **Museum of Macedonia.** *Old Bazaar. Open 10–6, closed Mon.*

For the third sight, you'll need to travel 6½ kilometers (4 miles) up the slopes of Vodno mountain to the church of **Sveti Pantelejmon** at Nerezi. It contains some of the most beautiful and best-known Byzantine frescoes in the country—among the first in the 12th century to demonstrate a new and powerful humanism. The grief on the face of Mary is almost tangible as she mourns over the body of Christ in *The Lamentation.* Just across the courtyard there is a good restaurant (*see* Dining).

About 80 kilometers (50 miles) southeast of Skopje, to the right of the main road, the ruins of the once great Roman city of **Stobi** lie scattered about the grassy plain of the Vardar valley. Its heyday extended from the 1st century until the Goths sacked it in the 5th; the earthquake of AD 518 completed the destruction. There's much more to be seen than first impressions might suggest, and guides are available to explain the site in meticulous detail. But there's a lot to be said for exploring alone and letting your imagination wander. Most of what you see is from the 4th and 5th centuries, including some of the most complete remains of early-Christian houses in the Mediterranean region. There are remains of churches, palaces, baths, and a fine amphitheater, but the highlights for most visitors are the outstanding mosaics totaling several thousand square yards. Time your trip for late April or after or you might miss out on them; they're protected by a covering of sand during the winter.

Just beyond Stobi, you turn right for the narrow, curving road over the 1,010-meter (3,260-foot) Pletvor Pass. Somewhat clogged by trucks, it leads to the tobacco-growing center of Prilep. From here the main road to Bitola streaks across the fertile plains of Bitolska Polje, full of tobacco, wheat, poppies, and grapevines. There's an even prettier deviation via **Kruševo,** a marvelous mountain town that you'll see long before you reach it, perched high above in a vivid splash of red roofs.

Kruševo was a hotbed of resistance against the Turks and even proclaimed itself a republic in 1903. Alas, the rebellion was short-lived, for after 12 days the populace was violently defeated. Not surprisingly, there isn't a mosque to be seen, but it's a living museum of urban architecture from the 19th and early 20th centuries, characterized by jutting upper stories, wood carving, and wrought ironwork.

Bitola was immensely important in Turkish times, as you might guess from some of the grand houses along Maršala Tita Street in the town center. Some are in need of spit and polish, but these were the houses of merchants who did business with the distant capitals of western Europe when Bitola was one of the most important centers in the Balkans. But its most famous sight lies just over one mile from the town. There are the ruins of the Greco-Roman settlement of **Heraclea Lyncestis,** which flourished up to the early Christian period. The setting against a mountainous backdrop is dramatic and, like Stobi, it has some superb mosaics. You'll find the most impressive in the vestibule of the Large Basilica: 120 square yards representing the universe with all its forms of life, including such graphic details as a leopard tearing at a fallen stag.

By the main road, it's 72 kilometers (45 miles) from Bitola to
Ohrid. A short and worthwhile side trip is up into the **Pelister
National Park,** 15 kilometers (9 miles) west of Bitola. The highest point of the Pelister massif is 2,645 meter (8,532 feet), but
the main attraction is its magnificent cloak of coniferous
forests—one of the few habitats of the molica pine—as well as a
great variety of plants, including rare crocuses. The combination of altitude and pinewoods makes for a heady cocktail of
unpolluted air.

A rash of modern building has changed the outskirts of Ohrid
beyond recognition in the past decade or so, but the lakeside
core of this marvelous little town has been carefully protected.
Of its complicated and often bloody history, the most important
facts to remember are that it was on the famed Roman road, the
Via Egnatia, linking the Adriatic and Aegean seas. In the 9th
century, it became a major seat of Christian learning, drawing
pilgrims and scholars from far and wide to study the new Sla-
vonic script, culture, and art. Churches sprang up, and artists
labored to cover almost every inch of their walls with frescoes
of a wondrous vitality. During the 500 years of Turkish rule,
most of the churches were turned into mosques or fell into dis-
repair, but a large proportion of the frescoes were covered with
whitewash, thus conserving them for later generations to discover.

Start down at the harbor and work your way uphill, by the main
thoroughfare of Car Samuil Street. Most of the houses, as opposed to the much older churches, are from the 19th and early
20th centuries, their jutting second and third stories all but
meeting over your head. Very soon, on your left, you'll come to
one of the greatest ecclesiastic monuments in Yugoslavia: the
Cathedral of **Sveta Sofija** (St. Sofia). It has taken a major rescue
operation to restore the shaky building and its whitewashed
frescoes (mainly those around the altar), some of which date
back to the 11th century and are among the best surviving examples of Byzantine art from that period. The *mimbar,* or
pulpit, is a reminder of the cathedral's days as a mosque.

At the top of Car Samuil Street, turn right into Ilindenska. A
Roman theater has recently been excavated on the left, and to
the right is the way to **Sveti Kliment.** This was never a mosque
and so became a repository for ecclesiastic treasures from many
other places. Among the few named artists from the early 14th
century were Mihailo and Eutihije; you'll find their initials in
several places on the magnificent frescoes here, including on
the bowl of *The Last Supper.*

Crowning the hill above old Ohrid are the imposing ruined fortress walls of Samuilo, emperor of the medieval Slav state of
Macedonia. From the walls, paths lead down through the
woods to an ancient complex, less visited than most but of particular significance. Though **St. Clement's Monastery** was later
to be completely obliterated by a mosque, its original foundations have now been excavated, revealing the site of one of the
world's first "universities," from which the earliest scholars of
the new Slav alphabet went out to spread the message of Christianity. It's a peaceful spot, high on a bluff above the tiny
fishing community of **Kaneo.** You can visit Kaneo by boat from
Ohrid harbor and clamber up to the small 13th-century church
of Sv. Jovan Kaneo, perched on the rocky bluff.

About 15 kilometers (9 miles) northwest of Ohrid is **Struga,** at the head of the lake. Saturday is the best day to visit. The market—one of the most colorful in the country—draws country folk in local costume from miles around with their rich variety of wares. Struga sits astride the fast-flowing river Crni Drim. On the return route to Skopje, you follow Crni Drim downstream toward Debar on the Albanian border. It's a dramatic road winding beneath the mountains, with villages clinging to steep slopes, some with baked-clay houses and slender minarets announcing their predominantly Albanian populations; others, with their square houses of rough and dressed stone, are typically Macedonian.

At **Debar,** the Crni Drim rushes off into Albania and the road turns away to follow the river Radika upstream between the Bistra and Korab mountain ranges. About 20 kilometers (12 miles) north of Debar, take a small road to the right and climb about a mile to the aptly named monastery of **Sveti Jovan Bigorski** (St. John of the Rocks). The views from here are stunning and the place itself enchanting, though mostly rebuilt in the early 19th century. The main sight is the iconostasis. If you've seen the one in Sveti Spas church in Skopje, you might recognize the masterly skill of the same craftsmen, the Filipovski brothers and Frčkovski from nearby Galičnik.

Galičnik is the setting for famous wedding festivities each July. At 1,426 meters (4,600 feet) the village is cut off by snow for several months. Even nowadays it's all but deserted except in summer. The only way to reach it by road is from the summer lakeside resort of Mavrovo, just off the road to Skopje. Now begins a long winding descent to Gostivar for the final stretch across a plain watered by the upper Vardar river.

The tobacco town of **Tetovo** is worth a halt for its 17th-century **Colored Mosque** (so-called because of the decorative painting on its outer walls) and the monastic complex of **Sersem Ali Baba.** The latter now houses a museum, a small hotel, and a restaurant from which you can look out over the gardens and ponder the frenetic rituals of the Whirling Dervishes whose home this was in the 18th and 19th centuries.

There are now only 40 kilometers (24 miles) to go, over the mountains and criss-crossing the river Vardar, before completing the Macedonian circuit.

Dining and Lodging

For details and price category definitions, *see* Dining and Lodging in Staying in Yugoslavia.

Kruševo
Lodging

Montana. A modern hotel built in 1974, the Montana stands on a hillside with lovely views over this very attractive town. *Tel. 77–121. 94 rooms with shower. Facilities: pool. AE. Moderate.*

Ohrid
Dining

Ohridska Pastrmka. Near the harbor and Old Town, this is the best place to try the special variety of salmon-trout found only in Lake Ohrid. It's cooked with onions, tomato juice, parsley, and slices of lemon. *Ul. Petar Čaule, tel. 096/23–827. Reservations accepted. No credit cards. Moderate.*

Orient. A little outside the Old Town, Orient also serves local fish specialties as well as more international fare. *Tel. 096/22–217. Reservations accepted. AE, DC, V. Moderate.*

Lodging **Gorica.** This hotel is in a lovely wooded setting above its own pebbled beach, 4.8 kilometers (3 miles) south of the resort. Built in 1970, it was renovated in the early '80s and the rooms are bright and comfortable. *Ul. Naum Ohridski 57, tel. 096/ 22–020. 131 rooms with bath. Facilities: pool, tennis. AE, DC, V. Expensive.*

Metropol. Eight kilometers (five miles) to the south of Ohrid, the Metropol is the best hotel in the area. A road separates it from the lakeshore and pebbled beach, but these are accessible by an underpass from the hotel that was built in 1975 and recently extended. *Dolnokonjsko bb, tel. 096/25–000. 200 rooms with bath. Facilities: saunas, pool, tennis. AE, DC, MC, V. Expensive.*

Skopje **Sveti Pantelejmon.** It's well worth the 4 mile trek up the moun-
Dining tainside to Nerezi for the stunning views over the city and the well-prepared national dishes. Try one of the lamb or kebab specialties. The restaurant is part of the old monastery compound. *Nerezi, tel. 091/258–045. Reservations advised. No credit cards. Moderate.*

Lodging **Bristol.** A town house dating from the '20s, renovated in 1985, the Bristol is a small, comfortable hotel in the center of the city. *Maršala Tito, tel. 091/239–821. 33 rooms with bath or shower. Facilities: nightclub. AE, DC, MC, V. Moderate.*

Grand Hotel Skopje. Centrally located, the Grand Hotel is by the river Vardar. Rooms are comfortable and some have river views. Its Ognjište cellar restaurant is a better choice than the somewhat bleak main restaurant. *Moša Pijade 2, tel. 091/239–925. 180 rooms with bath or shower. Facilities: 2 restaurants, disco. AE, DC, V. Moderate.*

Struga **Biser.** Here's a chance to get the feel of Macedonian adventure.
Lodging The Biser is built in attractive local style, set into a rock bluff adjoining Kalište Monastery, about 8 kilometers (5 miles) from Struga, near the Albanian border. Despite the atmospheric combination of history and mystery, the hotel is comfortable and well run. *Kalište, near Struga, tel. 72991. 51 rooms with bath or shower. Facilities: tennis. AE, DC, V. Expensive.*

Drim. Built in 1977 on the lakeshore near the Crni Drim river, Drim is a large and comfortable hotel. An attractive feature is its spacious, domed lobby with garden. *Kej. Boris Kidrić, tel. 72511. 325 rooms with bath or shower. Facilities: pool, tennis. AE, DC, V. Moderate.*

Conversion Tables

Distance

Kilometers/Miles To change kilometers to miles, multiply kilometers by .621.
To change miles to kilometers, multiply miles by 1.61.

Km to Mi	Mi to Km
1 = .62	1 = 1.6
2 = 1.2	2 = 3.2
3 = 1.9	3 = 4.8
4 = 2.5	4 = 6.4
5 = 3.1	5 = 8.1
6 = 3.7	6 = 9.7
7 = 4.3	7 = 11.3
8 = 5.0	8 = 12.9
9 = 5.6	9 = 14.5

Meters/Feet To change meters to feet, multiply meters by 3.28.
To change feet to meters, multiply feet by .305.

Meters to Feet	Feet to Meters
1 = 3.3	1 = .31
2 = 6.6	2 = .61
3 = 9.8	3 = .92
4 = 13.1	4 = 1.2
5 = 16.4	5 = 1.5
6 = 19.7	6 = 1.8
7 = 23.0	7 = 2.1
8 = 26.2	8 = 2.4
9 = 29.5	9 = 2.7

Weight

Kilograms/Pounds To change kilograms to pounds, multiply by 2.20.
To change pounds to kilograms, multiply by .453.

Kilos to Pounds	Pounds to Kilos
1 = 2.2	1 = .45
2 = 4.4	2 = .91
3 = 6.6	3 = 1.4
4 = 8.8	4 = 1.8
5 = 11.0	5 = 2.3
6 = 13.2	6 = 2.7

7 = 15.4	7 = 3.2
8 = 17.6	8 = 3.6
9 = 19.8	9 = 4.1

Grams/Ounces To change grams to ounces, multiply grams by .035.
To change ounces to grams, multiply ounces by 28.4.

Grams to Ounces	Ounces to Grams
1 = .04	1 = 28
2 = .07	2 = 57
3 = .11	3 = 85
4 = .14	4 = 114
5 = .18	5 = 142
6 = .21	6 = 170
7 = .25	7 = 199
8 = .28	8 = 227
9 = .32	9 = 256

Liquid Volume

Liters/U.S. Gallons To change liters to U.S. gallons, multiply liters by .264.
To change U.S. gallons to liters, multiply gallons by 3.79.

Liters to U.S. Gallons	U.S. Gallons to Liters
1 = .26	1 = 3.8
2 = .53	2 = 7.6
3 = .79	3 = 11.4
4 = 1.1	4 = 15.2
5 = 1.3	5 = 19.0
6 = 1.6	6 = 22.7
7 = 1.8	7 = 26.5
8 = 2.1	8 = 30.3
9 = 2.4	9 = 34.1

Clothing Sizes

Men *Suits*							
U.S./U.K.	36	38	40	42	44	46	48
Europe	46	48	50	52	54	56	58

Shirts	U.S./U.K.	14	14½	15	15½	16	16½	17	17½
	Europe	36	37	38	39	40	41	42	43

Shoes	U.S.	7½	8	8½/9	9½/10	10½/11	11½/12	12½
	Europe	40	41	42	43	44	45	46

Women Dresses and Coats	U.S.	4	6	8	10	12	14	16
	U.K.	28	30	32	34	36	38	40
	Europe	34	36	38	40	42	44	46

Blouses and Sweaters	U.S.	4	6	8	10	12	14	16
	U.K.	30	32	34	36	38	40	42
	Europe	36	38	40	42	44	46	48

Shoes	U.S.	5	6	7	8	9
	U.K.	3½	4½	5½	6½	7½
	Europe	35	37	38	39	40/41

Note that these sizes are not exact. You should *always* try on before buying.

Index

Help us evaluate hotels and restaurants for the next edition of this guide, and we will send you a free issue of Fodor's newsletter, TravelSense.

Title of this guide:

1 Hotel ❑   **Restaurant** ❑   *(check one)*

Name

Number/Street

City/State/Country

Comments

2 Hotel ❑   **Restaurant** ❑   *(check one)*

Name

Number/Street

City/State/Country

Comments

3 Hotel ❑   **Restaurant** ❑   *(check one)*

Name

Number/Street

City/State/Country

Comments

General Comments

Please complete for a free copy of TravelSense

Name

Number/Street

City/State/Zip

Business Reply Mail

First Class   *Permit Nº 7775*   *New York, NY*

Postage will be paid by addressee

Fodor's Travel Publications

201 East 50th Street
New York, NY 10022

Personal Itinerary

Departure *Date*

Time

Transportation

Arrival *Date*   *Time*

Departure *Date*   *Time*

Transportation

Accommodations

Arrival *Date*   *Time*

Departure *Date*   *Time*

Transportation

Accommodations

Arrival *Date*   *Time*

Departure *Date*   *Time*

Transportation

Accommodations

Personal Itinerary

Arrival	*Date*	*Time*
Departure	*Date*	*Time*
Transportation		
Accommodations		

Arrival	*Date*	*Time*
Departure	*Date*	*Time*
Transportation		
Accommodations		

Arrival	*Date*	*Time*
Departure	*Date*	*Time*
Transportation		
Accommodations		

Arrival	*Date*	*Time*
Departure	*Date*	*Time*
Transportation		
Accommodations		

Personal Itinerary

Arrival *Date*   *Time*

Departure *Date*   *Time*

Transportation

Accommodations

Arrival *Date*   *Time*

Departure *Date*   *Time*

Transportation

Accommodations

Arrival *Date*   *Time*

Departure *Date*   *Time*

Transportation

Accommodations

Arrival *Date*   *Time*

Departure *Date*   *Time*

Transportation

Accommodations

Personal Itinerary

Arrival *Date*   *Time*

Departure *Date*   *Time*

Transportation

Accommodations

Arrival *Date*   *Time*

Departure *Date*   *Time*

Transportation

Accommodations

Arrival *Date*   *Time*

Departure *Date*   *Time*

Transportation

Accommodations

Arrival *Date*   *Time*

Departure *Date*   *Time*

Transportation

Accommodations

Addresses

Name	*Name*
Address	*Address*
Telephone	*Telephone*
Name	*Name*
Address	*Address*
Telephone	*Telephone*
Name	*Name*
Address	*Address*
Telephone	*Telephone*
Name	*Name*
Address	*Address*
Telephone	*Telephone*
Name	*Name*
Address	*Address*
Telephone	*Telephone*
Name	*Name*
Address	*Address*
Telephone	*Telephone*
Name	*Name*
Address	*Address*
Telephone	*Telephone*
Name	*Name*
Address	*Address*
Telephone	*Telephone*

Fodor's Travel Guides

U.S. Guides

Alaska
Arizona
Atlantic City & the
New Jersey Shore
Boston
California
Cape Cod
Carolinas & the
Georgia Coast
The Chesapeake Region
Chicago
Colorado
Dallas & Fort
Worth

Disney World & the
Orlando Area
Florida
Hawaii
Houston &
Galveston
Las Vegas
Los Angeles, Orange
County, Palm Springs
Maui
Miami, Fort Lauderdale,
Palm Beach
Michigan, Wisconsin,
Minnesota

New England
New Mexico
New Orleans
New Orleans (Pocket
Guide)
New York City
New York City (Pocket
Guide)
New York State
Pacific North Coast
Philadelphia
The Rockies
San Diego
San Francisco

San Francisco (Pocket
Guide)
The South
Texas
USA
Virgin Islands
Virginia
Waikiki
Washington, DC
Williamsburg

Foreign Guides

Acapulco
Amsterdam
Australia, New Zealand,
The South Pacific
Austria
Bahamas
Bahamas (Pocket
Guide)
Baja & the Pacific
Coast Resorts
Barbados
Belgium & Luxembourg
Bermuda
Brazil
Britain (Great Travel
Values)
Budget Europe
Canada
Canada (Great Travel
Values)
Canada's Atlantic
Provinces
Cancún, Cozumel,
Mérida, the
Yucatán
Caribbean

Caribbean (Great
Travel Values)
Central America
China
China's Great Cities
Eastern Europe
Egypt
Europe
Europe's Great Cities
Florence & Venice
France
France (Great Travel
Values)
Germany
Germany (Great Travel
Values)
Great Britain
Greece
The Himalayan
Countries
Holland
Hong Kong
Hungary
India, including Nepal
Ireland
Israel

Italy
Italy (Great Travel
Values)
Jamaica
Japan
Japan (Great Travel
Values)
Jordan & the Holy Land
Kenya, Tanzania,
the Seychelles
Korea
Lisbon
Loire Valley
London
London (Great Travel
Values)
London (Pocket Guide)
Madrid & Barcelona
Mexico
Mexico City
Montreal &
Quebec City
Munich
New Zealand
North Africa
Paris

Paris (Pocket Guide)
Portugal
Rio de Janeiro
The Riviera (Fun on)
Rome
Saint Martin &
Sint Maarten
Scandinavia
Scandinavian Cities
Scotland
Singapore
South America
South Pacific
Southeast Asia
Soviet Union
Spain
Spain (Great Travel
Values)
Sweden
Switzerland
Sydney
Tokyo
Toronto
Turkey
Vienna
Yugoslavia

Special-Interest Guides

Bed & Breakfast
Guide: North America
Health & Fitness
Vacations

Royalty Watching
Selected Hotels of
Europe

Selected Resorts
and Hotels of the U.S.
Shopping in Europe

Skiing in North
America
Sunday in New York